Footprint

Caribbean Islands

Sarah Cameron

*I sang our wide country, the Caribbean Sea
who hated shoes, whose soles were as cracked as a stone,
who was gentle with ropes, who had one suit alone,
whom no man dared insult and who insulted no one,
whose grin was a white breaker cresting, but whose frown
was a growing thunderhead.*

Omeros by Derek Walcott (1990)

15th edition

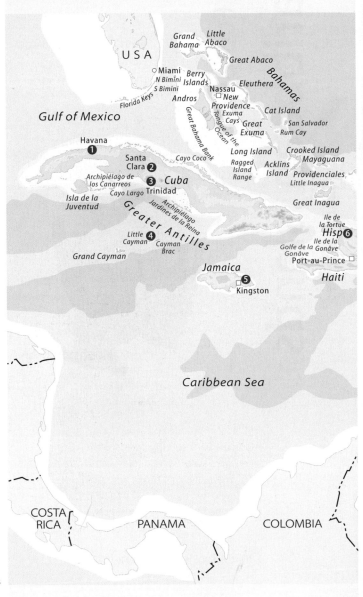

Caribbean Islands Highlights

See colour maps at back of book

❶ Havana
The capital city which never sleeps, rumba and salsa are its life blood

❷ Santa Clara
Tomb and monument to revolutionary hero Che Guevara

❸ Trinidad
A colonial city in a time warp, with cobbled streets and horse-drawn transport

❹ Little Cayman
A diver's paradise with virgin walls and reefs and excellent visibility

❺ Blue Mountains
Home of great coffee and forest hikes

❻ La Citadelle
Mountain-top fortress, symbol of the only successful black slave revolution

❼ Pico Duarte
The tallest mountain in the Caribbean and a mecca for hikers

❽ Bahía de Samaná
Great whale watching when humpbacks migrate

❾ British Virgin Islands
A sailors' playground; dozens of protected bays and islands

❿ Saba
A tiny Dutch outpost with glorious views and diving

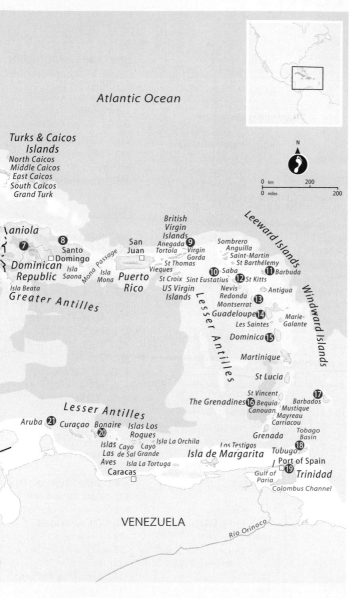

11 Barbuda
The world's largest breeding colony of frigate birds

12 Brimstone Hill Fortress
A UNESCO World Heritage Site built to deter invaders

13 Chances Peak
The volcano still rumbles but is now a tourist attraction

14 Parc Naturel
Hike the forest trails of the seventh largest national park in France

15 Morne Trois Pitons National Park
A mountainous reserve with Boiling Lake, rainforest, rushing rivers and abundant wildlife

16 The Grenadines
Tiny island retreats, glorious beaches and exhilarating sailing

17 Barbados
The holiday capital of the Caribbean

18 Tobago
Beaches and birdwatching, dining and diving, unspoilt and unrushed

19 Carnival
The best Mardi Gras in the world

20 Bonaire
Pristine underwater scenery, a divers' delight

21 Aruba Beaches
Windsurfing by day, casinos and partying by night

Contents

A foot in the door

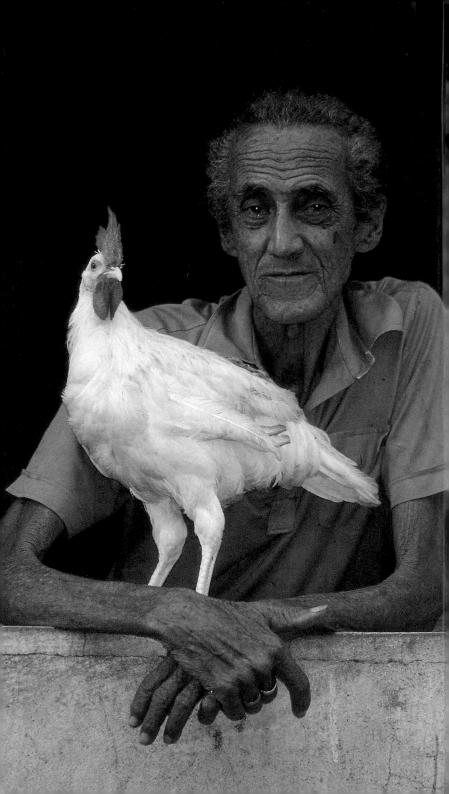

Introducing the Caribbean

Swaying palm trees, golden beaches, a hammock at siesta time, sunset rum cocktails… The heat of the tropical sun induces lethargy and all the conditions for a relaxing holiday. Sun, sea and sand are offered in abundance in the Caribbean and it is easy to adapt to the unhurried pace of island living. After dark when it is cooler, everyone comes out to play, to promenade, to sing and dance. This is the time to turn up a different sort of heat, take hold of a partner and gyrate your hips in time with the music, whether it be salsa, reggae, merengue or any other local dance. Islanders will be delighted to give you some hands-on tuition.The people of the islands are a diverse mix and their cultures vary according to their ethnic blend. Starting with different Amerindian tribes throughout the island arc, the melting pot has been added to by colonizers: the Spanish, French, English, Dutch, American, Swedish, followed by their slaves of various African tribes, indentured labourers from India or China and immigrants from Arab countries. Skin colour and features can differ greatly even within families, depending on their ancestors. Although there is now a huge US cultural and media influence everywhere except Cuba, most islands have kept their own identities and traditions based on their individual experience of immigration.You can enjoy Carnival in Trinidad, dance salsa in Cuba, hike the Caribbean's tallest mountain in the Dominican Republic, stay in the highest hotel in the Kingdom of the Netherlands in Saba, dive a sunken Russian frigate off Cayman Brac, worship in the oldest synagogue in the Western Hemisphere in Curaçao, watch African big drum music in Carriacou, visit an active volcano in Montserrat, immerse yourself in reggae in Jamaica, be initiated into the rites of voodoo in Haiti, go birdwatching in Tobago, ride the sugar train in St Kitts, or sample the local rum – everywhere.

Santiago de Cuba (opposite) *Watching the world go by*
The Grenadines (previous page) *Sailing is an excellent way to see the many islands and cays; bareboat and crewed yachts are available for wherever you want to go*

The Caribbean in a conch shell

Anguilla Anguilla is known for its luxury hotels and sandy beaches. It's one of the safest and most relaxing islands, but is not a low-budget option. Visitors amuse themselves in the water during the day and visit restaurants, bars and weekend beach parties at night. There's not much else to do on this low-lying coral island, but that's why people come here.

Antigua A family holiday destination with great beaches, watersports and safe swimming. Direct flights from Europe and the US and good transport links with other islands facilitate two-centre holidays or extensive island hopping. Yachts fill the historic bay at picturesque English Harbour, a popular staging post for centuries. Nelson's Dockyard is overlooked by the old battery on Shirley Heights, now better known for Sunday jump-ups and reggae.

Aruba Aruba is the smallest of the 'ABC' group of islands, only 25 km north of Venezuela. The coastal strip on the leeward side of the island with the best beaches is now wall-to-wall hotels, with all those of more than 300 rooms allowed to have a casino. A wide range of watersports are on offer, including excellent windsurfing, which is world class. On land there is a golf course among the sand dunes in the north which is very well regarded.

Barbados Barbados hasn't got the best beaches in the Caribbean, there are no volcanoes, no rainforest, no virgin coral reef, but visitors come back year after year. You can pay thousands of dollars for a hotel room and be truly cosseted or rent a moderate apartment and look after yourself. You can play any number of sports, or you can watch cricket, horseracing or polo. There is lovely walking along the rugged Atlantic coast, while watersports are offered along the more protected Caribbean beaches. For sightseeing, there are fortifications, plantation houses, museums, rum distilleries and gardens.

Bonaire The diving here is among the best in the Caribbean, with pristine reefs and wonderful visibility as there are no rivers to muddy the waters and it is out of the hurricane belt. Windsurfing is also excellent. The climate is dry and the vegetation little more than scrub and cactus but it is prized by birdwatchers.

British Virgin Islands The British Virgin Islands have a reputation for excellent sailing and there are many charter companies offering crewed or bareboat yachts. Windsurfing is also top quality and both sports organize international races and regattas. Races are accompanied by lots of parties and related activities typical of the yachtie fraternity. There are plenty of hotels, and a few really special places – popular with newly weds or the seriously rich.

Cayman Islands These three low-lying little islands south of Cuba are green with pine and mangroves, while underwater the reefs and walls offer some of the world's most thrilling dive sites. Conservation is top priority here, and there are a number of sanctuaries in the ponds and wetlands. Grand Cayman is busy with its offshore financial sector as well as tourism, whereas Cayman Brac and Little Cayman are quiet, unhurried places where you can escape the crowds and relax without giving up your creature comforts.

Cuba The largest island in the Caribbean, Cuba has rolling green sugar cane land or flat cattle plains, forested mountains, lakes, caves, beaches and swamps. Travellers come for the vibrant culture, music, dance, art and the people. The island's turbulent political past and its current communist stability is of interest to many. Colonial towns are unspoilt by advertising and American influence is minimal: Cuba is Cuban. You can laze on a beach, hike up a mountain, cycle the roads, wander around fortresses, historical monuments and museums or take to the water for excellent swimming, diving, snorkelling and fishing.

The Pitons (left) Thought to be volcanic plugs, the Pitons dominate the landscape in southwest St Lucia
Charlotte Amalie (below) The busy capital of St Thomas and the US Virgin Islands is a magnet for cruise ship shoppers

Trinidad (above) Celebrations for the world-famous carnival start warming up months before Mardi Gras
Marine turtles (left) Loggerhead, leatherback, hawksbill and green turtles are among the species paddling the Caribbean waters

Trinidad, Cuba (right) Many of the
well-known Caribbean and Latin
rhythms such as the son, rumba,
mambo, guajira, guaracha and
bolero have their roots in Cuba
Courland Bay (below) Fishing is
a way of life in Tobago; deep-sea charters
can be arranged, or you can watch (or
help) the locals pull in the nets
Treasure Beach (page 16) Siesta time
in Jamaica

Martinique (above) Gommier racing is just one of the many
sailboat races held throughout the Caribbean
Pink vase sponge (right) Invertebrates of all shapes and sizes live
on the reefs and walls of the Caribbean

Curaçao has some fine Dutch colonial architecture painted in a variety of pastel **Curaçao**
colours. It also has one of the most important historical sites in the Caribbean: a synagogue dating back to 1732. In the countryside there are several beautiful plantation
houses. An underwater park to preserve the reef has made diving very popular and
there are dive sites (and hotels) all along the leeward side of the island.

Dense forests, volcanic hills, rivers, waterfalls and the Boiling Lake, provide good hiking **Dominica**
and birdwatching opportunities. It is also a highly regarded diving destination and for
much of the year you can see whales and dolphins offshore. Hotels around the island
are small, intimate and low-key, greater development being deterred by the lack of
beaches. It is the only island where Caribs have survived and they still retain many of
their traditions such as canoe carving.

The Hispanic side of Hispaniola has some stunning scenery, with the highest mountain **Dominican**
in the Caribbean and some of the most beautiful beaches. It is green and fertile except **Republic**
in the southwest, which is a dry zone, and the southeast where huge cacti grow. The
capital, Santo Domingo, the first city in Spanish America, has some exceptional colonial architecture including the first cathedral and the first university. Hotels sprawl
along the coast for sun, sea and sand worshippers, but for anyone wanting action,
there's mountain biking, rafting, hiking, canyoning or horse riding. If you've still got
any energy after that for nightlife, the discos will be throbbing with merengue.

Grenada is known as the spice island because of the nutmeg, mace and other spices it **Grenada**
produces. It has a beautiful mountainous interior with many different ecosystems,
from dry tropical forest and mangroves on the coast, through lush rainforest on the
hillsides, to elfin woodland on the peaks. St George's, the capital, is widely acknowledged as the prettiest harbour city in the West Indies blending French and English
architectural styles with a picturesque setting on steep hills overlooking the bay.

This is France in the tropics: coffee, croissants, baguettes and delicious, spicy Creole **Guadeloupe**
food, which you can wash down with some very fine rum. Guadeloupe is really two
islands: Basse-Terre, to the west, which is mountainous and forested, with a huge
national park on and offshore, and Grand-Terre, to the east, which is smaller, flatter and
more densely populated with good beaches. The quiet outer islands of Les Saintes, La
Désirade and Marie Galante are within easily reach of Guadeloupe, but are quiet and
untouched by mass tourism.

The only country successfully to have carried out a slave rebellion, Haiti's religious **Haiti**
beliefs, music, dance and art stem directly from Africa with French influences from
colonial days. The most impressive fortification is the massive La Citadelle, built on top
of a 900-m peak to deter any French re-invasion. The capital, Port-au-Prince, is a seething mass of humanity where everyone plies their trade in the streets to eke out a living.
This is the poorest country in the Western Hemisphere and tourism is minimal.
Occupying the western third of the island of Hispaniola, it has little in common culturally with its neighbour, the Dominican Republic.

Isla de Margarita is the largest of Venezuela's 72 Caribbean islands. The beaches facing **Isla de**
east have excellent surfing and windsurfing. Excursions can be taken by boat to Islas **Margarita**
Los Roques, a national park treasured for long white beaches, snorkelling and diving
on the reef and many nesting sites for sea birds. Other more remote islands are best
visited by yacht, providing the freedom to explore without worrying where you are
going to sleep.

Jamaica A beautiful island with rolling hills and steep gullies, the spectacular Blue Mountains overlook a coastline indented with bays and coves. The vegetation is luxuriant, the colours are vibrant, and the people have a culture to match, from reggae and rastafarianism to English plantation houses and cricket. Music is everywhere and Jamaica is a hub of creativity in the Caribbean. Every conceivable watersport is on offer along the north coast, while in the south, mangroves are home to manatee and crocodiles.

Martinique Like Guadeloupe, this is a piece of France in the tropics, where language and customs have adapted to the climate. There is something for everybody: a variety of hotels; good beaches; watersports; historical attractions; beautiful scenery; hiking and birdwatching. Tourism is well developed in the south, but a large part of the more mountainous north is taken up by protected rainforest.

Montserrat The 'Emerald Isle', with its Irish influences, is recovering from the 1995 eruption of the volcano and volcano watching is now a tourist attraction, with a strategically placed observatory where scientists monitor activity. The southern part of the island, including the capital, Plymouth, is under a blanket of ash and has been evacuated. Houses have been built in the north and there is now a new airport and cricket pitch.

Puerto Rico The lovely old city of San Juan, the capital, still stands within its walls on a spit of land jutting out to sea. The sprawling, hideous new city is US-influenced, with shopping malls, industrial zones and wide highways. Large resorts, casinos, marinas and golf courses line the coast, but inland there are mountains, rainforest, caves and archaeological sites, while offshore the islands of Vieques and Culebra are quiet and unspoilt.

Saba This tiny Dutch island, an extinct volcano, rises out of the sea, green and lush. The underwater landscape is equally spectacular and divers treasure the marine park. Walking is rewarding too, and ancient trails weave their way around the island, the most stunning being the 1,064 irregular steps up Mount Scenery. Lodging is in small, friendly hotels, guesthouses and cottages, where you won't need a key – there is no crime.

St-Barthélemy Tiny St-Barts is easily reached by boat or a short air hop from St-Martin. It has gained a reputation as the place to go for the rich and famous. It is chic and expensive and its many beautiful beaches are dotted with luxury hotels and villas, designed for those who appreciate privacy. Gourmet French restaurants and Creole bistros can be found all over the island. This is a place to indulge yourself and be a part of the jet set.

Sint Eustatius Few tourists make the effort to visit this Dutch outpost which has a rich colonial history and a prosperous past, when some 3,500 ships visited each year. Having made its fortune in the 18th century out of the slave trade and commerce in plantation crops, it lost it in the 19th century and has never really recovered. The main town, Oranjestad, still has the fortifications and remains of warehouses from its heyday. There are walking trails up into the rainforest of the extinct volcano, the Quill, and diving is good in the marine park.

St Kitts & Nevis Slightly off the beaten track, St Kitts is developing its southern peninsula where there are golden sandy beaches, but most of the island is untouched by tourism. Rugged volcanic peaks, forests and old fortresses make for rewarding hiking, and a scenic railway meanders through billowing seas of cane, dotted with old sugar mills. Two miles away, the conical island of Nevis is smaller, quieter and very desirable. Here, plantation houses have been converted into some of the most romantic hotels in the Caribbean, very popular with honeymooners. Cycling or hiking along the old goat trails affords views across to other islands such as Montserrat, with its smoking volcano.

Very popular as both a family holiday destination and a romantic paradise for honey- **St Lucia**
mooners, St Lucia's beaches are golden or black sand, some with the spectacular setting of the Pitons as a backdrop, and many are favoured by turtles as a nesting site.
Offshore there is good diving and snorkelling along the west coast. Rodney Bay marina
is one of the best harbours in the West Indies, attracting yachts from around the region
and from across the Atlantic. The mountainous interior is outstandingly beautiful and
there are several forest reserves to protect the St Lucian parrot and other wildlife.
Sightseeing opportunities include sulphur springs, colonial fortifications and plantation tours.

Shared amicably between Holland and France, this island offers you two cultures **Sint Maarten/**
within easy reach of each other. Good international air transport links have encour- **St-Martin**
aged the construction of large resort hotels with casinos and duty-free shopping in the
Dutch part. The French part is considered more 'chic' and crowded with restaurants
dedicated to the serious business of eating well. Both sides have good harbours and
marinas and are popular with the sailing crowd. Heavily populated, there are not many
places on the island where houses have not been built, so this is not a place to come to
get away from it all, but it is ideal for a fun beach holiday.

St Vincent is green, fertile and very pretty, with fishing villages, coconut groves, banana **St Vincent &**
plantations and volcanic interior. However, it is also known for the superb sailing con- **the Grenadines**
ditions provided by its 32 sister islands and cays, and some very competitive regattas
are held throughout the year, accompanied by lots of parties and social events. The
Grenadines have a certain exclusivity, some of the smaller islands are privately owned
and Mustique is known for its villas owned by the rich, royal and famous. There are
some fabulously luxurious places to stay, but there are also more moderate hotels,
guesthouses and rental homes for those who don't want to spend all their time afloat.

Trinidad has a rich culture, largely a mixture of the traditions of African slaves and **Trinidad &**
Indian indentured labourers, brought together so spectacularly in the world's best car- **Tobago**
nival. Tobago, on the other hand, is a laid-back island where visitors appreciate the
clear, calm sea, the sandy beaches, the diving and snorkelling and the small, friendly
hotels and guesthouses. The two islands together are home to more species of birds
than any other island in the Caribbean, and birdwatchers have long been attracted to
the forests and swamps.

These flat, coral islands have miles of sandy beaches and are a water playground. **The Turks &**
Diving and snorkelling are superb among coral gardens, wrecks and walls which drop **Caicos Islands**
dramatically to the floor of the ocean. Most hotels are on the island of Providenciales,
spread along Grace Bay on the north shore, and there are lots of facilities. Grand Turk is
the seat of government but is a quiet, unhurried place with a few small hotels and
some pleasant colonial buildings. Other inhabited islands, North Caicos, Middle Caicos,
South Caicos and Salt Cay are good places to escape the crowds.

The three US Virgin Islands are very different from each other but are all very American. **US Virgin**
St Thomas attracts cruise ships and when several are in port the streets of town are **Islands**
heavily congested with shoppers. St John is dominated by the Virgin Islands National
Park, which has been in existence since 1956 and has some excellent trails for walkers.
St Croix is the poorest of the three but has a great deal to offer in the way of tourist
attractions. All three have good hotels and are popular with sailors.

Essentials

Planning your trip

Where to go

Holiday companies and travel agents tend to market the Caribbean as a homogenous tropical destination, but in reality each island has its own personality and what suits one person will not suit another. You have a choice between English, Spanish, French, American and Dutch islands, so language might be a consideration. Some islands are more difficult to get to than others. How much time do you want to spend travelling to your destination? Do you want to stay in one place or indulge in a spot of island-hopping? Do you like company and organized activities or would you prefer an empty mountain or deserted beach? Do you want to take it easy and relax or are you an active person who needs to face challenges?

Island hopping In general, you will not find a remote hideaway on islands like Antigua and Sint Maarten, which receive transatlantic charter flights. However, they are useful jumping-off points for smaller islands. If you have a tight budget, it is worth investigating where cheap flights go to from your country and then finding out which islands can be easily reached from there. For example, there are often cheap charter flights to Antigua, Sint Maarten or St Lucia from Europe, which connect with *Liat* flights to the British Virgin Islands and all the Leeward and Windward Islands. Connections are good between France and Guadeloupe and Martinique, which could combine with a visit to Les Saintes and Dominica. There are lots of flights from the USA to Puerto Rico, which again has inks with nearly all the other Caribbean Islands. *Air Jamaica* uses Montego Bay as its regional hub and is increasing the number of flights to other islands, including the Dutch Antilles. Only Cuba has rather poor inter-island links, both by air and by sea, but then there is enough to keep you busy on such a large island for you not to need to combine it with anywhere else.

Transport links between islands are fine if you want to fly everywhere, but after several hours in an aeroplane getting to the Caribbean from Europe, South or North America, you may prefer to travel by sea, which is usually cheaper but takes longer and can be either fascinating or unpleasant if you suffer from seasickness in rough weather. In the **Windward Islands** there is a ferry between Dominica, St Lucia and the French islands of Martinique and Guadeloupe, well used by local shoppers as well as tourists, offering you the chance of combining the nature tourism of Dominica and the beach resorts of St Lucia with the flavours of France in the Caribbean. You can travel from St Vincent down through the Grenadines to Grenada by mail boat, fishing boat and hovercraft, a cheaper alternative to chartering a yacht and doing it yourself. A car ferry links the **Dominican Republic** with **Puerto Rico** and there are ferries between the **US** and **British Virgin Islands** letting you visit a number of islands without having the work of sailing your own yacht. In the **Leeward Islands**, Sint Maarten/Saint-Martin is a useful hub for transatlantic flights from where ferries go out to Anguilla, St-Barts and Saba like spokes of a wheel, allowing you to sample English, French and Dutch islands. A few days on each island would be plenty, as they are small and compact. Links with **Venezuela** tend to come and go, but there is a ferry from **Trinidad** to Güiria.

One-week trip With only one week to spare it is best to stay on one island and take things easy. If you are basing yourself on an island with good links by ferry then a day trip to a neighbouring island would be plenty. For example, you could stay on Anguilla and hop across to the shops on St-Martin; base yourself on Providenciales and go sightseeing on any of the Caicos Islands; go to Antigua and fly over to Barbuda to see the frigate bird sanctuary or to Montserrat to see the volcano.

Two-week trip Two weeks gives you time to explore two or three small islands or a large one in depth. You need two weeks to see everything the Dominican Republic has to offer, for example, and you could see quite a lot of Cuba in a fortnight, too. You will probably have exhausted all there is to do on a small island in a week, so choosing a split destination is a good idea. For transport and immigration reasons this is usually easier if you choose places like Antigua and Barbuda, St Kitts and Nevis, Trinidad and Tobago, which are one country. Alternatively you could explore the British Virgin Islands or the Grenadines with a week ashore and a week on a yacht.

A month gives you serious time to get to know parts of the region. You could visit all the French islands, or all the Dutch islands; cover Cuba from top to toe; investigate both sides of Hispaniola: the Dominican Republic and its neighbour, Haiti. **One month**

The Caribbean is your oyster and where you go will be determined by the size of your budget. You could sail through the arc, stopping in where you felt like it and spending nights on shore at whim. There are those who have spent a couple of months cycling through the islands. Alternatively, set yourself a task: learn Spanish in the Dominican Republic and then put your skills to the test on any of the Spanish-speaking islands, or enrol on a salsa dancing course in Cuba and once you've mastered the art, you'll be in demand at all the bars and clubs as you travel around. **Two months**

Essentials

When to go

The climate everywhere in the Caribbean is tropical, with variations in rainfall. The volcanic, mountainous and forested islands attract more rain than the low-lying coral islands, so you can expect frequent showers in St Lucia but not on Bonaire. The driest and coolest time of year is usually December-April, coinciding with the winter peak in tourism as snow birds escape to the sun. Temperatures then can fall to 20°C during the day, depending on altitude, but are normally in the high 20°s, tempered by cooling trade winds. At other times of the year the temperature rises only slightly, but greater humidity can make it feel hotter if you are away from the coast. The main climate hazard is hurricane season (see page 42), which runs from June to November, although storms are rare before September. Islands south of Grenada are outside the hurricane belt although they can still receive storms and heavy rain at times. **Climate**

The huge popularity of Carnival in **Trinidad** has led many islands to develop new festivals to attract visitors and it is worth considering what events are planned when deciding where and when to go. Although Trinidad's Carnival is held pre-Lent, not all islands hold their Carnivals at this time and some, such as **St Lucia**, have actually moved theirs so as not to clash with Trinidad. **Jamaica** has one around Easter, recycling many of the Trinidadian songs and even the costumes, as well as much original material. Carnival in **Santiago de Cuba** is in July, taking in the anniversary of the Moncada rebellion as further cause for celebration. **Barbados'** Carnival celebrates the end of the sugar harvest, so Crop Over is in July, running over into the beginning of August on Kadooment Day, with lots of calypso, soca and other live music. **Festivals**

Music festivals, particularly jazz, are popular and usually a sell-out. Many are planned in low season, to try and even out the flow of tourists throughout the year. The **St Lucia Jazz Festival** in May is something to go out of your way for, and indeed most neighbouring islands lay on extra transport and package deals for that week. Most performances are open air, although fringe events can be found anywhere. **Grenada** follows it with a **Spice Jazz Festival** in May or June, which is increasing its international standing, but doesn't yet have quite the reputation of St Lucia. **Cuba's Jazz Plaza Festival** is in December, conveniently timed so that you can take in a Film Festival as well. **Jamaica** puts on **Reggae Sumfest**, in August, when, for five days you can listen to local and international reggae artistes until your head is throbbing, while **Santo Domingo**, in the Dominican Republic, hosts a **festival of merengue** in July with dancing in the streets late into the night until your hips hurt. A more high-brow cultural event is the **Holders Season** in **Barbados** in March, where you can catch drama, opera and comedy by performers from all over the world, held in a plantation house garden lit at night by of miles of fairy lights.

Tours and tour operators

Any travel agent can book you a holiday in the Caribbean, whether a package tour or tailor made, and just about all of them have benefited from 'fam trips' so they will probably be able to advise you from first hand experience.

In the UK, *Discovery Initiatives*, The Travel House, 51 Castle St, Cirencester, Gloucestershire GL7 1QD, T01285-643333, enquiry@discoveryinitiatives.com, are pioneers in special wildlife, marine and conservation interest groups and tailor-made ecotours. *Exodus Travels*, 9 Weir Road, London **Specialist tour operators**

▶ **Surfing the Caribbean**

The following is a list of general sites and a combination of official tourist office and private sector sites:

Anguilla www.anguilla-vacation.com, www.news.ai, www.anguillaguide.com

Antigua www.antigua-barbuda.com, www.antigua-barbuda.org, www.antiguanice.com

Aruba www.aruba.com www.arubatourism.com, www.visitaruba.com, www.aruba-travelguide.com

Barbados www.barbados.org, www.funbarbados.com, www.nationnews.com

Bonaire www.InfoBonaire.com, www.bonairereporter.com, www.bonairewebcams.com, www.bmp.org

British Virgin Islands www.bvitouristboard.com, www.b-v-i.com, www.islandsun.com
www.bviwelcome.com, www.britishvirginislands.com

Cayman Islands www.caymanislands.ky, www.cayman.com.ky www.cayman-islands.com

Cuba www.dtcuba.com, www.cubatravel.cu, www.cubaweb.cu www.cuba.cu

Curaçao www.curacao-tourism.com, www.curacao.com

Dominica www.ndcdominica.dm www.avirtualdominica.com

Dominican Republic www.dominicanrepublic.com, www.hispaniola.com,
www.dominicana.com.do, www.dr1.com, www.debbiesdominicantravel.com

Grenada www.grenadagrenadines.com, www.travelgrenada.com, ww.grenadahotelsinfo.com,
www.spiceisle.com, www.grenadines.net

Guadeloupe www.antilles-info-tourisme.com, www.guadeloupe-fr.com

Haiti www.haitionline.com, www.haiti.org, www.port-haiti.com, www.windowsonhaiti.com

Jamaica www.jamaicatravel.com, www.jamaicans.com,
www.go-jamaica.com, www.jamaicaobserver.com

SW12 0LT, T020-87723822, www.exodus.co.uk *Interchange*, Interchange House, 27 Stafford Rd, Croydon, Surrey CR0 4NG, T020-86813612, www.interchange.uk.com, specializes in Haiti, Cuba and Aruba. *Journey Latin America*, 12-13 Heathfield Terrace, Chiswick, London W4 4JE, T020-87478315, and in Manchester, T0161-8321441, www.journey latinamerica.co.uk, is good for Cuba (also flight only to Dominican Republic and Dutch Antilles), as are *Progressive Tours*, 12 Porchester Pl, Marble Arch, London W2 2BS, T020-74865704, *Regent Holidays*, 15 John St, Bristol BS1 2HR, T0117-9211711, and *South American Experience*, 47 Causton St, Pimlico, London SW1P 4AT, T020-79765511, www.southamerican experience.co.uk *Trips Worldwide Ltd*, 14 Frederick Place, Clifton, Bristol, BS8 1AS, T0117-3114400, www.trips worldwide.co.uk Tailor-made holidays to Latin America and the 'Alternative Caribbean'. *Mila Tours*, 100 S Greenleaf, Gurnee, Il 60031-3378, USA, T1-800- 3677378, www.milatours.com Covering Cuba and the Dominican Republic, Mila various tours from adventure, diving and scuba to culture, ecology and archaeology. Specialists in upmarket destinations include *ITC Classics/Caribbean Connection*, www.itcclassics.co.uk; *Caribtours*, T020-77510660, www.carib tours.co.uk; *Kuoni*, T01306- 747000, www.kuoni.co.uk; *Elegant Resorts*, www.elegantresorts.co.uk; *Hayes and Jarvis*, www.hayesand jarvis.co.uk; and *Virgin Holidays*, www.virginholidays.co.uk

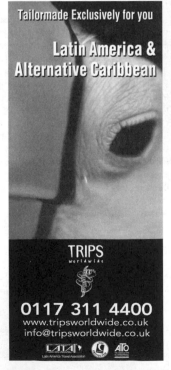

Martinique www.martinique.org www.touristmartinique.com
Montserrat www.visitmontserrat.com, www.mvo.ms, www.montserratreporter.org
Puerto Rico www.gotopuertorico.com, www.travelandsports.com, www.puerto-rico-tourism.com
www.culebra.org, www.vieques-island.com, www.viequespr.net
Saba www.sabatourism.com
St-Barthélémy www.antilles-info-tourisme.com, www.saint-barths.com, www.st-barths.com
St Kitts and Nevis www.stkittsnevis.net, www.stkitts-tourism.com, www.nevisisland.com
www.nevis1.com
St Lucia www.stlucia.org, www.stlucia.com
St-Martin/Sint Maarten www.stmartinstmaarten.com, www.st-martin.org
www.antilles-info-tourisme.com, www.st-maarten.com
St Vincent and the Grenadines www.svgtourism.com, www.vincy.com,
www.grenadines.net
Sint Eustatius www.statiatourism.com, www.netherlandsantilles.com/sinteustatius
Trinidad and Tobago www.visittnt.com, www.tidco.co.tt, www.discovertrinidad.com
Turks and Caicos Islands www.turksandcaicostourism.com
www.tcimall.tc, www.turksandcaicos.tc, www.wherewhenhow.com
US Virgin Islands www.usvi.net, www.usvitourism.vi
Venezuelan Islands www.terra.com.ve, www.auyantepuy.com
www.margaritaonline.com, www.islamargarita.com

Essentials

Finding out more

Each country has its own website, listed in the relevant chapter in this Handbook and in the box, page 20. In addition, the *Caribbean Tourism Organization* (CTO) has an umbrella site with links to individual islands: **www.caribtourism.com**, **www.onecaribbean.org**, or **www.doitcaribbean.com** Useful general websites and search engines for the Caribbean include **www.caribbean-on-line.com**, which has maps of most countries and cities.

Tourist information on the web

Language

In the majority of cases, **English** is widely spoken and understood. In the French Antilles and Haiti, **French** is the main language. However, in these last, and on English islands which at one time belonged to France, **Creole** is spoken. The population is bilingual, so on English islands the English-speaking traveller will have no problems with communication and on the French islands, knowledge of French is of great benefit. The Netherlands Antilles speak **Dutch**, English and **Papiamento**. English and **Spanish** are both spoken on Puerto Rico. The principal language in the Dominican Republic, Cuba and the Venezuelan islands is Spanish. If visiting non-English islands, a basic knowledge of the main language is an advantage. Language courses in Spanish, plus volunteer programmes and travel advice, are run in Puerto Rico and the Dominican Republic by *AmeriSpan Unlimited*, PO Box 58129, Philadelphia, PA 19106-0007, USA, T215-7511100, (1-800-8796640 in USA and Canada), www.amerispan.com Other courses are available with other companies in those islands and the universities run programmes in Cuba.

Disabled travellers

Pick your hotel carefully. The large, modern hotels will usually have a couple of specially adapted rooms to meet the needs of wheelchair users, but smaller hotels do not. It is worth checking whether the whole hotel is wheelchair friendly, or whether you will have to make a long detour to get to the restaurant or beach to avoid steps. Most activities are designed for able-bodied participants, but there are a few dive operators who will take you underwater, such as in the Cayman Islands. Transport also has to organized well in advance so that you can get a vehicle which is wheelchair accessible. One taxi company offering this service is *Dial-A-Ride* in St Thomas, T(340)7761277, F7775383. Streets and pavements can be difficult to negotiate as they are often made with storm drains. Potholes and loose paving stones compound the difficulties. However, don't be discouraged, disabled people have been travelling around the Caribbean for years, see *Touch the Happy Isles* by Quentin Crewe, for a first-hand account.

Gay and lesbian travellers

Several islands have in the past been homophobic, such as Cuba, where homosexuals were sent to labour camps to be 'rehabilitated' after the Revolution. However, times have changed and the

Essentials

tourist dollar is king. Although Grand Cayman turned away a gay cruise ship a few years ago, gay couples are accepted in hotels. Several hotels are openly gay friendly, such as *On the Beach* in St Croix and *Delfina* in St Maarten, but most prefer discretion and no open displays of affection. In 2003 *Sandals* hit the news when it became clear that their Couples resorts were for heterosexuals only, but the company declared that gays and lesbians were welcome at their other resorts.

Student travellers

International Student Identity Card (ISIC) If you are in full-time education you will be entitled to an ISIC, which is distributed by student travel offices and travel agencies in 77 countries. The ISIC gives you special prices on all forms of transport (air, sea, rail, etc), and access to a variety of other concessions and services. If you need to find the location of your nearest ISIC office contact: The ISIC Association, Herengracht 479, 1017 BS Amsterdam, Holland T+31-20-4212800, www.istc.org

Women travellers

Lots of women, including the author, travel around the Caribbean on their own or in pairs with no problems at all. However, you must be aware that men in many of the islands consider you fair game and there is the perception that you have travelled there specifically to find a gigolo. Hassling is unpleasant in Havana and a nuisance in the Dominican Republic, Jamaica and Tobago, but it can happen anywhere. Single women on the beach are a prime target. AIDS and sexually transmitted diseases are widespread and you will be taking an enormous risk if you go in for casual sex. A drink in a bar may seem harmless, but your new male friend may be expecting it to lead to something more and date rape is not unheard of. Make sure that someone knows where you are in case you don't come back. Do not disclose to strangers where you are staying.

Travelling with children

Some islands are more geared to children than others. Families are particularly welcome in Antigua, St Lucia and Barbados, but several exclusive resorts around the Caribbean limit the age of children allowed. Some of the all-inclusive resorts are geared towards couples and therefore kids are not accepted. At the cheaper end of the market there will be no restrictions. In the resort hotels there is a standard reduction for children or they go free if sharing a room with two adults. Several hotels offer kids' clubs which amuse the children all day and allow adults to go off and do their own thing. Babysitting services are usually available. If your children are young it might be best to pick a destination you can fly to direct, maybe flying on to a second island after a week when they have acclimatized. After a nine-hour transatlantic flight, children do not appreciate waiting for a connecting flight.

Food is not usually a problem as burgers, pizza, pasta or chicken and chips are available for fussy eaters. Bananas and avocados are safe, easy to eat and nutritious; they can be fed to young babies and most older children like them too. Buy what you can when you see it from farmers at the market or roadside stalls. If you are not in self-catering accommodation, there are many hotels with a kitchenette in the room so you can prepare snacks or light meals to fill a nagging hole. In restaurants you can ask for children's portions or divide one full-size helping between two children. It is advisable to take all your own baby food and nappies/diapers if travelling with babies, as in some islands, eg Cuba, you cannot rely on them being available.

Working in the Caribbean

For information on voluntary work and working abroad, try www.workingabroad.com, www.projecttrust.org.uk, www.gapyear.com. If you are looking for a paying job, visit the International Career and Employment Center, www.internationaljobs.org Cuba has over 1,600 solidarity organizations in some 120 countries, many of which organize work brigades, charity tours and donations of medical supplies and equipment to beat the US trade embargo. Try www.cubaconnect.co.uk, www.igc.apc.org/cubasoli, and www.global exchange.org For crewing in the Caribbean, see page 29, 32 and 38.

Exchange rates (June 2003)

Country	Currency	Abbreviation	Exchange Rate/US$
Anguilla	East Caribbean dollar	EC$	2.70
Antigua & Barbuda	East Caribbean dollar	EC$	2.70
Aruba	Aruban florin	Afl	1.79
Barbados	Barbados dollar	B$	2.00
Bonaire	Netherlands Antillies (NA) guilder	Naf	1.78
British Virgin Islands	US dollar	US$	1.00
Cayman Islands	Cayman dollar	CI$	1.22
Cuba	Cuban peso	$	1.00
		Market rate	25-30
Curaçao	NA guilder	Naf	1.78
Dominica	East Caribbean dollar	EC$	2.70
Dominican Rep	Dominican peso	RD$	30
Grenada	East Caribbean dollar	EC$	2.70
Guadeloupe	Euro	€	0.85
Haiti	Gourde		38.80
Jamaica	Jamaican dollar	J$	55.80
Martinique	Euro	€	0.85
Montserrat	East Caribbean dollar	EC$	2.70
Puerto Rico	US dollar	US$	1.00
Saba	NA guilder	Naf	1.78
St Barthélémy	Euro	€	0.85
St Kitts & Nevis	East Caribbean dollar	EC$	2.70
St Lucia	East Caribbean dollar	EC$	2.70
St Martin	Euro	€	0.85
St Vincent & the Grenadines	East Caribbean dollar	EC$	2.70
Sint Eustatius	NA guilder	Naf	1.78
Sint Maarten	NA guilder	Naf	1.78
Trinidad & Tobago	Trinidad dollar	TT$	6.13
Turks & Caicos	US dollar	US$	1.00
US Virgin Islands	US dollar	US$	1.00
Venezuela	Bolívar	Bs	1,600

Source:
www.oanda.com

See also Comparative cost of living table, page 26

Essentials

Before you travel

Getting in

North Americans, British and Commonwealth citizens in some cases need only show proof of identity, but it is always best to carry a **passport**. Immigration authorities are not keen on driver's licences or voter registration cards, even if technically they are adequate forms of identification. If you want to change travellers' cheques or hire a car you will need a passport anyway. If intending to visit Puerto Rico or the US Virgin Islands, or making connections through Miami or another US gateway, a **visa** for the United States will not be necessary if your home country and the airline on which you are travelling are part of the US Visa Waiver Program. A US consulate will supply all relevant details. Australians and New Zealanders should note that many islands impose strict entry laws on holders of the above passports. Satisfying visa and other requirements, if not done at home, can take at least a day, usually involve expense, and passport photographs will be needed: be prepared.

Documents
Individual island entry requirements are given in the relevant chapters under Essentials/ Touching down

▶ ## Comparative cost of living (US dollars)

Country	Coke in a bar	Beer/rum in a bar	Burger & chips
Antigua	1.10-2.00	2.25-3.00	3.00-7.50
Bonaire	1.50	2.00	4.00
Cuba	1.00	1.00	2.50
Cayman Islands	2.00	5.00	15.00
Dominica	0.50	0.60-1.20	4.50
Grenada	1.00	2.00-3.00	5.00-8.00
Guadeloupe	1.50	1.50	3.60-4.30
Haiti		1.00	2.00
Jamaica	0.75	1.75-2.00	3.75
Martinique	1.75	2.10	4.75
Montserrat	1.00-1.50	1.25-3.00	3.00-6.00
St Croix	1.80	2.50	7.50
St Kitts & Nevis	0.65-1.00	0.90-1.50	2.60-3.70
St Thomas	2.25	3.00	7.50
St Vincent & the Grenadines	0.40-0.75	1.15-2.00	3.00-9.50
Trinidad & Tobago	0.50-1.00	1.00-2.00	2.50-3.50
Turks & Caicos	1.50-3.00	3.50-6.00	7.50-9.50

On all forms, refer to yourself as a 'visitor' rather than a 'tourist'. If asked where you are staying and you have not booked in advance, say any hotel (they do not usually check), but do not say you are going to camp and do not say that you are going to arrange accommodation later.

Onward ticket Many islands insist that visitors have an air ticket to their home country before being allowed to enter; for non-US citizens travelling to the Caribbean from the USA, this means a ticket from the USA to their home country, not a ticket back to the USA. Tickets to other countries will not suffice. This becomes a problem if you are not going home for 12 months since airline tickets become void after a year. Some airlines sell tickets on the six- to 12-month extended payment plan; these can be credited when you have left the islands with restrictive entry requirements. Even if you propose to take some boat trips between islands, we recommend that you purchase flights in advance and refund those that have not been used later.

Passport You should carry your passport in a safe place about your person, or if not going far, leave it in the hotel safe. If staying in a place for several weeks, it is worth registering at your embassy or consulate. Then, if your passport is lost or stolen, it will be replaced quicker. It is also a good idea to keep photocopies of essential documents, as well as additional passport-sized photographs.

Insurance It's a very good idea to take out some form of travel insurance, wherever you're travelling from. This should cover you for theft or loss of possessions and money, the cost of medical and dental treatment, cancellation of flights, delays in travel arrangements, accidents, missed departures, lost baggage, lost passport and personal liability and legal expenses. Also check on inclusion of 'dangerous activities' such as climbing, diving, skiing, horse riding, even trekking, if you plan on doing any.

There are many insurance companies and policies to choose from, so it's best to shop around. Reputable student travel organizations often offer good value policies. Travellers from **North America** can try the *International Student Insurance Service* (ISIS), which is available through *STA*, T800-7770112, www.sta-travel.com Other recommended travel insurance companies include *Access America*, T800-2848300, *Travel Insurance Services*, T800-9371387, and *Council Travel*, T888-COUNCIL, www.counciltravel.com Companies

Daily special in a local restaurant/café	Local bus fare	Average salary/ month for Government worker	Average rent/ month on 1-2 bed-room apartment
7.50-15.00	1.00		
6.50	2.00	2,500	350-500
5.00-7.00	0.01	20	
15.00-20.00	2.50	6000	2500
3.75-9.25	1.10		
8.00	0.60		
6.50	1.00	715	285-360
3.00-5.00	5.00	0.25400-800	
4.25	0.45-0.65	800	175-375
7.00-8.50	0.90	750	285-500
3.50-7.00	0.75		
9.00	0.75-1.00	2,550	600
5.60-7.50	0.75	925	600-1,000
9.00	0.75-1.00	2,550	600
2.75-7.75	0.50	350	150
3.00-4.00	0.60	700	150-1,850
12.00	1.00	1,125	750-1,000

worth trying in **Britain** include *Direct Line*, T0845-2468744, directline.com, the *Flexicover Group*, T0870 990 9292, www.flexicover.net.uk, and *Columbus*, T020-7375 0011. Note that some companies will not cover those over 65. The best policies for older travellers are offered by *Age Concern*, T01883 346964.

What to take

High factor sun tan lotion, a hat and sunglasses are essential ingredients in anyone's suitcase. Mosquito repellent is also necessary at certain times of the year, or if there has been rain, but this is often provided wherever you are staying. It can even be found on the bar to accompany your sunset cocktail in that romantic outdoor location so loved by biting insects. Other useful items (which may or may not be available locally) are tampons, condoms and other contraceptives, disposable nappies if taking babies, reading and writing materials (bookshops are few and far between) photographic supplies, a torch and batteries. Lightweight clothing is adequate during the day but at night, especially up in the hills or in air-conditioned restaurants, a cover up is needed. All your medical requirements should be taken with you, see Health, page 48.

Money

Cost of visiting
Happy hours in bars often have free food; couples sharing costs can take advantage of Ladies' Night in bars or nightclubs, with free entry or cheap drinks

The Caribbean is not a cheap area to visit. Transport is expensive (unless you are staying in one place and using only buses), but if you book your flights in advance, taking advantage of whatever air pass or stopovers are suitable, that expenditure at least will be out of the way.

Accommodation is generally expensive, too, even at the lower end of the market. In a number of instances you can book all-inclusive packages which are often good value and let you know in advance almost exactly what your expenditure will be. However, you will not see much of your chosen island outside your enclave and organized excursions can be costly. To find cheaper accommodation you need mobility, probably a hired car. One option is renting a self-catering apartment, villa or house, the range of which is also vast, and here the advantage is that a group of people can share the cost (not so economical for single travellers).

Currency In general, the US dollar is the best currency to take, in cash or travellers' cheques. The latter are convenient and can be replaced if lost or stolen. On the most frequently visited holiday islands, euros and sterling can be exchanged without difficulty but at a poor rate, and US dollars are preferred. In some places, the US dollar is accepted alongside local currency (but make sure in which currency prices are being quoted). In others, only the local currency is accepted. On the French islands dollars are accepted, but the euro is the preferred currency. Credit cards are widely used. Remember to keep your money, credit cards, etc, safely on your person, or in a hotel safe. If your guesthouse has no safe in which to store money, passport, tickets, etc, try local banks.

Some peoplle recommend setting up two bank accounts before travelling. One has all your funds but no debit card; the other has no funds but does have a debit card. As you travel, use the internet to transfer money from the full account to the empty account when you need it and withdraw cash from an ATM. That way, if your debit card is stolen, you won't be at risk of losing all your capital. Also, by using a debit card rather than a credit card you incur fewer bank charges.

Getting there

Air

Airlines
See individual islands for major airlines flying to each one

In addition to the scheduled flights listed, there are a great many charter flights from Europe and North America. For details on both types of service, you are advised to consult a good travel agent. An agent will also be able to tell you if you qualify for any student or senior citizen discount on offer. From the USA, Puerto Rico and Antigua are the only islands to which student fares are available; it is worth checking these out since it may be cheaper to take a student flight then continue to your destination rather than flying direct to the island of your choice. If buying tickets routed through the USA, check that US taxes are included in the price. At certain times of the year, *Air France* have flights at very advantageous prices from several southern French cities and Paris to Guadeloupe and Martinique. *Air France* flights can also be combined with *Liat* air passes.

Baggage allowance Airlines will only allow a certain weight of luggage without a surcharge; this is normally 30 kg for first class and 20 kg for business and economy classes, but these limits may not be strictly enforced if the plane is not going to be full. *JMC Airways* (year-round charter from the UK) allows 40 kg, which is very popular with travellers visiting friends and relatives in the Caribbean. Weight limits for inter-island flights are often much lower; it is best to enquire beforehand. If you are transferring to a smaller plane for the second leg of your journey, you may find your luggage gets left behind and put on a later, less-crowded flight the next day.

Airline websites

ACES www.acescolombia.com
Aeropostal www.aeropostal.com
Air Canada www.aircanada.ca
Air Caraïbes www.st-barths.com/
     air-caraibes/index.html
Air France www.airfrance.com
Air Jamaica www.airjamaica.com
Air Lib (Air Liberté AOM) www.air-liberte.fr
Air Santo Domingo
     www.airsantodomingo.com
American Airlines www.aa.com
American Eagle www3.aa.com
Avianca www.avianca.com.co
British Airways www.british-airways.com
BWIA www.bwee.com
Caribbean Star Airlines
     www.flycaribbeanstar.com

Cayman Airways www.caymanairways.com
Condor www.condor.de
Continental Airlines www.continental.com
Copa www.copaair.com
Cubana www.cubana.cu
Delta www.delta-air.com
Dutch Caribbean
Airline/Express www.flydce.com
Iberia www.iberia.com
JMC www.jmc.com
KLM www.klm.com
Liat www.liatairline.com
Martinair www.martinair.de
Sky King www.skyking.tc
United Airlines www.ual.com
US Airways www.usairways.com
Virgin Atlantic www.virgin-atlantic.com

Essentials

Sea

Cruise lines & cargo ships

The most popular way of visiting the Caribbean by ship is on a cruise liner. It is possible to break your journey for a few days if you want to stay on an island but you will have to check with the company to see whether they can pick you up later. There are also sailing cruisers (eg the Windjammer and Star Clipper fleets) which allow flexible itineraries for cruising between the islands. *Windjammer Barefoot Cruises*, which operates five tall-masted ships (*Flying Cloud*, British Virgin Islands; *Legacy*, US and British Virgin Islands; *Mandalay* Leeward and Windward Islands; *Polynesia*, French West Indies; *Yankee Clipper*, Grenadines) and a supply ship (*Amazing Grace*), can be contacted direct in Florida, T305-6726453, www.windjammer.com The supply ship, MV *Amazing Grace*, sails every month from West Palm Beach, picking up southbound passengers in Freeport, Bahamas and visiting lots of islands as it meets up with the *Windjammer* tall ships, delivering monthly supplies, before turning round in Trinidad after two weeks and stopping at different ports from the southbound trip.

For cargo ships carrying passengers, it is recommended that you enquire in your own country. In general, it is very difficult to secure a passage on a cargo ship from Europe to the Caribbean without making full arrangements in advance. Round trips are easier to organize than one-way passages, although some companies are now offering a flight home. Fares range from about US$70-130 per person per day, cheaper than a passenger cruise, but without the continuous entertainment. **In the UK** Full details on this type of travel are available from *Strand Voyages*, London, T020-78366363, www.strandtravel.co.uk; *Cargo Ship Voyages Ltd*, Hemley, Woodbridge, Suffolk, IP12 4QF, T/F01473-736265. **In Europe**, *SGV Reisezentrum Weggis* Switzerland, T041-390 1133, www.reisezentrum-weggis.ch In the USA, contact *Freighter World Cruises*, T800-5317774, 626- 4493106, www.freighter world.com, or *Traveltips Cruise and Freighter Association*, T800-8728584, 718-0302400, www. travltips.com **On the web** www.contship.de, or the *Internet Guide to Freighter Travel*, **www.geocities.com/freighterman.geo/ mainmenu.html** Other websites are **www.freighter-cruises.com, www.navigator.com, www.atwtraveler.com/frei-fac.htm, http://members@aol.com/CruiseAZ/freighters.htm** *Reed Travel Group*, Dunstable, Bedfordshire LU5 4HB, UK, T0582-600111, publishes the *ABC Passenger Shipping Guide*, a monthly list of companies offering freighter transport for passengers.

Yacht crewing

For those with 1,000 miles offshore sailing experience, a cheap way to get to the Caribbean is crewing on a yacht being delivered from Europe or the USA to the region.

▶ ### How big is your Footprint?

Where possible choose a destination, tour operator or hotel with a proven ethical and environmental commitment; if in doubt, ask.

Spend money on locally produced (rather than imported) goods and services and use common sense when bargaining, your few dollars saved may be a week's salary to someone else.

Use water and electricity carefully, travellers may receive preferential supply while the needs of local communities are overlooked.

Learn about local etiquette and culture, consider local norms of behaviour and dress appropriately for local cultures and situations,   for example, while dress tends to

be casual, bathing suits are for the beach only; it is very offensive to locals to see bare chests and bellies, so cover up.

Protect wildlife and other natural resources: don't buy souvenirs or goods made from wildlife unless they are sustainably produced and are not protected under CITES legislation (CITES controls trade in endangered species).

Always ask before taking photographs or videos of people.

Consider staying in local accommodation rather than foreign-owned hotels, the economic benefits for host communities are far greater and there are ,many more opportunities to learn about local culture.

Touching down

Responsible travel

Travel to the furthest corners of the globe is now commonplace and the mass movement of people for leisure and business is a major source of foreign exchange and economic development in many parts of the Caribbean. In many areas it is the most significant economic activity.

The benefits of international travel are self-evident for both hosts and travellers: employment; increased understanding of different cultures; business and leisure opportunities. At the same time there is clearly a downside to the industry. Where visitor pressure is high and/or poorly regulated, adverse impacts to society and the natural environment may be apparent. Paradoxically, this is as true in undeveloped and pristine areas (where culture and the natural environment are less 'prepared' for visitors) as in major resort destinations.

The travel industry is growing rapidly and increasingly the impacts of this supposedly 'smokeless' industry are becoming apparent. These impacts can seem remote and unrelated to an individual trip or holiday (for example air travel is clearly implicated in global warming and damage to the ozone layer, resort location and construction can destroy natural habitats and restrict traditional rights and activities), but individual choice and awareness can make a difference in many instances, and collectively, travellers are having a significant effect in shaping a more responsible and sustainable industry.

In an attempt to promote awareness of and credibility for responsible tourism, organizations such as **Green Globe** (UK), T44-020-79308333, greenglobe@compuserve.com, and the **Centre for Environmentally Sustainable Tourism (CERT)** (UK), T44-1268-795772, now offer advice on destinations and sites that have achieved certain commitments to conservation and sustainable development. Generally these are larger mainstream destinations and resorts, but they are still a useful guide and increasingly aim to provide information on smaller operations.

Of course travel can have beneficial impacts and this is something to which every traveller can contribute. Many national parks are part funded by receipts from visitors. Similarly, travellers can promote patronage and protection of important archaeological sites and heritage through their interest and contributions via entrance and performance fees. They can also support small-scale enterprises by staying in locally run hotels and hostels, eating in local restaurants and by purchasing local goods, supplies and arts and crafts.

Since the early 1990s there has been a phenomenal growth in tourism that promotes and supports the conservation of natural environments and is also fair and equitable to local communities. This 'ecotourism' segment is probably the fastest-growing sector of the travel industry and provides a vast and growing range of destinations and activities in the Caribbean. While the authenticity of some ecotourism operators claims need to be interpreted with care, there is clearly both a huge demand for this type of activity and also significant opportunities to support worthwhile conservation and social development initiatives.

Organizations such as **Conservation International**, T001-202-4295660, www.ecotour.org, **The Eco-Tourism Society**, T001-802-4472121, http://ecotourism.org, **Planeta**, www.planeta.com, and **Tourism Concern**, T44-20-77533330, www.tourismconcern.org.uk, have begun to develop and/or promote ecotourism projects and destinations, and their websites are an excellent source of information and details for sites and initiatives throughout Latin America and the Caribbean. Additionally, organizations such as **Earthwatch**, T44-1865-311601, www.earthwatch.org, and **Discovery International**, T44-20-72299881, www.discoveryinitiatives.com, offer opportunities to participate directly in scientific research and development projects throughout the region.

The Caribbean offers unforgettable experiences – often based on the natural environment, cultural heritage and local society. These are the reasons many of us choose to travel and why many more will want to do so in the future. Shouldn't we provide an opportunity for future travellers and hosts to enjoy the quality of experience and interaction that we take for granted?

Where to stay

Your budget is likely to be the key determining factor in where you stay, but this will stretch further in some islands than others. The codes used in this book are for the price of a double room (rack rate) and take no account of the facilities offered. In some places a hotel in category **B** will be clean and simple, but in others it will represent the height of luxury. In many islands there are no hotels at all in the **F** category and those in **E** will be hard to find, often only on special offer. Youth hostels are non-existent, while camping is not a viable option in general although some islands, such as Puerto Rico or the French Antilles, have well-organized campsites; however, on many islands camping is actually forbidden.

See inside front cover for hotel price guide and guide to abbreviations used in listings

The cheapest accommodation can be found in guesthouses, small, privately run establishments which sometimes offer breakfast but do not rely on a full restaurant service. Many of these are not registered with the local tourist office and therefore difficult to find until you get there. They may be perfectly adequate if you are not very demanding, or they may be flea pits. You will soon find out why they have been left off the list.

Turning up at a cheaper place may not always yield a room because competition is great. Note also that, if booking ahead, tourist office lists may not include the cheapest establishments, so you may have to reserve one or two nights at a mid-price hotel for when you arrive and then ask around for cheaper accommodation if that is what you want. The longer you stay the better deal you will get, so negotiation is recommended. Remember also that high season runs from mid-December to mid-April and everything is more expensive then as well as being more heavily booked. The best deals can be found in – you guessed it – hurricane season.

The Dominican Republic and Cuba have the most hotel rooms in the Caribbean, so there is no real problem in finding a space there. The most popular form of accommodation for independent travellers in Cuba is to stay with a registered family in their home, a *casa particular*. In Havana they cost around US$25-30, but elsewhere they are about US$15-20. Food and lodging with families is far better value and much more rewarding than staying in a hotel, although it is not legal in the beach resorts of Varadero of Guardalavaca.

In Jamaica there are places costing less than US$20 but they are not to be recommended, the **E** range is more possible and **D** will be comfortable. Haiti is surprisingly expensive with most of the guesthouses charging rates in our **B-C** range unless you get right off the beaten track. The Dominican Republic, on the other hand, has a far greater range and **E-F** hotels can be found in fairly decent areas, although not beachfront properties. In the eastern Caribbean cheap places can be found in the **D-E** ranges in the capital cities, from where you can use public transport to get out to beaches and places of interest, but you will have to pay more if you want to be on the beach. Further south, Trinidad and Tobago have lots of good value places to stay, either in town or close to the beach, while Margarita is also relatively cheap.

Essentials

We assume that most of our readers are not interested in the all-inclusive resorts, although we include details of a few, partly to alert you if they predominate, such as in Ocho Rios in Jamaica or Playa Dorada in the Dominican Republic. We also include the super-luxury hotels, although we do realise that few will be able to afford Richard Branson's Necker Island at US$14,000 a day. Some, however, are within range for a special occasion, such as a honeymoon, and our **LL** range takes in everything from US$200 a night up to the stars.

Getting around

Air

The most extensive links between islands are by air, either with the scheduled flights on the regional and international carriers, or by chartered plane. If you are in a group, or family, the latter option may not cost very much more than a scheduled flight. It often has the advantage of linking the charter direct to your incoming or homeward flight.

Air passes
The regional carriers with most routes in the Caribbean are LIAT (headquarters in Antigua), BWIA (based in Trinidad), Caribbean Star (in St Kitts), and Air Jamaica (in Montego Bay)

LIAT has two passes called *Explorer tickets*: the *LIAT Explorer* costs US$300, valid for 21 days, maximum three stops between San Juan, Puerto Rico and Trinidad; the *LIAT Super Explorer* costs US$575 for a 30-day ticket, allowing unlimited stop overs in 18 destinations between San Juan and Caracas and Georgetown as well (do not overload your itinerary, a lot of time can be spent waiting at airports for flights). *LIAT* also operates an *Airpass* in which each flight costs US$98, valid for 21 days; minimum three stop overs, maximum six. These tickets may only be issued in conjunction with an international flight to a Caribbean gateway, the itinerary must be settled in advance, with no changes permitted, and no child discounts. A specialist travel agency may be able to book a return ticket with stopovers cheaper than the airpass, so it is worth enquiring. *LIAT's* phone number on Antigua is T268-4805600, or F4805625.

Try to book *LIAT* flights as far in advance as possible; planes are not large and fill up quickly. A golden rule when flying with *LIAT*: just because you are *not* booked on a flight it does not mean you will not get on (be patient and sweet-talking); just because you *are* booked on a flight it does not mean you will get on (never be last in the queue). Note also that *LIAT* is in financial difficulties and travel companies are warning clients that there can be no refunds once a ticket is issued, some also charge a booking fee. The airline is in negotiations to merge with *BWIA*.

Note that one-way tickets are hard to organize if you have not booked all your flights in advance. For instance if your transatlantic flight is to Barbados and back from Guadeloupe, *LIAT* will not let you buy (in Barbados) a ticket to St Lucia and will force you to buy the portion from St Lucia to Guadeloupe even if you are intending to take the ferry. Refunds are predictably hard to obtain as processing is done in Antigua.

BWIA's Caribbean airpass (Central House, Lampton Rd, Hounslow, Middlesex, London TW3 1HY, T0208 577 1100) covers all its destinations including Caracas and Paramaribo, but if you want to include any stop west of and including Kingston, Jamaica, it will cost more. A first-class unlimited mileage pass is US$750 (US$900 including Jamaica) and the economy pass is US$450 (US$550). There is a four-day pass for US$350 (US$450), but can only be bought in the UK, Europe, New Zealand and Australia. You can have any number of stopovers, but nowhere may be visited more than once, except for making a connection and the entire journey must be fixed at the time of payment (changes are subject to a US$25 surcharge); dates may be left open. This airpass is valid for 30 days, no refunds are given for unused sectors. It may not be used between 19 December and 6 January. *BWIA* also has a frequent flyer scheme for accumulating air miles.

Sea

Departure tax is payable on leaving each island; make sure you know what this is in advance

Island-hopping by boats with scheduled services is fairly limited. Boat services are more common between dependent islands, eg St Vincent and the Grenadines, Trinidad and Tobago. Again, full details are given in the relevant sections below. There are also good connections by sea in the French Antilles and with their neighbours, Dominica and St Lucia.

L'Express des Îles has a daily car ferry service between Fort-de-France and Pointe-à-Pitre and a high speed catamaran passenger ferry service five days a week between Martinique, Guadeloupe, Dominica and St Lucia. There are family rates, child, youth and senior citizen discounts and package deals. Remember that port taxes must be added for all destinations: www.whitchurch.com/express.htm or www.martinique.org/transportation.htm

Irregular passenger services on cargo boats (with basic accommodation, usually a hammock on deck, no meals supplied), schooners, crewing or hitching on yachts can only be discovered by asking around when you are in port. Crewing on yachts is not difficult in winter (in the hurricane season yachtsmen stay away). If you are looking for a job on a yacht, or trying to hitch a ride, it will be easier to make contact if you are living at the yacht harbour. Boat owners often advertise bunks for rent, which is a very cheap form of accommodation (US$10-30); ask around, or look on the bulletin boards. If arriving by sea, make sure you are aware of the island's entry requirements before setting out.

Essentials

Land

Bus Buses are cheap, but services tend not to be very convenient, and often involve a night away from the point of departure, even on small islands. This is because buses start in outlying towns in the early morning and return from the capital in the afternoon. Many smaller islands do not even have a bus service. The larger islands, such as Cuba, the Dominican Republic and Jamaica have good, long-distance services between major towns although outlying areas are usually served by minivans or *colectivos*.

Car hire Renting a car gives the greatest flexibility, but is also hardest on the pocket. You can expect to pay more than in the USA or Europe. A number of islands require drivers to take out a temporary, or visitor driver's licence (these are mentioned in the text). Some places will not issue a licence to those over 70 without a medical certificate. The minimum age for rental is usually 25. In small places, renting a motorcycle, scooter or bicycle is a good idea.

Taxi Taxis are plentiful, but generally not cheap. Some islands, eg Trinidad, have route taxis, which are inexpensive and travel only on set routes. On many islands, taxi fares are set by the tourist office or government.

Train Cuba is the only country in the Caribbean with a passenger rail service. St Kitts has a scenic railway using the sugar industry network, which runs in a circular route around the island.

Maps *See also Walking, page 44* An excellent source of maps is *Stanfords*, 12-14 Long Acre, Covent Garden, London WC2, T020-78361321, as well as 29 Corn St, Bristol, BS1, and 39 Spring Gardens, Manchester, M2, www.stanfords.co.uk

Keeping in touch

Post There are post offices in all the main towns but you can often buy stamps in hotels. Islands like Montserrat, the Cayman Islands and Nevis pride themselves on their philatelic issues, which are collectors' items. Postal service is not very efficient and for sending packages or parcels a courier service is recommended for speed and security.

Telephone, fax & internet Many airport lounges and phone companies in the region have *AT&T*'s USA Direct phones by which the USA and Canada may be called using a charge card (which bills your home phone account), or by calling collect. The service is not available to Europe, but the *BT* chargecard, for example, can be used on many of the islands (check with your phone company). Public card phones have been introduced by *Cable and Wireless* on those islands where it operates. This company offers discounts on evening rates for IDD calls from cardphones: 1800-2300 15%, 2300-0500 40%. Discounts do not apply to credit card calls (1-800-877-8000). Phone cards come in several denominations, with a tax added, and can be useful for local and international calls, as you avoid the extra charges made by hotels. Most countries have now cybercafés and the number is expanding all the time. Many hotels have business centres with terminals which can be used by their guests and are often open to the public. Often the local telephone office or post office will have a terminal you can use to send emails, but don't rely on it actually working.

Food and drink

As you might expect of islands, there is a wide variety of seafood on offer which is fresh and tasty and served in a multitude of ways. Fish of all sorts, lobster and conch are commonly available and are usually better quality than local meat. Beef and lamb are often imported from the USA or Argentina, but goat, pork and chicken are produced locally. There is no dairy industry to speak of, so cheeses are also usually imported. There is, however, a riot of tropical fruit and vegetables and a visit to a local market will give you the opportunity to see unusual and often unidentifiable objects as well as more familiar items found in supermarkets in Europe and North America but with ten times the flavour. The best bananas in the world are grown in the Caribbean on small farms using the minimum of chemicals, if not organic. They are cheap and incredibly sweet and unlike anything you can buy at home. Many of the wonderful tropical fruits you will come across in juices or in ice cream. Don't miss the rich flavours of the soursop, the guava or the sapodilla. Mangoes in season drip off the trees and those that don't end up on your breakfast plate can be found squashed in abundance all over the roads. Caribbean oranges are often green when ripe, as there is no cold season to bring out the orange colour, and are meant for juicing not peeling. Portugals are like tangerines and easy to peel. Avocados are nearly always sold unripe, so wait several days before attempting to eat. Avocado trees also provide a surplus of fruit and you will be doing everyone a favour if you eat as many as possible. Avocados have been around since the days of the Arawaks, who also cultivated cassava and cocoa, but many vegetables have their origins in the slave trade, brought over to provide a starchy diet for the slaves. The breadfruit, a common staple rich in carbohydrates and vitamins A, B and C, was brought from the South Seas in 1793 by Captain Bligh, perhaps more famous for the mutiny on the *Bounty*. The slaves were needed for work in the sugar plantations and sugar cane is still grown on some islands today, often ending up as rum, see box opposite.

Restaurants range from gourmet to cafés and all make the most of local ingredients. If you are economizing, find a local place and choose the daily special, which will give you a chance to try the typical food. See our Comparative cost of living table, page 26, for what you might expect to pay on each island. Fast food is also available, but you will be better off going to a local place serving chicken and chips or burgers, rather than the international chains. Trinidad has some of the best food around, drawing on the cultures of its many immigrants: Indian, African, Chinese, Syrian, etc, and fast food there is almost an art form. The *roti*, a thin chapatti wrap filled with spicy or curried meat, fish or vegetables is hugely popular and its success has spread to many other islands. Each island has its own specialities and these are described in the following chapters.

Top rum cocktails - author's addictions

There is nothing better at the end of a busy day than finding a pleasant spot overlooking the sea with a rum in your hand to watch the sunset and look out for the green flash. The theory is that the more rum you drink, the more likely you are to see this flash of green on the horizon as the sun goes down.

There are hundreds of different rums in the Caribbean, each island producing the best, of course. The main producers are Jamaica, Cuba, Barbados, Guyana, Martinique and the Dominican Republic, but other islands such as Grenada also produce excellent brands. The Bacardí family, the most important firm in Cuba for 100 years, no longer distils rum in Cuba, having moved to Puerto Rico and worldwide after the Revolution. Generally, the younger, light rums are used in cocktails and aged, dark rums are drunk on the rocks or treated as you might a single malt whisky. Cocktails first became popular after the development of ice-making in the USA in 1870, but boomed in the 1920s partly because of prohibition in the USA and the influx of visitors to Cuba, the Bahamas and other islands, escaping stringent regulations. People have been drowning their rum in cola ever since the Americans brought bottled drinks in to Cuba during the war against Spain at the end of the 19th century, hence the name, **Cuba Libre**. You can in fact adapt any cocktail recipe to substitute other spirits and incorporate rum. It makes an excellent **Bloody Mary**, the spicier the better.

One of the nicest and most refreshing cocktails is a **Daiquirí**, invented in Santiago de Cuba in 1898 by an engineer in the Daiquirí mines. The natural version combines 1½ tablespoons of sugar, the juice of half a lime, some drops of maraschino liqueur, 1½ oz light dry rum and a lot of shaved ice, all mixed in a blender and then served piled high in a wide,

chilled champagne glass with a straw. You can also have fruit versions, with strawberry, banana, peach or pineapple, using fruit or fruit liqueur.

Another Cuban favourite, drinkable at any time of the day or night, is the **Mojito**, once popular with Ernest Hemingway and his friends in Havana. Put half a tablespoon of sugar, the juice of half a lime and some lightly crushed mint leaves in a tall glass. Stir and mix well, then add some soda water, ice cubes, 1½ oz light dry rum and top up with soda water to taste. Garnish with mint leaves and serve with a straw.

Everybody has heard of the old favourite, **Piña Colada**, which can be found on all the islands and is probably the most popular of the fruit-based cocktails, ideal by the side of the pool. Combine and blend coconut liqueur, pineapple juice, light dry rum and shaved ice, then serve with a straw in a glass, a pineapple or a coconut.

Many Caribbean hotels offer you a welcome cocktail when you stagger out of the taxi, jet-lagged from your transatlantic flight. This is often an over-sweet, watered-down punch, with a poor quality rum and sickly fruit juice. You are more likely to find something palatable in the bar, but it always depends on which blend of juice the barman favours. In Grenada, **rum punch** is improved enormously with the addition of nutmeg sprinkled on top. The standard recipe for a rum punch is: 'one of sour, two of sweet, three of strong and four of weak'. If you measure that in fluid ounces, it comes out as 1 oz of lime juice, 2 oz of syrup (equal amounts of sugar and water, boiled for a few minutes), 3 oz of rum and 4 oz of water, fruit juices, ginger ale, or whatever takes your fancy. You could add ice and a dash of Angostura bitters from Trinidad, use nutmeg syrup from Grenada or Falernum from Barbados instead of sugar syrup, and garnish it with a slice of lime. Delicious!

Essentials

Festivals

Every island celebrates Carnival in some form or other, mostly as a pre-lenten event, but several countries schedule it for later in the year, partly to spread out the revelries. The biggest and best Carnival is in Trinidad, famous for its music and parades with lavish costumes and more spontaneity than its rival in Rio. For a full description and how to take part, see page 757. The common theme of all the carnivals is the masquerade, where masked and elaborately costumed dancers 'rush' through the streets, usually in the early hours of the morning on 'J'ouvert', Carnival Monday. Their disguises can be traced back to legends from Africa and colonial times and vary from country to country depending on their own histories. In the Dominican Republic they dress up as devils, piglets or bulls, with battles between rival factions, while in Carriacou, in the Grenadines, they celebrate Shakespeare Mas, where masked characters from Shakespeare's plays recite long speeches until they forget their lines and are beaten over the head by their rivals.

Even if you are not around for Carnival, you are sure to catch some other festivity. Each town celebrates its patron saint's day, often with a street party incorporating traditional food and drink, music and dance. There are several music festivals throughout the year, jazz being particularly popular in the eastern Caribbean, although Barbados stands out for offering an opera season. Regattas and all sorts of sailing activities inevitably end in parties and associated events in which visitors are welcome to participate.

Sport and activities

Information on sport is given under each island, but for those visiting the former British colonies, British dependencies and even the US Virgin Islands, an understanding of **cricket** is an advantage. It is more than a national game, having become a symbol of achievement and a unifying factor. Spectating at a match is entertaining both for the cricket itself and for the conversation that arises. **Baseball** and **basketball** serve much the same function in the Dominican Republic, Cuba and Puerto Rico, and if you are interested in the game, or just want to watch the crowd, it is worth finding out in advance about when the season is.

Watersports

See individual islands for detailed information

The crystal clear waters of the sunny Caribbean combined with the constant northeast trade winds make the islands a paradise for watersports enthusiasts. The great increase in tourism in the area has brought a corresponding development and every conceivable watersport is now available. Some of the best islands to head for are Barbados, Jamaica, Antigua, Martinique, the Bahamas, Cayman Islands, Puerto Rico and the Virgin Islands. On these islands you can find hobie-cats and sunfishes for rent, windsurfing, waterskiing, glass-bottomed boats plying the reefs, charter yachts and booze cruises, scuba diving, snorkelling and deap-sea fishing. Prices for such watersports vary from island to island and often increase by about 30% in the peak tourist season (December to April). It is worth knowing that prices can often be reduced for regular or long-term rentals and that bargaining with individual beach operators is definitely worth trying.

Swimming If all you want is sea and sand, these abound on nearly every island. The coral islands have the white postcard-perfect beaches and some of the islands of the Grenadines are nothing more than this. Swimming is safe on almost all Caribbean coasts, but do be careful on the exposed Atlantic coasts in the east where waves are big at times and currents rip. Swimming in the Atlantic can be dangerous and in some places it is actually forbidden.

Waterskiing This is widely available in developed resort areas and beginners are looked after well. If you are a serious waterskier it is worth bringing your own slalom ski as many boats only cater for beginners.

Surfing Good breaks for surfing and boogey-boarding can be found on the north shores of Puerto Rico, the Dominican Republic, Tobago and in Barbados. In both Puerto Rico and Barbados, custom- made surfboards can be bought and several competitions are organized every year. There are several good surf spots in Puerto Rico and the most consistent break in Barbados is at Bathsheba. In the Dominican Republic and Tobago, the sport is less developed. Waves tend to be bigger and more consistent in winter.

Fishing Sportfishing is excellent in many of the islands of the North Caribbean. Almost every variety of deep-sea game fish: marlin, swordfish, tuna, mackerel and dorado abound in the waters. In the reefs and shallows there are big barracuda, tarpon and bonefish. There are areas for all methods of fishing: surf fishing, bottom fishing or trolling. Spearfishing, however, is banned in many islands. Although most fish seem to run between November and March, there is no real off-season in most islands and local captains will know where to find the best fishing grounds.

Fishermen should beware of eating large predators (eg grand barracuda) and other fish which accumulate the ciguatera toxin

Cricket in the Caribbean

Test matches in the Caribbean are played, to date, in five countries: Jamaica, Barbados, Guyana, Trinidad and Antigua. Other first-class and one-day matches may be played in some of the smaller islands, part of either the Windward Islands or Leeward Islands teams, such as Grenada, Dominica, St Lucia, St Vincent, St Kitts and Nevis or Anguilla. The 2007 Cricket World Cup is to be held in the West Indies and work is being done to upgrade cricket facilities in traditional, yet out-of-date, venues. The six first-class teams are: Jamaica, Trinidad and Tobago, Barbados, Guyana, Windward Islands and Leeward Islands. Antigua is hoping to play separately from the Leeward Islands at some time in the future.

Large numbers of visitors go to the Caribbean to watch international matches. Book accommodation well in advance, particularly in Antigua. Note that it frequently rains in Guyana and that Barbados is expensive.

Huge and more relaxed entertainment can also be enjoyed by going to inter-island matches. Currently the one-day competition is being played before Christmas; it has suffered a lot of disruption from rain and this might not be the best time to go. The four-day competition, currently called the BUSTA Cup, runs from January to March. Unless West Indies are on tour at the time all the international players are required to play in the competition, so the standard is high.

Information about international matches can be obtained in the UK from the England and Wales Cricket Board (ECB), Lord's Cricket Ground, St John's Wood, London NW8 8QN, T020-74321200. However, finding out about the first-class matches between the islands is difficult. First ring the International Cricket Council (ICC), also at Lord's Cricket Ground (the Clock Tower) in London, T020-72661818, F020-72661777. They may give you the address and number of the West Indies Cricket Board which is based in Antigua. This is of little use, however, because the board does not answer letters and their number does not accept international calls! The best ploy is to ask someone at the ICC if they can help. (Don't ring up when a test match is being played.) They may give you the number of one of the local organizations, eg the Trinidad and Tobago or Windward Islands Board, or may even be prepared to ring themselves. If all else fails, a hotel or other organization in the Caribbean may be able to find out for you.

It is a lot of trouble but well worth it! Some useful websites for news, scores and statistics: www.caribbeancricket.com, www.windiescricket.com, http://uk.cricinfo.com, www.cwcricket.com (schedule for the Cable & Wireless Test Series, toll free West Indies ticket line 1-800-744-GAME).

Fishing is very well organized in such islands as Puerto Rico, especially in the area which has become known to the enthusiasts as Blue Marlin Alley. Fishing is also very good off the Cayman Islands, Jamaica and the US Virgin Islands. Hemingway made fishing off Cuba famous and it remains an exciting sport there. In many islands there are annual fishing tournaments open to all. Deep-sea fishing boats can be chartered for a half or full day and some are available on a weekly basis. Anglers can also pay individually on split charters. When arranging a charter, be careful to clarify all details in advance.

Exploring the Caribbean by boat has never been easier. New marinas and local communities near popular anchorages are catering to the increasing number of yachts which have made the Caribbean their home. The Caribbean islanders have coined the name 'yachties' to refer to those people who live and travel on their own boats as contrasted with those who visit the islands on their vacations on chartered boats, cruise ships or landbased resorts. While this information is directed toward the yachties, bareboat charterers will also find it useful.

Sailing
See individual islands for detailed information

From Europe to the Caribbean For boats crossing the Atlantic along the trade wind route, Barbados is the first landfall. Boats have the option of going on to Venezuela and Central America or through the Windward Islands of Grenada, St Vincent and the Grenadines. The Atlantic Rally for Cruisers offers support and entertainment for any sailors contemplating an Atlantic crossing. Departure is from Gran Canaria at the end of November and the yachts arrive in St Lucia to a warm welcome for Christmas.

From the USA to the Caribbean There are two routes from the USA to the Caribbean: from New England or Norfolk directly to the US Virgin Islands with the possibility of a stop in Bermuda; or island-hopping from Florida through the Bahamas across the 'Thornless Path' to windward described by Bruce Van Sant in his book *Passages South*. The Caribbean 1500 Rally organizes cruisers wishing to travel in a group to the Caribbean and depart from Newport, Rhode Island or Norfolk, Virginia, in late October arriving in St Thomas in the US Virgin Islands.

Ports of entry Arrive during weekday working hours to avoid overtime fees. Have the sun at your back to navigate through reefs, sand bars or other water hazards even if it means a midnight or late afternoon departure and an overnight sail. When making windward passages, overnight trips often mean lighter winds and seas.

Customs and immigration Yachties cross many countries and have to deal with more officials and procedures than tourists aboard cruise ships or travelling to resorts. No matter how many guidebooks are available, there will be at least one country with a change in procedures. Be careful to clear immigration on arrival as there are heavy fines for failing to do so. Plan to pay fees and to fill out paperwork in all countries. Occasionally, there are no fees. Different fees are often charged for charter boats and cruisers on their own boats who may wish to stay for a longer period of time.

Q Flag and courtesy flags Fly your 'Q' or quarantine flag until paperwork is completed. The captain should take ship's papers, passports and a list of the places you wish to stop and visit as in some countries you must be given specific clearance to stop and anchor. All crew should remain aboard until they have received clearance from the port authorities. Even though many of the islands are still a part of the British Commonwealth, they prefer to see their country's courtesy flag flown. (And fly it the right side up!)

Liveaboard community anchorages are found with a good, well-protected anchorage, provisions, water, laundry available in Luperón, Samaná and Puerto Plata in the Dominican Republic, Boquerón in Puerto Rico, Phillipsburg in Sint Maarten, Bequia in the Grenadines, Secret Harbour and Prickly Bay in Grenada, Chaguaramas in Trinidad, Porlamar, Margarita and Puerto la Cruz in Venezuela. Cruisers Net in Puerto la Cruz, Venezuela VHF 72 0745, during hurricane season in Porlamar, Margarita VHF 72 0800. Radio nets provide information about social activities, including Ladies' Lunches and especially Carnival activities in Trinidad, that might be of interest to tourists with extra time as well as cruisers.

Yacht charters Charter fleets operate from the US and British Virgin Islands, Antigua, Sint Maarten/St-Martin, Martinique, Guadeloupe, St Lucia, St Vincent and Grenada. One-way charters can often be arranged for an additional fee. Yachts can be chartered on a daily or term basis, either bareboat or with skipper and crew. Skippered day charters are now found in almost any area where there are land-based tourists.

Marinas Dry dock facilities for long-term boat storage are found in the Turks and Caicos, Puerto Rico, the Virgin Islands, St Martin, St Lucia, St Vincent, Antigua, Grenada, Trinidad and Venezuela. Marinas with slips of different types (slips, stern-to, pilings) are found in the majority of the islands and new ones are opening frequently. Most marinas will hold mail addressed to yachts for pick-up.

Hitching rides Hitching and working on yachts is another way to see the islands for the adventurous person with time on his/her hands. Many yachts charter in the Caribbean in winter and go north to the USA or Mediterranean for the charter season there. Other yachts are cruisers passing on their way around the world. Yachties are friendly people and if you ask in the right places, frequent the yachtie bars and put up a few notices, crew positions can often be found. Bulletin boards are found in Turtle Cove Marina (Turks and Caicos), Great Bay and Bobby's Marina in the Lagoon (Sint Maarten), Fort-de-France, Trois-Ilets and Le Marin (Martinique), Rodney Bay and Marigot Bay (St Lucia), English Harbour (Antigua), Admiralty Bay (Bequia) and Anchorage (Union Island) in the Grenadines, Secret Harbour and Spice Island Marina (Grenada), Porlamar (Margarita), any of the marinas in El Morro complex in Puerto la Cruz (Venezuela) where foreign yachties hang out, and any marina or yacht club in Chaguaramas in Trinidad. If you want to crew, check you have all necessary visas and documentation and confirm with the skipper that your paperwork is in order. Puerto Rico and the US Virgin Islands require visas for boat travellers as though you were travelling to the USA. To visit the USA from the Caribbean by yacht, many yachts leave Trinidad after Carnival in late February; boat deliveries back to the USA are also possible.

VHF nets In those areas where there are a substantial number of liveaboard sailors, VHF nets seem to spring up with volunteers taking turns providing weather information, arrivals and departures, information about services and announcements about local activities, sharing taxis or tours; guests returning home often offer to take mail back to the USA or Europe. **Email** access can be obtained by boats staying in a marina.

Fishing permits, park rules The Caribbean islands are becoming more ecoconscious. They are interested in preserving their natural resources and beauty and have established parks, marine preserves or national trust foundations. Some have mooring buoys, no-anchoring or anchoring limitations. Most prohibit the taking of coral or live creatures in shells; many prohibit the taking of shells. Don't anchor in areas where coral may be growing. Don't dispose of rubbish in enclosed anchorages. **Rubbish** is a problem on many of the smaller islands; don't give rubbish to boat boys as they often just take the money and throw the waste into the water. Try to dispose of edible waste at sea while travelling between islands in deep water; take paper, cans and bottles ashore to the town dump or a marina where they have waste disposal facilities.

Scuba diving Do not assume you can dive wherever you like even if you have all your own tanks and equipment. Several islands require divers to go with a local dive group and it is best to contact a local dive shop for advice. Many dive operators have special rates and packages for yachtie divers and will pick you up from your yacht.

Weapons Some countries want weapons and ammunition checked in ashore until you are ready to depart. Others will let you keep them locked on board and others don't really ask questions. Make sure clearance papers have the correct serial numbers and ammunition counts to avoid confusion when it comes to picking up the weapons that were checked ashore. Some areas even consider spearguns weapons and require them to be turned in until you leave.

Regattas or special activities Sailboat races of all types are held throughout the Caribbean during the entire year. Spectator boats may go out to watch the races, there may be crew sign-up lists for those who would like to sail and best of all, there are usually parties and other activities on shore. Most regattas have various different types of classes, even including liveaboard classes.

Guidebooks Julius Wilensky's guides have good sketch charts that are still useful even if not updated. *Yachtsman's Guide to the Bahamas and Turks and Caicos*, *Cruising Guide to Abaco*, Steve Dodge; *Cruising Guide to the Abacos* (2nd edition) Julius Wilensky; *Yachtsman's Guide to the Virgin Islands*, *Southern Waterway Guide* (covers Bahamas and Turks and Caicos), *Passages South*, Bruce Van Sant; *Guide to the Leeward Islands*, Chris Doyle; *VIP Cruising Guide* (Sint Maarten area), *Guide to the Windward Islands*, Chris Doyle; *Guide to Venezuela, Trinidad & Tobago*, Chris Doyle; *Guide to Trinidad and Tobago*, Chris Doyle; *Guide to Venezuela*, Chris Doyle; *Donald Street's Guides to the Caribbean* (Volumes I, II, III, IV). There are several 'yachting newspapers' that are distributed free around the Caribbean that have things to do, reports on regattas, tourist and sailing events: *Nautical Scene* (St Thomas to Venezuela), *The Compass* (Bequia and southern Caribbean), *All at Sea* (northern Caribbean), *The Boca* (Trinidad and Tobago) and *Mar y Tierra* (Venezuela).

The numbers of scuba divers has increased dramatically in recent years and the Caribbean is a scuba diver's paradise, for there is a conglomeration of islands surrounded by living reefs providing different types of diving to suit everyone. Unfortunately, as a result, some of the islands have become 'diving circuses', particularly in some of the more developed northern Caribbean islands where 30 or 40 divers are herded onto large dive boats and dropped on somewhat packaged dive sites where 'tame' fish come for handouts. However, other islands in the region are still virginal in the diving sense, which can lead to an exciting undersea adventure. On the more remote islands facilities are often unavailable and diving can be more difficult and basic.

Scuba diving
See individual islands for detailed information

Cayman Islands These are among the most developed for scuba diving and there is a fine organization of over 20 dive operations, including liveaboard boats. There is also a well-run decompression facility on Grand Cayman, which is an added safety factor. The Caymans are very conservation minded and it is a criminal offence to take ANY form of marine life while scuba diving. In fact, it is illegal on Cayman Brac, the smaller sister island, even to wear gloves while scuba diving. This helps ensure that divers will not hold or damage the delicate coral formations and other marine life.

Essentials

British Virgin Islands With some 50 coral islands, these islands are well worth a mention as the diving is exciting and varied. Both liveaboard and land-based operations are available with well-developed facilities for divers. Popular diving sites include the wreck of the *HMS Rhone*, a 310-ft British mail ship sunk in 1867 in a hurricane. She was the site for the Hollywood movie *The Deep*. Many sites lie in the string of islands to the south between Tortola and Virgin Gorda.

Saba, a tiny Dutch island, only 5 miles long, is truly one of the most protected places for divers. The entire reef surrounding the island was established as a marine park in 1987 and this conservation effort has led to an abundance of 'tame' fish. Saba diving is known for several deep pinnacles including Third Encounter, Twilight Zone and Shark Shoal. For the less adventurous and experienced, sites like Diamond Rock and Tent Reef offer the thrill of seeing large French angels swimming up to you. Land-based and liveaboard diving boat facilities are available, as well as a recompression chamber facility.

Dominica 'The Nature Island', or 'The Water Island', is a lush, mountainous island with rugged topside and underwater terrain. It is diving for the adventurous and not for the diver who wants it easy, although there are a few beginner sites. This is one of few islands left where black coral abounds along the wall drop-offs starting at 60 ft. For the more experienced the Atlantic east coast offers some spectacular wall dives.

Turks and Caicos Islands They consist of over 40 lovely sand islands and cays and are located on the Turks Island Passage, a 22-mile channel which is 7,000 ft deep connecting the Atlantic Ocean and the Caribbean Sea. This contributes to the abundance of marine life and large pelagic fish seen in these waters and spectacular wall diving in the channel. The islands are surrounded by coral reefs that cover over 200 sq miles. Visibility is usually 100 ft or more and marine life plentiful. A strong attitude towards conservation is reinforced by **Protection of Reefs and Islands from Degradation and Exploitation (PRIDE)**, based at the Sea Island Centre, a commercial conch farm. PRIDE is a US-based foundation which has helped in numerous conservation projects. There are several dive shops on Providenciales and Grand Turk, mostly catering for small groups of divers, and there are three or four liveaboard boats in the islands' waters at any one time.

St Vincent and the Grenadines Lying in the South Eastern Caribbean these islands offer pristine diving, although facilities are limited. **Grenada** and tiny sister island of **Carriacou** have several interesting sites, including a wrecked Italian cruise liner and an underwater volcano. Most of the islands have a dive shop or two, usually attached to a hotel.

Tobago An unspoiled destination well worth visiting. This small island is close to the South American coast and large marine life is encouraged by the flow of plankton-rich water from the continent's rivers. Manta ray are especially attracted by the plankton and at Speyside (also called Manta City) where currents meet they are seen on nearly every dive. Most diving is along the west and north coast.

Barbados Among the more developed islands in the Caribbean, though the surrounding reef life is not as unspoiled as on some of the less developed islands. However, there are some thriving reefs and within the last few years the island has become known as a wreck diving destination. Five shipwrecks have been intentionally sunk as diving sites, offering interesting underwater photography.

Bonaire Just off the South American coast Bonaire has long been known as a 'hot spot' for diving, and is one of the few islands (like the Caymans) which has devoted itself to scuba diving. A far-sighted government established a marine park way back in 1979 when conservation was not even being discussed by most diving destinations. Neighbouring Curaçao has now joined her in this reputation, with an expansion of diving facilities and exciting diving sites. Aruba is not likely to equal her sister islands as she lacks the reefs which surround Bonaire and Curaçao, although diving is available. Bonaire, being very experienced in offering diving, has a wide selection of about a dozen dive operations, including photo and marine life education facilities. Diving sites are also varied with reef, wreck and wall dives. In fact, the Marine Park Guide for Bonaire lists over 50 dive sites. The town pier, right off the capital, has long been a favourite night dive and the pilings are covered in soft sponges and invertebrate life.

Curaçao Offers the reef diving of Bonaire and a couple of wreck dives of interest. The freighter, *Superior Producer* (rather deep at 100 ft) is intact and has a variety of growth including beautiful orange tubastera sponges.

Aruba While the reefs may not be as prolific as her sister islands, there is an interesting wreck site, with which few other sites around the island compare in marine life. The *Antilla*, a 400 ft German ship, is in 70 ft (and less) of water. Her massive hull has provided a home for an amazing variety and size of fish life and night dives are truly a thrill. More wrecks are being sunk to create an artificial reef.

Safety Most Caribbean destinations offer some form of scuba diving, although not all operations are safety minded. While scuba diving is exciting and thrilling, it can also be dangerous, particularly for beginners who are not aware of what to look for in a safe diving operation. Proper instruction from a recognized scuba instructor is a must. Not all diving shops in the Caribbean adhere to the recommended safety standards, so it is important to enquire what level of training an instructor has and request to see certificates of instructor training if they are not displayed.

Good **health** is a must, but the myth that one needs to be a super man or super woman is not true. Important health aspects are healthy lungs, sinus and the ability to equalize your ears (by gently blowing air into the eustachian tube while blocking your nose). A medical exam by a physician trained in hyperbaric (diving) medicine is recommended and required by many instructors. A good basic swimming ability is necessary, although you do not need to be an Olympic swimmer. For female divers, smaller, lighter scuba tanks are available at some dive shops which makes the cumbersome, heavy gear easier to handle.

Most scuba training organizations offer several types of diving **courses**. A 'resort course' provides diving instruction in a condensed version (about three hours) with a minimum of academic knowledge, one confined water session (usually in a swimming pool) and one scuba dive. This type of course is done by many tourists who do not have the time to do a full certification course, which requires written exams, classroom lectures, several confined water sessions and several scuba dives. For the serious diver, however, a full certification course should be taken.

Windsurfing

For operators and associations, see individual islands

Whether you are an accomplished windsurfer or merely wishing to give it a try, the Caribbean offers warm clear water, trade winds and a wealth of locations to choose from. Throughout the Caribbean there are hundreds of pristine windsurfing locations, many undeveloped. Bring your own gear and have an adventure, or sail with the many schools across the islands. The strongest, steadiest winds are in June and July when the trade winds are at their most constant. Winter brings either howling winds or flat calm and is unpredictable. In summer the gentle breezes provide good learning conditions. Each island has different winds and conditions, there is something for everyone, even if you just want to sit on the beach and watch. Some islands now also offer kite surfing, a hugely exciting activity both to watch and do, but it is often limited to certain times of the day so that you don't clash with windsurfers or mow down swimmers. Both the Dominican Republic and Aruba have good facilities.

Antigua Steady winds and good locations, at present there is only one dedicated school, although hotels often have learner boards. Best wind November-February, June-July.

Aruba Well known as a centre for great windsurfing, flat waist deep water on the leeward side with strong wind make this an ideal location for learners and advanced windsurfers, the perfect family windsurf vacation. Best wind May-July.

Barbados Sun, sand, wind and waves make Barbados one of the favourite locations for many pro windsurfers on the World Tour. For those not willing to try the waves, flat water can be found at Oistins Bay. Best wind and wave conditions December-January and June.

Bequia Bequia is a beautiful island, but though the wind blows and the sun shines, there is only one windsurf school run by Basil, a Bequian with a big smile. Good location for learners or advanced sailors with flat water and wave sailing, well off the beaten track. Best winds November-February, June-July.

Bonaire Good winds and locations for all levels of sailors from flat water to gentle waves. Best winds December-August.

British Virgin Islands The centre for windsurf cruising, with over 50 small islands scattered within 40 miles and steady trades, the islands are perfect for flat water cruising and blasting.

Essentials

▶ Hurricane Season

See also box,
page 56

June too soon
July stand by
August it must
September remember
October all over

If only!

In recent years there have been several late storms and the 'October all over' proved a myth. There was little hurricane activity in the region from the 1950s until the late 1980s. Many of the islands were not affected by hurricanes and residents thought little of them. Homes were not built to withstand severe storms. In 1989 this all started to change when several violent storms roared through the islands and Hurricane Hugo did untold damage in the US Virgin Islands. The next few years were relatively quiet but 1995 struck with a bang (three names were 'retired' in deference to the dead and injured) and was the start of a five-year cycle that has gone down in history as the most active stretch on record for hurricanes: 41 developed with 20 major ones (Category 3 at 111 mph or more). 1996 brought nine hurricanes; 1997 gave the islands a breather with only three. 1998 was another active season with 10, one of which did much damage. On 25 September 1998 there were four hurricanes at the same time. 1999 brought eight hurricanes, five of which were Category 4 (130 mph or over) and two came late in the season, in October and November. In November 2001, both Central America and Cuba were badly damaged when hurricane Michelle (category 4) came calling, although thanks to emergency procedures the death toll was light.

In the daily weather forecasts, a **tropical depression** is an organized system of clouds and thunderstorms with a defined circulation and maximum sustained winds of 38 mph (33 knots) or less; a **tropical storm** is an organized system of strong thunderstorms with a defined circulation and maximum sustained winds of 39 to 73 mph (34 –63 knots); a **hurricane** is an intense tropical weather system with a well-defined circulation and maximum sustained winds of 74 mph (64 knots) or more.

A hurricane develops in warm waters and air, which is why the tropics are known for hurricanes. Powered by heat from the sea they are steered by the easterly trade winds and the temperate westerly winds, as well as their own ferocious energy. In the Atlantic, these storms form off the African coast and move west, developing as they come into warmer water. Around the core, winds grow to great velocity, generating violent seas. The process by which a disturbance forms and strengthens into a hurricane depends on at least three conditions: warm water, moisture and wind pattern near the ocean surface that spirals air inward. Bands of thunderstorms form and allow the air to warm further and rise higher into the atmosphere. If the winds at these higher levels are light, the structure remains intact and allows for further strengthening. If the winds are strong, they will shear off the top and stop the development. If the system develops, a definite eye is formed around which the most violent activity takes place; this is known as the eyewall. The centre of the eye is relatively calm. When the eye passes over land those on the ground are often misled that the hurricane is over; some even abandon safe shelter, not aware that as the eye passes the other side of the eyewall will produce violent winds and the other half of the hurricane. At the top of the eyewall (around 50,000 ft), most of the air is propelled outward, increasing the air's upward motion. Some of the air however, moves inward and sinks into the eye and creates a cloud-free area.

The word 'hurricane' is derived from the Amerindian 'Hurakan', both the Carib god of evil and also one of the Maya creator gods who blew his breath across the chaotic water and brought forth dry land. In the North Atlantic, Gulf of Mexico, Caribbean and the Eastern Pacific they are called hurricanes, in Australia, cyclones or 'willy willy', and in the Philippines, 'baguio'. In the Western North Pacific tropical

Already a popular yachting centre, the two sports fuse with international events such as the Hi Ho (hook in and hold on), a week long windsurf race and yacht cruise. Good sailing for all levels. Best winds December-January, June-July.

Grand Cayman Famous for its diving, Grand Cayman also offers good windsurfing, the east end is popular for beginners to advanced and everything in between, flat water on the inside and bump and jump further out. Best wind November-March.

cyclones of hurricane force are called typhoons. The first time hurricanes were named was by an Australian forecaster in the early 1900s who called them after political figures he disliked. During World War II US Army forecasters named storms after their girlfriends and wives. Between 1950-52 they were given phonetic names (able, baker, charlie). In 1953 the Weather Bureau started giving them female names again. Today individual names (male and female) are chosen by the National Hurricane Center in Miami and submitted to the World Meteorology Organization in Geneva, Switzerland. If approved these become the official names for the upcoming hurricane season. As a system develops and becomes a tropical depression (TD), it is assigned a name in alphabetical order from the official list.

There is very good information before hurricanes hit any land, thanks to accurate weather data gathered by the Hurricane Hunters from Keesler Airforce Base in the USA. During the storm season they operate out of St Croix in the US Virgin Islands, where they are closer to storms. This elite group of men and women actually fly through the eye of a hurricane in C130 airplanes gathering critical information on the wind speeds and directions and other data. This is sent to the Miami Hurricane Center where a forecast is made and sent to all islands in the potential path so they can prepare for the storm. Most of the island governments are now well prepared to cope with hurricanes and have disaster relief teams in place, while many of the island resorts, especially the larger ones, have their own generators and water supplies. Cuba has highly efficient evacuation procedures: over 705,000 people were evacuated from the path of Michelle in 2001, including tourists from Cayo Coco and Cayo Largo.

While a hurricane can certainly pose a threat to life, in most cases if precautions are taken the risks are reduced. Some of the main hazards are storm surge, heavy winds and rains. There is usually disruption of services such as communications, internal transport and airline services. The tourist may be left stranded while the roads and power lines are cleared. Communications home may be impossible for some days. Ideally, if a hurricane is approaching, it is better for the tourist to evacuate the island. During the hurricane, which is usually 6-36 hours, you have to be shut up inside a closed area, often with little ventilation or light, which can be stressful. Some tourists think a hurricane will be 'fun' and want to remain on island to see the storm. This is not a good idea. If you do remain you should register with your local consulate or embassy and it is a good idea to email home as soon as the warning is given to alert your family that communications may go down and that you will follow the rules of the emergency services. You should also be prepared to be inconvenienced in the ways already mentioned and even to help out in the clearing up afterwards. Team work in the aftermath of a disaster can be tremendous.

When there is potentially violent weather approaching, the local government met office issues advisories:

A tropical storm watch is an announcement to be on alert for a storm (winds of 39- 73 mph) which may pose threats to coastal areas within 36 hours.

A tropical storm warning is issued if the storm is expected within 24 hours.

A hurricane watch is given if hurricane conditions could be coming in 36 hours.

A hurricane warning is issued if the hurricane is expected within 24 hours.

One of the best internet sites for information and data from reporters on the islands during an actual hurricane is **www.stormcarib.com**

The website of the Hurricane Hunters is **www.hurricanehunters.com** (virtual reality flight with them into the eye of a hurricane on this site).

Miami National Hurricane Center **www.nhc.noaa.gov/**

Dominican Republic Voted by many top sailors as one of the most exciting places to sail in the Caribbean, Cabarete, on the north coast, offers everything a windsurfer could want: flat water for beginners and great wavesailing on the outside with thermally affected winds that mean you can take the morning off. Lots of schools and hotels on the strip of beach and some of the best gear in the Caribbean. Best wind January-March and June-August.

Essentials

Grenadines Great location with no facilities, take your own gear and hire a yacht out of Grenada or St Vincent, or visit Basil at Bequia (see above), the only rental centre in the area.

Nevis A windsurfer's paradise waiting to be discovered, good flat water and wavesailing, definitely no crowds, the island is small enough to offer all conditions for every skill level. Best wind December-January, June-July.

Puerto Rico Great wave-sailing spot, the Caribbean's answer to Maui. The location is The Shacks at Isabela on the northwest point of the island. Thermal winds make this a winter spot for the committed wave sailor, gentler sailing is offered in the San Juan area and in the summer. Best waves and wind December-April, slalom July-September.

St Barts Small exclusive island with some good windsurf spots for beginners and advanced, and it is quiet. Best wind December-February.

St Croix A great sailing spot. The guys here are good wave sailors and slalom racers as the island boasts all conditions at many locations. Best wind January-February and July.

St Lucia This beautiful destination offers uncrowded sailing for windsurfing and plenty to when not windy. Bring your own gear if you are an advanced sailor. Best winds December-June.

St Martin Orient Bay (Baie Orientale) has good winds and plenty of facilities. St Martin offers good learning and advanced slalom sailing. Best winds December-January and July.

St Thomas Everything you expect from a Caribbean windsurf vacation, with shopping malls. St Thomas boasts a lively local windsurfing community, flat water and lots of events to attend. Best wind December-January and July. Caribbean Team Boardsailing Championships in July.

Trinidad and Tobago In the prime trade wind zone, Tobago's Pigeon Point is the place to go, unexplored and beautiful with some excellent sailing spots. You will probably need to take your own gear. Best wind December-May.

Turks and Caicos Flat turquoise waters and steady winds make this an ideal learner and intermediate destination, perfect for a family diving and windsurf vacation. Best winds February-March intermediate, October-November for beginners.

Walking

See individual islands for further details

The Caribbean provides ideal conditions for medium-distance walking in the tropics. Small islands avoid the very high temperatures which are common in India, Africa or the South American mainland. Distances are manageable; a hard day's walk will take you from coast to coast on the smaller islands, and a few days is enough for a complete circuit. The scenery is varied, mountain streams and waterfalls, are perfect for bathing, and the sea is never far away. Nor are road transport, comfortable accommodation, rum shops and restaurants. Nevertheless, the illusion of remoteness can sometimes be complete. And much of the nastier *mainland* wildlife can't swim, so there are no large carnivores and few poisonous snakes on the islands.

Maps Good large scale maps (1: 25,000 or 1: 50,000) are available for all the British Commonwealth islands. These can be obtained from the local Lands and Surveys department on each island; and usually from **Stanfords** (see page 33, or **The Map Shop**, 15 High St, Upton-upon- Severn, Worcestershire, WR8 0HJ (T01684-593146), www.themapshop.co.uk The Ordnance Survey (Romsey Rd, Southampton, UK, T01703-792763, F01703-792404) publishes a series of colourful world maps including some holiday destinations. They contain comprehensive tourist information ranging from hotels and beaches to climbing and climate. Each map is produced in association with the country concerned. Relevant titles are: Barbados, St Lucia, Cayman Islands, British Virgin Islands, St Vincent, Dominica. There are also good large scale Serie Bleu maps of Guadeloupe and Martinique (1:25,000, seven maps of Guadeloupe, No 4601G-4607G) issued by the Institut Géographique National, Paris, which include all hiking trails. Footpath information on maps is not always reliable, however.

Hints

A small, collapsible umbrella may be useful and can also provide protection against the sun

Clothing Lightweight cotton clothing, with a wide-brimmed hat to keep off the sun. Shorts and short-sleeved shirts are comfortable, but can leave the legs and arms exposed to sunburn or sharp razor grasses. It is best to carry short and long, and change en route as appropriate. Wear a shirt with a collar to avoid sunburn on the back of your neck. Rain comes in intense bursts. Raincoats are not particularly comfortable. A better technique is to strip down to light clothes and dry off when the rain stops. There are many new fabrics on the market which are designed to wick away moisture from your body, keeping you cool, while drying rapidly if you are caught in a downpour. In the rainy season leather footwear is of little use as it will be permanently wet and muddy. Use trainers instead and be prepared to discard them at the end of your trip.

Timing An early start is ideal, preferably just before sunrise. This will give several hours walking before the sun becomes too hot or before rain sets in during the wet season. Public transport starts running surprisingly early in most places.

Water Carry a large thermos to keep water ice-cold through a full day. Refilling from mountain streams is generally safe with purification tablets, but be careful of streams *below* villages especially in islands like St Lucia and Martinique where there is some bilharzia, and of springs in cultivated areas where generously applied pesticides may have leached into the groundwater.

Sunburn Remember that the angle of the sun in the sky is what counts, not the temperature. So you may get burnt at midday even if you feel cool, but are unlikely to have trouble before 1000 or after 1500. Forearms can get burnt, and so can the back of your legs if you are walking away from the sun. It is a good idea to walk west in the morning and east in the afternoon to avoid strong sun on the face.

Snakes The only islands where these are a worry are Trinidad, St Lucia, and Martinique. Trinidad has several dangerous species, and also has African killer bees. All three islands have the venomous Fer de Lance. This snake is usually frightened off by approaching footsteps, so snakebites are rare, but they can be fatal. The Fer de Lance prefers bush country in dry coastal areas. Ask and accept local advice on where to go, and stick to well-marked trails. Some other islands have boa constrictors, which can bite but are not poisonous. In Trinidad, beware of the coral snake; visitors with children should take care because the snake looks like a colourful bracelet coiled on the ground. Most snakes will only attack in the breeding season if they feel the nest is threatened. Large centipedes (sometimes found in dry coastal areas) can also give a very nasty bite.

Marijuana farmers In remote mountain areas in most islands these people are likely to assume that outsiders have come either to steal the crop or as police spies. On most islands they are armed, and on some they set trap guns for the unwary. Again, the best way to avoid them is to keep to well-marked trails, and accept local advice about where to go. In some places, however, they assume you are a customer. One hiker was stopped by a farmer on his descent from a volcano. Although the machete was alarming, in fact he offered to sell him ganja. When the goods were politely declined, he offered to sell him guns instead.

Jamaica Spectacular scenery especially in the Blue Mountains and in the Cockpit country. Marijuana growers are a real problem in the remote areas, but the main trails in the Blue Mountains are safe. *Jamaica Camping and Hiking Association* and Ministry of Tourism have a useful *Hikers Guide to the Blue Mountains*.

Around the islands

Cuba Wonderful mountain scenery with several ranges in the east, centre and west of the island. There are trails and waterfalls to cool off in, but in the Sierra Maestra in the east the mountains are usually closed for security reasons except in a few areas for organized tours. Seek local advice.

Dominican Republic Home to the two highest peaks in the Caribbean (Pico Duarte and Pico La Pelona) in addition to many smaller mountains, it is one of the great places for hiking. A guide is mandatory in all the national parks. For information contact the Dirección Nacional de Parques, Av Máximo Gómez, Santo Domingo, Apto Postal 2487.

Haiti Another story altogether. Walking is the normal means of transport in rural areas, so there are masses of well-trodden trails, but it is better to walk with a group. Maps are rudimentary and small scale. Few people speak French in remote areas – try to pick up some Creole. Make sure you carry basic supplies, particularly water. Hiring a guide should be no problem.

Puerto Rico Although there is some lovely mountain scenery and several trails through forest reserves, this island is designed for the driver rather than the hiker. Long-distance hiking is difficult as far as food and lodging is concerned and accommodation is expensive when you get there.

Guadeloupe Network of waymarked trails on the mountainous half (Basse-Terre) in the Parc Naturel and up La Soufrière. Contact the *Organisation des Guides de Montagne de la Caraïbe* (Maison Forestière, 97120 Matouba, T590-800579) for a guide and/or the booklet *Promenades et Randonnées*.

Essentials

Martinique The *Parc Naturel Régional* (9 Blvd Géneral-de-Gaulle, T596-731930) organizes group hikes, usually on Sundays, and publishes a useful *Guide des Sentiers Pedestres à la Martinique*. Good trails on Mont Pelée and along the north coast.

Dominica Probably has the best unspoiled mountain scenery in the Caribbean. Some of the long-distance trails are hard to follow, though. Guides are readily available. Try the path via Laudat to the Boiling Lake.

St Lucia Very well-marked east-west trail through Quillesse forest reserve with excellent bird-watching. Other walks organized by the Forestry Department. See St Lucia chapter for details.

St Vincent Spectacular but sometimes difficult trail across the Soufrière volcano from Orange Hill to Richmond. Guide advisable. North coast trail past Falls of Baleine is spectacular, but hard to follow. Marijuana growers.

Grenada Very accessible mountain and rainforest scenery. Good network of signposted trails linking Grand Étang, Concord waterfall, and other points. The mountains to the southeast of the Grand Étang Forest Reserve are less well marked and you may need a local guide, but the walking is spectacular with marvellous views.

Barbados Very safe and pleasant walking, especially on the east coast, but little really wild scenery. *Barbados National Trust* (T246-4262421/4369033) organizes regular hikes.

Trinidad Some fine scenery, but marijuana growers are a problem, particularly in the Northern Range and you are advised always to walk in a group. Well-marked trails are safe. Those at the Asa Wright Nature Centre are recommended (T868-6674655, F6670493). *Trinidad Field Naturalists Club* (PO Box 642, Port of Spain, T868-6248017, evenings only) organizes long-distance hikes, and visits to caves, etc.

Tobago Safe and pleasant walking; distances are not too great. The scenery is varied: hills, woodland and unspoilt beaches.

Useful addresses For groups organizing a serious hiking/camping expedition in the Caribbean, contact the *Duke of Edinburgh's Award Scheme*, Bridge House, Cavans Lane, Bridgetown, Barbados (T246- 4369763). They may be able to provide advice and to supply the address of a local organization on most islands with expedition experience. In the UK the **Ramblers Association** has a subsidiary company *Ramblers Holidays*, T44-1707 331133, www.ramblersholidays.co.uk which offers walking holidays in Cuba and St Lucia.

Cycling

You can rent bikes on almost every island and because of the mountainous terrain and cool breezes, it is quite a comfortable way to get around. There has even been a Caribbean cup bike race, with bike clubs from each island travelling to different islands for the competition. Some of the islands have mountains as high as 3,000 m towering above the ocean, making the Caribbean one of the most exciting new mountain bike destinations in the world.

There is some exceptional cycling for a strong rider. Apart from on Barbados and Antigua there are plenty of hills and some fantastic scenery. However, away from the main tourist areas on each island, the tourist infrastructure is not well developed and the potential for crime is high. There are substantial social problems stemming from poverty and drug abuse and at times you can feel vulnerable in relatively remote areas on bicycles. Most West Indians are genuinely friendly and interested in your chosen mode of transport, but in many countries there is that small percentage of the population who openly display their dislike of the white tourist.

Antigua Has good bike shops, eg *Cycle Krazy*, and great single track, in addition to a local bike club. However the roads are generally flat, traffic moderately heavy and cycling is not as interesting as on some other islands.

Barbados Mountain biking on back-country roads with bike rental available. The east coast is best but elsewhere there is constant heavy traffic. Rush hour starts at 1600 everywhere.

Cuba Mountain bike tour companies, good terrain. Charity sponsored tours frequently organized. The west is the more popular part for touring, with gentle hills and plenty of places to stop. The centre can be flat and boring with miles of sugar cane or cattle lands. The Sierra Maestra in the east is demanding and very hot. Distances are huge, always start early and take a long lunch break. Roads are good and empty but poorly signed. Get to your destination before dark as street lighting is poor to non-existent.

Dominica A new attraction, with bike rental and tours offered. Roads are good for cycling, traffic is generally light with the exception of the stretch between Layou and Roseau. Canefield to Pont Casse is very steep, twisty and challenging. This is one of the most enjoyable islands to cycle due to the friendliness of the people, there are plenty of natural sites to visit and the coastal roads are quite easy even with gear (ie not so steep).

Dominican Republic Coined as the mountain bike mecca of the Caribbean, has a bicycle club with over 300 members with both mountain bike and road bike races held monthly. Bike shops throughout the island. *Iguana Mama* for tours. The north coast, the Cordillera Septentional and the slopes of the Cordillera Central are great places for scenery and challenging cycling. Exhilarating downhills.

Grenada Bike rental available. Parts (but no repairs) at *Ace Hardware*. Accommodation is strategically placed for cycling round the island. The cycle between Sauteurs and Victoria is a peaceful ride with spectacular views. The ride through the Grand Étang is rewarding but difficult, five to six hours with some steep hills but the beauty of the forest reserve and the small friendly communities are well worth it. **Carriacou** has great cycling. Many of the roads are in very poor repair giving it the semblance of off-road cycling. Traffic is light. Potential for lots of flat tyres in the dry season when the trail is overgrown with cactii.

Jamaica Bike rental and tour operators offering trips, excellent terrain, mountains, coastal routes, rolling hills. However, beware fast drivers on hairpin bends.

Martinique Do not attempt to cycle from the airport to either Fort-de-France or Trois-Ilets as the only route is via the main highway, four lanes each way with fast, heavy traffic and the shoulder is narrow to non-existent.

Montserrat The east coast is scenic with only light traffic to the former airport, which is the furthermost point you can travel. Immigration is strict and you have to leave a deposit to take bicycles in for a day trip from Antigua.

Puerto Rico Bike touring companies and rentals throughout the island, excellent terrain. Avoid the highways around San Juan, where traffic is very heavy.

St Croix Cycling tours of the forest or beach are offered by *St Croix Bikes & Tours*, while *VI Cycling* organize weekly rides and races.

St Kitts Bike rental and tours are available. Traffic is light.

St Martin *Frogs Legs* is a good bike shop in town, the owner David will take you out on rides.

St Lucia The best way to cycle the island is anti-clockwise. This will ensure long but gradual uphills and steep, fast downhills. Be extremely careful between Dennery and Castries. This is a drug-growing area and the locals are not particularly friendly. Those that are friendly will warn you not to stop. Castries to Soufrière is enjoyable with a fairly demanding but scenic section through the rainforest. Has the potential be to quite wet! Soufrière to Vieux Fort is another good ride and not so hard physically.

St Vincent and the Grenadines *Sailors* is a good cycle shop in Kingstown, also offering tours. The cycle between Layou and Richmond is a strenuous four hours one way, an absolutely spectacular ride, not to be missed, but expect long, steep hills and lots of them. The northern part of St Vincent is notorious for being a drug producing area, travel with caution. **Bequia** has really enjoyable cycling, lots of hills but not too steep and not a lot of traffic, great views and beaches scattered over the island.

Tobago Repairs and parts at *Número Uno* in Carnbee, can put you in touch with local riders for run road riding. Mountain bike needed for the trail between L'Anse Fourni and Charlotteville.

Trinidad *Geronimos* is an excellent bike shop owned by a retired professional cyclist.

Essentials

Health

Staying healthy in the Caribbean is straightforward. With the following advice and precautions you should keep as healthy as you do at home and most travellers experience no problems at all beyond an occasional upset stomach. Obviously this in part depends on how you are travelling: the beach tourist who stays in good hotels is much less at risk than the backpacker who slings his hammock in the back of beyond. Most of the islands have a tropical climate but this does not mean that tropical diseases as such are a great problem or even the main problem for visitors. Should you fall ill, remember that throughout the islands there are well-qualified doctors who speak good English (or French or Spanish). Medical practices may vary from those you are used to but there is likely to be better experience in dealing with locally occurring diseases. Most of the better hotels have a doctor on standby; ask at reception.

Before travelling

Ideally, you should see your GP or travel clinic at least six weeks before your departure for general advice on travel risks, malaria and vaccinations. Make sure you have travel insurance, get a dental check (especially if you are going to be away for more than a month), know your own blood group and if you suffer a long-term condition such as diabetes or epilepsy make sure someone knows or that you have a Medic Alert bracelet/necklace with this information on it.

Children   More preparation is probably necessary for babies and children than for adults and perhaps a little more care as children can become more rapidly ill than adults. Diarrhoea and vomiting are the most common problems, so take the usual precautions, but more intensively. Breast-feeding is best and most convenient for babies, but powdered milk is generally available and so are baby foods. Children get dehydrated very quickly in hot countries and can become drowsy and uncooperative unless cajoled to drink water or juice plus salts. Upper respiratory infections, such as colds, catarrh and middle ear infections are also common and if your child suffers from these normally take some antibiotics against the possibility. Outer ear infections after swimming are also common and antibiotic eardrops will help.

What to take   There is little control on the sale of drugs and medicines in some of the Caribbean. You may be able to buy any and every drug in pharmacies without a prescription. Be wary of this because pharmacists can be poorly trained and might sell you drugs that are unsuitable, dangerous or old. Many drugs and medicines are manufactured under licence from American or European companies, so the trade names may be familiar to you. This means you do not have to carry a whole chest of medicines with you (except in Cuba, where there are shortages) but remember that the shelf life of some items, especially vaccines and antibiotics, is markedly reduced in hot conditions. Buy your supplies at the better outlets where there are refrigerators, even though more expensive, and check the expiry date of all preparations you buy. Immigration officials occasionally confiscate scheduled drugs (*Lomotil* is an example) if they are not accompanied by a doctor's prescription.

   Mosquito repellents DEET (Di-ethyltoluamide) is the gold standard and must be applied every four to six hours, more often if you are sweating heavily. If a non-DEET product is used check who tested it. Validated products (tested at the London School of Hygiene and Tropical Medicine) include *Mosiguard*, Non-DEET *Jungle formula* and non-DEET *Autan*. If you want to use citronella remember that it must be applied very frequently (ie hourly) to be effective. If you are a popular target for insect bites or develop lumps quite soon after being bitten, carry an Aspivenin kit. This syringe suction device is available from many pharmacists and draws out some of the allergic materials and provides quick relief. **Sun Block** The Australians have a great campaign, which has reduced skin cancer. It is called Slip, Slap, Slop. Slip on a shirt, Slap on a hat, Slop on sun screen. **Pain killers** Paracetamol or a suitable painkiller can have multiple uses for symptoms. **Ciproxin** (Ciprofloaxcin) A useful antibiotic for some forms of travellers diarrhoea (see below). **Anti-malarials** Take specialist advice as to which type to take. General principles are that all except *Malarone* should be continued for four weeks after leaving the malarial area. *Malarone* needs to be continued for only seven days afterwards (if a tablet is missed or vomited seek specialist advice). The start times for the anti-malarials vary in that if you have never taken *Lariam* (Mefloquine) before it is advised to start it at least two to three weeks before the entry to a malarial zone (this is to help identify serious side-effects early). *Chloroquine* and *Paludrine* are often started a week before the trip to establish a pattern but *Doxycycline* and *Malarone* can be started only one or two days before entry to the malarial area. It is risky to buy medicinal tablets abroad because the doses may differ and there may be a trade in false drugs. **Immodium** A great standby for diarrhoea. It was believed that letting the bacteria or viruses flow out had to be more beneficial. However, with *Immodium* the bacteria still come out, just in a more solid form. **Pepto-Bismol** It certainly relieves symptoms of diarrhoea, but like *Immodium* it is not a cure for underlying disease. **MedicAlert** These simple bracelets, or an equivalent, should be carried or worn by anyone with a significant medical condition.

For longer trips involving jungle treks taking a clean needle pack, clean dental pack and water filtration devices are common-sense measures.

Polio and **Tetanus** recommended if you have not been immunised in the last 10 years; five doses of Tetanus vaccine provides lifetime innoculation. **Hepatitis A** recommended; the disease can be caught easily from food/water. **BCG** recommended for stays exceeding one month. **Yellow fever** Note that like India, the countries of the Caribbean Islands have no yellow fever and want to keep it that way; if you arrive from an infected country they will want to see your yellow fever certificate for almost all the islands . **Malaria** is limited to Haiti and western parts of the Dominican Republic that border Haiti, exclusively in the malignant (Pfalciparum) form (see below).

Vaccination & immunization

Websites Foreign and Commonwealth Office (FCO) (UK) www.fco.gov.uk This is a key travel advice site, with useful information on the country, people and climate, and lists the UK embassies/consulates. The site also promotes the concept of 'Know Before You Go'. And encourages travel insurance and appropriate travel health advice. It has links to the Department of Health travel advice site. **Department of Health Travel Advice** (UK) www.doh.gov.uk/traveladvice This excellent site is also available as a free booklet, the T6, from post offices. It lists the vaccine advice requirements for each country. **Medic Alert** (UK) www.medicalalert.co.uk This is the website of the foundation that produces bracelets and necklaces for those with existing medical problems. Once you have ordered your bracelet/necklace you write your key medical details on paper inside it, so that if you collapse, a medical person can identify you as someone with epilepsy or allergy to peanuts etc. **Blood Care Foundation** (UK) www.bloodcare.org.uk The Blood Care Foundation is a Kent-based charity "dedicated to the provision of screened blood and resuscitation fluids in countries where these are not readily available." They will dispatch certified non-infected blood of the right type to your hospital/clinic. The blood is flown in from various centres around the world. **Public Health Laboratory Service** (UK) www.phls.org.uk This site has up-to-date malaria advice guidelines for travel around the world. It gives specific advice about the right drugs for each location. It also has useful information for those who are pregnant, suffering from epilepsy or planning to travel with children. **Centers for Disease Control and Prevention** (USA) www.cdc.gov This site from the US Government gives excellent advice on travel health, has useful disease maps and details of disease outbreaks. **World Health Organisation** www.who.int The WHO site has links to the WHO Blue Book on travel advice. **Tropical Medicine Bureau** (Ireland) www.tmb.ie A good collection of general travel health information and disease risks.

Further information

Books *Travellers' Health: How to Stay Healthy abroad* by **Dr Richard Dawood**, ISBN 0-19-262947-6, is an excellent book updated in 2002. *The Travellers Good Health Guide* by **Dr Ted Lankester** by ISBN 0-85969-827-0. **Expedition Medicine** (The Royal Geographic Society) Editors *David Warrell* and *Sarah Anderson* ISBN 1 86197 040-4. International Travel and Health World Health Organisation Geneva ISBN 92 4 158026 7. *The World's Most Dangerous Places* by **Robert Young Pelton**, **Coskun Aral** and **Wink Dulles** ISBN 1-566952-140-9.

Essentials

Essentials

Leaflets *The Travellers Guide to Health* (T6) can be obtained by calling the Health Literature Line on 0800 555 777. Advice for travellers on avoiding the risks of HIV and AIDS (Travel Safe) available from Department of Health, PO Box 777, London SE1 6XH. The Blood Care Foundation order form PO Box 7, Sevenoaks, Kent TN13 2SZ, T01732-742427.

On the road

Flying If a trip to the Caribbean crosses time zones then jetlag can be a problem where your body's biological clock gets out of synchrony with the real time at your destination. On long-haul flights it is also important to stretch your legs at least every hour to prevent slowing of the circulation and the possible development of blood clots. Drinking plenty of non-alcoholic fluids will also help.

Diarrhoea & intestinal upset
This is almost inevitable. One study showed that up to 70% of all travellers may suffer during their trip

Diarrhoea should be short-lasting but persistence beyond two weeks, with blood or pain, requires specialist medical attention. *Ciproxin* (Ciprofloxacin) is a useful antibiotic and can be obtained by private prescription in the UK which is expensive, or bought over the counter in pharmacies on the islands. Take one 500 mg tablet when the diarrhoea starts; if there is no improvement in 24 hours, the diarrhoea is likely to have a non-bacterial cause and may be viral (in which case there is little you can do apart from keep yourself rehydrated and wait for it to settle on its own). The key treatment is to keep hydrated by taking the right mixture of salt and water. This is available as Oral Rehydration Salts (ORS) in ready-made sachets or can be made up by adding a teaspoon of sugar and a half-teaspoon of salt to a litre of clean water. Drink at least one large cup of this drink for each loose stool. You can also use flat carbonated drinks as an alternative. Immodium and Pepto- Bismol provide only symptomatic relief.

There is a simple adage that says wash it, peel it, boil it or forget it

To prevent diarrhoea, the standard advice is to be careful with drinking water and ice. If you have any doubts then boil it or filter and treat it. Be wary of salads (what were they washed in, who handled them), re-heated foods or food that has been left out in the sun having been cooked earlier in the day.

Malaria & insect bite prevention

Falciparum malaria can cause death within 24 hours. It may begin with flu-like symptoms; tiredness, lethargy, headaches. Or worse, fits may develop, followed by coma and then death. Whilst abroad and on return get tested as soon as possible, the test could save your life.

Treatment is with drugs and may be oral or into a vein depending on the seriousness of the infection. Remember ABCD: Awareness (of whether the disease is present in the area you are travelling in), Bite avoidance, Chemoprohylaxis, Diagnosis.

The Royal Homeopathic Hospital in the UK does not advocate homeopathic options for malaria prevention or treatment

Bite avoidance and chemoprophylaxis is the best prevention. Wear clothes that cover arms and legs and use effective insect repellents in areas with known risks of insect-spread disease. Use a mosquito net dipped in permethrin as both a physical and chemical barrier at night in the same areas. Guard against the contraction of malaria with the correct anti-malarials (see above).

Dengue fever This disease is an increasing problem throughout the Caribbean Islands. It can cause a severe flu-like illness which includes symptoms of fever, lethargy, enlarged lymph glands and muscle pains. It starts suddenly, lasts for two to three days, seems to get better for two to three days and then kicks in again for another two to three days. It is usually all over in an unpleasant week. The disease is self-limiting and forces rest and recuperation on the sufferer. The local people are prone to the much nastier haemorrhagic form of the disease, which causes them to bleed from internal organs, mucous membranes and often leads to their death. The mosquitoes that carry the Dengue virus bite during the day unlike the malaria mosquitoes. Which sadly means that repellent application and covered limbs are a 24-hour issue.

Sun protection The burning power of the tropical sun, especially at altitude, is phenomenal. Always wear a wide brimmed hat and use some form of suncream lotion on untanned skin. Normal temperate zone suntan lotions (protection factor up to seven) are not much good; you need to use the types designed specifically for the tropics or for mountaineers or skiers with protection factors up to 15 or above. Glare from the sun can cause conjunctivitis, so wear sunglasses, especially on tropical beaches, where high-protection factor sunscreen should also be used.

Hepatitis means inflammation of the liver. Viral causes of the disease can be acquired anywhere in South America and the Caribbean. The most obvious symptom is a yellowing of your skin or the whites of your eyes, prior to this you may notice is itching and tiredness. Depending on the type of hepatitis, a vaccine or immunoglobulin may reduce the duration of the illness. Pre-travel hepatitis A vaccine is the best prevention. Hepatitis B (for which there is a vaccine) is spread through blood and unprotected sex, both of these can be avoided. Unfortunately there is no vaccine for hepatitis C or the increasing alphabetical list of other Hepatitis viruses. **Hepatitis**

The range of visible and invisible diseases is awesome. Unprotected sex can spread HIV, Hepatitis B and C, Gonorrhea (green discharge), chlamydia (nothing to see but may cause painful urination and later female infertility), painful recurrent herpes, syphilis and warts, just to name a few. You can cut down the risk by using condoms, a femidom or avoiding sex altogether. Consider getting a sexual health check on your return home **Sexual health**

Remember to take your antimalarial tablets for six weeks after leaving the malarial area. If you have had attacks of diarrhoea it is worth having a stool specimen tested in case you have picked up amoebas. If you have been living rough, blood tests may be worthwhile to detect worms and other parasites. If you have been exposed to bilharzia (schistosomiasis) by swimming in lakes, etc, check by means of a blood test when you get home, but leave it for six weeks because the test is slow to become positive. Report any untoward symptoms to your doctor and tell the doctor exactly where you have been and, if you know, what the likelihood of disease is to which you were exposed. **When you return home**

Background

Pre-Columbian civilizations

Today's visitors to the Caribbean find an arc of islands whose culture has been determined by its immigrants: colonists, slaves, indentured labourers, from Europe, Africa and the East. It is easy to forget that there was a well-developed Amerindian society which was obliterated by Europeans in the 16th century.

The recorded history of the Caribbean islands begins with the arrival of Christopher Columbus' fleet in 1492. Our knowledge of the native peoples who inhabited the islands before and at the time of his arrival is largely derived from the accounts of contemporary Spanish writers and from archaeological examinations.

The Amerindians encountered by Columbus in the Greater Antilles had no overall tribal name but organized themselves in a series of villages or local chiefdoms, each of which had its own tribal name. The name now used, *Arawak*, was not in use then. The term was used by the Indians of the Guianas, a group of whom had spread into Trinidad, but their territory was not explored until nearly another century later. The use of the generic term Arawak to describe the Indians Columbus encountered, arose because of linguistic similarities with the Arawaks of the mainland. It is therefore surmised that migration took place many centuries before Columbus' arrival, but that the two groups were not in contact at that time. The time of the latest migration from the mainland, and consequently the existence of the island Arawaks, is in dispute, with some academics tracing it to about the time of Christ (the arrival of the Saladoids) and others to AD 1000 (the Ostionoids). **Tribes**

The inhabitants of the Bahamas were generally referred to as Lucayans, and those of the Greater Antilles as Taínos, but there were many sub-groupings. The inhabitants of the Lesser Antilles were, however, referred to as Carib and were described to Columbus as an aggressive tribe which sacrificed and sometimes ate the prisoners they captured in battle. It was from them that the Caribbean gets its name and from which the word cannibal is derived.

The earliest known inhabitants of the region, the *Siboneys*, migrated from Florida (some say Mexico) and spread throughout the Bahamas and the major islands. Most archaeological evidence of their settlements has been found near the shore, along bays or streams, where they lived in small groups. The largest discovered settlement has been one of 100 inhabitants in Cuba. They were hunters and gatherers, living on fish and other seafood, small rodents, iguanas, snakes and birds. They gathered roots and wild fruits, such as guava, guanábana and mamey, but did not cultivate plants. They worked with primitive tools made out of stone, shell, bone or wood, for hammering, chipping or scraping, but had no knowledge of pottery. The Siboneys were eventually absorbed by the advance of the Arawaks migrating from the south, who had made more technological advances in agriculture, arts and crafts.

The people now known as Arawaks migrated from the Guianas to Trinidad and on through the island arc to Cuba. Their population expanded because of the natural fertility of the islands and the abundance of fruit and seafood, helped by their agricultural skills in cultivating and improving wild plants and their excellent boat-building and fishing techniques. They were healthy, tall, good looking and lived to a ripe old age. It is estimated that up to eight million may have lived on the island of Hispaniola alone, but there was always plenty of food for all.

Society Their society was essentially communal and organized around families. The smaller islands were particularly egalitarian, but in the larger ones, where village communities of extended families numbered up to 500 people, there was an incipient class structure. Each village had a headman, called a *cacique*, whose duty it was to represent the village when dealing with other tribes, to settle family disputes and organize defence. However, he had no powers of coercion and was often little more than a nominal head. The position was largely hereditary, with the eldest son of the eldest sister having rights of succession, but women could and did become *caciques*. In the larger communities, there was some delegation of responsibility to the senior men, but economic activities were usually organized along family lines, and power was limited.

The division of labour was usually based on age and sex. The men would clear and prepare the land for agriculture and be responsible for defence of the village, while women cultivated the crops and were the major food producers, also making items such as mats, baskets, bowls and fishing nets. Women were in charge of raising the children, especially the girls, while the men taught the boys traditional customs, skills and rites.

Food & farming The Taínos hunted for some of their food, but fishing was more important and most of their settlements were close to the sea. Fish and shellfish were their main sources of protein and they had many different ways of catching them – from hands, baskets or nets to poisoning, shooting or line fishing. Cassava was a staple food, which they had successfully learned to leach of its poisonous juice. They also grew yams, maize, cotton, arrowroot, peanuts, beans, cocoa and spices, rotating their crops to prevent soil erosion. It is documented that in Jamaica they had three harvests of maize annually, using maize and cassava to make bread, cakes and beer.

Cotton was used to make clothing and hammocks (never before seen by Europeans), while the calabash tree was used to make ropes and cords, baskets and roofing. Plants were used for medicinal and spiritual purposes, and cosmetics such as face and body paint. Also important, both to the Arawaks and later to the Europeans, was the cultivation of tobacco, as a drug and as a means of exchange.

Arts & crafts They had no writing, no beasts of burden, no wheeled vehicles and no hard metals, although they did have some alluvial gold for personal ornament. The abundance of food allowed them time to develop their arts and crafts and they were skilled in woodwork and pottery. They had polished stone tools, but also carved shell implements for manioc preparation or as fish hooks. Coral manioc graters have also been found. Their boat-building techniques were noted by Columbus, who marvelled at their canoes of up to 75 ft in length, carrying up to 50 people, made of a single tree trunk in one piece. It took two months to fell a tree by gradually burning and chipping it down, and many more to make the canoe.

Religion The Arawaks had three main deities, evidence of which have been found in stone and conch carvings in many of the Lesser Antilles as well as the well populated Greater Antilles, although their relative importance varied according to the island. The principal male god was Yocahú, yoca being the word for cassava and hú meaning 'giver of'. It is believed that the Indians associated this deity's power to provide cassava with the mystery of the volcanoes, for all the carvings, the earliest out of shells and the later ones of stone, are conical. The Yocahú cult was wiped out in the Lesser Antilles by the invading Caribs, and in the Greater Antilles by the Spaniards, but it is thought to have existed from about AD 200.

The main female deity was a fertility goddess, often referred to as Atabeyra, but she is thought to have had several names relating to her other roles as goddess of the moon, mother of the sea, the tides and the springs, and the goddess of childbirth. In carvings she is usually depicted as a squatting figure with her hands up to her chin, sometimes in the act of giving birth.

A third deity is a dog god, named Opiyel-Guaobiran, meaning 'the dog deity who takes care of the souls of the immediately deceased and is the son of the spirit of darkness'. Again, carvings of a dog's head or whole body have been found of shell or stone, which were often used to induce narcotic trances. Many of the carvings have holes and Y-shaped passages which would have been put to the nose to snuff narcotics and induce a religious trance in the shaman or priest, who could then ascertain the status of a departed soul for a recently bereaved relative.

Sport

One custom which aroused interest in the Spaniards was the ball game, not only for the sport and its ceremonial features, but because the ball was made of rubber and bounced, a phenomenon which had not previously been seen in Europe. Catholicism soon eradicated the game, but archaeological remains have been found in several islands, notably in Puerto Rico, but also in Hispaniola. Excavations in the Greater Antilles have revealed earth embankments and rows of elongated upright stones surrounding plazas or courts, pavements and stone balls. These are called *bateyes, juegos de indios, juegos de bola, cercados* or *corrales de indios*. Batey was the aboriginal name for the ball game, the rubber ball itself and also the court where it was played. The word is still used to designate the cleared area in front of houses in the country.

The ball game had religious and ceremonial significance but it was a sport and bets and wagers were important. It was played by two teams of up to 20 or 30 players, who had to keep the ball in the air by means of their hips, shoulders, heads, elbows and other parts of their body, but never with their hands. The aim was to bounce the ball in this manner to the opposing team until it hit the ground. Men and women played, but not usually in mixed sex games. Great athleticism was required and it is clear that the players practised hard to perfect their skill, several, smaller practice courts having been built in larger settlements. The game was sometimes played before the village made an important decision, and the prize could be a sacrificial victim, usually a prisoner, granted to the victor.

Invaders

In 1492 Arawaks inhabited all the greater islands of the Caribbean, but in Puerto Rico they were being invaded by the Caribs who had pushed north through the Lesser Antilles, stealing their women and enslaving or killing the men. The Caribs had also originated in South America, from around the Orinoco delta. In their migration north through the Caribbean islands they proved to be fierce warriors and their raids on the Arawak settlements were feared. Many of their women were captured Arawaks, and it was they who cultivated the land and performed the domestic chores. Polygamy was common, encouraged by the surplus of women resulting from the raids, and the Arawak female influence on Carib culture was strong.

Despite rumours of cannibalism reported to Columbus by frightened Arawaks, there appears to be no direct evidence of the practice, although the Spaniards took it seriously enough to use it as an excuse to justify taking slaves. After some unfortunate encounters, colonizers left the Caribs alone for many years. The Arawaks, on the other hand, were soon wiped out by disease, cruelty and murder. The Spanish invaders exacted tribute and forced labour while allowing their herds of cattle and pigs to destroy the Indians' unfenced fields and clearings. Transportation to the mines resulted in shifts in the native population which could not be fed from the surrounding areas and starvation became common. Lack of labour in the Greater Antilles led to slave raids on the Lucayans in the Bahamas, but they also died or committed collective suicide. They felt that their gods had deserted them and there was nowhere for them to retreat or escape. Today there are no full-blooded Arawaks and only some 2,000 Caribs are left on Dominica (there has been no continuity of Carib language or religious belief on Dominica). The 500 years since Columbus' arrival have served to obliterate practically all the evidence of the indigenous civilization.

Flora and fauna

For many travellers, a trip to the Caribbean offers a first glimpse of the tropics, complete with luxuriant vegetation and exotic wildlife. Images of untouched beaches and rainforest form a major selling point of many travel brochures. In fact there is very little 'untouched' wilderness left and what visitors see is an environment that has been affected by the activities of man. Forestry, agriculture, fisheries and increasingly tourism have all helped to mould the modern landscape and natural heritage of the Caribbean. However, there is still much of interest to see, and it is true to say that small islands can combine a variety of habitats within a limited area. On many islands, it is possible to move between the coastal reefs and beaches through thorn scrub and plantation into rainforest within a matter of miles. Increasingly, the complexity and fragility of island ecosystems is being appreciated and fortunately most countries have recognized the value of balancing development and the protection of the natural environment and have begun to develop national parks and protected areas programmes. Many islands also have active conservation societies or national wildlife trusts (see page 30).

Over long periods of time, islands tend to develop their own unique flora and fauna. These endemic species add to the interest of wildlife and natural history tours. The St Lucia parrot and Dominica's sisserou have become a regular part of the tour circuit of these islands, and have undoubtedly benefited from the interest that tourists have shown in their plight. Details of National Parks and wildlife are included under the specific island chapter headings (Flora and fauna). This section provides a broad overview of the range of animals, plants and habitats that are to be found in the region.

Mammals Mammals are not particularly good colonizers of small islands and this has resulted in a general scarcity of species in the Caribbean. Many of the more commonly seen species (mongoose, agouti, opossum, and some of the monkeys) were introduced by man. Bats are the one exception to this rule and most islands have several native species. Mongoose were introduced to many islands to control snakes, they have also preyed on many birds, reptiles and other animals and have had a devastating effect on native fauna.

Of the monkeys, the green monkeys of Barbados, Grenada and St Kitts and Nevis were introduced from West Africa in the 17th century. Similarly, rhesus monkeys have been introduced to Desecheo Island off Puerto Rico. The red howler monkeys on Trinidad are native to the island as are several other mammals including the brocket deer, squirrel and armadillo. These species have managed to colonize from nearby Venezuela.

Sailors may encounter marine mammals including dolphin, porpoise and whales. Between November and December humpback whales migrate through the Turks and Caicos Passage on their way to the Silver Banks breeding grounds off the Dominican Republic. The manatee, or sea cow, can still be seen in some coastal areas in the Greater Antilles (especially Jamaica, Cuba – Zapata Peninsula – and Puerto Rico) although it is becoming uncommon.

Birds It is the birds perhaps more than any other group of animals that excite the most interest from visitors. Many islands have their own endemic species such as the Grenada dove, yellow-billed parrot and 24 other species in Jamaica and Guadeloupe woodpecker. The islands also act as important stepping stones in the migration of many birds through the Americas. As a result, the region is highly regarded by ornithologists and there are several important nature reserves.

Trinidad and Tobago demonstrate the influence of the nearby South American mainland. While they have no endemic species they still support at least 433 species and the Asa Wright Centre is regarded as one of the premier birdwatching sites in the world. There is also an important flamingo colony on Bonaire in the southern Caribbean.

Many of the endemic species have become rare as a result of man's activities. Habitat destruction, introduction of new species (especially the mongoose) and hunting for food and the international pet trade have all had an effect. Parrots in particular have suffered as a result of these activities. Fortunately, measures are now being undertaken to protect the birds and their habitats on many islands (eg Jamaica, Dominica, Puerto Rico and St Lucia).

Lizards and geckos are common on virtually all the islands in the region and may even be   **Reptiles**
seen on very small offshore islets. There are also a number of species of snakes, iguanas and
turtles scattered throughout the region. Many are restricted to one island and Jamaica has at
least 27 island endemics including several species of galliwasp. The vast majority of reptiles
found in the region are completely harmless to man although there are strong superstitions
about the geckos (*mabouya*) and of course the snakes. For example, the skin and fat of boa
constrictors (*tête chien*) are used for bush remedies on some of the Windward Islands.

The fer de lance snake (St Lucia, Martinique and also South America), deserves to be
treated with extreme caution; although the bite is not usually lethal, hospitalization is
required. It is found in isolated areas of dry scrubland and river valley. The best protection is
to wear long trousers and stout boots and to avoid walking in these areas at night. Local
advice should be sought if in doubt.

Iguanas are still found on many islands although they have declined as a result of hunting
throughout the region. In spite of their fearsome appearance, they are herbivorous and
spend much of their time in trees and low scrub feeding on leaves and trying to avoid man.

Marine turtles including the loggerhead, leatherback, hawksbill and green turtles are found
throughout Caribbean waters and they may occasionally be seen by divers and snorkellers.
Females come ashore on isolated sandy beaches between the months of May and August to lay
eggs. There may be opportunities for assisting natural history and wildlife societies (St Lucia Naturalists Society, Fish and Wildlife Dept in the US Virgin Islands) in their turtle watches, to record
numbers and locations of nests and to protect the turtles from poachers. There is a large commercial breeding programme for green turtles in the Cayman Islands. Freshwater turtles are also
found on some islands including Jamaica. Caiman have been introduced to Puerto Rico and are
also found on Cuba and the Dominican Republic.

Many species of reptile are now protected in the region and reserves have been specifically established to protect them. For example, the Maria Islands Nature Reserve on St Lucia
is home to the St Lucia ground lizard and grass snake. The latter is possibly the rarest snake in
the world with an estimated population of 150 individuals.

Frogs and toads are common in a variety of shapes and colours. There are generally more   **Amphibians**
species on the larger islands. The Cuban pygmy frog is described as the world's smallest frog,
while at the other end of the scale, the mountain chicken of Dominica and Montserrat is
probably the largest frog in the region. Its name relates to its supposed flavour. The call of the
piping frogs (*eleutherodactylus spp*) is often mistaken for a bird and these small animals are
common throughout the Lesser Antilles, becoming especially vocal at night and after rain.
The largest and most visible amphibian is probably the marine toad which has been introduced to islands throughout the region in an attempt to control insects and other invertebrate pests. The male toads use flat exposed areas from which to display, often roads.
Unfortunately, they have not evolved to deal with the car yet and as a result many are killed.

This group includes the insects, molluscs, spiders and a host of other animals that have no   **Invertebrates**
backbones. For first time travellers to the tropics, the huge range of invertebrates can seem
daunting and it is estimated that there are at least 290 species of butterfly in the Caribbean.
No one knows how many species of beetles, bugs or mollusc there are.

Of the butterflies, the swallowtails are the most spectacular, with several species found in
the Greater Antilles (especially Cuba). The other islands also have large colourful butterflies
including the monarch and flambeau which are present throughout the region. Another insect
of note is the hercules beetle, reportedly the world's second largest beetle with a large horn
that protrudes from its thorax, occasionally found in the rainforests of the Lesser Antilles.

Land and freshwater crabs inhabit a range of environments from the rainforest (eg bromeliad
crab from Jamaica) to the dry coastal areas (many species of hermit crab). Tarantulas are also
common, although they are nocturnal and rarely seen. Their bite is painful but no worse than a
bee sting. Of far more concern are the large centipedes (up to 15 cm long) that can inflict a nasty
and painful bite with their pincers. They are mostly restricted to the dry coastal areas and are most
active at night. Black widow spiders are also present on some of the islands in the Greater Antilles.
Fortunately they are rarely encountered by the traveller.

Essentials

▶ ## Disasters

If you live in the Caribbean you become accustomed to insurance companies taking a dim view of your prospects for a safe and untroubled life. **Hurricanes** are the most frequent sources of disaster, not only for the winds which can uproot trees, rip roofs from buildings and tear down power lines and telephone cables, but also for the rain, which often brings flooding and mudslides. Every year hurricanes rip through a selection of islands causing material damage to a greater or lesser degree. Although early warning systems have succeeded in cutting deaths to a minimum, damage to housing and infrastructure is usually costly. Some of the worst in recent years include Gilbert (8-20 Sep 1988), one of the strongest ever which tore through Jamaica, Hugo (10-25 Sep 1989), which damaged Montserrat (95% of houses were ruined), Puerto Rico and the Virgin Islands with winds of 140 mph, and Andrew, (16-28 Aug 1992), which charged through the Bahamas before hitting the USA, causing damage of over US$25 billion. In 1994, Tropical Storm Debbie dumped 26 inches of rain in seven hours on St Lucia, causing flooding and mudslides which wiped out much of the banana crop, while at the same time Guadeloupe was declared a disaster area because of drought. In 1995, two hurricanes in quick succession, Luis and Marilyn, wreaked havoc in the Leeward Islands, while in November 1999, Lenny took everyone by surprise by attacking from the Caribbean rather than the Atlantic, bringing strong winds and flooding and taking away normally protected beaches and buildings. In 2001, Michelle hurtled through Cuba and Central America, causing damage to housing, infrastructure and agriculture, but mass evacuation helped to avoid great loss of life. Hurricanes, however, are not the only problem. Since records began with colonization, earthquakes and volcanoes have also produced massive disasters in the region.

2002 marked the centenary of major eruptions of the **volcanoes** in St Vincent and in Martinique. On 6 May 1902, the Soufrière on St Vincent erupted, killing nearly 2,000 people and ruining farming in the area (see page 687). Activity continued until the end of March the following year, when the volcano returned to its slumbers. It awakened again in 1979, but the dangers were taken seriously

Environment

Beaches, coral reef, sea cliffs A diving or snorkelling trip over a tropical reef allows a first hand experience of this habitat's diversity of wildlife. There are a number of good field guides to reef fish and animals and some are even printed on waterproof paper. Alternatively, glass-bottomed boats sail over some sites (Buccoo Reef, Tobago), and there are underwater trails which identify types of corals and marine habitats.

Amongst the commonest fish are the grunts, butterfly, soldier, squirrel and angel fish. Tiny damsel fish are very territorial and may even attempt to nip swimmers who venture too close to their territories (more surprising than painful).

There are over 50 species of hard coral (the form that builds reefs) with a variety of sizes and colours. Amongst the most dramatic are the stagshorn and elkhorn corals which are found on the more exposed outer reefs. Brain coral forms massive round structures up to 2 m high and pillar coral forms columns that may also reach 2 m in height. Soft corals, which include black corals, sea fans and gorgonians, colonize the surface of the hard coral adding colour and variety. Associated with these structures is a host of animals and plants. Spiny lobsters may be seen lurking in holes and crevices along with other crustaceans and reef fish. The patches of sand between outcrops of coral provide suitable habitat for conch and other shellfish. Some islands now restrict the collection and sale of corals (especially black corals) and there are also legal restrictions on the sale of black corals under CITES. Overfishing has affected conch and lobster in places and there are reports of them being taken from the sea too small.

The delights of swimming on a coral reef need to be tempered by a few words of caution. Many people assume the water will be seething with sharks, however these animals are fairly uncommon in nearshore waters and the species most likely to be encountered is the nurse shark, which is harmless unless provoked. Other fish to keep an eye open for include the *and action was taken to prevent loss of life. Far worse than the St Vincent explosion was the eruption on Martinique when Mt Pelée burst into life on 8 May 1902 (see page 590). The pyroclastic flow swallowed up the chic and cultured city of St-Pierre, killing nearly 30,000 and leaving only one survivor, an inmate in the prison cells. More recently, the Soufrière Hills volcano in Montserrat began erupting in July 1995 and within two years the southern part of the island was covered in ash and lava and uninhabitable (see box, page 555). On 25 June 1997 the worst explosion yet trapped people who had returned to their homes and land to tend their crops and animals, killing 20. Although the volcano is still being monitored closely, activity has lessened and it seems to be starting to slumber again. The chain of dormant or active volcanoes runs down the eastern Caribbean all the way from Mt Liamuiga in St Kitts to the mud volcanoes of Trinidad. The volcano in the region which has erupted most frequently has in fact done the least damage. Kick 'em Jenny is an underwater volcano found in 1939, 8km north of Grenada. Since that date it is known to have erupted eleven times, and who knows how many times before then.*

*The islands are in a seismically active area and have had a number **earthquakes**. According to some, the 'sinful' town of Port Royal in Jamaica, known for its pirates and prostitutes, got its just rewards on 7 June 1692 when it was hit by an earthquake. Some 5,000 inhabitants were killed as the town slid into the sea, or perished in a subsequent fever epidemic (see page 198). Jamaica has had several earthquakes, one of which was in the disaster year of 1902, but most recently in 1993, when 5.3 on the Richter scale was recorded. In 1843 a massive earthquake struck the eastern Caribbean, affecting islands all down the chain from St Kitts to Dominica. The disaster was worst in Guadeloupe, where 5,000 people were killed and most buildings collapsed in Point-à-Pitre, but there were also 30 dead in Antigua, where much of English Harbour sank, and a handful of deaths on Montserrat and Dominica. The most recent earthquakes to have caused material damage to housing and other buildings were felt in the southern Caribbean, particularly Trinidad and Tobago, in April and July 1997.*

scorpion fish with its poisonous dorsal spines; it frequently lies stationary on coral reefs. Finally moray eels may be encountered, a fearsome looking fish, but harmless unless provoked at which point they can inflict serious bites. Of far more concern should be the variety of stinging invertebrates that are found on coral reefs. The most obvious is fire coral which comes in a range of shapes and sizes but is recognizable by the white tips to its branches. In addition, many corals have sharp edges and branches that can graze and cut. Another common group of stinging invertebrates are the fire worms which have white bristles. As with the fire coral, these can inflict a painful sting if handled or brushed against. Large black sea urchins are also common on some reefs and their spines can penetrate unprotected skin very easily. The best advice when observing coral reefs and their wildlife is to look, not touch.

Other coastal habitats that may have interesting wildlife include beaches and sea cliffs. Some islands, especially those in the southern part of the Caribbean, have spectacular cliffs and offshore islets. These are home to large flocks of sea birds including the piratical frigate bird which chases smaller birds, forcing them to disgorge their catch; another notable species is the tropic bird with its streamer like tail feathers. The cliffs may also provide dry sandy soils for the large range of Caribbean cacti, including prickly pear (*opuntia sp*) and the Turks head cactus.

Wetlands include a wide range of fresh and brackish water habitats such as rivers, marsh and mangroves. They are important for many species of bird, as well as fish. Unfortunately they are also home to an array of biting insects, including mosquitoes which are unpleasant and a serious problem where malaria or dengue are present. **Rivers, swamps, mangroves**

Important coastal wetlands include the Baie de Fort de France (Martinique), the Cabrits Swamp (Dominica), Caroni and Nariva Swamps (Trinidad), Negril and Black Morass (Jamaica). These sites all support large flocks of migratory and resident birds including waders, herons, egrets and ducks. In addition, some of the mangroves in the Greater Antilles also provide habitats for manatee, and the Negril and Black Morass has a population of American crocodiles. Large freshwater lakes are less common although Grenada, Dominica and St Vincent all have volcanic crater lakes and these are used by migratory waders and ducks as well as kingfishers.

Thorn scrub, plantations, rainforest There is little if any primary rainforest left in the Caribbean Islands, although there may be small patches in Guadeloupe. Nevertheless, many of the islands still have large areas of good secondary forest which has only suffered from a limited amount of selective felling for commercially valuable wood (eg gommier, balata and blue mahoe).

Martinique has some of the largest tracts of forest left in the Caribbean (eg rainforest at Piton du Carbet, cloud forest on Mt Pelée, dry woodland in the south). In Dominica, the Morne Trois Pitons National Park is a UNESCO World Heritage Site for its rare combination of natural features: volcanoes, fumaroles and hot springs, freshwater lakes, a 'boiling lake' and the richest biodiversity in the Lesser Antilles. Many other islands also have accessible forest, although you should always use a local guide if venturing off the beaten track.

The Caribbean rainforests are not as diverse as those on the South and Central American mainland, however they still support a large number of plant species many of which are endemic (Jamaica has over 3,000 species of which 800 are endemic). The orchids and bromeliads are impressive in many forests and it is not unusual to see trees festooned with both these groups. The wildlife of the rainforest includes both native and introduced species, although they are often difficult to see in the shady conditions. Agouti, boa constrictor, monkeys and opossum may be seen, but it is the bird life that is most evident. Hummingbirds, vireos, thrashers, todies and others are all found along with parrots, which are perhaps the group most associated with this habitat. Early morning and evening provide the best times for birdwatching.

Plantations of commercial timber (blue mahoe, Caribbean pine, teak, mahogany and others) have been established in many places. These reduce pressure on natural forest and help protect watersheds and soil. They are also valuable for wildlife and some species have adapted to them with alacrity.

Closer to the coasts, dry scrub woodland often predominates. The trees may lose their leaves during the dry season. One of the most recognizable of the trees in this woodland is the turpentine tree, also known as the tourist tree because of its red peeling bark! Bush medicines and herbal remedies are still used in the countryside although less so than previously. Leaves and bark can be seen for sale in markets.

Whale and dolphin watching

Whale and dolphin watching, long popular around North America, is starting to take off in the Caribbean too. There are three main attractions. The **humpback** whales, the acrobatic whale-watchers' favourite, who come to the Caribbean during the winter to mate, raise their calves and sing. The **sperm** whales are resident in various spots around the Caribbean but are easiest to see along the west coast of Dominica. Spotted and other **dolphin** species travel in large herds and are resident around many of the reefs, mangrove forests and offshore fishing banks. It is possible to see whales and dolphins from land and on some regular ferries, and even on air flights between the islands, but the best way to encounter them close-up is on boat tours. Some of these are general marine nature or even birding tours that include whales and dolphins. Others are specialized tours offered by diving, sportfishing or new eco-tourism ventures. Following is a guide to the best of whale and dolphin watching in the waters covered by this book.

Turks and Caicos Islands Humpbacks can be found offshore late January-early April with bottlenose and other dolphins sometimes seen close to shore. Contact *Blue Water Divers*, Grand Turk, T649-9462432; *Sea Eye Diving*, T649-9461407, F649-9461408; *Oasis Divers*, T/F649-9461128, www.oasisdivers.com

Puerto Rico Humpback whales and dolphins can be seen from land and occasional tours, particularly out of Rincón on the west coast of the island. Best lookouts are Aguadilla and from an old lighthouse near Punta Higuera, outside Rincón.

Dominican Republic The most popular and best-established whale watching in the Caribbean is found here. The industry is centred on humpback whales, but pilot whales and spotted dolphins can also be seen in Samaná Bay, and bottlenose, spinner, and spotted dolphins, Bryde's and other whales on Silver Bank. The season for both locales is January through March with whale watching tours in Samaná Bay 15 January-15 March. In recent years, more than 32,000 people a year have gone whale watching in the 20,000-sq-km marine sanctuary, most of them to Samaná Bay where the trips last two to four hours. The trips to Silver Bank are more educational and are usually arranged by specialist groups. In Samaná Bay, *Whale Samaná* is the oldest tour operator in the region and highly rated. There are about 40 registered boats; some specialize in speed, some in mass tourism and some in education and information. You will get a better view of the whales from a big boat, the smaller ones can get dwarfed by the waves. The national parks whale watch co-ordinator in Samaná can be contacted at T809-5382042, dnpballenas@yahoo.com Contact: Kim Beddall, *Whale Samaná*, Victoria Marine, PO Box 53-2, Samaná, Dominican Republic, T/F809-5382494, Kim.Beddall@usa.net Miguel Bezi, another operator, has five boats of different sizes. Contact: *Transporte Marítimo Minadiel*, Samaná Bay, Dominican Republic, T809-5382556, F5382098. For tours to see humpbacks on Silver Bank, some 50 miles north of Puerto Plata, contact: *Oceanic Society Expeditions*, Fort Mason Center, Bldg E, San Francisco, CA 94123-1394 USA, T415-4411106, www.oceanic-society.org; *Wild Oceans*, International House, Bank Rd, Kingswood, Bristol BS15 8LX, England, T0117-9848040, www.wildwings.co.uk; and *Bottom Time Adventures*, PO Box 11919, Ft Lauderdale, FL 33339-1919, USA, T831-8840122, F8840125.

For whale watching from land from January to March, but especially in February, try Cabo Francés Viejo, east along the coast from Puerto Plata, near Cabrera, as well as Punta Balandra light and Cabo Samaná (near Samaná). At Cueva de Agua there is a volunteer land-based whale watching project.

US Virgin Islands and **British Virgin Islands** They have periodic trips to see the 60-100 humpback whales that winter north of the islands. There are also spinner and other dolphins to be seen. The season is January through March. For a full-day catamaran sail contact Grethelyn Piper, *Environmental Association of St Thomas and St John* (EAST), PO Box 12379, St Thomas, USVI 00801, T340-7761976. In the BVI, humpback whale listening tours are offered from 30 December to 15 April on a 13-ft motor cruiser or a 30-ft sloop close to shore. The whales are rarely seen and never close-up, but their sounds fill the boat. Excellent tapes and CDs of whale songs are also sold. Departure is from Brewers Bay Campground, Tortola. Contact: Paul Knapp, Jr, PO Box 185, Road Town, Tortola, British Virgin Islands, T284-4943463.

St Kitts-Nevis From the island of Nevis, trips to see bottlenose dolphins and sometimes humpback whales can be arranged through dive boat operator Ellis Chaderton. Contact: *Scuba Safaris Ltd*, Qualie Beach, Nevis, T869-469 9518, F869-4699619.

Guadeloupe There are year-round half-day tours to see sperm and pilot whales and spotted dolphins offered by Caroline and Renato Rinaldi of *Association Evasion Tropicale*. Naturalists on board talk to passengers and collect scientific data. The whale watch runs from the dive centre Les Heures Saines in Malendure, about 4 km north of Bouillant on Basse-Terre. Contact: *Evasion Tropicale*, Courbaril, 971125 Bouillante, Guadeloupe, T590-571944, or *Les Heures Saines*, Rocher de Malendure, 97132 Pigeon, Guadeloupe, T590-988663, F590-987776.

Dominica Eight to 12 resident sperm whales delight visitors. You can also see spinner and spotted dolphins, pilot whales, false killer whales, and pygmy sperm whales. Occasional sightings are made of bottlenose, Risso's and Fraser's dolphins, orcas, dwarf sperm whales and melon-headed whales. The tours are run out of the *Anchorage Hotel*. Hydrophones are used to find and listen to the whales. The tours are three to four hours. *Anchorage Hotel & Dive Centre*, PO Box 34, Roseau, Dominica, T 767-4482638, F767-4485680. Tours are also offered by a well-equipped diving operator, Derek Perryman, next to the *Anchorage* at the *Castle Comfort Lodge* near Roseau. *Dive Dominica Ltd*, PO Box 2253, Roseau, Dominica, T767-4482188, F767-4486088. For land-based whale watching of sperm whales and others, Scotts Head, at the southwest tip of Dominica, overlooking Martinique Passage, is good most of the year.

St Lucia Sperm whales and various dolphins can be seen and on occasions humpback and pilot whales, Bryde's whales and orcas. The St Lucia Whale and Dolphin Watching Association is helping to organize and field enquiries for tours and to make sure that the whale watching is conducted with appropriate regulations. Contact *St Lucia Whale and Dolphin Watching Association*, c/o PO Box 1114, Castries, St Lucia, T758-452456,, www.geocities.com/slwdwa The 60-ft *Free Willy* offers three-hour morning trips all year round, but November to June is best when sperm whales and sometimes humpbacks are seen. Contact: *Captain Mike's Sport Fishing*, Pleasure Cruises and Whale Watching, PO Box GM617, Sunny Acres, St Lucia, T758-4527044/4501216, F758-4524845, www.captmikes.com Trips can also be arranged through *The Soufriere Water Taxi Association*, Bay St, Soufriere, St Lucia, T758- 4597239.

St Vincent Off the west coast, large herds of spinner and spotted dolphins are seen regularly. Sometimes bottlenose dolphins and pilot whales are also found and, sporadically, sperm and humpback whales. Tours go aboard the 36-ft sloop, *Sea Breeze*, or on a 28-ft power boat. Snorkelling and a trip to Baleine Falls can also be included. Almost year-round but avoid windy weather months of mid-December to mid-February. Best April to September when there is an 80% success rate. Trips depart from Calliaqua Lagoon on Indian Bay, southeast of Kingstown and Arnos Vale Airport. Cost for tours is US$30-40. Contact: Hal Daize, *Sea Breeze Tours/Guesthouse*, Arnos Vale Post Office, St Vincent, T784-4584969.

Petit Nevis Off Bequia, nine miles (15 km) south of St Vincent is the site of the old whaling station, once the hub of Caribbean whaling in this century. Access will require making arrangements locally.

Grenada From St George's Marina, Mosden Cumberbatch offers year-round whale watching. He takes up to 35 people for a four-hour trip to see humpbacks, which are often sighted from January through March. Other whales in the area from November to March include Cuvier's beaked whale, killer whales and the dwarf sperm whale, amongst others. The rest of the year you can see sperm whales, pigmy right whales, long and shortfinned pilot whales and others, as well as various dolphins. Contact: *First Impressions Ltd*, T/F473-4403678, www.catamaranchartering.com.

Conservation By watching whales and dolphins in the Caribbean, you can actually contribute to saving them. Many dolphins are still killed, mainly by fishermen, for food or fish bait. As well, pilot whales and even rare beaked whales are commonly harpooned, particularly in the eastern Caribbean. Almost every winter, over the past few years, two humpbacks have been killed off Bequia, nearly always a precious mother and calf. Mother and calf humpbacks have very high site fidelity on the mating and calving grounds and local whalers are effectively removing what could be a healthy whale watch industry. Whale and dolphin watching provides local people with another way to look at these intriguing animals – as well as a potentially more sustainable source of income.

Your support of whale watching may have the biggest impact in countries of the eastern Caribbean: Dominica, Grenada, St Lucia, and St Vincent and the Grenadines. Over the past few years, Japan has contributed to the development of these nations, by helping to build airports and adding fish docks and piers. In exchange, Japan has counted on the support of these four governments, all members of the International Whaling Commission (IWC), in its attempt to re-open commercial whaling. You can help conservation here by simply saying you enjoy seeing whales and dolphins in local waters. However, when referring to dolphins, use the word 'porpoises'. In most parts of the Caribbean, the word 'dolphin' means the dolphin fish. Best to specify that it is the mammal and not the fish that you want to see. And if you see whales and dolphins being killed at sea, express your views to local and national tourism outlets of the country concerned.

For more information contact the *Whale and Dolphin Conservation Society*, Alexander House, James Street West, Bath, BA1 2BT, UK, www.wdcs.org

Books

By no means all the writers of history, fiction, poetry and other topics will be found below. There is no room to talk of the many authors who have been inspired by aspects of the Caribbean for their fiction such as **Robert Louis Stevenson**, **Graham Greene**, **Ernest Hemingway**, **Gabriel García Márquez**. Nor can we detail travel writers, such as **Patrick Leigh Fermor**, *The Traveller's Tree*, **Quentin Crewe**, *Touch the Happy Isles*, **Trollope**, *Travels in the West Indies and the Spanish Main*, **Alec Waugh**, *The Sugar Isles*, **James Pope-Hennessy**, *West Indian Summer*, among others. This list is not exhaustive, concentrating mainly on books in English, published (or readily available) in the UK. For any favourites omitted, we apologize.

Other books have been suggested in culture, tourist information and other sections. See individual islands and page 44 for maps

Essentials

History
Of the histories of the region, **James Ferguson**, *A Traveller's History of the Caribbean* (1998), The Windrush Press. Concise and easy to dip in to. More academic is **J H Parry, P M Sherlock and Anthony Maingot**, *A Short History of The West Indies* (1987), Macmillan. Very accessible. Also **Eric Williams**, *From Columbus to Castro: The History of the Caribbean 1492-1969* (1970) Harper and Row.

Geography
James Ferguson, *Far from Paradise, An Introduction to Caribbean Development* (1990), Latin American Bureau. An introduction to the geography of the Caribbean, **Mark Wilson**, *The Caribbean Environment* (1989), OUP. Prepared for the Caribbean Examinations Council, a fascinating text book.

Field guides
The number of good books on Caribbean wildlife is slowly increasing. Look out for the following: **P Bacon**, *Flora and Fauna of the Caribbean*, Key Caribbean Publications, PO Box 21, Port of Spain, Trinidad. **J Bond**, *Birds of the West Indies*, Collins. **C C Chaplin**, *Fishwatchers Guide to West Atlantic Coral Reefs*, Horowood Books. Some printed on plastic paper for use underwater. **I Greenberg**, *Guide to Corals and Fishes of Florida, the Bahamas and the Caribbean*, Seahawk Press. **P Honeychurch**, *Caribbean Wild Plants and their Uses*, Macmillan. **Raffaele et al**, *A Guide to the Birds of the West Indies*, (1998) Princeton University Press. Thorough and rather heavy.

Macmillan also produce short field guides on *The Flowers of the Caribbean*, *The Fishes of the Caribbean*, *Fishes of the Caribbean Reefs*, *Marine Life of the Caribbean*, *Butterflies and Other Insects of the Caribbean*.

Economics
A study of Caribbean tourism and its impact on the economies and people is **Polly Pattullo's**, *Last Resort, The Cost of Tourism in the Caribbean* (1996), Cassell and Latin American Bureau, a new edition should be published in 2003. An economic study is **Clive Y Thomas**, *The Poor and the Powerless, Economic Policy and Change in the Caribbean* (1988), Latin American Bureau.

Literature
For an introduction to Caribbean writers and writers on the Caribbean, with extracts from numerous literary works, **James Ferguson**, *Traveller's Literary Companion to the Caribbean*, with chapters on Cuba and Puerto Rico by Jason Wilson (1997), In Print. Highly recommended. The work of a great many English-speaking poets is collected in *The Penguin Book of Caribbean Verse in English*, edited by **Paula Burnett** (1986) see also *Hinterland: Caribbean Poetry From the West Indies and Britain*, edited by **E A Markham** (1990) Bloodaxe, and *West Indian Poetry*, edited by **Kenneth Ramchand and Cecil Gray** (1989), Longman Caribbean. For a French verse anthology, see *La Poésie Antillaise*, collected by **Maryse Condé** (1977) Fernand Nathan. There are a number of prose anthologies of stories in English, eg *The Oxford Book of Caribbean Short Stories*, **Stewart Brown and John Wickham** (1999), *Stories from the Caribbean*, introduced by **Andrew Salkey** (1972) Paul Elek, or *West Indian Narrative: an Introductory Anthology*, **Kenneth Ramchand** (1966) Nelson. Heinemann's Caribbean Writers series publishes works of fiction by well-established and new writers. The *Story of English*, by **Robert McCrumb**, **William Cran** and **Robert MacNeil** (1986) Faber and Faber/BBC, has an interesting section on the development of the English language in the Caribbean.

General Finally, a generally excellent series of Caribbean books is published by Macmillan Caribbean; this includes island guides, natural histories, books on food and drink, sports and pirates, and wall maps (for a full catalogue, write to Macmillan Caribbean, Houndmills, Basingstoke, Hampshire, RG21 2XS, England).

Cuba

Introducing Cuba

Cuba's charms are as varied as they are fascinating. Most people spend some time relaxing and enjoying the sun and sand on Cuba's extensive beaches, but there is so much more to do. Go before Castro dies and see one of the last bastions of Communism and a culture which has denied itself the influences of the USA for so long. Visit the Spanish colonial cities, where the architecture is being beautifully preserved, go hiking or cycling in the countryside and see rural life in Cuba, take a ride in one of those famous 50s cars, go birdwatching or scuba diving, the list is endless. No one will leave the island without being affected by the pulsating rhythms of the music and dance and the racial mixture which has produced such creativity and exuberance in the arts and entertainment. And of course, you haven't lived until you've learned to dance the rumba.

Essentials

Before you travel

Visitors from the majority of countries need only a **passport**, return ticket and 30-day **tourist card** to enter Cuba, as long as they are going solely for tourist purposes. Tourist cards may be obtained from Cuban embassies, consulates, airlines, or approved travel agents (price in the UK £15 (agencies sometimes charge more), some other countries US$15-35). You have to fill in an application form, photocopy the main pages of your passport (valid for more than 6 months after departure from Cuba), submit confirmation of your accommodation booking and your return or onward flight ticket. Immigration in Havana Airport will only give you 30 days on your tourist card, but you can get it extended for a further 30 days at Immigration in Nuevo Vedado, Factor esq Final, open 0830-1200. Go early, it gets busy and there are queues.

The **US** government does not normally permit its citizens to visit Cuba. US citizens should have a US licence to engage in any transactions related to travel to Cuba, but tourist or business travel are not licensable, even through a third country such as Mexico or Canada. For further information on entry to Cuba from the USA and customs requirements, US travellers should contact the *Cuban Interests Section*, an office of the Cuban government, at 2630 16th St NW, Washington DC 20009, T202-7978518. Many travellers conceal their tracks by going via Mexico, the Bahamas, or Canada, when only the tourist card is stamped, not the passport. On your return be careful to destroy any evidence of having been in Cuba as US Immigration authorities frequently stop people at the border and threaten them with massive fines. A useful website for information and advice is at www.cubalinda.com

Documents

Personal baggage and articles for personal use are allowed in free of duty; so are 1 carton of cigarettes and 2 bottles of alcoholic drinks. Visitors importing new goods worth between US$100 and US$1,000 will be charged 100% duty, subject to a limit of 2 items a year. No duty is payable on goods valued at under US$100. You may take in up to 10 kg of medicine. It is prohibited to bring in fresh fruit and vegetables. On departure you may take out tobacco worth US$2,000 with a receipt, or only 50 cigars without a receipt, up to 6 bottles of rum and personal jewellery. To take out works of art you must have permission from the Registro Nacional de Bienes Culturales de la Dirección de Patrimonio del Ministerio de Cultura. More information is available at www.aduana.islagrande.com

Customs

Currency The monetary unit is the **peso cubano**. The official exchange rate is US$1=1 peso. There are notes for 3, 5, 10 and 20 pesos, and coins for 5, 20 and 40 centavos and 1 peso. You must have a supply of coins if you want to use the local town buses (20 or 40 centavos). The 20 centavo coin is called a *peseta*. In 1995 the government introduced a new '**peso convertible**' on a par with the US dollar, with a new set of notes and coins. It is fully exchangeable with authorized hard currencies circulating in the economy. Remember to spend or exchange any *pesos convertibles* before you leave as they are worthless outside Cuba.

Money

Exchange The 'peso convertible' is equal to the dollar and can be used freely in the country. The street exchange rate and official *casas de cambio* (CADECA) rates fluctuate between 19-27 pesos cubanos to the dollar and there is now virtually no black market. Food in the markets (*agromercados*), at street stalls and on trains, as well as books and popular cigarettes (but not in every shop), can be bought in pesos. You will need pesos for the toilet, rural trains, trucks, food at roadside cafeterías during a journey and drinks and snacks for a bus or train journey. Away from tourist hotels, in smaller towns there are very few dollar facilities and you will need pesos for everything. Visitors on pre-paid package tours need not acquire any pesos at all. Bring US$ in small denominations for spending money. US dollars are the only currency accepted in all tourist establishments but euros are accepted in Varadero, Cayo Coco, Cayo Largo, Cayo Santa María and at *El Colony*, Isla de la Juventud. **Travellers' cheques** expressed in US or Canadian dollars or sterling are valid in Cuba. Travellers' cheques issued on US bank paper are not accepted. Commission ranges from 2-4%. Don't enter the place or date when signing cheques, or they may be refused. There are **banks** and CADECAS (exchange houses) for changing money legally. Non-dollar currencies can be changed into dollars.

Banks and money changers are listed in individual town directories

Cuba

Cuba

▶ ## Cuban embassies overseas

Australia *Consulate: 18 Manwaring Ave, Maroubra NSW, 2035, T61-2-93114611, F931155112.*
Austria *Himmelhofgasse 40 A-C, A-1130, Vienna, T43-1-8778198/8778159, F8777703.*
Canada *388 Main Street, Ottawa, Ontario, K11E3, T1-613-5630141.*
France *16 rue de Presles 75015, Paris, T33-1-45675535, F45658092.*
Germany *Kennedyallee 22-24, Bad Godesberg 53175, Bonn, T49-228-3090, F309244.*
Italy *Via Licinia No 7, 00153, Rome, T39-06-5742347/5755984, F5745445.*
Netherlands *Mauritskade 49, 2514 HG The Hague, T31-70-3606061, F3647586.*

Portugal *Rua Pero Da Covilha No 14, Restelo, 1400, Lisbon, T351-1-3015318, F3011895.*
South Africa *45 Mackenzie St, Brooklyn 0181, Pretoria, PO Box 11605, Hatfield 0028, T27-12-3462215, F3462216.*
Spain *Paseo de La Habana No 194 entre Calle de la Macarena y Rodríguez, Pinilla, 28036, Madrid, T34-91-3592500, F3596145.*
Scandinavia *Karlavagen 49, 11449 Stockholm, T46-8-6630850, F6611418.*
Switzerland *Gesellsschaftsstrasse 8, CP 5275, 30112, Berne, T41-31-3022111/ 3029830 (Tourist Office), F3022111.*
UK *167 High Holborn, London WC1 6PA, T020-72402488/8367886, F78362602.*

Many restaurants are often reluctant to take credit cards

Credit cards The following credit cards are acceptable in most places: *Visa*, *MasterCard*, *Access*, *Diners*, *Banamex* (Mexican) and *Carnet*. No US credit cards are accepted so a Visa card issued in the USA will not be accepted. This includes, for example, a Virgin Mastercard issued by MBNA. *American Express*, no matter where issued, is unacceptable. You can obtain cash advances with a credit card at branches of the *Banco Financiero Internacional* and several other banks, but it is best to bring plenty of cash as there will often be no other way of paying for what you need. You will need to show your passport. Most financial institutions require a US$100 minimum withdrawal. It is usually quicker and easier to queue at a bank to get a dollar cash advance on your credit card than to trail around looking for a working ATM. There are no toll free numbers to call if your card is stolen, so bring a number from home for you to call. If you get really stuck and need money sent urgently to Cuba, you can get it transferred from any major commercial bank abroad direct to Asistur (see page 66) for a 10% commission.

Climate The high season is mid-Dec to mid-Apr, when there are more dry days and less humidity. Hurricanes and tropical storms begin in Aug and can go on until the end of Nov causing flooding and damage. It is hotter and drier in Santiago than in Havana, and wetter and cooler in the mountains than in the lowlands. Northeast trade winds temper the heat, but summer shade temperatures can rise to 33°C in Havana, and higher elsewhere. In winter, day temperatures drop to 20°C and there are a few cold days, 8°-10°C, with a north wind. Average rainfall is from 860 mm in the east to 1,730 mm in Havana; it falls mostly in the summer and autumn, but there can be torrential rains at any time.

Tourist information

Internet For lots of details and addresses of hotels, tour companies, car hire, etc, go to www.dtcuba.com They also have a weekly online newsletter, *Boletín Semanal DTC News*. For news, travel, politics, business, internet and technology, health, science, art and culture, festivals and events, you can try **www.cubaweb.cu** There is also a section, **Cocoweb**, where they will answer your questions by email, extremely useful and recommended. A small network of tourist information offices in Havana called *Infotur*, www.infotur.cu can be found in Old Havana, T333333, at Obispo entre Habana y Compostela, Obispo y San Ignacio, Obispo y Bernaza and the Terminal de Cruceros. In Playa at Av 5 y 112, T/F247036. At the airport at Terminal 1, T558734, Terminal 2, T558733, and Terminal 3, T666112, 666101. There is also an office serving the Playas del Este, at Av Las Terrazas entre 11 y 12, Santa María del Mar, T971261, F961111, open 0830-2030.

    Asistur, linked to overseas insurance companies, can help with emergency hospital treatment, robbery, direct transfer of funds to Cuba, etc. Main office in Miramar, Calle 4 110 entre 1 y 2, T2048835, F2048088, www.asistur.cubaweb.cu Also offices in *Hotel Casa del Científico*,

Cuban tourist offices overseas

◀

Canada, 440 Blvd René Levesque, Suite 1105, Montréal, *Quebec* H3Z 1V7, T1-514-8758004-5, mintur@generation.net 55 Queen Street E, Suite 705, *Toronto*, M5C 1R6, T1-416-3620700-2, cuba.tbtor@simpatico.ca
France, 280 Blvd Raspail, 75014 Paris, T33-1-45389010, ot.cuba@wanadoo.fr
Germany, Ander Hauptwache 7, 60313, Frankfurt, T49-69-288322-3, gocuba@compuserve.com

Italy, Via General Fara 30, Terzo Plano, 20124 Milan, T39-02-66981463, minturitalia@infuturo.it
Spain, Paseo de la Habana54-1, Izquierda, 28036 Madrid, T34-91-4113097, otcuba@otcuba.esp.com
Sweden, Vegagatan 6, 3rd floor, 113-29 Stockholm, augusto_h@hotmail.com
UK, 154 Shaftesbury Av, London WC2H 8JT, T44-020-72406655, cubatouristboard.london@virgin.net

Cuba

Paseo del Prado, entre Animas y Trocadero, Habana Vieja, for 24-hr service T338527, 338920, F338088, cellular Asis 2747; under *Hotel Casa Granda*, Santiago, T86128, Varadero, T667277; Cienfuegos, T6402; Guardalavaca, T30148.

Bring all medicines you might need as they can be difficult to find. Even painkillers are in very short supply. Many other things are scarce or unobtainable in Cuba, so take in everything you are likely to need other than food: razor blades; medicines and pills; heavy-duty insect repellent; strong sun protection and after-sun preparations; toilet paper; tampons; disposable nappies; photographic supplies; torch and batteries.

What to take

Getting there

The frequency of **scheduled** flights depends on the season, with twice-weekly flights in the winter being reduced to once a week/month in the summer. Most international flights come in to Havana, but the international airports of Varadero, Holguín (for Guardalavaca beaches), Santiago de Cuba, Ciego de Avila (for Cayo Coco), Cayo Largo, Santa Clara (for Cayo Santa María) and Camagüey (for Santa Lucía beaches) also receive flights. The state airline, *Cubana de Aviación* (www.cubana.cu), flies to Europe, Canada, Central and South America and to many islands in the Caribbean. It is cheaper than competitors on the same routes but the service is worse, seats are cramped and some travel agents do not recommend it. The main airlines offering scheduled flights are *Air France*, *Air Jamaica*, *Iberia*, *Air Europa*, *Spanair*, *Martinair*, *LTU*, *Condor* and *Aeroflot* from Europe, *Mexicana*, *Aerocaribe*, *Aeropostal*, *Lacsa*, *Tame*, *Copa* and *Lan Chile* from Latin America, *AeroCaribbean* and *Air Jamaica* from the Caribbean. Direct flights are available from Amsterdam, Bogotá, Buenos Aires, Cancún, Caracas, Curaçao, Fort-de-France, Frankfurt, Freeport, Grand Cayman, Guatemala City, Guayaquil, Kingston, Lima, London, Madrid, Managua, Mérida (Mexico), Mexico City, Milan, Montego Bay, Monterrey, Montréal, Moscow, Munich, Oaxaca, Panama City, Paris, Pointe-à-Pitre, Quito, Rome, San José, San Salvador, Santiago de Chile, Santo Domingo, São Paulo, Shannon, Toronto, Tuxtla Gutiérrez, Veracruz and Villahermosa. Connections have to be made from other parts of the world. There are **charters** from London, Manchester, Brussels, Frankfurt, Toronto, Vancouver, Montréal, Quebec, Halifax, Buenos Aires, Cancún and other cities to all the international airports in Cuba, and between Santiago de Cuba and Montego Bay, Jamaica. There are also regular charters between Cayo Largo and Grand Cayman and occasional charters between Providenciales, Turks and Caicos Islands and Santiago de Cuba. The Cuban air charter line *AeroCaribbean* has an arrangement with *Bahamasair* for a (nearly) daily service Miami-Nassau-Havana, changing planes in Nassau; the Cuban tourist agency *Amistur* organizes the service. *Gulfstream International*, T305-8711200, F305-8713540, operates a direct charter service Miami-Havana. *AeroCaribbean* flies from Montego Bay, Santo Domingo and Port-au-Prince, Haiti, to Santiago.

Air

Cuba

▶ ## Touching down

Hours of business Banks: 0830-1200, 1330-1500 Mon-Fri. **Government offices**: Mon-Fri 0830-1230, 1330-1730. Some offices open on Sat morning. **Shops**: 0830-1800 Mon-Sat 0900-1400 Sun. Hotel tourist (hard currency) shops open 1000-1800 or 1900.
Official time Eastern Standard Time, 5 hrs behind GMT; Daylight Saving Time, 4 hrs behind GMT.
Public Holidays Liberation Day (1 Jan), Labour Day (1 May), Revolution Day (26 Jul and the day either side), Beginning of War of Independence (10 Oct) and Christmas Day . Other **festive days** which are not public holidays are 28 Jan (birth of José Martí in 1853), 24 Feb (anniversary of renewal of War of Independence, 1895), 8 Mar (International Women's Day), 13 Mar (anniversary of 1957 attack on presidential palace in Havana by a group of young revolutionaries), 19 Apr (anniversary of defeat of mercenaries at Bay of Pigs, 1961), 30 Jul (martyrs of the Revolution day), 8 Oct (death of Che Guevara, 1967), 28 Oct (death of Camilo

Cienfuegos, 1959), 27 Nov (death by firing squad of 8 medical students by Spanish colonial government, 1871), 7 Dec (death of Antonio Maceo in battle in 1896).
  Jul is a good time to visit Santiago if you want to catch the **carnival**, although **New Year** is also lively with parades and street parties (Havana's **carnival** is in **Aug**, but it is not such an exciting affair). New Year is celebrated everywhere as the anniversary of the **Revolution**, so you can expect speeches as well as parties. Throughout the year there are lots of excuses for music and dancing in the street, washed down with quantities of rum and local food. Some towns even do it weekly, called a **Noche Cubana**. For a calendar of sporting and cultural events and festivals, see **www.buroconv.cubaweb.cu**
Voltage 110 Volts, 3 phase 60 cycles, AC. Plugs are usually of the American type.
Weights and measures The metric system is compulsory, but exists side by side with American and old Spanish systems.

Touching down

Airport information

On arrival Immigration can be very slow if you come off a busy *Iberia* DC10 flight but speedy off smaller *Cubana* aircraft. Cuba has several airports classified as international, but only Havana is of any size. Havana now has 3 terminals, the third and newest one being for international flights, with exchange facilities, snack bars, shops, etc. There is an ATM on the ground (arrivals) floor of Terminal 3.
On departure   Remember to reconfirm your onward or return flight 48 hrs before departure, otherwise you will lose your reservation. The airport departure tax is US$25. The seating in the Havana Airport is uncomfortable. The restaurant is poor to awful, but this will be your last chance to hear a live Cuban band while eating. The selection of shops is limited but there is lots of rum, cigars and coffee, a few books and magazines on sale. It is better to buy before you get to the airport.

Tourist information
For Havana tour operators, see page 98

Local tours Several state-owned tour companies offer day trips or excursion packages including accommodation to many parts of the island, as well as tours of colonial and modern Havana. Examples (from Havana, 1 day, except where indicated): Viñales, including tobacco and rum factories, US$44; Guamá, US$44; Cayo Coco (by air), US$143 overnight; Soroa, US$29; Varadero US$35 without lunch; Cayo Largo (by air), US$119 daytrip, US$170 overnight all-inclusive; Cienfuegos-Trinidad overnight US$115; Santiago de Cuba (by air) and Baracoa, US$159 including 1 night's accommodation, recommended, you see a lot and cover a lot of ground in 2 days. Tours can also be taken from any beach resort. Guides speak European languages; the tours are generally recommended as well-organized and good value. Actual departure depends on a minimum number of passengers (usually 6). Always ask the organizers when they will know if the trip is on or what the real departure time will be. Lunch is usually a poor-quality set meal.

Cuba had a reputation for prostitution before the Revolution and after a gap of some decades it has resurfaced. Behind every girl there is a pimp. In 2001 a German tourist was murdered by a pimp in Santiago for not paying the girl US$20 for sex. Despite government crackdowns and increased penalties, everything is available for both sexes if you know where to look. Be warned, you are likely to be fleeced. The age of consent is 18 in Cuba, so if you are introduced to a young girl you are in danger of being led into a blackmail trap. Hotels are not allowed to let Cubans enter the premises in the company of foreigners, so sexual encounters now often take place in *casas particulares*, private homes where there is little security and lots of risk. If you or your travelling companion are dark skinned, you may suffer from the exclusion policy in hotels as officials will assume he/she is Cuban until proved otherwise. If you are a man out alone at night in Havana you will find the market very active and you will be tugged at frequently, mostly by females.

Sex tourism
Cubans who offer their services (whether sexual or otherwise) in return for dollars are known as jineteros, or jineteras ('jockeys', because they 'ride on the back' of the tourists)

In general the Cuban people are very hospitable. The island is generally safer than many of its Caribbean and Latin neighbours, but certain precautions should be taken. Visitors should never lose sight of their luggage or leave valuables in hotel rooms (most hotels have safes). Do not leave your things on the beach when swimming. Guard your camera closely. Pickpocketing and bag-snatching are quite common in Havana and Santiago. Street lighting is poor so care is needed. Some people recommend walking in the middle of the street. Muggings in Havana have been reported to us, particularly in the dark, narrow streets of Chinatown at night. You must carry your passport and tourist visa everywhere. Never leave it in Havana with a *casa particular* owner while you visit other areas, this is a scam to get you to return to their house.

Safety

Where to stay

Tourists to Cuba often stay in rooms or apartments in private houses, known as *casas particulares*. Rates in private houses (US$15-30 per night) are per room, not per person, and many rooms sleep 3 or 4 people. You pay in US dollars for both accommodation and food, but prices are considerably less than in hotels while the service is more friendly and the food better quality and more plentiful. The casas must be registered to pay taxes for whatever services they offer. All legal *casas particulares* should have a yellow registration book you have to sign, and a sticker on their door of a blue triangle on a white background. There are thousands of *casas particulares* but only 40% of them are licensed. Taxes and licences are high at US$60-200 per room per month, depending on the region, plus 10% of earnings to be paid at the end of each year, so profit margins are tight. To offer food, Cubans have to buy another licence, US$30 per month, although many do not. Private homes vary considerably and can be extremely comfortable or very basic. Because of shortages things often don't work, there may be cold water only, once a day, and the lights often go off. A torch is useful. Rates can often be bargained down if you go directly to the owners, negotiate a package of bed, breakfast and evening meal, or stay for several nights. The owners pay US$5 per night per room for each client brought to them by a tout (who does not pay taxes) or recommended by another *casa* owner; this will inevitably end up on your bill, so avoid being taken to a house by anyone. If you are given a business card for a casa by someone selling bus tickets or a taxi driver, they will get their commission if you end up staying at that *casa*.

Casas particulares
This is currently the most popular form of accommodation for independent travellers and we have received hundreds of recommendations, not all of which we have space to include

All hotels are owned by the government, solely or in joint ventures with foreign partners. All *Cubanacán* hotels are 4-5 star and were finished after 1991; they are usually joint ventures. *Gaviota* hotels date from after 1990; *Gran Caribe* also has 4-5-star hotels, while *Horizontes* hotels are 3-star (mostly built in the 1940s and 50s) and *Islazul* has the cheaper end of the market, mostly for national tourism, but foreigners are welcome and many of their hotels are being upgraded. A 3-star hotel costs US$30-50 bed and breakfast in high season, US$25-35 in low season, while a 4-star hotel will charge US$80-90 and US$60-70 respectively. In remote beach resorts the hotels are usually all-inclusive.

Hotels

Getting around

Air There are **Cubana de Aviación** services from Havana to most of the main towns: Camagüey,

Tourists must pay air fares in US$ Holguín, Trinidad, Baracoa, Guantánamo, Manzanillo, Moa, Nueva Gerona/Isla de Juventud, Bayamo, Ciego de Avila, Las Tunas, Santa Clara, Santiago, Cayo Largo, Cayo Coco, Varadero, all have airports. Some places with airstrips are reached by Aerotaxi. Havana to Santiago costs US$100 1 way; it is advisable to prebook flights at home as demand is very heavy, although you can get flights from hotel tour desks as part of a package. It is difficult to book flights from 1 city to another when you are not at the point of departure, except from Havana; the computers are not able to cope. Delays are common. *Cubana* flights are very cold, take warm clothes and possibly some food for a long flight. *Aerotaxi* flights can also be cold, they are flying buses and you often get wooden bench seating in an old Soviet aircraft.

Bicycle For people who really want to explore the country in depth and independently, cycling is excellent, although you are advised to bring your own bike and all spare parts. *Iberia* and *Cubana* airlines both accept bicycles as normal luggage as long as you do not take more than 20 kg, but some charters, such as *Martinair*, charge extra. A good-quality bicycle is essential if you are going to spend many hours in the saddle. However, it does not have to be very sophisticated; most of Cuba is flat, the road network is good and there is little traffic. In cities there are *parqueos bicicletas*, where you can store your bike while walking around. Cycling can get very hot, so you are advised to do long distances early in the morning.

For organized cycling tours of Cuba contact **Blazing Saddles Travels**, in the UK, T020-84240483, saddles100@aol.com; **Havanatour UK**, 3 Wyllyots Pl, Potters Bar, Herts EN6 2JD, T01707-646463, F01707-663139; **Fietsvakantiewinkel**, Spoorlaan 19, 3445 AE Woerden, Holland, T31-3480-21844, F31-3480-23839. You may also be able to join a group of Cuban bikers (mostly English-speaking) through the **Club Nacional de Cicloturismo** (National Bike Club), Gran Caribe, Transnico Internacional, Lonja del Comercio Oficina 6d, La Habana Vieja, T969193, F669908, trans@mail.infocom.etecsa.cu They run tours of 1-28 days in all parts of the country, some with political themes. *Blazing Saddles Travels* also offers bike hire, ATB (mountain bikes) with 21 gears and pannier rack, US$12/day including puncture repair kit for a pre-arranged hire period. The bikes will be delivered to your hotel or *casa particular*.

Bus **Local** The local word for bus is *guagua*. In Havana there are huge double-jointed buses pulled by a truck, called *camellos* (camels) because of their shape, also irreverently known as 'Sat night at the cinema' because they are full of 'sex, crime and alcohol'. In the rush hours they are filled to more than capacity, making it hard to get off if you have managed to get on. The urban bus fare throughout Cuba is 20 centavos for *camellos* and 40 centavos for all others; it helps to have the exact fare.

Long distance For bus transport to other provinces from Havana there are 2 companies theoretically offering services in dollars to foreigners. **Astro** has a dollar ticket office in the Terminal de Omnibus Nacional, Boyeros y 19 de Mayo (third left via 19 de Mayo entrance), T703397, open daily 0700-2100. You don't have to book in advance but it is wiser to do so. It is becoming increasingly difficult for foreigners to use *Astro* and you may be turned away. The best service, and the one foreigners are encouraged to use, is **Víazul** (*Viajes Azul*), at Av 26 y Zoológico, Nuevo Vedado, T8811413, www.viazul.cu open 0900-2300. You have to pay in dollars, it is more expensive than *Astro*, and you will travel with other foreigners, but it is an efficient, punctual and comfortable service. The terminal is a long way from the centre so you have to get a taxi. In other cities *Viazul* and *Astro* use the same bus terminal. Tickets can also be booked through *Rumbos*, avoiding trips to the bus station. In 2003 *Víazul* had the following routes: Havana-Santiago, Havana-Varadero, Havana-Viñales, Havana-Trinidad, Varadero-Trinidad, Trinidad-Santiago and Baracoa-Santiago, stopping at all major towns along the way. There is a weight limit for luggage of 20 kg on all long-distance bus journeys and the bus-hoverfoil to Isla de la Juventud.

Car **Car hire** Rental companies are at the airport and most large hotels. Minimum US$40 a day (or US$50 for air conditioning) with limited mileage of 100 km a day, and US$8-20 a day optional insurance, or US$50-88 per day unlimited mileage; cheaper rates over 7 days. Credit cards accepted for the rental, or cash or TCs paid in advance, guarantee of US$200-250 required; you must also present your passport and home driving licence. In practice, you may find car hire rates prohibitively expensive when small cars are 'unavailable' and a 4-door sedan at US$93, unlimited km, insurance included, is your only option. It pays to shop around, even between offices of the same company. Cubans are not allowed to hire cars (although they may drive them), so even if you have organized a local driver you will have to show a foreign driving licence. If you want to drive from Havana to Santiago and return by air, try *Havanautos*, www.havanautos.cubaweb.cu They will charge at least US$80 to return the car to Havana, but most companies will not even consider it. *Vía Rent-a-Car* (*Gaviota*), www.gaviota.cubaweb.cu, charges US$160, calculated at US$0.18 per km on a distance of 884 km from Santiago to Havana, but this is reduced to US$0.09 if the car is hired for more than 15 days. If you hire in Havana and want to drop off the car at the airport, companies will charge you extra, around US$10, although this is sometimes waived if you bargain hard. Check what is required concerning fuel, you don't always have to leave the tank full, but make sure the tank is really full when you start. Fly-and-drive packages can be booked from abroad through *Cubacar*, part of the Grupo Cubanacán, www.cubacar.cubaweb.cu, who have a wide range of jeeps and cars all over the country and can even arrange a driver, pmando@cubacar.cha.cyt.cu Most vehicles are Japanese or Korean makes, Suzuki jeeps can be hired for 6 to 12 hrs in beach areas, US$11-22, plus US$8 insurance, extra hrs US$5. Watch out for theft of the radio and spare tyre; you will have to pay about US$350 if stolen unless you take out the costly extra insurance. Always remember to carry the rental agreement and your driving licence with you. Otherwise, you face an on-the-spot US$10 fine if you are stopped by the traffic police and a fine by the hire company when you return the vehicle. Another option is *Transautos*, www.transtur.cubaweb.cu Otherwise, there is more information at www.dtcuba.com/esp/transporte_tierra.asp

Moped rental at resorts is around US$8-10 per hr, cheaper for longer, US$25-30 per day, US$80 per week.

Taxi
See also page 99

There are 3 types of taxi: tourist taxis, Cuban taxis and private taxis (*particulares*). With dollar tourist taxis you pay for the distance, not for waiting time. On short routes, fares are metered. From the airport to Havana (depending on destination) costs US$12-18 with *Panataxi*, to Playas del Este US$30, to Varadero US$90. Cuban taxis, or *colectivos*, also operate on fixed routes and pick you up only if you know where to stand for certain destinations. Travelling on them is an adventure and a complicated cultural experience. Cubans are not allowed to carry foreigners in their vehicles, but they do; private taxis, *particulares*, are considerably cheaper than other taxis, for example airport to Havana centre US$8-12, from Santiago to the airport US$5. A *particular* who pays his tax will usually display a 'taxi' sign, which can be a hand-written piece of board, but have a private registration plate. Some have meters, in others you have to negotiate a price. If not metered, 10 km should cost around US$5. For long distances you can negotiate with official taxis as well as *particulares*, and the price should be around US$10 per hr. As a general rule, the cost will depend on the quality of your Spanish and how well you know the area.

Train

Travel between provinces is usually booked solid several days or weeks in advance and foreigners are frequently turned away. If you are on a short trip you may do better to go by *Víazul* bus or on a tour with excursions. Long delays and breakdowns must be expected. Be at the station at least 1 hr before the scheduled departure time. Fares have to be paid for in dollars, which will usually entitle you to a waiting area, seat reservation and to board the train before the big rush starts. There is a dollar ticket office in every station. Alternatively, the tourist desks in some of the larger hotels sell train tickets to foreigners, in dollars. Long-distance trains allow only seated passengers, they are spacious and comfortable, but extremely cold unless the air-conditioning is broken, so take warm clothes. A torch is useful for the toilet. All carriages are smoking areas. Bicycles can be carried as an express item only and often cost more than the fare for a person. Food service is inadequate so it is advisable to take food with you. If you are 15-16 hrs late you will be glad you took snacks and drinks.

Cuba

Cuba

Keeping in touch

Internet

Facilities are now more widespread, but expect long queues

Cubans are not generally allowed to access the internet, so facilities are limited to dollar-paying foreigners. You will be asked for your passport. The large, international 4- or 5-star hotels have business centres with computers for internet access (around US$5 for 30 mins). There are 'cybercafés' in the Capitolio, Havana, and the Café Las Begonias in Trinidad, where access costs US$3 for 30 mins and US$5 per hr. The telephone company, *Etecsa*, sells prepaid cards which give you an access code and a password code for when you log in and these cost US$15 for 5 hrs. In Havana you can use *Etecsa* cards at the International Press Center on La Rampa, Calle 23 entre N y O. In other towns *Etecsa* is installing mobile cabins (large blue telephone boxes) with international and national phone services and a computer for internet access, but there will be no internet access in small towns off the beaten tourist track. Telecorreos sells a different prepaid card for use in Post Offices, where you can send emails but not surf the internet. You will not be able to access your inbox via the internet and you will have to set up a new account. The Government plans to install computers in every post office soon.

Telephone

IDD code: 00-53

Cuba's communications are improving with help from foreign telecommunications companies but consequently numbers and codes are frequently changing

Many public phones take prepaid cards (*tarjetas*) which are easier than coins. For domestic, long-distance calls try and get hold of a peso phone card, eg 10 pesos, which works out much cheaper than the dollar cards. The furthest distance, Pinar del Río to Baracoa, costs 1 peso per min, but if you have a dollar phone card it will cost you US$1 per min. To phone abroad, dial 119 followed by the country and regional codes and number. Many hotels and airports have telephone offices where international calls can be made. Look for the *Telecorreos* or *Etecsa* signs. No 'collect' calls allowed and only cash accepted. In a few top-class hotels you can direct dial foreign countries from your room. Phonecards are in use at *Etecsa* callboxes, in different denominations from US$10-50, much cheaper for phoning abroad, eg US$2 per min to USA and Canada, US$2.60 per min to Central America and the Caribbean, US$3.40 to South America, US$4 to Spain, Italy, France and Germany and US$4.40 to the rest of the world. Mobile phones are commonly used in Cuba.

Media

Newspapers *Granma*, mornings except Sun and Mon; *Trabajadores*, Trade Union, weekly; *Tribuna* and *Juventud Rebelde*, also weekly. *Opciones* is a weekly national and international trade paper. *Granma* has a weekly edition, *Granma International* (in Spanish, English, French and Portuguese) and a monthly German edition, both on the Internet, www.granma.cu Av Gen Suárez y Territorial, Plaza de la Revolución, La Habana 6, T8816265, F335176.

Television There are 2 national channels: *Cubavisión* and *Tele Rebelde*, which broadcast morning and evening. The Sun Channel can be seen at hotels and broadcasts a special programme for tourists 24 hrs a day. Some of the upmarket hotels also have satellite TV.

Language

Spanish, with local variants in pronunciation and vocabulary. English, German, Italian and French are spoken by those in the tourist industry. There are **language courses** available at the universities of Havana, Cienfuegos and Santiago. They generally start on the first Mon of the month and you study Mon-Fri 0900-1300. There are different levels of study and Cuban cultural courses are also available. At the Faculty of Modern Languages at the University of Havana, latest prices are US$250 for 2 weeks, US$650 full board. A Spanish and popular dance course is US$300 for 3 weeks or US$670 full board. Spanish and Cuban Culture for 6 months is US$1,425 course only and US$4,692 full board. Contact Dr Jorge Núñez Jover or Lic Ileana Dopico Mateo, Dirección Postgrado, Calle J Pt 556, entre 25 y 27, Vedado, T334163, F335774. In Santiago, university accommodation is available for US$21 per person per day, contact Enrique Vallejo, T43186. Embassies abroad can also provide details. *Centro de Idiomas y Computación José Martí*, in Havana, is the only Ministry of Education school dedicated to teaching Spanish as a foreign language. 2-week Spanish courses with Cuban dance and a cultural programme are offered by *Càlédöniâ Languages Abroad*, The Clockhouse, Bonnington Mill, 72 New Haven Rd, Edinburgh EH6 5QG Scotland, T0131-6217721, www.caledonialanguages.co.uk

Food and drink

State-owned 'dollar' restaurants, recognizable by the credit card stickers on the door, serve meals for about US$10-25. Generally, although restaurants have improved in the last few years, the food in Cuba is not very exciting. There is little variety in the menu and menu items are frequently unavailable. Always check restaurant prices in advance and then your bill. Discrepancies occur in both the state and private sector. At the cheap end of the market you can expect poor quality, limited availability of ingredients and disinterested staff. For a cheap meal you are better off trying the Cuban version of fast-food restaurants, such as *El Rápido*, or *Burgui*, or one of Rumbos' *cafeterías*, of which there are many all round the island. As well as chicken and chips or burgers, they offer sandwiches: cheese, ham, or cheese and ham. A sandwich in a restaurant or bar in Havana costs around US$3, a coffee US$1. In a provincial town you can pay as little as US$2 for a sandwich and beer for lunch. All towns and cities have peso street stalls for sandwiches, pizza and snacks. You will be able to pay for food in pesos, but generally you will be charged in dollars.

Paladares are private houses operating as restaurants, licensed and taxed and limited to 12 chairs. A 3-course meal in Havana is US$15-25 per person, less than that outside the capital. If someone guides you to a *paladar* he will expect a commission, so you end up paying more for your food. The cheapest way of getting a decent meal is by eating in a *casa particular*, some of which pay tax to offer food and some don't, you will have to enquire. This is generally of excellent quality in plentiful, even vast, proportions, with the advantage that they will cook whatever you want. They usually charge US$5-7 for a meal, chicken and pork is cheaper than fish, while some *casa* owners seem to have access to all sorts of delicacies (illegal of course). Breakfast is usually US$2-3 and far better value than in a state hotel. You will get fresher food in a *casa particular* than in a restaurant or *paladar*, both of which have the reputation of recycling meals and reheating leftovers. As a result, the number of *paladares* has fallen from 1,562 in 1996 to only 200 in 2002.

For vegetarians the choice is very limited, normally only cheese sandwiches, spaghetti, pizzas, salads, bananas and omelettes. Even beans (and *congrís*) are usually cooked with meat or in meat fat. If you are staying at a *casa particular* licensed to serve food, or eating in a *paladar*, they will usually prepare meatless meals for you with advance warning. Always ask for beans to be cooked in vegetable oil.

The national dish is *congrís* (rice mixed with black beans), roast pork and yucca or fried plantain. Rice with kidney beans is known as *moros y cristianos*. Pork is traditionally eaten for the New Year celebrations. Seafood is largely found in the export and tourist markets. Most food is fried and can often be greasy and bland. Spices and herbs are not commonly used and Cubans limit their flavourings to onions and garlic. Salads are mixed, slightly pickled vegetables and not to everyone's taste. Cuba's range of tropical fruit and vegetables is magnificent. At the right time of year there will be a glut of avocados, mangoes, guavas or papaya. Cubans are hooked on ice cream, although it usually only comes in vanilla, strawberry or chocolate flavours. The ice cream parlour, *Coppelia*, can be found in every town of any size and is quite an experience, with long queues because of its popularity.

Rum is the national drink and all cocktails are rum-based. There are several brand names and each has a variety of ages, so you have plenty of choice. The locally grown **coffee** is good, although hotels often manage to make it undrinkable in the mornings. The most widely available **beer** throughout the island is *Cristal*, made by Cervecería Mayabe, in Holguín. From the same brewery is *Mayabe*, also popular, and *Bucanero*. *Tínimo* is from Camagüey. *Hatuey*, made in Havana, is named after an Indian chief ruling when the Spanish arrived. Cuba now also produces **wines** under the *Soroa* label, grown and produced in Pinar del Río, but you are better off buying something imported.

Flora and fauna

When the Spanish arrived at the end of the 15th century more than 90% of Cuba was covered with forest. However, clearance for cattle raising and sugar cane reduced this proportion: 75% of the land is now savannah or plains and 4% swamps. A reforestation programme aims to

Food
Food is not Cuba's strong point, although the supply of fresh food has improved

Drink

Cuba

increase Cuba's forests to 27% of the total area. Besides semi-deciduous woodland, vegetation types include rainforest, coastal and upland scrub, distinctive limestone vegetation found in the Sierra de los Organos and similar areas, savannah vegetation found on nutrient-deficient white silica sands, pine forests, xerophytic coastal limestone woodland, mangroves and other coastal wetlands. Cuba has extraordinarily high rates of biodiversity and endemism, particularly in four regions: the Montañas de Moa-Nipe-Sagua-Baracoa, which have the greatest diversity in all the Caribbean and are among the highest in the world, and 30% of the endemic species on the island; Parque Nacional Sierra de los Organos, the Reserva de la Biósfera Sierra del Rosario and the Reserva Ecológica del Macizo de Guamuhaya.

There are over 7,000 plant species in Cuba, of which around 3,000 are endemic and 950 are endangered, rare, or have become extinct in the last 350 years. Oddities in the plant world include the **Pinguicola lignicola**, the world's only carniverous epiphytic plant; the **cork palm** (*Microcycas colocoma*), an endemic living fossil which is a threatened species; and the **Solandra grandiflora**, one of the world's largest flowers, 10 cm across at the calyx and 30 cm at the corolla. There are around 100 different palm trees in Cuba, of which 90 are endemic. The **Royal palm** is the national tree and can be seen throughout the island. Cubans use the small, purple fruits to feed pigs, as they are oily and nutritious. There is one tiny orchid, *Pleurothallis shaferi*, which is only 1 cm, with leaves measuring 5 mm and flowers of only 2 mm.

Animal life is also varied, with nearly 14,000 species of fauna, of which 10 % could be on the verge of extinction. There are no native large mammals but some genera and families have diversified into a large number of distinct island species. These include mammals such as the **hutia**, **bats** and the protected **manatee** with more than 20 breeding groups, mostly in the Ciénaga de Zapata and north of Villa Clara. Reptiles range from 3 types of crocodiles

Cuba

♦ **National parks & reserves**

1 Parque Nacional
  Alejandro de Humboldt
2 Parque Nacional Turquino
3 Parque Nacional Desembarque
  de Granma
4 Parque Nacional La Bayamesa

5 Parque Nacional La Mensura
  Pilotos
6 Parque Nacional Pico Cristal
7 Parque Nacional Caguanes
8 Parque Nacional Viñales
9 Parque Nacional Punta Francés,
  Punta Pedernales

including the **Cuban crocodile** now found only in the Ciénaga de Zapata (although they are farmed) to iguanas and tiny salamanders. Cuba claims the smallest of a number of animals, for example the **Cuban pygmy frog**, 12 mm long, the **almiquí**, a shrew-like insectivore, the world's smallest mammal, the **butterfly** or **moth bat** and the **bee hummingbird**, 63 mm long, called locally the *zunzuncito*. The latter is an endangered species, like the **carpintero real woodpecker**, the **cariara** or **caracara**, the **pygmy owl**, the **Cuban green parrot** and the *fermina*, or **Zapata wren**. Less attractively, there is also a **dwarf scorpion**, 10 mm long.

The best place for birdwatching on the island is the Zapata Peninsula, where 170 species of Cuban birds have been recorded, including the majority of endemic species. In winter migratory waterbirds, swallows and others visit the marshes. The national bird is the forest-dwelling **Cuban trogon**, the *tocororo*, partly because of its blue head, white chest and red underbelly, the colours of the Cuban flag.

Protected areas cover 30% of Cuba including its marine platform. There are 14 national parks and 4 UNESCO biosphere reserves: **Guanahacabibes** in the extreme western tip of the island; the **Sierra del Rosario**, 60 km west of Havana; **Baconao** in the east and **Cuchillas del Toa**. However, not all legally established conservation areas have any infrastructure, personnel or administration in place.

Sport

Trekking, **hiking, rafting** and **birdwatching** are elements of adventure or nature travel which are still in their infancy in Cuba but are sure to be heavily promoted in the near future. The island's plentiful fauna and flora, its mountains, cays and wetlands, and its expanding system of national

Cuba

parks and other protected areas, are perfect for getting close to nature. Hunting and sport fishing are available, but in the last few years the emphasis has been on looking and not touching, as in birdwatching and scuba diving. The state travel agencies' specialist operations offer organized tours, with expert staff on hand to advise on biology, botany or forestry.

Cycling

An integral part of local culture with an estimated 2 million bicycles in Cuba

Cuba has an extensive network of tarmac and concrete roads, covering nearly 17,600 km. This impressive infrastructure means that the vast majority of the country is accessible to the cyclist, and there are some dramatic roads to climb and descend. There is total freedom of movement and the rewards can be immense. However, many of the roads are in poor condition, particularly in the rural areas. See page 70.

Diving

The main dive areas are Isla de la Juventud, Varadero, Faro de Luna, María La Gorda, Santa Lucía and Santiago de Cuba

Cuba's marine environment is pristine compared with many Caribbean islands. The majority of coral reefs are healthy and teeming with assorted marine life. The government has established a marine park around the **Isla de la Juventud** and much marine life is protected around the entire island, including turtles, the manatee and coral. There are 3 main marine platforms, the **Archipiélago del Rey** (Sabana-Camagüey), the **Archipiélago de la Reina** and the **Archipiélago de los Canarreos**. The first has the greatest diversity of marine species and is being explored and classified with the aim of making it a protected zone. There are believed to be some 900 species of fish, 1,400 species of mollusc, 60 species of coral, 1,100 species of crustacean, 67 species of shark and ray and 4 types of marine turtles around the island, as well as the manatee.

Fishing

Equipment can be hired, but serious fishermen will prefer to bring their own and large quantities of insect repellent

Cuba has been a fisherman's dream for many decades, not only for its deep-sea fishing, popularized by Ernest Hemingway, but also for its freshwater fishing in the many lakes and reservoirs spread around the island. **Freshwater fishing** is mostly for the largemouth bass (*trucha*), which grow to a great size in the Cuban lakes. *Horizontes* is the travel company to contact for fishing packages, which can be arranged all year round. The main places are Maspotón, in Pinar del Río; Laguna del Tesoro in the Ciénaga de Zapata; Presa Alacranes in Villa Clara province; Presa Zaza, in Sancti Spíritus and Lago La Redonda, near Morón in Ciego de Avila province. **Deep-sea fishing** can be organized at most marinas around the island, although most of the tournaments and the best facilities are at the Marina Hemingway, just west of Havana. The waters are home to marlin, swordfish, tarpon, sawfish, yellowfin tuna, dorado, wahoo, shark and a host of others. Varadero is a good point from which to go fishing and take advantage of the Gulf Stream which flows between Key West in Florida and Cuba, but records have been broken all along the northern coast in the cays of the Archipiélago de Sabana and the Archipiélago de Camagüey. There is also good fishing off the south coast around the Isla de la Juventud and Cayo Largo. **Bonefishing** is best done off the south coast in the Archipiélago de los Jardines de la Reina, or off Cayo Largo.

Sailing

There are marinas around the country offering moorings, boat rental and a variety of services, see www.cubanacan.cu   The largest is the Marina Hemingway in Havana, see page 101. Marinas are owned by Cubanacán Náutica, Puertosol and Gaviota. Before arriving in Cuban territorial waters (12 nautical miles from the island's platform), you should communicate with port authorities on channel HF (SSB) 2760 or VFH 68 and 16 (National Coastal Network) and 2790 or VHF 19A (Tourist Network). Not many 'yachties' (people who live and travel on their own boats) visit the island because of the political difficulties between Cuba and the USA. The US administration forbids any vessel, such as a cruise ship, cargo ship or yacht from calling at a US port if it has stopped in Cuba. This effectively prohibits anyone sailing from the US eastern seaboard calling in at a Cuban port on their way south through the Caribbean islands, or vice versa. It is better to rent a bareboat yacht from a Cuban marina and sail around the island, rather than include it in a Caribbean itinerary. Recommended is *The Cruising Guide to Cuba*, by Simon Charles (Cruising Guide Publications, 1017, Dunedin, FL 34697-1017, USA, T813-7335322, F813-7348179) before embarking.

Walking

A good pair of hiking books is essential. Good large-scale maps are non-existent

The 3 main mountain ranges are excellent for hill walking in a wide range of tropical vegetation, where many national parks are being established and trails demarcated. The highest peaks are in the **Sierra Maestra** in the east, where there are also many historical landmarks associated with the Wars of Independence and the Revolution. Unfortunately this area is often closed off for security reasons, so you should check locally before setting out. In any case you

> ### Things to do in Cuba
>
> - Go private, stay with a Cuban family, eat at a **paladar** for a taste of the real Cuba.
> - Work your way through your barman's list of **cocktails**: mojito, daiquirí, zombie, cubanito, or even a Cuba Libre.
> - Seek out the **Casa de la Trova** in any city for the best of traditional Cuban music.
> - Pay homage to **Che Guevara** at his mausoleum in Santa Clara.
> - Go back in time with a stroll through the cobbled streets of **Trinidad**.
> - For the ultimate party, hit **Santiago at Carnival** time in July.

will need a guide to accompany you in any National Park. A 3-day walk will take you from Alto del Naranjo up the island's highest peak, **Pico Turquino**, and down to the Caribbean coast at Las Cuevas, giving you fantastic views of the mountains and the coastline. The **Sierra del Escambray**, in the centre of the island, is conveniently located just north of the best preserved colonial city, Trinidad, and there are some lovely walks in the hills, along trails beside rivers, waterfalls and caves. The mountains of the west of the island, the **Sierra del Rosario** and the **Sierra de los Organos**, have some of the most unusual geological features, notably the large number of caves and the limestone *mogotes*, straight sided, flat topped hills rising from the midst of tobacco fields and looking almost Chinese, particularly in the early morning mist.

Health

Cuba has a high-quality national health service and is one of the healthiest countries in Latin America and the Caribbean. There are international clinics in tourist areas that charge in dollars (credit cards accepted). Visitors requiring medical attention will be sent to them. Emergencies are handled on an ad hoc basis. Check your insurance on coverage in Cuba and take a copy of your insurance policy with you. You cannot dial any toll-free numbers abroad so make sure you have a contact number. Take all prescription medicines and other remedies you might need as they may not be available in Cuba. The most common affliction of travellers is probably diarrhoea. Bottled water is widely available. Doctors will advise you to get hepatitis A and typhoid inoculations. Use plenty of insect repellent, dengue fever has been reported although the authorities spray regularly to keep mosquitos under control. Always carry toilet paper with you, it is not often available in public toilets and even some hotels do not have it.

Local health facilities are listed in individual town directories. See also main Health section page 48

Havana

Of all the capital cities in the Caribbean, Havana has the reputation for being the most splendid and sumptuous. Before the Revolution, its casinos and nightlife attracted the megastars of the day in much the same way as Beirut and Shanghai, and remarkably little has changed (architecturally) since then. There have been no tacky modernizations, partly because of lack of finance and materials. Low-level street lighting, relatively few cars (and many of those antiques), no (real) estate agents or Wendyburgers, no neon and very little advertising (except for political slogans), all give the city plenty of scope for nostalgia. Restoration works in the old part of the city are revealing the glories of the past, although most of the city is fighting a losing battle against the sea air – many of the finest buildings along the seafront are crumbling.

Havana is probably the finest example of a Spanish colonial city in the Americas. Many of its palaces were converted into museums after the Revolution and more work has been done (with millions of dollars of foreign aid and investment) since the old city was declared a UNESCO World Heritage Site in 1982. Away from the old city, there is some stunning modern architecture from the first half of the 20th century.

IDD code: 0053
Phone code: 7
Colour map 1, grid A2
Population: 2,204,300

Ins and outs

Getting there The José Martí international Airport is 18 km from Havana. **Taxi** fares range from US$15-20, but US$18 is commonly asked to the old city. No bus goes near the international terminal, but *Víazul* operates a transfer service from some hotels for US$4. The *Astro* **bus** terminal is very near the Plaza de la Revolución in Vedado, central and convenient for accommodation. *Víazul* dollar buses stop much further out and a taxi will be needed, US$5 to Habana Vieja or Centro. The **train** station is at the southern end of the old city, within walking distance of any of the hotels there or in Centro Habana, although if you arrive at night, take a taxi.

Getting around

See Transport, page 99, for further details

Buses involve complicated queuing procedures and a lot of pushing and shoving. *Camellos* are articulated double buses which cover the main arteries. Regular buses (blue) are being improved but all are hot and crowded. **Bicitaxi**, bicycle taxi, rates are negotiable but generally less than you would pay a normal taxi. Havana is very spread out along the coast. Those with really good walking boots can cover much of the city on foot, but the average visitor will be content with one district at a time, eg Habana Vieja one day, Vedado the next, and still feel well exercised. Car hire is not recommended in Havana.

Orientation The centre is divided into 5 sections, 3 of which are of most interest to visitors, **Habana Vieja** (Old Havana), **Habana Centro** (Central Havana) and **Vedado**. The oldest part of the city, around the **Plaza de Armas**, is quite near the docks. Here are the former **Palace of the Captains-General** and **Castillo de La Real Fuerza**, the oldest of all the forts. From Plaza de Armas run 2 narrow and picturesque streets, Calles Obispo and O'Reilly (there are several old-fashioned pharmacies on Obispo with traditional glass and ceramic medicine jars and decorative perfume bottles on display in shops that gleam with polished wood and mirrors). These 2 streets go west to the **Parque Central**, with its laurels, poincianas, almonds, palms, shrubs and gorgeous flowers. To the southwest rises the golden dome of the **Capitol**. From the northwest corner of Parque Central a wide, tree-shaded avenue with a central walkway, the **Paseo del Prado**, runs to the fortress of **La Punta**. At its north seaside end is the **Malecón**, a splendid highway along the coast to the west residential district of Vedado. The sea crashing along the seawall here is a spectacular sight when the wind blows from the north. On calmer days, fishermen lean over the parapet, lovers sit in the shade of the small pillars, and joggers sweat along the pavement. On the other side of the 6-lane road, buildings which from a distance look stout and grand, with arcaded pavements, balconies, mouldings and large entrances, are salt-eroded, faded and decrepit inside. Restoration is progressing slowly, but the sea is destroying old and new alike and creating a huge renovation task.

Further west, Calle San Lázaro leads directly from the monument to **General Antonio Maceo** on the Malecón to the magnificent central stairway of **Havana University**. A monument to **Julio Antonio Mella**, founder of the Cuban Communist Party, stands across from the stairway. Further out, past **El Príncipe** castle, is **Plaza de la Revolución**, with the impressive monument to **José Martí** at its centre and the much-photographed, huge outline of Che Guevara on one wall. The large buildings surrounding the square were mostly built in the 1950s and house the principal government ministries. The long, grey building behind the monument is the former Justice Ministry (1958), now the headquarters of the Central Committee of the Communist Party, where Fidel Castro has his office. The Plaza is the scene of massive parades (May Day) and speeches marking important events.

La Habana Vieja (Old Havana)

Castillo del Morro

The fortress stands on a bold headland, with the best view of Havana and is illuminated at night

Built between 1589 and 1630, with a 20-m moat, but much altered, it was one of the major fortifications built to protect the natural harbour and the assembly of Spain's silver fleets from pirate attack. The flash of its lighthouse, built in 1844, is visible 30 km out to sea. It now serves as a museum with a good exhibition of Cuban history since the arrival of Columbus. On the harbour side, down by the water, is the **Battery of the 12 Apostles**, each gun being named after an Apostle. ■ *Daily 0830-2030 (museum, 0900-2030). US$1 for the parque, US$3 for the Castillo, US$2 for photographs and US$2 for the lighthouse. T8637941. Access to the Castillo del Morro is from any bus going* through the tunnel (20 or 40 centavos), board at San Lázaro and Av del Puerto and get off at the stop after tunnel, cross the road and climb following the path to the left. Alternatively take a taxi, or a 20-min walk from the Fortaleza de la Cabaña.

Fortaleza de San Carlos de la Cabaña

Fronting the harbour is a high wall; the ditch on the landward side, 12 m deep, has a drawbridge to the main entrance. Inside are **Los Fosos de los Laureles** where political prisoners were shot during the Cuban fight for independence. Every night the cannon are fired at 2100 (El Cañonazo) in a historical ceremony recalling the closing of the city walls in the 17th century to protect it from pirates; this starts at 2045 so that the walls are closed at 2100. There are two museums here, one about Che Guevara and another about fortresses with pictures and models, some old weapons and a replica of a large catapult and battering ram. ■ *Daily 0900-2200. US$3 (US$5 1800-2100), extra charge for camera or video. T8620617. Access as for Castillo del Morro or via Casablanca.*

The **National Observatory** and the old station for (Hershey line) trains to Matanzas are on the same side of the Channel as the forts, at **Casablanca**. This charming town is also the site of a statue of a very human Jesus Christ, erected during the Batista dictatorship as a pacifying exercise. Go up a steep, twisting flight of stone steps, starting on the other side of the plaza in front of the landing stage, and you can walk from the statue to the Fortaleza (10 minutes) and then on to the Castillo del Morro. ■ *Left-hand ferry queue next to the Customs House, opposite Calle Santa Clara, 10 centavos.*

Castillo de la Real Fuerza
The second oldest fort in the New World

Built in 1558 after the city had been sacked by buccaneers and rebuilt in 1582, it is a low, long building, with a picturesque tower from which there is a grand view. Inside the castle is the **Museo de la Cerámica Cubana**, showcasing Cuban ceramic art dating from the 1940s onwards. ■ *Fortaleza: daily 0800-1900. US$2. T8615010. Museum: Mon-Sat 0830-1645. US$1, under 15 years free. Shop upstairs. T8616130. O'Reilly y Av del Puerto.*

Cathedral

Construction of a church on this site was begun by Jesuit missionaries at the beginning of the 18th century. After the Jesuits were expelled in 1767, the church was converted into a cathedral. On either side of the Spanish colonial baroque façade are bell towers, the left one (west) being half as wide as the right (east). The church is officially dedicated to the Virgin of the Immaculate Conception, but is better known as the church of Havana's patron saint, San Cristóbal, and as the Columbus cathedral. The bones of Christopher Columbus were sent to this cathedral when Santo Domingo was ceded by Spain to France in 1795; they now lie in Santo Domingo (Dominican Republic). ■ *Mon-Sat 0930-1230, Sun 0830-1230, Mass at 1030.*

Havana orientation

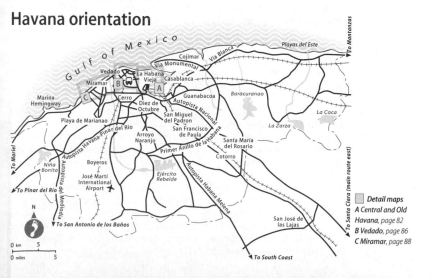

Detail maps
A Central and Old Havana, page 82
B Vedado, page 86
C Miramar, page 88

Plaza de Armas

In the Plaza de Armas there is a small, second-hand book market daily except Monday

The statue in the centre is of Carlos Manuel de Céspedes. In the northeast corner of the square is the church of **El Templete**; a column in front of it marks the spot where the first mass was said in 1519 under a ceiba tree. A sapling of the same tree, blown down by a hurricane in 1753, was planted on the same spot, and under its branches the supposed bones of Columbus reposed in state before being taken to the cathedral. This tree was cut down in 1828, the present tree planted, and the Doric temple opened. On the north side of the Plaza is the **Palacio del Segundo Cabo**, the former private residence of the Captains General, now housing the Feria Cubana del Libro. Its patio is worth a look. On the east side is the small luxury hotel, the *Santa Isabel*, and on the south side the modern **Museo Nacional de Historia Natural**. On the west side of Plaza de Armas is the former **Palace of the Captains General**, built in 1780, a charming example of colonial architecture with a beautiful courtyard with arcades and balconies and Royal palms. The Spanish Governors and the Presidents lived here until 1917, when it became the City Hall. It is now the **Museo de la Ciudad**, the Historical Museum of the city of Havana. There are no explanations, even in Spanish. 19th-century furnishings illustrate the wealth of the Spanish colonial community. The building was the site of the signing of the 1899 treaty between Spain and the USA. An extension to the museum is the **Casa de la Plata**, a silverware collection on Obispo entre Mercaderes y Oficios, fine pieces, jewellery and old frescoes. ■ *Daily 0900-1930. US$3 (includes Casa de la Plata); guided visit US$4; combined city and museum tour US$8; charge for photos US$2, video US$10.T8615779.*

The church & convent of San Francisco

Built in 1608 and reconstructed in 1730, this is a sombre edifice suggesting defence, rather than worship. The three-storey bell tower was both a landmark for returning voyagers and a look-out for pirates. The **Basílica Menor de San Francisco de Asís** is now a concert hall and the convent is a museum containing religious pieces. ■ *Daily 0930-1830. US$2 for museum and bell tower, photos US$2, video US$10, guide US$1.*

The Convento de Santa Clara

Founded in 1644 by nuns from Cartagena in Colombia, Santa Clara was in use as a convent until 1919, when the nuns sold the building. Restoration began in 1982, and is still continuing. The convent occupies four small blocks in Old Havana, bounded by Calles Habana, Sol, Cuba and Luz, and originally there were three cloisters and an orchard. You can see the cloisters, the nuns' cemetery and their cells. The first cloister has been carefully preserved; the ground floor is a grand porticoed stone gallery surrounding a large patio packed with vegetation, in it are the city's first slaughterhouse, first public fountain and public baths. The Sailor's House in the second cloister, reputedly built by a sailor for his love-lorn daughter, is now a *Residencia Académica* for student groups (and independent travellers if room, **D-E**, T863335, reaca@cencrem.cult.cu). ■ *Mon-Fri 0900-1500. US$2 for guided tour in Spanish or French. Entrance on Cuba.*

Parque Fraternidad

The park has been landscaped to show off the Capitol, north of it, to the best effect. At its centre is a ceiba tree growing in soil provided by each of the American republics. Also in the park is a famous statue of the Indian woman who first welcomed the Spaniards: La Noble Habana, sculpted in 1837.

El Capitolio

This is a copy, on a smaller scale, of the US Capitol in Washington DC

Opened in May 1929, the Capitol has a large dome over a rotunda. At the centre of its floor is set a 24-carat diamond, zero for all distance measurements in Cuba. The interior has large halls and stately staircases, all most sumptuously decorated. ■ *Entrance for visitors is to the left of the stairway, US$3 to go in the halls. Camera and video charge US$2. Tours available 0900-2000 daily, but often shuts early, restaurant. T610261.*

Cigar factory

The tour of **Partagas** is interesting but pricey. English-, Spanish- or French- speaking guides available. You are taken through the factory and shown the whole production process (explanation in Spanish only). Four brand names are made here; *Partagas, Cubana, Ramón Allones* and *Bolívar*. These and other famous cigars (and rum) can be bought at the shop. ■ *30-min tours, every 15 mines 0930-1200, 1330-1500, US$10. Shop 0900-1700. Calle Industria behind El Capitolio, T338060.*

A very pleasant park with a monument to **José Martí** in the centre. On its west side are the upmarket *Hotel Telégrafo*, the regal *Hotel Inglaterra* (built 1875, many famous foreign guests) and the **Gran Teatro de la Habana**, a beautiful building with tours of the inside. The north side is entirely occupied by the *Golden Tulip Parque Central*, while the *Hotel Plaza* is in the northeast corner. On the east side of the park is the **Museo Nacional Palacio de Bellas Artes**. After a five-year closure and extensive refurbishment estimated at US$14.5 million, Fidel Castro inaugurated this fantastic museum on 19 July 2001. There are two separate buildings. The 1954 Fine Arts Palace houses the collection of *Arte Cubano*, from colonial to the 1990s including a section on the post-Revolution Art Schools. The former Centro Asturiano houses European and ancient art, *Arte Universal*. This building, designed by the Spanish architect Manuel del Busto in the early 20th century, has been fabulously renovated with huge marble staircases giving access to five floors. The collection of European paintings, from the 16th century to the present, contains works by Gainsborough, Van Dyck, Velázquez, Tintoretto, Degas, et al. The museum also has Greek, Roman, Egyptian and Etruscan sculpture and artefacts, many very impressive. There are paintings from private collections left behind by rich Cuban families (including the Bacardí and Gómez Mena families) and members of the former dictator Fulgencio Batista's government who fled Cuba soon after the 1959 Revolution. ■ *Tue-Sat 1000-1800, Sun 0900-1300. US$5 entry to each museum for foreigners, but a same-day entrance to both sites is US$8. Arte Cubano is at Trocadero entre Zulueta y Monserrate, and Arte Universal is at San Rafael entre Zulueta y Monserrate. T8613858, www.museo nacional.cult.cu No photography permitted.*

Parque Central

This huge, ornate building, topped by a dome, was once the Presidential Palace, but now contains the Museo de la Revolución. The history of Cuban political development is charted, from the slave uprisings to joint space missions with the ex-Soviet Union. The liveliest section displays the final battles against Batista's troops, with excellent photographs and some bizarre mementoes from the Sierra Maestra campaign. The yacht *Granma*, from which Dr Castro disembarked with his companions in 1956 to launch the Revolution, has been installed in the park facing the south entrance, surrounded by planes, tanks and other vehicles involved, as well as a Soviet-built tank used against the Bay of Pigs invasion and a fragment from a US spy plane. ■ *Daily 1000-1700. US$4, guided tour 1030, US$10. Allow several hrs to see it all, explanations mostly in Spanish. Refugio entre Monserrate y Zulueta, facing Av de las Misiones. T8624091-6.*

Museo de la Revolución

Look out for the bullet holes as you walk up the stairs to the stuffed mule and stuffed horse used by Che Guevara and Camilo Cienfuegos

An 18th-century plaza, undergoing restoration since February 1996. Many of the buildings around the plaza boast elegant balconies overlooking the large square with a fountain in the middle. The former house of the Spanish Captain General, **Conde de Ricla**, who retook Havana from the English and restored power to Spain in 1763, can be seen on the corner of San Ignacio and Muralla. Known as **La Casona**, modern art exhibitions are held upstairs in the beautiful blue and white building. Note the friezes up the staircase and along the walls. There is a great view of the plaza from the balcony and trailing plants in the courtyard enhance the atmosphere. ■ *Muralla 107 esq San Ignacio, T8618544, www.artnet.com/casona*

La Plaza Vieja

Museo del Ron The Fundación Distilería Havana Club has a museum offering displays of the production of rum from the sugar cane plantation to the processing and bottling, with machinery dating from the early 20th century. Tours are available in several languages. There is a wonderful model railway which runs round a model sugar mill and distillery, designed and made by prize-winning Lázaro Eduardo García Driggs. At the end of the tour you get a tasting of a six-year-old Havana Club rum in a bar which is a mock up of the once-famous *Sloppy Joe's*. There is also a restaurant (excellent shrimp kebab) and bar (see below), a shop and an art gallery where present-day Cuban artists exhibit their work. ■ *Daily 0900-1700. US$5, under 15s free. Multilingual guides included. Av del Puerto 262 entre Sol y Muralla. T8618051, www.havanaclubfoundation.com*

Other museums

Cuba

Central & Old Havana

Straits of Florida

Av de Maceo

San Lázaro

Malecón

5   **6**

Av de Maceo

Gervasio

Escobar

Animas

Colón

Trocadero

Refugio

Genios

17

Concordia

Perseverancia

Blanco

19

Crespo

Industria

10

1

Neptuno

4

Campanario

15

Nuestro Señora
de Monserrate

Virtudes

Bernal

Animas

Morro

14

San Miguel

2

Manrique

San Nicolás

(Galiano)

Aguila

Amistad

Consulado

Paseo de Martí (del Prado)

San Rafael

CENTRO

Italia

26

2

Agramonte (Zulueta)

Main Police
Station

Pol

Neptuno

Museo Nacional
Palacio de Bellas Artes

8

Empedrado

Campanario

Manrique

San Miguel

4

San Rafael

21

17

San Juan

C

11 **22**

Chinese

12

Parque
Central

Museo Nacional
Palacio de Bellas Artes

13

O'Reilly

Nuestro Señora de
la Caridad del Cobre

Salud

Barcelona

24

Gran Teatro
de la Habana

San Martí (San José)

6

20

30

Obrapia

Av de Bolívar (Reina)

Rayo

Parque
El Curita

Partagás
Cigar Factory

El
Capitolio

Paseo de Martí

Monserrate

Bernaza

Cristo

Pl. del
Cristo

Santo Cristo
del Buen Viaje

14

Tenien

Angeles

D

Dragones

Parque
Fraternidad

Villegas

Aguacate

Muralla

Máximo Gómez (Monte)

Corrales

13

16

Sol

Indio

Apodaca

Aponte

Cienfuegos

Economía

Agramonte

Porvenir

E

Aguila

Revillagigedo

Gloria

Acosta

9

Misión

Jesús María

Esperanza

Arsenal

Av de Bélgica (Egido)

Merced

Alambique

Florida

Suárez

Factoría

Estación
Central

L. Pérez (Paula)

La Merced

San Isidro

F

Velazquez

Desamparados

A   **25**

A

B   **4**

C

1   **2**   **3**

Cuba

Sleeping

1 Caribbean *B3*
2 Carlos Luis
  Valderrama Moré *B1*
3 Conde de Villanueva,
  Hostal del Habano *D4*
4 Daisy y Jorge
  Castro Pérez *B1*
5 Deauville *A2*
6 Dr Alejandro Oses *B3*
7 Florida *D4*
8 Golden Tulip
  Parque Central *C3*
9 Gustavo Enamorado
  Zamora-Chez Nous *D4*
10 Hostal del Tejadillo *C4*
11 Hostal Valencia &
  Comendador *D5*
12 Inglaterra *C2*
13 Jesús y María *E3*
14 La Casa del
  Científico *B3*
15 Lincoln *B2*
16 Orlando y Liset *E3*
17 Plaza *C3*
18 Residencia Santa Clara *E4*
19 Rosa Artiles
  Hernández *B3*
20 Santa Isabel *D5*
21 Telégrafo *C2*

Eating

1 Al Medina *D5*
2 Bellomar *B2*
3 Cabaña *B4*
4 Café París *D4*
5 Cafetería Torre
  La Vega *D5*
6 Castillo de Farnés *C3*
7 D'Giovanni *C5*
8 Dominica *D5*
9 Don Lorenzo *E3*
10 Doña Blanquita *B3*
11 El Pacífico *C1*
12 El Patio *C4*
13 Floridita *C3*
14 Hanoi *D3*
15 La Bodeguita
  del Medio *C4*
16 La Divina Pastora *A5*
17 La Guarida *B1*
18 La Mina *D5*
19 La Moneda Cubana *C4*
20 La Zaragozana *C3*
21 Los XII Apostoles *A5*
22 Tien Tan *C1*
23 Torre de Marfil *D5*

Bars & clubs

24 Cabaret Nacional *C2*
25 Casa de la Trova *A1*
26 Casarón del Tango *C2*
27 Dos Hermanos *E5*
28 Fundación Distilería
  Havana Club *E5*
29 Lluvia de Oro *D4*
30 Monserrate *D3*

Casa de los Arabes   This lovely building with vines trained over the courtyard for shade, includes a mosque, jewels and rugs (as well as a bar and restaurant, *Al Medina*). *Daily 0930-1630. US$1. Oficios 16 entre Obispo y Obrapía, T8615868.*

Casa de Africa   Currently being restored, the majority of exhibits are being housed in Museo Humboldt until approximately the end of 2003, including the gallery of carved wooden artefacts and handmade costumes. Sculpture, furniture, paintings and ceramics from sub-Saharan Africa, including gifts given to Fidel by visiting African Presidents. Exhibit of elements of African-Cuban religions ■ *Mon-Sat 1030-1700, Sun 0930-1300. US$2, under 12s free. Obrapía 157, entre San Ignacio y Mercaderes, T8615798, africa@cultural.ohch.cu*

Museo de Automóviles   Vintage car museum with vehicles going back to the 1920s, due to be relocated. There are a great many museum pieces, pre-Revolutionary US models, still on the road especially outside Havana, in among the Ladas, VWs and Nissans. ■ *Daily 0900-1900. US$1. Oficios y Jústiz (just off Plaza de Armas).*

Casa de Guayasimín   Exhibition of works donated to Cuba by the late Ecuadorean artist Oswaldo Guayasimín (paintings, sculpture and silkscreens) occasionally other exhibitions. Guayasimín painted a portrait of Fidel Castro with his hands raised for his 70th birthday. ■ *Tue-Sat 0930-1630, Sun 0930-1430. Donations welcome. Obrapía 111 entre Mercaderes y San Ignacio, T8613843.*

Casa de México   Opposite the above, also called La Casa de Benito Juárez, the museum of Mexico is in a pink building marked with the Mexican flag. ■ *0930-1730 Tue-Sat, 0900-1300 Sun. US$1. Obrapía 116 entre Mercaderes y Oficios. T8618166.*

Casa de Simón Bolívar   Contains exhibits about the life of the South American liberator and some Venezuelan art. ■ *Tue-Sat 0930-1700, Sun 1030-1300. US$1. Mercaderes 158 entre Obrapía y Lamparilla, T8613998.*

Casa de la Obra-Pía   A beautiful yellow building dating from 1665, it contains furniture from the 18th and 19th centuries including collections from Asia. There is also an interesting exhibition on the life of the author, Alejo Carpentier, although his letters and books are at the Fundación Alejo Carpentier, Empedrado 215 entre Cuba y San Ignacio. ■ *Tue-Sat 0900-1630, Sun 0930-1230. Photos US$2. Obrapía 158 entre Mercaderes y San Ignacio, T8613998.*

Sights outside Old Havana

Plaza de la Revolución   In the base of the **Memorial José Martí** is a beautifully restored and impressive museum. The tower is the highest point in the city with good panoramic views of Havana. ■ *Mon-Sat 0930-1730, Sun 1000-1400. US$3. Lookout US$5 extra. T820906.* The **Museo Postal Cubano**, Ministry of Communications, tells the history of the postal service and stamps and the story books of José Antonio de Armona (1765). ■ *Mon-Fri 0900-1600. US$1. T705193.*

Vedado   **Museo Napoleónico** houses 7,000 pieces from the private collection of sugar baron, *See map page 86* Julio Lobo: paintings and other works of art, a specialized library and a collection of weaponry. Check out the tiled fencing gallery. ■ *Mon-Sat 1000-1800, Sun 0900-1230. US$3. San Miguel 1159 esq Ronda, T8791460.* **Casa de la Amistad**, in a beautiful 1926 former mansion with gardens, is now operated by ICAP (Cuban Institute for Friendship among the Peoples) and houses the *Amistur* travel agency (see page 98). It has a reasonably priced bar, cafetería and tourist shop (0930-1800). Cuban music nights are US$5 for tourists; good traditional music in a nice setting. Lots of Cubans go there too, but there is no soliciting. ■ *Bar and cafetería Mon-Fri 1100-2300 (son), Sat 1100-0200 (with Cuban bands). Paseo 406, entre 17 y 19, T8303114.* **Museo de la Danza** contains items from Alicia Alonso's personal collection and from the Ballet Nacional de Cuba. ■ *Tue-Sat 1100-1830. US$2, guided tour US$1. G (Presidentes) esq Línea, T8312198.* **Galería Haydée Santamaría**, alongside Casa de las Américas, is a good representation of mostly 20th-century styles by Latin American artists. ■ *Tue-Sat 1000-1630, US$2. G esq 5.* Visit the **Cementerio Colón** to see the wealth of funerary sculpture, including Carrara marbles; Cubans visit the sculpture of Amelia de Milagrosa and pray for miracles. ■ *US$1 entrance and US$1 for good map. Entrance on Zapata y 12. Rumbos bar opposite the cemetery gates.*

Museo de Artes Decorativas houses European and Oriental art from the 16th-20th century in a French Renaissance-style mansion originally designed by Alberto Camacho (1924-27) for José Gómez Mena's daughter. Most of the building materials were imported from France. In the 1930s the mansion was occupied by Gómez' sister, María Luisa, Condesa de Revilla de Camargo, who was a fervent collector of fine art and held elegant society dinners and receptions for guests including the Duke of Windsor and Wallace Simpson. The countess's valuable collections were found in the basement after the family fled Cuba following the Revolution in 1959. The interior decoration was by House of Jansen and her furniture included a desk that had belonged to Marie Antoinette. There are 10 permanent exhibition halls with works from the 16th-20th centuries including ceramics, porcelain (Sèvres, Chantilly and Wedgwood), furniture (Boudin, Simoneau and Chippendale) and paintings. The Regency-inspired dining room is recommended viewing. The attendants are knowledgeable and informative about the exhibits, but only in Spanish. ■ *Tue-Sat 1100-1830. US$2. Calle 17 502 esq E, T8308037.*

Maqueta de la Ciudad is a scale model of Havana and its suburbs as far out as Cojímar and the airport. Colonial buildings are in red, post-colonial pre-Revolution buildings in yellow and post-Revolution buildings in white. ■ *Tue-Sat 1000-1730. US$3, children US$1. Calle 28 113 entre 1 y 3, T332661.*

Miramar

Excursions

The former seaside village, now a concrete jungle, featured in *The Old Man and the Sea*, is an easy excursion (15 minutes by taxi) from central Havana. Hemingway celebrated his Nobel prize here in 1954 and there is a bust of him opposite a small fort.

Cojímar

Hemingway fans may wish to visit his house, **Finca Vigía,** 11 km from the centre of Havana, where he lived from 1939 to 1960 (called the **Museo Ernest Hemingway**). The signpost is opposite the post office, leading up a short driveway. Visitors are not allowed inside the plain whitewashed house, which has been lovingly preserved with all Hemingway's furniture and books, just as he left it, but you can walk all around the outside and look in through the windows and open doors. Since the end of 2002, US and Cuban researchers have been collaborating in going through the 9,000 books on the walls and thousands of photographs, manuscripts and letters in the cellar, all of which have been gathering dust where Hemingway left them in 1960. The garden is beautiful and tropical, with many shady palms. Next to the swimming pool (empty) are the gravestones of Hemingway's pet dogs. ■ *Mon, Wed-Sat 0930-1600, Sun 0900-1230. US$3, US$1 per person if you want a guide. T910809. No toilets. Photo permit US$5. Hemingway tours are offered by hotel tour desks for US$35.*

San Francisco de Paula

The **Jardín Botánico Nacional de Cuba** is well maintained with excellent collections, including a Japanese garden with tropical adaptations. A multilingual guide will meet you at the gate, no charge. You can take a 'train' tour along the 35 km of roads around the 60-ha site. This is an open-sided, wheeled carriage towed by a tractor, enabling you to see the whole garden in about two hours. Several inter-connected glass houses are filled with desert, tropical and subtropical plants, well worth walking through. There are only a few signs and so not as informative as it might be. There is a good **organic vegetarian restaurant** using solar energy for cooking. Only one sitting for lunch, but you can eat as much as you like from a selection of hot and cold vegetarian dishes and drinks for US$12. Water and waste food is recycled and the restaurant grows most of its own food. ■ *Daily 0900-1600, but you may not be allowed in after 1530. US$1, children US$0.50. T547278. Getting there: Km 3.5, Carretera Rocío, Calabazar, south of the city in Arroyo*

Botanic Gardens

Cuba

Cuba

Vedado

Feria del Malecón

C 1ra

C 3ra

Casa de las Américas

Galería Haydée Santamaría

5 14

C 5ta

Calzada (7ta)

Malecón

Swiss Embassy

C 9

Línea

Sagrado Corazón de Jesús

Museo de la Danza

C 11

Línea

Banco Metropolitano

C 13

3 9

C 15

Banco Financiero Internacional

Museo de Artes Decorativas

C 15

15

C 17

Av de los Presidentes (G)

C 17

C 17

4 8
24
11
10 2
23
21

Parque Víctor Húgo

12

10

4

C 19

Casa de la Amistad

Paseo

VEDADO

C 21

C 23

18

26
21

C 23 (La Ramp

16

C 25

13

C 27

C 29

Havana University

Monument to General Antonio Mell

Museo Napoleónico

Castillo del Príncipe

Universidad

Iglesia d Carmer

C 31

6

C 33

Zapata

Quinta de los Molinos

Carlos III

C 35

C 37

Lugareño

C 39

Teatro Nacional 14

Carlos Manuel de Céspedes

Museo Postal Cubano

Astro Bus Terminal

Pozos Dulces

Bruzón

Luaces

Requena

Plaza Carlos Barr

Av Carlos Manuel de Céspedes

Memorial & Museo José Martí

Plaza de la Revolución

Av Rancho Boyeros

Almendares

Calzada de Ayestarán

Calzada de Infanta

1 2 3 4

N

0 metres 200
0 yards 200

■ Sleeping

1 Adita *B3*
2 Armando Gutiérrez *C4*
3 Carmen y Ramón Fonseca Díaz *B2*
4 Familia Villazón *C3*
5 Gisela Ibarra y Daniel Riviero *A2*
6 Giuseppe y María Elena *E4*
7 Luís Cartaya y Alicia Horta *B4*
8 Marilys Herrera González *E5*
9 Martha Vitorte *B2*
10 Mercedes González *C3*
11 Nacional de Cuba *C5*
12 Natalia Rodés León *C3*
13 Pedro Mesa López y Tobias López Márquez *D2*
14 Presidente *A2*
15 Teresa Naredo *C1*
16 Tryp Habana Libre *C4*
17 Victoria *C4*

Eating

1 Amor *D1*
2 Centro de Prensa Internacional *C4*
3 Coppelia *C4*
4 El Conejito *C4*
5 Gringo Viejo *C2*
6 Hurón Azul *C5*
7 La Tasquita *D4*
8 La Torre *C4*
9 Le Chansonnier *B3*
10 Los Amigos *C4*
11 Nerei *C4*

Straits of Florida

Cuba

Naranjo, beyond Parque Lenin. Camello M6 and omnibus 88 every 30-40 mins. Many hotel tour desks now organize day trips including lunch for US$25, better value than going independently and probably less effort. Taxi from Old Havana US$15-18 1-way.

Essentials

Habana Vieja LL-L *NH Golden Tulip Parque Central* (Cubanacán), Neptuno entre Prado y Zulueta, T8606627, www.golden tuliphotels.nl/gtparquecentral, on north side of Parque Central. 277 rooms of international standard, excellent bathrooms with separate showers, business centre, Mediterranean and French à la carte restaurants, plush cigar-smoker's lounge, 2 bars, sweeping views of Havana from pool on top floor, fitness centre, charming and helpful multilingual staff. **LL-L** *Santa Isabel* (Habaguanex), Baratillo 9 entre O'Reilly y Narciso López, Plaza de Armas, T8608201, F338391. Renovated mansion, 17 rooms, 10 suites, busy with groups, height of luxury, very well-equipped bathrooms, rooms on 3rd floor have balcony overlooking plaza, pool, restaurant, central patio with fountain and greenery and lobby bar, great location. **L-A** *Conde de Villanueva, Hostal del Habano* (Habaguanex), Mercaderes 202 esq Lamparilla, T8629293, hconde@villanueva.ohch.cu 9 rooms and suites around peaceful courtyard, attractive red and green colour scheme, cigar theme with cigar shop, café, bar, good restaurant, highly regarded, friendly staff, named after Claudio Martínez del Pinillo, Conde de Villanueva (1789-1853), a notable personality who promoted tobacco abroad and helped to bring the railway to Cuba. **L-A** *Florida* (Habaguanex), Obispo 252 esq Cuba, T8624127, F8624117. Restored building dates from 1885, cool oasis, elegant restaurant, bar just off the street, serves great daiquirís, marble floors and pillars in courtyard, beautiful rooms with high ceilings, some balconies, some singles, overpriced and poor buffet breakfast, parking. **AL-A** *Telégrafo*, Prado y Neptuno, T8611010, F8614741. On the Parque Central and a great location. Reopened in 2001 after a luxury refit, the original building dates from 1860 but the 63 hotel rooms are modern, stylish and spacious with opulent bathrooms and soundproofing. **AL-B** *Inglaterra* (Gran Caribe), Prado 416 entre San Rafael y San Miguel, T8608595/7, F8608254. Built in 1875 next to

Sleeping
Several important hotel renovation projects have been completed in Old Havana and these are now elegant places to stay

12 Trattoria Marakas *C4*

● **Bars & clubs**
13 Cabaret Las Vegas *D5*
14 Café Cantante
  Mi Habana & El Delirio
  Habanero *E1*
15 Café El Gato Tuerto *C4*
16 Callejón de Hamel *D5*
17 Centro de Música
  Ignacio Piñeiro *B3*

18 Cine Riviera *C3*
19 Imágenes *B1*
20 Jazz Café *A1*
21 La Zorra y el
  Cuervo *C4*
22 Palmares *A2*
23 Salón Rojo *C4*
24 Sherezada *C4*
25 Teatro Mella *B1*
26 Tikoa *C4*
27 UNEAC *C2*

the *Teatro Nacional*, famous former foreign guests included Sara Bernhardt in 1887 and the authors Federico García Lorca and Rubén Darío in 1910. 86 rooms, colonial style, regal atmosphere, some single rooms have no windows, reasonable breakfast, lovely old mosaic tiled dining room, 1 of 4 cafés or restaurants with a variety of services and cuisines. **A-B** *Plaza* (Gran Caribe), Zulueta 267 esq Neptuno, or Ignacio Agramonte 267, T8608583/9, F8608869. 186 rooms, street-front rooms very noisy, ask for one in the inner courtyard, poor dinner, service generally poor. **AL-B** *Hostal del Tejadillo* (Habaguanex), Tejadillo 12 esq San Ignacio. Great location, comfortable rooms, high ceilings, tall wooden shuttered windows, fridge, good breakfast inside or in the courtyard, lively bar with entertaining barmen and music in the afternoon/evening. **A-C** *Hostal Valencia* (Habaguanex), Oficios 53 esq Obrapía, T8671037, reserva@habaguanexhvalencia.co.cu Joint Spanish/Cuban venture modelled on the Spanish *paradores*, suites and rooms named after Valencian towns, tastefully restored building, nicely furnished, pleasant courtyard with vines, music, good restaurant (see below), the **A-C** *Comendador*, next door, is a small hotel on 2 floors, same prices, separate but using the facilities of the *Valencia*. **D-E** *Residencia Santa Clara*, in colonial convent building dating from 1644, entrance on Sol y Cuba, T863335, reaca@cencrem.cult.cu, see page 80. Lovely atmosphere, spotless, can be noisy early morning, nice café, poor breakfast. Group discounts.

Centro C *Caribbean* (Horizontes), Paseo Martí (Prado) 164 esq Colón y Refugio, T8608233, F8609479. Remodelled, good security, convenient for the old town, 38 cold, sterile rooms, only 7 have windows, try and get 1 on 5th floor, fan and TV, popular with budget travellers, but avoid noisy rooms at front and lower floors at back over deafening water pump, 24-hr *Café del Prado* at street level for US$3,   pastas, pizzas and snacks, foreign-exchange services. **C-D** *Deauville* (Horizontes), Galiano y Malecón, T338812, F338148. 148 rooms, noise from Malecón but great view, balconies overlooking sea and fortress, renovated 1999, CP, pool, helpful *buró de turismo*. **C-D** *La Casa del Científico*, Prado 212 esq Trocadero, T8638103, F8600167. Beautiful colonial building with amazing original features, charmingly old-fashioned, shared or private bathroom,

Miramar

Straits of Florida

Maqueta de
la Ciudad

Av 1ra

Av 3ra

Av 5ta

MIRAMAR

Farmacia
Internacional

Cira García
Clinic

To

■ **Sleeping**	2 Calle 10	6 La Cocina	● **Bars & clubs**
1 Villa Babi	3 Casa de la Amistad	de Lilliam	10 Casa de la Cultura
	& Primavera	7 La Esperanza	de Plaza
● **Eating**	4 El Aljibe	8 La Fontana	11 Casa de la Música,
1 1830	5 El Tocororo	9 Pekin	Sala Te Quedarás

0 metres 200
0 yards 200

cheap breakfast, luxurious dining room and lounge in classic style, very pleasant atmo-sphere, friendly staff, reservations essential, often booked by groups, *Asistur* office on site. **D** *Lincoln* (Islazul), Galiano 164 esq Virtudes, T8610093. 135 mostly refurbished and good-value rooms, convenient location, friendly, TV with CNN, hot water, a/c, clean, guests are mostly Cuban, price includes breakfast on top floor, breezy, great view but no culinary experience.

Vedado LL-AL *Nacional de Cuba* (Gran Caribe), O esq 21, T333564, www.hotelnacionalde cuba.com 457 rooms, some renovated, good bathrooms with lots of bottles of goodies, some package tours use it at bargain rates, generally friendly and efficient service, faded grandeur, dates from 1930, superb reception hall, steam room, 2 pools, restaurants, bars, shops, business centre, exchange bureau, gardens with old cannon on hilltop overlooking the Malecón and harbour entrance. **AL** *Victoria* (Gran Caribe), 19 y M, T333510, reserva@gcvicto.gca.cma.net Good loca-tion, 32 standard rooms, 3 junior suites, small, quiet, intimate and pleasant, tasteful if conserva-tive, good bathrooms, small pool, parking, good cooking, in good order. Business oriented. **AL-B** *Presidente* (Gran Caribe), Calzada 110 y G (Presidentes), T551801, comerc@hpdte. gca.tur.cu Oldest hotel in Havana, refurbished, 160 rooms including 4 suites, 2 rooms are fully adapted for the disabled, ask for a room on the 10th floor (the Colonial Floor) which has sumptu-ous antiques, 2 restaurants, pool. **A** *Tryp Habana Libre* (Gran Caribe), L entre 23 y 25, T334011, www.solmeliacuba.com 572 rooms in huge block, 25 floors, prices depend on the floor number, most facilities are here, eg hotel reservations, excursions, Polynesian restaurant, buffet, 24-hr cof-fee shop, *Cabaret Turquino* 2200-0400, pool, shopping mall includes bank, airlines.

Casas particulares

La Habana Vieja E *Jesús y María*, Aguacate 518 entre Sol y Muralla, T8611378. Upstairs suite above the family and very private, a/c bedroom with twin beds, bathroom, living room and kitchenette with fan, fridge, also small outside sitting area, comfortable, clean. More

Only recent recommen-dations are Included here – there are many places to stay

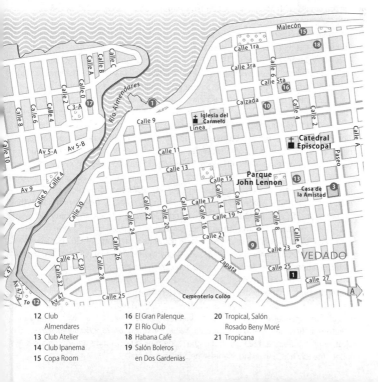

12	Club	16	El Gran Palenque	20	Tropical, Salón
	Almendares	17	El Río Club		Rosado Beny Moré
13	Club Atelier	18	Habana Café	21	Tropicana
14	Club Ipanema	19	Salón Boleros		
15	Copa Room		en Dos Gardenias		

modest and cheaper rooms off the courtyard downstairs. **E** *Orlando y Liset*, Aguacate 509 Apto 301 entre Sol y Muralla, T8675766. Lovely clean apartment, great view over La Habana Vieja from the terrace, garage, elevator, own entrance to guest room. Lisette is a university maths teacher. **E** *Gustavo Enamorado Zamora – Chez Nous*, Teniente Rey (Brasil) 115 entre Cuba y San Ignacio, T8626287, cheznous@ceniai.inf.cu 2 spacious double rooms, shared bathroom with original 1904 shower, hot water, fan, TV, balcony overlooking street, street noise, nice patio, parking, warm atmosphere, Gustavo (radio cultural correspondent) and Kathy (artist) are kind and helpful, French spoken, reservations essential.

Ask whether food is available. We do not mention which casas provide meals in case they are not paying taxes

Centro **E** *Dr Alejandro Oses*, Malecón 163, p1, entre Aguila y Crespo, T8637359. Best view in city from balcony of entire Malecón, from El Morro to *Hotel Nacional*, nice place to stay and one of the cheapest, helpful family, book ahead, always full. **E** *Carlos Luis Valderrama Moré*, Neptuno 404 entre San Nicolás y Manrique, 2nd floor, T8679842. Carlos and Vivian are former teachers, he speaks English, 1940s apartment above a shop, 2 rooms, front room has balcony overlooking street, good bathrooms, hot water. **E** *Giuseppe y María Elena*, Valle 205 entre Mazón y Basarrate, T8784763, giusepperosato@hotmail.com Colonial house with patio and terrace, fan, fridge, hot water, near University. **E** *Marilys Herrera González*, Concordia 714 altos entre Soledad y Aramburo, T8700608, www.casaparticular.tripod.com Bathroom with warm water, kitchen, fridge, kitchen, a/c, TV, all modern, clean and comfortable, laundry offered, Marylis is very kind and caring. **F** *Daisy y Jorge Castro Pérez*, Lealtad 308 entre Neptuno y San Miguel, T8785038, daisycastro@yahoo.com 2 rooms, a/c, hot showers, warm family atmosphere. **F** *Rosa Artiles Hernández*, Crespo 117 bajos entre Colón y Trocadero, T8627574. Excellent place, very clean and friendly, 3 rooms, 1 has private bathroom, other 2 share, hot water, shared use of fridge, a/c, fan, radio, separate entrance, own key, sitting area, beautiful car on ground floor, structural adjustments made to building to accommodate it, no food, son speaks English.

Vedado **E** *Armando Gutiérrez*, 21 62 entre M y N, Apto 7, 4th (top) floor, T/F8321876. Large a/c room with 2 beds, bathroom, hot water, Armando and his wife, Betty, and mother, Teresa, speak a little English and French. **E** *Carmen y Ramón Fonseca Díaz*, G 301 esq 13, Apto 13, T8324021, sandravigil76@yahoo.com Great view from balcony on 13th floor, 2 bedrooms, bathroom, use of kitchen and rest of apartment, English, French and German spoken, they offer their services as tour guides, translators and Spanish teachers. Salsa lessons can be organized. **E** *Familia Villazón*, 21 203 entre J y K, T8321066. Old colonial home with amazing high ceilings, antiques including antique swing chairs on front veranda, a/c, hot water, son speaks some English. **E** *Luís Cartaya y Alicia Horta*, Línea 53 entre M y N, Apto 9, T8328439. Friendly couple, both doctors, Spanish-speaking only, rooms cleaned daily, long stays possible, good view from 9th floor, popular so call in advance. **E** *Martha Vitorte*, G 301 Apto 14, 14th floor, entre 13 y 15, T8326475, high-rise building near corner with Línea, 1 apartment on each floor, referred to as 'horizontals', beautiful modern building, very spacious, en suite bathroom, a/c, security safe in bedroom, balcony on 2 sides for views of Havana, sea and sunsets, Martha is a retired civil servant and speaks some English and French. **E** *Mercedes González*, 21 360 Apto 2A, entre G y H, T8325846. 2 rooms, a/c, fan, good bathroom, hot water, airy rooms, balcony, smart, airport transfers, helpful and friendly, good location, near park. **E** *Natalia Rodés León*, 19 376 p11B, entre G y H, T8328909. 2 rooms, 1 bathroom, fridge, TV, friendly lady, fought with Fidel in the Sierra Maestra. **E** *Pedro Mesa López y Tobias López Márquez*, F 609 Apto 12 entre 25 y 27, T8329057. Quiet area, 3 rooms with attached bathrooms, fridge, a/c, only Spanish spoken by friendly couple in their 60s. **E** *Teresa Naredo*, 15 605 entre C y D, Apto 1, T8303382, alyogan@ hotmail. com Ground floor of low-rise block, balcony, clean and tidy, en suite facilities, a/c, hot water, quiet embassy residential neighbourhood, often booked for extended periods.**E** *Villa Babi*, 27 965 entre 6 y 8, T8306373, jlrc@informed.sld.cu Run by María del Carmen Díaz, second wife of the late Tomás Gutiérrea Alea, famed director of the movie, *Fresa y Chocolate*, the walls are covered with photos. Cheap, reservations essential. **E-F** *Adita*, 9 257 entre J y I, T8320643, whole of the top floor. Large double rooms, bathroom for each, own entrance, secret passageway to self-contained apartment, excellent value. **E-F** *Gisela Ibarra y Daniel Riviero*, F 104 altos, entre 5 y Calzada, T323238. Top of the range, high-quality rooms and decor, a/c, fans, fridge, friendly hosts, speaking Spanish a help but not essential.

Cuba

Eating

La Habana Vieja Expensive (US$30 and over) *Floridita*, Obispo esq Monserrate, next to the Parque Central, T8631060. Open 1130-2400. A favourite haunt of Hemingway, it is a very elegant bar and restaurant reflected in the prices (US$6 for a daiquiri), but well worth a visit to see the sumptuous decor and 'Bogart atmosphere'. *La Bodeguita del Medio*, Empedrado 207 entre Cuba y San Ignacio, near the cathedral, open 1030-0100, T8671374. Was made famous by Hemingway and should be visited if only for a drink (*mojito* – rum, crushed ice, mint, sugar, lime juice and carbonated water – is a must, US$6), food poor, expensive at US$35-40 for 2, but very popular.

State restaurants
All food tends to be greasy, although there does seem to be a tourist-oriented swing towards grilling, with a greater awareness of nutritional content

Mid-range (US$20-30) *Castillo de Farnés*, Monserrate 361 y Obrapía, T8671030. Tasty Spanish food, reasonable prices, good for *garbanzos* and shrimp, restaurant 1200-2400, bar open 24 hrs, Castro came here at 0445, 9 Jan 1959, with Che and Raúl. *D'Giovanni*, Tacón entre Empedrado y O'Reilly, T8671036. 1200-2300. Lovely building with patio and terrace, Italian, overpriced, often cold, pizza and spaghetti. *Dominica*, O' Reilly esq Mercaderes, T8662917. Italian, very smart, set menus US$25-30, pasta from US$6, pizza US$4.50-12 depending on size, vegetarian options, outdoor seating nice for lunch, credit cards. Open 1200-2400 daily. *El Patio*, San Ignacio 54 esq Empedrado, Plaza Catedral, T8618504. Expensive, small portions, appalling service, but has selection of national dishes, open 24 hrs, lovely location. *La Mina*, on Obispo esq Oficios, Plaza de Armas, T620216. Open 1200-2400, expensive, traditional Cuban food, sandwiches, pasta, liqueur coffees, tables and chairs outside with live Cuban music. *La Zaragozana*, Monserrate entre Obispo y Obrapía, T8671033. Oldest restaurant in Havana, international cuisine, good seafood and wine, 3 courses about US$25, good service but food nothing special. Open 1200-2400.

Cheap ($10-20) *Al Medina*, Oficios 12, entre Obrapía y Obispo, T8671041, 1200-2300. Arab food in lovely colonial mansion, dishes priced between US$4-11, try chicken in sesame, huge vegetarian combo, lovely fresh fruit juices US$1, good coffee, some seating on large cushions, show at 2130 Fri, Sat, also Mosque and Arab cultural centre off beautiful courtyard, *Gentiluomo*, Bernaza esq Obispo, T8671300. Pasta, pizza, US$3.50-8, reasonable food but don't expect them to have everything on the menu, friendly service, pleasant environment, a/c. Open 1200-2300. *Torre de Marfil*, Mercaderes, entre Obispo y Obrapía, T8671038, 1200-2200. Good, inexpensive Cantonese menu. Better than anything in Chinatown.

Seriously cheap (US$10 and under) *Cabaña*, Cuba 12 esq Peña Pobre, T335670, facing Av del Puerto. Bar and restaurant open 24 hrs. *Café París*, Obispo y San Ignacio. Serves good chicken for US$3.50, beer US$1, snacks and pizza around the clock, live music, lively in evenings, pity about the hassling from harmless but irritating *jineteros*. *Cafetería Torre La Vega*, Obrapía 114, next to the Casa de México. Open 0900-2100, does cheap breakfast, bland chicken and chips, salad and coffee for US$3, better value spaghetti US$0.65, beer US$1. *Hanoi*, Brasil 507 y Bernaza, T8671029. Open daily 0700-2400, Cuban food, 3 courses for US$6, *combinados* for US$2-2.50, *mojito* for US$1, plenty of food, live music, nice atmosphere, also good for breakfast. *La Dichosa*, Obispo esq Compostela. Good place for breakfast or a snack, US$2-4.

Vedado Expensive *La Torre*, 17 y M, at top of Edif Fosca, T8325650. Open 1200-2400, French chef, about US$40 per person but worth it, great views over Havana, a/c. *1830*, Calzada y 20, T553090. Open 1200-2400. Recently reopened after a revamp, wonderful setting at the mouth of the river, popular for weddings and *quinceañera* celebrations, international food at international prices, cabaret at 2200, T8339907, admission price depends on who is playing.

Mid-range *El Conejito*, M esq 17, T8324671. Open 1200-2400, specializes in rabbit in several different sauces, other meat options available, quite expensive but worth it, 24-hr bar attached for karaoke. In the *Habana Libre Hotel*, try *Polinesia*, (1200-2400) with access from the street, smart, dark and cool, a mix of Chinese and Indonesian dishes, US$12-20, and the *Bar Turquino* on the 25th floor (spectacular views of Havana which makes the food acceptable, service bad). Cabaret 2230-0430. Bar open 1030-0430.

Cheap *Trattoria Marakas*, O entre 23 y 25, T333640. Good Italian, great pizzas, US$3.95-5.75, pasta around US$5, even has mozzarella and olive oil. Plastic furniture, canteen atmosphere. Open 1200-2400. *Casa de la Amistad*, Paseo entre 17 y 19 (see above). 1100-2300, for chicken, snacks and pizza. Inside the main building is *Restaurant Primavera*, open 1200-2400, elegant furniture, antiques, good table service.

Along and near La Rampa there are some cheap pizzerías and self-service restaurants

Seriously cheap *Cafetería La Rampa*, at the *Habana Libre* with access from the street as well as the hotel, breakfast, sandwiches, pizza (US$3.50 plus toppings US$1-2) and pasta (US$2.20-6), burgers (US$4.50-6.50) and main meals. Open 24 hrs. *Centro de Prensa Internacional*, 23 2502 esq O. Basement bar open until 1900, good hamburgers for US$1, email access upstairs. *Pekin* 12 y 23, T8334020. Close to Cementerio Colon. Also at Calzada entre D y E. An unprecedented selection of 50 vegetable dishes. Clean, friendly and cheap, with informative run downs of the health benefits of veg. The catch is that it is all cold, tepid at best, there are normally huge queues, the service can be slow and by dinner time the options are limited.

Miramar Expensive *El Tocororo* (national bird of Cuba), 18 302 y Av 3, T2042209. Excellent food at US$40-60 a head, open Mon-Sat 1200-2400, old colonial mansion with nice terrace, great house band, no menu, ostrich steak, prices fluctuate widely but one of the best restaurants in town. Also has a *Salón Japonés*, with a Sakura sushi bar and saki. *La Cecilia*, 5 entre 110 y 112, T2041562. Good international food, mostly in open-air setting, good salsa from 2200, dancing outside until 0300, US$20 cover charge. Open 1200-2400.

Mid-range *El Aljibe*, 7 entre 24 y 26, T2044233. Open 1200-2300. Open framework design, nice and breezy, friendly atmosphere, popular with Cubans, chicken the house speciality, try *pollo al Aljibe*, delicious black beans, very generous portions, US$12-15 per person.

Casablanca Mid-range *La Divina Pastora*, Fortaleza de la Cabaña, open 1230-0200, T8623886. Expensive, fish restaurant, food praised. *Los XII Apostoles*, nearby on Vía Monumental, T638295. Open 1230-2300, fish and good *criollo* food, good views of the Malecón.

Parque Lenin Expensive *Las Ruinas*, 100 esq Cortina de la Presa in Parque Lenin, open 1200-2400, T578286. One of the best restaurants in Havana, the ruined plantation house has been incorporated into a modern structure, mosquitoes at dusk, great resident pianist, tours of Parque Lenin often include a meal here, otherwise take a taxi, US$15, try to persuade the driver to come back and fetch you, as otherwise it is difficult to get back.

Seriously cheap *La Casa del Dragón*, Cortina de la Presa y 100, off the main road to the right soon after entrance from Arroyo Naranjo, look out for the sign, T443026, ext 176. Chinese, small, only 4 tables, nice bamboo furniture, good food, reasonable prices, spring roll, sweet and sour pork, rice and salad US$6, beer US$0.85, open Tue-Sun 1200-2000, nice walks nearby.

Paladares
Prices refer to the cost of a full meal with a beer for one person

La Habana Vieja *Don Lorenzo*, Acosta 260A, entre Habana y Compostela. T8616733. 1200-2400. Dishes on offer include turtle steaks, protected species avoid, and crocodile (farmed). Good vegetarian options. Above the average paladar price bracket. Not far from Santa Clara. *Doña Blanquita*, Prado 158 entre Colón y Refugio. Run by English-speaking lawyer, simple but good food, pork, chicken or eggs, US$10, upstairs, inside with fan or on balcony if dry. *La Moneda Cubana* San Ignacio 77, entre O'Reilly y Empedrado. T8763852. Open 1200-2230. Limited choice, fried fish with salad, beans and rice with fried banana and bread around US$8.

Centro Mid-range *La Guarida*, Concordia 418 entre Gervasio y Escobar, T8624940. 1200-2300. Film location for *Fresa y Chocolate*, good food, international menu, fish a speciality, always busy, 'street guides' may not take you here because the owners do not pay commission to them. Reservations recommended.

Cheap *Bellomar*, Virtudes 169A esq Amistad, T8610023. 1130-2330. Good unassuming Cuban cooking, US$10 for fish, salad and rice. Friendly and obliging. Quirky festive setting with *Bodeguita*-style scribbles. *La Tasquita*, Jovellar (27 de Noviembre) entre Espada y San Francisco, T798647. 12002400. Wonderful food, great family atmosphere, traditional paladar setting, mammoth portions served with delicious rice and beans, plus good salads. Great cocktails.

Don't expect authentic food. Chop suey or chow mein is about as Oriental you'll get

Chinese market Seriously cheap At Zanja and Rayo, 1 block west of Galiano, are several *paladares* in a small street. Tables inside or outside, menus on view, you will be pestered for your custom. Meals around US$5. *Tien Tan*, open 1200-2100, always full but not good. *El Pacífico*. Impressive, looks like a Chinese temple, food can be good if it is open, if there is water, if there is cooking gas and if there is any food, problems which affect all the restaurants around here, all prices in pesos, therefore very cheap, around US$3-4 for 2, eg lobster chop suey for 13 pesos, lemonade 60 centavos, etc. *Tong Po Laug*, No 10. Cheap, pesos accepted.

Vedado Cheap *Amor*, 23 759 entre B y C, T8338150. Mon-Fri 1900-2400. Welcoming atmosphere, large eating area with elegant furniture, great food, good portions, fried turkey encrusted with peanuts, rice and beans, salad and beer for US$10. Try and go on the first Sun in the month when they have a musical gathering on the rooftop, the *Azotea de Elda Peña*. Local artists perform, great fun, entrance by donation to the local hospital. *Gringo Viejo*, 21 454 entre E y F, T8326150. Open Mon-Sat 1200-2400, nice atmosphere, good portions, main course US$8.50. *Hurón Azul*, Humboldt 153 esq P, T791691. International menu, works by local artists and photos of celebrity diners adorn the walls, open 1200-2400, a/c. Creative menu, but unsolicited bread and fruit basket will be charged extra. *Los Amigos*, M entre 19 y 21, opposite *Victoria*. Basic food, good mix of locals and tourists, main courses US$8, check your bill, open daily 1200-2400. *Le Chansonnier*, J 257 entre 15 y Linea, T8321576. 1900-2400. Beautiful colonial mansion, warm atmosphere, attentive service. Menu very meaty with just one fish choice. French 'inspired' dishes, including lamb with red wine and duck with pineapple and raison rauce. Substantial fruit and vegetable salad for vegetarians. *Nerei*, 19 esq L, T8327860. Open daily 1200-2400, good food, not everything is fried, main course US$11, porch dining, English spoken.

Miramar Mid-range *La Esperanza*, 16 105 entre 1 y 3, T224361. Open 1200-1600, 1900-2330, closed Wed. Small sign, very popular with Cubans and foreigners, traditional Cuban food, meal and drinks around US$15 per person, potent mango daiquirís, reservations advisable, run by Hubert and Manolo in their living room surrounded by their paintings. **Cheap** *Calle 10*, 10 314 entre 3 y 5, near Teatro Karl Marx, T296702. Open daily 1200-2400, good service, English spoken, main course plus beer US$10.50. Outdoor seating with open-air grill, tiki bar, strolling musicians expect hefty tip. *La Cocina de Lilliam*, 48 1311, entre 13 y 15, T296514. Open Sun-Fri 1200-1500, 1900-2200, closed Dec, good Cuban food with tables outside in lovely garden, fish, crab, popular with locals, reservations recommended, main course plus beer US$12, good service. *La Fontana*, 3-A 305 esq 46, T228337. Open 1200-2400, good Cuban food, French chef, extremely popular with Cubans, tourists and diplomats, ask for *menú de la casa* for non-inflated prices, under US$15, arrive early or make a reservation.

A visit to the *Coppelia* open-air ice cream parlour, 23 y L, Vedado, is recommended. The parlour found movie fame in *Strawberry and Chocolate*. The building, which occupies a whole block, has a capacity for 707 seated ice cream lovers. There are several separate outdoor areas to eat in, each with their own entrance and queue in the surrounding streets, or inside in La Torre. Open Tue-Sun 1100-2230, if you pay in pesos, you will almost certainly have to queue for an hour or so. Alternatively, pay in dollars to avoid the queue, in the upstairs section or the *Fuente de Soda* kiosks outside (said to be open 24 hrs but often closed after midnight. Bring your own plastic spoons for the tubs as they invariably run out. US$2 for small portion, many different flavours. *Bim Bom*, 23 y Calzada de Infanta, Vedado, is another ice cream shop, while several street stalls specialize in ice cream (*helado*), 21 esq K, near to *Coppelia* but no queues, 3 pesos per cone. **Ice cream parlours**

There are a rapidly growing number of fast food outlets in all parts of the city. *Pain de París*, several locations including Línea entre Paseo y A, next to *Teatro Trianón* and inside the Terminal de Omnibus, Plaza de la Revolución. 24-hr service, good coffee, *café cortadito* or *café con leche* US$0.65, croissants US$0.55 and *señoritas de chocolate* (custard slices) US$1.25, pizzas from US$1.25, take-out boxes provided. *El Rápido*, red logo, clean with fast service and numerous locations. *Burgui*, currently a handful of outlets, 23 entre G y H, Vedado, next to *Riviera* cinema, and Av de Italia (Galiano) esq Neptuno, Centro Habana, near to *Teatro América*, selling fast food (hamburger, fried chicken, fries, pizza, soft drinks and beer), freezing a/c. All *Burguis* are 24 hrs except for the one at Av 5 esq118, Miramar (1100-2300.) *DiTú*, prefabricated units springing up all over the city selling fried chicken by weight. *El Rapidito*, **Fast-food outlets**

Cuba

red logo, not to be confused with *El Rápido* chain. *Cadena Imágenes* and *Doña Yulla* serve fried chicken, pizzas, soft drinks and beer. There are many **street stalls** and places where you can pick up snacks, pizza, etc. Note that their prices are listed in pesos even though there is a $ sign posted. These can work out very cheap and are good for filling a hole at lunchtime, but don't expect a culinary masterpiece. Make sure you eat pizza fresh from the oven, 6 pesos a piece for cheese, 10 pesos for extra cheese or meat toppings. They are usually very greasy, take plenty of napkins. Very sweet juice drinks 2 pesos per glass.

Bars

La Habana Vieja

Musicians in most bars. Many play only a few songs, then come round with the collecting bowl trying to sell their CDs, and move on, to be replaced by another band who do the same thing

Bar Dos Hermanos, Av del Puerto esq Santa Clara, opposite the ferry terminals, T8613514. Good, down to earth bar, bohemian atmosphere, popular with Cubans, open 24 hrs, just off the tourist circuit so lower prices, chicken US$2.85, mojito US$1.50, local *son* band usually blast off after 2300, ask the barman who's playing. *Bar Monserrate*, Monserrate y Obrapía. 1100-0300. Beer US$1, cocktails US$3, food not recommended, interesting to sit and watch comings and goings, bar staff seem to have unwritten agreement whereby girls are allowed in with a foreigner, or if they buy a drink, but if girl-to-punters ratio gets too high, some of the girls have to leave. *Fundación Distilería Havana Club*, Av del Puerto 262 entre Sol y Muralla, T8618051. Rum museum, shop, art gallery, courtyard restaurant and 2 bars, 1 with nightly music, 1000-2400, good *Cuba Libre* and sometimes showcase quality live bands. The bar not to miss in the old town for Hemingway fans is *La Bodeguita del Medio* (see Eating, also for *La Floridita*), a favourite for tour parties. *Lluvia de Oro*, Obispo esq Habana. 0800-2400. Good place to drink rum and listen to loud rock music or salsa (full pelt in the afternoon), also food.

Vedado

The trendy place is the *Habana Café* in the *Meliá Cohiba*, T333636, which is now a 1950s theme place with old cars, Cubana plane hanging from the ceiling, memorabilia on the walls, Benny Moré music and large screen showing brilliant film of old Cuban musicians and artistes, entrance to the left of the main hotel entrance, open 1200-0200, live music at weekends 2230-0400, cover charge US$25 on Sun when top local bands, including NG La Banda, draw the crowds.

Music and dance

Radio Taíno FM 93.3, English and Spanish language tourist station, gives regular details of wide range of venues and Cuban bands playing, particularly in the programme El Exitazo Musical del Caribe from 1500-1800 presented by Alexis Nargona. Also Radio Ciudad de la Habana, 94.9 FM, 820 AM, in Spanish. Up-to-the-minute salsa programmes, Disco Fiesta 98, Mon-Sat 1100-1300, provides accurate information about musical events in Havana, Rapsodia Latina, Mon-Fri 1630-1730. The newspaper, *Opciones*, also has a listing of what's on and *Cartelera*, free, every Thu, is found at most hotel reception desks.

Centro

Callejón de Hamel, Hamel entre Aramburu y Hospital, Centro Habana. A fast, kicking *rumba* show with invited guests and community artists every Sun from 1200, a responsive audience and electric jam sessions make this a hot venue, recommended. *Casa de la Trova*, San Lázaro, entre Belascoaín y Gervasio, 1800-2400, where locals go to hear traditional Cuban music, open daily, session on Fri from 1800 thoroughly recommended. Equally recommended is the *Casa de la Trova* in **Guanabacoa**, Martí entre Versalles y San Antonio, T977687. A more authentic Cuban feel, few tourists, Mon-Fri 2000-2300 salsa dance group *Rumores del Omnibus*, Tue and Sun 1600 *campesina* music show, 2nd and 4th Thu every month 2200-0100 *filín* and *boleros* night, no entrance charge. Sat-Sun 2000-0200, salsa disco, 2 pesos, draws big local crowd of dance fanatics. *Casarón del Tango*, Neptuno 309 entre Aguila y Italia, T8630097. Sporadic opening hours. A museum to tango with memorabilia from the 1940s, octogenarians perform heart-wrenching tango here.

Vedado

Café El Gato Tuerto (One-eyed Cat), O entre 17 y 19, T552696. Open 2400-0500, US$5 *consumo mínimo*. Son, *trova* and *boleros* performed 2400-0500. Bohemian people and post-modern decor, funky, good restaurant on 1st floor, eat on balcony overlooking Malecón and *Hotel Nacional*. At the **Casa de la Amistad** (see Museums in Vedado, above), you are very unlikely to be hustled. US$3 admission plus US$2 *consumo mínimo*. A traditional son group, *La Peña del Chan Chan,* plays every Tue at 2100. Compay Segundo sometimes appears with the band, although following the huge success of the *Buena Vista Social Club* he is often on tour. Thu is trova night from 1800 and Sat is *Noche Cubana*, with son and guaracha. Dancing on the veranda or in the gardens after the show. Very limited toilet facilities. **Casa de la Cultura de Plaza**, Calzada y 8, Vedado. Concerts and shows, different artistes, different times. **Conjunto Folklórico Nacional de Cuba** performs traditional *rumba* and *Santería* music, outdoors, every Sat 1500-1600, US$5, recommended. **Cine Riviera**, 23 entre G y H, Vedado, T8309564. Third Fri of each month the cinema is given over to a live music event with an ecological theme, Cuban reggae and jazz bands, young, friendly and relaxed, mostly Cuban crowd, 1900-2300, 5 pesos. **Centro de Música Ignacio Piñeiro**, 17 y K, Vedado. The last Fri of every month, showcases new local salsa bands, young and very energetic crowd.

At the Teatro Nacional, Paseo y 39, Plaza de la Revolución, there is a piano bar **El Delirio Habanero**, T8335713, upstairs on the 5th floor (lift sometimes not working) where you can hear quality music, *nueva trova, bolero*, etc, 2230-0300. *Consumo mínimo* US$10. Resident band *Los Tres de la Habana* Thu and Sat. Great views of floodlit José Martí monument and Plaza de la Revolución. Take the big red sofa seats under the windows. Busy at weekends with a mostly Cuban crowd, phone to reserve the best tables. Recommended, Energetic clubbers leave here and head downstairs for the **Café Cantante Mi Habana**, T8796011, side entrance, down the stairs. Open nightly from 2230-0400, top live bands, US$10, sometimes it is US$15, depending on the band, well regarded and popular with Cuban musicians and other personalities. They also hold late afternoon (1600-1900) salsa and rock discos, *Tardes de Mi Habana*, sometimes with live local bands, entrance 10 pesos, very popular with young Cubans.

El Gran Palenque Bar plays host to *Patio de la Rumba*, 4 entre Calzada y 5, on Sat from 1500, US$5, when the Conjunto Folklórico Nacional puts on a rumba show. **Palmares**, Malecón y E, for *rumba* performances and disco dancing, 2100 until late. You can find *rumba* on Wed at the **Teatro Mella**, Línea entre A y B, T8335651, phone for programme details. **UNEAC**, Av 17 entre G y H, outside in the *Hurón Azul*. Bar, tables, chairs and small stage. *Rumba* (resident band *Clave y Guaguancó*) and *Trova* bands play alternate Wed 1700-2000. Crowded and can be difficult to get a drink from the bar. Sat, *Noche de Boleros*, 2000-0200. Both events charge US$5 entrance. Good atmosphere, friendly, popular with Cuban artists. Events listed at entrance.

Miramar *Club Almendares*, Márgenes del Río Almendares, 49C y 28, Kohly, Miramar, T244990. Open-air salsa disco, mosquitoes can be troublesome as you are in the Bosque de la Habana, Cuban crowd, daily 1900-2400, US$3, more if live band playing. For *bolero* admirers, try **Salón Boleros en Dos Gardenias**, with popular Chinese restaurant and bar, 7, esq 26, Miramar, T2042353. Daily 2230-0300, US$10, upmarket *bolero* venue, 2 live shows every night, elegant, well-dressed crowd. **La Cecilia**, 5 y 110, Miramar, T241562. Expensive restaurant, Thu-Sun features live *bolero* and salsa bands from 2130.

Jazz

All venues are in **Vedado**. During the annual *Jazz Festival* in **Dec** you can hear international as well as Cuban stars, free or US$5-10 per show, based at *Hotel Riviera* but in the 2 weeks before there are also events at the *Nacional* and the *Habana Libre*. Information from the *Instituto de la Música*, 15 452 entre E y F, T8323503-6, ask for schedule from Rita Rosa. Fri nights at **Meliá Cohiba** from 2100. **Hotel Riviera** sometimes features jazz sessions in the bar off the lobby, entrance after Copa Room, recommended, but phone first to check listing. **Jazz Café**, Galerías de Paseo, Primera entre A y Paseo, T553475, top floor of blue glass building. Open 1000-0200, US$10 *consumo mínimo*, live jazz bands from 2300 every night, including *Irakere*, *Chucho Valdés y su Grupo*, *Top Secret* and other top jazz bands, no cover charge, bar and restaurant, very popular, good atmosphere, can be hard to get a table, recommended. **La Zorra y el Cuervo** (the fox and the crow), 23 y O, T662402. Entrance through a very good reproduction British telephone box, US$5, opens 2100 for 1st set, 2nd set 2330, closes at 0400, very popular with locals and tourists, great jazz and salsa every night, get there before 2300 if you want a table with a good view of the stage or make a reservation, gets packed later. Good quality jazz club, Cuban bands often feature visiting US musicians, weekly listings at the entrance, highly recommended, beer US$2.50, Cuba libre US$3.

Nightclubs and cabarets

Amistur travel agency can help with nightclub and theatre bookings

Havana clubs are late night/early morning affairs with most Cubans arriving around midnight and staying late. Queues at the weekends. Cubans dress up for club nights and most clubs have a smart dress code, strictly enforced by the door staff. No one under 18 is admitted. The emphasis is on dancing, be it salsa and Latin styles, R and B, hip hop or rock. Many places are frequented by *jineteros/as* and lone travellers have reported feeling uncomfortable with unwelcome attention. Several venues now feature early shows, aimed at young Cubans, with entrance in pesos.

The *Cabaret Nacional*, San Rafael y Prado, entrance to the side of *Gran Teatro*, T8632361, is a cheap version of the *Tropicana*, 2200-0300, US$3 entry but expensive drinks. Shows at 2330 and 0130. Lots of prostitutes. *Macumba*, 222 esq 37, La Coronela, La Lisa, in *La Giraldilla* tourist complex in the western suburbs, T8330568. Open 2100-0500, small floor show, open-air, rated as a top Havana disco, very popular with Cubans and foreigners, queues, 2 large dance floors for salsa, *merengue* and R & B, Thu is carnival night, well-stocked cigar shop and smoking room (*humidor*). US$10 Sun-Thu, US$15 Fri-Sat, food not very good, dinner and show with bottle of rum and 4 cokes is US$35. *Tropicana* (closed Mon, 72 No 4504 entre 43 y 45, Marianao, 2100-0200) is internationally famous and open-air (entry refunded if it rains). It costs US$70 for the show and a 3-course meal, or US$60 for the show and a quarter bottle of rum and coke. Best to take a tour, which will include transport, as a taxi from La Habana Vieja costs US$12. Reservations are recommended, T270110, 279147, between 1000 and 1600. All the main hotels have their own cabarets, eg *Parisien* at *Hotel Nacional*, T333564/7, excellent show for US$30, lasts longer than *Tropicana* and of equivalent standard, Fri-Wed 2100-0230, make a reservation. *Salón Rojo* at *Hotel Capri* is recommended, at US$10 and longer show than *Tropicana* with disco afterwards until 0400, all drinks included. *Copa Room*, at the *Riviera*, Cuban cabaret *A lo Riviera* followed by resident salsa band. Glitzy cabaret, skimpy outfits and sequins, Thu, Fri, Sat 2030-0300, US$25 including cocktail, meal from US$50, T334051. The *Habana Libre Turquino* cabaret and *Euro* disco is on the 25th floor, T8334011. Amazing views, the roof opens and you can dance under the stars, US$10, if you are in a group 1 person needs a passport, drinks expensive. Top bands often play live, open every night 2230-0400, cabarets start at 2300 and 0100. *Cabaret Las Vegas*, Calzada de Infanta 104, T8707939. 2200-0500, minor salsa bands, entrance US$5, hot and raw. *Club Atelier*, 17 esq 6, corner of Parque John Lennon. Small L-shaped dance floor, pool table, beer US$1.50, various house styles from salsa to rap, every night 2200-0400, US$5. *Imágenes*, Calzada 602 esq C, T333606. Live *bolero* music, good karaoke set on Thu, Sinatra's *New York, New York* a favourite, minimum cover charge US$5, 1900-0400. *Sherezada*, Edificio FOCSA, M y 19, next to *Teatro Guiñol*, T8323042. Disco and show, US$2.50. Open 24 hrs. *Tikoa*, 23 entre N y O. Daily 2300-0300, US$2, at lower end of La Rampa along with several other similar-style discos, popular with tourists and young Cubans.

The *Casa de la Música, Sala Te Quedarás*, 20 esq 35, in Miramar, T2040447, open 1000-0300, is a great place with a solid salsa disco and live bands on stage in a beautiful old house. Entrance US$15-20 depending on which bands are playing. The latest Cuban bands play here and there is a well-stocked CD/music shop open 1000-2430. Afternoon *peñas* daily 1600-1900, entrance 10-15 pesos, popular with young Cubans. *Club Ipanema*, *Hotel Copacabana*, Av 1 entre 44 y 46, T241037. Every night 2400-0400, late starter, but gets very busy at weekends, large dance floor, salsa and western disco, Fri, Sat US$5, other nights US$10. *El Río Club*, A entre 3 y 5, T293389. Recently reopened, locals still refer to it as *Johnnie's Club*, its name before the Revolution. Salsa disco, hot and sweaty dance floor, current favourite with Havana's dance crowd, queue at weekends. *Tropical*, *Salón Rosado Beny Moré*, Av 41 y 46, T290985. Tue-Sun, with live salsa bands including top names on Fri-Sun 2100-0200, US$5. 'Third age' salsa activity Sun afternoons, outdoor location, very popular, mostly Cuban crowd. You will probably be directed to the upper section, where the entrance is in dollars, with a well-stocked bar and some tables, good views of the frenetic casino-style dancing downstairs, but if you really want to experience Cuban salsa first hand, head for the lower section, where the entrance is in pesos.

Entertainment

Comprehensive weekly listings of all films from Thu-Wed posted in cinema windows. Most have **Cinemas** a/c. *Yara*, opposite *Habana Libre* hotel, T8329430. From 1230, late showings at the weekends, 2 *Observe queuing* video lounges show recently released US films, 40 seats in each salon, but several are broken and *procedures to* sound quality is sometimes poor in Salon B. Often sold out at weekends. *Acapulco*, 26 entre 35 y *buy tickets* 37, Nuevo Vedado, T8339573, from 1630. *Chaplin*, 23 entre 10 y 12, T8311101. Arty films at 1700 and 2000, shop good for film memorabilia. *Payret*, Prado 503, esq San José, T8633163. Films shown continuously from 1230, and *La Rampa*, Rampa esq O, T8786146. 2 films from 1630, 900 comfortable seats, dodgy toilets. *Riviera*, 23 entre Presidentes y H, Vedado, T8309564. Many others, 2 pesos. *Annual Film Festival* in **Dec** (overlaps with Jazz Festival, above) in all cinemas. International films, no translations into English. Information in *Hotel Nacional*.

Teatro Mella, Línea 657 entre A y B, Vedado, T8335651. 8-10 pesos. Specializes in modern dance; **Theatres** more traditional programmes at *Gran Teatro de la Habana*, Prado y San José, on Parque Central next to *Hotel Inglaterra*, T8613078, bic@gth.cult.cu. Claims to be the oldest working theatre in the world, opened in 1837, building seats 1,500. The *Conjunto Folklórico Nacional* and *Danza Contemporánea* dance companies sometimes perform here. Highly recommended. US$10. **In Miramar**, *Teatro Karl Marx*, Av 1 entre 8 y 10, T2030801, renovated in 2000 and now famous for hosting the first rock concert by a Western band, *Manic Street Preachers*, who played there in 2001 in the presence of Fidel Castro. *Amadeo Roldán*, Calzada 512 y D, Vedado, T8321168. Newly renovated concert hall where you can hear the Orquesta Sinfónica Nacional. Pay in pesos.

Shopping

Original lithographs and other works of art can be purchased or commissioned directly from **Art** the artists at the *Galería del Grabado*, at the back of the *Taller Experimental de Gráfica de la* **& handicrafts** *Habana*, Callejón del Chorro 62, Plaza de la Catedral (open all day, closed Sun, T8620979). You *Shopaholics, be* can watch the prints and engravings being made and specialist courses are available. The *aware that Cuba is* *Taller Serigrafía* is another big workshop, on Cuba 513, making screen prints; again, you can *not going to satisfy* watch them being made and buy things. *La Victoria*, Obispo 366 entre Compostela y Habana, *your urges. There is* T627914. Open 1000-1900, is an art gallery with a large choice of paintings at good prices, and *little to spend your* books, owned by artist Natividad Scull Marchena. Reproductions of works of art are sold at *La* *money on without* *Exposición*, San Rafael 12, Manzana de Gómez, in front of Parque Central. You need documen- *a great deal of effort* tation to take works of art out of the country or you may have them confiscated at the airport; galleries will provide the necessary paperwork and even vendors in the market can give you the necessary stamp. The *Palacio de la Artesanía* is in the Palacio Pedroso (built 1780) at Cuba 64 entre Peña Pobre y Cuarteles (opposite Parque Anfiteatro), a mansion converted into boutiques on 3 floors with musicians in the courtyard. A large selection of Cuban handicrafts is available. It also has things not available elsewhere, such as American footwear (trainers), as well as clothing, jewelry, perfume, souvenirs, music, cigars, restaurant, bar and ice cream. Visa and Mastercard accepted, passport required. **Open-air markets** Handicraft and tourist souvenir markets, *feria de artesanías,* have sprung up. *Feria del Malecón* , Malecón, entre D y E, Vedado. Daily, except Wed 0800-1830, busy market, lots of homemade products, including shoes, jewellery, lamps and the ubiquitous booksellers. Che Guevara and religious *Santería* items lead the sales charts. Illegal cigar sellers operate here. *Feria del Tacón*, Av Tacón entre Chacón y Empedrado, Habana Vieja, Plaza de la Catedral end. Wed-Sat 0800-1900, Havana's largest craft market, a multitude of products and if they don't have what you want someone will know someone who does, tourist souvenirs, clothing, paintings, the list is endless. Also sold here are carvings, crochet, ceramics, boxes, jewellery, T-shirts, baseball bats and black coral (illegal to bring in to many countries, so avoid).

In the Palacio del Segundo Cabo, O'Reilly 4 y Tacón, is the **Instituto Cubano del Libro** and 3 **Bookshops** bookshops: *Librería Grijalba Mondadori*, excellent selection of novels, dictionaries, art books, children's books from around the world, all in Spanish; *Librería Bella Habana*, T8628091-3, Cuban and international publications, and *Librería UNESCO Cultura*, which stocks UNESCO publications, books on Cuba, a few thrillers in English and postcards. There are second-hand bookstalls outside on the Plaza de Armas where you can pick up a treasure if you know what to look for. *La Moderna Poesía*, Obispo esq Bernaza, modern design, literature, sciences, art materials, CDs, posters, cards, café, open until 2000. *Fernando Ortíz*, 27 160 esq L, T329653. Quite a wide selection, mostly in Spanish, and some beautiful postcards. *El Siglo de las Luces*, Neptuno esq Aguila, T8635321, near Capitolio. Good place to buy *son*, *trova* and jazz (rock) records. *Instituto Hidrográfico*, Mercaderes entre Oficios y Obispo, T8613625, F332869. Maps and charts, both national and regional, also prepaid phone cards.

Music & There is a good selection of CDs and other music at the *Casa de la Música EGREM* shop, 20
souvenirs 3308 esq 35, T2040447, see Nightclubs, above. *Artex* shop on L esq 23 has excellent music selection and tasteful T-shirts and postcards, T8320632, open Mon-Sat 0900-2100, Sun 1000-1600.

Food For food shopping, there is the *Focsa Supermarket*, or the *Amistad*, on San Lázaro, just below Infanta. The *Isla de Cuba* supermarket on Máximo Gómez entre Factoría y Suárez has the best selection of food in Old Havana. The *Caracol* chain, in tourist hotels (eg *Habana Libre*) and elsewhere, sell tourists' requisites and other luxury items such as chocolates, biscuits, wine, clothes, require payment in US$ (or credit cards: Mastercard, Visa). Bread is available at the French bakery on 42 y 19 and in the Focsa shopping complex on 17 entre M y N.

Markets Farmers are allowed to sell their produce (root and green vegetables, fruit, grains and meat) in free-priced city *agromercados*. You should pay for food in pesos. There are markets in Vedado at 19 y B and a smaller one at 21 esq J; in Nuevo Vedado, Tulipán opposite Hidalgo; in the Cerro district at the Monte and Belascoaín crossroads; and in Centro, the Chinese market at the junction of Zanja and Av Italia where you can eat at street food stalls (avoid Mon, not a good day). The last Sun of every month there is a large and very busy food market held in Paseo, between Calzada de Zapata and the *Teatro Nacional*.

Tobacco Tobacco is excellent, but all the best leaves go into cigar making rather than cigarettes. Buying cigars on the street is not legal, they are often not genuine, and may be confiscated at customs if you cannot produce an official receipt of purchase.

Tour operators There are bureaux in all the major hotels. Tours can be arranged all over Cuba by bus or air, with participants picked up from any hotel in Havana at no extra charge. Prices vary between agencies and you can negotiate a reduction without meals.

Amistur, Paseo 406 entre 17 y 19, T334544, amistur@ceniai.inf.cu, offers specialized visits for groups to factories and schools as well as places of local historical or community interest. *Cuba Deportes*, Calle 29 710 entre 7 y 9, Miramar, T2040945, F241914. Arranges all-inclusive sporting holidays. *Cubamar Viajes*, Paseo 306 entre 13 y 15, Vedado, T662523, cubamar@cubamar.mit.cma.net Some camping resorts, student groups and diving packages. *Cubanacán*, T337952, www.cubanacan.cu, has birdwatching and scuba diving tours, hunting and fishing tours. *Gaviota Tours*, hotels *Kohly* and *El Bosque* in Havana, T2044781, gavitour@gavitur.gav.cma.net and at all the Gaviota hotels. *Havanatur*, Edif Sierra Maestra, Av 1 entre 0 y 2, Miramar, T2047416, F2042074. Also branches in many hotels and separate offices in some towns, recommended for independent travellers who want tailor-made but reasonably priced tours. *Horizontes*, Calle 23 156 entre N y O, Vedado, Havana, T662004, www.horizontes.cu, run hotels which tend to be on the outskirts of towns and the chain provides activities for 'eco' tourists and hunters. Fly-drive tours can be arranged. *Islazul*, Malecón y G, Vedado, T325152, cmazul@Teda.get.cma.net, previously for Cubans only, is now moving into tourism for foreigners, offering more unusual and off-the-beaten track excursions. *Rumbos*, Calle O 108 entre 1 y 3, Miramar, Havana, T2049626, director@rumvia.rumb.cma.net, organize excursions and run bars and cafés. *Sol y Son*, Calle 23 64, La Rampa, Vedado, T333271, F333385. The travel company of *Cubana* airlines with offices in many hotels.

Agencies specializing in **marinas** and **diving**, including packages with accommodation and transfers, are: *Cubamar* (see above); *Ecotur*, Calle 98 y Av 5, Playa, T/F290230; *Gaviota* (see above), Av del Puerto 102, Edif La Marina, La Habana Vieja, T339780, gaviota@nwgaviot.gav.cma.net *Horizontes* (see above); *Marlin*, Calle 184 123, Reparto

Flores, Playa, T336675, F337020; *Marsub*, Calle B 310 esq 15, Vedado, T333055, F333481; *Puertosol*, Edif Focsa, Calle 17 y M, Vedado, T334705, F334703; *Club Náutico Internacional 'Hemingway'*, Av 5 y 248, Playa, T/F2041689.

Transport

Bicycle hire Check the bicycle carefully (take your own lock, pump, even a bicycle spanner and puncture repair kit; petrol stations have often been converted into bicycle stations, providing air and tyre repairs). Cycling is a good way to see Havana, especially the suburbs; some roads in the Embassy area are closed to cyclists. The tunnel underneath the harbour mouth has a bus designed specifically to carry bicycles and their riders. Take care at night as there are few street lights and bikes are not fitted with lamps.

Local
See also page 70

Buses There is a regular service on the *camellos*, long articulated buses on a truck bed, 20 centavos. They cover the main suburbs, M1 to Playa, M2 to the airport, M6 to Alamar, and mostly leave from Parque de la Fraternidad. Ask for the right queue. Other buses cost 40 centavos.

Taxis Taxis are plentiful, see page 71. One of the cheapest companies is *Panataxi*, a call-out service, T555555, *Panataxis* also wait just outside most hotels and at the airport, or ask your hotel to call one. They are yellow Citröen cars, so they are the most comfortable, reliable and still the cheapest dollar service, at under US$15 from the airport to Vedado. *Havanauto*, T2042424, is very competitive, US$0.53 per km. *Habanataxi* is a call-out taxi service, T419600. Others include *Gaviota*, T272727, *Taxi OK*, T2049518-9, 2041446, relatively expensive, *MiCar*, T2042444, and *Fénix*, T639720/639580. The cheapest taxis are the very smallest. Ask for the '*oferta especial*' or '*servicio económico*' and you will be charged less per km. For longer trips some companies charge by the hr and some by the km, eg for an excursion including Cojímar, Santa María del Mar and Regla, Panataxi quoted US$25 while Habanataxi quoted US$35. In Habana Vieja and Vedado, **bicycle or tricycle taxis** are cheap and readily available, a pleasant way to travel. A short journey will cost US$1, Old Havana to Vedado US$3, or pay around US$5 per hr, bargaining is acceptable. There is also the *cocomóvil*, quick and readily available if you can handle being driven around in a bright yellow vehicle shaped like a coconut shell on a 125cc motor bike. They take 2 passengers. The fare is fixed in dollars, but agree the fare before the journey. A typical fare from the *Hotel Nacional* to Old Havana is US$3. Less conspicuous are the *Rentar una fantasía* vehicles, using the same 125cc engine but designed as a pre-1920s motor car. For the real thing, *Gran Car*, T335647, rent classic cars (including Oldsmobiles, Mercury '54, Buicks and Chevvy '55) with driver, maximum 4 passengers, US$15 per hr or US$18 per hr for cars without roofs (go for the Oldsmobile '52).

Beware of private moonlighters (yellow licence plates, often identifiable by their harassment); they could charge you over the odds, generally are not paying any taxes and you have no come-back in the case of mishaps

Buses Terminal de Omnibus Interprovinciales, for *Astro* services, Av Rancho Boyeros (Independencia) by the Plaza de la Revolución, T703397. There are 2 ticket offices, the one painted blue is for foreigners and you pay in dollars. There is also a dollar tourist service, *Víazul*, which leaves from Av 26 entre Av Zoológico y Ulloa, Nuevo Vedado, T8811413, www.viazul.cu. See below under individual towns for details.

Long distance
See also page 70

Ferries There are ferries from Habana Vieja to Casablanca and Regla, which depart from San Pedro opposite Santa Clara. If you are facing the water, the Casablanca ferry docks on the left side of the pier and goes out in a left curve towards that headland, and the Regla ferry docks on the right side and goes out in a right curve.

Trains leave from the Estación Central on Ejido (Av de Bélgica) y Arsenal, Havana, to the larger cities. Get your tickets in advance as destinations vary, the departure time is very approximate. Tickets are easily purchased from *LADIS* (Ferrocuba) office on Arsenal y Aponte, open 0800-2000 daily, T614259, pay in US$, passport needed. There are 3 services to **Santiago de Cuba** and at least 1 train per day. They travel overnight and take 12-20 hrs, or so, with fares from US$30-62 1 way (first class, special and first special). Trains stop at every town along the way and have to give way for a goods train, so there are always delays. Take food

The Estación Central has what is claimed to be the oldest engine in Latin America, 'La Junta', built in Baltimore in 1842

and a torch as the toilets usually have no light. The best are the newly introduced French-built trains, freezing a/c, folding tables, clean toilets and comfortable with good lighting. If the train arrives more than 1 hr late, barring certain conditions, the cost of the ticket will be refunded. There are also daily trains to **Pinar del Río**, 2140 arrives 0310, US$6.50 and **Matanzas**, several from 0940, US$3. A long-distance bus or dollar taxi may well do the same journey in a fraction of the time, eg Havana-Pinar del Río, 2 hrs or less by taxi, 7-8 hrs by train. It is not unusual for the trains to break down, in fact Cubans refer to this as 'normal service'. It will be mended and carry on, but be prepared to spend a serious amount of time travelling. The 'Hershey' electric train with services to **Matanzas** no longer starts from the Casablanca station but from La Coubre, just round the corner from the main station.

Directory **Airlines** Most are in Havana, at the seaward end of Calle 23 (La Rampa), Vedado. *Cubana*, www.cubana.cu, for international sales, 23 64, esq Infanta, T334469/334950, for national sales, Infanta esq Humboldt, T8706714 and phone numbers above. *Aerocaribbean*, 23 esq P, T334543, F335016, or at the airport, T453013, F335017. *Air Europa*, Hotel Habana Libre, T666918-9, open 0900-1330, 1430-1800 Mon-Fri, 0900-1300 Sat. *Air France*, Hotel Habana Libre, T662644, open 0830-1200, 1300-1630 Mon-Fri, 0830-1230 Sat. *Air Jamaica*, Hotel Meliá Cohiba, T8662447, F662449, and at airport, Terminal 3, T330212. *Iberia*, 23 74 esq P, T3350412, F335061, at the airport T335234. *KLM*, 23 64, T333730, F333729. *LTU*, 23 64 esq Infanta, T333549, F332789, at the airport F335359. *Martinair Holland*, 23 esq P, T334364, F333729. *Mexicana de Aviación*, 23 esq P, T3335312, F333077, at the airport F335051.

Banks For dollar services, credit card withdrawals, TCs and exchange, *Banco Financiero Internacional*, Línea esq O, T333003, F333006, open Mon-Fri 0800-1500, last day of the month until 1200, in Old Havana at Teniente Rey esq Oficios, a branch in *Habana Libre* complex, T333429, F333795, same times, and another branch in Miramar, 18 111 entre 1 y 3, T332058, F332458, charges 3% commission for foreign exchange deals and gives credit card cash advances in US dollars. Exchange bureau in *Hotel Nacional*, open 0800-1200, 1230-1930, credit card cash advances. Buró de Turismo in *Tryp Habana Libre* also gives credit card cash advances. *Banco Metropolitano*, Línea 63 y M, T5531168, open Mon-Sat 0830-1500, cheapest (2%) for changing TCs, most hotels and airport cambios charge 4%. A Visa ATM in the lobby of the *Parque Central* issues convertible pesos to a certain limit. Credit card advances from exchange houses, *cadecas*, incur a standard 1.5% handling charge.

Communications **Internet**: access is available at the cybercafé in the Capitolio. Go in the main entrance and it is diagonally opposite to your right. There are 9 terminals, US$3 for 30 mins, US$5 per hr, open 0800-1800 (although 2000 is advertized but the Capitolio is shut by then). You may have to wait up to 45 mins for one to be free. The large hotels of 4 or 5 stars, such as the *Habana Libre, Nacional, Parque Central, Meliá Cohiba*, all have business centres with computers for internet access, as well as telephone, fax and telex facilities, but they charge a lot more, eg US$5 for 30 mins at the *Nacional* and US$7 for 30 mins at the *Parque Central* (business centre on 1st floor, ext 1911, 1833, open 0800-2000). The best value and most convenient facilities are in the bar of the *HotelTelégrafo* on Parque Central, US$2.50 per 30 mins, US$5 per hr. There are often queues, but the bar serves great daiquiris to ease the wait. The *Hotel Plaza*, Parque Central, also has internet facilities in the lobby, at US$6 per hr. The *Hotel Lido*, has one PC, Consulado 26 entre Animas y Trocadero, $6 per hr, but it is frustratingly slow. Prepaid Etecsa cards can be used in the International Press Center on La Rampa, Vedado, where there are also long queues. Several post offices have computers for the Telecorreos prepaid cards, including the post office under the Ministerio de Comunicaciones on Plaza de la Revolución (5 terminals including 1 for chat, US$4.50 per 3 hrs, 0800-1940 daily, 24-hr service planned with more terminals, long queues, sometimes of over an hr, popular with students, snack bar, clean toilets), and the post office at Línea y Paseo (same prices, 24-hr service also proposed here, 8 terminals, good equipment). **Post**: Oficios 102, opposite the Lonja, and in the *Hotel Nacional*, *Hotel Plaza* (5th floor, walk through dining area and turn right on to the terrace, open 0700-1900) and in the *Hotel Habana Libre* building. Also on Ejido, next to central railway station and under the Gran Teatro de La Habana. **Telephones**: *Empresa Telecomunicaciones de Cuba* (Etecsa) is on Av 33 1427 entre 18 y 14, Miramar, T332476, F332504.

Embassies and consulates All in Miramar, unless stated otherwise: **Austria**, 4 101, esq 1, T2042825, F2041235. **Belgium**, Av 5 7406 esq 76, T2042410, F2041318. **Canada**, 30 518, esq 7, T20425167, F2041069. **France**, 14 312 entre 3 y 5, T2042132, F2041439. **Germany**, B 652 esq 13, Vedado, T332569, F331586. **Italy**, Paseo 606 entre 25 y 27, Vedado, T333334, F333416. **Japan**, Av 3 esq 80, Centro de Negocios 5th floor, T2043508, F2048902. **Mexico**, 12 518 entre 5 y 7, T2042498, F2042294. **Netherlands**, 8 307 entre 3 y 5,

T2042511/2, F2042059. **Spain**, Cárcel 51 esq Zulueta, Habana Vieja, T338025, F338006. **Sweden**, 34 510 entre 5 y 7, T2042831, F2041194. **Switzerland**, Av 5, 2005, T2042611, F2041148. **UK**, 34, 702 y 704, T2041771, F2048104, embrit@ceniai.inf.cu Commercial Section, open Mon-Fri 0800-1530. **The US Interests Section** of the Swiss Embassy, Calzada entre L y M, Vedado, T333551, 334401.

Medical services *The Cira García Clinic*, 20 4101 esq 41, Miramar, T2042811/14, F2041633, payment in dollars, also the place to go for emergency dental treatment, the pharmacy (T2045051, open 24 hrs) sells prescription and patent drugs and medical supplies that are often unavailable in other pharmacies, as does the nearby *Farmacia Internacional*, Av 41, esq 20, Miramar (T2045051, open Mon-Fri 0900-1700, Sat 0900-1200).

Beaches around Havana

The beaches in Havana, at Miramar and Playa de Marianao are rocky, polluted and generally very crowded in summer. The beach clubs belong to trade unions and may not let non-members in. Those to the east, El Mégano, Santa María del Mar and Bacuranao, for example, are much better. To the west of Havana are Arena Blanca and Bahía Honda, which are good for diving and fishing but difficult to get to unless you have a car.

Off Avenida 5, 20 minutes by taxi from Havana, is the Marina Hemingway tourist complex, in the fishing village of **Santa Fe**. The Offshore Class 1 World Championship and the Great Island speedboat Grand Prix races have become an annual event in Havana, usually held during the last week in April, attracting power boat enthusiasts from all over the world. In May and June the marina hosts the annual Ernest Hemingway International Marlin Fishing Tournament, and in August and September the Blue Marlin Tournament. There arc 140 slips with electricity and water and space for docking 400 recreational boats. The resort includes the hotel *El Viejo y El Mar* (Cubanacán, 248 y Av 5, Santa Fé, T246336, F246823), restaurants, bungalows and villas for rent, shopping, watersports, facilities for yachts, sports and a tourist bureau.

Marina Hemingway

Watersports *Club Náutico Internacional 'Hemingway'*, *Residencial Turístico 'Marina Hemingway'*, Av 5 y 248 Playa, T/F2041689, 2046653. *Cubanacán Náutica 'Marina Hemingway'*, same address, T2041150-57, F2041149, VHF 16 and 72. Open Mon-Fri 0800-1700, boat trips, sport fishing, US$450 ½ day, motorized sports (waterskiing, banana boat), catamarans, sailing lessons in dinghies, windsurfing, diving and snorkelling. The dive centre, *Centro de Buceo La Aguja*, takes up to 8 divers on the boat.

Playas del Este

This is the all-encompassing name for a string of beaches within easy reach of Havana. East of the city is the pleasant little beach of **Bacuranao**, 15 km from Havana. At the far end of the beach is a villa complex with restaurant and bar. Then come **Tarará**, **El Mégano** and **Santa María del Mar**, with a long, open beach which continues eastwards to the beach at **Boca Ciega** and **Guanabo** (several train departures daily from La Coubre terminal, Estación Central, Havana, and from Matanzas, and buses from Havana), a pleasant, non-touristy beach 27 km from Havana, but packed with Habaneros at weekends. Cars roll in from Havana early on Saturday mornings, line up and deposit their cargo of sun worshippers at the sea's edge. The quietest spot is **Brisas del Mar**, at the east end. As a general rule, facilities for foreigners are at Santa María del Mar and for Cubans at Guanabo. The latter is therefore cheaper and livelier. Tourism bureaux offer day excursions (minimum six people) for about US$15 per person to the Playas del Este, but for two or more people its worth hiring a private car for the day for US$20-25.

Cuba

Cuba

Sleeping
Contact Horizontes for cheap all-inclusives, Islazul has hotels mainly for the Cuban market, cheap and basic

Casas particulares *Sra Eyda Iglesias Mora*, 494 A 5B10 entre 5B y 5C, T962903. **E** *Rosa López Rodríguez*, Quebec 53 entre Río de Janeiro y Montevideo, T963321. Quiet room, a/c, hot water, fridge, clean, private, 5 mins from beach. **E-F** *Hugo Puig Roque*, 5 Av 47203 entre 472 y 474, T963426. Choice of rooms, bathrooms fair, good location, friendly. Prices negotiable, depending on season and length of stay. **F** *Zoraida Ortega Amador*, Calle 470 305 entre 3 y 5, Guanabo, T965753. Warm and helpful family, some English spoken, nice patio area, 50 m from beach, meals available or use kitchen.

Eating
There are many paladares in Guanabo and elsewhere along the coast, reasonable prices

Restaurante Chino, Vía Blanco Km 19, one of the best Chinese restaurants in Cuba. *Cafetería Pinomar*, Santa María del Mar, fried chicken, US$2.50 for a ½, open 24 hrs, attractive. *Pizzería Al Mare*, 482, Guanabo, for pizza. *Café River Ristorante*, behind *Villa Playa Hermosa* entre 472 y 474. All dishes under US$3, beer US$0.85, open 1200-0200, cosy, funky. If you are self-catering, there is an excellent farmers' market in Guanabo selling fresh fruit and vegetables 6 days a week and a supermarket. Hotels in Guanabo have cheap food, with live music.

Watersports
The hotels provide some non-motorized watersports

Marina Tarará, run by Marinas Puertosol, Vía Blanca Km 19, T971462, F971333, VHF16, 19, 08, 72, has moorings for 50 boats, VHF communications and provisioning, yacht charters, deep-sea fishing (US$250-450 per day depending on type of boat) and scuba diving, all of which can be arranged through the hotel tour desks.

Transport
The 400 bus (40 centavos) from Ejido near the Estación Central de Trenes can get you to Bacuranao, Santa María and Guanabo, but getting back to Havana is problematic the longer you stay. The standard private taxi price is US$15 (fix the price before you set off), but getting a return taxi is more difficult. Cycling is a good way to get there. Use the *ciclobus* from Parque El Curita, Aguila y Dragones, to go through the tunnel under Havana Bay, or the 20-centavo ferry to Regla from near the Aduanas building, and cycle through Regla and Guanabacoa.

Directory
Medical services *Clínica Internacional Habana del Este*, Av de las Terrazas, between *Aparthotel Las Terrazas* and *Hotel Tropicoco* in Santa María del Mar.

West from Havana

A dual carriage highway runs to **Pinar del Río**, the major city west of Havana. It takes two hours to get to Pinar del Río on the *autopista*, with virtually no traffic except horse-drawn buses to nearby villages. The autopista passes through flat or gently rolling countryside, with large stretches of sugar cane, tobacco fields and some rice fields, scattered royal palms and distant views of the Cordillera de Guaniguanico. An alternative route is to leave the autopista at **Candelaria** or **Santa Cruz de los Pinos** for the Carretera Central, quite a good road which adds only 20 minutes to the journey. It passes through citrus and other fruit trees. Villages straggle along the road, with colonnaded single-storey traditional houses and newer post-Revolution concrete block structures.

Las Terrazas
Phone code: 8
Colour map 1, grid B2

On the autopista, 51 km west of Havana, the Sierra del Rosario appears on the right and a roadside billboard announces the turning to **Las Terrazas/Moka**, 4 km north of the autopista. However, after that there is little signposting. The **Biosphere Reserve** covers 260 sq km of the eastern Sierra del Rosario. ■ *Admission to the Reserve, US$3, unless you have a reservation at the hotel.* Las Terrazas was built in 1971 as a forestry and soil conservation station. It is a pleasant settlement of houses overlooking the lake of San Juan. In Las Terrazas there is a *paladar*, craft workshops, a gym, a cinema and a museum which sometimes holds *canturías* or folk music sessions. Following the death in a car accident of the popular singer, Polo Montañez in 2002, his house was also opened as a museum, run by his brother. In nearby San Cristóbal, a clay statue of the singer has been put on display. Once a woodcutter, he rose to fame as a singer/songwriter with many hits in the three years before his death, touring Latin America and Europe. The hills behind the hotel rise to the **Loma del Salón** (564 m). There are several easy hiking trails of 3-8 km or more demanding whole-day hikes. The cost of a day hiking with a professional guide is US$33-41 for one person, falling to US$14-18 with six people. Other activities include riding (US$6 per hour), mountain bikes (US$1), rowing (US$2 per hour) and fishing.

Sleeping Above the village is the 26-room **B** *Hotel Moka*, run in co-operation with the Cuban Academy of Sciences as an ecotourism centre, breakfast US$5, other meals US$15, transfer from Havana US$32, a/c, T/F335516. The hotel complex is beautifully designed and laid out, in Spanish colonial style with tiled roofs, gardens behind the hillside site have a tennis court and a pleasant swimming pool. This is an opportunity to stay in a nature reserve with tropical evergreen forests, 850 plant species, 82 bird species, an endemic water lizard and the world's 2nd smallest frog. **F** *Villa Juanita*, La Pastora 601, Cayajabos, Artemisa, 3 km from Las Terrazas. 2 rooms, small kitchenette, meals available, good food, very welcoming, no English but expressive, slow Spanish spoken.

If travelling by car, you can make a detour to Soroa, a spa and resort in the Sierra del Rosario, 81 km southwest of the capital, either by continuing 18 km west then southeast from Moka through the Sierra del Rosario, or directly from the autopista, driving northwest from Candelaria. As you drive into the area from the south, a sign on the right indicates the **Mirador de Venus** and **Baños Romanos**. Past the baths is the *Bar Edén* (open till 1800), where you can park before walking up to the Mirador (25 minutes, free on foot, US$3 on a horse) for fine views of the southern plains, the forest-covered Sierra and Soroa itself. There are lots of birds, butterflies, dragonflies and lizards around the path, and birdwatching is very popular here too.

Soroa
Phone code: 8

Further north is the **Jardín Botánico Orchidarium** with over 700 species of orchids, of which 250 are native to Cuba, as well as ferns and begonias. ■ *Guided tours daily 0830-1140, 1340-1555, US$3, birdwatching, hiking and riding US$3 an hr. Castillo de las Nubes restaurant (1200-1900, US$5-6). Alberto, at the desk, speaks good English and some French. There is an excursion to* **El Brujito**, *a village once owned by French landlords, where the third and fourth generations of slaves live.*

Beware of jineteros and hustlers at gas stations and junctions

Sleeping **C-D** *Horizontes Villa Soroa*, T852122. 49 cabins and 10 self-catering houses, a/c, phone, radio, some have VCR and private pool, restaurant *El Centro* (quite good), lunch US$8, dinner US$10, disco, bar, Olympic-sized swimming pool, bike rental, riding nearby and handicrafts and dollar shop. A peaceful place. The hotel runs 1-day, gently paced hikes around the main sights of the area with picnic for US$10, to caves for US$12. **E** *Casa Azul*, 300 m outside Soroa next to a primary school. One big room with private bath, hot water, balcony overlooking a huge garden, fruit trees, coffee bushes and mountains, free parking, meals available, daughter speaks some English.

Tour operators *Rumbos*, T771402, run by English-speaking Yania, open Mon-Fri 0800-1130, 1400-1700, Sat 0800-1200, aerotaxi and Víazul bookings, phone cards and tours.

Pinar del Río

The capital of Pinar del Río province is lively and attractive, and it gives a good taste of provincial Cuba. The centre consists of single-storey neoclassical houses with columns, some with other interesting architectural detail.

Phone code: 82
Colour map 1, grid B1

There is a **cigar factory**, one of the town's main tourist attractions, which reputedly makes the best cigars in Cuba. ■ *Mon-Sat 0800-1700. US$5 for a short visit. Avoid the youngsters selling cigars outside; buy from the shop opposite,* Casa del Habano, *and you'll get the genuine article, even if it is pricey.* The **rum factory** (Fábrica de Guayabita) on Isabel Rubio makes a special rum flavoured with miniature wild guavas, *Guayabita del Pinar*, which comes in either dry or sweet varieties. Between the two is the cathedral of **San Rosendo**. The **Museo Provincial de**

Cuba

Historia details the history of the town and displays objects from the wars of independence. ■ *Mon-Sat 0800-1700. US$0.25. Martí 58.* The **Casa de la Cultura Tito Junco**, on Martí esquina Rafael Morales, is in a huge, recently renovated colonial house and includes an art gallery, a hall for parties and seven classrooms for teaching dancing, painting, singing, etc. ■ *Mon-Sat 0800-1800. Evening activities according to scheduled programmes.* Another renovated building on Martí opposite the Wedding Palace, is the **Palacio de Computación**, inaugurated by Fidel Castro in January 2001. ■ *Mon-Sat 0800-2100. Theatre, cafeteria and classrooms.*

Sleeping

A mafia of youths offer their assistance in taking you to the casa. They are after a commission and sometimes say that they are from Formatur, the tourism school

As you leave the autopista on the north side of José Martí, but within walking distance of the city centre, is the **C** *Hotel Pinar del Río*, José Martí final, T50707. Staff are friendly and helpful, swimming pool, nightclub, car hire, in need of updating, beds too soft, sheets too short, hot water evenings only, poor lighting, no bedside light, poor TV reception, poor breakfast. **Casas particulares F** *Bertha Báez*, Pedro Téllez 53 entre Ormani Arenado e Isidro de Armas, T4247. 1 room, hot and cold shower, a/c, fans, garage US$1. **F** *Hospedaje Torres*, Adela Azcuy 7 entre Gerardo Medina y Isabel Rubio, no phone. Run by nice young lady, room with fan or a/c, clean and safe. **F** *José Antonio Mesa*, Gerardo Medina 67 entre Adela Azcuy y Isidro de Armas, T3173. Attractive colonial building, 8 rooms, spacious, nice family but involved in paying commissions so unpopular with other renters. **F** *Noelia Pérez Blanco*, Gerardo Medina 175 entre Ceferino Fernández y Frank País, T3660. Run by elderly lady, most of the house is used by tourists although there is only 1 bedroom, 2 beds, fan or a/c, TV, hot water, garage US$2, roof with table and chairs, a little English spoken. **F** *Salvador Reyes y Ana María*, Alameda 24 entre Volcán y Avellaneda, opposite phone company, T773146. 1 room, a/c, fan, hot shower, nice terrace, English and German spoken, nice family and atmosphere. **F** *Traveller's Rest*, Primero de Mayo 29 entre Isidro de Armas y Antonio Rubio, Apto 16, sign outside, T5681 (neighbour, please phone 1200-1400, 1800-2100), http://geocities.com/travellers_rest_pinar/ Hot shower, a/c or fan, 2 small rooms, bicycle rental, excursions, salsa lessons, garage US$1 a day. Run by Juan Carlos Otaño, also known as 'The Teacher', he speaks English, French, some Italian and German, very friendly and helpful. **F** *Villa Lolo*, Martí 57 entre Isabel Rubio y Colón, sign outside. 1 room sleeps up to 4, private, a/c, fan, hot and cold shower, little English spoken, watch out for hustlers seeking commission. **F** *Zunilda Rodríguez Hernández*, Acueducto 16 entre Méndez Capote y Primera Rpto Celso Maragota, T4639. 2 a/c rooms, private bath, hot water, garage, her husband Julio fought with Che and Fidel, interesting.

Eating

The state-run *Rumayor*, 2 km on Viñales road. Specializes in *pollo ahumado* (smoked chicken), US$6.50, neat toilets, open 1200-2200, closed Thu, cabaret at night, see below. *La Casona*, Martí esq Colón. Charges in dollars, service slow but food good, a trio plays *boleros*, bar at the back, many *jineteros*. *El Mesón*, Martí, opposite the Museo de Ciencias Naturales. A *paladar* run by Rafael, a former teacher, nice place, lunch or dinner US$6-7, open Mon-Sat 1100-2400. *Mar Init*, José Martí, opposite Parque de la Independencia, T4952. Open Tue-Sun 1930-2130, pay in pesos, fish is the speciality of the house. *Vueltabajo*, Martí y Rafael Morales. Open 0930-2000, food available, also bar selling rum, beer, soft drinks. *Coppelia*, Gerardo Medina. Open daily 0800-2330, ice cream can be bought in pesos, very cheap. *Terrazina*, Antonio Rubio y Primero de Mayo. Open 1130-1500, 1800-2200, pay in pesos, pizza, spaghetti, beer, you can eat for less than US$1. *Pinar Café*, Gerardo Medina, opposite *Coppelia*. Open daily 1800-0200, expensive restaurant, US$5 for soft drink, beers, bottle of rum and potato chips, also a show at 2130, Afro-Cuban show Tue. Beware of theft here. *La Taberna*, Coro 103 opposite La Paquita amusement park for children. Open daily from 1800, pesos only, very cheap, dinner around 50-60 pesos, beer 8-10 pesos, bar and patio. The best peso pizzas are on Gerardo Medina opposite *Doña Neli* bakery, 6-10 pesos, Mon-Sat 0900-1700.

Entertainment

Music The town is very lively on Sat nights, and to a lesser extent on Fri. There is live music everywhere, salsa, son, Mexican music, international stuff. During the day in Parque Roberto Amarán you can hear traditional music (Mambo, Rumba, Cha-cha-cha, Danzón) Wed and Sat 1400-1520, Sun 0900. *Disco Rita*, on González Coro, is an open-air venue popular with teenagers, where they play loud, US-style disco music, entry 2 pesos, the only drink on sale is neat rum at 25 pesos a bottle. *Bar La Esquinita*, on Isabel Rubio, 2000-0200, has live music, usually guitarist. *Rumayor*, see Eating above, identification required for this top tourist attraction. Cabaret show at 2230-2400, followed by recorded music, US$5. The classy night life, however, is the disco in the *Hotel Pinar del Río*, US$1, 2000-0400, Thu-Sun, very popular, full every night, young crowd. The *Casa de la Cultura* has a band playing every Sun evening with a dance contest for the elderly, fantastic, free, photos allowed. *La Picaula*, at the back of the Teatro Milanés, Sat, Sun 2100 for the best bands and a fashion show, 10 pesos. **Nightclubs** *Artex*, Martí 36, opposite *Photo service*, open daily 0900-0200. *The Wedding Palace*, Martí 125, bar open Tue-Fri 0800-2400, Sat-Sun 1000-0200, beer, rum, snacks, TV, a/c, a lovely place.

Cubatur, Martí 51, esq Ormani Arenado, T78405, 0800-1700, tour guide Dora Pendas. **Tour** *Rumbos*, Martí, next to *La Casona*, Mon-Fri 0800-1700, Sat 0800-1200, T771802, **operators** arumcupr@ip.etecsa.cu Excursions to beaches, tobacco plantations, etc, maps and phone cards for sale, car rental.

Local Car hire: *Havanautos* and *Transautos* both have offices in *Hotel Pinar del Río*. **Transport**

Long distance Air: The airport is on the road to La Coloma, 8 km from town, T5545. To Isla *Distances from Pinar* de la Juventud,Tue and Thu 1240, US$22 1-way, rather like a flying bus, DC3 taking 20 *del Río are 157 km* Cubans and 10 foreigners. Reservations at *Rumbos* on Calle Martí or call Cristino, T5545. **Bus**: *to Havana, 159 km* The bus station is on Colón, north of José Martí, near Gómez. *Víazul*, T2571, 5255, daily from *to María La Gorda,* Havana to Viñales at 0900. It stops on request at Las Terrazas (US$6) and San Diego de los *103 km to Las* Banos (US$8), and gets to Pinar del Río (US$11) at around 1120 with no stops. The return bus *Terrazas, 88 km* leaves Viñales at 1330, stopping in Pinar del Río around 1400 and getting to Havana at 1645. *to Soroa, 25 km* There is also a daily *Astro* bus at around 1700, which is cheaper at US$7 but unreliable. Pinar *to Viñales* del Río to Viñales in a state taxi is US$10, although locals can hire a taxi for the same distance for about US$5. To Viñales by bus 1 peso on route for Bahía Honda, La Palma or Puerto Esperanza, but your name has to be on the list. **Train**: The railway station in Pinar del Río is on Av Comandante Pinares, T2106. From **Havana** at 2140, arriving at 0310. Take a torch, hang on to your luggage, don't sleep, noisy, train stops about 29 times, very slow. Trains to Havana leave at 0900 on alternate days, and cost US$7.

Banks *Banco Financiero Internacional* (BFI), Gerardo Medina, opposite *Coppelia*, T78183, F78213. Open **Directory** Mon-Fri 0800-1500. *Cadeca*, *Gerardo Medina, next to Coppelia*. Open 0830-1800. Also on Martí 50 next to Artex bar. *Banco Popular de Ahorro*, Martí 113. Mon-Fri 0800-1700, cash on credit cards. **Communications Internet**: US$15 for 5 hrs with *tarjeta* Telecorreos in *Hotel Pinar del Río*. **Post office**: Martí esq Isabel Rubio, Mon-Sat 0800-1700. Email 0800-2000, US$1 to receive and US$1.20 to send overseas (appr@esipr.cu). Fax service abroad US$8 per page. At Telecorreos in *Hotel Pinar del Río* US$10.20 a page. **Telephone**: *Etecsa* is at Av Alameda IIA, T4585-7, Parque de la Independencia. A 24-hr phone centre is at Gerardo Medina esq Juan Gualberto Gómez, domestic and calls abroad, phone cards for sale.

Península de Guanahacabibes

The Península de Guanahacabibes, which forms the western tip of Cuba, is a Natural *Phone code: 8* Biosphere Reserve. It is made up of very recent limestone, with a rocky surface and *Colour map 1, grid B1* patchy soil cover. There are fossil coastlines, caves and blue holes; but with dense woodland on the south coast and mangrove on the north, the peninsula is uninviting for the casual hiker. There are 12 amphibian species, 29 reptiles including iguana species, 10 mammals (including *carabalí* and *jutia conga*) and 147 bird species, including nine of the 22 which are endemic to Cuba. Permits are required for entering the 1,175-sq-km reserve. There is a scientific station at La Bajada. The Science Academy, T3277, offers a Safari Tour with an English-speaking guide, Osmani Borrego, for US$6 per person. You can climb to the Radar for US$1 for a good view of the forest and the sea.

F *Science Academy Lodge*, La Bajada, 100 m from the sea, T3277. 4 rooms with a/c and bath- **Sleeping** room, food is difficult to get and awful but worth it for the location. Call in advance.

María La Gorda In the middle of nowhere, and reputedly the best diving centre in Cuba, María La Gorda is an idyllic spot for relaxing or doing nothing but **diving**. *Cubamar* and *Puertosol* organize a package including accommodation, food, diving (US$100 per person a day, minimum 2 people) and transfers from Havana (US$70 each way, 4-5 hrs). The sea is very clear, very warm and calm, even when it is too rough to dive anywhere else in Cuba. There is good snorkelling too with small coral heads close to the white-sand beach, or you can go out on the dive boat.

Sleeping C-D *María La Gorda*, T/F5382. Jul-Aug are most expensive, Nov-Easter high season, 3 meals US$31 per person, nowhere else to eat. Lovely location, rooms open onto the beach, hammocks between palm trees, excellent value, nicely decorated, simple but comfortable, a/c, hot water, minibar, TV. 20 new cabañas have been built inland in the forest, but these attract mosquitoes. Good service, friendly staff, buffet meals, bar, shop, *Telecorreos*, dive shop on site with doctor specializing in hyperbaric medicine, US$30 per dive if not on a package.

Transport *Víazul* runs a minibus from Pinar del Río to María la Gorda, timed to leave after the bus from Havana has arrived in Pinar del Río, returning 1500, US$9. Or visitors come on package tours with US$70 transfers from Havana or rented car. For visitors arriving by yacht, María La Gorda is a port of entry. There are 4 moorings, maximum draft 2 m, VHF channels 16, 19, 68 and 72.

Viñales

Phone code: 8
Colour map 1, grid B1

North of Pinar del Río, the road leads across pine-covered hills and valley for 25 km to Viñales, a delightful, small town in a dramatic valley in the **Sierra de los Organos**. The valley has a distinctive landscape, with steep-sided limestone mountains called *mogotes* rising dramatically from fertile flat-floored valleys, where farmers cultivate the red soil for tobacco, fruits and vegetables. An area of 132 sq km around Viñales has been declared a National Monument. There is a visitors' centre near *Hotel Los Jazmines*. Viñales itself is a pleasant town, with trees and wooden colonnades along the main street, red-tiled roofs, a main square with a little-used church and a **Casa de Cultura** with an art gallery. The **Mural de la Prehistoria**, 2 km west, was painted between 1959 and 1976 by **Lovigildo González**, a disciple of the Mexican Diego Rivera. It is generally disliked as a monstrous piece of graffiti. You can see the paintings from *Restaurant Jurásico* (bar open 0800-1630), 100 m before the mural, and there is a swimming pool nearby. The **Cueva del Indio**, 6 km north of Viñales, is a cave which you enter on foot, then take a boat (US$3 for foreigners) with a guide who gives you a description, very beautiful. There is a restaurant nearby where tour parties are given a lunch of *lechón* (suckling pig).

As in so much of rural Cuba, horses, pigs, oxen, zebu cattle and chickens are everywhere, including on the main road

Sleeping C *Los Jazmines* (Horizontes), Carretera de Vinales Km 23.5, 3 km before the town, in a superb location with travel brochure view of the valley, T936205, F936215, book through *Horizontes* in Havana, T334042, F333722. 62 nice rooms and 16 *cabañas*, nightclub, breakfast buffet US$5 if not already included, lunch US$10, dinner US$12, restaurant, bar with snacks available, shops, swimming pool (US$5 including towels for day visitors and US$5 in vouchers for bar drinks), riding, transport. C *Horizontes La Ermita*, Carretera de la Ermita Km 2, 3 km from town with magnificent view, T893204. 62 rooms, a/c, phone, radio, shop, tennis court, wheelchair access, pool (not always in use), nicer public areas and food better than at *Los Jazmines*, CP, lunch US$10, dinner US$12. D *Horizontes Rancho San Vicente*, Valle de San Vicente, near Cueva del Indio, T893200. 40 a/c *cabañas*, bar, restaurant, CP , lunch US$8, dinner US$10, nightclub, shop, tourist information desk, pool, open to day visitors, spa with sulphurous waters, mud baths, full-body massage.

Casas particulares F *Doña Inesita*, Salvador Cisneros 40, T93297. Inés Núñez Rodríguez and her husband, both in their 80s, offer an upstairs apartment with own entrance, 2 bedrooms each sleep 3, sitting room, aged bathroom, cold water, balcony, terrace, a/c, but cheaper without, substantial breakfast US$5, vast dinner US$8, fruit, eggs and meat from their own garden,

There are a huge number of registered casas particulares and people meet you off the buses

even coffee is home-grown and roasted, the energetic couple are friendly and welcoming. **F** *Elisa Jaime*, Rafael Trejo 37, T93602. Private bathroom, hot water, patio in back yard where Elisa serves beautiful meals. **F** *Estevan Orama Ovalle*, Orlando Nodarse 13, T93305. Very knowledgeable and friendly hosts, big room, clean and safe, excellent breakfast and dinner, good *mojitos*. **F** *Garden House*, Salvador Cisnero 44, T93297. 1 room, terrace overlooking big garden, garage US$1, meals available. **F** *Manuela Martínez Rodríguez*, Villa El Coral, Joaquín Pérez 25, T93217. Warm, friendly family, daughter Danay speaks English, husband Amable makes a mean *mojito*. Private bath, fantastic food and large portions, US$3-10. **F** *Marcelino y Yamile Arteaga González*, Salvador Cisneros 6, near the *Cupet* station, road to the cemetery, no phone. Welcoming and kind, great breakfast US$3 and tasty dinner US$6. **F** *Silvia Guzmán Collado (Berito)*, Camilo Cienfuegos 60A, T93245, 936205. 1 room, sleeps up to 6, fans, private, hot shower, garden, English spoken, meals available, try 'Berito's chicken', drinks (beer, *mojito*). **F** *Villa Azul*, km 25 Carretera Pinar del Río, T93288 (neighbour). Large room for up to 5 people, private bath, parking, fruit and coffee from own garden overlooked by terrace. **F** *Villa Blanca*, Salvador Cisneros, Edif Colonial 2 Apto 12, T93319. Friendly hostess, excellent cook and she makes a terrific *mojito*, 2 bedrooms, fans, shared bathroom, balcony, breakfast and dinner. **F** *Villa Chicha*, Camilo Cienfuegos 22. Charming single-storey house with rocking chairs outside, 1 adequate room, a/c, private bathroom, good-value accommodation and meals, entertaining family. **F** *Villa José*, Salvador Cisnero 23, T936026. Dr José López Camargo and his wife, Danalys, are both doctors and work in the hospital opposite. The house has a large garden full of interesting plants, José is very knowledgeable about the area and has a beautiful collection of snails. **F** *Villa Mirtha*, Rafael Trejo 129. Run by Martha Fernández Hernández, double room with 2 double beds, bathroom, hot water, breakfast included, dinner US$6 for fish, beans, rice and salad, son David speaks French. **F** *Villa Nenita*, behind the polyclinic, T93367/93319 (neighbours) emiliadiaz2000@yahoo.es 2 rooms, 1 sleeps 6 (US$20, a bargain), spacious, fan, a/c, quiet, the other room sleeps 4, free garage, meals and drinks available, Emilia (Nenita) Diaz is very welcoming. **F** *Villa Neyda*, Camilo Cienfuegos 41. Comfortable rooms, wonderful hospitality, good food, Neyda's sister, at Camilo Cienfuegos 42, also rents rooms, same quality. **F** *Villa Yolanda Tamargo*, Salvador Cisneros 186, T93208. 1 room sleeps up to 5, hot and cold shower, fan, colonial architecture, parking US$1, terrace overlooking garden with fruits and orchids, nice place, meals available. **F** *Yolanda y Pedro Somonte Pino*, Interior 7A (behind the *Secundaria*), no phone. Nice family, quiet, relaxing, little garden, 1 room with 2 beds, fan, bathroom, hot water, simple but clean, good breakfast with fruit from the garden, dinner available.

Eating

Las Brisas, formerly *Valle Bar*, T93183, on the main street. Small, friendly, recommended, *pollo frito* US$4, spaghetti US$2.50, steak, or just have a beer, US$1, and listen to the live music in the evening, talk to Osmany Paez Arteaga who plays percussion in the band, helpful advice on local attitudes and information. Also licensed is **Casa Cocero**, which takes pesos. **Casa de Don Tomás** is the oldest house in Viñales (1879), state-owned, features in *Horizontes* brochure. Unexciting paella, OK for US$8 but cocktails a bargain at US$0.90. **Casa Dago**, popular restaurant/bar with good jazz salsa band, run by extraordinary character with impressive 1927 Ford Chevrolet, food indifferent, but once the music gets going and the rum starts flowing you could be dancing all night. There is a bakery close to the farmers' market.

Entertainment

Music *Palenque de los Cimarrones*, 4 km north of Viñales at Km 32 Carretera a Puerto Esperanza. *Rumbos*-run, show Mon-Sat 2230-2400, US$5 for foreigners. Disco at **Los Jazmines**, 2000-0300, US$5. **Artex**, Salvador Cisneros, bar open 24 hrs, shop 1000-2200, live music.

Tour operators

Agency on Salvador Cisnero 63C, next to the bus terminal, 0800-1700, also does motocross rental, US$30 per day, phone cards, lodgings, car rental. **Cubanacán**, T936262, vinales@cimex.com.cu Safari to Cayo Levisa, departs Mon, Wed, Fri, Sun 0800 from *Los Jazmines*, picking up at *La Ermita*, Viñales bus terminal and *Rancho San Vicente*, returning 1700, minimum 3 passengers, US$28-58, depending on what you want to do, eg a boat trip is offered.

Transport

Bus Bus terminal at Salvador Cisneros 63A. *Viazul* daily from Havana via Pinar del Río at 0900, US$12, arrives 1215, returns 1330, arrives in Havana at 1645 depending on the number of stops.

Cuba

Astro from Havana 0900 via Pinar del Río, returns 1430, arrives in Havana 1820, US$8, cheaper but less comfortable and unreliable. Local buses from Pinar del Río to Puerto Esperanza, La Palma and Bahía Honda all pass through Viñales. **Car hire** *Transtur*, Ceferino Fernández 6 entre Salvador Cisneros y Final, T936060, cars from US$45 a day, fuel extra. Transtur also rents **bicycles**, US$2 per hr, US$0.75/hr for more than 5 hrs or US$10 per day, gears sometimes work, and **scooters**, US$23 per day plus fuel. Moped hire from *Casa de Don Tomás* US$20 per day. **Taxi** *Transtur* has a taxi service, US$0.40 per km, with waiting time of US$4 per hr. Viñales to Cayo Jutías US$40, Palma Rubia for Cayo Levisa US$22, Cuevas de Santo Tomás US$8.

Directory **Banks** *Bandec* does not do card transactions, but next door is *Banco Popular de Ahorro*, which does, Mon-Fri 0800-1200, 1330-1630. *Cadeca*, Salvador Cisnero 92, open Mon-Sat 0800-1800.

North coast The coast north of Viñales is worth a visit if you have transport. The best and closest beach, 50 km, is at **Cayo Jutías**, near Santa Lucía. A Km 6.7 the cay is reached by a causeway. ■ *US$5 entrance.* Rumbos *bar/restaurant.* Further east is **Cayo Levisa**, with a long, sandy beach and reef running parallel to the shore, with good snorkelling and scuba diving. Cayo Levisa is 15 minutes by boat from Palma Rubia. The jetty is on the south side and you follow a boardwalk through the mangroves to get to the hotel on the north side. Take insect repellent. Day trips or longer stays (20 cabins on the beach) are organized by *Horizontes*; you can even visit by helicopter.

East of Havana

The main road along the coast towards Matanzas and Varadero is called the **Vía Blanca**. There are some scenic parts, but you also drive through quite a lot of industry. The **Hershey Railway** runs inland from Havana, more or less parallel to the Vía Blanca, and is an interesting way to get to Matanzas. This electric line was built by the Hershey chocolate family in 1917 to service their sugar mill, at what is now the Central Camilo Cienfuegos. Some 60 km east of Havana is **Jibacoa** beach, which is good for snorkelling as the reefs are close to the beach and it is also a nice area for walking. It is pretty, with hills coming down to the sea. *Víazul* bus Havana-Varadero will drop you off at the beach, US$7 (ask for the Playa, not the hotels).

Matanzas

Phone code: 52
Colour map 1, grid A2
Population: 115,000

Matanzas is a sleepy town with old colonial buildings and a busy, ugly industrial zone. Both the rivers Yumurí and San Juan flow through the city. Most of the old buildings are between the two rivers, with another colonial district, Versalles, to the east of the Río Yumurí. This area was colonized in the 19th century by French refugees from Haiti after the Revolution there. The newer district, Pueblo Nuevo, also has many colonial houses. The industrial zone runs along the north shore of the bay, with railways running inland and around the bay.

Although you will now find numbers written on the streets, locals still refer to names. Streets running north-south in the old town have even numbers, while streets running east-west have odd numbers

The town dates from 1693, but became prosperous with the advent of sugar mills in the 1820s, followed by the railway in 1843. Most of the buildings date from this time and by the 1860s it was the second largest town in Cuba after Havana. The **Galería de Arte Provincial** is on the Plaza de la Vigía. ■ *Mon 0900-1700, Tue-Sat 0900-1800. US$2.* Next door is **Ediciones Vigía**, where you can see books being produced. These are all handmade and in first editions of only 200 copies, so they are collectors' items. Also on Plaza de la Vigía is **Teatro Sauto**, a magnificent neoclassical building dating from 1862-63 and seating 775 people in three-tiered balconies. The floor can be raised to convert the auditorium into a ballroom. ■ *Tue-Sun. US$2. Tickets for Cubans are 15 pesos but foreigners pay US$4 for a performance.*

Museums The **Museo Farmacéutico**, which contains the original equipment, porcelain jars, recipes and furnishings of the *Botica La Francesa*, opened in 1882 by the Triolet family, is worth visiting. It was a working pharmacy until 1964, when it was converted into a fascinating museum, believed to be unique in Latin America. ■ *Mon-Sat 1000-1700, Sun 0800-1200. US$2. Milanés 4951 entre Santa Teresa y Ayuntamiento, on the south side of Parque Libertad, T23197.* The **Museo Provincial** is a large museum in the former **Palacio del Junco**, built by a wealthy plantation owner and dating from 1840. The historical exhibits include an archaeological display and the development of sugar and slavery in the province. ■ *Mon-Sat 1000-1700, Sun 0800-1200. US$1. Milanés entre Magdalena y Ayllón, T23195.*

Sleeping

D-E *Canimao*, km 4 Carretera Matanzas a Varadero, T668021. 120 rooms on hill above Río Canímar, pool (empty) with loud music all night, nightclub, good restaurant, excursions on the river or to caves. **D-E** *El Valle*, T53300/53118, 7 km northwest of Matanzas, in woodland in the Valle del Yumurí. Built 1985, 42 rooms, some with shared bath, pool, bowling alley, riding, good walking. **D-E** *Louvre*, 19th-century building on south side of Parque Libertad, T4074. Variety of rooms and prices, opt for the a/c room with bathroom and balcony overlooking the square, beautiful mahogany furniture, rather than the small, dark, cupboard room in the bowels of the hotel, water shortages, no toilet paper, friendly, lush garden in patio.

Eating

La Ruina. Very attractive *Rumbos* restaurant converted from sugar warehouse, open 24 hrs, dinner US$2.50-10, delicious pastries, great ice cream, pesos and dollars accepted, live music at weekends. *Pekin*, 83 entre 292 y 294. Daily 1200-1400, 1800-2100, foreigners pay in dollars. *Año 30*, 272 entre 75 y 77. Mon-Sat 1200-1400. *Café Atenas*, 83 y 272 on Plaza La Vigía. Open 24 hrs, snack food, modern design, strong lighting. *Paladar El Reloj*, 135 y 298. Collection of old clocks, big *criollo* meal US$5. Cheap food at *Mercado Central*, complete meal for less than US$2, pay in pesos, eg *Parillada Las Mariposas*, C 300 entre 95 y 97. Outdoor tables. Around the corner, *Shanghai*, standard cheap Chinese. These and others serve whatever the market is selling, seasonal fruit and vegetables.

Nightlife

The Plaza Vigía is the place to go in the evenings; locals congregate here to chat, play dominoes or draughts, or make music. The *Casa de la Trova* here, near the bridge, was where the *Muñequitas de Matanzas*, a famous rumba band, was formed. The *Sala de Conciertos José White de Matanzas*, on 79 entre 288 y 290, was formerly the *Lyceum Club* and is famous for being the place where the *danzón* was danced for the first time in 1879; music is performed here and all events are free. *Teatro Sauto* usually has live performances at the weekends.

Transport

Bus The long-distance bus station is at 131 y 272, Calzada Esteban esq Terry, while the interprovincial terminal is at 298 y 127, both in Pueblo Nuevo. *Víazul*, T916445, passes through on its Havana-Varadero route, leaves Havana 0800, 0830, 1600, 2 hrs, US$7, departs for Varadero (and airport) 1010, 1035, 1810, 50 mins, US$6. Returns from Varadero 0800, 1600, 1800. *Astro* from Havana at 0910 arrives around midday, US$4. **Train** The 3-4-hr journey via the Hershey Railway, the only electric train in Cuba, is memorable and scenic if you are not in a hurry. Those who wish to make it a day trip from Havana can do so, long queues for return tickets, best to get one as soon as you arrive. 5 trains daily, from La Coubre terminal, Havana Central Station to a station north of the Río Yumurí in Versalles. The station south of the town at 181, Miret receives regular and *especial* trains from Havana to Santiago.

Directory

Banks *Banco Financiero Internacional*, 85 y 298, for exchange facilities and cash advances on credit cards. *Banco Nacional* at 83 (Milanés) y 282. **Communications** Post office: 85 y 290. **Telephone:** office on 83 y 288, open 0630-2200 every day. **Medical services** Facilities for foreigners are available in Varadero, but there is a pharmacy here, open 24 hrs, at 85 y 280.

Varadero

Cuba's chief beach resort, Varadero, is built on the Península de Hicacos, a 20-km sandspit, the length of which run two roads lined with dozens of large hotels. Development of the peninsula began in 1923 but the village area was not built until the 1950s. The

Phone code: 5
Colour map 1, grid A2

Du Pont family bought land, sold it for profit, then bought more, constructed roads and built a large house, now the *Xanadú* clubhouse for the new golf course. Varadero is still undergoing large-scale development with the aim of expanding capacity to 30,000 rooms. Despite the building in progress it is not over-exploited and is a good place for a family beach holiday. The beaches are quite empty, if a bit exposed, and you can walk for miles along the sand, totally isolated from the rest of Cuba.

Museo Municipal, with some indigenous artefacts and history of Varadero. The house itself is interesting as an example of one of the first beach houses. Originally known as Casa Villa Abreu, it was built in 1921 and restored in 1980-81, with a lovely timber veranda and wooden balconies all round, designed to catch the breeze. ■ *Tue-Sat 0900-1800, Sun 0900-1200. US$1. 57 y Av de la Playa.* There is a small artesanía market outside. Towards the end of the peninsula, halfway between Marina Chapelín and Marina Gaviota, is a cave, **Cueva de Ambrosio**, where dozens of indigenous drawings were discovered in 1961. ■ *Tue-Sun 1000-1200, 1400-1600. US$2, but may be unattended unless a tour party is booked in to visit.* At the far end of the peninsula the land has been designated the **Parque Natural de Varadero**. It is an area of scrub and cactus, with a lagoon where salt was once made, and several kilometres of sandy beach.

Beaches &
watersports
You can indulge in almost any form of watersports, including windsurfing, parasailing, waterskiing, jet skiing and non-motorized pedalos and water bikes

Varadero's sandy beach stretches the length of the peninsula, broken only occasionally by rocky outcrops which can be traversed by walking through a hotel's grounds. Some parts are wider than others and as a general rule the older hotels have the best bits of beach. However, the sand is all beautifully looked after and cleaned daily. The water is clean and nice for swimming, but for good **snorkelling** take one of the many boat trips out to the cays. There are three **marinas** (see below), all full-service with sailing tours, restaurants, fishing and diving. All their services can be booked through the tour desks in hotels. **deep-sea fishing** costs around US$250 for four people for half a day, but prices vary according to what exactly is on offer.

Dive shops

Barracuda (Cubanacán), Av 1 entre 58 y 59, T667072; *Marina Gaviota* (Gaviota Group), T667755; and *Dársena de Varadero* (Puertosol), T668063. Average diving prices are US$35 for a single dive, US$70 for 2 tanks. A 5-day ACUC certification course costs US$365.

Excursions
All hotels, restaurants and excursions must be paid for in US dollars. Don't bother to buy pesos for your stay here. Book excursions at any hotel with a tour agency office

Cárdenas is usually visited as a day trip from Varadero. It was founded in 1828 and attractive, in the traditional 19th-century Spanish colonial style of houses with tall windows, intricate lattices, high ceilings inside, ceramic-tiled floors and interior gardens. Cárdenas was a wealthy sugar town in the 19th century. The Cuban flag was first raised here in 1850 by the revolutionary **General Narciso López**, a Venezuelan who tried unsuccessfully to invade Cuba by landing at Cárdenas with an army of 600 men (only six of whom were Cuban). **Plaza Molokoff** has a decaying 19th-century iron market building, on Avenida 3 oeste y 12. It was built in the shape of a cross and

Varadero

	Sleeping	4 Kawama	7 Varazul
	1 Acuazul	5 Pullman	8 Villa La Caleta
	2 Dos Mares	6 Varadero	9 Villa La Mar
	3 Herradura	Internacional	10 Villa Sotavento

the two-storey building is surmounted by a 15-m dome made in the USA. *Víazul* will drop you in Cárdenas on request on their Trinidad-Varadero route, US$6 from Varadero, US$10 from Santa Clara, US$18 from Trinidad. Alternatively, *Astro* from Havana 0845, US$6, returns to Havana 1340 via Varadero and Matanzas.

There are **sailing tours** to the offshore cays around US$70 including lunch and open bar, several stops for snorkelling or beaches.   **Cayo Mono** lies five nautical miles north northeast of Punta de Morlas. During the nesting season in mid-year it becomes a seagull sanctuary for the 'Gaviota Negra' (*Anous stolidus*) and the 'Gaviota Monja' (*Sterna fuscata* and *Annaethetus*), during which time you can watch them through binoculars. Other cays visited by tour boats include Cayo Blanco, Cayo Romero and Cayo Diana.

Varasub I, a Japanese semi-submersible carrying 48 passengers, has six daily departures, adults US$25, children US$20. Reservations can be made with Havanatur representatives or the Varasub offices: Avenida Playa 3606, entre 36 y 37, T667279, and others. The *Mundo Mágico* submarine goes down to a depth of 35 m with 46 passengers for 55 minutes. It leaves from the Dársena Marina, T668060-5. You can also see underwater by taking a trip on the glass-bottomed boat, *Martín*, which does a 3-hour tour over the reef, open bar and snorkelling equipment.

Cuba

Marinas

Marina Chapelin is at Carretera Las Morlas, km 12.5, T667550/565, VHF 16 and 72. Moorings for 20 boats, maximum draft 30 m, boat rental, laundry, fishing. *Marina Dársena de Varadero*, is at Carretera de Vía Blanca km 31, T63730, 63133, 62363, VHF 16, 19, 68, 72. Moorings for 70 boats, maximum draft 5 m, boat rental, showers, laundry, restaurants, bars, fishing, shops, day charters, diving, liveaboard for 20 people. *Marina Gaviota Varadero*, Península de Hicacos km 21, T667550/565, VHF 16. 10 moorings, 3 m draft, showers, laundry, restaurant, bar, seafaris, yacht rental, fishing, dolphinarium, diving.

Sleeping

The building and renovation of hotels is continuing all along the Varadero peninsula, with *Beaches, Gran* and *Paradisus Varadero* encroaching on the edge of the nature reserve at the extreme end. A bunch of hotels is springing up from around Calle 64 up to the golf course, where there is a cluster of Sol Meliá Hotels. Unless you want an all-inclusive beach holiday in an international hotel (*Sandals, Superclubs, Club Med* and others are all here), it is best to stay in the mid-town area, where restaurants, bars and shops are within walking distance, hotels are smaller and more intimate and the beach is just as good.

Many hotels offer all-inclusive rates, these can be disappointing with lack of variety in food and drinks. Private accommodation is not legal in Varadero but it exists

AL-A *Varadero Internacional* (Gran Caribe), Av Las Américas, T667038/9, F667246. Formerly the *Hilton*, renovated 1999 2000 when many of its period features were obliterated and instead of the garish pink it is now painted in tasteful shades of cream. With tennis, pool, sauna, massage, watersports, restaurant, cabaret, Cuban art gallery, and best bit of beach on whole peninsula.

A-C *Kawama* (Gran Caribe), Carretera de Kawama y O, T614416-9. On the beach, 202 double rooms and 30 triples, a/c, balcony or terrace, minibar, bathroom, TV, phone, safe in room,

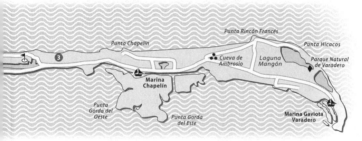

● Eating
1 El Mirador at LTI Bella Costa Resort
2 Habana Café at Sol Club Las Sirenas
3 Oshin at Sol Club Palmeras

Cuba

snack bar, buffet and restaurant, entertainment, watersports, pool, tennis, gym, sauna, massage, hairdresser, medical services, laundry, PO, cambio, fax and email services, bicycle, moped and car rental, taxis, tourism bureau. **B** *Acuazul*, Av 1 entre 13 y 14, T667132-4. 156 rooms, with pool, older style, not on beach. **B-C** *Herradura* (Horizontes), Av Playa entre 35 y 36, T613725. Rather run-down, although looks better from the sea than from the road. MAP, well-equipped suites, balconies overlook sea, right on narrow bit of beach, restaurant, bar built up above sand, shop, *buró de turismo*, massage US$10 for 30 mins. **C** *Pullman*, Av 1 entre 49 y 50, T667161. Small, not directly on the beach, but low key, a/c, TV. **C** *Dos Mares*, Calle 53 y Av 1, T612702, F667499, carpeta@ dmares.hor.tur.cu One of the oldest hotels, dating from 1940, small, friendly and full of character, across the road from the beach, CP, rooms adequate, some good-sized bathrooms, others small, low water pressure, a/c, TV (CNN), safe, bar, restaurant with average food. **C** *Villa La Caleta* (Gaviota), 20 y Av 1, T667080-1, F3291. 46 a/c rooms with baths, phone, TV, minibar, restaurant, room service, pizzeria, grill, bar, pool, scooter and bike hire, parking, convenient for nightlife. **C** *Villa La Mar*, Av 3 y 29, T613910, 612181. Convenient for *Víazul* bus but not the nicest beach, a/c, TV, hot water, clean, pool, bar, excursions, cheap hotel for package deals booked from abroad. **D** *Varazul*, Av 1 entre 14 y 15, T667132-4, F667229. Aparthotel, 69 rooms, quiet. **D** *Villa Sotavento*, 13 between Av 1 and Av Playa, T667132-4. 130 rooms, next to beach, clean, with bath, breakfast, US$5, buffet, very good.

Eating

Most charge between US$9 and US$15 for a main dish, food is nothing special here, very mediocre quality

In the hotels: *Oshin*, Chinese, in grounds of *Sol Club Palmeras*. Open 1200-1500, 1800-2300, popular, reservations essential. *Habana Café*, at Sol *Club Las Sirenas*, T668070, a copy of *Habana Café* at *Meliá Cohiba* in Havana. 1950s atmosphere, car, photos, music, open 1800-0200, snacks, cocktails, international food. *El Mesón del Quijote* at *Villa Cuba*, Carretera Las Américas, T63522. Spanish, open 1200-2300. *Las Américas*, Av Las Américas, T63856. International food, beautiful setting, food good 1 night, inedible the next. Open 1200-2215. *El Mirador*, at *LTI Bella Costa Resort*, on cliff overlooking the sea. Lovely fish restaurant, lobster US$18.50, shrimp US$14, open 1200-2300.

Along Camino del Mar: *La Cabañita* Camino del Mar esq 9, T62215. Meat and seafood, open 1900-0100. *Mi Casita* (book in advance), Camino del Mar entre 11 y 12, T63787. Meat and seafood, open 1800-2300. *Halong*, Camino del Mar esq 12, T63787. Chinese, open 1900-2300.

Heading east on Av Primera and Playa: *Deportivo Kiki's Club*, Av 1 y 8. Open 1200-2345, sports theme, Italian food, sports shop and sporting exhibitions. *La Sangría*, snack bar on sea front, Av 1 entre 8 y 9, T62025, open 24 hrs. *Castelnuovo*, Av 1 y 11, T667794. Open 1200-2345, Italian. *Lai-Lai* Av 1 y 18, T667793. Bar/restaurant, Oriental, Open 1200-0300. *La Vega*, Av Playa entre 31 y 32. New, smart building with wooden decking all round, dishes US$5-10, lobster US$19. *El Aljibe*, Av 1 y 36, T614019. Open 1200-2400, chicken and more chicken. *Bodegón Criollo*, Av Playa esq 40, T667795. Open 1200-0100, pleasant atmosphere, copy of *Bodeguita del Medio* in Havana with graffiti on walls, popular, music, no vegetarian food. *Coppelia*, Av 1 entre 44 y 46, T612866, open 1000-2245, in town centre, ice cream US$0.90. In Parque Josone are: *El Retiro*, T667316, international; *Dante*, T667738, Italian; *La Campana*, T667224, *criollo* and *La Casa de las Antigüedades*, T667329, meat and seafood. *Albacora*, at the end of 59 off Av Playa. Open 1200-2400, seafood, terrace with tables and dance area under sea grapes with sea views, day package US$12 including lunch, kayaks, water bicycles, sunbed, room for changing in with shower and towel, day trippers from Havana come here, food described as disappointing. *Mallorca*, Av Playa y 64, T667711. Seafood, spaghetti, pizza, snack bar. *La Fondue*, also called *La Casa del Queso Cubano*, Av Playa y 64. Open 1200-2300, now has no cheese or fondue on the menu, concentrating on steak and lobster. *Villa Sirena*, 64 y Playa, on the seafront, T614562. Mediterranean, run by an Italian, smart and pricey with pleasant outdoor seating, seafood US$7-15, lobster US$25, even frogs legs on the menu, excellent wine list and good house Chilean, entertainment. Next door the same Italian runs a bistro offering good-value snacks such as smoked salmon bagels, spring rolls, Canadian imported burgers and the ubiquitous rice and beans, average US$3.50.

Entertainment

Cinema *Cine Varadero*, Av Playa entre 42 y 43. Shows Cuban and foreign films. **Discos** Most large hotels have one including: *La Patana*, Canal de Paso Malo, T667791, open 2200-0500, floating disco at entrance to the balneario; *La Bamba*, hottest in town at *LTI-Tuxpán*, biggest, most popular, T667560, open 2200-0400. **Nightclubs** *Cabaret Continental* at *Hotel Internacional*. US$40 with dinner, 2000, show and disco US$25, open Tue-Sun, 2100-0330, reservations T667038. *Cabaret Cueva del Pirata*, show in a cave, Autopista Sur km 11,: T667751. Open 2200-0300, closed Sun. *Mambo Club*, next to *Gran Hotel*. The *Orquesta Tarafa* plays here, they were famous in the 1950s. *Palacio de la Rumba*, Av Las Américas, km 4, T668210. Open daily 2200-0500, US$10 entrance, includes bar, live salsa bands at weekends, Cubans are allowed in.

Handicraft **markets** offer all manner of souvenirs, from elaborately decorated wooden *humedores* to keep your cigars temperature controlled, to T-shirts and keyrings which are easier to pack. There are several stalls lining the road to the Museo Municipal, but the main market area is in the Parque Central and on the other side of the road around *Coppelia* in the Parque de las Mil Taquillas. Do not buy black coral. It is protected by CITES and it is illegal to take it into your home country.

Shopping

The **golf** course on Av Las Américas Km 8.5, T667788, F668180, golf@ate/nas.inf.cu, was upgraded in 1996-98 to 18 holes, par 72. The original 9 holes were set out by the Du Ponts around their mansion, built in 1928-30, which is now the *Xanadú Club House*, and the new ones extend along the *Sol Meliá* resorts. Golf lessons are offered and there are 2 putting greens and a driving range. 3-8-day packages are available with accommodation in the clubhouse. Pro-shop and equipment rental at *Caddie House*. Bookings can be made, 24 hrs in advance, direct or through hotel tour desks.

Sports
For watersports, see page 110

Most hotels have a tour agency on-site offering local and national excursions, boat trips, multilingual guides, transfers, booking and confirmation of air tickets, air charters, car rentals, reception and representation service. A day trip to Havana is usually US$55, Guamá US$53, Matanzas, riding in the Yumurí Valley and snorkelling in the Saturno Cave US$31, to Elguea via the Che Memorial in Santa Clara with mud baths and lunch US$45.

Tour operators

Local Car hire: *Havanautos*, agency in Varadero at Av 1 y 31, T63733, F667029, T63630 at airport, or through many hotels. *Cubacar* at: *Hotel Sol Palmeras*, T667359; *Hotel LTI-Tuxpan*, T667639; *Hotel Meliá Varadero*, T667013 ext 8191. *Transautos*, Av 2 y 64, T667336, or Av 1 entre 21 y 22. *Nacional* at 13 entre Av 2 y Av 4, T63706, T/F667663. **Moped rental**: US$9 per hr, US$15 for 3 hrs, extra hrs US$5, a good way to see the peninsula but you will have no insurance and no helmet. **Bicycle-hire**: from hotels, US$1 per hr. **Horse-drawn vehicles** act as taxis, usually just for a tour around town. **Taxis** (cars) charge US$0.50 per km. They usually wait at hotels for fares. *Transagaviota*, T619761-2; *Turistaxi*, T613763/377; *Taxi OK*, T612827. Beware of being fleeced on arrival at the bus station. A 2-min taxi ride can cost US$3 and up for the innocent newcomers.

Transport
Hot tip: hire a car rather than jeep to avoid having your spare wheel stolen, insurance covers four wheels, not the spare (see page 70)

Long distance Air The **Juan Gualberto Gómez Airport** (VRA), T613016, 23 km from the beginning of the hotel strip, receives international scheduled and charter flights. *Cubana* or *Sansa* have domestic flights from Baracoa, Cayo Coco, Cayo Largo, Havana, Holguín, Santiago and Trinidad. Bus from airport to hotels US$10pp. Flights to Trinidad, 0900, 1630, leave from Kawama airstrip, just across the bridge on the mainland. **Bus** The interprovincial bus station is at Autopista Sur y 36, T63254, 62626. *Víazul*, T614886, has 3 daily buses Havana-Varadero via Matanzas and Varadero Airport, 0800, 0830, 1600, 3 hrs, US$10 (returning 0800, 1600, 1800), and there is a regular Astro bus twice a day (0805 and 1600) from Havana to Varadero, via Varadero Airport, US$8, reserve 1-2 days in advance. *Víazul* Varadero-Trinidad 0730, 6 hrs, US$20, with stops in Cárdenas US$6, Coliseo US$6, Jovellanos US$6, Jagüey US$6, Santa Clara US$11 and Sancti Spíritus US$16, returns from Trinidad 1430.

Airlines All at the airport: *Aerocaribbean*, T53616; *Aerogaviota*, T613018; *Air Canada*, T612010; *Air Europa*, T613016; *AOM*, T613016; *Cubana*, T613612-14; *LTU*, T53611; *Martinair*, T53624. *Aerotaxi* is at 24 y Av 1, T612929. Cubana has an office at 9 esq 1, T667593. **Banks** *Banco Financiero Internacional*, Av Playa y 32, cash advance service with credit cards available 0900-1900, office open 0900-1500 Mon-Fri, last working day of month 0900-1200. **Communications** Most hotels have post offices. Phone and fax services usually available. The *Centro Internacional de Comunicaciones* is at 64 entre

Directory

Av 1 y Av 3, T612103/612356, F667020. *Etecsa* is at 18 y Av 3, T667070, F667050 with cabinas in other locations such as the corner of Av 1 y 30 and Av 1 y 54, where computer terminals for internet with prepaid cards are being introduced. **Medical services** *Policlínico Internacional*, Av 1 y 61, T668611, 667710-1, F667226, clinica@clinica.var.cyt.cu International clinic, doctor on duty 24 hrs, a medical consultation in your hotel will cost US$25. The clinic has an excellent **pharmacy**, T667226. Recompression chamber at the *Centro Médico Sub Acuática* at the **Hospital Julio M Arístegui**, just outside Cárdenas. **Useful addresses** Immigration and **Police**: 39 y Av 1, T116. Immigration is open Mon-Fri 0800-1130, 1300-1600, Sat 0800-1130 for visa extensions.

Peninsula de Zapata

Phone code: 459
Colour map 1,
grid B2

Hurricane Michelle ripped through the Zapata Peninsula and its tourist attractions in November 2001, with lots of houses and the sugar mill damaged or destroyed

The whole of the south coast of Matanzas province is taken up with the Zapata Peninsula, an area of swamps, mangroves and beaches. It is the largest ecosystem in the island and contains the **Laguna del Tesoro**, a 9.1 sq km lagoon over 10 m deep, an important winter home for flocks of migrating birds. There are 16 species of reptile, including crocodiles. Mammals include the jutia and the manatee, while there are over 1,000 species of invertebrate, of which more than 100 are spiders.

There is a **crocodile farm** in Boca de Guamá, where they breed the native Rhombifer (*cocodrilo*). They also have turtles (*jicotea*), *jutía* and what they call a living fossil, the manjuari fish/alligator. There are shops, a bar and restaurant, occasional live bands and a ceramics factory. It's all a bit touristy; hotels and tourist agencies from Varadero, Havana and other places organize day excursions including lunch, a multilingual guide and a boat ride on the lagoon through the swamps to **Villa Guamá**, a replica Indian village. On one of the islets a series of life-size statues of Indians going through their daily routines has been carved by the late Cuban sculptor Rita Longa. Birdwatchers will see most at dawn before the tour buses arrive. Take insect repellent. ■ *If you go on your own, entrance to the crocodile farm 0900-1630 is US$5, US$3 for children, and the boat trip from Boca de Guamá to Villa Guamá is US$10, US$5 for children. The big boats leave 1000-1200, 45 mins, speed boats keep running 0900-1800. Life jackets are on board.*

The road south across the peninsula meets the coast at **Playa Larga**, at the head of the **Bahía de Cochinos** (**Bay of Pigs**). The US-backed invasion force landed here on 17 April 1961 but was repelled. There is a small monument but most of the commemorative paraphernalia is at Playa Girón (see below). The beach is open and better than that at Playa Girón. The **Laguna de las Salinas**, 25 km southwest, is the temporary home of migratory birds from December-April. The rest of the year it is empty. ■ *Tours go from the Hotel Playa Larga, Mon and Wed mornings, US$15.*

West of Playa Larga, a track leads to **Santo Tomás** where, in addition to waterfowl, you can see the Zapata wren, the Zapata rail and the Zapata sparrow. The park also runs a number of rare bird- (Cuban parrots and Cuban parakeets), turtle- and fish-breeding programmes. Not far from the *Hotel Playa Larga* there is a good site for watching birds such as hummingbirds and the Cuban trogon. ■ *Park headquarters are near the Hotel Playa Larga, in the Empresa Municipal Agropecuaria, T7249. Here you can get permission to enter and pay the admission fee of US$10 per person as well as find a guide (obligatory), about US$50. Insect repellent essential.*

The resort at **Playa Girón** is isolated and small. The beach is walled in and therefore protected, but the sea is rocky. The **diving** and **snorkelling** is excellent and you can walk to the reef from the shore. There is a **museum** at the site of national pilgrimage where, in 1961 at the Bay of Pigs, the disastrous US-backed invasion of Cuba was attempted. ■ *Museum open daily 0800-1700. US$2.*

Sleeping

Playa Larga D *Villa Horizontes Playa Larga*, T7294, F7167. Sometimes fully booked with tour groups, 59 a/c spacious rooms in basic 1- or 2-bedroomed bungalows with bath, fridges, radio, TV, water goes off at night, restaurant, bar, nightclub, shop, tour desk open 0800-1300, birdwatching and watersports. Most people travel on to stay at **Playa Girón C-E** *Villa Horizontes Playa Girón*, T4110, F4117. 287 rooms in bungalows or blocks of rooms, a/c with bath, buffet meals, bar, pool, diving, disco, tourist information desk, shop, car rental (no gas station nearby).

Casas particulares Playa Larga E *Roberto Mesa Pujol*, Barrio Caletón, Playa Larga, T7210. Double rooms, a/c, bathroom shared, hot water, garage, marvellous waterfront location, garden opens onto white-sand beach where you can swim, palm trees, volleyball net. E *Ernesto Delgado Chirino*, Roberto's cousin, another waterfront property, same details. F *Fidel Silvestre Fuentes*, Caletón, T7233, fidelsf@cubasi.cu A/c, hot water, *comida criolla*. F *Mirta Navarro González*, T7286. Clean house, nice family with 3 children, 2 double rooms, 1 bathroom, a/c, US$3 for rather poor breakfast. **Playa Girón** There are 15 in houses and 2 blocks of apartments in Playa Girón. Coming from Cienfuegos, the 1st block is edif 2, the one behind, at an angle, is edif 1. Note that there are roosters behind the blocks for early morning wake-up call. E *Hostal Luís*, Carretera a Cienfuegos esq Carretera a Playa Larga, www.cuba.tc/cuplayagiron.html Owned by Luís A García Padrón, 1 bedroom, a/c, hot water, parking, very clean and friendly. E *José García Mesa (Tito) y Yaquelín Ulloa Pérez*, Frente al edif 2. Room with bathroom, hot and cold water 24 hrs, parking, secure, very nice people. **E-F** *Mayra Ortega Mejías*, edif 1, Apto 19, neighbour's phone T4252. 2 rooms, 1 triple, a/c, TV, 1 with 2 double beds, no a/c, share family bathroom. **E-F** *Victoria Ugaldes y Roberto León*, T4186. 2 rooms, shared bathroom, hot water, good cooking, nice people. E *Maritza López Flores*, edif 1, Apto 21, neighbour's phone T4266. Dinner, bed and breakfast, package deal, good food, double bed, clean, nice lady, share her bathroom. F *Miguel A Padrón y Odalys Figueredo*, behind edif 1, T4100. New house, exceptionally clean, fan, helpful.

Cuba

Eating On the road to Playa Larga is *Rumbos' La Casa del Mar* bar and grill, open 1000-1800, near here is a place to swim. Ask at the *casas particulares* about eating in private homes. Lobster and crocodile on the menu.

Transport **Bus** Guagua to Playa Larga from edif 2, 0630, 30-40 mins, 1.45 pesos. In high season, *Víazul* runs a daily bus Varadero-Guamá-Girón-Cienfuegos, US$16, 4½ hrs, departing Varadero 0830, returning from Cienfuegos 1400. *Astro* to Havana, Fri, Sat, Sun, 10.50 pesos, passes through Playa Larga.

Cienfuegos

Phone code: 432
Colour map 1, grid B3

Cienfuegos, on the south coast, is an attractive seaport and industrial city, sometimes described as the pearl of the south, and there is a very Caribbean feel to the place. French immigrants at the beginning of the 19th century influenced the development and architecture of the city, which is a fascinating blend of styles.

There are interesting colonial buildings around the Parque José Martí. On the east side on Calle 29 is **La Catedral Purísima Concepción**, built in 1868, which has a somewhat neo-Gothic interior with silvered columns. ■ *Mass is at 0730 and the church is open until 1200*. On the north side, on Avenida 56, is the **Teatro Tomás Terry**, built in 1889 after the death of the Venezuelan Tomás Terry, with the proceeds of a donation by his family. It was inaugurated in 1890 with an audience of 1,200. The lobby has an Italian marble statue of Terry and is decorated with fine paintings and ornate gold work. The interior is largely original with wooden seats. Note the ceiling with exquisite paintings. ■ *Daily 0900-1800. US$1 including guided tour*. On the west side is the **Palacio de Ferrer**, now the **Casa de Cultura Benjamín Duarte**, a beautiful building dating from 1894, with a magnificent tower on the corner designed to keep an eye on the port and shipping. Worth seeing for the marble floor, staircases and walls, carved in Italy and assembled at the palace. ■ *Mon-Sat 0830-1900. US$0.50 (including the tower, great views), guided tours in Spanish*.

Excursions On the road to Trinidad between the villages. ■ Daily *0800-1700. US$2.50, children US$1. Bar for drinks. Look out for 2 rows of palm trees leading to the garden from the entrance at the road. Bus from Cienfuegos stops outside, 20 centavos.* **Playa Rancho Luna** is about 14 km from Cienfuegos, near the *Hotel Rancho Luna*. The beach is quite nice but nothing special. The *Centro de Buceo Faro Luna* runs the diving here. If you continue along the road past the beach you get to the *Hotel Pasacaballo*. There is a jetty here and another further along a rough track to the left, from where you can get a little ferry

(US$1) across the mouth of the Bahía de Cienfuegos to the village on the western side, site of the **Castillo de Jagua**. The castle was built at the entrance to the bay in 1733-45 by Joseph Tantete, of France. There is only one entrance via a drawbridge across a dry moat. ■ *Daily 0800-1700. US$1 includes a tour. Ferries also from Av 46 in Cienfuegos harbour, US$0.50, several stops, 45 mins.*

Sleeping   **A-D** *Jagua* (Gran Caribe), Punta Gorda, 37 1, T551003, F551245. 149 a/c rooms with view over bay, singles, doubles and triples available, 2 suites and 1 room for the handicapped, 4-star, comfortable, small pool, DHL office in hotel. **A** *Boutique La Unión* (Cubanacán), Av 31 esq 54, T/F551020, comercial@union.cfg.cyt.cu Built in 1869, newly restored, upmarket, 36 double rooms and 13 suites, CP, a/c, safe box, satellite TV, business centre, car rental, gym, pool, restaurant and bars. **B-C** *Faro Luna* (Cubanacán), Carretera Pasacaballo km 18, Playa Faro Luna, T548030, F548062. 70 rooms, CP, 3-star, nice, clean, hot water, TV, some staff friendly, aimed at individual travellers who want to dive and sail. **C-D** *Villa Guajimico*, Carretera a Trinidad km 42, Cumanayagua, T540947, best to book through Cubamar, in Havana, T662523-4, F333111, cubamar@cubamar.mit.cma.net Overlooks mouth of Río La Jutía, surrounded by cliffs, caves, coral reefs and beaches accessible only by boat. 3-star, 51 cabins, some triples, a/c, bathroom, pool, restaurant, bar, parking, hobicats, good for excursions, a great dive resort, 3 (average) meals US$31, diving US$25, sailing US$10.

Numerous casas all down 37 to Punta Gorda, too many to list here. We list only those recently recommended   **Casas particulares**   **E-F** *Delíz y Pedro Sierra*, 37 3806 entre 38 y 40. 5 a/c rooms (avoid the first room on the ground floor, uncomfortable bed), private bathroom, TV, fridge, 24-hr hot and cold water, meals on request, parking, fantastic view of bay from balcony on first floor, English spoken by well-educated health professionals who are very knowledgeable about their country. **E-F** *Marta González González*, 39 6401 entre 64 y 66, T3268. 2 a/c double rooms, simple but clean, bathroom, hot water, nice family, cosy atmosphere, breakfast and dinner available, Spanish only. **F** *Alina Alonso Araña*, Av 56 4106 entre 41 y 43, T518609. Two double bedrooms upstairs in a separate part of the house with nice roof terrace. **F** *Isabel Martínez Cordero y Pepe*, Av 52 4318 entre 43 y 45, T518276. A/c, private bathroom, garage nearby, very good vegetarian option. **F** *María Núñez Suárez*, Av 58 3705 Altos entre 37 y 39, T7867. A/c room with adjoining bathroom. Ask her husband and friends to tell you stories about when they were young, fighting with Che in the Sierra Maestra, at the Bay of Pigs or working in Ethiopia. **F** *Maritza Guedes Brito*, 39 2202B entre 22 y 24, T3388. 2 a/c rooms independent of the rest of the house, shared bathroom, hot water, fridge, garage, owner is a gynaecologist.

Eating   The place to go for its style, if not for the food, is *Palacio de Valle*, by *Hotel Jagua*, a building dating from 1894 in a mixture of architectural styles but with Arab influences predominating, incredibly ornate ceilings and other decorations. Open 1145-2300 for food, from 1000 for drinks, meals US$10-22, speciality seafood, upstairs on the roof is a bar with good views and another restaurant in the garden. On 37, adjacent to the hotel, is *Los Laureles*, where meals are cheaper. Also on 37, opposite the hotel, is *Cueva del Camarón*. Nice place to eat, clean, open 1200-2300, meals around US$10-25. Nearby is *Covadonga*, on 37. Paella restaurant. *37 y 42*, 37 4204 entre 42 y 44, T6027. Open 1100-0100 or 0200, meals around US$6-10. *El Criollito*, 33 5603 entre 56 y 58, T5540. Open 24 hrs, meals US$7-8 include salad, chips, rice and coffee, tasty fish, live music. *El Cochinto*, Prado y 4. Not a great choice but you pay in pesos, open 1900-2100. *1819*, Av Prado. Limited choice, menu in dollars or pesos. Plenty of *paladares* on the Prado. *Coppelia* ice cream, on Prado y 53, open Tue-Sun 1100-2300. *Helados Alondria*, known as *Terry Sodería*, between Terry Theatre and Colegio San Lorenzo. Open 0900-2300, of ice cream delights.

Tour operators   *Rumbos*, Av 20 3905 entre 39 y 41, T1231, F1175. Trips to waterfalls and other local attractions.

Transport   **Local   Coches**: horse-drawn carriages operate in Cienfuegos. **Car hire**: *RentaCar* is in *Hotel Jagua* car park. *Havanautos* and *Servi Cupet Cimex* is at 37 entre 15 y 17.

Long distance   Bus   Terminal at 49 (Gloria) esq Av 56, T62170. Tickets may be purchased 1 hr or so in advance from the small office with a brown door, next to the Salón Reservaciones.

Astro to **Havana**, 5 daily, 5 hrs, US$14. To **Santiago de Cuba**, every other day, 1700, US$31. To **Trinidad**, 0630, 1230, 5-6 hrs, US$3. To **Santa Clara**, 0700, 0900, 1¼ hrs, US$1.50. *Astro* has a daily 1430 service to **Matanzas**, US$14, via Cárdenas and Varadero, but check if it is running. Sun is a good day with people returning to work in Varadero. *Viazul*, T8114/5720, passes through here on its Havana-Trinidad route. In high season, *Víazul* runs a service Varadero-Guamá-Girón-Cienfuegos, US$16, leaving Varadero 0830, 4½ hrs, returning from Cienfuegos 1400. **Train** Terminal at 49 esq Av 58, T3403, 5495. All services generally slow and uncomfortable.

Banks The *Banco Financiero Internacional* is on Av 54 esq 29, T/F335603, open 0800-1500 Mon-Fri, 3% commission on TCs. Cash advances on credit cards. **Communications** Internet: *Etecsa* internet access opposite *Hotel La Unión*, Calle 31 entre 54 y 56. **Medical services** *International Clinic*, Punta Gorda on 37 202, opposite the *Hotel Jagua*, T/F8959, offering 24-hr emergency care, consultations, laboratory services, X-rays, pharmacy and other services. Pharmacy on Prado esq Av 60, open 24 hrs.

Directory

Cuba

Santa Clara

Santa Clara is a pleasant university city in the centre of the island best known for being the site of the last and definitive battle of the Revolution and the last resting place of Che Guevara. The northern coast is low lying and there are mangroves and swamps, but it is fringed with coral cays with sandy beaches and crystal clear water.

Phone code: 42
Colour map 1, grid B3
Population: 200,000
300 km from Havana

In December 1958, before Castro entered Havana, Batista sent an armoured train with military supplies including guns, ammunition and soldiers, to Santiago de Cuba to counter-attack the revolutionaries. However, **Che Guevara** and his troops were hiding in the outskirts of Santa Clara, waiting for the train. On 28 December 1958 it was ambushed in the afternoon. The soldiers on the train surrendered quickly and the fighting for the train was soon over. However, the battle for the city lasted nearly four days, until 1 January 1959 when news spread that Batista had fled the country.

Heading east on Calle Independencia towards Camajuaní, between Río Cubanicay and the railway line, is the **Monumento a la Toma del Tren Blindado**, where four of the carriages of Batista's troop train are preserved. There is a museum inside the wagons showing weapons and other things carried on the train. ■ *Tue-Sat 0900- 1200, 1500-1900 (1800 in winter), Sun 0900-1200. US$1.* There is also a monument on top of **El Capiro**, the hill where Che and his troops waited to attack the train. You can get an excellent view of the city from here, just as Che did in 1958.

A monument to Che has been built in the **Plaza de la Revolución Ernesto Guevara**, with a huge bronze statue of Che on top of a large concrete plinth, a bas-relief scene depicting Che in battle and an inscription of a letter from him to Fidel. Under the monument is a **Mausoleum**. The remains of Che and his comrades who fell in Bolivia have been interred here. Beside the mausoleum is the **Museo Histórico de la Revolución**, with good displays in Spanish and sometimes a video about Che's life and role in the Revolution, as well as displays of the battle in Santa Clara. Recommended. ■ *Tue-Sun 0900-1700. Free. Prolongación Marta Abreu after the Carretera Central forks to the north; look out for La Victoria service station, entrance on Rafael Tristá, which runs parallel. Bicitaxi US$1 from the centre.*

C *Villa La Granjita* (Cubanacán), outside town at Km 2.5 on Maleza road, T218190, F218192, aloja@granjita.vcl.cyt.cu 75 rooms in thatched cabañas among fruit trees, cable TV, a/c, phone, pool, bar, shop, buffet restaurant, horses, night-time entertainment around the pool. **D** *Los Caneyes* (Horizontes), Av de los Eucaliptos y Circunvalación, T218140, 204512. Thatched public areas with 91 cabins, a/c, hot showers, TV, facilities for disabled people, pool, disco, evening entertainment by the pool, good buffet, supper US$12, breakfast US$4, excellent value, car rental, medical services, shop, tourism bureau, hairdresser, game shooting and fishing can be arranged, popular hotel for tour parties and hunters.

Sleeping

Cuba

Most casas offer breakfast US$3, dinner US$7-8, recommended, better than restaurants

Casas particulares E-F *Casa Mercy*, San Cristóbal (Machado) 4 entre Cuba y Colón, T216941, iselmm@yahoo.es Run by Omelio y Mercedes Moreno, 2 good rooms, 1 bathroom, upstairs, private but noise from road, double bed, a/c, fan, 1 room has fridge and balcony, TV in ante-room, towel and soap provided, iron, friendly family with dog, very central. **E-F** *Hostal Florida Center*, Candelaria (Maestra Nicolasa) 56 entre Colón y Maceo, T208161. Delightful colonial house with 2 rooms opening on to verdant garden in patio where there are parrots, a dog and cats. Rooms have double bed with extra single bed, basin in room, 1½ bathrooms between them, a/c, TV, fridge and minibar, antique furniture, hospitable host Angel Martínez speaks some English, French and a little Italian. Beware *jineteros* outside who may tell you the house is full and offer to take you somewhere else, or concoct some other story. Ring the bell and get the facts from someone inside. **E-F** *Orlando García Rodríguez*, Buen Viaje 7 entre Parque y Maceo, T206761. 2 rooms, a/c, fan, shared fridge, shared bathroom, lovely house, eating area on the roof, guitar/singer, excursions arranged. **E-F** *María and Jorge García Rodriguez*, Cuba 209, Apdo 1, entre Serafín García (Nazareno) y E P Morales (Síndico), T202329, garcrodz@yahoo.com 2 a/c rooms, clean, comfortable, owners very helpful and informative. **E-F** *Hostal Mauricio*, Martha Abreu 58 altos entre Zayas y Villuendas. Owner is Belgian and speaks Spanish, English, French, German and Dutch, good location, 1 min from Parque Vidal. **F** *Eduardo Alvarez Chaviano*, Colón 170 entre Nazareno y San Miguel, T206190. Eduardo is a geography teacher and speaks English. The room is clean, a/c, private bathroom. **F** *Ernesto y Mireya*, Cuba 227 altos entre Pastora y Síndico, opposite Iglesia La Pastora, T273501. 2 double rooms with shared bathroom, Ernesto is funny and helpful, will arrange collection from bus station if you pay for taxi. **F** *Mariela Consuelo Ramos Rodríguez*, Independencia 265 Este Apto 1 entre Pedro Estévez (Unión) y M Gutiérrez (San Isidro), T202064. Ernesto's cousin, English spoken, huge room with 2 double beds and bathroom, Miriam Consuelo is a 1-person tourist office, she knows everything, large family and comedy dog. **F** *Mercedes*, Máximo Gómez 51 altos, entre Independencia y Martí. Central, 3 rooms, each with own bathroom, 2 with own terrace, the cheapest one at the top is the most private, friendly family, Mercedes practices *Santería*, high standard.

Eating

Begging can be persistent if you eat outside at a street café

1878 Colonial, Máximo Gómez 8, near the Boulevard, T22428. Offers a variety of *criollo* dishes, mainly pork in different styles, bar in the patio, drinks limited to rum, priced in pesos so may mysteriously run out. *Mandarín*, Chinese, Carretera Central beyond bus stations, reservations needed with Islazul on Calle Lorda, or T91010, open 1830-2230. *Casa del Gobernador*, Boulevard, in old, colonial building, open Tue-Sun for lunch 1200-1500, *merienda* (tea/snacks) in the patio 1500-1800, dinner 1900-2200, on Sat-Sun there is a night club 2100-0200. *La Casona*, Carretera Central 6 entre Padre Chao y Marta Abreu, just by Río Bélico, T205027. Very tasty, nice old house with beautiful tiled floor but no tables or chairs, food served at standing counter to avoid *paladar* regulations, like a takeaway service, friendly hosts, open Sat-Thu1200-1600, 1900-2300. *Coppelia* ice cream, Colón esq Mujica just off Parque Vidal, T206426, 1000-2330, closed Mon. *La Marquesina*, 24-hr café next to theatre, pleasant place for a drink, popular with young people at night. Another dollar cafeteria is *Europa* on the corner of Boulevard and Colón. A good place to sit and watch shoppers and drink a cool beer, Cristal US$0.85.

Entertainment

Cartelera is a pamphlet with what's on in Santa Clara, Remedios, Caibarién

Club Mejunje (mishmash), 2½ blocks west from Parque Vidal, Marta Abréu 107 entre Alemán y Juan Bruno Zayas, cultural centre and *Casa de la Trova* in a backyard full of artefacts and graffiti-covered walls, opens Tue-Fri 2200 , Sat 1700 and 1600 and 2200 on Sun, 2 pesos, pay for rum in pesos, composers, singers, musicians and friends sing, play and drink together, friendly, welcoming, enjoyable. Rock night Tue, *Trovuntivitis* Thu, *filín* Sat, something on most nights and Sun during the day. Larger events are staged in the courtyard, wide variety ranging from concerts to theatre, from shows for kids to shows for gays, US$1 for foreigners, 5 pesos for Cubans. *Bar Club Boulevard*, Independencia 225 entre Maceo y Unión, T216236. Nightclub, very trendy, small, also used for social occasions, birthdays, etc, open 1300-1900, 2100-0330, US$2, bar, music and show (Carishow, US$1) with different acts, singers, comedians, etc. *Piano Bar*, Luis Estévez 13 entre Independencia y Parque, T215215. The restaurant is open 0900-0100, *comida criolla*, the piano bar opens 2100-0400, live music with the pianist Freyda Anido and band, invited singers, national and international music, taped music, drinks and snacks, closed Tue. *El Bosque, Centro Cultural*, Av Sandino y Carr Central, Vigía, T204444, is an outdoor venue for live and taped music and nightlife, cabaret, 80 pesos, US$4, including bottle of rum and 4 colas and table for the show, patio bar and cafeteria, open 24 hrs, pay in dollars. There is a cinema on the ground floor of the *Hotel Santa Clara Libre* on Parque Vidal and the best local disco is in the basement, *El Sótano*, good for young crowd, noisy, opens Tue-Sun 2230-0400, US$5. The disco on the 10th floor has a reputation for prostitution; pimps entice tourists with underage prostitutes and then blackmail them.

Local Horse-drawn **coches**, or **taxi-buses**, go all over town and down Marta Abreu to the bus stations, 1 peso. There are also some **buses**, 40 centavos. **Bicitaxi** costs US$1 to most places in town, fix a price beforehand or they will overcharge you, lots of complaints. The best **taxi** company is *Cubataxi*, T202691, 206903, good drivers, reasonable prices, about US$60 for a whole day's tour to the cays and Remedios. **Long distance   Air** Airport about 8 km north of Santa Clara near La Granjita, for transporting tourists to the cays, T286183. **Bus** The municipal bus station for destinations within Villa Clara is on Marta Abreu esq Pichardo, T206284, 1 km from centre. The intermunicipal bus station for long distances is 1 km further out on Carretera Central (Av Cincuentenario) Km 483 entre Independencia y Oquendo, T292113-4, 291572. *Víazul*, T92113/91572. Buses on the Varadero-Trinidad route stop here, also buses Havana-Santiago. *Astro* to most towns, cheaper, slower and less frequent. **Train** The Martha Abreu railway station, T202895, is north of Parque Vidal on Estévez and is much more central than either of the bus stations. The *especial* stops here, heading east at 2148 (US$41 first class, US$33 second class, 10 hrs), and west at 0304 (US$21 first class, US$17 second class, 4 hrs). There are trains to Bayamo, Manzanillo, Camagüey, Sancti Spíritus, Holguín and other towns, timetables are unreliable and the train may not even appear at any time.

Transport

Banks The *Cadeca* office for changing currency and TCs (4% commission) is at Parque Vidal on the corner of Rafael Tristá and Cuba, T205690, open Mon-Sat 0830-1800, Sun 0830-1230. *Bandec*, on the corner of Vidal and Tristá and Cuba, Visa and MC, open Mon-Fri 0800-1400, Sat 0800-1100. *Banco Financiero Internacional*, on Cuba 6 entre Tristá y E Machado, just down from Parque Vidal, T207450, F208115, is open Mon-Fri 0800-1500, also Visa and MC. **Communications** Post office: Colón 10 entre Parque y E Machado, just off Parque Vidal, opposite *Coppelia* ice cream parlour, open 0800-2200 Mon-Sat, email service with prepaid cards. **Telephones**: *Etecsa* has a cabina on the corner of Cuba and Machado (San Cristóbal) for domestic, foreign calls and internet with the prepaid *tarjetas*, open 0730-2230.

Directory

Trinidad

Trinidad, 133 km south of Santa Clara, is a perfect relic of the early days of the Spanish colony: beautifully preserved streets and buildings and hardly a trace of the 20th century anywhere. It was founded in 1514 by Diego Velázquez as a base for expeditions into the 'New World' and Cortés set out from here for Mexico in 1518. The five main squares and four churches date from the 18th and 19th centuries and the whole city, with its fine palaces, cobbled streets and tiled roofs, is a national monument and since 1988 has been a UNESCO World Heritage Site.

Phone code: 419
Colour map 1, grid B3
Population: 60,000

On the Plaza Mayor is the cathedral, **Iglesia Parroquial de la Santísima Trinidad**, built between 1817 and 1892. It is the largest church in Cuba and is renowned for its acoustics. On the left of the altar is a crucifix of the brown-skinned Christ of Veracruz, who is the patron of Trinidad. ■ *1100-1300 for sightseeing and photos; mass daily at 2000 and on Sun at 0900. Casa Parroquial at Fco J Zerquera 456, opposite the church, T3668, F6387.*

Sights

Begging has become persistent, mainly children and old women asking for dollars, soap, skin cream

The **Museo Romántico** has an excellent collection of romantic-style porcelain, glass, paintings and ornate furniture, which belonged to the Conde de Brunet family and dates from 1830-60. ■ *Fri-Wed 0900-1700. US$2, no cameras allowed. Hernández 52, next to the church of Santísima Trinidad on the main square, T4363.* **Museo Municipal de Historia**, an attractive building but rather dull displays in eight rooms of scientific, historical and cultural displays, walk up the tower for a

Trinidad

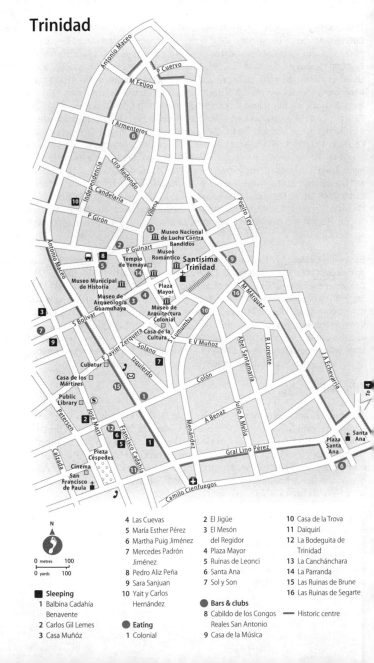

Sleeping
1 Balbina Cadahía Benavente
2 Carlos Gil Lemes
3 Casa Muñóz

4 Las Cuevas
5 María Esther Pérez
6 Martha Puig Jiménez
7 Mercedes Padrón Jiménez
8 Pedro Aliz Peña
9 Sara Sanjuan
10 Yait y Carlos Hernández

Eating
1 Colonial

2 El Jigüe
3 El Mesón del Regidor
4 Plaza Mayor
5 Ruinas de Leonci
6 Santa Ana
7 Sol y Son

Bars & clubs
8 Cabildo de los Congos Reales San Antonio
9 Casa de la Música

10 Casa de la Trova
11 Daiquirí
12 La Bodeguita de Trinidad
13 La Canchánchara
14 La Parranda
15 Las Ruinas de Brune
16 Las Ruinas de Segarte

— Historic centre

good view of Trinidad. ■ *Sat-Thu 0900-1700. US$2. Simón Bolívar 423, T4460.*
Other museums worth visiting include: the **Museo de Arqueología Guamuhaya**, a
general view of developments from precolumbian to post-conquest times.
■ *Sat-Thu 0900-1700. US$1. Simón Bolívar 457, esq Villena, Plaza Mayor, T3420.*
Museo de Arquitectura Colonial exhibits specifically on the architecture of Trini-
dad. ■ *Sat-Thu 0900-1700. US$1. Ripalda 83, T3208.* **Museo Nacional de Lucha
Contra Bandidos**, housed in the old San Francisco convent, exhibits about the
post-revolutionary campaign in the Escambray mountains. ■ *Tue-Sun 0900-1700,
US$1. Hernández esq Piro Guinart, T4121.*

Inland from Trinidad are the beautiful, wooded Escambray mountains, whose high- **Excursions**
est point is **Pico San Juan**, also known as La Cuca, at 1,140 m. Rivers have cut deep
valleys, some of which, such as the Caburní and the Guanayara, have attractive
waterfalls and pools where you can swim. The **Parque Natural Topes de Collantes**
is a 110 sq km area of the mountains which contains many endemic species of fauna
and flora. There are several paths in the area and walking is very rewarding with
lovely views and lush forest. There is no public transport but day trips are organized
to Topes de Collantes by *Cubatur* or *Rumbos* by jeep or truck, which take in swimming in a waterfall. You can see lots of wildlife, butterflies, hummingbirds and the
tocororo. A great day out. Private tours do not go to the same places as jeep tours,
whatever anybody tells you. ■ *US$6.50.*

   Rumbos will also take you to the **Torre de Manaca Iznaga** in the village of the same
name about 15 km from Trinidad on the road to Sancti Spíritus, or you can hire a private car to take you for about US$10 or you can catch a train heading to Meyor or
Condado, US$7 return, to Manaca Iznaga. The tower, built between 1835 and 1845 is
43.5 m high, has seven floors and 136 steps to the top. It was built as a lookout to watch
the slaves working in the valley at the sugar mills. It has UNESCO World Heritage status alongside Trinidad city. There is a great view of the surrounding countryside,
including the **Valle de los Ingenios** (Valley of the Sugar Mills) and the Escambray
Mountains as well as the roof tops of the village below. ■ *0900-1600 or 1700. US$2.*

B *Las Cuevas* (Horizontes), Finca Santa Ana, T6133, F6161, reservas@cuevas.co.cu On a hill 10   **Sleeping**
mins' walk from town (good road), with caves in the grounds, view of the sea. Recently remodelled, 109 comfortable rooms and mini suites in chalets and apartments with a/c, phone, radio,
hot water, very clean, 2 swimming pools, bar with excellent daiquirís and great view, disco
2230-0200 Fri, Sat, 2130-2400 other days, in cave below reception, entrance US$10, dollar shop,
post office, exchange facilities, tour agencies (*Cubatur* and *Rumbos*), restaurant with poor buffet
meals, breakfast US$4, evening meal US$12. **C** *Finca María Dolores*, Carretera Circuito Sur, T6481,
also called *Casa de Campesino*, 3 km from Trinidad on the road to Cienfuegos. Garden setting near
Río Guaurabo, 12 brick cabañas and 26 bungalows with kitchen, recently renovated, a/c, shower,
clean, restaurant, shop, pool bar, quiet spot but noisy in the evening as it is an all-dancing,
all-singing tour group destination, horse riding, volleyball, basketball, fishing, river excursions.

Casas particulares E *Casa Muñóz*, José Martí 401 entre Fidel Claro y Santiago Escobar,   *Only casa owners*
T/F3673, trinidadjulio@yahoo.com Very friendly, English speaking, run by Julio César   *waiting for*
Muñóz Cocina and Rosa Orbea Cerrillo, great house, built in 1800, 2 rooms with 2 double   *pre-booked tourists*
beds, new bathrooms, a/c and fans, roof terrace, parking, very popular so book in advance.   *are allowed at the*
Julio is a photographer and can arrange workshops and study groups,   *bus station, no touts*
www.trinidadphoto.com **E** *Víctor Valmuseda Díaz*, Frank País 381 entre Simón Bolívar y   *allowed, although*
Zerquera, T4157. Self contained apartment, kitchen, bathroom, 2 bedrooms, balcony, ter-   *it happens*
race, sitting room, a bargain for 4 people, clean, central, good.

F *Balbina Cadahía Benavente*, Maceo 355 entre Lino Pérez y Colón, CP 62600, T2585.
Extremely nice family, old colonial house, hot water shower, will arrange trips, friendly, good
reports. **F** *Carlos Gil Lemes*, José Martí 263 entre Colón y Fco J Zerquera, T3142, next to library.
Beautiful late-19th century house with sumptuous tile decoration, English spoken, 2 rooms

with shared bath, hot water, fans, garden courtyard, neighbour has a garage for rent, US$1 per night. **F** *Casa de Hospedaje El Fausto*, Simón Bolívar 220 entre Clemente Pereira y Frank País, T3466. Exceptionally clean, nice room with fan and bathroom. Several terraces around the house to sit and relax. **F** *Gisela Borrell Bastida*, Frank País (Carmen) 486 entre Fidel Claro y Santiago Escobar, opposite *Gaviota*, about 200 m from bus station, T4301. Bedroom with double and 2 single beds on ground floor, bathroom with hot shower, use of own dining room, sitting room, own entrance, lots of space. **F** *Hospedaje Yolanda*, Piro Guinart 227 entre Izquierdo y Maceo, opposite the bus station. Very nice rooms in enormous colonial house including 1 up a spiral staircase with 2 double beds, terrace and views of sea and mountains, hot water shower, a/c. **F** *Hostal La Candelaria*, Antonio Guiteras (Mercedes) 129 entre P Zerquera y A Cárdenas, T4239. Run by Elvira and Eddy, both teachers but no English spoken, friendly and generous, humble accommodation, but spotlessly clean, 2 rooms, hot water, a/c, fans, nice garden. **F** *Hostal La Rioja* , Frank País 389 entre Simón Bolívar y Fco J Zerquera, T4177. Run by Teresa Leris Echerri, 3 rooms with bathrooms, 2 with noisy a/c, 1 with fan and cooking facilities, hot water, garage, some French and English spoken, several good reports. **F** *Hugo P Bastida*, Maceo 539 (Gutiérrez), entre Santiago Escobar (Olvido) y Piro Guinart (Boca), T3186. Name above the door, nice room, a/c, bathroom, hot water, very friendly dog, Sr Bastida speaks good English and his wife is an excellent cook. **F** *Dr Manuel Lagunilla Martínez*, a retired lawyer, he lives at Maceo 455 but rents rooms at José Martí 327. Colonial house, 3 rooms each with bathroom, hot water all day, English spoken, has pictures of pre-Revolution Havana. **F** *María Esther Pérez*, Francisco Cadahía 224 (Gracia) entre Colón y Lino Pérez, T35258. Nice extension with 2 rooms attached to old colonial house, antique beds in both, 1 communal bathroom, a/c or fan, porch area, small kitchen, bike hire US$3 per day, can arrange cheap taxi tours to Topes de Collantes, parking 5 doors away. **F** *Martha Puig Jiménez*, Francisco Cadahía 236, entre Colón y Lino Pérez, T2361. Speaks fluent English, free coffee, house and courtyard spotlessly clean, fans, shared bathroom, hot water, friendly, informative, car parking arranged. **F** *Mercedes Padrón Jiménez*, Manuel Solano 7 (Pimpolo), T3068. 2 rooms, 1 with own bathroom, more privacy than some, owner is former teacher and speaks the kind of Spanish that even people who don't speak Spanish can understand, phone ahead, popular. **F** *Pedro Aliz Peña*, Gustavo Izquierdo 127 (Gloria) entre Piro Guinart y Simón Bolívar, T3776/3025, just by bus station where *Víazul* buses stop. Old house with high ceilings, patio, quiet, 2 spacious rooms, fans, simple but clean, new bathrooms, hot water, Pedro and Teresa are sociable and helpful, only Spanish spoken. **F** *Sara Sanjuan*, Simón Bolívar 266 entre José Martí y Frank País, T3997. 3 rooms, sleep 3, a/c, colonial building, quiet courtyard with rocking chairs and roof terrace. **F** *Yait y Carlos Hernández*, Independencia 35 entre Pablo Pichs Girón y Conrado Benítez, T3362. Close to bus station, 2 rooms, bathroom and kitchen, can rent whole house or just a room, friendly young couple, a/c, hot water, good for families, Yait will babysit, bring own soap and towels.

Eating

Most people eat in casas particulares where the food is excellent even if not strictly legal. Breakfast is usually US$2-3 and dinner US$5-7

Colonial, Maceo 402, esq Colón. Open daily 0900-2200, US$7-8, nice place, locally popular. *El Jigüe*, Real 69 esq Guinart, T6476. Open 0900-2230, live music, good food and atmosphere, most dishes US$7-8, chicken special US$12, lower prices for groups of over 10 people. A *Rumbos* restaurant is *El Mesón del Regidor*, Simón Bolívar 426 entre Ernesto V Muñoz y Villena, opposite Toro, T6572/3. Open 0900-1800 daily, US$7-8, also in the complex is a bar, internet terminal and 4 rooms to rent. *Las Begonias*, Maceo esq Simón Bolívar. Open 0900-2200, the only café in town with the added attraction of 6 computer terminals for internet access. Fast food dishes around US$5-8, ice cream a speciality, 2 pool tables. Also ice cream parlour opposite. *Plaza Mayor*, Villena 15, just off Plaza Mayor. Elegant setting, very smart, buffet dinner US$8 and *parrillada* with local specialities and international dishes, open 1200-2200. *Restaurante Don Antonio*, Izquierdo 118 entre Piro Guinart y Simón Bolívar, T6548. Open 1130-1700, in nice old colonial house with ornate columns and tiled floor, meals around US$6-8. *Ruinas de Leonci*, Gustavo Izquierdo 106 entre Simón Bolívar y Piro Guinart. Bar and restaurant open 0900-2300, cosy small garden, pleasant wooden tables and chairs inside, live music every night at 2100. *Santa Ana*, on Plaza Santa Ana. Open 0900-2200 every day, house special pork US$4.65, other dishes US$5-6, pool table, souvenir shop with food. The price of beer in some restaurants drops from US$2 to US$0.60 after 1700 when the tourist tours leave, but all the state-run places shut then too. *Sol y Son*, Simón Bolívar 283 entre Frank País y José Martí. Run by English-speaking ex-architect Lázaro, open 1200-1500, 1900-2300, in 19th-century house, nice decor, courtyard, mixed reports, some say it is the best food in Cuba, others that it is overpriced with average food, vegetarian special, excellent pork, tasty stuffed fish around US$10 with drinks. Sit-down pizza restaurant where tourists can pay in pesos on Martí at Parque Céspedes. Lots of pizza stalls on Lino Pérez entre Martí y Maceo, but the best on Francisco Cadahía y Lino Pérez.

Bar Daiquirí, Lino Pérez entre Cadahía y José Martí. Open 0800-1900, fast food beer US$1, mojito **Bars** US$2, zombie US$4. *Bar Las Ruinas de Segarte*, Alameda entre Márquez y Galdós, in ruined courtyard. Open 1000-2400, also does fried chicken for US$1.50 or other fast food, traditional music, live bands play in the day, Afro-Cuban dance, variety show at 2100. The *Círculo Social de Obreros*, on Martí, serves rum in pesos, tourists welcome, an authentic drinking experience. *La Bodeguita de Trinidad*, Colón entre Martí y Maceo. Open 0900-2400. Not as legendary as its Havana namesake, but a nice music bar and restaurant, open courtyard and with sheltered booths for couples, *trova* group every night, 2100-2400, entry free, beer US$1, cocktails US$2.

Music and dance *Casa de la Música*, up the steps past the church in Plaza Mayor, popular **Entertainment** disco, full of tourists and Cubans, open 2130-0130 daily, disco, salsa, live performers at week- ends. *Casa Fisher (Artex)*, Lino Pérez 306 entre Cadahía y José Martí. In a nice old colonial house built in 1870, outdoor bar 0900-0100, show at 2130 with dance, live music and karaoke. *Coppelia*, still open after everything else is closed, music, popular with Cubans. Open for break- fast at 0700, restaurant food 1000-2100, disco at 2200, special show Sat, Sun at 2300, US$1 for show and disco. *La Escalinata*, on the terrace leading up the steps next to the church, open 1000-2400, live bands all the time but not when it rains. 1 block from the church is the *Casa de la Trova*, open weekend lunchtimes and daily in the evenings, 0900-2400, entry US$1 at night, but sometimes free. Excellent live Cuban music with a warm, vibrant atmosphere. There are mostly Cubans here, of all age groups, and it's a great place to watch, and join in with, the locals having a good time. All drinks paid for in dollars, quite expensive. *Cabildo de los Congos Reales*, Fernando H Echerri entre *La Escalinata* y Casa de la Trova. Bar open 1000-2400, during the day there are sometimes groups playing and at 2200 there is an Afro-Cuban show. Another venue for live music is *La Canchánchara*, Villena 70. Open 0900-2100, cocktails, no food, serves a drink of the same name created out of rum, honey and lime in small earthenware pots. More touristy than *Casa de La Trova* (cigar and souvenir shop), but good traditional music at lunchtimes. *La Parranda*, Villena 59 in the patio of the Templo de Yemaya, just off Plaza Mayor. An outdoor bar/music venue, very ad hoc farmyard atmosphere, but excellent live music every night, good place to learn salsa, watched from semi-circle of seats, cocktails US$2, dancing, open 0900-2400. The disco at *Las Cuevas* (see under Sleeping) is good, dance merengue and salsa with Cubans between the stalactites in a cave below reception, from 2200, entrance US$510. *Las Ruinas de Brunet*, Maceo entre Colón y Francisco Javier Zerquera. Open 0900-2330. Nightly Afro-Cuban show at 2100 for tourists in ruined colonial courtyard, very tacky and unauthentic, also trova from 1600 and percussion classes 0900-1200.

Lots of people offer 'unofficial' salsa lessons for about US$4 an hour; Trinidad is a good place to learn and you'll soon be dancing with Cubans in local bars

Rumbos Cuba office is on maceo esq Simón Bolívar, T6404, open daily 0900-1800, can arrange **Tour operators** tours and excursions and find out any information for travellers, will renew tourist cards, book flights from Trinidad and deal with Cubana enquiries. Staff speak French, English, German and Italian. *Cubanacán*, in the Universo store on Martí entre Rosario y Colón, T6142, open Mon-Sat 0800-1900, Sun 0800-1400, tours to waterfalls with horses or jeeps, catamaran and other off- shore excursions. *Cubatur*, Maceo esq Zerquera, T/F6314, open 0900-1200, 1300-1800, much the same tours and prices as *Rumbos* and hotel reservations. In the office there is also a bank, T6310, and the office of *Transtur Rent a Car*, T6110. *Havanatur*, T/F6183, tour operator and **Veracuba**, T6317 (*Cubacar, Taxi OK*), are in the same building at Lino Pérez entre Maceo y Cadahía. *Paradiso*, Lino Pérez 306 y Martí (Casa Fisher), T6486, F6308, paradiso@artextdad.co.cu, is a tour operator specializing in promoting cultural tourism. **Excur- sions** are all much the same price, for example: US$12 for a city tour; US$25 for a sea safari from Playa Ancón marina. Bicycles and horses are for hire. Try and use the legal operators as you will be better covered in case of emergency and the horses and bikes will be better quality.

Cuba

Transport **Local Car hire**: *Transtur*, Maceo esq Zerquera, T5314, cars and buses. *Rent a Car Via* (Gaviota), at the airport, T6388. There is also car hire at *Hotel Las Cuevas* and *Hotel Ancón*. *Havanautos*, at ServiCupet on the way out of Trinidad towards Casilda, T/F6301. *Transautos*, T5336. Cupet station on Frank País esq Zerquera. **Taxi** *Cubataxi*, T2214, at the bus station. *Taxi OK*, T6302. *Transtur*, T5314. *Cubataxi* to Playa Ancón, up to 5 people, from the bus terminal US$10 1 way, 15 mins. To Topes de Collantes, up to 4 people, US$25 return with 3-hr wait there. **Bicycles** and scooters can be hired from *Ruinas de Brunet*, see above.

Long distance **Air** Flights to Havana, Tue, Thu, Sat, 0955 (and 1630 via Cienfuegos, Varadero, Cayo Largo), US$50. **Bus** Terminal entrance on Gustavo Izquierdo, near the corner with Piro Guinart, office open 0600-1700, T4448. *Víazul* from Havana 0815, 1300, via Cienfuegos, arriving 1400, 1800, US$25, returning 0700, 1515; from Varadero via Santa Clara and Sancti Spíritus at 0730, arriving 1405, US$20, returning 1440. *Víazul* also runs Trinidad-Santiago 0815, 12 hrs, US$33, via Sancti Spíritus, Jatibonico, Ciego de Avila, Florida, Camagüey, Sibanicú, Guáimaro, Las Tunas, Holguín, Bayamo and Palma Soriano, returning from Santiago at 1900 overnight. *Astro* daily services to Havana, Sancti Spíritus, Cienfuegos, Santa Clara, cheaper, slower, less comfortable. Ticket office open daily, 0800-1200, 1330-1700. **Train** The station is south of the town, walk south straight down Lino Pérez until you get to the railway line and turn left. The old building once used for the trains has been renovated as the School of Art; the office is now about 100 m to the right, T3348. Local services only. Tourists can take a trip on a 1907 steam train daily at 0930, US$10. Best to buy ticket at an agency (*Rumbos*, *Cubatur*, etc).

Directory **Banks** *Bandec* is on José Martí 264 entre Zerquera y Colón, T2405, open Mon-Fri 0800-1700, Sat 0800-1600, will change TCs for dollars and cash advances on credit cards. *Cadeca* on Martí 164, T6262/3, half a block from Parque Céspedes, open Mon-Sat 0830-1730, Sun 0830-1200. There are *cambios* in *Hotel Las Cuevas*, *Hotel Ancón* and *Hotel Costa Sur*. **Communications** **Internet**: Access is available at *Las Begonias*, Maceo entre FJ Zerquera y Simón Bolívar, 4 terminals, US$1 for 10 mins, US$5 per hr, passport required, open 0900-1300, 1500-2100 Mon-Fri, 0900-1300 Sat-Sun. *Etecsa*, in Parque Céspedes, also has email facilities using the prepaid card system. **Post office**: Antonio Maceo 418 entre Zerquera y Colón, also for international **telephones**, open Mon-Sat 0900-1800, Sun 0900-1700. Another small post office and *Etecsa* telephone/fax/internet office on Gral Lino Pérez, Parque Céspedes, beside Iglesia San Francisco, open 0700-2300. **Medical services** *Clínica Internacional*, Lino Pérez 103 esq Anastasio Cárdenas, T6492, F6240, modern, with out-patient consultations, laboratory tests, X-rays, pharmacy, dentistry, massage and 24-hr emergency care. A consultation fee is US$25, a call out fee US$50. After 1600 prices rise.

Playa Ancón The best beach resort near Trinidad is Playa Ancón, not a town as such, just three resort hotels of varying quality, none of them recommended. The beach is white sand and clean turquoise water, but sand flies appear after 1600. The best part of the beach is right in front of the *Hotel Ancón*, where there are straw sunshades and beach loungers. The rest of the beach has little shade. People are sometimes disappointed when they come here and expect something more spectacular, but it is very pleasant for a day trip out of Trinidad. There is good **diving** and **snorkelling** less than 300 m offshore; US$42 for one dive with all equipment, US$55 for two, boat trip to the reef for snorkelling US$8 for 45 minutes.

Transport There is a yellow bus, called *Tren Turístico*, with 2 carriages, US$2 (pay on board), 15 mins, 0815, 1030, 1230, 1600, from outside *Cubatur* in Trinidad and other stops. Returning from *Hotel Ancón* and intermediate hotels at 0900, 1115, 1400, 1630. Cancelled if it rains. Taxis usually charge US$6-8 one way, cocotaxis US$4 one way. To La Boca is half the fare to Ancón.

Sancti Spíritus
Phone code: 41
Colour map 1, grid B4
Population: 80,000

Sancti Spíritus, the provincial capital, is about 80 km northeast of Trinidad and 90 km southeast of Santa Clara. Like Trinidad, the town was founded by Diego Velázquez in 1514 and is one of Cuba's seven original Spanish towns and has a wealth of buildings from the colonial period. The **Iglesia Parroquial Mayor del Espíritu Santo**, on Plaza Honorato, dates from 1522 when it was a wooden construction. Fray Bartolomé de las Casas gave his famous sermon here, marking the start of his campaign to help the indigenous people. The present building, of stone, replaced the earlier one in 1680, but it is acknowledged as the oldest church in Cuba because it still stands on its original foundations. The church is a National Monument, but it is not always open so you may not be able to look inside. The **Puente Yayabo** is considered a particular feature of Sancti Spíritus and is the only one of its type left on the island. The bridge was built in 1815 with five arches made of lime, sand and bricks. It is now also a National Monument. The river itself has given its name to the *guayaba*, or guava, which grows along its banks, and also to the *guayabera*, a loose man's shirt without a tail worn outside the trousers and without a tie. The former **Teatro Principal** next to the bridge was built in 1839 and was the scene of all the major cultural, social and political events of the city.

Ciego de Avila was founded in 1849, and is an agricultural market town with a large thermal electricity plant. The main road from Havana to Camagüey passes straight through the middle of town; most people just keep going. The main square is the **Parque Martí**, with a church and the former town hall, **Ayuntamiento**, built in 1911, and now the provincial government headquarters. There are a couple of basic hotels, *casas particulares*, and the usual crop of low quality state run restaurants if you have to spend the night. There is an airport at **Ceballos**, 24 km north of Ciego de Avila, Aeropuerto Máximo Gómez (AVI), which receives weekly scheduled flights from European cities, as well as twice weekly flights from Havana with *Cubana*. Charter flights also use this airport to get holiday-makers out to the resort hotels on Cayo Coco.

Ciego de Avila
Phone code: 33
Colour map 1, grid B4
Population: 85,000

Cayo Coco is a large island, 374 sq km, of mostly mangrove and bush, which shelter many migratory birds as well as permanent residents. The island is connected to the mainland just north of Morón by a 27-km causeway across the Bahía de Perros. The Atlantic side of the island has excellent beaches, particularly **Playa los Flamencos**, with some 5 km of white sand and shallow, crystalline water. At certain times of the year you will see flamingos, after whom the beach is named. A nature reserve, **El Bagá**, opened in 2002 and great emphasis is placed on preserving the wide variety of flora and fauna species, many of which are endemic to the zone. Cayo Coco is very isolated and nearly all foreigners are here on an all-inclusive package of a week or so and do not go far. Marina Puertosol offers deep-sea fishing and there is good diving. There are large, luxury resorts and plans to build an average of 1,000 hotel rooms a year, all four or five star, until Cayo Coco has 16,000 and the other cays have a further 6,000. In 2003 there were 11 hotels with 3,300 rooms in Coco and Guillermo. A golf course and marina for 400 yachts are also in the works.

Cayo Coco
Phone code: 33
Colour map 1, grid B4

Cayo Guillermo, a 13-sq-km cay with 5 km of beach, is connected to Cayo Coco by a causeway and there are plans to build a 35-km causeway to link it with Cayo Santa María to the west. Cayo Guillermo is protected by a long coral reef which is good for diving with plentiful fish and crustaceans, while on land there are lots of birds. Sand dunes, covered in palms and other vegetation, are believed to be in the highest in the Caribbean.

Only tour buses go to Cayo Coco, there are no public buses and a checkpoint at the beginning of the causeway effectively prevents Cubans without permission from visiting the cay. The new, Jardines del Rey international airport was inaugurated in December 2002, the eleventh international airport in the country.

Camagüey

Camagüey has been politically and historically important since the beginning of the 16th century and still has a lot of well-preserved colonial buildings, most dating from the 18th and 19th centuries. Many generations of revolutionaries have been associated with Camagüey and several key figures are commemorated, the most notable being Ignacio Agramonte, who was killed in action in 1873.

Phone code: 32
Colour map 1, grid B4
Population: 772,000

Until 9 June 1903,
the town was
called Puerto Príncipe

The village of Santa María de Puerto del Príncipe was first founded in 1515 at Punta del Guincho in the Bahía de Nuevitas but moved several times until it was finally established between the Río Tínima and the Río Hatibonico. Moving inland was no protection against pirate attacks. It was the target of the Englishman Henry Morgan in 1668 and of French pirates led by François Granmont in 1679. Architects took the precaution of designing the layout to foil pirate attacks. No two streets run parallel, to create a maze effect, which is most unlike other colonial towns built on the grid system.

Nuestra Señora de la Merced, a National Monument on Avenida Agramonte on the edge of the Plaza de los Trabajadores, was built in 1747 as a church and convent, the catacomb can still be seen. The original wooden cross on the bell tower was moved into the catacombs in 1999. On the walls are 17th and 18th-century paintings, but the most important treasure in the church is the Santo Sepulcro constructed in 1762 with the donation of 23,000 silver coins. **Nuestra Señora de la Soledad**, on República esquina Agramonte, is the oldest church in town. In 1697-1701 a hermitage was built. In 1733 the current church was started, although construction was not finished until 1776. **San Juan de Dios**, another National Monument, was built in 1728 as a church with a hospital attached, the first hospital in the village for men which also contained a home for the aged. Apparently this is the only church in Latin America which has the Holy Trinity as its central image. **Nuestra Señora del Carmen**, on Plaza Carmen, was started in 1732 but soon demolished for being too far out of town. It was later the site of the women's hospital of Nuestra Señora del Carmen, which was finished in 1825. A church was built alongside the hospital, with a second tower added in 1846, making it the only two-towered church in Camagüey. Part of the church collapsed in 1966 but restoration started in January 2001. The whole of the Plaza del Carmen is being renovated, a task which will include housing as well as opening smart new restaurants and tourist shops.

The **Museo Casa Natal Ignacio Agramonte** is for serious students of revolutionary history. Ignacio Agramonte y Loynaz, one of the national heroes of the struggle against the Spanish, was born here on 23 December 1841. The top floor is a museum dedicated to his life. ■ *Tue-Sat 1000-1800. US$2. Av Ignacio Agramonte 49, T297116.*

Sleeping **C-D** *Gran Hotel* (Islazul), Maceo 67, entre Ignacio Agramonte y General Gómez, T292093-4, comazul@teleda.get.cma.net. Colonial style, built 1939, renovated 1997, very smart now, central, breakfast included, a/c, fan, cable TV, fridge, good bathroom, best rooms with balcony overlooking Maceo, security box rental, car hire, small swimming pool with children's area, restaurant on top floor, good view, also piano bar, snack bar (see Entertainment). **D** *Colón* (Accor/Islazul), República 472 entre San José y San Martín, T283346, 283368, no fax. Old style built in 1920s, beautifully painted blue and white, marble staircase, long thin hotel on 2 floors round central well, rocking chairs overlook patio bar and restaurant, rooms with 1 or 2 beds, a/c, TV, phone, good bathroom, TV, lobby bar, friendly staff. **F** *América* Avellaneda at the intersection with San Martín, T82135. Small, cosy hotel with a/c, nice variety of dishes in the restaurant, bar.

Rooms cost US$15-20,
depending on
commission, breakfast
usually US$2-3, dinner
US$5-7 if available

Casas particulares **F** *Caridad García Valua*, Oscar Primelles 310 A entre Bartolomé Masó y Padre Olallo (Pobres), T291554. 2 rooms with private bathrooms, a/c or fan, fridge, garden, clean and nice. **F** *Casa Manolo*, Santa Rita 18 (El Solitario) entre República y Santa Rosa, T94403. Run by Migdalia Carmenates y Manolo Rodríguez, 3 rooms, a/c, fan, 2 share bathroom, 1 en suite, hot shower, garden, laundry US$2, garage US$2, nice house, newly painted, positive atmosphere, extremely helpful landlady. **F** *Casa Rosello*, Carlos M de Céspedes 260 (Hospital) entre Hnos Agüeros y San Ramón, T92143/96879, ask for Pedro. 2 beautiful rooms, bathroom, owner practices *Santería* and will show you some interesting things, garage opposite, US$1 per night. **F** *El Hostal de Lita*, Padre Olallo (Pobres) 524, entre Ignacio Agramonte y Montera, T291065. Beautiful colonial house, good reports. **F** *Hospedaje Colonial Los Vitrales*, Avellanada 3 entre Gral Gómez y Martí, T295866. Run by Rafael Requejo, an architect, and his family, 2 rooms sleep 2-3, garage for 3 cars, Rafael has great plans for improving the house and courtyard. **F** *Jorge Saéz Solano*, San Ramón 239 entre San Martín y Heredia, T286456. 2 rooms each with double and single bed, shared good bathroom between them, communicating doors, a/c, fan, bedside light, sheets rather small, hot water if turned on 15 mins in advance, laundry on request, friendly family, no *chicas* allowed, don't touch the Dobermann.

Renovation of colonial buildings has led to a proliferation of smart, overpriced, state-run restaurants with fairly mediocre food but in very attractive locations. On the Plaza de San Juan there are the *Parador de los Tres Reyes* and the *Campana de Toledo*, 2 small colonial-style Rumbos restaurants serving Spanish food, live music. The latter has tables overlooking the square or in the courtyard, chicken/fish US$5-6, moros y cristianos US$1.50. At the entrance to Plaza del Carmen is *El Ovejito*, T292524. Main course US$10-30, moros y cristianos US$4, mojito an extortionate US$5.50. *Don Ronquillo*, at the back of Cubanacán Galería Colonial, Ignacio Agramonte esq República. Used by tour parties with set lunch and live music for US$10, reasonably priced, most dishes US$5-10, beer US$1, *mojito* US$1. At the cheap end of the scale are *Rancho Luna*, on east side of Plaza Maceo, open 1200-1400, 1800-2200, and *La Volanta*, on Parque Agramonte, open 1200-2300, both of which offer basic Cuban food, no frills, and you will be asked to pay in dollars. You can pay in pesos at *Pizzería La Piazza* on Agramonte on the corner with Maceo, but there may be a queue at lunchtime. Near the railway station there is *El Paradero* cafetería and bar open 24 hrs and a bakery and cafetería also open 24 hrs. There are several shops to buy food, but to find out how the locals cope, go to the Agromercado near the river. As well as fruit and vegetables there is a small place where you can order cooked food an buy snacks.

Eating
Restaurants have a reputation for reheating leftovers, paladares can be expensive, casas particulares are best for fresh, wholesome cooking

Every Sat night a *Noche Camagüeya* is held along República, when the street is closed to traffic and there is music everywhere and traditional food. On Sun morning there are activities in Parque Casino Campestre, including live music. Folk music is played at the *Casa de la Trova*, on the west side of Parque Agramonte between Martí and Cristo, closed Mon. It has a courtyard and bar, while at the entrance is a souvenir shop where you can buy music. The *Gran Hotel*, has several bars with entertainment: *Piano Bar Marquesina*, US$5 for 2 people Mon-Fri, US$10 per couple on Sat, Sun, includes 2 meals and beer or rum; *Bar Piscina 1920*, US$3 per person (US$1 entrance, US$2 drinks), or US$10 Sat, Sun per couple including meal, beer/rum, with *ballet acuático* at 2130; *Bar El Mirador*, US$1 per person. *Disco Labarra*, República entre O Primelles (San Estéban) y Santa Rita, opposite the Cadeca, popular with younger crowd. *Disco Café*, Independencia entre Martí y Plaza Maceo, good late night place. Also cabaret/disco in *Hotel Camagüey*, and night club in *Puerto Príncipe*. *Galería Colonial*, Ignacio Agramonte y República, has cabaret 3 times a week. Can be rented for private functions. The **Ballet de Camagüey**, ranked 2nd in the country after Havana's ballet company, often performs at the Teatro Principal, on Padre Valencia 64, T293048. There are 3 cinemas: *Casablanca*, T292244, *Guerrero*, T292874 and *Encanto*, T295511.

Entertainment

Local Car hire: *Havanautos* is at *Hotel Camagüey*, T272239 and at airport T287068. There are Servi Cupet gas stations by the river on Carretera Central with Av de la Libertad, and a couple of blocks further south on the other side of the Carretera Central. **Taxi:** *Cubataxi*, T281247/298721.Bicitaxis charge about US$1 per person, fix price in advance.

Transport

Long distance Air Ignacio Agramonte International Airport (CMW) is 9 km from the centre on the road to Nuevitas, T261010. *Cubana* flies daily from Havana. There are also charter flights from Toronto and Europe depending on the season. **Bus** The Interprovincial bus station is southwest of the centre along the Carretera Central Oeste, esq Perú. *Astro* T271668. *Víazul*, T272346/271646, stops here on its Havana-Santiago and Trinidad-Santiago routes.

Train Railway station, T292633/281525. Train ticket agency, T283214. Foreigners pay in dollars at Ladis office upstairs above the main ticket office opposite *Hotel Plaza*. Trains to/from **Havana** daily, usually in the night.

Airlines *Cubana*, República 400 esq Correa, open Mon-Fri 0815-1600, T292156, 291338. **Banks** *Banco Financiero Internacional*, Plaza Maceo, T294846. There is a *cadeca* on República entre Primelles y Santa Rita, T295220. *Bandec,* Plaza de los Trabajadores, open 0800-1400 Mon-Fri, 0800-1200 Sat, Visa accepted. **Medical services** 24-hr pharmacy, Avellaneda esq Primelles.

Directory

Playa Santa Lucía

Cuba

Phone code: 32
Colour map 1, grid B5

Santa Lucía is a beach resort 112 km northeast of Camagüey, where the sand stretches some 20 km along the northern coast. You can sometimes see dolphins and there are flamingos in the salt flats (*saliñas*) inshore. This is a beautiful beach, protected by a reef which contains over 50 species of coral and is much sought after by divers. There are 37 dive sites at depths of 5-40 m in the area including a daily shark-feeding site where up to 20 sharks congregate; some of them swim in between the divers. Contact *Shark's Friends Dive Centre* T336404, who charge US$70. It is a lovely place to come and relax but it is remote, there is no real town, and people who stay here are on all-inclusive package tours. **Playa Los Cocos**, 8 km from Santa Lucía, is even better than Santa Lucía. There is a broad sweep of beach with a fishing village, La Boca, at one end and beach bars at the other end by the channel which leads to Nuevitas. There are lots of coconut palms after which the beach gets its name. The sand here is very white and the water crystal clear. Across the channel, west of Playa Los Cocos, is **Cayo Sabinal**, reached by road from Nuevitas or by boat from Santa Lucía. There are beautiful beaches of white sand which are practically deserted and the cay is a wildlife reserve housing the largest colony of pink flamingos in the Caribbean, plus many other birds which are rare or endangered elsewhere.

Sleeping
It is possible to stay in casas particulares at Playa Santa Lucía and Playa Los Cocos, but they are illegal

The resort is part of the Cubanacán group (www.cubanacan.cu), including joint venture hotels, restaurants, shopping centre, watersports, discos, tennis and other land sports and activities. All the hotels are all-inclusive and prices are per person sharing a double room. **A-C** *Club Cuatro Vientos*, T336360, F334533, aloja@cvientos.stl.cyt.cu 404 rooms and 8 suites, thatched and a bit tatty but supposedly 4-star, marina, scuba diving. **B** *Club Mayanabo*, T365168, F365176, aloja@mayanabo.stl.cyt.cu One of the older hotels, 3-star, 212 rooms and 13 suites. **B-C** *Vita Club Caracol*, T336402-3, secre@vitaclub.stl.cyt.cu In large gardens, 3-star, 150 2-storey cabañas with sea view. **B** *Club Santa Lucía*, T365146-8, aloja@coral.stl.cyt.cu Newish, low buildings and cabins, considered one of the best, 108 rooms on the beach, 144 garden rooms and 108 suites. **D** *Villa Tararaco*, T365184, 336310. The oldest, cheapest and furthest north, 2-star, 30 rooms.

Eating
Las Brisas, near the junction in the residential area, T322340, Creole, and *Luna Mar*, at the Centro Comercial, T326284, Italian. There are also *paladares* where you can eat for at a reasonable price.

Transport
Air International flights use the airport near Camagüey, but there is a small airstrip, Joaquín de Agüero, for Aerotaxi services. *Cubana*, in *Club Mayanabo*, T365352.

Bus *Víazul*, runs a minibus from Camagüey to Playa Los Cocos for day trips to the beach according to demand, picking you up at your hotel or *casa particular*, leaving Camagüey at 0900, returning at 1600, 1hr 40 mins, US$12 return, phone the driver, Jesús, T283988, to see if he is going. **Car hire** Rental desks at the hotels or just outside them. *Servi Cupet* fuel station at the junction as you arrive at Playa Santa Lucía. **Taxi** *Cubataxi*, Av Principal La Concha, T336196. Horse drawn carriages are used for local taxi journeys.

Directory
Banks *Bandec*, in the residential area where the workers live; hotels will change money if you need it. Only US dollars accepted here. **Communications** Post office and *Etecsa* are by *Servi Cupet* at the main junction. Email is available. **Medical services** *Clínica Internacional*, T365292,336203.

Holguín

Phone code: 24
Colour map 1, grid B5
Population: 250,000

Holguín was founded in 1545, but most of the architecture dates from the 19th and 20th centuries. It is known as the 'city of the parks', four of which, **Parque Infantil**, **Parque Carlos Manuel de Céspedes** (also known as Parque San José), the **Plaza Central** (Plaza General Calixto García) and **Parque José Martí**, lie between the two main streets, Antonio Maceo and Libertad (Manduley). There is a statue of **Carlos**

Manuel de Céspedes in the park named after him. He is remembered for having freed his slaves on 10 October 1868 and starting the War of Independence. **General Calixto García Iñiguez** (statue in the centre of Plaza Central) was born in Holguín in 1839 and took part in both wars of Independence. He captured the town from the Spanish in 1872 and again occupied it in 1898 after helping the US forces defeat the colonial power in Santiago de Cuba. His birthplace on Calle Miró 147, one block from the plaza, is now a National Monument and a museum, **Casa Natal de Calixto García**. ■ *Mon-Fri 0800-1700, Sat 0800-1300. US$1.* On the north side of the square is the **Museo Provincial**, built between 1860-1868 and now a National Monument. The most important item on display here is the Hacha de Holguín, a pre-Columbian axe head carved with the head of a man, found in 1860 on one of the hills around the city and believed to be about 500 years old. It has become the symbol of Holguín. ■ *Mon-Fri 0900-1700, Sat 0900-1300, US$1. US$3 with camera.* Renovation work is taking place to restore the **Plaza de la Maqueta** southwest of the Plaza Central between Mártires and Máximo Gómez. The old market building is being reconstructed in the centre and shops, galleries and a hotel are in progress around the outside.

Above the city is **La Loma de la Cruz**, a strategic hill which used to have a cross on top until Hurricane Georges blew it down in 1998. On 3 May 1790, a Franciscan priest, Antonio de Alegría, came with a group of religious people and put up the cross. In 1929 stone steps were begun up the hill, which were finished 3 May 1950. Every 3 May locals celebrate the Romerías de la Cruz de Mayo. They light candles and offer coins.

Sleeping

D-E *Pernik* (Islazul), T481011. Near Plaza de la Revolución on Av Jorge Dimitrov y Av XX Aniversario. 202 rooms, mostly overnighters passing through, shops, bar, restaurant, empty swimming pool, TV, a/c, nice view from top floor rooms, blue furniture, small bathrooms, adequate. **D-E***Villa El Bosque* (Islazul), T481012, just off Av Jorge Dimitrov. 69 rooms in spread out villas, patio garden, fridge, basic shower room, TV, a/c, also 2 suites, **C**, good security, car rental, large pool, *El Pétalo* disco, popular. **D-E** *El Mirador de Mayabe* (Islazul), T422160, T/F425347, outside the town, 24 rooms in cabins under the trees, tiled floors, a/c, TV, wooden furniture, fridge, hot water, adequate bathroom, quiet, also a suite and **C** 4 rooms in a house at the top of the hill with a fantastic view. Popular for a day trip, for lunch and to see Pancho, the beer-drinking donkey.

Casas particulares E-F *José Pavón*, José A Cardet 180-F-1, T422687. Family runs restaurant but has an apartment to rent. **F** *Antonio Ochoa*, Morales Lemus 199 entre Martí y Frexes, T423659. Spanish-style house with courtyard, light and airy, 2 rooms with bathrooms, one has independent access through garage, 3 generations live here, English spoken by Antonio's sons, welcoming family, discounts for long stays, a/c, fan, hot water, towels, laundry. **F** *Evaristo Bofill and Mirtha Lago*, Luz Caballero 78 Altos entre Miró y Morales Lemus. 2 large rooms, very clean, private bathroom, a/c, terrace, friendly and helpful family who make you feel at home and like a good laugh. **F** *Luís Turbay y Marya Ferrás*, Agramonte 68 entre Progreso y Río Marañón, T461000. The whole of the first floor is to let, including 2 bedrooms, huge kitchen, 2 bathrooms, a/c, TV, VCR, great place but often booked by long-stay guests, welcoming owners. **F** *Rolando Torres Cardet*, José Antonio Cardet 202 entre Frexes y Aguilera, T425619. Very clean, a/c, free coffee, central. **F** *Rosalía Días V*, Frexes 176 entre Miró y Morales Lemus, T423395. Excellent location, big room with bathroom, a/c, run by charming elderly lady.

Ask if food is available, not all families pay tax to provide food

Eating

There are several *paladares*. *Jelly Boom*, on Martí, near the cemetery. *La Malagüeña*, Martí entre Maceo y Mártires. 4 tables, can get very busy at weekends, long queue, accepts pesos or dollars. *Las Galicias*, Martí entre Fomento y Cervantes, in front of *Turquino*. 4 tables, small, criollo food. *Ramón*, Rastro 57 entre Frexes y Pérez Zorilla, next to the telephone *cabina*. Ramón is the owner, good food. *El Cauto*, Martí esq Morales Lemus. On the corner, pleasant, reasonable criollo food, beer, rum, pizza, open 1200-2400, accepts pesos and dollars. *1720*, Frexes esq Miró. Rumbos restaurant, bar, shows, information, souvenirs, in nicely restored blue and white building. *La Begonia*, is a Rumbos *cafetería* on the Plaza Central. Outdoors under a flowering creeper, very pretty, good for a Mayabe beer, meeting place for *jineteras*. *El Tocororo*, across the

Cuba

square, also Rumbos but toasted sandwiches are cheaper here, open 24 hrs, wooden sculpture above door. *Cafetería Cristal*, corner of plaza with Libertad. On 3 floors, cafetería on ground floor, open 24 hrs, usual range of fastish food, disco *Diskaraoke* on first floor, restaurant *Isla Cristal* on top floor, open 1200-1545, 1830-2245. For ice cream, **Coppelia** is on Parque Peralta. *La Crema*, on Libertad just north of Plaza Central, is a bakery and sweet shop.

Entertainment   *Casa de la Trova* on Plaza Calixto García between *Casa de la Cultura* and *La Begonia*, open daily except Mon, good music and dance, notice board outside announcing what's on that night, small stage, bar, salón, you can hear it all from the plaza outside. *Cabaret El Nocturno*, on road to Las Tunas, show with different Latin American music followed by salsa and disco. *Bolera*, Parque Infantil, bowling, electronic games and other indoor games, US$0.50 entrance.

Transport   **Local** There is very little motorized public transport. The city is choked with *bicitaxis*, or *The family vehicle* horse-drawn buses and taxis, charging 50-80 centavos. **Long distance   Bus**: The interurban bus *is a bicycle* terminal is on Av de los Libertadores after the coffee-roasting plant and opposite the turning to *with side car* Estadio Calixto García. The interprovincial bus terminal is west of the centre on the Carretera Central. You can walk along Frexes from the centre, but it is hot with luggage. A *bicitaxi* costs US$2. *Astro* and *Víazul* (T461036/422111) buses stop here. Daily services on the Havana-Santiago route.

Directory   **Airlines** *Aerotaxi*, T462512. *Cubana* is in Edif Pico de Cristal, Libertad esq Martí, Policentro, T425707, F46811. *LTU* at the airport, F335360. **Banks** *Bandec*, Arias 159, open Mon-Fri 0800-1500. *Cadeca*, just south of Cristal building on Libertad, Visa, Mastercard. *Banco Financiero Internacional*, on Libertad just north of the Plaza Central, open Mon-Fri 0800-1500, last working day of the month 0800-1200, Mastercard, Visa, Tran$card. *Bancrédito*, on south side of Parque Céspedes, open Mon-Fri 0800-1500, Visa, Mastercard. **Communications   Post office and internet**, Maceo, opposite Parque Céspedes. 2 terminals for email with prepaid *tarjetas*. Small post office with telephones and *DHL* on Libertad, Plaza Central, open Mon-Fri 1000-1200, 1300-1600, alternate Sat 0800-1500, 1 computer terminal for email access with prepaid *tarjetas*.

Guardalavaca

Phone code: 24   Guardalavaca has been developed as a tourist resort along a beautiful stretch of coast-*Colour map 1, grid B6* line, indented with horseshoe bays and sandy beaches. The resort is in several sections: the older part is rather like a village, apartments for workers are here and there are a few shops, discos, bank, restaurant and bus stop, while newer hotels further west on the beaches Estero Ciego (also referred to as Playa Esmeralda), Playa Pesquero Viejo and Playa Pesquero Nuevo are very isolated and there is nothing to do outside the hotels. There is a reef offshore for diving, which is very unspoilt and has a lot to offer.

Excursions   The lagoon in the **Bahía de Naranjo** has a small marina, where sailing trips and fishing expeditions can be arranged. Near the mouth of the lagoon is an aquarium, 10 minutes by boat from the dock, with dolphins and a sea lion, and a restaurant. At the mouth of the bay on the west side, is **El Birancito**, a replica of where Fidel Castro was born. A few km from Guardalavaca on a hill with a wonderful view, is the **Museo Aborigen Chorro de Maita**, a small but well-presented museum displaying a collection of 56 skeletons dating from 1490-1540, exactly as they were found. One is of a young Spaniard of about 22 years of age with his arms crossed for a Christian burial, but the rest are Amerindians, buried in the Central American style, lying flat with their arms folded across their stomachs. ■ *Mon-Fri 0900-1700, Sun 0900-1300. US$2 entrance, US$1 per photo, plus US$5 per film, US$5 video. Small shop with souvenirs.* Also here is a replica of a Taíno village, with statues of Indians going about their daily activities. ■ *US$5.* The **Museo Indocubano Bani**, in **Banes** has a good collection of pre-Columbian artifacts, probably the best in Cuba. The town of Banes was originally the site of the Bani chieftancy and the museum contains treasures discovered by the many archaeological digs in the area. ■ *Tue-Sat 0900-1700, Sun 0800-1200, US$1. Gen Marrero 305 y Av José Martí.*

On Playa Guardalavaca: **L-B** *Delta Las Brisas* (Cubanacán), T30218, F30018, reserva@ deltsbsa.gvc.gyt.cu All-inclusive, 349 good sized sea view or inland rooms, 84 mini-suites, non-motorized watersports, small beach, pool, entertainment, gym, tennis, bicycles, kids camp, tour desk, car rental. **AL-C** *Atlántico* (Cubanacán), T30180/30280, F30200, recep@ hatlant.gvc.cyt.cu Best position right on beach, 264 rooms with shower, long dark corridors, adequate but nothing special for the price, good food, set meal times, bicycles, windsurfing, pedalos, sailing, diving, snorkelling, gym, entertainment, shops, pool, tennis. **A** *Villa Turey*, opposite bus stop. Not on beach, spread out villas and apartments around pool, 136 rooms, 3 suites (with 2 bedrooms, 2 bathrooms upstairs, sitting room, kitchenette and toilet downstairs), short walk to beach through other hotels. **AL-C** *Club Amigo Guardalavaca* (Cubanacán), T30121, F30221, recep@hguard.gvc.cyt.cu 234 rooms, TV, renovated 2001, tennis courts.

On Playa Esmeralda: 3 all-inclusive hotels in the Sol Meliá group. **On Playa Pesquero Viejo and Playa Pesquero Nuevo**: several more all-inclusive hotels, including the largest in Cuba, the *Playa Pesquero* (Gaviota) with 944 rooms, which opened in 2002, *Sol Club Playa Pesquero*, *Superclubs Breezes*, *LTI Costa Verde Beach Resort*. A *Club Med* is being built. **At Playa Blanca**: **D** *Club Amigo Don Lino* (Cubanacán), T4977. Recently renovated. Good for the price, clean, good beach, reasonable food, price, CP. Cubans come here on holiday and there are *cabañas* for rent.

Bayamo

Bayamo is the capital of the province of Granma. It was the second town founded by Diego Velázquez in November 1513 and has been declared a Ciudad Monumento Nacional. It was burned to the ground in 1869 as an act of rebellion against the colonial Spanish, so there is little colonial architecture. The **Iglesia de Santísimo Salvador** in the Plaza del Himno Nacional is a 16th-century church which was damaged by the 1869 fire, but is currently under restoration. **Casa Natal de Carlos Manuel de Céspedes** is a museum dedicated to the life of the main campaigner of the 1868 independence movement, who was born here. ■ *Tue-Sat 0900-1700, Sun 0900-1200. US$1. On Maceo.*

Public relations officers at the *Hotel Sierra Maestra* are very helpful with information on all tours in this area, whether you take one of their organized ones or not. There is a trip to the **Parque Nacional Sierra Maestra**, taking you by truck from *Villa Santo Domingo*, 20 km south of Bartolomé Masó, to **Alto de Naranjo**, then a 3-km walk to the **Comandancia de la Plata**, Castro's mountain base prior to the Revolution. Photographs are not allowed here. Although this part of the mountains is usually open, from time to time the national park is closed for environmental or security reasons. Check with Islazul or the Campismo reservations office in town (General García 115 entre Lora y Masó, T424200) for latest reports. There is a chain across the road. **Pico Turquino** can also be visited on this route if access is permitted. If doing it independently, you can hike, cycle or drive from Bartolomé Masó to Santo Domingo, high in the Sierra Maestra.

C *Sierra Maestra* (Islazul), Carretera Central via Santiago de Cuba, T481013, 2 km from city centre. 204 rooms, delightful post-Revolution 1960s building, thoroughly kitsch interior, avoid rooms overlooking noisy pool, plenty of nightlife, 3 bars, disco, mostly Cubans, helpful staff, car hire, credit cards accepted. Cheaper is *Villa Bayamo* (2-star) on the Carretera Manzanillo km 5.5, T423102/423124. 34 rooms, 1 km from city centre. **E** *Royalton* (Islazul), on Maceo y Joaquín Palma, very central location, T422224. 33 rooms, a/c, private bathrooms, phones, restaurant, lobby bar and terrace bar open each night, toilets just beyond reception. **Casa particular F** *Ramón Enrique Alvarez Sánchez*, Pío Rosado 22 entre Ramírez y Av Fco Vte Aguilera, T423984. Enormous rooms, a/c, private bathroom, wife Carolina is a good cook.

Restaurante 1513, Gen García esq Gen Lora, T425921. Open 1200-2200, small but recommended. *La Casona*, Plaza del Himno Nacional, behind the church. Nice bar, cheap pizzas or spaghetti, courtyard at the back completely covered with flowering vine, open 1300-2200. *Tropicrema*, Parque Céspedes. Cake and ice cream, 1.80 pesos, good and popular.

Nightlife *Casa de la Trova* on the corner of Maspote and José Martí has shows during the afternoon and every night, quite touristy in high season. **Cabaret Bayamo** opposite *Hotel Sierra Maestra*, on Carretera Central, T421698. Open 2100-0200. Every Sat there is a *Noche Cubana*, when the whole of Gen García fills with stalls, ad hoc bars, pigs on spits, and the restaurants all put tables on the road. Everything is sold in pesos, even in the established bars.

Tour operators *Islazul* office on Gen García 207. Open 0830-1700, also tourist information in *Hotel Sierra Maestra* and occasionally maps, but they do not cater for many foreign visitors.

Transport **Local** Horse and cart, 7 pesos from bus station to *Hotel Sierra Maestra*. **Car hire**: the *Havanautos* office is in Cupet Cimex gas station next to the bus station, on road to Jiguaní, T423223.

Long distance **Air** Carlos Manuel de Céspedes Airport is 4 km out of town; flight to Havana 3 times a week. **Bus** The terminal is on the corner of Carretera Central and Jesús Rabi, T424036. *Víazul*, T424036, stops here for 5 mins on its Havana-Santiago route. There are also daytime buses to Santiago and to Guantánamo, occasionally there is a direct bus, otherwise change at Santiago. **Train** Station is at Saco y Línea. Daily trains to Santiago and Havana.

Directory **Banks** *Banco Nacional de Cuba*, Saco y Gen García. *Bandec*, Gen García 101. Visa and MC, open Mon-Fri 0800-1500. **Medical services** *Farmacia Principal Municipal*, 24-hr at Gen García 53.

Santiago de Cuba

Phone code: 226
Colour map 1, grid B6

Santiago de Cuba is one of the oldest towns on the island, protected from the sea in an attractive bay surrounded by mountains. It is a lively city with plenty of music and other cultural activities and the place to come for carnival in July, a raw, ebullient celebration. Santiago, Cuba's second city, is not a colonial gem along the lines of Havana or Trinidad, but it does have an eclectic range of architectural styles from colonial to art deco. The city centre is cluttered, featuring many beautiful pastel coloured buildings in better condition than many of those in the capital. There is a very Caribbean feel to life here, hot and steamy, both during the day and in the discos and bars as you dance the night away.

Getting there & around
See also page 140

Santiago can be reached by air, train or bus. International and domestic *Cubana* flights arrive at the **Antonio Maceo Airport** (SCU), 8 km south of the city on the coast. Taxis around US$5-8, depending on the company and the distance. The long-distance bus terminal is to the north of the city, by the Plaza de la Revolución. Outside are taxis, *colectivos*, trucks, buses and horse-drawn *coches*. The new railway station is more central, opposite the rum factory on Av Jesús Menéndez, and within walking distance of many *casas particulares* and some hotels.

Urban buses cost 20 centavos. There are also *coches*, 1 peso, motorbikes, US$1, and *bicitaxis*, US$0.50, for short journeys around town. Plaza Marte is a central hub for lots of local transport.

History Santiago de Cuba was one of the seven towns (*villas*) founded by Diego Velázquez. It was first built in 1515 on the mouth of the Río Paradas but moved in 1516 to its present location in a horseshoe valley surrounded by mountains. It was Cuba's capital city until replaced by Havana in 1553 and was capital of Oriente province until 1976. During the 17th century Santiago was besieged by pirates from France and England, leading to the construction of the Castillo del Morro, still intact and now housing the piracy museum. Because of its location, Santiago has been the scene of many migratory exchanges with other countries; it was the first city in Cuba to receive African slaves, many French fled here from the slaves' insurrection in Haiti in the 18th century and Jamaicans have also migrated here. Santiago is more of a truly ethnic blend than many other towns in Cuba. It is known as the *Ciudad Héroe* (heroic city) or *Capital moral de la Revolución Cubana*. One of Cuba's foremost revolutionaries of the 19th century, **General Antonio Maceo**, is honoured in the **Plaza de la Revolución**, to the northeast of the centre, with a dramatic monument made of galvanized steel in searing, solid Soviet style, and a gargantuan bronze statue of the general on horseback surrounded by huge iron machetes.

Parque Céspedes is in the centre of town and everything revolves around it. Most of the main museums are within easy walking distance. The *Hotel Casa Granda* flanks the east side of the small park. The **Cathedral**, Santa Iglesia Basílica Metropolitana, is on the south side, entrance on Félix Peña. The first building on the site was completed in 1524, but four subsequent disasters, including earthquakes and pirate attacks meant that the cathedral was rebuilt four times. ■ *Daily, 0800-1200.*

Sights

The **Cementerio Santa Ifigenia**, northwest of the city, features **José Martí's** mausoleum, a huge structure with a statue of Martí inside, designed to receive a shaft of sunlight all morning. Martí is surrounded by six statues of women, representing the six Cuban provinces of the 19th century. Also in the cemetery is the grave of **Frank País**, a prime mover in the revolutionary struggle and other notable figures such as Céspedes, the Bacardí family and the mother and widow of Maceo. There is a monument to the Moncada fallen and the tomb of Cuba's first president, Tomás Estrada Palma. Well worth a visit. ■ *US$1, extra US$1 to take pictures, price includes guided tour in Spanish and English. Av Crombet, Reparto Juan G Gómez.*

Of the several museums, the best is the **Museo de Ambiente Histórico Cubano**, at Diego Velázquez' house (the oldest in Cuba, started in 1516, completed 1530). Velázquez lived on the top floor, and the ground floor was a contracting house and a smelter for gold. Each room shows a particular period, featuring furniture, porcelain and crystal. ■ *Mon-Sun 0900-1700. US$2, with guided tour in English, French or German, camera fee US$1 per photo. At the northwest corner of Parque Céspedes, Félix Peña 612, T52652.*

Museums

The **Museo Emilio Bacardí**, was named after industrialist Emilio Bacardí Moreau, its main benefactor and collector of much of the museum's contents. This was the second museum founded in Cuba and has exhibits from prehistory to the Revolution downstairs, one of the most important collections of Cuban colonial paintings and the archaeology hall has mummies from Egypt and South America. ■ *Tue-Sat 1000-2000, Sun 1000-1800, Mon 1200-2000. Guided tour in English. US$2. 2 blocks east of the Parque, opposite the Palacio Provincial, entrance on Pío Rosado esq Aguilera, T28402.*

The **Museo Histórico 26 de Julio**, formerly the Moncada Garrison, was attacked (unsuccessfully) by Castro and his revolutionaries on 26 July 1953. When the Revolution triumphed in 1959, the building was turned into a school. To mark the 14th anniversary of the attack, one of the buildings was converted to a museum, featuring photos, plans and drawings of the battle. Bullet holes, filled in by Batista, have been reconstructed on the outer walls. ■ *Tue-Fri 0900-2000, Sat, Mon 0900-1700, Sun 0900-1300. US$1. Guided tour in English, French, Italian. Camera fee US$1, video camera US$5. Av Moncada esq Gen Portuondo, T20157.* The **Museo Casa Natal de Frank País**, is in the birthplace of the leader of the armed uprising in Santiago on 30 November 1956, who was shot in July 1957. ■ *Gen Banderas 226 y Los Maceos, T52710.* The **Museo de la Lucha Clandestina** highlights the support given by the local urban population during the battle in the Sierra Maestra. Exhibits revolve around Frank País, from his early moves to foment a revolutionary consciousness to his integration into the Movimiento 26 de Julio under Fidel Castro. ■ *0900-1900 Tue-Sat, 0900-1700 Sun. US$2. At the top of picturesque Padre Pico (steps) and corner of Santa Rita and Jesús Rabí, T24689.* The **Casa Natal de Antonio Maceo**, built between 1800-1830, was the birthplace, on 14 June 1845, of Antonio Maceo y Grajales, one of the greatest military commanders of the 1868 and 1895 wars of independence. The museum houses his biography and details of his 32 years' devotion to the struggle for independence. ■ *Mon-Sat 0900-1700. US$1. Los Maceo 207 entre Corona y Rastro, T23750.*

The **Museo del Carnaval** exhibits a collection of instruments, drums and costumes from Santiago's famous July carnival. If you are not going to be there in July, this is the best way to get a flavour of the celebrations. ■ *Tue-Sat 0900-1800, Sun 0900-1200. US$2. Daily dance show 1545. On Heredia esq Pío Rosado.* The **Casa del Caribe** is a

Cuba

world-renowned cultural centre. In *Santería* (see page 153) there is a musical and religious ceremony at 0930 on Wednesdays. ■ *Off Av Manduley on 13 esq 8.* The **Museo de la Religión** displays religious items particularly concerning *Santería*, but there are no written explanations of the exhibits, best to ask for a guide. ■ *Mon-Sat 0830-1700. Free. 13 206, esq 10.*

Santiago de Cuba

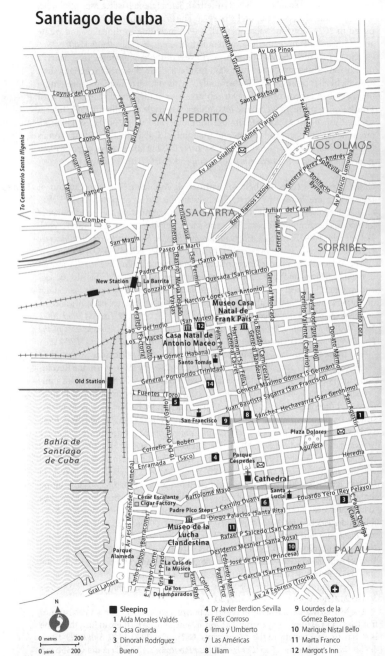

■ **Sleeping**
1 Aída Morales Valdés
2 Casa Granda
3 Dinorah Rodríguez Bueno
4 Dr Javier Berdion Sevilla
5 Félix Corroso
6 Irma y Umberto
7 Las Américas
8 Liliam
9 Lourdes de la Gómez Beaton
10 Marique Nistal Bello
11 Marta Franco
12 Margot's Inn

South of Santiago The Ruta Turística runs along the shore of the Bahía de Santiago to the **Castillo del Morro**, a clifftop fort with the **Museo de la Piratería**, a museum of the sea, piracy and local history, charting the pirate attacks made on Santiago during the 16th century. Pirates included the Frenchman Jacques de Sores and the Welshman Sir Henry Morgan, and you can see many of the weapons used in both

Santiago de Cuba centre

attack and defence of the city. From the roof you can admire the thrilling views over the Bay of Santiago and Cayo Granma and you can follow some 16th-century steps almost down to the waterline. ■ *US$4, cameras US$1. T91569. Restaurant on a terrace with a great view, main dish US$6. Turistaxi to El Morro, US$10 round trip with wait. Bus 212 from Plaza Marte or opposite the cinema Rialto, Parque Céspedes, stops in front of embarkation point for Cayo Granma.*

East of Santiago Excellent excursions can be made to the **Gran Piedra** (26 km east) a viewpoint from which it is said you can see Haiti and Jamaica on a clear day, more likely their lights on a clear night. It is a giant rock weighing 75,000 tonnes, 1,234-m high, and reached by climbing 454 steps from the road (only for the fit). The view is tremendous and buzzards circle you. ■ *US$1 to climb. There are no buses but a private car will charge you about US$15 there and back (hotel tour desks will arrange a tour, good value).*

Some 2 km before La Gran Piedra are the **Jardines de la Siberia**, on the site of a former coffee plantation, an extensive botanical garden; turn right and follow the track for about 1 km to reach the gardens. The **Museo La Isabelica** is at Carretera de la Gran Piedra Km 14, a ruined coffee plantation once owned by French emigrés from Haiti, the buildings of which are now turned into a museum housing the former kitchen and other facilities on the ground floor with farming tools and archaeological finds. Upstairs is the owners' house in 19th-century style. ■ *Tue-Sat 0900-1700, Sun 0900-1300. US$2.*

On the Carretera Siboney at Km 13½ is **La Granjita Siboney**, the farmhouse used as the headquarters for the revolutionaries' attack on the Moncada barracks on 26 July 1953. It now has a museum of uniforms, weapons and artefacts used by the 106 men who gathered here the night before, as well as extensive newspaper accounts of the attack. ■ *Tue-Sun 0900-1700. US$2. T9836.*

Siboney, 16 km east of the city, is the nearest beach to Santiago with a reef just offshore which is great for snorkelling. ■ *Take bus 214 from near bus terminal or truck from Av de los Libertadores outside the maternity hospital, 1 peso. Very crowded at weekends.* At Km 24 is the **Valle de la Prehistoria**, a huge park filled with life-size carved stone dinosaurs and stone age men. Great for kids but due to the total absence of shade it is like walking around a desert. Take huge supplies of water and try to go early or late. ■ *US$2, extra US$1 to take photos.*

Watch out for the touts; probably best to offer 50 cents or some pesos, otherwise they will be waiting for you when you leave the church

West of Santiago **El Sanctuario de Nuestra Señora de la Caridad del Cobre** ('El Cobre'), 10 km west of Santiago and home to the shrine of Cuba's patron saint, the Virgen de la Caridad del Cobre, is built over a working copper mine. The story goes that in the 17th century, three fishermen were about to capsize in Nipe Bay, when they found a wooden statue of the Virgin Mary floating in the sea. Their lives were saved and they brought the statue to its current resting place above the altar. Downstairs there are many tokens of gratitude left by Cubans who have been helped by the Virgin in some way. There is a pilgrimage here on 12 September. ■ *There is no bus, so either hire a car and driver, about US$8, or get on a truck at the bus station for a few pesos. Cover your shoulders or hire a coverall.*

Essentials

Sleeping **L-A** *Casa Granda* (Gran Caribe/Accor, managed by Sofitel), Heredia 201 entre San Pedro y San Félix, on Parque Céspedes, T686600, F686035. Elegant building opened in 1914 and patronized by many famous people. 4-star, a/c, laundry, car hire, satellite TV, pool, post office, 1 room for handicapped people, *Havanatur* and *Asistur* offices. **AL** *Meliá Santiago de Cuba* (Cubanacán), Av Las Américas entre 4 y M, Reparto Sueño, T687070, F687170, dircom@santiago.solmelia.cma.net 5-star, 302 rooms and suites, clean, good service, excellent breakfast buffet US$9, lots of bars and restaurants, good view of city from roof top bar, swimming pools open to day visitors for US$10, tennis, sauna, car hire, has business centre with internet access, post office, will change almost any currency into dollars, staff exceptionally helpful and friendly. **B-C** *Las Américas* (Horizontes), T642011, F687075, Av de las Américas esq Gen Cebreco, easy bus/truck access to centre, taxis around bus stop opposite hotel. Rebuilt, 68 rooms, 2 mini-suites, lively, high-quality restaurant, variety of dishes, non-residents may use pool where they have cultural shows every night, nice reception staff, safety deposit, *Cadeca*, shop, car and bicycle hire. **B-C** *Hotel San Juan* (Horizontes), km 1 Carretera a Siboney, T687200, F686137, hotel@sanjuan.scu.cyt.cu, out of town but nice location, *turistaxi* US$3.95, private car US$2. A complex with cabins, 110 very nice rooms, large, clean, hot water, large pool, bar, restaurants, good breakfast, accepts pesos, queues at weekends and during festivals, car hire, private car into town US$2. **D** *Villa Santiago de Cuba* (Gaviota), Av Manduley 502, entre 19 y 21, Reparto Vista Alegre, T641368/641346, F687166. 3-star, car hire, tourist office, nearby pool for guests, quiet, no credit cards. **E-F** *Rex*, Av Garzón 10, T626314. Clean, with toilet paper and towels, but the a/c is noisy and the water is not always on.

Casas particulares In the centre: **E-F** *Marta Franco*, Corona 802 bajos entre San Carlos y Santa Rita, T651882, very central, about 100 m west of Cathedral, apartment on ground floor of fairly modern block. 2 rooms, 1 with a/c, bathroom between them, hot shower, breakfast US$3, dinner US$6, meals taken in family room, very good food, helpful and friendly family. **E-F** *Manrique Nistal Bello*, Princesa 565 entre Carnicería y Calvario, T651909, abarreda@abt.uo.edu.cu 1 room with 1 bed, another with 2 beds, bathroom, fridge, good food in large portions, some English spoken. **E-F** *Irma y Umberto*, Santa Lucía 303 entre San Pedro y San Félix, T622391, close to Parque Céspedes. Brother and sister, live in huge house with their respective families, large room sleeps 3, private bathroom, patio. Umberto has a private taxi although he used to be a radiologist, very hospitable, caring people. **F** *Migdalia Gámez Rodríguez*, Corona 371 entre San Germán y Trinidad, T624569. Large, private room with shower, fan, quiet, friendly, great food. **F** *Margot's Inn*, San Fermín 207 entre Maceo y San Mateo. Quiet neighbourhood. Margot is in her 70s and lives with her son, Tony, an English teacher, nice people, 1 room sleeps 3, shower, hot water, a/c, fridge. **F** *Dinorah Rodríguez Bueno and William Pérez*, Diego Palacios (Santa Rita) 504 entre Reloj y Clarín, T625834. Dinorah speaks a little English, independent room with en suite bathroom, a/c, good food, patio, William and Dinorah are excellent sources of information and very helpful, 10-min walk from Parque Céspedes. **E-F** *Félix Corroso*, San Germán 165 entre Rastro y Gallo, T653720. Known as Garden House, 2 rooms, a/c, fan, nice garden, breakfast US$3, dinner US$6-8. **F** *Nercy y Oscar Montoto*, San Jerónimo 560, T652192. Self-contained, luxurious 1-bedroom modern apartment. Opposite is **F** *Marisloe y Ernesto*, San Jerónimo 555, same phone number, T652192. Private 1-bedroom apartment with traditional features, beautiful tiled floor, stained-glass windows, comfortable, friendly. **F** *Aída Morales Valdés*, Enramada 565 entre San Agustín y Barnada, T628612. Room with private bathroom, a/c, very good food, friendly family, central, only 1 block from Plaza Marte. **F** *Dr Javier Berdion Sevilla*, Corona 564 Apto B entre Enramadas y Aguilera, T622959. 2 rooms, double bed, a/c, hot water, shared bathroom, fridge, balcony, terrace, great view of the bay. **F** *Miriam Osorio Fonseca*, Aguilera 606 entre Barnarda y Plácido, T624723. 2 rooms with en suite bathrooms, fan, hot water, terrace. **F** *Lourdes de la Gómez Beaton*, Félix Peña 454 entre San Jerónimo y San Francisco, T654468. Large old house with patio, excellent accommodation in 2 rooms, bathroom, hospitable hostess. **F** *Liliam*, Hechavarría (San Jerónimo) 308 entre Hartmann (San Félix) y Lacret (San Pedro), T627236. Small, independent apartment, 2 bedrooms with twin beds, kitchen and bathroom, owner lives downstairs. **F** *Maraima Sánchez*, Hartmann entre Sagarra y Máximo Gómez, T652728. 2 double rooms, shared bathroom, use of kitchen, family atmosphere, very clean.

East of Ferreiro: **E-F** *Rubén Rodes Estrada*, 10 410 entre 15 y 17, Vista Alegre, T642611. Run by great (gay) couple, house painted red and yellow, giant cactus outside and inside, hot water, good food, US$5 huge breakfast and US$10 evening meal even bigger. They also have a good self-contained flat for the same price. **F** *Ana María González y César Falagón*, 12 308 entre 11 y 13, Rpto Vista Alegre, T642968. 2 lovely rooms, independent of the rest of the house, shared bathroom, nice residential area, owner is a doctor, elderly Dobermann for security. **F** *Laysol Matos Hernández*, Raúl Pujol 102 esq Aguilera, Rpto Terraza, T6627616. Large, modern house, a/c, hot water, private bathroom, fridge,

Touts hang around Parque Céspedes, also near all hotels and at the railway terminal exit

Cuba

pleasant terrace. **F** *Vicente Piñeiro González*, Bravo Correoso 407½ entre 11 y 12, Santa Bárbara. A/c bedroom, living room, private bathroom, hot water, use of kitchen, very nice couple. **F** *Omar Frómeta*, Anacaona 194 entre Alfredo Zayas y Bravo Correoso, Santa Bárbara. Nice apartment, a/c, hot water, terrace, balcony, private bathroom, fridge.

Eating In local restaurants the main dish is chicken, usually fried but sometimes with a garlic and onion sauce. A half chicken with fried green plantain (*tostones*), sweet potatoes (*boniato*) or chips costs 25 pesos, rice and beans (*congrí*) 2 pesos, salad 3 pesos, beer 10 pesos. You can find this sort of meal at the *Doña Yuya* chain, where they also serve things like smoked pork chops (*chuletas de cerdo ahumado*), veal (*ternera*) or thin steak (*bistec de palomilla*), costing around 25 pesos. Down town, *Santiago 1900*, San Basilio entre San Félix y Carnicería, also offers these basic meals.

Restaurants 3 restaurants run by *Rumbos* (*Combinado* is the collective name) on Plaza Dolores (known as Búlevar locally), Italian, Chinese (dodgy food, stomach troubles reported) and Creole food, quite expensive and low on local atmosphere; opposite them is *Matamoros*, which is better although prices are high with a system of US$1=1 peso; also *Las Enramadas*, Búlevar. Good atmosphere, cheap, basic food, nice setting. *La Taberna de Dolores*, Aguilera esq Reloj, T623913. Spanish food, 1900-2400, reasonable at around US$5 for main course.

Paladares Lots of good *paladares* (official ones have sign) around Calles Heredia and Aguilera, and in Reparto Vista Alegre, near hotels *Santiago*, *Las Américas* and *San Juan*. *Doña Cristina*, Padre Pico. Good reports. *El Balcón*, Independencia 253, Reparto Sueño, T627407. Good food, US$3, open 24 hrs, popular with locals. *Terrazas*, 5 50 entre M y Terraza, Ampliación de Terraza, T641491. On the upper floor, daily 1000-2400, tasty food, nicely presented, chicken US$6, pork US$5. If the gate is locked, whistle.

Street stalls Usually only open until early evening, some only at lunchtime. Snacks sold in pesos. Most things cost 1 peso. Avoid *fritos*, they are just fried lumps of dough; most reliable thing is cheese, pork or egg sandwich; pizza is usually a dry bit of dough with a few gratings of cheese. Lots of stalls along 'Ferreiro' or Av Victoriano Garzón, these are open later than others, especially up near *Hotel Las Américas*. Also lots around bus station on Libertadores and a few along the bottom part of Aguilera, between Parque Céspedes and Plaza Dolores.

Cafés The *Terrace Coffee Bar* at the *Casa Granda* is open 24 hrs and is a pleasant place for a drink, but the service ranges from bad to appalling, the *Roof Garden* at the top of the same hotel is open 2000-0300, *mojitos* US$1.65. *Café Ajedrez*, Enramada y Santo Tomás. open-air café in cool structure designed by Cuban architect, Walter A Betancourt Fernández. Coffee served only. *Casa del Té*, Aguilera esq Lacret. Grow their own herbs, cheap herbal tea available. *Coppelia* ice cream on Félix Peña under the cathedral, open Mon-Fri 1000-2100, Sat-Sun 1100-2200, no queuing if you have dollars, also at Av de los Libertadores y Victoriano Garzón. *Helado Alondra*, Garzón near junction with *Hotel Santiago*. Great ice creams and milk shakes, 0900-2200. *Isabelica*, Aguilera esq Plaza Dolores. Open 24 hrs, serves only coffee, US$0.85, cigars rolled, bohemian hangout, watch out for hustlers, serious hassling by *jineteros/as*.

Bars *Kontiki*, a popular dark bar, Enramada esq San Pedro. Terrace bar in *Hotel Casa Granda*, overlooking Parque Céspedes. *Las Columnitas*, outdoor dollar bar and café, 1 block from Enramada, San Félix y Callejón del Carmen. *Baturro*, Aguilera esq San Félix. Snacks, bar, reliable prices. The local speciality *Rocío del Gallo* is coffee and rum – ask for it at *Café Isabelica*, see above.

Entertainment
Check locally for cinema programmes and theatre performances

Cabaret San Pedro del Mar, Carretera del Morro, Islazul-run, US$5 taxi, US$5 entrance, reasonable food. *Club Tropicana Santiago*, Autopista Nacional Km 1.5, T643036, (restaurant 1200-2200). Local show with emphasis on the Caribbean and Santiaguerans, different from Havana's version and considered one of the best shows in Cuba, dancing on the stage after the show, open 2000-0300, closed Mon, US$50. There is a restaurant with a limited menu and drinks aren't cheap. Taxi, US$8-10. *Buró de Información Cultural*, Plaza Marte, has poetry, dance, live music in its patio bar, *Los Dos Abuelos*, 2230-0200. *Casa de la Música*, Corona 564 entre Aguilera y Enramada, F686225. Live Cuban music every night 2000-0300, US$5 entrance, sale of CDs and tapes, worth trying. *Casa de las Tradiciones*, also known as *La Casona*, Rabí entre José de Diego (Princesa) y García (San Fernando), large colonial house with central patio, live music for listening and dancing to, small bar, open 2030-0100, closed Tue, US$1. *Casa de la Trova*, Heredia 206, around the corner from *Casa Granda*. *Casa del Caribe* on 13 154 esq 8, T642285, great, authentic, Afro-Cuban music and dance at weekends, recommended if you like *folklórico*. *Casa de los Estudiantes*, Heredia, near *Casa Granda*. Live music Sun 1330, always popular, US$1. 2 daily shows of music, morning and evening, traditional, acoustic son music, open until 2400, US$1 and worth it, nice venue in beautiful building with patio where the bands play at night, also bar. Very friendly and welcoming, the bands are excellent and dancing is encouraged, particularly at night when you can expect hassling from locals wanting to dance with you. *Club La Iris*, Aguilera entre Paraíso y Barnarda. Disco daily 1000-1600, 2200-0400, snack bar, 24 hrs. *Sala de Conciertos Dolores* on Plaza Dolores has classical and choral concerts. Lively disco in *Santiago* and *Las Américas* hotels, to which Cubans are welcome, American disco music, hardly any salsa, *jinetera* pick-up places. *Disco Las Américas* closed Wed, entrance US$4 includes a drink. *Disco Santiago* and *Café Cantante* in the *Hotel Santiago*, daily 2000-0200, US$6, every drink including bottled water costs US$6. *Disco Bar/Club 300*, Aguilera entre San Félix y San Pedro, closed Wed, 1000-1800, 2200-0400, live and recorded music, snack bar. *El Patio de Artex*, Heredia 304. Home of painters, Félix and José Joaquín Tejada Revilla, often live music with fantastic local bands, lots of dancing, friendly. *Grupo Folklórico del Oriente*, San Francisco y San Félix, folk groups play daytime till lunchtime, then again in the evening. *Ballet Folkórico Cutatumba*, Enramada, 2 blocks west of Plaza Céspedes. There is a superb show Sun 1030, US$3.

Festivals

The *Festival de Baile* takes place in the streets **15-19 May**. The *Festival del Caribe* begins in the first week **Jul** with theatre, dancing and conferences, and continues later in Jul to coincide with the Moncada celebrations on **26 Jul**.

The *Carnival*, already in full swing by then (as it was in 1953, the date carefully chosen to catch Batista's militia drunk and off-guard and use the noise of the carnival to drown the sound of gunfire), traditionally stops for a day of more serious celebration, then continues on 27 Jul. Carnival always lasts 1 week between **18-27 Jul**, taking in Santiago's patron saint's day, 25 Jul. This Carnival is well worth seeing. Wear no jewellery, leave all valuables behind. Each *municipio* organizes different activities, music, dancing, cabaret, etc in different parts of the city, even in the sea, with beer, food and kiosks. There are competitions and parades, with rivalry between the *comparsas* (congas) and *paseos* (dance groups). The whole city is covered in lights and all the doors are decorated. The parades and floats are judged from 2100 and pass down Garzón where there are seats for viewing. To get a seat go to the temporary *Izlazul* office behind the seating area on the south side of the road between 1800-2000. It starts at 2100, US$2 for a tourist seat. Good views possible if you queue early. *Festival del Pregón*, also known as *Fruta del Carey*, a festival of song in **Sep** when people dress up in traditional costumes and sell fruit in the street while singing; *Festival de la Trova*, a festival of folk music is held in **Sep or Oct**. On **New Year's Eve** you will find son bands playing in Plaza Marte and surrounding streets. Just before midnight everyone moves toward Parque Céspedes and sings the National Anthem. On the stroke of midnight the Cuban flag is raised on the Casa de Gobierno, commemorating the anniversary of the first time it was flown in 1902 when the Republic of Cuba was proclaimed. Then there's all night drinking and dancing on the streets and in local bars.

Shopping

Casa de la Artesanía, under the cathedral in Parque Céspedes, T23924. Open 0800-1730, also on Lacret 724 entre San Basilio y Heredia, T24027. *Cubartesana* on Félix Peña esq Masó under the cathedral. *Salón Artexanda* on Heredia 304 entre Pío Rosado y Calvario. Handicrafts are sold on the street on Heredia entre Hartmann y Pío Rosado. **Music** *Casa de la Trova* sells CDs and tapes. *Artex* on Aguilera sells CDs, tapes and videos for dollars. *Enramadas* and *Siglo XX*, both on Enramada, are stores with stalls selling records, books, clothes, jewellery, ornaments etc in pesos. On Enramada there is a second hand record shop. Several dollar stores can be found in the Parque Céspedes area, ask for 'shopping', especially on Saco. There is a good **bread** shop (dollars) called *Doña Neli* on Aguilera at Plaza Marte. *Panadería El Sol* is on Plaza Marte entre Saco y Aguilera. *Casa de Miel*, Gen Lacret, sells honey. *La Bombonera* is a dollar store selling **food** near Parque Céspedes on Aguilera entre Gen Lacret y Hartmann, open Mon-Sat 0900-1800, Sun 0900-1200. Food market on Ferreiro opposite *Hotel Las Américas*.

Cuba

Cuba

Tour operators *Rumbos Cuba* is on Heredia opposite *Casa Granda* hotel, open 0800-1700 for tours and later for car hire. Organized city tours with guide, also day trips to all destinations around Santiago. Prices vary according to season and number of people; also flights and trips to Jamaica and Santo Domingo. *Havanatur* main office is near La Maison on Av Manduley, T43603, with another office under the *Hotel Casa Granda*, offering the same as Rumbos but slightly more expensive. *Cubatur*, Victoriano Garzón y 4, is very helpful with knowledgeable guides and excellent value. All the main hotels have tour agencies.

Transport **Local Bus**: 20 centavos, run to the suburbs and outskirts. If there is no sign of a bus, catch a truck, ask driver the destination, pay flat rate 1 peso. Horse-drawn *coches* are also 1 peso. **Car hire**: At the airport: *Transautos*, T92245; *Havanautos*, T91873, 86161; *Vía Rent a Car* in *Rumbos* office opposite *Casa Granda*, T24646, also at Carretera del Caney y Calle 15, Reparto Vista Alegre, T41465, US$192 for 4 days plus US$40 for insurance. On return beware of US$10 charge for dirty exterior, US$20 for dirty interior and US$16 for scratches on the paint work caused by flying stones. These and other agencies in main hotels. *Havanautos* also has an agency at La Punta service station, T39328. **Taxis**: there are 3 types: *Turistaxi* most expensive, eg US$8 from airport to town centre; *Taxis OK* also expensive; *Cubataxi*, T51038/9, cheapest (name on windscreen), eg airport to town US$5. You can also get a private taxi, lots of them hanging around Parque Céspedes and Plaza Marte, but they will charge about the same as a Cubataxi. For a longer journey, you can negotiate a price. However, get a written quote if possible as even *Cubataxis* have been known to renegue on their agreements. Motorbike transport can be arranged at Plaza Marte for about US$1. *Bicitaxis* cost US$0.50.

Long distance Bus: Terminal near Plaza de la Revolución at the top of Av de los Libertadores/Carretera Central. Buy ticket in advance at *Astro* office on Yarayo (the 1st street on the left going north from the terminal), open daily 0600-1400. *Víazul*, T28484, is in an office to the left of the bus departure area, with a blue door, open 0700-2100, closed Sun pm but if you turn up 30 mins before departure you can buy a ticket. For an overnight journey wear trousers and a sweater if you have one, as the a/c is very cold and even *Víazul* is not comfortable at night. To Havana, 1500, 2000, arrive 0720, 1130, US$51, from Havana 1500, 2000, arrive 0650, 1130. To Baracoa 0730, via El Cristo, La Maya, Guantánamo, San Antonio and Imías, arriving 1215, US$15, returning from Baracoa 1415, arriving Santiago 1900. Note that the buses to Baracoa are only 9-seater minibuses and demand can be great in high season. Get your ticket the day before (or Sat for a Mon journey). Once a busload of tickets has been sold no more will be sold that day but if you turn up at 0500 the next morning they usually put on more buses depending on demand. On your return you can only buy tickets on the day of travel because the number of seats depends on how many buses have come from Santiago, but queue early. Trucks are available outside terminal to most destinations, drivers shout destination prior to departure, pay in pesos. For a long journey avoid trucks without any kind of cover. **Train**: The station is opposite the rum factory on Av Jesús Menéndez. Book tickets in advance from basement office in new terminal. Train travel is not as reliable or comfortable as bus travel. Take sweater for Havana journey, freezing a/c.

Directory **Airlines** *Cubana* office on Félix Peña 673 entre Heredia y San Basilio, near the cathedral, open Mon-Fri 0900-1700, Sat 0900-1400, T24156/51579/22290. *Aerotaxi* at the airport, T91410 ext 2019. *Aerocaribbean* office under *Hotel Casa Granda*. Local and inter-Caribbean (some destinations) flights can also be booked in *Rumbos* or *Havanatur*. **Banks** *Banco Financiero Internacional*, Parque Céspedes at Santo Tomás 565 entre Enramada y Aguilera, T22101, open Mon-Fri 0800-1600, dollar cash on Visa, change foreign currency and TCs. *Banco de Crédito y Comercio*, Parque Céspedes, Santo Tomás entre Aguilera y Heredia and Lacret esq Aguilera, efficient service for changing TCs in European currencies into dollars, US$2.5% commission. *BICSA*, Enramada opposite Plaza Dolores, for changing foreign currency and TCs. *Banco Popular de Ahorro*, Plaza Dolores, 0800-1500, Visa and Mastercard, ATM, prompt service, also a newly-built branch on Victoriano Garzón esq 3. TCs can be changed in any hotel except those in the Islazul chain; commission is usually 2-3%. *Hotel Santiago* will change virtually any cash currency into dollars. TCs can be changed in the Havanatur office in *Casa Granda*. In the Asistur office under *Casa Granda* you can get cash advance on all major credit cards including American Express and Diners Club; they will also change American Express TCs, the only place who will do so in all Cuba. **Communications** **Post office and internet**: main post office is on Aguilera y Clarín, open 0700-2000, where you can make phone calls within Cuba and buy international phone cards. There is email service but no internet access. *DHL*, opposite the bar, *El Baturro*, near Plaza Céspedes, has **email** facilities. The business centre at the *Santiago* will help you make international phone calls and has internet access, US$5 per hr. **Telephones**: *Etecsa* is on Aguilera, just before Plaza Dolores, open 24 hrs. For calls outside Santiago, Centro de Comunicaciones Nacional e Internacional, Heredia y Félix Peña, by the cathedral. **Medical services** *Clínica Internacional*, Av Raúl Pujol esq 10, T642589. Outpatient appointments, laboratory, dentist, 24-hr emergencies, international pharmacy. especially for tourists, everything payable in dollars, US$25 per consultation, the best clinic to visit to be sure of immediate treatment. **Useful addresses** **Immigration**: Inmigración y Extranjería on Av Raúl Pujol y 1, Reparto Santa Bárbara, open Mon, Fri 0900-1200, 1330-1630, Tue, Wed, Thu 0900-1200, in summer holiday mornings only. Go to *Bandec* on Parque Céspedes y Aguilera and buy special stamp (sello) for US$25, then return to Immigration for paper work (15 mins). **Asistur**: *Hotel Casa Granda*, Heredia esq San Pedro, T86600, for all health, financial, legal and insurance problems for foreign tourists.

Guantánamo

Guantánamo is the most easterly and most mountainous province on the island. The range of the Montañas de Nipe-Sagua-Baracoa runs through the province, ending in the Atlantic Ocean on the northern coast and the Caribbean Sea to the south. The area is notable for its many endemic species of fauna and flora. Guantánamo, the provincial capital, had a large influx of Haitian, French and Jamaican immigrants in the 19th century. The architecture has much less of a Spanish colonial feel; the narrow, brightly coloured buildings with thin wooden balconies and wrought ironwork are more reminiscent of New Orleans than Madrid. This is also reflected in the local musical rhythms, notably the Tumba Francesa.

Phone code: 21
Colour map 1, grid B6
Population: 205,000

The **US naval base** of Guantánamo (which cannot be easily visited from Cuba) was established at the beginning of the 20th century in the area known as Caimanera. The base is so little a part of the town that you will not come across it unless you make a specific trip to Mirador de Malones to view it through binoculars. In 2002, al-Qaida and Taliban prisoners were transferred there from Afghanistan under heavy guard to await military trial. Huge metal cages were built to incarcerate the prisoners and security at the base was tighter than ever.

The **Zoológico de Piedra** is an outdoor museum of stone animals, just outside of town, set in a beautiful hillside location with tropical vegetation. Many are bizarre, from tiny stone lizards to huge bison. All are carved directly from the rocks in their natural setting and you can buy miniature replicas from the sculptor on the way out.

Sleeping E *Guantánamo* (Islazul), Ahogados, esq 13 Norte, Plaza Mariana Grajales, Reparto Caribe, T381015, F382406, 15 mins' walk from the centre. 3-star, 112 rooms, 12 cabins, pool, clean, a/c, 2 bars and busy restaurant, food average, disco, mostly Cuban clientele, staff pleasant and helpful. **E** *La Lupe* (Islazul), Carretera del Salvador km 2, T326168/326180. 2-star but much nicer than *Guantánamo*, a bit far out of town, nice pool, peaceful atmosphere, 50 rooms, mostly cabins, sports area, a/c, restaurant, bar. **E** *Casa de Los Ensueños*, Ahogados esq 15 Norte, Reparto Caribe, T326304. 3 rooms, a/c, TV, bar, 24-hr room service. **F** *Osmaída Blanco Castillo*, Pedro A Pérez 664 entre Paseo y Narciso López, T325193. 1 room has no windows, but there are other, more pleasant rooms, just ask. Outside sitting areas.

Eating *Restaurante Caribe*, on top of a tower block near *Hotel Guantánamo*. Local food, pay in pesos. Plenty of *paladares*, most of whom charge in pesos but will accept dollars. Price should be about 45 pesos per person, but some raise it for tourists. 2 *paladares* on Av de los Estudiantes (Paseo) and a number of street stalls selling pork sandwiches for 5 pesos, some are there every day, all of them at weekends. Other *paladares* off Plaza Martí in the centre.

Tour operators Peter Hope, public relations officer at the *Hotel Guantánamo* (Room 117, Mon-Sat), is the fount of all tourist information in the area and runs guided *Islazul* and *Havanatur* tours for foreigners, including to Mt Malones, to see the US base through Soviet binoculars. He speaks English, German and French. *Islazul* office is on Los Maceo entre Narciso López y Paseo.

Cuba

Transport **Local Car hire** *Havanautos* office is at Cupet Cimex gas station at the beginning of the Baracoa road. **Long distance Air** Aeropuerto Mariana Grajales (GAO) is 16 km from Guantánamo, off the Baracoa road. Daily (except Mon) scheduled flight at 0600 from Havana, returning 0855, plus a Sat flight at 0845 (1140). **Bus** The bus terminal, T326016, is 5 km southwest from the centre. Taxis run from the train and bus station to *Hotel Guantánamo*/town centre, US$1. Daily bus to **Havana**, 4 buses to **Santiago**, 1 bus to **Baracoa**. *Víazul* stops here on its Santiago-Baracoa route. **Train** The station is in the centre on Calixto García. Daily trains to **Santiago** and **Havana**.

Directory **Banks** *Banco de Crédito* at Calixto García esq Carretera, changes TCs into dollars.

Baracoa

Phone code: 21
Colour map 1, grid B6

Close to the most easterly point of the island, Baracoa is an attractive place surrounded by rich, tropical vegetation and the perfect place to come and spend a few relaxing days on the beach. It was the first town founded in 1512 by Diego Velázquez, and for three years it was the capital of Cuba. Up until the 1960s it was really only accessible by sea until the viaduct, La Farola was built. This is a spectacular road, 30 km long, joined to the mountain on one side and supported by columns on the other. It is well worth the trip from Santiago (150 km, 4 hours' drive) for the scenery of this section of road, which winds through lush tropical mountains and then descends steeply to the coast.

The area is a UNESCO biosphere, with more than 10 rivers, including the **Río Toa**, 120 km long and the widest river in Cuba. Whitewater rafting is possible down the Río Toa, with different levels of difficulty. The **Río Yumurí**, 30 km east of Baracoa, is the most spectacular of Baracoa's rivers, running through two deep canyons. You can take an organized tour (US$28), rent a private car (US$10) or take a *colectivo* taxi or truck to the Río Yumurí where the road ends. A canoe will ferry you across or you can hire one to take you upriver for US$1. You can continue walking upriver and swim; it's very quiet and peaceful.

Christopher Columbus arrived in Baracoa on 27 November 1492. He planted a cross, now housed in the church, **Iglesia de la Asunción**, and described a mountain in the shape of an anvil (*yunque*) which was thereafter used as a point of reference for sailors. The first maps of Cuba drawn by an Englishman showed the **Yunque de Baracoa** mountain, copies of which can be seen in the museum. Between 1639 and 1742, Baracoa's three forts were built. The oldest, **El Castillo**, was destroyed in 1652 by the French. The others were **Fuerte de la Punta**, now restaurant *La Punta*, and **Fuerte Matachín**, now the Museo Municipal. ■ *Daily 0800-1800. US$2.*

Baracoa has 56 archaeological sites, with many traces of the three Indian groups who lived there: the Siboney, the Taíno and the Guanturabey. There is one surviving community of 300 Indians, called the **Yateras**, dating back to the Spaniards' arrival. They are integrated with the rest of society but only marry among themselves and maintain their traditions. They live in an isolated region along the shores of the Río Toa, but a visit can be organized through the Museo Municipal.

Sleeping **A-D** *Porto Santo* (Gaviota), T43511, 43590, F86074. 53 rooms, 3 suites, a/c, bath, TV, restaurant, bar, shop, beautiful swimming pool, car hire, next to airport, beach, peaceful atmosphere, friendly. **C-D** *El Castillo* (Gaviota), Calixto García, Loma del Paraíso, T42147, F86074. 35 a/c rooms with bath, phone, TV in lobby lounge, pool (US$2 for use by non-residents), parking, friendly staff, food OK, excellent views, very good breakfast. **E-F** *La Rusa* (Islazul), a bright yellow building on the Malecón, Máximo Gómez 13, T43011, islazul@gtmo.cu Named after the Russian lady, Magdalena Menasse, who used to run the hotel and whose photos adorn the walls, famous guests have included Fidel Castro, accommodation now basic, food average, nice location, good *paladar* opposite.

Casas particulares F *Casa Ernesto*, Libertad 13 entre 1 Abril y M Grajales, 5 mins' walk from Plaza Independencia towards *Hotel Porto Santo*. Room with a/c, big breakfast included, dinner US$3-4, traditional food from the region (fish in coconut milk), bike rental US$2 per day. **F** *Daniel Pérez Carcasses* , Coroneles Galana 6 entre Flor Crombet y Martí, T43274. Near the sea, private roof and room with new shower and a/c, nice family, good cooking. **F** *Ikira Mahíquez Machado*, Maceo 168-A entre Céspedes y Ciro Frías, T42466. 2 rooms, also a separate part of the house with kitchen and garage, nice building, friendly family. **F** *Inés Morgado Terán*, Maceo 51 entre Peralejo y Coliseo, T43292. Room with private bathroom, a/c, no English spoken but Inés and her husband are warm and helpful. **F** *Miriam Zolla Montoya*, Martí 301, T43529. Extremely hospitable, comfortable, a/c, good food offered. **F** *Neida Cuenca Prada*, Flor Crombet 194 esq Céspedes, T43178. Upstairs rooms better than the one downstairs, kind and generous family, wonderful food and reasonably priced. **F** *Nelia y Yaquelín*, Mariana Grajales 11 entre Julio A Mella y Calixto García, T42652. 3 generations of a delightful family offer a simple but comfortable place to stay, sea views, new private bathroom, small room, breakfast US$2, dinner US$5, both delicious and more than you can eat. **F** *Pedro Jiménez Martínez*, Flor Crombet 213 entre Coroneles y Reyes. Extremely nice family, great food, will cook anything you want, huge portions. **F** *Dr Sánchez Rosell*, Maceo 123 entre Frank País y Maravi, T43161. Friendly couple, private bathroom, fan, extremely clean, breakfast and dinner, on main road. **F** *Tatiana Borges*, Rodney Coutin 46 entre Abel Días y Moncada, T43674. Nice room with balcony and your own entrance, friendly hosts, dinner available. **F** *Williams Montoya Sánchez*, Martí 287, T42798. Very hospitable, a/c, car parking, US$1, car cleaning US$2, available to non-guests. **F** *Yamilet Selva Bartelemy*, Frank País 6 entre Máximo Gómez y Flor Crombet, T42724. Sea view from 2 rooms with bathrooms in hospitable household with charming couple, secure, comfortable.

There are alleged to be 200 casas particulares in Baracoa now

The isolation of Baracoa has led to an individual local cuisine, mostly featuring coconut milk and fish. 80% of Cuba's coconuts are grown here. Don't miss the *cucurucho*, a delicious mixture of coconut, fruit and sugar served in a cone of palm leaves and sold at roadsides for about 3 pesos. *La Colonial*, José Martí 123, T43161. Extensive menu. *Tropical*, José Martí 175. Good local specialities, calalú, vegetarian options, fish in coconut, book ahead for advance preparation of some dishes. The fort at La Punta, which juts out into the bay west of the town, has been converted to a pleasant, breezy, open-air restaurant, *La Guama*, although everyone refers to it as La Punta. Nice setting, Creole food, main courses (described on the menu as 'mean' plates) US$3-5.50. *Casa de Chocolate*, José Martí, near bus terminal. Local version of hot chocolate with water and salt.

Eating

Lots of paladares, most offer pork, chicken, fish, turtle (endangered, don't eat), some offer lobster

Casa de la Trova, José Martí 149. Traditional music, Tue-Sun from 2100, US$1, good *son* and friendly atmosphere. *Casa de la Cultura*, Maceo 122. Live music. Nightly show of Afro-Cuban music by Yambú Akalé at *La Punta*, highly recommended, US$4. *Dancing Light* on Maceo just before Parque Central, disco for young Cubans although tourists will not feel out of place, drinks in dollars for tourists, small but lively, check out breakdancing show nightly by local youths. *Cuatro ochenta cinco (485)*, Félix Ruenes, bar with live band every night, US$1, great fun. Live music at *Porto Santo* and *El Castillo*, the former is livelier. *Noche Cubana* on Sat, when Antonio Maceo fills up with food and drink stalls and there is dancing to street musicians.

Nightlife

Gaviota, from *Hotel Castillo* (T43665, Antonio (Tony) Mas) or *Hotel Porto Santo* (T43590, Wilder Laffita). Baracoa city tour US$4, Saltadero (35-m waterfall) US$8, El Yunque US$18, Playa Maguana US$7, Toa US$8. Duaba US$8 (Toa and Duaba, peasant farms and boat trips), Yumurí US$12 (fishing village, cocoa plantation and boat trip). Taxi drivers will also take you to Playa Maguana and Río Yumurí via cocoa and coffee plantations. When you arrive all the guys will want to be your guide and all the girls will want to cook you lunch.

Tour operators

Local Car hire: at the 24-hr Servi Cupet station, Guantánamo road Km 4. **Long distance Air**: Airport 100 m from *Hotel Porto Santo*. There are 3 scheduled *Cubana* flights a week from Havana, on Tue (0645), Sat (0645) and Sun (0620), with the Sun flight via Santiago (0925). All times subject to frequent change. **Bus**: Main bus terminal at the end of Martí near Av de los

Transport

Cuba

Mártires, T42239, 43670, for buses to Havana, Santiago, Guantánamo. Reserve in advance at busy times and ensure your name is on the list, *plano*, otherwise your reservation will not be valid. Trucks to Guantánamo, Moa and other destinations from 2nd bus terminal on Coroneles Galana.

Directory **Banks** *Banco Nacional de Cuba* is on Maceo but will change only TCs, you can not get cash advance on credit cards. *Porto Santo* and *El Castillo* hotels both change TCs.

Isla de la Juventud

Colour map 1, grid B2

There are three good reasons for visiting the Isla de la Juventud: diving, birdwatching and checking out Cuban provincial life away from tourist resorts. The island is a good place to go for a weekend out of Havana, although if you plan to see the whole island you will need more time. In recent decades its population has been swelled by tens of thousands of Cuban and Third World students, giving rise to the modern name of Isle of Youth. From the 19th century until the Revolution its main function was as a prison and both José Martí and Fidel Castro served time there.

Nueva Gerona
Phone code: 61

The capital, Nueva Gerona, dates from the 19th century and remains the only substantial settlement. Surrounded by small hills, it is a pleasant country town with a slow pace. As most development has taken place post-1959, there are few historical buildings. The **Río Las Casas** runs through the town heading northwards out to sea, and this has traditionally been the main route to the Cuban mainland. The boat which served as a ferry from the 1920s until 1974, *El Pinero*, has been preserved by the river at the end of Calle 28.

The **Museo Municipal** building was once the Casa de Gobierno, built in 1853, one of the oldest on the island. It is on the south side of the Parque Central and has a small historical collection of items. ■ *Tue-Sat 0800-1700, Sun 0900-1300. Calle 30.* The **Museo de la Lucha Clandestina**, near *Coppelia*, has a collection of photos and other material relating to the Revolution. ■ *Tue-Sat, 0900-1700, Sun 0800-1200. Calle 37 y 30.* The **Planetario y Museo de Historia Natural** has exhibits relating to the natural history, geology and archaeology of the island. ■ *Tue-Thu 0800-1900, Fri 1400-2200, Sat 1300-1700, Sun 0900-1300. US$2. Calle 41 y 52.* Outside the town, 3 km west just off the road to La Demajagua, is **Museo Finca El Abra**. This is where José Martí came on 17 October 1870, to spend nine weeks of exile and labour quarrying marble in the Sierra de las Casas before being deported to Spain. You can see the contents of the house and kitchen and some of Martí's belongings. ■ *Tue-Sun 0900-1700.*

Excursions

The **Presidio Modelo** (the Model Prison), 4 km east of Nueva Gerona in Reparto Chacón, was built by the dictator Machado to a high-security 'panopticon' design first developed by Jeremy Bentham in 1791 to give total surveillance and control of the inmates. It is a sinister and impressive sight; wander around the guard towers and circular cell blocks, and see the numbered, tiered cells. Inmates have included many fighters in the independence struggle, Japanese Cuban internees in the Second World War, and Fidel Castro and fellow Moncada rebels imprisoned from 1953 to 1955. Castro closed the prison in 1967. ■ *Mon-Sat 0800-1700, Sun 0800-1300. US$2, cameras US$1.*

The **Cueva del Punta del Este** contains paintings attributed to the original Siboney inhabitants. They were discovered in 1910 by a shipwrecked French sailor and contain 235 pictures on the walls and ceilings, painted long before the arrival of the Spanish. They are considered the most important pictographs in the Caribbean and have been declared a national monument. It is believed that they might represent a solar calendar. ■ *The only way to get there is by organized excursion. US$92 flat rate divided between however many passengers there are.*

The **Cocodrilo** crocodile farm is a one-hour drive south and west from Nueva Gerona, including several kilometres of dirt road. There are guided tours (in Spanish) of the hatchery and breeding pens where the crocodiles stay for four or five years until released. ■ *US$3.*

C-E *El Colony* (Marinas Puertosol), T98282. 40 mins by road from Nueva Gerona's small airport, very isolated, diving centre with access to 56 buoyed diving locations. Swimming and snorkelling not great because of shallow water and sea urchins, you have to wade a long way before it is deep enough to swim, but beach is white sand. 77 a/c rooms in main block and cabañas, in need of renovation, single and triple available, discounts for stays of over a week, TV. Lovely setting, pool, 3 restaurants, snack bar, store, basket ball, volleyball, tennis and squash courts, horse riding, disco Sat 2100-0600, excursions, busy with package tourists, so accommodation could be hard to find. **E** *Villa Gaviota* (3-star) on the outskirts of Nueva Gerona on the road to La Fe beside the river, T23290. 20 rooms, single and triple available, extra cots for children, a/c, fridge, TV, phone, pool where national swimming team trains, good service at poolside bar, restaurants, squash court and gymnasium, disco Thu-Sun 2130-0400, techno music, young crowd, dance and aerobics classes advertised, the nicest dollar place to stay if you are not diving or on a package. **Casas particulares** *Roberto Figuerero Rodríguez*, 35 1809, entre 18 y 20, Apto 1, T4892. Friendly, help with cars and drivers and information in general. **F** *Andrés Corbello Pino*, 24 5305 entre 53 y 55. A/c, food available, US$7 dinner including drinks.

El Tocororo, opposite the park on Calles 39 y 16. Cuban dishes, pay in pesos, breakfast 0700-0900, lunch 1200-1400, dinner 1800-2000, but times seem flexible. *El Cochinito*, 39 y 24. State run, open 1400-2200, specializes in pork. *Cabaret El Dragón*, 39 y 26. Also state-run but Chinese and Cuban food, restaurant and bar, open 1600-2200, Mon-Thu, 1600-0030 Fri-Sun, cabaret at weekends, deluxe atmosphere, upscale crowd; there is a *Mercado Agropecuario* at 41 y 40, fresh fruit and vegetables, and there are a few basic places to eat in this area where you can pay in pesos. For ice cream, *Coppelia* is at 37 y 32.

Casa de los Vinos, 20 y 41. Open Mon-Wed 1400-2200, Fri-Sun 1400-2400, popular peso drinking spot with grapefruit, melon, tomato and grape wines in earthenware jugs, drink orders finish at 2300, advisable to take glasses, avoid the snacks. *Taberna Gerona*, 39 y 22. Open daily 1100-2100, Cuban food and pub atmosphere, very friendly, strictly pesos.

El Patio, 24 entre 37 y 39. Open 2100-0300, cabaret, 2 shows nightly at weekends, at 2200 and 0100, entry US$3, lots of Cubans and popular. *La Movida* disco, 34 entre 18 y 20. Outdoors, US$3, Cubans pay in pesos, young student crowd, starts at 2200. *Villa Gaviota* disco, Thu-Sun, 2130-0400, entry US$1, cave-like atmosphere, picks up after midnight, young crowd, techno music. *Casa de la Cultura*, 37 y 24, check the schedule posted outside for dance events; beside the Servi Cupet petrol station on 39 y 30, no sign outside, café where you can dance, open 24 hrs, total mix of music, comfortable and friendly, best place.

Local Travel can be difficult although nearly every car will turn into a taxi on request. Fares within Nueva Gerona are about US$2. The best way to see the island is to hire a private car with a driver/guide, which costs about US$40-60 a day. Motorbike hire from the hotels is US$7 per hr. Local transport is often by horse and cart. **Car hire**: *Havanautos* 32 y 39, T24432, but the dollar hotels also have car hire desks. **Bus** Buses run to **La Fe**, the *Hotel Colony*, **Playa Bibijagua**, and bus marked 'Servicio Aereo', between the airport and the cinema, but don't rely on any of these to run on a regular basis.

Long distance Air The Rafael Cabrera Airport (GER) is nearly 5 km from town and there are 2 or 3 scheduled 40-min flights a day from Havana so you could do a day trip if you wanted. Fare US$22 1-way, book in advance. *Aerotaxi* to Pinar del Río US$22, like a flying bus. **Sea** An interesting way of getting to the island is by the 106-passenger *kometa* (a vintage Soviet hydrofoil), from Surgidero de Batabanó on the mainland south coast. There is a morning crossing and an evening crossing, which take 2 hrs, US$15. Connecting bus from **Havana** to Surgidero de Batabanó, 1 hr, from bus terminal on Boyeros at 0700 and 1300. Book a couple of days in advance at the terminal at the far end of the Boyeros entry, between 0600-1200, 2 pesos, at the office in the terminal. On the *kometa* try for Salón A, the only one with a view.

Sleeping
Hotels can be booked through Amistur; many are not advertised in tourist literature and it can be difficult to book or verify whether they are open

Eating
Private restaurants are few and aimed mainly at locals. It is best to eat in people's homes, where you can get an excellent meal for US$5-6

Bars

Nightlife

Transport

Cuba

Those paying in dollars are usually directed to Salón C, with freezing a/c. Snacks available in pesos and beer at US$1. Customs entry both ways, remember 20-kg weight limit. Alternatively, a ferry crosses on the same route Wed, Fri and Sun at 1930 from Havana train station and takes 6 hrs, US$10. In Havana tickets are sold at the station office. In Nueva Gerona the terminal is on the Río Las Casas at the end of Calle 22 and the ticket office is open daily 0600-1300. Fares in dollars, take your passport.

Directory **Airlines** *Cubana* at 39 1415 entre 16 y 18, Nueva Gerona, T061-22531/24259. *Aerotaxi* at Siguanea Airport, T98282, 98181. **Banks** *Banco Nacional*, 39 y 18, open Mon-Fri 0800-1400, Sat 1300-1500. Best to bring enough cash from the mainland. **Medical services** Pharmacy at 39 y 24, open Mon-Fri 0800-2200, Sat 0800-1600. Take plenty of insect repellent, particularly for the Ciénaga or the *Hotel Colony*.

Cayo Largo

Phone code: 5
Colour map 1, grid B2

Cayo Largo is at the eastern end of the Archipiélago de los Canarreos, 114 km east of Isla de la Juventud and 80 km south of the Península de Zapata. It is a long, thin, coral island, 26 km long and no more than 2 km wide. There are beautiful white sandy beaches protected by a reef, all along the southern coast which, together with the cristal clear, warm waters of the Caribbean, make it ideal for tourism. A string of hotels lines the southern tip of the island. The northern coast is mostly mangrove and swamp, housing hungry mosquitoes as well as numerous birds (pelicans being the most visible) and iguanas. Turtles lay their eggs at Playa Tortuga in the northeast, and there is a turtle farm at Combinado northwest of the airstrip.

Beaches & watersports
Watersports include windsurfing, kayaking, jet skis, catamarans, and banana rides

The best beach on the island is the 2-km white-sand **Playa Sirena**, which faces west and is spared any wind or currents which sometimes affect the southern beaches. Snorkelling and scuba diving can be done here, 10 minutes' boat ride from the hotels and at **Playa Los Cocos**, which you can reach by bicycle. **Scuba diving** is good around the island. There is an extensive reef with gorgonians, sponges and lots of fish, while north of the island you will find large pelagics. **Sailing** is popular and there is a bareboat yacht charter fleet. The Marina Cayo Largo del Sur at Combinado has 50 moorings for visiting yachts, who don't have to buy a tourist card to come here if they are not going on to anywhere else in Cuba, because the island is a free port. To clear customs, call the marina on VHF 6, or maritime security (*seguridad marítima*) on VHF 16. There is **deep-sea fishing** for marlin and other big fish, with international fishing tournaments held here.

Sleeping & eating
There is no private accommodation on the island and you will not need any pesos. You will not find any paladares here but there is lots of lobster

There are several hotels, all in the Gran Caribe chain and grouped together under the name of the *Isla del Sur Hotel Resort*, T548111-8, F548201. All facilities shared and included in the package cost, which can be as low as US$185 per person for 2 day/1 night or US$400 per person for 4 nights, including air and ground transport from Havana, 3 meals and free use of all water sports and other activities such as tennis, horse riding and volleyball. Medical facilities, entertainment, disco, laundry, post office and fax services available. The hotels and the thatched *cabañas* are low-lying and pleasantly spread out in gardens by the beach, all rooms are a/c, with private bath, telephone and satellite TV. There are several buffet restaurants and thatched snack bars (*ranchones*) attached to the hotels, as well as 2 à la carte restaurants which have to be booked.

Transport
Package tours from Havana might fly you on a 60-year-old Antonov bi-plane, at an altitude of 3,500 ft

Local Car hire: *Havanautos* and *Transautos* at the *Hotel Pelícano*. Motorcycles, bicycles, and jeeps are also available. **Long distance Air** There are several charters and scheduled international flights to Cayo Largo del Sur Airport (CYO). *Aerogaviota* flies from Aeropuerto Playa Baracoa, **Havana**, a former military air base. There are also flights from **Varadero**, or by light plane or boat from **Isla de la Juventud**. *Aerotaxi* at the airport, T793255.

Background

History

Cuba was visited by Cristóbal Colón (Christopher Columbus) during his first voyage to find a westerly route to the Orient on 27 October 1492, and he made another brief stop two years later on his way from Hispaniola to Jamaica. Columbus did not realize it was an island when he landed; he hoped it was Japan. He arrived on the north coast of 'Colba', but found little gold. He did, however, note the Indians' practice of puffing at a large, burning roll of leaves, which they called 'tobacos'. Cuba was first circumnavigated by Sebastián de Ocampo in 1508, but it was Diego de Velázquez who conquered it in 1511 and founded several towns, called *villas*, including Havana. The first African slaves were imported to Cuba in 1526. Sugar was introduced soon after. Tobacco was made a strict monopoly of Spain in 1717. The coffee plant was introduced in 1748. The British, under Lord Albemarle and Admiral Pocock, captured Havana and held the island in 1762-63, but it was returned to Spain in exchange for Florida. Towards the end of the 18th century Cuba became a slave plantation society. By the 1860s Cuba was producing about a third of the world's sugar and was heavily dependent on slaves to do so, supplemented by indentured Chinese labourers in the 1850s and 1860s. An estimated 600,000 African slaves were imported by 1867.

Spanish conquest

Independence from Spain became a burning issue in Cuba as Spain refused to consider political reforms which would give the colony more autonomy. The first war of independence was in the eastern part of the island between 1868 and 1878, but it gained little save a modest move towards the abolition of slavery; and complete abolition was not achieved until 1886. One consequence of the war was the ruin of many sugar planters. US interests began to take over the sugar plantations and the sugar mills, and Cuba became more dependent on the US market.

Independence movement
Many national heroes of this period have become revolutionary icons in the struggle against domination by a foreign power

From 1895 to 1898 rebellion flared up again in the second war of independence under the young poet and revolutionary, José Martí, together with the old guard of Antonio Maceo and Máximo Gómez. José Martí was tragically killed in May 1895 and Maceo in 1896. Despite fierce fighting throughout the island, neither the Nationalists nor the Spanish could gain the upper hand. However, the USA was now concerned for its investments and its strategic interests. When the US battleship *Maine* exploded in Havana harbour on 15 February 1898, killing 260 crew, the USA declared war on Spain. American forces were landed, a squadron blockaded Havana and defeated the Spanish fleet at Santiago de Cuba. In December peace was signed and US forces occupied the island for four years.

The Republic of Cuba was proclaimed in 1902 and the Government was handed over to its first president. However, the Platt Amendment to the constitution, passed by the US Congress, clearly made Cuba a protectorate of the USA. The USA retained naval bases and reserved the right of intervention in Cuban domestic affairs but, to quell growing unrest, repealed the Platt Amendment in 1934. The USA formally relinquished the right to intervene but retained its naval base at Guantánamo on a 99-year lease.

Around two thirds of sugar exports went to the USA under a quota system at prices set by Washington; two thirds of Cuba's imports came from the USA; foreign capital investment was largely from the USA and Cuba was effectively a client state. Yet its people suffered from grinding rural poverty, high unemployment, illiteracy and inadequate health care. Politics was a mixture of authoritarian rule and corrupt democracy. From 1924 to 1933 the 'strong man' Gerardo Machado ruled Cuba. He was elected in 1924 on a wave of popularity but a drastic fall in sugar prices in the late 1920s led to strikes; nationalist popular rebellion was harshly repressed. The USA tried to negotiate a deal but nationalists called a general strike in protest at US interference, and Machado finally went into exile. The violence did not abate, however,

Dictatorship

Cuba

Cuba

and there were more strikes, mob attacks and occupations of factories. In September 1933 a revolt of non-commissioned officers including Sergeant Fulgencio Batista, deposed the government. Batista then held power through presidential puppets until he was elected president himself in 1940. He pursued nationalist and populist policies, set against corruption and political violence. In 1940 a new Constitution was passed by a constituent assembly dominated by Batista, which included universal suffrage and benefits for workers such as a minimum wage, pensions, social insurance and an eight-hour day. In 1944 Batista lost the elections but corruption continued. Batista, by then a self-promoted general, staged a military coup in 1952. Constitutional and democratic government was at an end. His harshly repressive dictatorship was brought to a close by Fidel Castro in January 1959, after a three-year campaign, mostly in the Sierra Maestra, with a guerrilla force reduced at one point to 12 men.

Revolution Fidel Castro, the son of immigrants from Galicia and born in Cuba in 1926 saw José Martí as his role model and aimed to follow his ideals. In 1953, the 100th anniversary of José Martí's birth, Castro and a committed band of about 160 revolutionaries attacked the Moncada barracks in Santiago de Cuba on 26 July. The attack failed and Castro and his brother Raúl were later captured and put on trial. Fidel used the occasion to make an impassioned speech denouncing corruption in the ruling class and the need for political freedom and economic independence. In 1955 the Castros were given an amnesty and went to Mexico. There Fidel continued to work on his essentially nationalist revolutionary programme, called the 26 July Movement, which called for radical social and economic reforms and a return to the democracy of Cuba's 1940 constitution. He met another man of ideas, an Argentine doctor called Ernesto (Che) Guevara, who sailed with him and his brother Raúl and a band of 82 like-minded revolutionaries, back to Cuba on 2 December 1956. Their campaign began in the Sierra Maestra in the east of Cuba and, after years of fierce fighting, Batista fled the country on 1 January 1959. Fidel Castro, to universal popular acclaim, entered Havana and assumed control of the island.

Communism & the 1960s From 1960 onwards, in the face of increasing hostility from the USA, Castro led Cuba into socialism and then communism. Officials of the Batista regime were put on trial in 'people's courts' and executed. The promised new elections were not held. The judiciary lost its independence when Castro assumed the right to appoint judges. The free press was closed or taken over. Trade unions lost their independence and became part of government. The University of Havana, a former focus of dissent, and professional associations all lost their autonomy. The democratic constitution of 1940 was never reinstated. In 1960 the sugar *centrales*, the oil refineries and the foreign banks were nationalized, all US property was expropriated and the Central Planning Board (Juceplan) was established. The professional and property-owning middle classes began a steady exodus which drained the country of its skilled workers. CIA-backed mercenaries and Cuban emigrés kept up a relentless barrage of attacks, but failed to achieve their objective.

1961 was the year of the Bay of Pigs invasion, a fiasco which was to harden Castro's political persuasion. Some 1,400 CIA-trained Cuban émigrés landed in the Bahía de Cochinos (Bay of Pigs), but were stranded on the beaches when the Cuban air force attacked their supply ships. Two hundred were killed and the rest surrendered within three days. In his May Day speech, Fidel Castro confirmed that the Cuban Revolution was socialist. The US reaction was to isolate Cuba, with a full trade embargo. Cuba was expelled from the Organization of American States (OAS) and the OAS imposed economic sanctions. In March 1962 rationing had to be imposed.

In April 1962, President Kruschev of the USSR decided to send medium-range missiles to Cuba, which would be capable of striking anywhere in the USA. This episode, which became known as the 'Cuban Missile Crisis', brought the world to the brink of nuclear war, defused only by secret negotiations between John F Kennedy and Kruschev. Without consulting Castro and without his knowledge, Kruschev eventually agreed to have the missiles dismantled and withdrawn on condition that the west would guarantee a policy of non-aggression towards Cuba.

Economic policy during the 1960s was largely unsuccessful in achieving its aims. The government wanted to industrialize rapidly to reduce dependence on sugar. However, the crash programme, with help from the USSR, was a failure and had to be abandoned. The whole nation was called upon to achieve a target of 10 million tonnes of sugar by 1970 and everyone spent time in the fields helping towards this goal. It was never reached and never has been. Rationing is still fierce, and there are still shortages of consumer goods. However, the Revolution's social policies have largely been successful and it is principally these achievements which have ensured the people's support of Castro and kept him in power. Education, housing and health services have been improved and the social inequalities of the 1940s and 1950s have been wiped out.

Cuba became firmly entrenched as a member of the Soviet bloc, joining COMECON in 1972. The Revolution was institutionalized along Soviet lines and the Party gained control of the bureaucracy, the judiciary and the local and national assemblies. A new socialist constitution was adopted in 1976. Cuba's foreign policy changed from actively fomenting socialist revolutions abroad (such as Guevara's forays into the Congo and Bolivia in the 1960s) to supporting other left-wing or third-world countries with combat troops and technical advisers including Angola, Ethiopia, Nicaragua, Jamaica and Grenada. In September 1979, Castro hosted a summit conference of the non-aligned nations in Havana, a high point in his foreign policy initiatives.

1970s Soviet domination

By the 1980s, the heavy dependence on sugar and the USSR, coupled with the trade embargo, meant that the expected improvements in living standards were not being delivered as fast as hoped and the people were tiring of being asked for ever more sacrifices. In 1980, the Peruvian embassy was overrun by 11,000 people seeking political asylum. Castro opened the port of Mariel for a mass departure of some 125,000 by sea in anything they could find which would float.

Before the collapse of the Soviet system, aid to Cuba from the USSR was estimated at about 25% of GNP. Cuba's debt with the USSR was a secret; estimates ranged from US$8.5 bn to US$34 bn. Apart from military aid, economic assistance took two forms: balance of payments support (about 85%), under which sugar and nickel exports were priced in excess of world levels, and assistance for development projects. About 13 mn tonnes of oil a year were supplied by the USSR, allowing 3 mn to be re-exported, providing a valuable source of foreign earnings. By the late 1980s up to 90% of Cuba's foreign trade was with planned economies. The collapse of the Communist system in Eastern Europe, followed by the demise of the USSR, nearly brought the end of Castro's Cuba.

1980s dissatisfaction

Economic difficulties in the 1990s brought on by the loss of markets in the former USSR and Eastern Europe, together with higher oil prices because of the Gulf crisis, forced the Government to impose emergency measures and declare a special period in peace time. Rationing was increased, petrol became scarce, the bureaucracy was slashed. In 1993, Cuba was hit by a storm which caused an estimated US$1bn in damage. In mid-1994, economic discontent flared and Cubans began to flee for Florida in a mass exodus. It was estimated that between mid-August and mid-September 30,000 Cubans had left the country. Eventually the crisis forced President Clinton into an agreement whereby the USA was committed to accepting at least 20,000 Cubans a year, plus the next of kin of US citizens, while Cuba agreed to prevent further departures.

As the economic crisis persisted, the government adopted measures which opened up many sectors to private enterprise and recognized the dependence of much of the economy on dollars. The partial reforms did not eradicate the

1990s crisis & change

imbalances between the peso and the dollar economies, and shortages remained for those without access to hard currency. Cuba intensified its economic liberalization programme, allowing farmers to sell at uncontrolled prices once their commitments to the state procurement system were fulfilled. Importantly, the reforms also allowed middlemen to operate.

US pressure in the 1990s Before the Revolution of 1959 the USA had investments in Cuba worth about US$1 bn, covering nearly every activity from agriculture and mining to oil installations. Today all American businesses have been nationalized; the USA has cut off all imports from Cuba, placed an embargo on exports to Cuba, and broken off diplomatic relations. Prior to the 1992 US presidential elections, President Bush approved the Cuban Democracy Act (Torricelli Bill) which forbade US subsidiaries from trading with Cuba. Many countries, including EC members and Canada, said they would not allow the US bill to affect their trade with Cuba and the UN General Assembly voted in favour of a resolution calling for an end to the embargo.

In 1996, US election year, Cuba faced another crackdown by the US administration. In February, Cuba shot down two light aircraft piloted by Miami émigrés allegedly over Cuban air space and implicitly confirmed by the findings of the International Civil Aviation Organization (ICAO) report in June. The attack provoked President Clinton to tighten and internationalize the US embargo on Cuba and on 12 March he signed into law the (Helms-Burton) Cuban Freedom and Democratic Solidarity Act. This legislation allows legal action against any company or individual benefiting from properties expropriated by the Cuban government after the Revolution. It brought universal condemnation: Canada and Mexico (Nafta partners), the EU, Russia, China, the Caribbean Community and the Río Group of Latin American countries all protested that it was unacceptable to extend sanctions outside the USA to foreign companies and their employees who do business with Cuba.

Recent events 1997 was the 30th anniversary of the death of Che Guevara, whose remains were returned from Bolivia to Cuba in July. During a week of official mourning for Che and his comrades in arms, vast numbers filed past their remains in Havana and Santa Clara, where they were laid to rest on 17 October. In December 1998 the remains of 10 more guerrillas killed in Bolivia in 1967 were also interred in the Che Guevara memorial in Santa Clara.

In January 1998 the Pope visited Cuba for the first time and held open-air masses around the country. The Pope preached against Cuba's record on human rights and abortion while also condemning the US trade embargo preventing food and medicines reaching the needy. The visit was a public relations success for both Castro and the Pope. Shortly afterwards, 200 prisoners were pardoned and released.

In November 1999 a six-year-old boy, Elián González, was rescued from the sea off Florida, the only survivor from a boatload of illegal migrants which included his mother and her boyfriend. He was looked after by distant relatives in Miami and quickly became the centrepiece of a new row between Cuban émigrés, supported by right-wing Republicans, and Cuba. The US Attorney General, Janet Reno, supported the decision by the US Immigration and and Naturalization Service (INS) on 5 January 2000, that the boy should be repatriated and reunited with his father in Cuba by 14 January, but she postponed the deadline to allow for legal challenges. Mass demonstrations were held in Havana in support of Elián's return but legal manoeuvres by US politicians stalled progress and caused further disputes. Amid enormous controversy, the US authorities siezed Elián on 22 April and reunited him with his father, who had travelled to the USA earlier in the month with his second wife and baby. The family finally took him home, amid celebrations in Cuba, where the boy had become a symbol of resistance to the USA.

The election of George W Bush to the US presidency was bad news for any prospects of a thaw in relations with the USA. A crackdown on spies was ordered and in June 2001, five Cubans were convicted in a US Federal Court in Miami. Castro referred to them as 'heroes', who he said had not been putting the USA in danger but had been infiltrating Cuban-American anti-Castro groups and defending Cuba. However, 2001 did see the first commercial export of food from the USA to Cuba, with a shipment of corn from Louisiana and the debate on the lifting of sanctions was fueled by the visit of former US President Jimmy Carter in 2002.

Towards the end of 2002 lobbying intensified in the USA for an end to the embargo and travel restrictions while farmers enthusiastically embraced trade with Cuba. However, the thaw came to a grinding halt in 2003 when Castro had three ferry hijackers executed and imprisoned 75 journalists, rights activists and dissidents, many of whom had allegedly been encouraged by the head of the US Interests Section in Havana. Amid universal condemnation, the EU announced a review of its relations with Cuba and curtailed high-level governmental visits.

Geography

The island of Cuba, 1,250 km long, 191 km at its widest point, is the largest of the Caribbean islands and only 145 km south of Florida. Gifted with a moderate climate, afflicted only occasionally by hurricanes, not cursed by frosts, blessed by an ample and well-distributed rainfall and excellent soils, it has traditionally been one of the largest exporters of cane sugar in the world.

Old coral reefs have been brought to the surface, so that much of the northern coast consists of coral limestone cliffs and sandy beaches. By contrast the southern coastline is being gradually submerged, producing wetlands and mangroves. Limestones of various types cover about two-thirds of the island. In most areas, there is a flat or gently rolling landscape. There are three main mountain areas in the island. In the west, the Cordillera de Guaniguanico is divided into the Sierra del los Organos in the west, with thick deposits of limestone which have developed a distinctive landscape of steep-sided flat-topped mountains; and the Sierra del Rosario in the east, made up partly of limestones and partly of lavas and other igneous rocks. Another mountainous area in central Cuba includes the Escambray mountains north of Trinidad, a double dome structure made up of igneous and metamorphic rocks, including marble. The Sierra Maestra in east Cuba has Cuba's highest mountains, rising to Pico Turquino (1,974 m) and a rather different geological history, with some rocks formed in an arc of volcanic activity around 50 million years ago. Older rocks include marble, and other metamorphics. Important mineral deposits are in this area; nickel is mined near Moa.

Government

In 1976 a new constitution was approved by 97.7% of the voters, setting up municipal and provincial assemblies and a National Assembly of People's Power. The membership of the Assembly is now 609, candidates being nominated by the 169 municipal councils, and elected by direct secret ballot. Similarly elected are members of the 14 provincial assemblies, both for five-year terms. In the latest elections, in January 2003, 8.1 mn of the 8.2 mn registered voters cast ballots and support for the candidates reached 97% of votes cast. All Cubans over 16 may vote. The number of Cuba's provinces was increased from six to 14 at the First Congress of the Communist Party of Cuba in December 1975. Dr Fidel Castro was elected President of the Council of State by the National Assembly and his brother, Major Raúl Castro, was elected First Vice-President. There are five other vice-presidents.

Economy

Following the 1959 Revolution, Cuba adopted a Marxist-Leninist economic system. Almost all sectors of the economy were state controlled and centrally planned, the only significant exception being agriculture, where some 12% of arable land was still privately owned. The country became heavily dependent on trade and aid from other Communist countries, principally the USSR (through its participation in the Council of Mutual Economic Aid), encouraged by the US trade embargo. It relied on sugar, and to a lesser extent nickel, for nearly all its exports. While times were good, Cuba used the Soviet protection to build up an impressive, but costly, social welfare system, with better housing, education and health care than anywhere else in Latin America and the Caribbean. The collapse of the Eastern European bloc, however, revealed the vulnerability of the island's economy and the desperate need for reform. A sharp fall in GDP of 35% in 1990-93, accompanied by a decline in exports from US$8.1 bn (1989) to US$1.7 bn (1993), forced the Government to take remedial action and the decision was made to change to a mixed economy.

Transformation of the heavily centralized state apparatus has progressed in fits and starts. The Government initially encouraged self-employment to enable it to reduce the public sector workforce, but Cuban workers are cautious about relinquishing their job security. Some small businesses have sprung up, particularly in tourism, but numbers of registered tax payers have fallen. Free farm produce markets were permitted in 1994 and these were followed by similar markets at deregulated prices for manufacturers, including goods produced by state enterprises and handicrafts. Cubans are now allowed to hold US dollars. The US trade embargo and the associated inability to secure finance from multilateral sources has led the Government to encourage foreign investment, principally in joint ventures. All sectors of the economy are now open to foreign investment and in some areas majority foreign shareholdings are allowed.

Sugar is the major crop, and earns around US$430 mn in foreign exchange. However, the industry has consistently failed to reach the targets set, with output falling from 8mn tonnes in 1990 to 3.2 mn tonnes in 1998, the lowest for 50 years. Poor weather and shortages of fertilizers, oil and spare parts cut output. In 2002, 71 of the country's 156 sugar mills were closed and the land under production cut by 60%, with consequent severe job losses. **Tobacco** is a traditional crop, but this too has suffered from lack of fuel, fertilizers and other inputs. Production is recovering with the help of Spanish investment and credits and importers from France and Britain.

Diversification away is a major goal, with the emphasis on production of **food** for domestic use because of the shortage of foreign exchange for imports. The supply of food for the capital has greatly improved, partly with the introduction of city vegetable gardens, *agropónicos*, but the main staple, rice, is still imported to make up a shortfall in domestic production caused by inefficiencies. The beef herd declined in the first half of the 1990s because of the inability to pay for imports of grains, fertilizers and chemicals. Production is now less intensive and numbers are beginning to rise again. Similarly, milk production is also increasing.

The sudden withdrawal of **oil** supplies when trade agreements with Russia had to be renegotiated and denominated in convertible currencies, was a crucial factor in the collapse of the Cuban economy. Although trade agreements involving oil and sugar remain, Cuba has had to purchase oil from other suppliers with limited foreign exchange. As a result, Cuba has stepped up its own production: foreign companies explore for oil on and offshore and investment has borne fruit, with over 92% of electricity generated by domestic oil and gas and half of all consumption met by domestic production, but shortages of fuel remain.

Mining is attracting foreign interest and in 1994 a new mining law was passed. Major foreign investors include Australian (nickel), Canadian (gold, silver and base metals) and South African (gold, copper, nickel) companies. About half of nickel and cobalt production comes from the Moa Bay plant, a Canadian/Cuban joint venture.

Tourism is now a major foreign exchange earner and has received massive investment from abroad with many joint ventures. New hotel projects are coming on stream and many more are planned. Most of the development was initially along the Varadero coast, where large resort hotels attract package tourism, but Guardalavaca, Cayo Coco, Cayo Guillermo and other north coast cays are undergoing major construction. Despite political crises, numbers of visitors rose steadily from 546,000 in 1993 to 1.7 mn in 2002, generating revenues of US$1.85 bn. The target is for 7 mn tourists a year by 2010, bringing earnings of about US$11.8 bn. It is estimated that if the travel ban were lifted in the USA, some 1 mn American tourists would immediately book holidays in Cuba.

Culture

Church and State were separated at the beginning of the 20th century. The domination of the USA after that time encouraged the spread of Protestantism, although Catholicism remained the religion of the majority. Nevertheless, Catholicism was not as well supported as in some other Latin American countries. After the Revolution relations between the Catholic Church and Castro were frosty. Most priests left the country. By the late 1970s the Vatican's condemnation of the US embargo helped towards a gradual reconciliation. A ban on religious believers joining the Communist Party has been lifted and Protestant, Catholic and other Church leaders have reported rising congregations. In 1996 Fidel visited Pope John Paul II at the Vatican and the Pope visited Cuba in January 1998. Castro has stated in the past that there is no conflict between Marxism and Christianity and has been sympathetic towards supporters of liberation theology in their quest for equality and a just distribution of social wealth.

Religion

From the mid-16th century to the late 19th, hundreds of thousands of African slaves were brought to Cuba. The most numerous and culturally most influential group were the Yoruba-speaking agriculturalists from of Southeast Nigeria, Dahomey and Togo, who became known collectively in Cuba as *lucumí*. It is their pantheon of deities or *orishas*, and the legends (*pwatakis*) and customs surrounding these, which form the basis of the syncretic **Regla de Ocha** cult, better known as **Santería**. Though slaves were ostensibly obliged to become Christians, their owners turned a blind eye to their rituals. The Catholic saints thus spontaneously merged or syncretized in the *lucumí* mind with the *orishas* whose imagined attributes they shared. Some two dozen regularly receive tribute at the rites known as *toques de santo*. *Santería* is non-sectarian and non-proselytizing, co-existing peacefully with both Christianity and the **Regla Conga** or **Palo Monte** cult brought to Cuba by *congos*, slaves from various Bantu-speaking regions of the Congo basin. Indeed many people are practising believers in both or all three. The **Abakuá Secret Society** is not a religion but a closed sect. Open to men only, and upholding traditional *macho* virtues, it has been described as an Afro-Cuban freemasonry, though it claims many non-black devotees. Also known as **ñañiguismo**, the sect originated among slaves brought from the Calabar region of southern Nigeria and Cameroon, whose Cuban descendants are called *carabalí*.

Afro-Cuban religion

The Cuban Revolution had perhaps its widest cultural influence in the field of **literature**. Many now famous Latin American novelists (like Gabriel García Márquez, Mario Vargas Llosa and Julio Cortázar) visited Havana and worked with the Prensa Latina news agency or on the *Casa de las Américas* review. Not all have maintained their allegiance, just as some Cuban writers have deserted the Revolution. One such Cuban is Guillermo Cabrera Infante, whose most celebrated novel is *Tres tristes tigres* (1967). Other established writers remained in Cuba after the Revolution: Jorge Lezama Lima (*Paradiso*, 1966); Edmundo Desnoes (*Memorias del subdesarrollo*); and Alejo Carpentier, who invented the phrase *lo real maravilloso* (marvellous realism) to describe the different order of reality which he perceived in Latin America and the Caribbean and which influenced many other writers from the region (his novels include *El reino de este mundo, El siglo de las luces, Los pasos perdidos*, and many more). Of post-revolutionary writers, the poet and novelist Miguel Barnet is worth reading, especially for the use of black oral history and

Literature

traditions in his work. After 1959, Nicolás Guillén, a black, was adopted as the national poet; his poems of the 1930s (*Motivos de son, Sóngoro cosongo, West Indies Ltd*) are steeped in popular speech and musical rhythms. In tone they are close to the work of the *négritude* writers (see under Martinique), but they look more towards Latin America than Africa. The other poet-hero of the Revolution is the 19th-century writer and fighter for freedom from Spain, José Martí.

Music   Music is incredibly vibrant on the island. It is, again, a marriage of African rhythms, expressed in percussion instruments (batá drums, congas, claves, maracas, etc), and the Spanish guitar. Accompanying the music is an equally strong tradition of dance. There are four basic elements out of which all others grow. The *rumba* (drumming, singing about social preoccupations and dancing) is one of the original black dance forms. By the end of the 19th century, it had been transferred from the plantations to the slums; now it is a collective expression, with Saturday evening competitions in which anyone can partake. Originating in eastern Cuba, *son* is the music out of which *salsa* was born. *Son* itself takes many different forms and it gained worldwide popularity after the 1920s when the National Septet of Ignacio Piñeiro made it fashionable. The more sophisticated *danzón*, ballroom dance music which was not accepted by the upper classes until the end of the 19th century, has also been very influential. It was the root for the *cha-cha-cha* (invented in 1948 by Enrique Jorrin). The fourth tradition is *trova*, the itinerant troubadour singing ballads, which has been transformed, post-Revolution, into the *nueva trova*, made famous by singers such as Pablo Milanés and Silvio Rodríguez. The new tradition adds politics and everyday concerns to the romantic themes. There are many other styles, such as the *guajira*, the most famous example of which is the song *Guantanamera*; *tumba francesa* drumming and dancing; and Afro-Cuban jazz, performed by internationally renowned artists like Irakere and Arturo Sandoval. Apart from sampling the recordings of groups, put out by the state company Egrem, the National Folklore Company (Conjunto Folklórico Nacional) gives performances of the traditional music which it was set up to study and keep alive. The international explosion of Cuban music, old and new, has led to a trend in Cuban musical documentaries. The film that has made the greatest impact in recent years is without a doubt Wim Wender's documentary *Buena Vista Social Club* (Cuba/Germany, 1998), a nostalgic reconstruction of the lives and times of the band of the same name, whose original members are now in their eighties and nineties. Rubén González's piano playing, Ibrahim Ferrer's crooning, accompanied by Ry Cooder on guitar (with his soon Joaquín Cooder, on drums) practising for two gigs in Amsterdam (April 1998) and New York (July 1998) and – above all – the stunning colour photography are quite unforgettable. Two Grammy Award winning Cds are available: *Buena Vista Social Club* (WCD050) and *Buena Vista Social Club Presents Ibrahim Ferrer* (WCD055).

Cayman Islands

Introducing the Cayman Islands

These three low-lying little islands south of Cuba are green with pine and mangroves. Seven Mile Beach along the west side of Grand Cayman provides a welcome break for workers in the offshore financial centre. Nature conservation is top priority here, both on land and under water and there are a number of sanctuaries in the ponds and wetlands. The sister islands of Cayman Brac and Little Cayman are quiet, unhurried places where you can escape the crowds and relax without giving up your creature comforts. A dive destination ranked among the world's best, the islands offer a variety of thrilling dive sites. Famous too for their underwater scenery, there are tropical fish of all kinds in the waters surrounding the islands, especially in the coral reefs, and green turtles are now increasing in numbers, having been deliberately restocked by excess hatchings at the Cayman Turtle Farm.

USA

Atlantic
Ocean

Bahamas

Cuba

CAYMAN ISLANDS

Little
Cayman   Cayman
Grand   Brac
Cayman

Haiti

Jamaica

Caribbean
Sea

HONDURAS

NICARAGUA

Essentials

Before you travel

Passports or birth certificates and photo ID (but not voter registration card) but not visas are **Documents**
required for citizens of the USA, Canada, UK and British Dependent Territories. Passports are
required for visitors of all other countries. Everyone also needs a return or onward airline ticket.
Visas are not required for citizens of Commonwealth countries, Andorra, Argentina, Austria,
Bahrain, Belgium, Brazil, Chile, Costa Rica, Denmark, Ecuador, El Salvador, Finland, France, Germany, Greece, Guatemala, Iceland, Irish Republic, Israel, Italy, Japan, Kuwait, Liechtenstein, Luxembourg, Mexico, Monaco, Netherlands, Norway, Oman, Panama, Peru, Portugal, San Merino,
Saudi Arabia, Spain, Sweden, Switzerland and Venezuela. If you are from any of these countries
you may be admitted to the Cayman Islands for a period of up to six months. Resident aliens of
the USA who show a valid US Alien Registration Card (Green Card) may enter and remain in the
Cayman Islands for 30 days. **Visas** are required by all countries not included in the above list
and should be applied for at the nearest British Consulate or High Commission Office. Temporary work permits are available for business people on a short visit; these can be obtained in
advance from the Department of Immigration, PO Box 1098 GT, Grand Cayman, T9498052. If
you want to work in the country you may not accept a job unless you have a govern-
ment-issued work permit. No attempt should be made to take drugs into the country.

The legal **currency** is the Cayman Islands dollar (CI$). The **exchange rate** is fixed at CI$1 to **Money**
US$1.20, or CI$0.80 to US$1, although officially the exchange rate is CI$0.84 to US$1. US cur-
rency is readily accepted throughout the islands (although all change will be returned in CI$)
and Canadian and British currencies can be exchanged at all banks. There is no exchange control. **Credit cards** are accepted nearly everywhere. Personal cheques are not generally welcome. Travellers' cheques are preferred. Most of the major international **banks** are represented
in George Town, Grand Cayman but not all are licensed to offer normal banking facilities. Those
which do include *Bank of Nova Scotia, Barclays Bank International, Canadian Imperial Bank
of Commerce* and *Royal Bank of Canada*. Commercial banking hours are 0900-1600 Mon-Thu,
and 0900-1630 Fri. The *Cayman National Bank* has a branch on Cayman Brac.

The Cayman Islands lie in the trade-wind belt and the prevailing northeast winds moderate **Climate**
the temperatures, making the climate delightful all year round. Most rain falls May-Oct, but *Average temperatures*
even then it only takes the form of short showers. Hurricane season is Jun-Oct but the *are 24°C in winter and*
Cayman Islands have had little trouble since Hurricane Gilbert in 1988. *26°-29°C in summer*

Getting there

From Europe *British Airways* flies from London via Nassau, so 2-centre visits are possible. **Air**
There are also daily *BA* flights to Miami, which connect with *Cayman Airways* and only take an *All international*
hour longer. **From North America** The number of routes and destinations increases in *flights land in Grand*
winter, but the following are year-round: the national flag carrier, *Cayman Airways*, has reg- *Cayman. Cayman*
ular services from Houston, Miami and Tampa in the USA. *American Airlines* flies from Miami *Airways and Island Air*
and New Orleans. *US Air* flies from Charlotte, New York, Philadelphia. *Continental* flies from *connect the sister*
New York (Newark). *Delta* flies from Atlanta and New York (JFK, Dec-Apr). *Air Canada* flies *islands, Cayman Brac*
from Toronto. *Sunworld* from Cincinnati. **From the Caribbean** *Air Jamaica* and *Cayman* *and Little Cayman*
Airways share a service from Kingston; *Air Jamaica* also has services from Montego Bay *Isleña*
flies from La Ceiba, Honduras. *Aerocaribbean* and *Cayman Airways* fly to/from Havana, Cuba
twice a week (Sun and Fri, contact *Lily Tours* T9450871 or *Cayman Airways*, T9492311).

No more than 4 cruise ships may be in port at any given time, or 6,500 passengers, whichever is **Sea**
greater. The islands are not served by scheduled passenger ships but there are cargo services *30 major cruise lines*
between the islands, Kingston in Jamaica, Honduras and Costa Rica and Miami and Tampa in *visit Grand Cayman*
the USA. The port at George Town comprises the south wharf and the west wharf. The port at *with 600 calls to port*
Creek, Cayman Brac, can handle the same vessels but Little Cayman only has a small facility. *each year bringing*
over 1 million visitors

Cayman Islands

▶ ## Tourist offices overseas

Canada *234 Eglinton Av East, Suite 306, Toronto, Ontario, M4P IK5 T416-4851550, info-canada@caymanislands.ky*
Germany/Austria/Switzerland *Johanna-Melber-Weg 12, D-60599, Frankfurt, T69-6032094, msi-germany@t-online.de*
UK *6 Arlington St, London SW1A 1RE, T020-74917771, www.caymanislands.co.uk The London office is also the European headquarters for Cayman Airways,*

providing air reservations and tickets as well as a hotel reservations service (free).
USA *8300 NW 53rd St, Suite 103, Miami, FL 33166, T305-5999033; 9525 W Bryn Mawr, Suite 160, Rosemont, Illinois 60018, T847-6786446; 2 Memorial City Plaza, 820 Gessner, Suite 170, Houston, Texas 77024, T713-4611317; 3 Park Av, 39th Floor, New York, NY 10016, T212-8899009, info-usa@caymanislands.ky*

Touching down

Airport information Air communications are good and there are 2 international airports, the **Owen Roberts International Airport** on Grand Cayman and the **Gerrard Smith Airport** on Cayman Brac. **Owen Roberts International Airport** is situated less than 2 miles from the centre of George Town and only 10 minutes' drive from most of the hotels on Seven Mile Beach. In a plaza outside the terminal there are car hire companies and a café, open 0600-1800.

Airlines *Cayman Airways*, T9492311 on Grand Cayman, T9481221 on Cayman Brac, www.camanairways.com *Island Air*, for flights to the sister islands, T9490241 (charters), T9495252 (reservations), F9497044, online reservations can be made at www.IslandAir Cayman.com *Air Jamaica*, T9492300. *American Airlines*, T9490666. *Northwest Airlines*, T9492955/6. *US Air*, T9497488. Charter companies: *Executive Air Services*, T9497775.

Tourist information Information may be obtained from the **Cayman Islands Department of Tourism**, The Pavilion, Cricket Sq, Elgin Av, George Town, Grand Cayman, BWI, T9490623, toll free 1800-3463313, 0830-1700, www.cayman islands.ky The *Cayman Islands National Trust* has a lot of historical and environmental information about the islands, T9490121, www.caymannationaltrust.org
  The Cayman Islands Government Information Services (The Pavilion, Cricket Sq, Grand Cayman, T9498092, F9498487) publishes a series of booklets including *Marine Parks Rules and Sea Code in The Cayman Islands* and several on banking, captive insurance, company registration, residential status, work permits, living in the Cayman Islands, etc. The Department of Tourism publishes *The Rates and Facts Guide to the Cayman Islands* annually, giving hotel and transport prices as well as other useful information. The tourist office also has a list of books about the Cayman Islands which can be bought in the islands.
  Maps The *Ordnance Survey* produces a 1:50,000 scale map of the Cayman Islands with an inset map of George Town. For information contact *Ordnance Survey*, Romsey Rd, Maybush, Southampton SO16 4GU, T08456-050505, F02380-792615, www.ordnancesurvey.co.uk

Where to stay

A government tax of 10% is added to the room charge and most hotels also add a 10-15% service charge to the bill in lieu of tipping. The winter season, running from 16 Dec-15 Apr, is the peak tourist season. Visitors intending to come to the islands during this period are advised to make hotel and travel arrangements well in advance. There are substantial reductions during the rest of the year, with cut rates or even free accommodation for children under 12. Most hotels offer watersports, scuba diving and snorkelling, and many have tennis courts, swimming pools and other facilities. Accommodation is plentiful and varied, ranging from resort hotels on the beach to small, out of the way, family-run guesthouses, but it is not cheap and you will not get a double room for less than US$60 on any of the islands. There is also a wide variety of cottages, apartments (condominiums) and villas available for daily, weekly or monthly rental, which can work out more economical if you are in a group.

Touching down

Business hours Banks: Mon-Thu 0900-1600, Fri 0900-1630; **Offices:** 0830-1600; **Shops:** 0900-1700.
Currency The Cayman Islands dollar (CI$). US currency is readily accepted throughout the Islands (although all change will be returned in CI$). Credit cards are accepted nearly everywhere.
Departure tax US$25/CI$20 for all visitors aged 12 and over included in the price of your airline ticket.
Emergency numbers T911.
Media The Caymanian Compass is published Mon-Fri with a circulation of 25,000. Online you can get news and information with Cayman Net News at www.caymannetnews.com
Official time Eastern Standard Time,

5 hrs behind GMT, for the whole year.
Public holidays New Year's Day, Ash Wed, Good Fri, Easter Mon, Discovery Day (third Mon in May), the Mon following the Queen's official birthday (Jun), Constitution Day (first Mon in Jul), the Mon after Remembrance Sun (Nov), Christmas Day and Boxing Day.
Safety The Cayman Islands are safe to visit and present no need for extra security precautions. However, drugs-related offences have increased. The islands remain a major trans-shipment point. Care must be taken when walking on a road, especially at night; they are narrow and vehicles move fast.
Voltage 110 voltage, 60 cycles.
Weights and measures Imperial.

Cayman Islands

Getting around

Air Cayman Airways and Island Air provide inter-island services from Grand Cayman to Cayman Brac and Little Cayman and return (see Airlines above). There are 4 flights a day from Grand Cayman to Cayman Brac and Little Cayman with Island Air. You can have a full day on either sister island by booking flight 6131, departing Grand Cayman 0745, arriving Cayman Brac at 0825 and Little Cayman at 0845. The last return flight 6314 departs Cayman Brac at 1725, Little Cayman at 1745, arriving back in Grand Cayman at 1830. Fares are US$110 day trip Grand Cayman to Little Cayman or Cayman Brac (US$40 day trip Cayman Brac to Little Cayman); US$77 (US$20) one way; US$154 (US$40) ordinary return. A child's day trip fare is US$89, T9495252. A US$5 per passenger facility charge is added to fares from Grand Cayman.

Keeping in touch

Post The Philatelic Bureau releases 6 stamp issues a year. Stamps are sold separately or as a First Day Cover from CI$0.10 to 2.00. Airmail postal rates are divided into 3 groups. **Group A**: the Caribbean, USA, Canada, Central America and Venezuela, first class 30 cents, second class, post cards, airletters 20 cents. **Group B**: Europe, Scandinavia, West Africa, South America, first class 40 cents, others 25 cents. **Group C**: East Africa, the Arabian sub-continent, Asia and the Far East, first class 60 cents, others 30 cents.

Telephone & internet
IDD code: 1-345
The Cayman Islands have a modern automatic telephone system operated by *Cable and Wireless*. International telephone, email and facsimile facilities are available. Public international telephone booths and a telegram counter are at the *Cable and Wireless* offices at Anderson Sq. Open Mon-Thu 0815-1700, Fri 0815-1600, Sat 0815-1300. *Communication Station* is behind *Colombian Emeralds International* in George Town by the harbour. There are 32 telephones, 5 internet kiosks, a photocopier, fax machine and phone cards for sale. 0830-1700 Mon-Sat. Many hotels offer internet access for guests. The international code is followed by a 7-digit local number. For overseas credit card calls (Visa and Mastercard) dial 0 for operator and follow instructions.

Food and drink

Caymanian recipes use seafood predominantly

The range of restaurants is wide and all styles are available from fast food to gourmet. Check your bill as gratuities are sometimes added. Cayman-style fish is sautéed with tomato, onion, pepper and piquant seasoning. Conch is available as chowder, fritters or marinated. Try Caymanian rum cake for dessert. The *Tortuga Rum Company*, T9497701, has many outlets plus a 2,500-sq ft bakery (open to visitors daily 0730-1700) where up to 5,000 rum cakes are baked daily for shipment worldwide. While the recipe remains a family secret, a key component is the use of *Tortuga Gold Rum*, which is not sold to the public. You can visit and sample the varieties of rum cake, purchase the rum blends or other locally made items such as fudge, hot pepper sauce, steak sauce or flavoured coffee. The *Stingray Brewery*, Red Bay, east of George Town, T9476699, can also be visited. This microbrewery makes 1,500 barrels of beer for island consumption, every year. Gift shop and brewery Mon-Sat 0900-1800. Tours on request with free samples of dark and premium beer. *Icoa Chocolates*, 127 North Church St, George Town, T9451915, is the only chocolate shop, making delicacies blended with local ingredients such as Caribbean spice, Cayman honey and coconut (Mon-Fri 0900-1700, Sat 1130-1700).

Shopping

As a free port, there is duty-free shopping and a range of British glass, crystal, china, woollens, perfumes and spirits are available. US citizens are entitled to a US$400 exemption after being away from the USA for 48 hours

Black coral carvings and **jewellery** are widely available. Note that since the 1978 Cayman Islands Marine Conservation Law prohibited the removal of coral from local waters, manufacturers turned to Belize and Honduras for their supply. All the Central American countries are now members of CITES, so if you must buy it, check the source in case it has been procured illegally. **Caymanite** is a semi-precious gem stone with layers of various colours found only in the Cayman Islands. Local craftspeople use it to make jewellery.

At *Churchill's Cigar Store*, T9456141, you can buy **Cuban** seed tobacco, rolled and packaged in the Cayman Islands so it can be legally imported into the USA, look for Cayman Crown and Cayman Premium. The day's **fish** catch can be bought from the fishermen most afternoons opposite the Tower Building just outside central George Town..

Useful for **arts** and **crafts** is the *National Gallery of the Cayman Islands* (T9458111) comprehensive 'Art Trail' map which highlights the location of artists, studios, galleries, craftsmen's homes and retail outlets, related establishments and points of interest in the Cayman Islands. The Gallery is temporarily located at Harbour Place, George Town, due to move to Harquail Bypass by 2004. They have a stall in central George Town, Grand Cayman, selling work by local artists and craftsmen, run as a cooperative called *Native Done*. *Pure Art*, T9455633, on South Church St (also at *Hyatt Regency*), sells the work of over 100 local artists and craftsmen and women; paintings, prints, sculptures, crafts, rugs, wallhangings, etc. Open daily 0900-1700. *Kennedy Gallery*, T9498077, in the West Shore Centre off West Bay Rd, exhibits all types of art including functional sculpture. Open Mon-Sat 1000-1800. *Kensington Lott Gallery*, T9469696, in Harbour Place, George Town, is devoted to the work of many talented local artists. Open 1100-1900. *The National Museum* on the waterfront in George Town has a popular, well-stocked gift shop for prints, posters, books and crafts. Open Mon-Fri 0900-1700, Sat 0900-1400, T9498368. The *National Trust House* headquarters on Courts Rd, T9490121, ntrust@candw.ky, open Mon-Fri 0900-1700, has a gift shop featuring locally made gifts, Cayman-related books and Trust materials, including posters of the red-footed booby and the endangered blue iguana. *Caribbean Charlie's* in Northside, near Rum Point, offers a wide assortment of tropical crafts with handmade, custom designed and signed work, T9479452. On Cayman Brac, *NIM Things* sells items made locally, including caymanite jewellery, straw bags and crochet. Open 0900-1900, T9480461, at Spot Bay, east-end of the Main North Side Rd, but not always open. *Joe Tourist*, T9465638, is 'Made in Cayman' casual wear and **accessory** line. The children's range is decorated with stingrays, blue iguanas and green sea turtles. *Joe Tourist* products are available only in the Cayman Islands, although you can order them on-line at www.joetourist.com *The Book Nook* (which sells *Caribbean Islands Handbook* among other **books**, **toys**, **gifts** and games), is at Galleria Plaza, West Bay Rd, T9474686, Mon-Sat 0900-1800, and Anchorage Centre, T9497392, PO Box 1551, Grand Cayman, F9475053, Mon-Fri 0900-1600.

Flora and fauna

Birds that inhabit the islands include the Antillean grackle, the smooth-billed ani, the green-backed heron, the yellow-crowned night heron and many other heron species, the snowy egret, the common ground dove, the bananaquit and the Cayman parrot. The endangered West Indian whistling duck can be seen on Grand Cayman and Little Cayman. If you are interested in birdwatching, go to the mosquito control dykes on the West Bay peninsula of Grand Cayman, or walk to the Cistern at East End. A former Governor was a keen birdwatcher and in 1993 he set up a fund to establish the **Governor Michael Gore Bird Sanctuary** on 3½ acres of wetland on Grand Cayman, where you can see 60 local species. There are nesting colonies of the red-footed booby and the magnificent frigate bird on Little Cayman. There is a parrot reserve on Cayman Brac on 197 acres of land donated to the National Trust by Donald Pennie. The **Brac Parrot Reserve** is the nesting ground for the endangered endemic Cayman Brac parrot, numbering about 400 birds. The reserve covers pristine ancient woodlands on a very rough and rocky terrain with a diversity of native trees, including species not present on Grand Cayman or Little Cayman. A 1-mile nature trail has been established through part of the reserve. The trail forms a loop which passes through several different types of terrain, from old farm land now under grass, past mango trees on red soil and through thickets and mature woodlands, a startling mixture of hardwoods and cacti. Signs and information boards are placed at strategic points along the trail and a brochure is available. *Birds of the Cayman Islands*, by PE Bradley, published by the British Ornithologists Union, is a photographic record; it costs £35. **Cardinal D's Park** on the outskirts of George Town, and the beginning of Seven Mile Beach, has four acres of natural lakes and woodlands. The bird sanctuary includes parrots, macaws, whistling duck and turtles. ■ *Mon-Fri 1000-1800, Sat-Sun 1200-1800. US$ 6, children US$3. T9498855.*

Indigenous animals on the islands are few. The most common are the agouti, non-poisonous snakes, iguana and other small lizards, freshwater turtle, the hickatee and two species of tree frog. Several animal sanctuaries have been established, most of which are RAMSAR sites where no hunting or collecting of any species is allowed. On Grand Cayman there are sanctuaries at Booby Cay, Meagre Bay Pond and Colliers Bay Pond; on Cayman Brac at the ponds near the airport and on Little Cayman at Booby Rd and Rookery, Tarpon Lake and the Wearis Bay Wetland, stretching east along the south coast to the Easterly Wetlands. The National Trust, T9490121, ntrust@candw.ky, has set up a Land Reserves Fund to buy environmentally sensitive land and protect natural resources.

Oncidium calochilum, a rare orchid, indigenous to Grand Cayman with a small yellow flower about ½ in long, is found only in the rocky area off Frank Sound Drive. Several other orchid species have been recorded as endemic but are threatened by construction and orchid fanciers. There is protection under international and local laws for several indigenous species, including sea turtles, iguanas, Cayman parrots, orchids and marine life. For a full description of the islands' flora see George R Proctor, *Flora of the Cayman Islands*, Kew Bulletin Additional Series XI, HMSO (1984), 834 pages, which lists 21 endemic plant taxa including some which are rare, endangered or possibly extinct.

The **Queen Elizabeth II Botanic Park** (which was officially opened by the Queen in 1994), is off Frank Sound Rd, Grand Cayman. A mile-long woodland trail has been cleared and an entrance garden created. In 1997 a second phase brought a Floral Colour Garden and a Heritage Garden, with endemic plants, within the park. The gardens are very beautiful now , so much so that they have become very well-established and are recommended for a day away from the beach even for those who know nothing about botany. Over 200 plants have been labelled so far, several of which are rare. Orchids bloom in May-Jun and there are breeding areas for the Grand Cayman blue iguana, the Grand Cayman parrot, the Cayman rabbit and the Cayman anole lizard. More gardens and sections are planned for the future. There are special events, which are sometimes held, such as an orchid show, in Feb, and a mango morning in Aug. There is a Visitor Centre, café and giftshop and a typical Caymanian cottage and garden has been built. ■ *Daily 0900-1730, last admission 1630. US$7.50, children 6-12 US$5. T9473558 (information line), 9479462, F9477873, www.botanic-park.ky*

There are around 200 species of bird on the islands

Cayman Islands

Diving and marine life

The best months for diving are April to October

Since 1986, a Marine Parks plan has been implemented to preserve the beauty and marine life of the islands. Even before then, however, a moorings project was in place. This has been highly successful in marine conservation and critical in protecting Cayman's fragile coral reefs and marine life from destruction by boat anchors. Permanent moorings have been installed along the west coast of Grand Cayman where there is concentrated diving, and also outside the marine parks in order to encourage diving boats to disperse and lessen anchor damage to the reefs. Make sure you check all rules and regulations as there have been several prosecutions and convictions for offences such as taking conch or lobsters. The import of spearguns or speargun parts and their use without a licence is banned. Divers and snorkellers must use a flag attached to a buoy when outside safe swimming areas. For further information call *Natural Resources (Department of Environment)*, T9498469.

Many of the better reefs and several wrecks are found in water shallow enough to require only mask, snorkel and fins; the swimming is easy and fish friendly

Although boats take snorkellers to many sites, you can snorkel quite happily from the shore. However, each island has a wall going down to extraordinary depths: the north wall of Cayman Brac drops from 60 to 14,000 ft, while the south wall drops to 18,000 ft. The deepest known point in the Caribbean is the Cayman Trench, 40 miles south of Cayman Brac, where soundings have indicated a depth of 24,724 ft. *The Dive Sites of the Cayman Islands*, by Lawson Wood, latest edition published by McGraw-Hill in 2001, describes 260 dive and snorkel sites aroundthe islands, together with beautiful underwater photographs mostly taken by the author. One site is the Russian frigate (a Brigadier Type II Class), brought from Cuba and deliberately sunk in 1996 to provide good wreck diving off Cayman Brac. The 330-ft relic of the Cold War was sunk on a sloping bed of sand 27-72 ft deep and only 90 ft from the shore, good for snorkellers as well as divers. It has been renamed the *MV Captain Keith Tibbetts*, after a popular resident of Cayman Brac, and its sinking was supervised by Jean Michel Cousteau, who stood on the bridge and 'went down with the ship'. Mounted underwater cameras will monitor the growth of coral, etc.

The dive-tourism market is highly developed in the Cayman Islands and there is plenty of choice, but it has been often described as a cattle market with dive boats taking very large parties. Many companies offer full services to certified divers as well as courses designed to introduce scuba diving to novices; there are many highly qualified instructor-guides. There is a firm limit of a depth of 100 ft for visiting divers, regardless of training and experience and the 69 member companies of the CIWOA will not allow you to exceed that. A complete selection of diving and fishing tackle, underwater cameras and video equipment is available for hire. The tourist office has a full price list for all operators. There is also the liveaboard *Cayman Aggressor IV* (US$1,795-2,095 per week all-inclusive, 5½ days' diving, 4-5 dives daily), which accommodates 18 divers and cruises around Grand Cayman, Cayman Brac and Little Cayman, depending on weather conditions. Contact *Aggressor Fleet Limited*, T9495551, www.aggressor.com

Festivals

2003 was the 500th anniversary of the colonization of the island and there were lots of Quincentennial festivities year round, see www.cayman500.ky *Pirates' Week* is the islands' national festival and takes place in the **last week of Oct**. Parades, regattas, fishing tournaments, treasure hunts, historical and cultural 'district days' in Grand Cayman's 5 districts and on Little Cayman, are all part of the celebrations, which commemorate the days when the Cayman Islands were the haunt of pirates and buccaneers (T9495078, www.piratesweekfestival.com). *Batabano* is Grand Cayman's costume carnival weekend, with street parades, music and dancing, which takes place in the **last week of Apr** or **beginning of May**. Cayman Brac has a similar celebration, known as *Brachanal*, which takes place in **Jun**. Everyone is invited to dress up and participate, and there are several competitions. *Cayfest*, the islands' national arts festival, takes place through most of **Apr**, with exhibitions, displays, dance and drama. The *Queen's Birthday* is celebrated in **mid-Jun** with a full-dress uniform parade, marching bands and a 21-gun salute. At the **end of Apr** is an 8-day *International Fishing Tournament*, with big prizes for catches of blue marlin, yellowfin tuna, wahoo and dolphin fish, contact tournament HQ T9453131 , www.fishcayman.com for details. In **mid-Jun**, *International Aviation Week* attracts private pilots and flight demonstrations over Seven Mile Beach. The **first weekend in Jul** the Cayman Islands Restaurant Association holds an annual food festival: the *Taste of Cayman*, with lots of food and outdoor activities. Christmas brings the Parade of Lights by boat on the waterfront, the Rotary Club's Annual Christmas Tree Lighting and Radio 3-99's 'Wacky House Light Tour'.

Health

Medical care on Grand Cayman is good and readily available. There is a 128-bed **Cayman Islands Hospital** in George Town (T9496066), with accident and emergency unit. For 24-hour ambulance and paramedic service on Grand Cayman, T911 or 555. The hospital is affiliated with the Baptist Hospital of Miami for patient referrals involving advanced care or treatment. A 2-person, double-lock recompression chamber is located by the hospital and supervised by a physician experienced in hyperbaric medicine. Out-patients pay a fixed charge per visit. There is a 12-bed hospital in Cayman Brac (T9482243/2245) and a clinic on Little Cayman (T9480072) staffed by a registered nurse. Open Mon-Fri 0900-1300, or on call 24 hrs. A doctor visits Wed.

Grand Cayman is sprayed frequently though it is advisable to bring insect repellent to combat mosquitoes and sandflies. Little Cayman is sprayed every two weeks

Grand Cayman

Grand Cayman is a prosperous island with a British feel despite the huge American influence on tourism. The island is green with luxuriant vegetation, especially at the East End with the pastures and grazing cows. North Sound is a 40-square mile lagoon with mangroves, although dredging schemes and urban growth threaten the mangrove habitat and the reefs. Some low-key but sophisticated development has taken place along the north coast around Cayman Kai, which has lovely beaches and good swimming and snorkelling. Most of the tourist development is along Seven Mile Beach on West Bay, where there are hotels, clubs, sports facilities, banks, restaurants and supermarkets.

IDD code: 345
Colour map 1, grid C2
Population 37,083

Ins and outs

See page 157 for details of flights from London, Toronto and US cities as well as from neighbouring islands.

Getting there

Driving is on the left and the roads are in good order. The Public Transportation Board offers a recorded information service at T9455100, giving details on buses, taxis, limousines and tour buses, including routes and fares. There is a bus service all over the island with marked stops. If you stand by the road minibuses will toot their horns to see if you want a ride. Be careful of buses whose doors open into the centre of the road. Island tours can be arranged at about US$60 for a taxi, or US$10 per person on a bus with a minimum of 20 people. Check with your hotel for full details.

Getting around
See Transport, page 173 for more details

Diving and marine life

Snorkelling and dive sites abound all round the island and include shallow dives for beginners as well as highly challenging and deeper dives for the experienced. Off the west coast there are three wrecks, arches, tunnels, caves, canyons and lots of reef sites close to shore which can be enjoyed by snorkellers and divers. Along the south coast the coral reefs are rich and varied with depths ranging from 15 ft to thousands of feet. The **East End wall** has pinnacles, tunnels and a coral formation known as **The Maze**, a 500-ft coral formation of caverns, chimneys, arches and crevices. There are several wrecks here also. Snorkelling is good near the *Morritt's Tortuga Club* at the East End, also all along **Seven Mile Beach**, **North Sound**, **Smith Cove** in South Sound and off **Eden Rock**, near George Town. Along the north coast you can dive the **North Wall**. Near **Rum Point Channel** experienced divers can dive the Grand

Dive sites

Cayman Islands

> ### ★ Things to do in the Cayman Islands
>
> - The **National Museum** gives an excellent introduction to the history of the islands and the way of life of the people.
> - Feel the thrill of **touching a stingray** at Stingray City.
> - Hike through the **Parrot Reserve** on Cayman Brac, one of the many Heritage Sites on the island.
> - Kayak to **Owen Island** off Little Cayman for peace and tranquillity.
> - **Dive the wall**, and then do it again, and again.

Canyon, where depths start at 70 ft. The canyons, collapsed reefs, are 150 ft wide in places. Other sites in this area towards **Palmetto Point** include the aptly-named **Eagle Ray Pass**, **Tarpon Alley** and **Stingray City**.

Dive centres The tourist office lists 32 dive operations on Grand Cayman, offering a wide range of courses and dive sites. For a full list of dive operators and sites, see www.divecayman.ky Many are at more than one location, attached to hotels. All are of a high standard but you may want to make your choice according to the number of divers per boat. The popular and accessible dive sites are off South Sound or North West Point, where the wall or mini walls are close to shore. Boat dives go to the many sites along Seven Mile Beach or the North Wall, which is much more dramatic but generally a little rougher. Prices for a certification course start at US$300, rising to US$500; for qualified divers, a 2-tank dive costs US$50-75 and a Stingray City dive US$40-60, depending on how far the boat has to come. Snorkelling trips are also available, US$20-40.

Grand Cayman is host to a revolutionary product for youngsters under 12 who are too young to use standard scuba equipment. Children as young as 4 can now snorkel with a SASY (approved by PADI and NAUI). Supplied Air Snorkelling for Youth (SASY) is a scuba unit customised to fit children, allowing the child to float safely on the surface and view the marine world below without danger of being submerged. SASY units are available at all Red Sail Sports locations in Grand Cayman (www.redsail.com).

An additional refinement, *Atlantis* submarines, T9497700, operate a 20-ft research submarine, *Deep Explorer 1000* (2 passengers, fare US$395 per person, 5 dives a day Mon-Sat) to the 800-ft deep Cayman Wall or to the wreck of the *Kirk Pride* at 780 ft, while a larger submarine, with room for 48 passengers dives to 100 ft along Cayman Wall; fares are US$69 for a 1-hr day or night dive (children 4-12 half price). For US$24 you can take a 1-hr ride in *Seaworld Explorer*, an underwater observatory for 35 people, down 4 ft. A diver will attract fish within view by feeding them (Don Foster's – *Subsee* – Ltd, T9498534). The Nautilus Semi-Submersible is a 110-ft hulled vessel, which seats 60 people 5 ft below the surface.

Grand Cayman

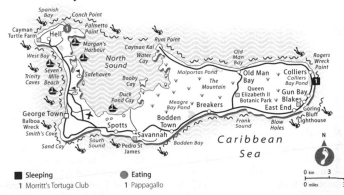

■ Sleeping	● Eating
1 Morritt's Tortuga Club	1 Pappagallo

Stingray City

◀

Stingray City is a popular local phenomenon, where it is possible to swim with and observe large groups of extremely tame rays in only 12 ft of water. Stingray City is better dived but half a mile away is the sandbar where stingrays also congregate, usually over 30 at a time, although there are thought to be around 250 in the area. The water here is only 1-3 ft deep and crystal clear, so you hop out of your boat and the rays brush past you waiting to be fed. Their mouths are beneath their head and the rays, 3 ft across, swim into your arms to be fed on squid. They can give your arm quite a suck if they miss the food in your hand. Unfortunately the sandbar can get too popular. Thousands of cruise ship passengers crowd into a small area and there are no limitations on the number of boats allowed to visit. A glass-bottom boat leaves from the Rum Point Club to the sandbar and a nearby reef, 1100-1230, 1500-1630, US$28. From Morgan's Harbour boats charge US$35.

There are at least 14 companies on Grand Cayman offering fishing. The tourist office can give you a full list with prices, which depend on the type of boat you choose. Deep-sea fishing boats can be chartered for a half day (US$350-700) or full day (US$500-1,500). Reef and bone fishing is about US$400-700 for a full day including all equipment, bait and lunch. There is an **Angling Club**, call Donna Sjostrom, T9497099, fishing@candw.ky   **Fishing**

Cayman Islands

Beaches and watersports

West Bay Beach, now known as **Seven Mile Beach**, has dazzling white sand and is lined by hotels, tall Australian pines and silver thatch palms, the national tree. Beaches on the east and north coasts are equally good, and are protected by an offshore barrier reef. On the north coast, at **Cayman Kai**, there is a superb public beach with changing facilities; from here you can snorkel along the reef to **Rum Point**. The beaches around Rum Point are recommended for peace and quiet, with shallow water safe for children. *Red Sail Sports* at Rum Point also ensure lots of entertainment, with wind surfers, sail boats, wave runners and waterskiing as well as glass-bottomed boat tours to see the stingrays and scuba diving. There are hammocks, sunbeds, lockers, changing rooms, showers, restaurants, bar and Thomas the tabby cat. You can cross the North Sound by ferry from the *Hyatt Regency* to *Rum Point Club* (also under Hyatt management). ■ *T9499098. US$15 round trip, children 5 to 12 years half price, under 5s free. 120 passengers, 30 mins, departs 0930, 1200, 1400, 1600, returns 1100, 1300, 1500, 1700, 2130. The timetable is subject to change depending on the time of year.* Around Rum Point at Water Cay and Finger Cay there are picnic sites on the lagoon. Take insect repellent. South of George Town there are good beaches for swimming and snorkelling at **Smith's Cove** and **Sand Cay**. In Frank Sound, **Heritage Beach**, just west of Cottage Point, is owned by the National Trust.

For information about sailing contact the **Cayman Islands Yacht Club**, Grand Cayman, T9454322, F9454432, with docking facilities for 154 boats, 7 ft maximum draft. *Aquanauts* at Morgan's Harbour, T9451990, F9451991, also offers 15 slips accommodating boats of 6½ ft draft and the usual facilities. For a social sailing club there is the **Grand Cayman Sailing Club**, Red Bay Estates, T9477913.   **Sailing**

Cayman Windsurf, a BiC Centre, is at *Morritt's Tortuga Club*, East End, T9477492, cawin@candw.ky, with a full range of BiC boards and UP sails and instruction available. On Seven Mile Beach, *Surfside Aquasports*, T/F9491068, windsurf@candw.ky, also offer rental and instruction, this is a Mistral certified school. Windsurfing at the East End is highly rated for people of all abilities. Beginners are safe within the reef, while outside the reef experienced sailors can try wave jumping or wave riding. Winds are brisk nearly all the year, with speeds of 15-25 knots. Lots of hotels' watersports operators offer windsurfing, sunfish, wave runners and other equipment.   **Windsurfing**

George Town

IDD code: 345
Colour map 1, grid C2
Population:
over 18,000

The largest town and capital of the islands is George Town, which is principally a business centre dominated by modern office blocks. However, many of the older buildings are being restored and the government is trying to promote museums and societies to complement beach and watersports tourism. When cruise ships come in the town can be exceptionally crowded, but at other times it is a quiet place where people work rather than live.

Sights The **Cayman Islands National Museum**, in the restored Old Courts Building in George Town, opened in 1990 and is well worth a visit. There are exhibits portraying the nation's seafaring history, an audiovisual presentation and a natural history display, as well as temporary exhibitions. The newest feature is a CD-ROM interactive exhibit, where you can touch the screen and access nearly 400 images of traditional sand yards, provision gardens and other features of typical Caymanian life as it used to be. There are also audio segments where you can touch and hear accounts by older Caymanians about backing sand, caboose cooking, tending provision gardens, making grounds and sharing the harvest with neighbours. ■ *Mon-Fri 0900-1700, Sat 1000-1400. US$5, children 6-18 US$2.50. T9498368, www.museum.ky There is a museum shop and* The Cool Caboose *for refreshments.*

Four of the older buildings which are being preserved are the work of a local boat-builder, Captain Rayal Brazley Bodden, MBE, JP (1885-1976). He was called upon to build the **Elmslie Memorial Church** (Presbyterian, on Harbour Drive, opposite the docks) in 1923. He put in a remarkable roof, with timbers largely salvaged from shipwrecks. Such was the general admiration that he was asked to design the **Town Hall**, a peace memorial for the First World War. It now looks tiny, but when it was opened in 1926 it was considered a grandiose folly, far too big for the island. Then came the **Public Library** nearby, with its beautiful hammer-beam roof and painted British university heraldic shields. Lastly came the **General Post Office**, 1939, which once housed all the colony's departments of government. Bodden surrounded the main façades of the building with art deco tapered columns. All his buildings have an inter-war flavour. They are one-storey, made of carefully shaped concrete blocks, poured to give a rustic, deep-grooved effect.

Cayman Islands

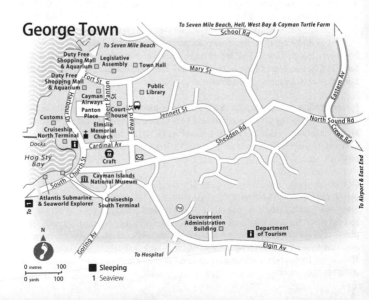

George Town

To Seven Mile Beach, Hell, West Bay & Cayman Turtle Farm
School Rd
To Seven Mile Beach
Duty Free Shopping Mall & Aquarium
Legislative Assembly
Town Hall
Mary St
Duty Free Shopping Mall & Aquarium
Fort St
Public Library
Eastern Av
Cayman Airways
Albert Panton St
Panton Place
Court-house
Jennett St
Customs
Edward St
North Sound Rd
Cruiseship North Terminal
Elmslie Memorial Church
Shedden Rd
Crewe Rd
Docks
Cardinal Av
Hog Sty Bay
South Church St
Craft
Cayman Islands National Museum
Atlantis Submarine & Seaworld Explorer
Cruiseship South Terminal
Pol
Government Administration Building
Department of Tourism
Goring Av
Elgin Av
To Hospital
To Airport & East End

N

0 metres 100
0 yards 100

■ **Sleeping**
1 Seaview

An archaeological dig on the waterfront on the site of **Fort George** has been sponsored by the Cayman National Trust. Unfortunately only a small part of the walls remain, much was demolished in 1972 by a developer who would have destroyed the lot if residents had not prevented him. The National Trust has designed a walking tour of George Town to include 28 sites of interest, such as Fort George, built around 1790, the Legislative Assembly, the war and peace memorials and traditional Caymanian architecture. A brochure and map (free) is available from the National Trust, T9490121, or the tourist office. Walking tours are also available for West Bay and Bodden Town.

There is a new duty-free shopping mall close to George Town harbour containing a 12,000-gallon saltwater aquarium, stocked with colourful fish, sharks, eels and stingrays. Educational lectures and fish feedings at 1100 and 1300. Close by are a *Hard Rock Café*, a new art gallery and a *Tortuga Rum* factory shop.

Around the island

Interesting places to visit in Grand Cayman are included in a *Heritage One* passport, with discounts of 25% to the Museum, Turtle Farm, Pedro St James and Queen Elizabeth II Botanic Garden. The green and blue passports are stamped at each site but have no expiry date. They are available at each attraction, US$20 adults, US$11 children.

The **Cayman Turtle Farm**, at Northwest Point, houses over 16,000 green turtles and is the only commercial turtle farm in the world. Most of the turtles are used for meat locally since the USA banned the import of turtle meat, but some 28,000 turtles have been released into the wild to replenish native stocks. They are released as yearlings weighing 3-6 lbs. Those at the farm range in size from 2 oz hatchlings to breeding stock weighing an average of 38.5 lbs. Polished turtle shells are sold here for about US$100, but their import into the USA is prohibited. A flora and fauna section of the farm includes the Cayman green parrot, a macaw called Crackers, a freshwater turtle, ground iguanas and agouti (known as the Cayman rabbit). In November 2001, a surge storm associated with Hurricane Michelle seriously damaged the farm's sea walls allowing 275 breeding turtles to escape. A few have been recovered but it was decided that relocation was essential to prevent it happening again. Work has started on a new farm across the road, which will be laid out better for visitors and turtles, with more space also for the other animals, such as iguanas, and a nature trail. There will also be an application to CITES for the registration of the Cayman Turtle Farm for captive breeding status. ■ *Daily 0830-1700. US$6, free for children 12 and under. PO Box 645GT, T9493893/4, www.turtle.ky Taxi from George Town US$20.*

West Bay is a colourful area with houses dating back to the seafaring days. The National Trust has a self-guided walkers' booklet of the area, directing you along lanes and paths with illustrated information about the district. The Pink House, built in 1912, is included in tour itineraries as a typical Caymanian home. Originally home to the Bothwell family, it is now open to the public. Its sand yard is raked every morning according to custom. **Hell**, situated near West Bay, is a rock formation worth visiting. Have your cards and letters postmarked at the sub-post office there. ■ *The post office and gift shop is open Mon-Fri 0800-1700, Sat 0830-1130.*

On the south coast at Savannah, just off the main coastal road, **Pedro St James** has been restored and developed into a national landmark. On 4 December 1831 a historic meeting was held here at which it was decided to split the island into districts with representation, and democracy was introduced. The site has the oldest known existing stone structure in the Cayman Islands. The original building is believed to have been built of quarried native rock around 1780 by William Eden, a plantation owner, and are the only known remains of a late 18th-century residence on the island. The upper floors are of mahogany with a fine balcony. There are a number of outbuildings and traditional activities which recreate plantation life. The Steadman Bodden house, a 100-year-old wattle and daub cottage was relocated in 1995 from the cruise ship landing at Spotts. An impressive Visitors' Centre has been built as a gateway to the Great House and grounds, offering the opportunity to learn about the history of the site before beginning the tour. The main attraction is a state-of-the-art multimedia theatre featuring a 20-minute show (1000-1600, every hour on the hour) that brings to life the people, their dramas and the conditions in which they struggled, including a storm. ■ *Daily 0830-1700. US$8, children 6-12 US$4. T9473329, www.pedrostjames.ky*

There are caves in **Bodden Town**, believed to have been used by pirates, where you can see bones and stocks, and a line of unmarked graves in an old cemetery on the shore opposite, said to be those of buccaneers. Bodden Town was once the capital of the island and all shipping came here. Continuing east just after Half Moon Bay you will see blowholes: waterspouts that rise above the coral rock in unusual patterns as a result of water being funnelled along passages in the rock as the waves come rolling in. At the east end of the island there is a good viewing point at the **Goring Bluff lighthouse**. A trip to **Gun Bay** at the east end of the island will show you the scene of the famous 'Wreck of the Ten Sails', which took place in 1788 (see page 178).

A drive along the north coast to **Rum Point** (see page 165) is picturesque, with views of the sea through the vegetation. There are lots of villas and plots of land for sale along the coast and all development is upmarket. The return journey can be made via the Botanic Park (see page 161) to make a circular trip.

The National Trust organizes guided village walks and has opened a nature trail, the **Mastic Trail**, a two-mile walk through farmlands, woodlands and mangroves. It starts near the south coast and ends near the north coast, from where a van will carry you back to the start. It takes about 2½ hours, moderate fitness recommended, US$30 per person. *Silver Thatch Excursions* is the only tour operator offering the National Trust escorted hikes along the trail and is highly recommended, T9456588.

For a pleasurable day's outing, arrange a boat trip to **North Sound** for US$35 or so. This will include snorkelling, fishing and a good look at marine life on a barrier reef. Your guide will cook fish, fresh marinated conch or lobster, for you, delicious and highly recommended. You can also take a moonlit cruise aboard the *Jolly Roger* or the *Valhalla*, T9498988. ■ *Sunset buffet dinner cruise US$60; cocktail cruise US$40, daily, weather permitting.*

Essentials

Sleeping

There are about 50 hotels along Seven Mile Beach; all the major chains are represented, offering all types of luxury accommodation

Seven Mile Beach **LL** *Grand Cayman Marriott Beach Resort*, T9490088, www.marriott.ky Right on the beach, 309 rooms, comfortable, pleasant, friendly service, 2 miles from George Town, watersports, tennis. **LL** *Westin Casuarina Resort*, T9453800, www.westin.com 341 rooms, a/c, TV, phone, mini-bar, fan, marble bath, 2 pools, swim-up bar, tennis, dive shop, watersports, next to golf course. **LL-L** *Hyatt Regency Grand Cayman*, T9491234, www.grandcayman.hyatt.com 236 rooms, 55 villas, overlooking golf course and private waterway, lots of facilities, access for the disabled, an all-suite 5-storey tower is directly across the road from the main Hyatt complex, 53 1 or 2 bedroom apartments, lots of amenities, all with sea views and concierge. **LL-L** *Comfort Suites and Resort*, West Bay Rd, just south of the *Marriott*, T9457300, www.caymancomfort.com On the beach side of the road but not beachfront, about 300 ft from sea behind condos, 110 suites, studios and spacious 1-2 bedroom suites with full kitchens, some accessible for wheelchair guests, phones, restaurant, *Stingers* bar, meeting room, fitness centre, child care facilities, pool, scuba and watersports rental on site, dive packages available. **LL-L** *Holiday Inn*, West Bay Rd, T9464433, www.holiday-inn.com 230 standard rooms and 1 penthouse suite in 5-storey block, wheelchair accessible, non-smoking rooms available, a/c, TV, pool, dive and watersports operation, beach bar, lobby bar, massage, fitness centre, shops, restaurant and meeting room, access to beach. **L-AL** *Indies Suites*, T9455025, indiessuites@worldnet.att.net Off West Bay Rd. 2 mins' walk from Seven Mile Beach. Just far enough off the beaten track to give this resort an intimate feel. Pool, jacuzzi, dive shop. Rooms have private patios, sundecks and kitchens.

Elsewhere **LL** *Beach Club Colony*, T9498100, F9455167, bchclub@candw.ky 41-room beachfront hotel, 3 miles from George Town, tropical in ambiance and decor, full range of facilities including bar, restaurant, a/c, internet access, TV, watersports and dive shop. **LL** *Royal Reef Resort*, East End, Colliers Bay, T9473100, www.royalreef.com 90-room beachfront hotel, tranquil setting in the less crowded East End, full facilities including beauty salon, floodlit tennis courts, pool and dive shop. **LL-AL** *Cobalt Coast Resort & Suites*, north of Seven Mile Beach, past the Turtle Farm on Boatswains Bay, T9465656, www.cobaltcoast.com Built in the style of a Great House, small and intimate, 18 rooms in 1-2 bedroom suites and villas sleeping up to 6, kitchens, *Duppies* restaurant, pool, jacuzzi, dock, dive shop on site. **At North Sound:** **LL-L** *Grand Caymanian Beach Club and Resort*, T 9493100, www.grandcaymanian.ky 5-star, full-service resort, studios, 1 to 2 bedroom suites, grand villas, all with lots of luxury facilities, kitchens, jacuzzis, pool, barbecues, children's playground, Kid's Club, fitness centre, gift shop, concierge, watersports. **At East End:** **LL-AL** *Morritt's Tortuga Club*, T 9477449, www.morritt.com Upmarket, suites and town houses, on beach, excellent windsurfing, pool with waterfalls and bar, full dive operation, packages available. **L-AL** *Cayman Diving Lodge*, T9477555, www.divelodge.com 12 rooms, including 2-3-tank boat dive and 3 meals, photo centre, great diving, snorkelling, bicycles, hammocks, internet access. **At Bodden Town:** **L-AL** *Turtle Nest Inn*, T9478665, www.turtlenestinn.com On a quiet, protected beach with excellent snorkelling, 8 smart 1-bedroom apartments with sofa beds, TV, phone, a/c, fans, laundry room, maid service, gas barbecue, pool, internet access. **South of George Town:** . **LL-AL** *Sunset House*, T9497111, www.sunsethouse.com 59 rooms, dedicated dive hotel on rocky shoreline, good shore diving, a bronze statue of a mermaid called Amphitrite (Poseidon's wife, queen of the sea) has been sunk in 50 ft of water for snorkellers and divers to enjoy. **L-A** *Eldemire's Guest House*, South Church St, T9495387, www.eldemire.com A friendly 'home away from home' atmosphere, room, studio or apartment, 1 mile from town, ½ mile from beach, bicycles, internet, hammocks, wheelchair accessible. **AL** *Annie's Place*, 282 Andrew Drive, Snug Harbour, Seven Mile Beach, behind Grand Pavilion office, T9455505, www. anniesplace.ky 2 bedrooms, CP, a/c, fan, TV, fridge, no smoking, 2 sitting rooms, one with TV and library, beach chairs and towels. **AL-A** *Seaview Hotel and Dive Centre*, T9450558, www.seaviewdivers.com Pleasant small hotel, 15 rooms, a/c, fans, saltwater pool, hammocks, internet access, piano bar, restaurant, excellent snorkelling and offshore diving, credit cards accepted. **A-B** *Adam's Guest House*, 84 Melmac Av, ½ mile south of George Town, T9492512, F9490919. Run by Tom and Olga Adams, excellent accommodation, 6 rooms, US$15 additional person, a/c or fan, very helpful, about 300 yd from *Parrots Landing* dive shop, TCs or credit cards accepted. **A-B** *Wild Orchid Inn*, 120 Northward Rd, Bodden Town, T/F9472298, orchidinn@ candw.ky CP, a/c, kitchen, TV, jacuzzi, internet access.

Self-catering Basic cottages may cost US$900-1,000 a week per house. For those wishing to stay longer, 2-bedroom, furnished houses can be found away from the tourist areas in areas such as Breakers or Bodden Town for US$700-1,000 a month. Luxury villas and apartments, beachfront properties, can be rented through *Cayman Villas* (**L**), T9454144, F9497471, www.caymanvillas.com Situated all round the island, along Seven Mile Beach and North Side, including the exclusive resort area of Cayman Kai.

There are about 200 restaurants on Grand Cayman ranging from gourmet standards, to smaller places serving native dishes. In George Town, there are many restaurants catering for the lunchtime trade of the office workers and a number of fast-food places, takeaways and delicatessens. Eating out is not cheap, but you pay for what you get, and food is usually excellent. Prices obviously vary according to the standard of restaurant, but for dinner, main courses start at about US$10 and range upward to US$60 or more for a full meal including wine. Lunch prices can be around US$7 to 15 and breakfast from about US$5. Excellent Sun brunch buffets, all you can eat, with orange juice and sparkling wine, at the *Hyatt* (recommended for meat, spit roasts) and the *Westin* (recommended for fish and sushi, but it also has pasta, spit roast, oyster and seafood bar, salads, fruit and cheese, you can stay there from 1100 to 1400 and visit the buffet as many times as you want) for about US$55 per person. For

There are guesthouses catering for divers in the suburbs south of George Town

Cayman Islands

Eating
The opening times generally refer to the times between which meals are served, although the restaurants often stay open later

the less affluent, most bars have a Fri happy hour with free food. All-you-can-eat lunch buffets are good value at the *Thai Orchid*, Queen's Court, West Bay Rd, T9497955 (Tue, Thu, 1145-1430), *Bella Capri*, T9454755 (Fri, 1145-1430), and *Gateway of India* , T9462815 (Mon-Fri, 1130-1430), both next to the Strand shopping centre, West Bay Rd. During the high season it is advisable to reserve tables for dinner. People tend to eat early so if you reserve a table after 2000 you are likely to finish with the restaurant to yourself, although many restaurants have adjoining bars that stay open until later. There is a restaurant delivery service called *Fine Dine-In*, T9463463, ken@candw.ky which you can call daily 1730-2300 for all sorts of cuisines from 22 restaurants on the list (and growing). They also do video rental, drinks, etc, for a real night in.

Prices refer to the cost of a main course **Expensive** (US$30 and over) **George Town** *Brasserie*, Cricket Sq, T9451815. Off the beaten path, undiscovered by many visitors, sophisticated menu, excellent wine selection, tapas bar daily, open for lunch and dinner, excellent value Sun dinner menu for 2. Open 1130-1430, 1730-2200. *Grand Old House*, South Church St, T9499333, www.grandoldhouse.com Restored waterfront home, top-notch service and seafood specialities. Mon-Fri 1145-2130, Sat-Sun 1800-2130. *The Wharf*, on the outskirts of George Town on the way to Seven Mile Beach, T9492231. Bar open for happy hour 1700-1900, dinner daily 1800-2200, beautiful waterfront setting, quite a large restaurant, tarpon feeding nightly at 2100. **West Bay Road** *Bamboo Lounge*, at the *Hyatt*, T9478744. Not your normal hotel restaurant, By far the best sushi on the island, sashimi, riqiri and specials, also vegetarian menu, Japanese chef with flair, creative, generous portions, intimate and relaxing atmosphere, staff professional and friendly, popular with locals and visitors. Daily 1700-0100, except Sat 1700-2400. *Pirate's Buffet* at the *Marriott*, T9490088. Fri nights, all you can eat, music, fire eater, limbo dancer, reservations required. Daily 1800-2100. *Ragazzi*, Buckingham Square, off West Bay Rd, T9453484, ragazzi@candw.ky Generally agreed to be the best Italian on the island, extremely popular. Open daily 1130-2300. *Reef Grille*, at *Royal Palms Beach Club*, T9456358, www.reefgrill.com One of the hottest dining and entertainment spots, dinner daily 1800-2200, inside or out on the patio, wheelchair-accessible, American bistro, live bands Wed-Sat in May-Nov, Mon-Sat in Dec-Apr and special occasions at the *Royal Palms*, also watersports centre and beach facility open daily. **West Bay (Northwest)** *Pappagallo*, Barkers, T9491119. Italian cuisine, expensive, on 14-acre bird sanctuary overlooking natural lagoon, eat inside the haphazardly thatched building or in outside screened patio, excellent food and extensive wine list, reservations essential, open daily 1800-2230. **South Coast** *The Lighthouse* at Breakers T9472047, www.lighthouse.ky 20 mins' drive east of George Town, seafood and Italian cuisine, idyllic setting with dock dining and a stunning ocean view, one of the finer spots to dine on the island. Open 1130-1630, 1730-2200. **North Coast** *Cecil's Restaurant*, *Kaibo Yacht Club* at Cayman Kai, T9479975. Cajun and New Orleans food, beach bar downstairs open daily 1100-1800, upstairs open Tue-Sat 1800-2230 for dinner and Sun for brunch featuring New Orleans classics like crawfish étouffée, jambalaya, red beans and rice, shrimp creole plus fresh Louisiana oysters, fresh local seafood always on the menu.

Mid-range (US$20-30) **George Town** *Almond Tree*, North Church St, on the waterfront, T9450155, www.almond treehouse.com The thatched hut is a landmark, macaws and iguanas, opposite *Kirk's* supermarket, open-air dining, 1100-2300, tarpon feeding 2030, the *Tree House Beach Bar* is here too. Daily 1100-2200. *Casanova Restaurant*, Old Fort Building, T9497633, www.casanova.ky. Excellent, Italian, on the waterfront. Mon-Sat 1130-2200, no lunch Sun. *Paradise Bar & Grill* on waterfront, South Church St, T9451444. Good outdoor dining and regular drink specials. Open 1000-2200. **West Bay Road** *Bed Restaurant*, near Harquail Bypass, just opposite cinemas, T9497199, www.bed.com.ky whimsically appointed like a lady's boudoir, popular, continental food with Thai and Mediterranean influences, the adjoining lounge is a favourite late-night hang-out. Restaurant open 1800-2300, lounge Mon-Fri 1800-0100, Sat-Sun 1800-2400. *Decker's*, T9456600, www.deckers.ky. Built around a double decker bus, which serves as the bar, moderate prices, bistro style, nightly music, daily happy hours. Dinner 1730-2230, Bar open till 0100. *Hook's Seafood Grotto*, next to *Treasure Island Resort*, T9458731. Looks like pirate's hideaway, breakfast (all you can eat buffet), lunch and dinner, seafood and steak, cheerful. Free punch and nibbles on Mon evening to go with its brass band concert. Open 0700-2300. *La Bodega Latin Lounge & Grill*, Westshore shopping centre, T9468511. A fresh Latin ambiance with excellent Caribbean fusion cuisine. Salsa classes on Wed. Lunch 1130-1500, dinner 1700-2300, bar open until 0100, except Sat 2400. *Naked Fish*, *Seaview Hotel*, T9450558. Beautiful ocean-front setting, casual friendly atmosphere and continental food. Daily 1100-2200. *Neptune's*, Trafalgar Square, West Bay Rd, T9468709. Chefs from countries as diverse as India and Italy, good and varied menu, welcoming atmosphere, popular locally, booking advisable. *Pirate's Den*, Galleria Plaza, T9497144. Popular with ex-pats, breakfast, lunch and dinner, great Sun brunch buffet, open Mon-Fri 0700-0100, Sat-Sun 1100-2400. **West Bay (Northwest)** *Calypso Grill*, Morgan's Harbour, T9493948. Lunch and dinner, 3-tiered dining area with panoramic view of North Sound, seafood and beef or salads and good desserts. Lunch 1130-1500, dinner 1800-2200.*Cracked Conch*, Northwest Point Rd, T9455217. Near Turtle Farm, popular stopping place for excursions, very nice setting and atmosphere, lively, conch is the speciality, takeaways very popular. Lunch and dinner 1130-2200.

Cheap (US$10-20) **George Town** *Champion House, I* and *II*, both on Eastern Av, George Town, T9492190, open 1000-2400 (*I*), T9497882, open 0730-2400 (*II*), cheap, local food. Recommended. *Welly's Cool Spot*, North Sound Rd, T9492541. Native food at reasonable prices. Mon-Thu 1130-2100, Fri 1130-2330, Sat 1130-2230. **West Bay Road** *Chicken! Chicken!*, West Shore Centre, T9452290. Tasty spit-roasted chicken with assorted accompaniments, CI$20 for whole chicken plus 'fixin's', eat in or takeaway. Open 1000-2200. *Cimboco*, next to cinema, T9472782, www.cimboco.com This 'Caribbean Café' is good value for good food. Daily 1100-2200. *Eats Diner*, Cayman Falls, West Bay Rd, T9455288. American diner food, for breakfast, lunch and dinner. **South coast** *Crow's Nest*, about 4 miles south of George Town, T9499366. A locals' favourite, small, glorious position, dining on the patio overlooking the sea or inside, reservations essential. Lunch 1130-1500, dinner 1730-2200. *Durty Reids Sports Bar*, Red Bay Plaza, Red Bay Rd, near Savannah, T9471860. With possibly the most amusing menu of all time, this bar is reminiscent of the US Midwest, and a popular beer-drinking, football-watching, local hangout. Wed and Fri all you can eat buffet. Open 1000-2200, bar open later depending on demand.

On the harbour side near Eden Rock on Friday nights a temporary stall sells takeaway jerk pork and chicken dinners, huge, delicious helpings, excellent value

Seriously cheap (US$10 and under) **George Town** *Breadfruit Tree Café*, Eastern Av and Coconut Place, T9452124. Best spot for local delicacies, no alcohol, busiest very late, serves cowfoot, fish tea, curry goat, jerk pork, jerk chicken, etc, quaint, garden-like atmosphere in decor, best prices in town. Mon-Sat, 1100-0300, only place open that late. *Carib Bean Coffee House*, upstairs at Harbour Place off South Church St, T9452326. Very popular with locals, view of the Harbour, serves a wide range of coffees, sandwiches, cakes and bagels. Daily 0700-1600. **West Bay Road** *Azurro*, Buckingham Square, opposite *Hyatt*, T9467745. Italian coffee, sandwiches on freshly baked focaccia and delicious handmade pastries. Daily 0630-1800. *Coffee Grinder*, Seven Mile Shops, T9494833. A bakery, open 0700-1700. *Seymour's* has 2 'stands', one in front of *The Planet*, off West Bay Rd, the other outside the Racquet Club near Cricket Sq, both open 2000-0100 for late crowds. Sells Mannish Water, a local concoction of goats' parts rumoured to give a man extra potency, not sold to women, popular Fri, Sat night, couples line up to get a taste and eat great jerk pork and chicken. **South coast** *Willy's Fruit and Juice Stall*, Red Bay Rd between George Town and Savannah. Fresh fruit and freshly made juice from this roadside stall. Daily 1200-1900.

Due to licensing laws, the vast majority of bars are attached to restaurants that stay open until 0100, or 2400 Sat. Some of the most popular are in *Bamboo*, *Bed* and *La Bodega* and all have live music at least twice a week. **George Town**: for local colour visit *Farmers*, off Eastern Av, near the school. In downtown George Town, on North Church St, *Captain Bryan's Seaside Patio*, T9496163. Patio overlooking the harbour. *Rackham's Pub*, North Church St, T9453860. Good rum-based drinks, light meals, view of harbour, food good value. *The Tree House Beach Bar*,T9450155, is an open-air bar right on the beach on North Church St. Thatched hut, pleasant tropical atmosphere, tarpon feeding at 2000. *Lone Star Bar and Grill*,

Bars

Cayman Islands

next to the *Hyatt Hotel*, West Bay Rd, T9455175. Favourites with sports fans, showing international sporting events nightly, Tex-Mex food, happy hour Mon-Fri 1700-1830. *Stingers*, T9453000, is a friendly bar behind *Comfort Suites* on West Bay Rd.

Nightlife The opening hours of clubs are subject to frequent change due to difficulty with licensing laws, but are usually Sun-Fri 2200-0300, Sat 2200-2400. The 3 main nightclubs on the island are: *The Matrix*, in the Islander Complex, West Bay Rd, T9497169. The type of music and the crowd in the above 3 places depends on the theme for that particular night (Latino, hip hop, retro, etc); *Next Level*, on West Bay Rd opposite the Marriott, T9466398, www.nextlevel.ky slightly more upmarket; and *O Bar*, Queens Court, West Bay Rd, T9436227, www.obar.ky *Benjamin's Roof*, Coconut Place, Tue-Sat 1930-2300, T9454080. Big screen TV in sports room, family dining room and Irish pub room. Paraguayan harpists play for dinner guests Mon-Sat at *The Wharf*, T9492231. Hear jazz at *The Bed Restaurant*, Mon evenings, T9497199. *Apollo II Club*, North Side, T9479568, local groups such as Cayman Edition, as well as rock, reggae and other Caribbean music. *McDoom's Club Inferno*, Hell, West Bay, T9493263. *The Barefoot Man*, a local artist playing calypso and a dash of country music at Rum Point on Mon and Fri nights. *The Cayman National Cultural Foundation*, T9495477, puts on plays and musicals at the Harquail Theatre on West Bay Rd. The Cayman Drama Society uses the Prospect Play House, a small theatre on the road to Bodden Town. There is a **cinema** on West Bay Rd with 2 screens, 2 showings a night Mon-Sat, CI$6 adults, CI$2.75 children, T9494011.

Sports
For diving and watersports, see pages 163 and 165

Golf Jack Nicklaus has designed the *Britannia Golf Course* for the *Hyatt-Regency Grand Cayman Resort & Villas*. There is a 9-hole Championship course, an 18-hole executive course and an 18-hole Cayman course played with a special short-distance Cayman ball, but it can only be laid out for 1 course at a time; the executive has 14 par 3s and 4 par 4s, so it is short, while the short-distance ball with local winds is a tourist gimmick. T9498020 for starting times. To play the executive course with hire of clubs and compulsory buggie will cost you about US$75, the regulation course US$90 for 18 holes. *The Links*, the 18-hole championship golf course, is at Safehaven, with a par 71 course and a total yardage of 6,605 from the championship tees, although every hole has 5 separate tee areas to accommodate all levels of players. The club house is open daily with restaurant and bar open to golfers and non-golfers. Practice facilities include an aqua range, 2 putting greens, sand trap and pitching green (night lights). T9495988, F9495457, 0700-1800. 18 holes with cart/buggie costs US$110/120 summer/winter. You can hire clubs, US$1 per club, US$15-35 for a whole set, take lessons or just practice, US$6 per 50 balls (you can buy balls at the bar if the clubhouse is closed). *Sunrise Family Golf Centre* is a 9-hole par 3 layout ideally suited for junior and beginning golfers looking to sharpen their iron and short-game skills. Located at the end of Hirst Rd in Savannah, the longest hole is 160 yd while the shortest is 57 yd. There is also a 300-yd driving range, practice chipping and putting green. Rental clubs and PGA professional on site for lessons. Daily 0730-1800, US$15 for 9 holes, US$22 for 18 holes. Buckets for the driving range are US$4 small and US$6 large. T9474653, www.sunrisecayman.com

There are 3 **squash** courts at the *Cayman Islands Squash Racquets Association* at South Sound, T9499469. Most of the larger hotels have their own **tennis** courts but the *Cayman Islands Tennis Club* next door to the squash courts at South Sound has 6 floodlit tennis courts and a club pro. For match information contact Scott Smith (T9499464). For **soccer**, contact the *Cayman Islands Football Association*, T9495775. **Cricket** matches are played at the Smith Road Oval near the airport (although location may change with extension of runway); there are 5 teams in the *Cayman Islands Cricket Association's league*. **Rugby** is played every Sat between Sep and May at the *Cayman Rugby Football Club* at South Sound, T9497960. **Horse riding** with *Nicki's Beach Rides*, T9455839, on trails and beaches in the northwest, with *Pampered Ponies*, T9452262, or with *Coral Stone Stables*, T9164799, estones@candw.ky.

Motorcycling *Eagles Nest Cycles* runs *The Harley Davidson Club*, T9494866, specializing in Harley Davidson motorcycles and souvenirs. **Motocross** is popular in Grand Cayman and **stock car races** are held on the first Sun of each month at the *Lakeview Raceway* (also known as Jay Bodden's Marl Pit) in George Town at 1300, CI$5 admission.

The *Cayman Motorsports Association's* annual International Challenge Cup attracts racing drivers from Jamaica, Colombia, Canada and the USA. The association has built a new 30-acre racetrack, with a 20-acre family recreation area and 15-acre nature reserve, T9497135. No alcoholic beverages allowed.

Bowling You can go bowling at the *Stingray Bowling Centre and Arcade*, T9454444, at the Greenery on Seven Mile Beach, just north of the Strand Shopping Centre on West Bay Rd. The centre has 10 lanes with Qubica automatic scoring, CI$4 per game with adult rental shoes for CI$3 and junior rental shoes for CI$2.50. Up to 6 people can play each lane and lanes can be rented by the hr for CI$24. There is also a pro-shop, you can have lessons, there is a snack bar, 4 satellite TVs and an arcade with video games. No alcohol, children under 12 must be accompanied by an adult. Mon-Fri 1500-2300, Sat-Sun 1200-2330.

Children If you want to entertain small children out of the sun (or rain), *Smyles* is an indoor play centre at the Islander complex just off the Harquail Bypass, T9465800, with more than 3,200 sq ft of tunnels, ball pit, snack bar, soft play area, arcade, games. Tue-Thu 0900-2000, Fri 0900-2200, Sat 1000-2200, Sun 1100-2000 CI$5.50. *Scholars Park*, on Stadium Drive opposite the Stadium in West Bay, offers a large outdoor play area. All children must be accompanied by an adult. Daily 0700-1900. For further information on children's play areas and activities call the Department of Youth and Sport, T9497900.

Bus Public buses run on 8 colour-coded routes from terminal next to Public Library on Edward St, George Town. All routes run 0600-2300 Sun-Thu, 0600-0100 Fri-Sat. Route 1 (yellow) and 2 (lime green) to West Bay every 15 mins 0600-1800, then every 30 mins, CI$1.50. Route 3 (blue) to Bodden Town runs hourly, same price. Route 4 (purple) to East End and route 5 (red) to East End and North Side, every hr, CI$2. Route 6 (dark green) North Side to West Bay. Route 7 (green, white numbers) around George Town. Route 8 (orange) to North Side. Hotline T9455100.

Transport

Car hire Avis, *National* and *Hertz* are represented and there are a number of good local companies as well, many of which are at the airport. Rental firms issue visitors with driving permits on production of a valid driving licence from the visitor's country of residence. Most car hire firms have boxes in the airport departure lounge where you can drop off your car keys prior to departure, having left the car in the company's car park. *Ace Hertz*, T9492280, F9490572, compact car US$25-52; *Andy's Rent A Car Ltd*, West Bay Road, opposite *Marriott*, T9498111, F9498385, cheapest automatic car US$35 in winter, US$25 in summer, weekly rates US$210 or US$150; *Just Jeeps*, West Bay Rd, T9497263, F9490216, US$45-65; *Cico Avis*, T9492468, F9497127, smallest standard car US$46/37 winter/summer, jeeps and automatics available. *Coconut Car Rentals Ltd*, T9494037, F9497786, from US$50/35 a day winter/summer or US$295/195 a week, jeeps US$50/55, US$320/250. Collision damage waiver US$14 a day. **Bicycle hire** (cheapest US$10/day), **scooters** (US$20-25/day) can also be rented, from *Cayman Cycle Rentals*, T9454021, at *Coconut Place*, *Hyatt Regency* and *Treasure Island*, US$15 a day. *Soto Scooters & Car Rentals*, Seven Mile Beach, T9454465, at Coconut Place, scooters US$25/day, bicycles US$15/day, mountain bikes and tandems available. Bicycles are also available at Rum Point. **Taxis** are readily obtainable at hotels and restaurants. In George Town there are always lots of taxis at the dock when the cruise ships come in, otherwise hailing a taxi is most easily done in the vicinity of the post office. Fares are based on a fixed place-to-place tariff rather than a meter charge and vary according to how many people there are and how much luggage there is. For going a long distance (ie across the island) they are expensive. From the airport to George Town is US$12, based on up to 4 passengers with 2 pieces of luggage each; to West Bay US$23-29; to East End, US$49; to Rum Point US$60. *Burton's Taxi Service*, T9472274, and *AA Chauffeur and Transportation Services*, T9497222, F9455823, offer standard taxi service plus island tours.

The minimum hiring age is 21 at some places, 25 at others; ask around

Cayman Islands

Cayman Brac

IDD code: 345
Colour map 1, grid C3
Population 1,822

Settlement on Cayman Brac has been determined by the Bluff, which rises from sea level at the west end to a sheer cliff at the east end. Most building first took place on the flatter land in the west, where the sea is a little calmer, and then spread along the north coast where the Bluff gives shelter. A number of Heritage Sites, linked by hiking trails, are being promoted, including bat caves, the old lighthouse and a place to watch the sunset. Cayman Brac is blessed with spectacular reef and wall diving with excellent visibility. The **tourist office** can be contacted at PO Box 194, Stake Bay, T9481649, F9481629.

Diving & marine life

Most of the sites are around the west end, with both shallow reef snorkelling, with beautiful coral gardens and lots of fish, and diving and deeper wall diving a bit further out. There are also a few wrecks among the 40 or so named dive sites including a newly-sunk Russian frigate (see page 162), which is within snorkelling distance of the beach and rises to about 10 ft from the surface. On the north coast road, go west past the airport turning to Robert Foster Lane, which leads to the sea. You can locate the wreck by the buoys for dive boats.

Dive centres *Reef Divers*, T9481642, www.bracreef.com, offers diving at both Cayman Brac and Little Cayman sites, certification and resort courses, photo/video services and equipment rental. A 2-tank dive costs US$75, snorkelling trips are US$10-15. *Brac Aquatics*, T9481429, www.candw.ky/users/Cay3931, charges US$70 for a 2-tank dive. *Dive Tiara* at *Divi Tiara Resort*, T9481553, US$60 for 2-tank dive and US$10-20 for snorkel trips.

Around the island
www.nature cayman.com for information on birdwatching and nature tourism

The recently introduced Heritage Sites and Trails include 35 attractions and hikes to entice visitors away from the water and discover what is on land. It is not possible to drive all round the island because of the Bluff. The road linking the north and south coasts is roughly half way along the island. There are three roads running east-west, one along the north shore, one along the south coast and a third (unpaved) in the middle which runs along the top of the Bluff to the lighthouse. Although lots of roads have been built up on the Bluff, they are to service houses which have not yet been built, and do not lead anywhere. There are several, rather poor, farms and cows wander on the road. At the top of the Bluff it is sometimes possible to spot various orchids and there is a 197-acre **Parrot Reserve** (see page 161). A hiking trail has been cleared by the Cayman Brac National Trust, only for the able bodied as it is rocky, but there is a great view from the Bluff at the end of the path. You are only likely to see parrots at dawn or dusk, but it is a nice walk anyway through the bush.

Cayman Brac

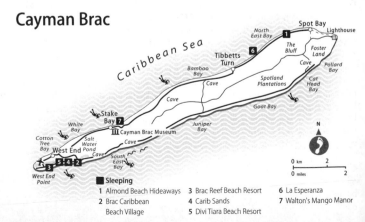

Sleeping
1 Almond Beach Hideaways
2 Brac Caribbean Beach Village
3 Brac Reef Beach Resort
4 Carib Sands
5 Divi Tiara Beach Resort
6 La Esperanza
7 Walton's Mango Manor

From the airport the north shore road leads to **Cotton Tree Bay**, where in 1932 a hurricane flooded the area, killing more than 100 people and destroying virtually every house. The coconut groves were devastated and many people left the island at this time. Demand for turtle shell went into decline as the use of plastic increased and many men found that the only opportunities open to them were as sailors, travelling around the world on merchant ships.

Stake Bay is the main village on the north coast and it is well worthwhile visiting the small, but interesting **Cayman Brac Museum**. ■ *Mon-Fri 0900-1200, 1300-1600. Free. T9482622.* Further east at Creek, *La Esperanza* is a good place to stop for refreshment, in a glorious setting with good views and welcome sea breeze. At **Spot Bay** at the extreme east, follow a track up towards the lighthouse. Here you will find Peter's Cave and a good viewpoint. From the end of the north coast road you can walk through the almond trees to the beach, from where you get an excellent view of the Bluff from below.

Along the south coast, the best beaches are at the west end, where there are two dive resorts. There is a pleasant public beach with shade and toilets at **South East Bay**. Bat Cave and Rebecca's Cave are in this vicinity and can be visited. When you get to the end of the road, walk along the ironshore to the end of the island. There is a blow-hole, lots of beachcombing opportunities and if you look for stripes in the cliff you may find caymanite, which is only found here and at the east end of Grand Cayman. Holiday homes have been built along this coast. Tourism is now the main-stay of the economy but construction of homes for foreigners has pushed up the price of land out of the reach of many local families. Most young adults leave the island for a career in financial services or government on Grand Cayman or other jobs further afield.

Rock climbing is popular along this coastline. There are 66 recognized climbing sites

The 3 best resorts are **LL-L** *Brac Caribbean Beach Village*, on the south coast, West End, T9482265, www.866thebrac.com A condominium development, a/c, fans, on beach, reef protected, credit cards accepted, 16 2-bedroom condos, restaurant, pool, dive packages, laundry, maid service available, satellite TV, child and teenage discounts. **LL-L** *Carib Sands*, T9481121, www.866thebrac.com 34 1-4 bedroom condos, nicely furnished, in 2 pink blocks by the sea, full kitchens, balconies, pool, bicycles, dive packages, pier for pick up by dive boat, restaurant *Captain's Table*. **L-AL** *Divi Tiara Beach Resort*, Stake Bay, T9481553, www.diveresorts.com 71-room beachfront hotel, located on a picturesque beach. Various accommodation levels available. Diving is the main attraction, PADI 5-star diving centre as well as full diving facilities. At West End Point: **AL** *Brac Reef Beach Resort*, T9481323, www.bracreef.com 40 rooms, packages available, comfortable, nice beach, some sea grass, lovely dock with lookout tower, conference centre for large and small groups, internet access.

Smaller, individual properties include **L** *Almond Beach Hideaways*, Spot Bay, T9480470, www.almondbeachhideaways.com On beach, good snorkelling, 2 villas with 2 bedrooms, 2 bathrooms, sofa bed in living room, a/c, fans, hammocks and sunbeds. **AL-B** *La Esperanza*, Stake Bay, T9480531, esperan@candw.ky Condos and house on north side, access to private beach on south side, restaurant, snorkelling, hammocks, bicycles. The only B&B is **A** *Walton's Mango Manor*, Stake Bay, T/F9480518, www.waltonsmangomanor.com CP, 5 rooms, antiques, veranda, hammocks, a/c, fans, TV, kitchenettes, great snorkelling.

Sleeping
Accommodation is mostly self-catering in condos and villas. www.thebrac.com for a listing

Mid-range (US$20-30) *The Captain's Table*, at *Brac Caribbean Beach Village*, T9481418. The best dining on the island, lobster, seafood and steaks. Lunch 1130-1500, dinner 1800-2200. Bar open 1200-2400. *La Esperanza*, Stake Bay, T9480531, seafood, one of the nicest, tables at water's edge as well as a/c dining room, music, bar, active at weekends, transport available, open Mon-Sat 0800-2100, Sun 0900-2100.

Eating

Cheap (US$10-20) *Aunt Sha's Kitchen*, T9481581. Ocean view, island style, local dishes, conch fritters, key lime pie, open daily 0730-2300, breakfast, lunch, dinner, also takeaway, TV, billiards, darts, *Coral Isle*, next door, is one of the few nightspots on the island. *G&M Diner*, open 0730-1430 and 1830-2030, for breakfast, lunch and dinner, local dishes and seafood,

Cayman Islands

no alcohol. Closed Wed. *Sonia's*, White Bay, T9481214. Island food, special diets catered for, takeaway available. Mon-Sat 0830-1330. *Cozy Kitchen*, West End, casual, local lunch only, eat in or takeaway. *Blackie's*, at the Youth Centre, South Side, T9480232. Good ice cream, fried chicken, lunch only. There are 3 supermarkets in the west end, you may need to shop at all 3 to find what you want, the supply boat comes in only once a week and things can run out.

Transport *Cayman Airways* and *Island Air* fly from Grand Cayman and Little Cayman. There is no inter-island ferry service, so you have to catch a small plane, used like a bus service. There are no buses on the island, so taxis or car hire or walking are the only options. Taxi An island tour by taxi costs about CI$15, *Elo's Taxi and Tours*, T9480220, recommended, *Hill's Taxi and Tours*, T9480540, *Maple Edward's Taxi and Tours*, T9480448. **Bike** and **moped hire** *B&S Motor Ventures*, T9481646 www.bandsmv.com. **Car hire** *Brac Rent-A-Car*, T9481515, F9481380, at the airport, compact car US$42/35 winter/summer. *Seaview Car Rentals*, T9482847, F9482329 and *Four D's*, T/F9481599, about US$35-40 per day for a car.

Little Cayman

IDD code: 345
Colour map 1,
grid C3
Population: 115

Little Cayman is small and low-lying with large areas of dense mangrove swamps, ponds, lagoons and lakes. The diving is excellent. Underwater visibility averages 100-150 ft all year. Bloody Bay wall, a mile-deep vertical drop, is one of the major dive sites worldwide and is highly rated by marine biologists and photographers.

Diving & marine life
There are dive sites all round the island, but the most popular spot is in the Marine Park in **Bloody Bay**, a two-mile stretch between Spot Bay and Jackson's Point off the north coast. Unlike the walls around the other islands, which begin at a depth of about 65 ft and drop down about a mile, the Bloody Bay wall begins at 15-20 ft, meaning you can snorkel over the drop-off. This is spectacular, with coral canyons and caves before you get to the outer reef. There is also a Marine Park off the south coast opposite the airport, with *Pirate's Point Dive Resort* at one end. Shore diving from **Jackson's Point** is also spectacular, with coral heads rising from a 40-ft sandy bottom to about 10 ft of the surface. Along the south coast you can snorkel or kayak out to **Owen Island**.

Dive centres Diving can be arranged with *Pirate's Point*, *Sam McCoy's* (at the west end of Spot Bay) or *Southern Cross Club* (voted best dive resort in the Caribbean in 2001 by *Scuba Diving Magazine*), usually as a package deal with accommodation, but there are dive operations at each of the other resorts. A 2-tank dive costs US$65-80 including weights and tanks.
Fishing The bonefishing around Little Cayman is some of the best. The 15-acre Tarpon Lake

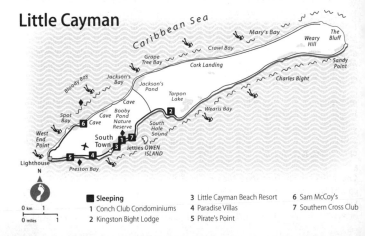

Little Cayman

Caribbean Sea

Mary's Bay · Weary Hill · The Bluff
Crawl Bay
Grape Tree Bay · Cork Landing · Sandy Point
Jackson's Bay · Jackson's Pond · Charles Bight
Bloody Bay
Cave
Tarpon Lake
Spot Bay · Cave · Booby Pond Nature Reserve · Wearis Bay
Cave
West End Point · South Town · South Hole Sound
Jetties · OWEN ISLAND
Lighthouse · Preston Bay

N

0 km   1
0 miles   1

■ **Sleeping**
1 Conch Club Condominiums
2 Kingston Bight Lodge
3 Little Cayman Beach Resort
4 Paradise Villas
5 Pirate's Point
6 Sam McCoy's
7 Southern Cross Club

is home to the game fish from which the pond gets its name. Fishing is offered at *Sam McCoy's* and at *Southern Cross Club*. Rates on request, but generally US$160/half day, US$300/full day for bonefishing and twice that for deep-sea fishing.

Little Cayman's swamps, ponds, lagoons and lakes make an ideal habitat for red-footed boobies and iguanas. **Booby Pond Nature Reserve**, T9481010, attracts about 3,500 nesting pairs of red-footed boobies and 100 pairs of frigate birds. On the edge of the pond, the other side of the road from the museum, is the **National Trust House**, where you can look through a telescope or strong binoculars to watch the birds. ■ *The house is open Mon-Sat 1500-1800, but you can use the veranda any time.* Further east is **Tarpon Lake**, another good spot for seeing wildlife. A boardwalk has been built out into the lake and if you are lucky you might see some tarpon.

Around the island

The beaches by the hotels on the south coast are good, with fine sand, but the swimming is marred by huge swathes of sea grass in the shallow water. Many of the other beaches around the island are more gritty, but you will have them to yourself. The best beach for swimming and snorkelling is at **Sandy Point** at the east tip of the island. Look for a red and white marker opposite a pond, a sandy path leads down to the beach. Other beaches are at **Jackson's Point** on the north side and on **Owen Island** in South Hole Sound. This privately owned island, 200 yd offshore, is freely used by residents and visitors alike and is accessible by row boat or kayak. Snorkelling is good just to the west of *Pirate's Point Resort*, where the water is shallow just within the reef.

Blossom is by the airstrip, and there you will find the post office. ■ *Mon-Fri 0900-1100, 1300-1500, Sat 0900-1100.* Car hire, a grocery and hardware store, bank (open Wednesday) and the **Little Cayman Museum**. The museum is in a typical wooden house and has a small, but nicely presented, collection of local artefacts and antiques. ■ *Mon-Fri 1500-1700. Free. T9481072.* Little Cayman Baptist Church is the only church. ■ *Services Sun 1100, 1930, Wed 1930.*

Sleeping

Accommodation consists of small hotels, diving lodges, a few private cottages and homes

LL (per person) *Southern Cross Club*, T9481099, www.southern crossclub.com Includes all meals, packages for scuba and/or fishing, cabins on sandy beach, view of Owen Island, friendly, excellent staff, good food served family-style, indoor and outdoor bar, pool, internet access, one of the nicest places to stay, relaxed, laid back, barefoot elegance. **LL** *Conch Club Condominiums*, Blossom Village, T9481033, www.conchclub.com 8 units with 2 or 3 bedrooms, beachfront, pool, jacuzzi, diving, snorkelling, tennis, photo centre, restaurant. **LL-L** *Pirate's Point*, Sefton Bay, T9481010, www.piratespointresort.com. Rooms in cabins, simple luxury, lovely big bathrooms, all inclusive with or without diving, 42-ft dive boat, 5 instructors, fishing, a/c, fan, TV, phone, small deep pool and 10-person jacuzzi, bar decorated with driftwood signs made by guests, owned by a cordon bleu chef, very relaxing, friendly. **LL-AL** *Little Cayman Beach Resort*, Blossom Village, T9481033, www.littlecayman.com The only real hotel on the island and seems huge, 40 rooms, a/c, TV, on beach, dock facilities, spa, tennis, basketball, volleyball, pool, jacuzzi, diving, facilities for the handicapped, all-inclusive dive packages available. **L-AL** *Paradise Villas*, T9480001, www.paradisevillas.com Small, duplex, 1-2- bedroom cottages with kitchens, on the shore, restaurant *Hungry Iguana* next door. For villas contact *Cayman Villas*, T9454144, F9497471, www.caymanvillas.com (**AL** per person) *Sam McCoy's*, T9480026, www.mccoyslodge.com.ky Includes transport, 3 meals, **L** includes 2-tank morning dive and shore diving, fishing costs extra (see above), small scale, simple and low key, 8 rooms, tiny pool with jacuzzi jets, hammocks, small beach, internet access. **AL** *Kingston Bight Lodge*, T9481015, kblodge@candw.ky A small personal lodge with four 4-bedroom units, snorkelling, diving, fishing, bar and restaurant.

Eating

Mid-range (US$20-30) *Hungry Iguana*, T9480007, in the village at *Paradise Villas*, is the only independent restaurant, indoor or outdoor dining, good food, pizza on Sat, popular, shrimp, lobster often on menu, open daily, lunch 1200-1430, dinner 1730-2100, takeaway available.

Cayman Islands

Transport

There is no public transport, a 25 mph speed limit and frequent signs for iguana or duck crossings

Air *Island Air* has small planes for island hopping from Grand Cayman and Cayman Brac (see page 159). The airport consists of a wooden shack and a grass runway.

Car hire Jeep and compact car hire (US$50-75 per day) is available here with *McLaughlin Rentals*, T9481000, F9481001, daily and weekly rates, prices vary due to length of rental. The office is 100 yd away from the airport. Roads are unpaved around the east half of the island but the main road goes all the way round the edge. You cannot often see the sea because of seagrape and other vegetation lining the shore.

Background

History

The islands were first sighted by Columbus in May 1503 when he was blown off course on his way to Hispaniola. He found two small islands (Cayman Brac and Little Cayman) which were full of turtles, and he therefore named the islands Las Tortugas. A 1523 map of the islands referred to them as Lagartos, meaning alligators or large lizards, but by 1530 they were known as the Caymanas after the Carib word for the marine crocodile which also lived there. The first recorded English visitor to the Caymans was Sir Francis Drake in 1586, when he reported that the *caymanas* were edible. But it was the turtles which really attracted ships in search of fresh meat for their crews. Generations of sailors stocked up on turtle meat here, keeping the creatures alive on board ship for later use. The islands were ceded to the English Crown under the Treaty of Madrid in 1670, after the first settlers came from Jamaica in 1661-71 to Little Cayman and Cayman Brac. The first settlements were abandoned after attacks by Spanish privateers, but British privateers often used the Cayman Islands as a base and in the 18th century they became an increasingly popular hideout for pirates, even after the end of legitimate privateering in 1713. In November 1794, a convoy of 10 ships was wrecked on the reef in Gun Bay, on the East End of Grand Cayman, but with the help of the local residents there was no loss of life. Legend has it that there was a member of the Royal Family on board and that in gratitude for their bravery, King George III decreed that Caymanians should never be conscripted for war service and Parliament legislated that they should never be taxed.

From 1670, the Cayman Islands were dependencies of Jamaica, although there was considerable self-government. In 1832, a legislative assembly was established, consisting of eight magistrates appointed by the Governor of Jamaica and 10 (later increased to 27) elected representatives. In 1959 dependency ceased when Jamaica became a member of the Federation of the West Indies, although the Governor of Jamaica remained the Governor of the Cayman Islands. When Jamaica achieved independence in 1962 the islands opted to become a direct dependency of the British Crown.

In 1991 a review of the 1972 constitution recommended several constitutional changes to be debated by the Legislative Assembly (see Government). The post of Chief Secretary was reinstated in 1992 after having been abolished in 1986 and members of the executive committee are called ministers.

The first three families of settlers arrived on Cayman Brac in 1833, followed by two more families in 1835. These five families, Ritch, Scott, Foster, Hunter and Ryan, are still well represented on the island today. They made a living from growing coconuts and selling turtle shells and from the 1850s started building boats to facilitate trading. In 1886 a Baptist missionary arrived from Jamaica and introduced education and health care.

The first inhabitants of Little Cayman were turtlers who made camp on the south shore. After them, at the beginning of the 20th century, the population exploded to over 100 Caymanians living at Blossom on the southwest coast and farming coconuts. Attacks of blight killed off the palms and the farmers moved to the other two islands. In the 1950s, some US sport fishermen set up a small fishing camp on the south coast known as the *Southern Cross Club*, which is still in operation today as a diving/fishing lodge. A handful of similar small resorts and holiday villas have since been built but the resident population remains tiny.

Geography

Grand Cayman, the largest of the three islands, lies 150 miles south of Havana, Cuba, about 180 miles northwest of Jamaica and 480 miles south of Miami. Grand Cayman is low-lying, 22 miles long and four miles wide, but of the total 76 sq miles about half is swamp. A striking feature is the shallow, reef-protected lagoon, North Sound, 40 miles square and the largest area of inland mangrove in the Caribbean. None of the islands has any rivers, but vegetation is luxuriant, the main trees being coconut, thatch palm, seagrape and Australian pine. George Town, the capital of the islands, is located on the west side of Grand Cayman. Cayman Brac (Gaelic for 'bluff') gets its name from the high limestone bluff rising from sea level in the west to a height of 140 ft in the east. The island lies about 89 miles east northeast of Grand Cayman. It is about 12 miles long and a little more than a mile wide. Little Cayman lies five miles west of Cayman Brac and is 10 miles long and just over a mile wide with its highest point being only 40 ft above sea level. Owen Island, an islet off the southwest coast of Little Cayman, is uninhabited but visited by picnickers.

People

The total population of mixed African and European descent is estimated at 36,500, of whom around a third are foreigners on work permits. Nearly everyone lives on Grand Cayman, most of them in George Town, or the smaller towns of West Bay, Bodden Town, North Side and East End. The population of Cayman Brac is only 1,200. Little Cayman is largely undeveloped with only about 120 residents. The Cayman Islands are very exclusive, with strict controls on who is allowed to settle. Consequently the cost of living is extremely high. On the other hand, petty crime is rare and the islands are well looked after (described as 'a very clean sandbank'). Although Caymanians have considerable affection for Britain and do not seek independence, their way of life is Americanized. Higher education and advanced health care are usually sought in the USA and their geographical proximity influences travel choices.

District days during Cayfest in April and Pirates' Week in October are good times to meet local people

Government

A Governor appointed by the British Crown is the head of Government. The present Constitution came into effect in 1993 and provides for an Executive Council to advise the Governor on administration of the islands. The Council is made up of five Elected and three Official Members and is chaired by the Governor. The former, called Ministers from February 1994, are elected from the 15 elected representatives in the Legislative Assembly and have a range of responsibilities allocated by the Governor, while the latter are the Chief Secretary, the Financial Secretary, and the Attorney General. The Legislative Assembly may remove a minister from office by nine votes out of the 15. There is no Chief Minister. There have been no political parties since the mid-1960s but politicians organize themselves into teams. There are three teams, the National Team, Team Cayman and the Democratic Alliance Group. The Chief Secretary is the First Official Member of the Executive Council, and acts as Governor in the absence of the Governor.

Economy

The original settlers earned their living from the sea, either as turtle fishermen or as crew members on ships around the world. In 1906 more than a fifth of the population of 5,000 was estimated to be at sea, and even in the 1950s the government's annual report said that the main export was of seamen and their remittances the mainstay of the economy. Today the standard of living is high, with the highest per capita income in the Caribbean. The islands' economy is based largely on offshore finance and banking, tourism, real estate and construction, and a little local industry. Apart from a certain amount of meat, turtle, fish and a few local fruits and vegetables, almost all foodstuffs and other necessities are imported. The cost of living therefore rises in line with that of the main trading partners. The economy is highly dependent upon the fortunes of the US economy, with interest

The Cayman Islands is the largest offshore financial centre and the fifth largest financial centre in the world

Cayman Islands

rates rising and falling according to those of US instruments. Tourism revenues have risen sharply in recent years although income still fluctuates according to the strength of the US economy. In the 1990s cruise ship visitors soared with the introduction of calls by the cruise liner *Ecstasy* which carries 2,500 passengers. Cruise ship passengers outnumber stayover visitors by two to one, but the latter account for 90% of revenues. Nearly three quarters of all stayover visitors are from the USA.

Jamaica

Introducing Jamaica

Jamaica has been called the Island of Springs, and Xaymaca, the name used by its pre-Columbian inhabitants, the Taínos, meant 'land of wood and water'. It is indeed a beautiful island, with rolling hills and steep gullies, and the spectacular Blue Mountains overlooking a coastline indented with bays and coves. Rain falls freely, water is abundant, the vegetation is luxuriant and colours are vibrant. The people have a culture to match, from reggae and rastafarianism to English plantation houses and cricket. The place lives and breathes rhythm: music is everywhere and Jamaica is a hub of creativity in the Caribbean.

Every conceivable watersport is on offer in the resort areas on the north coast, where the beaches are safe for swimming. The south coast, though having fewer beaches, is richly endowed with natural attractions such as Black River Safari and YS Falls and is fast becoming the destination for nature lovers.

Essentials

Before you travel

Canadian and US citizens do not need passports or visas for a stay of up to 6 months, if they **Documents** reside in their own countries and have proof of citizenship with photo ID (i.e. a birth certificate or certificate of citizenship). Residents of Commonwealth countries (except Nigerians, who need a visa), the EC, Scandinavia and Switzerland, Turkey and Germany, need a passport and an onward ticket for a stay not exceeding 6 months. Japanese visitors need a passport and a visa if staying more than 30 days. Citizens of all other countries must have a **visa**, **passport** and **onward ticket**. Immigration may insist on an onward address, before issuing an entry stamp. Hotel rooms can be booked at the airport tourist office. For visa extensions, apply to Ministry of Social Security and Justice, Kingston Mall, 12 Ocean Boulevard, Kingston, T9220800. No vaccinations required unless you have visited Asia, Africa, Central or South America, Dominican Republic, Haiti, Trinidad or Tobago within 6 weeks of going to Jamaica.

Currency The Jamaican dollar (J\$) is the local currency but foreign currency up to US\$100 is **Money** legal tender for purchases of goods and services, with change given in J\$.

Exchange The Jamaican dollar floats on the foreign exchange market. The only legal *Rates in Negril can* exchange transactions are those carried out in commercial banks, or in official exchange *be worse than in* bureaux in major hotels and the international airports. It is illegal to buy, sell or lend foreign *Montego Bay* currency without a licence. Banks pay slightly more for US\$ travellers' cheques than for cash. Retain your receipt so you can convert Jamaican dollars at the end of your stay. Most banks and exchange bureaux, including at the airport, will not accept US\$100 bills because of forgeries. If using credit cards the transaction will be converted into US\$ before you sign; be sure to verify the exact rate being used, often a 5-10% adjustment can be instantly obtained.

In the mountains, the temperature can fall to as low as 7°C during the winter season. Tem- **Climate** peratures on the coast average 27°C, rising occasionally to 32°C in Jul-Aug and never falling below 20°C. The humidity is fairly high. The best months are Dec-Apr. Rain falls intermittently from about May, with short daily tropical showers in Sep, with Oct-Nov being the rainy season.

Getting there

From Europe *British Airways* (Gatwick) and/or *Air Jamaica* (Heathrow) fly direct, between **Air** London and Kingston and Montego Bay with lots of connections from other European cities. *Air Europe* and *Lauda Air* fly from Milan. *Condor* flies weekly from Frankfurt to Montego Bay. There are many charter flights from Europe which change according to the season, check with travel agent. **From North America** *Air Jamaica* has services to Kingston and/or Montego Bay from Atlanta, Baltimore, Boston, Chicago, Fort Lauderdale, Houston, Los Angeles, Miami, New York, Orlando, Philadelphia. *Air Canada* flies from Toronto to Kingston and Montego Bay. *American Airlines* flies to Kingston and/or Montego Bay from Dallas, Houston, New York and Miami, with lots of connections from other cities through Miami. *US Air* flies to Montego Bay from Charlotte, New York, Philadelphia and Pittsburg. *Northwest Airlines* from Memphis and New York to Montego Bay. **From the Caribbean** Regional airlines have services to Kingston from Antigua, Barbados, Curaçao, Grand Cayman, Havana, Nassau, Port-au-Prince, Port of Spain, St Maarten and Santo Domingo, and to Montego Bay from Barbados, Bonaire, Curaçao, Grand Cayman, Grenada, Havana, Holguín, Nassau, Port-au-Prince, Providenciales, Punta Cana, St Lucia and Santo Domingo. Flights are timed to connect with intercontinental arrivals and departures.

It is extremely difficult to book a passage by ship to other Caribbean islands. About 9 cruise **Boat** lines call at Ocho Rios or Montego Bay weekly, mostly from Florida ports.

Tourist offices overseas

Canada *303 Eglington Ave East, Suite 200, Toronto, Ontario M4P 1L3, T416-4827850, jtb@jtbcanada.com.*
France, Belgium, Luxembourg *32 rue de Ponthieu, 4th Floor, 75996 Paris, T331-45634201, jamaicaf@worldnet.fr.*
Germany, Austria, Switzerland *Postfach 900437, 60444 Frankfurt, T4961-84990044, jtbgermany@t-online.de.*
Italy, southern Europe *c/o Sergat Italia, Via Nazionale 230, 00184 Roma, T3906-48901255, sergat@rmnet.it.*

Japan *3-1-8 Shibuya, Shibuya-ku, Tokyo 105-0002, T813-34868851, info@jamaica.co.jp.*
UK *1-2 Prince Consort Rd, London SW7 2BZ, T020-72240505, jamaicatravel@btconnect.com*
USA *New York: 801 2nd Av, 20th Fl, New York, NY10017, T212-8569727, F8569730; Suite 1101, 1320 South Dixie Highway, Coral Gables, Miami, FL 33146, T305-6650557, F6667239; 3440 Wilshire Blvd, Suite 805, Los Angeles, CA 900010, T2133841123, F3841780. www.jamaicatravel.com, jamaicatrv1@aol.com*

Touching down

Jamaica

Airport information
See pages 191 and 210 for further details

There are 2 international airports: the **Norman Manley** in Kingston and **Donald Sangster** in Montego Bay. Montego Bay airport is the only one really within walking distance of most hotels. The Kingston domestic airstrip is at **Tinson Pen**, 3 km from the centre of town on Marcus Garvey Drive; those at Ocho Rios and Port Antonio are a long way out of town. At Kingston's Norman Manley Airport you can change back excess Jamaican dollars into US$ at the bank in the departure lounge. There are also several reasonable shops there which will accept Jamaican currency (except for duty-free goods). Allow 3 hrs to check in for a flight; there are 4 separate security, baggage or documentation checks.

Airlines

Air Jamaica, passenger information and reservations, Kingston office, 72 Harbour St, Kingston, or frequent flyer at 4 St Lucia Av, Kingston 5, ticket office and sales in Montego Bay at 9 Queens Drive, other offices in Negril, T9574210, Ocho Rios, T9742566. Montego Bay is its regional hub. *Air Jamaica Express*, reservations and information, 9 Queens Drive, T888-9524300. *British Airways* is in The Towers, Dominica Drive, Kingston 5, T9299020, 9400890 (Montego Bay). *BWIA*, 19 Dominica Drive, Kingston 5, T9293770, 9248364 (airport), 9524100 (Montego Bay). *American Airlines*, T9208887 (Kingston), 888-3592247 (Montego Bay).

Tourist information
For Tour operators, see page 197

The 'Meet the People' programme can introduce you to Jamaicans with your interests and hobbies

Local tourist office **Helpline** T0888-995-9999, www.jamaicatravel.com Head office at Pan Caribbean Building, 64 Knutsford Blvd, Kingston 5, T9299200, F9299375. Circulates detailed hotel lists and plenty of other information. Other offices in Jamaica: at the international airports; Cornwall Beach Complex, Montego Bay, T9524425 or T9522462, airport, nights, holidays, F9523587; Ocean Village Shopping Centre, Ocho Rios, T9742582 or T9742570, F9742559; City Centre Plaza, Port Antonio, T9933051, F9932117; Coral Seas Plaza, Negril T9574243, F9574489; Hendricks Building, 2 High St, Black River, T9652074, F9652076.

Maps The *Discover Jamaica* road map (American Map Corporation) is widely available free from tourist offices. It has plans of Kingston, Montego Bay, Negril, Mandeville, Ocho Rios, Port Antonio and Spanish Town. Good clear series of 1:50,000 maps covering Jamaica in 20 sheets from Survey Department, 23½ Charles St, Kingston, T9224443.

Security
While most areas are generally safe, advice should be sought on the most appropriate routes and means of travel. If possible, travel in groups

The per capita crime rate is lower than in most North American cities, but there is a lot of violent crime. This is particularly concentrated in downtown Kingston (90% of violent crime takes place in four Kingston police districts), but can be encountered anywhere. Do not walk about in downtown Kingston after dark. There are large areas of west Kingston where you should not go off the main roads even by day. The motive is robbery so take sensible precautions. Gang warfare has been exacerbated by the US policy of deporting Jamaican criminals back to Kingston.

Beware of pickpockets and be firm but polite with touts. Do not wear jewellery. Do not go into the downtown areas of any towns at night. Avoid arriving in a town at night. Take a taxi

Touching down

See also Directory, page 197

Boat information Port Antonio Marina opened in 2002 with 24-hr Customs and Immigration, 32-slips for yachts of up to 350 ft, as well as facilities for fishing boats. Fuel, provisioning, power and 3 phone lines for each berth, restaurant, bar, pool, internet access, laundry, showers and storage. Full-service boatyard for repairs and maintenance, haul-out for vessels up to 80 tons, 50-bay storage for vessels up to 50 ft across the harbour from the marina.

Business hours Banks: Mon-Fri 0900-1500 or 1530 (some local variations). **Offices**: Mon-Fri 0830-1630. **Shops**: Mon-Sat 0830 or 0930 -1600 or 1730, depending on area; half-day closing (1200) on Wed in Down Town Kingston, on Thu in uptown Kingston and Montego Bay, and on Fri in Ocho Rios.

Clothing Light summer clothing is needed all the year round, with a sweater for cooler evenings. Some hotels expect casual evening wear in their dining rooms and nightclubs, but for the most part dress is informal. Bathing costumes, though, are only appropriate by the pool or on the beach.

Departure tax J$1,000, payable in Jamaican or US dollars for stays of 24 hrs or more. Cruise ship passengers pay US$15. Airport improvement taxes are included in the cost of your ticket.

Drugs Marijuana (ganja) is widely grown in remote areas and frequently offered to tourists. Cocaine (not indigenous to Jamaica) is also peddled. Possession of either drug is a criminal offence. On average over 200 foreigners are serving prison sentences in Jamaica at any given moment for drug offences. The police stop taxis, cars, etc in random road checks. Airport security is tight with sniffer dogs, scans, etc.

Emergency numbers Fire/Ambulance 110, Police 119.

Health In general, health care is good with average life expectancy of 75 years. Declining government spending on health and social programmes has led to falling standards and a rise in private hospitals and clinics with rising costs. The growing rate of HIV infection among Jamaicans is a serious concern. St James parish, which includes Montego Bay, has the highest incidence of AIDS in the country, with 198 cases per 100,000 population, compared with the national average of 83 per 100,000.

Official time Eastern Standard Time, 5 hrs behind GMT and 1 hr behind the Eastern Caribbean.

Public holidays New Year's Day, Ash Wed, Good Fri, Easter Sun, Easter Mon, Labour Day (23 May), Independence Day (first Sun in Aug), Emancipation Day (6 Aug), National Heroes Day (20 Oct), Christmas Day, Boxing Day.

Tipping Hotel staff, waiters at restaurants, barmen, taxi drivers, cloakroom attendants and hairdressers get 10-15% of the bill. When service is included, personal tips are often still expected. In some areas you may be expected to tip when asking for information.

Voltage 110 volts, 50 cycles AC; some hotels have 220 volts.

Weights and measures Metric.

Jamaica

from bus stations to your hotel. Travellers have reported being threatened for refusing to buy drugs, as well as incidents where Jamaicans have become aggressive over traffic accidents, however minor. Take the obvious precautions and you should have no problem. The vast majority of Jamaicans welcome tourists and want to be helpful but the actions of the minority can leave you with the impression that tourists are not wanted. Crimes against tourists have fallen and there are frequent military patrols to reinforce security in tourist areas. Harassment of tourists in downtown Montego Bay has been greatly reduced as a result of increased police patrols on bikes, and community involvement. Still, exercise caution when shopping and especially at nights.

Where to stay

All-inclusive resorts are extremely popular in Jamaica, and include **SuperClubs** (www.super clubs.com) and **Sandals** (www.sandals.com), with hotels mainly along the north coast; some allow children but most are for couples only. As a result of their popularity, other hotels have been forced to discount their rates. Chris Blackwell's **Island Outpost**, www.islandoutpost.com, now has several luxury hideaways, popular with the rich and famous.

Larger hotels have introduced strict security to prevent guests being bothered by hustling

Accommodation is subject to a 15% General Consumption Tax, check whether it is included in room rates

Aim to arrive at Montego Bay rather than Kingston because the former is the island's tourism capital with a greater variety of affordable accommodation. However, if you can arrange to fly out from Kingston you will have a chance to get the flavour of the Jamaican experience in both cities. Get hold of the tourist board's list of hotels and guesthouses offering rates and addresses, and also a copy of *Jamaica Vacation Guide* (both free). Many small hotels and inns have grouped themselves as the 'Insider's Jamaica'. The tourist board has their brochure, or visit www.insidersjamaica.com

The *Jamaica Association of Villas and Apartments* (JAVA), Pineapple Place, Ocho Rios, Box 298, T9742508, F9742967, represents over 300 private houses, villas and apartments. For villas go to www.villaconnections.co.uk or www.villasofjamaica.com Renting a villa may be an attractive option if you do not intend to do much travelling and there are 4/6 of you to share the costs (about US$1,800-2,000 per week for a nice villa with private swimming pool and fully staffed). You will, however, probably have to rent a car as you will have to take the cook shopping, etc. You can go even more upmarket and pay US$3,000-14,000 a week for a fully staffed luxury villa.

Cultural homestays can be arranged if you would like to experience local hospitality with professional or retired professional hosts. Contact Hilary Burke, T613-2374658, hilary.burke@pointtopointbooks.com English-language tuition also offered.

Getting around

Air

All fares attract US$2.50 stamp duty

Air Jamaica Express (T9224661, www.airjamaica.com/express) flies to the 2 international airports, Boscobel Aerodrome at Ocho Rios, Negril, Tinson Pen in Kingston and Ken Jones Aerodrome at Port Antonio. Charges are reasonable but using this method of travel is not very satisfactory unless you can arrange to be met at your destination. Fares Kingston-Negril, US$80 one way, US$157 return, Kingston-Montego Bay, US$75 one way, US$153 return.

Bus

Public road transport is mostly by minibus. The transportation system was reorganized in 2001 and is now more convenient and safe for travel. This form of travel is cheap and fast as buses operate on a schedule enforced by the transport authority officials located at bus terminals. Help may be obtained from the uniformed conductor or conductress on the bus.

Car

Drive on the left

Most petrol stations open on Sunday; note that fuel is paid for in cash

Distances and driving times of major routes: Kingston to Montego Bay 193 km (3½ hrs), to Ocho Rios 90 km (2 hrs), to Port Antonio 109 km (2 hrs); Montego Bay to Negril 80 km (1½ hrs), to Ocho Rios 108 km (2 hrs); Ocho Rios to Port Antonio 108 km (2½ hrs). A new highway linking Negril, Montego Bay and Ocho Rios has shortened travel times along the north coast. The speed limit is 50 kmph in built-up areas, 80 kmph on highways. A North American driving licence is valid for up to 3 months per visit, a British licence 12 months and a Japanese licence 1 month. Try to avoid driving outside towns at night. Roads are often twisty and potholed, especially in mountainous areas, where there are no guard rails. Plan ahead because it gets dark early. Sections of the northern coastal road from Kingston to Port

Antonio are in a particularly bad condition. Breath tests for drunk driving and speed traps are now in effect. Traffic congestion is to be expected in all large towns and jams are the norm in rush hour. Traffic is particularly slow and heavy between Kingston and Spanish Town.

Car hire Undoubtedly a rented car is the most satisfactory, and most expensive, way of getting about. All the major car rental firms are represented both at the airports and in the major resort areas. There are also numerous local car rental firms which are mostly just as good and tend to be cheaper. The tourist board has a list of members of the *Jamaica U-Drive Association*, Newlin St, Ocho Rios, T9742852. Be prepared to pay considerably more than in North America or Europe (starting from about US$112 per day plus CDW of US$25 and tax of 15%). Many companies operate a three-day minimum hire policy. *Island Car Rentals* is a well-known firm, airport office T9248075, Montego Bay T9255771, Kingston T9268861. *Praise Tours & Auto Rentals Ltd*, 72 Half Way Tree Rd, Kingston 10, T9290215, F9296962, good deals on longer rentals, no trouble with refunds, airport transfers, recommended. *Don's Car Rental*, headquarters 1 Worthington Av, New Kingston, Kingston 5, T9262181, F9260866, also offices at Negril Aerodrome, T9574366, Trident Hotel, Port Antonio, T9932241. In the resort areas of Montego Bay, Ocho Rios and Negril, jeeps are available for about US$80-90 a day, motorbikes and scooters from US$30 and bicycles from US$5.

There are taxis, with red PPV (Public Passenger Vehicle) licence plates, in all the major resort **Taxi** areas and at the airports. Some have meters, most do not. Only the JUTA taxis have officially authorized charges to all destinations. With others (Yellow Cab, Checker Cab etc), the important point is to ask the fare before you get in. It can be around US$4-5 for a short hop, US$6-7 from New Kingston to Down Town, US$8 from Down Town to Mona Campus. All taxis should charge the same to the airport, US$18-23 from New Kingston. The tourist information centres should also be able to help in this respect. Some 'non-tourist' taxis operate like minibuses, that is, they have a set route and can be flagged down at the bus stop. They will carry about 4-5 passengers in a Nissan, Hyundai or Lada, but if you do not want to share you can hire it all for yourself at a higher cost. Negotiate the fare in advance. To take a taxi for a long distance is expensive; a JUTA taxi from Kingston to Ocho Rios for example could cost US$125-145, rather more than a day's car hire, although you could negotiate a fare of less than half that with a smaller taxi company.

Keeping in touch

Additional phone lines have been installed and internet access is now available in several **Internet** post offices around the country.

There are post offices in all main towns. The sorting office on South Camp Road, Down Town **Post** Kingston, has a good and helpful philatelic bureau.

Cable, telephone and fax services are operated by *Cable & Wireless Jamaica Ltd*. 'Time and **Telephone** charge' phone calls overseas cost the same in hotels as at the phone company, but there is a *IDD code: 876* 15% tax and a service charge that varies. In fact, making an international call is often easier from a hotel. Phone cards may be obtained from Cable and Wireless, gas stations, supermarkets and various stores, available in J$50, J$100, J$200, J$500 and J$1,000 denominations, plus 15% tax. Check that the year is valid for use. Two new telecommunications companies have entered the cellular service market: Digicel and Centenial.

The daily paper with the largest circulation is *The Daily Gleaner*, which also publishes an **Newspapers** evening paper, *The Star*, and the *Sunday Gleaner*. *The Jamaica Herald* is a livelier daily than *The Gleaner*, also the *Sunday Herald*. The other daily is the *Observer*. *Money Index* is a financial weekly, in Montego Bay *The Western Mirror* is weekly. *Lifestyle* is a monthly glossy magazine, *Jamaica Journal* is a quarterly with interesting but academic articles.

Jamaica

Food and drink

Food There are many unusual and delicious vegetables and fruits such as sweetsop, soursop and sapodilla. National specialities include saltfish (salt cod) and ackee, saltfish fritters and curried goat. Jerked pork is highly spiced pork which has been cooked in the earth covered by wood and burning coals. Chicken is cooked in the same way. Patties, sold in specialist shops and bars, are seasoned meat, vegetables or lobster in pastry, and very good value. Curried lobster is a delightful local speciality. The closed season for lobster fishing is Apr-Jun, so if lobster is on the menu during those months check where it has come from. Stew peas is chunks of beef stewed with kidney beans and spices and served with rice. Along the coast, fish tea is a hotch potch of the day's catch made into a soup, US$1-1.50 a cup.

Drink Local rum is combined with local fruit juices to create cocktails, or mixed with *Ting*, a local carbonated grapefruit soft drink. Red Stripe lager, with which, the locals say, no other Caribbean beer compares, is about US$1.10 at roadside bar, considerably more in a hotel. Try the Irish Moss natural drink. All rums are very cheap duty free, typically US$13 for a 3-pack.

Shopping

Some shopkeepers offer a 10-15% discount on all goods and there is a 15% tax added to all goods. Street vendors never add tax

In the craft markets and stores you can find items of wood (by Rastafarians, Maroons and other craftsmen), straw, batik (from a number of good textile companies) and embroidery; the hand-knitted woollen gold, red, green Rasta caps (with or without black dreadlocks affixed) are very cheap. Jewellery from *Blue Mountain Gems*, near Rose Hall, Montego Bay area. For art and ceramics, *Devon House Gallery*, *Chelsea Galleries* on Chelsea Rd, *Gallery 14*, *Old Boulevard Gallery*, *Grosvenor Gallery*, *Contemporary Art Centre* in Liguanea. Blue Mountain coffee is excellent, cheaper at airport duty-free shop than in supermarkets or tourist shops.

Check with legislation (and your conscience) before buying articles made from tortoiseshell or crocodile skin, and certain corals, shells and butterflies. Many of these creatures are protected and should not be bought as souvenirs. It is illegal to take or possess black or white coral in Jamaica; sea turtles are protected and you should refuse to buy products made from their shells.

Jamaica

Flora and fauna

The 'land of wood and water' is a botanist's paradise. There are reported to be about 3,000 species of flowering plants, 827 of which are not found anywhere else. There are over 550 varieties of fern, 300 of which can be found in **Fern Gully**. There are many orchids, bougainvillea, hibiscus and other tropical flowers. Tropical hardwoods like cedar and mahogany, palms, balsa and many other trees, besides those that are cultivated, can be seen. Cultivation, however, is putting much of Jamaica's plant life at risk. Having been almost entirely forested, an estimated 6% of the land is virgin forest. A great many species are endangered.

The national flower is the dark blue bloom of the lignum vitae

This is also a land of hummingbirds and butterflies (see page 203). Sea cows and the Pedro seal are found in the island's waters, although fewer than 100 sea cows, or manatee, survive. There are crocodiles, but no large wild mammals apart from the hutia, or coney (an endangered species), the mongoose (considered a pest since it eats chickens) and, in the mountains, wild boar. There are, however, lots of bats, with 25 species recorded. Most live in caves or woods and eat fruit and insects, but there is a fish-eating bat which can sometimes be seen swooping over the water in Kingston Harbour. The Jamaican iguana (*Cyclura collei*) was thought to have died out in the 1960s, but in 1990 a small group was found to be surviving in the Hellshire Hills. There are 5 species of snakes, all harmless and rare, the largest of which is the yellow snake (the Jamaican boa), which can grow up to 3 m.

Good sites for bird watching are given in the text below; the 3 main areas are the **Cockpit Country**, the **Blue Mountains** and **Marshall's Pen**. The national bird is the red-billed streamertail hummingbird (*Trochilus polytmus*), also known as the doctor bird or swallow tail hummingbird. The male has a long, sweeping tail much longer than its body, and is one of Jamaica's endemic species. Other endemic birds are the yellow-billed parrot and the black-billed parrot, found in the Cockpit Country or Hope Zoo. There are 25 species and 21 subspecies of endemic land birds which are found nowhere else. A good place to see Jamaica's birds is the **Rocklands Feeding Station**, near Montego Bay. On weekday evenings you can watch the birds being fed and even offer a hummingbird a syrup and get really close. Many migratory birds stop on Jamaica on their journeys north or south. One of the best references is *Birds of Jamaica: a photographic field guide* by Audrey Downer and Robert Sutton with photos by Yves-Jacques Rey Millet Cambridge University Press (1990).

Jamaica

In 1989 the Government established two pilot national parks under the Protected Areas Resource Conservation (PARC) project. The **Blue Mountain/John Crow Mountain National Park** encompasses almost 81,000 ha of mountains, forests and rivers. Efforts are being made to develop the area for ecotourism and provide a livelihood for local people. The **Montego Bay Marine Park** aims to protect the offshore reef from urban waste, over-fishing and hillside erosion leading to excessive soil deposition. Several initiatives on protected areas are under way, including the Negril Environmental Protection Area and the Negril Marine Park, Ocho Rios, Port Antonio Marine Park along the northern coast and the Portland Bight Protected Area and the Canoe Valley National Park along the south coast. All coral reefs are now protected. Hunting of the American crocodile, the yellow- and black-billed parrot and all species of sea turtle is banned. See shopping above.

Diving and marine life

There are marine parks in Montego Bay, Port Antonio and Negril. The **Montego Bay Marine Park** stretches from the east end of the airport to the Great River and contains three major ecosystems: seagrass bed, mangroves and coral reefs. Non-motorized watersports such as diving, snorkelling and glass-bottom boat tours are permitted, but you are not allowed to touch or remove anything. There are several conservation groups involved in marine ecology. In St Ann, *Friends of the Sea* is a non-profit, non-governmental organization, which concentrates on education and public awareness and draws attention to what is happening on land that might affect what happens underwater. The *Negril Coral Reef Preservation Society* has installed permanent mooring buoys for recreational boats and works on educational programmes with schools. The Negril marine park set up in conjunction with protected coastal and terrestrial habitats, aims at protecting the coral reefs and improving fish stocks.

Around Negril there are many reef sites and a huge variety of marine life: coral, sponges, invertebrates, sea turtles, octopus, starfish and lots of fish. Off Montego Bay and Ocho Rios there is wall diving quite close to shore and a few wrecks. Off Port Antonio fish are attracted to freshwater springs which provide good feeding grounds. The best wreck diving is off Port Royal and Kingston where you can also explore the city that slid into the sea in the 1692 earthquake.

Dive centres Nearly all dive operators are based at hotels along the north coast. Licensed by The Jamaica Tourist Board, most are members of the *Jamaica Association of Dive Operators* (JADO). They offer courses at all levels. Contact the tourist board for a full list of operators and map of dive sites. Diving can be included in a hotel package. A 2-tank dive costs on average US$65. Dives are limited to 30 m. There are hyperbaric chambers at Discovery Bay and Port Royal.

Fishing Deep-sea fishing for white marlin, wahoo, tuna and dolphin fish can be arranged at north coast hotels. A half-day charter costs US$400 for up to 6 people, plus a 10% tip for the crew, who will expect to keep half the catch. There is a blue marlin tournament at Port Antonio and others at Montego Bay, Falmouth and Discovery Bay, as well as a James Bond Oracabessa Marlin Tournament. Contact the *Montego Bay Yacht Club* for details, T9798038, mbyc@infochan.com

Holidays and festivals

Dancing for six hours a night for seven nights is the best way to get fit!

Carnival (www.jamaicacarnival.com) has come only recently to Jamaica and is held around Easter time, at various locations around the island, attended by thousands. Byron Lee, the leading Jamaican calypsonian, spends a lot of time in Trinidad over Carnival period and then brings the Trinidad calypsos back to Jamaica. The *Calabash Literary Festival* is held in **May**. Events leading up to the festival are held in Kingston while the event culminates in a weekend in Treasure Beach, www.calabash.org The 5-day annual festival, *Reggae Sumfest*, is held in **Aug** with local and international musicians, contact the office, T9520889, F9797437, info@reggaesumfest.com The celebrations around *Independence Day*,1 **Aug**, last a week, ending with a street dance at Half Way Tree. The *Jamaica Film and Music Festival* is held at the Wyndham Rosehall, Montego Bay, in **Nov**. Film makers, musicians and artistes gather for discussions, culminating in an awards ceremony, www.jamericanfilmfest.com The tourist board

★

Things to do in Jamaica

- Enjoy a sunset seafood dinner at **Fisherman's Inn** followed by a boat tour of the bioluminescent lagoon just east of the historic town of **Falmouth**, said to be the most active bioluminescent lake in the world.
- Catch the dawn with a **Blue Mountain sunrise**, not a cocktail, but still likely to give you a high as the mist surrenders quietly to the rising sun and the golden hue of dawn sweeps across the eastern sky, tinting cloud layers far below.
- Experience the culture of reggae and rastafarianism with a visit to the **Bob Marley Museum** in Kingston.
- Buy **jerk pork, chicken** or **fish** at the roadside. This delicious and tasty Jamaican speciality is excellent, washed down with a cold Red Stripe beer.

publishes a calendar of events which covers arts and sports festivals, www.jamaicatravel.com/events There is also www.whatsonjamaica.com, a guide to events, sports, entertainment and theatre. Cultural events are organized by the *Jamaica Cultural Development Commission* (JCDC) at theatres, T9265726, www.jcdc.org.jm

Jamaica

Kingston

Jamaica's capital since 1870 and the island's commercial centre, Kingston has one of the largest and best natural harbours in the world. Following the earthquake of 1907 much of the lower part of the city (Down Town) was rebuilt in concrete. On the waterfront there are some notable modern buildings including the Bank of Jamaica and the Jamaica Conference Centre, which also houses the National Gallery. Most of the new shops and offices are in the Parish of St Andrew, although visitors and even locals are often not aware of where one parish ends and the next begins. Crossroads and Halfway Tree (St Andrew) are referred to as midtown areas. Many shopping plazas are further north again along the Constant Spring Road and east along Old Hope Road to Liguanea. The old racecourse was redeveloped in the 1960s as the New Kingston district, which contains most of the big hotels and many banks and financial institutions. Kingston and the adjoining parish of St Andrew (Corporate Area) are busy urban areas with traffic congestion. It is a place to work rather than vacation, although there are some important places of interest. A city tour could extend as far as Devon House and the nearby Blue Mountains and beaches at Hellshire and Lime Key, followed by several nightclubs. Reggae lovers should visit the Bob Marley Museum, but reggae can be heard anywhere with frequent blasts from buses, bars and cars.

IDD code: 876
Colour map 1, grid C5
Population: 750,000

Ins and outs

The international airport for Kingston is the **Norman Manley** (restaurant, good tourist office), 17 km away, up to 30 mins' drive, on the peninsula opposite Kingston across the bay. There is also an airstrip for domestic flights on Tinson Pen, 3 km from the centre. If you have flown in to Montego Bay on the north coast you can get to Kingston by air or overland by frequent bus.

Getting there
See Transport, page 183, for further details

Bus travel in Kingston costs between US$0.43 and US$0.65. Travelling by bus is safe and convenient as the transport system is now operated by the Government and monitored by the Transport Authority. Crossroads, Pechon Street and Half Way Tree are the main bus stops. Addresses in the Parish of St Andrew have a numbered zone, eg Kingston 10, while those in the Parish of Kingston have no zone number and the address is just Kingston.

Getting around
It's best to go to a hotel to order a taxi

The tourist office is at Pan Caribbean Building, 64 Knutsford Blvd, T9299200.

Tourist information

Sights

Among older buildings of note in the Down Town area are **Gordon House** (on Duke Street), which dates from the mid-18th century and houses the Jamaican legislature. Visitors are allowed into the Strangers' Gallery but must be suitably dressed (jackets for men and dresses for women). There is also the early 18th-century parish church south of Parade, where Admiral Benbow is buried. **Parade** (Sir William Grant Park) is at the heart of the city centre; it is an open oasis amid the densely packed surroundings. The name derives from the British soldiers' parades here during colonial rule. Now it is

Kingston orientation

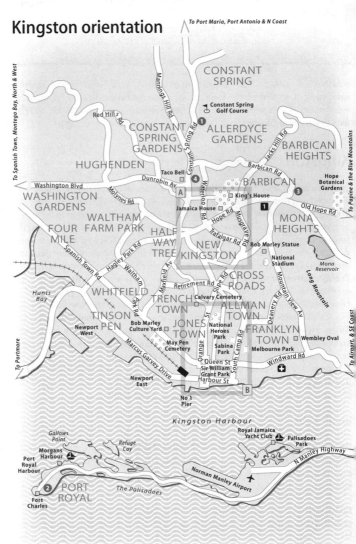

Related maps:
A New Kingston, page 194
B Downtown, Kingston, page 196

■ **Sleeping**	● **Eating**
1 Christar Villas	**1** Fish Place

 2 Guilt Trip/ Village Café/ Village Grill

 3 Susie's Bakery & Coffee Bar

Jamaica

at the junction of the main east-west route through the Down Town area (Windward Road/East Queen Street-West Queen Street/Spanish Town Road) and King Street/Orange Street, which runs north to Cross Roads. At Cross Roads, the main route forks, left to Half Way Tree (recently renamed Nelson Mandela Park), straight on up Old Hope Road to Liguanea. These two roads encompass New Kingston.

The Parish Church at St Andrew at **Half Way Tree** dates from 1700. Half Way Tree was a half-way stage on the road between Spanish Town, the then capital, and the hills. It is a busy traffic junction which takes some negotiating in a car. This area is known as the **Corporate Area** (Kingston being that section of the Corporate Area south of the National Heroes Circle/Park) and most modern development is here. Hope Road, on the north edge of New Kingston, runs east from Half Way Tree. Just off it is **Devon House**, built like a 'great house', by Jamaica's first millionaire in the 1880s, at the corner of Trafalgar and Hope roads. Now renovated, it houses a museum of antique furniture. ■ *Tue-Sat 1000-1700. US$5 for a guided tour, but the craft shops and restaurants in the grounds are open to all and well worth a visit. T9260829.* Not far away is **King's House**, the official residence of the Governor-General and, nearby, **Jamaica House**, the office of the Prime Minister.

About 10 blocks east of Devon House, off Hope Road, is the **Bob Marley Museum**. The house where Marley used to live traces his story back to the time of his childhood and family, with paintings, newspaper cuttings, posters and other memorabilia. He died tragically of brain cancer in 1981 at the age of 36, having survived a controversial assassination attempt (the bullet-holes in the walls have been left as a reminder). There is a gift shop selling Jamaican and African artefacts. Marijuana plants grow profusely throughout the grounds and ganja is smoked openly by staff. ■ *Mon, Tue, Thu, Fri 0900-1700, Wed, Sat 1230-1730. US$10 including obligatory 1-hr guided tour and 20-min audio visual presentation. 56 Hope Rd, T9782991.*

Photography is allowed, but no videotaping within the museum and grounds

Further east, along Old Hope Road, are the **Hope Royal Botanical Gardens**. The land was first acquired by Major Richard Hope in 1671 and 200 years later the Governor of Jamaica, Sir John Peter Grant, bought 81 ha and created the gardens. ■ *0830-1830.* In 1961 a **zoo** was opened alongside the gardens, now a showcase for the different habitats of Jamaica and its indigenous animals. ■ *Daily 1000-1700. J$10.*

West of downtown Kingston, near the May Pen Cemetery, is the **Bob Marley Culture Yard**, a project started by the *Trench Town Development Association* (TTDA), a community-based NGO, to boost the inner-city community of Trench Town, concentrating on the reggae heritage of Bob Marley and other great musicians who came from the area. Culture Yard is an attraction in the making, based on restoring the home and belongings of the reggae superstar to be opened for visitors. ■ *Trench Town Development Association, 6 Lower First St, Trench Town, Kingston, T9484455, and 18 Collie Smith Drive, Kingston 12, T7576739.*

The swimming at Kingston is not good and the sea at Gunboat beach, near the airport, is dirty. Swim at Port Royal (see below) instead. 'Hellshire', south of Port Henderson, is a locals' favourite, but is about 15 to 20 minutes out of Kingston depending on traffic. *Bammy* (made from cassava root) and *festival* (a Jamaican appetizer) with fish are prepared along the beach strip.

Beaches

Essentials

Up in the hills overlooking Kingston Bay is Island Outpost's **LL** *Strawberry Hill*, now a 12-villa luxury retreat but formerly a coffee and fruit plantation house, sadly destroyed by Hurricane Gilbert in 1988. Recommended weekend brunch of jerk meats, salt fish, etc, washed down with champagne and orange juice, US$45, T9448400, www.islandoutpost.com

LL-L *Hilton Kingston*, 77 Knutsford Blvd, Kingston 5, T9265430, www.hilton.com 303 rooms, usual *Hilton* facilities. **LL-L** *Jamaica Pegasus*, 81 Knutsford Blvd, T9263690, www.meridien jamaica.com 350 rooms, pleasant service and atmosphere but nothing special. **L** *Terra Nova*, 17 Waterloo Rd, T9269334, www.cariboutpost.com/terra_nova 35

Sleeping
Morgan's Harbour is near the airport and has transport there and back; all the other main hotels are in or near New Kingston

Jamaica

rooms, popular with business travellers, pool, bar, café and restaurant. **AL** *Knutsford Court*, 16 Chels ea Av, Kingston 5, T9291000. Formerly *Sutton Place*, now refurbished and re-branded. 177 rooms and suites, a/c, TV, balcony, smoking or non-smoking floors, CP, room service, restaurant, pool, business centre, laundromat or laundry service, meeting rooms. **AL-A** *Christar Villas*, 99A Hope Rd, Kingston 6, T9787864, christar@n5.com.jm 32 1 or 2-bedroom suites and studios with kitchenettes, pool, bar, restaurant, small gym. **AL-B** *The Gardens Liguanea*, 23 Liguanea Av, Kingston 6, T9275957, www.forrespark.com Town houses, with 2 rooms, private bathrooms and shared living and dining room downstairs, rent a room or the whole house, CP, homely service, convenient location within walking distance of Sovereign Shopping Mall and the bus route, also close to the university. **A** *Altamont Court*, 1-5 Altamont Terr, T9294497, www.cariboutpost.com, 55 rooms, pool, restaurant, a/c, TV, facilities for the disabled. **A-B** *Four Seasons*, 18 Ruthven Rd, T9297655, www.hotelfourseasonsja.com Run by Mrs Stockhert, German, long-time knowledgeable resident, in a converted Edwardian house and gardens, 76 rooms, pool, bar, conference room, business centre, good cooking. **B-C** *Mayfair*, 4 West King's House Close, Kingston 10,

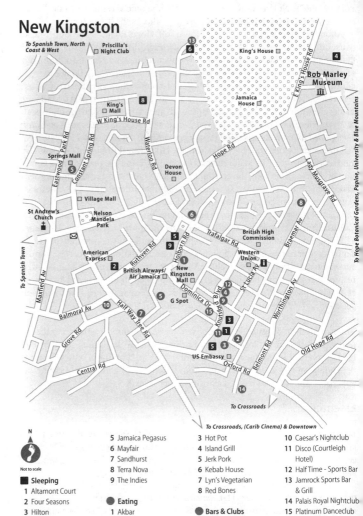

New Kingston

To Spanish Town, North Coast & West

Priscilla's Night Club

King's House

Bob Marley Museum

King's Mall

W King's House Rd

Jamaica House

Springs Mall

Hope Rd

Devon House

Village Mall

St Andrew's Church

Nelson Mandela Park

Devon House

American Express

British High Commission

Trafalgar Rd

Western Union

British Airways/ Air Jamaica

New Kingston Mall

G Spot

Balmoral Av

Half Way Tree Rd

US Embassy

Oxford Rd

Central Rd

To Spanish Town

To Hope Botanical Gardens, Papine, University & Blue Mountains

To Crossroads

To Crossroads, (Carib Cinema) & Downtown

N Not to scale

■ **Sleeping**
1 Altamont Court
2 Four Seasons
3 Hilton
4 Johnson Holborn Manor

5 Jamaica Pegasus
6 Mayfair
7 Sandhurst
8 Terra Nova
9 The Indies

● **Eating**
1 Akbar
2 Heather's

3 Hot Pot
4 Island Grill
5 Jerk Pork
6 Kebab House
7 Lyn's Vegetarian
8 Red Bones

● **Bars & Clubs**
9 Asylum Nightclub

10 Caesar's Nightclub
11 Disco (Courtleigh Hotel)
12 Half Time - Sports Bar
13 Jamrock Sports Bar & Grill
14 Palais Royal Nightclub
15 Platinum Danceclub

Jamaica

T9261610, F9297741. Beautiful setting (adjoining the Governor General's residence), balconies look towards mountains, 32 good rooms, also 8 houses, pool, food and service. **B** *The Indies*, 5 Holborn Rd, T9262952, indies@discoverjamaica.com 15 rooms, television US$6 extra, breakfast and lunch available, comfortable, pleasant patio, garden, helpful owners. Next door is the popular **D** *Johnson Holborn Manor*, 3 Holborn Rd. CP, fan, clean, safe and quiet, very convenient for business in New Kingston, 3 good places to eat within 50 m, luggage storage available, friendly, new annex. **B** *Sandhurst*, 70 Sandhurst Cres, Kingston 6, T9277239. 35 rooms, a/c or fan, restaurant. **D-E** *Retreat Guest House*, 8 Devon Rd, T9262565. 4 rooms, among the cheapest, safe area after dark. The *YMCA*, opposite Devon House on Hope Road, has a good swimming pool, many sports facilities and a cheaply priced restaurant. The tourist board can arrange B&B for you, usually US$25-60 a night.

Expensive (over US$20) *Red Bones Blues Café*, 21 Braemar Av, Kingston 10, T9786091. 'Nouvelle Jamaican cuisine', quite expensive but lovely garden and blues music. At *Devon House* (see page 193), there is a plush expensive restaurant, a reasonably priced snack bar and delicious ice cream at *I Scream*. *Kebab House*, 40 Trafalgar Rd, Kingston 5, T9680790. Specializes in Mediterranean food, open 1200-2300, belly dancing Wed and Sat.

Eating
There are many places, plush and modest, to eat in Downtown Kingston, New Kingston and the Half Way Tree area

By the waterfront most places close at 1700

    Mid-range (US$10-20) *The Fish Place*, 136 Constant Spring Rd, Kingston 8, T9244063, or the Mall Plaza, 20 Constant Spring Rd, Kingston 10. Jamaican restaurant specializing in seafood, the best place in town for fish in all styles, prices around US$10-15, easy-going, relaxed atmosphere, popular after-work dining and weekend stop for families and friends, live music sometimes. *Island Grill*, Shop 28, Twin Gates Plaza, 25½ Constant Spring Rd, Kingston 10, T9205016, and Sovereign Centre (Shopping Mall), Shop 16, 106 Hope Rd, Kingston 6, T9783535. *Real Jamaican Jerk*, Jamaican restaurant serving very tasty fast foods, affordable prices, several branches now appearing, jerk chicken and fish are popular, with a variety of side orders. *Akbar*, 11 Holborn Rd. Very good Indian food, good service, nice atmosphere, US$20 for 3-course dinner and drinks for 2. On Chelsea Av is *Jerk Pork*, popular with locals. Nearby are Mexican and Indian restaurants, both very good but not cheap. *The Lychee Gardens*, Shop 34, New Kingston Shopping Mall, Dominica Drive, T9298619. Serves excellent Chinese food, moderately priced. Several other eating places here, from takeaway pattie bakery to upmarket restaurant. *Heather's Garden Restaurant*, 9 Haining Rd, Kingston 5, T9607739. Middle Eastern and Jamaican dishes, US$3.25-9. *Lyn's Vegetarian Restaurant* and Performing Arts Auditorium, 7 Tangerine Pl, Kingston 10, T9293842, 9683487. *Guilt Trip Restaurant and Patisserie*, 20 Barbican Rd, Kingston 6, T9775130. Italian-influenced menu and delicious pastries and desserts. *Susie's Bakery & Coffee Bar*, Southdale Plaza and in the Orchid Village, 20 Barbican Rd, T9685030. Recommended for light lunches, pastry and coffee. *Village Café*, Orchid Village, 20 Barbican Rd, T9775851, robsvillage@hotmail.com Delicious finger foods with alternative live entertainment, often referred to as 'Kingston's living room' because of its relaxed atmosphere. Tue live music, poetry reading and young talent exposure, Wed bikini contest, Thu 70s and 80s music, Fri after work jam, Sat 'Sat night hype' disco and dancing. Under the same roof is the *Village Grill*, T9704861. Open Tue-Sat 1700 until late, finger food such as Ma Lou's wing ding (chicken wings) and sandwiches. *Ashanti Oasis*, Hope Gardens, Old Hope Rd. Vegetarian meals and cool jazz on Sun afternoons, open daily from 1300.

    Cheap (under US$10) *Hot Pot*, 2 Altamont Terr, Kingston 5, T9293906. Very cheap, serves good Jamaican food in a pleasant patio, also a take-out box for just over US$1; difficult to find – ask for directions. On Knutsford Blvd there are lots of vans selling a satisfying lunch for US$1-1.50, often less, depending on what you eat. Many outlets of international takeaway chains all over the city, *Burger King* and *Kentucky Fried Chicken*, etc, as well as Jamaica's own variation, *Mothers*, also widespread. *The Tastees* chain serves good-value takeaway patties and cakes, branches on Knutsford Blvd, Liguanea, Manor Park and Papine. In the grounds of the University of Technology at Papine is *Lillian's*, T9702224. Staffed by trainees, good cheap lunch for about US$3.

For the impecunious, meat patties may be had at US$0.43 each

Unless they have Jamaican friends, tourists are strongly advised not to probe too deeply into real Jamaican nightlife, at least in towns. For genuine local dances and songs, see the advertisements in the local press. The *Jamaica Vacation Guide* (at hotels, tourist offices) has the latest

Nightlife
Most hotels have dancing at weekends

information. Clubs and discos include **Asylum**, 69 Knutsford Blvd, Kingston 5, T9061828, the number one young adult disco, closed Mon, Ladies' Night Tue (ladies free before 2300), oldies' night Wed, Dance Hall night Thu, after-work jam and disco Fri, international music Sat, disco night Sun. **Turntable**, Red Hills Rd. **Courtleigh Hotel** , 85 Knutsford Blvd, Kingston 5, T9299000, www.courtleigh.com A popular nightclub and disco, with food and drink, regular hangout for consultants and young professionals, karaoke on Thu, Escapade 'After Work Jam' on Fri, Latin night on Sat popular with cross-section of party goers. **Half Time Sports Bar**, 61 Knutsford Blvd, T9061452, and **Jamrock Sports Bar & Grill**, 69 Knutsford Blvd, downstairs from **Asylum**, T7544032. Young crowd, music, TV, pool. **Devon House** is a good place for a quiet evening drink under the trees. **Centre Pole** at Mary Brown's Corner on Constant Spring Rd is rowdy and raunchy but fairly safe. **Palais Royal**, 14 Ripon Rd, Kingston 5, T9061828 and **Caesar's**, 5 Balmoral Av, Kingston 10are both wild and exciting if you like dancing girls in costumes that leave as much to the imagination as hair on a turtles's shell, but safe and comfortable and an interesting aspect of Jamaican culture. **Priscilla's**, 103 Constant Spring Rd, Kingston 5, T9699638. **Platinum Dance Club**, Dominica Drive, Kingston 5, T9081143, exotic dancers from Russia, closed Sun. **Rae Town**, just east of downtown Kingston, is primarily a fishing community on the coast, but it is a very popular inner-city hangout for locals and visitors, especially on Sun nights, offering a secure experience of street dance urban entertainment 'ghetto style', with typically heavy Dance Hall music from huge sound systems, and a variety of Jamaican food and drink from roadside bars and restaurants.

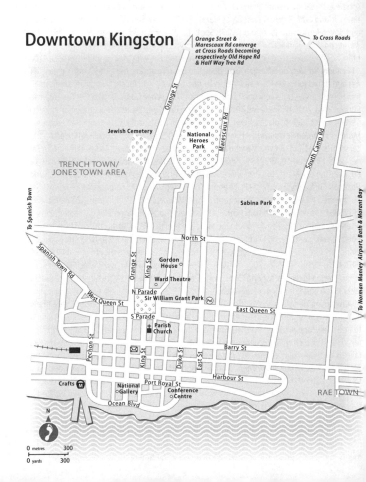

Downtown Kingston

The *Edna Manley School for the Visual and Performing Arts* produces graduates of a very high **Entertainment**
standard and there are several very active theatre and dance companies. *National Dance*
Theatre Comapny is well known internationally. Theatres include *Ward Theatre* (North
Parade), *Little Theatre* (St Andrew, T9266129), *The Barn*, *New Kingston Playhouse*, *Green*
Gables, *Phillip Sherlock Creative Arts Centre*. Watch the press for details of performances.

In downtown Kingston, the *Jamaica Crafts Market*, at the corner of Ocean Blvd and Port Royal **Shopping**
St and many shops at west end of Port Royal St have local crafts. The market is a must for souve-   *There are various*
nir hunters, craft items are reasonably priced and there is a wide range of traditional Jamaican   *duty-free concessions*
handicrafts. Off West Queen St is an interesting local market, selling fish, fruit and general pro-   *for visitors*
duce. Downtown is where Jamaicans shop for bargains, but be careful, particularly in the market; it can be dangerous, even if you do not get robbed. Most shops are in the plazas along
Constant Spring Rd and in Liguanea. There is a smart little shopping centre in New Kingston.
Reggae music shops can be found close together along Orange St, just north of Parade. For
books, try *Kingston Bookshop*, at 70B King St, T9224056, the Pavilion Shopping Mall, 13 Constant Spring Rd, T9684591, and at The Springs, 15-17 Constant Spring Rd. *Bookland* on
Knutsford Blvd has a wide range of US magazines and newspapers and also *The Times*.

Cricket is the island's main spectator sport, although it was overtaken by soccer in 1998 **Sport**
when Jamaica qualified for the World Cup. Test matches are played at Sabina Park. For details   *For diving and*
on matches ring *Jamaica Cricket Association*, T9670322, F9673976,   *fishing, see*
www.greatvacations.com **Football** Phone *Jamaica Football Federation*, T9290484. **Golf**   *page 190*
is played at the *Constant Spring* (18 holes, green fee US$38 week days and US$46 weekends,
T9241610) and *Caymanas Clubs* (18 holes, green fee US$38 week days and US$48 weekends, T9223386, c/o *Liguanea Club*). The *Jamaica Golf Association* has information on tournaments, T9252325, jamaicagolf@cwjamaica.com **Horse racing** at Caymanas Park,
T9257780/9253312, every Wed and Sat and most public holidays. **Polo** International tournaments are held at *Caymanas Polo Club*. For information, contact Shane Chin, T9525586,
chilly@colis.com **Tennis** can be played at the *Eric Bell Tennis Centre*.

Caribic Vacations, T9529874, F9533463. *Juta Jamaica*, T9520813, F9525355. *Sun Venture* **Tour operators**
Tours, 30 Balmoral Av, Kingston 10, T9606685, F9208348, www.sunventuretours.com
Activities for nature lovers away from the beach, hiking, caving, safaris, birdwatching and
educational tours, managed by Robert Kerr. *UTAS Tours*, T9523820, F9793465. For sched-
uled or charter flights to neighbouring islands, try *Apollo Travel Services*, 14 Dominica Drive,
New Kingston, T9298483, F9687214, also at 28 Main St, May Pen, T9864270, and Shop No 3,
Spanish Town Shopping Centre, T9845040, IATA members.

Bus Fares from Kingston are: US$3 to Mandeville, US$5.60 to Montego Bay, US$1.50 to **Transport**
Negril, US$2.80 to Ocho Rios, US$3 to Port Antonio. The buses are invaded by touts as they
approach the bus station. **Local** The Government bus service, *Jamaica Urban Transit Com-*
pany (JUTC), has largely replaced the old bus franchise services with a fleet of newly acquired
buses and a much more efficient service, significantly improving travel times and comfort
around the Corporate Area. Tickets are US$0.43 for the first 2 stages and about US$0.65 for 3
stages. Buses and shared taxis to/from North Parade for the airport, US$0.45. The upgraded
bus service has improved buses and timetabling, but allow waiting time during rush hour.
The buses are well marked with destinations and numbers.To get to New Kingston by bus,
change bus (to No 27) downtown. The recognized service between town and airport is JUTA,
taxi/minibus, which charges US$21 to New Kingston (taxi dispatcher gives you a note of fare
before you leave, can be shared). Alternatively, if travelling light, take taxi to Port Royal,
US$13, ferry to Kingston (see below, Port Royal) and then taxi to New Kingston, US$6-7.

Banks *National Commercial Bank of Jamaica*, 77 King St, Kingston, and branches all over the **Directory**
island; *Bank of Nova Scotia Jamaica Ltd*, head office: Duke and Port Royal Sts, Kingston. *Citibank*,
63-67 Knutsford Blvd, Kingston; and other local banks. **ATMs** are widespread. Immediate money
transfers; *Western Union Bank*, behind the *National Commercial Bank* at the top of Knutsford Blvd.

Embassies and consulates Australia (High Commission), 9263550. **Canada** (High Commission), 30-36 Knutsford Blvd, T9261500, kngtn@kngtn01.x400.gc.ca **Denmark**, T9235051. **France**, 13 Hillcrest Av, T9780210, www.ambafrance-jm.org **Germany**, T9266728. **Israel**, T9268768. **Italy**, 9781273, **Japan**, 9297534. **Japan**, 2 Oxford Rd, 6th floor, T9293338. **Netherlands**, 926- 2026. **Norway**, 9235541. **Spain**, 9296710. **Sweden**, 9237114. Switzerland, 9223347. **UK** (High Commission), 26 Trafalgar Rd, T9269050, bhckingston@cwjamaica.com **US**, 2 Oxford Rd, 3rd floor, T9294850.

Port Royal

Population: 2,000   Port Royal, the old naval base, lies across the harbour from Kingston. It was founded in 1650, captured by the English and turned into a strategic military and naval base. Merchant shipping developed under naval protection and the town soon became prosperous. It also attracted less reputable shipping and in 1660-92 became a haven for pirates such as Henry Morgan, with gambling and drinking dens and brothels protected by the six forts and 145 guns. The 'wickedest city in the world', with a population of 8,000, soon provoked what was thought to be divine retribution. On 7 June 1692 an earthquake hit east Jamaica, coursing along the Port Royal fault line and bringing with it massive tidal waves. The port, commercial area and harbour front were cut away and slid down the slope of the bay to rest on the sea bed, while much of the rest of the town was flooded for weeks. About 5,000 people died (of drowning, injuries or subsequent disease) and the naval, merchant and fishing fleets were wrecked. The town was gradually rebuilt as a naval and military post but has had to withstand 16 hurricanes, nine earthquakes, three fires and a storm (which in 1951 left only four buildings undamaged).

Nelson served here as a post-captain from 1779 to 1780 and commanded **Fort Charles**, built in 1655, key battery in the island's fortifications. The former British naval headquarters now house the **Fort Charles Maritime Museum**, with a scale model of the fort and ships. ■ *Mon-Thu 1000-1700, Fri 1000-1600, US$1. Part of the ramparts, known as Nelson's Quarterdeck, still stands. US$2.* The Giddy House was the Royal Artillery store, built in 1888 but damaged by the 1907 earthquake, which caused it to tilt at an angle of 45°. The Victoria Albert battery complex was a boiler house and underground armoury with late 19th-century guns to protect the harbour and tunnels. The old naval hospital was built in 1819 of prefabricated cast-iron sections brought all the way from England, one of the earliest constructions of this type and built on a raft foundation. The old gaol can also be seen. This dates from the early 18th century and was used as a women's prison in the 19th century. **St Peter's Church** is of historic interest, though the restoration is unfortunate. The **National Museum of Historical Archaeology** is little more than one room and the Fort Charles remains are more informative and substantive. ■ *US$0.30. Getting there: beyond the international airport, some 24 km by excellent road. Can also be reached by boat from Victoria Pier; 7 daily, 20 mins, US$0.30.*

Beaches &   Boats may be hired for picnics on the numerous nearby cays or at Port Henderson.
watersports   **Lime Cay** (about the size of a football field) is the most popular, offering a
For diving and fishing,   white-sand beach and crystal clear water. A seafood restaurant and bar provides
see page 190   tasty fried fish and chicken meals. There is a full service marina at *Morgan's Harbour* with customs clearance, 24-hour security and fishing boats for hire.

Sleeping   **L** *Morgan's Harbour* at Port Royal is a favourite holiday centre, T9678075 , F9678073. 40 rooms, 5 suites, sea view, seminar rooms, scuba diving (packages available with *Buccaneer Scuba Club* at the marina, T9678061, F9678073), with waterskiing, fresh and saltwater swimming pools, beach cabins, a good seafood restaurant, and dancing, closest hotel to airport.

Spanish Town

Spanish Town, the former capital, founded in 1534 and some 23 km west of Kingston (bus from Half Way Tree and from Orange Street), is historically the most interesting of Jamaica's towns and in desperate need of funds for renovation. Some money has been secured and restoration has started on sections of the fine Georgian main square. Its English-style architecture dates from the 18th century. Well worth seeing are the **Cathedral Church of St James**, the oldest in the anglophone West Indies, dating back to 1714. The square houses the ruins of the **King's House**, built in 1762 (Governor's residence until 1872 when Kingston became the capital) and burnt down in 1925. The façade has been rebuilt and within it is the **Archaeological Museum**, containing exhibits excavated here and a site history of 1534-1872. In the old stables is the **Jamaican People's Museum of Craft and Technology**. ■ *US$0.20. Mon-Fri, 1000-1700.* Also on the square are a colonnade (paint peeling off) and statue commemorating Rodney's victory at the Battle of the Saints, the **House of Assembly** and the **Courthouse**. There is a museum with interesting relics of Jamaican history and an accurate portrayal of the life of country people. The **park** in the centre is overgrown with weeds and the gates are padlocked. Outside town, on the road to Kingston is the **White Marl Taíno Museum**. ■ *Mon-Fri 1000-1600. US$0.10.*

Miami, Cumberland Rd, near the market area; food is delicious, especially the pumpkin soup. **Eating**

Eastern Jamaica and the mountains

Behind Kingston lie the Blue Mountains, with Blue Mountain Peak rising to a height of 2,256 m. This is undoubtedly one of the most spectacular and beautiful parts of Jamaica and an absolute must for keen bird watchers and botanists and also for those who like hiking. It is possible to explore some of the Blue Mountains by ordinary car from Kingston via **Papine**. After leaving Papine and just after passing the *Blue Mountain Inn* (good restaurant and nightclub), turn left to Irish Town and thence to **Newcastle**, a Jamaica Defence Force training camp at 1,219 m with magnificent views of Kingston and Port Royal. The road to **Catherine's Peak** (1,585 m) directly behind the camp is about an hour's climb for the moderately fit. **North from Kingston**

Beyond Newcastle lie **Hardwar Gap** and **Holywell National Park**, a recreational area within the Blue and John Crow Mountains National Park. Managed by the Jamaica Conservation and Development Trust (JCDT), the Park offers nature trails, campsites and picnic areas. ■ *Entry US$10.00, children US$5.00, Jamaicans US$1.00. Oately Mountain Trail is a commercial trail within the Holywell Park for which there is a separate user fee of US$10.00, children US$5.00, including entry into the park and guided tour. Bookings can be made through the JCDT, 1st floor, Workforce Development Building, 22b Old Hope Rd, Kingston 5, T9208278-82, jcdt@kasnet.com* **Holywell National Park to Buff Bay** *This whole area is full of mountain trails with innumerable birds, some unique to Jamaica*

The picturesque little community of **Section** is at the junction of three roads and is a travel halt. There the road from Holywell intersects with the Silver Hill to Buff Bay Road. A left turn from Holywell takes you to Buff Bay and a turning off to the right to Silver Hill Gap. Section is the most popular spot on the north side of the Blue Mountains for purchasing genuine Blue Mountain coffee. A coffee tour is offered which includes a demonstration of the traditional way of growing, preparing and roasting Blue Mountain coffee, as it has been done for 200 years.

The road from Silver Hill Gap to the left turn-off to Clydesdale (about a 4-km drive) has mostly been repaired and the route is passable. The road to Clydesdale and the **Cinchona botanical garden** is unpaved and very steep between Clydesdale and Cinchona (4WD required, or walk, about one hour uphill but well worth it). The route from Silver Hill Gap continues past the turn-off to Clydesdale to **Content**

Gap, passing en route *Pine Grove Guest House*. Content is a three-road junction; coming from Clydesdale the left turn goes to Gordon Town and Kingston whereas the right goes to Mavis Bank and Blue Mountain Peak.

Sleeping and eating In Holywell National Park, **B** 3 log cabins, 2 sleep 4 and 1 sleeps 6 people. at **Silver Hill Gap**, **B** *Starlight Chalet*, T7989868, office T9603070, www.jamaicamarketplace.com/starlight Recently built, with a spa, bar guesthouse, and a growing clientele. At **Hardwar**, *The Gap Café*, T9237078, has spectacular views and serves real Blue Mountain coffee.

Around Blue Mountain

You should avoid all major rivers whenever flood warnings have been issued or during very heavy rains

To go towards **Blue Mountain Peak** from Kingston (Corporate Area) via Papine, drive straight on at *Blue Mountain Inn* (instead of turning left), through Gordon Town and on through **Mavis Bank** for 6.5 km to **Hagley Gap**, if the Mahogany Vale ford is passable. The community and the National Park have constructed a flat bridge that has made passage more secure even during the rainy season. However, you will almost certainly not be able to get a car up to the starting point for the walk to the Peak. Public transport up the Blue Mountains is infrequent. There are some buses to Mavis Bank from the square in Papine, US$1, but you will need to ask. Taxis from Papine to Mavis Bank are about US$7.50. Only 4WD vehicles are advisable after Mavis Bank (no shortage of people offering to take you), and there are no petrol stations en route. There are two walking possibilities from Mavis Bank: either look for a 4WD to Hagley Gap and walk from there to the starting point of the trail to the Peak (5.5 km uphill through villages), or walk the short cut (6.5 km) from Mavis Bank. You may need to be guided for the first part (plenty of guides, including Linford Morrison, who lives near the Police Station), across two small rivers and on to the path, which is then straightforward – a reasonably hard but lovely two-hour walk. Keep going when you eventually reach the village. Ask for *Whitfield Hall* or *Wildflower Lodge* (see below), the turning is just beyond Penlynecastle School, by

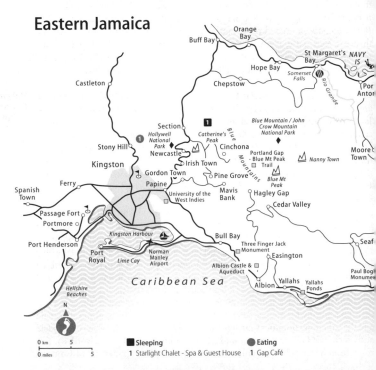

Eastern Jamaica

Sleeping	Eating
1 Starlight Chalet - Spa & Guest House	1 Gap Café

the Post Office. Land Rovers are available from *Whitfield Hall* (John Allgrove, T9270986) and *Wildflower Lodge* (Eric Leiba, T9295395). *Sun Venture Tours* (see page 197) provide complete tour services for Blue Mountain Peak, with transfers from anywhere on the island to Penlynecastle, meals, accommodation and guides.

B-C *Forest Park Guest House* on the main road near the Mavis Bank Coffee Factory, T9275957, run by Jennifer Lyn. Cabins and cottages are provided and 4WD transport can be arranged with a guide to the Blue Mountain Peak. There are 2 lodges close to the point where the Blue Mountain Peak trail begins. John Algrove (8 Almon Crescent, Kingston 6, T9270986) owns *Whitfield Hall Hostel*, a large wooden lodge with no electricity but paraffin lamps, **F** per person, capacity 40, hostel or **D** private room, cold showers only. No meals unless you order them in advance, but kitchen with gas stoves and crockery, for guests' use. Very peaceful and homely with comfortable lounge, log fire and library (visitors' books dating back to the 1950s), friendly and helpful staff. If the hostel is full, camping is permitted. Just before *Whitfield Hall* is *Wildflower Lodge*, known locally as the White House, T9295394/5, or write 10 Ellesmere Rd, Kingston 10. Same prices as *Whitfield Hall*, but a bit more modern and better food, breakfast US$3, evening meals US$5 but hard to tell the difference, substantial and excellent vegetables from the garden. Both lodges will arrange 4WD transport from Kingston or Mavis Bank and offer guides and horses for walking or riding excursions.

Mountain lodges

The Blue Mountains play a symbolic role for Jamaicans. Jamaican poet Roger Mais (1905-55) wrote a moving poem called 'All Men Come to the Hills' about men's desire to rest finally in the hills, wherever or however they have spent their lives. The walk to **Blue Mountain Peak** (10.5 km from Whitfield Hall) takes three or four hours up and two or three hours down. The first part is the steepest. Some start very early in the morning in the hope of watching the sunrise from the Peak. The thrill of victory takes on new meaning once you've climbed Jacob's Ladder and posed atop the Trig Station on the highest point, Middle Peak (2,256 m), waiting anxiously ...

Climbing the peak

braving the bitter cold... to catch that first faint glow of sunlight. As often as not, though, the peak is shrouded in cloud and rain in the early morning, a disheartening experience. You can leave in early daylight and almost certainly reach the top before it starts clouding over again (mid to late morning). In this case you do not need a guide, as the path is straightforward. The trail winds through a fascinating variety of vegetation: coffee groves and banana plantations on the lower, south slopes, to tree ferns and dwarf forest near the summit (with some explanatory and mileage signposts). The doctor bird (a beautiful swallow-tailed hummingbird, national bird of Jamaica) is quite common. Quite hard to spot, at first recognizable by its loud buzz, especially near the many flowering bushes. Take your own food and torch (spare set of batteries and bulb), sweater and raincoat if you set out in the darkness. There is one hut on the peak (an empty concrete building with no door) where you can stay overnight in some discomfort. However, the National Park authorities discourage overnighting at the Peak due to the absence of toilet facilities and inadequate waste disposal. There is a campsite with cabins (bunk beds and floor space rental), pit latrines, water and a shower at Portland Gap, about one hour up. Snacks and drinks are available at the ranger station; the rangers are very helpful. Another trail, to **Mossman Peak**, starts at Portland Gap, but is currently overgrown after 15 minutes, not having recovered from Hurricane Gilbert. In high season up to 500 people walk up Blue Mountain Peak every day, while in low season there will be only a handful. Considering the numbers, it is remarkably unspoiled and the views are spectacular.

Southeast coast The A4 road runs east out of Kingston, all along the south coast through Bull Bay, Yallahs, Morant Bay and Port Morant, before turning up on to the north coast to Port Antonio, Buff Bay and Annotto Bay, where it ends at the junction with the A3 running directly north from Kingston. Just beyond **Bull Bay** on the way to Yallahs, there is a plaque in memory of '**Three-Finger Jack**', Jack Mansong, one of Jamaica's legendary highway men and a folk hero-villain in the mould of Robin Hood. From the marker you get a magnificent view of Kingston harbour to the southwest, while to the north are the dry forested hills of the Port Royal Mountains, once the territory of Jack. He fought a guerrilla war single-handedly against the British military and the plantocracy. It is not known whether he was born in Africa or Jamaica in 1780-81. He is thought to have lost two fingers in a battle with a maroon called Quashee who later killed Jack in another fight, whereupon he cut off his head and three remaining fingers as trophies. Legends about Jack proliferated, books about him became popular and then came a musical, or pantomime. *Obi-* or *Three-Fingered Jack* had a run of some nine years at the Covent Garden, Haymarket and Victoria Theatres in London. (Further reading: L Alan Eyre, *Jack Mansong, 'Bloodshed or Brotherhood'.*)

About 300 m from the junction of the A4 with the roads to Easington and Yallahs at Albion are the overgrown ruins of the **Albion Great House and Aqueduct**, often referred to as **Albion Castle**. Of the remaining structures the great house and the waterwheel are the most impressive. Descendants of those who worked on the estate as slaves still occupy the 'slave house' today. In colonial times the estate was the leading producer of sugar in Jamaica and its crystal sugar was known as 'Albion Sugar'. On emancipation in 1838 there were about 450 slaves at Albion producing 400 hogsheads of sugar and more than double that quantity of rum was being at the end of the century. Its waterwheels were supplied by a large aqueduct transporting water from the Yallahs River several kilometres away. One of the wheels had a diameter of 9.6 m and supported 88 buckets. These and other innovations in the milling and drying process made Albion Estate a leader in sugar production technology. Access to the property is through the estate gate just up the road. There is usually a caretaker in the old 'slave house' or someone to help you gain access.

Yallahs is famous for jerk chicken (drum roasted) and its main street must have more jerk chicken stands than anywhere else

Yallahs is one of the major towns in St Thomas. No one is quite sure where the town got its name, but it may have been named after a privateer, or buccaneer, called Captain Yhallahs, who operated in the area around 1671. On the other hand it may have been a corruption of Hato de Ayala, the name of one of the large cattle ranches run by the Spanish when they occupied the island. Yallahs Salt Ponds stretch for about 5 km, providing an outstanding landmark. Legend has it that two brothers argued over the sub-division of a piece of land and the argument became so fierce that the two plots of land sank, forming two of the three salt ponds. The hyper-saline ponds have created a unique ecosystem and several scientific discoveries have been made here. They are also good spots for bird watching. A 4WD vehicle is recommended for visiting the beach side of the ponds, ask directions in town, best at *Miss Johnson's A&I Bar & Restaurant* in the centre, or contact the Yallahs Community Development Fund, T9825021. The dumping of wrecked cars spoils the first part of the journey but beyond that it is great going.

Morant Bay, the capital of St Thomas, has a colourful and legendary past. On 11 October 1865, it was the scene of the Morant Bay Rebellion. A group of farmers and other disaffected citizens led by farmer and Baptist Deacon, Paul Bogle, marched to the Courthouse to complain about high taxes, the collapse of the sugar industry and the economic downturn, which had been exacerbated by drought and outbreaks of smallpox and cholera. The Government was not sympathetic to the views of the people, the Courthouse was burned down and the uprising assumed dangerous proportions. The military rounded up the protestors and killed or sentenced to death hundreds of men and women who had allegedly taken part, burned nearly 1,000 homes and flogged members of the surrounding communities. Today there is a statue to Paul Bogle at Morant Bay, and the monument is in remembrance of Bogle, George William Gordon and 437 martyrs who fought and died for justice. The artist was Edna Manley, the wife of national hero Norman Washington Manley, and mother of the Hon Michael Manley, a former Prime Minister.

North of Port Morant at the east end of the island, **Bath** is another place from which to access the **John Crow Mountains** (named after the ubiquitous turkey buzzards). There is a modest but cheap hotel, *Bath Spa,* dating from 1727, where the main attraction is the natural hot water spring baths, which are most relaxing at the end of a long day. Two passes above Bath, the **Cuna Cuna Pass** and the **Cornpuss Gap** lead down to the source of the Rio Grande River on the north slopes of the mountain range. Both are tough going particularly the Cornpuss Gap. It is absolutely essential to take a local guide. The north slopes of the mountain range are the home of the unique and extremely rare Jamaican butterfly, *Papilio homerus,* a large black and yellow swallowtail. It is the second-largest butterfly in the world and the largest in the Americas, and is protected under international law (CITES) regulating the trade in endangered species. This butterfly is very spectacular in flight and easily recognizable because of its size. It can best be seen in May and June.

East of Port Morant, but not easily accessible, is the magnificent **Pera** beach between Port Morant and Morant Lighthouse. Near the lighthouse is another good beach. Just before reaching Manchioneal a road off to the left leads to the **Reach Falls** or **Manchioneal Falls** (about 5 km). Well worth a visit if you have a car or are prepared to walk (45 minutes with views of rolling forested hills) from the main road. There are no facilities at the falls, but there may be an entry charge. Pretty tiers of smooth boulders, the highest fall about 4.5 m, tumble through a lush, green gorge. Buses from main road to Port Antonio are infrequent, every one or two hours. Further along the coast from Manchioneal to Long Bay cottages and guesthouses have been built on the beach.

Nearly all the beaches along the east coast round to Port Antonio have a dangerous undertow in certain spots

Port Antonio

Once the major banana port, where many of the island's first tourists arrived on banana boats, Port Antonio dates back to the 16th century. Its prosperity has for many years been in gentle decline and it is now run-down, but it has an atmosphere unlike any other town in Jamaica, with some superb old public buildings. It is an excellent base from which to explore inland or along the coast. Boston Bay, Fairy Hill Beach (also known as Winnefred Beach), San San Beach, the Blue Lagoon (also known as the Blue Hole) and Frenchman's Cove Beach are notable beauty spots to the east of the town. **Boston Bay** is renowned for its local jerk food pits; several unnamed places by the roadside serve hot spicy chicken, pork or fish, chopped up and wrapped in paper, cooked on planks over a pit of hot coals, very good and tasty.

Population: 14,000

The rainfall in this part of the island is very high and in consequence the vegetation very lush

For diving and fishing, see page 190

The **tourist office**, upstairs in City Centre Plaza on Harbour Street, T9933051, F9932117, is quite helpful, with timetables for local buses ('soon come'), which leave regularly when full, but at uncertain hours, from seafront behind Texaco station.

Also worth visiting are **Somerset Falls**. ■ *Daily 0900-1700. US$3. Getting there: bus to Buff Bay (any westbound Kingston bus) and 5 mins' walk.* About 30 minutes' walk around the bay from town are the **Folly Ruins**, an elaborate, turn-of-the-century mansion built in the style of Roman and Greek architecture, now in ruins (partly because the millionaire American's wife took an instant dislike to it). It is a ghostly, crumbling old mansion in an open field with lovely views shared with

For information on Port Antonio Marina, see page 185

Jamaica

grazing cows. ■ *Fork right off the path before going into a clump of trees on the peninsula (leading towards lighthouse inside military camp)*. At **Nonsuch Cave**, a few kilometres to the southeast, there are fossils, stalactites and evidence of Taíno occupation. ■ *Daily 0900-1600. US$5. Gift shop and lunch area. No public transport, return taxi fare US$10 including waiting time.*

Navy Island
Ferry 0700-2200 daily, US$3 return

In the harbour you can visit the 28-ha **Navy Island**, at one time owned by Errol Flynn, which has beaches (one nudist) and a moderately expensive restaurant. Accommodation at the **AL** *Navy Island Marina Resort*, reservations, T9932667, F9932041. Rooms (14) or individual villas, restaurant, pool and bar open to non-guests, open view of bay. 'Errol Flynn Gallery' has display of movie stills and screenings of his golden oldies. The beaches on the island all belong to the resort but are open to non-guests. Snorkelling available (at the nudist beach), US$2 for half-day hire, but there are strong currents and not many fish.

Rafting on the Rio Grande
Because of frequent problems between raftsmen and the concessionaire contact the Port Antonio tourist office to find out whether the service is operational

Flynn saw the bamboo rafts which used to bring bananas down the Rio Grande as a potential tourist attraction. If you turn up at Berrydale there are now always expert rafters ready and willing to take you down the river. Each raft (US$45 per raft from the ticket office, but if you arrive before it opens at 0830 or if you arrive by local bus, you can sometimes negotiate a fare of as little as US$25 with a rafter) takes two passengers. The trip takes 1½ to two hours (depending on the river flow) through magnificent scenery and there is an opportunity to stop en route. Before you start make it clear who is buying the drinks. A driver takes your car down from the embarkation point to the point of arrival, Rafter's Rest, on the main coastal road, recommended as a place to have a pleasant, moderately priced lunch or drink, even if you are not proposing to raft. The return taxi fare is US$10; there are also buses, US$0.25, back to Berrydale, the setting-off point, though infrequent. Returning from St Margaret's, downstream, is easier as there are plenty of buses passing between Annotto Bay and Port Antonio.

The Maroons

The Rio Grande valley is also well worth exploring, including a trip to the Maroons (descendants of escaped slaves) at **Moore Town**, but the roads are rough and public transport minimal. Ask for Colonel Harris, there who is the leader of the Maroons and is recommended for guided tours. There is no telephone contact nor accommodation, return taxi fare US$15. To the west of the Rio Grande lie the north slopes of the Blue Mountains. **Nanny Town**, the home of the Maroons, was destroyed by the British in 1734 and then 'lost' until the 1960s. There is recent archaeological evidence at Nanny Town to suggest that the Maroons originally took to the mountains and lived with (and possibly later absorbed) Taíno peoples. There have been some dramatic discoveries of Taíno wooden carvings which are now on display at the National Gallery.

Sleeping

Port Antonio LL *Trident Villas and Hotel*, T9932602, www. tridentjamaica.com 26 rooms/suites with sea view, MAP, antique furniture, tennis, croquet, pools, restaurants. **L** *Jamaica Palace*, Williams Field, T9932020, F9933459. 65 rooms, a/c, beach, pool, wheelchair accessible, watersports. **Titchfield Hill**, 5 mins' walk from the town: **C-D** *De Montevin Lodge*, 21 Fort George St, T9932604. CP, shared bath, more expensive rooms have private bath, old Victorian house, restaurant serves set meals, US$8-10, good value. **C-E** *Ivanhoe* nearby. Some rooms with shared bath, patio with bay view. Several nearby private houses take guests. In the centre **D** *Triff's Inn*, 1 Bridge St, T7156890. Modern, clean, 17 rooms, restaurant, bars.

Port Antonio has a Guesthouse Association offering good-value lodging, excursions and transfers, www.go-jam.com

Outside Port Antonio LL-L *Goblin Hill Villas* at San San, reservations c/o 11 East Av, Kingston 10, T9258108, F9256248. 44 rooms in 1- or 2- bedroomed villas, kitchen, restaurant or housekeepers available, cheaper with no sea view, tennis, short walk to beach, pool, car hire, bar, TV room. **LL-AL** *Dragon Bay Beach Resort*, T9938514, F9933284. Attractive resort, villas or rooms on secluded bay, diving, snorkelling, pool, beach volleyball, tennis, good restaurant. **L-B** *Fern Hill Club* at San San, T9937374, F9937373. 31 rooms and spa suites, cottages, all-inclusive available including tours, 4 pools, jacuzzi, restaurant, golf, tennis, windsurfing, sailing, diving, snorkelling, horse riding. At **Frenchman's Cove**, **LL-L** *Mocking Bird Hill*, Port Antonio,

Jamaica

T9937134, www.hotelmockingbirdhill.com 15 mins from town, 5 mins' walk from beach, 10 rooms in Caribbean-style villa in 3 ha of parkland, pool, gardens, nature trail, restaurant with Jamaican and international cuisine, Gallery Carriacou and gift shop exhibits owner's art, German, French, English and Spanish spoken. 19 km west of Port Antonio just after Hope Bay at Rodney Hall, Black Hill, is **C-D** *I-tal Village*, T9130917, www.italvillage.com 5 rooms with shared facilities, CP, dinner, fruit and juices all day US$15-20, Jamaican and Italian organic vegetarian food, locally grown, weekly rates available.

Blue Lagoon, Fairy Hill, T9938491. Built over the water, great swimming in the deep blue water, Jamaican food, jerk specialities, fresh lobster, try the blue cocktail, live music and entertainment at weekends, open Mon-Wed 1100-1700, Thu-Sun 1100-2200. *Huntress Marina* on a jetty in the harbour, T9933053. Mainly a bar popular with yachting fraternity, but good breakfast, evening meals also served, cold beer. *Barracuda*, 1 Bridge St, T7156111. Variety of seafood and Jamaican cuisine at affordable prices, central and easily accessible. *Coronation Bakery*, near Musgrave Market on West St. Good for cheap patties and spice buns. *Cream World*, good for ice cream, cakes and cheap snacks. *Stop Group Jerk Centre* on the bay out of town towards the Folly. Bar and jerk pork, chicken and fish, also music and dance until late. *Best Kept Secret*, on road coming into Port Antonio from the west, little blue and yellow shack perched on a cliff, T8096276. Alvin Dickie Butler and his wife Joy offer fine dining, reservations only, breakfast, lunch and high tea, great home cooking and flavours, Dickie's famous clientele have included Errol Flynn, the Duke of Edinburgh, Winnie Mandela and Princess Margaret. **Eating**

Roof Club, 11 West St, T9933817 (may not work), disco and night spot where everything happens, with sign outside saying 'no drugs, no firecrackers, don't destroy furniture'. Popular with all social classes and types, melting pot of excitement, advisable for women to be escorted or in a group, weekends best nights. *Renny*, also known as 'Old Hits Corner' on Somers Town Rd near Police Station, popular at weekend with locals and visitors, its selection of 'oldies' offers an alternative from the dance hall and hip hop rhythms. **Nightlife**

Between Port Antonio and the Buff Bay area there are several roads into the interior from places such as Hope Bay and Orange Bay. Just to the east of Buff Bay is **Crystal Springs**, and from there the road goes on to Chepstow and thence to **Claverty Cottage** and **Thompson Gap**; spectacular scenery, waterfalls in the valleys and very remote. It is possible to walk from Thompson Gap over the Blue Mountains via Morces Gap and down to Clydesdale, but the trails are very overgrown and would require extensive bushing for access. This is a full day's trip and only to be undertaken with an experienced local guide (problem with getting transport to meet you at Clydesdale). Consult the staff at the Cinchona Gardens before planning your trip. It is also possible to take a bus for part of the way up the Buff Bay valley and then walk on either to Clydesdale or over the Hardwar Gap to Newcastle. Both trips are very long and only for the really fit. **Port Antonio to Buff Bay**

The north coast

The Kingston to Port Maria road (the Junction Road) passes through **Castleton Botanical Gardens** (in a very tranquil setting, well worth a visit). The journey takes about two hours and there are plenty of minibuses. **Port Maria** itself is a sleepy and decaying old banana port not without charm and with lots of goats.

Sleeping East of Port Maria in **Robin's Bay**, on the beach, is **AL-C** *Sonrise Beach Retreat*, standard or 'deluxe' cabins (sleep 5-6) with or without bath and tent sites, **F**, bath house, T/F9997169, 3 km from village, transport essential or arrange pick-up with resort, meal plans and ecotour packages available, restaurant, nature trails, trampoline, volleyball, ping pong. A few kilometres to the west of Port Maria, the **D** *Casa Maria* hotel has seen better days, T9942323, F9942324, www.nwas.com/casamaria 20 rooms, beach, restaurants, bars.

Noel Coward's homes Close by the hotel is *Firefly*, Noel Coward's Jamaican home, now owned by the Jamaican National Trust. It is evocative of a stylish era and a highlight if you are interested in the theatre or film stars of that period. Magnificent view. ■ *0830-1700 daily except Fri, US$10, T9940920*. Noel Coward's other property, *Blue Harbour*, is about 1 km from the hotel; this is where he used to entertain film stars, royalty etc. It is now a **B-C** guesthouse with accommodation for up to 15 in the Villa Grande (two bedrooms), the Villa Chica (one bedroom) and the Villa Rose (four bedrooms), all much as Coward left it despite some hurricane damage and it is dilapidated. Saltwater pool, coral beach, good snorkelling and scuba, gardens, lovely views, T9942262.

Ian Fleming's home **Oracabessa** is another old banana port with a half-completed marina and *Golden Eye*, the house where **Ian Fleming** wrote all the James Bond books. The house is now a **LL** retreat owned by Chris Blackwell's Island Outpost, www.islandoutpost.com The James Bond beach is in front of the house, it is small but highly recommended, as safe and child-friendly. Bars and fish meals available. To the west of Oracabessa is Boscobel, where the airstrip for Ocho Rios is located. Opposite the airstrip there are numerous houses for rent.

Ocho Rios

Colour map 1, grid C5 Ocho Rios stands on a bay sheltered by reefs and surrounded by coconut groves, sugar cane and fruit plantations. The town has become very popular, with many cruise ships making a stop here. It is 103 km east of Montego Bay and claims some of the best beaches on the island. The beach in town, safe and well organized with facilities, is 200 m from Main Street where most of the shops and vehicle hire companies

Ocho Rios & surroundings

Sleeping
1 Casa Maria
2 Firefly
3 Hibiscus Lodge
4 Jamaica Inn
5 Little Pub Inn
6 Plantation Inn

Eating
1 Acropolis Nightclu
2 Shakey's Pizza

can be found. A landscaped and paved boardwalk, the 'One Love Trail', leads from Dunn's River Falls and the surrounding attractions to the town of Ocho Rios, Dolphin Cove (Seaquarium, T9745335, www.dolphincove.com, US$15.00) and Island Village shopping and entertainment complex (music, cinema, art, beach and gaming), developed and operated by Island Outpost. **Shaw Park Gardens** are an easy walk from the town centre, up the hill on the edge of town. Nice gardens, recommended. ■ *Daily 0800-1700. US$4. T9748888.* The tourist office is at Ocean Village Shopping Centre, T9742582/3.

Excursions

The scenery of the surrounding area is an added attraction. Most spectacular are the beauty spots of **Roaring River Falls**, and **Dunn's River Falls**, tumbling into the Caribbean with invigorating salt- and freshwater bathing at its foot. ■ *Daily 0900-1700. US$6, locker US$1, bath shoes US$5 (rental) but not necessary if you move with care. Get there early before the coach parties arrive. 5-min bus ride, US$0.20, from Ocho Rios, or 1-hr drive from Montego Bay (beware of pseudo guides who hang around and take you somewhere totally different, then try to sell you marijuana).*

The journey from Kingston to Ocho Rios follows a spectacular route, up the gorge of the **Rio Cobre**, then across Mount Diablo. **Faith's Pen**, right on the top, is an enormous collection of huts selling food and drink, and great for a stop. Near Moneague is *Café Aubergine*, T9730527, an upmarket and tasteful restaurant in an 18th-century house, about US$25 per person. The last section of road whizzes round a series of blind corners as you go through **Fern Gully**, a marvel of unspoilt tropical vegetation. Driving time is 1 hour 50 minutes by bus. Alternatively, take a minibus from the Texaco petrol station on Da Costa Drive, Ocho Rios, for US$0.30 to Fern Gully. There are lots of minibuses for the return journey.

Historical attractions in the area include **Sevilla Nueva**, some 14.5 km to the west, the place where the Spanish first settled in 1509. The ruins of the fort still remain. The Great House and property is managed by the Jamaica National Heritage Trust as a museum. Guided tours are professional and informative and give you a good understanding of the island's heritage. ■ *Daily 0900-1700, last tour 1600. US$4, children US$2. T9729407.* Offshore, marine archaeologists are investigating the **St Ann's Bay** area for sunken ships. Salvaged timbers are believed to have come from two disabled caravels, the *Capitana* and the *Santiago de Palos*, abandoned at Sevilla Nueva probably in 1503 during Columbus' last visit to Jamaica. **Mammee Beach**, which is beautiful and less crowded than Ocho Rios, though there is no shade.

There are numerous **plantation tours**. Details are widely publicized. Probably the most attractive and informative, and certainly the most accessible, is the *Prospect Plantation Tour*, a short distance to the east of Ocho Rios nearly opposite the *Sans Souci Lido*. ■ *1030, 1400, and 1530 daily. US$12. T9742058.* Another, just southwest of St Ann's Bay, is *Circle B*, owned by former senator, Bob Miller. Very good tour of working plantation. ■ *Welcome drink and sample fruits of Jamaica, lunch can be included, T9722988.* **Harmony Hall** art gallery just east of Ocho Rios is worth a visit. There are frequent exhibitions of paintings and sculpture in a classic gingerbread house, as well as crafts, clothes and other gifts to buy. ■ *1000-1800. T9754222, www.harmonyhall.com There is also an Italian restaurant,* Toscanini's, *open 1000-2200, closed Mon evenings, T9754785.* **Wassi Art** pottery workshop, Great Pond, T9745044, is delightful; there is a good selection in the salesroom and you can visit each artist. Ask your taxi driver to wait as it is several kilometres away. If you have your own transport you could combine a visit to Harmony Hall with some time on **Reggae Beach**, 2 km east of White River Bridge in a little cove between Little Bay and Frankfort Bay. A bright sign on the seaward side of the main road marks a somewhat inconspicuous entrance leading to a long, shaded driveway and then a beach hideaway bustling with activity. It is an easy going spot with clean water and a nice beach, but you also get jerk chicken, roasts at festivals, reggae music, dominoes and Red Stripe beer to complete the picture.

Sleeping

The coast is dominated by many huge, all-inclusive resorts, usually booked from abroad

LL *Jamaica Inn*, T9742514, www.jamaicainn.com 45 rooms, seaview, FAP, pool, private beach, jacket and tie for men in the evenings, Winston Churchill used to stay here and Noel Coward drank here. **AL-A** *Hibiscus Lodge*, 83 Main St, T9742676, mdoswald@cwjamaica.com 26 rooms in gardens overlooking sea, man-made beach, pool, jacuzzi, tennis, *Almond Tree* restaurant. **B-C** *Little Pub Inn*, 59 Main St, T9742324, littlepub@ infochan.com CP, small rooms, a/c, nightly entertainment, games room, shopping, restaurants and bars. **C** *La Penciano Guest House*, 3 Short Lane, T9745472, run by Lloyd Thomas. Rooms with shared or private bath, fan, TV, in centre and noisy, but clean and safe, friendly, bar (open Fri and Sat night) has views over Ocho Rios. About 1.5 km from town centre, you can camp at Milford Falls, **F**, by the waterfall, take Kingston road out of Ocho Rios, turn right at sign to Shaw Park Gardens then fork left up Milford Rd, stop at *George Barnes' shop* on right, he will take you there and provide you with information, food and drink, he has a tent or a rustic cabin with 1 bed to rent.

Eating

On Main St there are lots of restaurants offering Jamaican, international or seafood cuisine, including *The Almond Tree*, the restaurant at the *Hibiscus Lodge*, T9742813. *The Lobsterpot*, Chinese, US$19-21 for lobster supper. *Jerk Pork*, same price for barbecued pork, fish or chicken. *Shakey's Pizza*, Main St. Nice bar and patio, fast, friendly service, smallest pizza from US$5.50. *Little Pub*, 59 Main St. Jamaican food and entertainment. *Bill's Place* on Main St.

Nightlife

The *Lion's Den* is a friendly club frequented by Rastafarians; rooms available, good food, clean. There is much fashionable nightlife in and around Ocho Rios. *Amnesia Night Club*, 70 Main St, T9742633. *The Acropolis* nightclub is lively and fairly safe.

Sport

Golf *Sandals Ocho Rios Resort & Golf Club*, formerly known as *Upton* 18 holes, green fee US$70, golf and restaurant free for *Sandals* guests, T9750119/22. **Polo** is played on Sat afternoons at Drax Hall, near Ocho Rios and at the *Polo and Equestrian Club of Oakbrook*, T9228581 for match details. International tournaments are held at Chukka Cove. For information, contact Shane Chin, T9525586, chilly@colis.com **Riding** lessons and trail rides also available at Chukka Cove, which has probably the best facilities, T9722506.

Tour operators

Blue Mountain Bicycle Tours, Main St, T9747075, bmtours@infochan.com Tours include an 29-km downhill trip through the forest to a waterfall, but don't expect much from the bikes.

West to Falmouth

Continuing west along the coast is **Runaway Bay**, an attractive and friendly resort. It is named for the Spanish governor Ysasi, who left quickly for Cuba in a canoe when he saw the English coming. Only 8 km away is **Discovery Bay** where Columbus made his first landing. The **Columbus Park**, an outdoor museum, has exhibits and relics of Jamaican history. From Runaway Bay, the Runaway Caves can be visited (there is an underground lake in the Green Grotto), but the place is littered with beer bottles and is not recommended. ■ *0900-1700.*

Sleeping Among the hotels in this area is the **A** *Runaway Bay HEART Hotel*, T9736671, runaway.heart@cwjamaica.com, which has an adjoining hotel training centre and overlooks the golf club. There are several **LL** all-inclusive resorts here too.

Sport Golf: *Breezes Golf Beach Resort* 18 holes, green fee US$58, free for guests at *Breezes Runaway Bay*, the only golf school open to the public, T9732561.

For diving and fishing, see page 190

Falmouth

Falmouth is a charming small town about 32 km east of Montego Bay. It is the best example of a Georgian town and the Jamaica National Heritage Trust has declared the whole town a National Monument. It has a fine colonial courthouse, a church, some 18th-century houses with wrought-iron balconies, and *Antonio's*, a famous place to buy beach shirts. There is good fishing (tarpon and kingfish) at the mouth of the Martha Brae, near Falmouth, and no licence is required. It is possible to go rafting from **Martha Brae** village. Expert rafters guide the craft very gently for the one-hour trip to the coast. ■ *0900-1600. US$42 on 2-person raft. Take local bus from Montego Bay to Falmouth, US$0.50, hitchhike or walk 9.5 km to upper station; end station is about 5 km from Falmouth.* **Jamaica Swamp Safaris** is a crocodile farm where you can see lazy crocodiles with equally laid-back guides. Bar and restaurant. Two James Bond films were made here. ■ *US$6 for adults.* Some 10 miles inland, the 18th-century plantation guesthouse of **Good Hope** set among coconut palms offers deluxe accommodation, as well as day tours and horse riding – some of the best riding in Jamaica – and its own beach on the coast. ■ *Daily 1200-1600. US$10. T9543289.*

A little-known but exciting attraction, 2.5 km east of Falmouth, is a bioluminescent lagoon, known locally as the **Luminous Lagoon**, where the water comes alive at night with sparkling blue-green lights from marine micro-organisms called dinaflagellates. The lagoon is said to be the most active bioluminescent lake in the world. A dark, moonless night, a local guide with typical Jamaican sense of humour, and a small power launch, all of which can be booked through *Fisherman's Inn*, are all that you need. Alternatively, the *Glistening Waters Restaurant* next door, offers regular boat tours after dark (see below). Less than five minutes out, the pitch-black water behind the boat begins to illuminate, leaving a blue-green-white trail in its wake. When the boat stops, streaks of light flash intermittently in every direction, caused by small fry jumping out of the water. Larger fish tunnelling through the water carry a wake of luminescence with them.

Collect some of the water from the lagoon in your hand and shake it to see it sparkle for several seconds

Sleeping and eating AL-A *Fisherman's Inn*, T9543427 (rooms with 2 single or 2 double beds), on the main road, heading to St Ann. You can have an excellent seafood sunset dinner on the deck followed by a 25-minute lake tour. *Glistening Waters Restaurant*, next door, T9543229. Open Mon-Sat 1000-2130, Sun 1200-2130, boat tours are daily every 30 mins, 1900-2100, US$15 adult, US$7.50 children, 50% discount if you eat in the restaurant. On Tue and Sat evenings a local Mento band plays delightful Jamaican folk songs.

Cockpit Country

This is a strange and virtually uninhabited area to the south of Falmouth. It consists of a seemingly endless succession of high bumps made of limestone rock. The tourist office and hotels in Montego Bay organize day trips (about US$50) to **Maroon Town** and **Accompong**, the headquarters of the Maroons who live in the Cockpit Country area. An annual festival is held here at the beginning of January with traditional music and dance, to commemorate the treaty with the British giving the Maroons lands and autonomy, T9524546, Kenneth Watson. Older locals can accurately describe what happened at the last battle between the Maroons and the British forces. Ask to see the **'Wondrous Caves'** at Elderslie near Accompong. If you have a car take the road on the east side of the Cockpit Country from Duncans (near Falmouth) to Clark's Town. From there the road deteriorates to a track, impassable after a few kilometres even for 4WD vehicles, to **Barbecue Bottom** and on to Albert Town. The views from Barbecue Bottom are truly spectacular (the track is high above the Bottom) and this is wonderful birding country. If you wish to walk in the Cockpit Country make your way (no public

Jamaica

transport) to the **Windsor Caves** due south of Falmouth. They are full of bats which make a spectacular mass exit at dusk. There are local guides. The underground rivers in the caves run for miles, but are only for the experienced and properly equipped pot-holer. A locally published book called *Jamaica Underground*; details the many caves and good walks in the area. It is possible to walk from the Windsor Caves across the middle of the Cockpit Country to Troy on the south side (about eight hours). It is essential to have a local guide and to make a preliminary trip to the Windsor Caves to engage him. Make sure that he really does know the way because these days this cross-ing is very rarely made even by the locals. It is also vastly preferable to be met with transport at Troy because you will still be in a pretty remote area.

Tour operators   For **caving**, contact Mike Schwartz of *Windsor Great House*, T9973832, windsor@cwjamaica.com, where there is rustic accommodation. *Sun Venture Tours* (see page 197) offer tailor-made tours of the Cockpit Country Crossing (Troy to Windsor the preferred route).

Montego Bay

Population: 92,000   *About 193 km from Kingston, on the island's northwest coast, Montego Bay is Jamaica's principal tourist centre with all possible watersports amenities. Known familiarly as Mo'Bay, it has superb natural features, sunshine most of the year round, a beautiful coastline with miles of white sand, deep blue water never too cold for bathing and gentle winds that make sailing a favourite sport. Doctor's Cave is the social centre of beach life. Gloucester Avenue, by Doctor's Cave, is one of the busiest streets for tour-ists, lined with duty-free shops, souvenir arcades, hotels and restaurants.*

Ins and outs

Getting there   The **Donald Sangster International Airport** is only 3 km from the town centre, taxi US$7, or
& around   20-min walk to Doctor's Cave. JUTA and JCAL are licensed taxis.
See Transport, page   The **Soon Come Shuttle** bus operates on 2 routes: Central Route (every 15 mins) and East-
183 for further details   ern Route (every 45 mins), stopping at hotels and some shops. Tokens (US$1) are purchased at hotels and special outlets; 2 tokens on Eastern Route, 1 token on Central Route 1000-2400. The **tourist office** is on Cornwall Beach, T9524425.

Sights

Forts &   Of interest to the sightseer are the remaining battery, cannons and powder magazine
churches   of an old British fort, **Fort Montego**, with landscaped gardens and crafts market (free), and the 18th-century church of **St James** in Montego Bay, built in 1778 and restored after earthquake damage. There are a few Georgian buildings, such as the *Town House Restaurant*, 16 Church Street (local art gallery next door), and the Geor-gian Court at the corner of Union and Orange Streets. The centre of town is **Sam Sharpe Square**, named after the slave who led a rebellion. The Burchell Memorial Church, established by the Baptist missionary, Thomas Burchell, was where Samuel Sharpe served as a deacon. The recently opened **Heritage Museum of Montego Bay** displays artefacts from pre- and post-independent Jamaica in the restored Old Court-house in the civic centre on Sam Sharpe Square. ■ *Tue-Sun 0900-1700. US$3.*

Beaches   **Doctor's Cave** has underwater coral gardens, so clear that they can be seen without effort from glass-bottomed boats. ■ *Daily 0900-1800. US$1.70, children under 12 half price.* Doctor's Cave is the beach for relaxed sunbathing, while **Cornwall** is more sun 'n' fun, or beach 'n' boogie, with beach contests, etc. ■ *Daily 0900-1700. US$1.* The **Walter Fletcher** beach has been converted to the **Aqua Sol** theme park, the latest addition to the list of attractions, offering rides and sports facilities.

Margueritaville (see Nightlife, page 213) offers a mix of bar, restaurant, rides, slides and various forms of entertainment. Scuba diving can be arranged through about a dozen operators, several of which have outlets at more than one hotel. Single dive, US$45, a snorkelling trip US$25.

If you are staying in town, rather than at the hotel strip, there are beaches close by, either public with no services or private, with food, drinks, tennis, boat hire, snorkelling, shower, changing rooms, etc. Walk from the traffic circle in the middle of town towards the hotels and the beach will be on your left. ■ *US$0.50-2.*

Mosquitoes are a problem at certain times of the year; take repellent and coils

Jamaica

Montego Bay

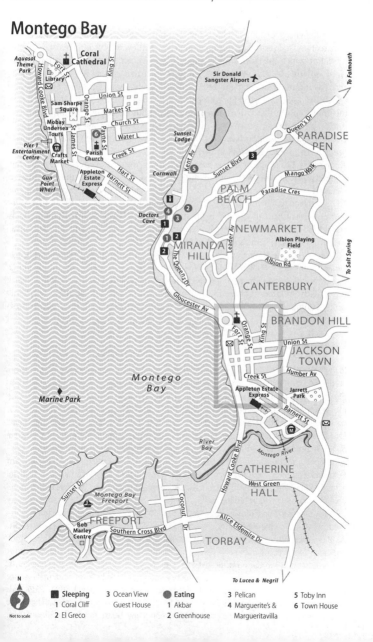

■ **Sleeping**	3 Ocean View	● **Eating**	3 Pelican	5 Toby Inn
1 Coral Cliff	Guest House	1 Akbar	4 Marguerite's &	6 Town House
2 El Greco		2 Greenhouse	Margueritavilla	

Not to scale

Excursions

Out of town, to the east, are two great houses. **Greenwood** was built in 1780-1800 by the forefathers of the poet Elizabeth Barrett Browning. It has a colourful avenue of bougainvillea and mimosa and a panoramic view over the coast from the veranda. ■ *Daily 0900-1800. US$10.* **Rose Hall** was started in 1770 by John Palmer. A lively legend of witchcraft surrounds the wife of one of his descendants, Anne Palmer. ■ *Daily 0900-1800. US$15. Rose Hall Beach Club daily 1000-1730. US$55 includes lunch, drinks, entertainment, watersports.*

Southeast of Montego Bay is the Taíno rock carving at Kempshot

Inland, 1 km from Montego Bay off the Maroon Town road (turn off east 1 km before the village of Johns Hall), is the recommended **C-F** *Orange River Lodge*, an old great house overlooking the **Orange River Valley**, guest rooms, hostel accommodation with bunk beds, and camping (bring own tent), beautiful location, excellent food, friendly staff, excursions, shuttle service to Montego Bay. Good walking, river swimming, canoeing and birdwatching, in the area, T9792688 at Lodge, or T9527208, F9526241 at 34 Fort Street, Montego Bay. Southwest of Montego Bay is the unmissable bird sanctuary at **Anchovy, Rocklands Feeding Station**, where the doctor bird humming birds will even perch on your finger. ■ *Daily 1400-1700. US$8.50. Members of birdwatching societies will be admitted any time. No children under 5.* The road to Anchovy is too rough for ordinary cars. Five kilometres west of Anchovy is **Lethe**, the starting point for rafting down the Great River. Sixteen kilometres from Montego Bay on the Savanna-La-Mar road is the **Montpelier Great House**, on the site of the old Montpelier sugar factory, destroyed during the 1831 rebellion, call Pat Ottey, T9524299, for bed and breakfast (**E-F**) children welcome. South of Anchovy, about 40 km from Montego Bay, is **Seaford Town**, which was settled by Germans in the 1830s. About 200 of their descendants survive. Write to Francis Friesen, Lamb's River Post Office.

Tamarind Lodge serves excellent Jamaican food. LL *Tryall Golf Tennis and Beach Club*, T9565600/5, F9565673, expensive, deluxe villas, 1-2 beds. Continuing along the island's west end, the road passes through **Green Island** before reaching Negril (29 miles from Lucea, a charming spot on the north coast), where there are several pretty fishing villages, such as Cousins Cove, with small guesthouses and seaside cottages for rent.

Essentials

Sleeping

There are over 40 all-inclusive hotels, guesthouses and apartment hotels listed by the tourist board and many more which are not

In the super-luxury range are LL *Round Hill Hotel and Villas*, 10 mins west of Montego Bay on 40-ha peninsula, T9567050, www.roundhilljamaica.com Originally a coconut and pineapple plantation, it opened in the 1950s with the help of Noel Coward, celebrity owners include Paul McCartney, Ralph Lauren, Lord Rothermere. LL *Half Moon Golf, Tennis and Beach Club*, on 162 ha adjoining beach, T9532615, www.halfmoon.com.jm 340 rooms and 5 to 7-bedroomed villas with staff, golf, tennis, riding stables, squash, fitness centre, spa, theatre etc. **LL-L** *Coyaba Beach Resort and Club*, T9539150, www.coyabaresortjamaica.com 50 rooms and suites, gardens, pool, jacuzzi, private dock, tennis, fitness room, hammocks on the shore, family-owned. **L-A** *Coral Cliff*, 365 Gloucester Av, T9524130, www.coralcliffjamaica.com Remodelled to allow slot machines, entertainment fantasyland, jungle theme, rooms variable, food reasonable, bar, pool and friendly service.

There is a YMCA at Mount Salem with sports facilities available to members

AL-A *Montego Bay Club*, Gloucester Av, T9524310, F9524639. Dominant 12-storey apartment hotel in centre of tourist area overlooking Doctor's Cave Beach, pool, tennis. **AL-B** *Cariblue*, Ironshore, T9532020, www.caribluehotel.com A dedicated dive resort, lots of packages, 24 a/c rooms, pool, deep-sea fishing, sailing, snorkelling, windsurfing, glass-bottom boats, day sails. **B** *The Guest House*, 29 Gloucester Av, T9523121, F9793176. Beautiful house with wide balcony overlooking sunset in the bay, rooms at back are away from traffic noise, includes huge nutritious breakfast, run by Irish and Canadian, very friendly. **B-D** *Ridgeway Guest House*, 34 Queen's Drive, T9522709, F9791740. 5 mins' walk from airport, with bath and fan, friendly, clean, family atmosphere. **C-D** *Ocean View Guest House*, 26 Sunset Blvd,

T9522662. 10 mins' easy walk from the airport, cheaper without a/c, many rooms overlook the bay, all clean, with bath, back-breaking mattresses, no advance bookings, but on arrival, ask tourist board to phone the hotel who will arrange free transport from the airport.

Self-catering AL *El Greco*, Queens Drive, T9406116, www.elgrecojamaica.com, has 64 1-bedroom and 32 2-bedroom suites on hillside overlooking bay, CP, direct elevator access to Gloucester Av and Doctor's Cave Beach, grocery store, pool, beach towels, tennis, laundry, cook and nanny on request.

Service at restaurants can be begrudging but the food is excellent. On the way into town from the airport there are several reasonably priced restaurants. Recommended is the *Pork Pit* next to *The Guest House*, 27 Gloucester Av, T9521046. Jerk chicken, pork and ribs sold by weight, service basic, and the *Toby Inn*, very good for cheap barbecued chicken and pork, cheap drinks, live band, romantic atmosphere. *Baba Joe's* (Barbara Joe's), Kent Av, near airport on way to Whitehouse Village, just past *Sandals*. Excellent fish, local style, about US$8 for meal with beer. *Orlan Caribe Vegetarian Restaurant*, 71 Barnett St. Tidy, comfortable, low prices, rather out of the way, open 1000-1600. The *Pelican*, Gloucester Av, T9523171. Excellent breakfasts, good value. *Akbar*, Gloucester Av, T9790113. *Patsy's Place*, 100 m from *The Guest House*. Small, good local dishes, excellent curried goat, cheap. *Walter's Bar and Grill*, 39 Gloucester Av, T9529391. Local food, nice garden, good value. *The Greenhouse*, T9527838, opposite St James Place shopping arcade. Good food, and inexpensive, Jamaican/American. *Marguerite's*, T9524777, on the seafront, 2 restaurants, one posh with a/c and *Margueritaville* next door on a patio, sports bar and grill. *Le Chalet*, 32 Gloucester Av, T9525240. Clean, friendly, Chinese, Jamaican (good curried goat), European menu at a quarter of the price of neighbouring restaurants, free hotel transfers. *Town House*, 16 Church St (see above), T9522660. Mildly pungent, tasty stuffed lobster US$42, other dishes also good, US$17-27. *Natives Jerk Centre*, Market St. Garden, outside bar, jerk chicken or pork, fish dishes with rice 'n' peas, about US$7 for meal with beer. *Scotchie's Jerk Place*, in Coral Gardens near the *Holiday Inn*, T9533301. Just about as good as jerk gets. Finger-licking jerk pork, chicken and fish available with just the right amount of spice, served wedded to roasted breadfruit, potato, yam or festival, open 1100-2300. *Smokey Joe's*, St James St. Good local restaurant, about US$6 for soup, main course, beer.

Eating
Most restaurants are happy for guests to bring wine and provide chillers and glasses. Rum is cheaper here than at airport duty-free shops

Harassment of tourists has reduced, still exercise caution when shopping and at night *Margueritaville Caribbean Bar & Grill*, Gloucester Av, T9524777. Now quite an institution, very popular, 52 flavours of Margaritas and 32-oz 'bong of beer', sport on big TVs, Nintendo and kids' menu, waterslide from roof to sea, DJ at night, open daily from 1000, cover charge US$9 Fri-Sat. Disco on Cornwall Beach with volleyball on beach at night. Lots of hotels have discos and clubs. *The Garage* sports bar at the end of Union St, close to Sam Sharpe's Sq, is the place to be, entertaining music.

Nightlife

Golf *Ironshore Golf and Country Club*, T9532800. A *Sandals* course, free for guests, 18 holes, green fee US$45. *Half Moon Golf Club*, T9532731, advance booking necessary for this championship course, 18 holes, green fee US$95, also **tennis** and **squash**. *Wyndham Rose Hall Golf Club*, east of Montego Bay, T9532650, 18 holes, green fee US$60. **Horse riding** Hotels can arrange riding with local stables and there are good facilities at the *Equestrian Centre* at *Half Moon* Club. A 3-hr beach ride costs about US$55.

Sports
For diving and fishing, see page 190

Air The **Donald Sangster International Airport** is *Air Jamaica*'s regional hub and there are good connections with lots of airlines landing here. There is a transfer service to Kingston by Martins minibus, 5 hrs. To get to the **Norman Manley Airport**, Kingston, take the minibus from the town centre to Pechon St, Kingston, from where the airport buses leave.

Transport
Don't buy at the airport duty-free shop; everything is half the price in town

Road Bicycle rentals through *Montego Bike Rentals*, T9524984, and *Tropic Ride Car and Bike Rental*, T9527096. **Bus** The bus station for Kingston and Ocho Rios is behind Courts (Electrical). The bus station for Negril is off Barnett St (beware pickpockets). There is no need to take the expensive tourist buses, except that the regular buses get crowded. They depart

Jamaica

Jamaica

when full. The regular buses are fast, very frequent and cheap, about US$2 to Negril with a 30-second transfer in Lucea. There are more buses Montego Bay-Lucea than Lucea-Negril, which often causes a bottleneck. Buses from Kingston depart from Pechon St, roughly every hr from 0600 to 1500, US$5.60. It is possible to get to Montego Bay from Port Antonio all along the north coast, a scenic journey involving changes in Annotto Bay (then shared taxi, US$1 per person, mad rush to squeeze into clapped-out Ladas, the locals giving no quarter to slow tourists), Port Maria US$1, and Ocho Rios. Ochos Rios-Montego Bay by bus takes 2 hrs. **Taxi** *JUTA* are usually found outside hotels. *JCAL*, T9527574/8277, charges US$10 to Gloucester Av from *Sandals Montego Bay*, US$15 from *Wyndham*. Lucea-Negril about US$20. *UTAS Tours*, T9523820, F9793465, offer 12-hr day trip to Kingston via Dunns River Falls and Ocho Rios, US$60 in a/c car; also 9-hr tour to Negril, US$21, with sunset drink at *Rick's Café*.

Negril

Negril, on a seven-mile stretch of pure white sand on the west end of the island, is far less formal than other tourist spots but is still a one-industry town. The town is at the south end of Long Bay; at the north is the smaller Bloody Bay, where whalers used to carve up their catch. The Negril Area Environmental Protection Trust (NEPT) hopes to have the coastal area declared a national marine park and a grant has been awarded by the European Union (for information T9574473). The main part of the town has resorts and beaches but no snorkelling and you have to take a boat. In the West End of the town are beautiful cliffs and many fine caves, with great snorkelling but no beaches. In between is an area with neither beaches nor cliffs. Behind the bay is the Great Morass, which is being drained for development but remains a protected area as a natural wetland. The local **tourist office** is in Coral Seas Plaza, T9574243.

Negril

Beaches & sports

There is clothes-optional bathing at certain hotels, quite rare in the Caribbean

There are toilets and showers (US$0.30)

Hawkers ('higglers'), pushing their drugs, hair braiding, aloe, etc, on the beach, are annoying and reported to be worse than at Montego Bay. Politely decline whatever they are offering (if you do not want it). Fruit is readily available although not ready to eat; ask the vendor to cut it up and put it in a bag for you. To avoid the worst of the higglers go to the end of the beach near the crafts market where there are no stalls or bars.

By the *Poinciana Beach Resort* is the **Anancy Park** with boating lake, mini-golf, go-karts, fishing pond, nature trail, and historical exhibitions. ■ *Tue-Sun 1300-2200. US$1-3.*

Dive centres

There is a dive shop at *Hedonism II*, T9574200, free for guests, and *Sundivers Negril*, a PADI 5-star facility at *Poinciana Beach Resort*, diving lessons 0900 and 1200, resort course US$60, guided boat dives 3

Sleeping
1 Charela Inn
2 Mariner's Inn

Eating
1 Rick's Café

times daily, US$30 single tank, US$45 for 2 tanks (also at *Rock Cliff Resort*). **Negril Scuba Centre** is at *Negril Beach Club*, T9574425, neg.scuba.centre@toj.com There are also dive operations at *Swept Away* and *Sandals*.

L-A *Firefly Beach Cottages*, Norman Manley Blvd, on the beach and therefore not very private, T9574358, www.jamaicalink.com From a basic cabin for 2 or studios, to 1 to 3-bedroomed cottages or luxury villas, clothes optional, gymnasium, minimum 1 week rental in winter, 3 nights in summer. **L-AL** *Charela Inn*, on the beach, T9574277, F9574414. 49 rooms, family-owned and run, Sunfish, sailboards, restaurant, bar. **L-AL** *Negril Cabins*, Norman Manley Blvd, on Bloody Bay, across the road from the beach, T9575350, www.negril-cabins.com 70 rooms in cabins on stilts, or more expensive rooms, pool, swim-up bar, private beach, restaurant, piano bar, children's programme, security guards keep away 'higglers'.

L-A *Rockhouse*, West End Rd, T/F9574373, www.rockhousehotel.com On cliffs at Pristine Cove, just north of *Rick's Café*, 11 octagonal villas by the sea with fans, indoor bathrooms, outdoor showers, built of timber, stone and thatch, or 17 studios in thatched blocks in the garden, cliff-edge pool, restaurant above the water serving 'new Jamaican cuisine', open 0700-2300, no beach but steps down to sea, snorkelling and kayak rental, quiet, restful, Australian-owned, no children under 12 because of potentially dangerous cliffs. **AL-B** *Mariner's Inn and Diving Resort*, West End, T9570393, F9570391. On cliffs, 52 rooms, PADI and NAUI instructors for diving, kayaking, riding, volleyball. **A-C** *Ocean Edge Resort*, also on cliffs, T9574362, F9570086. 30 rooms. **A-C** *Heart Beat*, T9574329, heartbeat@cw jamaica.com, on West End cliffs. 9 rooms, 1- 2- or 3-bed cottages and efficiencies, run by Valerie Brewis, cafés and music nearby, great sunset watching from veranda. **C** *Emerald Hotel*, Westland Mountain Rd, T9574814, F9570708. Chalets, small pool, CP, TV, gardens with hammocks, short walk to beach. **C-E** *Tigress 1*, West End Rd. Cheaper rooms with fan, no hot water, shared bathrooms, higher- priced rooms with a/c, hot water, private bath, all with kitchen facilities, good security, bar and pool in gardens, 20 mins' walk to beach and walking distance from town centre, friendly, clean, lots of repeat business. Accommodation **D** available at the *Yacht Club*, West End Rd, T9995732. **D-F** *Lighthouse Park* on cliffs. Campsite, cabins, tent site.

The northern end is the more expensive part of town, but there are a few cheap cabins: **E** *Roots Bamboo* is very neat. **F** *Coconut International*, on the beach. Basic cabin, dirty, no fan. Next door is *Gloria's Sunset*, Jamaican family run, clean, friendly, helpful, security guards at night, variety of accommodation, bar, restaurant. This whole beach is lined with clubs and is noisy. None of the cabins has any services, nor do they provide blankets, but they are on the beach. When choosing cabin check to see whether it has a fan, whether there is a mesh or screen to keep out mosquitoes, and whether it looks safe (many get broken into). Locals living along the beach will often let you camp on their property.

Rick's Café, full ocean view from clifftop setting but pricey with it, Red Stripe beer or cocktail US$3, plastic bead money used, full restaurant next door, expensive, with good view of sunset. *Cool Runnings*, with a chef/owner, is also recommended. *The Office*, on the beach, open 24 hrs, provides a good choice of Jamaican food, reasonably priced and friendly service, a good place to meet the locals. *The Pickled Parrot*, West End Rd, T9574864, on the cliffs, call for free pick-up. Serves Mexican, Jamaican and American food, large portions, also reached by snorkelling and catamaran cruises with dancing and limbo competitions en route, entertainment includes cliff diving, rope swing and waterslide over the rocks into the sea, US$1, Norman Manley Blvd, just before you get to Negril Tree House, unless you are on a tour. *Juicy J*, T9574213. Jamaican restaurant and bar. *Hunan Garden*, T9574347. Fine and authentic Chinese cuisine served in a very charming setting, free shuttle and take away service, open daily 1000-2200. Eating cheaply is difficult but not impossible. The native restaurant-food stalls are good and relatively cheap; the local patties are delicious. Street hawkers will sell you jerk chicken for US$4-5. *The Bread Basket*, next to the banks at the mall in town is recommended, but even better is the *Fisherman's Club* supermarket, just off the beach in the main part of town near *Pete's Seafood*, which is a restaurant as well as a market and serves good, local, filling meals for about US$4.

Sleeping

Several large all-inclusives, but no hotel is allowed to be taller than the tallest palm tree to minimize the visual and environmental impact of tourism

Hotels to the west of centre, about 10-20 mins' walk, are better for mixing with Jamaicans

Eating

Festivals *Negril Reggae Marathon*, is an annual event in Dec (6 Dec 2003), starting at 0515. Well supported marathon and half marathon, begins and ends at Long Bay Beach Park, www.reggaemarathon.com

Nightlife Live reggae shows in outdoor venues most nights, featuring local and well-known stars. Entrance is usually US$5-7, good fun, lively atmosphere, very popular. Nice bars are located along the beach, usually with music, unnamed bar next to *Coconut International* recommended, friendly service. For beautiful surroundings try the bar at the *Rock Cliff Hotel* on the West End Rd, friendly barman who mixes great fruit punches and cocktails. **Compulsion Disco**, Shop 24, Negril Plaza, T9574735. **Jungle Disco**, Norman Manley Blvd, across from Rondel Village, T9573283. Open daily from 2200 until dawn, Ladies' Night Thu, Dance Hall Night Fri, restaurant and bar, lots of high spirits, recently expanded its entertainment centre and gaming area, giving even more room to rumble, gaming room open from 1500 until the club closes.

Shopping Times Square, for jewellery, perfume and gifts. The **mall** in downtown Negril offers much the same but at slightly higher prices. The **Craft Market** is overwhelming, with 200 stalls of sarongs and wood carvings, not much in the way of variety and everyone wants your attention.

Sport
For diving and fishing, see page 190

Golf *Tryall Golf, Tennis and Beach Resort*, between Montego Bay and Negril, T9565681/3. Par 71, 6,328 m in 890-ha resort complex, green fee US$125. The *Tryall* course is probably the best known and hosts the annual *Johnny Walker World Championship*. Advance bookings are essential. Inland, up in the hills near Negril, is the **Negril Hills Golf Club**, T9574638, F9570222. Par 72, 5,790-m, 18-hole course with clubhouse, restaurant, pro shop and tennis. Green fees US$58. **Horse riding** *Babo's Horseback Riding Stable* and *Country Western Riding Stables* have facilities for tennis and riding, daily 0800-1700, US$30-35. **Road races** The Reggae marathon and half marathon starting at the Negril UDC playing field to Green Island and return, www.reggaemarathon.com

Transport Licensed, unmetered taxis have red licence plates with PP before the numbers. Avoid unlicensed taxis. Local buses operate between Negril and Montego Bay stopping frequently. JUTA-operated tour buses typically charge US$20 per person with a minimum charge US$60 per trip between Montego Bay and Negril. From the Donald Sangster Airport minibuses run to Negril; you must bargain with the driver to get the fare to US$5-7. Lots of companies do bike rental.

Directory **Banks** *National Commercial Bank* and *Nova Scotia* and several *cambios* in town including one at the *Hi-lo-Supermarket*.

The south coast

Savanna-La-Mar
No good beach, or good-quality restaurants or accommodation

About 29 km east of Negril, on the coast, is Savanna-la-Mar, a busy, commercial town with shopping and banks, but no major attractions for tourists. Regular concerts are held at *St Joseph's Catholic Church*, T9552648. Local musicians play under the auspices of Father Sean Lavery, formerly a professor of music at Dublin University. Easily reached by minibus from Negril, there are hourly buses from Montego Bay (US$2). The Frome sugar refinery, 8 km north of Savanna-la-Mar, will often allow visitors to tour their facilities during sugar cane season (November-June). Another interesting outing is to the 9.5-km **Roaring River** and the organic **Ital Herbs and Spice Farm**, owned by an American, Ed Kritzler. There is a cave at Roaring River and the farm is about half a mile on, 3 km north of Petersfield, from where it is well signposted. It is a scenic area with interesting walks and streams suitable for bathing. A restaurant serves fish and vegetable dishes at the farm, and it is best to order lunch before exploring. Basic hut accommodation is available and popular, but try to look before you book.

Jamaica

Outside Savanna-la-Mar, the main south coast road (A2) passes by Paradise Planta- **Bluefields**
tion, a private estate with miles of frontage on **Bluefields Bay**, a protected anchorage
with reefs and wetlands teeming with birds. At Ferris Crossroads, the A2 meets up
with the B8 road, a well-maintained north-south connection and about 40 minutes'
drive to Montego Bay via Whithorn and Anchovy. For the next 6.5 km the A2 hugs the
coast along road to Bluefields, where there is a white-sand beach mainly used by locals.
There is no mass tourism either in Bluefields or in the adjacent village of **Belmont**. The
local **tourist office** is in Hendricks Building, 2 High St, T9562074.

Sleeping In Belmont there are a few expat homes sometimes available for rent: *Oristano*, the
oldest home in west Jamaica, dating back to the 1700s, is owned by the Hon William Fielding,
PO Box 1, Bluefields, Westmoreland Parish. **A-D** *Ashton Great House*, higher up hillside,
T/F9652036. Pool, restaurant, free ride from Bluefields, 24 rooms. **C-D** *Casa Marina*, in Cave, 3.2
km from Bluefields. Friendly owner Manley Wallace, restaurant, private pier and gazebo.

The south coast is known as the best part of Jamaica for deep-sea fishing and boat **East of**
trips go out from Belmont to the reefs or to offshore banks. Snorkelling is also good **Bluefields**
because the sea is mainly calm in the morning. The **Bluefields Great House**, now
privately owned, was the place where Philip Gosse lived in the 1830s and wrote his
book, *Birds of Jamaica*. It reportedly contains the first breadfruit tree planted in
Jamaica by Captain Bligh after his expedition to the South Pacific. The next 9.5 km of
coast southeast of Bluefields covers a beautiful, unspoiled coastal stetch. A
258-room *Beaches Whitehouse* resort is being built in the Culloden district, for completion in Dec 2003. A bird sanctuary and turtle nesting area has been designated.

Sleeping and eating **B** *Natania's*, a guesthouse and seafood restaurant at Little Culloden,
Whitehouse, has been praised. It is on the sea and has 8 rooms, food is good and reasonably
priced. The owner is Peter Probst. Transport from Montego Bay can be arranged, as can local
tours, deep-sea fishing and watersports.

Black River

Black River is one of the oldest towns in Jamaica. It had its heyday in the 18th century *The first car imported*
when it was the main exporting harbour for logwood dyes. Along the shore are some *into Jamaica was*
fine early 19th-century mansions, some of which are being restored. At Black River, *landed here*
you can go by boat from across the bridge up the lower stretches of the Black River,
the longest river in Jamaica. ■ *Daily 0900, 1100, 1230, 1400, 1600. US$15 per person,
drinks included, 16 km, 1½-2 hrs, 3 boats, 25 people per boat. Contact South Coast
Safaris, run by Charles Swaby in Black River, T9620220, F9652086.* You should see
crocodiles, mostly at midday basking on the river banks, and plenty of birdlife in
tranquil surroundings. To avoid large tour parties, go with a local, whose boats are
through the fish market. The boats are smaller, slower, quieter and go further up
river. They stop at a 'countryside bar' rather than the one the tour companies use. ■
2 hrs, US$27 for 2 including boatman and guide.

D-E *Waterloo Guest House*, in a Georgian building (the first house in Jamaica with electric **Sleeping**
light). Old rooms in the main house, or more expensive in the new annex, all with showers,
very good restaurant (lobster in season). 3 km east of Black River is the **D** *Port of Call Hotel*,
136 Crane Rd, T9652360. A bit spartan but on the sea, a/c, pool. **D** *Bridge House Inn*, Crane
Rd, T9652361, F2652081. 14 rooms, a/c, fan, kitchen facilities, shady garden with hammocks
leads down to beach, good Jamaican food, US$8-10 for a meal, staff friendly, bar, TV, lounge,
ask for odd-numbered room at front to avoid noise from club on the beach.

Bayside, near bridge. Excellent steamed fish with rice and peas for US$6, usually all gone by **Eating**
1300. *Caribbe*, near bus station. Very good steamed fish and curried goat for US$6 with beer.
Superbus, an old bus near bus station. Good cheap food, eg fried chicken with trimmings and

beer for US$3. *Riverside Dock* , water's edge, T9659486, 6343333, F6343388. Just up Black River from the coast, exquisite Japanese, Chinese and international seafood dishes, outside bar, pool tables, swings and slides for children, karaoke and local music. Safari rides up the Black River can be arranged through the restaurant with one of the local tour operators.

Transport **Road** To get to Black River from Mandeville by bus involves a change in Santa Cruz.

The road to Mandeville

On the south coast past Black River is **Treasure Beach**, a wide dark-sand beach with body-surfing waves, in one of the most beautiful areas on the island. It is largely used by local fishermen as it is the closest point to the Pedro Banks. There is one small grocery shop and a bakery. A van comes to the village every day with fresh fruit and vegetables. This area is quite unlike any other part of Jamaica and still relatively unvisited by tourists. The local people are very friendly and you will be less hassled by higglers than elsewhere. You can take a daytime or moonlight tour to Sunny Island (Alligator Reef) from *Jake's*, T9652472. To the east of Treasure Beach lies **Lovers' Leap**, a beauty spot named after the slave and his lover (his owner's daughter) who jumped off the cliff in despair. ■ *Daily 1000-1800. US$3.* At **Alligator Pond** on the coast, you can eat at on the beach at Blackie's *Little Ochie*, fish restaurant, everything freshly caught, six ways of cooking lobster, US$10. East of Alligator Pond is **Gut River**, where you can sometimes see alligators and manatees. Boat and fishing trips can be made to **Pigeon Island**, with a day on the island for swimming and snorkelling.

Sleeping **On the beach AL** *Treasure Beach Hotel*, T9650110, www.treasurebeachjamaica.com, 36 rooms. **A** *Jake's Place*, T9650635, www.islandoutpost.com, part of Island Outpost chain, run by Jason Henzell. 14 rooms in small and exclusive, brightly painted cottages, arty, CP, good food, saltwater pool, riding, cycling and hiking can be arranged, yoga and massage, music. **D** *Four M's Cottage*, T/F9652472, T9650131. 4 rooms. Several houses can be rented: *Sparkling Waters*, *Folichon*, *Caprice*, and *Siwind*, PO Box 73, Black River, which has its own cove.

Sport The Treasure Beach Off-Road **Triathlon** in May, involves swimming, mountain biking and running. Contact Jason Henzel, T9650636, F9650552, jakes@cwjamaica.com.

Bamboo Avenue Inland on the A2 is Middle Quarters, on the edge of the Black River Morass, hot pepper shrimp are sold by the wayside, but make sure they are today's catch. Just after Middle Quarters is the left turn which takes you to **YS Falls** (pronounced Why-Ess), an unspoiled spot in the middle of a large private plantation. You can bathe but there are no changing rooms or shelter. ■ *Tue-Sun 0930-1530, closed public holidays. US$9. 15-min walk from car park.* Further along the A2 is the impressive 2½-mile long Bamboo Avenue. North of Bamboo Avenue is **Maggotty**, on the (closed) railway line from Montego Bay to Kingston and close to the **Appleton Estate**, where tours of the rum factory are offered. ■ *Mon-Fri 0900-1600. US$12. Jamaica Estate Tours Ltd, T9976077, F9632243, or T9526606, Montego Bay.* Opposite the Maggotty train depot is the *Sweet Bakery*, run by Patrick and Lucille Lee, who can arrange accommodation in a great house (**D**) or at a rustic campsite (**F**), very friendly and helpful, local trips organized.

Mandeville

Population: 50,000 After Bamboo Avenue, the A2 road goes through Lacovia and Santa Cruz, an expanding town on the St Elizabeth Plain, and on up to Mandeville, a peaceful upland town with perhaps the best climate on the island. It is very spread out, with building on all the surrounding hills and no slums. In recent years, Mandeville has derived much of its prosperity from the bauxite/alumina industry (outside the town). There are lots of expensive homes and the town is congested.

Jamaica

The town's centre is the village green, now called **Cecil Charlton Park** (after the ex-mayor, whose opulent mansion, Huntingdon Summit, can be visited by prior arrangement). The green looks a bit like New England; at its northeast side stands a Georgian courthouse and, on the southeast, **St Mark's parish church** (both 1820). By St Mark's is the **market** area (busiest days Monday, Wednesday and Friday) and the area where buses congregate. West of the green, at the corner of Ward Avenue and Caledonia Road, is the *Manchester Club*, T9622403, one of the oldest country clubs in the West Indies (1868) and the oldest in Jamaica. It has a nine-hole golf course (18 tee boxes, enabling you to play 18 holes) and tennis courts (you must be introduced by a member). Also, horse riding can be arranged, Ann Turner on T9622527.

Although some way inland, Mandeville is a good place from which to start exploring **Excursions** both the surrounding area and the south coast. In fact, by car you can get to most of Jamaica's resorts, except those east of Ocho Rios or Kingston, in two hours or less. Bird watchers and those interested in seeing a beautiful 'great house' in a cattle property should contact Ann Sutton at **Marshall's Pen**. Even after her husband's death in 2002, Ann carries on organizing birding tours and accommodating visitors. ■ *T9622260, US$10 for great house tour by appointment only.* Also around the town you can visit the **High Mountain Coffee** (■ *Mon-Fri, free*) and **Pioneer Chocolate Factories**, a factory making bammy (a delicacy from cassava root), the Alcan works, and local gardens.

From Mandeville it is about 88.5 km east to Kingston on the A2, bypassing May Pen, through Old Harbour then on to Spanish Town and Kingston. Before the May Pen bypass, a road branches south to **Milk River Bath**, the world's most radioactive spa. The baths are somewhat run-down, but the medical properties of the water are among the best. ■ *Daily 0700-2100. US$1.40, 15 mins. T9024657. Restaurant and hotel.* Five kilometres from the baths is a marine conservation area, **Alligator Hole**, where manatees (sea cows) can sometimes be seen. Local boatmen do their best to oblige.

AL-C *Astra Country Inn*, 62 Ward Av, T9623725. Some way from town centre. 22 rooms, **Sleeping** pool, sauna, entertainment, natural health fitness programme, tour desk. In the centre is the **AL** *Mandeville Hotel*, 4 Hotel St, T9622138, www.mandevillehotel.com TV, spacious, pool, restaurant, excursions arranged, good. **C** *Kariba Kariba*, Atkinson's Drive, near New Green roundabout on Winston Jones highway, first right off New Green Rd, 45 mins' walk from centre, on bus route, T9623039. Bath, fan, 5 rooms or suites, CP, TV lounge, bar, dining room. The owners, Derrick and Hazel O'Conner, are friendly, knowledgeable and hospitable, they can arrange for you to meet local people with similar interests and offer tours. Derrick is developing a 5-ha farm at Mile Gully (opportunity for work if you wish) and plans to develop a small campsite, bar, accommodation and other facilities there.

Bloomfield Great House, 8 Perth Road, T9627130, bloomfield.g.h@cwjamaica.com Ori- **Eating** ginally a coffee estate, part of its land was used to build the town, 200 m above Mandeville, panoramic views. The Georgian great house has also been used as a hotel, a dairy, a private home and more recently, Bill Laurie's Steak House, now owned by Ralph Pearce (Australian) and his wife Pamela Grant (Jamaican). Open for lunch and dinner, varied menu, fish 'n' chips, filet mignon, beer-batter shrimp, homemade pasta, smoked marlin, cheesecakes are a speciality. *Pot Pourri*, on 2nd floor of the Caledonia Mall, just north of the Manchester Club. Clean and bright, good food and service. *International Chinese Restaurant*, Newport Rd. *Hungry Hut*, 45 Manchester Rd. Cheap, excellent food and service (owner, Fay, grew up in England).

The *Eclipse Disco*, Ward Av near the *Manchester Club*. The main disco, patronized by younger **Nightlife** crowd, but good mix of music, closed Mon, Tue, after-work jam on Fri, Dance Hall night and live entertainment Sat, karaoke until 2200 and then oldies on Sun.

Jamaica

Sport   **Golf** *Manchester Country Club*, T9622403, 9-hole, green fee US$16. There are several **road races** during the year, including the *High Mountain Coffee* 10- km and 5- km races at Williamsfield, Manchester, which usually attract around 450 runners (contact John Minott, T9634211, sanco@colis.com).

Background

History   When Columbus landed on Jamaica in 1494 it was inhabited by peaceful Taíno Indians. Under Spanish occupation, which began in 1509, the race died out and gradually African slaves, were brought in to provide the labour force. In 1655 an English expeditionary force landed at Passage Fort and met with little resistance other than that offered by a small group of Spanish settlers and a larger number of African slaves who took refuge in the mountains. The Spaniards abandoned the island after about five years, but the slaves and their descendants, who became known as Maroons, waged war against the new colonists for 80 years until the 1730s although there was another brief rebellion in 1795. Some of their descendants still live in the Cockpit Country, where the Leeward Maroons hid, and around Nanny Town where the Windward Maroons hid.

After a short period of military rule, the colony was adopted with an English-type constitution and a Legislative Council. The great sugar estates, were planted in the early days of English occupation when Jamaica also became the haunt of buccaneers and slave traders. In 1833 slave emancipation was declared, although an apprenticeship system remained until 1838, and modern Jamaica was born. The framework for Jamaica's modern political system was laid in the 1930s. Norman W Manley formed the People's National Party (PNP) in 1938 and his cousin, Sir Alexander Bustamante, formed the Jamaica Labour Party (JLP) in 1944. These two parties had their roots in rival trade unions and have dominated Jamaican politics since universal adult suffrage was introduced in 1944. In 1958, Jamaica joined the West Indies Federation with nine other British territories but withdrew following a national referendum on the issue in 1961. On 6 August 1962, Jamaica became an independent Commonwealth member.

After 23 years as leader of the PNP, eight of them as Prime Minister in the 1970s and three as Prime Minister from 1989, Michael Manley, son of the party's founder, retired in March 1992 because of ill health. During Manley's first two terms in office between 1972 and 1980 he endorsed socialist policies at home and encouraged South-South relations abroad. He antagonized the USA by developing close economic and political links with Cuba. Manley's government focused on state-led income distribution to the poorer classes at the expense of private sector support and increased productivity. Failure to deliver economic stability and growth led to his defeat in the 1980 elections. The conservative Edward Seaga (JLP), held office for the next nine years. By 1989 however, Manley's political thinking had changed dramatically and he was re-elected with policies advocating the free market. He was succeeded by the Party Chairman, former Deputy Prime Minister and Finance Minister P J Patterson. Patterson promised to maintain Manley's policies and to deepen the restructuring of the economy.

General elections were held early, on 30 March 1993, and the incumbent PNP was returned for a second term with a larger than expected majority, winning 55 of the 60 seats. Despite the landslide victory, the elections were marred by violence that led to 11 deaths, malpractices and a turnout of only 58%. The JLP boycotted parliament for four months while it demanded electoral reform and an inquiry into the election day events. It also refused to contest by-elections, two of which were held in the next 12 months and won by the PNP. Concessions were made by the Government, including a reorganization of the police force to remove direct political control and the postponement of local government elections pending electoral reform. The reform drafted by the Electoral Advisory Committee was completed in time for general elections in December 1997.

The 1997 elections gave the PNP a third consecutive term in office. The PNP won 50 seats while the JLP won 10 and the National Democratic Movement (NDM), a new party formed by dissident JLP members in 1995, failed to win any. There was less violence than in previous campaigns, with only two deaths, but there were some electoral inefficiencies because of the new

Dreadlocks to reggae

◀

Followers of the Rastafarian cult are non-violent, do not eat pork and believe in the divinity of the late Emperor of Ethiopia, Haile Selassie (Ras Tafari). Haile Selassie's call for the end of the superiority of one race over another has been incorporated into a faith which holds that God, Jah, will lead the blacks out of oppression (Babylon) back to Ethiopia (Zion, the Promised Land). The Rastas regard the ideologist Marcus Garvey (born 1887, St Ann's Bay) as a prophet of the return to Africa (he is now a Jamaican national hero). In the early 20th century, Garvey founded the idea of black nationalism, with Africa as the home for blacks, whether they are living on the continent or not.

The music most strongly associated with Rastafarianism is reggae. According to OR Dathorne, "it is evident that the sound and words of Jamaican reggae have altered the life of the English-speaking Caribbean. The extent of this alteration is still unknown, but this new sound has touched, more than any other single art medium, the consciousness of the people of this region" (Dark Ancestor, page 229, Louisiana State University Press, 1981). The sound is a mixture of African percussion and up-to-the-minute electronics; the lyrics a blend of praise of Jah, political comment and

criticism and the mundane. The late Bob Marley, the late Peter Tosh, Dennis Brown and Jimmy Cliff are among Jamaica's most famous reggae artists. Over the last few years, traditional reggae has been supplanted by Dance Hall Reggae, which has a much heavier beat, with new artists such as Grammy winners Shabba Ranks and Junior Gong, son of Bob Marley. Also closely related to reggae is dub poetry, a chanted verse form that combines the musical tradition, folk traditions and popular speech. Its first practitioner was Louise Bennett, in the 1970s, who has been followed by poets such as Linton Kwesi Johnson, Michael Smith, Oku Onora and Mutabaruka. Many of these poets work in the UK, but their links with Jamaica are strong.

Two novels which give a fascinating insight into Rasta culture (and, in the latter, Revival and other social events) are Brother Man, *by Roger Mais, and* The Children of Sysiphus, *by H Orlando Patterson. These writers have also published other books that are worth investigating, as are the works of Olive Senior (eg* Summer Lightning), *and the poets Mervyn Morris, the late Andrew Salkey and Dennis Scott (who is also involved in the theatre).*

Jamaica

register and a few irregularities leading to re-run elections in a couple of constituencies. When he was sworn into office, Prime Minister PJ Patterson promised that it would be the last time that the Government would swear allegiance to the British monarchy. The PNP proposes an executive president but the JLP advocates a ceremonial president with a Prime Minister.

The 2002 general elections resulted in the ruling PNP winning 35 seats and the JLP 25. Massive expenditures on infrastructure projects, involving island-wide road repairs and construction in the months leading up to the elections, secured victory in a keenly contested poll. The other minor parties made insignificant showings, receiving less than 1% of the vote in each case. Politically motivated violence was considerably reduced and the elections were judged well run and markedly free from corruption. Local government elections, after several postponements, will be held in late 2003.

Geography Jamaica lies some 145 km south of Cuba and a little over 160 km west of Haiti. With an area of 10,992 sq km, it is the third-largest island in the Greater Antilles. It is 235 km from east to west and 82 km from north to south at its widest, bounded by the Caribbean. Like other West Indian islands, it is an outcrop of a submerged mountain range. It is crossed by a spectacular range of mountains which rises to 2,256 m at Blue Mountain Peak in the east and descends towards the west, with a series of spurs and forested gullies running north and south. The luxuriance of the vegetation is striking. Tropical beaches surround the island. The best are on the north and west coasts, though there are some good bathing places on the south coast too.

People With a population 2.5 million, the island is a fascinating blend of cultures from colonial Britain, African slavery and immigrants from China, India and the Middle East. Reggae and Rastafariansim have become synonymous with Jamaica, and Bob Marley and Peter Tosh are just two of the greats to have been born here. Over 90% of Jamaicans are of West African descent. Because of this, Ashanti words still figure very largely in the local dialect (patois). There are also Chinese, East Indians and Christian Arabs as well as those of British descent and other European minorities. There is considerable poverty on the island, which has created social problems and some tension, although Jamaicans are naturally friendly, easy-going and international in their outlook (more people of Jamaican origin live outside Jamaica than inside).

The predominant religion is Protestantism, but there is also a Roman Catholic community, as well as followers of the Church of God, Baptists, Anglicans, Seventh Day Adventists, Pentecostals, Methodists and others. The Jewish, Moslem, Hindu and Bahai religions are also practised. Jamaicans are a very religious people and it is said that Jamaica has more churches per square mile than anywhere else in the world. To a small degree, early adaptations of the Christian faith, Revival and Pocomania, survive, but the most obvious local minority sect is Rastafarianism (see box above).

Economy   Once one of the more prosperous islands in the West Indies, Jamaica went into recession in 1973 and output declined steadily throughout the 1970s and 1980s. At the core of Jamaica's economic difficulties lay the collapse of the vital bauxite-mining and alumina-refining industries. Jamaica is the world's third-largest producer of bauxite after Australia and Guinea, but despite rising production of bauxite and alumina, earnings have slumped because of lower prices.

Manufacturing and mining contribute over 23% to GDP, while agriculture accounts for only 8%. Garments exported to the USA and other miscellaneous manufactured articles have seen considerable decline due to competition from Mexico and other NAFTA member states, and from imports due to market liberalization. Sugar is the main crop, and most important export after bauxite and alumina, but production costs are high and the industry insolvent. Other export crops include bananas, coffee, cocoa and citrus fruits. Jamaica is famous for its Blue Mountain coffee, first produced in 1757, commands a high premium in the world market.

Tourism is the largest foreign exchange earner, contributing about 20% of GDP. Combined stopover and cruise arrivals passed the million mark in 1987 and the two million mark in 2002, resulting in earnings of over US$1,200 mn for the industry. Further increases are forecast for 2003, barring any unexpected shocks to the sector. Remittances from Jamaicans abroad remain the second largest source of foreign exchange income, growing from US$331 mn in 1993 to over US$958 mn in 2001. The support, whether in cash, clothing, food or cars, is a significant source of welfare income, especially for those in the lower economic and social strata.

The Government turned to the IMF for support in 1976 and was a regular customer until 1995. In compliance with IMF agreements, the Government reduced domestic demand commensurate with the fall in export earnings, by devaluing the currency and reducing the size of its fiscal deficits. Jamaica rescheduled its debt to creditor governments and foreign commercial banks. Some debt forgiveness was granted. The foreign exchange market was deregulated, and interest rates and credit ceilings kept high to reduce consumption, close the trade gap and rebuild foreign reserves.

Debt servicing remains a heavy burden, with amortization and interest payments accounting for 67% of budget expenditure. Although inflation has been reduced to single digits, the Government appears unable to sustain the macro-economic stability achieved at the turn of the century, as increasingly high interest rates not only exacerbate the debt situation but also undermine the productive sector. The continuing slide in the value of the Jamaican dollar and the growing difficulty in raising affordable money on the international capital markets, have raised the spectre of another crisis in the financial sector such as occurred in the mid 1990s.

Turks and Caicos Islands

Introducing the Turks and Caicos Islands

Similar to the southern Bahamas islands, to which they are geographically linked, these flat, coral islands are a British Overseas Territory. Miles of sandy beaches attract sun-loving tourists to a water playground. Diving and snorkelling are superb among coral gardens, wrecks and walls which drop dramatically to the floor of the ocean. Most hotels are on the island of Providenciales (also known as 'Provo'), spread along Grace Bay on the north shore, and there are lots of facilities for sailing, diving and fishing. Grand Turk is the seat of government but is a quiet, unhurried place with a few small hotels and some pleasant colonial buildings. Other inhabited islands, North Caicos, Middle Caicos, South Caicos and Salt Cay, have tiny populations and are good places to escape the crowds.

Essentials

Before you travel

US and Canadian citizens need only a birth certificate and photo ID such as a driving licence to enter the Turks and Caicos. Other nationalities need a valid passport; a visa is not necessary except for nationals of former eastern bloc and communist countries. An onward ticket is officially required. Visitors are allowed to stay for 30 days, renewable once only for a fee of US$50.

Documents

The official **currency** is the US dollar. Most banks will advance cash on **credit cards**. Most hotels, restaurants and taxi drivers will accept travellers' cheques, but personal cheques are not widely accepted. There are **banks** on Grand Turk and Providenciales (and South Caicos on Wed) but not on the other islands. Take lots of cash and small denomination US dollars when visiting an island without a bank, as it is often difficult to get change from big notes. As well as domestic banking there is a growing offshore banking industry, regulated by the UK.

Money

Temperatures average 75-85°F from Nov to May, reaching into the 90s from Jun to Oct, but constant tradewinds keep life comfortable. Average annual rainfall is 21 ins on Grand Turk and South Caicos but increases to 40 ins as you travel westwards through the Caicos Islands where more lush vegetation is found. Several hurricanes have caused damage in the last 20 years.

Climate
Hurricane season is normally June-November, with August and September being the peak

Getting there

Ports of entry for aircraft are Providenciales, South Caicos and Grand Turk, but the major international airport is on Providenciales. There are also airstrips on North Caicos, Middle Caicos, Pine Cay and Salt Cay. Flights from Miami, New York (*American Airlines* www.aa.com) and Charlotte (US Air), Jamaica (*Air Jamaica Express* www.airjamaica.com), Bahamas (*Bahamas Air* www.bahamasair.com), the Dominican Republic, Haiti (*TCI Sky King* www.skyking.tc) and the UK (*British Airways* www.british-airways.com) come in to Providenciales and then, if you are not staying on Provo, you get a connecting flight to your destination on a small plane. See each island's Transport section for details.

Air
There are weekly BA flights to Provo from London via Nassau. Other flights from Europe connect with AA in the USA

There is no scheduled passenger service (cargo comes in regularly from Florida) and no port is deep enough to take cruise ships although some occasionally stop outside the reef and shuttle in passengers for half a day.

Boat
Evening weather report on VHF radio from Blue Water Divers on Grand Turk; Mystine on SSB

Ports of entry (British flag) Providenciales: Turtle Cove Marina, Caicos Marina & Boatyard, Leeward Marina, South Dock/Sapodilla Bay; Grand Turk; South Caicos; Salt Cay. Clear in and out with customs and immigration, VHF 16. On arrival, customs will grant seven days immigration clearance. Go to town to the Immigration Office (closed 1230-1430) to obtain a US$50 30-day extension. Fuel and alcoholic drink may be purchased duty free with clearance to leave the country. The Customs Office is at Airport Rd, Provo, and there are Customs Officers at the airport all day too.

There are no bareboat charters

Marinas There are 5 marinas on Provo. **Leeward Marina** at Leeward Going Through, T9465553, marina@tciway.tc gas/diesel sales only, restaurant; **Turtle Cove Landing**, Sellar's Pond, T9464307, long-term dockage for boats up to 70 ft, 5-ft draft; **Turtle Cove Marina**, Sellar's Pond, T9413781, tcmarina@ provo.net full service, all-weather anchorage, 6-ft draft, 100 new slips (still under construction), RO, water and ice, premium prices; **South Side Marina**, T9464747, dockside T9464200, hamilton&pratt@ tciway.tc, diesel, gas, oil, water, 4½ ft controlling depth, call for reservations; **Caicos Marina & Boatyard**, Long Bay, T9465600, SSB 4143.6, (fuel, ice, dry storage, machinist/diesel mechanic). South Caicos also has a marina.

▶ ## Tourist offices overseas

Canada *c/o RMR Group, 512 Duplex Av, Toronto, Ontario M4R 2E3, T416-4400212.*
UK *c/o Morris Kevan International Ltd, Mitre House, 66 Abbey Rd, Bush Hill Park, Enfield, Middlesex EN1 2RQ, T020-83501017, www.mki.ltd.uk*

USA *Trombone Associates Inc, 420 Madison Av, New York NY 10017, T212-2232323, T1-800-2410824. TCI Tourist Board, 11645 Biscayne Blvd, Suite 302, North Miami, FL 33181, T305-8914117, T800-2410824, tcitrsm@bellSouth.net*

Touching down

Airport information
It is worth checking in early when returning to Miami from Provo, to avoid long queues

Scheduled service airlines are *TCA* (on Provo, T9464255, domestic emergency T9415353); *American Airlines* (T1-800-4337300, T9415700); *US Air* (T1-800-6221015, T9415837, Provo office hours 1115-1530 Mon, Wed, Fri, Sat) *British Airways* (on Provo T1-800-2479297),*TCI Sky King* (T9461520 on Grand Turk, T9415461/4 on Provo, King@tciway.tc); *Bahamasair* and *Lynx Air* (to Grand Turk only). Charter airlines are *Global Airways*, run by the Gardiner family (T9413222 on Provo, T9467093 on North Caicos, www.globalairways.com); *Interisland Airways* (Provo T9415481, Grand Turk T9461667, www.interislandairways.com); *Provo Air Charter* (T9465578).

Tourist information

Local tourist office Turks and Caicos Islands Tourist Board, Grand Turk, Turks and Caicos Islands, T9462321/2322, www.turksandcaicostourism.com On Provo the tourist office is at Diamond Stubbs Plaza, on the low road leading to *Sibonné*, T9464970. Various maps and guidebooks have been published including *Where, When, How, Providenciales; Your Monthly Entertainment Guide*, distributed in hotels and selected shops, free of charge; *Times of the Islands; International Magazine of the Turks and Caicos*, quarterly, US$4. Special Edition publishes a large, user-friendly road map of Providenciales each year, indicating the location of advertisers, pay/card phones, fuel stations and other information, contact Kathi Robertson, F9465122, brad@tciway.tc Useful websites with lots of information on lodgings, particularly on the smaller islands are **www.tcimall.tc** and **www.wherewhenhow.com**

Local tour operators *Marco Travel Services*, Town Centre Mall, Down Town, T9464393, www.marcotravel.tc, for reconfirmation of tickets, emergency cheque cashing, travel services, TC sales, Amex representative. *Provo Travel Ltd*, run by Althea Ewing, at Central Sq, Leeward Highway, T9464035, helpful. On Grand Turk: *T & C Travel Ltd*, at *Hotel Osprey Beach*, T9462592, run by Daphne James, friendly, reliable.

Where to stay

There is a 10-15% service charge and 10% bed tax added to the bill

Hotels on Provo are aiming for North American standards and so they are expensive. Rack rates will not include tax and service, so be sure to check what you are quoted. Most hotels on Provo are all-inclusive or condominium-style. Grand Turk, Salt Cay, South Caicos and North Caicos are better bets for inexpensive, charming, more 'islandy' lodgings. **Camping** is possible on beaches on most islands but not encouraged (no water or sewage facilities). Contact the District Commissioner's office on each island for permission. If planning to stay on a deserted island take everything with you and leave nothing behind.

Getting around

Air
Taking a small plane between islands is a delightful experience as you fly low over the coral cays, reefs and sea

Several airlines provide flying bus services between the islands. The main ones are *Turks & Caicos Airways (TCA)*, *InterIsland Airways*, *SkyKing* and *Global Airways*. Flight time from Grand Turk to the furthest island (Provo) is 35 mins. Sample round trip fares: Provo to North Caicos is US$60, to Middle Caicos US$80, to South Caicos US$110, to Grand Turk US$125 and to Salt Cay US$110. Grand Turk to South Caicos US$70. Private charters are readily available within the island group and can easily be arranged by asking around at Grand Turk or Provo

Touching down

◀

Business hours On Provo **Banks**: Mon-Thu 0900-1600, Fri 0900-1630; **Offices**: 0830-1600; **Shops** 0900-1700. On other islands hours are more erratic.

Currency The official currency is the US dollar.

Clothing Dress is informal and shorts are worn in town and on the beach, but some restaurants are more formal, ask when making a reservation. Nudity is illegal although topless is condoned by Club Med on Grace Bay. The islanders find it offensive and flouting local protocol may elicit stares and remarks.

Departure tax US$25.50 including US$2.50 US security tax. All but the US$2.50 is included in the price of your ticket.

Emergency numbers In an **emergency** anywhere T999/911.

Official time GMT minus 4 hrs.

Public holidays New Year's Day, Commonwealth Day in Mar, Good Fri, Easter Mon, National Heroes Day (end May), the Queen's birthday (2nd week in Jun), Emancipation Day (beginning Aug), National Youth Day (end Sep), Columbus' Day and International Human Rights' Day (both in Oct), Christmas Day and Boxing Day.

Safety Providenciales is not as safe as it was before it became a tourist and offshore banking destination, but it is still safer than most Caribbean islands. It is definitely not advisable to walk around alone at night or on deserted beaches. On Provo, take precautions about leaving valuables in your room or on the beach. Traffic is fast and aggressive, causing many accidents. Personal security is much better on Grand Turk and the other islands.

Useful addresses Chief Secretary (Grand Turk), T9462702 (Provo), T9464258, 9415123; Customs (Grand Turk) T9462993/4, (Provo) T9464214; Immigration (Grand Turk) T946-2939 (Provo) T9464233.

Voltage 110 volts, 60 cycles, as in the USA.

Weights and measures Imperial.

See also Directory, pages 237 and 248

Turks & Caicos Islands

airport, as charter pilots meet incoming international flights and wait to see if they can fill a plane in the mornings. They often hold up boards showing which island they are flying to. If you pre-book you may sit for 2 or 3 hours waiting for a particular plane; similarly if travelling to the outer islands, do not buy a return ticket, whatever the airlines tell you, as you may have to pay twice if you come back with someone else. Your hotel or guesthouse can help you arrange your return flight when you are ready to leave (this does not include package tours). *TCA* does not fly on Sun.

Bicycles and motor scooters can be rented from some hotels but can be relatively expensive compared with cars. Helmets are not mandatory but should be worn. Tourists invite trouble riding in bathing suits and bare feet and at night.

Bicycle

Numerous cramped mini-vans serve as buses on Provo for about US$1 per trip.

Bus

Rental cars are available on Grand Turk, North and South Caicos and Provo, although demand often exceeds supply on Provo. Most roads are fairly basic, although those on Provo have been upgraded and paved, and all parts are easily accessible. In Jan 2003 construction work began on widening Leeward Highway to 4 lanes, an 18-month project likely to disrupt traffic. Gasoline was US$3.96 a gallon in 2003 and rising. Maximum speed in urban areas is 20 mph and outside villages 40 mph, but on Provo driving is erratic and no one (except visitors) pays heed to speed limits, not even the Traffic Department. Local drivers do not dim their headlights at night. Pedestrians and cyclists should be careful on the roads because of the speeding drivers and heavy construction vehicles.

Car
Drive on the left. Watch out for donkeys on Grand Turk

Taxis charge a basic fare of US$2 per mile, although drivers are not always consistent. Complaints are frequent. Taxis can be hired for island tours, agree the price beforehand.

Taxi

Keeping in touch

Internet There are 2 internet cafés on Provo: *TCI Online* in Ports of Call, Grace Bay area, T9414711, and *The Computer Guy's Internet Café*, Leeward Highway, Central Provo, T9464152.

Post On Grand Turk the post office is on Front St near *FirstCaribbean International Bank*, T9462801. *Federal Express*, T9462542 (Grand Turk), T9464682 (Provo); *DHL*, T9464352 (Provo); *UPS* agent, T9462030, incoming only package delivery, Cee's Building, Pond St, Grand Turk and on Provo through *Provo Travel*, T9464080. Postage for postcards US$0.50 to USA, US$0.60 Canada/UK, US$0.80 Europe, US$1.10 Africa. Letters each half an ounce US$0.60, US$0.80, US$1, US$1.25 respectively.

Telephone
IDD code: 649
Grand Turk, Provo and South Caicos have a modern local and international telephone service, with Cable and Wireless offices in Grand Turk and Provo. Telephone services on the North and Middle Caicos and Salt City are improving. There are 5 exchanges, 946 and 941 for land lines, 231 for post pay cell phones and 241 and 242 for prepaid cell phones. Local directory assistance T118, international operator T115; credit card calls T111, 1-800-8778000, 3 mins minimum. The small volume of international calls means that costs are higher than in the USA. The local phone book has a list of charges to anywhere in the world. Pay phones take phone cards, which are available from Cable and Wireless and from many outlets including Provo Airport in US$5, US$10 and US$20 denominations plus 10%. The Cable and Wireless Public Sales Office in Grand Turk and Provo has a public fax service, F9462497/4210. Paging service is popular among businesses and cell phones are widely used. Many visitors bring their own cell phones, or you can rent one while on the islands. Local calls made from or to a cell phone are US$0.50 a minute, billed to the caller. International calls from cell phones cost the same as from a regular phone. Internet service is also

Turks & Caicos Islands

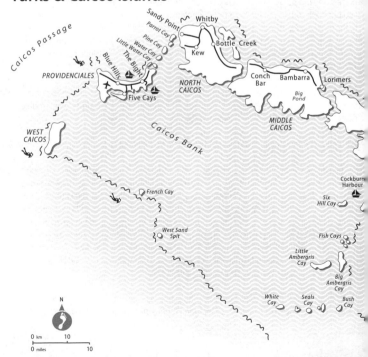

available. There is a telephone directory published by Olympia Publishing (saunders@tciway.tc) with lots of useful information about the TCI, more useful than the Cable and Wireless directory.

Food and drink

Expensive to mid-range meals in restaurants and bars will usually be of good quality. Watch out for specials with no posted prices. Wine by the glass is US$4.50-8.50 while beer ranges from US$3.50-6. With over 50 restaurants and delis on Provo alone, prices are maily expensive but local restaurants with native cuisine are reasonable. Many restaurants feature vegetarian meals and low-fat cooking. All food is imported (except seafood) from Miami, occasionally from the Dominican Republic, and therefore not cheap. Many restaurants charge a 10% gratuity in addition to the 10% government tax. Restaurants owned and operated by the islanders, or 'Belongers', do not have to charge tax because they serve the local market. Some do not charge for service. Check your bill carefully and tip, or not, accordingly.

Seafood, lobster, conch with peas 'n' rice is standard island fare

Entertainment

There are a few night spots on Providenciales, but on the other islands you will find only occasional live music after dinner at a restaurant. Local bands play mostly calypso, reggae and the traditional island music with its Haitian and African influences. Bands from the USA and UK are sometimes invited in high season. On Provo, ask hoteliers and residents when and where live bands are playing. Latin influence in discos, featuring soca, reggae and latino, loudly! Check cover charges before you go. Nightlife does not start until 2200-2300.

Flora and fauna

The islands support 175 resident and migrant species of birds, including flocks of greater flamingos, frigate birds, ospreys, brown pelicans, the ruby-throated humming bird, the belted kingfisher, white-billed tropic birds, black-necked stilts, snowy plovers, peregrine falcons, red-tailed hawks, northern harriers, Baltimore orioles and scarlet tanagers, and many others. *Birds of the Turks and Caicos*, by Richard Ground (Chief Justice in 2003), is available through the National Trust office, tcnattrust@tciway.tc There are lizards, iguanas, 2 species of snake, including a pygmy boa, and 2 species of bat. The south parts of North, Middle and East Caicos have been designated an internationally important wetland under the Ramsar Convention for the protection of waterbirds, lobster, conch, flora and a fish nursery.

The National Environment Centre, in the Bight, Provo, is open to the public. It is also home to the Coastal Resources Management Project, T9415122.

The islands boast 11 national parks, four sanctuaries, 10 nature reserves and seven historical sites; entrance to sanctuaries by permit only

Turks & Caicos Islands

(map)

Atlantic Ocean

Drum Point
EAST CAICOS
Columbus Passage
SOUTH CAICOS
GRAND TURK
Cockburn Town
Gibbs Cay
...g Cay
Long Cay
Penniston Cay
Cotton Cay
Martin Alonza Pinzon Cay (East Cay)
Balfour Town
Salt Cay
Big Sand Cay
Endymion Rock
South Rock

Diving and marine life

The sea is often rough between February and March

The islands have become one of the most highly regarded diving locations in the region, with excellent visibility, unspoilt reefs, unpolluted waters and uncrowded dive spots. Great care has been taken in the past to conserve the reefs and the coral is in very good condition. However, a new cruise ship dock to be built by 2004 in front of the town in Grand Turk is predicted to damage much of the famous wall on the west side of that island. Marine life is varied and beautiful and can be enjoyed by snorkellers and sailors as well as scuba divers. Colourful fish and grouper can be seen on the coral, and close to the shore there are green and loggerhead turtles and manta and spotted eagle rays. Beyond the reef are the game fish such as tuna, blue marlin, wahoo, snapper, bill fish and barracuda. Dolphins are commonly seen playing in the wake of dive boats and there is a friendly bottlenose dolphin named Jo Jo, which has been declared a National Treasure. He is not seen so frequently now, but he used to visit the Princess Alexandra Marine Park where he played with people in the sea, often coming in very close to shore. For more information contact Jo Jo's warden at VHF 'Sea Base' channel 68 or 73, or T/F9415617, www.jojo.tc In Jan-Mar, humpback whales migrate through the deep Turks Island Passage on their way south to the Silver and Mouchoir Banks breeding grounds north of the Dominican Republic (see box page 344). Whale watching is co-ordinated by the Department of Environmental Heritage and Parks, which has drawn up rules to protect the whales, and several dive operators offer whale watching tours in the season, Jan-Mar. The best months for diving are Apr-Nov. Some of the best diving is off the wall at Northwest Point, West Caicos and French Cay. Do not remove live coral, sea fans or other marine life. The use of spearguns is prohibited.

Dive centres

There is a recompression chamber at Associated Medical Practice on Provo, T9464242, DAN insurance is accepted

On **Provo** there are 9 land-based dive operations offering courses (resort course approximately US$130, full certification US$400) and dive packages. The standard cost of a 2-tank dive is US$100. Several companies are based at **Turtle Cove**: *Flamingo Divers*, at *Turtle Cove Landing*, Providenciales, T/F9464193, www.Provo.net/flamingo, caters for small groups, PADI and SSI instruction; Art Pickering's *Provo Turtle Divers*, T9464232, provoturtledivers@provo.net, at Turtle Cove Marina and at *Ocean Club Resort*, and *Comfort Suites*, Grace Bay, is also recommended for small groups of experienced divers at similar prices; *Ocean Vibes*, T9413141, oceanvibes@tciway.tc, also at Turtle Cove Marina does small dive groups and other watersports; *Caicos Adventures*, South Side Marina, T/F9413346, www.caicosadventures.com, has a comfortable 52-ft motor catamaran for dive trips to West Caicos, French Cay for small groups, NAUI/CMAS. On **Grace Bay** *Dive Provo*, at the *Allegro Resort*, T9465029/5040, www.diveprovo.com, has three boats, windsurfing, kayaks, shop in Ports of Call. At **Leeward Marina** is *Big Blue Unlimited*, T9465034, www.bigblue.tc, which specializes in eco-adventures, small groups, private charters; *J&B Tours*, T9465047, www.jbtours.com, has 24-ft dive boat, courses, 1 tank US$60, 2 tanks US$85 and *Silver Deep*, T9465612, www.silverdeep.com, private dives, 3 divers US$280 including tanks, 4-6 divers US$85 per person including tanks. The newest dive operation with the latest in hi-tech diving is *O2 Technical Diving*, T/F9413499.

There are 2 live-aboard boats based in Provo for those who want to spend a week doing nothing but diving. *Sea Dancer* (Peter Hughes Diving, T800-9-DANCER or 305-6699475, whatever@tciway.tc) operates from Sellar's Pond, Turtle Cove, has accommodation for 18 people and offers 5 dives a day around French Cay, West Caicos and Northwest Point. For the *Turks and Caicos Aggressor*, T2311322 or contact the Aggressor Fleet Limited, T800-3482628, www.turksandcaicosaggressor.com

The three dive shops on Grand Turk also offer whale watching in season, see Whale and dolphin watching, page 58

Grand Turk The highlight of diving is the wall off Cockburn Town, which drops suddenly from 40 ft to 7,000 ft only a quarter of a mile offshore. There are 25 moored sites along the wall where you can find coral arches, tunnels, canyons, caves and overhangs. A mile east of Grand Turk is **Gibbs Cay**, where snorkellers are taken for a great day trip, suitable for all the family. As well as a pristine sandy beach and beautifully clear water, there are friendly sting rays which will come right up to you and nose around. Picnics are usually provided and conch is often caught along the way to make a really fresh conch salad. There are 3 very experienced dive organizers who have been diving these waters for decades and can offer a range of courses, full accommodation and diving packages. All 3 have retail outlets and offer photographic services with equipment rental. Rates are US$35-50 for a single-tank dive, US$60-75 for 2 tanks, depending on whether you have pre-booked, although there are extra charges for long distance trips such as to South Caicos, which is an hour there and 2 hours on the way back. *Blue Water Divers Ltd* is on Front St, next to the museum, T/F9462432, www.grandturkscuba.com, the only PADI 5-star operation on the island. *Sea Eye Diving*, run by Cecil Ingham and Connie Rus, has a range of watersports on offer. They have NAUI and PADI instruction, frequent cay trips, T/F9461407, www.reefnet.on.ca/grandturk *Oasis Divers* is run by Everette Freites (see whale watching) and Dale Barker, T9461128, www.oasisdivers.com, taking small groups aboard 28-ft dive boats.

Salt Cay *Reef Runners*, T9466901, www.reefrunnerssc.com, has a 24-ft Carolina skiff which takes you to the main dive site in 5 mins. A 1-tank, 1-day dive package is US$80, but most people take a 7-night, 5-days diving package for US$999 including accommodation, transfers, 3 meals and 3 dives a day. Another operator is *Salt Cay Divers*, T9466906, www.saltcaydivers.tc, with 3 Carolina skiffs and a yacht for non-diving activities, accommodation and diving packages. A 2-tank morning diving session is US$60, a single dive US$35. There are 7 moored dive sites and off Great Sand Cay lies a British shipwreck from 1790, now a National Monument, the *Endymion*, still loaded with cannon. A wall chart telling her story is on sale at gift shops on the islands and at the museum on Grand Turk. She was found in 1991 by Brian Sheedy with the help of a local historian, Josiah Marvel. It is thought that this is the only unsalvaged 18th-century wreck in the world which the diving public can visit. The wreck lies in about 25 ft of water with the remains of 2 other ships nearby: a Civil War steamer and a ship dating from around 1900. The coral is prolific and the fish are plentiful.

South Caicos and Long Cay On the west side of the Columbus Passage the wall along the east shores of South Caicos and Long Cay drops gradually or steeply from a depth of about 50 ft, with many types of coral and a variety of fish of all sizes. Snorkelling is rewarding with several shallow reefs close to the shore, but the diving is really for advanced divers, as it is best on the windward side where there are strong currents and surges. On South Caicos *South Caicos Ocean Haven* T9463444, www.oceanhaven.tc, offers excellent diving and snorkelling with eagle rays about 10 mins offshore, packages available. Alternatively join an excursion with one of the dive operators on Grand Turk.

Don't be alarmed if you meet sharks; there have been sightings of black tip, reef, bull, tiger and hammerhead sharks as well as manta rays

Beaches and watersports

Grace Bay on Provo is the longest stretch of sand, at 12 miles, and despite the hotels it is possible to find plenty of empty space, but *no* shade. There is rarely any shade on the beaches except umbrellas supplied by resorts, usually for their guests only. Most watersports can be arranged through the hotels or tour operators.

230 miles of white-sand beaches and coral surround the islands

Several tour operators represent all **day sails**, **scuba dives** or **snorkelling trips** or you can contact the captains direct or through your hotel. Sailing and beach cruising trips from Provo include: *Sail the Trade Winds* Schooner, *Atabeyra*, anchored at Leeward Marina, offering Pirates Cay full- and half-day sails and ecology tours, cold drinks and snorkelling gear included, call *Sun Charters* T9415363; *Beluga*, Leeward Going Through, T/F9464396, VHF 68, 37-ft catamaran, private, full- and half-day sails; *Phoenix*, a 62-ft catamaran and *Arielle*, a 52-ft catamaran, offer full- and half-day cruises, snorkelling, trips arranged by *Sail Provo*, T9464783, www.sailprovo.com Also at Leeward Marina, *Catch the Wave Charters*, T/F9413047, www.tcimall.tc/catchthewave, has a 26-ft Bowrider, comfortable and roomy, and a 27-ft World Cat, both with shade tops. They specialize in private charters and offer bonefishing, flyfishing, waterskiing, beach cruising, reggae sunset cruises; *J & B Tours* (see page 230) offers beach and snorkelling excursions, barbecues, waterskiing, island getaways, trips to Conch Farm, caves on Middle Caicos, glo-worm cruises, fishing and scuba;

Day sails

Turks & Caicos Islands

Silver Deep (see page 230) offers similar beach cruises, glo-worm charters, secluded get-aways, trips to Middle and North Caicos. Exclusively at Sapodilla Bay, *Ocean Outback*'s 'Ulti-mate Getaway', all-day adventure by 18-ft or 24-ft runabouts visiting settlers' ruins, pirate caves and rock carvings, snorkelling, beach BBQ, snacks, beers, round-trip transportation included, T9410824, www.Provo.net/OceanOutback. *Ocean Obsession* offers day charters and sunset cruises aboard its 55-ft motor yacht, T9465011. *Windsurfing Provo* at *Ocean Club*, Grace Bay, T9465649 and evenings T9465490, windpro@tciway.tc, offers hobie waves, hobie cats, small motor boats and kayaking as well as **windsurfing**. Owner Mike Rosati is an expert and an excellent teacher.

Fishing

Two international billfishing tournaments are held annually, T9413781; they are big events with lots of parties

Fishing is popular and May is the prime time. Provo and Pine Cay have the best bonefishing though it is also possible at South Caicos, Middle Caicos, North Caicos and Salt Cay. Fisher-men have not organized themselves into offering packages, so you have to find your own accommodation and fishing guide. Shop around because visiting experienced fishermen have reported a lack of skill, professionalism and simple amenities among local guides. A US$16 sport fishing licence, for pole fishing only, is required from the Fisheries Department, Grand Turk, T9462970, or South Caicos, T9463306, or Provo, T9464017. Ask your guide whether the fishing licence is included in his package. Spear fishing is not allowed.

On **Providenciales**, the choices are: *Captain Barr Gardiner's Bonefish Unlimited* (Box 241, T9464874, bonefish@provo.net), *Light Tackle and 'Black Diamond' Fishing and Boat Tours* (T9464451), Earl Musgrove. Leeward Going Through Marina is the best place to find and talk to fishermen, or try to reach them on the radio, VHF 16. *J & B Tours* (see above) will arrange full- and half-day fishing. *Gilley's* restaurant will cook your catch. *Silver Deep* (see above) includes bone, fly, light tackle and night fishing in its itinerary. There are 2 deep-sea sport fishing operators in Turtle Cove Marina: *Gwod Phrienz* (Good Friends), contact Algie Dean, T9464342, reservations@tciway.tc; *Gwendolyn*, 45-ft Hatteras sportfisher, T9465321, www.fishingtci.com Rates approximately US$400 half day, US$750 full day. On **Grand Turk** fishing can be arranged through Ossie (Oswald) Virgil, of Virgil's Taxis at the airport, T9462018. Ossie also arranges an annual game fishing tournament in Aug. The record catch is a 460-lb marlin caught in 1998 by Art Pickering of Provo. On **Middle Caicos** fishing and boating is arranged through the District Commissioner's Office, T9466100, with Dotis Arthur and her husband, Cardinal. On **South Caicos**, bonefish specialist Julius 'Goo the Guide' Jennings, US$20 per hr, can be contacted through the *South Caicos Ocean Haven*. On **North Caicos** call *Beach Cruisers*, T9467113.

Other activities

Parasailing with *Turtle Parasailing*, *Turtle Cove Inn*, costs US$60 a flight, T/F9415389, parasail@tciway.tc *Ocean Obsessions* also offers parasailing and its Leeward Marina Office is T6495011. **Jetskis** are banned from any of the marine parks, although they may be used in parts of Leeward Channel and on the Banks or rented from *Sun and Fun Seasports* at Lee-ward Marina, T9465724.

Holidays and festivals

New Year's Day is celebrated with a *Junkanoo Jump-Up* from midnight to sunrise on most of the islands, with lots of noise and masquerades. Most events are linked to the sea and land-based activities are tacked on to regattas or fishing tournaments. In Providenciales the *Billfishing Tournament* (see page 232) is a big event with lots of partying. *Provo Day Sum-mer Festival* held over a weekend at the end of **Jul**, sees the crowning of Miss Turks and Caicos. In **Oct** there is an *Annual Amateur Open Golf Championship*; tourists are welcome to participate. On Grand Turk a *Conch Carnival* is held in **Jun**, with island music and dancing, competitions, snorkelling treasure hunts, lots of conch fritters, etc, while the *Heineken Game Fishing Tournament* (with beach parties every evening) and the *Cactus Fest* are held in **Aug**; the latter has competitions for sports, costumes, bands and gospel, a float parade, dancing and an art exhibition. *Guy Fawkes Bonfire Night* is celebrated on **5 Nov**. *Museum Day* is at the end of **Nov**, celebrating the anniversary of the opening of the museum with music, cho-ral singing, children's events. In **Dec**, '*Run Turks and Caicos*' (first week), is followed by the

> ### Things to do in the Turks and Caicos Islands
>
> - Explore the huge and beautiful **caves** on Middle Caicos, formerly home to Taíno Indians, and walk or bicycle the **Crossing Place Trail** along the beautiful north coast.
> - See the **carvings in stone** dating back to the 17th century on the hill behind the old Mariner Inn on Provo.
> - Go to the abandoned old **salt cellars** under the houses on Salt Cay.
> - Don't miss the excellent **museum** on Grand Turk.
> - Walk for miles along the deserted beach west of **Whitby**, North Caicos.

Christmas Tree-lighting Ceremony in the second week and then the *Anglican Church Bazaar* a week before Christmas. The Methodist Church holds a fair on **Boxing Day**. On North Caicos, *Festarama* is in **Jul**; on Middle Caicos, *Expo* is in **Aug**, with traditional sailboat races and a procession along the Crossing Place Trail; the oldest festival in the islands, on South Caicos, the *Regatta*, with power boat and sail boat races and associated activities, takes place on the weekend closest to **24 May**.

Health

There are no endemic tropical diseases and no malaria, no special vaccinations are required prior to arrival. Aids cases have been reported. See main Health section on page 48.

Grand Turk

Grand Turk is not a resort island although there are a few struggling hotels and dive operations that concentrate mostly on the wall just off the west coast. It is a wonderfully laid-back place to come for a holiday but the atmosphere may change with the advent of cruise ships to the new port to be built during 2003. The vegetation is mostly scrub and cactus, and wild donkeys and horses roam freely. Behind the town and around the island are old salt pans, with crumbling walls and ruined windmills, where pelicans and other waterbirds fish. The east coast is often littered with tree trunks and other debris which have drifted across from Africa, lending credence to the claim that Columbus could have been carried here, rather than further north in the Bahamas chain. There are great sea views from the 1852 lighthouse at the extreme north of the island. Grand Turk is the seat of government and the second-largest population centre, although it has an area of only 7 sq miles.

IDD code: 649
Colour map 2, grid A2
Population: 2,000

Ins and outs

Airlines and schedules tend to change often. Most visitors arrive in Provo and then shuttle over on a small aircraft. There are frequent inter-island flights and it is possible to turn up on the day you want to travel and catch the next flight. A taxi from the airport will cost US$4 to the *Osprey Beach*, the first hotel you come to in Cockburn Town. If coming by yacht, the harbour is in North Creek.

Getting there
See Transport, page 236, for further details

Taxis are the only form of public transport. Jeeps, cars and bicycles can be rented. Distances are not great and if you are based in Cockburn Town you may not need a vehicle.

Getting around

Around the island

Cockburn Town, the capital and financial centre, has some attractive colonial buildings, mostly along Duke Street, or Front Street, as it is usually known. The government offices are in a small restored square with cannons facing the sea. The

Cockburn Town

post office and government buildings are painted in blues, ranging from deep turquoise to almost white, nicely matching the ocean. Despite opposition from divers and other conservationists, a plan to build a cruise ship dock has been approved and should be built by 2004. The jetty will extend about 2,000 ft from shore, including a T at the end, and will accommodate two 980-ft ships, each carrying about 2,000 passengers, equivalent to the local population.

The oldest church on Grand Turk is **St Thomas' Anglican church** (inland, near the water catchment tanks), built by Bermudan settlers. After a while it was considered too far to walk to the centre of the island and **St Mary's Anglican church** was built in 1899 on Front Street. This is now a pro-Cathedral with the southern Bahamas and is the first cathedral in the islands. The **Victoria Library**, built to commemorate 50 years of Queen Victoria's reign, is also an interesting building. **Odd Fellows Lodge**, opposite the salt pier, is thought to be one of the oldest buildings on the island and was probably the place where the abolition of slavery was proclaimed in 1832.

The Tourist Board office is in a renovated town customs building and warehouse, built in the old Bermudan architectural style. It sits on the water at the north end of Cockburn Town and is a pleasant place to stop off.

The **Turks and Caicos National Museum** is in the beautifully renovated Guinep Lodge. The exhibition on the ground floor is of the early 16th-century wreck of a Spanish caravel found on the Molasses Reef between West Caicos and French Cay in only 20 ft of water. The ship is believed to have been on an illegal slaving mission in the islands, as evidenced by locked leg irons found on the site. A guided tour is highly recommended although not essential. Upstairs there is an exhibition of local artefacts, photos, stamps, coins, a few Taíno beads, figures and potsherds. A local historian, the late Herbert Sadler, compiled many volumes on the theory of Columbus' landfall and local history. A **Science Building** has been completed beside the museum, which houses a conservation laboratory, the only one of its kind in the English-speaking Caribbean. The most recent find was a Taíno paddle buried in the peat bottom of North

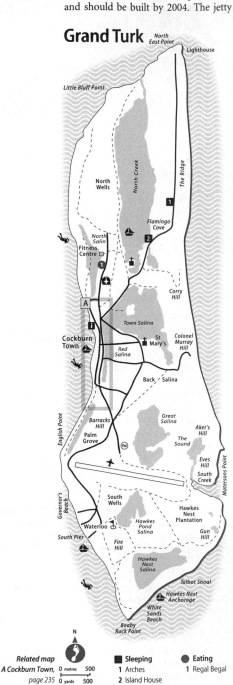

Grand Turk

North East Point

Lighthouse

Little Bluff Point

North Wells

North Creek

The Ridge

Flamingo Cove

North Salin
Fitness Centre

Corry Hill

Town Salina

Cockburn Town

St Mary's

Colonel Murray Hill

Red Salina

Back Salina

English Point

Barracks Hill
Palm Grove

Great Salina

Aker's Hill

The Sound

Eves Hill

South Creek

Matersons Point

Governor's Beach

South Wells

Hawkes Nest Plantation

Waterloo

Hawkes Pond Salina

Gun Hill

South Pier

Fire Hill

Hawkes Nest Salina

Talbot Shoal

Hawkes Nest Anchorage

White Sands Beach

Boaby Rock Point

N

Related map
A Cockburn Town,
page 235

0 metres 500
0 yards 500

■ **Sleeping**
1 Arches
2 Island House

● **Eating**
1 Regal Begal

Creek, which has been carbon dated to AD 1100. Also beside the museum is a new and delightful garden of native plants. The original building on the site was destroyed by fire, but the oven from the old slave kitchen and the water catchment tank have been renovated and preserved as garden features. ■ *Mon-Fri 1000-1600, Sat 1000-1300. US$5 for non-residents, US$2 residents, US$0.50 students. T9462160.*

The Governor's residence, **Waterloo**, south of the airport, was built in 1815 by a Bermudan salt merchant as a private residence and acquired for the head of government in 1857. Successive governors and administrators have modified and extended it, prompted partly by hurricane damage in 1866 and 1945, and by the Queen's visit in 1966. In 1993 the building was again renovated and remodelled; the works were so extensive they constituted a near rebuilding of the historic residence. Governor's Beach is one of the nicest beaches and excellent for snorkelling, with isolated coral heads rising out of the sand and a wide variety of fish and invertebrates.

Further south is an ex-USAF base, known as **South Base**, which is now used as government offices, and beyond there some pleasant beaches on the south coast, with good snorkelling at White Sands beach by the point. US Navy, NASA and Coast Guard bases were once important for the economy of Grand Turk; John Glenn, the first American to orbit the earth, splashed down off Grand Turk in the 1960s.

The cays southeast of Grand Turk are a land and sea national park, sheltering Turks Head cacti on **Martin Alonza Pinzon Cay**, frigate birds on **Penniston Cay** and breeding sooty terns, noddy terns and other seabirds on **Gibbs Quay**. The lagoons and red mangroves of South Creek are also a national park, with a nursery for fish, crabs and other sea life, as well as a reserve for birds.

Essentials

Cockburn Town

Sleeping

Osprey Beach
Salt Raker Inn

Eating

3 Turks Head Inn

1 Courtyard Café
2 Poop Deck

LL-L *The Arches*, on North Ridge, T/F9462941. 4 townhouses each with 2 bedrooms, 2 bathrooms, balconies with views east and west for sunrise and sunset, can sleep 6 if you're good friends or family, a/c, fan, kitchen, pool, bicycles, dive gear storage and washing area, housekeeping and food available, new, clean and spacious, but some distance from the beach. **LL-L** *Osprey Beach*, T9462232, www.ospreybeachhotel.com 28 standard or deluxe beachfront rooms, those on ground floor open directly onto the sand, suites available with kitchenette, a/c, TV, fan, fridge, pool, lots of packages available for divers or non-divers, including 2-centre with *South Caicos Ocean Haven*, Mitch Rolling from Blue Water Divers plays and sings poolside some nights (CD available). **L-A** *Salt Raker Inn*, T9462260, www.microplan.com/bluerake.htm/, is an old Bermuda-style building on Duke St, built by Bermudan shipwright Jonathon Glass in the 1840s, facing the beach. It is very friendly, relaxed and unpretentious. 10 rooms, 3 suites, sea or garden view, balconies or patios, a/c, fan, fridge, TV. **AL-A** *Turks Head Inn* on Duke St, T9462466, www.grand-turk.com Built in 1869 by Jonathon Glass first as a private house and

Sleeping
All hotels offer dive packages with local dive companies

▶ ## The Battle of Waterloo

Former Governor John Kelly was a keen golfer and when he took over the Governor's residence, Waterloo, in 1996, he soon had designs on the 20 acres of wilderness surrounding his new home. The overgrown land was attacked by a battalion of volunteer kindred spirits to create a nine-hole, par three course. The acacia thorn bushes and vines fought back as trees not seen for years were exposed and park land appeared. The wilderness was finally dominated by a team from Her Majesty's

Prison and some heavy equipment operators who uprooted the big thorn trees. The opening of the golf club was planned for June 1997, the anniversary of the Battle of Waterloo, but actually took place in January 1998, with 43 players in the Governor's Trophy competition. Visitors may pay their green fee at the Governor's office – a slightly unusual arrangement. T2312515 and speak to the former president of the ' golf club', Clifford Wilson, or try Moses Britton, T2415184.

later used as a doctor's dispensary, the American Consulate and a guesthouse for the British Government, it is set back from the beach surrounded by tall trees. Renovated and decorated in period style, 7 rooms, with wooden floors, beds and balconies, phone, minibar, 2 family rooms, outside dining and upstairs dining deck, pizza ovens, barbecue night with live local music, weekly dive slide show (Oasis Divers).

North of town on Lighthouse Rd, **L** *Island House*, T9461519, www.islandhouse-tci.com Price includes tax and service, golf cart and airport transfers for stays of 4 nights, 8 different suites or studios with kitchen and barbecue, spacious, fully equipped, TV, phone, a/c, fan, on edge of North Creek, pool, free laundry facilities, maid service, bicycles available, fishing can be arranged, popular with people who like to spend a month or two on the island in the winter, attentive and welcoming management, contact Colin or Donna Brooker.

Eating

The best restaurants and bars are at the hotels

The *Courtyard Café* is in the courtyard of the *Osprey Beach* across the road from the beach, surrounded by trees. Phyllis Hayward serves breakfast from 0700 and lunches until 1500, excellent, freshly prepared meals, pastas and salads and home-made desserts, nothing fried. *Peanut's* snack bar at the airport. Hot snacks, peanuts and drinks. The *Poop Deck* is a tiny bar, set back from the road in the centre of town by the sea, local food and hamburgers at lunchtime, chicken and chips in the evenings. *Regal Begal* serves local food, on the road north of town on the west side of North Creek, a favourite lunch place. The outdoor *Salt Raker Inn* is recommended for good food and pleasant company. It is a popular meeting place with live music and a sing-along some nights. The *Turks Head Inn* is a gathering place with a friendly bar and good food. Their barbecue night is Fri when they have live music. For local food and lunch specials try *Touch of Class* on the road south out of town, a/c, TV, bar, filling, tasty portions. *Water's Edge*, T9461680, offers a very cheerful, informal atmosphere for lunch and dinner with ample portions served and a reasonably priced menu, lots of conch. Mitch entertains here on Sat. Scooter rental available.

Nightlife

Grand Turk is not an island where you will find lots of nightlife. Most of the evening activity takes place when people get together for meals and drinks at the small inns and restaurants, with live music some nights. Do not expect a lot of action.

Sports

See also watersports, page 231

Golf The former Governor created a 9-hole golf course on Grand Turk in the grounds of his residence (see box on page 236). There is a small **fitness centre** next to South Primary School.

Transport

Long distance Air *Lynx Air* flies once a week, Sat, from Fort Lauderdale, T954-7729808, 1995 West Commercial Blvd, Ft Lauderdale (T9461971 on Grand Turk). *TCA* flies from Cap Haitiën, Middle Caicos, North Caicos, Providenciales, Salt Cay and South Caicos. *Sky King* (T9461520 on Grand Turk) has scheduled flights from Provo and South Caicos and will fly to Cuba, the Dominican Republic, Bahamas and Haiti on request. *Interisland Airways*,

Turks & Caicos Islands

T9461667, has scheduled services throughout the Turks and Caicos (6 daily flights to Provo, 3 a week to Salt Cay and South Caicos) and chartered flights to Cuba, Cap Haïtien, Puerto Plata and other Caribbean destinations.

Local Jeeps or cars can be rented from *Tropical Auto Leasing*, US$55 per day, everything included except fuel, T9461000 *Sunshine Auto Leasing*, by airport, T9461588; *Dutchie's Car Rental*, Airport Rd, T9462244; *C J Car Rental*, T9462744. If you rent a bicycle, jeep or car, note that the islanders completely ignore the 20 mph speed limit in town (and 40 mph outside), particularly on Pond St, recommended to stay on Front St/Duke St route through town and exercise caution elsewhere. Fatal accidents have occurred. **Boat** There is a safe harbour and marina at Flamingo Cove, North Creek, T9462227.

Banks *FirstCaribbean International Bank*, T9462831; *Turks & Caicos Banking Co Ltd*, Grand Turk, T9462368; *Scotiabank* at Harbour House, T9462506. **Medical services** There is a small, understaffed **hospital** on the north side of town, T9462333, and a government clinic in town, T9462328, open 0800-1230, 1400-1630. The other islands organize emergency air evacuation to Grand Turk hospital. **Directory**

Salt Cay

Seven miles south of Grand Turk, Salt Cay is out of the past, with windmills, salt sheds and other remnants of the old salt industry and little else. The island was first visited by the Bermudans in 1645; they started making salt here in 1673 and maintained a thriving salt industry until its collapse in the 1960s. Production ceased all together in 1971. The main village is **Balfour Town**, divided into North Side and South Side, noted for its Bermudan buildings and pretty cottages with stone walls around the gardens. The **White House**, which dominates the skyline, was built in the 1830s of Bermudan stone brought in as ballast by the Harriott family during the height of the salt industry. The **Methodist Church** nearby, one of several churches on the island, is over 130 years old. Snorkelling is good and diving is excellent; there are 10 moored dive sites along the wall, with tunnels, caves and undercuts. Between January and March you can often see the humpback whales migrating through the channel as they pass close to the west coast. The island has been designated a UNESCO World Heritage Site.

IDD code: 649
Population: 208

Plant life was curtailed during the salt raking days to prevent rainfall. Look into some of the ruined houses and you will find salt still stored in the cellars

Turks & Caicos Islands

Salt Cay

Northeast Point
North Beach
Northwest Point
Grey Salina
WHALE ISLAND
Whale House Bay
Deanes Dock
Town Salinas
Taylor Hill
Long Bay
D C's Office
Methodist
White House
North Creek
Balfour Town
South Creek
South Point

■ **Sleeping**
1 Castaways
2 Mount Pleasant Guest House
3 Pirates Hideaway
4 Sunset House
5 Sunset Reef
6 Tradewinds
7 Windmills Plantation

● **Eating**
1 Island Thyme

N
km   1
miles   1

The most expensive and exclusive hotel is the **LL** *Windmills Plantation* on a 2½ mile beach, T9466962, www.saltcaysite.com It appeals to people who want to do nothing undisturbed, 7 suites, including all food and drink, meals taken family style, local recipes, saltwater pool, no children. **L-AL** *Castaways*, T9466921 or 315-5360737, www.vikingresort.com 6 1-bedroom villas along the beach north of *Windmills Plantation*, available for rent Nov-Apr, self-catering, take supplies with you. **L-AL** *Pirates Hideaway*, Victoria St, T/F9466909, www.pirateshideaway.com 4 rooms in cottage, 'Blackbeard Quarters', or rent whole house, or suite, 'The Crow's Nest', sea views, balcony, fans, meals on request, complimentary bikes and kayaks, boat trips, ask about the workshops held here by

Sleeping
All hotels can arrange dive packages

eminent international artists if you are keen on painting. **L-AL** *Tradewinds*, Victoria St, T9466906, www.tradewinds.tc 5 1-bedroom suites each sleep 4, new, kitchenettes, on the beach surrounded by casuarina trees, screened patios, deck for whale watching, hammocks, barbecue, walking distance from the dock, bicycles. **L** *Sunset Reef*, in USA T410-8893662, www.sunsetreef.com 1 or 2-bedroom villa with en suite bathrooms, on the beach with wonderful view from the deck, look out for whales in season, all amenities, well-equipped and comfortable, golf cart or bicycle rental. At the other end of the scale is the cheerful **AL-A** *Mount Pleasant Guest House*, T9466927, www.mtpleasant.tc Standard rooms or deluxe with private bath and a/c, video/TV, library, bicycles, outdoor restaurant/bar with some of the best food on the island, dive packages, very laid-back, relaxed, run by long resident Brian Sheedy. He also has a 7-room, 5-bathroom house on the waterfront for rent to groups. **AL** *The Salt Cay Sunset House*, Victoria St, Balfour Town, T/F9466942, seaone@tciway.tc Former 1832 plantation home run by Michelle, Paul and lots of cats, high ceilings, 3 bedrooms with bath, fans, comfortable, veranda with *Blue Mermaid Sunset Café*, meal packages available, special needs catered for, good food, sea view.

Eating See *Blue Mermaid Sunset Café* and *Mount Pleasant Guest House,* above. Also *Island Thyme*, T9466977, www.islandthyme.tc A pleasant, screened restaurant and bar, limited seating so reservations advised, mostly seafood, some chicken, pasta, lots of cocktails, run by Porter and Haidee Williams, open Fri-Wed for lunch US$7-10, 1200-1400, early bird special 1700-1800, dinner 1900-2100, entrées US$16-28, 3-course meal about US$35, cocktails US$4-8, wine US$30-80, closing at 2200, breakfast US$9-15 on request, no credit cards. For full meals, drinks and snacks, try the *Smuggler's Tavern* at *Pirate's Hideaway*.

Transport
There is a paved airstrip for small aircraft, around which a fence has been erected to keep out the donkeys. A day trip is possible from Grand Turk or Provo

The island is served by *TCA* (T9466968 on Salt Cay), with 2 5-min flights Mon, Wed, Fri from Grand Turk, 1 at 0645 and 1 at 1715, returning immediately. *InterIsland Airways* also flies from Grand Turk Mon, Wed, Fri, 0900 and 1650, returning 0920 and 1700. They fly from Provo daily. Alternatively, charter a flight, or get a seat on someone else's charter, which costs the same if you can fill the aircraft, or contact the District Commissioner's Office on Salt Cay (or *Mount Pleasant Guest House*, who cross regularly to do shopping) for details of ferries. The only public transport on the island is the taxi van run by Nathan Smith (T9466920), airport pickup and touring; there are very few vehicles of any sort, only a few golf carts.

South Caicos

IDD code: 649
Population: 1,198
The beaches going east and north are totally deserted. You can walk for miles beachcombing along the east shore

The nearest Caicos island, 22 miles west of Grand Turk, South Caicos was once the most populous and the largest producer of salt in the region. It is now the main fishing port, having benefited from the most naturally protected harbour in the islands and is also known as East Harbour, or the 'rock'. As a result, yachts frequently call here and a popular annual regatta is held at the end of May. There is excellent diving along the drop-off to the south and the best snorkelling is on the windward side going east and north. Boat trips can be organized with fishermen to the island reserves of **Six Hill Cays** and **Long Cay**. Further south are the two **Ambergris Cays**, Big and Little, where there are caves and the diving and fishing are good.

According to legend, the rock formation at the entrance to the harbour is a sea monster, Sassy Sam, who guarded pirates' treasure on the island and was turned to stone

Cockburn Harbour is the only settlement and is an attractive, if rather run-down, little place with lots of old buildings, a pleasant waterfront with old salt warehouses and boats. The District Commissioner's house, currently unoccupied, stands atop a hill southeast of the village and can be recognized by its green roof. The **School For Field Studies** is in the 19th-century *Admiral's Arm Inn*, and attracts undergraduate students from abroad to the island to study reef ecology and marine resources, but otherwise there are very few visitors. Wild donkeys, cows and horses roam the island and several have made their home in an abandoned hotel construction site along the coast from the Residency. The **salinas** dominate the central part of the island and there is a 'boiling hole', connected to the sea by a subterranean passage, which was used to supply the salt pans. It makes an interesting walk and you may see flamingos.

AL *South Caicos Ocean Haven*, in town, T9463444, www.oceanhaven.tc Not luxurious, but a clean, quiet dive lodge, a top location for pristine diving and world class bonefishing, 22 rooms, a/c, diving packages available, saltwater pool, ocean kayaks, windsurfing, restaurant. **B** *Mae's Bed & Breakfast*, Forth St, T9463207. 3 rooms, laundry service, no credit cards. *Love's*, local dishes. *Muriel's*, Graham St, T9463535, native dishes. *Pond View*, T9463276, native dishes. *Dora's Lobster Pot* at the airport, T9463247.

Air See Getting around, page 226. There are a few taxis on the island, US$4 from the airport to *South Caicos Ocean Haven* hotel.

Sleeping & eating

Transport

Banks *FirstCaribbean International Bank* opens on Wed.

Directory

East Caicos

East Caicos has an area of 18 sq miles which makes it one of the largest islands, and Flamingo Hill, at 156 ft, is the highest point in the Turks and Caicos. A ridge runs along the north coast, but the rest of the island is swamp, creeks, mangrove and mudflats. Jacksonville, in the northwest, used to be the centre of a 50,000-acre sisal plantation and there was also a cattle farm at the beginning of the 20th century. The island is now uninhabited except for mosquitoes and wild donkeys. There is an abandoned railway left over from the plantation days and feral donkeys have worn paths through the scrub and sisal. Caves near Jacksonville, which were once mined for bat guano, contain petroglyphs carved on the walls and there is evidence of several Lucayan settlements. Splendid beaches include a 17-mile stretch on the north coast. Off the north coast, opposite Jacksonville, is **Guana Cay**, home to the Caicos iguana. There is no official transport to East Caicos, although people occasionally sail there.

Originally named Guana by the Lucayans

Middle Caicos

Also known as **Grand Caicos**, this is the largest of the islands, with an area of 48 sq miles. Its coastline is more dramatic than some of the other islands, characterized by limestone cliffs along the north coast, interspersed with long sandy beaches shaded by casuarina trees or secluded coves. The south part of the island is swamp and tidal flats. There are three settlements linked by the paved King's Road: **Conch Bar**, where there is an airstrip, a primary school, beach and guesthouses, **Bambarra** and **Lorimers**. A visit to the caves between Bambarra and Lorimers is a must. Originally used by Amerindians as dwelling places, they were later mined for guano. They are huge, complex and beautiful with bats, stalactites, stalagmites and underwater salt lakes with pink shrimps. Day tours are available from Provo at around US$145, including transport from Leeward, lunch, drinks, snorkelling and beachcombing. Archaeological excavations have uncovered a Lucayan ball court and a settlement near Armstrong Pond, due south of Bambarra, but these are not easily accessible. Evidence of the Lucayan civilization dates back to AD 750. Loyalist plantation ruins can also be explored. Bambarra beach is an empty, curving sweep of white sand, fringed with casuarina trees. Middle Caicos regatta is held here, but there are no facilities. A sand bar stretches half a mile out to **Pelican Cay**, which you can walk on at low tide. A pretty and popular cove is **Mudjeon Harbour**, just west of Conch Bar, protected by a sand bar and with shade under a rocky overhang. The reef juts out from the land here, and this can be spectacular in the winter months with the crashing waves. South of Middle Caicos is a nature reserve comprising a frigate bird breeding colony and a marine sinkhole with turtles, bonefish and shark. The blue hole shows up on the satellite photo of the islands on display in the museum in Grand Turk.

IDD code: 649 Population: 272

Turks & Caicos Islands

For tour information;
District
Commissioner's office,
T94661000
Wear strong
walking shoes

The **Crossing Place Trail** was a path worn by Lucayan Indians and later by slaves travelling between plantations. It is well marked and runs for 12 dramatic and beautiful miles (seven can be cycled) along the north coast, connecting Lorimers, Bambarra and Conch Bar. Developed by the National Trust to encourage ecotourism, the trail takes in beaches, coastal cliffs, Conch Bar, Indian Caves and the Blowing Hole. Tours from Provo and Grand Turk are available.

Sleeping   **LL-L** *Blue Horizon Resort* above Mudjeon Harbour beach, T9466141, www.bhresort.com 1- or 2-bedroomed cottages, screened porches, well-equipped, light and airy, on 50 acres (land for sale), weekly rental available, bicycles, fishing, tours arranged, bring your own groceries or ask for accommodation to be stocked with your requirements. **LL** *Dreamscape Villa*, Bambarra beach, T802-2952652 in the USA, T9466175 in the TCI (Ernest Forbes Jr), www.middlecaicos.com. 3 bedrooms, 2 bathrooms, outside shower, large veranda, 80 ft from water, hammock on deck. **L** *Seascape Villa*, www.caicosvilla.com On 2 acres of beachfront, view of reef and gardens from screened veranda, only 6 houses on this 5-mile stretch of shore, 2 miles, 30-min walk to Bambarra, sleeps 8, 2 bedrooms, a/c on first floor, 2 queen size beds in a/c loft, well-equipped kitchen, barbecue, games, books, caretakers. In Conch Bar: Stacia and Dolphus Arthur run **C** *Arthur's Guesthouse* next to Arthur's Store, T9466122. 1 double, 1 twin-bedded room, private bath, kitchen.

Eating   Canned foods and sodas are available from the few small stores in Conch Bar and fresh food arrives weekly on the ferry from Provo. However, it is advisable to bring your own food. Annie Taylor is known for her cooking and runs a restaurant on demand in her house. *Johnson's Bar* is open in Conch Bar most afternoons and evenings for cold beer, dominoes and music. *T&J Boutique* in Conch Bar has ice creams, cold drinks and fried chicken on Fri. *Daniel's Café*, Middle Caicos Co-Op, T9466132, serves native specialities for breakfast, lunch and dinner. *Elshaadi's*, at the airport, T9466136, snacks, burgers, conch fritters and drinks. *Shanique's Kitchen*, Conch Bar, T9466128. Reservations only, catering service for breakfast, lunch and dinner.

Transport   **Air**   See Getting around page 226.   **Road**   You have to take a taxi from the airport to where you are staying. Carlton Forbes runs a taxi service and fares are based on US$2 per mile for 2 people, eg Conch Bar to Bambarra US$14, to Lorimers US$20, about US$20-24 to *Seascape Villa*. **Bicycle**   *Sports Shack* in Conch Bar sells, rents and repairs bicycles. **Ferry**   A ferry service for cargo and passengers runs between Middle and North Caicos on Sat (Fri evening and Sun by appointment), starting from Middle at 0800, 30 mins, until early afternoon. The ferry carries 2 cars or 1 truck, US$20 per vehicle round trip, passengers US$2 round trip.

North Caicos

IDD code: 649
Population: 1,275

The lushest of the islands, North Caicos has taller trees than the other islands and attracts more rain. As on Middle and East Caicos, the south part of the island comprises swamp and mangrove.

There is one nature reserve at **Dick Hill Creek** and **Bellefield Landing Pond**, to protect the West Indian whistling duck and flamingos, and another at **Cottage Pond**, a fresh/saltwater sinkhole, about 170 ft deep, where there are grebes and West Indian whistling duck. **Pumpkin Bluff Pond** is a sanctuary for flamingos, Bahamian pintail and various waders. Flocks of flamingos can also be seen on **Flamingo Pond**, but take binoculars. There is a viewing point at the side of the road, but at low tide they can be a long way off. There is good snorkelling at **Three Mary's Cays** (a sanctuary for flamingos and an osprey nesting site) and **Sandy Point beach** to the west is lovely. The rough road to Three Mary's Cays is suitable for jeeps. The beaches are good along the north coast where the hotels are, although the best is a seven-mile strip west of Pumpkin Bluff, where there has been no development so far. It can be reached by walking along the beach or via a dirt road past the *Club Vacanze* (an Italian all-inclusive) car park. A cargo ship foundered on the reef in the 1980s, and is still stuck fast, making it of snorkelling interest. Construction of a new deep-water harbour has begun and when finished it will extend from Pine Cay to Bellefield Landing and over Dick Hill Creek.

Kew, in the centre, is a pretty little village with neat gardens and tall trees, many of them exotic fruit trees, to provide shade. There are three churches, a primary school, a shop and two bars. A lookout tower has been built to give 360° views. **Bottle Creek**, in the east, has a high school, clinic and churches. The paved road ends here and a rough road requiring 4WD continues to Toby Rock. **Whitby**, on the north coast, is rather spread out along the road, and this is where the few hotels are. Several expatriates have built their homes along Whitby Beach. **Sandy Point**, in the west, is a fishing community. North Caicos is the centre of basket making in the islands and there are several women who are experts in their craft, making beautiful bags and baskets using many colours and designs. Prices do not vary much from those in the shops in Providenciales. **Wades Green Plantation**, just to the west of Kew, is the best example of a Loyalist plantation in the islands, with many ruins, including a courtyard and a prison.

Sleeping

LL *Datai Villa*, www.datai-villa.com New in 1999, on beach, 2 separate buildings open on to patio with large deck, master bedroom in 1, 2 further bedrooms in the other, sleep 2-6 people. **LL-AL** *Ocean Beach*, T9467113. 10 units in condominiums, room only or suites, with up to 3 bedrooms, dining room/lounge, freshwater swimming pool, diving on site and excursions with Beach Cruiser Charters. **LL-AL** *Pelican Beach Hotel*, T9467112, www.tcimall.tc/pelicanbeach Friendly, few facilities, 14 rooms, 2 suites, the older rooms face the beach, packages available, run by Clifford and Susan Gardiner. **L-AL** *Bottle Creek Lodge*, T9467080, www.bottlecreeklodge.com Run by Howard and Cheryl Gibbs, members of Ecotourism Society, lodge room or detached cabin, on top of small ridge on north-east side of Flamingo Pond, all rooms sea view, composting toilets, fans, special diets catered for, CP, kayaks, bicycles. **L-AL** *Whitby Beach Hideaway*, T/F9467301, joannesbnb@tciway.tc 3 bedrooms, 2 en suite bathrooms, large, bright, airy, comfortable, screened veranda, secluded, 300 ft from beach, all rooms ocean view. Under same ownership is **AL-A** *Jo Anne's Whitby Plaza Bed & Breakfast*, T/F as for *Whitby Beach Hideaway*. Large rooms or suites with bath, hot water, fans, king, queen or twin beds, private entrances and veranda, also 4-room housekeeping unit, short walk to Whitby Beach, bicycle, kayak and canoe rental, *Papa Grunt's* on premises. **A** *Hollywood Beach Condos*, Whitby, T9467185. 4 1-bed units with kitchen on the beach, transportation, fishing, diving arranged, bring your own food. **A** *North Caicos Villas*, T/F9467308. 1 1,200-sq ft and 1 800-sq ft villa, all watersports, transportation arranged, bring your own food.

All accommodation is in the Whitby Beach area on the north coast. Sandflies can be a problem, particularly if there is not enough wind; take insect repellent

Eating

Simple local restaurants include *Club Titter's Restaurant and Bar*, near the airport, *Super D's*, in the airport itself, *Taylor's Bar* and *Big Josh's* in Kew (beer US$2), *The Anchor Inn*, T2414658, and *Bernie's* in Bottle Creek. Italian at the private *Club Vacanze*, T9467119, reservations necessary. *Pelican Beach Hotel* serves good food but is only open if there are guests at the hotel. *Papa Grunt's Restaurant*, Whitby Plaza, 0830, Sun 1100-1400 for lunch. Credit cards accepted, indoor or screened veranda dining, native and American cuisine, fresh seafood, lots of conch, sandwiches with home-made bread US$5.75, pizza, salads, vegetarian platter.

Sports

Watersports *Beach Cruiser* at the *Ocean Beach Hotel*, T9467113, offers snorkelling, diving (US$50 for 1-tank dive, US$80 for 2-tank dive, minimum 4 people, packages and equipment hire available), fishing (US$275 a half-day or US$425 a whole day, maximum 4 people), and sailing (20-ft pontoon 'flat top' boat offering trips of 1 hr, half-day or full day, picnics, snorkelling, etc, island hopping and visits to see iguanas on Little Water Cay). **Tennis** There are courts at *Club Vacanze*.

See also watersports, page 231

Transport

Air See Getting around, page 226. **Road** For day trips or overnight stays you can rent a cruising bicycle at *Papa Grunt's* restaurant at Whitby Plaza, island map supplied. Rates are US$15 per person per 24 hrs, for weekly rates seventh day free, credit card deposit required,

Turks & Caicos Islands

▶ **The Turks and Caicos National Trust**

The National Trust is a non-profit, non-governmental conservation organization, working in co-operation with the Government, the World Wildlife Fund, The Nature Conservancy and local people to preserve the natural and historical heritage of the islands and develop sustainable tourism to keep the Turks and Caicos Islands 'beautiful by nature'. Projects completed include: an exhibition on national parks, endangered animals and the islands' history in the departure terminal at Provo Airport; a historically oriented public park around the Cheshire Hall plantation ruins near downtown Provo; public access to the 100-acre Bird Rock Point Natural Area on the northeast tip of Provo for walking and birdwatching; a fund-raising campaign and work with the Government on a financial framework for the long-term management of the national parks. For information or to become a member or volunteer, contact Ethlyn Gibbs-Williams, the National Trust of the Turks and Caicos Islands, Providenciales, T9415710.

T/F9467301. There are car hire facilities on North Caicos with **Saunders Rent A Car**, VHF Channel 16 'Sierra 7', or **Gardiners Auto Service**, US$35 for half-day, US$70 for full-day, plus US$10 tax. A taxi costs US$10 from the airport to Whitby for 1 person, US$12 for 2, US$15 for 3. Taxi from Sandy Point to Whitby is US$20. A tour of the island by taxi costs US$80-100, the drivers are friendly and knowledgeable but some do tend to run their own errands while working. **Scooter** getaway to North Caicos with **Provo Fun Cycles**, T9465868.

Directory **Banks** You are advised to bring small-denomination US dollar notes as there is no bank and it is difficult to cash US$50 or US$100, TCs or money orders around the island. **Communications** Phone, fax and email service offered in the office area.

Parrot Cay Cotton used to be grown on Parrot Cay and there are the remains of a plantation house, protected wetlands and mangroves.

Sleeping LL *Parrot Cay Resort*, T9467788, www.Provo.net/ParrotCay, is a luxury 56-room hotel, opened in 1998 on this 1,300-acre private island. It has already attracted the rich and famous, with a guest list that includes Paul McCartney and Bruce Willis, and it is frequently featured in glossy magazines and TV travel shows. It has beautiful landscaping and the largest freshwater pool in the TCI. The furniture is Indonesian, some of the staff are Asian and the food is Asian-influenced. You can have a Thai, Balinese or Swedish massage at the award-winning Shambala Spa, and there are tennis courts.

Dellis Cay Dellis Cay is uninhabited but frequently visited for its **shells**. You can be dropped off there for the day for shelling by a local charter boat out from Leeward Marina, on Providenciales.

Pine Cay

A hurricane in 1969 left Pine Cay 5 ft under water for a while and since then houses have been built back from the beach and many are on stilts

Pine Cay is an 800-acre private resort owned by a group of homeowners who also own the exclusive 12-room **LL** *Meridian Club* (November to June. Resorts Management Inc, T800-3319154, 212-6964566, locally T/F9465128). Children under six years are not allowed to stay in the hotel and there are lots of restrictions on where they are allowed if brought to a villa. The homes, which are very comfortable, with spectacular views, can be rented. There is a fairly well-stocked commissary or you can eat in the hotel; golf carts are used to get around the island. Day trippers are not encouraged although visitors may come for lunch at the restaurant by prior reservation as long as they do not use the facilities; the homeowners value their privacy and put a ban on visitors if they feel there have been too many. Pine Cay benefits from a few freshwater ponds and wells, so water is no problem and it is greener than Provo. On the other hand mosquito control is a constant problem.

Nature trails have been laid out around the ponds and through the trees. There are tennis courts. There is an airstrip as guests usually charter a flight, and a dock if they prefer to come in with the *Meridian Club's* exclusive shuttle boat.

Water Cay is a nature reserve and, although classified as a separate island, is joined to Pine Cay by sand dunes created during the 1969 hurricane. **Water Cay**

Little Water Cay, the nearest island to Provo is inhabited by iguanas. The endangered Turks and Caicos rock iguana is now protected from threatening human presence by boardwalks, which protect their burrows and nesting chambers, and by strict rules that stop visitors feeding them. A visitor's fee is charged to support the protection programme. (Most tour operators have day trips, see page 231.) **Little Water Cay**

Providenciales

'Provo' is 25 miles long and about 3 miles wide. A surge of building work since the early 1990s has changed Grace Bay, on the north shore, beyond all recognition, but despite the many hotels and condominiums you can still walk along the beach and snorkel without feeling crowded. Away from the smart hotels, condos and villas, however, the island is dry, scrubby and nothing like as pretty as the underwater world surrounding it. The reef is superb and attracts thousands of divers every year.

IDD code: 649 Population: over 10,000

Ins and outs

Provo has the main airport for the islands and international flights come in here. There are no scheduled boat services and cruise ships do not call. **Getting there**

Most roads are paved, contributing to fast, erratic driving by residents; speed limits (40 mph highway, 20 mph in town) are not observed, dangerous overtaking is common. Hired cars are generally not well serviced, and may have to be exchanged for another. Taxis charge US$2 per mile, a ride for 1 person from the airport to the *Allegro* is US$12-15, and a round trip to a restaurant or Downtown can be US$40. Tours and shopping trips about US$25 per hr. Complaints have not lowered the rates. There are usually taxis at the large hotels. **Getting around** *See page 225 for international air services and other transport details*

Around the island

Development of the island began in 1967 although it had been settled in the 18th century and there were three large plantations in the 19th century growing cotton and sisal. The three original settlements, **The Bight** (meaning Bay), **Five Cays** and **Blue Hills**, are fragmented and have not grown into towns as the population has increased. Instead shopping malls and offices have been built along the Leeward Highway (Market Place, Plantation Hills, Central Square, Provo Plaza). The Office of the Chief Secretary, Customs Office, banks, law firms, supermarkets and travel agents are **Down Town**. **Turtle Cove** calls itself 'the heart of Provo', with a couple of hotels, a marina, dive operators, boat charters, deep-sea fishing, restaurants and the tourist office.

On the south side of the island, **South Dock** is the island's commercial port and here you will find the Harbourmaster. **The Caicos Marina and Boatyard** on the south coast is many miles from shopping supplies. Also on the south side is the small **South Side Marina**. To the west, **Sapodilla Bay** offers good protection for yachts in all winds west through southeast. It is open to the south through southwest. **Chalk Sound**, a national park inland from Sapodilla Bay, is a shallow lagoon of marvellous turquoise colours, dotted with rocky islets.

Turks & Caicos Islands

Northwest Point, a marine park offshore, has good beaches, diving and snorkelling. In 1993 a French television company shot a series of underwater game shows here and a treacherous road was bulldozed through to the beautiful beach. They left several tiki huts which offer much-needed shade for a day on the beach. Two good places to snorkel in the **Grace Bay** area are just to the east of Turtle Cove, where grouper rays and turtles can be seen on Smith's Reef near the entrance to the marina, just west of *Treasure Beach Villas*, and in front of *Coral Gardens Resort*. The **Princess Alexandra Marine Park** along Grace Bay incorporates the reef offshore. At the northeast end, a deep channel known as **Leeward Going Through** is a natural harbour and a marina with fuel, water and ice, and a restaurant has been built here. There is a conch farm at the **Island Sea Centre** near Leeward. ■ *Hatchery tours 0900-1700. US$6, children under 12 US$3. T9465330, gift shop.*

Inland, along Seasage Hill Road in Long Bay, is **The Hole**, a collapsed limestone, water-filled sinkhole next to a house called *By the Hole*. A tunnel to the right-hand side gives access to the main pool. Do not attempt to descend. Ruins of Loyalist and Bermudan settlers' plantations and houses can be seen at **Cheshire Hall**, Richmond Hills and along the Bight road. On the hill overlooking the *Mariner Hotel* (closed) at Sapodilla Bay a pole marks the location of stones engraved with initials and dates in the 17th century possibly by shipwrecked sailors or wreckers. The view, even with the commercial dock in the foreground, is quite lovely, and it is free.

Providenciales

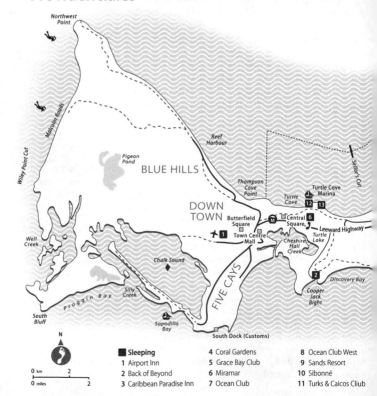

Sleeping		
■	4 Coral Gardens	8 Ocean Club West
1 Airport Inn	5 Grace Bay Club	9 Sands Resort
2 Back of Beyond	6 Miramar	10 Sibonné
3 Caribbean Paradise Inn	7 Ocean Club	11 Turks & Caicos Club

Essentials

There is still a lot of construction in progress, with a *Yacht Club* being built at Turtle Cove and several resorts in various stages of completion.

LL *Grace Bay Club*, on beach, T9465757, www.gracebay.com Luxury accommodation, 22 elegant condos, a/c, phone, TV, watersports, tennis, pool, jacuzzi, all amenities, French restaurant, beach bar. **LL***The Sands Resort*, T9465199, www.thesandsresort.com On the beach, 105 suites and rooms in 5 buildings, 2 pools, extensive landscaping. **LL** *The Turks & Caicos Club*, T9465800, www.turksandcaicosclub.com 21 luxury suites and gourmet restaurant, pool, ocean views. **LL-L** *Ocean Club and Ocean Club West, Beach and Golf Resort*, T9465880, oceanclb@tciway.tc Condos on the beach, comfortable, well-equipped, balconies, some with good views the length of Grace Bay, spacious deck around pool with daytime snack bar, next to Provo Golf Club, packages available, free transport to airport, bike rentals. **LL-L** *Sibonné*, T9465547, www.sibonne.com 26 rooms and *condos*, golf packages, restaurant, lovely bougainvillea in the courtyard, pool. **LL-L** *Turtle Watch*, Turtle Cove area, 2 mins' walk to north shore beaches, T9464362, turtlewatch@tciway.tc Linda and Mike St Louis run a 2-bedroom guesthouse or whole house rental with CP, kitchen facilities, including taxes and airport transfers, delightful landscaping, pool. **LL-AL** *Back of Beyond*, Discovery Bay, T9414555, backofbeyond@tciway.tc 9-bedroom adobe-style guesthouse with bar and restaurant. **LL-AL** *Caribbean Paradise Inn*, T9465020, www.paradise.tc 200 m from beach, by *Grace Bay Club*, 15 rooms, ocean or pool view, CP, snacks available, new, popular, dive gear storage, German-owned and managed. **LL-AL** *Coral Gardens Resort and White House Villa* on Grace Bay, T/F9413713, coralgardens@tciway.tc Best snorkelling site, now 30 'boutique residences' for sale or rental, 1-2 bedrooms or junior suite. **LL-A** *Turtle Cove Inn*, T9464203, tcinn@tciway.tc 3 rate schedules, special weekly packages, 30 rooms, poolside or ocean view, smallish rooms but comfortable, suite with kitchenette available, not on beach, all watersports at the marina, cable TV, 2 restaurants.

L-A *Miramar Resort* (formerly *Erebus Inn*), on hillside overlooking Turtle Cove, T9464240, www.themiramarresort.com 26 rooms, larger than those in other hotels, and a few basic chalets with wonderful views liked by divers, dive packages available, all watersports at the marina, gym and fitness centre on site, pool, tennis, 2 rooms fully equipped for ham radio operators. **B** *Airport Inn*, T9464701/9413514, airport@tciway.tc 2 mins to airport, close to banks, groceries, restaurants, 25 rooms, 24-hr service, shops and restaurant on site, a/c, TV, special rates for pilots, 15% discount if you book room and rental car.

Sleeping
When confirming rates and availability, check whether tax and service are included. There are plenty of self-catering condos and villas around the island

Turks & Caicos Islands

12 Turtle Cove Inn
13 Turtle Watch

● **Bars & clubs**
14 Club Mediterranée

Eating

Dinner with wine at an expensive restaurant can easily cost US$200 for two

Turtle Cove Expensive (over US$40 per person) *Baci Ristorante*, T9413044. Fine Italian dining indoors and on the terrace overlooking the Pond, 1200-1430, 1800-2200, daily. *Magnolia Restaurant and Bar*, at the *Miramar Resort* overlooking Turtle Cove, T9464240, info@themiramarresort.com Spectacular view, serving New Age Asian and Caribbean cuisine to popular acclaim, 0730-1030, 1800-2200, bar from 1500, closed Mon. **Mid-range** (US$20-40 per person) *Banana Boat*, dockside at Turtle Cove marina, T9415706. Caribbean bar and grill, colourful, cheerful, daily 1130-2200. *Sharkbite Bar and Grill*, Admiral's Club, on the water, T9415090,1100-2400, happy hour 1700-1900, nightly specials and events. *The Aqua*, T9464763, 1130-1500, 1800-2200, closed Sun. 'Creative' conch, seafood, lunch, dinner. *Tiki Hut*, at the *Turtle Cove Marina* landspit, T9465341, daily 0700-2200. Chicken or ribs every Wed night, US$10, popular with ex-pats.

Down Town and on Airport Road you'll find the least expensive, but not necessarily cheap meals, catering to islanders and office workers in town

Down Town Cheap (under US$20) *Club Latino Bar and Grill*, behind Ward Construction building, open 24 hrs, slots, chicken 'n' ribs, nightclub and disco after 2000. *Denny's Express*, in Butterfield Plaza, offers fast food and some native dishes, 0700-2000, closed Sun. *Hole in the Wall*, on Old Airport Rd, T9414136. Formerly *Nyammings*, native food with Jamaican twist, daily 0800-2200 and Tue and Fri until 2300. *Lamont's*, T9416115, Mon-Sat 0600-2300, Sun 0900-2300. Pink building, native and 'absolutely-everything-American' menu, to go. *Sweet T's Meals On Wheels*, next to *Texaco* service station, 0600-2200, closed Sun. Native dishes, proprietor Mary Simmons. *Tasty Temptations*, next to the dry cleaners, T9464049, daily 0630-1500. French breakfasts, sandwiches, fresh salads for lunch, good coffee, deli.

Airport Road Cheap Within walking distance from the airport is *Fast Eddie's*, open 0830-1900. Excellent native food, no alcohol on premises, reservations for groups. *Frances Place*, T9464472, 0600-2200. Family dining, Jamaican touch, TV, slots, closed Sun. *Gilley's*, daily 0600-1930, is the only place to eat at the airport, a/c, noisy, local hangout, indifferent service and menu. *Rolling Pin Hotte Shoppe Restaurant*, 5-min walk from airport, no phone, indoor or outdoor seating, Trinidadian and native food, curry and roti, salads, 0900-2100, at Airport Plaza near *Airport Inn*. *Where It's At*, T9464185, 0700-0100. Jamaican specialities by Yvette, curried goat and Presidente beer, generous portions, daily specials, nightclub next door.

Restaurant hours change with the season so call first to avoid disappointment

Leeward Highway Mid-range *Hey José Cantina*, Near the Tourist Shoppe, Central Square Shopping Centre, T9464812. 1200-late, closed Sun. Great food, Mexican/American, tacos, huge pizza, etc, takeaways. *Angela's Top O' The Cove Deli*, next to Napa auto at Suzie Turn, order lunch by T/F9464694. 0630-1700, Mon-Fri, 0630-1500 Sat, 0630- 1400 Sun. 'Little bit of New York-style deli', subs, bagels, beer, wine, picnic food. *Dora's Restaurant and Bar*, near PPC power station, T9464558, open from 0730 until late. Local recipes, eat in or take away. *Go Fish*, at Provo Plaza, east of WIV, T9414646. Mon-Fri 1000-1900, Sat 1000- 1500. Great fish and chips, chicken, wine and beer, indoors or shaded on the patio. Satellite TV. **Cheap** At Market Pl, *Mackie's Café*, T9413640, 0900-2100, closed Sun. Native-style, stewed fish and Johnny cake, fresh seafood. *Pizza Pizza*, T9413577, Tue-Thu 1130-2130, Fri-Sat 1130- 2200, Sun 1700-2130. New York-style pizza, eat in or takeaway, recommended. *Club Sodax*, opposite *Dora's*, T9414540. Nice new sports bar. *Chinson Pastry & Restaurant*, T9413533. Jamaican breakfast and lunch, closed Sun.

Hotel restaurants are open to all, but visitors to all-inclusives must have a day/evening pass

Grace Bay (west to east) Expensive *Mango Reef*, in *Royal West Indies Resort*, T9468200. Indoor and poolside dining, great food, good service. *Anacaona* restaurant and bar on the beach, east of *Allegro Resort*,T9465050, daily1200-1500, 1900-2100. Thatched roof elegance, nouvelle cuisine with Caribbean flair, exclusive and expensive, live music some evenings, reservations recommended. *Coco Bistro*, past *Caicos Café*, east of *Allegro* near *Club Med*, behind Sunshine Nursery in palm trees, T9465369, Mon-Sat 1800-2130, closed Sep-Oct. Indoor dining/bar, or outdoors under the palms, Mediterranean cooking, specials every night reservations advised, expensive, congenial hosts and service. *Bella Luna Ristorante*, in the *Glass House*, west of *Allegro*, T9465214. Dinner 1800-late, nightly specials, reservations recommended, closed Mon. *Bay Bistro*, at *Sibonné*, T9465396. Open Wed-Mon 0700-2200, ocean front dining, international cuisine, very nice. *Coyaba* at *Coral Gardens*, T9465186. The name means 'heavenly' in Arawak and so is the food, 1800-2200, closed Tue. Adjacent to *Ocean Club*, *Gecko Grille*, Ocean Club Plaza, T9465885. Bar opens 1630-2400, dining 1800-2130, closed Mon. Pretentious, expensive, opt for garden dining as indoors is noisy. *Seaside Café*, at *Ocean Club*. Open for breakfast and lunch daily and dinner Thu-Tue, tropical dishes, great view. **Mid-range** *Barefoot Café*, in *Ports of Call*, T946-JAVA, daily 0700-2130 but no dinner Sun, Bagels, subs, cappuccino, ice cream or dinners. *Cuba Bella*, T9414528. Lunch 1100-1800 Mon-Sat, dinner daily 1800-2200, a taste of Cuba, pleasant. *Ripples by the Sea*, at *Coral Gardens*, T9465186. Caribbean grilled delicacies, great sushi and sashimi, open daily for breakfast and lunch. *Caicos Café and Grill*, next to *Ports of Call*, T9465278. Daily Jan-Apr 1200-1530, 1800-2200, closed Sun dinner other months, closed totally Sep-Oct. Homemade pasta, grilled fish and seafood, go early or late to avoid crowds, open-air. *Fairways Bar and Grill*, opposite *Ocean Club*, Provo Golf Course Clubhouse, T9465991. Daily 0700-1500 and Tue-Sat 1800-2200, Wed lunch specials, Fri happy hour. At the Ports of Call shopping centre across the street from *Allegro*, *Lattitudes*, Tex Mex, T9465832. 1700-late, daily. Seafood and more. *Hemingway's*, at *The Sands Resort*, T9465199. Ocean-view dining and good service.

Leeward going through Mid-range At the east end of Providenciales is *Gilley's at Leeward*, T9465094, open 0800-2100, except Thu, Sun 0800-1800. By the marina, breakfast, lunch specials, good food, friendly, superb service, meet local fishermen, arrange outings, boat trips, elegant, romantic dinners.

Blue Hills settlement Mid-range *Caribbean Mack* (formerly *Roadrunner*). Nightly till late. Soca, reggae, latino. *Conch House*, Mon-Sat 1100-late. *Smokey's On the Bay*, T9414453, 1030-2300 daily. Not to be missed, indoor or tiki hut dining on the beach, great native dishes, lobster, conch, buffets, sometimes live band. *Three Queens Bar and Restaurant*, T9415984, open 1130-2100 Mon-Sat, 1130-1600 Sun. Excellent, reasonably priced, local seafood lunches and dinners, by reservation only.

Entertainment

Provo is not a party place, people come here for relaxation and to enjoy the water, not for the nightlife

Casino Small casino in the *Allegro Resort*, open Mon-Sat 1900-0100. **Cinema** *Village Cinemas* is a new 2-screen movie theatre complex which will seat 370 people, tickets US$10 adults, US$7 children under 12, T9414108. **Disco** *Casablanca Disco*, immediately west of *Club Med*, open weekends, nothing ever happens until after midnight, loud music. Latin influence in discos such as *Club Latino* , Down Town, and *Caribbean Mack* in Blue Hills, featuring soca, reggae and latino, loudly! Live entertainment, Fri nights, Ports of Call courtyard. *Club Med* has nightly dinner/show for guests and visitors who phone for reservations (T9465500), US$40 including dinner Fri, US$30 other nights. Arrive 1830-1930 to get in. *Where It's At Disco*, on Leeward Highway, T9415475, 1600-0100, loud 'island' music, DJ, drinks.

Sports

For watersports, see page 231

Golf An 18-hole championship course (black tees 2,928 m, white tees 2,620 m), owned by the water company, T9465991, www.provogolfclub.com, is located within walking distance of the *Club Med*, *Allegro Resort*, *Grace Bay Club* and *Ocean Club*. Most hotels offer 3- to 5-day packages of green fees and mandatory carts. Licensed snackbar. An amateur open golf championship is held in Oct. *Island Network* sports and **fitness centre** with aqua/land aerobics is at Ports of Call across from *Allegro Resort*, contact Darlene, T9464240. *Fun & Fit Health Club*, at the *Miramar Resort*, offers weights and machines, aerobics, pool, tennis, personal training and nutrition advice. There is a certified fitness trainer, T9413527, ask for Lisa. **Horse riding** on quiet roads and Long Bay Beach, Provo, is available with Provo Ponies, T9465252. Suitable for novice or experienced riders, very popular, the only tuition is for kids on Sat. Transport included in price of ride, US$45 for 45 mins, US$65 for 80 mins. **Tennis** There are courts on Provo at several of the larger hotels. A small but active **squash** community welcomes visitors and can be contacted at *Johnston Apartments*, Kings Court, T9465683.

Turks & Caicos Islands

Turks & Caicos Islands

Transport **Bus** *Stafford Morris' Blue Bus*, VHF16, pick-up and delivery almost anywhere, including the
Be careful on the airport, US$3 each way, say Down Town to Grace Bay, T9413598 or flag him down. *Pelican*
roads; Leeward *Bus Service*, T9464092, VHF 67. **Car and bike hire** An economy car, quoted at US$39 per
Highway is day will work out to US$61.50 with taxes and insurance. Deposits are at least US$400. A 'gold'
especially risky credit card qualifies for an exemption of US$11.95 per day CDW. *Provo Rent A Car*, T9464404,
rentacar@provo.net, at the airport, T9465610, a/c vehicles, jeeps, vans, recommended.
Hertz, Central Leeward Highway, T9413910. *Budget*, Down Town, Town Centre Mall, open
Mon-Sat 0800-1700, Sun 1000-1600, T9464709, worldwide reservations T800-5270700,
Suzukis, Mitsubishis, 1 day free for weekly rental. *Tropical Auto Rental*, Tropicana Plaza at
Grace Bay, T9465300. *Turks and Caicos National Car Rental*, Airport Rd, T/F9464701, not
always reliable vehicle delivery. *Rent-a-Buggy*, Leeward Highway, T9464158, Suzuki jeeps,
and VWs. *Provo Fun Cycles* at Ports of Call across from *Allegro*, single scooters US$25 per day,
doubles US$39, packages, can take them to North Caicos on the ferry, Honda motorcycles,
also bicycles and jeeps, T9465868, Provofuncycles@Provo.net; *Sunrise Auto Rental*, jeeps
and scooters, Leeward Highway and *Club Med*, T9469730; *Avis* at airport and Bayview
Motors, Leeward Highway, T9464705, at *Club Med*, T9469730, Avis@provo.net, affiliated with
Sunrise Auto Rental; *Scooter Bob's*, Turtle Cove Marina, T9464684, vans, scooters and bicycles,
Mon-Sat 0900-1700, Sun 0900-1200. **Taxi** *Paradise Taxi Co*, T9413555; *Nell's Taxi*,
T9413228; *Island's Choice Taxi*, T9410409; *Provo Taxi Association*, T9465481.

Directory **Banks** *FirstCaribbean International Bank*, Butterfield Sq, Provo, T9464245; *Scotiabank*, Town Centre
Mall, T9464750. **Medical services** *MBS Group Medical Practice*, Leeward Highway, Jon Delisser
Building, Mon-Fri 0830-1700, Sat 0830-1200, recompression chamber; *Grace Bay Medical Clinic* is a
private clinic in the plaza on the road to the *Allegro* from Leeward Highway, Dr Sam Slattery, T9415252,
T2310525 (mob). The government clinic on Provo is *Myrtle Rigby Health Complex*, Leeward Highway,
near Down Town, T9413000, open daily. **Ambulance** services available and emergency medical air
charter to USA or Nassau, full life support can be arranged, T999 or any doctor. There is no anaesthetist on
Provo so surgery is done on Grand Turk, in Nassau or Miami. **Pharmacy** *Island Pharmacy*, T9464150.

West Caicos Rugged and currently uninhabited but worth visiting for its beach on the northwest
Once frequented coast and diving offshore. Parcels of this island are being developed as a luxury
by pirates, there resort/retirement resort with a dredged marina to accommodate mega-yachts.
are many wrecks Advertised as 'The Isle of West Caicos'. The east shore is a national marine park.
between here Inland there is a saltwater lake, Lake Catherine, which rises and falls with the tides
and Provo and is a nature reserve, home to migrant nesting flamingos, ducks and waders. The
ruins of Yankee Town, its sisal press and railroad are a surface interval destination
for scuba divers and sailors.

French Cay An old pirate lair, now uninhabited, but with exceptional marine life, and on the diving circuit (see page 230), French Cay has been designated a sanctuary for frigate
birds, osprey and nesting seabirds. There is no official transport but tour and dive
operators will go there on demand.

Background

History The islands' first dwellers were the peaceful Taínos, who left behind ancient utensils and little
The islands were else. By the middle of the 16th century not one Lucayan, as Columbus named them, remained.
named after the Like the Lucayans in the Bahamas islands, they were kidnapped for use as slaves or pearl divers,
Turk's Head 'fez' while many others died of imported diseases. The discovery of the islands, whether by Colum-
cactus found bus in 1492 or later by Ponce de León, is hotly disputed. There is a very convincing argument
growing here. The that Columbus' first landfall was on Grand Turk, not Watling Island in the Bahamas, now offi-
name Caicos comes cially named San Salvador. The infamous Caicos Banks, south of the Caicos group, where in the
from the Lucayan, space of 1 km the water depth changes from 1,830 m to 9 m, claimed many of the Spanish
caya hico, meaning ships lost in the central Caribbean from the 16th to the 18th century.
'string of islands'

The Bermudan traders who settled on the islands of Grand Turk, Salt Cay and South Caicos in the 17th century used slaves to rake salt for sale to British colonies on the American mainland, and fought pirates and buccaneers for over 200 years. During the American Revolution, British loyalists found refuge on the islands, setting up cotton and sisal plantations with the labour of imported slaves. For a while, cotton and sisal from the islands were sold in New York and London, solar salt became the staple of the economy, and the Turks and Caicos thrived, but all these products encountered overwhelming competition from elsewhere. The thin soil was an added disadvantage and a hurricane in 1813 marked the demise of cotton plantations.

Following an alternation of Spanish, French and British control, the group became part of the Bahamas colony in 1766. Attempts to integrate the Turks and Caicos failed, rule from Nassau was unpopular and inefficient, and abandoned in 1848. Links with Jamaica were more developed, partly because London-Kingston boats visited frequently. The Turks and Caicos were annexed to Jamaica in 1874. After Jamaica's independence in 1962, they were loosely associated with the Bahamas for just over 10 years until the latter became independent. At that point, the Turks and Caicos became a British Crown Colony (now a Dependent Territory). The Anglican Church maintained its links with the Bahamas, which is where the Bishop resides.

The main political parties were established in 1976: the People's Democratic Movement (PDM) and the Progressive National Party (PNP). From time to time independence is raised as a political issue but does not have universal support.

The isolation of the Turks and Caicos and the benign neglect of the British government led to increasing use of the islands as refuelling posts by drug smugglers *en route* from South America to Florida. Constitutional government was suspended in 1986 after it was discovered that several Ministers were involved and direct rule from the UK was imposed while investigations continued into malpractice by other public officials. The Chief Minister and the Minister of Development were imprisoned for accepting bribes to allow drugs planes to refuel on South Caicos. The islands are still being used for trans-shipment of cocaine and other drugs.

In 1988, general elections restored constitutional government. These were won by the PDM. The April 1991 elections brought the PNP back to power, but economic austerity measures and civil service job cuts cost the PNP its mandate. The PDM, under the leadership of Derek Taylor, held power from 1995 until 2003. Declining popularity of the government led to hotly contested elections in April 2003. Initial results gave the PDM 7 seats and the PNP 6, but three seats were contested in court and there were rumours of illegal dealings. In June it was announced that by-elections for the contested seats would be held in August.

Geography
Only eight islands are inhabited

The Turks and Caicos comprise about 40 low-lying islands and cays covering 193 sq miles, and surrounded by one of the longest coral reefs in the world. The islands are separated by the Columbus Passage, a 22-mile channel over 7,000 ft deep, which connects the Atlantic and the Caribbean, contributing to the area's profusion of marine life. Generally, the windward sides of the islands are made up of limestone cliffs and sand dunes, while the leeward sides have greener vegetation. The south islands of Grand Turk, Salt Cay and South Caicos are very dry, having had their trees felled by salt rakers long ago to discourage rain. The other islands have slightly more rain but very little soil and most of the vegetation is scrub and cactus. The islands lie directly east of Inagua at the south tip of the Bahamas and north of Hispaniola.

People

The main islands of the Turks group, Grand Turk and Salt Cay, shelter 20% of the colony's 7,901 'belongers', as the islanders call themselves, but only 15% of the total resident population of 19,000 (a census was taken in August 2001 but results have still not been released), which includes many Haitians, Dominicans and ex-pat North Americans and Europeans. The rest of the population is scattered among the larger Caicos group to the west: South Caicos, Middle Caicos, North Caicos and Providenciales, the most populous, known locally as 'Provo'.

Government

The Turks and Caicos are a British Overseas Territory. The British monarch is Head of State, represented by a Governor. The Executive Council chaired by the Governor is formed by six ministers, the Financial Secretary, the Attorney General (British Government appointment) and the Chief Secretary. Mrs Cynthia Astwood is Chief Secretary, the first native Turks Islander to be appointed to the position. The Legislative Council has 13 elected members and two party-appointed members.

Economy   The traditional economic activity, salt production, ceased in 1964, and for two decades there was little to generate legal income apart from fishing, government employment and some tourism. Natural resources are limited, even water has to be strictly conserved. Agriculture is almost non-existent. Practically all consumer goods and most foodstuffs are imported. The lack of major employment activities led in the 1960s and 1970s to thousands of local people emigrating to the nearby Bahamas or the USA to seek work. This trend has now been reversed as the economy has improved and the population is rising. Belongers have returned to work in the tourist industry and professionals trained abroad are returning to work as lawyers, accountants, etc. Poorly paid skilled and unskilled labour, much of it illegal, comes from Haiti and the Dominican Republic.

There is no income tax, company tax, exchange control or restriction on the nationality or residence of shareholders or directors. New legislation and the creation of the Offshore Finance Centre Unit (OFCU) were designed to regulate the growth of offshore finance and encourage banking, insurance and trust companies.

Haïti

Introducing Haiti

Haiti is famous for being the only country to have had a successful slave revolt: whites have not governed here for two centuries and the bicentenary of independence will be celebrated 1 January 2004 with great fanfare. African customs persist strongly, most noticeably in language, art, music, dance and religion, with voodoo being widely practised. Nevertheless, the influence of former French colonists and merchants is still evident, particularly in architecture, with many old buildings enhanced by the gingerbread style of elaborate fretwork, balconies and decorated gables. Language also reflects the French colonial past, with everybody speaking a French-based Creole. Haiti is the poorest country in the western hemisphere and the capital, Port-au-Prince, is a seething mass of humanity with crowds of people plying their trade in the streets to eke out a living. This is the most mountainous island in the Caribbean, but pressure for the land has led Haitians to cut down all their trees for fuel, leaving the hillsides bare. There is no mass tourism and exploring the country is a rewarding experience for the independent and adventurous of spirit. Fortifications and other historical landmarks dot the countryside, but the most impressive is the massive La Citadelle, built on top of a 900-m peak in order to deter any French invasion.

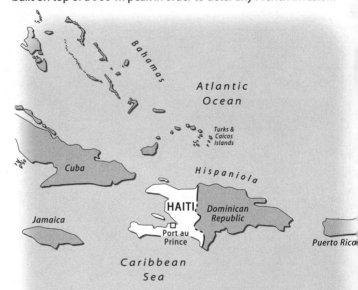

Essentials

Before you travel

All visitors need **passports** valid for at least 6 months after your departure date from Haiti. **Documents**
Visas are not needed for anyone staying under 90 days, but everyone must have an onward ticket. All visitors, except cruise ship passengers, must complete an embarkation/ disembarkation card on the plane; this is valid for 90 days, and may be extended. Don't lose the yellow card (exit visa) because you will need it when you leave. Keep your passport with you as identification for police controls when travelling in the interior. Baggage inspection and drug-enforcement laws are strict. There is no restriction on foreign currency and no export limitations.

Currency The unit is the gourde (Creole: goud), divided into 100 centimes (Creole: kòb). **Money**
Coins in circulation are for 5, 10, 20 and 50 centimes, notes for 1, 2, 5, 10, 25, 50, 100, 250 and *Try to break*
500 gourdes. Some 100-gourde notes are plastic, faded, smeared and look like forgeries; *down large notes*
they are not. They have 'American Banknote Company' printed on them. Small denomina- *whenever possible*
tion notes are in appalling condition and there is always a shortage of them. 500-gourde notes are next to useless unless you can break them down at a bank or spend them at expensive hotels; ask for smaller denominations. Coins are few and far between.

    Exchange The gourde was tied at 5 to the US dollar during the US occupation. In the 1980s it began to trade at a slightly lower value on a parallel market, but the official rate was kept until 1991, when the Aristide government severed the tie and let the gourde float. From 7.5 to the dollar at the time of the Sep 1991 coup, it fell to 38 to the dollar in May 2003. So far, so good. Now it gets complicated. Haitians routinely refer to their own money as dollars, based on the old 5 to 1 rate. Thus, 5 gourdes is called a dollar, 10 gourdes is 2 dollars, 25 gourdes is 5 dollars, etc. Prices in shops are usually in Haitian dollars, therefore multiply by 5 to get the price in gourdes. Visitors must constantly clarify whether the price being quoted is in Haitian or American dollars, or gourdes, now increasingly used on bills.

    The best exchange rate is obtained from money changers, whether those on the street or those working out of offices. It is perfectly legal but not recommended, for safety reasons. The rate in banks is not far behind and it is therefore better to trade with one of the many banks. It is foolish to come to Haiti with any currency other than US dollars, although euros are accepted. Currencies such as sterling can be changed, but only at a massive loss. Travellers' cheques are difficult to change in some banks. **Credit cards** Visa, Mastercard and American Express are widely accepted. Beware, card users will not get a good rate and are often charged a premium.

The climate is generally very warm but the cool on and offshore winds of morning and eve- **Climate**
ning help to make it bearable. In coastal areas temperatures vary between 20 and 35°C, *Haiti has two*
being slightly hotter in Apr-Sep. The driest, coolest months are Dec-Mar. In the hill resorts the *rainy seasons:*
temperature is cooler. *April-May and*
September-October

Getting there

From Europe: there are no direct flights, but *Air France* flies from Paris via Guadeloupe and **Air**
Martinique. **From North America**: *American Airlines* flies from New York Miami daily. Other airlines from Miami include *Dutch Caribbean Express* and *Air France*. *Air Canada* flies from Montréal. **From Central America**: *Copa* flies from Panama City with connections from neighbouring capitals. **From the Caribbean**: *Dutch Caribbean Express* from Curaçao and Sint Maarten; *Air France* from Fort-de-France, Pointe-à-Pitre, Port of Spain; *Air Jamaica Express* from Kingston and Santo Domingo; *AeroCaribbean* from Santiago de Cuba; *Dominair* from Santiago (Dominican Republic). **From South America**: *Air France* from Cayenne, French Guiane; *Suriname Airways* from Paramaribo.

    Flights from Miami are frequently overbooked and you should be at the airport at least 2 hrs in advance. You may be asked to give your seat to another passenger in return for credit vouchers to be used on another flight within 12 months. Your original ticket will still be valid for the next flight, or for transfer to a different flight.

Touching down

See also Directory, page 266

Business hours *Banks: Mon-Fri 0900-1300; Government offices: Mon-Fri 0700-1200, 1300- 1600 (Oct-Apr 0800-1200, 1300-1800); Shops and offices: 0700-1600 (an hour later Oct-Apr).*

Clothing As in most other countries in the Caribbean, beachwear should not be worn away from the beach and poolside.

Departure tax Visitors leaving by air must pay a US$25 departure tax in US currency and a 10-gourde security tax in Haitian currency. Do not buy international flight tickets in Haiti, especially not at the airport. Sales tax is very high and the application of exchange rates may be very arbitrary.

Emergency numbers Observe the US Embassy travel warning: Haitian authorities are unlikely to respond to requests for assistance; you are advised to call your consulate in an emergency.

Official time Eastern standard time, 5 hrs behind GMT; 4 hrs behind early Apr-late Oct.

Safety Despite all the political turmoil since 1986, security is not a major problem for the foreign visitor. In fact, Haiti has much less crime than most Caribbean countries. Take normal precautions. Carry handbags securely and do not leave belongings in sight in a parked car.

During any political unrest it is advisable to limit your movements in the daytime and not to go out at night. Streets are usually deserted by 2300. Foreigners are not normally targeted at such times, but seek local advice.

Tipping Budget travellers, particularly outside Port-au-Prince, are a rarity. Expect to be the subject of much friendly curiosity, and keep a pocketful of small change to conform with the local custom of tipping on every conceivable occasion. Even cigarettes and sweets are accepted. Hotels generally add 10% service charge. Baggage porters at hotels usually get US$0.50 per bag. Do not fail to reward good service since hotel and restaurant staff rely on tips to boost their meagre salaries. Nobody tips taxi, publique, camionette or taptap drivers, unless exceptional service has been given.

Voltage 110 volt, 60 cycle AC. Electricity supply is unpredictable as there are insufficient funds to maintain the service. Only if sufficient rain falls to operate the hydroelectric facility will the capital have power and water. Only the best hotels have powerful generators to make up the deficiency. As the Oloffson is on the same circuit as the Presidential Palace, it is never blacked out.

Weights and measures Metric.

Sea Cruise ships stopped calling at Port-au-Prince years ago, partly because of passenger reaction to begging. Some cruise lines have leased private beaches near Cap-Haïtien for 1-day stopovers, and they have renewed their visits.

Road

See page 293 and check with the Dominican Consulate to see if you need a visa

There is a one-hour time difference between Haiti and the Dominican Republic

Travel to the Dominican Republic *Taptaps* (converted pick-ups) and trucks ply the road to the border of the Dominican Republic at Malpasse/Jimaní, 1 hour from Port-au-Prince. The Ouanaminthe/Dajabón crossing in the north is easily reached from Cap-Haïtien and is straightforward. On leaving Haiti by bus or car you have to pay US$13 plus 15-30 gourdes per person. It is US$15 plus 20 pesos to re-enter Haiti from the Dominican Republic. If you are travelling by bus you pay at the bus terminal. These rates are variable and change frequently. It is advisable to put aside US$50 to cover all taxes both ways. Mopeds ferry you between the Haitian and Dominican border posts for US$1. There are lots of money changers on both sides. The easiest way to get to Santo Domingo is with *Terra Bus* or *Caribe Tours*, both Dominican companies, who deal with all immigration and other formalities so all you have to do is get off the bus to take care of Dominican customs. Excellent service, efficient, comfortable a/c buses which show at least 2 movies, snacks and drinks provided, recommended. *Terra Bus*, T2237882, is handled by *Chatelain Tours*, T2232400, 2225664, in Port-au-Prince. Fare US$50 one way, US$75 return or US$80 open return, child reductions, departs Mon 0800, arrives Santo Domingo 1530, other days except Sat departs 1400, arrives 2000, leaves from Tabarre, between Pétion-Ville and the airport, US$20 by taxi from town centre. *Caribe Tours* is in Pétion-Ville, T2579379, and departs from the corner of rue Clerveaux and Gabart, daily at 0730, US$75 return, leaves Santo Domingo at 1100 for the return journey. *Luz Tours*, T2231059 and *Kenya Express* (same number) have weekly buses to Santo Domingo. Haitian travel agencies sometimes offer 3- or 4-day inclusive bus tours into the Dominican Republic. There are regular buses from the Dominican

Travel hints

Haiti is especially fascinating for anyone who is avid for off-the-beaten-track experience. The following hints should help you to make the most of your visit.

Although it is one of the poorest countries in the world, with most citizens suffering from one kind of oppression or another, Haiti is proud of having been the only nation to have carried out a successful slave rebellion.

Haitians at all levels are very sensitive to the way they are treated by foreigners, commonly called 'blanc'. If you treat them with warmth and consideration, they will respond with enthusiasm and friendship. There is no innate hostility towards 'blancs'; if you feel threatened it is probably the result of a misunderstanding. For example if someone looks at you and draws one finger across his neck, it does not mean he wants to cut your throat. Rather, it means he is hungry and is asking for a dollar.

Eye contact is very important; it is not avoided as in some other countries.

Humour plays an important role in social interactions; Haitians survive by laughing at themselves and their situation.

It is important to recognize the presence of each person in a social encounter, either with a handshake or a nod. When walking in the countryside, you usually wish bonjour (before 1200) or bonsoir to anyone you meet. Salud is another common greeting, at any time of day. Coffee or cola are often offered by richer peasants to visitors.

Do not expect straight answers to questions about a peasant's wealth, property or income.

It is assumed that every 'blanc' is wealthy and therefore it is legitimate to try to separate foreigners from their riches. Treat such attempts with humour, indignation or consideration as you feel appropriate.

Haiti

frontier town of Jimaní to Santo Domingo (6 hrs) and from Dajabón via Montecristi and Santiago de los Caballeros. Rental cars are not allowed to cross the border, but you could safely leave one at the border for a few hours during a quick excursion to Jimaní. Cheaper Dominican buses leave Port-au-Prince most mornings for their return trip to Santo Domingo via Malpasse, but they have no fixed time or departure point (the trip can take up to 10 hrs, with 2 hrs at the border). Ask at the Hotel Palace on rue Capois, where many Dominicans stay. Buses also leave from rue du Centre, between Auberge Port-au-Prince and rue des Miracles, around 3-4 per day, mostly 25-seater a/c Mitsubishis, US$20.

Touching down

On arrival at Port-au-Prince and after emerging through Customs, you will be crushed by a throng of porters and taxi drivers eager to take your bags. It is best to have a plan of action before leaving Customs. The information office at the airport is very helpful. The downstairs snackbar is cheap and friendly. The public area has a bookstore and a handicraft shop. Duty-free goods and more crafts are on sale in the area reserved for departing passengers.

Airport information

Airlines *Air Canada*, T2460441/2; *Air France*, T2221700/1086, T2462085 at airport, 11 rue Capois, corner rue Ducoste, near *Le Plaza*; *American Airlines*, T2231314, 2460100, Av Pie XII, near post office, always packed with people (also T2460110 at the airport); *Copa*, 35 Ave Marie Jeanne, T2232366, or airport T2460946.

Information overseas The Embassy of Haiti, 2311 Massachusetts Av NW, Washington DC 20008, USA, T202-3324090, embassy@haiti.org Mon-Thu 0900-1600, Fri 0900-1500. The following websites are useful for finding out more: www.haiti-org, iwww.haititourisme.com, www.haitiglobalvillage.com, www.port-haiti.com, www.uhhp.com

Tourist information
See also page 261

Guides Young men and boys offer their services as guides. In some places it's worth taking them up on it – it is easier to get about, you can visit places off the beaten tourist track and avoid some of the frustrations of the public transport system – though generally you can get by without one. Most guides speak English or pidgin English. **Chauffeurs-guides** are cab drivers who cater to foreign visitors. Usually found outside the biggest hotels such as the *Le Plaza*, or at the airport, their cars can be used like regular taxis or hired by the hour, half-day, day or for a

Guides expect you to buy them food if you stop to eat

tour. The drivers usually speak French, plus a little English. They can be booked through the *Association des Chauffeurs-Guides*, T2220330, 18 Blvd Harry Truman. You usually have the option of having a driver when hiring a car, US$15 a day in Port-au-Prince, more if you go out into the country and you pay for his food and accommodation. A recommended private guide/driver is Lionel Elie, rue St Surin 20 Bis, Pétion-Ville, T2572968, also an artist, used by visiting writers and film crews, speaks English, Spanish and a little German. Price negotiable depending on the job and whether you have your own transport. Max Church, a pastor who has been training English/French/Creole-speaking guides, can be called on 2342622, Port-au-Prince. An English-speaking guide named Ed can be found on the corner of rue José de San Martin and Av Panamericaine in Pétion-Ville. He is protective and can help you do things like take a taptap to Port-au-Prince and visit the Iron Market, excursions that you might not feel brave enough to do on your own. Guides cost about US$15-30 per day, depending where you go, and you should also buy them food and drink. Bear in mind that most guides are 'on commission' with local shops and stall-keepers. If you ask them to bargain for you, you will not necessarily be getting a good price. Nor will they necessarily go where you want to go. If you don't want a guide, a firm but polite *Non, merci* gets the message across. It is best to ignore altogether hustlers outside guesthouses, etc, as any contact only makes them persist.

Where to stay

Hotels There are a few good hotels in Pétion-Ville, up the hillside from Port-au-Prince, mostly designed for businessmen, and a couple of international-standard beach hotels along the Côte des Arcadins, northwest of the capital. Elsewhere, however, lodgings can be idiosyncratic, poor value, and variable in the quality of furnishings and service. In Port-au-Prince only the most expensive hotels and guesthouses have a/c plus sufficiently powerful in-house generators able to cope with the long electricity blackouts in the city. Some have a generator to give partial power to the bar but not to guest rooms. Water is also rationed, and many of the cheaper, central hotels lack both water and electricity much of the time. Check rooms in advance in the cheaper hotels, where service may be deficient. Tax, service charge and energy surcharge are usually added to hotel bills. These extras have been included in the prices given here, which are very approximate because of exchange rate vagaries. While hotels are accommodating UN and NGO personnel, prices are usually quoted in US dollars and in consequence are high. Where possible, it is cheaper to pay in gourdes. Paying by credit card is more expensive. The *Association Hotelière et Touristique d'Haïti* is at Choucoune Plaza, Pétion-Ville, T2574647.

Camping This is an adventure in Haiti. The dramatic scenery is very enticing but access to much of it is
Offer to pay a small amount for use of the land over rough terrain and there are no facilities. Campers have to take everything, and create or find their own shelter. Peasant homes dot the countryside and it is almost impossible to find a spot where you will be spared curious and suspicious onlookers. It is best to set up camp or lodging before dark. To prevent misunderstanding, it is important to explain to the locals your intentions, or, better still, talk to the local elder and ask assistance or protection.

Getting around

Air *Tropical Airways d'Haiti* has regular scheduled services linking Port-au-Prince with Cap Haïtien, Jérémie and Port-au-Paix. There are less regular domestic services with *Mission Aviation Fellowship* (T2463993) and *Caribintair* (T2460737). Book and pay through travel agents. Flights leave from Aviation Générale, a small domestic airport 1 km east of the international airport. *Caribintair* also operates as a charter/air taxi company. *Marien Air*, T2620527, an air taxi service run by Paul Takeo Hodges, flies anywhere in Haiti. It also offers flights to Port-au-Prince, the Dominican Republic, Turks and Caicos, Bahamas and Jamaica.

Road **Bus** Fairly conventional-looking buses (Creole: *bis*) or colourfully converted trucks and pick-ups (*taptap*) provide inter-city transport. There are no fixed departure times. Buses leave the 'stations' when they are packed. Roads are bad and journeys are long and uncomfortable. In trucks, it is worth paying more to sit with the driver.

Car Driving in Haiti is a hazardous free-for-all which some find exhilarating. The streets are narrow, with many sharp bends, and full of pedestrians in the towns. Outside the towns you have to look out for animals, potholes, sleeping policemen and police roadblocks. In wet weather, city streets and main highways all get clogged with traffic and become impassable. Haitians use their horns constantly to warn pedestrians of their approach. Vehicles swerve unexpectedly to avoid potholes. Cars often don't stop in an accident, so, to avoid paying the high insurance excess, keep a pen and paper handy to take down a number if necessary. Fuel (leaded, unleaded or diesel) is usually available in the big provincial towns, but power cuts may prevent stations from pumping. For driving to Cap-Haïtien, Les Cayes and Jacmel, an ordinary car is fine, but for Jérémie, Port-de-Paix or Hinche, a 4WD is necessary. Foreigners may use an international driving licence for 3 months, then a local permit is required.

For car hire, see page 265

Hitchhiking Many young Haitian men stick out a thumb asking for a 'roue libre', especially from foreigners. Use your discretion.

Dangerous and not advisable

Keeping in touch

Always bad, the telephone system deteriorated even more during the 1991-94 embargo and now fewer than a third of calls get through. The Haitian international operator (dial 09) is hard to raise. However, Teleco offices in major cities are central and easy to use and the operators are helpful. Expect queues. The *Oloffson*, *Le Plaza*, *Montana* and *El Rancho* hotels have AT&T 'USA Direct' telephones for collect calls to the USA or calls anywhere in the world with an AT&T credit card, but even these connections can be problematic. Email service is very limited. The postal service is slow and poor.

Telephone, internet & post
IDD code: 509

Newspapers *Le Nouvelliste* is the better of the 2 daily French-language newspapers. It is conservative, but tries to be impartial. 3 weekly newspapers are published in French, all very one-sided, but on different sides. The pro-Aristide weekly *Libète* is the only Creole newspaper. **Radio** Radio stations use a mix of French and Creole. *Metropole* and *Tropic* are best for news. *Radio France Inter* is re-broadcast locally on FM 89.3. The *BBC World Service* can be heard on 15220 (early morning) and 7325 (evenings). *Voice of America* is on 11915 (mornings) and 9455 evenings. **Television** A commercial TV station, *Télé-Haiti*, re-transmits American, French, Canadian and Latin American stations (including CNN, CBS, NBC, ABC, HBO, etc) to cable subscribers, electricity permitting.

Media

Haiti

Food and drink

Most restaurants offer Creole or French cuisine, or a mixture of both. Haiti's Creole cuisine is like that of its Caribbean cousins, but more peppery. Specialities include *griot* (deep-fried pieces of pork), *lambi* (conch, considered an aphrodisiac), *tassot* (jerked beef) and rice with djon-djon (tiny, dark mushrooms). Fried plantains appear on every menu. As elsewhere in the Caribbean, lobster is widely available. Pétion-Ville has many good French restaurants. Some are French-managed or have French chefs. Haiti's wide range of micro-climates produces a large assortment of fruits and vegetables. It is popular to buy these in the regions where they grow and are freshest (prices can be bargained). The French influence is obvious in butcher shops where fine cuts of meat, charcuterie, pâté and cheeses can be bought. American influence is felt in the supermarkets, where you can find almost everything. Vegetarians will find Haiti extremely difficult. Haitians cook nearly everything in pig fat, so even beans are to be avoided. One traveller survived on a diet of cornflakes, boiled eggs and fruit. Only the expensive restaurants and hotels will have a vegetarian option on the menu. A health/vegetarian shop on the corner of rue Grégoire and Louverture, in Pétion-Ville, stocks soya milk, a variety of spices, grains, pulses and some organic products.

Food
Bakeries sell French croissants, baguettes, cakes and pastries, together with Creole bread and meat pasties

Haiti's *Barbancourt* rum is excellent. The 5-star is particularly recommended and a bottle sells for only US$7; if you buy it at the airport on departure you can get a case of 5 bottles for about US$30. The distillery is in Damians and can be visited. Rum punch is popular but often

Drink
Haitian coffee is drunk strong and sweet, Rebo is the best brand

over-sweet. The local beer, *Prestige*, may be too sweet for some palates but is an acceptable alternative to sugary, fizzy drinks. The Dominican beer *Presidente* is the best of the foreign beers sold in Haiti, which all cost around US$0.75-1.50 depending on the brand. Soft drinks include *Séjourne*, *Couronne* and *Sékola* (banana).

Entertainment Until the mid-1980s, Haiti used to be a very good place for nightspots. With the drop in tourism and Haitians hesitating to be out late in uneasy times, many places have had to close or curtail their level of entertainment. The few that survive offer a good night out; evening entertainment starts at about 2030-2100. Nightclubbing starts around 2330.

Flora and fauna

There are no poisonous snakes or insects in Haiti Deforestation and soil erosion have destroyed habitats. Haiti is therefore poor in flora and fauna compared with its eastern neighbour. Lake Saumâtre, 90 mins east of the capital, is worth visiting. Less brackish than Enriquillo, across the Dominican border, it is the habitat of more than 100 species of waterfowl (including migratory North American ducks), plus flamingos and American crocodiles. The north side of the lake is better, reached via the town of Thomazeau (see page 271).

Also worthwhile and relatively easy to reach is Parc La Visite, about 5 hrs' hike from the hill resort of Kenscoff behind Port-au-Prince. On the high Massif de la Selle, with a mixture of pine forest and montane cloud forest, it has 80 bird species and 2 endemic mammals, the Hispaniolan hutia (*Plagiodontia aedium*) and the nez longue (*Solenodon paradoxus*). North American warblers winter there. It is also a nesting place for the black-capped petrel (*Pteradoma hasitata*). See page 271. Harder to reach is the Macaya National Park, at the tip of the southwest peninsula, site of Haiti's last virgin cloud forest. It has pines 45 m high, 141 species of orchid, 102 species of fern, 99 species of moss and 49 species of liverwort. Its fauna include 11 species of butterfly, 57 species of snail, 28 species of amphibian, 34 species of

Haiti

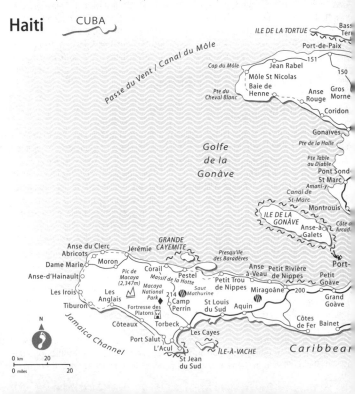

reptile, 65 species of bird and 19 species of bat. As well as the hutia, nez longue and black-capped petrel, its most exotic animals are the grey-crowned palm tanager (*Phaenicophilus poliocephalus*) and the Hispaniolan trogan (*Temnotrogan roseigaster*). The endangered peregrine falcon (*Falco pergrinus*) winters in the park. From Les Cayes, it takes half a day to get to a University of Florida base on the edge of the park which has basic camping. Allow 2 days each way for the 2,347 m Pic Macaya (see page 275). Paul Paryski (T2231400/1), a UN ecosystems expert, will give advice.

Leaf doctors, voodoo priests and sorcerers have a wealth of knowledge of natural remedies and poisons to be found in Haiti's surviving plant life. They do not share their knowledge readily. In his book *The Serpent and the Rainbow*, Harvard ethnobotanist Wade Davis gives a racy account of his attempts to discover which natural toxins sorcerers are thought to use to turn their victims into *zombis*. Almost any tree is liable to be chopped down for firewood or charcoal; a few very large species are not because they are believed to be the habitat of *loas* (spirits). Chief among them is the silkcotton tree, called *mapou* in Creole.

Shopping

The iron markets sell only food items, charcoal, knick knacks, etc, and sometimes paintings if there is a tourist market. The iron market in Port-au-Prince would be a fascinating place to visit but for the hustlers who will latch on to you and make the experience hell. It is also extremely narrow and dirty; it is important to be careful, go with a group and do not carry valuables. Try out your bargaining skills at the iron markets in Jacmel and Cap-Haïtien. Haitians may tell you that many of the items for sale in the few tourist shops can be bought far cheaper in markets. That may be true for them, but market vendors jack up prices for the foreigner, who will have to haggle skilfully to bring them down. See page 264 for best buys, and under towns for individual establishments.

People always ask for a discount in shops, except at food shops

Haiti

Holidays and festivals

Atlantic Ocean

The standard of the **Port-au-Prince Carnival** has fallen since the Duvaliers left (see page 284). Nowadays few people wear costumes and the floats are poorly decorated. There is a cacophony of music blaring out from both stands and passing floats. Excitement is provided by the walking bands (*bandes-à-pied*), cousins of the *Rara* bands that appear after carnival (see below). Circulating on foot, drawing a large, dancing, chanting crowd in their wake, they specialize in salacious lyrics and political satire. When crowds move in different directions there is boisterous pushing. The safest place to watch is from one of the stands near *Le Plaza*. Safer still and more peaceful are the Carnival celebrations in **Pétion-Ville**. Carnival climaxes on the 3 days before Ash Wed, but the government lays on free open-air concerts in different parts of the city during the 3 or 4 weekends of pre-carnival. Many people prefer the Carnival a week earlier at **Jacmel**, 2-3 hrs from the capital, where the tradition of elaborate, imaginative masked costumes still thrives. If you plan to stay in Jacmel you must book accommodation weeks, if not months, in advance, as it gets packed.

Festivals

Leave your money and valuables in the hotel safe; pickpockets are everywhere and there are occasional knife fights

I January 2004 is the 200th anniversary of independence from France

Port-au-Prince Carnival is immediately followed by **Rara**, dubbed the 'peasant carnival'. Every weekend during Lent, including Easter weekend, colourfully attired Rara bands emerge from Voodoo societies and roam the countryside. They seek donations, so be ready with a few small notes. Beating drums, blowing homemade wind instruments, dancing and singing, some bands may have a thousand or more members. A good place to see it is the town of Léogâne on Easter Sun. Beware, the drinking is heavy and fights are common.

The **Gede** (pronounced gay-day) are *loas* (spirits) who possess Voodooists on 1-2 Nov (*All Saints'* and *Day of the Dead*). They can be seen in cemeteries or roaming the streets, dressed to look like corpses or undertakers. The Lords of Death and the Cemetery, they mock human vanity and pretension, and remind people that sex is the source of life. They do this by dancing in a lewd fashion with strangers, causing much hilarity. For pilgrimages, see **Saut d'Eau**, **Plaine du Nord** and **Limonade** in the text below.

Health

See also main Health
section in Essentials
chapter, page 48

Prophylaxis against **malaria** is essential. Tap water is not to be trusted (drink only bottled, filtered or treated water) and take care when choosing food. The local herb tea can help stomach troubles; diarrhoea is often known as 'Haitian Happiness'! Hepatitis is common in some areas. Good professional advice is available for the more common ailments. Ask at the hotel desk for referrals to a doctor suited to your requirements. Office hours are usually 0730-1200, 1500-1800. A consultation costs about US$15-20. Hospital care and comfort varies. See page 266 for hospital listings in Port-au-Prince. Pharmacies can fill out prescriptions and many prescription drugs may be bought over the counter.

There is currently a red alert in Haiti over HIV/AIDS. The infection rate is over 6% of the population. There are no laws in Haiti to suppress prostitution. Activity seems to be evident only at night with the commonly known areas being along the main roads in Carrefour and street corners in Pétion-Ville. After hours the prostitutes move into the dive-type joints, targeting foreigners.

Port-au-Prince

IDD code: 509
Colour map 2, grid B2
Population: 846,247
Metropolitan area:
2,000,000

What Port-au-Prince lacks in architectural grace, it makes up for with a stunning setting. Steep mountains tower over the city to the south, La Gonâve island lies in a horseshoe bay to the west, and another wall of mountains beyond a rift valley plain rises to the north. The city has overflowed its original waterfront location, swollen by a rural exodus, and has climbed into the mountains behind. Most of the city is very poor, but the worst bidonvilles (shantytowns) are in a marshy waterfront area north of the centre. There are crowds of people everywhere, spilling off the sidewalks into the streets, moving to a cacophony of horns and engines.

Ins and outs

Getting there
The so-called
'supervisors' at the
airport are in fact
taxi drivers touting
for business

The airport is on the northern edge of Delmas, 13 km outside Port-au-Prince, T2410516. Arrival can be pandemonium especially if more than one flight is being dealt with. Just get on with your affairs and try not to get distracted. Once through the squash inside you emerge into a squash outside, of taxi drivers and people awaiting friends. A knowledge of French is useful. Porters charge US$0.50 per bag. A taxi into town is US$20-25 depending on how hard you bargain, or take a seat in a taptap (open-backed truck), extra charged for large bag. To get to the airport cheaply take a shared taxi from the turning off Av St-Martin (see map, formerly Av François Duvalier) for 3-4 km to rue Haile Sellassie where taptaps marked 'Airport' gather; US$0.15 from here, 10 km. For those coming by bus from the Dominican Republic, see page 253.

Things to do in Haiti

- Catch the beat with the writhing, twirling, dancing **Rara bands** each Sunday in Lent, a follow-up to Carnival but emanating from voodoo.
- Get a feel for the beauty of the countryside with a trek to **Bassin Bleu** and cool off in the pools at the foot of the green-blue waterfall.
- Head for the southwest to the tip of the peninsula for undisturbed beaches and the quiet life. **Anse du Clerc** has a small guesthouse on the beach with excellent food and buckets of tranquillity.
- Spend Thursday evening at the charming and idiosyncratic *Oloffson Hotel* in Port-au-Prince, setting for Graham Greene's *The Comedians*. Live music performed by RAM, a 'voodoo beat' band with a large following.

Getting around
For further details see Transport, page 265

A regular taxi is hard to find

Shared taxis (called **publiques** or simply taxis) are flagged down. They charge a basic fare (Creole: *kous*) of US$0.20 that may double or treble (*de kous*, *twa kous*) depending on how far off the beaten track you go. A red ribbon tied to the inside rear-view mirror identifies them. French is needed. They stop work at about 1930. **Camionettes** (minibuses) and **taptaps** (open-backed pick-ups with a brightly painted wooden superstructure) have fixed routes and fares (about US$0.15). They rarely circulate after 2030. They are difficult to manage with luggage. Camionettes to Pétion-Ville leave from Av John Brown, US$0.20.

Tourist information

Haiti

The Tourism Secretariat, upstairs at 8 rue Légitime, T2232143, F2235359, half a block from the Musée d'Art Haïtien, has poor information and no maps or brochures. Extra information may be found at the **Haitian Association for the Tourism and Hotel Industry** in Choucoune Plaza, Pétion-Ville, T2574647, at the *Hotel Montana*, or from travel agencies. **ISPAN** (Institute for the Protection of the Nation's Heritage), corner of Av Martin Luther King and Cherlez, Pont Morin, T2453220/3118, has information on forts and plantation houses. Also at rue 15-B, Cap-Haïtien (T2622459).

Safety
Watch out for pickpockets in markets, bus terminal areas and inside buses

Shantytown dwellers don't welcome sightseers and people with cameras. The area between the Champs de Mars and the waterfront is deserted after dark and should be avoided. It is safe to go to most places by car or taxi at night, but don't go about on foot. Political violence means that even in Pétion-Ville, generally considered safer than Port-au-Prince, it is not recommended that you go out after dark, or certainly not on the streets after 2100. Remember that frequent power cuts can plunge entire neighbourhoods into darkness. Drivers must always carry a licence as police blocks are common at night. Be careful of traffic when walking around town. Street vendors crowd the pavements, which forces pedestrians into the path of vehicles and many people have been knocked down and injured.

Sights

Several major thoroughfares have two names, the official one used for maps and the telephone book, and the one commonly used in speech. Often taxi drivers only know the second

The commercial quarter starts near the port and stretches inland about 10 blocks. It lacks charm or interest, except the area beside the port that was remodelled for the city's 1949 bicentennial. Known as the **Bicentenaire** (more formally, Cité de l'Exposition), it contains the post office, foreign ministry, parliament, American Embassy and French Institute. It is now very run down. The central reference point is the large, irregularly shaped park called the **Champs de Mars**, which begins to the east of the commercial quarter. The northwest corner is dominated by the white, triple-domed presidential palace. It was built in 1918 on the site of a predecessor that was blown up in 1912 with its president inside. In the 1991 coup, President Aristide made a stand inside the present building. Just to the northeast is the colonnaded, white and gold army high-command building, where soldiers nearly lynched Aristide after dragging him out of the palace. (He was saved by the French Ambassador, the American Ambassador or General Cedras, depending on whose story you believe.) Immediately behind the palace, to the south, is a large, mustard-yellow army garrison that was once the fief of the ill-famed Colonel Jean-Claude Paul, indicted in Miami in 1987 for drug smuggling and poisoned the following year.

Immediately to the east of the palace, on **Place des Héros de l'Independence**, the subterranean **Musée du Panthéon National (MUPANAH)** houses historical relics, including the rusted anchor of Columbus' flagship, the *Santa María*. It is not a very big museum, but worth the stop to learn a little about Haitian history and see some art displayed. Don't miss an 1818 oil painting of King Henri Christophe by Welshman Richard Evans, director of Christophe's Fine Arts Academy at Sans Souci. ■ *Mon-Fri 0900-1600, Sat 1000-1300. US$3. T2228337.* Two blocks north and west, at the corner of Avenue Mgr Guilloux and the busy rue Pavée, the **Sainte Trinité Episcopal Cathedral**, T2230814, has astounding biblical murals created in 1949 by the greatest naive artists, including Philomé Obin, Castera Bazile and Riguaud Benoit. The adjoining complex has a gift shop and a school whose students give excellent choral and classical music concerts.

At the intersection of rues Capois and Champ de Mars, the **Musée d'Art Haïtien** has Haiti's finest naive art collection, plus a craft shop and a small café in its garden. The collection is not large and there is no recent art. ■ *From 1000. US$0.50. T2222510.* The **Maison Défly**, built by an army commander in 1896, is in the Victorian 'gingerbread' style, characterized by steep roofs and gables, round turrets, high ceilings, balconies and rich fretwork embellishment. Not a distinguished example, it contains a museum with period furniture.

■ *Mon-Sat 0900-1300. 7 Av John Paul II, T2224081.* The rue Capois has several hotels, restaurants and shops. At the southern end, 1 km from the Champs de Mars, is the *Hôtel Oloffson*, a much more imposing example of a gingerbread. West of rue Capois are leafy neighbourhoods climbing into the foothills where prosperous 19th-century gingerbread house residences abound.

Port-au-Prince orientation

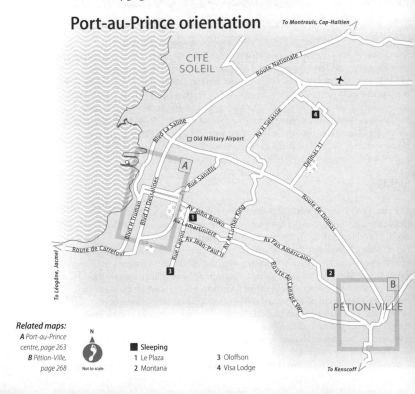

Related maps:
A *Port-au-Prince centre, page 263*
B *Pétion-Ville, page 268*

N
Not to scale

■ **Sleeping**
1 Le Plaza
2 Montana
3 Oloffson
4 Visa Lodge

Essentials

Hotels L-B *Le Plaza* (formerly *Holiday Inn*), 10 rue Capois, central location on Champs de Mars, T2239800/93. Jungly gardens, pool, tolerable restaurant, own generator, price includes taxes and electricity, children under 18 free if sharing room, all rooms a/c. **AL-B** *Oloffson* (see above), rue Cadet Jérémie at intersection with rue Capois, T2234000, www.oloffson.com. Model for *Hotel Trianon* in Graham Greene's *The Comedians* and eccentrically managed by Haitian-American musician Richard Morse, this is Haiti's most charming hotel. However, you pay for the atmosphere and carefully cultivated faded grandeur. The smaller rooms were built as a hospital and maternity wing by the US marines. Haunt of writers, journalists and film makers. Thu buffet and live music with RAM band playing, well worth the money, pool, never lacks electricity, most rooms a/c, CP. **A** *Visa Lodge*, rue des Nimes, Rte de l'Aéroport, T2491202/3/4, 2462662. Businessman's hotel in industrial zone near airport, pool, good restaurant, own generator, EP. **B** *Prince*, corner of rue 3 and Av N, Pacot, T2452764. Quiet hillside neighbourhood 15 mins' walk from taxis, own generator, all rooms a/c. **B** *Villa St-Louis*, 95 Bourdon, on the way to Pétion-Ville, T2456417, F2457949. CP, weekly rates, studio apartments, fridge, phone, TV. **B-C** *Park*, 25 rue Capois, near *Le Plaza*, T2224406, www.parkhotel.homestead.com Cheaper to pay in gourdes, safe, central, be prepared to wait an age for breakfast, no generator. **E-F** *Auberge Port-au-Prince*, 148 rue du Centre, where buses from Dominican Republic disgorge their passengers amid hordes of vendors, very basic rooms with bath or inside room, fan, management surly, ground floor bar serves lunch but closes around 1900, good view from roof.

Guesthouses B *La Griffonne*, 21 rue Jean Baptiste, Canapé Vert, T2454095/3440. Quiet neighbourhood 5 mins' walk from Av John Brown, own generator, rooms with private bath and a/c, MAP. **B** *Sendral's*, rue Mercier, Bourdon, near *Hotel Villa St-Louis*, T2456502. Own generator, rooms with private bath and fan, CP. **C** *May's Villa*, 28 Debussy, T2451208. Quiet neighbourhood at top of Av John Paul II, 10 mins' walk from taxis, view, has generator, but room lights come on with city power at about 2100, rooms with bath and fan, CP.

Almost the only decent places to eat out at night in Port-au-Prince are the *Oloffson* or *Le Plaza*, or a row of terrace cafés selling barbecued chicken at the southeast corner of the Champs de Mars (starting near Rex theatre). Bars in this area will probably try and short-change you. Well-off Port-au-Princiens go up to Pétion-Ville to dine out. The following restaurants are open during the day and close at about 1600: *Café Terrasse*, rear of *Air France* Bldg, 11 rue Capois and rue Ducoste, T2225468. Excellent lunch, favoured by international aid agency staffers. *Tiffany*, Blvd Harry Truman, Bicentenaire 12, north of Télé-Haiti, T2220993. Haitian, French and American food. *Chez Yvane*, 19 blvd Harry Truman, south of Télé-Haiti, T2220188. Creole lunch in a/c premises. *La Perle*, 80 rue Pavée, between Dessalines and rue des Miracles. Pleasant, cool, enormous sandwiches, also spaghetti, omelettes. *Paradis de Amis*, 43 rue Pavée, between Centre and Dessalines. Club sandwiches, omelettes, ice cream, a/c, popular with locals, cheap, large

Haiti

portions, spaghetti costs US$2. *Les Jardins du Musée*, at the *Museé d'Art Haïtien*, T2238738, is a small oasis, but a bit pricey, popular with 'blancs', particularly French embassy staff at lunchtime, slow service.

Drinks such as cold beers, water, juice, rum at the *Supermarket de la Bonne Foie*, 52 rue Dr Marselly Seide. Mon-Sat 0730-1600, small, friendly, English spoken. *Supermarket Express* up on the hill on John Brown. Cold beer and *Guinness*, UN customers.

Entertainment Voodoo beat band RAM performs Thu at the *Oloffson*, the place to be. Otherwise, the best nightlife is to be found in Pétion-Ville (see below). There is a red-light district on the southwest Carrefour Rd that has been badly affected by AIDS and political turmoil. The central part of the establishments consists of spacious, breezy, outdoor discos. The Dominican beer on offer is excellent and cheap, but the Dominican prostitutes and loud Dominican merengue music may have scant appeal. The city's western limits, around Mariani, have several ill-lit waterfront nightclubs, such as *Le Lambi*, where couples dance groin-to-groin to live *compas* bands and the men eat plate after plate of spicy, freshly caught *lambi* (conch) to boost their virility.

Cinemas Cheap and interesting: the best are *Imperial* (a/c), Delmas; *Capitol* (a/c), 53 rue Lamarre; *Paramount*, Champs de Mars. Non-French films are dubbed into French.

Shopping **Art and craft** Some galleries have a near-monopoly on certain artists, so don't expect to see a cross-section of all the major artists in any one good gallery. The paintings hung at the *Oloffson* are for sale. *Galerie Carlos Jara*, T2457164, has a fine collection at 28 rue Armand Holly, Pacot, 10 mins' drive uphill from the *Oloffson*. *Le Centre d'Art*, 58 rue Roy, Pacot, T2222018. In a beautiful but crumbling old house, 2 floors of artwork with stacks of paintings, upstairs, founded 1944, open Mon-Fri 0930-1300, 1430-1600, Sat 0930-1230. The *Nader* family has 2 galleries: one in Pétion-Ville (see page 269); the other at 18 rue Bouvreuil, T2450565/4524, in the leafy Croix Desprez neighbourhood, is now principally a museum; *Galerie Issa*, T2223287, 17 Av du Chili (300 m from *Oloffson*) is more like a wholesale warehouse, but cheap if you know what you are looking for. *Damballa Art Gallery*, rue 3, Pacot, next to Comité Artisanal Haïtien, open Mon-Fri 0800-1800, Sat 0800-1500. Mass-produced copies of the Haitian masters are sold cheaply around the post office, near the port. If you want to buy paintings, you are advised to

Haïti

Port-au-Prince centre

N
Not to scale

To Léogâne, Jacmel

■ Sleeping
1 Aubergue Port-au-Prince

Voodoo

Seeing a Voodoo ceremony or dance during a short visit is likely to get easier since Voodoo was recognized as an official religion in 2003. However, they are not announced in newspapers or on the radio. Never go unless accompanied by a Haitian, or someone already known there. Most middleclass Haitians do not attend ceremonies. They won't know where or when they are happening and they may even be discomforted by your interest. Instead, tell poor, working-class Haitians about your interest. You may strike lucky. To increase your chances, time your stay to coincide with 2 November (Day of the Dead), Christmas, New Year or the Epiphany (6 January), when there are many ceremonies. If invited, take a bottle or two of rum or whisky and be ready to give generously if there is a collection. Sometimes, on the contrary, a wealthy oungan *(priest) or* mambo *(priestess) will insist on lavishing drinks and food on a visitor. Don't refuse. Before taking pictures with a still camera or video, ask permission. You may be asked to pay for the privilege. TV crews are usually asked to pay substantial amounts. An* oungan *may always be consulted in his* ounphor *(temple) even if there is no ceremony; plead poverty if the sum requested seems exorbitant.*

Max Beauvoir (T2342818/3723), an oungan *intellectual with fluent English, has initiated foreigners. Purists questioned the authenticity of the regular Voodoo dances he laid on for tourists, but he is unquestionably an authority and talks readily to visitors. Aboudja (T2458476, or through the Oloffson), an English-speaking TV news cameraman and voodoo consultant for visiting journalists and TV crews, has been initiated as an* oungan *although he does not practise regularly.*

take your time, look around, and be prepared to bargain. You will learn which patterns are imitations or mass-produced just by seeing them repeatedly. Vendors sell first-class Voodoo flags outside the Musée d'Art Haïtien. Souvenir sellers also set up close to the *Holiday Inn*.

Comité Artisanal Haïtien, 29 rue 3, Pacot (near *Oloffson*), T2228440. A co-operative selling handicrafts (no paintings) from all over Haiti at good prices, open 0900-1600 Mon-Fri, 1000-1200 Sat. **Ambiance**, 17 Av M, Pacot, T2452494. Haitian jewellery and pottery. **The Rainbow**, 9 rue Pierre Wiener, Bourdon, T2456655/6039. Sells handicraft and paintings. **Fanal**, 124 Av Christophe, corner of rue Waag, T2451948. Antiques, handicrafts, toys, open Mon-Fri 1000-1700, Sat 1000-1400.

Local Bus Pick-up trucks with seats in the back, known as *Publiques* are the common form of public transport. They stop on demand and are usually overcrowded and uncomfortable. Most of the bus *stations* for out-of-town destinations are somewhere on or between Blvd Jean-Jacques Dessalines and the waterfront.

Transport
See also Ins and outs and Getting around, pages 256 and 261

Car hire A small Japanese car with a/c, rents for about US$50 per day, US$280 per week, plus 10% sales tax, unlimited mileage. A basic 4WD starts at US$510 per week with US$500 deposit and excess of US$1,000 for damages. Chauffeurs cost as little as US$15 a day in Port-au-Prince and US$25 a day if you go elsewhere in the country, although you will have to pay for his meals and accommodation. **Avis**, T2464161, **Hertz**, T2460700, **Dollar**, T2491800, and **Budget**, T2461366, all have bases near the airport; *Avis* is opposite the airport terminal, open 0800-1700, *Hertz* is in the Dynamic Entreprise Building and *Dollar* in the Firestone Building. Smaller companies include **Sunshine Jeep**, T2491155, **Secom**, 564 Route de Delmas, T2571913, www.secomhaiti.com, and **Sugar**, T2463413. *Hertz* is the only company with a base in Cap-Haïtien.

Taxis *Nick's Taxis*, T2577777, based at 31 rue Panaméricaine, in Pétion-Ville, is the only radio taxi company. It charges according to the meter. A new, reliable company in Pétion-Ville is **Sunny Taxi Services**, rue Lambert between rue Clervaux and rue Rebecca, T5107000. A passing *Publique* that is empty can be persuaded to do a private job (Creole: *flete*). The driver removes the red ribbon.

Agence Citadelle, 35 Place du Marron Inconnu, T2225900, F2221792, www.agence citadelle.com Mon-Fri 0800-1300, 1400-1630, Sat 0830-1230, also offices in Pétion-Ville and

Tour operators

Haïti

Cap Haïtien. Sightseeing tours in a/c buses, airport shuttle (US$15 per person, min 2 people), travel and tours to Dominican Republic and Cuba, as well as specializing in travel to South, Central America and the Caribbean islands (owner Bobby Chauvet is a leading Haitian ecologist). *ABC Tours*, 156 rue Pavée, near Sainte-Trinité, T2220335, F2231855. Courteous, helpful. *Voyage Chatelain*, rue Geffrard, T2220130, F2235065. Handles Terra Bus to Santo Domingo including immigration formalities. Because of the collapse of tourism, sightseeing tours are set up only on request. For boat trips try Bernard, T2572399, who can arrange custom-made excursions on a boat sleeping 4-6, although for day trips 8 are taken, price up to US$50 per person per day, sailing to Les Cayemites and Pestel is recommended, with good beaches.

Directory **Banks** *Promobank*, T2222461, corner of Lamarre and Av John Brown, also a branch at Blvd du Quai and rue Eden. *Scotiabank*, Route de Delmas (beneath Canadian Embassy) and branch on rue des Miracles near corner of Blvd Dessalines. *Citibank*, T2462600, Route de Delmas. Also several Haitian banks such as *Sogebank*, T2295000, and *Banque de L'Union Haïtienne*, T2230499. There are long queues in most banks for any kind of service. **Exchange** Street money changers (*cambistes*) can be found on rue Pavée, at the airport, or near the market in Pétion-Ville. It is perfectly legal but they will try and make as much as possible out of you. Check the rate on page 2 of the daily Le Nouvelliste newspaper. You may prefer to go in a car and do it through the window. The *cambiste* hands over the agreed sum in gourdes for you to count before you surrender the equivalent US dollar amount. They take only cash. If possible, use a *cambiste* you have seen regularly at a particular spot; never allow yourself to be steered to a cambiste by an informal guide. Banks or currency dealers working out of offices give almost as good a rate. They also take TCs. Try Daniel Fouchard (T2231739), 14 rue des Miracles, Banque de Boston Building. Many importers and big retailers give a good rate for cash, TCs and even personal cheques on US bank accounts. Try Didier Rossard (T2225163), upstairs at 115 Place Geffrard; M or Mme Handal at Express Market, Av John Brown, 6 blocks down from Villa St-Louis. (See also page 253.) **Communications** Internet: US$3 per hr at Centre de Formation JRC Software, Av Magny 16, T2222632, jrcardozo@aol.com Mon-Sat 0800-1900, Sun 0800-1200. **Embassies** Canada, T2232358, F2238720, Bank of Nova Scotia Bldg, Delmas 18; **Cuba** (T2576626), 18 rue E Pierre Péguy-Ville, Pétion-Ville; **Dominican Republic**, T2571650, F2579215, 121 rue Panaméricaine (50 m down rue José de San Martín), Pétion-Ville; **EC Delegation** (T2490141, T2490246), Delmas 60, Impasse Bravé 1, rue Mercier Laham; **France** (T2220951, F2239858), 51 Place des Héros de l'Indépendance, on rue Capois at the southwest corner of the Champs de Mars, near Hotel Palace; **Germany** (T2573128), 17 rue Edmond Mangonès, Berthé, Pétion-Ville; **Japan** (T2455875, F2458834), Villa Besta Vista, Impasse Tulipe 2 Desprez; **Spain** (T2454410, F2453901), 54 Pacot; **US** (T2220200, F2231641), Blvd Harry Truman, Bicentenaire; **US**, T2237011, 104 rue Oswald Durand, Mon-Wed, Thu 0730-1400, Thu 0730-1100, emergencies T2230955, acspap@state.gov. **Medical services** *Hospital Canapé Vert*, rue Canapé Vert, T2451052/3/0984. *Adventiste de Diquini*, Carrefour Rd, T2342000/0521. *Hospital Français de Haiti*, rue du Centre, T2222323. *St François de Salles*, rue de la Révolution, T2222110/0232.

Pétion-Ville

Pétion-Ville was once the capital's hill resort, lying just 15 minutes from Port-au-Prince, but 450 m above sea level and therefore cooler. Now it is considered a middle-class suburb, with restaurants and boutiques. Three roads lead up from Port-au-Prince. The northernmost, the Route de Delmas, is ugly and dusty. Preferable to this is the Panaméricaine, an extension of Avenue John Brown (Creole: Lali), which is serviced by camionettes. The southernmost, Route du Canapé Vert, has the best views. In Pétion-Ville, the main streets, Lamarre and Grégoire, are parallel to each other, one block apart, on the six blocks between the Panaméricaine and the Place St Pierre. Most of the shops, galleries and restaurants are on or between these two streets or within a couple of blocks of them.

Sleeping   **Hotels LL-A** *El Rancho*, rue José de San Martín, just off the Panaméricaine, T2574928,
Most of the larger   F2574134, elrancho@msn.com Very pleasant, painted white with tiled roofs, rooms and
hotels with pools will   suites, balconies, beautiful view, 2 pools, fitness centre, tennis, 2 restaurants, bars, casino,
let non-guests use   nightclub, sauna, spa, EP, a/c. **LL-A** *Villa Créole*, just beyond the *El Rancho* on José de San
their facilities for the   Martín, T2571570/1, www.villacreole.com Tennis court, pool, good view, rooms and suites,
day for a small charge   some connecting, a/c, TV, internet access. **L-A** *Montana*, rue Cardozo, a turning off the

Panaméricaine at the entrance to Pétion-Ville, T2574020, F2576137, htmontana@aol.com An oasis of luxury, best views over Port-au-Prince, especially from poolside restaurant, EP, a/c, phone, TV, airport transfers, conference facilities, built on hillside with lots of stairs, elevators, non-guests can use the pool for US$3. **AL-B** *Kinam*, at the corner of rue Lamarre and rue Moise, facing Place St-Pierre, T2570482, www.hotelkinam.com. Mock gingerbread house, 38 rooms, 3 suites, a/c, phone, TV, good restaurant, bar, small pool, handy location. Under same ownership is **AL** *Le Ritz*, corner rue Panaméricaine and rue José San-Martin, T2576520/1, F2576508. Aparthotel, studios, good for business groups, conference facilities. **AL-B** *Ibo Lele*, at the upper side of Pétion-Ville, towards Montagne Noire, T2575668. Slightly cheaper than Kinam, with pool. **A-B** *Caraïbe*, central, 13 rue Leon Nau, Nerette, T2572524, F2570625. 12 rooms with large baths, a/c, restaurant, TV lounge, pool, built in 1920s, charming, friendly, helpful, family-run, French, English, Spanish spoken.

Guesthouses **D-E** *Doux Séjour*, 32 rue Magny (quiet street 5 blocks from Place St Pierre), T2571560, F2576518. Weekly rates, apartments or nice rooms with 2 beds, fan and bathroom, pizza restaurant alongside. *Marabou*, 72 rue Stephen Archer, just behind St Pierre church, T2571934. Haggle for good rate for long stay. **C** *Ife*, 30 rue Grégoire, a busy street by

Pétion-Ville

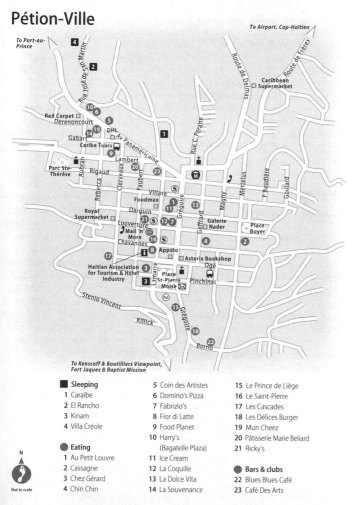

N

Not to scale

Haïti

the market, T2570737. Some a/c, CP. **C** *Villa Kalewes*, 99 rue Grégoire (at the upper, quiet end of the street), T2570817. CP, pool. **D** *St Joseph's Home for Boys Guest House*, Delmas 91, T/F2574237, or write to Michael Geilenfeld, Lynx Air, PO Box 407139, Fort Lauderdale, FL 33340, USA. Rates include breakfast and dinner, vegetarian meals on request, laundry, bottled water, money exchange, security. For a fee the boys will escort you, give drum lessons, the home can also provide guides, translators, Creole lessons, airport pick-up. Some of the boys perform in the Resurrection Dance Theatre, self-written dances based on their experiences when they lived on the street. Revenue from guests helps to pay for the boys, aged 8-18, who live and work as a family, running the guesthouse when not at classes. Founder Michael Geilenfeld was a brother with Mother Theresa before starting the home in 1985.

Eating **Mid-range** (over US$10) *Chez Gérard*, 17 rue Pinchinat, T2571949. Beautiful setting with outside veranda and lush greenery growing everywhere, only items written on menu board are available, about 16/day, prices relatively high, appetizers US$4.50-16, entrées US$14-25, rum US$2.75-3.40, beer US$1.80. *Hotel Kinam*, see above, French/Creole cuisine, very good, lovely ambiance, *lambi* in Creole sauce recommended, prices around US$9-23. *La Dolce Vita*, 59 rue Geffrard, T2571133. Excellent Italian, home-made pasta, US$8-13 main course, Italian beer and wine, dinner only, advance booking recommended. *La Souvenance*, 8 rue Gabart at the corner of Aubran, T2577688. Gourmet French cuisine. Recommended. Pricey. *Les Cascades*, 73 rue Clerveaux, T2577589. Open Mon-Sat 1200-2300, long-established, good French food, a place for lunch, dinner, brunch, cocktail, buffet, takeaway, wedding receptions, etc.

Cheap (US$5-10) *Cassagne*, at the corner of Louverture and Mettelus. Beautiful old home converted into a restaurant, outdoor and indoor seating, bar, stage, live DJ at weekends with dancing from 2300, very nice owner, Haitian/Creole cuisine, moderate prices, food on grill US$6-10, seafood a bit more expensive. *Fabrizio's*, 126 rue Louverture, T2578433, fabrizio@ haitiworld.com Really good Italian restaurant with some tasty dishes, meals from US$6-12, desserts, takeaway and delivery available, beer US$2.25, rum US$3.20-4.50 a glass. *Fior Di Latte*, Choucounne Plaza, corner of rue Lamarre and rue Chavannes, T2568474. Excellent, especially thin-crust pizzas, small US$7-10, medium (for 2 people) US$7-10, home-made ice cream, US$0.75 per scoop, cappuccino US$2, shady outside seating, popular, open Tue-Sat 1000-2200, Sun 1400-2200. *La Coquille*, 42 rue Lamarre, T2572542. Buffet place with good food, mainly Creole, US$6.85, open 1200-1800, beer US$1.85-2.25, rum US$3. *Le Prince de Liège*, 89 rue Grégoire, T2578522. New in 2002, Belgian-owned, nice atmosphere, reasonable prices, steak US$8, *lambi* quiche US$4.50, huge shish kebab US$9, cheese tray US$6, good food, Cuban and Dominican cigars, open Mon-Sat 1900-2300. *Le Saint-Pierre*, corner of rue Lamarre and rue Chavannes, T2572280. Small outside seating area overlooking street and indoors with 3 TVs for sports fans, Canadian-owned, pizzas, wings, Creole dishes and *poutine* (fries with cheese and gravy, a Canadian speciality), open daily 1100-2330. *Plantation*, Impasse Fouchard, turning off rue Borno, T2570979. Excellent French chef, good wine. Recommended. *Coin Des Artistes*, 59 rue Panaméricaine, beneath Festival Arts Gallery, T2572400. Grilled fish and lobster, moderate prices. *Au Petit Louvre*, rue Grégoire, north of rue Darguin. Creole and Middle Eastern food, moderate prices, good but not everything on the menu is always available, try their *kibbis*. On the Kenscoff Rd the *Altitude 1300*, 67 Laboule, T2559719 is the place where the bourgeoisie go at weekends, with the best of Creole cuisine. *Station 39*, 39 rue Lamarre. Boasts the best Creole food, breakfast from US$1-2.75, sandwiches and pasta dishes for lunch US$1-3.50, meat and seafood for dinner US$4.50-9. *Chin Chin*, 49 rue Geffrard, T2573155. Bar-pizzeria-restaurant, not very clean, but prices low, beer US$1.40-2.25, rum US$1.60, Coke US$0.90, pizza US$5-12.50, also some Middle Eastern dishes. *Harry's*, 97 Av Panaméricaine, inside Bagatelle Plaza, T2571885. Bar, restaurant, pizzeria, small US$5.25, medium US$7.25, large US$9, ice cream, sandwiches, American and Haitian food, low to moderate prices.

Seriously cheap (under US$5) *Ricky's Restaurant*, 34 rue Faubert, T2578524. Mostly Creole dishes, US$4.50 buffet Mon-Sat 1200-1500 or 1600 depending on when they run out of food, beer US$1.60, rum US$1.80, also have great artwork on display from the Gallery Valcin II. **Fast food** *Domino's Pizza*, 91 Av Panaméricaine, T2575151. Very clean and you can sit inside, also delivery, prices slightly higher than in North America, but if you have to have pizza... Small US$7.25, medium US$12, large US$17. *Food Planet*, 79 rue Lambert. American-type fast food with some Haitian dishes, open daily until 2100. *Les Délices Burger*, 97 rue Grégoire, T2578468. Very good and large hamburgers, taste American, US$2.50-3.50, mini-pizza, nuggets and fries. *Mun Cheez*, Av Panaméricaine on the corner of rue Rebecca, T2562177. Open daily until 2200 except Sun 1400, mostly snack foods such as subs, burgers, pizza, salads, egg rolls, fries, also home delivery. *Star Mart/Tiger Mart* are gas/petrol stations that also sell snack foods and usually very good pizza and sandwiches, found around the Av Panaméricaine and also on rue Canapé Vert. **Cafés** *Presse Café*, 28 rue Riaud. Small, coffee and cake, US$1.15 for an expresso, sit and read, magazines and newspapers for sale, mostly in French. *Ice Cream*, 25 rue Darguin. Quite good and tasty ice cream with 6-10 different flavours, also hot dogs, milkshakes and beer, cheap. **Bakery** *Pâtisserie Marie Beliard*, on corner of rue Lambert and rue Faubert. Great bread, cakes, pâtés and French pastries.

Nightlife *Ada Club*, 16 rue Rigaud, '*Resto Dansant*', dancing club and eatery. *Bash*, in the *Hotel El Rancho*, also Sat evening live jazz. *Blues Blues Café*, rue Borno between rue Grégoire and Mettelus. Good setting, bar, live music, restaurant and small boutique, but the food is not great, mix of things and nothing spectacular, moderate prices. *Café Des Arts*, 19 rue Lamarre (same house as *Galerie Monnin*), T2577979. Open 1900 until late, dining and sometimes live music at weekends, large bar, beautiful setting, mostly French cuisine, grill US$9-14, pastas US$7.25-12, speciality entrées US$11-15. Upstairs is *Full Moon*. *Cheers*, 14 rue Villatte. Great pina colada or food in a relaxed environment, ask in advance and you can rent videos and a room in which to watch them with friends. *Guess Who*, rue Grégoire. Pleasant terrace, often have concerts. *Harry's*, (next to *Coin des Artistes*), T2571885. Food OK, good value, 2 pool tables, often live music, latin and dance music, popular with families. *Sunset Bar*, 58 rue Grégoire, T2576236. Run by Canadian Paul, good music, not too much compa, darts and table football, open late, relaxed atmosphere, mixed clientèle.

Shopping *La Promenade* at the intersection of Grégoire and Moise (southeast corner of Place St-Pierre), a garden turned into a small shopping promenade with an outdoor café, 1000-1800. **Art and handicrafts** *Expressions*, 55 rue Mettelus, south of rue Ogé, T2563471, expregal@haitiworld.com One of the Nader family galleries, English-speaking owners, beautiful gallery, excellent and large selection of paintings. *Festival Arts Gallery*, 1 bis, rue Gabart, T2577956. Haitian artists who have moved on from primitivism. *Fleur De Canne*, 34 bis, rue Gabart, T2574266. Good-quality craft in a charming store. Place St-Pierre is a good place to find street vendors selling handicrafts, paintings, carpets, sculptures, plants, flowers etc, remember to bargain. *Galata*, 57 rue Faubert, T2572124. Mainly handicrafts, especially weavings, metalwork. *Galerie Bourbon-Lally*, 23 rue Lamarre, corner of rue Villate, T2576321/3397. Owned by Englishman Reynald Lally, good choice of naive art. *Galerie Marassa*, 11 rue Lamarre, T2571967. Hand-painted boxes, trays, art exhibitions. *Galerie Monnin*, 19 rue Lamarre, in same house as *Café des Arts*, T2574430. *Galerie Nader*, 50 rue Grégoire, T2575602, 2570855. The most expensive, but has an exceptional range of naive and other modern Haitian artists, also exhibitions. *Galerie Valcin II*, corner of rue Rigaud and Faubert. Paintings, crafts and souvenirs. *La Galerie*, 37 rue Clerveaux, T2570216. Great selection of paintings and cheaper than the 2 galleries above. *The Red Carpet*, 86 rue Panaméricaine, opposite turnings for *El Rancho* and *Villa Créole*, T2572048, F2573324. Large art collection, pizza restaurant attached.

Books *Asterix*, corner of rue Ogé and rue Grégoire, the place to get good French books, magazines (some in English), stationery. **Photography** Lots of places for photo processing, including one on rue Louverture between Lamarre and Grégoire, owned by Philippe, who speaks English and French, good quality, considerably cheaper than in the USA.

Food *Foodmax*, corner of rue Darguin and rue Lamarre, is a supermarket which carries a lot of 'Western' items. *Royal Supermarket*, rue Clerveaux, just north of rue Louverture, also full of imported goods. *Appolo*, rue Grégoire just north of Place St-Pierre, best place to buy fresh meat. *Caribbean Supermarket*, Delmas 95, the biggest supermarket with the most varieties.

Haiti

Tour operators   *Voyages Plus*, La Promenade St, T2573868. You can book *Caribe Tour* buses to the Dominican Republic here. *Multivision*, Angle rues Lambert and Clerveaux, T2579771. English spoken. *Jacqualine Labrom*, T4013742, ljacqui@haitiworld.com English-speaking, Jacqui can book packages to Cap and trips all over Haiti. *Agence Citadelle*, branch at Complexe Promenade, Angle rues Grégoire et Moise, T2570944, vppvl@agencecitadelle.com Open 0900-1300, 1400-1730 Mon-Fri, 1000-1400 Sat.

Directory   **Banks** *BUH* and *Capital* are on rue Lamarre. Open Mon-Fri 0900-1700, Sat 0900-1300, very slow and bureaucratic. *Sogébank*, on rue Grégoire, on rue Louverture and on rue Lamarre gives faster service. *Promobank* is on the corner of rue Rigaud and Faubert. *CitiBank* has an affiliate on rue Louverture between rue Faubert and rue Clerveaux. **Communications** *Téléco* is at the corner of rue Magny and rue Rigaud. All calls go through an operator. Faxes can be sent through *Speedy Fax* on rue Louverture, between rues Faubert and Clerveaux. *Mail 'n More*, 107 rue Louverture, photocopying, email, fax, UPS, calling cards, new and clean building. *DHL* is at 21 rue Gabart, T2576192, 2578446.

Côte des Arcadins

Beaches
Haiti's best beaches are far from the capital, on the Caribbean and Atlantic coasts

The Gulf of La Gonâve beaches, the only ones that can be reached within an hour's drive, are not particularly good compared to the ones on the north coast of the island, but popular for a day trip out of the capital at weekends. Those west of the capital are poor. The first beaches you get to are rather gritty, but they improve as you go further north. The backdrop is of arid, deforested mountainside but the calm, clear, shallow water is excellent for children. The Côte des Arcadins, a 20-km stretch of beach, begins 60 km north of the capital. The few hotels have bars and restaurants, and charge admission to day visitors. They may be crowded with wealthy Port-au-Princiens or aid agency staff at weekends. There are also public beaches with no hotels. The **Musée Colonial Ogier-Fombrun** (see *Moulin Sur Mer*, below), in a stone 18th-century plantation building, has a model of the original house and buildings, also museum pieces outside. ■ *Daily 1000-1700. US$2, students and children US$1.* **The Arcadins** are three uninhabited, sandy cays 3 km offshore, surrounded by reef. The diving is excellent. **Isle La Gonâve** is also visible and dive boats visit the wall offshore.

Sleeping
Overnight stays at weekends are popular, you may need to book ahead, very calm at night, beautiful stars

Heading north along the Côte des Arcadins in geographical order: **C** *Kyona*, T2576850. Basic rooms in bungalows or newer block, cold water, thatched open-air restaurant, volleyball, hotel dates from early 1960s. Daily admission US$9 adults, US$$1.50 children, curved, gritty beach, loungers and tables in shade, lots of trees, locals selling paintings, turtle shells, black coral. **AL** *Kaliko Beach Club*, at Km 61, T2984607, kaliko@haitiworld.com All-inclusive, smart blue and white plantation-style resort, popular with French Canadians, this is the noisiest of the resorts with music playing all the time, but it also has the most facilities to offer, 55 rooms (sleep 4) with fan or a/c, and growing, day pass US$40 with 2 meals, US$15 lunch only, pleasant beach but not spectacular, pool, tennis, gardens, entertainment, Creole lessons, boat cruises, conference facilities, excursions. **A-B** *Wahoo Bay*, T2229653. Day pass US$10, 20 large, clean rooms, CP, a/c, upstairs rooms with balcony and view of La Gonâve, good showers, delicious food with generous portions, pool, small but sandy beach, good swimming, loungers and tables with shade, windsurfing, horse riding, tennis, some new rooms. **C** *Ouanga Bay*, at Km 65, T29831556, F2224422. Day pass US$3.50 until 1900, food and drinks extra, small sandy beach with man-made reef, quiet and private, loungers, restaurant built over the water, 27 rooms and apartments right on beach, large beds, fan or a/c, TV and phones, bathrooms adequate, English-speaking owner, friendly, watersports include snorkelling, windsurfing, pedalos and glass-bottom boats with electric motors, diving arranged. After Montrouis, at Km 77, is **L-AL** *Moulin Sur Mer*, T2221918, www.moulin surmer.net, reached through the extensive gardens of the Musée Colonial Ogier-Fombrun (see above), with palms, peacocks, geese and ducks, beautiful setting on sandy beach. 65 rooms, FAP, Haitian furniture and art, a/c, hot water, tiled floors, phones, suites for families, also beach rooms for day use, 2 restaurants, vegetarian food available, tennis, volleyball, ping pong, pool, mini golf, playground, watersports including pedalos, kayaks, windriders, diving arranged, golf carts. A day pass costs US$10.

Diving Just along the beach from the *Kaliko Beach Club* is *Pegasus Diving*, T2383140: snorkelling trips at Les Arcadins, US$20, Anse à Pirogues, US$35, and La Gonâve, US$50. Diving for certified divers only to Les Arcadins, US$70 including gear, and the wall at Isle La Gonâve, US$80, 30 mins on dive boat. **Fishing** also available, US$200 for 2 people, half day, including gear, Captain, drinks and boat rental. **Sports**

East of Port-au-Prince

The asphalt road to Kenscoff, in the mountains behind Port-au-Prince, starts just to the west of the Pétion-Ville police station, on the Place St-Pierre. After 10 minutes, there is a turn-off on the right at **United Sculptors of Haiti**, which sells good wood carvings. It skirts a huge quarry and climbs to **Boutilliers**, a peak topped by radio and television masts that dominates the city. Great view but you will be promptly greeted by handicraft vendors and good-natured pestering. In about 20 minutes, the main Kenscoff road reaches **Fermathe** where the large Baptist Mission has a restaurant selling sandwiches, hot dogs, fries, pizza, ice cream, etc, with fine views south, and a store selling handicraft and souvenirs (taptaps and camionettes from near the market in Pétion-Ville). There is also a museum of the 'history of this land, of this people and of serving Satan'. Voodoo is seen by the museum as the cause of all poverty in Haiti. Near the mission is *Le 3 Decks*, 3 bis, Fermathe 54, on the Kenscoff road, T5103722, 2557499, a lovely and very peaceful restaurant in the hills, with a beautiful view, main courses US$10-22 (Tue-Sun 1200-1800). A turn-off near the Mission leads to **Fort Jacques** and **Fort Alexandre** (10 minutes by car or an 45 minutes' walk), two forts on adjoining summits built after the defeat of Napoleon. The views over the Cul de Sac plain are breathtaking. Fort Jacques has been restored.

Kenscoff is a hill resort where, just 30 minutes (15 km) from Pétion-Ville, but 1,500 m above sea level, members of the élite retire to their country homes in July and August to escape the heat. A camionette from Pétion-Ville is US$0.30. **D** *Hotel Florville* is fairly basic and not especially friendly but provides refreshments and meals in a nice dining room. Market day is on Friday. You can drive just beyond **Furcy**, from where you can hike to the summit above Kenscoff (about one hour), or the summit just to the west, called Morne Zombi. The ridge just to the east of the radio mast can be reached by a surfaced road in poor condition. It offers views south over a rugged, dark massif that boasts Haiti's highest peak, the 2,674-m **La Selle**.

From the ridge, a four to five-hour hike (at a comfortable pace) along a trail heading towards the village of **Seguin** brings you to **Parc La Visite**, a nature park covering part of the massif. It has pine woods, montane cloud forest at higher altitudes, dozens of big limestone caves (one 10 km long), and strange karst-formation rocks locals call 'broken teeth' (Creole: *kase dan*) (see page 258). A guide is required. Camp at a disused saw mill (Creole: *siri*) by the trail, where water is available from a fountain. Bring thick clothes and sleeping bags; temperatures can fall to freezing at night. A waterfall is a short hike away. For longer hikes and fine views, head east with a guide and climb the 2,282-m **Pic Cabaio** or the 2,100-m **Pic La Visite** (another camping site). The park keeper, Jean-Claude, rents horses. Seguin lies on a sloping plateau on the massif's southern face, about one hour beyond the park. **C** per person hostal/guesthouse, MAP. Book in advance through the restaurant *Yaquimo* in Jacmel (see below), they will send a guide with a mule/horse to carry your luggage and show you the way. You can walk there in less than three hours. From Seguin, a five-hour hike gets you to the south-coast village of **Marigot**, from where you can bus back to Port-au-Prince via Jacmel in four hours.

Lake Saumâtre (see page 258) is at the eastern end of the Cul de Sac plain near the Dominican border. The newly improved road from Croix-des-Bouquets to the border crossing at Malpasse skirts the lake's southern side. The northern side offers more chance of seeing its wildlife. On Route Nationale 3, heading northeast from Port-au-Prince towards Mirebalais, fork right at the Thomazeau turn-off to the lakeside villages of Manneville and Fond Pite. It takes 90 minutes.

Haiti

South of Port-au-Prince

Set off on the Route Nationale 2, the highway heading west toward Les Cayes. The lush, densely populated coastal Léogâne Plain, 45 minutes west of the capital, offers a look at rural life. East and west of the town of Léogâne, the plain is dotted with small villages and criss-crossed by bumpy lanes. After Léogâne, at the Dufort junction, fork left. The road climbs steeply, winding through the mountains with good views.

Jacmel

The name Jacmel derives from an Indian word meaning 'rich land'

The run-down port of Jacmel is Haiti's prettiest city at the head of a 3 km wide horseshoe bay. A quiet place, Jacmel has changed little since the late 19th century, when it was a booming coffee port and its wealthy merchants built New Orleans-style mansions using cast-iron pillars and balconies imported from France or the United States. Its charming Victorian streets wind down three small hills to a palm-fringed, black-sand beach. A hurricane swallowed up most of Jacmel's beach and what is left is dirty, with pigs rooting around in the debris.

The best views can be had from the south-facing upper veranda of the **Manoir Alexandre**, a late 19th-century patrician home that is now a guesthouse. The main square is pleasant and busy with vendors; the *Hôtel de la Place* restaurant is a good place to have lunch and watch the world go by. One block to the east opposite the church is an iron market built in 1895. Saturday is market day. The street below the *Manoir Alexandre*, rue Seymour Pradel, has another old residence, now an art gallery called **Salubria-Brictson Galleries**. Owner Bob Brictson is in residence only a few months of the year, but if you knock you will be shown his collection of worldwide art. Closer to the beach, on rue du Commerce, more 19th-century homes have been turned into galleries or handicraft stores. The Boucard family residence at the corner of Grand' Rue and Commerce, is especially fine. At the other end of rue du Commerce, near the wharf, note the Vital family warehouse dating from 1865. The nearby prison was built in the 18th century. Jacmel's handicraft speciality are objects painted with colourful parrots or flowers. There are lots of artists painting and selling their work along Portail Léogane.

Sleeping, eating & nightlife

B *La Jacmelienne*, T2883451. A modern, 2-storey hotel on the beach with pool, MAP, fans, no a/c, often no water either, all rooms with balcony and sea view, restaurant open-air and pleasant at night. **B-C** *Hotelflorida*, rue du Commerce 29, near the post office, T2882805, F2883182. Breakfast available, cosy living room, also **AL** suite with 4 beds. Next to the hotel is a French patisserie with bread, pizza etc, where you can eat in the backyard. **C** *Hôtel de la Place*, 3 rue de l'Église, T2882832, overlooks Place d'Armes. Good location, very central with lots to see and interesting people-watching, functional rooms with bathrooms, clean, pleasant restaurant, reasonable food. **D** *Manoir Alexandre*, rue d'Orléans, T2882711. Large untended garden, faded grandeur, lots of character but shared bathroom has seen better days, lovely view from veranda, sunset-watching, CP available. **E** *Guy's*, 52 Grand' Rue, T2883421. 10 rooms, CP, breakfast, 2 rooms with bathroom, fans, clean, popular, good value. *Yaquimo Nightclub and Restaurant* is 100 m west of the wharf. Fairly good food, good atmosphere, live bands. Book here for the guesthouse in Seguin.

Transport

In Port-au-Prince, buses leave from the station Jacmel on Dessalines, a couple of blocks the other side of Chareron, 2½-3 hrs, US$1.50, lovely route, very crowded. In Jacmel buses leave from the gas station at the junction of Portail Léogane and Av de La Liberté.

Directory

Exchange *BMH*, 60 Grand' Rue, between bus station and *Guy's Guest House*, good rates, changes TCs. You can also change money at *La Jacmelienne*, but don't expect a good rate.

Beaches

Beaches on the south coast tend to have a slight undertow

A good dirt road leads east to fine white-sand beaches. The first is **Cyvadier**, a tiny cove down a side road at Km 7. The shade around the beach prevent much sunbathing, but the water is clean and pleasant, although the surf can be rough at times. Fishermen cast their nets from the beach. At Km 15, just before Cayes Jacmel, is

Haiti

Raymond-les-Bains, a beach alongside the road. No facilities except showers. Beware of the slight undertow in the sea. Just after Cayes Jacmel, at **Ti Mouillage**, the road runs beside two beaches. The first has a basic restaurant. From Marigot, a pretty coastal village 10 km further on, a 4WD can climb a rough trail to the village of Seguin and Parc La Visite (see page 271).

Sleeping and eating AL-A *Cyvadier Plage*, T2883323. A quiet hotel and restaurant offering rooms and 3 meals with ceiling fans, balcony, private bath with water and electricity, meals take up to 2 hours to be served, so order early, mostly seafood, fruit and vegetables, all fresh and local, swimming pool, secure, gates locked at night.

A 12-km track into the hills west of Jacmel leads to Bassin Bleu, a series of natural pools and waterfalls descending a limestone gorge in tiers. The biggest, deep, blue-green pool is framed by smooth rocks and draped with creeper and maidenhair fern. Jump in for a cool swim. It takes 1½-2 hours each way on foot or horseback (horses for hire in Jacmel or in the village up the hill on the other side of the river from Jacmel, about US$6-7, depending on the quality). Take a guide, fixing a price in advance, and water to drink. If it has not rained, the road is fine for a 4WD for three-quarters of the way. The Jacmel guide hands over to a local guide for the last kilometre which is a rough path and, at one point, requires the aid of a rope. This means an additional small fee. Guides here can be a problem, only one with the rope is needed, but you will find that you may be accompanied by others who will later demand payment. The diver who plunges from the uppermost rock into the pool also expects to be paid for his 'show'. In sum, this is a very rewarding excursion and highly recommended, but you need deep pockets with lots of small change for tips.

Bassin Bleu
There are excellent views over Jacmel bay on the way

West of Port-au-Prince

The southwestern peninsula is the greenest and most beautiful part of Haiti. Its rugged western tip has forests, rivers, waterfalls and unspoilt beaches. The Route Nationale 2 to Les Cayes is very scenic but is frequently almost non-existent and where there is any surface it is often seriously potholed.

For the first 92 km the Route Nationale 2 runs along the north coast of the peninsula. There are rooms to let near **Grand Goâve** on Taïno Beach: **F** *Christian Ravanetti*, 80 rue Janty, T4056962. Meals are US$10, sailing and fishing trips can be organized, good view of Île de la Gonâve. At Km 68 is the town of **Petit Goave** (Creole: Ti Gwav). Visit the *Relais de l'Empereur*, once the residence of Emperor Faustin I (1849-56). The hotel is no longer operating, but the caretaker will show you around. ■ *T2229557.*

Just 2 km down a turn-off at Km 92 is the smugglers' port of **Miragoane**, a town of narrow streets that wind around a natural harbour or climb a hill capped by a neo-Gothic church. The town is dirty, dusty, crowded and poor, bars and restaurants no longer function and the hotel is for sale. Activity has moved up to the main road where there is a large market. In the centre of the market is a good café with parking space and charging medium prices. A 4WD is needed for the dirt road that continues along the north coast, fording rivers and passing fishing villages, as far as Petit Trou de Nippes. At Petite Rivière de Nippes, 15 km from Miragoane, a three-hour trek inland on foot or horseback (take a guide) brings you to one of Haiti's four great waterfalls, **Saut de Baril**.

After Miragoane, the main road crosses the peninsula's spine and reaches the southern, Caribbean coast at Aquin (Km 138), where you can bathe in several rivers. At **Zanglais**, 6 km further on, there are white-sand beaches. Just beyond Zanglais a ruined English fort is visible on a small offshore island, with the remains of a battery emplacement opposite.

Beware of slight undertow at any beach on the south coast

Haiti

Les Cayes

Lying on a wet, coastal plain 196 km west of Port-au-Prince, Haiti's fourth city, Les Cayes (Creole: Okay), is quiet but not without charm. The Fête de Notre Dame around 15 August is recommended. Spend the day swimming, eating, drinking and watching people, and at night until 0200 the crowd moves to the *musique racine*, which is irresistible. Some people sleep on the beach because hotels are usually packed. Advance booking is necessary at this time. Buses or taptaps leave Port-au-Prince in the mornings from the same area as those for Jacmel, on Blvd Dessalines, for the four-hour trip (US$4). Visible from the waterfront is **Île-à-Vache**, a 20 km-long island with a population of 5,000 that was Henry Morgan's base for a 1670 raid against Panama. It has Indian remains and good beaches on the southern side near La Hatte, the biggest village. Visit it by renting a motor boat (about US$25 for the day) or take the daily ferry, leaving at around 1600, and pay to sleep in someone's home. Or camp, after asking permission. A more regular service goes to **Port Morgan**, a wonderful small resort/marina run by a French couple, Didier and Françoise Boulard, T2861600, www.port-morgan.com They have their own boat service to Les Cayes, US$10, and offer tours to local villages for markets and other activities. There are some beautiful hikes in the area. As well as accommodation (see below), showers, laundry, fuel and internet access are available for visitors to the marina. Very knowledgeable and helpful hosts, willing to help with travel arrangements on the mainland.

Excursions **Fortresse des Platons**, a huge ruined fortress built in 1804 at Dessalines' behest on a 600-m summit overlooking the coastal plain, can be visited in a one-day excursion from Les Cayes. Take the coast road southwest out of the city. Just after Torbeck, a rough road heads inland up a river valley via Ducis to the village of Dubreuil (trucks from Les Cayes). From Dubreuil, the fortress is a two- to three-hour hike up a steep trail with great views. Carry on the same trail via Formond to enter the **Macaya National Park**, which has Haiti's last virgin cloud forest surrounding the 2,347-m Pic Macaya. See page 258. A University of Florida base at Plaine Durand (two hours beyond the fortress) has basic camping facilities. Hire guides for hikes into the lower montane rainforest. Only the very fit should attempt the hike to the top of the Pic Macaya. It entails climbing a 2,100-m ridge and then descending to 1,000 m before tackling the peak itself. Allow at least two days each way and take a guide.

Beyond Torbeck, the coast road goes as far as **St Jean du Sud** where a small offshore cay is suitable for camping. Before St Jean du Sud, fork right at L'Acul for **Port Salut**, a 90-minute drive from Les Cayes (two buses a day, also some trucks). This small village (birthplace of President Aristide) has a wild, 800 m-long, palm-lined beach that is one of the most beautiful in Haiti. The town is a haven of paved roads and laid-back people. The beaches are beautiful and totally empty. There is a pleasant waterfall, 10 minutes' drive, 30 minutes' walk away, where you can swim.

Sleeping **In Les Cayes C** *La Cayenne*, T2860379, by the beach, on the main street. Some rooms with
& eating a/c, pool, the only restaurant in town, poor service. **C** *La Concorde*, rue Gabions des Indigènes, T2860277. Rooms with bath, fan, EP, not always open, very comfortable. At the end of the village is a **E** *Village Touristique*, BP 118, comfortable bungalows with shower, big bed, mosquito screens, nice, quiet, right on beach, water but not always electricity, candles supplied, contact Maurice, the caretaker; or rent rooms from locals. **In Port Morgan B-C** per person in immaculate bungalows includes 3 meals, delicious French food, restaurant open for visitors too, breakfast US$5, 0730-0930, lunch from US$9, 1200-1500, dinner from US$13.50, 1700-1800, reserve before noon and tell them whether you are vegetarian or vegan. Happy hour at the beach bar is 1700-1800. **In Port Salut**, *Village*, booking through the *P'tit Bistro* in Pétion-Ville, T2573042. A 20-min walk beyond the former *Arada Inn*, now closed, leads to a good and noisy restaurant, US$3 for breakfast, US$6.25 for fish or lobster.

The adventurous can take the coastal route from Les Cayes to **Jérémie**, around the **West coast** peninsula's tip, a remote, rugged, lush region that has changed little in 200 years. It **road** has wild rivers, sand beaches, mountains falling steeply into the sea, and some of Haiti's last rainforest. Allow four days. Les Cayes buses or taptaps may go as far as **Les Anglais**, depending on the state of the road. A 4WD may even get to **Tiburon**. Thereafter, you must hike to **Anse-d'Hainault** or even **Dame Marie** before finding a road good enough to be serviced by taptaps out of Jérémie. Alternatively, take your life in your hands and try getting a ride on sloops that carry merchandise and passengers along the coast. Villagers all the way will cook meals and rent beds for a few dollars. *Pripri*, rafts made of bamboo lashed together and steered by a pole, ply the rivers. Anse-d'Hainault and Abricots (25 km west of Jérémie) have good beaches.

The scenic, hair-raising, 97-km mountain road from Les Cayes to Jérémie, across the Massif de la Hotte, takes three hours, but it may be impassable after rain and must be done in daylight. One hour's drive brings you to **Camp Perrin**, a hill resort at the foot of Pic Macaya. Here there are several guesthouses. Hire horses for a two-hour ride to **Saut Mathurine**, Haiti's biggest waterfall. There is good swimming in the deep, green pool at its base.

Fork right off the Jérémie road at the Kafou Zaboka intersection for **Pestel**, a picturesque port dominated by a French fort. It is worth seeing especially during the Easter weekend regatta, when many Rara bands come. The town is pretty with old wooden houses and a hotel with nice rooms and a friendly owner. Charter a boat to tour nearby fishing villages such as **Les Basses** (Creole: Obas) on the Baradères peninsula and **Anse-à-Maçon** on the offshore island of **Grande Cayemite** with its splendid view of the Massif de la Hotte. The beaches are very beautiful and totally empty.

Sleeping and eating: 5 mins from Pestel there is the *Café de la Gare* restaurant run by a Frenchman and his son (dancing in the evenings, happy hr Sat evening), and a few **C** *bungalows* for rent by the sea which are basic but OK, for 2-4 people.

With crumbling mansions overgrown by rampant vegetation, Jérémie is famed for **Jérémie** its poets, eccentrics and isolation. Although the road is bad, some buses are still running from Port-au-Prince, leaving from Jean-Jacques Dessalines near rue Chareron (US$8). The 12-hour overnight ferry is not recommended. In February 1993 at least 800 people (maybe as many as 1,500) drowned when an overloaded ferry, the *Neptune*, sank on its way to Port-au-Prince. The quickest and easiest way of getting there is to fly with *Tropical Airways* from Port-au-Prince, T2563626-8, US$89. They may be booked up to 10 days ahead. **Anse d'Azur**, 4 km west of the town, is a white-sand beach with a rocky headland at one end, and a big cave into which you can swim. The road west continues to the beaches of Anse du Clerc and Abricots (see above).

Sleeping   On a hill above the town, with a shady garden, is **D** *Hôtel La Cabane* (MAP). Out of town, 20 km west, about 1½ hrs' drive from the airport, depending on the state of the road, is **D per person** *Anse-du-Clerc Beach*, along the coast on the way to Abricots, T2463519 in Port-au- Prince (ask for Jean Charles). The owners (Michel and Danielle Bonhomme, Haitian and Canadian) will collect you from Jérémie airstrip. 7 rooms in small bungalows, MAP, shared bathroom, warm water, on a beach of polished pebbles. The seabed is sandy, so once you are in the water you can stand easily. It is a very peaceful spot. Food excellent, local ingredients.

North of Port-au-Prince

The seaboard north of the capital is arid or semi-arid most of the way to Gonaïves, and all round the northwest peninsula as far as Port-de-Paix. This area was hit by drought and famine in the 1990s and severe ecological damage has occurred. From Port-de-Paix to the Dominican border, it is quite lush and green. Route Nationale 1 hugs the coast for most of the first 85 km skirting the foot of the Chaine des Matheux mountains.

RN 1 is asphalted to
Cap-Haïtien, but is
badly potholed for
65 km between Pont
Sondé and Gonaïves

Cabaret (Km 35) is the former Duvalierville. Its modernistic buildings and pretensions to become Haiti's Brasilia were lampooned in *The Comedians*. **L'Arcahaie** (Km 47) is where Dessalines created the blue and red Haitian flag by tearing the white out of the French tricolor. Outside L'Arcahaie, just before the highway crosses the small Mi Temps river, a road heads east high into the Chaine des Matheux to a region where coffee was grown in colonial times. Sailboats leave mid-morning from Montrouis (Km 76) for the 22-km crossing to **Anse-à-Galets** (one guesthouse), the main town on barren **La Gonâve Island**. In 1997 a ferry capsized just off Montrouis as it was docking. At least 172 died when passengers all fell to one side, causing the boat to turn over only 50 m from the shore. At Km 96, after the Côte des Arcadins beaches, the Route Nationale 1 reaches the port of **St Marc** (**F** *Hotel Belfort*, 166 rue Louverture, clean, basic). There are several gingerbread houses on streets to the east of the main street. A pretty valley runs inland southeast as far as Goavier.

The highway crosses the Artibonite river at **Pont Sondé**, entering a region of rice paddies irrigated by canals. Fork right at the Kafou Peyi intersection, 2 km north of Pont Sondé, for **Petite Rivière de L'Artibonite** (Creole: Ti Rivyè), a picturesque town built by King Henri Christophe on a steep-sided ridge overlooking the river Artibonite. Its Palace of 365 Doors was Christophe's provincial headquarters. In 1802, there was a key battle at the Crète-à-Pierrot fort (five minutes' walk above the town) in which Leclerc sacrificed 2,000 men to dislodge a force of 1,200 led by Dessalines.

About 8 km after **L'Estère**, a right turn-off runs southeast 25 km to **Marchand**, a town at the foot of the Cahos mountains that was briefly Dessalines' capital. Hike into the surrounding hills to visit seven big ruined forts built by Dessalines. Near the town is a spring with a natural swimming pool. Dessalines told his soldiers that bathing here made them immune to French bullets. The house of Dessalines' wife, Claire Heureuse, still survives in the town. You can also see the foundations of his own home. After Marchand, the RN1 crosses a semi-desert called Savane Désolée.

Gonaïves

Amid salt pans and arid lowlands, Gonaïves at Km 171 is an ugly, dusty town of 70,000 (Haiti's third-largest). It is called the City of Independence because Dessalines proclaimed Haiti's independence here in 1804. The unrest that toppled Jean-Claude Duvalier in February 1986 also began here and there have often been labour disputes here which have had a national impact.

Sleeping, eating and transport D *Chez Elias*, rue Egalité, opposite Téléco, T2740318. Safe, clean guesthouse, fan, bathroom, MAP. *Chez Frantz*, Av des Dattes, T2740348. Rooms often taken by long-term residents, but food is Gonaïves' best. *Rex Restaurant*, rue Louverture, half a block from the market, has Creole food and hamburgers. **Buses** (US$3, 4 hrs) leave Port-au-Prince mornings from the intersection of Blvd La Saline and Jean-Jacques Dessalines. **Taxis** In Gonaïves, mopeds operate as taxis, charging US$0.20 a ride.

Limbé &
Le Borgne

After Ennery at Km 201, the Route Nationale 1 climbs steeply up to the Chaine de Belance watershed and enters the green, northern region. Limbé at Km 245, has the **Musée de Guahaba**, created by Dr William Hodges, a Baptist missionary doctor who runs the local hospital and supervises archaeological digs along the north coast (see La Navidad on page 280). The museum is not always open but you can ask for admission from his family who work at the Limbé hospital nearby. **Fort Crète Rouge**, above Limbé, is one of the many fortresses built by Christophe.

A rugged road from Limbé down to Le Borgne (Creole: Oboy) on the coast offers spectacular views. The 20 km either side of Le Borgne abound with white-sand beaches. The green mountains behind add to their beauty, but the coast is densely inhabited and the beaches are used as a public latrine. From Le Borgne to St Louis du Nord, the road is bad but not impassable for 4WD. After Limbé, the highway descends quickly, offering fine views over **L'Acul Bay**, where Columbus anchored on 23 December 1492, two days before his flagship sank.

Cap-Haïtien

Cap-Haïtien, Haiti's second city, has a dramatic location on the sheltered, southeast side of an 824-m-high cape, from which it gets its name. It was the capital in colonial times, when it was called Cap-Français. Its wealth and sophistication earned it the title of 'Paris of the Antilles'. The colony's biggest port, it was also the commercial centre of the northern plain, the biggest sugar-producing region. It was burned to the ground three times, in 1734, 1798 and 1802, the last time by Christophe to prevent it falling intact into the hands of the French. It was destroyed again by an 1842 earthquake that killed half the population. The historic centre's architecture is now Spanish-influenced, with barrel-tile roofs, porches, arcades and interior courtyards.

Nowadays it as usually referred to simply as Cap, or Okap in Creole

Vertières, an outlying district on the Port-au-Prince Road, is the site of the battle at which Dessalines' army definitively routed the French on 18 November 1803, forcing them to leave the island for good 12 days later. There is a roadside monument.

Cap appears to be more relaxed than Port-au-Prince and you will see people out on the streets at night. It is well worth visiting for its buildings and its surroundings but the people are not accustomed to tourists (*blancs*). The streets are filthy with streams of foul-smelling water running down them. The municipal government functions rarely and its services, such as street cleaning, are moribund.

A-B *Beck*, on the mountainside, residential Bel-Air district, T2620001. Woodland setting, 2 pools, constant water, own generator, private beach at Cormier, German owner, rooms with private bath and fan, MAP. **A-C** *Mont-Joli*, on the hillside above town, T2620300, MontJoli@aol.com Includes breakfast and tax, a/c, TV, hot water, rooms have a beautiful view, free internet access in the lobby, pool, tennis court, good restaurant, sandwiches US$7, shrimp or lobster meal US$14, bar opens 2000, own generator. **C** *Les Jardins de l'Océan*, Blvd de Mer, T2621169, F2622277. Small hotel, nice terrace with sea view, good food à la carte, steak, pizza, lobster, shrimp, friendly atmosphere, cosy rooms all with bathroom, fan. **C** *Roi Christophe*, T2620414, corner of 24 and B. Central location in colonial house first built in 1724 as the French Governor's palace (Pauline Bonaparte stayed here), lush gardens, pool, own generator (not big enough for a/c) runs 0600 until city power comes on, more expensive with a/c, cheaper with fan, CP. **F** *Brise De Mer*, 4 Carenage (on waterfront at northern edge of town), T2620821. Friendly but reportedly not very safe, own generator, rooms with private bath and fan. **F** *Columbia*, rue 5, 3-K. Fan, clean, safe, very helpful owner speaks English, friendly, even when there is no water or electricity. Beer, soft drinks and spaghetti on request.

Cap 2000, rue 5 and Blvd (not far from waterfront). Sandwiches, ice cream. A popular and cheap restaurant, good basic food, on Av L just past the corner with rue 1, near *Hotel Columbia*.

Sleeping & eating
Cap-Haitien gets electricity only 1900-2300. Do not drink the water, or even use it to clean your teeth

Ateliers Taggart, T2621931, rue 5 near Blvd (by *Cap 2000*). Handicrafts, especially weavings and metalwork, Mon-Fri 1000-1700. *Galerie Des Trois Visages*, excellent art gallery next to *Ateliers Taggart*. A tourist market by the port has handicrafts and naive paintings. Bargain hard. There is a supermarket, *Marina Market*, on the Blvd with rue 13. Most shops close between 1700-1800.

Shopping

Cap Travel, 84 rue 23A, T2620517. *Agence Citadelle*, rues 11 and A, T2620484, vpcap@agencecitadelle.com Mon-Fri 0800-1300, 1400-1600 Sat 0900- 1300.

Tour operators

Air *Tropical Airways d'Haiti* daily from Port-au-Prince and Port-de-Paix. *TCI Sky King* from Providenciales, Turks and Caicos. There are also air taxi services. **Buses** Buses leave Port-au-Prince from the station Au Cap opposite the big Texaco garage at the junction of Delmas and Blvd La Saline between 0630 and 0830, when full. The 274-km trip usually takes 6-7 hrs. Fare US$6. It may be necessary to change in Gonaïves, 3½ hrs, US$2. There are 2 principal taptap stations in Cap: **Barrière Bouteille** at southern end of town, for all destinations to Port-au-Prince (taptaps go during the morning, buses at night), and **Port Metalique**, at A2, also south end of town, cross bridge for station for all destinations to Milot (outside *Hôtel Bon Dieu Bon*), Hinche, Fort Liberté, Ouanaminthe and the border. **Car hire** *Hertz*, T2620369. Check price quotes very carefully. Don't leave your passport as deposit.

Transport

Haiti

▶ ## Shiver me timbers

The buccaneers who settled on the north coast of Hispaniola were a mixed bunch of runaways and renegades. Some were escaped indentured labourers, who fled the gruelling life of the plantation; others were marooned sailors or deserters. Most were European, but there were a few blacks among them. Although some had a background in piracy, this was not their principal means of subsistence. What kept them alive and gave them their name were the cattle that roamed in the deserted northern plains of the island. These they rounded up and slaughtered, cooking the meat over wooden fires known as boucans. From these early barbecues came the English word 'buccaneer'.

The disappearance of the indigenous population together with thriving herds of feral cattle and pigs, introduced by the Spanish in the early days of settlement, ensured a viable, if not comfortable, lifestyle. The buccaneers would hunt cattle in the interior, tanning hides and curing meat on their boucans. Accompanied by dogs and armed with muskets, they collected enough of their bloody merchandise to return to the coast, where occasional trading exchanges took place with passing pirate or smuggling ships. So covered in blood were the buccaneers after their expeditions that contemporary observers thought they were covered in ship's tar.

In return for meat and hides, the buccaneers wanted alcohol, tobacco and weaponry. These were among the few manufactured essentials in an otherwise rudimentary way of life. They lived in basic stilted shacks with palm roofs, modelled on the indigenous ajoupa, and wore rough cotton trousers and shirts with home made caps, belts and shoes of rawhide.

The 'brethren of the coast', as they were called by the French historians Dutertre and Labat, inhabited a world without women. Many entered into same-sex marriages, known as matelotage. These relationships probably had legal foundations, ensuring that the surviving member of a pair would inherit the other's assets on his death. Death in the wilds of northern Hispaniola and nearby Tortuga Island was commonplace, through violence, malaria and other tropical hazards.

Although they were not first and foremost pirates, most buccaneers were not averse to a little casual predation. As their numbers grew, they occasionally set out to attack coastal traders, mostly Spanish, in long dugout canoes. After seizing whatever was on board, they would normally throw the crew into the sea before returning to their bases in the captured ship. Loot was scrupulously shared out, with extra quotas going to those who had been injured in the adventure.

Over time, the buccaneers seem to have tired of piratical activity, and many began to farm smallholdings of coffee and sugar cane. As the French staked a claim to the western side of Hispaniola, so the forces of law and order arrived, discouraging brigandage and supporting more sustainable economic pursuits. The buccaneers eventually disappeared as a distinct community, some moving on to other pirate havens such as Port Royal, Jamaica, others remaining in Hispaniola as small farmers and hunters.

Directory **Banks** *BNP*, changes TCs; also *Banque Union Haïtien* changes TCs, open until 1300. **Communications** **Internet**: internet café opposite church, US$1.40/hr. **Post office**: Av B at rue 17.

Excursions from Cap-Haïtien

The rich, alluvial plain to the south and east of Cap boasted a thousand plantation houses during the last years of the colonial period. *ISPAN*, rue 15 and rue B in Cap, T2622459, is a good source of information on these nearby colonial ruins, as well as on Sans Souci and the Citadelle.

The **beaches** in Cap itself are dirty and lack charm, but excellent beaches can be reached in 20 minutes by car from Cap. The first is **Cormier Plage**. Five minutes further west (30 minutes on foot) is **Labadie**, or **Labadee**, a fenced-off sandy peninsula used by Royal Caribbean Cruise Lines as a private beach for its cruise ships two days a week. Passengers are taken on snorkelling trips to L'Îlet, renamed by RCCL as Amiga Island, they can jet ski or take a banana boat ride and there is a craft market within the beach compound and a couple of bars. They are not, however, taken beyond the compound to sites in Haiti. In fact they are not even told they are on Haiti, the destination is marketed as the 'private island of Labadee'. On other days the public may use the empty beach and watersports for US$3.

Just beyond this beach, about 30 minutes' walk, are steps down to **Belli Beach**, a small sandy cove with a hotel. Boats, some with outboards, can be rented here to visit nearby Labadie village, dramatically located at the foot of a cliff, and other beaches further along the coast, for example Paradise beach, 30 minutes, US$6, no facilities. Fix a price before boarding. Labadie village (about US$3 by boat, also reachable by scrambling over the rocks) has guesthouses. Excursions can be arranged, ask Arnold at *Kayanol Village Labadee* about going to the Citadelle, beaches and water taxi.

Cormier Plage   A-B *Hotel Cormier Plage*, T2621000. Simple chalets or rooms overlooking the sand and sea, MAP, excellent food, freshly caught seafood, own generator turned on 0730-1100 and 1630-2330, airport transfers. Scuba diving with good wrecks and coral reefs. Run by a charming French couple, Jean-Claude and Kathy Dicqueman. Book ahead, because tour groups from Dominican Republic sometimes fill the place up. Take mosquito repellent. **Belli Beach E** Nice rooms, WC, shower, fan, mosquito nets, they will cook good fish à la Créole for US$5.50. Drinking water costs 2.50 gourdes, but if they run out you will be offered small cans of Coca Cola for 20 gourdes. **Labadie   C-E** *Kayanol Village Labadee* (*Arnold's Place*), T4316659, www.kayanol.com 10 rooms on a hill overlooking Labadie, a/c, TV, VCR/DVD, 24-hr electricity, bar, games room, becomes a dance hall at night. There is usually a DJ, but sometimes a live band and folklore show. The restaurant and garden have an ocean view. **F** *Dessa Motel* and **F** *Maison Amitié*, with basic rooms on the beach. Employees will buy and cook food for a price to be negotiated. From the end of the road you can also take a boat round the cove (US$10 one way) to **C** *Norm's Place*, T2620400, 2620866, an old French fortress, refurbished by an American who is very hospitable and runs it as a guesthouse, 8 basic rooms, no screens but beds have mosquito nets, no shower curtains, no hot water, not much of a beach, accessible only by boat. Lots of nice excursions by boat to small islands and other beaches, about US$6, cheaper for more people. Norm's wife is a good cook, but offers no choice, breakfast US$8, lunch US$10, dinner US$12, beer US$2-3. About 1½ hrs' walk along the coast (or by boat) is **A** *Habitation Labadie*, T2235900, hablab@hotmail.com MAP, delicious food, good for lunchtime excursion, lobster US$8, 24 rooms, TV, beach, pool.

Sleeping & eating

Taptaps US$0.60 to Labadie from Cap leave frequently in the morning from Champs de Mars, 10 mins' walk up rue 22 away from the centre and the waterfront towards the mountains, ask if you get confused, it looks a bit rural. Taptaps will drop you at the gate to Coco Beach.

Transport

The mountain-top fortress of La Citadelle was built by King Henri Christophe to deter any French reinvasion (see page 284). It has walls up to 40 m high and 4 m thick, and covers 10,000 sq m. It is perched atop the 900-m Pic La Ferrière, overlooking Cap and the northern plain, and controlling access to the Central Plateau. Its 5,000 soldiers (plus the royal family and its retinue) could have held out for a year. Restoration work is ongoing. Behind the fortress, at the end of a 1.5-km level ridge with sheer drops on both sides, is the **Site des Ramiers**, a complex of four small forts which controlled the rear access.

La Citadelle
Haitians call this the eighth wonder of the world. It is indeed impressive, with breathtaking views

To get to the fortress take the 25-km asphalt road south from Cap to the village of Milot in a publique (US$1) or taptap (US$0.30). Taptaps leave Cap in the morning. Hotels like the *Mont Joli* offer jeep tours for about US$60 per person, but don't count on the guide's information being correct. From Milot it is a steep 5-km hike through Sans Souci Palace and lush countryside up to the fortress (about 1½ hours, start early to avoid the heat; wear stout shoes and protect yourself from the sun). Horses can be rented for about US$7 plus a tip for the man who leads the horse (dangerous in wet weather). Hire a guide even if you don't want one, just to stop others importuning and to make you feel safer (fix the fee in advance, US$10 for two, or more, for the walk). Several speak fluent French and English making the visit more interesting. Prices of refreshments at the Citadelle are higher than elsewhere (US$0.80 for a Coke), but then someone has had to carry them up there. Those with a car can drive to a car park two-thirds of the way up, reducing the walk to 1½ km (this last part is the hardest). Horses available here too, US$3.50 plus tip. *US$5 admission to the Citadelle and Sans Souci but they will try and sell it to you for more including guide.*

Sans Souci
The admission to the Citadelle also covers Sans Souci

No buses or taptaps back to Cap after 1700

At Milot itself are the ruins of Christophe's royal palace, Sans Souci. More than a palace, it was an embryo administrative capital ranging over 8 ha in the foothills beneath the Citadelle. Christophe sited his capital inland because of the difficulty of defending coastal cities against the overwhelming naval might of France and Britain. The complex included a printing shop, garment factory, distillery, schools, hospital, medical faculty, chapel and military barracks. Begun in 1810, inaugurated in 1813 and ransacked after Christophe shot himself in the heart with a silver bullet in 1820, it was finally ruined by the 1842 earthquake that destroyed Cap. ■ *Closes at 1700.*

Morne Rouge
An uprising planned in this area directly led to Haiti's independence

Morne Rouge, 8 km southwest of Cap, is the site of Habitation Le Normand de Mezy, a sugar plantation that spawned several famous rebel slaves. Leave Cap by the RN1 and take a dirt road running north from a point about 75 m west of the turn-off to the town of Plaine du Nord. Its ruins include two aqueducts and bits of walls. Voodoo ceremonies are held under a giant tree in the village. Among its rebel progeny was Mackandal, an African chief's son who became an *oungan* and led a band of maroons. After terrorizing the entire northern plain by poisoning food and water supplies, he was captured and burned alive in January 1758. **Bois Caiman** was the wood where slaves met secretly on the night of 14 August 1791 to hold a Voodoo ceremony and plan an uprising. (It is near the Plaine du Nord road, about 3 km south of the RN1. Ask locals to guide you once you are in the area.) Their leader was an *oungan* and slave foreman from Le Normand de Mezy called Boukman. The uprising a week later was the Haitian equivalent of the storming of the Bastille. Slaves put plantation houses and cane fields to the torch and massacred hundreds of French settlers. It began the only successful slave revolt in history and led to Haiti's independence. Little is left of the wood now except a giant ficus tree overgrowing a colonial well credited with mystic properties.

Plaine du Nord

The town of Plaine du Nord, 12 km southwest of Cap, becomes a pilgrimage centre on 24-25 July for the Catholic festival of St James, who is identified with Ogou. Voodoo societies come from all over Haiti, camp in the streets and spend the two days in drumming and dancing. On 26 July, the feast day of St Anne, they decamp to nearby **Limonade**, 15 km southeast of Cap, for another day and night of celebrations. A dirt road on the northwest side of Limonade leads to Bord de Mer de Limonade, a fishing village where Columbus' flagship, the *Santa María*, struck a reef and sank on Christmas Day 1492. Columbus used wood from the wreck to build a settlement, **La Navidad**, which was wiped out by Taíno Indians after he left. Its location was discovered by American archaeologist William Hodges while digging at the site of Puerto Real, a city founded years later on the same spot. The untrained eye will detect nothing of either settlement now, but the Hodges museum in Limbé, see page 276, has relics.

Fort Liberté

Fort Liberté, 56 km east of Cap, is a picturesque, French-designed town on a large bay with a narrow entrance. It is dotted with French forts that can be reached by boat. The best is Fort Dauphin, built in 1732. The bay was the site of the Caribbean's largest sisal plantation until nylon was invented. There are direct taptaps from Cap to Fort Liberté, but it may be easier to return to Cap from the main road, which is 4 km from the centre of Fort Liberté.
Sleeping and eating D *Bayaha*, rue des Bourbons, by the sea, great view, terrace, quiet, MAP, good food, basic rooms, no a/c, cold water.

Border with Dominican Republic

Ouanaminthe is northern Haiti's chief border crossing. Accommodation is available at *Hotel Paradis* on the main street. The Dominican frontier town, Dajabón, is just 2 km from the Ouanaminthe taptap station. Taptaps for US$2 from the Station Nordest in Cap; US$1.10 from Fort Liberté. The crossing is straightforward and the

Haiti

Haitian border office is very helpful. Buses leave Dajabón for many Dominican cities. The river Massacre, which forms the border, had this name long before the massacre of thousands of Haitians in the neighbouring part of the Dominican Republic under Trujillo in 1937, when the river was said to have been red with blood for days. The bridge across the river is packed with money changers and *motoconchos* (not necessary for transport to Haitian border post, which is about 1 km from Dominican side). The Dominican side of the border has been described as an armed camp, with a heavy military presence controlling the flow of Haitian labour. The Haitian side, on the other hand, is more like a gypsy camp, with a thicket of tents and shacks.

The dirt road forking left 5 km before Milot could be a rugged alternative, two- to three-hour route back to Port-au-Prince via Hinche and the Central Plateau (see page 282) by 4WD. By public transport it takes much longer – up to two days. Vehicles tend to be old, it is very dusty and the worst stretch is from near Milot to Hinche. The first town is **Grande Rivière du Nord**, where another of Christophe's fortresses, Fort Rivière, sits atop a ridge to the east. It was used by the Cacos guerrillas who fought the US occupation from 1918-20. The Americans captured the Cacos leader Charlemagne Peralte near here. **Dondon** has caves inhabited by bats. One is close to the town. The other, 90 minutes away on foot or horseback up a river bed to the west of the village, has heads carved in relief on its walls, presumably created by the original Indian inhabitants. In the rainy season, cars cannot ford the river near St Raphaël, but you can walk, with locals helping for a small fee.

South of Cap-Haïtien

The Northwest

Except for Tortuga Island and a coastal strip running east from Port-de-Paix, the northwest peninsula is Haiti's driest, most barren region. In recent years, especially since the 1991 coup, it has teetered on the brink of famine and toppled over in 1997 when international agencies had to bring aid.

The 86-km mountain road from Gonaïves to Port-de-Paix via Gros Morne fords several rivers and the trip takes four hours in a 4WD, needed for travel anywhere in the northwest. (Minibuses from Gonaïves, big buses from Port-au-Prince, leaving from beside the station Au Cap.) Port-de-Paix once made an honest living exporting coffee and bananas. Now it specializes in importing contraband goods from Miami. Vendors tout the wares on all its unpaved streets. In 1992-93, its small freighters also ferried illegal immigrants into Miami. Despite the smuggling, it is safe.
Sleeping D *Hotel Brise Marina*, about 10 mins from the town centre northeast along the coast. The best in the area, clean, basic rooms with bathroom, pool, restaurant OK, nice view over the sea. **E** *Holiday Beach*, in the town centre, basic.West to Môle St Nicolas

Port-de-Paix

A coast road runs west from Port-de-Paix along the north coast of the peninsula as far as Môle St Nicolas and then returns to Gonaïves via the south coast. **Jean Rabel** is a tense town which was the site of a peasant massacre in July 1987. At least 150 died in the clash, said to have been engineered by local Duvalierist landlords seeking to crush the attempts of Catholic priests to organize landless peasants. From Jean Rabel round to Baie de Henne, the landscape is arid, windy and dusty. Old people say they can remember when it was still green and forested.

Columbus first set foot on the island of Hispaniola at **Môle St Nicolas**. It has several ruined forts built by the English and French. General Maitland's surrender of Môle to Toussaint in 1798 marked the end of a five-year British bid to gain a toehold on this end of the island. Strategically located on the Windward Passage, just 120 km from Cuba, Môle was long coveted as a naval base by the USA. The hinterland has Haiti's lowest rainfall and little grows. The main occupation is making charcoal and shipping it to Port-au-Prince. Because few trees are left, charcoal makers now dig up roots. The peninsula's south side, especially from Baie de Henne to Anse Rouge, is a mixture of barren rock and desert, but the sea is crystal clear. There are few inhabitants. With salt pans on either side, Anse Rouge ships sacks of salt instead of charcoal.

Tortuga Island
Population 30,000

A 30-minute drive to the east of Port-de-Paix takes you to **St Louis du Nord**, a pretty coastal town from where sailing boats cross the 10-km channel to Tortuga Island, the Caribbean's biggest pirate base in the 17th century. Nearly 40 km long, 7 km wide and 464 m above the sea at its highest point, its smooth rounded shape reminded seafarers of the back of a turtle (*tortuga* in Spanish and La Tortue, its Haitian name, in French).

The biggest south-coast villages, **Cayonne** and **Basse-Terre**, are less than 1 km apart. A ferry boat leaves Cayonne for St Louis du Nord at 0800 and returns at about 1000, charging locals US$0.50 each way. Foreigners may have to pay up to US$10, depending on their negotiating skills. Boats crossing at other times charge more. From Cayonne there is a narrow cement road up to **Palmiste** serviced by a single taptap, one of the few cars on the island. From Palmiste, the biggest village on the rounded spine, there are spectacular views of the corniche coastline stretching from Cap to Jean Rabel, and the towering mountains behind. The best view is from the home of French Canadian priest Bruno Blondeau (T2685138/6709), the director of a Catholic Church mission who has effectively governed the island since 1977. He runs 35 schools and has built all 55 km of its roads. His order also operates a small, basic hotel (**F**, EP).

The best beach, 2 km long, is at **Pointe Saline**, at the western tip (34 km from Palmiste, two hours by car). This is also the driest part of the island and there is little shade. **La Grotte au Bassin**, 6 km east of Palmiste, is a large cave with a 10 m high pre-Columbian rock carving of a goddess. There are two other big caves: **Trou d'Enfer**, near La Rochelle ravine, and **La Grotte de la Galerie**, 1 km east of Trou d'Enfer. The largest ruin is a 15-m-high lime kiln (*four à chaux*), built at the end of the 18th century. **Fort de la Roche**, 1639, was once Tortuga's biggest fortress (70 m high). Its masonry foundations can be seen at a spring on the hillside above Basse-Terre. Three cannon and a bit of wall remain from **Fort d'Ogeron**, built in 1667.

Northeast of Port-au-Prince

Grandly called the Route Nationale 3, the 128-km dirt road northeast from Port-au-Prince to Hinche requires a 4WD and takes at least five hours (much longer by public transport). It crosses the Cul de Sac plain via Croix-des-Bouquets, where a road branches off southeast through a parched, barren region, skirting Lake Saumâtre (see pages 258 and 271) before reaching the Dominican border at Malpasse (see page 254). On the north side of the plain, the Route Nationale 3 zig-zags up a steep mountainside called Morne Tapion (great views back over Port-au-Prince) to reach **Mirebalais**, a crossroads at the head of the Artibonite valley, and Haiti's wettest town. The road east leads to Lascahobas and the frontier town of Belladère, the least used of Haiti's three border crossings into the Dominican Republic. The road west heads down the Artibonite valley. A left turn-off leads up into the hills to the charming village of **Ville-Bonheur** which has a church built on the spot where locals reported an appearance of the Virgin in a palm tree in 1884. Thousands of pilgrims come every 15 July. The Voodooists among them hike 4 km to visit the much-filmed **Saut d'Eau** waterfall. Overhung by creepers, descending 30 m in a series of shallow pools separated by mossy limestone shelves, the fall seems enchanted. The Voodooists bathe in its waters to purify themselves and light candles to enlist the help of the ancient spirits who are believed to live there.

The Route Nationale 3 heads north out of Mirebalais on to the Central Plateau, where the military crackdown was especially harsh after the 1991 coup because peasant movements had been pressing for change. After skirting the Peligre hydroelectric dam, now silted up and almost useless, the road passes Thomonde and reaches the region's capital, **Hinche**. In Port-au-Prince, buses leave from the station Au Cap at the intersection of Blvd La Saline and Route de Delmas. East of Hinche, **Bassin Zim** is a 20-m waterfall in a lush setting 30 minutes' drive from town (head east on the Thomassique Road, then fork north at Papaye). The cascade fans out over a rounded, sloping, limestone rockface. At its foot is a 60-m wide natural pool with deep, milky-blue water that is perfect for swimming.

Sleeping in Hinche F *Foyer d'Accueil* is an unmarked guesthouse above a school behind the blue and white church on the east side of the main square, basic, fan, rarely any power, EP. **F** *Hotel Prestige*, also unmarked, at 2 rue Cité du Peuple, near the market, is worse.

Background

History

Columbus visited the north coast of Hispaniola, modern Haiti, on his first visit to the West Indies, leaving a few men there to make a settlement before he moved on to Cuba. Columbus traded with the native Taínos for trinkets, which were to seal the Indians' fate when shown to the Spanish monarchs. A second voyage was ordered immediately. Columbus tried again to establish settlements, his first having been wiped out. His undisciplined men were soon at war with the native Taínos, who were hunted, taxed and enslaved. Hundreds were shipped to Spain, where they died. When Columbus had to return to Spain he left his brother, Bartolomé, in charge of the fever-ridden, starving colony. The latter sensibly moved the settlement to the healthier south coast and founded Santo Domingo, which became the capital of the Spanish Indies. The native inhabitants were gradually eliminated by European diseases, murder, suicide and slavery, while their crops were destroyed by newly introduced herds of cattle and pigs. Development was hindered by the labour shortage and the island became merely a base from which to provision further exploration, being a source of bacon, dried beef and cassava. Even the alluvial gold dwindled and could not compete with discoveries on the mainland. The population of some 400,000 Taínos in 1492 fell to about 60,000 by 1508. In 1512 the Indians were declared free subjects of Spain, and missionary zeal ensured their conversion to Christianity. A further 40,000 were brought from the Turks and Caicos, the Bahamas and Venezuela, but by 1525 the Indian population had practically disappeared. Sugar was introduced at the beginning of the 16th century and the need for labour soon brought African slaves.

Hispaniola

In the 17th century the French invaded from their base on Tortuga and colonized what became known as Saint Domingue, its borders later being determined by the Treaty of Ryswick in 1697. The area was occupied by cattle-hunting buccaneers and pirates, but Governor de Cussy, appointed in 1684, introduced legal trading and planting. By the 18th century it was regarded as the most valuable tropical colony of its size in the world and was the largest sugar producer in the West Indies. However, that wealth was based on slavery and the planters feared rebellion. After the French Revolution, slavery came under attack in France and the planters called for more freedom to run their colony as they wished. In 1791 France decreed that persons of colour born of free parents should be entitled to vote; the white inhabitants of Saint Domingue refused to implement the decree and mulattos were up in arms demanding their rights. However, while the whites and mulattos were absorbed in their dispute, slave unrest erupted in the north in 1791. Thousands of white inhabitants were slaughtered. Soon whites, mulattos and negroes were all fighting, with shifting alliances and mutual hatred.

Birth of a colony

Out of the chaos rose a new leader, an ex-slave called François-Dominique Toussaint, who created his own roaming army after the 1791 uprising. When France and Spain went to war, he joined the Spanish forces as a mercenary and built up a troop of 4,000 negroes. However, when the English captured Port-au-Prince in 1794 he defected with his men to join the French against the English. After four years the English withdrew, by which time Toussaint was a leader among the black population. He then turned against the mulattos of the west and south, forcing their armies to surrender. Ordered to purge the mulatto troops, Toussaint's cruel lieutenant, **Jean-Jacques Dessalines**, an African-born ex-slave, slew at least 350. Mulatto historians later

Toussaint Louverture

Haiti

claimed that 10,000 were massacred. The same year, torrential rain broke the irrigation dams upon which the prosperity of the area depended. They were never repaired and the soil was gradually eroded, creating a wilderness. By 1800 Toussaint was politically supreme. In 1801 he drew up a new constitution and proclaimed himself Governor General for life. However, Napoleon had other plans, which included an alliance with Spain, complicated by Toussaint's successful invasion of Santo Domingo, and the reintroduction of the colonial system based on slavery. In 1802 a French army sent to Saint Domingue defeated Toussaint and shipped him to France, where he died in prison. The news that slavery had been reintroduced in Guadeloupe provoked another popular uprising which drove out the French.

19th-century revolution
For a fictionalized account of this period, read Alejo Carpentier's El reino de este mundo (The Kingdom of This World)

The new revolt was led by Dessalines, who had risen to power in Toussaint's entourage and was his natural successor. In 1804 he proclaimed himself Emperor of an independent Haiti, naming the country after the Taíno word for 'high land'. Dessalines was assassinated in 1806 and the country divided between his rival successors: the negro **Christophe** in the north, and the mulatto **Pétion** in the south. The former's rule was based on forced labour and he managed to keep the estates running until his death in 1820. He called himself **Roi Henri Christophe** and built the Citadelle and Sans Souci near Milot. Pétion divided the land into peasant plots, which became the pattern all over Haiti and led to economic ruin with no sugar production and little coffee. Revolution succeeded revolution as hatred between the blacks and mulattos intensified. Constitutional government rarely existed in the 19th century.

US intervention

In 1915, the USA intervened for geopolitical and strategic reasons, provoked by the murder and mutilation of a President. Occupation brought order, the reorganization of public finances, health services, water supply, sewerage and education, but there was still opposition to it, erupting in an uprising in 1918-20 which left 2,000 Haitians dead. By the 1930s the strategic need for occupation had receded and the expense was unpopular in the USA. In 1934 the USA withdrew, leaving Haiti poor and overpopulated with few natural resources. Migrants commonly sought work on the sugar estates of the neighbouring Dominican Republic, although there was hatred between the two nations. In 1937 about 10,000 Haitian immigrants were rounded up and massacred in the Dominican Republic (see Further reading).

Duvalier Dynasty

In 1957 **François (Papa Doc) Duvalier**, a black nationalist, was elected President and succeeded in holding on to power. He managed to break the mulattos' grip on political power, even if not on the economy. In 1964 he became President-for-Life, a title inherited by his 19-year-old son, **Jean-Claude (Baby Doc) Duvalier**, in 1971. The Duvaliers' power rested on the use of an armed militia, the **Tontons Macoutes**, to dominate the people. Tens of thousands of Haitians were murdered and thousands more fled the country. Repression eased under Jean-Claude, but dissidence rose, encouraged partly by US policies on human rights. Internecine rivalry continued and the mulatto elite began to regain power, highlighted by the President's 1980 marriage to Michèle Bennett, the daughter of a mulatto businessman. Discontent erupted with the May 1984 riots in Gonaïves and Cap-Haïtien, and resurfaced after the holding of a constitutional referendum on 22 July 1985 giving the Government 99.98% of the vote. Several months of unrest and rioting gradually built up into a tide of popular insistence on the removal of Duvalier, during the course of which several hundred people were killed by his henchmen. The dictatorship of the Duvaliers (father and son) was brought to a swift and unexpected end when the President-for-Life fled to France on 7 February 1986.

Democracy & the army

The removal of the Duvaliers left Haitians hungry for radical change. The leader of the interim military-civilian Government, **General Henri Namphy**, promised presidential elections for November 1987, but they were called off after Duvalierists massacred at least 34 voters early on polling day with apparent military connivance. New, rigged elections were held in January 1988, and **Professor Leslie Manigat** was handed the presidency only to be ousted in June when he tried to remove Namphy as army commander. Namphy took over as military President, but four months later he himself was ousted in a coup that brought **General Prosper Avril** to power. Dissatisfaction within the army resurfaced in April 1989, when several coup attempts were staged within quick succession and lawlessness increased as armed gangs,

Haiti

including disaffected soldiers, terrorized the population. Nevertheless, the USA renewed aid, for the first time since 1987, on the grounds that Haiti was moving towards democratic elections, promised for 1990, and was making efforts to combat drug smuggling. Under General Namphy, cocaine worth US$700 million passed through Haiti each month, with a 10% cut for senior army officers. However, Avril's position was insecure; he moved closer to hardline Duvalierists, and arrests, beatings and murders of opposition activists increased. Foreign aid was cut off in January 1990 when Avril imposed a state of siege and the holding of elections looked unlikely. In March, Avril fled the country. Following his resignation, Haiti was governed by an interim President, Supreme Court judge **Ertha Pascal-Trouillot**.

Despite poor relations between Mme Pascal-Trouillot and the 19-member Council of State appointed to assist her, successful elections were held on 16 December 1990. The presidential winner, with a landslide 67% of the vote, was **Father Jean-Bertrand Aristide**, who was sworn in on 7 February 1991. His denunciations of corruption within the government, church and army over the previous decade had won him a vast following. One of his immediate steps on taking office was to start investigations into the conduct of many officials, to seek the resignation of six generals, to propose the separation of the army and police and to garner urgently needed financial assistance from abroad. Aristide's refusal to share power with other politicians, his attacks on the interests of the armed forces and the business elite, and the actions of some of his militant supporters provoked his overthrow by the army on 30 September 1991. Aristide fled into exile. Harsh repression was imposed; at least 2,000 people were said to have died in the first six months, almost 600 during the coup itself. People began fleeing in small boats to the US Guantánamo naval base on Cuba in an exodus that had reached 38,000 by May 1992. The USA brought it to an end by immediately repatriating everyone without even screening claims for political asylum.

1990 elections & coup
Aristide ('Titide'), a Roman Catholic priest, was expelled from the Salesian order in 1988 for 'incitement to hatred, violence and class struggle'

International condemnation of the coup was swift, with the Organization of American States, led by the USA, imposing an embargo. The EU and other nations suspended aid and froze Haitian government assets. The sanctions hurt, but not sufficiently to promote a formula for Aristide's return; this was partly because of Washington's misgivings about his radical populism. The election of Bill Clinton to the US Presidency in 1992, with the prospect of more decisive US action on restoring Aristide to power, prompted UN involvement. With Washington making it clear it was ready to step up sanctions, the UN envoy persuaded the army commander, **General Raoul Cedras**, to agree in February 1993 to the deployment of 250 civilian UN/OAS human-rights monitors throughout Haiti. Further UN pressure was applied in June 1993 with the imposition of an oil embargo and a freeze on financial assets. As a result, an accord was reached in July whereby Aristide would return to office by 30 October, Cedras would retire and Aristide would appoint a new army chief and a Prime Minister.

International pressure

As the 30 October deadline approached, it became clear that Aristide would not be allowed to return. In mid-October, the Haitian rulers humiliated the USA by refusing to allow a ship to dock carrying a 1,300-strong UN non-combat mission. Aristide supporters continued to be killed and harassed. Aristide's appointed cabinet resigned in mid-December as the regime showed no signs of weakening. As smuggled fuel from the Dominican Republic flowed in, Cedras and his collaborators set their sights on staying in power until the end of Aristide's term of office, February 1996.

Meanwhile, tensions between Aristide and the Clinton administration grew as the USA appeared unable, or unwilling, to break the impasse. Pressure from the US Black Caucus and from Florida politicians eventually persuaded Clinton to take more positive action. The policy of returning boat people was stopped. Tough worldwide sanctions, including a cessation of commercial flights, were initiated in May 1994 and the Dominican Republic was approached to control sanctions breaking. These measures led to a state of emergency in Haiti, but not to an end to defiance.

Despite the lack of wholehearted support in the USA, an occupation of Haiti by 20,000 US troops began on 19 September 1994. Aristide returned to the presidency on 15 October to serve the remainder of his term, aided first by a 6,000-strong US force, then by 6,000 UN troops who replaced the Americans in March 1995. General Cedras and his chief-of-staff, General Philippe Biamby, were talked into exile in Panama, while the third leader of the regime, police chief Michel François, fled to the Dominican Republic. Aristide set about reducing the influence of the army

Aristide's return

and police and the USA began to train recruits for a new police force, but by April 1995, the absence of a fully trained police force and of an adequate justice system had contributed to a general breakdown of law and order. Many people suspected of robbery or murder were brutally punished by ordinary Haitians taking the law into their own hands. 'Zenglendo' thugs, often thought to be demobilized soldiers, were involved in the killing of political figures and others.

The fear of violence disrupted preparations for legislative and local elections, held over two rounds in 1995. These gave overwhelming support to Aristide's Lavalas movement in the Senate (all but one of the seats up for election) and the Lower House (71 of the 83 seats), but the turn-out was very low and the results were bitterly contested. Of the 27 competing parties, 23 denounced the election because of irregularities reported by international observers.

Economic reform under Aristide was slow and there was dissent within the cabinet. Progress on judicial reform progressed but investigations into killings stalled. The US Senate consequently blocked disbursement of aid. Mob violence and extra-judicial killings continued, with the new police force unable to cope.

René Préval

For the first time power was transferred from one elected Haitian President to another

Presidential elections were held on 17 December 1995. René Préval, a close aide of Aristide's, won a landslide victory with 87% of the vote, although only 25% of the electorate turned out and most opposition parties boycotted the event. He was inaugurated on 7 February 1996. Agreement on a structural adjustment programme was reached with the IMF in May but was hampered by a hostile Congress and not approved until October. Haiti was treated as a political football in the US Senate, which was absorbed in its own presidential race. Aid only dribbled in; civil servants and police were unpaid and there was mounting violence in the streets. The UN Peacekeeping Force was asked to stay for longer as the new police force was unready to take over. Some arrests were made as the Government attempted to move against widespread corruption but nothing could be done about the nationwide violence.

Rivalries within the ruling coalition, the Lavalas Political Organization, spilled into the open at the end of 1996 when Aristide launched a new group, the Lavalas Family (Fanmi Lavalas), which became a political party in time for the senatorial and local elections, held in April 1997, at which less than 10% of the electorate voted. The major opposition parties boycotted the poll, claiming that the electoral council was controlled by Aristide, and later called for the results to be annulled. The second round of the senatorial elections was postponed indefinitely. It was feared that if the Lavalas Family gained control of the Senate, the reform package would be blocked.

In June, Prime Minister Rosny Smarth resigned. He blamed elements of Lavalas for stirring up political unrest and the electoral council for not annulling the April elections, which were marked by fraud. His departure increased concern in Washington that the faltering political and economic recovery programme would be brought down. Smarth remained in office until October pending the appointment of a successor, but he had still not been replaced a year later. The two opposing factions of the Lavalas movement were unable to resolve their quarrel over the April 1997 elections. Local elections were completed in mid-October, allowing the formation of an electoral council, which was dominated by Aristide supporters. In November 1997, about 1,200 UN troops began to withdraw, leaving 300 police instructors in place for another year and 400 US troops, who were engaged in construction and health care. Violence and murders continued. The Organisation Politique Lavalas changed its name to Organisation du Peuple en Lutte (OPL) to distance itself from Fanmi Lavalas (FL), and in February 1998 it dropped its demands to have the April 1997 elections annulled, but other parts of a political deal collapsed within a week. International donors held up millions of dollars of aid with a brake on growth and poverty alleviation.

In July 1998, Education Minister Jacques Edouard Alexis was nominated as head of Government. He had the support of the OPL but political infighting delayed his appointment. In January 1999, President Préval declared Alexis Prime Minister and announced he would no longer recognize parliament as its term had expired under the law governing the delayed 1995 elections. Nevertheless, amid violence and demonstrations, the Chamber of Deputies continued to meet, claiming it was entitled to sit for four years from October 1995. A new government was finally sworn in on 26 March 1999 and a provisional electoral board two days later. The much-delayed legislative and municipal elections were held in May 2000 and were won overwhelmingly by the FL. Foreign observers described the elections as flawed but credible, but opposition parties denounced the results. Murder and harassment of candidates and their supporters before and during the vote did not prevent the USA and the UN praising the generally peaceful voting process, but certain results were disputed.

Opposition parties boycotted the presidential elections in November 2000 because of the flawed May elections and for the same reason the USA, Canada and the EU refused to send observers. Six candidates were found to stand against Aristide, but none of them campaigned because of pre-election violence. Aristide himself was rarely seen in the years he was out of office, preferring to stay at his walled compound in Tabarre in the north of Port-au-Prince. Official results gave Aristide 92% of the vote and he was inaugurated in February 2001. His party now holds 28 of the 29 Senate seats, over 80% of the seats in the Legislature and nearly all the mayoralties and municipalities. Violence has not stopped, however. Despite post-election declarations by Aristide for peace and democracy, his supporters have continued to carry out violent anti-opposition protests, while the opposition continues to question the legitimacy of the electoral process. There was an attack on the National Palace in December 2001, after which the former police chief of Cap Haïtien was arrested for his part in an alleged coup attempt. He later fled to the Dominican Republic, protesting his innocence. In March 2002, former Senate President Yvon Neptune became Prime Minister, following the resignation of Jean-Marie Cherestal, who was criticized for not doing enough to help the poor.

In an attempt to release blocked aid funding of around US$500 mn, in May 2003 Haiti agreed to cut spending and stabilize its currency in a deal with the IMF. However, US$60 mn of payment arrears to the InterAmerican Development Bank and the World Bank had to be paid off before new loans from those institutions to eradicate poverty could be disbursed.

Geography and people

Haiti is the Caribbean's most mountainous country. Except for a few small, mainly coastal plains and the central Artibonite River valley, the entire country is a mass of ranges. The highest peak is the 2,674-m La Selle, southeast of the capital. Little remains of Haiti's once-luxuriant forest cover, cut down for fuel or to make way for farming. With soil erosion and desertification far advanced, Haiti is an ecological disaster. The main regions still regularly receiving abundant rainfall are the southwest peninsula and the eastern two-thirds of the northern seaboard.

Haiti is a Taíno word meaning 'high ground'

About 95% are of almost pure African descent. The rest are mostly mulattos, the descendants of unions between French masters and African slaves, and some are of Arabic descent, who tend to be merchants and shop owners. The Haitian culture is a unique mixture of African and French influences. Haiti was a French colony until 1804 when black slaves revolted, massacred the French landowners and proclaimed the world's first black republic. Throughout the 19th century Haitians indulged in a succession of bloody, almost tribal wars. Even today African cults, particularly voodoo, play a large part in everyday life like nowhere else in the Caribbean. The country is desperately poor and the standard of living is the lowest in the Americas. According to UNICEF, only 20% of children reach secondary school. Illiteracy is believed to be about 80% of the population, with unemployment at around the same level. With per capita income running at US$400 a year, 62% are underfed, the third-worst level in the world, exceeded only by Somalia and Afghanistan. Infant mortality is 93 per 1,000 live births (2002) and life expectancy is only 49.5 years. The incidence of HIV/AIDS was running at 6.1% of the population in 1999, with 23,000 AIDS related deaths that year. Since then things have got worse. The UN has highlighted the deteriorated state of the infrastructure in urban areas, where the roads are very poor and there is a lack of electricity and potable water, as well as a badly degraded environment. Such problems have all attributed to political chaos and the resulting scarcity of international aid.

Government

Under the terms of the 1993 UN-brokered agreement to restore democracy, Haiti has two legislative houses, a 27-seat Senate and an 83-seat Chamber of Deputies. The parliament, with the elected President as chief of state, came into effect in October 1994. Senators are elected for a 6-year term. Deputies are elected for a 4-year term; the next elections are due in 2004. The President is elected for a 5-year term which expires in 2005.

Economy

Haiti is the western hemisphere's poorest country and among the 30 poorest in the world; 80% of the people fall below the World Bank's absolute poverty level (1998). It is overpopulated. It lacks communications, cheap power and raw materials for industry. Its mountainous terrain cannot provide a living for its rural population.

Until the embargo, the main economic problem was low agricultural productivity, compounded by low world commodity prices. Just 1% of the population controls 40% of the wealth. The average farm size is less than 1 ha. Only a third of the land is arable, yet most of the people live in the country, using tools to grow maize, rice, sorghum and coffee. Deforestation has played havoc with watersheds and agriculture. Only a fraction of the land is now forested, yet charcoal continues to supply 70% of fuel needs. Agriculture generates 30% of the GDP but employs two thirds of the workforce. Coffee is the main cash crop, providing 8% of exports. Sugar and sisal output has slumped as population pressure has forced farmers to switch to subsistence crops. A land reform programme was begun in 1997 in the Artibonite Valley to give land to families in an area where violent land disputes have been common. Agriculture was badly hit by a drought in the northwest in 1997, causing famine in that area. In 1998 Hurricane Georges killed around 100 people and left many homeless. The devastation was intensified because of the lack of trees and ground cover, which meant flooding and erosion.

Industry and commerce are limited, and heavily concentrated in Port-au-Prince. Until the embargo, assembly operations turned out baseballs, garments and electronic parts for export to the USA. After the lifting of the embargo, factories were slow to reopen because of civil unrest and electricity shortages. A 40% increase in the minimum wage, to US$2.57 per day, made Haiti's pay level marginally higher than that of the Dominican Republic, to which many offshore companies had relocated. Vegetable oils, footwear and metal goods are still produced for domestic consumption. Manufactured goods make up two-thirds of total exports. Tourism has all but disappeared, at first because of AIDS, then because of the political instability.

Culture

Although Haiti wiped out slavery in its 18th-century revolution, the country's society still suffers from slavery's legacies of racial, cultural and linguistic divisions. Toussaint's tolerant statesmanship was unable to resist Napoleon's push to reimpose slavery. It took the tyranny and despotism of Dessalines and Christophe. Haitian despots stepped into the shoes of the French despots. The new mulatto ruling class considered its French language and culture superior to the blacks' Creole language and Voodoo religion, which it despised. The corruption and despotism of the black political class created by Duvalier suggest that, despite its profession of *noirisme*, it internalized the mulatto contempt for its own race.

Religion Voodoo (French: Vaudou) is a blend of religions from West Africa, above all from Dahomey (present-day Benin) and the Congo River basin. Like Cuba's Santería and Brazil's Candomblé, it uses drumming, singing and dance to induce possession by powerful African spirits with colourful personalities. These spirits, called *loas* in Haiti (pronounced *lwa*), help with life's daily problems. In return, they must be 'served' with ceremonies, offerings of food and drink, and occasional animal sacrifice in temples known as *ounphors*. The essence of Voodoo is keeping in harmony with the *loas*, the dead and nature. Magic may be used in self-defence, but those in perfect harmony with the universe should not need it. Magic in the pursuit of personal ambitions is frowned upon. The use of black magic and sorcery, or the use of attack magic against others without just cause, is considered evil. Sorcerers, called *bokors*, exist but they are not seen as part of Voodoo. The *loas* punish *oungans* (Voodoo priests) or *mambos* (priestesses) who betray their vocation by practising black magic. Many Haitians believe in the existence of *zombis*, the living-dead victims of black magic who are supposedly disinterred by sorcerers and put to work as slaves.

Voodoo acquired an overlay of Catholicism in colonial times, when the slaves learned to disguise their *loas* as saints. Nowadays, major ceremonies coincide with Catholic celebrations such as Christmas, Epiphany and the Day of the Dead and lithographs of Catholic saints are used to represent the *loas*.

The role of attack and defence magic in Haiti's religious culture expanded during the slave revolts and the independence war. Many rebel leaders were *oungans*, including Mackandal, who terrorized the northern plain with his knowledge of poisons from 1748 to 1758, and Boukman, who plotted the 1791 uprising at a clandestine Voodoo ceremony. Belief in Voodoo's protective spells inspired a fearlessness in battle that amazed the French. As a result, many Haitian rulers saw Voodoo as a threat to their own authority and tried to stamp it out. They also thought its survival weakened Haiti's claim to membership of the family of 'civilized' nations. François Duvalier enlisted enough *oungans* to neutralize Voodoo as a potential threat. He also co-opted the hierarchy of the Catholic Church. He had less success with the Catholic grass roots which, inspired by Liberation Theology, played a key role in his son's 1986 fall and Aristide's election in 1990. After several ruthless campaigns against Voodoo, most recently in the early 1940s, the Catholic Church has settled into an attitude of tolerant coexistence. Now the militant hostility to Voodoo comes from fundamentalist Protestant sects of American origin, which have exploited their relative wealth and ability to provide jobs in order to win converts. In 2003 President Aristide recognized Voodoo as an official religion, thereby allowing *oungans* legally to accept money for the services they provide as well as to counter the Protestant missionary zeal.

Language

Haitian Creole is the only language of 85% of inhabitants. It evolved from French into a distinct language. The other 15% speak Creole and French

Haitian Creole is the product of the transformation of French in Saint Domingue by African slaves who needed a common language, one that the slave-owners were forced to learn in order to speak to their slaves.

More important is the way in which Creole and French are used now. All Haitians understand Creole and speak it at least part of the time. Use of French is limited to the élite. The illiterate majority of the population understand no French at all. There is almost no teaching in Creole and no attempt is made to teach French as a foreign language to the few Creole-only speakers who enter the school system. Since mastery of French is still a condition for self-advancement, language perpetuates Haiti's class divisions. All those pushing for reform in Haiti are trying to change this. Radio stations have begun using Creole in the last 10 years and musicians now increasingly sing in Creole. The 1987 constitution gave Creole equal official status alongside French and even élite politicians have begun using Creole in speeches. Aristide's sway over the people is due in part to his poetic virtuosity in Creole. A phonetic transcription of Creole has evolved over the last 50 years, but little has been published in the language except the Bible, some poetry and a pro-Aristide newspaper, *Libète*. Creole is famed for its proverbs voicing popular philosophy and reflecting Haiti's enormous social divisions. The best teach-yourself book is *Ann Pale Kreyòl*, published by the Creole Institute, Ballentine Hall 602, Indiana University, Bloomington IN 47405, USA. It is hard to find in Haitian bookshops.

The arts

Haitian handicraft and naive art is the best in the Caribbean. Even such utilitarian articles as the woven-straw shoulder bags and the tooled-leather scabbards of the peasant machetes have great beauty. The *rada* (Voodoo drum) is an object of great aesthetic appeal. Haiti is famed for its wood carvings, but poverty has pushed craftsmen into producing art from such cheap material as papier maché and steel drums, flattened and turned into cut-out wall-hangings or sculpture. Haitian naive art on canvas emerged only in response to the demand of travellers and tourists in the 1930s and 40s, but it had always existed on the walls of Voodoo temples, where some of the best representations of the spirit world are to be found. Weddings, cock fights, market scenes or fantasy African jungles are other favoured themes. Good paintings can range from 100 to several thousand dollars. Mass-produced but lively copies of the masters sell for as little as US$10. Negotiating with street vendors and artists can be an animated experience, offering insights into the nation's personality.

Exposure to white racism during the US occupation shook some of the mulatto intellectuals out of their complacent Francophilia. Led by Jean Price Mars and his 1919 pioneering essay *Ainsi parla l'oncle* (Thus Spoke Uncle) they began to seek their identity in Haiti's African roots. Peasant life, Creole expressions and Voodoo started to appear together with a Marxist perspective in novels such as Jacques Romain's *Gouverneurs de la rosée* (Masters of the Dew). René Depestre, now resident in Paris after years in Cuba, is viewed as Haiti's greatest living novelist. Voodoo, politics and acerbic social comment are blended in the novels of Gary Victor, a deputy minister in the Aristide Government before the coup.

Music & dance   Nigel Gallop writes: The poorest nation in the western hemisphere is among the richest when it comes to music. Its most popular religion worships the deities through singing, drumming and dancing. The prime musical influence is African, and, while European elements are to be found, there are none that are Amerindian. Music and dance can be divided into three main categories: Voodoo ritual, rural folk and urban popular. Voodoo rituals are collective and profoundly serious, even when the *loa* is humorous or mischievous. The dance is accompanied by call-and-response singing and continuous drumming, the drums themselves (the large *manman*, medium-sized *seconde* and smaller *bula* or *kata*) are regarded as sacred.

During Mardi Gras (Carnival) and Rara (see below), bands of masked dancers and revellers can be found on the roads and in the streets almost anywhere in the country, accompanied by musicians playing the *vaccines* (bamboo trumpets). Haitians also give free rein to their love of music and dance in the so-called Bambouches, social gatherings where the dancing is *pou' plaisi'* (for pleasure) and largely directed towards the opposite sex. They may be doing the Congo, the Martinique or Juba, the Crabienne or the national dance, the Méringue. The first two are of African provenance, the Crabienne evolved from the European Quadrille, while the Méringue is cousin to the Dominican Merengue. Haitians claim it originated in their country and was taken to the Dominican Republic during the Haitian occupation of 1822 to 1844, but this is a matter of fierce debate between the two nations. In remote villages it is still possible to come across such European dances as the Waltz, Polka, Mazurka and Contredanse.

Haitian music has not remained impervious to outside influences during the 20th century, many of them introduced by Haitian migrant workers returning from Cuba, the Dominican Republic and elsewhere in the region (as well as exporting its own music to Cuba's Oriente province in the form of the Tumba Francesa). One important external influence was that of the Cuban Son, which gave rise to the so-called 'Troubadour Groups', with their melodious voices and soft guitar accompaniment. Jazz was another intruder, a result of the US Marines' occupation between 1915 and 1934. In the 1950s two equally celebrated composers and band leaders, Nemours Jean-Baptiste and Weber Sicot, introduced a new style of recreational dance music, strongly influenced by the Dominican Merengue and known as Compact Directe (*compas*) or Cadence Rampa. Compas dominated the music scene until the past few years, when it has become a much more open market, with Salsa, Reggae, Soca and Zouk all making big inroads.

A number of Haitian groups have achieved international recognition, notably Tabou Combo and Coupé Cloué, while female singers Martha-Jean Claude and Toto Bissainthe have also made a name for themselves abroad. Also highly recommended is the set of six LPs titled *Roots of Haiti*, recorded in the country. Finally, no comment on Haitian music would be complete without reference to the well-known lullaby *Choucounne* which, under the title *Yellow Bird*, is crooned to tourists every night on every English-speaking Antillean island.

Mike Tarr adds: A musical revolution came with 'voodoo beat', a fusion of Voodoo drumming and melody with an international rock guitar and keyboard sound. Its lyrics call for political change and a return to peasant values. With albums out on the Island label, and US tours behind them, Boukman Eksperyans is the most successful of these bands. People who have ignored Voodoo all their life are seemingly possessed at Boukman concerts. Other 'voodoo beat' bands of note are RAM, Boukan Ginen, Foula, Sanba-Yo and Koudjay, and new bands are springing up all the time RAM remains very popular, as are T-Vice, Sweet Micky, King Posse and Kompa Kreyol.

Books

History   *The Black Jacobins*, by CLR James (about Toussaint); *Papa Doc and the Tontons Macoutes*, by Bernard Diederich and Al Burt. **Voodoo**   *The Drum and the Hoe*, by Harold Courlander; *Divine Horsemen* by Maya Deren; *The Serpent and the Rainbow* by Wade Davis; *Mama Lola* by Karen McCarthy Brown. **Travelogue**   *Bonjour Blanc: A Journey Through Haiti* by Ian Thomson, Hutchinson, 1992; *The Rainy Season: Haiti Since Duvalier*, by Amy Wilentz, Jonathan Cape, 1989. **Fiction**   *The Comedians* by Graham Greene; *The Kingdom of This World* by Alejo Carpentier (about Mackandal and Christophe); *Hadriana dans tous mes rêves*, by René Depestre, Gallimard 1988, Haiti's best-known living writer who grew up in Jacmel where the story is set; *The Farming of Bones*, by Edwidge Danticat, Soho Press 1998, a fictional account of the massacre of Haitians in the Dominican Republic in 1937. Also worth reading are *Krik! Krak!* and *Breath, Eyes, Memory*.

Dominican Republic

Introducing the Dominican Republic

The Dominican Republic, occupying the eastern two-thirds of Hispaniola, has some spectacularly beautiful scenery. The country is mountainous and has the highest peak in the Caribbean, the 3,175-m Pico Duarte. It is green and fertile and has many more forests than its neighbour, Haiti. Within a system of widespread food production are large sugar and fruit plantations and cattle ranches. The Republic has built up its tourist trade, and has much to offer in the way of natural beauty, old colonial architecture, attractive beaches, adventure sports, modern resorts and native friendliness. Public transport is good and it is easy and rewarding to explore by bus or hired car. Its Spanish-speaking population is mostly a mixture of black, white and mulatto.

Essentials

Before you travel

All visitors (except US and Canadian) require a **passport** and most need a green **tourist card**, US$10, purchased from consulates, tourist offices, airlines on departure, or at the airport on arrival before lining up in the (long) queue for immigration. Citizens of Argentina, Chile, Ecuador, Iceland, Israel, Japan, Liechtenstein, Peru, South Korea, Uruguay do not need a tourist card to enter. The time limit on tourist cards is 90 days, but if necessary extensions are obtainable from Immigration, Huacal Building, Santo Domingo (T6852505/2535). The easiest method of extending a tourist card is simply to pay the fine (variable) at the airport when leaving. You should have an outward ticket, although not always asked for.

Documents
US and Canadian citizens may enter with birth certificate or voter registration card and photo ID, but will need pass- port to cash TCs, hire a car or make large credit card purchases

You should be up to date with your typhoid, tetanus and polio inoculations. The vaccine against infectious hepatitis is a good idea. Malaria prevention is recommended, as it is present in the southwest and the west of the country. There is also dengue fever: the Aedes mosquito breeds in urban areas and is more prevalent when there has been lots of rain. There is no cure, so prevention is essential. There is rabies, so if you are at high risk get yourself vaccinated before you travel. In any case, if you are bitten seek medical help immediately.

Vaccinations

Duty-free import permitted of 200 cigarettes or one box of cigars, plus 2 litres of alcoholic liquor and gift articles to the value of US$1,000. Military-type clothing and food products will be confiscated on arrival. Currency in excess of US$10,000 may not be taken out of the country without special permission. Airport police are on the lookout for illegal drugs. It is illegal to bring firearms into the country.

Customs

Currency The Dominican peso (RD$) is the only legal tender. The peso is divided into 100 centavos. There are coins in circulation of 25 and 50 centavos, 1 peso and 5 pesos, and notes of 5, 10, 20, 50, 100, 500, 1,000 and 2,000 pesos. However, you will hardly ever see 25-centavo coins and people tend to round up or down to the nearest peso.
Exchange The exchange rate fluctuates against the dollar. A banking fraud scandal led to volatility in the exchange rate in 2003 and the rate dropped from RD$20=US$1 to RD$27=US$1 in 5 months, provoking the *Central Bank* to intervene to stabilize the currency. Banks and exchange houses *(casas de cambio)* are authorized to deal in foreign exchange. Cambios often give better rates than banks. You will be given a receipt and, with this, you can change remaining pesos back into dollars at the end of your visit (maximum 30% of dollars changed; cash obtained against a credit card does not count). There is sometimes a buyback charge. Do not rely on the airport bank being open. The US dollar is the best currency to bring. Sterling and the euro can be changed at the *Banco de Reservas* (and some other banks); Scandinavian currencies are very hard to change. If stuck at weekends, most hotels will change money; cash only. ATMs are an easy way to get cash and you will get close to the market rate, plus a commission of up to 5%. They are sometimes out of action at weekends and holidays and in small places they suffer from lack of maintenance and often do not work. If you bring travellers' cheques they should be denominated in US dollars. In Santo Domingo and tourist places you will not have much trouble changing them, but in Santiago, only the *Banco Popular* on Calle del Sol is authorized to change TCs.

Money
In the countryside away from major centres, it can be difficult to change anything higher than a 100-peso note

Credit cards Nearly all major hotels, restaurants and stores accept most credit cards. Several banks will give cash against Visa, Mastercard or American Express cards, usually with 5% commission. However, Amex is not much used on the north coast. It is advisable to inform your bank or credit card company before you use your card in the Dominican Republic. Some companies will put a stop on your card after you have used it twice. This is for your own protection as the Dominican Republic has a high rate of credit card fraud.

Banks The commercial banks are *Scotiabank* (Santo Domingo, Santiago, and Puerto Plata), *Chase Manhattan* (Santo Domingo and Santiago), *Citibank* (Santo Domingo and Santiago),

Dominican Republic

▶ ## Tourist offices overseas

Argentina *Marcelo T de Alvear 772 (1058), Buenos Aires, T5411-43122203, argentina@sectur.gov.do*

Belgium *Louizalaan 271, 8th floor, 1050 Brussels, T322-6461300, benelux@sectur.gov.do*

Canada *2080 rue Crescent, Montréal, Québec, H3G 2B8, T514-4991918, montreal@sectur.gov.do; 26 Wellington Street East, Suite 201, Toronto, Ontario M5E 1S2, T416-3612126, toronto@sectur.gov.do*

Colombia *Oficina 513 de la Torre A Edif, Teleport Business Park, Calle 114 9-01, Bogotá, T571-6291818, F6291830, colombia@sectur.gov.do*

France *11 rue Boudreau, Paris 75009, T331-43129191, francia@sectur.gov.do*

Germany *Kaiserstr 13, 2nd floor, D-60311 Frankfurt am Main 1, T49-69-91397878, alemania@sectur.gov.do*

Haiti *rue Faubert 43, Pétion-Ville, Port-au-Prince, T509-2566196, haiti@sectur.gov.do*

Italy *Piazza Castello 25, 20121 Milan, T3902-8057781, italia@sectur.gov.do*

Puerto Rico *Av Ashford 809, Local C-3, Condado, San Juan, PR 00940, T787-7220881, puertorico@sectur.gov.do*

Spain *general Yague 4, Puerta 12, Madrid, T3491-4177375, espana@sectur.gov.do*

Sweden *Turistbyra, Vastmannagartan 37, 11325 Stockholm, T468-4422242, F233445, suecia@sectur.gov.do*

UK *20 Hand Court, High Holborn, London WC1V 6JF, T44-20-72427778, inglaterra@sectur.gov.do*

USA *136E 57 Street Suite 803, New York, NY 10022, T212-5881012/4, newyork@sectur.gov.do; 561 West Diversey Building, Suite 214, Chicago, IL 60614-1643, T773-5291336/7, chicago@sectur.gov.do; 248 NW Le Jeune Rd, Miami, Florida 33126, T305-4444592/3, miami@sectur.gov.do; 12174 Greenspoint DH, Houston, TX 77060, T281-8751959, houston@sectur.gov.do; 25 Caribbean Court, Laguna Niguel, CA 92677, T949-3638520, california@sectur.gov.do*

Venezuela *Av 2, Edif Uslar 62, piso 6, Urbanización Montalbán 1 Caracas, T581-212-4711172, venezuela@sectur.gov.do*

Banco de Reservas, Banco Popular, Banco Metropolitano, Banco Central, Bancrédito, Baninter, Banco Dominicano Hispano, Banco del Progreso and others. Money can be sent via *Western Union*, which operates through *Vimenca* but the exchange rate is up to 20% more than banks.

Climate   Rainfall is greatest on high ground, reaching more than 2,500 mm in parts of the Cordillera Septentrional, which faces directly into the northeast trade winds. The valleys between the mountain ranges are dry rain-shadow areas; some parts of the southwest are virtual semi-deserts. In winter, the northern parts of the island are affected by cold fronts which move down from the North American continent; these can bring heavy rain, grey skies, and squally northern winds. The average temperature is around 25°C. There is not much seasonal variation, although north coast winter temperatures can be cool during cold fronts. Altitude is an important influence, with an average fall of 6°C for each 1,000 m above sea level. Below-freezing temperatures have been recorded on Pico Duarte. The Dominican Republic lies within the hurricane belt. Storms can strike at any time from Aug-Nov, but 60% of the hurricanes that have hit the Dominican Republic since 1871 have done so in Sep. Hurricane David devastated the country in 1979, killing 1,000 people and causing widespread disruption. The most recent direct hit was from Hurricane Georges in 1998, which had maximum wind speeds of close to 200 kmph.

Getting there

Air   The main gateways are Santo Domingo, Puerto Plata and Punta Cana although there are
In addition to   other international airports with limited services. Punta Cana is only worth flying to if you are
scheduled flights   staying at one of the all-inclusive hotels along the eastern coast. If you want to start your trav-
there are hundreds of   els on the south coast, including the capital, then fly to Santo Domingo. For the north coast
charter flights from   use the airport outside Puerto Plata. It is possible to fly in to one and out of the other,
North America, Europe   although that will obviously cost a little more. For details of airlines see Transport sections.
and South America

Touching down

◀

See also Directory
page 321

Business hours *Offices: 0830-1230, 1430-1630; some offices and shops work 0930-1730 Mon-Fri, 0800-1300 Sat. Banks: 0830-1700 Mon-Fri. Government offices 0730-1430.* **Shops:** *normally 0800-1900, some open all day Sat and mornings on Sun and holidays. Most shops in tourist areas stay open through the siesta and on Sun.*

Clothing *Light clothing, preferably cotton, is best all year round. It is recommended to take one formal outfit since some hotels and nightclubs do not permit casual dress.*

Currency *The dominican peso (RD$) is the only legal tender.*

Departure tax *US$10.*

Emergency numbers *T911.*

Official time *Atlantic Standard Time, four hours behind GMT, one hour ahead of EST.*

Public holidays *New Year's Day (1 Jan), Epiphany (6 Jan), Our Lady of Altagracia (21 Jan), Duarte Day (26 Jan), Independence Day (27 Feb), Good Fri (although all Semana Santa is treated as a holiday), Labour Day (1 May), Corpus Christi (60 days after Good Fri), Restoration Day (16 Aug), Our Lady of Las Mercedes (24 Sep), Christmas Day (25 Dec).*

Tipping *In addition to the 10% service and 12% VAT charge in restaurants, it is customary in the nicer, sit down restaurants to give an extra tip of about 10%, depending on service. Porters receive US$0.50 per bag; taxi drivers, público drivers and garage attendants are not usually tipped.*

Voltage *110 volts, 60 cycles AC current. American-type, flat-pin plugs are used. There are frequent power cuts, often for several hours, so take a torch with you when you go out at night. Many establishments have their own (often noisy) generators.*

Weights and measures *Officially metric, but business is often done on a pound/ yard/US gallon basis. Land areas in cities are measured by square metres, but in the countryside by the tarea, one of which equals 624 sq m.*

Boat

Many passenger cruise lines from the USA, Canada and Europe call at the Dominican Republic on itineraries to various ports on Caribbean islands or the mainland. *Ferries del Caribe* has a car and passenger ferry between the Dominican Republic and Puerto Rico, with a capacity for 250 vehicles and 550 passengers. The *Millennium Express* (known as *El Ferry*) departs Mayagüez Mon, Wed, Fri, 2000, 10-12 hrs, departs Santo Domingo Tue, Thu, Sun, 2000, prices from US$141 return, Mon-Fri, including port tax each way of US$11.50, US$161 at weekends, sleeper cabins for up to 4 people, US$68 superior, US$58 standard and US$48 económica (without bathroom). Discounts are available. In Santo Domingo, T809-6884400, F6884963, in Puerto Rico, T787-8324800, F8311810 www.ferriesdelcaribe.com You can arrange onward transport by bus from Mayagüez to San Juan and from Santo Domingo to *Terrabús* destinations in the Dominican Republic and Haiti.

Ports of entry

Santo Domingo, Luperón, Puerto Plata, Samaná, Punta Cana (with 24 hrs' notice). **Boat documents** Customs fees US$10 per person. 30 days' immigration clearance. Declare weapons and check in with Customs officials ashore at each port of entry. Do not depart from anchorage before sunrise after picking up weapons. You have to clear Customs and Immigration at each port. The port captain will come on board with a group of officials, each of whom have been reported by yachties to ask for 'tips' of US$20-25 to expedite the paperwork.

Travel to Haiti
Remember there is a one-hour time difference between Haiti (GMT-5) and the Dominican Republic (GMT-4) in summer

Air *Caribair* has 2 flights daily Mon-Sat at 0830 and 1330 and one flight Sun at 1000 from Herrera Airport, returning from Port-au-Prince at 1130 and 1530 Mon-Sat and 1530 Sun, for US$180 return, T5426688. **Bus** By far the easiest way is with *Terrabús*, which has a service between Santo Domingo and Pétion-Ville, US$50 one way, US$75 return, US$80 open return, T4721080, terminal at Av 27 de Febrero esq Anacaona, Plaza Criolla, Sat-Mon departs 1200, arrives 0500, Wed-Fri departs 0600, arrives 1200, they deal with all border formalities for you (except customs). *Caribe Tours* also has a service to Haiti, departing daily at 1100, arriving in Port-au-Prince at 1400, US$75 return. The return bus leaves Port-au-Prince at 0700 (see Haiti chapter). There are cheaper options but they take longer and are less comfortable. A syndicate of Dominican operators runs 30-seat buses from outside the Haitian embassy, 33 Av Juan

Dominican Republic

Sánchez Ramírez, just off Av Máximo Gómez between Independencia and Bolívar. 3-4 leave every morning Mon-Fri 1100-1200 and take about 7 hrs or longer to Port-au-Prince, depending on the amount of merchandise to be inspected by Customs at the border. They return next day from rue du Centre between Pavée and des Miracles at around the same time. Your passport must be processed in the embassy before boarding the bus. Be quick on arriving at the embassy, get through the gates, ignoring hangers on and cries of 'passport', unless you want to wait in the street and pay someone else US$10 to take your passport in. All the passports are processed together. Payments may be required. Do not wear shorts. Alternatively, take a minibus to Jimaní from near the bridge over the Río Seco in the centre of Santo Domingo, 6-8 hrs; get a lift up to the Haitian border and then get overcharged by Haitian youths on mopeds who take you across 3 km of no-man's-land for US$3. From Haitian immigration take a lorry-bus to Port-au-Prince, 3-4 hrs, very dusty. You can also take Dominican public transport to Dajabón, cross to Ounaminthe and continue to Cap Haïtien. If driving to Haiti you must get a vehicle permit at the Foreign Ministry (T5331424). Hire cars are not allowed across the border. The drive from Santo Domingo to Port-au-Prince takes about 6 hrs. Buy gourdes from money changers outside the embassy, or at the border, but no more than US$50-worth, rates are much better in Haiti. Also take US$25 for border taxes, which have to be paid in dollars cash.

Touching down

Airport information

Details of airports are given in the text below. There are several: **Las Américas**, Santo Domingo, T5490450/80, **Herrera**, Santo Domingo, T5673900, **Gregorio Luperón**, Puerto Plata, T5860219, **Arroyo Barril**, Samaná, **Cibao**, Santiago, T5824894, **Punta Aguila**, La Romana, T5565565, **Punta Cana**, Higüey, T6868790, and **María Montéz**, Barahona, T5247010). A new domestic airport is being built to replace Herrera, 40 mins north of the centre of Santo Domingo in the Higuero sector.

Tourist information

You are more likely to notice private sector operators and get information from tour companies or guesthouses

The head office of the Secretaría de Estado de Turismo is in the Edificio de Oficinas Gubernamentales, Av México esq 30 de Marzo, Ala 'D', near the Palacio Nacional (T2214660, F6823806, sectur@codetel.net.do) There are no facilities for dealing with the general public. Although there are small tourist offices in most towns. There are offices at **Las Américas International Airport**, in Santo Domingo in the colonial city on the first floor of the Palacio Borgella near the Cathedral (T6863858), **Gregorio Luperón Airport** at Puerto Plata, in Puerto Plata (Malecón 20, T5863676), in Santiago (Ayuntamiento, T5825885), Barahona (T5243650), Jimaní (T2483000), Samaná (T5382332), Boca Chica (T5235106), San Pedro de Macorís (T5293644), La Romana (T5506922), Baní (T5226018), San Cristóbal (T5283533), Pedernales (T5240409), Higüey (T5542672), El Seíbo (T5523402), Sosúa (T5712254), Cabarete (T5710962), Gaspar Hernández (T5872485), Río San Juan (T5892831), Nagua (T5843862), Las Terrenas (T2406363), Luperón (T5718303), Monte Cristi (T5792254), La Vega (T2421289), Bonao (T5253941), Constanza (T5392900).

Useful websites

www.dominicana.com.do Secretaría de Turismo website; www.dr1.com Daily news and weather service; www.thedominicanrepublic.net Listings of businesses with no paid advertising; www.domrep.ch News and information; www.zonacolonial.com Concentrates on the old city of Santo Domingo with some country-wide information; www.hispaniola.com A good general site; www.DRpure.com Great for adventure sports with background information too; There are a few other local sites, such as www.samana.com, www.cabarete.com and www.puertoplataguide.com

See also Tour operators, page 319

Guides *The Asociación de Guías de Turismo de la República Dominicana* (Asogiturd) can be contacted at Calle Vicente C Duarte 3, Apdo Postal 21360, Santo Domingo, T6820209. Nearly all their members speak English and other languages. A 2-hr tour of colonial Santo Domingo will cost about US$15, or US$50 for a full day, depending on the number of people and what they want to do. Outside the historic buildings in Santo Domingo, on the beaches and at other tourist attractions, visitors will be approached by unofficial English-speaking guides, sellers of rum, women or drugs. The only value in taking an unofficial guide is to deter others from pestering you. Unofficial guides often refuse to give prices in advance, saying 'pay what you want' and then at the end, if they are not happy with the tip, they make a scene and threaten to tell the police that you had approached them to deal in drugs, etc.

Maps *Gaar,* on Arzobispo Nouel esq Espaillat, Santo Domingo, open Mon-Fri 0830-1900, Sat 0930-1500. *Berndtson & Berndtson* publish a good road map, 1:600,000, with detail on Santo Domingo, Puerto Plata and Santiago, available locally for US$5. *Scheidig* publishes the *Mapa Geográfica de la República Dominicana*, which is approved by the Instituto Geográfico Universitario and available at *Gaar* for US$7. There are several other good maps of the country including *Hildebrand*, *Nelles* and *Texaco*.

It is advisable to take at least one smart outfit with you so that you can dress up in the evening. Shorts are not permitted in the cathedral in Santo Domingo. It is polite to ask before taking photos of people. Normally they will agree cheerfully, but some may ask for a payment.

Local customs & laws
Swim wear is for the beach only

On no account change money on the streets. Banks and cambios offer the market rate and are safer. Be careful with 'helpers' at the airports, who speed your progress through the queues and then charge US$15-20 for their services. Single men have complained of the massive presence of pimps and prostitutes. Be prepared to say 'no' a lot. These problems do not occur in rural areas and small towns, where travellers have been impressed with the open and welcoming nature of the Dominicans. Violent crime against tourists is rare but, as anywhere, watch your money and valuables in cities late at night and on beaches. The streets of Santo Domingo are not considered safe after 2300. Purse snatchers on motorcycles operate in cities. Keep away from anything to do with illegal drugs. You may be set up and find yourself facing an extended stay in a Dominican prison. Beware of drug-pushers on the Malecón in Santo Domingo and near the Cathedral in Puerto Plata.

Safety

Politur, the Tourist Police, has a toll-free phone 1-200-3500, or at the office in Santo Domingo T6868639. There are also Politur offices in Puerto Plata, Luperón, Sosúa, Cabarete, Río San Juan, Las Terrenas, Samaná, Jarabacoa, Barahona, Boca Chica, Juan Dolio, La Romana, Bávaro, and Las Américas international airport. If you have anything stolen go to a police station to report the crime and get a signed, stamped declaration for your insurance company.

Dominican Republic

Where to stay

There is a wide range of accommodation, from the 4-5 star, all-inclusive beach resorts run by international companies, to simple lodgings for local travelling salesmen. The cheaper all-inclusive hotels usually offer buffet food and local alcoholic drinks (rum and beer), which can get boring after a few days, you get what you pay for. In Santo Domingo the string of 4-5 star hotels along the Malecón are designed to cater for businessmen, diplomats and politicians and are of international standard, with business centres, elegant restaurants, casinos and conference centres. Note that 5-star hotels charge an average of US$140 room only, plus 22% tax. In aparthotels, the average price is US$130 for 2, but this can be negotiated down for long stays. There are plenty of nice places to stay in the **B-C** range, which offer peace and quiet, good food and comfortable rooms in pleasant locations. In more modest guesthouses, a weekly or monthly rate, with discount, can be arranged. Hotels with rooms for US$10-15 will be basic with erratic plumbing and electricity; check the lock on the door.

All hotels charge the 22% tax; the VAT component is 12%

Getting around

Air Santo Domingo, Av 27 de Febrero 272, esq Seminario, T6838006, has regular flights between Santo Domingo (Herrera, T6836691, and Las Américas, T5491110) and Puerto Plata (US$56, daily, T5860385), Punta Cana (US$56, daily, T2211170), Arroyo Barril and El Portillo, Samaná (US$55, Mon-Sat, T2406571); also flights from Puerto Plata to Punta Cana (US$66, daily).Fly drive available from around US$100. Several companies offer air taxi or charter services within the Republic, all

Air

based at Herrera Airport. *Caribair*, T8426688, F5677033, caribair.sa@codetel.net.do has offices in all national airports and a fleet including air ambulance and helicopters. *Alas Nacionales*, T5426688; *Transporte Aéreo SA*, T5674549; *Coturisca*, T5677211. *Dorado Air* (T6861067) flies between Santo Domingo and Puerto Plata several times a day on Fri and Sat. Air taxis charge around US$185 per plane to Samaná and US$285 to Punta Cana.

Road

Fares increased significantly in 2003, but an initial fall in the peso cushioned the rise in dollar terms

Bus Long-distance bus services are very good, with a wide network and several different companies. The 3 most comfortable and reliable are *Metro, Caribe Tours* and *Terrabús*. Services from Santo Domingo: *Metro Expreso*, first class (T5667126, F5419454) operate from Calle Hatuey esq Av Winston Churchill, near 27 de Febrero and have buses to La Vega (US$3), Santiago (US$4.70), Puerto Plata (US$6), Nagua (US$5), Moca (US$4.50), San Francisco de Macorís (US$4), Sánchez/Samaná (US$5.60) and Castillo (US$4.50) daily. In Puerto Plata, T5866063, Santiago, T5839111, Nagua, T5842259. *Caribe Tours* (T2214422) operates from Av 27 de Febrero at Leopoldo Navarro; the bus terminal, with ticket office, café, information desk, ATM (Visa, Electron, Plus), cambio and waiting area with TV; most of their services are in a/c buses, with video and toilet, punctual, good service, no smoking (US$3 to Bonao, US$3.30 to La Vega, US$4.70 to Jarabacoa, US$4 to Santiago, US$4.30 to Barahona, US$5.70 to Dajabón, Puerto Plata or Monte Cristi, US$6 to Sosúa, US$5.30 to Sánchez, Samaná or Río San Juan); they run to all parts except east of Santo Domingo. *Terrabús*, Plaza Criolla, Anacaona 15, T4721080, is an international company with services to Haiti and Puerto Rico (via the ferry, see above), but it also has linked domestic routes to Santiago (T5873000), Puerto Plata (T5861977) and Sosúa (T5711274). Their buses are very comfortable, offering TV, snacks, pillows and blankets, while their terminals have food shops, toilets, television and children's play area. *Transporte del Cibao*, T6857210, opposite Parque Enriquillo in Santo Domingo, to Puerto Plata, cheaper at US$3.60, to Santiago US$3. *Transporte Espinal* (4 blocks north of Parque Enriquillo) US$4 to Santiago, US$3 to La Vega, US$3 to Bonao. *La Covacha* buses leave from Parque Enriquillo (Av Duarte and Ravelo) for the east: La Romana, Higüey, Nagua, San Pedro de Macorís, Hato Mayor, Miches, etc. *Astrapu* does the same routes. *Expresos Moto Saad*, Av Independencia near Parque Independencia runs 12 daily buses to Bonao, La Vega and Santiago. *Línea Sur* (T6827682) runs to San Juan, Barahona, Azua and Haiti. Offices in other towns, see text.

Bus services between most towns are efficient and inexpensive. In rural areas it can be easy to find a *guagua* (minibus or pick-up) but they are usually filled to the point where you cannot move your legs and luggage is an uncomfortable inconvenience. There are also cars (*carros*) on some of these routes, which are equally dilapidated and crowded. It is possible to buy an extra seat in a *carro* or *guagua* to make yourself more comfortable.

Local drivers can be erratic; be alert. Hand signals mean only 'I am about to do something', nothing more specific than that

Car A valid driving licence from your country of origin or an international licence is accepted for 3 months. Dominicans drive on the right. Many of them do not have licences. The Autopista Duarte is a good, 4-lane highway between Santo Domingo and Santiago, but dangerous. It is used by bicycles and horse-drawn carts as well as motorized vehicles, while drivers switch from one lane to the other without warning. Lots of shopping opportunities by the roadside contribute to the hazards, with vehicles swerving on and off the road. The Autovía del Este is an excellent road from Santo Domingo out to the east, with good access roads to Higüey, Punta Cana Airport, Hato Mayor and Sabana de la Mar. Minor roads and many city streets are in poor condition with lots of potholes. The speed limit for city driving is 40 kmph, for suburban areas 60 kmph and on main roads 80 kmph. Service stations generally close at 1800, although there are now some offering 24-hr service. Gasoline prices rose sharply in 2003, but in dollar terms are around US$2 for super unleaded, US$1.50 for diesel. Most police or military posts have 'sleeping policemen', speed humps, usually unmarked, outside them. In towns there are often 'ditches' at road junctions, which need as much care as humps. At night look out for poorly lighted, or lightless vehicles. Many *motoconchos* have no lights. There are tolls on all principal roads out of the capital: RD$15, exact change needed. Road signs are very poor: a detailed map is essential, plus a knowledge of Spanish for asking directions. Expect to be stopped by the police at the entrance to and exit from towns (normally brief and courteous), at junctions in towns, or any speed-restricted area.

Car hire Avoid the cheapest companies because their vehicles are not usually trustworthy. Prices for small vehicles start at US$40 per day but can be as much as US$90. Weekly rates are better value. Credit cards are widely accepted; the cash deposit is normally twice the sum of the contract. The minimum age for hiring a car is usually 25, although some companies will rent to 20 year olds; maximum period for driving is 90 days. Mopeds and motorcycles are everywhere and are very noisy. Most beach resorts hire motorcycles for between US$15 and US$35 a day. By law, the driver of a motorcycle must wear a crash helmet, but very few do; passengers are not required to wear one.

Taxi If travelling by private taxi, bargaining is very important. In Santo Domingo, *Apolo Taxi*, T5377771, is recommended if you need to call a taxi, cheap, friendly and efficient. Motorcyclists (*motoconchos*) also offer a taxi service and take several passengers on pillion. In some towns, eg Samaná, *motoconchos* and cyclists pull 4-seater covered rickshaws. During the day a short distance costs RD$10 for 1 passenger, although if it is less than 1 km they sometimes drop the fare to RD$5. For longer journeys negotiate fare first. During the night fares double. There are usually fixed *público* rates (see under Santo Domingo) between cities, so inquire first. They can take 2 passengers in front and 4 on the back seat, regardless of the size of the car, so the ride is often uncomfortable, but friendly.

Motoconchos can be found on all the main streets and near the beaches

Keeping in touch

Internet *Codetel* offices in most towns have a computer for internet access, but don't expect it to work, RD$11, 15 mins, RD$0.55 additional mins. *Tricom* has internet access at Las Américas Airport and a few centres in Santo Domingo, RD$8.99 15 mins, RD$0.55 additional mins. Cybercafés are now opening in tourist areas such as Cabarete and Las Terrenas, but, again, service is often down.

Post Don't use post boxes, they are unreliable. The postal system as a whole is very slow. A letter to Europe is RD$15; to North America and the Caribbean, RD$10; to South and Central America, Australia and Asia, RD$28. You can buy postal envelopes without stamps but with pictures of tourist sites, issued by the Instituto Postal Dominicano. It is recommended to use *entrega especial* (special delivery, with separate window at post offices), for RD$2 extra, on overseas mail, or better still a courier service (see under Santo Domingo).

Telephone Operated by the *Compañía Dominicana de Teléfonos* (Codetel, T2201111, www.codetel.net.do), or *Tricom* (T4766000 in Santo Domingo, T4718000 in Santiago). Call centres usually open 0800-2200. Through Codetel you call abroad either person-to-person or through an operator (more expensive, but you only pay if connected). Calls and faxes may be paid for by credit card. Pre-paid calling cards are available. For phone boxes you need 25-centavo coins. Phone calls to the USA cost RD$9.40 per min, to Europe RD$23.80, to Australia RD$25.90, Puerto Rico RD$7.80, Haiti RD$10.90 and the rest of the Caribbean RD$12.90.

IDD code: 809 Emergency number: 911

Media **Newspapers** There are 8 daily papers in all, 6 in the morning, 2 in the afternoon. *Listín Diario* (www.listin.com.do) has the widest circulation; among the other morning papers are *La Nación*, *El Nuevo Diario*, *El Caribe*, *Hoy* (www.hoy.com.do), *El Siglo* (has good foreign coverage, www.elsiglord.com.do). In the afternoon, *Ultima Hora* (www.ultimahora.com.do) and *El Nacional* (www.elnacional.com.do) are published. *Primicias* is a Sun paper. *Touring* is a multilingual tourist newspaper with articles and adverts in English, German, French, Spanish and Italian. *La Información*, published in Santiago on weekdays, is a good regional paper carrying both national and international stories. **Radio and television** There are over 170 local radio stations and 7 television stations. Cable television is available. *Cadena de Noticias* transmits news programmes 24 hrs a day. *Caribbean Travelling Network* (CTN) has news of tourist sites, good for visitors.

Language The official language is Spanish, although English, German, French and Italian are spoken in tourist resorts by guides and some hotel employees. English is the language most commonly taught to tourism workers. If you are planning to travel off the beaten track, a working knowledge of Spanish is essential.

Dominican Republic

Food and drink

Food Like most Caribbean cooking, local food tends to be calorific and spicy. The usual starches, rice, yams and plantains, underpin most meals, while chips/fries are usually also available. Dominicans like their food well seasoned, so sauces include a good deal of chilli, garlic, pepper and oregano. Strangely, the staple of *comida criolla* (Creole cooking) is the dish known as *bandera dominicana* (the Dominican flag), a colourful arrangement of stewed beef, rice, plantains and red beans, which is actually rather unspicy. More exotic and challenging is the legendary *sancocho* or *salcocho prieto*, a hearty stew made of 6 or 7 different types of meat as well as vegetables. Even traditional Dominican breakfasts can be a serious affair. The dish *mangú* is mashed plantain, drizzled with oil and accompanied by fried onions. Goat meat is a great favourite and usually comes either as roast (*chivo asado*) or stewed (*chivo guisado*). A *locrio* is a rice dish, accompanied by meat, chicken or sausages, and the formidable *mondongo* is a tripe stew. Another local speciality is the *asopao*, somewhere between a soup and a pilau-style rice dish (sometimes unappetizingly translated as soupy rice) that is served with fish or chicken. The ubiquitous street snacks such as *pastelitos* (pasties or turnovers filled with minced beef, chicken or cheese) are fried according to demand, as are *quipes* (cracked-wheat fritters with a meat filling) or *platanitos* (hot plantain crisps). *Tostones*, or twice-fried slices of plantain, are often served as a side dish.

Most Dominican restaurants assume their customers to be carnivorous and the number of vegetarian restaurants is still limited. Fresh fruit is plentiful all year round and changes according to season. *Lechoza* (papaya) is commonly served at breakfast, as is *guineo* (sweet banana). More unusual are *jagua* (custard apple), *caimito* and *mamey*. Many *cafeterías* serve delicious fresh milk shakes (*batidas*), made out of any of these fruits, water and milk (optional, *con leche*).

Drink
Wine is imported and often indifferent and pricey, but locally produced drinks are extremely cheap

Statistics reveal that Dominicans account for one of the world's highest per capita consumptions of alcohol, and a look around any *colmado* (corner store) will confirm this fact. The Presidente brand of lager beer comes in 2 sizes (*pequeño* or *grande*) and seems to enjoy a near monopoly. Other beers such as Quisqueya and Bohemia are much less visible. *Mamajuana* is a home-made spiced rum mixed with honey and sweet wine, sold in markets and on street corners, frequently called the Dominican viagra. There are many rums (the most popular brands are Barceló, Brugal, Bermúdez, Macorix, Siboney and Carta Vieja). Light rum (*blanco*) is the driest and has the highest proof, usually mixed with fruit juice or other soft drink (*refresco*). Watch out for cocktails mixed with 151° proof rum. Amber (*amarillo*) or gold (*dorado*) is aged at least a year in an oak barrel and has a lower proof and more flavour, while dark rum (*añejo*) is aged for several years and is smooth enough, like a brandy, to be drunk neat or with ice and lime. Brugal allows visitors to tour its bottling plant in Puerto Plata, on Av Luis Genebra, just before the entrance to the town, and offers free daiquiris. In a discothèque, *un servicio* is a ½ litre bottle of rum with a bucket of ice and *refrescos*. In rural areas this costs US$3-4, but in cities rises to US$15. Despite being a major coffee-producer, the country does not always offer visitors good coffee, and much of what is served in hotels is either American-style watery instant or over-stewed and over-strong. Good coffee is available in small *comedores*, *cafeterías* and even from street vendors, who sell a small, dark shot for barely more than a peso.

Shopping

What to buy
If you are taken into a shop by a guide you can expect to pay a premium so that he gets his commission

The native **amber** is sold throughout the country. Do not buy amber on the street, it will as likely as not be plastic. Real amber fluoresces under ultra violet light (most reputable shops have a UV light); it floats in saltwater; if rubbed it produces static electricity; except for the very best pieces it is not absolutely pure, streaks, bits of dirt, etc, are common. **Larimar**, a sea-blue stone found only in the Dominican Republic, and red and black coral are also available (remember that coral is protected). Other souvenirs are **leather goods**, **basketware**, **weavings** and **onyx** jewellery. The ceramic *muñeca sin rostro* (faceless doll) has become a sort of symbol of the Dominican Republic. Paintings and other **art work** are on sale everywhere, but beware of the mass-produced Haitian-style naive art. Thousands of these brightly coloured, low-quality paintings are churned out for sale to tourists. Good Dominican art is for sale in the Santo Domingo galleries or you can buy direct from artists in Jarabacoa. There are excellent **cigars**, **rum** and **coffee** at very reasonable prices. Bargaining is acceptable in markets but rarely in shops. You will not get much of a discount but it is worth a try, particularly if you are buying in bulk.

Flora and fauna

The Dominican Republic offers luxuriant vegetation and exotic wildlife, combining a variety of habitats within a limited area. It is possible to move between the coastal reefs and beaches through thorn scrub and plantation into rainforest within a matter of miles.

Varied plant life is found within several tropical zones, from the arid tropical forest found in the west, where scrub and cactus predominate, to the subtropical forest on the slopes of the mountains and in the valleys and the mountain forests in the highlands where pine trees predominate. There is no primary rainforest left, but there are large areas of secondary forest which have suffered from only a limited amount of selective felling. There are many palm trees, including the royal palm (*Roystonea regia*) and the coconut palm (*Cocos nucifera*), as well as other tropical species such as Hispaniolan mahogany (*Swietenia mahogoni*), West Indian cedar (*Cedrela odorata*) and American muskwood (*Guarea guidonia*). The most common pine tree is the Creole pine (*Pinus occidentalis*). The national plant is the *caoba* (mahogany). Along parts of the coast there are red (*Rhizophora mangle*), white (*Laguncularia racemosa*) and button (*Conocarpus erectus*) mangroves which provide a habitat for migrating birds and the manatee as well as fish, shrimp, mosquitoes and other biting insects. You can see large flocks of sea birds including the frigate bird and the tropic bird with its streamer-like tail feathers.

There is some confusion over which is the national bird. Some have it as the *sigua palmera* or palm chat (*Dulus dominicus*), an olive brown bird in the thrush family with bold streaks of white and brown on its underparts. It usually makes its nest high up in a palm tree in a communal structure with passages to the eggs in an inner chamber. Others name the *cotica* or Hispaniolan parrot (*Amazona ventralis*), which is green, very talkative and a popular pet although it is protected. Among other birds that can be seen are the *periquito* or Hispaniolan parakeet (*Aratinga chloroptera*), which is also green but with some red feathers, the *guaraguao* or red-tailed hawk (*Buteo jamaicensis*), and todies, known locally as *barrancolí*, which behave rather like fly catchers but nest in burrows. There are several hummingbirds (*zumbador*) throughout the country, including the Hispaniolan emerald (*Chlorostilbon swainsonii*), the Antillian mango (*Anthracothorax dominicus*) and the tiny Vervain hummingbird (*Mellisuga minima*). The Hispaniolan trogon (*Temnotrogon roseigaster*) is worth looking out for, with its green upper parts, grey breast, red underbelly and long tail streaked with white. It is known locally as a *papagayo*, or *cotorrita de sierra*, and although it is found chiefly in the mountains, it is also seen in mangroves. The Hispaniolan woodpecker, the *carpintero* (*Melanerpes striatus*) is found only on Hispaniola.

Indigenous mammals are few. There are two, rare and endangered species, however, which you are unlikely to see in the wild. They are both nocturnal. The *jutía*, or hutia (*Plagiodontia aedium*), is a small rodent which lives in caves and tree trunks. The *solenodonte*, or solenodon (*Solenodon pardoxus*), is an insectivore with a long nose, round ears and long tail, with the appearance of a large rat, which grows to about 30 cm and can weigh 1 kg. Similarly in peril is the *manatí*, sea cow or manatee (*Trichechus manatus*), which lives in mangroves and seagrass beds. The Taíno used to eat the manatee, which are slow moving and therefore easy prey, as did the pirates who hid in the waterways where they live. There are also lots of bats, many of which live in the plentiful caves found around the island.

There are 2 species of iguana found in the Dominican Republic, the rhinoceros iguana (*Cyclura cornuta*) and the Ricord iguana (*Cyclura ricordi*), both found in the hot, dry area in and around Lake Enriquillo where the terrain is rocky and cactus, scrub and thorn bushes such as acacia grow. They are best seen at the hottest time of the day as they disappear when it gets cool. In this area you can also find the American crocodile (*Crocodylus acutus*), one of the largest wild crocodile populations in the world.

National parks The government has adopted 6 generic categories for environmental protection: areas for scientific research, national parks, natural monuments, sanctuaries, protected areas and wildernesses. The total number of protected areas (including panoramic routes, recreational areas and ecological corridors) is about 70. All are under the control of the Dirección Nacional de Parques (DNP). Armando Bermúdez and José del Carmen Ramírez National Parks, both containing pine forests and mountains in the Cordillera Central, are the only remaining areas of extensive forest in the Republic; since the arrival of Columbus, two-thirds of the virgin forest has been destroyed. The Reservas Científicas include lakes, patches of forest and the Banco de la Plata (Silver Banks), to which humpback whales migrate yearly from the Arctic for the birth of their young. Silver Banks lies some 140 km north of Puerto Plata but there is a proposal to include it in a Biosphere Reserve which would stretch as far as Los Haitises. The reserve protects fish, coral and several species of sea turtles as well as the whales. It is a rather dangerous area for shipping, with depths changing from 20 m to 1,800 m giving the wildlife added protection.

Dominican Republic

◆ **National parks**

1 Armando Bermúdez	6 Isla Cabritos	10 La Vega Vieja
2 Cabo Francés Viejo	7 Jaragua	11 Loma Quita Espuela
3 Del Este	8 José del Carmen	12 Los Haïtises
4 El Choco	Ramírez	13 Monte Cristi
5 Isabel de Torres	9 Lagunas Redonda y	14 Sierra Baoruco
	Limón	15 Submarino La Caleta

Diving and marine life

There is good diving all round the island despite there being relatively few underwater parks. The coral in most places is in good condition and the underwater landscape is varied and interesting. Offshore, the tropical reef provides a diversity of wildlife which you can see by scuba diving, snorkelling or taking a glass bottomed boat trip. There are over 50 species of hard coral (the form that builds reefs) with a variety of sizes and colours. Among the most dramatic are the staghorn and elkhorn corals which are found on the more exposed outer reefs. Brain coral forms massive round structures up to 2 m high, while pillar coral forms columns which reach a similar height. Soft corals, which include black corals (protected by CITES), sea fans and gorgonians, colonize the surface of the hard coral adding colour and variety. Associated with these structures is a host of animals and plants. The quantity of fish varies from place to place, depending on the local fishing industry, as some areas have depleted stocks because of spearfishing. Nevertheless, in Dominican waters you can see whales, dolphins, grouper, barracuda and other large pelagics, as well as lots of colourful reef fish, turtles and invertebrates.

Snorkelling is good and many dive boats offer snorkelling excusions

In the Puerto Plata area of the north coast, the diving is best around Sosúa. It is particularly good for first time divers, with sandy spots, reefs and interesting rock formations, while for more experienced divers there are tunnels, chimneys, overhangs and walls. Some sites are virgin, but many are fished out. In places the coral has been badly damaged and broken by overdiving. The best time of year is usually May-Sep, when the sea is calm and the visibility good. In high season, Dec-Apr, there can often be winds and rain which stir up the sand, reduce visibility and bring in a lot of rubbish which litters the dive sites. More conservation-minded divers should head further east to Río San Juan, where there are plans to make the area offshore of the Laguna Grí Grí an underwater park. There are varied dive sites for beginners or intermediate divers and the coral is in good condition. Lots of reef fish can be seen, and if you go over the wall you are likely to spot larger life such as barracuda. At the beginning of the year whales are sometimes seen, usually humpbacks during their migration and breeding season. The Samaná peninsula offers rewarding diving on its north side and there are several dive shops at Las Terrenas and one at Las Galeras. In season some of them offer whale watching as well as diving. There are dive sites all around the bays and headlands, including wrecks, caves, drop-offs and reefs.

Bayahibe on the southeast coast is good for independent divers as there is reasonable, cheap accommodation and a good, German-run dive shop offering tailor-made programmes into the National Park. There are also several all-inclusive resorts with their own dive shops if you want to stay in

From Puerto Plata to Cabarete there are 16 or 17 dive operations, but you need to ask lots of questions to establish their safety record, standard of equipment and teaching ability

16 Valle Nuevo

19 Villa Elisa

♦ **Scientific reserves**

17 Del Ebano Verde

18 Samaná Bay Marine Sanctuary

Dominican Republic

more upmarket lodgings. The National Park offers some of the best diving in the country; the reef is in good condition, and although local fishermen are still going in and spearfishing, it is not overfished. There are nice dive sites all along the coast to Saona island, in the Park, with plentiful and colourful underwater life. Catalina island, with its wall and coral gardens, is a big attraction here but there is also Catalinita, north of Saona island, about 1 hr by boat from Bayahibe, where you can find sharks and rays, while dolphins will accompany you on your route. Nearer to Santo Domingo is La Caleta underwater park which has good reef and wreck diving, with 2 deliberately-sunk boats close to each other. There are no dive shops at La Caleta, most divers come on trips from nearby Boca Chica or from Santo Domingo.

Dive operators Most dive operations in the Dominican Republic offer tuition in a variety of languages. PADI is the most widely offered instruction, although CMAS and others are available. A PADI Open Water certification can cost anything from US$290 to US$400, while a 2-tank boat dive for qualified divers varies from US$50 to US$75, so it is worth shopping around. In case of emergencies, those with DAN insurance will be flown out to Miami. There is a recompression chamber in Santo Domingo, but there is no one to operate it, so the nearest is in Puerto Rico. A chamber is planned for the new hospital in the Punta Cana/Bávaro area.

Beaches and watersports

Beaches According to UNESCO, the Dominican Republic has some of the best beaches in the world: white sand, coconut palms and many with a profusion of green vegetation. They vary enormously in development, cleanliness, price of facilities, number of hawkers and so on. Boca Chica and Juan Dolio, for instance, are very touristy and not suitable for anyone seeking peace and quiet (except mid-week out of season). The best-known beaches are in the east of the Republic, including: Boca Chica, Juan Dolio, Guayacanes and Villas del Mar in San Pedro de Macorís; Minitas (*Casa de Campo,* La Romana), Bayahibe, Macao, Bávaro and Punta Cana in the far east, all taken up by resort hotels. Cayo Levantado, an islet with one hotel where the beach is used by day-trippers, Las Terrenas, Playa Bonita, Playa Rincón, Playa Portillo and Las Galeras, are all on the Samaná peninsula and hardly ever crowded. On the north coast, Playa Diamante at Cabrera, Playa Grande and Laguna Grí-Grí at Río San Juan, where you can also visit the lovely beaches of Puerto Escondido, Punta Preciosa in the Bahía Escocesa and Cabo Francés Viejo. East of Puerto Plata, recommended, although fully developed, beaches include Cabarete, Sosúa and Playa Dorada. West of Puerto Plata are Costambar, Cofresí, and several smaller beaches. Towards the northwest and the Haitian border there are uncluttered beaches at Bahía de Luperón, Playa El Morro, Punta Rucia, Cayos los Siete Hermanos and Estero Hondo. In the southwest the best beaches are Las Salinas, Monte Río, Palmar de Ocoa, Najayo, Nigua, Palenque, Nizao and those south and west of Barahona. This area is rather neglected as far as tourism is concerned but popular with people from Santo Domingo and at weekends the beaches can get busy and noisy with those escaping the capital. Watersports are available on most beaches east of Santo Domingo and along the north coast, but you are less likely to find facilities in the southwest except in certain places like Las Salinas, where windsurfing is popular.

Windsurfing
A useful website for windsurfing in Cabarete is www.hispaniola.com/ Cabarete/windsurf. html, it has information on schools, events and daily wind and wave reports

Cabarete, near Sosúa, is one of the best windsurfing places in the world, attracting international competitors to tournaments there. Other centres are Playa Salinas (Baní), Boca Chica and Puerto Plata, while most beach hotels offer windsurfing facilities. Cabarete is the place to be in Jun, when the town is taken over by serious windsurfers. For the annual **World Cup Windsurfing Competition** and then **Cabarete Race Week**, www.cabarete raceweek.com The winds are at their best at this time of year attracting both professional and amateur racers. There are lots of competitions, fiestas and other events, contact Vela, T5710805, for information. Although the strength of the wind varies throughout the year, windsurfing is nearly always possible. Generally the mornings are calm, but by the afternoon the bay is full of sails flitting about like butterflies on a puddle. The windsurfing schools are all good, with excellent equipment. They do not all stock the same, so if you have a preference it is worth contacting them in advance to see what they can supply. Most of them stock other watersports equipment too, such as surf boards and kayaks.

Guibia is a great surfing beach, but it is full of garbage and oil from the ships going to Ozama. **Surfing**
Other surf beaches include Baoruco and Playa Pato in Barahona, La Preciosa, La Pasa and
Playa Grande in Río San Juan, El Encuentro and El Canal in Cabarete, Sosúa Bay and La Boca in
Sosúa, La Puntilla in Puerto Plata, Cofresí west of Puerto Plata, and El Macao near Bávaro in
the east.

For renting boats and yachts, contact the Secretaría de Turismo. There are no charter fleets at **Sailing**
present. The *Punta Cana Resort* has a brand new marina and so does *Casa de Campo*,
www.casadecampomarina.com Most beach resorts have small craft for rent by the hour or
the half day. For independent yachtsmen the Dominican Republic is an excellent place to
reprovision if cruising the islands.

Several international fishing tournaments are held each year, the catch being blue marlin, **Fishing**
bonito and dorado. There is an annual deep-sea fishing tournament at Boca de Yuma, east of
La Romana, in Jun. For information about fishing contact Santo Domingo Club Náutico, Lope
de Vega 55, T5661682, or the Clubes Náuticos at Boca Chica, T6854940, Cabeza de Toro, near
Bávaro, and at Monte Cristi. However, these clubs are for members only, so you will need to
know someone who is a member if you want to visit. For instruction contact Actividades
Acuáticas at Boca Chica, T5234511.

Jarabacoa is the centre for adventure sports, being blessed with 3 main rivers, the Río Yaque **River sports**
del Norte, the Jimenoa and the Baiguate, and their many tributaries. There are 3 companies *Information can*
active in watersports: *Aventuras del Caribe, Get Wet* and *Máxima Aventura*. **Canyoning** is *be found at*
done on the Río Jimenoa amidst beautiful scenery, unless the river is too full, as you can't do *www.DRpure.com,*
it at high water. Advanced level athletes can also go canyoning at La Damajagua near Imbert. *www.hispaniola.com/*
Cascading is done at El Salto de Jimenoa and El Salto de Baiguate, elsewhere it can be done *whitewater and*
at the Cascada Ojo de Agua near Gaspar Hernández. The Río Yaque del Norte is a level 3-4 *www.rancho*
river for **rafting**. There are several short rapids in gorges with lots of rocks and boulders to *baiguate.com*
negotiate, followed by calmer sections of river. The rainy season (Nov and May) is more exciting than the dry season because the more water there is the faster it flows. The rainy season is
also the favoured time of year for **tubing**, the best rivers being the Río Yaque del Norte, the
Río Jamao and the Río Isabela. **Kayaking** is offered for beginners and advanced level by
Aventuras del Caribe, which has all the equipment for class 5-6 rivers, found on the tributaries
of the Río Yaque del Norte. Beginners are taken to the lower Yaque del Norte, the Río Yasica
and the lower Río Bao, which are class 2.

Other sports

The Dominican Republic has miles of dirt roads and endless mule trails, making it a paradise **Cycling**
for mountain bikers. There is also some good road biking if you don't mind sharing the roads *The scenery is*
with trucks, mules, motorbikes and *guaguas*. There are hundreds of great rides in the moun- *breathtaking and the*
tains and along coastal routes. These can change after hurricanes and rain storms. For exam- *locals are so friendly*
ple after Hurricane Georges in 1998, you could not drive a car over the road from Constanza *that you may have*
to San José de Ocoa. It is now a great bike ride, but if they fix the road it will not be as good. *a hard time making*
The best time of year to mountain bike on the island is Jun-Oct. It tends to be dry and more *any great distance*
single track is open, but you can bike all year round. It is hottest between 1200-1500, so if you *in one day, due to*
want to cover large distances get an early start and take a long lunch break. In the mountains *constant photo stops*
it is hot during the day, but gets cool at night, so dressing in layers and having warm clothing *and invites for coffee*
for after sunset is important. Good rain gear is also recommended. Carry at least 2 water bottles and make sure you drink more than you think you need.

  Bike rental There are only a few places to rent mountain bikes, including *Iguana Mama*
based in Cabarete, and *Rancho Baiguate* in Jarabacoa. Sometimes some of the local bike shops
have bikes to rent. Equipment at hotels is often not well maintained; this doesn't mean that
they are not great bikes for a coastal cruise, but anyone wanting a real mountain bike adventure should not be fooled into thinking that they have a suitable bike at their hotel.

Dominican Republic

Golf

Golf is big business here, with swathes of the coast east of Santo Domingo and along the north coast devoted to the sport

There are 23 golf courses with more being built or renovated, many more than any other country in the Caribbean. All the biggest and newest resorts have a golf course attached and golf is included in many package holidays. The 3 most famous golf courses are the **Teeth of the Dog**, at *Casa de Campo*, **Playa Grande**, near Río San Juan, and **Playa Dorada**, near Puerto Plata. The first is a Pete Dye designed masterpiece with 8 holes right on the sea and judged one of the most beautiful courses in the world. (Golf shop T5232480, F5238800, green fee US$175 including cart, par 72 Championship course.) Next to it is **The Links**, par 71, green fee US$125, and the **Romana Country Club** (members only, par 72, green fee US$135 including cart, T5238600, F5238479) and a new par 72 course at **Altos de Chavón**. **Playa Grande** was designed by Robert Trent Jones Sr and has 10 of its holes along the coast on top of cliffs but none is far from the sea. (Golf shop T2485313, F2485314, green fee US$81 including cart, par 72 course.) **Playa Dorada** was also designed by Robert Trent Jones Sr as part of a complex of all-inclusive hotels outside Puerto Plata. (Golf shop T3726020, F3202773, open 0700-1730, green fee US$45, including cart, extra charge for mandatory caddy, par 72 Championship course.) There are many courses around Santo Domingo, of the country club variety, offering tennis and swimming and social activities for their members. Other 18-hole courses include **Las Aromas** in Santiago, which is hilly, with lovely views of the Cibao valley, wide fairways and lots of trees. (Golf shop T2765396, green fee US$13, par 70) In the **Bávaro** area there are 4 courses at the resort hotels and at **Punta Cana** a new Pete Dye course runs between the *Punta Cana Beach Resort* and the *Club Med* (T2212262, F6883951, www.puntacana.com).

The Dominican Golf Association organizes tournaments all year round, T4764898. For information about courses, tournaments, holidays, tours, pros, club membership etc, T2485263, F2482287.

Hiking

Walking sticks are advised, particularly if it has been raining and the tracks are slippery or muddy

The Dominican Republic provides ideal conditions for medium-distance walking in the tropics. Distances and temperatures are manageable. Road transport, accommodation, restaurants and rum shops are all within convenient reach. Nevertheless, the illusion of remoteness can sometimes be complete. The 2 highest peaks in the Caribbean are here: Pico Duarte (3,087 m) and La Pelona (3,082 m), side by side in the Cordillera Central. Hiking up Pico Duarte is now a major attraction with 3,500 people making the ascent in 1999. Although most start from the park entrance at La Ciénaga, there are other, longer routes you can take. There is a fee of RD$50 to enter any national park in the Republic and you must always be accompanied by a guide, who will bring food and water and mules to carry your bags and the provisions. The guides are well-trained and highly experienced, but they only speak Spanish. Other areas for rewarding hiking are around Jarabacoa, Constanza and in the Valle Nuevo national park, while easy climbs can be done up Pico Yaque, Mt Isabel de Torres outside Puerto Plata, or in the Sierra de Bahoruco in the southwest. Wherever you are in the country you will be able to find walking opportunities in the many ranges of hills and mountains, or even along the beach for a few kilometres. In rural areas farms and villages are reached by dirt tracks, rather than roads, which are proving popular with mountain bikers, horse riders and hikers. You may be greeted as a curiosity by local children but everyone will be pleased to see you and refreshments can usually be sought at a *colmado*, the village shop and bar. There are no large scale, reliable maps for walkers, although you can pick up regional maps from people like *Iguana Mama* in Cabarete (see opposite). If you are walking in the national parks you will, in any case, have to have a guide. You will need to carry plenty of water. Do not drink from the rivers unless you have a purification system with you.

Riding is available in several places, but like cycling, the mountains descending to the north coast are especially rewarding. No previous experience of riding is necessary as Dominican horses are placid and well behaved. Complaints from tourists have led to improvements in their care, but you still need to keep an eye out for a healthy horse and check there are no sores, particularly in the saddle area. You should also make sure that your saddle is well made and comfortable, for your own benefit as much as the horse's. If you are going to be in it for hours, you will suffer on a wooden saddle with no padding. Riding is western style, with a raised pommel on the saddle to hang on to.

Horse riding
No one wears a hard hat, so check your insurance policy before setting out along mountain trails. It's not far to fall, but rocks are hard from any height

The national sport is **baseball**. The Dominican Republic has produced a phenomenal number of great players and the game has become known as a way out of poverty, with thousands of boys hoping to be plucked out of obscurity by team selectors and paid a fortune to play their favourite game. The best players are recruited by US and Canadian teams who maintain feeder academies in the Republic; about half of the 300 professional Dominican players in the USA come from San Pedro de Macorís. The regular season starts on the last Fri in Oct and runs until end-Dec, with national and big league players participating. At the beginning of Jan for 3 weeks, round robin semi-final matches are held, after which the 2 best teams compete in the Serie Final in the last week of Jan.

Spectator sports

    Basketball is the second sport, played on an amateur basis in the Olympic centre, the Palacio de los Deportes, and in sports clubs around the country, also matches at the Club San Lázaro and Club San Carlos. Every town has a good outdoor court where they play every evening and anyone can join in. The talent is good, there are a lot of Dominicans in the NBA. Be careful of slippery courts and keep your elbows out! In Santo Domingo **cockfights** take place at the Coliseo Gallístico de Santo Domingo, Av Luperón, near Herrera Airport, T5653844, fights Sat, Sun, tickets from US$2, but the spectacle can equally well be seen at any rural town or village. Sun is the big day for cockfighting, although you will often see them practising on other days. **Polo** matches are played at weekends at Sierra Prieta, 25 mins from Santo Domingo, and at Casa de Campo, T5233333. **Horse racing** takes place at the Hipódromo V Centenario at Km 14.5 on the Autopista de las Américas, T6876060, grandstand ticket US$1. **Dog racing** at the Canodromo El Coco, off Autopista Duarte north of Santo Domingo, T5674461. Boxing matches take place frequently in Santo Domingo at the new Gimnasio-Coliseo de Boxeo (with a capacity to seat 7,000 but capable of holding 10,000 spectators) next to the baseball stadium, the Carlos Teo Cruz Coliseum, hotels and sports clubs, where you can also see **fencing**, **judo**, **karate** and **table tennis**. **Bowling** has now become hugely popular pastime. The Sebelén Bowling Centre (Bolera), Av Abraham Lincoln, esquina Roberto Pastoriza in a large commercial plaza in Santo Domingo. Built to host the 1997 Panamerican Bowling Games, it is said to be the world's most hi-tech bowling alley, open 1000-0200, T5400101.

Holidays and festivals

New Year is celebrated in the capital on Av Francisco Alberto Caamaño Deñó (formerly Av del Puerto) beside the river. The major bands and orchestras of the country give a free concert, which attracts thousands of people. The celebration ends with fireworks and the whole area becomes a huge disco. On **21 Jan** the day of the *Virgen de la Altagracia*, spiritual mother of the Dominicans, is celebrated with *'velaciones'*, or night-long vigils, and African-influenced singing and music, found in many towns. Higüey is the site of a mass pilgrimage and huge all-night party. *Carnival* (www.carnaval.com.do) is at the end of **Feb**, notable in Santo Domingo for the parade along the Malecón. Carnival in Santiago de los Caballeros is very colourful; its central character is the piglet, which represents the devil. On Sun in **Feb** at Monte Cristi there are the festivals of the *Toros* versus the *Civiles*. La Vega also celebrates for several Sun prior to Lent.

Dominican Republic

Things to do in the Dominican Republic

- **Whale watching** in the **Bay of Samaná** is an absolute must in January-March, the ultimate thrill to see humpback whales breaching in front of your boat.
- Anyone who likes **windsurfing** should spend a few days at Cabarete, great winds, flat water and the beach bars to go with it.
- Indulge yourself by staying in one of the **restored colonial mansions** in the heart of old **Santo Domingo**, even the cheap hotels are elegant and atmospheric while the expensive ones are luxurious.
- **Hiking up Pico Duarte** must be a highlight for anyone fit enough to tackle the highest mountain in the Caribbean, the scenery is spectacular, forests, rivers, wildlife and, in the distance, the shining blue sea of the silver coast.
- The north coast beaches are among the best in the world, try the deserted **Playa Rincón** on the Samaná peninsula if you want to get away from hotels.

There are other parades on *Restoration Day*, **16 Aug**. Each town's saint's day is celebrated with several days of festivities known as *patronales*. Based in Catholicism, everyone gets involved and has a party. *Holy Week* is the most important holiday time for Dominicans, when there are processions and festivities such as the *guloyas* in San Pedro de Macorís, the mystical-religious *ga-ga* in sugar cane villages and the *cachúas* in Cabral in the southwest.

The *Festival Presidente de Música Latina* is held in **Jun** in the Olympic Stadium, featuring musicians from all over Latin America. The *Merengue Festival* in **Jul** (see Culture), includes festivals of gastronomy, cocktails, and exhibitions of handicrafts and fruit. Puerto Plata has a similar, annual *Merengue Festival* at the beginning of **Oct** on the Malecón La Puntilla, as does Sosúa, in the last week of **Sep**.

Santo Domingo

IDD code: 809
Colour map 2,
grid B3
Population: 4,000,000

Travellers have been marvelling at this city since the beginning of the 16th century, when its streets, fortresses, palaces and churches were the wonder of the Caribbean and conquistadores set off from the port on the river to discover new territory for Spain in the Americas. Santo Domingo, the first European city in the Western Hemisphere, is now the capital and business centre of the Dominican Republic. Busy and modern, it sprawls along the Caribbean coast and inland along the banks of the Río Ozama. Restoration of the old city on the west bank of the river has made the area very attractive, with open-air cafés and pleasant squares near the waterfront. Those who have wealth flaunt it by building ostentatious villas and driving German cars, but the slums are some of the worst in the Caribbean.

Ins and outs

Getting there
Aeropuerto Las Américas, east of Santo Domingo, is the international airport for the capital, receiving flights from North and South America and Europe. **Las Herreras**, on the western outskirts of town is for domestic and commercial flights, although many of these also go from Las Américas, so you should check. See Airport for details of taxis and buses. If you are arriving in the capital by bus, you will come in to that company's bus terminal. There is no central bus station. Taxis wait outside to take you to your hotel or other destination.

Getting around
See Transport, page 320 for further details
If you are limiting yourself to the colonial city, you will be able to walk around all the places of interest. Further afield, however, distances are great. Public transport is varied: there are government-run buses on the arterial routes in and out of town for commuters; shared or privately hired taxis called *públicos*, radio taxis and motorcycle taxis, known as *motoconchos*. Car hire is not recommended for the capital. There is a **tourist office** in the colonial city in the Palacio Borgella, Isabel la Católica, near Plaza Colón, T6863858, and at Las Américas Airport, T5491496.

History

The first wooden houses were built in 1496 by Christopher Columbus' (Cristóbal Colón) brother Bartolomé on the eastern bank of the Río Ozama after the failure of the settlement at La Isabela on the north coast. In 1498 the Governor, Nicolás de Ovando, moved the city to the other side of the river and started building with stone, a successful move which was continued by Diego Colón, Christopher's son, when he took charge in 1509. It then became the first capital city in Spanish America. For years the city was the base for the Spaniards' exploration and conquest of the continent. Santo Domingo holds the title 'first' for a variety of offices: first city, having the first Audiencia Real, cathedral, university, coinage, etc. In view of this, UNESCO has designated Santo Domingo a World Cultural Heritage site. However, Santo Domingo's importance waned when Spain set up her colonies in Peru and Mexico with seemingly limitless silver and gold to finance the Crown. Hurricanes managed to sink 15 ships in 1508, 18 in 1509 and many more in later years. 1562 brought an earthquake which destroyed much of the town; 1586 brought Sir Francis Drake, who attacked from inland where defences were vulnerable, looted and pillaged and set the city alight. He was the first of many British and French pirates and privateers who attacked in the 16th and 17th centuries and rebuilding works were continually in progress.

In the 1930s, the dictator Rafael Leonidas Trujillo renamed the city Ciudad Trujillo and embarked on a series of public works. After his assassination in 1961 the city immediately reverted to the title of Santo Domingo, but his successor, Joaquín Balaguer, continued to build on a monumental scale. Prestigious projects such as the Faro a Colón took pride of place over social spending on education, health and housing for the poor. Governments since the 1960s have been criticized for concentrating on the capital and ignoring the provinces. As a result, migration to the capital has surged and little has been done to prevent the growth of slums and poor barrios. However, tourism is booming and it is a lively and vibrant place to spend a few days.

Sights

The colonial city is now only about 1% of the total area of Santo Domingo but it is the first port of call for visitors, holding almost all the sights of historical interest. **Calle Las Damas**, which runs alongside the Fortress, is the oldest paved (cobbled) street in the New World and is where the wife of Diego Colón and the ladies of the court would take their evening promenade. **Plaza España** lies at the end of Calle Las Damas and has lovely views over the river. At night time there are often cultural events laid on, such as music, folk dancing or theatre. **Calle El Conde** runs the length of the colonial city from the entrance gate, **Puerta El Conde** in the west, to the Fortaleza Ozama and the river in the east. It is a pleasant pedestrian boulevard with shops, bars and cafés.

Colonial city
Zona Colonial
Ciudad Vieja

Fortification of Santo Domingo began in 1503, with the construction of a tower to protect the entrance to the port. The city walls, only partially restored, were started in 1543 by the architect, Rodrigo de Liendo. All along the walls they built 20 defensive positions, six of them gates to the city and the others forts or bastions reserved for the military. The most important and largest fort was the **Fortaleza Ozama** or Fortaleza de Santo Domingo, overlooking the river and now bounded by the Avenida Francisco Alberto Caamaño Deñó, or Avenida del Puerto, running beneath it at the water's edge. It is the oldest fortress in America, constructed 1503-07 by Nicolás de Ovando.

Just to the west, is the **Catedral Basílica Menor de Santa María**, Primada de América, Isabel La Católica esquina Nouel, the first cathedral to be founded in the New World. Its first stone was laid by Diego Colón in 1514 (although there is some dispute and some people think it was after 1520); the first architect was Alonzo Rodríguez, but there were several. It was finished in 1540 and dedicated in 1542. The alleged remains of Christopher Columbus were found in 1877 during restoration work. In 1892, the Government of Spain donated the tomb in which the remains lay,

Little remains of the original interior decoration, because when Drake sacked the city in 1586 his men removed everything of value

a neo-Gothic wedding cake of a monument, behind the high altar, until their removal to the Faro a Colón (see below). The cathedral was fully restored for 1992, the 500th anniversary of Columbus' first voyage, with new gargoyles and sculptures at the gates showing the indigenous people when Columbus arrived. Ther are 14 chapels with multilingual boards explaining each one. ■ *Mon-Sat 0900-1630, Sun for services. No shorts allowed, women may be asked to wear skirts, not trousers.*

Parque Colón is outside the Cathedral, on its north side, next to Calle El Conde. A statue to Christopher Columbus (Cristóbal Colón) is in the middle, with a Taíno woman at his feet, a symbol now considered rather politically incorrect. The **Museo de Ambar**, El Conde 107 on Parque Colón, is upstairs, with a shop on the ground floor selling amber, larimar, protected black coral, local gold and pearls. ■ *T6864471.* There is also a **Museo de Larimar** on Isabel la Católica, where you can see examples of this lovely pale blue stone found only in the Dominican Republic. ■ *Mon-Fri 0830-1800, Sun 0900-1300. Free. T6896605.*

A cluster of historical buildings lies either side of Las Damas running north from the Fortaleza Ozama. The first is the **Casa de Don Rodrigo de Bastidas**, built in to the city

Santo Domingo

wall on Calle Las Damas in 1510. This was the house of the royal tax collector and mayor, who went on to colonize Colombia. It is built around an inner courtyard with arches around all four walls and enormous caucho trees. ■ *Mon-Fri 0930-1700. Free.* Beside it is the **Casa de Ovando**, the home of the man who did most to build the city. It is being developed into a hotel, the *Hostal Nicolás de Ovando.*

The **Casa de Francia**, opposite the *Hostal Nicolás de Ovando*, was built in the early 16th century. Next door is the **Convento de San Ignacio de Loyola**, Las Damas between Mercedes and El Conde, a Jesuit monastery and church. Finished in 1743, it has been the **National Pantheon** since 1958. The central nave forms a cross with the lateral chapels and a bronze lamp donated by the Spanish government (General Franco) hangs in the intersection. It contains the tombs of, or memorials to, many of the country's presidents, heroes and an ornate tomb built before his death for the dictator Trujillo, the 'Benefactor of the Fatherland', but after his assassination he was not given the honour of being buried here. ■ *Mon 1330-1800, Tue-Sun 0800-1800. Free.* Cross the street again for the **Capilla de Nuestra Señora de Los Remedios**, built in the early 16th century as the private chapel of the Dávila

Dominican Republic

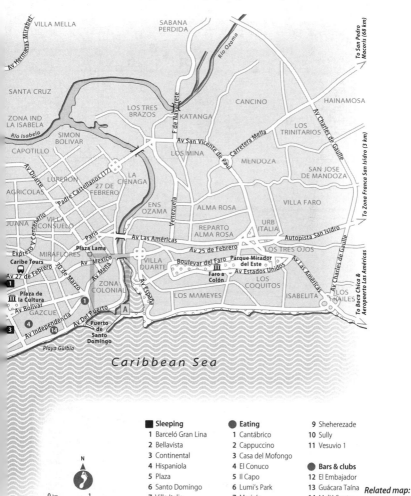

■ Sleeping	● Eating	9 Sheherezade
1 Barceló Gran Lina	1 Cantábrico	10 Sully
2 Bellavista	2 Cappuccino	11 Vesuvio 1
3 Continental	3 Casa del Mofongo	
4 Hispaniola	4 El Conuco	● Bars & clubs
5 Plaza	5 Il Capo	12 El Embajador
6 Santo Domingo	6 Lumi's Park	13 Guácara Taína
7 Villa Italia	7 Mario's	14 Meliá Santo
	8 Mesón de la Cava	Domingo

Related map:
A *Zona Colonial*
page 312

N

0 km   1
0 miles   1

family. By its side the Reloj de Sol (sundial) was built in 1753, near the end of Las Damas, so that court officials could tell the time.

One of the most significant historical buildings in this area is the **Museo de las Casas Reales**, in a reconstructed early 16th-century building which was in colonial days the Palace of the Governors and Captains-General, and of the Audiencia Real

Zona Colonial

N

0 metres 100
0 yards 100

■ **Sleeping**
1 Aída
2 Conde de Peñalba
3 El Palacio
4 Francés
5 Hodelpa Caribe Colonial
6 Hostal Nicolás Nader
7 Mercure
8 Bettye's Plaza Toledo
9 Saint-Amad

○ **Walls & fortresses**
1 Fortaleza Ozama/
  Fortaleza de Santo
  Domingo

2 Fuerte de San José
3 Fuerte de San Gil
4 Puerta de la Misericordia
5 Fuerte de Santiago
6 Puerta del Conde
7 Fuerte de la Concepción
8 Convento de San
  Ignacio de Loyola/
  Fuerte de la Caridad
9 Fuerte de San Lázaro
10 Fuerte de San Miguel
11 Fuerte de San Francisco
12 Fuerte de San Antón
13 Fuerte de Santa Bárbara
14 Fuerte del Angulo
15 Fuerte de la Carena
16 Puerta de las Atarazanas
17 Batería del Almirante
18 Puerta de San Diego
19 Fuerte de San Diego
20 Fuerte Invencible
21 Torre del Homenaje

22 Alcázar de Colón

✝ **Religious buildings**
1 Capilla de San Andrés
2 Iglesia del Carmen
3 Convento
  Regina Angelorum
4 Capilla de la Tercera
  Orden
5 Convento de los
  Dominicos
6 Iglesia Santa Clara
7 Catedral Basílica Menor
  de Santa María
8 Panteón Nacional
9 Capilla de Nuestra
  Señora Los Remedios
10 Iglesia de Santa Bárbara
  (ruins)
11 Capilla de San Antón
12 Monasterio de San
  Francisco

13 Iglesia de la Altagracia
14 Hospita-Iglesia del San
  Nicolás de Bari
15 Iglesia de las Mercedes
16 Iglesia de San Miguel
17 Iglesia de San Lázaro
18 Iglesia San Carlos
19 Capilla de la Virgen del
  Rosario

🏛 **Museums**
1 Museo de Ambar
2 Museo de la Familia
  Dominicana
3 Museo de Larimar
4 Museo de las
  Casas Reales
5 Museo Mundo
  de Ambar
6 Museo Nacional
  de las Atarazanas

Dominican Republic

and Chancery of the Indies. The Audiencia Real was a supreme court made up of three judges, designed to check the power of the Governor, and its power extended to the rest of the Caribbean and the mainland coast around the Caribbean basin. It is an excellent colonial museum (often has special exhibits), with many items salvaged from ships sunk in local waters as well as furniture, art and military items. ■ *Daily 0900-1700. RD$20. Calle Las Damas. T6824202.*

The **Alcázar de Colón** at the end of Las Damas and Emilio Tejera, is a fortified house constructed without any nails by the first Viceroy, Diego Colón, in 1510-14 to house his court and his wife, María de Toledo. It was the seat of the Spanish Crown in the New World until the family left for Spain in 1577 and in 1770 the building was abandoned. Now completely restored, it houses the interesting **Museo Virreinal** (Viceregal Museum), with religious art and colonial artefacts. ■ *Mon-Sat 0900-1700, Sun 0900-1600. RD$50.* **La(s) Atarazana(s)**, the Dockyards, near the Alcázar, are a cluster of 16th-century buildings which served as an arsenal, warehouses and taverns for the sailors in port, now restored to contain shops, bars and restaurants. The **Museo Naval de la(s) Atarazana(s)** at the end, contains recovered treasure from several shipwrecks, namely the *Concepción*, *Nuestra Señora de Guadalupe* and *Conde de Tolosa*. There are accounts of the many attempts to raise numerous 17th- and 18th-century ships which sank around the island and exhibits show what life was like on board ship at that time. ■ *Daily 0900-1700. RD$15. T6825834.*

Near the end of Isabel La Católica lies the only joint church and fort in Santo Domingo, the **Iglesia de Santa Bárbara**, just off Avenida Mella. Built in 1574 on the site of the city quarry, it was sacked by Drake in 1586, and destroyed by a hurricane in 1591. It was reconstructed at the beginning of the 17th century. Its design is rather lopsided and haphazard, its two towers being of completely different size and style and bearing little relation with the main entrance with its triple arches. Behind the church are the ruins of its fort, where there are good views and photo opportunities.

Santa Bárbara is the patron saint of the military

Don't miss the **Museo Mundo de Ambar**, Arzobispo Meriño 452, esquina Restauración, in a restored 17th-century building, which has a fascinating display of scorpions, butterflies and plants fossilized in amber, with microscopes and videos. A guided tour is recommended but not essential. The staff are very informative and will teach you how to tell real from fake amber. Craftsmen polish and shape raw amber for sale in an adjoining room. ■ *Mon-Sat 0800-1800, Sun 0000-1300. RD$15. T6823309.*

Round the corner and up the hill, the **Monasterio de San Francisco** (ruins), Hostos esquina E Tejera, was the first monastery in America, constructed in the first half of the 16th century, although dates vary. Sacked by Drake and destroyed by earthquakes in 1673 and 1751, it was repeatedly repaired or rebuilt. For about 50 years until the 1930s it was used as an asylum for the insane, and there are still metal brackets in places where patients were restrained with leg chains. A hurricane closed it down for good and the ruins are now used for cultural events.

Walk south down Hostos to the **Hospital-Iglesia de San Nicolás de Bari** (ruins), Hostos between Mercedes and Luperón, begun in 1509 by Nicolás de Ovando, completed 1552, was the first stone-built hospital in the Americas. In a cruciform plan, the three-aisled Gothic-vaulted church was used for worship while two-storey wings were used for wards to cure the sick. Also plundered by Drake, it was probably one of the best-constructed buildings of the period, it survived many earthquakes and hurricanes. In 1911 some of its walls were knocked down because they posed a hazard to passers-by; also the last of its valuable wood was taken. It is now full of pigeons.

The **Museo de la Familia Dominicana** has a collection of furniture, antiques and memorabilia from the 19th century. It is housed in the **Casa de Tostada**, an early 16th-century mansion with a Gothic-Isabelline double window on its northern façade. The house was the home of the writer, Francisco de Tostada, the first native professor at the university, who was killed when Drake set about destroying the city in 1586. ■ *Mon-Sat 0800-1600. RD$20. Calle Padre Billini esq Arz Meriño T6895000.* One block further down Padre Billini is the **Convento de los Dominicos**, built in 1510. Here in 1538 the first university in the Americas was founded.

Dominican Republic

▶ The mystery of Columbus' bones

After his death in 1506, Columbus was buried in Valladolid, Spain. In 1509 his body was apparently removed to Sevilla, then together with that of his son Diego to Santo Domingo sometime in the 1540s. When France took control of Hispaniola in 1795, Cuba (still part of Spain) requested Columbus' remains. An urn bearing the name 'Colón' was disinterred from beneath the altar, sent to Havana and then back to the cathedral in Sevilla in 1898, when Cuba became independent. In 1877, however, during alterations and repairs in Santo

Domingo cathedral, the cache of urns beneath the altar was reopened. One casket bore the inscription 'Almirante Cristóbal Colón', both outside and in. Experts confirmed that the remains were those of Columbus; the Spanish ambassador and two further experts from Spain were dismissed for concurring with the findings. A second pair of Spanish experts denied the discovery, hence the confusion over where the admiral's bones lay. The urn that was opened in 1877 is that which is now given pride of place in the Faro a Colón.

East of the Río Ozama The **Faro a Colón** (Columbus Lighthouse), built at great cost (and not without controversy) in the **Parque Mirador del Este**, is in the shape of a cross. Where the arms of the cross intersect is the mausoleum containing the supposed remains of Columbus. Spotlights project a crucifix of light into the night sky, spectacular on a cloudy night. One of the rooms inside the lighthouse is a chapel, in others, different countries have mounted exhibitions (the British exhibit concentrates on the entries for the competition to design the lighthouse: the competition was won by a British design). Slums were cleared and some of the 2,000 families evicted received a paltry sum of US$50 before losing their homes. Some 100,000 people are believed to have been adversely affected by the construction work, road building and slum clearance. In the light of the controversy the King and Queen of Spain declined an invitation to attend the 1992 celebrations and the Pope withdrew his acceptance to officially open the building. Two days before the ceremonies were to begin, President Balaguer's sister, Doña Emma, to whom he was devoted, inspected the Faro and hours later, she died, inspiring further belief that Columbus brings bad luck and that there was a curse, or *fukú* on the building. Balaguer, who had been held responsible for the whole enterprise and who was criticized for his megalomania, also stayed away from the ceremony, while he mourned his sister. ■ *Daily 0900-1700. RDS20, children, RD$5. T5911492. Photography inside permitted, but no photos in the museums, no smoking, eating, drinking or pets; guides are free, but tip; shorts above the knee not allowed.*

At the entrance vendors sell artesanías made from stalactites (light colour) and stalagmites (dark colour), an ecological horror

East of the Lighthouse in the **Parque Mirador del Este** are the *cenotes* (limestone sinkholes) **Tres Ojos** (Three Eyes), a popular tourist attraction. They used to be public bathing pools in the times of the Taínos, and Anacaona, the wife of Enriquillo, would bathe here, but now 'Tarzan' is the only person allowed to swim. A local man, he has been doing it since 1958 and is a tourist attraction in himself. ■ *Daily: RD$30 adults, RD$10 children and students. Ferry to the furthest lake RD$10 adults, children RD$5. Toilets. Guagua from Parque Enriquillo.*

West of the Río Ozama **Gazcue** is a quiet, attractive residential area with expensive homes built in the 1930s and 1940s, stretching west of the Zona Colonial as far as Avenida Máximo Gómez. The coral pink **Palacio Presidencial** with a neoclassical central portico and cupola, built by Trujillo, is at the intersection of Doctor Delgado and Manuel María Castillo. It is used by the President, but guided tours of the richly decorated interior can be arranged. ■ *T6958000.* Opposite the Palacio's grounds, at Avenida México y 30 de Marzo, are the government offices. The 1955/56 World's Fair (Feria de Confraternidad) buildings now house the Senate and Congress.

The modern city to the west is very spread out because, until recently, there was no high-rise building. Avenida George Washington (also known as the Malecón) runs parallel to the sea; it often becomes an open-air discothèque, where locals and foreigners dance the merengue. The annual merengue festival is held here in July. The **Plaza de la**

Cultura, founded by Presidente Joaquín Balaguer on Avenida Máximo Gómez, contains the country's major museums alongside the national library and the ultra-modern, white marble **National Theatre** ■ *T6873191 (you will have to go to the ballet or opera to see the lavish interior, although you can go to the restaurant at the back of the building for a wonderful buffet at lunchtime)*. The **Museo del Hombre Dominicano** traces the development of the modern Dominican, from the Amerindians, in pre-Columbian times, who were hunters and gatherers, to the Spanish conquerors and the African slaves. There were about 400,000 Taínos on the island in 1492, but only 60,000 in 1508 and they had nearly all died by 1525. Despite their rapid annihilation their influences live on in Dominican life today, all explained here. There is a large display of carnival costumes and a Dominican vodú altar. ■ *1000-1700, closed on Mon. RD$20. T6873622.* The **Museo de Arte Moderno** contains a huge amount of 20th-century Dominican art on four floors. ■ Tue-Sun 0900-1700, RD$10, T6852154. The **Museo de Historia Natural** is of more use to Dominican schoolchildren learning about science, than to visitors wanting to find out about the natural history of the Republic, although there are some exhibits of interest. ■ *Tue-Sun 1000-1700. RD$20. T6890106.* The **Museo de Historia y Geografía** has a few Taíno exhibits, but most of the displays are from the 19th and 20th centuries, starting with the Haitian invasion and following on to the American occupation. A great deal of space is taken up by artefacts belonging to Trujillo, illustrating his wealth and vanity. The museum organizes ecological excursions to different parts of the country. ■ *Tue-Sun 0900-1630. RD$5, children RD$3. T6866668.*

Among the attractive parks are the **Centro Olímpico**, JF Kennedy and Máximo Gómez, in the city centre, **Parque Mirador del Este** (Autopista de las Américas, a 7-km-long alameda) and **Parque Mirador del Sur**. The Centro Olímpico is a public park, but the sporting facilities are technically only for Dominicans. The Paseo de los Indios at Parque Mirador del Sur is a 7-km-long trail, popular for walking, jogging, cycling and picnics. Avenida Anacaona runs along the north side and many desirable residences overlook the park. On Avenida José Contreras are many caves, some with lakes, in the southern cliff of Parque Mirador del Sur. Along this cliff is the Avenida Cayetano Germosén, giving access to a number of caves used at one time by Taíno Indians. Caves are also the setting for the *Mesón de la Cava* restaurant and the *Guacara Taíno* nightclub. The road, lined with gardens, links Avenidas Luperón and Núñez de Cáceres. **Parque Mirador del Norte** has been constructed on the banks of the Río Isabela, near Guarícano and Villa Mella. There is a boating lake, picnic areas, restaurants, jogging and cycling trails. ■ *Tue-Sun 0900-1800. RD$10.*

Parks

The **Jardín Botánico Nacional** has a full classification of the Republic's flora. Plants endemic to the island are grown here. There are 300 types of orchid and a greenhouse for bromeliads and aquatic plants, highly recommended, especially the beautifully manicured Japanese Garden; a small train tours the extensive grounds. ■ *Daily 0900-1700. RD$15, children RD$10. Av República de Colombia, Urbanización Los Ríos, T3852611.*

Essentials

For cheap rooms in *casas de pensión*, or for apartments for rent for longer stays in or outside the capital, look in the classified section of daily paper, *Listín Diario*. There are many cheap hotels around the Mercado Modelo; those on Av Duarte are usually used by prostitutes.
Zona Colonial L *Francés* (Sofitel), Las Mercedes esq Arzobispo Meriño, T6859331, F6851289. Restored colonial mansion, 19 luxury rooms, lovely furnishings, restaurant in beautiful courtyard with fountain or indoors, superb French food, expensive but recommended. **L-A** *Hodelpa Caribe Colonial*, Isabel La Católica 159, T6887799, www.hodelpa.com 54 rooms and suites, art deco style, smart, good location, a/c, TV, fridge, bar, restaurant, internet access. **AL** *El Palacio*, Duarte 106 y Ureña, T6824730, www.hotel-palacio.com Colonial mansion with new extension at rear with pool, heavy wooden furniture, tiled floors, no restaurant. **AL-B** *Hostal Nicolás Nader*, Duarte y General Luperón, T6876674. Includes taxes, colonial mansion, 10 rooms, best upstairs,

Sleeping
Prices listed are high season rates and do not include taxes, normally 23%

Dominican Republic

beautifully furnished with lots of modern art for sale, friendly, personal service, pleasant. **A** *Mercure*, El Conde esq Hostos, T6885500, F6885522. Renovated by the French group, Accor, to a high standard, CP, good for business travellers, desk, internet connection, phone, fridge, TV, good bathrooms. **B** *Saint-Amad*, Arzobispo Meriño 353, T6871447, F6871478. 14 rooms in colonial house, a/c, TV, charming restaurant and bar area, room service, internet connection, all beautifully renovated. **B-C** *Conde de Peñalba*, corner of El Conde and Arzobispo Meriño facing Parque Colón, T6887121, www.condepenalba.com Great location, newly decorated rooms with TV, suites have balconies with lovely views, interior rooms have no windows, US$10 for additional person, bar, restaurant. **C** *El Beaterio*, Duarte 8, T6878657. Guesthouse with 11 rooms, all different, CP, roof terrace and patio, wonderful renovation, owners speak English. **D-E** (per person) *Bettye's Plaza Toledo*, Isabel la Católica 163, T6887649, www.dominican-rep.com/toledo.html Run by Bettye Marshall, private or dormitory-style rooms, good for groups, clean and comfortable, breakfast included, restored colonial house, shae also runs an art gallery. **E** *Aída*, El Conde 464 and Espaillat, T6857692, F6889350. A/c rooms have no windows, rooms with fan have balcony, some rooms sleep 3, family-run, very nice, no smoking, fairly quiet at night, but record shop below may be noisy in day, very central, popular, often full, Amex accepted. **F** *Independencia*, Estrella y Arzobispo Nouel, near Parque Independencia, T6861663. Price for single room, soap, towels etc provided, clean, convenient location, some rooms without windows, also has a club, bar (noisy all night), language school (across the street) and art exhibitions.

North of the Zona Colonial **E** *Caribeño*, Av Duarte y 27 de Febrero, T6853167. Fully a/c, small pool, good restaurant, *guaguas* leaving to north and west across the street. **D** *Señorial*, Av Presidente Vicini Burgos 58 (Parque Eugenio María de Hostos), T6874367, F6870600. Swiss-run, a/c, good electricity and water supply, TV, friendly, clean and informal, good Italian food, popular with Swiss-Italian visitors, see the 1952 map on the wall. **F** *Ferdan*, Francisco Henríquez 107 y Carvajal, T2217710, just off Av Duarte. Buses to Boca Chica and to airport 2 blocks away, large clean rooms with bath, foreigners given rooms with windows, large discounts for long stays but you will be given room on top floors where generator does not reach and suffer power cuts.

Away from the old city along the Malecón are the modern international-style hotels with business centres and entertainment, Hotel V Centenario Intercontinental, Meliá Santo Domingo and Renaissance Jaragua

Business travellers can often get cheaper rates than posted by requesting 'la tarifa comercial'

Gazcue **C-D** *La Casona Dorada*, Independencia 255 y Báez, in Gazcue, near *Jaragua*, T2213535, casonadorada@codetel.net.do. 25 rooms, some sleep 3, a/c, TV, laundry and dry cleaning, small pool, 24-hr room service, courteous staff, secure parking. **C-D** *Duque de Wellington*, Av Independencia 304, T6824525, www.hotelduque.com 28 budget rooms, TV, fridge, bar and restaurant, convenient. **F** *La Llave del Mar*, Av George Washington 43, esq Santomé, T6825961. 10 rooms, restaurant with aquarium tables, live piano music nightly. **E** *Palmeras del Caribe*, Cambronal 1, T3335510. Nice rooms but small, pleasant garden, use of fridge, adjoining café.

Near the university **L-AL** *Santo Domingo*, Av Independencia y Av Abraham Lincoln, T2211511, F5354050. Colonial style, plush and charming, main restaurant open 5 days a week for lunch, otherwise for receptions, *Café Tal*, less well-staffed. Opposite is its sister hotel **L-AL** *Hispaniola*, Av Independencia y Abraham Lincoln, T2217111, F5350976. Pleasant public areas, noisy, glitzy, casino off reception, bedrooms and corridors showing their age, bathroom adequate, very clean, good service, repairs carried out quickly, pool, disco. **B-C** *Continental*, Av Máximo Gómez 16, T6891151, F6878397. Includes taxes and breakfast, pleasant area, pool. **B-C** *Villa Italia*, Av Independencia 1107 casi esq Alma Mater, T6823373, F2217461, hotel.villa@codetel.net.do 25 rooms, 3 suites, 1 apartment, a/c, phone, TV, jacuzzi on terrace, sea view, wooden furniture colour washed green, restaurant, fridge available for extra charge, attractive but service found lacking.

Near the Centro Olímpico **L-B** *Plaza*, Av Tiradentes, T5416226, F5497743. Suites with kitchenette, very comfortable, pool, gym, gourmet restaurant, coffee shop. **L** *Barceló Gran Hotel Lina*, Av Máximo Gómez y 27 de Febrero, T5635000, h.lina@codetel.net.do Good restaurant, well equipped, 217 rooms, casino, convenient for *Caribe Tours* terminal, painted orange and pink, internet access.

Near Parque Mirador del Sur **B** *Delta*, Av Sarasota 53, T5350800, F5356448. 73 rooms, restaurant, bar and pool, easy access to main avenues. **E** *Bellavista*, Dr F Defilló 43, Ens Bella Vista, T5320412, hotelbellavista@codetel.net.do Good, large, clean rooms.

Expensive (US$20 and above) **Zona Colonial**: *La Briciola*, Arzobispo Merino 152, T6885055. Recommended Italian cuisine in spectacular setting in courtyard of colonial house. *Caribbean Blue*, Hostos 205 with El Conde, opposite *Mercure*, T6821238.Latin-Caribbean fusion dishes, great style. *Coco's*, Padre Billini 53, T6879624.Excellent food and service, menu changes daily, highly recommended, open Tue-Sat 1830-2400, Sun 1200-1500, dinner for 2 with wine costs about US$75. In the Plaza España is *Museo de Jamón*, La Atarazana 17, T6889644, ceiling covered with hams, also delicious selection of tapas. **West of the Zona Colonial**: *Fellini*, Roberto Pastoriza 504, esq Winston Churchill, T5405330. Mediterranean cuisine. *Sully*, Av Charles Summer 19 y Calle Caoba, T5623389. Lots of seafood in Dominican, French and Italian styles, full dinner for 2 about US$50, closed Mon. *Spagghettíssimo*, Paseo de los Locutores 13, entre A Lincoln y W Churchill, T5653708. Italian, fish, seafood, meat, pasta, open-air jazz on Wed, also home delivery. *Vesuvio I*, Av George Washington, T2211954. For a long time, the place to go in Santo Domingo for an expensive meal.

Mid-range (US$15-20) **Zona Colonial**: *Palmito Gourmet*, Arzobispo Portés esq Santomé, T2215777, restaurant and bar, mix of Dominican and Italian dishes, good atmosphere. *Mesón de Barí*, corner of Hostos and Arzobispo Nouel, T6874091 Open daily, 1200-0100, great place for typical Dominican dishes, on 2 levels, merengue music at weekends, unusual collection of artwork. **West of the Zona Colonial**: *Mesón de la Cava*, Parque Mirador del Sur, T5332818, in a natural cave. Good steaks, live music, dancing, great experience, very popular so reserve in advance, open daily 1130-1700, 1730-2400. *Asadero los Argentinos*, Av Independencia between Av Abraham Lincoln and Máximo Gómez. Excellent Argentine food. *Cappuccino*, Av Máximo Gómez 60, T6898600. Italian-owned restaurant and café, great Italian food, suave, prices to match, Italian murals. *Les Fondues*, Av Winston Churchill, esq Sarasota, T5355947. All types of fondue including chocolate, run by Swiss. *Il Capo*, Jardines del Embajador, Av Sarasota, Centro Comercial Embajador, T5346252. Italian cuisine, excellent pizza.

Mid-range-cheap (US$10-15) **Zona Colonial**: *La Atarazana*, La Atarazana 5, T6892900. Popular for Creole and international cuisine, good seafood. Several restaurants to choose from in this area, including *Rita's Café*, international food, paella, Mexican, meat and seafood, overlooking river, open from 1000 daily. Also *Mesón La Quintana*, La Atarazana 13, T6872646.Spanish dishes, closed Mon. *Campo de Francia*, Calle Las Damas, esq El Conde, T6890583. French-run, authentic regional French dishes, open from 1100. **West of the Zona Colonial**: *Restaurant Cantábrico*, Av Independencia 54, T6875101. Recommended fresh seafood, Spanish and criollo. *Payan Barra*, 30 de Marzo 140, T6896654. Sandwiches and tropical juices, a Dominican favourite. *Sheherezade*, Roberto Pastoriza 226, T2272323. Arabian and Mediterranean food. *Samurai*, Av Lincoln 902, T4723442. Very good Japanese, try the Sun brunch. *Chino de Mariscos*, Av Sarasota 38, T5335249, 5328350. Very good Chinese seafood. *TGI Friday*, Av Winston Churchill, Plaza Acropolis, 3rd floor. Bar area has floor to ceiling windows, large crowd for happy hour. *La Esquina de Tejas*, Av 27 de Febrero 343, T5606075. Spanish cuisine. *Boga Boga*, Plaza Florida, Av Bolívar 203, T4720950. Spanish, good jamón serrano and chorizo, US$15-20 for a meal. *Mario's*, Av 27 de Febrero 299, T5624441. Very popular, smart and formal, good Chinese food and also international dishes. Seasons, Roberto Pastoriza 14, T5652616. Spanish, hot and cold tapas. *Vesuvio II*, Av Tiradentes 17, T5626060. Italian and international cuisine, better value than Vesuvio I. *Lumi's Park*, Av Abraham Lincoln 809, T5404584. The place to be, outdoor seating under canvas, 'steak park', *churrasco*, excellent *mofongos*, full dinner for 2 with rum or beer US$30, open until dawn, also takeaway or local delivery.

Cheap (US$10 and under) **Zona Colonial**: *Anacaona*, El Conde 101, corner of Isabel la Católica, T6828253. Bar restaurant owned by Martine and Jean-Pierre Boutte, excellent location and menu, outdoor seating. *Bariloche*, El Conde 203. Self-service food from about 1145, look at what is on offer then buy ticket at cash register, lasagne only US$1, *menú del día* US$3, huge portions. **West of the Zona Colonial**: *Bagels'n More*, Fantino Falco, T5402263. New York bagel sandwiches, soups, salads and muffins. *El Conuco*, Casimiro de Moya 152 y José Joaquín Pérez, road running off behind Jaragua, T6860129. *Comida criolla, sancocho, chivo guisado, la bandera dominicana* and other typical dishes, home cooking, large portions, decorated like a thatched barn in the country, music in the evening. *Maniquí* Pedro Henríquez Ureña in the

Eating
Many hotels have 'bufet ejecutivos' at lunchtime and gourmet restaurants for evening meals

The Asociación Nacional de Hoteles y Restaurantes, Asonahores, T5404676, publishes a guide to the best restaurants in the capital, 'Guía de Restaurantes'

There are numerous pizzerias, burger bars and American fast food chains. Cafeterías around the Mercado Modelo serve local lunches

Dominican Republic

Plaza de la Cultura, T6882854. Busy at lunchtime, try the crab in coconut, vegetarian dishes. Good for the local dish *mofongo*, *Palacio del Mofongo*, Av George Washington 509, T6888621, or *Casa del Mofongo*, 27 de Febrero y Calle 299, T5411121 (a long way from the centre). *Lincoln Road*, Av A Lincoln 949. T5493020. Fast food restaurant serving dishes of the day.

Vegetarian 2 good vegetarian restaurants are *Ananda*, Casimiro Núñez de Moya 7, Gazcue, T6827153, cafetería style, and *Lotus Vegetarian Restaurant*, Av 27 de Febrero, T5353319, a bit far from the city centre.

Cafés   **Zona Colonial** *La Cafetería Colonial*, El Conde 253, T6827114. Good for coffee after meal elsewhere, freshly ground. A good place for snacks and drinks is *La Panadería*, Isabel la Católica 251. Mon-Fri 0630-2030, Sat 0700-1700, Sun 0800-1300. *La Crêperie*, La Atarazana 11, Plaza de España, T2214734. Nice outdoor seating on the plaza. **West of the Zona Colonial** *France-Croissant*, Av Sarasota 82 y Dr Defilló, French bakery, tastiest pastries in the country, unsweetened wholemeal bread available, small café. **East of the Zona Colonial** *Café del Río*, Plaza la Marina, overlooking the Ozama River. Good place for a cold beer, near the Sugar Cane Monument on eastern side of river. Try a chimichurri (spiced sausage), throughout the city stalls sell sandwiches, chimichurris, hot dogs and hamburgers. Several small restaurants specialize in roast chicken, *pollo al carbón*, with a tasty wasa kaca sauce. The best of these is *Provocon IV*, Santiago 253, Gazcue, T2212233. Also other locations around the city.

Discos,   The top hotels have the top dance floors, with admission prices of US$2-10, depending on
nightclubs   whether there is a live band that night or recorded music. Things get going after midnight and
& casinos   they close around 0400. Dominicans dress up smartly to go dancing, so no jeans, T-shirts or
It is not a good   trainers. Taxi drivers know all the best places. In the area west of the Colonial Zone along the
idea to walk around   Malecón where all the international hotels are you will find: *Salón La Fiesta* in the *Jaragua*
town after about   *Hotel*, also *Jubilee*, T6888026, Dominican music. *Maunaloa Night Club* in the Centro de los
2300, take a taxi,   Héroes also has live music and comedians, dancing every night to Dominican music. *Club 60*,
street lighting is not   Máximo Gómez 60. Rock, merengue and ballads. *El Embajador* has live piano music nightly in
always good   the lobby. Hotels *Meliá Santo Domingo* and *Jaragua* have orchestras every night, free. Live music in many of these hotels coincides with happy hour, which is a pleasant way to get the evening's entertainment started. To hear *pericos ripiaos*, go on Fri or Sat night to the *colmados* near the Malecón in Ciudad Nueva; the groups move from place to place.

     Further west *Guácara Taína*, Paseo de los Indios, Avenida Cayetano Germosén, T5330671, has shows of Taíno dancing in a deep natural cave with stalactites and indigenous pictographs, spectacular setting, huge, can fit over 2,000 guests, from 2100-0200, US$4-12 (also disco, all types of music, a/c, 2 dance floors, happy hours and fashion shows). For daytime tours of the cave T5302662 (0900-1700), or T5331051 (1700-2100), reserve 24 hrs in advance. *Beer House*, Gustavo Mejía Ricart esq Winston Churchill, stocks about 30-40 beers from around the world, great to get something other than Presidente, live bands (often jazz) in the middle of the week, decent, casual ambiance.

     In the Zona Colonial *Momentos*, Hostos 202. Downmarket with lots of merengue.

     In Villa Consuelo *El Rincón Habanero*, Sánchez Valverde y Baltazar de los Reyes. Working class enthusiasts of Cuban son dance between tables to old records of the 1940s and 1950s. *Secreto Musical Bar*, 1 block away, Baltazar de los Reyes and Pimentel, similar, headquarters of Club Nacional de los Soneros, rock, merengue, salsa and ballads.

     Gay discos *Aire Club*, Mercedes 313. Open Wed-Sun, from 2200, in colonial house with large patio and open garden area. *Atlantis Disco*, Av George Washington 555. Open Thu-Sun, from 2300, different shows every night with male strippers, transvestites, drag queens, etc. *Bar Phoenix*, Polvorín 10 in the colonial zone. Neighbourhood bar, friendly, run by gays. Sex tourism is rife in Santo Domingo and you will be taking a risk if you participate. Remember the age of consent is 18 and many foreigners end up being blackmailed for having sex with a minor. Pickpocketing is common. In any bar or disco, unattached men will be approached by girls (*chicas*), while unattached women are considered fair game. Girls in brothels are checked for sexually transmitted diseases, but those on the street are not.

     Casinos In several of the hotels and *Maunaloa Night Club*, Centro de los Héroes.

Theatres *Teatro Nacional*, Plaza de la Cultura, Av Máximo Gómez, T6873191, for tickets. *Palacio de Bellas Artes*, Av Independencia and Máximo Gómez, T6872494. *Casa de Teatro*, small drama workshop, Arzobispo Meriño 110, T6893430. Cinemas In the Diamond Plaza mall, Av de Los Próceres, Plaza Central mall, 27 de Febrero, Bella Vista Mall, Av Sarasota and Plaza Acrópolis, Av Winston Churchill.

Entertainment

Mercado Modelo, Av Mella esq Santomé, open Mon-Sat 0900-1230, 1430-1700, gift shops, handicrafts, paintings, foodstuffs; bargain to get a good price, most prices have been marked up to allow for this. Guides appointed to assist tourists get a 5-10% commission from the vendor. There are also 'speciality shops' at larger malls. Prices will be higher than in the Mercado Modelo, but the quality will be better. The shop at the Museo del Hombre Dominicano sells ceramics, Taíno reproductions and works of anthropological interest. Calle El Conde, now reserved to pedestrians, is the oldest shopping sector in Santo Domingo; Av Mella at Duarte is good for discount shopping. A flea market, *Mercado de las Pulgas*, operates on Sun in the Centro de los Héroes and at the Parque Mirador del Sur at Av Luperón. Cigars can be bought at *La Casa del Fumador*, Fco Prats Ramírez 159, T5413390, F5414896, open Mon- Sat 1030-1400, 1530-2030, *Santo Domingo Cigar Club*, in the *Hotel Jaragua* and in the restaurant *Ambrosía*.

Shopping
Duty-free at Centro de los Héroes, La Atarazana, shops in large hotels; departure lounge at airport; all purchases must be in US dollars

Art galleries The best gallery is the *Galería de Arte Nader*, Calle Rafael Augusto Sánchez 22, Torre Don Roberto, Ens Piantini T5440878. The Nader family are hugely influential and stock collecters' items of Haitian, Dominican and other Latin American works of art, see also Sleeping above and Haiti chapter. *Ramírez Conde Centro de Arte y Antiguedades*, Av Roberto Pastoriza 704, Evaristo Morales, T5675613, promovideo@codetel.net.do Exhibitions of Dominican art are held frequently in Santo Domingo galleries, for example the Voluntariado de las Casas Reales, Galería Nader, Museo de Arte Moderno, El Pincel, La Galería, and others. Street sellers of Haitian or Dominican copies of Haitian naif art are not representative of what is going on in the Dominican art world and are merely gaudy paintings for tourist consumption. For details on contemporary Dominican painters, consult *Arte Contemporáneo Dominicano*, by Gary Nicolás Nader.

Bookshops *Tienda Macalé*, Calle Arzobispo Nouel 3, T6822011, near cathedral. Open daily including Sun, has a wide selection of books, especially on the Republic's history. *New Horizons Book Shop*, Av Sarasota 51, T5334915, and 3rd floor of Bella Vista Mall, T2550676. *Centro Cuesta del Libro*, 27 de Febrero esq Lincoln. *Thesaurus*, Av Abraham Lincoln esq Sarasota, sofas, reading areas, café, play area, cultural events with Dominican authors, some English language books, large by Dominican standards.

Music *Music Box*, Plaza Central. *Tiagos*, Calle El Conde. *Musicalia*, El Conde, T2218445, Tiradentes esq Gustavo Mejía Ricart, T5622878. *CD Mania*, Unicentro Plaza, esq 27 de Febrero and Abraham Lincoln. *CD Stop*, Plaza Central, T5495640. *Karen Records*, El Conde 251, T6860019.

Jewellery As well as the shops in the amber and larimar museums (see above) there is *Ambar Nacional*, Calle Restauración 110, T6865700, which sells amber, coral and larimar, at lower prices than the museums. *Centario*, Arzobispo Merino 304 in the colonial zone, 16872933, has a large selection at good prices, with fairly good quality.

A tour service covers the major sites of the city, in *merenguaguas parranderas*, buses without seats with names like La Gallera, La Monumental, La Criolla, La Bachatera, T5327154. There are several tours of the city, taking in the duty-free shops, nightlife, etc. Recommended travel agents in Santo Domingo for sightseeing tours include: *Metro Tours*, Av 27 de Febrero, T5444580. *Domitur*, Av N de Cáceres 374, T5307313. *Prieto Tours*, Av Francia 125, T6850102. *Coco Tours*, T5861311, www.cocotours.com, city tour Thu US$49 including lunch, shopping tour Sat US$25. *Turinter*, T6864020, F6883890, www.turinter.com city tour US$41 not including lunch, Santo Domingo by night, US$39 at *Museo del Jamón* and *Guácara Taína*.

Tour operators

Sunshine Tours, Las Terrenas, T2406164, offer tours on the Samaná peninsula and further afield, from hiking to whale watching. *Espeleogrupo Santo Domingo*, T6821577, is an educational organization working to protect many anthropological and geological sites, to which they also arrange technical and non-technical excursions, specifically Las Cuevas de Pomier in San Cristóbal and the Cuevas de las Maravillas in La Romana. The *Museo de Historia y Geografía* in Santo Domingo organizes archaeological and historical tours in the Republic, tours are announced in the newspapers. The co-ordinator is Vilma Benzo de Ferrer, T6886952.

Dominican Republic

Transport   **Air** From North America: Boston, Miami, New York and Philadelphia with connections from other US cities, with *American Airlines, USAirways, Continental* and smaller airlines which tend to come and go. **From Europe:** Amsterdam (*Martinair*), Madrid (*Iberia* with connecting flights from most European and Spanish cities, *Air Europa*), Milan (*Lauda Air*), Paris (*Air France*). **From the Caribbean:** Direct flights from Aruba, Barbados, Curaçao, Fort-de-France, Havana, Kingston, Mayagüez, Montego Bay, Pointe-à-Pitre, Port-au-Prince, St Maarten, San Juan and Santiago de Cuba, and connections with other islands with a variety of regional and international airlines. **From Central America:** *Copa* from Panama City, San José, Guatemala City, Managua. **From South America:** from Caracas, *Aserca* and *Aeropostal*; other capital cities are connected through Miami or Panama City.

Airport Aeropuerto Las Américas, 23 km out of town, T5491253, very clean and smart. Immediately on arrival there is a tourist office on your right (helpful, will make bus reservation if you want to go straight out of Santo Domingo), and next to that an office selling tourist cards, a blackboard indicates who needs a card. Check if you need a card, or else the long queue to get through immigration will be wasted. Banco de Reservas for currency exchange is in the customs hall open Sun and at night, while Baninter is outside the customs hall by car hire. Car hire offices are numerous as you come out of the customs hall. Remember you will need 15 pesos for the toll (peaje) if you drive in to Santo Domingo. On departure, the queue for check-in can be long and slow for large aircraft (eg Iberia to Madrid), allow plenty of time. In the departure area are lots of duty-free shops, cafés, and limited seating. Upstairs there are good facilities with burger restaurants which have plenty of seating and a good view of the airport.

Leaving the airport on the ground floor, you find the expensive, individual taxis. (Upstairs, outside departures, *colectivo* taxis cram up to 6 passengers into the vehicle; much cheaper.) The drive from Las Américas International Airport to Santo Domingo should take no more than 30 mins, but allow an hr, and cost no more than US$20 during the daytime although it varies between companies and US$25 is usual. From the capital to the airport for the return journey prices range from US$15 (*Alex Taxi*) to US$20 (*Apolo Taxi*). Most large hotels have a taxi or limousine service with set fares throughout the city and to the airport. Alternatively you can get from the airport to the colonial city for about US$1 if you walk, or take a *motoconcho* (motorcycle taxi), to the *autopista* (main road) and then catch a *guagua* (minibus) to Parque Enriquillo. On your return, catch any bus to Boca Chica or towns east and get a *motoconcho* from the junction; only really feasible if you are travelling light. If arriving late at night it may be better to go to Boca Chica (see page 348), about 10 km from the airport, taxi about US$20. Various tour agencies also run minibuses to the airport; check with your hotel.

Local Bus: *OMSA* buses run along the main corridors (corredores), Avs 27 de Febrero, Luperón, Bolívar, Independencia, John F Kennedy, Máximo Gómez and the west of the city, RD$5. **Long distance buses** For bus information see Essentials page 297.

Car hire: many places at the airport, on the road to the airport and on Malecón. There are more agencies, here are a selection: *MC Auto Rent-A-Car* (Av George Washington No 105, T6886518, F6864529, www.mccarrental.com), branches also at Las Américas Airport (T5498911) and Boca Chica (T5234414); *Nelly* (Av Independencia 654, T6877979, from US$45 a day); *Dollar* (Av Independencia, T2217368, from US$47 a day); *Hertz* (Av Independencia 454,T2215333); *Payless* (Gustavo Mejía Ricart 826, T5634686).

Taxi: *Carros públicos*, or *conchos*, are shared taxis normally operating on fixed routes, 24 hrs a day, basic fare RD$5. *Públicos* can be hired by one person, if they are empty, and are then called *carreras*. They can be expensive (US$3-4, more on longer routes); settle price before getting in. Fares are higher at Christmas time. *Públicos/conchos* also run on long-distance routes; ask around to find the cheapest. You can get to just about anywhere by bus or *público* from Parque Independencia, but you have to ask where to stand. *Conchos* running on a shared basis are becoming scarcer, being replaced by *carreras*. Radio taxis charge between US$3-5 on local journeys around Santo Domingo (US$10 per hr) and are safer than street taxis, call about 20-30 mins in advance: *Taxi Anacaona*, T5304800; *Apolo Taxi*, T5377771; *Taxi Express*, T5377777; *Taxi Oriental*, T5495555; *Alex Taxi*, T5403311; *Taxi Hogar*, T5682825; *Tecni Taxi*, T5672010; *Maxi Taxi*, T5440077; *Taxi Raffi*, T6860385. Motorcycle taxi service, *motoconchos*, RD$10, sometimes take up to 3 passengers on pillion.

Dominican Republic

Airline offices *Air Century*, Herrera Airport, Local 1, T5660888; *Air Europa*, Av Winston Churchill 459, **Directory**
T6838020; *Air France*, Av Máximo Gómez 15, T6868432; *Air Santo Domingo*, Av 27 de Febrero 272,
T6838006, information and reservations, T6838020, at Herrera Airport T6836691, at Las Américas T5491-
097, at Punta Cana T9592473, at Puerto Plata T5860391; *American Airlines*, Edif IN TEMPO, Av W Churchill,
T5622030; *Aserca*, Av Gustavo Mejía Ricart 93, esq Roberto Pastoriza, T5635400; *Caribair*, Av Luperón,
T5426688; *Condor*, Av George Washington 353, T6853125; *Continental*, Av Winston Churchill, T5626688;
Copa, 27 de Febrero, T4722233; *Cubana*, Av Tiradentes, T2272040; *Iberia*, Lope de Vega 63, T5080188;
Lufthansa, Av George Washington 353, T6899625; *Martinair*, M Gómez y Juan S Ramírez, T6886661.

Banks Many along Isabel La Católica, but check which banks accept which TCs, see page 293.
Casa de Cambio La Catedral, Sánchez, off El Conde, gives a slightly better rate than banks.

Communications Internet: *Centennial Dominicana* offices allow you to walk in and use their
internet computer stations for free. Offices at corner of Winston Churchill and Gustavo Mejía Ricart
(Edificio Grouconsa), corner of Máximo Gómez and Av Bolívar (Plaza de los Libertadores), and Carretera
Mella Km 8.5 next to the Ferretería Haché. Open Mon-Sat 0800-1900. Reserve in advance to use the
internet service at the *Codetel* offices in Unicentro Plaza, T2204721, Cacique, T2207411 and Oficina Torre
Cristal, T2205312. Codetel is among the cheapest, at US$0.75 for 15 mins, US$2 per hr. *Cibercafé*, Av
Máximo Gómez 49, T6872888. In the Zona Colonial: *Abel Brown's Internet World*, El Conde 359,
T3335604, 0900-2100 Mon-Sat, 1000-1600 Sun; *Servir*, El Conde 351 esq José Reyes, T6228537,
0800-2200 Mon-Sat, 0800-2000 Sun; *Codetel*, El Conde 202, T2201111, 0800-2000 Mon-Sat, 0800-1400
Sun. **Post office:** *Correo Central* is in La Feria, Calle Rafael Damirón, Centro de los Héroes. Open
0800-1600, Mon-Fri; 0800-1200, Sat. *Lista de correo* (poste restante) keeps mail for 2 months. There are
post offices in *Hotel Embajador*, T2212131, Plaza Central, T4726777, Isabela La Católica, Zona Colonial,
T6894721 and Av George Washington, T6823439. To ensure the delivery of documents worldwide, use a
courier service: *American Airlines* (T5490043). *DHL Dominicana*, T5437888, *Universal Courier Services*,
T5497398; *UPS Dominicana*, T5665177; *Federal Express*, T5679547; *Internacional Bonded Couriers*,
T5425265. **Telephone:** international and long distance, also fax: *Codetel*, Av 30 de Marzo 12, near Parque
Independencia, and 11 others throughout the city (open 0730-1800 Mon-Fri, 0800-1300 Sat). Cheaper
for phone calls is the *Tricom* office on Av Máximo Gómez between Bolívar and Independencia. In the
Zona Colonial: *Codetel*, El Conde 202, T2201111, *Tricom*, El Conde, T4766000.

Embassies and consulates Austria, Gen Román Franco Bidó 11, T5080709; **Belgium**, Abraham
Lincoln 504, T5621661, F5623383; **Canada**, Capitán Eugenio de Marchena 39, T6851136,
sdmgo@dfait-maeci.ge.ca   **France**, Calle Las Damas 42, T6875621, ambatrance.sd@codetel.net.do
Germany, Lope de Vega esq Rafael Augusto Sánchez, T5658811; **Haiti**, Juan Sánchez Ramírez 33,
T4127112-5, Amb.haiti@codetel.net.do; **Israel**, P Henríquez Ureña 80, T5418974; **Italy**, Manuel
Rodríguez Objío 4, T6820830; **Japan**, Winston Churchill, Torre BHD, piso 8, T5668023; **Netherlands**,
Max Enrique Ureña 50 esq Av Lincoln, T2620300, std@minguza.nl **Spain**, Independencia 1205,
T5356500; **Switzerland**, Recodo 2, Edificio Monte Mirador, Bella Vista, T5333781, F5323781; **UK**, 27 de
Febrero 233, Edificio Corominas Pepín, 7th floor, T4727111, F4727574; **USA** César Nicolás Penson esq
Leopoldo Navarro, (embassy) T2212171, (consulate) 2215511, F6856959;

Medical services *Clínica Abréu*, Av Independencia y Beller 42, T6884411, and adjacent *Clínica
Gómez Patiño* are recommended for foreigners needing treatment or hospitalization. Fees are high
but care is good. 24-hr emergency department. For free consultation and prescription, *Padre Billini
Hospital*, Calle Padre Billini y Santomé, Zona Colonial, efficient, friendly. **Pharmacies:** *Farmacia San
Judas Tadeo*, Independencia 57 esq Bernardo Pichardo, T6858165, open 24 hrs all year, home delivery.

North to Santiago

*The Autopista Duarte, a four-lane highway, runs northwest from Santo Domingo to
Santiago de los Caballeros, with the Cordillera Central on one side and the Cordillera
Septentrional on the other. From there it reduces in size, becoming the Carretera
Duarte, and follows the length of the Cibao Valley alongside the Río Yaque del Norte to
its outlet on the coast at Monte Cristi. This is the main artery through the country, used
by cars, trucks, motoconchos, cows, horse-drawn vehicles and others. The first town of
any size just west of the Autopista Duarte is Bonao, 85 km from the centre of Santo
Domingo and surrounded by rice paddies. To the east is the Falconbridge ferronickel
mine, a large employer and major contributor to the region's economy. After Bonao on
the Autopista Duarte, on the left, is the main road to Constanza.*

Dominican Republic

Constanza

Population: 80,000
Altitude: 1,300 m

The Garlic Festival is held in June

High up in the mountains, set in a circular valley formed by a meteor, is Constanza. Dubbed the Alps of the Dominican Republic, the mountains provide a spectacular backdrop for what is a fairly ordinary town with no buildings of note. The scenery is some of the best in the country, with rivers, forests and waterfalls and there are lots of good hikes in the area. In winter, temperatures can fall to zero or lower and there may be frosts at night, but during the day it is pleasant and fresh. In the 1950s, the dictator, General Trujillo brought in 200 Japanese families to farm the land and the valley is famous for food production, potatoes, garlic, strawberries, mushrooms and other vegetables, and for growing ornamental flowers. The main street is Calle Luperón, which runs east to west. Most of the cheap hotels and restaurants are here or nearby. La Isla gas station is at the east end, where taxis and *motoconchos* congregate. The local **tourist office** is beside Radio Constanza on Matilde Viñas esquina Abreu, www.constanza.net

Good bird-watching country

With a good, tough, 4WD you can visit the **Parque Nacional Valle Nuevo**, through which passes the very poor but spectacular road from Constanza to San José de Ocoa, see below. Wonderful views and you pass the geographical centre of the island, marked by four small pyramids at the Alta Bandera military post about 30 km south of Constanza. The park's alpine plateau is at an altitude of about 2,640 m and has a large number of plants which are unique to the island in pine and broadleaf forests. There are also thermal springs, three Amerindian cemeteries and the **Aguas Blancas** waterfall about 15 km south of town, so you can walk it if you want. The waterfall falls in three stages with a maximum drop of 87 m to a large pool at the bottom. At weekends or holidays it is very busy and lots of litter accumulates.

Sleeping **C-D** *Hotel Rancho Constanza & Cabañas de la Montaña*, east of town towards Colonia Kennedy, T5393268, cabaranchcons@hotmail.com Modern, rustic, Alpine-style hotel, rooms or suites with kitchens, also dark, basic cabins, good for families, playground and volley ball, lovely setting, tours arranged to waterfalls and hikes up into the mountains behind the hotel. **C-F** *Alto Cerro*, east of town, T6960202, c.matias@codetel.net.do Highly thought of, camping, hotel rooms and 2-bedroom villas, strung along a rise, great view of fields in valley, excursions on horse back, quad bike rental, very popular at weekends, grocery, restaurant serving home-grown meat, fruit and veg, playground. **B-E** *Mi Cabaña*, Carretera Gen Antonio Duvergé, Colonia Japonesa, T5392930, micabana@hotmail.com At entrance to *Hotel Nueva Suiza*, small townhouses sleep 4, kitchenettes, pool, bar, volleyball court, loud music, breakfast but no restaurant. In town there are several basic hotels, check whether they have hot water. **F** *Mi Casa*, Luperón y Sánchez, T5392764. 7 single rooms, 3 double rooms, 1 suite sleeps 4, hot water, restaurant/comedor, great strawberry juice and strawberry jam.

Eating

All the food here is wonderfully fresh, with local ingredients such as guinea fowl and rabbit

*L*os Niveles, town centre, upstairs. Open 1100-1600, 1800-2300. The poshest restaurant in town, serving steak, rabbit, guinea fowl, goat and fish, most dishes US$4-6.50, wine by the glass or bottle, special events held here. *Lorenzo's*, Luperón 83, T5392008. Excellent Dominican food, try the guinea fowl or rabbit cooked in wine, also sandwiches, pizza and pasta, most dishes under US$5, open for breakfast, lunch and dinner, TV. *Pizzería Antojitos d' Lauren*, Duarte 16 beside the Red Cross, T5392129. Casual, plastic tables, plastic cups, open 0800-2300, chicken, sancocho, local specialities, popular at night for pizza. *Comedor Gladys*, Luperón, T5393625. Open 0700-2230, menú del día US$2.25, plenty of food and freshly cooked, fish, goat or ask for something different, pastry counter popular with kids after school.

Transport **Road** There are direct buses from Santo Domingo, Línea Cibao, San Martín 197 esq Máximo Gómez, T5657363, and Línea Gladys, San Martín 194, T5651223, US$4.50, 0500, 0600, 1300. The last direct bus back to Santo Domingo leaves at 1200. Also buses from Santiago, La Vega and Bonao. *Expreso Dominicano*, Av Independencia, 100 m west of Parque Independencia, Santo Domingo, to La Vega every hr 0700-1800, get off at junction for Constanza. You can get to/from the Autopista Duarte by taking a *público* or *guagua* (US$1.50) to/from

Constanza. There is a poor, part paved, part dirt road from Jarabacoa to Constanza, passable with an ordinary car in dry weather, but 4WD recommended for safety, 1½-2 hrs. Constanza can also be reached from the south coast via San José de Ocoa. Sturdy 4WD essential, with 2 spare tyres, food, drink and warm clothing in case you break down. Much of the road has been washed away by Hurricane Georges and other storms, leaving huge holes and cracks.

Banks There is an ATM (Plus, Visa).

Directory

La Vega

Further north up the Autopista Duarte is La Vega, a quiet place in the beautiful valley of La Vega Real. After the declaration of independence on 27 February 1844, La Vega was the first place to raise the national flag, on 4 March. It was also the first town to embrace the Restoration Movement in 1863. The town is nothing special and most people only come here to change *guaguas* or buses or to visit the local archaeological sites (see below), which can be reached by hiring a taxi in the Parque Central or at the bus stations.

Population: 200,000

La Vega's **carnival** is one of the most colourful pre-Lenten festivities in the country, with elaborate masks (*caretas*) of devils (*diablos cojuelos*), made mostly of papier maché. Activities are held on six Sundays in February-March, in the afternoons from 1500-1800. *Comparsas*, sponsored music groups, compete and there are competitions for the best costumes. Materials are brightly coloured and hundreds of little bells are sown into the costumes. There are currently over 90 'groups' of between 5-40 members, and it is estimated that some 1,500 people dress up every Sunday. It is a huge, rowdy affair. A collection of masks can be seen in the **Casa de la Cultura**, on Calle Independencia, which also puts on temporary art exhibitions. ■ *Mon-Fri 0930-1200, 1400-1700. Free.*

Watch out for the local custom of hitting people with vejigas, balls on ropes, traditionally made from cows' bladders

About 5 km north is the turn for **Santo Cerro**, an old convent where the image of Virgen de las Mercedes is venerated and pilgrims come every 24 September to pray to Nuestra Señora de las Mercedes. Legend has it that Columbus raised a cross on the summit of the hill in 1494. Inside the brick church on the hill is a hole in which the cross is supposed to have stood. If you continue along the road to the other side of the hill and into the valley the ruins of **La Vega Vieja** (Old La Vega) can be seen. It was founded by Columbus in 1494 but destroyed by an earthquake on 2 December 1562. Bartolomé de las Casas said the first Mass here and the first baptisms of Taínos took place here, on 21 September 1496. The first protest against the treatment of Indians was also made here in 1510, by Fray Pedro de Córdoba. La Vega Vieja is now a National Park and the foundations of the fortress, church and a few houses can be seen. ■ *Mon-Sat 0900-1200, 1400-1700. US$2.*

There are some basic hotels, **F**, in town on Calle Cáceres, but they are not recommended, and slightly better accommodation, **E**, along the highway. There is a *Codetel* office and an ATM on the Parque Central. *Caribe Tours* (T5733488), *Metro* (T5737099) and *Vegano Express* (T5737079) are on Carretera La Vega, the road coming in to town from the autopista, but *guaguas* can be found on the corner of 27 de Febrero y Restauración.

Essentials

Jarabacoa

The road from the Autopista Duarte to Jarabacoa winds through some beautiful pine forests. The climate is fresh, with warm days and cool nights. It is an important agricultural area, growing coffee, flowers, strawberries, watercress and other crops. The town itself is quite modern. Everything is in walking distance and most things can be found along the main street, Calle Mario Nelson Galán. Several notable artists and sculptors live in the area and are willing to receive visitors to their studios or give classes.

Jarabacoa is the place to come for adventure sports

Dominican Republic

Mountains, rivers and waterfalls are spectacular features in this area

The three main rivers are the **Río Jimenoa**, the **Río Baiguate** and the **Río Yaque del Sur**. The Baiguate flows into the Jimenoa and the Jimenoa then flows into the Yaque. There are several other tributaries which are being explored for new white-water rafting locations. The Jimenoa waterfalls are worth seeing, 10 km from town, although they are often crowded with tour parties. Hurricane Georges wreaked havoc in 1998, washing away the power plant and bridge by the falls. A new walkway has been made, with wobbly suspension bridges (avoid too many people on them at any one time). The falls are large, with a tremendous volume of water and consequent noise. The last wall is used for canyoning. ■ *0800-1800. US$0.50 (which goes towards the upkeep of walkways).* There is another waterfall dropping 75 m over a cliff on the Río Jimenoa, which is more difficult to get to and unsigned, off the road to Constanza, so you will have to ask for directions locally or go with a group. Closer to town, off the Constanza road, are the Baiguate falls, 3½-4 km, an easy walk, there is a signpost to the falls, fourth turn on the right after *Pinar Dorado*. A path leads from the road around the hillside, hugging the side of the gorge, until you get to some steps down to a sandy river beach and the rocks beneath the falls. There are usually lots of tours to the falls by jeep or horse. The local **Tourist Office** is on Parque Duarte.

Sleeping **B-C** per person, FAP, *Rancho Baiguate*, T5746890, F5744940, www.ranchobaiguate.com.do, owned and managed by Omar and Estela Rodríguez. Lovely countryside setting beside river, extensive gardens, 27 rooms from standard to luxury, or small, medium and large, hot water, good bathrooms. Also 2 dormitories with 9 bunk beds in each for students/groups (the hotel started out as a summer camp). Bracing unheated pool, soccer and basketball court, quad bikes, horse riding and Maroma's Parcours, an adventure playground for adults, helpful staff and management, friendly, English spoken, good place for buffet lunch, lots of tour parties come for the day. Free transport into town until 2200, if there are not many guests you eat supper at the *Rancho Restaurant*. **C-D** *Gran Jimenoa*, out of town on Av La Confluencia, Los Corralitos, T5746304, hotel.jimenoa@codetel.net.do 28 rooms in lush countryside beside the river, safe for bathing when there isn't too much water, great location, new and in good condition, comfortable, pool, jacuzzi, indoor games, TV, room service, good restaurant with river view, local meats, packed with Dominicans at weekends. **F** *California*, on road to Constanza, Calle José Durán E 99, T5746255, i.lupo@codetel.net.do Owned by Dutchman Jan Sheffers and his Dominican wife, 9 simple rooms, bathroom, hot water, fan, breakfast, bar, small pool, popular, friendly, best in season when the owners are there, standards go down in their absence. **D** *Brisas del Yaque*, Luperón esq Peregrina Herrera, T5744490. New, small rooms but good bathrooms, small balcony, TV, a/c, brick and wood decor, tiled floors. **F** *Hogar*, Mella 34, T5742739. Central, 5-mins' walk from *Caribe Tours* terminal, 8 rooms, twin beds, cold water, clean, huge old trees in patio.

Eating *Rancho Restaurant*, opposite Esso station. Criollo and international, good food using locally grown ingredients, belongs to *Rancho Baiguate*. The walls are lined with the work of several local artists (who often dine there with the owners). *El Trebol*, small outdoor bar/restaurant under leafy canopy, sandwiches, hamburgers, tacos, *plato del día* US$2.50, specials on Sun US$3, vegetarian options. Several other *comedores* and *cafeterías*, including *D'lo Ultimos*, in town centre, best *batidas* (milk shakes) and *pastelitos* (stuffed pastries). *Vistabella Club Bar & Grill*, off road to Salto Jimenoa, 5 km from town, also part of *Rancho Baiguate*. Pleasant setting overlooking valley and president's new country mansion, pool, bar and excellent food, specialize in goat, guinea fowl, pigeon, duck, US$5-9, or for a snack ask for a plate of mixed *longaniza, carne salteada* and *tostones*, great with a cold beer, popular for lunch at weekends but often quiet at night. Buy strawberries beside the road, locally grown, but restaurants hardly ever have them.

Festivals There is a carnival in Feb, similar to that in La Vega, but on a smaller scale, rather chaotic with lots of music and rum all month.

Sport Whitewater rafting, canyoning, tubing, kayaking, rock climbing, horse riding, mountain biking, quad bikes, jeep safaris, paragliding and hiking are all on offer here. It is one of the starting points for climbing Pico Duarte. *Rancho Baiguate's* **Aventura Máxima** is the biggest adventure sports centre and has a small army of Dominican and international specialist guides and instructors for each activity. They have also taken over *Get Wet*, still run as a separate operation, which offers river activities. A third company, *Aventuras del Caribe*, T/F5742669, franz.lang@codetel.net.do, is run by Franz Lang, an Austrian. He deals with small groups, is recommended for canyoning and kayaking and is very safety conscious.

Road *Conchos* in town US$0.60. *Motoconcho* to *Rancho Baiguate* US$1.20. *Jarabataxi* opposite *Esso*, beside *Rancho* restaurant, T5744640. To Santo Domingo, *Caribe Tours*, T5744557, from its own terminal off the main street, 0700, 1000, 1330, 1630, arrive 30 mins in advance (even earlier for the 0730 Mon bus), tickets sold only on day of departure, US$4.66, 2½ hrs. To La Vega by *guagua*, US$1.20; if you want to go to the capital or Santiago, they will let you off at the right place to pick up the next *guagua*. To Constanza, you can get a 2-cabin pick-up truck via a very poor road over the mountains, but most people go back down to La Vega and up the Constanza road 10 km before Bonao. All transport can be found opposite the gas station.

Transport
No transport anywhere after 1800, very little after 1500

Banks *Banco de Progreso* by the Palacio Municipal near the bus stop. No ATMs in town. 5 banks on Mario Galán. **Communications** *Codetel* about ½ km on the road to La Vega beyond the gas station. In town, *Tricom* is at Sánchez y Libertad. *Televimenca* and *Western Union* are at Herrera y Independencia, Mon-Sat, 0900-1200, 1400-1700. The *Centro de Copiado y Papelería*, a stationery shop on Calle Duarte 53, T5742902, has 6 computers for internet access, US$2.30 per hr, open 0800-1300, 1400-1900. **Medical services** *Clínica César Terrero*, at the junction, T5744397. *Farmacia San Miguel*, 16 de Agosto y Libertad, T5746536, Mon-Sat 0900-1200, 1400-1700.

Directory

Pico Duarte

In the Cordillera Central near Jarabacoa and Constanza is Pico Duarte, at 3,087 m the highest peak in the Caribbean, but only just. Its neighbour, La Pelona, is only 5 m lower at 3,082 m. During the Trujillo dictatorship, when Pico Duarte was inevitably named Pico Trujillo, one of his geographers erroneously added to the height of the mountain, allegedly to impress his *jefe* (boss). To this day, most maps have Pico Duarte at 3,175 m. There are several popular hiking routes, requiring differing degrees of stamina. Some of the routes take in other mountains as well. You will see a wide selection of native flora and birds, rainforest and pine forest, and several different ecosystems. It is very beautiful landscape and a great experience. If you are not shrouded in cloud there is a fantastic view looking down on clouds and other mountain peaks. The most popular routes are the 46-km trail from La Ciénaga near Jarabacoa, and the 90-km trail from Mata Grande near San José de las Matas. Whichever route you take you will have to pay a RD$50 National Park fee (passport or copy required) and hire a guide, US$11 per day. They speak only Spanish and you must pay them as well as feed them and tip them. You are not allowed to set off on your own. There are other walks in the Parque Nacional Armando Bermúdez and the adjoining Parque Nacional José del Carmen Ramírez, but they all involve some steep climbing. Guides are available at the park entrance.

The driest time is December-February, but March-November is still good

At La Ciénaga the DNP has set up a nice little camp ground. You can sleep here and there is a tap in the yard for washing but facilities are very basic. Mules are definitely recommended for the average hiker, US$5.50-7 per day; you can carry all your gear and water if you want, but the guide will want a mule for his gear. The hike is moderate, for intermediate to advanced hikers, but very hard indeed for those who are not in regular training for hill climbing. Allow three days and two nights (or more if it rains, the paths turn to mud). ■ Guagua *from Jarabacoa to La Ciénaga US$3, or hitch (very little traffic). On your return, the last carro for Jarabacoa leaves at 1600.* Iguana Mama, *in Cabarete and Rancho Baiguate in Jarabacoa (see page 323) both offer tours of three to nine days, or a custom-designed trek is possible if they have nothing else arranged. Walking sticks/hiking poles are highly recommended, particularly for the journey down, which can be hard on the knees and dangerous if wet and muddy. Take adequate clothing with you; it can be cold (below 0°C) and wet; also take a torch and matches.*

La Ciénaga route
Allow US$60 for National Park entry fee, guide and mule hire for three days

Dominican Republic

Santiago de los Caballeros

Population: Santiago de los Caballeros is the second largest city in the Republic and chief town of
690,000 the Cibao valley. The streets of the centre are busy, noisy, with lots of advertising signs;
east of the centre it becomes greener, cleaner and quieter. The Río Yaque del Norte
skirts the city with Av Circunvalación parallel to it. There are few sites of tourist interest, this is a modern, working city, although there are some old buildings. In the colonial part look out for tiles on the walls at street corners, with the old names of the
streets, put there in 1995 to mark the 500th anniversary of the founding of the city.

Ins & outs **Getting there** There are good links by road from Santo Domingo (4-lane highway all the
See Transport, way) and Puerto Plata on the coast. Several bus companies have services to the city. There is
page 327, for also an airport for domestic flights. **Getting around** The long distance bus terminals are
further details scattered around the city and you will probably have to get a taxi to your destination. You
can walk round the centre of the city but suburbs and outlying areas are best reached by bus
or *carro público*. Calle del Sol is the main commercial street, with both vendors and the main
shops. In the newer part of the town, Av Juan Pablo Duarte and Av 27 de Febrero have shopping plazas, banks and fast food restaurants, very much in the US style. **Tourist office** There
is a tourist office in the basement of the Town Hall (Ayuntamiento), Av Juan Pablo Duarte; it
has little information available, only Spanish spoken.

Sights On **Parque Duarte** are the **Catedral de Santiago Apóstol**, a neoclassical building
(19th-century) containing the tombs of the tyrant Ulises Heureux and of heroes of
the Restauración de la República; the **Museo del Tabaco**, a pink colonial building
with large green rotting wooden doors. ■ *Tue-Sat 0800-1200, 1500-1800;* the
Centro de Recreo (one of the country's most exclusive private clubs) with Moor-
ish-style arches and the **Palacio Consistorial** (1895-96). Also on Parque Duarte is
the **Plaza de la Cultura y Oficina Regional de Patrimonio Cultural**, which is now
the **Museo de la Villa de Santiago** and holds cultural and art exhibitions. ■ *Closes
1230 on Sat.* **Fortaleza San Luís**, overlooking the Río Yaque del Norte, is not open to
the public as it is a military zone.

Other places worth visiting are the **Pontífica Universidad Católica Madre y
Maestra** (founded 1962) and the **Monumento a los Héroes de la Restauración**, at
the highest point in the city (panoramic views of the Cibao valley, commissioned by
Trujillo in his own honour and remodelled in 1991 to include a mirador). You can
climb up to the top of the monument for a panoramic view of the city, the valley and
the mountains. Behind the monument is a **theatre** built by Balaguer in the 1980s, a
rather impenetrable rectangular block with lots of Italian marble. This area is popular at weekends and fiestas and there are lots of bars and restaurants around the park.
At carnival or any other outdoor celebration, this is the place to come. Rum shops
sprout all over the open spaces and parades and parties occupy roads and squares.
Along Av 27 de Febrero is the León Jiménez tobacco factory, established in 1903. As
well as 18 mn Marlboro cigarettes a day, the workers turn out 20,000 hand-rolled
cigars, which you can watch being made. Each cigar maker has a target of 100 cigars a
day and earns about US$70 a week. The free tour is interesting and ends with a free
drink and shopping opportunities if you like cigars.

Sleeping **A-C** *Aloha Sol*, Calle del Sol 150, T5830090, F5830950. Rooms and suites, smart, upmarket,
cool, restaurant *D'Manon* with local and international food. **B** *El Gran Almirante*, Av Estrella
Sadhalá 10, Los Jardines, on road north, T5801992, F2411492. Popular with business visitors,
quite good, casino, Spanish restaurant and tapas bar. **B-C** *Hodelpa Centro Plaza*, Calle Mella
54 esq del Sol, T5817000, F5824566, Apdo 459. Smart, modern, good restaurant, disco club
Tarari next door, no parking facilities. **B-C** *Matum Hotel & Casino*, Las Carreras opposite
Parque Monumento, T5813107, F5818415. 47 rooms, new ones with 2 beds, fridge, TV,
phone, smart, old ones still a mess, pool. **C-D** *Don Diego*, Av Estrella Sadhalá, on road north,
T5754186. Restaurant and nightclub. **C-E** *Ambar*, also on Av Estrella Sadhalá, T5751957. On

Av Salvador Cucurullo in the centre there are 4 cheap hotels between 30 de Marzo and España: **F** *Dorado*, No 88, T5827563. With bath, basic, friendly. Opposite and better is **F** *Colonial*, No 115, T2473122. Small clean rooms with a/c and fan, good bathrooms, very hot water, fridge, TV, small cheap restaurant, friendly, luggage store. Also *Monterey*, No 92, T5824558 and *Lima*, on the corner, 30 de Marzo 57 esq Cucurullo, T5820620.

Pez Dorado, Calle del Sol 43 (Parque Colón), T5822518. Chinese and international, good quality food in generous portions, very popular for Sun lunch. At the upper end of the price range is *El Café*, Av Texas esq Calle 5, Jardines Metropolitanos. The favourite of businessmen and upper class society. *Los 3 Café*, Calle R, César Tolentino 38, T2765909. Specializes in *comida criolla*. Fresh homemade Italian food at *Ciao Ciao*, Av María R Sánchez, Los Jardines 13, T5831092. Run by an eccentric, entertaining Italian. Another Italian restaurant is *Il Pasticio*, behind the *Supermercado Nacional*. Eclectic place, great for late night drinks, a time when the owner, Paolo, is frequently there for conversation. There are several restaurants around the monument on Av Francia and Calle del Sol, popular on Sun. *La Brasa* has barbecued chicken. *Kukara Macara* has a rustic decor, cowboy style, lots of steak including Angus, prices up to US$20 for a huge, top class piece of meat, also seafood, tacos, sandwiches and burgers, open daily 1100-0300. *Los Tablones* on Calle del Sol has a good view of the monument, open-air dining. Next door, *Puerto Sol* is cheaper and popular with a slightly younger crowd. *Maroma*, opposite *Mr Movies* on Calle Metropolitana. New, for elegant and trendy dining. *Olé* JP Duarte esq Independencia, restaurant and pizzería.

For the most spectacular view across the Cibao Valley, try *Camp David Ranch*, T6260578. Drive (or take a taxi, fare about US$10) to Km 7 on Carretera Luperón, the turn-off is on the right, unsigned, before the *El Económico* supermarket; a 10-min climb up a winding, paved road to the ranch. The food quality is erratic, but the view is breathtaking. Next door is *El Generalísimo*, a piano bar decorated with classic cars from the Trujillo era. Some 10 bedrooms and suites reasonably priced in our **E** range. At the foot of the hill leading up to *Camp David Ranch* is *Rancho Luna Steak House*, Carretera Luperón Km 7.5, T5813136, F5813145, definitely not recommended for vegetarians. There is also *Cigar Ranch* on the way to *Rancho Luna* out of Santiago, a nice dining experience.

Santiago is the home of *perico ripiao* (see Music and dance), a folk style of merengue, which can be heard in bars and clubs alongside more modern merengue, salsa, bachata and US disco music. Things start late and go on until dawn. The monument is always a great place to hang out. *Metropolis Billards*, Estrella Sadhalá, in front of the PUCMM University in Plaza Alejo, has a cool bar and pool tables. *Dalí*, Av Juan Pablo Duarte, is also a good spot. **Discos** *La Nuit*, in *Hotel Matum*; *El Alcázar*, in basement of *El Gran Almirante* hotel; *Ambis I* and *Ambis II*, Autopista Duarte Km 2, side by side; *Antifas*, Don Pedro 50, gay club, live shows; *La Antorcha*, 27 Febrero 58; and *Las Vegas*, Autopista Navarrete Km 9. All modern. *Champion Palace* is a huge disco for 2,000 people, open daily. **Casino** The *Matum* and *Gran Almirante* hotels both have casinos open until 0400. **Theatre** *The Gran Teatro del Cibao*, T5831150, seats 15,000 in its main auditorium, sometimes shows opera, while merengue concerts and plays are put on in the smaller concert hall.

Santiago's **carnival** is a pagan celebration surrounding Independence and Easter. Working class *barrios*, particularly La Joya and Los Pepines, have developed rival themes of Los Lechones and Los Pepines and there is much competition between them. The *lechones* have papier maché masks of stylized pigs, while the *pepines* have pointed horns on their masks, often hugely decorated. Parades start the weekend before *Independence Day*, 27 Feb, moving off from Las Carreras and ending up at the Monumento a los Héroes de la Restauración.

Mercado Modelo Turístico. Calle del Sol and Av España. Cheap amber at Calle del Sol 60. Outside town, on Autopista Duarte, are many potteries where ceramics are cheap.

Air *American Airlines* fly daily from Miami and New York. *North American Airlines* and *Continental* also fly from New York. *American Eagle* flies from San Juan, Puerto Rico and *Dominair*, from Port-au-Prince. See page 297, for domestic flights.

Eating

Entertainment

Festivals

Shopping

Transport

Dominican Republic

Bus Local OMSA buses on main routes, as in Santo Domingo. All *carros públicos* have a letter indicating which route they are on; *carros* cost US$0.25, *guaguas* US$0.25. Many congregate at La Rotunda de las Pinas at the intersection of Estrella Sadalhá and Av 27 de Febrero. **Long distance** *Caribe Tours* (Av 27 de Febrero, Las Colinas, T5760790) bus to Puerto Plata US$2.66 every hr; it is easier to take *Caribe Tours* than *Metro* to Puerto Plata or the capital because *Metro* only takes passengers on standby on their Santo Domingo-Puerto Plata route. *Metro* terminal, Maimón y Duarte, T5829111, a block or so towards the centre on Duarte from the roundabout at Estrella Sadalá (opposite direction from *Codetel*); 6 buses daily Santo Domingo-Santiago. *Terrabus* has its terminal at the junction of Calle del Sol and Av Francia by the monument. Service to Santo Domingo with connections for the ferry to Puerto Rico or the bus to Haiti. Other companies from the capital with good, a/c buses include *Cibao* (from Parque Enriquillo) and *Transporte Espinal* (4 blocks north of Parque Enriquillo). To Samaná, go to Puerto Plata and take *Caribe Tours* from there. *Guaguas* to San José de las Matas leave from the Puente Hermanos Patiño, by the river not far from the centre. *Guaguas* for La Vega, US$1.20, go from the park at the corner of Restauración y Sabana Larga. Many other *guaguas* leave from 30 de Marzo with Salvador Cucurullo, average US$1.30, eg Puerto Plata 2 hrs, not recommended if you have lots of luggage. *Transporte del Cibao*, Restauración almost with the corner of J P Duarte, runs buses up to Dajabón in the northwest near the Haitian border, 2½ hrs.

Directory **Banks** *Scotiabank* on Parque Duarte, others on Calle del Sol between San Luís and Sánchez include *Banco Popular* (ATM), *Baninter*, *Citibank*, *Bancrédito* (ATM), *Banco del Progreso*, and *Banco de Reservas* (ATM). There are also a *Banco de Reservas*, *Bancrédito* and *Banco del Progreso* on Av 27 de Febrero. The only place you can change travellers' cheques is the *Banco Popular* on Calle del Sol esq Mella. **Communications** Post office: on the corner of Calle del Sol and San Luís. **Telephone**: *Codetel* is at San Luís between Restauración and Independencia, and further out at the junction of Estrella Sadhalá and J P Duarte; take Carro A from the Parque. *Tricom* is on San Luís between Restauración and Beller, also on Av 27 de Febrero next to *Bancrédito*.

The north coast

The north coast boasts a stretch of shoreline of immense beauty, with sandy beaches, cliffs, coves and mangroves sandwiched between clear, blue sea and picturesque green mountains. It is home to the historic port of Puerto Plata, fishing villages, all-inclusive resorts and guesthouses. To the west the climate is dry and the vegetation predominantly scrub and cactus, while to the east it is wetter and the vegetation lush, with the ubiquitous coconut palms towering above the beaches and greener than green golf courses.

The north coast

Puerto Plata

Puerto Plata, sandwiched between Mt Isabel de Torres and the sea, is the main gate- Population: 200,000
way on the northern coast, but the town itself is not much visited. The old town centre comprises dilapidated wooden houses and other colonial buildings behind
warehouses and the power station alongside the docks. There is some renovation
and some new building taking place. The seafront drive, the Malecón, sweeps along
the beach for about 5 km, between the San Felipe fortress to the west on the point
protecting the harbour and Long Beach to the east.

Getting there Domestic and international flights to the Gregorio Luperón International **Ins & outs**
Airport, 15 mins by road from town, there are many domestic flights from Santo Domingo
and other airports. Taxis are for hire at the terminal, or you can walk to the main road if you
have not much luggage and hail a *guagua*. *Caribe Tours, Metro* and many other bus companies pass through or terminate at Puerto Plata and transport links are good. **Getting
around** The old city and the fortress can be toured on foot as it is quite compact. For longer
distances you can hop on a *motoconcho* or take a safer taxi. There are buses if you've got
plenty of time and know where you are going. **Tourist office** At the far east end of the
Malecón in the little park in the same building as the Tourist Police, T5865000, F5863806.

Puerto Plata, was founded by Nicolás de Ovando in 1502, although Columbus had **History**
sailed past the bay and named it the silver port because of the way the sun glistened
on the sea. For many years it was used as a supply stop for the silver fleets on their
way from Mexico to Spain, but it was prone to pirate attacks and it was eventually
supplanted by Havana. Buccaneers then roamed the hills hunting wild cattle and
pigs and selling the hides and meat. After the War of Restoration in the 1860s,
tobacco became the supreme commodity. The profitable trade attracted merchants,
many of them from Germany, and they built luxury mansions, some of which still
stand. Tobacco waned at the beginning of the 20th century, but by 1910 Puerto Plata
was experiencing a boom in sugar prices and more building. Boom turned to bust
with the Great Depression in the USA in the 1930s. In the 1960s investment in tourism and the construction of the Playa Dorada all-inclusive complex, provided thousands of jobs and is the mainstay of the region's economy.

The old city is contained within Av Colón, the Malecón and Calle José Ramón **Sights**
Torres. The hub of the old town is the **Parque Central**. In the centre is an early 20th-
century gazebo, or bandstand, and on the south side, the **San Felipe cathedral** is
worth a visit. Also on the Parque Central is the **Patrimonio Cultural** in a majestic
building dating from 1908 where there are interesting art exhibitions. The **Museo
del Ambar**, Amber Museum, Duarte 61 esquina Emilio Prud'home, houses a collection of rare amber in a renovated house built by a German tobacco merchant in
1918. The main museum is on the second floor containing amber from the Cordillera Septentrional, the mountains behind Puerto Plata, which contain the world's
richest deposits of amber. ■ *Mon-Sat 0900-1700. US$2. T5862848. Amber Museum
Shop also at Playa Dorada Plaza, T3202215.*
    A visit to the colonial fortress, **Fortaleza de San Felipe**, the oldest in the New
World, on a promontory at the west end of the Malecón is recommended. Once the
era of pirates and privateers was ended the fortress was long used as a prison. Juan
Pablo Duarte was locked up here in 1844. The museum contains rusty armoury and
photos of the excavation and renovation of the fortress, which was built in 1540. The
museum is not especially interesting but if you climb the turrets you get a wonderful
view of the coast and ships coming into the harbour. Outside there is a statue and
monument to General Gregorio Luperón on a prancing horse. ■ *US$0.60. Guided
tours available but not really necessary.* Nearby is the restored iron **lighthouse**, first
lit on 9 September 1879, now surrounded by bits of fortress walls and cannon.

Dominican Republic

Sleeping

Cheap hotels can only be found in the town centre

D *Sofy's Bed & Breakfast*, Calle Las Rosas, T/F5866411, gillin.n@codetel.net.do Run by Canadian Noelle Gillin (and Sofy the dog), look for sign of La Batera between the baseball stadium and the police station on Av Luis Ginebra, go down that street and the house is the third to last on the left, 3 rooms, great American breakfast on the terrace, popular with ex-pats, airport transfers are included if you stay a week. **D-F** *Sunshine Hotel*, Manolo Tavárez Justo 78, T5861771, on main road. Good for public transport, 19 rooms, a/c or fan, TV, balcony, hot water, some rooms better than others, bathrooms adequate, lumpy pillows, sheets don't fit, parking, restaurant, open 0700-2400. **E** *Hotel/Restaurant El Indio*, Plaza Anacaona, 30 de Marzo 94-98, T/F5861201. CP, fan, clean, restaurant serves good breakfast and fish, very good value, Mexican music on Sat, a patio with native plants, palm trees and hummingbirds. **E** *Portofino*, Hermanas Mirabal 12, T5862858. Long Beach residential area, small pool, 18 rooms, a/c, cable TV, hot water, own generator, children's play area, parking, pizza restaurant. **E-F** *Castillo*, José del Carmen Ariza 34, near Parque Central, look for the red awning of *Sam's Bar & Grill*, T5867267, sams.bar@codetel.net.do One-bedroom furnished apartment or rooms with private or shared bathroom, weekly and monthly rates available, own generator, hot water, TV, internet access, the first hotel in town, dating from 1890s. **E** *Aparta-Hotel Lomar*, Malecón 8, T3208555. 18 large rooms, warm water, cable TV, a/c or fan, some rooms with balcony overlooking sea, good value. **F** *Victoriano*, San Felipe 33 esq Restauración, T5869752. Central, a/c, cable TV, fan or a/c, 1 or 2 beds, clean, friendly, own generator, hot water.

Eating

Acuarela, Prof Certad 3 esq Pres Vásquez, T5865314. Open 1800-0200, garden café, in old wooden house, excellent restaurant. *Aguaceros*, Malecón edif 32, near fire station, T5862796. Open from 1700, steaks, seafood, burgers, Mexican, tables on sidewalk, bar. *Café Cito*, on the highway towards Playa Dorada, open Mon-Sat 1030-2400, away from the hustle and bustle, jazz music, very good food, popular with the ex-pat crowd. *Comacho*, Circunvalación Norte (Malecón), T6856348. Good Dominican restaurant. *Jardín Suizo* , Malecón 32, T5869564. Run by Swiss James and his Dominican wife, excellent food. *Jungle Bar*, Plaza Turisol 12, T2613544. English run with English menu, come here for chip butties, curry or fried breakfast, open 1000-2200 for food, later for the bar, happy hour 1700-1900, popular with ex-pats, particularly on quiz nights. *Sam's Bar and Grill* on José del Carmen Ariza 34, near Plaza Central, T5867267, sams.bar@codetel.net.do American-run, good American food, satellite TV, meeting place, notice board, internet, rooms also available, see *Hotel Castillo*, above.

Nightlife

On Sun nights there is open-air dancing on the Malecón, with huge sound systems on the road and street vendors selling drinks. Most of the nightlife is in Playa Dorada, see below.

Shopping

The Mercado Viejo is at Ureña and Separación and sells mostly hardware and furniture, although there is also a *botánica*, items relating to syncretist religion, witchcraft, voodoo and folk healing. The Mercado Nuevo, at Isabela de Torres and Villanueva, sells handicrafts, rum, Cuban cigars, Haitian art and other souvenirs.

Transport

For domestic flights, see Essentials, Getting around

Air From North America: *American Airlines* from Miami and New York. *Continental* also from New York. **From Europe:** *Martinair* from Amsterdam; *Condor* and/or *LTU* from Berlin, Düsseldorf, Frankfurt, Leipzig and Munich. **From the Caribbean:** *TCI Sky King* from Providenciales; *American Eagle* from San Juan. Some flights are seasonal.

Airport Gregorio Luperón International Airport, T5860219/5860106, serves the entire north coast. It is 15-20 mins from Puerto Plata, 7 mins from Sosúa and 20 from Cabarete. Taxi from airport to Puerto Plata or Cabarete US$20, to Sosúa US$10. Small bank for exchange (closed weekends), car hire agencies and a few shops. Proper tipping for baggage handlers (in overalls) is about US$2 per bag and they will expect you to pay something even just for picking up a bag.

Local *Motoconchos*, US$0.60 almost anywhere in town, negotiate a fare for longer distances. *Guaguas*, leave Parque Central, more frequently, from the hospital on Circunvalación Sur to destinations along the north coast. Taxis charge US$5 from Puerto Plata to Puerto Dorado. They can be found around the Parque Central, at Long Beach near the *Ahmsa Puerto*

Plata Beach Resort, or on Circunvalación Sur near *Caribe Tours*. **Long distance Bus** *Metrobus* (T5866062, Beller y 16 de Agosto), and *Caribe Tours* (T5864544, at Caribe Centro Plaza, Camino Real, just off the Circunvalación Sur) run a/c coaches to/from Santo Domingo, 4 hrs, US$6. To Santiago, every hr on the hr, 1000-1800, US$3. *Caribe Tours* also run buses to Samaná (US$6) via Sosúa (US$1.60) and Cabarete, 0700, 1600 daily, 3½ hrs. To La Vega US$4. Alternatively you can use the *guagua* system, changing at each town, but this will take much longer, be more uncomfortable and more costly. **Car hire** Best arranged at the airport, more choice than in town. *Avis*, airport, T5860496. *Honda*, Carrera Luperón 2½ km, T5863136, at the airport, T5860233. *Puerto Plata Rent a Car*, Beller 7, Puerto Plata, T5863141. *Nelly Rent a Car*, Puerto Dorada, T3204888, at the airport, T5860505.

Banks *Banco Popular* (24-hr ATM) on José del Carmen Ariza esq Duarte, opposite the cathedral, **Directory** *Banco Mercantil* (T5868977) and *Banco del Progreso* (T3200504) are on the other side of the square on Separación, either side of Beller. *Banco BHD* J F Kennedy, T3207919; *Banco de Cambio Vimenca*, Av L Ginebra, T5864022; *Banco de Reservas*, J F Kennedy 16, T5862518, and at Playa Dorada, T3204830; *Banco Intercontinental*, Pte Castellanos, T5862350; *Banco Metropolitano*, José del Carmen Ariza, T3200714. **Communications** Internet: *Comp.Net*, Calle 12 de Julio 77, T5864104, US$3 per hr. *Hotel Castillo/Sam's Bar & Grill*, US$3 per hr, credit given for time not used. **Post office** On 12 de Julio 42 esq Separación, T5862377. **Telephone:** *Codetel* is on Beller 48 esq Padre Castellanos, T5863803, and 27 de Febrero, T5863311, for domestic and international calls. *Tricom* long distance call centre is at 27 de Febrero 75, T4715005. Cheaper is *All American Cable & Radio* (AACR), on J F Kennedy 40, T5862660. **Medical services** *Hospital Ricardo Limardo*, J E Kunhardt, T5862210/5862237. There are several doctors with clinics. **Useful addresses** Immigration: Dirección General de Migración, 12 de Julio 33, T5862364.

Excursions from Puerto Plata

Just 1 km past Puerto Plata, a *teleférico* (cable car) runs to the summit of Loma Isabel de Torres, an elevation of 779 m. A statue of Christ looks out over all of Puerto Plata, rather like the one in Rio de Janeiro; it also houses craft shops, a restaurant and there are beautifully manicured botanical gardens with a lovely view of the coast and mountains. ■ *Daily except Wed with last trip about 1900 depending on the time of year. US$6 round trip. Entrance is south of the Circunvalación del Sur on a paved road marked* teleférico. Hiking tours up the mountain can be arranged with *Iguana Mama, in Cabarete. Hiking alone is not recommended. It is a moderate to hard hike, being quite steep in parts, and takes about three hours to get up to the top.*

Just 6 km east of Puerto Plata, 4 km from the airport, is the beach resort of **Playa Dorada** with an exceptional golf course, and other sporting facilities. The Playa Dorada Resort is an umbrella name for a complex of 14 large all-inclusive hotels with over 4,000 rooms, offering similar services, eg pool, tennis, golf, best booked as part of a package from abroad. Not all of them are beachfront. There is a central shopping mall, the Playa Dorada Centro Comercial, and lots of nightlife including discos and casinos. The beach is a glorious sweep of golden sand around the promontory on which stand most of the hotels, while the golf course weaves in and out of the hotels not on the beach.

The food is good at all the main hotels; there is every variety of cuisine. In the Playa Dorada **Eating** shopping mall is *Hemingway's Café*, T3202230. Predictable nautical, sport fishing theme. Good food and music, a/c, good service, open from 1100, fun at night and during the day, live bands at weekends, karaoke some nights.

On the main road, 5 mins' walk from the entrance to Playa Dorada, is *Pat's Rum Runners Bar*, **Bars &** on the roadside. Makes a change from the hotel complex, pool table, sports TV, live music and **nightclubs** karaoke at weekends. *Andromeda* in *Heavens Hotel* (the most popular club), *Charlie's* in *Jack Tar Village Casino* and *Crazy Moon* in *Paradise Beach Resort*; all three are popular and offer a mix of merengue, salsa and international pop music. All have cover charges, about US$2.

Dominican Republic

Entertain- There are 3 **casinos**. *Jack Tar Village*, *Occidental Playa Dorada Hotel*, *Ahmsa Paradise*
ment *Beach Club* with slot machines, black jack, craps, roulette and poker. **Cinema** Recently
released US films with Spanish subtitles in Centro Comercial.

Shopping The Playa Dorada complex has the first real shopping mall on the north coast, called the *Playa*
Dorada Plaza or *Centro Comercial*. Prices are slightly inflated, but the quality of all items, especially the locally-made ceramics, jewellery, and clothing, is superior to most sold by beach or
street vendors. The mall includes a *Bennetton*, a selection of Tiffany lamps and some very original jewellery. Cigars, leather goods, amber, larimar, coffee and rum can all be found here.

Sport Golf is the main attraction here at the *Robert Trent Jones Golf Course*, T3204262/3803,
www.playa-dorada-golf.com which is right in the middle of the resort, see Sport, page 305.
If you are staying at one of the resort hotels, green fees with caddy are about US$33, outsid-
ers pay about 10% more. The hotels offer lots of sports for their all-inclusive guests and activities away from Playa Dorada, like horse riding, are easily arranged. Most watersports are also
on offer through the hotels, but for scuba diving go to Sosúa.

Directory **Banks** At the Centro Comercial are *Banco Popular* and *Banco BHD*, both of which have ATMs.
Communications Internet: *Hot.com C@fé* in the Playa Dorada Plaza, T3425500,
hot.com@codetel.net.do Tour agencies in the Centro Comercial offer free internet access if you buy a
tour, otherwise US$2 for 30 mins.

West of Puerto Plata

To the west of Puerto Plata and within easy striking distance of the city, is
Costambar, which has a long stretch of sand with few waves, making it perfect for
children. There are restaurants beside the beach and supermarkets if you want to
cater for yourself. This is the best place to look for self-catering accommodation,
there are lots of villas and condos, some for as little as US$100 a week, excellent value
if you are in a group.

This is a good area   **Cofresí** beach has several hotels, villas and cabins and is busy at weekends. An
to stay in if you   enormous dolphinarium has been built here despite opposition from conservationists
don't want to get   and environmentalists (see also Antigua, Anguilla, British Virgin Islands chapters). A
caught up in the   huge hotel and marina come as part of the investment package, changing the character
all-inclusive style of of the village entirely.
holiday offered at   Further west at **Bahía de Maimón**, 9 km from Puerto Plata, are two all-inclusive
Playa Dorada, but hotels, *Mambo* and *Merengue*.
would rather be on   **Luperón** is a typical Dominican village, with several markets selling fish, meat and
the beach than vegetables, basic restaurants and baseball field. The jetty in the village is in a lagoon
in the city surrounded by mangroves and is a safe harbour for yachts and other boats. 3 km from
the village is **Puerto Blanco Marina**, T2994096, surrounded by more mangroves providing a pretty setting and good protection for yachts. *Motoconchos* charge less than
US$1 from the village, and taxis US$3. The marina is the place to be. The bar is popular, with a happy hour at 1700-1900 and live music some nights. The restaurant is
known for its seafood and the food is cheap. Rooms are available, **E**, with a/c and hot
water. Watersports include snorkelling, fishing and scuba diving. Catamaran tours are
recommended as a great way to see the coast and snorkel in some lovely secluded spots
where the coral is alive and healthy. *Cat's Sailing Adventure* charges US$45 per person
for its daily catamaran trips, T/F2612046, catsail@hotmail.com

Sleeping **Cofresí D** *Plaza Taíno*, 100 m from sand, T9702719, F9707504. Small, family-run hotel,
& eating orthopaedic beds, a/c. There are also comfortable, fully staffed villas, contact *Vacation Villa*
Always ask for *Referral Center* (14 Rolling Rd, Wynnewood, Pennsylvania, USA 19096-3521, T610-8965815,
bottled water and www.puerto-plata.com *Chris & Mady's* is a thatched restaurant and bar overlooking the
be careful with ice ocean, within walking distance of the *Hacienda* complex. Good seafood at reasonable prices
and you can watch sports on TV.

Bahía de Maimón 2 all-inclusive hotels, *Mambo* and *Merengue*, T3204000, www.riuhotels.com Nearly 1,000 rooms between them, on the beach, all the usual facilities on land and in the water, shopping complex and *Pacha* disco.

Luperón A-B *Luperón Beach Resort*, T5718303, www.besthotels.es. Excellent value, no other hotel close by, on lovely beach, comfortable rooms decorated daily with flowers, a/c, TV, fridge, fan, terrace, some connect to make a suite, 3 restaurants, Italian, Brazilian and Mexican, bars, pools and jacuzzis, lots of watersports, tennis, riding (check horses' condition), bicycles, ping pong, billiards, gym and sauna, children's activities. **F** *Hotel Casa del Sol*, T5718403. Rooms clean, with bathroom. **F** *Dally*, 27 de Febrero 46, T5718034, F5718052. On the main road, popular, 8 rooms, renovated in 2002, clean, fan, hot water, good restaurant (see below), disco behind, *The Moon*. There are lots of Dominican restaurants which are best found by just walking around town. *La Yola*, German-owned and well known for its seafood. *Restaurante Dally*, 27 de Febrero 46, T5718034. Specializes in seafood, fresh daily, good value. *Los Almendros*, T5718121. Good sea food. *Casa del Sol*, T5718403. Also with good sea food.

Communications Internet: *Punto Internet Café*, at *Farmacia Vanessa*, Independencia 7 esq Hugo Kunhart, US$2 per hr. **Medical services** There are 2 pharmacies, *Vanessa*, T5718201, see above, and *Alejandra*, Duarte 121, T5718135.

Directory

West of Luperón is La Isabela, now a Parque Nacional Histórico. Here, on his second voyage, on 29 May 1493, Columbus landed with 1,500 men on 17 ships. He founded the first European town in the Americas, with the first *ayuntamiento* and court, and here was said the first mass on 6 January 1494 by Fray Bernardo Boil. Only the layout of the town is visible. The story goes that Trujillo ordered the place cleaned up before an official visit, but his instructions were misunderstood and workers bulldozed the whole site, pushing the ruins into the sea. The restoration and archaeological excavation of La Isabela has uncovered a variey of ruins as well as Taíno and Macorix pottery and the first Hispanic ceramics. The Guayacán tree found growing around La Isabela was there before Columbus landed. The wood is very hard and the Guayacán is used to carve replicas of Taíno artefacts. ■ *Daily 0800-1745. RD$50. Take a tour from Puerto Plata, or a carro público from Villanueva y Kundhard, Puerto Plata, to La Isabela village, US$3.50, then a motoconcho to the ruins, US$7.25 return including wait at ruins, a lovely trip. There is a small museum with labels in Spanish and a brief description in English, a café, toilets and small gift shops selling artesanías. Guides are available.*

La Isabela
Bring lots of insect repellent, 20 mosquitoes counted feasting on one leg!

Monte Cristi

At the far northwestern tip of the Dominican Republic is Monte Cristi, a 19th-century town with a Victorian feel to it, while the sea around it is believed to hold the treasures of 179 sunken galleons. Carretera Duarte runs from Santiago to Monte Cristi, passing first through rice paddies and tobacco plantations in the valley, but about 50 km from the town the area becomes arid, with cactus and other desert plants, home to a multitude of goats. A large land and marine park stretches either side of the town along the coast, protecting the mouth of the Río Yaque del Norte, with mangroves, a lagoon and lots of channels. Its proximity to the Haitian border means that transport links are good. There are several lovely old wooden houses in sore need of renovation. Just beyond the *Banco de Reservas*, on Calle Duarte, which was the first theatre, is a large old house formerly the home of one of Trujillo's mistresses. Another, called Doña Emilia's house, is huge, with lovely fretwork and verandas. Both are due to be renovated. The town has an interesting, big old clock on the **Parque Central**, or Parque Reloj, made in France, but brought here on the train *Lavonia* on 11 March 1895. You can visit the house of **Máximo Gómez**, the Dominican patriot who played an important role in the struggle for Cuban independence and in the Dominican Restoration. Inside are pictures and mementoes of Máximo Gómez, a library with a detailed atlas of Cuba and a lot of

Population: 22,000

Dominican Republic

books relating to Cuba, but very few about the Dominican Republic. ■ *0900-1200, 1500-1900. Av Mella, opposite Helados Bon*. Between the town and Playa Juan de Bolaños there is a monument to José Martí (a rather lugubrious head of Martí on a stick), the Cuban poet and independence fighter who came here in September 1892 before sailing with Máximo Gómez to liberate Cuba. The beach is nothing special and backs on to salt pans, but the coast is dominated by a large flat-topped mountain known as El Morro. Steps have been built up the hillside, making an extremely testing climb to a windy viewpoint.

Sleeping **E** *Chic Hotel Restaurant*, Benito Monción 44, T5792316. 50 rooms sleep 1-4, nice hotel, only Spanish spoken, TV, hot water, phone, shag carpet or tiled, decor different in each room, good food but slow service, avoid dodgy ice in water. **E-F** *Don Gaspar*, Pte Jiménez 21 esq Rodríguez Camargo, T5792477, F5792206. Price depends on a/c, cable TV (with porn channel), hot water, Tony the receptionist is funny and informative, with exceptional English. **B** *Cayo Arena*, Playa Juan de Bolaños, T5793145, F5792096. 2-bedroomed apartments on the beach, sleep 4, basic bathroom and kitchen, small pool, bar, security, parking. **D** *Los Jardines*, next to *Cayo Arena*, T5792091, hotel.jardines@codetel.net.do Run by Hervé and Dorca, 2 bungalows each with 2 basic rooms, fan or a/c, no food or cooking facilities, good bathrooms, quiet, parking, beach chairs, boat excursions to the mangroves and **Cayos Siete Hermanos**, English and French spoken, jeep and bicycle hire, owner will collect you from *Caribe Tours* if you call, or a *motoconcho* costs US$0.30.

Eating *Don Gaspar Restaurant & Hotel*, Pte Jiménez 21 esq Rodríguez Camargo, T5792477,
Chivo picante F5792206. Also a disco with a variety of music and requests, good breakfast menu, eggs,
(spicy goat) *mangú*, juice and coffee for less than US$4, Dominican and Spanish dishes. *El Bistro*, San
is sold at Fernando 26, T5792091. Same ownership as *Hotel Los Jardines*, set in lovely courtyard on a
roadside stands corner with big wooden doors, white furniture and rocking chairs, seating in open-air or under cover, seafood, lobster, goat, as well as sandwiches, salads and pasta, 3 blocks from the clock, open Mon-Fri 1100-1430, 1800-2400, Sat-Sun 1000-2400. *Comedor Adela*, Juan de la Cruz Alvarez 41, T5792254. Family atmosphere, lots of choice, good food, parking available, open for lunch and dinner. *Cocomar,* by the monument to José Martí, T5793354. Good breakfast, if a little greasy, also lunch and dinner, meals range from US$3-50 per person, with the top price for the *Paella Marinera* or seafood platter, they will make what you want if they have the ingredients.*Helados Bon*, Av Mella, opposite the house of Máximo Gómez.

Festivals Monte Cristi is famous for its *pre-Lenten fiesta* in **Feb**. On Sun the *toros* and the *civiles* compete against each other in the streets. The *toros* are people dressed in costumes with elaborate bull masks, wielding whips with a ball.

Watersports Scuba diving is excellent in the area, with over 9 shipwrecks to explore, but there is no organized dive operation. **Fishing** is popular. Contact the *Club Náutico*, T5972530. Offshore there are barracuda, tuna, marlin, dorado and carite. If you are **sailing** in the lagoon or channels, be aware that when the tides change the water can rise or fall by about 1½ m. There is one channel in the lagoon, which apparently has some 50 different entrances but only 1 exit.

Transport **Local** Taxis and *motoconchos* collect at the corner of Mella and Duarte. **Long distance** *Caribe Tours* is on Rodríguez Camargo esq Mella, services to Dajabón (34 km, border town opposite Ounaminthe in Haiti, 5 buses daily from Santo Domingo via Monte Cristi) and Santiago.

Directory **Banks** *Banco de Reservas* is on Duarte 38, T5792392. **Casa de Cambio Frías** is on Duarte 40, T5792388. **Communications** Telephone: *Codetel* at Duarte 56, T5793021. **Medical services** *Hospital Padre Fantino* is on J Cabrera, T5792401. Pharmacies: *Sol*, Mella 1a, T5792404, *San Juan Bosco*, Benito Monción 49, T5792327, *Clara Nidia ,* Duarte, T5791180, and *Pueblo*, Duarte 41, T5792394.

East of Puerto Plata

The coast east of Puerto Plata has some of the most beautiful beaches in the world, with a green backdrop of mountains descending to a narrow coastal plain, with palm trees, pale sand stretching for miles and sea of all shades of blue. Sosúa, Cabarete and Río San Juan are the main beach destinations, Cabarete being one of the best windsurfing locations in the Caribbean. From all these places you can get quickly up into the mountains for hiking, cycling, horse riding or whatever you fancy away from the beach.

Sosúa

Sosúa is a little town with a beautiful and lively 1-km beach. Vendors' stalls and snackbars line the path along the back of the beach and you will be offered anything from sunbeds to toilets. There is a smaller public beach on the east side of town, referred to as the 'playita', or Little Beach, where you will be less bothered by vendors. The main street (correctly named Calle Pedro Clisante, but only ever referred to as Main Street, or Calle Principal in Spanish) is lined with a variety of shops, restaurants and bars. Little or no attention is paid to street names or numbers. The **El Batey** side of town (the side that houses most of the hotels and restaurants) was founded by German-Jewish refugees who settled here in 1941. A synagogue and memorial building are open to the public. The western end of the town is referred to as **Los Charamicos** (the two ends are separated by the beach); this is the older side of town, where the Dominicans themselves generally live, shop and party. The **Tourist Office**, T5792254, F5792100, is at Pedro Clisante 12, T5713433.

28 km east of Puerto Plata

AL-B *Sosúa-by-the-Sea*, T5713222, www.sosuabythesea.com CP, owned and operated by Austrian-Canadians, 91 rooms and suites sleep 2-4, on cliff above Little Beach, immaculate, a/c rather inefficient in the rooms/studios, water pressure can be a problem, kitchenette, good restaurant, pool, beach loungers and towels, bar, good food and service, although you may get bored with the limited choice. **A** *Pier Giorgio Palace Hotel*, La Puntilla 1, T5712626, www.piergiorgiohotel.com. On cliff-top, owned by Italian designer who fell in love with the property and built a hotel to fit with Victorian-style building, now a restaurant. 28 rooms, all have balconies with sea view, 24-hr electricity, excursions, white stretch limo for airport transfers, boat or bus shuttle to beach 1000-1600, good snorkelling under the cliffs with steps down to the water, 2 pools and jacuzzi, all very smart, comfortable and great position. **C** *On the Waterfront*, Dr Rosen 1, El Batey, T5712670. 27 cabins, clean but rather thin walls, extra charges for drinking water, fridge, on a cliff overlooking the sea, 5 mins to beach. **C-D** *Condos Dominicano*, T5712787, F5713430, www.condo4u.net Studios, 1- and 2- bedroom apartments, 20 units, daily, weekly or monthly rates, full kitchen, TV, garden, pool, generator, security guard, close to beach and shops. **C-D** *JJ's Auberge*, Dr Rosen, El Batey, T5712569, F5712865, auberge.jj@codetel.net.do 8 rooms around a pool, a few blocks from the beach, secluded, in trees, clean, a/c, friendly, informative service. **C-D** *Tropix*, T/F5712291 www.tropixhotel.com 200 m uphill from Texaco station. US-owned, but one is a descendant of the original Jewish settlers, clean, 10 rooms, including 4 suites sleeping 5, a/c or fan, minibar, some traffic noise, beautiful pool and landscaped garden, impeccable service, good food, use of kitchen facilities, horses for guests' use. **E-F** *Yaroa*, Dr Rosen, T5712651, F5713814, info@hotelyaroa.com Central, good value, discounts for long stays, 24 rooms, CP, a/c, fan, balcony, 2 beds, phone, safety boxes for rent, pool, bar/restaurant, Dutch management. **E** *Coco Hotel*, Alejo Martínez, T/F5712184, cocohotel@codetel.net.do Only 12 rooms, simple but nice, several languages spoken, breakfast US$3, 3-course dinner US$10, bar at the pool but not noisy. **F** *Koch's Guest House*, El Batey, down a dirt side street, ocean front, no beach. Use of kitchen, breakfast extra. There are many other hotels, guesthouses and villas for rent, ask around locally.

Sleeping
There are several all-inclusives not listed here including the new luxury Sosúa Bay Hotel at the El Batey end of the beach

Dominican Republic

Eating

There are fewer restaurants than there used to be, probably due to the increase in all-inclusive hotels

La Puntilla de Pier Giorgio, Calle La Puntilla 1, T5712215. Right on cliff edge, part of hotel, see above, gourmet Italian restaurant, very pretty, lovely views, possibly the nicest place in town for a romantic meal, somewhere special. *On the Waterfront*, Calle Dr Rosen 1, El Batey, T5713024. Fish, seafood, snacks, happy hour 1600-1800, excellent food and a spectacular sunset overlooking the sea, all-you-can-eat barbecue on Fri night. Ask for one of the speciality coffees, the waiter puts on an excellent fire show with the rum and they taste amazing. Pleasant entertainment nightly, on the lookout point. For an equally good view over the water go the other side of the bay to Los Charamicos to *Atlántico*, T5712878, on the cliff road from the beach. Open 1200-1500, 1900-2300, closed Thu, seafood and steak interesting menu, main dishes US$8-15, seafood platter for 2 US$17.50, lobster US$15 per lb. There are several restaurants on Main St serving international, French, Italian food, walk around and see what takes your fancy, they change frequently. Also several eating places along the beach, some with lobster tanks, OK for lunch. For Dominican food go to Los Charamicos where there are *comedores*. *Central*, is a nice fish restaurant on the main street here, very cheap, carry on to one of the *colmados* afterwards for cheap rum and beer with bachata and merengue, best Fri, Sat evening. *Dundee's Burgers*, Calle Alejo Martínez, in-front-of-school yard, open 1900-0700, the place to go after a night of revelling, Dundee, the American-Dominican owner, is a local fixture. *Hotel Sosúa-by-the-Sea* serves the best value buffet breakfast in town. For delicious baked products go to the *German Bakery (Panadería Alemán)*, in Villas Ana María, residential area.

Bars & nightclubs

Lots going on in Main Street

Merengue Club, huge open-air club, open until 0300, no charge; next to it the *Hotel Central* has a pub, *Toff Toff*; *Tucan* disco is on the other side of the street. *La Roca*, last spot on Main St before the beach, Sosúa's oldest bar/disco/eatery, now a sports bar, big screen. *Copacabana* also has girls working. Elsewhere, *High Caribbean*, T5712129, disco by the casino at the east end of town, has a terrace and small indoor and outdoor swimming pool. *Copacabana* and *High* are international-style discos with a/c, modern disco lighting and sound systems, fairly smart, 80% tourists, the rest usually locals dancing with tourists and showing off their skills. *Eddie's Sports Bar* has 4 satellite dishes, can get anything, near *Super Super Supermarket*.

Watersports

Diving There are lots of dive operations, in town and on the beach, offering tuition and boat dives. There is no jetty and no large dive boats, so you must be prepared to wade out to a small boat, with probably no shade, and be capable of getting back into the boat without a ladder after your dive, which can be tricky if it is rough. A recommended and long-established dive shop is *Northern Coast Aquasports/Diving*, Pedro Clisante 8, T5711028, www.northerncoastdiving.com Lots of courses, multilingual staff, several boats normally taking 4-6 divers, good with novice or experienced divers, probably the most professional operation on this stretch of coast. **Swimming** *Columbus Aqua Park*, 3 mins from the airport, Km 18, T5712642. Open 1000-1800, US$10 adults, US$3 children, with water toboggans, 3 large pools, a lazy river, children's water play area, diving tower, restaurants, gift shops, bars, discos, etc.

Transport

Local In Sosúa, transport congregates by the *Texaco* station and the junction of Calle Dr Rosen and the Carretera. *Motoconcho* (motorcycle taxi), RD$5 (RD$10 at night) to anywhere in town. A taxi to/from Puerto Plata costs US$17, a *guagua* US$0.60 and a *carro público* US$7 if you take the whole car. Car and bike rentals are everywhere, shop around for prices. *Asociación de Renta Moto* Sosúa Cabarete, US$28-35 for 1-2 days, US$5-7.25 hourly, depending on type. *Pilar*, Pedro Clisante 1, T5713281. Friendly, Carretera Sosúa-Sabaneta, T5713575. **Bus** *Caribe Tours* from Santo Domingo, US$5.30. In Sosúa, T5713808.

Directory

Banks *Banco Popular* (ATM outside) on the small square at Calle Dr Martínez and Duarte. *Bancrédito* (ATM outside) T5711204 is further along on Duarte. *Banco de Reservas*, Urb Tavárez, T5713836, F5713181. *Banco del Progreso*, Pedro Clisante 12B, T5712815. *Vimenca*, Duarte 2, T5713800. **Communications** Internet: On Duarte is an internet café, @, also *Tricom*, on the corner near *Bancrédito*. Post office: E Kunhardt 8, T5712222. Telephone: *Codetel*, Calle Dr Alejo Martínez, near corner with Dr Rosen, T2203697, F5712456 (also in Charamicos, T5712601, F5712900). **Medical services** The main hospital for the area is in Puerto Plata, but there are several clinics and pharmacies in Sosúa.

Dominican Republic

Cabarete

Cabarete, famous for world-class windsurfing, is 14 km east of Sosúa. Although it has grown considerably since French-Canadian windsurfers first staked their claim on this small fishing village it still maintains its small town character. There is a wide range of places to stay, eat and dance the night away. Cabarete offers a variety of adventure sports: mountain biking, horse riding, whitewater rafting and scuba diving are within easy reach. International **windsurf** competitions are held annually in June, www.CabareteRaceWeek.com Wind conditions vary according to season: in summer (mid-June to mid-September) there are constant trade winds but few waves, in winter there is less wind, but the waves can be tremendous. Winds are light in the mornings, but get strong in the afternoon, when hundreds of sails flit about on the water like butterflies.

It is the windsurf capital of the world, having hosted many World Cup events

  Kitesurfing has taken Cabarete by storm. It takes place about 1 km downwind of the windsurfers on the aptly named **Kite Beach**, where there is flat water for the first 500 m and then a reef with waves. On the outskirts of town is El Encuentro, a surfing beach, with a consistent 'break' off the right and left. **Waterskiing** and **wakeboarding** (like waterskiing but with a surfboard) take place on the **Río Yásica**. Contact *The Tropical Wakeboard Centre*, T7070048, tropicwake@hotmail.com they offer coaching for beginners or advanced. **Scuba diving** is popular and there are many dive schools in the area. *Northern Coast Diving* in Sosúa covers the Cabarete area (see above); also *Dolphin Dive*, T5710842 and *Caribbean Divers*, T5710218.

Cabarete now hosts the Kitesurfing World Cup each June, www.kiteboarding.com

  The local **Tourist Office** can be contacted on T5710950. An alternative and better place for information is *Iguana Mama* (see Tour operators below).

Windsurfing Boards rent for US$50 per day, US$200 per week, with variations, make sure insurance is available. Highly recommended is the *Carib Bic Center*, T5710640, www.caribwind com It has excellent windsurfing gear for rent, with professional and experienced instructors, the nicest surf shop in town and a restaurant. They have a full watersports centre with sea kayaks, boogie boards, surfboards, hobiecats, laser sailboats and snorkelling gear for rent. Other windsurfing schools include *Vela/Spin Out*, T5710805; *Club Nathalie Simon* (French speaking), T5710848; *Happy* (German and English speaking), T5710784 and *Club Mistral*, T5710770.

Watersports

  The *Carib Bic Centre* (see above) offers lessons and equipment rental through *Cabarete Kitesurfing School*, www.cabaretekite.com, on Kite Beach. Another school is *Kite-Excite*, T5719509. Private lessons are US$300 for 3 days, less for more people. After that you can rent equipment, US$45-60 a day, weekly rates available for kites and boards. *Surf & Sport* surfing school, run by long-time local surfer, Markus Bohm, offers daily lessons, US$25, for all ages and levels, T5710463. Other surf schools include *No Work Team*, T5710820, and *Del Mar*, T3602576, www.delmarcabarete.com, at El Encuentro Beach. Surf boards rent for about US$15 per half day.

There are 2 high seasons: Dec-Apr as usual and then mid-Jun to mid-Sep when the winds are strong and attract the windsurfing and kitesurfing crowd. **L-A** *Nänny's Estate*, T5710744, nanny.state@codetel.net.do A bit out of town and therefore quieter, a condo-hotel, 2-bedroom apartments built on 2 floors like town houses, with sun deck on the roof, on the beach, pool, tennis. **L-B** *Palm Beach Condos*, T5710758, CPBCondos@codetel.net.do Spacious, deluxe condos, 2 bedroom, 2 bathroom, fully equipped kitchens, patios with ocean views, pool, on the beach, perfect for families and windsurfers, nannies and cooks available, central but quiet. **L-B** *Velero Beach Resort*, Calle La Punta 1, T5719727, www.velerobeach.com Luxurious new 4-star hotel right at the east end of the beach, rooms and suites can be combined to make apartments with kitchens sleeping up to 6, neat lawns and small pool giving view of whole bay, beach bar but no restaurant, eating places in walking distance, excellent value out of season. **L-B** *Villa Taína*, T5710722, www.villataina.com On the beach in town centre, windsurf centre alongside, a/c, balcony or terrace, some rooms larger than others, comfortable, phone, CP, restaurant. **L-B** *El Magnífico*, T/F5710868, hotel.magnifico@codetel.net.do 10 luxury apartments, ocean view, a/c, classic Caribbean design and amazing art deco. **L-C** *Windsurf Aparthotel*, T5710718, www.windsurfcabarete.com Studio and 2-bedroom condos, satellite TV, phone,

Sleeping

Low-rise hotels, condos and guesthouses line the 2-km bay. Contact Home Key Management, www.cabarete villas.com for rental properties

a/c, restaurant, all watersports, central, very good, across the street from Carib Bic centre. **A-C** *Cita del Sol*, T5710720, cita.delsol@codetel.net.do French-Canadian, restaurant, across the road from the beach, computers for internet access, pool.

B-C *Albatros*, T5710841, h.albatros@codetel.net.do 11 condos which can be divided, big airy apartments, coconut palms, tropical garden, 150 m from beach and centre of Cabarete. **B-C** *Caracol Aparthotel*, T5710788, F5710665, only steps from the beach, 5 mins from Cabarete centre. Terrace overlooking ocean, 2 pools, fully equipped kitchenettes. **B-C** *La Punta*, T5710897, lapunta@codetel.net.do 12 apartments on the beach, quiet, wonderful restaurant, *Otra Cosa*. **B-D** *Caribe Surf Hotel*, T/F5710788. New, modern, clean, reasonably priced, 22 rooms, comfortable, clean, not fancy but quiet, small pool, restaurant. **B-E** *Wilson Beach House*, T5710616, gaby_reiners@yahoo.com Big house with terrace, the nicest view of the bay, on the beach, rooms and apartments with kitchen. **B-F** *Casa Blanca*, T/F5710934. On main road, seaview, 9 rooms, some singles, 7 apartments with kitchenette, clean, friendly, German owned and managed. **C-D** *Kaoba*, T5710837, h.kaoba@codetel.net.do Fan, hot water, reductions for over 2 weeks, rooms, apartments, good value, separate restaurant for breakfast and evening meal, across the road from the beach, pool. **C-D** *Ali's Apartments & Cabarete Surf Camp*, T5710733, www.cabaretekitesurfhotel.com Studios and apartments with kitchen, pool. **D-F** *Residencia Dominicana*, T/F5710890, resdom@hispaniola.com Excellent value, studios, some with kitchenettes, apartments, pool, tennis, movie screen, 3 films a week, TV/VCR rental, breakfast buffet US$3.25, evening restaurant, special price for long stays. **E-F** *Banana Boat*, T5710690. Finnish/Canadian owned, quiet, central, kitchen facilities, laundry. **F** *Laguna Blu*, behind the shops, across the road from the beach. Good budget option, a place to sleep with no frills, fan, hot water, quiet except for the chickens and canaries, 26 rooms, 1 or 2 beds.

Eating
Wide range of places to eat and drink, lots of beach restaurants and bars, varied cuisine. Restaurants change hands frequently

Blue Moon, T2230614, 20 mins outside town in a village called Los Brazos. Excellent Indian food served on banana leaves, reservations required, make up a group for best results. *La Casita*, middle of town, beachfront, near *Onno's*. Excellent seafood, large portions, open 1200-2400. *La Casa del Pescador*, T5710760. Excellent seafood. *Las Brisas*, beachfront, east side, beside *Iguana Mama*, T5710614. Buffet-style dinners, affordable food, open 0700-0400. *Lax*, west side, on the beach, near *La Casa del Pescador*. Good pizza and sushi, huge calamari salad for US$8.50, relaxed atmosphere, open 1100-0100. Next door to *Lax* is *Cabarete Blu*, T5719714. Elegant and refined dining. *Miros*, T5710888. Excellent dinners on the more expensive side. *José Oshay's Irish Beach Pub*, beachfront, go through the *José Oshay's Shopping Village*, near *Miros*, T5710775. Serves one dish every night, open 0800-0100. *Tropicoco*, 5 mins west of Cabarete towards Sosúa, T5710647. Fantastic Sat night buffet, fabulous Thai food Thu, open 1700-2400. *Otra Cosa*, T5710897, at *La Punta*, around the eastern point, beach side. French-Caribbean food, dinner only. Next to *Otra Cosa* is *Toma La Luna*, T7765176, a Sicilian gourmet restaurant. *Vento*, T5710977, on the beach next to *La Casita*. Italian food, dinner only, open until around 2400. *Ho La La*, town centre, T5710806. French, international food, good seafood, good pizza, open 0700-2300. *La Dolce Vita*, in *Windsurf Resort*, on the street, east end of town, T5710718. Italian food, buffet Tue and Fri nights, Dominican buffet Thu night. *The Castle Club*, T2230601, castleclub@hotmail.com 20 mins from Cabarete in the mountains. Unique gourmet dining experience, private dinner parties for 4-10 guests, reservations need to be made at least 2 days in advance. *Onno's*, T3831448. In the centre of town on the beach, access by *Harrison's* jewellers, relaxed ambience, open approximately 1100-0600. Next to *Onno's*, *Barrio Latino*, offers daily specials with a tropical environment during the evening (owned by *Onno's* and *Vento*). *Pitú*, on the beach, next to *Carib Bic Centre*. Friendly atmosphere, daily specials, open 0900-0100. **Cheap** Dominican food is available at *Sandros*, on the street on the west side of town, rough and ready but nice people, good fun and good food, open 0830-1700. *Willy's Seafood Restaurant*, next to *Planet Photo* in front of Tricom, T13745889, serves inexpensive local fish daily. If you go just out of town on the same road that goes to the caves (turn at the National Park El Chocó sign and follow the dirt road), in a small village (Callejón) there are 6 or 7 excellent, cheap, Dominican restaurants, *Mercedes* and *Loly* being the best. *Panadería Dick's* bakery, west end of town, near *La Casa Rosada* grocery store, T5710612, serves you the best coffee in town and fabulous breakfasts, open 0630-1800.

Many of the beach restaurants double as bars in the evening: *Pitú, Onno's, Las Brisas, José Oshay's Irish Beach Pub, Lax*. Live bands play certain nights of the week. *Tiki Bar* on the street side, opposite the Kodak photo shop, is the only place you will find a live DJ and house music, open around 1200-0400. Ask any local and they will point you in the direction of the party that night.

Bars & nightclubs

Cabarete hosts an international sandcastle competition every **Feb**, when visitors construct fantastic mermaids, flowers, fruit and even the *Titanic*. *Cabarete Race Week* (windsurfing) and a *World Kiteboarding Cup* event are in **Jun**, there is a *Jazz Festival* in **Oct** and an *International Surf Competition* in **Nov**.

Festivals

Bike rental *Iguana Mama* (see below) on the main street at the east end of town next to *Fanatic Windsurf School*, rents well-maintained Specialized Stump Jumpers, Rock Hoppers and Cannondale bikes, US$30 per day, US$140 per week. All have front suspension and some have full suspension. They include helmets, water bottles, repair kit and spare tubes and bike insurance with all bike rentals. They offer a 10-day **Coast to Coast** package tour for US$1,850, a 5-day Dominican Alps trip for US$950, and a variety of whole-day and half-day tours ranging from US$40-85. Highly recommended are the **Cibao Downhill** US$55 half-day or US$85 full-day tours. The company is friendly and helpful and the multilingual staff know the country inside out. They pride themselves on giving something back to the country and 20% of income goes to local people and parks.

Sports
See also pages 303, 304 and 305

Iguana Mama, T5710908, or in the US, toll free, T800-8494720, www.iguanamama.com, is the only licensed biking tour operator on the north coast. Guided daily mountain biking, hiking and cultural tours as well as several multi-day tours, including Pico Duarte hike and whale watching in Samaná. Also contact them for whitewater rafting, canyoning and cascading, they will put you in touch with the best companies. *Iguana Mama* donates 20% of its profits to local schools. *Rancho Al Norte*, T2230660, horse riding and tubing with refreshments, light meal, transport, US$75. *Rancho Montana*, T2485407, riding along dry river beds and through mountains, snacks, drinks, transport, US$65.

Tour operators

Taxi Cabarete-Sosúa US$8-9, airport US$20, Puerto Plata US$40. Always check price with driver before setting off. *Guagua* to Sosúa US$0.60. *Motoconcho* US$0.60 anywhere in town, negotiate price for anywhere further, price doubles at night.

Transport

Banks *Banco del Progreso*, Carretera Luperón, T5710625. *Banco BHD*, Carretera Cabarete, T5710662. *Banco Popular*, Plaza Popular, just before Callejón de la Loma, T5710903. *Baninter*, in front of Iguana Mama on main street, T5710292. All banks have ATMs outside. **Communications** Internet: *Codetel*, Plaza Don Pepe, in same office as Western Union, T5710998. Internet access US$2 per hr. *Tele-cabarete*, in front of *Onno's*, T/F5710975, calls at RD$14 per min to Europe, RD$5 to USA, internet access RD$1 per min, open 0900-0400. *Internet Gallery*, beyond *Fanatic*. Calls to Europe RD$15 per min, to USA and Canada RD$10 per min, internet RD! per min, printer, scanner, USB reader and CD burning available. *Tricom* long distance and local, next to *Tiki Bar*, T5719757. **Medical services** *Servi-Med* medical centre, open 24 hrs, Carretera Cabarete 6, T5710413, close to *Helados Bon*.

Directory

Río San Juan

Further east along the north coast, Río San Juan is a friendly town in an area now quite a tourist attraction. The **Tourist Office** can be reached at T5892831, F5892964. One major site of interest is a lagoon called **Laguna Grí Grí**. Boats take visitors through the mangrove forests into the lagoon and to see caves and rocks, notably the **Cueva de las Golondrinas**, formed by an 1846 rockslide. It is several kilometres long and filled with swallows, from which it gets its name. Expect to pay about US$25 per person on a boat trip taking up to 20 people.

The main attraction here is the beach called **Playa Grande**, 5 km east of Río San Juan. Great swathes of pale sand make it one of the most beautiful beaches on the island. Sadly, it now being developed with large hotels, most of them all-inclusives.

It is packed with people at weekends. There is public access to the beach, which is one of the longest white-sand beaches on the north coast. When the swell is up in winter this is the place to be for good surfing and is a seventh heaven for golfers with one of the best courses in the country (see Sport, page 305), designed by Robert Trent Jones Sr with 10 of its tees at the edge of the ocean.

Playa La Preciosa was so named by surfers who come here to surf because of its beauty. It is a great place for photos and a lot more secluded than Playa Grande. *National Geographic* took one of their cover shots at this beach. It is the next left turn east after Playa Grande at the headland of the **Parque Nacional Cabo Francés Viejo**.

Sleeping

Several large all-inclusives have been built in the area, offering lots of facilities

C *Club Costa Verde*, T2485555, F2485557. 94 rooms, a/c, pool, tennis, open bar, buffet restaurant, small disco, access to small beach in front of the hotel or free transfer to Playa Grande, 10 mins' drive, friendly service, lots of tours. **E** *Bahía Blanca*, Gastón F Deligne 5, T5892563, www.bahiablancahotel.com. Lovely location right on rocks above the sea, beach 75 m away, wonderful views, 3-floor, well-maintained, white building, 30 rooms open out onto balcony, from where you get a great view of the coast and lovely colours of the fabulously clear water, hot water, good water pressure, no pool, no TV, no a/c, restaurant open for breakfast and dinner, meal plans available, no evening entertainment but near local bars and disco. **E** *Coral Inn*, T2485435, F2485437. Italian-Canadian owned, cliff view, pool, CP, food reflects owners' nationalities. **E-F** *Santa Clara*, Padre Billini y Capotillo, opposite Mini Market. With or without bath and fan, electricity and water often off and then very hot. **F** *La Casona*, Duarte 6, T5892597. 2 rooms with 3 more planned, exceptionally clean, hot water, cable TV, mini fridge, purified water, very friendly, restaurant serves their famous empanadas, fresh juices, good value.

Sports

See also pages 303 and 304

Scuba diving is offered by *Grí Grí Divers*, Gaston Deligne 4, near the *Hotel Bahía Blanca*, T/F5892671, D.McEachron@codetel.net.do Staff at the dive centre speak English, Spanish, German and French and are helpful and friendly. PADI courses are offered, from a US$65 resort course to full certification at US$350 and advanced open water at US$265. A single dive is US$40, 2 dives on the same day US$70. There are about 20 dive sites ranging in depth from 8-40 m and some are spectacular, including caves, coral, and underwater mountains called the Seven Hills. Grí Grí Divers are trying to get the area declared an Underwater National Park.

Transport

Guagua from Sosúa, 1¼ hrs, may have to change in Gáspar Hernández. Transport stops at the junction of Duarte and the main road. *Caribe Tours* T5892633, to Puerto Plata US$6.30, to Samaná 0830 US$3.10, 3 hrs, to Santo Domingo 0730, 1500.

Directory

Banks *Agencia de Cambio e Inversiones Río San Juan*, Duarte 34, T5892455. *Banco Metropolitano*, Duarte 38, T5892383, F5892493. *Banco Popular*, Bahía Príncipe, T2263234. **Medical services** There is a cardiology unit here, *Centro de Cardiología y Especialidades*, M Alejandro, T5892807, also 2 clinics. Also several pharmacies on Billini and Duarte. **Useful addresses** Police: T5892298.

The Samaná Peninsula

The Samaná Peninsula is in the far northeast of the country, geologically the oldest part of the island, a finger of land which used to be a separate island. In the 19th century the bay started to silt up to such an extent that the two parts became stuck together and the resulting land is now used to grow rice. Previously the narrow channel between the two was used as a handy escape route by pirates evading larger ships. A ridge of hills runs along the peninsula, green with fields and forests. There are several beautiful beaches, which have not been overdeveloped or 'improved', fringed with palm trees and interspersed with looming cliffs. They have become popular with Europeans, many of whom were so attracted by the laid-back lifestyle they set up home here, running small hotels and restaurants. Whale watching is a big attraction here, January-March, when the humpbacks come to the Bahía de Samaná to breed. This is one of the best places in the world to get close to the whales and a well-organized network of boats takes out visitors to see them.

Samaná

The town of **Santa Bárbara de Samaná**, commonly known just as Samaná, is set in a protected harbour, within the Bahía de Samaná. Columbus arrived here on 12 January 1493, but was so fiercely repelled by the Ciguayo Indians that he called the bay the Golfo de las Flechas (the Gulf of Arrows). Nowadays two small islets offshore are linked by a causeway to the mainland, providing a picturesque focal point when looking out to sea and added protection for yachts. The town itself is not startling, there are no colonial buildings, no old town to wander around, but the location is most attractive and it is a lively place particularly in whale watching season.

Getting there

Sánchez is the gateway town to the peninsula and all road transport passes through here. A good road runs along the southern side of the peninsula to Samaná with a spur over the hills from Sánchez to Las Terrenas on the north side. There are good bus services from Santo Domingo and from Puerto Plata and towns along the north coast. An airport outside Samaná at Arroyo Barril handles domestic flights. If coming from the east of the island you either have to fly, or go to Santo Domingo and get a bus from there, or head for Sabana de la Mar and get the ferry across the bay. There is no road connection through the Parque Nacional Los Haïtises.

Getting around

Samaná is a small town and it is easy to walk around most of the places of interest. For short excursions you can take a *motoconcho*, some of which have been fitted with tricycles like rickshaws. There are also *guaguas*, or minibuses, for a safer ride. There is no tourist office in Samaná. Samaná Tourist Service, T5382451, on the Malecón, sells tours but will also provide information; alternatively, call T5382206 (Ayuntamiento), or 5382210 (Governor's office).

Sights

The present town of Santa Bárbara de Samaná was founded in 1756 by families expressly brought from the Canary Islands. The city, reconstructed after being devastated by fire in 1946, shows no evidence of this past, with its modern Catholic church, broad streets, new restaurants and hotels, and noisy motorcycle taxis. Any remaining old buildings were torn down by Balaguer, in the 1970s as part of his grand design to make the Samaná peninsula into a huge tourist resort. When he was defeated in the 1978 elections his plans were discarded and Playa Dorada was developed instead. In contrast to the Catholic church, and overlooking it, is a more traditional Protestant church, white with red corrugated-iron roofing, nicknamed locally 'La Churcha'. It came originally from England, donated by the Methodist Church. They started the custom of holding harvest festivals, which still take place today. The Malecón waterfront road is the main street in the town, lined with restaurants, bars and tour operators. The dock is here, for the ferry to Sabana de la Mar, some whale watching tours and private yacht services. A causeway links two islands in the bay, which can be reached by taking the road to the *Hotel Cayacoa*.

Dominican Republic

Samaná Peninsula

See box, page 344
for more details

Humpback whales return to Samaná Bay at the beginning of every year to mate and calve. Various half-day tours go whale watching, certainly worthwhile if you are in the area then. This is recognized as one of the ten best places in the world to see whales and is very convenient for the average tourist as they are so close to the shore.

Sleeping **L** *Gran Bahía*, T5383111, F5382764, h.granb@codetel.net.do 110-room, charming luxury all-inclusive resort on coast road, 10 mins, 8 km east of town, also 8 villas with pool, all facilities available, less in low season, small beach, good food and service, compact 9-hole golf course, watersports, tennis, horse riding, heliport, shuttle service to Cayo Levantado. **E-F** *Nilka*, Santa Bárbara y Colón, T5382244. 11 rooms, with hot water, popular. **E** *Cotubanamá*, T5382557, go west along the Malecón to the roundabout and turn right, the hotel is one block up on the left. Clean, adequate, fan, bedside light, make sure your bedroom door locks properly, hot water sometimes, doesn't last long. **F** *Docia*, overlooking La Churcha, T5382041. New, basic lodging, hot water, fan, rooms upstairs have bigger windows and are lighter and brighter with more breeze, also great view of harbour from balcony. **F** *Paraíso*, Av Francisco del Rosario Sánchez 53, T5382648. Near *rotunda*, central but quiet, modern, good and clean, good cold shower. There are other **F** hotels, eg *Casa de Huéspedes*, T5382475 and *Ursula*, T5382402.

Eating **Going east along the Malecón**: *L'Hacienda*, T5382383. Grill and bar open from 1200, the best in town, excellent specials, main dishes US$8-10, closed Wed. *Bar Le France*, T5382257. Café style. *Le Café de Paris*, brightly painted, good crêperie, ice cream, breakfast, cocktails, loud rock music, very slow service when busy, can take 45 mins to get the bill. *La Mata Rosada*, T5382388, opposite the harbour. French-run but lots of languages spoken, popular with ex-pats, not always open, seafood, about US$10 per person. *Camilo's*, T5382781. Local and not-so-local food, reasonable (takes credit cards). *Chino's*, on hill behind *Docia*. Beautiful view, run by immigrants, doing very well.

The local cuisine is highly regarded, especially the fish and coconut dishes

Bars & There is a nightclub above *L'Hacienda* restaurant but it is more of a brothel. *La Loba* by the
nightclubs roundabout is better. A disco above *Victoria Marine* opens and closes sporadically. Outdoor nightlife can be found along the Malecón, where several stalls are set up as bars at weekends and fiestas. There is usually music at one or other of the restaurants, whether live or recorded.

Festivals Traditional dances, such as *bambulá* and the *chivo florete* can be seen at local festivals (4 Dec, the patron saint's day; 24 Oct, San Rafael).

Transport **Long distance** **Air** An airport for the peninsula is at Arroyo Barril (8 km from town, good road, only 25 mins flying time from Santo Domingo), which is being upgraded to take international traffic. There is also an airstrip east of Las Terrenas at El Portillo. **Sea** There is a ferry across the bay from Sabana de la Mar to Samaná run by *Transporte Marítimo Tom Phipps*, T5382289. Morning crossings are usually calmer than the afternoon, when the sea can be choppy and rough. A pier for a car ferry has been built at Sabana de la Mar and the boat is waiting to be put into operation some time in 2002. Many yachts anchor at Samaná. The Port Captain comes on board when you arrive, with a group of officials, each of whom may expect a tip to expedite the paperwork. It can be particularly bad at weekends and holidays.

Local *Concho* or *guagua* in town US$0.25; *carreras* US$3.50-4. *Guagua* to Sánchez from market place US$2. **Car hire** *Rentacar* is on the Malecón, next to *Mata Rosada* restaurant and opposite *Metro*. *Fabrizio y Daniele*, T2535727, have motorbikes and run moto tours. **Bus** From the capital either via San Francisco de Macorís (where *Caribe Tours* has a terminal, 5 hrs with ½ hr stop), Nagua and Sánchez, or via Cotui, Nagua and Sánchez (*Caribe Tours* and *Metro*, 4 hrs). Alternatively from the capital by bus or *público* to San Pedro de Macorís, then another to **Sabana de la Mar** and take the ferry across the bay. Return to Santo Domingo, *Caribe Tours*, T5382229, 5 daily. US$6. *Metro*, T5382851, at 0800, 1500, via Sánchez US$3, Nagua US$3, San Francisco de Macorís US$4.40, to Santo Domingo US$6. *Caribe Tours* from Samaná to Puerto Plata (US$6) via Sánchez, Nagua, Cabrera, Río San Juan, Gáspar Hernández, Cabarete (US$4) and Sosúa daily 1600, 4 hrs. *Línea Gladys* to Santiago, US$4.50, from traffic lights west of town.

Dominican Republic

Dominican Republic

Banks *Banco del Cambio*, behind *Samaná Tours*, changes TCs. *Baninter* has ATM inside, gives cash against Visa, 6% commission, open 0830-1500 Mon-Fri. Also *Banco de Reservas*, but no ATMs. **Communications** Internet: *Compucentro* in the same building as Codetel but round the corner on Calle Lavandier, has email facilities, T5383146, compucentro@hotmail.com open 0900-1230, 1500-1800 Mon-Fri, US$2.75 per hr, minimum charge US$1. **Post office**: behind *Camilo's*, just off Parque. **Telephone**: *Codetel*, Calle Santa Bárbara, 0800-2200 daily for phone, fax and email. **Medical services** *The Clínica Vicente*, T5382535, is the most advanced in Samaná, with ultrasound and X-rays.

Directory

Excursions from Samaná

Across the bay is the Los Haïtises National Park, a fascinating area of 208 sq km of mangroves, humid subtropical forest, seagrass beds, cays, *mogotes* and caves, which were used by the Taínos and later by pirates. The irregular topography of bumpy, green hills was caused by the uplifting of the limestone bedrock and subsequent erosion. There are anthropomorphic cave drawings and other pictures, best seen with a torch, and some carvings. Wooden walkways have been constructed through the caves and into the mangroves in a small area accessible to boats and tourists. The park is rich in wildlife and birds. Many of the caves have bats, but there are also manatee and turtles in the mangroves and inland the endangered solenodon (see Flora and fauna, page 301). ■ *Visits to the Park can be arranged by launch for US$45 including lunch, with departures from Sánchez and Samaná on the north side of the bay, and Sabana de la Mar on the south side; various companies organize tours (eg Amilka Tours, T5527664, daily from Sánchez, takes large tour parties and is the most regular but does not always have the best guides). It takes longer to get there by boat from Samaná, so it is better to start from Sánchez. Sabana de la Mar is even closer, but excursions are informal. The DNP, from whom permits must be obtained, also organizes tours, US$35 per person for 12 passengers (in Sabana de la Mar, T5567333).*

Parque Nacional Los Haïtises

The offshore island, Cayo Levantado, is a popular picnic place, especially at weekends when the beach is packed. The white-sand beach is nice, though, and there are good views of the bay and the peninsulas on either side. Public boats go there from the dock in Samaná (US$6-8 return, buy ticket at Malecón No 3, not from the hustlers on the pier, lots of boats daily outward 0900-1100, return 1500-1700); alternatively, take a *público* or *motoconcho* 8 km out of town to Los Cacaos (US$3) to where *Transportes José* and *Simi Báez* run boats to the island.

Cayo Levantado
Often included as a lunch and swim stop after a whale watching tour

At the eastern end of the peninsula is **Playa Galeras**. The 1-km beach is framed by the dark rock cliffs and forested mountains of **Cape Samaná** and **Cape Cabrón**, now designated a National Park. The village is popular with Europeans, several of whom have set up small hotels and restaurants. There is a fair amount of weed on the beach and some coral, so rubber shoes are a good idea, but it is 'unimproved', with trees for shade. If you walk east along the beach you come to the biggest hotel so far, *Casa Marina Bay*, set among masses of coconut palms. The beach here is sandy with no coral and very safe for children.

Las Galeras
There are very few vendors and the beaches are hassle-free

20 mins away by boat, or 40 mins by jeep (not suitable for cars) along a rough 8-km track more suited to horses is **Playa Rincón**, dominated by the cliffs of 600-m high Cape Cabrón. The sand is soft and there are few corals in the water, which is beautifully clear. A campground is being cleared on the hillside of the Cabo Cabrón National Park overlooking the beach. **Playa Frontón**, at the foot of Cape Samaná and part of the National Park, can be reached only by boat, but despite this an eco-tourist project is in progress. Many beaches are accessible only by boat. Others are reached by a dirt road, negotiable by ordinary cars. Check before swimming at deserted beaches where there can be strong surf and an undertow. Drownings have occurred near El Valle.

▶ ## Humpback whales

A fully grown humpback whale (Megaptera novaeangliae) measures 12-15 m and weighs 30-40 tonnes. It is dark grey, or black, with a white belly and long white flippers. On its nose and flippers it has large nodules, not perhaps an attractive feature, but the hairs coming out of the lumps on its nose are used like a cat uses its whiskers. All humpbacks can be identified by the markings on their tails, or flukes, as no two are the same, and scientists have recorded thousands of them so that they can trace and monitor them. They even give them names. Humpbacks are famous for their singing. Only the males sing and they all sing the same song, repeating phrases over and over again, sometimes for hours, but each year they have a new refrain, a variation on the theme, which they develop during the journey. Maybe to keep the kids amused along the way, but more likely to attract a mate. The humpback is a baleen whale, which means that it scoops up huge gulps of water containing small fish or krill, then sieves it, squeezing the water out between the baleens, retaining the food. When they are in the Bahía de Samaná, Banca Navidad (Navidad Bank) or the Banca de Plata (Silver Bank), they do not feed for the three months of their stay. The water is too warm to support their type of food, although a perfect temperature in which to give birth without harming the calf, which is born without any protective fat to ward off the cold. This fat is soon built up, however, in time for the return journey north to the western north Atlantic and Iceland, by drinking up to 200 litres a day of its mother's milk and putting on weight at a rate of 45 kg a day.

The Dominican Republic has the most popular and well established whale watching in the Caribbean. The industry is centred on humpback whales, but pilot whales and spotted dolphins can also be seen in Samaná Bay, and bottlenose, spinner and spotted dolphins, Bryde's and other whales on Silver Bank. The season for both locales is January through March with whale watching tours in Samaná Bay 15 January-15 March. Whale watching started in 1991 and in 1999 32,000 people went on tours, most of them to Samaná Bay where the trips last 2-4 hours. The trips to Silver Bank are more educational and are usually arranged by specialist groups. There are currently about eight companies offering tours of up to a week.

The whole of Samaná Bay, Silver Bank and Navidad Bank is now a National Marine Sanctuary. The aim is to include the peninsula and Los Haïtises National Park and have it all declared a Biosphere Reserve by UNESCO. During the season the Dirección Nacional de Parques monitors the whale watching and has four vigilantes, recognizable by their green caps, of which three are in Samaná and one at Silver Bank. They can be contacted at the offices of the Centre for the Conservation and Ecodevelopment of Samaná Bay (CEBSE), T5382042. A set of rules and guidelines has been drawn up by CEBSE, the DNP and the Association of Boat Owners in Samaná to regulate the activities of whale watching boats, including limits on how close they can get to whales and how long they can remain watching them. Data has been collected on the impact on breeding of whale watching, to see if this new tourist attraction has been affecting the humpbacks. There has, however, been no change since 1987, with mothers and calves and singers still in the same area, although more studies are to be undertaken on dive intervals, to see if they are being forced to stay down longer. For whale watching tours see Whale and dolphin watching, page 58.

Sleeping **AL-A** *Villa Serena*, next to the shore, T5830000, www.villaserena.com Croatian-owned, painted turquoise, pink and white, cool, plantation-style, 21 huge, stylish rooms, private terrace overlooking sea and little islet, rocky coast but small, sandy beach, gourmet restaurant, tours organized, free bicycles, snorkel gear for hire. **A** *Club Bonito*, T5380203, club.bonito@codetel.net.do the first hotel on the right along the beach track, orange building. Very central, Italian restaurant *Il Pirata*, with seafood specialities, bar, boutique, pool. **C** *Moorea Beach*, T5380007. 12 rooms, CP, seaview, 200 m from beach, in palm trees, painted white, in good order, pool, quiet but close to village centre, bar, restaurant, Dominican specialities, run by Bernard (German) and Eleni (Greek). **C** *El Marinique*, T5380262, www.elmarinique.com 5 cabañas and restaurant under palm trees, CP, sea view from restaurant, excellent food, on water's edge but no beach, simple, clean, in nicely decorated cabins, mosquito screens and coils, small bathrooms with no door, water pressure poor, relaxed atmosphere, run by Andy and Nicole, the latter is a wonderful cook, papaya crêpes with maple syrup recommended for breakfast, Andy has a country and western pizza bar and can take you fishing, tackle provided. Horses and boat trips also offered, meal and activity packages available. **E** *El Paradiso*, owned by Peter Traubel of *Dive Samaná*, T5380210. Cabins on main street, close to beach and dive shop. **F** *Villa Marina*, 800 m north of beach on road to Samaná. Italian-owned, 11 basic rooms with fan and bathroom, CP, excellent meals (fish platters or Italian food), served at reasonable prices under supervision of Vittorio Grillo, T/F5382545.

Good food at the hotels. Behind the dive shop is *Jardín Tropical*, restaurant and bar, daily **Eating** specials US$5. *L' Aventura*, good pizza for US$4.50. *Chez Denise*, T5380219. French food, crêpes, salads, from US$3.50. *El Marinique* (see above). Locals eat at the mini-*comedores* on the beach at the end of the road where the *guaguas* stop, not recommended for hygiene but plenty of local colour. You can find boatmen here for trips to other beaches.

Diving *Dive Samaná*, T/F5380001, at the end of the road on your left by the beach, run by **Watersports** Peter Traubel, boat *Highlander* takes 24 passengers or 12 divers, great diving, CMAS, no jetty, no service so load your own gear, no shade on board, good new rental equipment. Peter goes to 15 dive sites around the bay and the headland west to Puerto Escondido. Also coastal excursions, snorkelling trips, boat transfers and whale watching US$40 in season.

Las Galeras is 1 hr, US$1.75 by *guagua*, from either the market or the dock in Samaná, **Transport** US$4.50 by *motoconcho*. All transport congregates where the road ends at the beach, by the *comedores* on the sand. *Guaguas* leave when more or less full but you won't have to wait long. Jeep and motorbike rental on the road to *Hotel Moorea Beach*.

Banks There is a *Western Union Cambio* are by the Spanish restaurant *El Pescador*. **Directory** **Communication** *Codetel* is on the main road next to *De Todo Un Poco*.

Las Terrenas

On the north coast of the peninsula is Las Terrenas, with some of the finest beaches *Insect repellent is* in the country, from which, at low tide, you can walk out to coral reefs to see abun- *necessary at dawn* dant sea life. The beaches seem to go on for miles, fringed by palm trees under which *and dusk to combat* are hidden a large number of small hotels and restaurants, often run by Europeans, *the sandflies* attracted by the lifestyle. It is a quiet, low key resort and never crowded, partly because it takes a while to get there; the beaches are mostly clean and remain beautiful. It is reachable by a 17-km road from Sánchez which zig-zags steeply up to a height of 450 m with wonderful views before dropping down to the north coast. The road Samaná-Las Terrenas via Limón is also a pretty route although perhaps not so spectacular from the top.

Where the road reaches the shore, at the cemetery in Las Terrenas village, a left turn takes you along a sandy track that winds between coconut palms alongside the white-sand beach for about 5 km, past guesthouses and restaurants. At the end of the beach, walk behind a rocky promontory to reach **Playa Bonita**, with hotels, guesthouses and restaurants. Beyond the western tip of this beach is the deserted **Playa Cosón**, a magnificent 6-km arc of white sand and coconut groves ending in steep wooded cliffs (1½-hour walk or US$1 on *motoconcho*).

A right turn at the waterfront in Las Terrenas takes you along a potholed road about 4 km to the largest hotel in the area, *El Portillo*, which looks rather out of place, being a large multistorey building. The airstrip is behind it on the other side of the road. 10 km further on is **El Limón**, a farming village on the road across the peninsula to Samaná. From El Limón you can ride or hike for an hour into the hills to a 40-m high waterfall on the Arroyo Chico and swim in a pool of green water at its foot, a highly recommended excursion. The **Cascada del Limón** (or El Salto de Limón) is a National Monument. Behind the falls is a small cave. There are four different access routes to the falls from the Samaná road, from the communities of

Rancho Español, Arroyo Surdido, El Café and El Limón, from all of which you can hire horses, buy food and drinks and local produce. If taking a guide to the falls, fix the price in advance (the falls can be deserted, do not take valuables there). Access to the falls is regulated to prevent erosion and other damage; visits are only permitted during the day on foot or horseback. *Motoconcho* from Las Terrenas to El Limón US$2.50, but they will try to charge US$5-10.

Sleeping

Most hotels on the beach have prices up to 'B', but in town or behind those on the beach can be cheaper All-inclusives are not listed here

In Las Terrenas A-D *Playa Colibri*, west end of Las Terrenas, T2406434, F2406917, www.playacolibri.com 45 studios, 1-bedroom and 2-bedroom apartments, a few sleep 6-8, daily, weekly or monthly rates, kitchenette, pool, jacuzzi, parking, all clean and new, comfortable, sea view through the palm trees. 200 m east is **B-C** *Las Cayenas*, T2406080. Nice hotel run by Swiss-French lady, Marie Antoinette Piguet, rooms with or without balcony, CP, also large room for 4, good value. **C** *Tropic Banana*, T2406110. 25 rooms, CP, tennis, coaching available, pool, fans, screened windows, balconies, one of the larger guesthouses, good value food, popular bar with live merengue nightly. **C-D** *Kanesh*, at end of west track to beach, T2406187, F2406233. Run by Tamil/Swiss, some rooms cheaper, clean, hot water, large rooms with balconies and sea view, good food, help with excursions. **E** *Aloha*, T2406287. Just off the beach road, quiet, hot water, clean, beautiful garden, run by Spanish, cheerful staff and friendly cats, breakfast included. **E-F** *L'Aubergine*, T2406167, F2406070. Price depends on room and number of people, run by French-Canadians, near *Cacao* and beach, quieter than hotels on beach, very good, restaurant closed Sun. **C-E** *Villa Caracol*, along from *L'Aubergine*. Clean, friendly, quiet. **E** *Casa Robinson*, set back from beach, 200 m from village centre, T2406070. Rather noisy, double rooms with shower and terrace or small suites with kitchenettes and balconies. **E** *La Louisiane*, T2406223, F2406070. French-run, 5 rooms, some with kitchen, good value, reduced rates for long stays. **E** *Casa Nina*, turn right for 800 m along the beach in Las Terrenas. Renovated, cosy cabins. **F** *Casa de los Tres Locos*, on the way to Playa Bonita. Nice bungalows in huge garden, Austrian-run.

On Playa Bonita are **B-C** *Atlantis*, T2406111, hotel.atlantis@codetel.net.do CP, French-run with excellent French cuisine, chef used to work for President Mitterand. **C-D** *Acaya*, Playa Bonita, T2406161, F2406166. 2 buildings on the beach, 16 rooms, hot water, fan, terrace, dive shop, good breakfast and thatched restaurant, international menu with specialities like meat and fish fondue. **C-D** *Coyamar*, 1st hotel at Playa Bonita, German-run, 12 rooms, nice, cosy, beachfront, friendly, helpful. **E** *Casa Grande*, right on beach. Friendly, French-run, good kitchen, nice location. **E** *Papagayo*, T2406131, on beach road. Rather noisy beside disco, CP, good, bath, clean, fans, screened windows, small bar and restaurant, dive shop on site. **E** *Casas del Mar*, run by French, Mme Guislaine, CP. **E** *El Rincón de Abi*, El Torcido 2, T2406639, dtaza@hotmail.com, 100 m inland, take turning by *Pizzería al Coco*.Guesthouse in quiet neighbourhood, 6 rooms, CP, meals available US$6-10, local recipes, kitchen facilities for guests, run by Giselle and Jordi Taza, friendly, French and English spoken. **E-F** *Paraíso*, Av Franciso del Rosario Sánchez 53, T5382648. Safe, helpful, very clean, good. **F** *Fata Morgana*, near French school off Fabio Abreu, inland, T8365541, editdejong@hotmail.com Budget option for backpackers, rooms sleep 1-4, bathroom, kitchen, laundry, book exchange, Dutch-run.

Eating

The restaurant in *Hotel Palo Coco* on main road is Spanish-run with daily menu for US$5.50 with glass of wine and dessert. *Pizzería al Coco*, Playa Bonita. Good pizzas, Swiss-run, excellent Swiss food, nice atmosphere, also **C** bungalows to rent for 1-3 people. By the beach in the grounds of *Hotel Las Cayenas*, but independent, is *Morea Beach*, friendly, good food, open air or under thatched roof, also bar; *La Campanina*, next to *Hotel Aligio*. Good Italian food. *Aubergine*, next to *Hotel Cacao Beach*. Canadian-run, excellent seafood, fine French cuisine, also pizzas and some Chinese dishes. *Casa Boga (Iñaki & Isabel)*, between *Salsa* and *Casa Papón*, in the *Pueblo de los Pescadores*, best fish and seafood in town, fresh daily, nice little restaurant right by the sea, friendly, owners are Basque. *Dinny*, beachfront. Serves excellent breakfast with *jugos* and lots of fresh fruit. *Indiana Café*, next to *Casa Boga*. Meeting point, nice seafront spot with good atmosphere. *Casa Azul*, Dominican-run, sandwiches, salads, Spanish tortilla, hamburgers, good for breakfast, lunch or dinner, on beach by main junction. *Casa Papón*, right by the sea. Good food. *La Salsa*, thatched roof restaurant on the beach near *Trópico Banana*. French-owned, expensive. *Suni*, Dominican food, cheap and good on Calle Principal. Small places along main street may have only 1-2 items on menu but food is usually good and cheap. *Sucresale*, at the main road. French bakery, breakfast and pastries. Also *Pizza Playa*, very good pizzas and other dishes.

Nuevo Mundo is a popular disco although tourists pay more than Dominicans. There is often music at the bars and restaurants for less energetic entertainment. At weekends there is quite a lot going on, particularly along the beach road, with street sellers of food and drinks and impromptu drum music, but this is not Ibiza.

Bars & nightclubs

There are several **dive** shops, including one at *Tropic Banana*, T5899410, courses available, one of the best for watersports. **Windsurfing** and **sailing** are mostly only available at the all-inclusive resorts but equipment can be rented at the Pura Vida office, between the cemetery and *Paco Cabana*. Diving schools at the *Kanesh Hotel*, the *Castello Beach* (Alex Abbas) and the *Bahía Las Ballenas* hotel, Playa Bonita. **Tennis** lessons at *Tropic Banana*, 0900-1100, US$13.50 1 hr, US$20 2 hrs, sparring partner US$6.50 per hr. **Horse riding** can be arranged through *El Portillo* or *Tropic Banana* (stables run by Luc, who is Swiss) on healthy, well-schooled animals, for beach or mountain rides.

Sports
See also pages 303, 304 and 305

For tourist information, domestic flights and hotel booking service go to *Sunshine Services*, Calle del Carmen 151, T2406164, sunshineservice@gmx.net, run by Mara and Urs (Swiss); Spanish, English, German, French and Italian spoken. Lots of information and help, also car and motorbike rental, excursions (about 25), fishing and boat trips. *La Casa de las Terrenas*, Calle Principal, T/F2406251, casater.resa@codetel.net.do, can also help with information, tours, bookings, etc.

Tour operators

Local *Motoconchos* whizz up and down the road through the village and weave their way along the beach track, US$1, depending on how far you go. **Bus** *Caribe Tours* stops in Sánchez (T5527434) on the way to Samaná, from Santo Domingo or Puerto Plata. You will be met by *motoconchos*, US$3 to the *guagua* stop, up to US$4.50 to a hotel further along the beach. A taxi (minibus) Sánchez-Las Terrenas costs US$20, Samaná-Las Terrenas US$47. Note that *guaguas* which meet arriving *Caribe Tours* buses in Sánchez overcharge for the journey to Las Terrenas (US$4.75-9.50). **Car hire** Lots of car, jeep, *moto* hire. Motorbikes (US$15-25) and mountain bikes (no brakes) can be hired. Jeep rental US$60. There is a petrol/gasoline station.

Transport

Banks *Baninter* in *centro comercial* in the middle of the village. *Banco del Progreso* has an ATM but it is not always working. *Crediprogreso* in the centre Paseo down by the cemetery. *Agencia de Viajes Vimenca*, Remeses Vimenca, on the main road. *Western Union* for fast money transfers, exchanges money at the best rates in town. **Communications** Telephone: *Codetel* has a phone, internet and fax office, open daily 0800-2200, credit cards accepted.

Directory

Dominican Republic

East of Santo Domingo

The eastern end of the island is generally flatter and drier than the rest, although the hills of the Cordillera Oriental are attractive and provide some great views. Cattle and sugar cane are the predominant agricultural products and this is definitely cowboy country. However, much of the sugar land has been turned over to more prosperous activities such as tourism, the Casa de Campo development being a prime example. The main beach resorts are Boca Chica, Juan Dolio, Casa de Campo, Punta Cana and Bávaro, but there are several other smaller and more intimate places to stay.

Boca Chica
Do not visit at the weekend as it can be packed with people from the capital

About 25 km east of Santo Domingo (RD$5 toll on autopista, past international airport) is the beach town of Boca Chica, the principal resort for the capital. Its days of being a quiet fishing village are long gone. It is set on a reef-protected shallow lagoon, with a wide sweep of white sand and the water is perfect for families. Tourist development has been intensive and there are many hotels, aparthotels and restaurants of different standards with lots of bars and nightlife. All-inclusive resorts, of which there are several, are best booked as a package if you want a good deal. Vendors line the main road, selling mostly Haitian paintings of poor quality but they are colourful. The main street is closed to traffic at night and the restaurants move their tables on to the road. The local tourist office is near *Coral Hamaca* at end of Calle Duarte, upstairs with Politur.

Sleeping
The cheapest guesthouses are away from the beach up by the autopista

B-C *Calypso Beach Hotel*, Caracol esq 20 de Diciembre, T5234666, F5234829. Not on beach, but close, some rooms overlook small pool, new, well kept, pleasant, lots of plants, small bar, restaurant, higher price includes breakfast, billiards. On Calle Duarte at eastern end of town is **C-D** *Mesón Isabela*, T5234224, F5234136. Price for a room, more in apartment without tax, French-Canadian and Dominican owned, bar, pool, family atmosphere, quiet, personal service, breakfast, light lunches on request, across road to beach, cookers in some rooms. Next door is **C-D** *Neptuno's Club Guest House* (for restaurant, see below), with bath, free coffee, very satisfactory. **C-D** *Villa Sans Souci*, Juan Bautista Vicini 48, T5234461, F5234327. Includes tax, clean, beautiful, pool, restaurant, excellent French-Canadian food, bar by pool, no a/c, airport transfers with advance notice. **C-D** *Las Kasistas del Sol*, Primera y 2 de Junio, away from beach, T5234386, F5236056. Pool, restaurant, clean, beautiful setting, good service, friendly. **C-D** *Mango*, near Calle Juan Bautista Vicini, T5235333. Fan, TV, pool, nice garden. **C-F** *Villa Don*, Calle Juan Bautista Vicini 11, T/F5234679. Variety of rooms, private or shared bathroom, hot water, apartment with kitchen, discounts for long stays, some with TV, a/c, fridge, one or 2 beds, clean, cheap rooms are basic but adequate, small pool, right by road, bar, credit cards accepted, price for longer stay negotiable. **D** *Costalunga*, Av del Sur, T/F5236883. Short walk to beach, Italian-run, clean, a/c, TV, fridge, cooker, wall safe, bathroom, parking, pool, beauty salon, restaurant, travel agency and fax service, excellent value, security guard at night but no one to check you in if you've had a late flight. **D-E** *La Belle*, Calle Juan Bautista Vicini 9, T5235959, F5235077, on corner of highway. Very nice, a/c, pool, TV, permanent water and electricity (but may be turned off in low season when quiet). **F** *Don Paco*, Duarte 6, T5234816. Central, clean, friendly, own generator but not always on, ask for it to be turned on. **F** *Pensión Alemania*, Calle 18, T5235179. Quiet, clean and good value.

Eating
On the beach fritureras sell typical dishes

L'Horizon is excellent and *Buxeda* is good for seafood, especially *centolla* (crab). *Neptuno's Club*, T5234703, F5234251, east of *Coral Hamaca*. Built over water, with pier, good fish watching, swimming rafts, seafood, German-owned, menu is German and English, 0900-2230, closed Mon, reservations essential, now has replica of the *Santa María* for trips along the beach. Other good restaurants are *Casa Marina*, *Porto Fino* and *Pequeña Suiza*.

Nightlife

There are numerous bars for couples on Calle Duarte. Mostly safe at night although poor street lighting can be alarming. *Mad House* has rock music, not too loud, you can talk. In the same area is plenty of variety for unattached males, female prostitutes are provocatively dressed, but beware of pickpockets and AIDS.

Sport

Diving with *Treasure Divers* on the beach in front of *Hotel Don Juan*.

Road Taxi: Santo Domingo-Boca Chica US$25 (can be only US$15 from Boca Chica to Santo **Transport**
Domingo), US$15 from the airport. **Bus** *Guagua* US$1 from either Parque Enriquillo or
Parque Independencia, or the corner of San Martín and Av París but not after dark; *Boca
Chica Express*, US$1, 30-40 mins, stops running around 2100. **Car** If driving from the capital,
look carefully for signposts to whichever part of Boca Chica you wish to go. Numerous park-
ing attendants will offer spots along the beach.

Banks *Banco Popular* has an ATM and will change TCs at good rates. There are several exchange **Directory**
houses. **Communications** Phone calls can be made from *Televimenca/Western Union*, on main
street, also *Codetel*, near *Coral Hamaca*.

Los Guayacanes, Embassy and Juan Dolio beaches, east of Boca Chica, are also pop- **Juan Dolio**
ular, especially at weekends when they can be littered and plagued with hawkers
(much cleaner and very quiet out of season). The whole area is being developed in a
long ribbon of holiday homes, hotels and resorts, and a new highway is improving
access. **Los Guayacanes** has a nice little beach and the village is less overcrowded
than Boca Chica. Buses going along the south coast will drop you, and pick you up
again, at the various turn-offs to the beaches. **Juan Dolio** village is low key, with
hotels, apartments, a few small bars, a tour agency and dive shop. Tourist taxis from
the Juan Dolio hotels charge US$44 for a return trip to Santo Domingo with a
three-hour wait. Taxi to the airport US$20 one-way (T5262006).

Los Guayacanes C (per person) *Playa Esmeralda*, Paseo Vicini, T5263434, **Sleeping &**
www.playa-esmeralda.com All-inclusive, nice gardens, pool, quiet, low key, but beach can get **eating**
busy at weekends with Dominicans from the capital, diving. **C-D** *Sol-y-Mar*, Calle Central 23,
T5262514.CP, very clean big rooms, own beach, helpful, French-Canadian-run, overpriced restaurant. **C-D** *Woody's Guesthouse & Deli*, Calle Central, T5261226. Small beach, restaurant,
Swiss owner. Cheaper is **D-E** *Las Brisas*, family-run, also on Calle Central. Lots of apartments
and hotels along the newly-paved beach road. *El Refugio de los Desperados*, near *Sol-y-Mar*.
Basic but excellent cooking, try fresh lobster with pasta for US$4.50.

Juan Dolio All the large hotels are all-inclusive and offer pools, sports facilities, restaurants,
bars and entertainment. On the poor road between the beach and highway is **C-D** *Ramada
Guesthouse*, T5263310, F5262512. Meals US$18.50 FAP, pool, disco bar, watersports; opposite
is *Marco's* restaurant and bar. There is a selection of modern, modestly-priced apartments for
rent, by day, week, month or year, eg *Yamina*, T5261123 (operated by Villas del Mar Realty).
   East of Juan Dolio is the resort of **Villas del Mar** and the beach area of **Playa Real**, with
some 8 all-inclusive resorts. There are also several apartment developments.

East of San Pedro de Macorís is La Romana. The town is dominated by its sugar fac- **La Romana**
tory, which can be seen all along the coast. There are still railways here which carry *Population: 101,350*
sugar to the Central La Romana and the trains' horns can be heard through the
night. The town is very spread out, mostly on the west bank of the Río Dulce, which
reaches the sea here.

Off La Romana is Isla Catalina (also called Serena Cay). Although inland the south- **Isla Catalina**
east part of the island is dry, flat and monotonous, the beaches have fine white sand.
The reef provides protected bathing and excellent diving. Tours for US$30-68
including lunch, supper and drinks. Cruise ships also call, disgorging some 100,000
passengers in a winter season. The island is under the permanent supervision of the
Dominican Navy and the Ministry of Tourism. All works that may affect the vegetation have been prohibited. The Río Chavón area east of La Romana and Casa de
Campo is a protected zone to safeguard a large area of red and black mangroves.

Dominican Republic

Casa de Campo

Many famous people have stayed here, including Michael Jackson and Lisa Marie Presley when they got married in the Dominican Republic in 1994

Just east of La Romana on the road to Higüey you pass the entrance to Casa de Campo. This is the premier tourist centre in the Republic. The resort was built in 1974 by Charles Bluhdorn, the founder of *Gulf & Western*, which originally grew sugar cane on the land. After he died the Cuban-American family Fanjul bought it and opened it to paying guests in the 1980s. It is kept isolated from the rest of the country behind strict security. It has its own airport and is totally self-contained. Covering 7,000 acres, it is vast, exclusive, with miles of luxury villas surrounded by beautifully tended gardens full of bougainvillea and coleus of all colours. It has won numerous awards and accolades from travel and specialist sporting magazines. A Marina and Yacht Club with Customs on site is at the mouth of the Río Chavón, from where you can take boat trips up the river.

Sport is the key to the resort's success. There are lots of activities on offer and they are all done professionally and with no expense spared. The tennis club has 13 courts where you can have lessons with a pro or knock up with a ballboy, the club is busy from early in the morning to late at night. The riding school has some 150 horses for polo, showjumping, trail riding, or whatever you want to do. The polo is of a particularly high standard and international matches are held here. For those with a keen eye, there is a world-class Sporting Clays facility developed by the British marksman, Michael Rose, with trap, skeet and sporting clays. Above all, however, guests come here for the golf. There are two world-class 18-hole courses designed by Pete Dye: 'The Links' and 'Teeth of the Dog'. The latter, ranked number one in the Caribbean, has seven water holes which challenge even the greatest players.

Sleeping LL *Casa de Campo*, 10 km to the east of La Romana, T5233333, www.casadecampo.cc Operated by Premier Resorts & Hotels. Hotel, villas, bars, restaurants and country club. Lots of different packages for families, golf, tennis, etc.

Transport La Romana International Airport, across the road from Casa de Campo, receives *American Airlines* flights from Miami and *American Eagle* from San Juan. *Lauda Air* flies from Milan. Charter transfers can be arranged from Santo Domingo's International Airport, Las Américas. *Carros públicos* from La Romana to *Casa de Campo* US$0.20.

Altos de Chavón

Altos de Chavón is an international artists' village in mock-Italian style built by an Italian cinematographer, in a spectacular hilltop setting above the gorge through which flows the Río Chavón. Students from all over the world come to the art school, but the village is now a major tourist attraction and is linked to *Casa de Campo*. There are several restaurants of a variety of nationalities, expensive shops and a disco. The Church of St Stanislaus, finished in 1979 and consecrated by Pope John Paul II, contains the ashes of Poland's patron saint and statue from Krakow. It is a perfect spot for a wedding with a lovely view of the river and great photo opportunities. An amphitheatre for open-air concerts seating 5,500 was inaugurated with a show by Frank Sinatra (many international stars perform there, eg Julio Iglesias, Gloria Estefan, as well as the best Dominican performers). There is also an excellent little **Museo Arqueológico Regional**, with explanations in Spanish and English and lots of information about the Taínos.

Transport Free bus every 15 mins from *Casa de Campo*. Taxi from La Romana US$15-20. Most people arrive on tour buses or hired car.

Bayahibe

About 25 km east of La Romana

Bayahibe is a fishing village on a small bay in a region of dry tropical forest and cactus on the edge of the **Parque Nacional del Este**, a great place to stay, with excursions, diving, budget lodgings and cafés. Its proximity to the park and offshore islands has made it popular with divers it is considered it the best dive destination in the country. Small wooden houses and church of the village are on a point between the little bay and an excellent, 1½ km curving white-sand beach fringed with palms. There are lots of rooms and cabañas to rent and several bars and restaurants for low-budget travellers. Plenty of fishing and pleasure boats are moored in the bay and it is from here that boats depart for Isla Saona. At the end of the bay is one of the all-inclusive resorts built along the coast, east and west of the village, pushing at the boundaries of the national park to the east.

Isla Saona is a picture book tropical island with palm trees and white sandy beaches, set in a protected national park. However it is also an example of mass tourism, which conflicts with its protected status. Every day some 1,000 tourists are brought on catamarans, speed boats or smaller *lanchas*, for a swim, a buffet lunch with rum on the beach and departure around 1500 with a stop off at the 'swimming pool' a patch of waist-deep water on a sand bank, where more rum is served. The sea looks like rush hour when the boats come and go. If you arrange a trip independently on a *lancha*, a smaller, slower boat, the local association of boat owners assures uniform prices.

Sleeping E-F *Hotel Bayahibe*, T7073684, F5564513. Best in village but staff from *Casa del Mar* stay here and its often full, rooms have 2 beds, bathroom, hot water, a/c, fan, balcony, kitchenette, right by the water and dive boats. **E-F** *Llave del Mar*, T8330081, F8330088. Basic but adequate, 25 rooms with 1-2 beds, fan, fridge, a/c and balcony in more expensive rooms, pine furniture, small bathroom but OK for the price, cold water, TV. *Cabañas* for rent, for as little as US$10, ask around, don't expect hot water.

There are five all-inclusive hotels not listed here, mostly booked from abroad

Eating There are lots of small bars and restaurants, which frequently change hands. *Casa Eva*, Calle Principal 1, casa_eva@yahoo.com Open 0830-1500, 1800-2400, on the waterfront, serving plato del día or salads, pasta, breakfast, also internet café, US$1 for 15 mins. *Big Sur*, on the beach, Italian-owned, great food. *Restaurante La Punta*, seafood. *Café Caribe*, breakfasts and other meals. *Adrian café* and restaurant. *La Bahía*, fish dishes, international calls, main street, on the beach. *Cafetería Yulissa*, good breakfast, recommended. *El Oasis*, good for breakfast.

Sport Diving The all-inclusive resorts have their own dive operations, but there is an independent dive shop in Bayahibe, *Scubafun*, run by Germans, Werner and Martina Marzilius, T18330003, www.scubafun.info. Their clients range from *Casa de Campo* guests to backpackers, beginners to experienced divers. They are very flexible and will do almost anything on request. Wear shoes when you go in the water as there is broken glass. Some of the best diving in the country is in this area, in the National Park, and although local fishermen are still spearfishing, the reef is in good condition and there are plenty of fish, more in some areas than others. Dolphins are often seen from the boat, while underwater you find sharks and rays off Catalinita Island, east of Saona, reef sharks at La Parguera, west of Saona, the wreck of *St George* close to the *Dominicus* and freshwater caves inland for experienced divers. 2-tank dives with a beach stop cost US$56-75, depending on the distance, a trip to Saona, Catalina or Catalinita, including national park fees, drinks and snacks, costs US$75-100. Day trip to Saona Island costs US$44.

Transport Take the road which turns off the highway from La Romana to Higüey. A *carro público* La Romana-Bayahibe is US$2.50, or take a Higüey bus to the turn-off and take a *motoconcho*, US$1. A taxi from La Romana costs about US$10.

The main town in the far east of the island is the modern, dusty and concrete Higüey. The **Basílica de Nuestra Señora de la Altagracia** (patroness of the Republic) can be seen for miles away. It is a very impressive modern building, to which every year there is a pilgrimage on 21 January; the statue of the Virgin and a silver crown are in a glass case on the altar and are paraded through the streets at the end of the fiesta. According to legend, the Virgin appeared in 1691 in an orange tree to a sick girl. Oranges are conveniently in season in January and huge piles of them are sold on the streets, while statues made of orange wood are also in demand. The Basilica was started by Trujillo in 1954, but finished by Balaguer in 1972. The architects were French, the stained glass is French. The Italian bronze doors (1988) portray the history of the Dominican Republic.

Higüey

Dominican Republic

Punta Cana

Julio Iglesias and Oscar de la Renta have built villas in Los Corales

Punta Cana, on the coast due east from Higüey, has some beautiful beaches, good diving and an international airport. The area is not particularly pretty, the land is flat and the vegetation is mostly scrub and cactus, except for the palm trees along the beach. There are two resorts but no small hotels. The *Club Med* opened in 1981, followed by the *Punta Cana Beach Resort* in 1988 and a golf course runs between them. Independent visitors find it difficult to find a public beach as the hotels will not allow non-residents through their property. The Marina Punta Cana has a capacity for 22 yachts and eight other sailing boats, immigration and customs services provided by officers at the Punta Cana Airport (24 hours' notice required if arriving by sea). There is also a championship bowling alley in the residential area, with 18 lanes, billiards, internet and cafeteria.

Flights vary according to season

Transport Air From North America: *Lan Chile* and *American Airlines* from Miami and *American Airlines* from New York. **From Europe**: Amsterdam (*Martinair*), Madrid (*Air Europa*), Paris (*Air France*), *Condor* and/or *LTU* from Berlin, Düsseldorf, Frankfurt, Hamburg, Leipzig, Munich. and *Lauda Air* from Milan. **From the Caribbean**: San Juan (*American Eagle*). **From South America**: Santiago (*Lan Chile*).

Bávaro

Continuing round the coast, there are many other beaches with white sand and reef-sheltered water. The area now known as Bávaro was once a series of fishing villages, but they have disappeared under the weight of hotels which contrast with the shacks still hanging on in places. All the hotels are usually booked from abroad as package holidays and most of them are all-inclusive, run by international companies such as Barceló, Meliá, Occidental, Fiesta or Riü.

The southwest

The far southwest of the Republic is a dry zone with typical dry-forest vegetation. It also contains some of the country's most spectacular coastline and several national parks. It is a mountainous area with great views and scary roads and the closer you get to the Haitian border the poorer and more deforested the country becomes. Tourism is not big business here yet, although there are some fascinating places to visit, such as Lago Enriquillo, a saltwater lake below sea level and three times saltier than the sea, or the mines for larimar, a pale blue semi-precious stone used in jewellery. The towns and villages are unremarkable and unpretentious but give a fascinating insight into rural and provincial life in the Republic.

San Cristóbal

The birthplace of the dictator Rafael Leonidas Trujillo, San Cristóbal is 25 km west of Santo Domingo. Most of sites of interest are related to his involvement with the town. He was on his way to San Cristóbal to visit a mistress when he was gunned down. A busy industrial and commercial centre, San Cristóbal does not have great charm, you can bypass it by taking the road via Nigua from Haina or Hatillo.

As well as fine beaches, the region of San Cristóbal has several sites of natural and historical interest. The caves at **El Pomier** are some 15 km north out of town (buses from Parque Central) on the same road as the **Casa de Caoba**, Trujillo's home. It is a long, hot walk from the gate that marks the entrance to the Reserva Antropológica. A guide leads a tour of the caves, pointing out the faint white pictograms in the first cave, which is also inhabited by thousands of bats. Unfortunately, neglect and graffiti has led to considerable damage to some of the images. ■ *0930-1700 except Sun. US$3 for tour. Wear solid footwear and bring a torch.* Two other caves, Borbón and Santa María, are not open to the public, but on public holidays, and on the local saint's day festival (6-10 June) religious ceremonies take place around the caves, with a mix of supposedly Taíno ritual and Aftican-influenced stick and drum festivals. Nearby are La Toma natural pools, for swimming. ■ *Mon-Fri 0900-1800, Sat-Sun 0700-1930. US$1.30.*

South of San Cristóbal, the beaches at **Palenque, Nigua** and **Najayo** (*públicos* leave regularly from San Cristóbal's Parque Central) are mostly of grey sand. On a hill over-looking Najayo beach are the ruins of Trujillo's beach house. These beaches are popular as excursions from Santo Domingo and at weekends and holidays can be packed. There are lots of beach bars serving finger-licking fried fish and local food, washed down with ice cold beer. The music can be overbearing at times with personal sound systems com-peting against each other on the beach, but at Palenque the dark sand beach is deserted at the far end and you don't have to walk far to get away from the crowds. Good swimming at Palenque, rougher at Najayo but there is an artificial wave breaker.

From San Cristóbal the road runs west through sugar cane country to Baní. Baní is   **Baní** the birthplace of Máximo Gómez, the 19th-century fighter for the liberation of Cuba. The **Casa de Máximo Gómez** is a museum with a mural in his memory, set in a shady plaza within walking distance of the main Parque Duarte, the centre of the town and a pleasant spot. ■ *0900-1700, closed Sun. Free. Ask for directions from the main Parque.* Another attraction is the **Museo del Café Dominicano**, which is informative about the Dominican coffee industry. ■ *0900-1700, closed Sun. US$1.20. Opening times erratic.*

Of the two roads west out of Baní, take the one to Las Calderas naval base for **Las Salinas**. There is no problem in going through the base (photography is not allowed); after it, turn left onto an unmade road for 3 km to the fishing village of Las Salinas, passing the unique sand dunes of the **Bahía de Calderas**, now a national monument and an inlet on the Bahía de Ocoa, shallow, with some mangroves and good windsurf-ing and fishing. The dunes, the largest in the Caribbean, can be reached from the road, but there are no facilities and little shade. The views are spectacular, however.

Sleeping In the village is **C-D** *Las Salinas High Wind Centre*, T3108141. Run by Jorge Domenech, 24-room hotel, clean, restaurant with Dominican cuisine and wonderful seafood including lobster caught locally, bar, pool, windsurf centre, great dock house where you can relax out of the sun. Also in the area on the coast is **C-D** *Boca Canasta Caribe Beach Club Hotel*, T2230664, F5225210. Run by Don Vito Rallo and Hans Dieter Riediger, 40-room hotel on the beach, a/c, hot water, café, bar, restaurant, massage room, diving, tennis, basket and volleyball, fishing, horse riding, windsurfing, sailing, waterski, jetski, car hire.

Barahona

Barahona is a comparatively young town, founded in 1802 by the Haitian leader,   *Population: 100,000* Toussaint Louverture, when he was briefly in control of the whole of Hispaniola. Its economy initially rested on the export to Europe of precious woods, for example mahogany. In the 20th century the sugar industry took over. The large sugar mill at the northern end of town is surrounded by the shanty town district of Batey Central and is currently closed pending privatization negotiations. The main attractions of this rather rundown grid-system town revolve around the seafront Malecón, where most hotels and restaurants are to be found. The Parque Central, five blocks up, is the com-mercial hub of the town and a pleasant spot to sit (although tourists are liable to be pes-tered). The small, public beach at Barahona frequently has stinging jelly fish. It is also filthy, as is the sea, and theft is common. The best beach near town is called El Cayo and is reached by passing the sugar mill and surrounding slums and doubling back on to the sandy peninsula with palms (visible from the *Brisas del Caribe* restaurant).

E *Hotel Caribe* Av Enriquillo, T5244111. Excellent open-air restaurant (*La Rocca*) next door. **Sleeping** **E** *Hotel Guaracuyá*, T2330748, on its own beach nearer the town centre. Rather gloomy, but good value, with a/c. In town, **E** *Micheluz*, Av 30 de Mayo 28, T5242358. A/c, cheaper with fan, cold water, restaurant. **F** *Gran Hotel Barahona*, Calle Jaime Mota 5, T5423442. Fan, res-taurant. **F** *Hotel Cacique*, Av Uruguay (behind Parque Infantil), T5244620. Basic, clean.

Dominican Republic

In Baoruco, 16 km from Barahona, **L-B** *Barceló Bahoruco Beach Resort*, T5241111, www.barcelo.com All-inclusive, 105 large rooms in 5 blocks, all facilities, stony beach, rough waves, good pool, only one restaurant, serves buffet food with good variety. **B-C** *Casa Bonita*, T6960215, F2230548, on hillside overlooking coast. 12 rooms in bungalows with gardens, small pool, fan, no a/c, TV or phone, expensive restaurant.

Eating   *Brisas del Caribe* seafood restaurant at northern end of Malecón, T5242794. Excellent food and service, reasonable prices, pleasant setting, popular at lunchtime. *El Curro Steak House*, Calle Luperón, opposite cinema, T5243645. Meat and fish specialities, good value, outside sitting area, owner speaks English. *La Rocca*, next to *Caribe Hotel* on Malecón. Great breakfast menu, inexpensive. *D'Lina Pizza* , Av 30 de Mayo. Cheap and very large portions. *Panadería del Sur*, Uruguay y Luperón. Fresh bread, breakfasts and snacks.

Nightlife   *Costa Sur* disco with restaurant almost opposite *Riviera Beach*

Tour operators   *The Barahona Ecological Society* welcomes enquiries from Spanish-speaking visitors and offers ecotourism advice and possibly guides. Contact Roberto Dominici, T5245081, r.dominici@codetel.net.do *Julio Féliz* is an English-speaking local guide who specializes in ecotourism and birdwatching, fees negotiable, T5246570, F5243929.

Transport   **Air** The international **María Montéz Airport**, opened in 1996. There should be daily connections with Santo Domingo and Port-au-Prince, but really there are few flights. **Bus** Journey time from the capital is 3 hrs. Minibus fare is US$3, *público* US$4, *Caribe Tours* runs 4 buses a day. To Jimaní 2½ hrs, US$3.30. *Concho* or *guagua* in town RD$5; *carrera* RD$5-6.

Directory   **Banks** *Banco Popular* on Parque Central has an ATM (Plus, Visa). **Communications** *Codetel* across the square from *Banco Popular*, open daily 0800-2200.

Excursions from Barahona

Beaches south of Barahona   Those with a car can visit remote beaches from Barahona (public transport is limited to *públicos*). The coast road south of Barahona, runs through some of the most beautiful scenery in the Republic, mountains on one side, the sea on the other, leading to Pedernales on the Haitian border (146 km). All along the southern coast are many white-sand beaches with some of the best snorkelling in the Republic. The first place is the pebble beach of **El Quemaito**, where the river comes out of the beach, the cold freshwater mixing with the warm sea; offshore is a reef. **B** *Hotel El Quemaito*, T/F2230999. Small Swiss-run beach resort, pleasant gardens, good restaurant.

Larimar is mined only in the Dominican Republic and is mostly used for jewellery   At the end of the village of **Las Filipinas**, about 14 km from Barahona, turn right on to a dirt road. Inland about 15 km into the hills along a very poor track (4WD essential, especially after rain, ask directions at the nearby *colmado)* are the open-cast mines where the semi-precious mineral, larimar, is dug. The primitive mines are worth a visit but they will be closed if it rains as the mines flood. Miners or local boys will sell you fragments of stone, usually in jars of water to enhance the colour, for US$5-10, depending on size and colour. When dry, larimar is a paler blue.

Back on the main road, you pass through **Baoruco** (see Sleeping above) and La **Ciénaga** (small stony beaches and rough tides). The road comes right down to the sea before **San Rafael** (about 40 minutes from Barahona) where a river runs out onto a stony beach. The forest grows to the edge of the beach. Where the road crosses the river is a *pensión* with a cold water swimming hole behind it (the swimming hole is safer than the sea as enormous waves surge onto the beach). Construction is under way here. At weekends it gets very crowded. The refreshing cold water *balneario* is free and there are normally a number of stalls selling drinks and fried fish. It is also possible to climb up the mountain alongside the river, which has small waterfalls and pools. At **El Paraíso**, 31 km from Barahona, are a Texaco station and **F** *Hotel Paraíso* (T2431080, big rooms with bath, clean, TV). *Paola* restaurant, on the main road, is recommended and cheap.

At **Los Patos** another river flows into the sea to form a cool bathing place; a great place to spend the day at a weekend to watch Dominicans at play, with excellent swimming and lots of family groups. There are cool, freshwater lagoons behind several of the other beaches on this stretch of coast. **Laguna Limón** is a flamingo reserve. It is dangerous to drive at night. Roads are impassable without 4WD after rain.

Note that most of these beaches have domestic animals, so there are droppings on the sand

Enriquillo, 54 km south of Barahona (F *Hotel Dayira*, on main road, no phone, basic; **F** *Dormitorio Juan José*, even more primitive, no phone), is the last place for fuel until Pedernales, 80 km away, but no unleaded is available. After Enriquillo the road turns inland up to Oviedo and then skirts the Parque Nacional Jaragua as it runs a further 60 km to Pedernales. Oviedo, with the atmosphere of a desert settlement, has no hotels or decent restaurants and is one of the hottest places in the country.

Pedernales is the most westerly town of the Republic, on the Haitian border. This is a major crossing point for migrant Haitian workers who come over to work in the sugar cane plantations and in construction. There is no immigration office so in theory only Haitians may enter Haiti here. However, this prohibition is frequently flouted, as border guards are willing to turn a blind eye in return for a small sum (US$10 or so). It is advised, however, that you make yourself known at the Anse-à-Pitres police station on the Haitian side and that you return within a few hours. If there is a change of personnel at the border station, you may find yourself paying another 'tip'. There is no road link, but the crossing can be done on foot if the stream that divides the countries is not too high, or you can hire a *motoconcho*. Every Friday there is an informal market in the no man's land at the border crossing, where Haitians sell cheap counterfeit clothing brands, smuggled spirits and a vast array of plastic kitchenware.

Pedernales

Sleeping There are few decent hotels in Pedernales. The best is **C** *Caribe Sur*, on nearby Playa Pedernales, a/c, hot water. **F** *Rossy*, no phone, is extremely basic. Rudimentary *comedores* in town.

Parque Nacional Jaragua is the largest of the Dominican Republic's national parks. This area of subtropical dry forest and inhospitable prickly scrub also contains a marine zone, in which lie the uninhabited islands of **Beata** and **Alto Velo**. The vegetation is largely cactus and other desert plants, but there are also mahogany, frangipani and extensive mangroves. Of particular interest is the **Laguna Oviedo** at the eastern end of the Park, which is easily accessible from Oviedo. Here there are the country's largest population of flamingos as well as herons, terns, spoonbills and frigate birds. Animals include the Ricord iguana, the rhinoceros iguana and several species of bat. The lagoon is reached via the National Park office just outside Oviedo (0830-1630 daily) where an entrance permit must be bought. Turn right on a rough track after the office to reach a hut, where *Blanco Tours* offers a highly recommended boat trip around the lake. An ex-soldier, Blanco is a knowledgeable guide (Spanish only), who will point out birds and iguanas and will take visitors to inspect a couple of Taíno cave sites with pictograms. ■ *Entry RD$50. A tour normally costs around US$50, but up to six people can take part for that price.*

Parque Nacional Jaragua

Near the Haitian border, is the 200 sq km **Lago Enriquillo**, whose waters, 30 m below sea level, are three times saltier than the sea. Once linked to the bay of Port-au-Prince and the Bahía de Neiba, the lake was cut off from the sea by tectonic movements some million years ago and the surrounding beaches and the islands are rich in ancient seashells and coral fragments. Wildlife includes some 500 American crocodiles, iguanas and flamingos. Three islands in the lake, together with the lake and surrounding shoreline, make up the **Parque Nacional Isla Cabritos**. You need to purchase a Dirección Nacional de Parques (DNP) permit (RD$50) at the ranger station east of La Descubierta (0700-1630) to visit the island and only groups with a guide are permitted to go there. The 30-min boat trip to the island is offered by

Parque Nacional Isla Cabritos
There is no accommodation on the lake shore but basic lodging can be found at La Descubierta

Dominican Republic

various local boatmen, who are recommended by the DNP staff at La Descubierta. There are usually one or two boats waiting to take parties over, and they will wait for other passengers if you are on your own, since the price of about US$50 is payable by one or up to six passengers. **Isla Cabritos** is a flat expanse of parched sand, with cactus and other desert vegetation. It is extremely hot and oppressive around midday (temperatures have been known to rise to 50°C) and visitors are recommended to arrive as early as possible and to take precautions against sunburn. This barren island is home to the rhinoceros iguana and the Ricord iguana, both of which have become quite tame, even aggressive, and approach boat parties in search of treats. The two smaller islands are **Barbarita** and **La Islita**. To visit the lake it is best to have one's own transport because, even though public transport runs both on the north and south shores, there is no guarantee of travelling on (or returning) the same day. Note that there is a filling station in Duvergé but no fuel elsewhere in this area.

Jimaní Jimaní, at the western end of the lake (not on the shore), is about 2 km from the Haitian border. The space in between is a no man's land of rocky terrain crossed by an extremely hot road, which fortunately has a constant coming and going of *guaguas* and *motoconchos*. Jimaní is an authorized crossing point for foreigners in general (as is Dajabón) and it is possible to leave the Dominican Republic here and cross into Haiti (see Travel to Haiti, above). Customs officers in Jimaní are not above taking items from your luggage. The immigration office closes at 1800 (or before). There is a semi-permanent market in the no man's land, in which Haitian merchants display vast quantities of mostly shoddy and/or counterfeit goods, Barbancourt rum and perfumes. Jimaní itself is a spread out town of single-storey housing which swelters in temperatures of up to 50°C.

Sleeping and eating E *Hotel Jimaní*, T2483139, on road east out of town, appears to be converted military accommodation, no hot water, little service but nice pool, decent restaurant and ice cold beer. *Restaurant Los Lagos*, Duarte y Restauración, excellent *chivo y gandules* (goat and beans), stays open late as town's main meeting place, also has disco *Krystal*.

Background

History

The colony Although the Spanish launched much of their westward expansion from Santo Domingo,
See page 283 for their efforts at colonizing the rest of the island were desultory. Even Santo Domingo soon
more on Columbus' declined in importance, overwhelmed by the onslaught of hurricanes and pirate attacks.
colonization of Drake sacked Santo Domingo in 1586 and the rebuilding costs were more than the fledgling
Hispaniola colony could bear. The French invaded in the 17th century from their base on Tortuga and colonized what became known as Saint Domingue in the west. The French colony, the largest sugar producer in the West Indies, soon became the most valuable tropical colony of its size in the world, while the Spanish colony was used mostly for cattle ranching and supplying ships from the Old World to the New.

By the mid-18th century, the number of Spaniards in the eastern part of the island was only about one-third of a total population of 6,000. Since there was little commercial activity or population of the interior, it was easy prey for Haitian invaders fired with the fervour of their rebellion at the turn of the 19th century. Between 1801 and 1805, followers of **Toussaint L'Ouverture** and **Dessalines** plundered the Spanish territory. Sovereignty was disputed throughout the beginning of the 19th century with frequent incursions and occupations by Haitian forces. In 1822, Haiti's army took control for a further 22 years. This occupation lives on in the country's mythology as its lowest point, with the ruthless Haitians expropriating land and raising taxes. It was a very anti-Spanish and anti-white régime and many of the Spanish hierarchy left the island. Santo Domingo descended into poverty.

In February 1844 pro-independence forces led by three men, the writer **Juan Pablo Duarte**, the lawyer **Francisco del Rosario Sánchez** and the soldier **Ramón Mella**, defeated Haitian troops in Santo Domingo. The independent nation was called the Dominican Republic, supposedly free and independent of all foreign domination. However, the new leaders were not a cohesive group and once in power they soon succumbed to infighting. Duarte was sent into exile and the country underwent yet another period of instability, including more Haitian incursions. In November 1844, the strongman, **Pedro Santana**, assumed the presidency. He wanted to make the Republic a protectorate of France, Spain or Britain, but with no luck. The other leader, or *caudillo*, at this time, Buenaventura Báez, also favoured annexation and the USA was also approached.

Independence

In 1861, Santana finally achieved re-annexation with Spain in the first and only recolonization in the Americas. Spanish bureaucrats were incompetent, the clergy was once again dominated by reactionary Spaniards and military rule was repressive and contemptuous of the Dominicans. There was a hatred of Spain and an increasing number of guerrillas took to the hills to fight a war of attrition. Spain resented the money it had to spend on suppressing revolts and reinforcing its garrison, depleted by yellow fever.

A Spanish colony again

The resurrection in the countryside proved successful and became known as the **War of Restoration** (la Restauración), ending in 1865 when Queen Isabella II abrogated the treaty of annexation and evacuated Spanish officials and troops. The Restoration is remembered as a great moment in Dominican history, but governments still pursued the idea of annexation as the answer to their problems. They wooed the USA, but the US Senate could not muster enough support and a vote for the proposal was defeated. However, Germany became deeply involved in the economy, with its traders and bankers supporting the tobacco crop. German warships were sent on occasion to collect debts and the USA was becoming increasingly apprehensive about Germany's motives.

The Restoration

The USA intervened to prevent a European power gaining control of the country's customs on behalf of creditors. Roosevelt put the Dominican customs into receivership and under an agreement signed in 1905, the US authorities would collect import and export duties and distribute 55% to the country's creditors and 45% to the Dominican government. In 1907 a formal receivership treaty was signed, heralding the start of the USA's financial leverage in the region. Peace was not assured, however, and in 1916, when the presidency appeared to collapse in chaos, US marines were landed. During the US occupation Dominican finances improved dramatically and the country became creditworthy again, but the American occupiers were deeply resented. Guerrilla fighters were suppressed by US troops. In 1920 the new Land Registration Act dispossessed peasant farmers who had held land communally in traditional holdings known as *terrenos comuneros*, in favour of private ownership, allowing Dominican and US investors to buy up land titles and purchase huge areas on the cheap. Some of the dispossessed small scale farmers formed armed bands, known as *gavilleros*, and waged intermittent guerrilla warfare against the Guardia Nacional and US forces. In 1924 US troops were withdrawn, although the administration of the customs remained under US control.

US intervention

In May 1930 elections were won by the armed forces commander, **Rafael Leonidas Trujillo Molina**, who became president. Thus began one of the most ruthless dictatorships ever seen in the Dominican Republic. With either himself or his surrogates at the helm (Héctor Trujillo, 1947-60, and Joaquín Balaguer, 1960-62), Trujillo embarked on the expansion of industry and public works and the liquidation of the country's debts. Nevertheless, his methods of government denied any form of representation and included murder, torture, blackmail and corruption. For 30 years he ruled supreme, dispensing favours or punishment as he deemed appropriate. During his reign, in 1937, an estimated 10,000 Haitian immigrants were rounded up and slaughtered, prolonging the hatred between the two republics. The economy prospered with the expansion of the sugar industry and an influx of US capital, but much of the wealth ended up in the bank accounts of the Trujillos, as the General appropriated companies and land. In 1961 Trujillo was assassinated and another power vacuum was created.

The Trujillo dictatorship

Dominican Republic

The Balaguer presidencies

Joaquín Balaguer had been part of Trujillo's government since 1930 and was nominally president at the time of the murder, although without any real power or legitimacy. He tried to hang on to the presidency, but there was violence and the military intervened. A Council of State was set up in 1962 which, with US approval and finance set the country on the path to some sort of representative democracy. The first free elections for 40 years were held on 20 December 1962 in which Balaguer was defeated by **Professor Juan Bosch** of the Partido Revolucionario Dominicano (PRD). Bosch was a left-wing intellectual who had formed the social democratic PRD in exile. The party's policies for land reform with the redistribution of the vast estates held by the Trujillo family, together with an attack on unemployment and poverty, were overwhelmingly supported by the electorate. He took office in February 1963 but after seven months he was ousted by a military coup and sent into exile. A three-man civilian junta was installed with martial law and new elections were promised, but instability ruled, with several changes of government. With civil war raging in the capital and memories of Communist Cuba still fresh, the USA dispatched 23,000 troops on 28 April 1965 to control the country. The USA supported another provisional government, but there followed several months of fighting with the loss of some 3,000 lives. Finally, new elections were held in June 1966. They were won by Balaguer, returned from exile in New York. The economy was in tatters and US aid was crucial in rebuilding the country. The US peace keeping force returned home, calm descended for a while and Balaguer concentrated on imposing austerity and bolstering the country's finances. He retained power in the 1970 elections, and remained in office with the help of a secret paramilitary force known as *La Banda*, the gang, until 1978, forging closer links with the USA, but not without facing coup attempts, right-wing terrorism and left-wing guerrilla incursions.

The PRD boycotted elections in 1970 and 1974, but the declining popularity of Balaguer led it to challenge him in 1978. A PRD President was returned: **Antonio Guzmán**, a wealthy land-owner and former minister in Juan Bosch's brief government, whose chief aims were to reduce army power and eliminate corruption. His election was achieved after the intervention of President Carter of the USA, who prevented a military takeover when it became clear that the PRD was winning. Guzmán's successor, **Dr Salvador Jorge Blanco**, also of the PRD, presided over severe economic difficulties which led to rioting in 1984 in which 60 people died. The party split over the handling of the economy, helping Joaquín Balaguer to win a narrow majority in the 1986 elections giving him a fifth presidential term. The 1990 elections were contested by two octogenarians, Dr Balaguer (83) and Dr Juan Bosch (80), now of the Partido de la Liberación Dominicana (PLD). Dr Balaguer won a sixth term of office by a narrow majority, which was subjected to a verification process after Dr Bosch alleged fraud had taken place in the capital. The May 1994 elections had the same outcome, after Balaguer had decided late in the campaign to stand for re-election. His chief opponent was **José Francisco Peña Gómez** of the PRD, who was subjected to blatantly racist campaign abuse because of his dark skin and alleged Haitian ancestry. First results gave Balaguer the narrowest of victories. Peña Gómez, supported by many outside observers, claimed that fraud had taken place and the election was reviewed by a revision committee appointed by the Junta Central Electoral (JCE). The committee found irregularities, but its findings were ignored by the Junta which awarded victory to Balaguer. To defuse the crisis, Balaguer signed a pact with Peña Gómez allowing for new elections in November 1995; Congress rejected this date, putting the new election back six months to 16 May 1996.

1996 election campaign

Almost at once campaigning began for the 1996 presidential election. The PRD selected Peña Gómez again while the PLD chose **Leonel Fernández** as its candidate, to replace Juan Bosch who had retired. Within the PRSC, jockeying for the candidacy was beset by scandals and power struggles, exacerbated by the absence of an appointment by Balaguer himself. In the first round of the 1996 elections, Peña Gómez received 46% of the vote, compared with 39% for Leonel Fernández. However, in the second round, Balaguer gave his support to Fernández, in an effort to keep Peña from the presidency, and he won 51% of the vote. Balaguer continued to influence the new government's policies through Congress. The PLD was in a minority in both houses, holding only one Senate seat, compared with 15 for the PRSC and 14 for the PRD, and 13 congressional seats, compared with 58 for the PRD and 48 for the PRSC.

President Leonel Fernández was sworn in on 16 August 1996 and appointed a cabinet **The Fernández** largely from his own party, after a cooling of relations with Dr Balaguer. His comparative **administration** youth signalled a breath of fresh air despite the continuing influence of the old *caudillos*. He pledged to fight poverty, modernize the economy and fight corruption. In 1997 relations with the PRSC deteriorated rapidly because of investigations into land purchase scandals involving members of the previous administration. Land which was in national parks or in protected areas of special scientific interest, or expropriated under the agrarian reform programme for distribution to small farmers, was found to have been allocated to PRSC officials and sold on for profit, mostly for tourism development. There was also a shake up in the top ranks of the military and police, with some linked to drugs offences, others to unsolved murders and disappearances.

José Francisco Peña Gómez died of cancer in May 1998. Six days later, his party, the PRD, won a landslide victory in the mid-term congressional and municipal elections.

Presidential elections in 2000 were keenly fought between the 93-year-old Balaguer for the **2000** PRSC, Danilo Medina for the ruling PLD and **Hipólito Mejía** for the PRD. The government **elections** was credited with achieving economic growth, but it was perceived that the benefits had not been widely enough distributed and corruption within the administration was alleged. Despite his age, blindness and other infirmities, Balaguer was seen as an influential power broker and a force to be reckoned with. Mejía won 49.87% of the vote, Balaguer 24.6% and Medina 24.9%. As no one achieved the 50% required for an outright win, a second round was technically necessary, but after both other candidates visited Balaguer, both he and Medina pulled out of the race, leaving Mejía the victor. Joaquín Balaguer died in 2002.

Government

The Dominican Republic is a representative democracy, with legislative power resting in a bicameral Congress: a 30-seat Senate and a 149-seat Chamber of Deputies. Senators and deputies are elected for a four-year term, as is the President.

Economy

The largest foreign exchange earner is tourism, with annual receipts exceeding US$2 bn. The industry generates 20% of gdp and employs about 5% of the labour force, 50,000 in direct jobs and 110,000 indirectly. The number of hotel rooms is around 55,000, compared with 11,400 in 1987, and more than any other Caribbean country. Nearly half of hotel rooms are sold on an all-inclusive basis.

There are six main agricultural regions: the north, the Cibao valley in the north central area, Constanza and Tiero, the east, the San Juan valley, and the south. Cibao is the most fertile and largest region, while the eastern region is the main sugar-producing area. Sugar was traditionally the main crop and times of prosperity have nearly always been related to high world sugar prices, but diversification out of sugar cane, the conversion of some cane lands into tourist resorts, the expulsion of Haitian cutters and a slump in productivity led to lower volume and value of sugar production. Other traditional products grown for export include sugar, coffee, cocoa and tobacco, but they now account of only a third of total exports. Non-traditional products have been gaining in importance. These include fruit and vegetables, plants and cut flowers, marine products, processed foods, cigars and other agroindustrial products. Growth of the cigar industry has put the Dominican Republic in competition with Cuba, with sales of around US$400 mn a year.

Since 1975 gold and silver mining has been of considerable importance. Large gold, silver and zinc deposits have been found near the Pueblo Viejo mine, where the oxide ores were running out, and a major gold and silver deposit has been discovered in the Haitian border area, which could mean a joint operation to establish an open cast mine. The country also produces ferronickel, which has overtaken sugar as the major commodity export earner. Reserves are estimated at 10% of total world deposits.

Dominican Republic

Despite the tourist economy roughly half the population lives in poverty, with a third lacking secure employment. Two thirds of the people live in urban areas and many depend on the informal economy to survive. Remittances from relatives in the USA are the life blood of many families and even whole villages. Inequalities in income are glaring, with the poorest 20% receiving less than 5% of the national income. The rich live in luxury villas driving large cars and the oligarchy continues to dominate the economy as since colonial times. From sugar cane and coffee, the powerful families (among them Bermúdez, Barceló and Jiménez) have moved into tourism and export manufacturing.

Culture

Literature As with all facets of Dominican culture, the US occupation of 1916-24 proved a turning-point in the search for authentic forms of expression. But no sooner had a radical generation of nationalist writers begun to find their voice to protest against the imposition of North American values than the long period of the Trujillo dictatorship was under way. For 30 years the régime tolerated no criticism whatsoever, stamping on any literary originality and encouraging only absurd paeans of praise to 'the Benefactor'. Two of the 20th century's most prominent Dominican writers chose exile. The opposition leader, Juan Bosch, wrote polemics against Trujillo, historical studies and, most readable, two collections of short stories that revealed a formidable grasp of narrative technique. Probably the greatest of the country's poets, Pedro Mir, also lived and wrote abroad until the late 1960s, producing *Hay un país en el mundo* (There's a Country in the World, 1949), an epic poem that tells of an imaginary but recognizable country's history of suffering and exploitation. In 1978, Mir published *Cuando amaban las tierras comuneras* (When They Loved the Communal Lands), a powerful fictional critique of the US occupation and its expropriation of traditional communal land. The conservative Joaquín Balaguer who remained on the island, wrote poetry, historical fiction and a biography of Juan Pablo Duarte. With the assassination of Trujillo in 1961, the exiles were able to return and politically committed writing was again allowed. Authors such as Manuel del Cabral wrote incisively about the social turmoil of the 1960s in books like *La Isla ofendida* (1965), while Freddy Prestol Castillo's *El Masacre se pasa a pie* (1973) was a damning account of the 1937 massacre of Haitians ordered by Trujillo.

Curiously, the dictatorship itself, although stifling literary creativity for three decades, has inspired some of the country's most interesting recent writing. One of the country's most successful writers, Julia Alvarez, situates her *In the Time of the Butterflies* (1994) around the political assassination of the three Mirabal sisters by Trujillo's henchmen. The brutal methods and bizarre megalomania of the dictator have also caught the imagination of foreign writers, notably the Peruvian Mario Vargas Llosa, whose *La Fiesta del chivo* (The Feast of the Goat) was published in 2000 to great critical acclaim. Dramatizing the worst excesses of the Trujillo period and the build-up to the dictator's assassination, the novel caused unease and controversy in Santo Domingo, where memories are long. Alvarez, together with Junot Díaz, typifies the new generation of Dominican writers, who have been as much shaped by their experience of life in the USA as in their parents' homeland. Both write in English as easily as in Spanish, and Díaz in particular has mastered the tough street-wise vernacular of young Dominicanyorks, the distinctive community of migrant Dominicans in New York and other US cities. His collection of short stories, *Drown* (1996) received rapturous reviews for its unsentimental and sometimes shocking portrayal of alienation and cultural displacement in the Dominican diaspora. Julia Alvarez has also written about the tensions and contradictions experienced by those with double lives. *How the García Girls Lost Their Accents* (1991), looks at a Dominican family in New York and their relationship with *la isla*.

Music & dance The most popular dance is the merengue, which dominates the musical life of the Dominican Republic and has spread across the water with migrants to colonize New York as well. Merengue is believed to have developed in the mid-19th century as a local version of European dances for couples, such as *contredanse*. An Afro-Caribbean flavour was added with lively rhythms and lyrics to reflect social commentary. It was the music of the people, from cane-cutters to dock workers, and frowned upon by the upper classes but, with regional variants it survived as a sort of folk music. There would be four musicians, playing the *cuatro*, similar to a guitar, the *güira*, a cylindrical scraper of African origin but akin to the Indian gourd scraped with a forked stick, the *tambora*, a double-headed drum using male goatskin played with the hand on one head and female goatskin played with a stick on the other, and the *marimba*, a wooden box with plucked metal keys. Despite the regional variations, the merengue of the Cibao Valley around Santiago developed most strongly and became known as the *merengue típico*. In the 1920s, it was played with an accordion, introduced by the Germans, a *güira*, *tambora* and *marimba*, with the accordion being the most important. Over the years, other instruments have been added, such as the saxophone, horn or electric bass guitar. A merengue would have a short introduction, *paseo*, then move into the song, or merengue, followed by a call and response section, the *jaleo*. Although similar to some Cuban or other Latin music and dance, the steps of the merengue have always been simpler, with a basic two-step pattern, but at a fast tempo with a suggestive hip movement.

The other main music style you will find in the Dominican Republic is bachata, which also emerged from the peasant and shanty town dwellers. It was music for the soul, for the poor and downtrodden, the dispossessed farmers who were forced off the land in the 1960s and flooded into the urban slums with their guitar-based *canciones de amargue*, songs of bitterness. The traditional group had one or two guitars, maracas, bongo and *marimba*, with a solo male singer, who sang songs based on the Cuban *son*, Mexican *ranchera*, merengue and boleros. The songs expressed the frustrations of the newly-urban male, a *macho* without a cause, who was often unemployed and often dependent on a woman for his income. The sudden rise in popularity of bachata was principally due to Juan Luis Guerra, who experimented with the romantic, sentimental genre and sensitively created a poetry which appealed to everyone, particularly women. Most bachata songs are similar to boleros, with the guitar, the rhythm and the sentimentality, but faster than usual and with one singer rather than three.

There is a merengue festival in the last week of July and the first week of August, held on the Malecón in Santo Domingo. Puerto Plata holds its merengue festival in the first week of October and Sosúa has one the last week of September. Salsa is also very popular in dance halls and discos (every town, however small, has a discothèque).

People

About one million legal and illegal Dominican immigrants live in the USA, mostly in New York

African slaves began to arrive in Santo Domingo from the 1530s. Although the proportion of slaves in the colony never matched that of Saint-Domingue, blacks nevertheless formed an important part of the colonial population. As the indigenous Taíno inhabitants were exterminated within half a century of European colonization, African slaves and their descendants became the largest non-European group. From the mixing of Africans and Europeans emerged the coloured or mulatto population to which the majority of Dominicans nowadays belong. Successive governments tried to attract non-African settlers, especially after independence, when fears of Haitian territorial ambitions were at their highest and the 'whitening' of the population was deemed desirable. Some Canarian and Italian migrants took up the offer of government-assisted relocation schemes, while an important community from the Middle East, mostly Syrians but known generically as *turcos*, arrived to establish businesses. Another group of immigrants, known as *cocolos*, left the English-speaking Caribbean islands of Tortola, Anguilla and St Kitts to work in the Republic's sugar plantations. Their descendants still live around San Pedro de Macorís. Under Trujillo, there was even an attempt to settle Japanese farmers near the border with Haiti, presumably as a deterrent to would-be smugglers and rustlers. This racial policy is no longer on the agenda, but it shows how the country's leaders have traditionally viewed the nation as white, Hispanic and Christian.

Conventional demographic surveys suggest that about 15% of Dominicans are white, 15% black and 65% mixed-race or mulatto (the rest being of Middle Eastern or other origins). A whole vocabulary exists to describe skin colour and ethnic identity: most desirable, of course, is to be *blanco* (white), followed by *trigueño* (olive-skinned). Further down the hierarchy come *mulatto* and *moreno* (meaning dark or swarthy), and at the bottom is the term *negro*, sometimes used affectionately but more normally a mark of disapproval or even an insult. Perhaps the most idiosyncratic racial category is that of the *indio*. The island's indigenous Taíno population was effectively extinct only 50 years after the arrival of the first European colonists. Yet the term is used to describe non-white Dominicans, and many identity cards describe their bearers as

Dominican Republic

Indians, colour-coded as *oscuro* (dark), *quemado* (burnt), *canelo* (cinnamon) or *lavado* (washed). An *indio oscuro* may therefore be a dark-skinned individual of mixed ethnic background. There is a certain aspiration towards the Indian; this can be seen not only in the use of the original name for the island, Quisqueya (and Quisqueyanos), but in place names (San Pedro de Macorís, from the Macorix tribe) and in given family names (Guainorex, Anacaona, etc). Recent research into DNA in the Dominican Republic and Puerto Rico has shown that claims of Taíno ancestry are not fanciful and that much of the population does indeed carry Amerindian genes passed down by enslaved Taína women before full-blooded Indians were wiped out.

Afro-Caribbean religious beliefs have significant numbers of followers in the Dominican Republic. Mixing reconstructed Taíno rituals, Catholic saints and African divinities, believers worship archetypal lúas or gods, such as Anaísa, the goddess of love (based loosely on Santa Ana) or the Barón del Cementario (equivalent to the Christian San Elías), the guardian of the graveyard. Ceremonies involve music, dancing, trances and spirit possession, and often take place at what are thought to be holy Taíno sites or during rural village fiestas. Other well-known venues for *vodú dominicana* are the mostly black, inner-city barrios of Villa Mella and the western mountain town of San Juan de la Maguana. A connected phenomenon is the widespread Dominican interest in *brujería* or witchcraft. *Brujos* are thought to have supernatural powers, both benevolent and malevolent, and are consulted by a wide cross-section of people in search of cures for broken hearts, financial problems and the difficulties caused by *mal de ojo* (the evil eye). Market place stalls and so-called *botánicas* (shops selling religious paraphernalia of all sorts) testify to the country's fascination with spiritual and supernatural forces.

Geography

The western part of the Dominican Republic is dominated by four mountain ranges which run roughly northwest to southeast. The most impressive is the Cordillera Central, which rises to twin peaks of La Pelona and Pico Duarte, and at 3,082 m and 3,087 m are the highest mountains in the Caribbean. The eastern half of the country is flatter, bar the hills of the Cordillera Oriental which run roughly parallel to the northeast coast. There is a tropical limestone landscape in part of the Cordillera Oriental, to the south of Sabana de la Mar. The northern boundary of the Caribbean plate lies just north of Hispaniola. The whole island is an active seismic zone, and there have been eight major earthquakes since 1751, the most recent in 1953. The island is moving slowly east, while Cuba and the Bahamas are moving to the west; what is now Hispaniola was attached to southeastern Cuba around 20 million years ago. The mountain ranges of the western Dominican Republic are associated with strong faulting close to a slight irregularity in the plate boundary.

Puerto Rico

Introducing Puerto Rico

Puerto Rico may be part of the USA but its music and dance is a combination of both Spanish and African rhythms. The country, as a result, is a mixture of the very new and the very old. It exhibits an open American way of life yet retains much of the more formal Spanish influences. This is reflected in the architecture, not just the contrast between the colonial and the modern in urban areas but also in the countryside, where older buildings sit side by side with concrete schools and dwellings; it is found in the cuisine, a plethora of fast food restaurants together with local cooking which has its roots in a hybrid Caribbean culture; and it is found in the music, where rock and salsa are played in beach resorts but where, in the hilly interior, rustic songs of Puerto Rican folklore can still be heard. However, be warned: if you do not stray beyond the tourist areas on the coast, you will have a very one-sided experience of this paradoxical dependent territory.

Puerto Rico

Essentials

Before you travel

All non-US residents need a US visa, or a US visa waiver for participating countries. All **Documents** requirements are the same as for the USA.

Currency United States dollar. Locally, a dollar may be called a *peso*, 25 cents a *peseta*, 5 **Money** cents a *bellón* (but in Ponce a *bellón* is 10 cents and a *ficha* is 5 cents). Most international and US credit cards are accepted. **Exchange** Currency exchange at *Banco Popular*; *Caribbean Foreign Exchange*, 201B Tetuán, Old San Juan, T7228222, and at the airport; *Deak international* at the airport; *Scotia Bank* exchange only Canadian currency; *Western Union* for cable money transfer, Pueblo Supermarket, Old San Juan. **Banks** *Banco Popular*; *Banco de San Juan*; *Banco Mercantil de Puerto Rico*; and branches of US and foreign banks.

Tradewinds make the temperatures of 82-86°F bearable in the summer. Temperatures in the **Climate** winter drop to the range 70-79°F and the climate all the year round is very agreeable. Rain falls mainly May-Oct, with most precipitation Jul-Oct.

Getting there

From Europe *Condor* from Frankfurt; *Iberia* from Barcelona and Madrid; *US Air* from Lon- **Air** don Gatwick and Manchester via Philadelphia. **From Latin America** Most South and Central American countries are connected via Miami or Panama City, most Central American capital cities via Panama City (*Copa*). **From the Caribbean** Just about every island is connected with direct or indirect flights with *LIAT*, *American Eagle* and others. *Seaborne Airlines*, has a seaplane service from Piers 6-7 in Old San Juan to St Croix and St Thomas. **From the USA** A great many US cities are served by *American Airlines, Delta, Continental, US Air, United Airlines* and others. Lots of flights have connections at JFK and Miami.

Cruise ships call at San Juan and Ponce. *Ferries del Caribe* run a passenger and car (no hire cars) **Boat** ferry service to/from the Dominican Republic from Santo Domingo to Mayagüez (Tue, Thu, Sun, 2000, arrives 0800, returns Mon, Wed, Fri, same times) with a bus link across the island to San Juan (T8324800), see page 295. There is a weekend passenger launch on the *Caribe Cay* between Fajardo and St Thomas, 1¾ hr, Sat 0830, US$70 return, T8608809. **Ports of entry** Mayagüez, Ponce, Fajardo, San Juan (not Boquerón). **Boat documents** Clearance required from Customs, Immigration and Agriculture. Foreigners must meet same entry requirements as into USA (US$90 if you arrive without a visa). US vessels must pay a US$25 annual customs fee (a sticker). US citizens must clear into Puerto Rico when coming from USVI. Do not bring in fruit, vegetables or garbage into the USA/Puerto Rico. Boats and firearms must be registered after 60 days. **Marinas** There is a liveaboard community at Boquerón. Ponce is a good place to provision, with wholesale houses, *Sears*, *Walmart*, nearby. Fajardo is headquarters for marinas, boat supplies and haul-out. Puerto del Rey marina has 750 slips, transient rate US$1 per foot per day (includes water, electricity, cable TV); Palmas del Mar, 40 slips, also many houses on the water have space to rent with water and electricity. Small anchorage area has cleaner water than stagnant marina. Nothing nearby, car rental needed. **Anchorages**: Boquerón, La Parguera, Guánica, Ponce, Fajardo, Vieques, Culebra has many (see Bruce Van Sant's *Guide to the Spanish Virgin Islands*). Ponce Yacht Club (members) allows one night free to other Yacht Club members. Get **weather** from VHF weather, VI Radio or local AM station.

Touching down

There are airport limousines to a number of hotels. Set rates for *Taxi Turístico*: Zone 1, Luis **Airport** Muñoz Marín Airport to Isla Verde, US$8; Zone 2, airport to Condado/Miramar, US$12; Zone 3, **information** airport to Pier area in Old San Juan, US$16. Between and beyond the zones rates are metered.

Drivers prefer going to beach areas than old San Juan

Puerto Rico

▶ ## Tourist offices overseas

Canada, 41-43 Colbourne St, Suite 301, Toronto, Ontario, M5E 1E3, T416-3682680, F3685350.
France, Express Conseil, 5 bis, rue du Louvre, 75001 Paris, T331-44778800, F42600545.
Germany, Eifelstrasse 14a, 60529 Frankfurt, T49-69-350047, F350040.
Italy, Piazza Caiazzo 3, 20124 Milano, T39-0266-714403.
Spain, Calle Serrano, 1-2° izda, 28001, Madrid, T3491-4312128, 800-898920, F5775260.
UK, 8 Anarth Court, Oatlands Drive, Weybridge, Surrey KT13 9JQ, T44-(0)1932-253302.
USA, 666 5th Av, 15th floor, New York, NY 10103, T1-800-8667827, 212-5866262, F212-5861212; 901 Ponce de León Blvd, Suite 101, Coral Gables, Fl33134, T305-4459112, F4459450; 3575 W Cahuenga Blvd, Suite 405, Los Angeles, CA90068, T323-8745991, F8747257.
Venezuela, Piso 6 Oficina 65, Centro Profesion del Este Calle Villaflor, Sabana Grande Caracas 1050, Venezuela Oficina 619, Chuao, T58212 7613865, F7617929.

Airlines *ACES*, T800-8462237, www.aces.com.co; *Air Caraïbes*, T877-7721005, *Air St Thomas*, T800-5223084; *American Airlines* and *American Eagle*, T800-4337300; *American Trans Air*, T800-2252995; *COPA*, T800-3592672; *Continental*, T800-2310856; *Delta*, T800-2211212; *Iberia*, T800-7724642; *Isla Nena*, T877-8125144; *LIAT*, T7913838; *Northwest Airlines*, T800-3747747; *Seaborne Airlines*, T888-3598687; *United Airlines*, T800-2416522; *Vieques Air Link*, T888-9019247.

Tourist information **Local tourist offices** The *Puerto Rico Tourism Company*, San Juan 00902-3960, www.prtourism.com, www.gotopuertorico.com publishes lots of brochures and booklets including *Travel and Sports Planner*, www.travelandsports.com, and *Qué Pasa!* which comes out every 2 months and has a useful tourist directory. Information centres also at the international airport, (T7911014, next to the *Condado Plaza Hotel*, T7212400 (ext 2280); *La Casita*, near Pier One, Old San Juan, T7221709, open Mon-Wed 0830-2000, Thu, Fri 0830-1730, Sat, Sun 0900-2000; Rafael Hernández Airport, Aguadilla, T8903315; Citibank Building, 53 McKinley East, facing plaza, Mayagüez, T8315220; *Casa Armstrong-Proventud*, Plaza Las Delicias, Ponce, T8405695.

Regional tourist offices Adjuntas, T8292590; Añasco, T8263100 ext 272; Bayamón, T7988191; Cabo Rojo, T8517015; Camuy, T8982240; Culebra, T7423291; Dorado, T796-5740/1030; Fajardo, T8634013; Guanica, T8212777; Jayuya, T8285010; Luquillo, T8892851; Naguabo, T8740389; Rincón, T8235024; Vieques, T7415000. Out in the country, tourist information can be obtained from the town halls, usually found on the main plaza. Hours are usually Mon-Fri, 0800-1200, 1300-1430.

Maps The *Rand McNally* road map is recommended; the *Gousha* road map is sold at Texaco stations. The tourist office distributes an *Official Transportation Map* with town maps of San Juan, Caguas, Ponce, Mayagüez, Aguadilla and Arecibo.

Where to stay

The summer season runs from 16 Apr to 14 Dec and is somewhat cheaper than the winter season. An 11% tax is charged on the room rate in hotels with casinos, 9% in those without casinos, 7% in *paradores*. There are many large, resort hotels managed by international chains but smaller, more intimate hotels and guesthouses can be found around the island. Cheap hotels are very hard to find, there is nothing under about US$45 double, and single rates are often non-existent. Campsites (see below) are the only budget option, but you will probably need a hired car to reach them, which will increase the cost of your holiday.

There are 18 **Paradores Puertorriqueños** to put you up while touring, some old, most new, some quiet and peaceful (for example *Coamo, Gripiñas, Juanita, Casa Grande*), some used by local families for boisterous entertainment, with prices at US$55-100. The majority are to the west of San Juan; for reservations T7212884 or from the USA T1-800-4430266. Many *paradores* are not what the average traveller wants, so do some research first. They are

Touching down

◀

Business hours Banks: 0830-1430, some have extended hours. **Shops**: mostly Mon-Sat 0900-2100, Sun 1100-1700.
Currency US dollar.
Emergency numbers Tourist Zone Police, Vieques St, Condado, T7220738, 7245210, can help you settle problems with taxis. Emergency T911.
Language Spanish is the first language with less than 30% of the population speaking English fluently.
Official time GMT minus 4 hrs.
Public holidays Everything is usually closed on public holidays. These are: New Year's Day, Three Kings' Day (6 Jan), De Hostos' Birthday (11 Jan), Washington's Birthday (22 Feb), Emancipation Day (22 Mar), Good Fri, José de Diego's Birthday (16 Apr), Memorial Day (30 May), St John the Baptist (24 Jun), Independence Day (4 Jul), Muñoz Rivera's Birthday (17 Jul), Constitution Day (25 Jul), Dr José Celso Barbosa's Birthday (27 Jul), Labour Day (1 Sep), Columbus Day (12 Oct), Veterans' Day (11 Nov), Discovery of Puerto Rico (19 Nov), Thanksgiving Day (25 Nov), Christmas Day.

Safety We have received several warnings from travellers. Of all crimes 65% are related to drugs trafficking. La Perla is known as San Juan's most dangerous slum and the end of Calle Tanca should be avoided as it is a favourite drinking and drug-dealing area for residents. Female tourists should avoid the Condado beach areas at night and all areas of San Juan can be dangerous after dark. Take precautions against theft from your person and your car, wherever you are on the island. Hiking on mainland beaches is not a good idea; never stay on a beach if you are alone, beautiful areas such as Carite or Route186 above El Verde look like great hiking spots but do not always attract people with good intentions. Safety in numbers. Take advice locally.
Tipping Service is usually included in the bill, but where no fixed service charge is included, it is recommended that 15-20% is given to waiters, taxi drivers, etc.
Voltage US system, 110 volts AC.
Weights and measures Imperial.

Puerto Rico

convenient places to stay when on the road, but lack the old charm of their Spanish counterparts. The cheapest lodging is in motels, but these are generally use by 'couples'.

Camping is permitted in the forest reserves; you usually have to get a permit in advance (see below) although often they are available at the sites themselves. Camping is also allowed on some of the public beaches. Government agencies expect everyone to arrive or call before 1500. You can take *públicos* to some of the camping places, but with difficulty, car rental is advised.

Camping
Forest reserves campsites are safer than beach ones; large groups are recommended

The Government agency **Fomento Recreativo** (T722-1551 for reservations, PO Box 9022089, San Juan, PR 00904-2089) administers the following campgrounds and cabins: Luquillo Beach, Seven Seas (Fajardo), Punta Guilarte (Arroyo), Monte del Estado (Maricao), Boquerón, Tres Hermanos (Anasco), Rincón. 2-bedroom cabins and villas are offered on 5 of their beaches, villas are newer and nicer. The **Negociado del Servicio Forestal** (part of the Departamento de Recursos Naturales y Ambientales – DRNA) administers 8 campgrounds and cabins and Mona Island, PO Box 9066600, Puerta de Tierra, San Juan, Puerto Rico 00906-6600, T7243724, F7215984, www.drnapr.com You need a permit and reservation, fee US$4 per person per night (cabins in Guilarte US$20), easiest to go to their office at Club Náutico by the marina at the Dos Hermanos bridges on the way to Old San Juan. They will also help you plan an itinerary. Permits and changes to reservations can be made at regional offices Their camp grounds are: Carite Forest, Toro Negro Forest Reserve, Guilarte Route 131 and 518, Coamo Hot Springs, Lago Luchetti, Susua Dry Forest, Guánica Forest, Guajataca Forest, Río Abajo Forest, Cambalache Beach. El Yunque rain forest is administered by the **US Forest Service**, T8881880, www.fs.fed.us and ask for camping information, or get free permit at El Portal, Route 191, north side, before 1600. The **Autoridad de Conservación y Desarrollo de Culebra** (ACC) administers the Flamenco Beach campgrounds on Culebra, PO Box 217, Culebra, PR 00775, T7420700, US$10 per tent per night, they often accept walk-in reservations in winter but in summer, especially at weekends, it is like a zoo.

Getting around

Air Several local airlines operate services within Puerto Rico, including *American Eagle* and *Vieques Air Link*, and have offices either at the **Luis Muñoz Marín International Airport**, or the **Isla Grande** Airport. There are 3 daily *American Eagle* flights between San Juan and Ponce and several to Mayagüez. Some charter or interisland flights leave from the Isla Grande Airport.

Bus
City buses run to a 30- or 45-minute schedule and cost US$0.25. Many don't operate after 2200

Bus stops are marked *Parada*, or *Parada de guaguas*. From the terminal near Plazoleta del Puerto in Old San Juan, **B21 goes along the upper road along the ocean (near** *Caribe Hilton*) to Condado (Condado Plaza, El Canario) then up Avenida de Diego to stop 18 on Ponce de León, and then to Plaza las Américas Shopping Mall. **A5 goes along to Ponce de León and then down Avenida de Diego to Isla Verde** (*El San Juan, Ritz Carlton*, etc) and to Iturregui terminal. To get to the airport by bus from Old San Juan is complicated. Take **A5 bus to Isla Verde terminal, then C45 or B40 to the airport. From Condado take B21 to Avenida de Diego, then A5, then as above. Metrobus 1 (US$0.50) goes from Old San Juan along the upper road along the ocean to Avenida Ponce de León and then to Río Piedras. Metrobus E goes to Río Piedras via the express way to Hato Rey. Long-distance buses run to all the major towns, leaving from their own bus stations in San Juan.**

Car
The best and easiest form of transport if you want to see the island; public transport is not always easy and finishes early

There are many car rental agencies, including at the airport: *Hertz*, T800-6543131, www.hertz.com; *Budget*, T800-5270700, www.budget.com; *AAA*, T7912609, www.aaacar rental pr.com; *Leaseway*, T800-4682647, www.leaswaypr.com. *Target*, T7281447, www.targetrentacar.com), not at airport, among the cheapest, will negotiate rates, open Mon-Sat 0900-1900, Sun 0800-1700. *Charlie's Rental*, T800-2891227, www.charliecars.com, in Condado and Isla Verde among the cheapest, 24-hour service. *L & M*, T800-6660807, www.lmcarrental.com, free pick-up, make sure you get it even for day hire, open daily 0600-2400. For the less mobile, *Wheelchair Getaway*, T7264023, 800-8688028, has vehicles which can accommodate a wheelchair, daily 0800-2200. A small car may be hired for as little as US$25 (not including collision damage waiver, US$12.50, insurance is sometimes covered by your credit card) for 24 hr, unlimited mileage (national driving licence preferred to international licence), but rates vary according to company and demand.

A good map is essential because there are few signs to places, but frequent indications of Route numbers and intersections. Avoid driving in the San Juan metropolitan area as traffic can be very heavy. Car theft and burglar damage is a major problem in the San Juan area. Make sure you use all the security devices given you by the rental company. Many people actually recommend that you do not stop at red lights after 2200, because of hold-ups; just pause, look and go. Best not to drive at night at all; lock car doors.

Taxi All taxis are metered, charge US$1 for initial charge and US$0.10 for every additional 1/3 mile; US$0.50 for each suitcase; US$5 reservation charge, surcharge 2200-0600 US$1. Minimum fee US$3. Taxi drivers sometimes try to ask more from tourists, so beware, insist that the meter is used, and avoid picking up a taxi anywhere near a cruise ship. If they refuse, tell them you will call Puerto Rico Tourist Zone Police, T7220738, or the Public Service Commission, T7515050, ext 253. They can revoke a taxi licence. White tourist taxis with a logo on the side offer fixed rates to and from tourist sites, for example airport, San Juan Pier, but outside those areas they are metered. **Zone 4**, Piers to Old San Juan, US$6; **Zone 5**, Piers to Puerta de Tierra, US$8; **Zone 6**, Piers to Condado/Miramar, US$10; **Zone 7**, Piers to Isla Verde, US$16.

Be prepared to wait a couple of hours for the car to fill up

Públicos There are also shared taxis, usually *Ford* minibuses (*carros públicos*) which have yellow number plates with the letters P or PD at the end and run to most parts of the island from one main plaza to the next. They usually carry about 10 people and are not particularly comfortable. The Río Piedras *terminal de públicos* handles all departures to the east. Many *públicos* for the west leave from *puntos* near parada 18 in Santurce. Also some leave from the main post office and others collect at the airport; elsewhere, ask around for the terminal. They do not usually operate after about 1600 and some connections do not operate after 1500, for example Río Piedras-Fajardo. They are also very scarce on Sun and public holidays. *Público* to Caguas costs US$1.25; Río Piedras-Fajardo 1½ hr (US$3); to Ponce takes 2 hrs (US$6-7). A service referred to as *línea* will pick up and drop off passengers where they wish. They operate between San Juan, and most towns and cities at a fixed rate. They can be found in the phone book under *Líneas de Carros*.

A 17.2-km urban rail service has been constructed in San Juan and trains are supposed to start running from Santurce to Bayamón in late 2003.

Train

Keeping in touch

Inside the post office in Hato Rey, on Avenida Roosevelt is a separate counter for sales of special tourist stamps. In Old San Juan, the post office is on Cruz and Fortaleza. Stamps may be bought at hotels and the airport. *Poste restante* is called General Delivery, letters are held for 9 days.

Post
www.usps.com

Numbers with area code 800, 888, 877 or 866 are toll free from Puerto Rico or the USA. Most hotel systems are compatible with dial-up modems and there are internet cafés in San Juan.

    Local calls from coin-operated booths cost US$0.10, or US$0.25 from a private pay phone, but from one city to another on the island costs more (for example US$1.25 Ponce-San Juan). Local calls from hotel rooms cost US$2.60 and often a charge is made even if there is no connection. Payphones now charge a fee of US$0.25, either deducted from your prepaid card or with a coin. The cheapest way to phone abroad is from *Phone Home*, 257 Recinto Sur, Old San Juan, T7215431, F7215497, opposite the post office by Pier 1, US$0.36 per min to the USA, discounts on all other calls abroad, no 3-min minimum charge, faxes also sent and received. Overseas calls can be made from the *AT&T* office at Parada 11, Avenida Ponce de León 850, Miramar (opposite *Hotel Excelsior*, bus T1 passes outside, a chaotic place), from an office next to the Museo del Mar on Pier One, and from the airport. 3 mins to New York, US$1.50 and to the UK, US$3. For Canada Direct, dial 1-800-4967123 to get through to a Canadian operator.

Telephone & internet
IDD code: 787
To call outside San Juan from the metropolitan area dial 1-787 and then the number

Newspapers *San Juan Star* is the only daily English paper. There are 2 Spanish daily papers of note, *El Vocero* and *El Nuevo Día*. **Radio** There are 7 radio stations: WDAC-FM, 105.7FM Alfa Rock 106; WKAQ-FM, 104.7FM KQ105; WIOA-FM 99.9FM Cadena Estereotempo; WMEG-FM, 106.9FM La Mega Estación; WDOY-FM, 96.5FM Y-96; WOYE-FM, 94.7FM Cosmos 94; WOSO-AM, 1030AM Radio Woso.

Media

Puerto Rico

Food and drink

Good local dishes are the mixed stew *asopao*, (chicken, seafood, etc). *Mofongo*, mashed plantain with garlic served instead of rice, is very filling. *Mofongo relleno* is the *mofongo* used as a crust around a seafood stew. *Sancocho* is a beef stew with various root vegetables, starchy but tasty. *Empanadillas* are similar to South American *empanadas* but with a thinner dough and filled with fish or meat. *Pasteles* are yucca, peas, meat, usually pork, wrapped in a banana leaf and boiled. *Tostones* are fried banana slices. Rice is served with many dishes; *arroz con habichuelas* (rice with red kidney beans) is a standard side dish. *Provisiones* are root vegetables and are worth trying. *Comida criolla* means 'food of the island', *criollo* refers to anything 'native'. Some local fruit names: *china* is orange, *parcha* passionfruit, *guanábana* soursop, *toronja* grapefruit; juices are made of all these, as well as guava, tamarind and mixtures. *Papaya* in a restaurant may not be fresh fruit, but *dulce de papaya* (candied), served with cheese.

Mesones Gastronómicos, a network of 42 restaurants outside San Juan, serve Puerto Rican dishes

Local beers are *Medalla* (a light beer), *Gold Label* (a premium beer) and *Indio* (a dark beer); a number of US brands and *Heineken* are brewed under licence. Rums include *Don Q*, the local favourite, *Palo Viejo*, *Ron Llave* and the world-famous *Bacardi* (not so highly regarded by puertorriqueños). *Ron Barrilito*, a small distillery, has a very good reputation. *Maví* is a drink fermented from the bark of a tree and sold in many snack-bars. Home-grown Puerto Rican coffee is very good.

Drink

Shopping

Many of the tourist shops in the old city sell Andean goods

Puerto Rico is a large producer of rum, with many different types (see above). Hand made cigars can be found in Old San Juan and Puerta de Tierra. There is a place in the bus station complex in San Juan where cigars are rolled using Dominican leaf, which is better than local leaf. Shopping malls include *Plaza las Américas* in Hato Rey (the largest in the Caribbean with 300 stores, 21 cinemas, restaurants and other services, open 0900-2100 Mon-Sat, 1100-1700 Sun), others include *Plaza Carolina* in Carolina, *Río Hondo* in Levittown, *Plaza del Carmen* in Caguas and *Mayagüez Mall* in Mayagüez. There are many souvenir shops in Old San Juan. Local artesanías include wooden carvings, musical instruments, lace, ceramics (especially model house fronts, for example from *La Casa de Las Casitas*, Cristo 250), hammocks, masks and basketwork. It is more interesting to visit the workshops around Puerto Rico. Contact the *Centro de Artes Populares*, T7246250, or the *Tourism Company Artisan Office*, T7212891, for details of the 681 artisans on the list.

Flora and fauna

Although less than 1% of the island is virgin forest, there are several forest reserves designed to protect plants and wildlife. At the highest altitude you find dwarf cloud forest, with palms, ferns and epiphytes. On exposed ridges it has a windswept appearance. Below the dwarf forest is the rainforest and below that the subtropical wet forest, with open-crowned trees and canopy trees such as *Cyrilla racemiflora*, which is large with reddish bark. Classifications below this include the lower wet forest (Tabanuco) and the subtropical moist forest zone, which covers most of Puerto Rico, and dry forest, found along the south coast and the eastern tip of the island.

In **El Yunque Tropical Rain Forest** (called The Caribbean National Forest) there are an estimated 240 types of tree (26 indigenous), and many other plants, such as tiny wild orchids, bamboo trees and giant ferns. The total area is 11,270 ha and 75% of Puerto Rico's virgin forest is here. Several marked paths (quite easy, you could walk 2-3 in a day, no guide needed), recreational areas and information areas have been set up. It is also home to the Puerto Rican parrot, but there are only 30 left. The whole forest is a bird sanctuary. (*Las aves*

Puerto Rico

○ **Forests**	4 Carite / Guavate	8 El Yunque	12 Jobos
1 Aguirre	5 Casa Pueblo	9 Guajataca	13 Maricao
2 Boquerón	6 Ceiba	10 Guánica	14 Piñones
3 Cambalache	7 Cerrillos	11 Guilarte	15 Río Abajo

0 km   10
0 miles   10

de Puerto Rico, by Virgilio Biaggi, University of Puerto Rico, 1983, US$12.95, and Herbert Raffaele's *Guide to the Birds of Puerto Rico and the Virgin Islands* is recommended.)

Mangroves are protected in **Aguirre Forest**, on the south coast near Salinas, at the Jobos Bay National Estuarine Research Reserve, at the west end of Jobos Bay from Aguirre, and at Piñones Forest, east of San Juan. Unlike the north coast mangroves, those on the south coast tend to die behind the outer fringe because not enough water is received to wash away the salt. This leaves areas of mud and skeletal trees which, at times of spring tide, flood and are home to many birds. In winter, many ducks stop on their migration routes at Jobos. Also at **Jobos Bay**, manatees and turtles can be seen. A short boardwalk runs into the mangroves at Jobos, while at Aguirre a man runs catamaran trips to the offshore cays, and there are some good fish restaurants; take Route 7710. For Jobos Bay take Route 703, to Las Mareas de Salinas (marked Mar Negro on some maps). Before going to Jobos, contact the office at Jobos, Box 1170, Guayama, Puerto Rico 00655, T8640105, or 7248774 in San Juan.

The largest number of bird species can be found at the 655-ha **Guánica Forest**, west of Ponce, which is home to 700 plant species of which 48 are endangered and 16 exist nowhere else. Guánica's dry forest vegetation is unique and the forest has been declared an International Biosphere Reserve by UNESCO. There are 10 marked trails through the forest, but it may be advisable to contact the wardens for directions before wandering off. It can be hot in the middle of the day so don't be too ambitious in which trail you choose. The Ballena Trail is quite short and you will see lizards, snakes, birds and a 700-year old guayacán tree, very gnarled and not as big as you might expect. If you want to head for the beach, Playa de Ventanas is within the Reserve. ■ *Daily 0900-1700. No admission charge; wear protective clothing and take drinking water. T7231770.* The **Punta Ballena Reserve** is next to the Guánica Forest and included in the Biosphere Reserve because of coastal ecosystem. It contains mangrove forest, manatees, nesting sites for hawksbill turtles, and crested toads. Beach access off Route 333.

The Río Camuy runs underground for part of its course, forming the third largest subterranean river in the world. Near Lares, on Route 129, Km 9.8, the **Río Camuy Cave Park** has been established by the Administración de Terrenos (PO Box 3767, San Juan, T8983100), where visitors are guided through 1 cave and 2 sinkholes. Wed to Sun, and holidays 0830-1600, last trip 1545, US$10 for adults, U$S7 for children, highly recommended, very

Puerto Rico has some of the most important caves in the western hemisphere

Puerto Rico

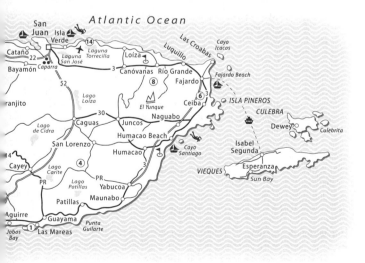

16 Susua
17 Toro Negro
18 Vega   **PR** Panoramic Route

easy, but entry is limited. The trip takes 2 hrs and you may have to wait an hour beforehand, so allow plenty of time. There are fine examples of stalactites, stalagmites and, of course, plenty of bats. Keen photographers should bring a tripod for excellent photo opportunities. A recently opened part of the Río Camuy cave system is named Cathedral Cave Wild Adventure. You have to rappel down 150 ft into a vaulted cave, where there are lots of pre-Columbian petroglyphs, then exit through interlinked caves to the valley floor before hiking back to the rim of the canyon. Advance reservations essential as the trip is organized only twice a week and depends on the weather. Several caving tour specialists can take you to a different and undeveloped part of the cave system. Offered in three degrees of difficulty, they explore underground caves, pre-Columbian petroglyphs, rivers and sinkholes. No prior knowledge needed but you need to be in good physical shape as you will have to travel on a hot-line, rappel and body raft, about US$85 for a day's adventure starting at dawn, returning to San Juan by 1800. See page 381 for tour agents. Also close is the privately owned **Cueva de Camuy**, Route 486, Km 1.1; much smaller and less interesting, with guided tours, the area also has a swimming pool and waterslide, amusements, café, ponies, go-karts, entertainments. ■ *Daily 0900-1700 (till 2000 Sun). US$1, children US$0.50*. Nearby is **Cueva del Infierno**, to which 2-3 hr tours can be arranged by phoning 8982723. About 2,000 caves have been discovered; in them live 13 species of bat (but not in every cave), the *coquí* (tiny frog), crickets, an arachnid called the *guavá*, and other species. Contact the Speleological Society of Puerto Rico (Sepri) for further details.

Other forest reserves, some of which are mentioned below are Aguirre, T8640105, Boquerón, T8517260, Cambalache, T8811004, Carite, T7474545, Casa Pueblo Forest T8524440, Ceiba, T8524440, Cerrillos, T7243724, Guánicam, T8215706, Guajataca in the northeast, T8721045, Guilarte, T8295767, Maricao, T7243724, Mona Island, T7243724, Piñones, T7917750, Río Abajo, T8806557, Susúa, T7243724, Toro Negro, T8673040, Vega, T8332240, these can also be contacted through the Central Office in San Juan, T7243724, or at prforests@hotmail.com

Diving and marine life

The shallow waters are good for snorkelling and while a boat is needed to reach deeper water for most scuba diving, divers can walk in at Isabela. Visibility is not as good as in some other islands because of the large number of rivers flowing out to the sea, but is generally around 70 ft. However, an advantage is that the freshwater attracts a large number of fish. Manatees can occasionally be seen and humpback whales migrate through Puerto Rican waters in the autumn.

Dive centres There are many companies all round the island offering boat dives, equipment rental and diving instruction, including *Caribbean School of Aquatics*, diving out of San Juan and Fajardo, T7286606, NAUI, PADI, Greg Korwek has 40 years' experience here, leader in safety standards, knows every reef; *Caribe Aquatic Adventures*, T7241882, based in San Juan, local diving and snorkelling excursions as well as to Fajardo. Diving also at some of the larger hotels. Companies in San Juan and to the east also dive Culebra and Vieques, but there are dive shops on those islands if you want to avoid long boat rides. Check how many divers are taken on the boats, some companies cater for small groups of 6-7 divers, but several of the larger operations take out parties of 40 or 80. Look for instructor's certificate, motor boat operator's licence and coast guard inspection sticker on the boat. If any are missing you will not be insured. The inspection sticker on the boat specifies how many paying passengers are allowed.

Snorkelling
Always be aware of jet skis and other motorized craft: they will be oblivious of you

Luquillo Beach has 2 snorkelling spots: in town, off the point between the surfers' beach, **La Pared** and **Blue Beach** (the beach in front of the tallest condos), and at the point of the Balneario Luquillo, past the 'no swimming' signs (beware of current, and jet skis at weekends). **Seven Seas Beach** has some good snorkelling right off the beach and there are reefs to the east. *Caribe Kayak Tours & More*, near Fajardo, specialize in small groups for snorkelling and kayaking (ocean and Lagoon) starting from Seven Seas Beach, US$40, 4½ hr, includes lunch and equipment, T8897734. Many dive shops will also take you snorkelling.

Beaches and watersports

Swimming from most beaches is safe; the best beaches near San Juan are those at **Isla Verde** in front of the main hotels; **Luquillo** to the east of San Juan is less crowded and has a fine-sand beach from where there are good views of El Yunque (controlled car parking, US$2 per car all day, if arriving by *público* from San Juan, ask to get off at Balneario Luquillo, which is 1 km west of the town). There are showers, toilets and lifeguards, food kiosks and souvenir shops, it is peaceful during the week but noisy at weekends. The north coast Atlantic sea is rougher than the east and south waters, particularly in winter; some beaches are semi-deserted. There are 13 *balneario* beaches round the island where lockers, showers and parking places are provided for a small fee. Some have cabins, tent sites or trailer sites. *Balnearios* are open Tue-Sun 0900-1700 in winter and 0800-1700 in summer. Puerto Rico is aiming for the award of Blue Flag status for the beaches of Carolina, Escambron, Luquillo and Flamenco.

Surfing & windsurfing

The most popular beaches for surfing are the **Pine Beach Grove** in Isla Verde (San Juan), **Jobos** (near Isabela in the northeast, not the south coast bay), **La Pared** in Luquillo, officially listed as dangerous for swimming but used for surfing tournaments, **Surfer** and **Wilderness** beaches in the former Ramey Field air base at Punta Borinquén, north of Aguadilla and **Punta Higuero**, Route 413 between Aguadilla and Rincón on the west coast. Several international surfing competitions have been held at Surfer and Wilderness.

The **Condado lagoon** is calm with steady winds and is popular for windsurfing, as is **Boquerón Bay**, off Isla Verde beach, and **Ocean Park beach**. Only experts can cope with conditions on the northeast shore near Aguadilla: **Jobos**, **Wilderness** and **Surfer** beaches, where the winds are good and the waves break with excellent shape. **Rincón** is the same. **La Parguera** is great for slalom conditions, a great sail to Cayo Enrique on waters with lots of wind.

Day sails

Puerto Rico's coastline is protected in many places by coral reefs and cays which are fun to visit and explore. **La Cordillera** is a nature reserve of cays and rocks off the northeast tip of Puerto Rico, including Icacos, Diablo, Ratones and Las Cucarachas, which have a rich coral reef, clear water and sandy beaches. There is an abandoned limestone quarry on the south side of Icacos. The cays are easily accessible by boat from Las Croabas or Fajardo. There are many sailboat excursions from Fajardo with snorkelling, lunch and drinks, usually US$55 per person on catamarans (also known as cattlemarans taking 49 people), more on the monohulls. Also sailboats from Marina del Rey, San Juan and **La Parguera**.

Sailing

There are 4 marinas at **Fajardo, Puerto del Rey**, the **Club Náutico** at Miramar and another at **Boca de Cangrejos** in Isla Verde (both in San Juan) and one at the *Palmas del Mar Resort* near Humacao. There is a marina for fishing boats at **Arecibo**. Sailing is popular, with winds of about 10 15 knots all year round. Craft of all sizes are available for hire. There are several racing tournaments. Power boats appeal to the Puerto Rican spirit and there are a lot of races, held mostly off the west coast from Mayagüez Bay to Boquerón Bay. A huge crowd collects for the Caribbean Offshore Race, with professionals and celebrities participating.

Fishing

Deep-sea fishing is popular and more than 30 world records have been broken in Puerto Rican waters, where blue and white marlin, sailfish, wahoo, dolphin, mackerel and tarpon, to mention a few, are a challenge to the angler. An international bill fish competition is held in Aug at the Club Náutico de San Juan (T7220177), one of the biggest tournaments in the Caribbean and the longest consecutively held big game fishing tournament in the world. Fishing boat charters are available: for example *Mike Benítez Fishing Charters Inc*, at the Club Náutico de San Juan, T7232292 (till 2100), 7246265 (till 1700), www.mikebenitezfishing.com, US$490 per half day, US$850 full day. Also *Caribbean Outfitters*, T3968346, www.fishingin puertorico.com Others around the island are mentioned in the text below. Contact the Department of Natural Resources, T7248774, ext 445 for details.

Other sports

There are 19 **golf** courses around the island, many of which are professionally designed championship courses. The *Hyatt Cerromar* and *Hyatt Dorado* hotels in Dorado have 4 excellent

Puerto Rico

36-hole championship golf courses, T7968915, www.hyatt.com; among the 18-hole courses, *Berwind Country Club* (T8763056) accepts non-members on Tue, Thu and Fri, *Palmas del Mar* (Humacao, T2852221, www.palmasdelmar.com), **Westin Riomar** (Río Grande, T8886000), and Punta Borinquén (Aguadilla, 9 holes, T8902987) all have golf pros and are open to the public. Over 100 **tennis** courts are available, mostly in the larger hotels. There are also 17 lit public courts in San Juan's Central Park, open daily, with tennis pro, T7221646. The *Palmas del Mar* resort, at Humacao, has 20 courts. **Cockfighting** season is from 1 Nov-31 Aug and is held at the new, a/c *Coliseo Gallístico* in Isla Verde, near the *Holiday Inn* (Route 37, Km 1.5) on Sat, 1300-1900, T7911557. Admission from US$4-10. **Horse racing** at *El Comandante*, Route 3, Km 15.3, T8762450, www.elcomandante.com Canóvanas is one of the hemisphere's most beautiful race courses. Races are held all the year round (Wed, Fri, Sun and holidays, 1415-1730). Wed is Ladies' Day. Children under 12 not admitted. **Riding** is a good way to see the island. Puerto Rico also prides itself on its paso fino horses. There are over 7,000 registered paso fino horses on the island and several horse shows are held. The 2 best known are the **Dulce Sueño Fair**, Guayama, the first weekend in Mar, and the **Fiesta La Candelaria**, Manatí, the first weekend in Feb. At *Palmas del Mar*, Humacao, there is an equestrian centre T8528888 with beach rides and riding and jumping lessons. *Tropical Trails Rides*, Route 4466, Km 1.8, Isabela, beach, forest and cliff trails, Craig Barker has 20 beautiful paso fino horses, about 1½ hr west of San Juan, US$35 for 2 hrs, T8729256, www.home.coqui.net/barker At the *El Conquistador Resort* complex, T8631000, ask for Richard and the ferry to the horses on Isla Palominos. **Polo** is popular and the *Ingenio Polo Club* hosts the *Rolex Polo Cup* on its 25-acre grounds by the Loiza River in Mar.

Popular **spectator sports** are boxing and baseball (at professional level, also a winter league at San Juan stadium, US$4 for a general seat, US$5 box seat, Tue is Ladies' Night), basketball, volleyball and beach volleyball.

Holidays and festivals

Festivals
There is a festival somewhere every week in Puerto Rico

Everything is usually closed on public holidays. One of the most important is **24 Jun**, though in fact the capital grinds to a halt the previous afternoon and everyone heads for the beach. Here there is loud *salsa* music and barbecues until midnight when everyone walks backwards into the sea to greet the Baptist and ensure good fortune. *Día de la Constitución*, **25 Jul**, takes place at a weekend and it is almost impossible to get a hotel room. Reserve in advance. Every town/city has local holidays for *crop-over festivals* (pineapple, tobacco, sugar cane, etc) and for celebration of the town's saint. These festivals can be great fun, especially the Carnival in Mayagüez late **May**. For lovers of classical music, there is the annual *Casals Festival* in **Jun**, which brings orchestras from all over the world for a couple of weeks of concerts at the Luis A Ferré Performing Arts Center. The festival was founded in 1957 by Pablo Casals, who created the Puerto Rican Symphony Orchestra and the Musical Conservatory. Tickets range from US$20-40, with a 50% discount for senior citizens, while children under 12 are free if accompanied by an adult, T7217727 for information, www.artes-musicales.com Another annual music festival in **May/Jun** is the *Puerto Rico Heineken JazzFest*, held in the open-air Tito Puente Amphitheatre, T2779200, www.prheinekenjazz.com Founded in 1990, this also attracts international artists in Latin and contemporary jazz.

Health

See also Health, page 29

'La monga' is a common, flu-like illness, nothing serious, it goes away after a few days. Avoid swimming in rivers; bilharzia may be present. There has been dengue fever, so take care not to get bitten by mosquitoes; the northeast coast is particularly risky.

Puerto Rico

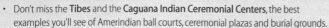

Things to do in Puerto Rico

- Don't miss the **Tibes** and the **Caguana Indian Ceremonial Centers**, the best examples you'll see of Amerindian ball courts, ceremonial plazas and burial grounds.
- Get back to nature on **Mona Island** with huge iguanas and sea birds, once home to Taínos and then pirates.
- Head underground to explore the caves, sinkholes and underground **Río Camuy**, where you can find bats and pre-Columbian petroglyphs as you travel on a hot-line, rappel and body raft.
- For after dark-entertainment visit **Phosphorescent Bay** in Vieques Island.
- Chill out on beautiful **Flamenco Beach** on the island of Culebra, where the water is a clear turquoise and the sand pristine white.

San Juan

Founded in 1510, San Juan, the capital, spreads several kilometres along the north coast and also inland. The nucleus is Old San Juan, the old walled city on a tongue of land between the Atlantic and San Juan bay. It has a great deal of charm and character, a living museum, lovingly restored. The narrow streets of Old San Juan, some paved with small grey-blue cobblestones which were brought over as ships' ballast, are lined with colonial churches, houses and mansions, in a very good state of repair and all painted different pastel colours. Although the old city is lovely, the rest of San Juan is modern, sprawling, without a semblance of planning and devoid of attractive features. The beach resorts are massive, high rise, expensive and international in character.

IDD code: 787
Colour map 2, grid B5
Population:
about 1 million

Ins and outs

Getting a taxi from the airport is your best bet; buses from the airport to San Juan and back are complicated. There is a despatch desk for *públicos* at the airport. See also page 365. **Getting there**

Small yellow buses, or trolleys, run around the old city all day 0600-2200, free, *paradas* (stops) are marked. They start from La Puntilla and Covadonga public car parks. There is also a trolley service in the Isla Verde beach area from Punta Las Marías. There is a city bus (*guagua*) service with a fixed charge of US$0.25 for standard route, US$0.50 for longer. They have special routes, sometimes against the normal direction of traffic, in which case the bus lanes are marked by yellow and white lines. Bus stops are have white and orange signs or yellow and black notices on lampposts '*Parada*'. Up until the 1950s tramcars ran between Río Piedras and Old San Juan along Avs Ponce de León and Fernández Juncos. To this day directions are given by *Paradas*, or tram stops, so you have to find out where each one is. **Getting around**

Sights

Some of the restored and interesting buildings to visit include **La Fortaleza**, the Governor's Palace, built between 1533 and 1540 as a fortress against Carib attacks but greatly expanded in the 19th century. It is believed to be the oldest executive residence in continuous use in the Western Hemisphere. Access to the official areas is not permitted. ■ *Mon-Fri 0900-1600. Guided tours in English on the hour, in Spanish every 30 mins. T7217000 ext 2211.* The **cathedral** was built in the 16th century but extensively restored in the 19th and 20th. The body of Juan Ponce de León rests in a marble tomb. ■ *Daily 0630-1700.* The tiny **Cristo Chapel** with its silver altar, was built after a young man competing in 1753 in a horse race during the San Juan festival celebrations plunged with his horse over the precipice at that very spot. ■ *Tue 1000-1600.* Next to it is the aptly named **Parque de las Palomas**, where the birds perch on your hand to be fed. This practice is best avoided, however, as we have heard of people contracting a lung virus and ending up in hospital. **San Felipe del Morro** was built in 1591 to defend the entrance to the harbour, and the 11ha **Fort San Cristóbal** was completed in 1772 to support El Morro and to defend the landward side of the city, with its five independent units connected by tunnels and dry moats, rising 46m above the ocean. Good views of the city. ■ *Both open daily 0900-1700. Free. Tours of El Morro in English at 1100 and 1500, tours of San Cristóbal in English at 1000 and 1400. T7296777, www.nps.gov/saju* Next to El Morro is the **St Mary Magdalene** cemetery, also called the San Juan cemetery, which is beautiful and well worth a visit, though crowded. The **Plaza del Quinto Centenario**, inaugurated on 12 October 1992 to commemorate the 500th anniversary of Columbus' landing, is a modernistic square on several levels with steps leading to a central fountain with hundreds of jets (good view of El Morro, the cemetery and sunsets). The restored **Cuartel de Ballajá**, once the barracks for Spanish troops and their families, was also inaugurated 12 October 1992 with the **Museum of the Americas** on the second floor tracing the cultural development of the history of the New World. ■ *Mon-Fri 1000-1600, Sat-Sun 1100-1700. Free. T7245052. Guided tours available weekdays 1030, 1130, 1230 and 1400.* The **Dominican Convent** built in the early 16th century, later used as a headquarters by the US Army, is now the office of the Institute of Culture, with a good art gallery. Cultural events are sometimes held in the patio, art exhibitions in the galleries. ■ *Wed-Sun 0900-1200, 1300-1630. T7240700.* The 16th-century **San José** church, originally a Dominican chapel, is the second oldest church in the Western Hemisphere and once the family church of Ponce de León's descendants. Ponce was buried here until moved to the Cathedral in the 20th century. ■ *Mon-Sat 0830-1600, Sun mass at 1200.* The early-18th-century **Casa de los Contrafuertes** believed to be the oldest private residence in the old city, now has periodic art exhibitions on the second floor and a small pharmacy museum with 19th-century exhibits on the ground floor. ■ *Wed-Sun 0900-1630. T7245949.* The **Casa Blanca** was built in 1523 by the family of Ponce de León, who

San Juan orientation

Related map:
A Old San Juan, page 380
Not to Scale

N

■ **Sleeping**
1 Aleli By the Sea
2 Beach Buoy Inn
3 Best Western Pierre
4 El Canario Inn
5 El Canario by the Lagoon
6 El Canario by the Sea
7 Embassy
8 Excelsior
9 Green Isle Inn

lived in it for 250 years until it became the residence of the Spanish and then the US military commander-in-chief. It is now a historical museum which is well worth a visit. ■ *Tue-Sun 0900-1200, 1300-1630. US$2, children, US$1 children. 1 Calle San Sebastián, T7244102. Guided tours Tue-Fri by appointment*. The **Alcaldía**, or City Hall, was built 1604-1789. ■ *Mon-Fri 0800-1600 except holidays. T7247171, ext 2391*. The **naval arsenal** was the last place in Puerto Rico to be evacuated by the Spanish in 1898. ■ *Wed-Sun 0900-1200, 1300-1630. T7245949*.

Apart from those in historic buildings listed above, there are the **Pablo Casals Museum** in an 18th-century house beside San José church, with Casals' cello and other memorabilia. ■ *Tue-Sat 0930-1730. US$1, children US$0.50. T7239185*. The **San Juan Museum of Art and History**, Norzagaray y MacArthur, built in 1855 as a marketplace, now a cultural centre with exhibition galleries. ■ *Tue-Sun 1000-1600. T7241875*. The **Casa del Libro** is an 18th-century house on Calle Cristo, has a collection of rare books, including some over 400 years old. ■ *Tue-Sat, except holidays, 1100-1630. T7230354*. **Museum of the Sea** on Pier One, a collection of maritime instruments and models. ■ *Open when the pier is open for cruise ships. T7252532*. The **Indian Museum** at Calle San José 109 on the corner of Luna concentrates on Puerto Rican indigenous cultures, with exhibits, ceramics and archaeological digs. ■ *Tue-Sat 0900-1600. No admission charge. T7245477*. Another museum in the old city is a military museum at **Fort San Jerónimo**. ■ *Wed-Sun 0930-1200, 1300-1630. T7245949*.

Museums

The metropolitan area of San Juan includes the more modern areas of Santurce, Hato Rey, and Río Piedras. In **Santurce** a new museum opened in 2000, the **Museo de Arte de Puerto Rico**, showcasing 500 years of Puerto Rican sculpture, painting, drawing, photography and graphic arts. There are also temporary exhibitions, films and classes. The west wing contains the last remnant of the former Municipal Hospital and has a permanent collection in 18 exhibition halls. The east wing is a modern, 5-storey structure, designed by local architects, Otto Reyes and Luis Gutiérrez, containing an

Metropolitan San Juan

Puerto Rico

10 Hostería del Mar
11 La Casa Mathieson
12 Numero Uno on the Beach

atrium, a conservation laboratory, an interactive family gallery and ActivArte, a computer learning centre, as well as studios and workshops, museum shop, restaurant and café. ■ *Tue-Sat 1000-1700, Sun 1100-1800; the gallery is open Wed until 2000 for special interactive and educational programmes. US$5, concessions US$3. 300 de Diego Av, Santurce, T9776277, www.mapr.org* The **Sacred Heart University** with the **Museum of Contemporary Puerto Rican Art** is in Santurce. ■ *Tue-Sat 0900-1600, Sun 1100-1700. T2680049.* The **Centro Bellas Artes Luis A Ferré** (Fine Arts Centre), opened in 1981, with theatres and halls at the corner of De Diego and Ponce de León. ■ *Mon-Fri 0800-1700. T7244747, www.centrobellasartes.com*

Río Piedras was founded in 1714 but became incorporated into San Juan in 1951. On the edge of Río Piedras, the gardens and library of the former governor, Luis Muñoz Marín, are open to the public, with a museum showing his letters, photos and speeches. ■ *Tue-Sat 0900-1300. T7557979.* The **University of Puerto Rico** at Río Piedras is in a lovely area. The **University Museum** has archaeological and historical exhibitions, and also monthly art exhibitions. ■ *Mon-Fri 0900-2100, Sat-Sun 0900-1500. T7640000, ext 2452.* The **Botanical Garden** at the Agricultural Experiment Station has over 200 species of tropical and subtropical plants, a bamboo promenade (one variety can grow 4 ft in a day), an orchid garden (over 30,000 orchids), and an aquatic garden. ■ *Daily 0800-1630. T7634408, www.upr.clu.edu*

Hato Rey is the financial district of San Juan nicknamed 'the Golden Mile'. The **Luís Muñoz Marín Park** on Avenida Jesús T Piñero covers 35ha, which can be toured by a 1 km cable car. ■ *Open Tue-Sun 0900-1700.* The residential area **Miramar** has several moderately priced hotels as well as some expensive ones. Miramar is separated from the Atlantic coast by the **Condado lagoon** and the Condado beach area, where the luxury hotels, casinos, nightclubs and restaurants are concentrated. From Condado the beachfront is built up eastwards through Ocean Park, Santa Teresita, Punta Las Marías and Isla Verde along the narrow strip beyond Isla Verde, between the sea and the airport.

Excursions A ferry, Old San Juan (Pier Two) – Hato Rey, Cataño, crosses every 30 minutes, 0600-2200, weather permitting, T7881155, US$0.50, to Cataño. In 1999 an enormous statue of Columbus made by a Georgian, Zurab Tsereteli, was assembled in sections here as a major tourist attraction. From Cataño waterfront you can catch a *público* (US$1 per person), or bus C37 to about five blocks from the **Bacardí rum distillery** where there are free conducted tours around the plant, travelling from one building to the next by a little open motor train. ■ *Mon-Sat 0830-1630, every 30 mins. Closed for Christmas holidays. Route 888, Km 2.6, T7881500, www.bacardi.com*

On Route 2, shortly before Bayamón, is the island's earliest settlement, **Caparra**, established by Ponce de León in 1508. Ruins of the fort can still be seen and there is a museum, **Museo y Parque Histórico Ruinas de Caparra**. ■ *Daily 0900-1600. T7814795.*

Essentials

Sleeping Most of the large San Juan hotels are in **Condado** or **Isla Verde** and overlook the sea, with swimming pools, nightclubs, restaurants, shops and bars. They are mostly part of international chains, such as *Hilton, Marriott, Radisson, Ritz Carlton, Wyndham*, and are not listed here. To get value for money, it may be advisable to avoid the luxury hotels on the sea front. There are beachfront apartments at reasonable prices for stays of a week or more, and the further away from the beach you go, the cheaper they will become; look in the local newspaper, *El Nuevo Día* for notices, usually quote monthly rates but available for shorter stays.

Condado L *Best Western Pierre*, 105 De Diego, T7211200, www.hotelpierresanjuan.com Designed for business travellers or families. Good value are the 3 Canario hotels, B&B, www.canariohotels.com: **L-AL** *El Canario by the Lagoon*, 4 Clemenceau, T7228640, 40 rooms , 1 block from beach. **AL** *El Canario by the Sea*, 4 Condado Av, T7228640, 25 rooms, close to beach, comfortable. **AL** *El Canario Inn*, 1317 Ashford, T7223861. Near beach. **AL-C** *Embassy,*

1125 Sea View, T7258284, home.att.net/~embassyguesthouse 20 rooms, good bathroom, TV, a/c, fan, pool and jacuzzi on the beach, some rooms have kitchenette. **A-B** *Aleli By The Sea*, 1125 Sea View St, T7255313, F7214744, on seafront. Kitchen facilities, no pool, parking. **A-B** *Casa del Caribe*, 57 Caribe, T7227139, F7232575. 1 block from beach, CP, a/c, TV, phone, patio and garden, 13 rooms, convenient for restaurants and nightlife.

Ocean Park LL-AL *Numero Uno on the Beach*, 1 Santa Ana, T7265010, roman@caribe.net. 14 rooms, a/c, fan, CP, safe, good beach but not safe after dark, with pool, gay friendly. **LL-B** *Hostería del Mar*, 1 Tapia St, T7273302, www.prhtasmallhotels com, on the beach. 20 rooms, restaurant. **B-C** *Beach Buoy Inn*, 1853 McLeary, T7288119, F2680037. Also safe behind barred doors and high walls, but on busy road so some traffic noise, windows sealed in some rooms, no restaurant, parking, shopping close by, beach towels.

Isla Verde A-B *La Casa Mathieson*, Uno 14, T7268662, and *Green Isle*, Uno 36, T7264330, are jointly owned, greeninn@prtc.net Both charge the same, both near airport, and have swimming pools, cooking facilities, friendly, free transport to and from airport, restaurant. **A-B** *Green Isle Inn*, 36 Calle Uno, Villamar, T7264330, F2682415. 21 rooms, some with kitchenette, TV, functional but comfortable, lots of repeat guests, convenient location. **A-B** *El Patio*, Tres Oeste 87, Bloque D-8, Villamar, T7266298. 14 rooms, swimming pool, use of kitchen, laundry, short walk to beach. **A-B** *Mario's*, 2 Rosa St, T7913748. From US$60 for a single or double this is one of the cheapest you are likely to find. Has the necessities but not much else, convenient, only 5 mins' drive from airport, rooms always available mid-week, a/c, TV, live music sometimes.

Old San Juan LL *El Convento Hotel & Casino*, a converted Carmelite nunnery at Cristo 100, T7239020, www.elconvento.com A charming hotel with a Spanish atmosphere and the dining room is in the former chapel, exclusive, very good service, 58 rooms, swimming pool, nice garden in which to have a drink, unfortunately the plaza opposite is a nocturnal campsite for junkies/alcoholics and stray cats. **LL-A** *Galería San Juan*, Norzagaray 204, T7236515. 300-year-old rambling house with inner courtyards, artist's residence and studio, art, antiques, views everywhere, labyrinth, rooms and suites. **AL-B** *Milano*, Fortaleza 307, T7299050, www.hotelmilanopr.com 19th-century building on 3 floors with restaurant and bar on roof giving views of harbour and cruise ships, 30 rooms, CP, most expensive at the front, cheapest in the middle of the building, 2 rooms for the disabled, comfortable, TV, phones, mini-fridge. **AL-B** *153 O'Donnell*, 153 O'Donnell. T8396399 (at *Caribe Playa*, see The Southeast below), www.caribeplaya.com 6 1-bedroom apartments and a 2-bedroom penthouse, in beautiful colonial building, whitewashed walls, tiled floors, Moorish arches, sleep 3-4, a/c, phone, TV, new, clean and well-equipped, some have balconies. **AL-C** *The Caleta*, 11 Caleta de las Monjas, T7255347, www.thecaleta.com Furnished studios and apartments, some with kitchens or kitchenettes, most have a/c, TV and phone, run by Michael Giessler, minimum 3-night stay, weekly, monthly and long term rates, coin laundry.

Picturesque area, hilly cobbled streets, ocean views but no beach swimming

Miramar L *Excelsior*, 801 Ponce de León, T7217400, hotelexcelsior@worldnet.att.net 140 rooms, studios and 2-room suites with kitchenettes, popular gourmet restaurants, *Café de Paris* and *Agostino's*, bar, pool, rooms overlooking freeway are noisy, business-type hotel with dataport in rooms but with attention to families, Nintendo games provided, facilities for the handicapped, fitness room, transport to beaches. **B** *Olimpo Court*, 603 Av Miramar, T7240600, hotelolimpocourt@hotmail.com 45 rooms and studios with kitchenettes, a/c, TV, phone, *Chayote* restaurant, parking. **B** *Miramar*, 606 Av Ponce de León, T7226239, F7231180. 'Not chic', but OK, business travellers on a budget, a/c, pool, sea view from 5th floor front, dirty carpets, ask for room without carpet, longer stays possible.

Residential area, easy bus to old San Juan, but not great at night

Old San Juan *Al Dente*, 309 Recinto Sur, T7237303. Posh Italian, US$15-20 main course, live entertainment, reservations required, open for lunch and dinner, valet parking. *Amadeus Café*, 106 San Sebastián, T7216720, amadeuscafé@world net.att.net European cuisine with Caribbean touches, tasty vegetarian options and puddings, popular, lively, friendly, lunch and dinner, bar, live entertainment, parking. *Café Berlin*, 407 San Francisco, T7225205. Breakfast, lunch and dinner, local produce, some organic, vegetarian dishes, also chicken and fish. *Ché's*, Coaba 35, Punta Las Marías, T7267202. The place for meat lovers, Argentine parrilladas, churrascos and chimichurri, lunch and dinner, parking. *La Bombonera*, San Francisco 259, T7220658. Restaurant, bar and pastry shop, good value breakfast, 1960s atmosphere, antique coffee

Eating

Puerto Rico

machine, try the *mallorcas*, a pastry dusted with sugar, sandwiches or full meals, 0730-2030 daily. *La Danza*, corner of Cristo and Fortaleza, T7231642. Eat inside or outside, opposite Capilla de Santo Cristo, Puerto Rican food but paella a speciality, live entertainment 1430-1700 Tue, Fri, Sat, open 1200-2030, closed Thu. *La Mallorquina*, San Justo 207, T7223261. The oldest restaurant in San Juan, Puerto Rican food, 1130-2200 Mon-Sat. *Patio de Sam*, 102 San Sebastián on Plaza San José, T7238802. Facing the plaza, serving everything from burgers to gourmet, kids menu, live entertainment, bar, very good for local drinks (happy hour 1600-1900), 1100-2400 daily. *Yukiyu*, Recinto Sur 311, T7221423, www.yukiyupr.com Sushi bar, Teppan Yaki and Japanese restaurant, open Mon-Fri 1200-1430, 1730-2230, Sat 1800-2200, Sun 1700-2100, takeaway available daily 1200-1430, also 1700-2100 Sat, Sun.

Condado There is a huge selection of restaurants in Condado, from the posh to all the fast food chain restaurants. *Ajili Mojili*, 1052 Ashford Av, T7259195, www.icepr.com/ajili-mojili Fine dining, Puerto Rican cuisine, elegant, US$15-20 main course, live music Sun, 1145-1500 daily, also 1800-2200 Mon-Thu, 1800-2300 Fri, Sat, reservations required, valet parking. *Don Andrés*, 1350 Ashford Av, T7230223. Mexican, live entertainment Thu-Sat evenings, moderate prices, casual, 1130-2300 Tue-Wed, 1130-2400 Thu-Sat, 1700-2400 Sun, valet parking. *José José*, 1110 Magdalena Av, T7258546. Named after 2 owner chefs, José Garden and José Abreu, international food with Caribbean flair, gourmet, 1200-1500, 1830-2300 Tue-Fri, 1830-2300 Sat, 1200-2130 Sun, valet parking. **Isla Verde** is well served by the fast-food fraternity; on the beach at Isla Verde is *The Hungry Sailor* bar and grill. Sandwiches, tapas, burgers, with a snack bar next door. *Bagelfields Inc*, 6070 Isla Verde Av Food Court, T2533663. Types of bagels baked daily, lots of deli and healthy fillings, wraps and sandwiches, pastries, coffee bar, wines and beer, good for breakfast. Parking.

Hato Rey *Frida's*, Av Domenech 128, Hato Rey, T7634827, www.letsdine.com/fridas Mexican, around US$12, quite upscale, good, dinner only, parking. *Jerusalem*, O'Neil St, G-1, T2818232. Middle Eastern food, belly dancing Fri, Sat nights, lunch and dinner.

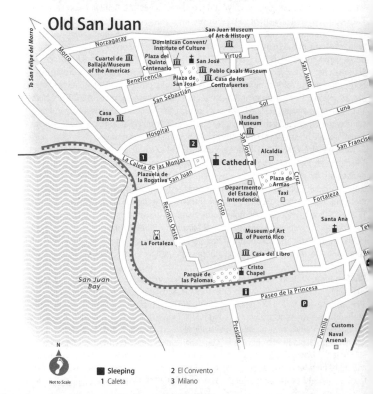

Old San Juan

Sleeping
1 Caleta
2 El Convento
3 Milano

Not to Scale

Puerto Nuevo *Allegro Ristorante*, Av Roosevelt esq Duero 1350, T7930190. High class Italian, 1200-1500, 1800-2200 Tue-Fri, 1800-2200 Sat, 1200-1800 Sun, parking. *Aurorita Mexican Restaurant*, Av de Diego 303, T7832899. Authentic Mexican, Mole Poblano, Margaritas, Mariachi band Wed-Sun, takeaway, parking, 1130-2200 Tue-Thu, 1130-2230 Fri-Sun.

Fondas For breakfast or lunch seek out the *fondas*, not advertised as restaurants but usually part of a private home, or a family-run eating place serving *criollo* meals which are filling and good value. Recommended in San Juan are: *Macumba*, 2000 Loíza. *Casa Juanita*, 242 Av Roosevelt, Hato Rey. Try chicken asopao or pork chops con mangú. *Cafetería del Parking*, 757 José de Diego. Interior, Cayey (specialities include *mondongo*, and *boronia de apio y bacalao* – cod and celery root). *D'Arcos*, 605 Miramar, Santurce. Speciality is roast veal with stuffed peppers and white bean sauce, also try *pega'o* (crunchy rice).

In Old San Juan, Calle San Sebastián has lots of bars and clubs making it a lively street after dark. *Bachelor's*, Av Condado 112, T7252734. Gay club, dance and techno music, casual, 2300-0500 Tue-Sun. *Club Lazer*, Cruz 251, T7257581. Bar on first floor, then above is the dance floor with state-of-the-art light show and above that is the roof terrace, 2000-0500 Mon-Sat, themed nights. *Jazz at The Place*, Fortaleza 154 in old San Juan. No admission charge, drinks about US$2. *Neons Videotech*, Tanca 203, T7243426. Music, dance, live rock Sun, from 2000 Thu, from 2100 Fri, Sat, from 1900 Sun. *Rumba*, San Sebastián 152, T7254407. Live guaracha and salsa Thu-Sat, open daily from 1930, casual. *Shannons Irish Pub*, Bori esq San José de Diego, Condado. Bus from airport passes it, don't miss St Patrick's Day, live music (rock and roll) Wed-Sun, beer US$2.50, open until 0100 Sun-Tue, 0230 Wed-Sat. *The Gallery Café*, Fortaleza 305, T7258676. Open from 2100 onwards, DJs play dance and electronic music, casual. *Caribe Hilton* is a favourite nightspot, also the other 4-5-star hotels have nightclubs. In **Isla Verde**, *Area 51*, or *The Dome*, Av Isla Verde, D-11, T7283780. Dance music, electronic and rave, UFO-shaped building, smart casual, 2100-0400 Fri-Sat. *The X Club*, Calle Rosa 7, T2533050. DJs playing rock and dance, daily from midnight, casual. *Dunbar's*, 1954 McCleary St, Ocean Park, T7282920. Bar and restaurant with live music weekends, happy hour 1700-1900, open until 0100. Several places in **Santurce**, *Asylum*, Av Ponce de León 1420, T7233416. Converted theatre, from 2100 onwards Thu-Sat, invited DJs on Fri, usually drum, bass, trance. *Stanley's E-Net Club*, Av Ponce de León 1515, T9770770, www.stanleysenc.com Unlimited free use of Play Station, Dream Cast and internet as well as invited DJs, live bands, music is varied, pop, lounge, breakbeats, trance, house, Thu-Sat from 2100 onwards. *Stargate*, Av Roberto H Todd 1, T7254664. House DJs play dance music, Thu, Sat 2130 onwards, Fri, Sun from 1700, smart casual. *Eros*, Av Ponce de León 1257, T7221131. Gay club, tribal house music, Tue-Sat from 2200, Sun from 2000, dress creatively. And then there are the casinos…

Nightlife
Check age limits, some clubs are for 18 and over but others for 21 and up

Countryside Tours, 1048 Las Palmas Av, Suite 1101, T7239691, angelfire.com/super/san juan/index.html Customized tours, to the University of Puerto Rico, the first Governor's house in Trujillo Alto and a (hard to find) typical lunch, pointing out typical plants and

Tour operators

Puerto Rico

trees along the way, delightful cultural experience, recommended to get to know Puerto Rico, daily 0800-2000. *Hillbilly Tours*, day trips from San Juan into the hills, run by Edwin Betancourt, T7605618, www.hillbillytours.com Helpful with information, open 0700-1900. *Northwestern Land Tours*, T6449841, www.puertoricoexcursions.com Andrés Alicea offers day trips to the Indian ceremonial centre, Guanica Forest, El Yunque, Ponce, Río Camuy Caves, etc. *Aventuras Tierra Adentro*, 272B Av Pinero, University Gardens, Río Piedras, PR 00927, T7660470, www.aventurastierraadentro.com Rappelling, rock climbing, body rafting, canyoning, ziplines, outdoor sport shop, caving and team building, Tue-Sat 0900-1800. *Encantos Ecotours*, El Muelle Shopping Center, T8080005, www.ecotourspr.com, bikes and kayaks, tours and rentals, also surf rafting in Piñones, internet café.

El Yunque

El Yunque (see also page 370), or **Caribbean National Forest**, is a tropical forest and bird sanctuary, the largest rain forest in the US forest service system. The forest is divided into north side and south side, with no road connection. After a series of landslides everyone has given up and Route 191 is permanently closed in the middle; you have to drive all the way around to get to the south side or hike (a bit tricky to get past the landslides). There are concrete trails to the various peaks: El Yunque (The Anvil) itself, Mount Britton, Los Picachos, as well as to waterfalls and lookout towers giving excellent views. There are 13 trails in all, covering 37 km. The **Baño Grande** is the shortest, taking about 45 minutes and passing a large man-made pool built by the Civilian Conservation Corp in the 1930s. The **Big Tree Trail** is about the most strenuous, taking 1¾ hours and ending at La Mina waterfall. ■ *Caribbean National Forest, PO Box 490, Palmer, PR 00712, T8881810, F8885622, www.r8web.com/caribbean Getting there: via Route 3 from San Juan towards Fajardo, and then right on Route 191 at Palmer. The Palma de Sierra Picnic Grounds have parking, tables, water and shelters. El Portal, Centro Forestal Tropical, at the entrance on Route 191, has exhibitions, educational and conservation material, patios where you can relax and admire the view, 100-seat theatre showing a 30-min documentary film on El Yunque, in Spanish followed by an English version. US$3 adults, US$1.50 children and older people. Daily 0900-1700. The Park Service publishes a good map.*

The south side of the forest is approached from Naguabo up Route 191. No facilities have yet been developed. The soil and weather here is different from the north. The north is red clay (and soggy) and the south is almost sandy (fine granite), while it is less humid and cooler. It is also quieter, with no tour buses or parking lots.

Sleeping
For camping, see page 367

South side *Robin Phillips* has several rustic cabins, **D**, and tent sites on his fruit farm. Robin and Sita will guide you through the forest or to the petroglyphs. Terrific views to the sea. Robin is full of information. T8742138 or write to *Adventures with Nature*, HC1, Box 4449, Naguabo, PR 00718 Also 2 excellent B&Bs on Route 191 through Naguabo, wonderful views of forest, rivers, waterfalls: **A** *Casa Cabuy*, T8746221. Fabulous views, built on hillside overlooking forest, close to Río Cabuy, 9 rooms, family-style lunch and dinner on request.

Eastern tour

An interesting round trip through the east half of the island can be done by a series of *públicos* from San Juan – Río Grande – Luquillo – Fajardo – Humacao – Yabucoa – Guayama – Cayey – Aibonito – Barranquitas – Bayamón – San Juan. If travelling by car, a variant between San Juan and El Yunque takes you on Route 187 from Isla Verde, outside San Juan, to Loíza along a stretch of the north coast, which includes the **Piñones State Forest**, a sand blown and palm-lined road. There are some huge resorts and golf clubs in the Río Grande area.

Luquillo

Luquillo was founded in 1797 when a group of colonizers led by Cristóbal de Guzmán moved from San Juan to escape frequent British naval attacks. The town was named after the Indian cacique Loquillo, who died a few years after the last Indian rebellion of Boriquén that took place following the seizure of the Spanish settlement of Santiago by the shores of the Río Daguao in 1513. In honour of the anniversary of its founding, in 1997 a new landscaped plaza municipal was inaugurated with a statue of Loquillo. There is a beach in town and a *balneario* west of town (see page 373); just by the latter is a row of restaurants on the slip road off the dual carriageway (Route 3). *Públicos* from San Juan to Luquillo are marked Fajardo, US$3, no return *públicos* after 1500.

Fajardo is a boating centre with several marinas and a public beach at Seven Seas; beyond Seven Seas is Las Croabas beach. Offshore is an uninhabited, but much visited, coral island, Icacos. **Las Cabezas de San Juan** is a nature reserve on the headlands (three promontories) north of Fajardo on Route 987, Km 6. A 19th-century lighthouse contains a nature centre and its observation deck has a great view of El Yunque and surrounding islands. There are trails and boardwalks, guides and explanatory signs of the different ecological habitats. ■ *Fri-Sun US$5, US$2 children. Tours, reservations required. T7225882, or T8602560 at weekends, www.fideicomiso.org* Off Humacao Beach/Balneario is a tiny cay called **Cayo Santiago**, also known as **Monkey Island**. It is inhabited by over 500 tiny monkeys, which are protected. The island is closed to the public although there are sightseeing tours which get you close enough to see the monkeys through binoculars.

Sleeping
For camping, see page 367

There are several mega resorts in the area and construction continues: the new *Inter-Continental Cayo Largo Resort*, *El Conquistador Resort & Country Club*, west of Fajardo on the hill and *Palmas del Mar*, further south. **AL-A** *Fajardo Inn*, Route 195, Parcelas Beltrán 52, Puerto Real, T8606000, www.fajardoinn.com 75 rooms, a/c, TV, phone, computer services, restaurant, also guesthouse alongside, *Scenic Inn*, both with great views of El Yunque and the coast from on top of the hill. **B** *Martorell* at Luquillo, 6A Ocean Drive, T8892710, F8894520. Close to beach, CP, kitchen, shared bath. You pay for the location, advisable to reserve in advance here at any time. **B** *La Familia*, on Route 987, Km 4, Las Croabas, Fajardo, T8631193, www.hotellafamilia.com 27 rooms, rather small, a/c, bath, TV, CP, pool, restaurant, 2 mins from beach, next to *El Conquistador*. **B** *Anchor's Inn*, Route 987 Km 27, Fajardo, T8637200, www.anchorsinn.homestead.com/anchorsinn.html Nice rooms, a/c, TV, good facilities but no breakfast, bar/restaurant expensive, part of Mesones Gastronómicos programme.

Eating

Rosa's Seafood in Fajardo, Route 195, Tablazo 536, T8630213. Puerto Rican food and steak. *Lighthouse*, near Roosevelt Rds. Inexpensive meals. *Plaza Caliente Seafood*, on the beach at Puerto del Rey Marina, T8609162.

Watersports
Lots of companies offer day sails, snorkelling, diving and fishing

Marinas Isleta Marina, Playa Puerto Real, T6432180 (*Ventajero Sailing Charters*, T8631871, domingoj@coqui.net, day sails and overnight charters); Marina Puerto Chico, Route 987, Km 2.4, T8630834; Marina Puerto Real, Playa Puerto Real, T8632188; Puerto del Rey Marina, Route 33, Km 51.4, T8601000, www.puertodelrey.com (*Sea Ventures Dive Center*, PADI 5-star, T800-7393483, www.divepuertorico.com, *East Wind* catamaran with underwater windows, 1000 departure to islands for beaches and snorkelling, T8603434, sailcats@hotmail.com); Sea Lovers Marina, Route 987, Km 2.3, T8633762; Villa Marina Yacht Harbour, Route 987, Km 1.3, T8635131 (*Club Nautico Powerboat Rentals*, T8602400, boatrent@coqui.net, *Caribbean School of Aquatics*, T7286606, catamaran for cruises and day sails, dive boat for snorkelling and diving); El Conquistador Marina, 1000 El Conquistador Av, T8636594 (*Palomino Island Divers*, T8631000, Tropical Fishing & Tournaments, T2664524, deep-sea sport fishing). Lots of other companies offering day sails, snorkelling, diving and fishing.

The southeast

One of the prettiest parts of Puerto Rico, lies south of Humacao, between Yabucoa and Guayama. Here are the villages of **Patillas** (*público* from Guayama) and

Puerto Rico

Maunabo (*público* from Patillas, and from Yabucoa). There are a number of restaurants in this area, especially on the coast, which sell good, cheap food. **Yabucoa** is the east starting point of the Panoramic Route which runs the length of the island. There is an extension to the Route around the Cerro La Pandura and the Puntas Quebrada Honda, Yaguas and Toro; this affords lovely views of the Caribbean coast and Vieques island. **Guayama**, the cleanest town in Puerto Rico, it claims, has a delightful square, on which are the church and the **Casa Cautiño**, built in 1887, now a museum and cultural centre. Route 3, the coastal road around the east part continues from Guayama to Salinas (see below), where it joins Route 1 for Ponce.

Sleeping Near **Patillas** is **AL-B** *Caribe Playa*, Route 3, Km 112, right on the Caribbean, T8396339, F8391817, www.caribeplaya.com 32 beachfront rooms, sleep 4, a/c, fan, TV, patio or balcony, comfortable, rather noisy road runs behind rooms, pool and whirlpool, children's pool, open-air restaurant (order dinner in advance), library, sea bathing and snorkelling in a small, safe area, barbecue, hammocks, boat trips for fishing, diving, snorkelling, very friendly and helpful. Near **Maunabo**, is **C** *Playa Emajaguas Guest House*, off the Ruta Panorámica, Route 901, Km 2.5, T8616023. Lovely view, short walk down private path to empty beach (rough sea, currents), owned by Victor Morales and Edna Huertos, 7 apartments with kitchens, friendly, helpful, tennis court, pool table, horses. Good seafood restaurants nearby. At **Yabucoa**, **AL-A** *Palmas de Lucía*, Route 901 at Route 9911, T8934423, F8930291, www.palmasdelucia.com New parador, 29 rooms, balconies with sea view, clean, basketball court, pool, restaurant, waves can be rough at nearby Lucía beach. At **Punta Guilarte**, near Arroyo, there are cabins, **B**, on the beach, no camping, T8393565. Inland, north of Barranquitas is **AL-B** *Hacienda Margarita*, Route 52, Km 1.7, T8570414, F8571265. 27 rooms, balcony, view of El Yunque, useful for people following the Panoramic route.

Carite Forest The Carite Forest lies west of Yabucoa on the Panoramic Route. Covering an area of 2,428 ha, its highest peak is Cerro La Santa at 903 m. The Forest Supervisor, (Km 20 Route 184), is very helpful and can tell you what there is to do including kayaks to rent on the lake. Bring permit from San Juan or Servicio Forestal regional office in Guayama, T8643262. There are two camping areas: Charco Azul and Guavate (the latter closer to the forestry office, phone and supplies) with bathrooms. If you have a car you will be given a key to get it into the campsite. By *público*, from Río Piedras terminal, San Juan, occasionally direct to Barrio Guavate, Carite, otherwise to Caguas and change. The *público* will drop you quite close to the office where you check in.

The south and west

A round trip through the west half of the island would take in Ponce, the second city (reached by motorway from San Juan via Caguas), Guánica, Parguera, San Germán, Boquerón, Mayagüez (the third city), Aguadilla, Quebradillas and Arecibo, with side trips to the Maricao State Forest and fish hatchery, the Río Abajo State Forest and Lake Dos Bocas, the pre-Columbian ceremonial ball-park near Utuado, and the Arecibo observatory.

Baños de Coamo Off the motorway which runs from San Juan to Ponce is Baños de Coamo, which was the island's most fashionable resort from 1847 to 1958; legend has it that the thermal spring was the fountain of youth which Juan Ponce de León was seeking. Take Route 153 from the motorway and then 546. About 45 minutes southeast of Coamo is **Salinas**, a fishing and farming centre. There are several good seafood restaurants on the waterfront. The Marina de Salinas offers transport to islands and accommodation, T7528484, F7687676, jarce@coqui.net

Sleeping A-B *Baños de Coamo* at the end of Route 546, Coamo, Puerto Rico 00640, T8252186, F8254739, www.banoscoamo.com Thermal water springs (maximum 15 mins) and an ordinary pool (spend as long as you like), 48 rooms, bar, restaurant with limited hrs.

Ponce

The city is now very pleasant to walk around. Much renovation has taken place in the *www.ponceweb.org*
heart of the city; the Casas Villaronga and Salazar-Zapater have been restored (the
latter to accommodate the Museo de Historia de Ponce), other houses are being
repainted in pastel shades, streets have been, and the large, air-conditioned market
on Vives and Atocho (north of the plaza) has been remodelled.

The **Puerto Rico Tourism Co** is on Route 1, west of Route 52, south side,
T8430465. **The Ponce Tourism office** is on the first floor inside *Citibank* at the
Plaza Las Delicias in front of the Parque Bomberos, open Monday to Friday
0800-1630, T8418160.

The cathedral is worth a look, and so is the black and red fire station, built for a fair in **Sights**
1883. Both buildings stand back to back in the main square, **Plaza Las Delicias**, which
has fountains and many neatly trimmed trees. Also on the plaza is the **Casa
Armstrong-Poventud** (or Casa de las Cariatides), facing the cathedral, with the
Instituto de Cultura Puertorriqueño (Región Sur) and tourist information centre.
■ *Mon-Fri 0800-1200, 1300-1630; the Instituto is open Tue-Sun 0900-1200,
1300-1600.* East of the plaza is the **Teatro La Perla**, painted cream, white and gold, the
city's cultural centre (19th century), restored in 1990, as was the Alcaldía on the Plaza.

Ponce has a very fine **Museo de Arte de Ponce**, donated by a foundation estab-   *There are three*
lished by Luis A Ferré (industrialist, art historian and Governor 1968-72) in a mod-   *gardens here, one*
ern building designed by Edward Durrel Stone, with a beautiful staircase, now   *Spanish,*
famous. It contains a representative collection of European and American art from   *one American and*
the third century BC to the present day. As well as an extensive Baroque collection   *one Puerto Rican*
and fine examples of pre-Raphaelite painting, there is a small collection of
precolumbian ceramics. Art Nouveau glass. Most of the best Latin American painters are exhibited and there are often special displays. ■ *Daily 1000-1700. US$3, chil-
dren under 12 US$2. T8480511, www.museoarteponce.org*

The **Museo de la Historia de Ponce** on Calle Isabela 51-53, near La Perla,
opened in 1992 and has 10 exhibition halls with photographs, documents and memorabilia provided by locals, as well as models and other exhibits chronicling the
city's history. Guided tours in English, Spanish or French. ■ *Wed-Mon 0900-1700
(Jun-Aug Sat-Sun 1000-1800). US$3, children US$1. T8447071.* The **Museo de la
Música Puertorriqueña** is next door at Isabela 45, in the neoclassical former home
of the Serralés-Nevárez family, with music videos and history of local music.
■ *Wed-Sun 0900-1630, catalogue US$3, T8487016.*

On **El Vigía** hill is the **Observation Tower**. ■ *Tue-Thu 0900-1800, Fri-Sun
0930-1830. US$0.50.* The **Museo Castillo Serrallés** is also on El Vigía hill. This fine,
1930s mansion has been restored by the Municipio. ■ *Tue-Sun 0900-1800. US$3,
children US$1.50. Groups must reserve in advance. T2591774.*

Outside the town by the **Yacht and Fishing Club**, T8429003, is a good place to be
at the weekend having a vibrant atmosphere. A wooden broadwalk, La Guancha,
has been built along the edge of the harbour. There are kiosks selling *pinchos* and
other local treats, simple meals, cold beer and drinks. At one end is an open-air stage
for live music or DJs with big sound systems. The music is ear-splittingly loud, especially at weekends. A two-storey building houses a restaurant, small theatre, tourist
office and police substation. There is also an observation tower you can climb up.

A short drive away on Route 503, Km 2.1, in the outskirts of the city, is the **Tibes Indian   Excursions**
Ceremonial Center**. This is an Igneri (AD 300) and pre-Taíno (AD 700) burial ground,   *All the ball courts*
with seven ball courts (*bateyes*) and two plazas, one in the form of a star, a replica of a   *and plazas are said to*
Taíno village and a good museum. The site was discovered in 1975 after heavy rain   *line up with solstices*
uncovered some of the stone margins of the ball courts. Under the Zemi Batey, the lon-   *or equinoxes*
gest in the Caribbean (approximately 100 by 20 m), evidence of human sacrifice has
been found. Underneath a stone in the Main Plaza, which is almost square (55 by 50 m),

Puerto Rico

the bodies of children were found, buried ceremonially in earthenware pots. In all, 130 skeletons have been uncovered near the Main Plaza, out of a total on site of 187. The park is filled with trees (all named), the most predominant being the higuera, whose fruit is used, among other things, for making maracas (it's forbidden to pick them up though). ■ *Tue-Sun (and Mon holidays, when closed Tue) 0900-1600. US$2; bilingual guides give an informative description of the site and a documentary is shown. T8402255.*

Hacienda Buena Vista, at Km 16.8 on Route 123, north of the city, is another recommended excursion. Built in 1833, converted into a coffee plantation and corn mill in 1845 and in operation till 1937. All the machinery works (the metal parts are original), operated by water channelled from the 360 m Vives waterfall; the hydraulic turbine which turns the corn mill is unique. ■ *Fri-Sun, tours at 0830, 1030, 1330 and 1530; groups of 20 or more admitted Wed and Thu. US$5, children under 12 US$1. T7225882 (weekends 8487020), www.fideicomiso.org Reservations are necessary for the 2-hr tour (Spanish or English).*

At weekends trips can be made to the beach at **Caja de Muerto**, Coffin Island, the ferry (if still running) leaves from La Guancha at 0900, returns 1600. There is a fishing pier, barbecue area, information office and beautiful beach with clear water. A trail to the 1880 lighthouse leads from White Beach where the dock is. Very good snorkelling. ■ *US$5.50 return, children US$3.50. T8484575.*

Sleeping   **LL-L** *Ponce Hilton & Casino*, 1150 Caribe Av, on the beach, T2597676, F2597674, www.ponce. hilton.com 153 rooms, convention centre for 1,500, all the business and sporting facilities you expect of a *Hilton*. **L-AL** *Ponce Holiday Inn & Tropical Casino*, Route 2, Km 221.2, west of the city on the bypass, T8441200, F8418683, www.hidpr.com 116 rooms, tennis, pools, and golf arrangements made. **AL-A** *Meliá*, 2 Cristina, just off main plaza, T8420260, F8413602, home. coqui.net/melia Run by Meliá family since 1920s, 77 rooms, CP, a/c, TV, roof top and garden terraces. **B** *Bélgica*, 122 Villa, in old centre, next to Plaza Delicias, on free trolley route for touring city, T8443255, F8446149, www.hotelbelgica.somewhere.net Tasteful, clean, 20 huge rooms with balcony overlooking city hall, friendly, on trolley route. West of Ponce at **Guayanilla**, is **AL-A** *Pichi's* , Route 132, Km 204, T8353335, www.pichis.com, next to *McDonalds*. 58 big rooms, a/c, TV, phone, pool, seafood and steak restaurant, bar, meeting rooms and banqueting facilities.

Eating   The restaurant of the *Meliá hotel*, **Mark at the Meliá** is good and the award-winning chef, Mark French, is on the Puerto Rican National Team. *Canda's*, Alfonso XII esq Bonair, T8439223. Menu with seafood, 1100-2200 Mon-Fri, 1100-2400 Sat-Sun. Fast food places on main plaza.

Tour operators   A **tourist trolley bus** makes a tour of the city, 0900-2130, 1¼ hrs on eastern route, 1¾ hrs west, 1½ hrs north. Free tour of city and out to La Guancha boardwalk on **Chu Chu Tren**, Sat, Sun 0900-1700, T8418160. There are also **horses and carriages**, 1000-1800 Thu-Sun.

Transport   Several flights daily from San Juan. *Público* from San Juan, US$6-7, 2 hrs. *Públicos* serve outlying districts if you have not got a car. Most *carros públicos* leave from the intersection of Victoria and Unión, 3 blocks north of the plaza. To Guayama, either direct or via Santa Isabel, US$3.

Guánica

For details on the Guánica Forest see page 370

Going west from Ponce is Guánica, the place where American troops first landed in the Spanish-American war. It has an old fort from which there are excellent views. Although Guánica has a history stretching back to Ponce de León's landing in 1508, the first of many colonist landings in the bay, the town was not actually founded here until 1914. Outside Guánica is a *balneario* with a large hotel alongside, *Copamarina*. Scuba diving and other watersports are possible here; the wall is close to the shore and there are drop-offs and canyons. You can get to **Gilligans Island** by 15-minute water taxi. Go past *Balneario Caña Gorda* on route 333, turn right towards Punta Jacinto and the pier. There is a fishing pier, barbecue area, information office and beautiful beach. ■ *0900-1700, closed Mon (or Tue if Mon is a holiday).*

LL-L *Copamarina Beach Resort*, Route 333, Km 6.5, T8210505, F8210070. Set in 6.5-ha tropical estate, 106 rooms, also villas sleeping 6, a/c, TV, balcony, 2 pools, tennis, watersports, PADI dive centre, tour desk, restaurants, on eelgrass beach but good swimming on Gilligans Island.

Further west is La Parguera, originally a fishing village and now a popular resort with *paradores*, guesthouses, fish restaurants, fast food outlets. Noisy on holiday weekends. Fishing, kayaking, mountain biking and other activities are offered. **Phosphorescent Bay** is an area of phosphorescent water, occurring through a permanent population of minescent dinoflagellates, a tiny form of marine life, which produce sparks of chemical light. 1-hour boat trips round the bay depart 1930-2230, every 30 minutes, US$12. It is best to go on a very dark night or even when it is raining. Mosquito Bay on Vieques is much better.

Sleeping and eating AL-A *Villa Parguera*, Route 304, T8997777, F8996040, www.villaparguera.com 70 rooms, sea view, by docks, rent boat to get to mangrove canals and cays for good swimming and snorkelling, restaurant, live music and dancing at weekends. **A-B** *Posada Porlamar*, Route 304, Km 3.3, T8994015, F8995558, www.posadaporlamar.com 24 rooms, TV, phone, on the canals, dock, watersports arranged, dive shop on site, dive packages available. **A-B** *Estancia La Jamaca* , Route 304, T/F8996162, inland. 8 rooms, quiet, country noises at night.

Watersports *Parguera Divers* are at *Posada Porlamar*, T8994171, www.pargueradivers.com for wall diving. *Parguera Fishing Charters*, T8994698, hometown.aol.com/mareja, will take you reef fishing or out to catch marlin, dorado and tuna.

Inland from La Parguera, off the main Route 2, San Germán has much traditional charm; it was the second town to be founded on the island and has preserved its colonial atmosphere. It is an excellent base from which to explore the mountains and villages of southwest Puerto Rico. The beautiful little **Porta Coeli** chapel on the east plaza contains a small museum of religious art. ■ *Wed-Sun 0830-1200, 1300-1630*. On the west plaza, **San Germán de Auxerre** is another beautiful church. A university town, it can be difficult to get cheap accommodation in term time.

Sleeping B-C *Oasis*, 72 Luna, T8921175, F8924546, has 52 rooms in old colonial mansion, a/c, TV, restaurant, pool, parking.

Sleeping

La Parguera

San Germán

Boquerón

On the south side of the west coast is Boquerón, in Cabo Rojo district, which has an excellent beach for swimming. It is very wide and long, admission US$1, camping, changing rooms, beach and first 30 m of sea packed with bodies on holiday weekends. About 1½ km away across the bay is a beautiful, deserted beach, but there is no road to it. The small village is pleasant, with typical bars, restaurants and street vendors serving the local speciality, oysters.

South of the town is **Boquerón Lagoon**, a wildfowl sanctuary; also the **Cabo Rojo Wildlife Refuge**, with a visitors' centre and birdwatching trails. The **Cabo Rojo lighthouse** (Faro), at the island's southwest tip is the most southerly point on the island with a breathtaking view; the exposed coral rocks have marine fossils and, closer inshore, shallow salt pools where crystals collect. The vegetation is dry scrub and you can find the slow growing hard wood, lignum vitae. Popular beaches in this area are **El Combate** (miles of white sand, undeveloped, but now a favourite with university students), south of Boquerón, and **Joyuda** (Isla de Ratones, a small island just offshore offers good snorkelling and swimming, but beach itself not spectacular) and **Buyé** to the north. At Joyuda you can go fishing, snorkelling or take a trip to Mona Island with Tour Marine Adventures, on the beach near *Perichi's*, T8519259, www.tourmarinepr.com

This is one of the cheapest spots on the island because it is a centre for the Compañía de Fomento Recreativo providing holiday accommodation for Puerto Rican families

Puerto Rico

Sleeping & eating C-D *Canadian Jack's Guest House*, T8512410. Private bathroom, colour TV, clean and comfortable but noisy on Fri, Sat nights when the streets are crowded with people partying, fantastic spot. Jack also rents hammocks overlooking the water. **A-B** *Boquemar*, end of Route 100, Int 101, Gil Bouye St, T8512158, F8517600, www.boquemar.com 75 rooms, a/c, bar, restaurant, pool, facilities for disabled, parking. At Cabo Rojo, **B** *Punta Aguila Villas*, T7254659, past the salt flats and *Agua El Cuello* restaurant. On shallow eelgrass beach but near 2 good swimming beaches, good hiking area, gazebos, jacuzzi, pool, 2 bedrooms. Next door is **AL-A** *Parador Bahía Salinas*, Route 301, Km 11.5, T2541212, F2541215, www.bahiasalinas.net Lovely setting, 24 rooms, most with porch for sunset watching, pool, kayaking, sailing, diving, fishing. **AL-B** *Perichi's*, Route 102,Km 14.3, Playa Joyuda, T8513131, F8510560, perichi@tropicweb.net 41 rooms, well-run, with good award-winning restaurant, walking distance to beach. **B** *Centro Vacacional de Boquerón*, run by Fomento Recreativo, fully self-contained, with barbecues, beach cabins. Foreigners are welcomed, but it is so popular with Puerto Ricans that you may have to make an application up to 3 months in advance. There are other hotels and a *parador*, **A-B** *Joyuda Beach*, Route 102, Km 11.7, T8515650, F2553750, www.joyudabeach.com 41 rooms, restaurant. **Camping** *Villa Plaza* (Denigno Ojeda Plaza) on the road to Cabo Rojo lighthouse, Route 301, Km 6.6, T8511340. Cabins, pool, electricity, security, US$25 per tent per night, US$20 for more than 1 day, take insect repellent.

Joyuda is famous for seafood restaurants on the beach; inexpensive food, good quality, nice atmosphere, whole, grilled fish is a must, especially snapper (*chillo*).

Mayagüez Founded in 1760, Mayagüez is now the third largest city, but crowded with little of interest to the tourist unless you want to go to the Tropical Agricultural Research Station (T8313435) or the **zoo**. ■ *Wed-Sun 0830-1600, T8348110*. There are some historic buildings around the Plaza Colón, including the City Hall and church. One block away, the **Teatro Yagüez** has been restored as the main cultural centre for the west of the island. It is not far to get to beaches or into the hills and is the western end of the Panoramic Route.

Sleeping **L-AL** *Mayagüez Resort & Casino*, Route 104, Km 0.3, T8317575, F2653020. 140 rooms in 20 acres, view of harbour, business hotel and resort of international standard, pool. **A-C** *Embajador*, 111 Ramos Antonini, Este, T8333340, F8347664. 29 rooms, central, phones, TV, restaurant, facilities for wheelchair visitors, laundry room. **A-B** *El Sol*, 9 Santiago R Palmer E, T8340303, T/F2657567. 52 rooms, CP, TV, fridge, phone, hair dryer, bar, restaurant, pool, modern block in city centre. **C** *Colonial*, Iglesia 14 Sur, T/F8332150, www.hotel-colonial.com 29 rooms for 1-4 people, CP, TV, building dates from 1920s and was once used as a convent. North of Mayagüez at Tres Hermanos, Bahía de Añasco, at Route 115 Km 5, is a **campground** with beach and pool, **B** cabins sleep 6, camping with water and electricity US$10 per tent per night.

Eating *Vegetarian Restaurant*, José de Diego. Open 1100-1400. *Fuente Tropical*, same street. Run by Colombians, good fruit shakes and hamburgers. *Recomeni*, Vigo. Good inexpensive food, open all hrs, eat in or takeaway.

Transport *Públicos* leave from a modern terminal in Calle Peral. Bus to San Juan US$10. Trolley bus service around town is free.

Mona Island
Colour map 2, grid B/C 5

Mona Island, 80 km west of Mayagüez, is fascinating with its turquoise sea and white sand. Originally inhabited by Taíno Indians and then by pirates and privateers, it is now deserted except for its wildlife. Here you can see 1-m iguanas, colonies of seabirds and bats in the caves. Cliffs, 60-m high, are dotted with caves, ascending to a flat table top covered with dry forest. The surrounding waters are teeming with fish, turtles, dolphins and, in the winter, whales, with excellent visibility and great diving.

Sleeping and eating The island is managed by the Department of National Resources (permit required, T7221726), who have cabins to rent with prior permission. **Camping** is allowed at Sardinera Beach, where there are bathrooms. Take all your food and water with you and bring back all your rubbish.

Tour operators *Eco Aventuras*, T8865309. Karina Zuñiga has specialized trips about 5 times a year, providing meals, transport, tents, permits, information and planning, US$175 per person for 7 days with 20 people, US$135 per person for 4 days with 4 people. *Aventurisla*, T7907816. Ricardo Otero offers much the same trip only you bring your own tent. *Tour Marine*, T8519259, 3752625, www.tourmarinepr.com Mona Island charters for parties of 6-12, take your own tents.

Transport Boats from Boquerón or Cabo Rojo 4 hrs, US$1,200 for 20-person boat, less for 14-person boat, leave before dawn. Contact Captains Porfirio Andujar, T8517359, Ramón Peña, T2552031; Catalino Lallave, T2855129; David Rodríguez, T8511885; Luís Ortiz, T8516276. Check with the PR Forestry Service or Vieques Air Link (Coptco Aviation T7290000 for private charter).

Going north from Mayagüez, you come to Rincón, on the westernmost point of the island. Here the mountains run down to the sea, and the scenery is spectacular. For a great panoramic view visit the **Punta Higuera Lighthouse**, built on a cliff overlooking the surf where the Atlantic and Caribbean meet. The town itself is unremarkable, but the nearby beaches are beautiful and the surfing is a major attraction. The beaches are called Steps, Domes (named after the nearby nuclear storage dome) and the Public Beach, with lifeguard. Pools, Sandy Beach and Antonio's are north of Punta Higuera and popular with winter surfers. Domes and María's are further south and offer good waves. Excursions can be arranged to the island of **Desecheo**, 19 km off the coast of Rincón. Desecheo is near Mona Island, but is smaller with terrific diving offshore.

Rincón
Humpback whales visit in winter and can be seen playing in the surf. Divers sometimes see them

Sleeping and eating LL *Horned Dorset Primavera*, Route 429, Km 0.3, T8234030, www.horneddorset.com No children under 12, no TV, no organized activities, 30 luxury suites in colonial Spanish style, private, good restaurant, beach not good for swimming, pool. **L-AL** *Villa Cofresí*, Route 115, Km 12.3, T8232450, www.villacofresi.com 63 rooms in modern blocks, on the beach, TV, kitchens, restaurant, bar, outdoor restaurant, watersports. **AL-A** *Villa Antonio*, alongside it, also at Route 115, Km 12.3, T8232645, www.villa-antonio.com 61 rooms (1 or 2 bedrooms) on a good beach for swimming and near good surfing beaches, a/c, volleyball, tennis, pool, kitchen, TV, parking, bar and restaurant close by. **AL-A** *The Lazy Parrot Inn and Restaurant*, Route 413, Km 4.1, Barrio Puntas, T8235654, www.lazyparrot.com In La Cadena hills overlooking coast, 11 rooms, sleep 4 in family room, also honeymoon suite, a/c, cable TV, fridge, restaurant closed Mon. **A-B** *Sandy Beach Inn*, Route 413, Km 4.3, T8231146, www.sandybeachinn.com On hillside with great view of Mona Passage, humpback whales can sometimes be seen from restaurant on roof, basic rooms and more comfortable apartment, imaginative menu, great fish and salads, main courses US$15-20, also burgers, sandwiches and wraps, vegetarian by prior arrangement.

Transport Rincón can be reached by *público* from Mayagüez or (less frequent) from Aguadilla. Public transport is scarce at weekends.

North of Rincón the road leads to Aguadilla, another good spot for sunset watching. **Crash Boat Beach** is a popular surfing and diving beach just to the north and lots of watersports are on offer. North again are more surfing beaches, **Gas Chamber** and **Wilderness**. *Aquatica Underwater Adventures*, Route 110, Km 10, T8906071, www.aquatica.cjb.net, offers diving and fishing and trips to Desecheo.

Aguadilla

Sleeping and eating L-B *La Cima*, Route 110, Km 9.2, Barrio Maleza Alta, T8902016, F8902017, www.lacima.com 40 rooms in 2-storey block around pool, a/c, TV, phone, exercise room, within reach of 6 beaches and golf. **AL-B** *Parador J B Hidden Village*, Route 416, Barrio Piedras Blancas, Aguada, T8688686, F8688701. 36 rooms built in 1990, a/c, bar, restaurant, pool, parking, facilities for disabled. **A-B** *Parador El Faro* , Route 107, Km 2.1, T8828000, F8913110, www.ihppr.com 75 rooms, built 1990, TV, phone, *Tres Amigos* restaurant for Puerto Rican and international food. **A-B** *Hacienda El Pedregal*, Route 111, Km 0.1, T8822865, F8822885, www.hotelelpedregal.com 27 rooms, view of ocean and sunsets, attractive rooms, TV, phone, parking, restaurant, bar, pools.

Puerto Rico

North coast road

Route 2, the main road in the north, runs from Aguadilla through Quebradillas to Arecibo, then through urban areas to some extent from Arecibo and completely from Manatí to San Juan. South of Quebradillas in the Montañas Aymamón is the **Bosque Estatal de Guajataca**, a dry forest with a large number of bird species, on Route 446. There are over 40 walking trails with 40 km of maintained footpaths through the Karst region, three picnic areas and two camping areas with tent sites (see page 367). South of Arecibo in the Karst country is the **Bosque Río Abajo**, a 2,023-ha reserve off Route 10. It contains 70 trails and dirt roads, ideal for viewing plant and birdlife, 15 commercial plantations (teak, mahogany, maga trees), two new campsites, two natural springwater swimming pools and some amazing bamboo near the end of the road. There is also a private campsite at Dos Bocas: *T J Ranch*, a coffee farm run by Tony and Juanita, pool, toilets, no electricity, US$5 per person, breakfast on request, go over the dam on Route 146, first left straight up to the top, past phone booth, then at intersection turn left (small sign for T J Ranch), T8801217, HC02 Box 14926, Arecibo, PR 00612.

Arecibo is famous for the **Observatory**, the world's largest radio radar telescope, south of the town, operated by Cornell University. There is a Visitors' Centre which puts on exhibitions for all ages. ■ *Mon-Fri 1200-1600, Sat-Sun 0900-1600. T8782612, www.naic.edu Route 625*. **The Arecibo Lighthouse** is also worth a visit, particularly if you have children. It has been fully restored in a recreation park with play area and replica sailing ships, together with museum, restaurant and sports facilities. ■ *Mon-Thu 0900-1800, Fri-Sun 0900-2100. Arecibo Dock, T8807540, www.arecibolighthouse.com Route 655.*

If you have the time it is much nicer to drive along the coast then along Route 2. Take Route 681 out of Arecibo, with an immediate detour to the Poza del Obispo beach, by Arecibo lighthouse. Here a pool has been formed inside some rocks, but the breakers on the rocks themselves send up magnificent jets of spray. The bay, with fine surf, stretches round to another headland, **Punta Caracoles**, on which is the **Cueva del Indio** (small car park on Route 681, US$1 charge if anyone is around). A short walk through private land leads to the cave, a sea-eroded hole and funnel in the cliff. There are Taíno/Arawak drawings in the cave. *Públicos* run along Route 681 from Arecibo. Rejoin Route 2 through Barceloneta. The State Forest of Cambalache is between Arecibo and Barceloneta. Cambalache Beach has two camping areas, La Boba and La Rusa, with water and showers, see page 367

The coast road is not continuous; where it does go beside the sea, there are beaches, seafood restaurants and some good views. Route 165, another coastal stretch which can be reached either through **Dorado** on the 693 (where there are three large *Hyatt* hotels and several golf courses, www.hyatt.com), or through Toa Baja, enters metropolitan San Juan at Cataño.

Sleeping & eating Near **Isabela** (www.isabelapr.com) on the coast is **LL** *Villa Montana*, Route 4466, Km 1.2, T8729554, www.villamontana.com Nice resort, tranquil spot, miles of sand dunes and surf, protected area for swimming, tennis, restaurant by pool bar, villas with kitchens, not much else, lots to do during the day but nothing at night. **AL-A** *Villas del Mar Hau*, T8722627, www.villahau.com Beachfront cabins set in palm and pine trees, some with a/c, some with fans, a few tent sites, US$10, private farm on beach, horse riding nearby, bike rental. **B** *Ocean Front Hotel*, Route 4466, Km 0.1, T8720444. Right on the beach with verandas overlooking the sand and the waves lapping feet away. 13 rooms with ocean view and excellent restaurant. At **Arecibo** there are several hotels and guesthouses around the main square, **D** *Hotel Plaza*. Near **Quebradillas**, Route 2, Km 103.8, are **A-B** *El Guajataca*, T8953070, www.elguajataca.com Beautifully located on a beach (dangerous swimming). 38 rooms, pool, entertainment, restaurant, bars. On the other side of the road, and higher up the hill at Km 7.9, Route 113, is **AL-B** *Vistamar*, T8952065, www.paradorvistamar.com 55 rooms, also with pool, restaurant and bar with view down to ocean, live music Sat.

Camping *Punta Maracayo Camping*, next to Sardinera beach, Km 84.6 on Ruta 2, T8200274. Owned by Hatillo Municipality, surreal with concrete dinosaurs, elephant etc next to campsite, small sheltered cove, calm water, good swimming, sand average, pool, cabins US$135 for 2 nights, US$25 additional nights, tent sites US$50 for 2 nights, US$20 additional nights, guard, fenced in, busy at weekends and in summer.

Panoramic Route

Heading east from Mayagüez is the Panoramic Route which runs the whole length of Puerto Rico, through some of the island's most stunning scenery. It passes through the Cordillera Central, with large areas of forest, and there are several excursions to various countryside resorts. Despite the fact that you are never far from buildings, schools or farms, the landscape is always fascinating. In the evening the panoramas are lovely and you can hear the song of the *coquí*. No trip to the interior should miss at least some part of the Panoramic Route, but if you want to travel all of it, allow three days. The roads which are used are narrow, with many bends, so take care at corners. From Maricao to Adjuntas there is no accommodation and no public transport. The **Maricao State Forest** (Monte del Estado) is the most westerly forest on the Route. It is a beautiful forest with magnificent views, an observation tower and a fish hatchery. ■ *Visitors' areas open 0600-1800. T7243724.*

In this part of the island it rains. Get your walking done in the morning as far as possible

A good three or four hour walk is to Las Marías, a cheery little town on a hill north of Maricao. You climb through banana and coffee plantations to a high ridge; views to the east show the degree of deforestation caused by coffee growing and building. For dedicated hikers, six hours of hard walking separates Las Marías from Lares ('captain of the mountains', see below). The countryside is lovely, you pass through forests, up large hills, down deep valleys and across wide rivers.

If you're very lucky it won't rain

Sleeping and eating AL-A *Parador Hacienda Juanita*, Route 105, Km 23.5, Maricao, T8382550, www.haciendajuanita.com 21 modest rooms, MAP, part of an old coffee plantation, bar, restaurant, pool, volleyball, tennis, basketball, gardens, walking trails, parking, facilities for disabled, cool at night. The only accommodation in Las Marías is **B-D** *Gutiérrez Guest House,* ½ mile east of town centre perched on top of a hill, Route 119, Km 26.1, T8272087/8273100. Essential to book ahead otherwise it may be closed, 13 rooms, big kitchen, pool, bar. Lares has nowhere to stay and the closest place is **B-C** *El Castillo*, on the road to San Sebastián, Route 111, Km 28.3, Barrio Eneas, T8962365. New building, good rooms, a/c, TV, pool, games room, barbecue and kitchen for guests' use, also cabins with jacuzzi, parking.

South of the Panoramic Route between Sabana Grande and Yauco on Route 371 is the **Bosque Estatal de Susua**, a dry forest with recreational areas, a river, 40 tent sites and showers (see page 367). As it approaches Adjuntas and the transinsular Route 10 (now the 123), the Panoramic Route goes through the **Bosque de Guilarte**, again with fine views, flowering trees, bougainvillaea, banks of impatiens (busy lizzie, *miramelinda* in Spanish), and bird song (if you stop to listen).

Susua & Guilarte

Adjuntas is a pleasant town with a picturesque plaza, surrounded by hills. Not much English is spoken at the tourist office on the main square, Plaza Aristides, T8293310, Mon-Fri 0800-1630, Sat 1000-1400. Roads around Adjuntas are confusing because new roads and road numbers may not be on your map. The old Route 10 to Ponce is now the 123, and there is a new road, Route 6. A big day out from Adjuntas is to climb up **Monte Guilarte** (1,205 m). To walk, leave town on the old Route 10 off the square, turn right on the 518 (unmarked). Three hours walking, past the lake, brings a park ranger station at the junction with the 131. From here a path takes nearly 30 minutes through eucalyptus trees to the summit, from where there are fantastic, breathtaking views. The path is easy and lovely but can be slippery coming down. If walking, this is what you have come to Puerto Rico for. At the bottom of the path is a small restaurant. Camping is available a few hundred metres away (see Camping, page 367).

Officially the coolest place in Puerto Rico, a good place for hikers to rest and burst blisters

Puerto Rico

Sleeping and eating LL-A *Parador Villas de Sotomayor*, Route 10, Km 36.3, Barrio Garzas, T8291717, F8295105, www.villassotomayor.com In valley west of town, 34 rooms, TV, tennis, volleyball, basketball, barbecue, bicycles, pool. **C** *Hotel Monte Río*, 2 blocks from Plaza in Adjuntas, Calle César González 18, T/F8293705, melo@coqui.net. Pool, economical, convenient, a bit old-fashioned but cheerful, daytime restaurant and bar.

Toro Negro After Adjuntas, the road enters the **Toro Negro Forest Reserve**, which includes the highest point on the island, **Cerro de Punta** (1,338 m). This is a smaller area than El Yunque, with fewer rivers. There are many very tall eucalyptus trees along the road. Lago El Guineo and Lago de Matrullas are Puerto Rico's highest lakes. The reserve has five trails, one to an observation tower with views of the mountains and lakes. You can see all too clearly the destruction of the forests by house building and coffee planting. A camping area (14 tent sites), has showers and toilets, see page 367.

Jayuya Just north of the Panoramic Route is Jayuya, overlooked by Cerro de Punta and Tres Picachos in a beautiful mountain setting, but the town is rather ramshackle It is known as the indigenous capital of Puerto Rico and is named after the Indian cacique Hayuya. Two monuments commemorate the Taíno heritage: a statue of Hayuya sculpted by Tomás Batista in 1969, and the Tumba del Indio Puertorriqueño, containing a Taíno skeleton buried in the foetal position. *Público* to San Juan at 1730, 3 hours, US$10, Línea San Juan, T7661720, César Ragan, will drop you anywhere around Río Piedras.

Sleeping and eating AL-A *Parador Hacienda Gripiñas*, Route 527 Km 2.7, T8281717, F8281719. About 1 hr's walk from town, 19 rooms in a coffee plantation house built in 1858, set in lovely gardens, friendly, pleasant, MAP, bar, restaurant, pool, parking, facilities for disabled. **A-B** *Posada Jayuya*, Guillermo Esteves 49, T8287250, F8281466. The only hotel in town, hideous building, conference facilities, can organize excursions, no food, helpful staff.

Cañon San Cristóbal
You can see the canyon from the top from a dirt road off Route 162; very impressive

After this high, lush forest with its marvellous vistas, the Panoramic Route continues to Aibonito, around which the views and scenery are more open, mainly as a result of deforestation (**C-E** *Swiss Inn Guest House*, Route 14 Km 49.3, T7358500, run by Gregory Muñoz, 8 rooms with shower, fans, balcony, TV, microwave, fridge, price negotiable for longer stays, very friendly and helpful, up in the mountains). Thence to Cayey and, beyond, to another forest, Carite (also known as Guavate, see page 384). Finally the road descends into the rich, green valley which leads to Yabucoa. Between Aibonito and Barranquitas is the Cañón San Cristóbal, where you can climb down a mountain trail between steep walls to the bottom, where the temperature is considerably warmer, four-hour trip. ■ *Call Félix Rivera, T7355188, for a guide, you will need one to find the way. He usually meets people at* La Piedra *restaurant, on Route 7718, one of Puerto Rico's gastronomic delights*.

From various points on the Panoramic Route you can head north or south; for example Route 10/123 goes south from Adjuntas to Ponce, or north to Utuado and then on to **Río Abajo State Forest** where there are a swimming pool and various picnic spots. ■ *0600-1800*. It is approached through splendid views of the karst hills and the **Dos Bocas Lake**. Free launch trips are offered on this lake at 0700, 1000, 1400 and 1700; they last two hours and are provided by the Public Works Department. Route 10 reaches the north coast at Arecibo.

Caguana Indian Ceremonial Park The Caguana Indian Ceremonial Park, west of Utuado, dates from about AD 1100, and contains 10 Taíno ball courts, each named after a Taíno *cacique* (chieftain). The courts vary in size, the longest being about 85 m by 20 m (Guarionex), the largest 65 m by 50 m (Agueybana). These two have monoliths in the stones that line the level 'pitch', and on those of Agueybana there are petroglyphs. A path leads down to the Río Tanamá. The setting, amid limestone hills, is very impressive. It is believed to be a site of some religious significance and has been restored with a small museum in the

13-acre landscaped botanical park containing royal palm, guava, cedar and ceiba. ■ *It is on Route 111 to Lares, Km 12.3. 0900-1700 (gate to the river closes at 1630). Free.*

Sleeping and eating A *Casa Grande*, Barrio Caonillas, Utuado, Route 612, Km 0.3, T8943939, www.hotelcasagrande.com 20 rooms in attractive mountain setting, former coffee plantation, hammocks, yoga, kayaking, bar, *Jungle Jane's* restaurant, pool.

Vieques

Vieques, a peaceful, relaxing, low-key island of rolling hills, is 11 km across the sea from Puerto Rico. It has been catapulted into the limelight since 1999 when islanders began a campaign for the removal of the US military from their bases at the east and west ends of the island. The island is about 34 km long and the inhabitants are mostly concentrated in the main town of Isabel Segunda. It was named Graciosa by Columbus, after a friend's mother, but was then better known as Crab Island by pirates.

Colour map 2, grid B6
Population: 9,400

Ins and outs

Fajardo is the closest sea and air port. Catch the ferry from Fajardo or a plane from San Juan or Fajardo. *Vieques Air Link* (T7413266) have flights from Fajardo (10 mins, T8633020), San Juan International (30 mins, T7223736), and Isla Grande and St Croix (30 mins, T7789858) many times a day. *Isla Nena*, T7411577, and the charter airline, *Air Culebra*, T2686951, also fly to Vieques.

Getting there
See Transport, page 395, for further details

Públicos meet you at the airport and ferry dock, posted rates (none higher than US$3), but some drivers will try to overcharge you, ask the price first, or let your hotel/guesthouse arrange transport for you. Car hire is widely available.

Getting around

Sights

There is an excellent historical museum in Isabel Segunda at the beautifully restored fort, **El Fortín Conde de Mirasol** which was the last fort begun by the Spanish in the Western Hemisphere. ■ *Wed-Sun 1000-1600. Week days by appointment,* T7411717 (7418651 evenings), www.vieques-island.com There is another interesting exhibit at the **Punta Mulas Lighthouse**. ■ *Daily 0800-1630. T7415000.*

The small beach town of **Esperanza** is the main area of guesthouses and tourist related restaurants, bars, dive companies (*Blue Caribe Dive Center*, SSI facility, full service, T7412522, PO Box 1574), etc. The **museum** in Esperanza has archaeological and natural history exhibits. ■ *Tue-Sun 1100-1500, T7418850.*

The biggest 'action' is on Sat night in Esperanza. Everyone promenades along the sea front dressed in their finest, talking and flirting, before going to a nightclub or bar

The US Military owns two-thirds of the island. The bases are theoretically open to the public upon presentation of any photo identification except on days when the red flag is up. However, since December 1999 Naval security guards have prevented tourists gaining any access to beaches although they can still be reached by boat. The Navy's reaction was as a result of the establishment of a protest camp at the gates. The US Navy is under pressure to leave and return the land. In 1999 the Governor requested an end of US weapons training on the island after a civilian was killed (see page 398). The military is heard but not seen, planes and helicopters fly low but since only a few personnel are permanently stationed on the island, it does not have a base town atmosphere.

Vieques has over 52 beaches in secluded coves. Public **Sun Bay** has picnic and camping areas (no shade in camping area, lots of petty theft). Small, hardy, island horses, most with paso fino blood lines (that means smooth gaits with no bouncing), are still used as transport, and wild horses roam the island. Renting a horse is an exciting way to explore the island.

Puerto Rico

Mosquito Bay, also known as **Phosphorescent Bay**, is a large, but very shallow bay, surrounded by mangrove trees and full of bioluminescent organisms. The organisms glow when disturbed. The glow generated by a 13 cm fish is about a 39 cm circle of light brighter than a light bulb. Swimming in this glow is a wonderful experience. Sightseeing trips go at night. ■ *US$15-18. Clark, T7417600, has a small boat; Sharon Grasso at* Island Adventures, *T741-0717/0720, www.bio bay.com, has an electric boat, naturalist, US$23 for night-time tour;* Blue Caribe Divers, *T7412522, night-time kayak tours, US$23, and night scuba dives. This is the only dive shop on the island, charging US$90 for a 2-tank dive with equipment rental.*

Essentials

Sleeping
www.vieques-island.com
www.viequespr.net
www.enchanted-isle.com
www.goto.com

Esperanza LL-L *Inn on the Blue Horizon*, Route 996, Km 4.2, T7413318, www.innonthebluehorizon.com, on the beach west of Esperanza. Run by Billy Knight and James Weis, from New York, 9 rooms, pool, popular bar and restaurant. **A** *La Casa del Francés*, T7413751, www.enchanted-isle.com/lacasa, Route 996. 18 rooms, classical sugar plantation Great House, designated historical landmark, bar, restaurant, pool, 5-min walk out of Esperanza. **A-B** *Amapola*, Flamboyan 144, T7411382, F7413704, www.enchanted-isle.com/amapola Five a/c rooms with private baths, restaurant. **C-D** *Bananas Guest House*, T7418700, facing the ocean. Some rooms a/c. **D** *Tradewinds*, owned by Janet and Harry Washburn, T7418666. Bar, restaurant. Smaller and cheaper guesthouses include: *La Central* (T7410106), *La Concha* (T7412733). *Acacia Apts*, 236 Acacia St, T/F7411856. Owned by Jürgen Meuser and Manfred Kissel, clean.

Isabel Segunda A-B *Ocean View*, 751 Calle Plinio Peterson, T7413696, F7411793. Concrete block hotel right on water's edge next to ferry dock, 31 rooms with balconies, Chinese restaurant next door under same ownership, car rental for guests. **B-C** *Sea Gate*, near the fort, T7414661, www.seagatehotel.com 16 rooms high up on hill, good views, pool, tennis, beach shuttle, horse riding. **C** *Posada Vistamar*, T741 8716. 6 rooms, a/c, fan, basic but adequate, excellent food, mosquitoes. **Inland** is **LL-L** *Hacienda Tamarindo*, T7418525, www.enchanted-isle.com/tamarindo 16 rooms and suites, CP, no children under 15, sea views, pool, run by Burr and Linda Vail. **L-B** *Crow's Nest*, T7410033, www.crowsnestvieques.com 16 rooms CP with kitchenettes or 2-bedroom suites with living areas, pool, restaurant. For villa rentals contact *Connections*, T7410023.

Vieques

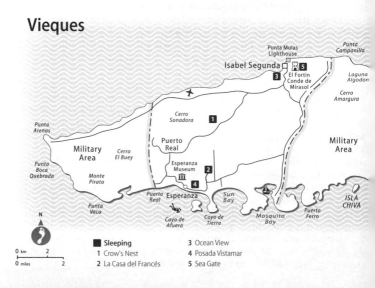

Sleeping
1 Crow's Nest
2 La Casa del Francés
3 Ocean View
4 Posada Vistamar
5 Sea Gate

Esperanza *Inn on the Blue Horizon* has *Café Blu* for fine dining, open Wed-Sun 1800-2200, lunchtimes Sat, Sun, reservations recommended, T7413318, and *Blu Bar* with happy hour 1600-1800 every day and lighter food 1200-2145, bar until 0030. *Bananas*, T7418700, Flamboyán St. Pub food and pizzas, beachfront, food until 2200-2300, late bar. *La Sirena*, T7414462. Waterfront French Caribbean, delicious 3-course dinner with wine US$30-35. *Crabwalk Café*, next to *Tradewinds*. Sandwiches, salads, open from 0800. *Trapper John's*, T7411325. Food until 2400, frozen drinks US$5. *La Central*, T7410106. For Puerto Rican food, *empanadas*. *Eddie's* for dancing, rum and beer, live music last weekend every month. *Chef Michael's*, 134 Flamboyan, T7410190. Good deli for picnic provisions or if you are self-catering. **Isabel Segunda** *Café Mar Azul*, bar on ocean front, T7413400. Open 0900-0100, happy hour 1700-1800. *Posada Vistamar* (see above), great Puerto Rican food with modern interpretation, full meal with wine around US$30. *Café Media Luna*, 351 AG Mellado, T7412594. In yellow colonial house, food a fusion of Puerto Rican and Indian, run by a Puerto Rican from New York and his wife from Bombay, choose a variety of dishes, tapas style, allow US$50 per person with wine. *Taverna Española*, T7411175. Spanish food, seafood, cheap and cheerful, around US$15 for meal with wine.

Eating
Almost all of the island's restaurants are part of a hotel or guesthouse

Ferry From Fajardo, the car, cargo and passenger ferries leave Mon-Fri 0400 (cars), 0930 (passengers), 0930 (cars), 1300 (passengers), 1630 (passengers and cars), Sat, Sun 0930, 1500, 1800, no car ferries. Vieques-Fajardo Mon-Fri at 0600 (cars), 0700 (passengers), 1100 (passengers), 1330 (cars), 1500 (passengers), 1830 (cars), Sat, Sun 0700, 1300, 1630, in Fajardo call the Port Authority office to transport a car, T8630852, 900-4622005, in Vieques T7414761, open for reservations 0800-1100, 1300-1500, reservations needed for cars only, book 2-3 weeks in advance, US$26 average return, passenger fare is US$2.25 one way, crossing takes 1½ hrs. At weekends the ferries are often full and advance reservations are recommended.

Transport

Road Car rentals available at *Maritza's Car Rental*(T7410078, www.islavieques.com/maritzas), *Island Car Rentals* (T7411666), *Fonsin*(T7418163) or *Vieques Car and Jeep Rental* (T7411037, www.viequescarrental.com). Bicycle rental through *DYMC*(T3162617) and *La Dulce Vida Mountain Bike Rental*, Calle Orquideas 69, T6172453, www.bikevieques.com

Culebra

Culebra has a climate and landscape similar to that of the Virgin Islands, with tropical forest on the hills and palm groves near the beaches. It is even better than Vieques, with less petty theft, better accommodation, more peace and more beautiful beaches, though the island is poor, with very high unemployment; most people who have jobs work for the municipality or in construction. It is about 11 km long and 5 km wide. Contact the **tourist office** on T7423291, F7420111; www.culebra.org, is an independent website.

Colour map 2, grid B6
Population: 3,500

The main village, **Dewey** (called Pueblo by the locals) is attractively set between two lagoons. A visitors' information centre is in the City Hall. About 40% of the land is park or national reserve, including many beaches. The **Culebra National Wildlife Refuge**, T7420115, 600 ha, comprising 23 offshore islands and four parcels of land on Culebra, protects large colonies of sea

Puerto Rico

birds, particularly terns, red-billed tropic birds and boobies, as well as nesting sea turtles: hawksbill, leatherback, loggerhead and green. Volunteers are welcomed (Apr-Aug) to help Wildlife Refuge rangers count and protect nests and hatchlings. Contact *Culebra Leatherback Project*, PO Box 617, Culebra, PR 00775, T7420050.

Flamenco Beach is 1½ km long with white sand and exquisitely beautiful clear turquoise water, a reef at one end and waves at the other. It is almost deserted except for a few guesthouses at the far end selling a limited amount of drinks, but it becomes a zoo at summer weekends. **Culebrita** and **Luís Peña** are two small cays offshore with beaches. Both are wildlife sanctuaries.

Sleeping **LL-AL** *Villa Flamenco Beach*, on the beach, 2 miles from town, T7423275. Range of studios, 3-bedroom villas, nice place to stay, some with ocean view. **L-AL** *Club Seabourne Mini Resort*, Fulladoza Bay, T7423169, seabourne@gobeach.com Villas and rooms, CP, restaurant, bar, pool, view, 1 mile from town, car hire needed. **L-AL** *Tamarindo Estates*, T7423343, www.tamarindoestates.com Pool, dock, private bay, snorkelling, dirt access road with potholes, 2 miles to town, car hire needed, restaurant open occasionally. **AL** *Rustic Eco-Cottages*, on the hill at Mosquito Bay, T7423136. 1 cottage sleeps 2, the other 4, CP, minimum 1 week rental, open Dec-Apr, solar power, composting toilets, no kitchens, no hot water, jeep rental needed, 2 mins down lovely trail to beach, good swimming and snorkelling, kayaks to rent, have to eat lunch and dinner out. **AL-A** *Villa Boheme*, Ensenada Honda, T/F7423508, on edge of town, harbour front. Family place, well-managed, clean, a/c, fans, 8 rooms with communal kitchen, 4 apartments with private kitchens, lovely breeze. **AL-A** *Villa Boheme*, Ensenada Honda, T/F7423508, on edge of town, harbour front. Family place, well-managed, clean, a/c, fans, 8 rooms with communal kitchen, 4 apartments with private kitchens, lovely breeze. **A** *Culebra Beach Resort*, T7420319. Run by Max and Esmeralda, next to *Villa Flamenco*, on the beach, nice, simple, clean rooms with kitchen, pleasant, helpful, lots of repeat business. **A-B** *Posada La Hamaca*, 68 Castelar, T7423516, www.posada.com Well kept, only 10 rooms, private bath, beach towels, book in advance, next to *Mamacitas* on the canal. **B** *Arynar Villa*, T7423145, www.enchantedisle.com/villaaarynar 2 rooms in lovely house on hill, CP, less than a mile to town. **B-C** *Mamacitas Guest House*, T7420090. With or without kitchens. **B-C** *Villa Fulladoza Guest House*, T7423576, on the bay. Best value, kitchens, short walk to town, usually booked up. **C-D** *Kokomo*, T7420719, opposite ferry dock. Some rooms a/c. *Casa Katrina*, T7423565, in town. Weekly rates. *Pelican Enterprise & Culebra Island Realty*, T7420052, www.culebrais landrealty.com, do house rentals, island-wide.

Camping *Culebra Campgrounds* are government-run, US$10 per site, up to 6 people per tent, 2-night minimum, 140 tent sites, bathrooms and water provided but that's all. Not crowded during winter months, just turn up, office open 0700-1800, T7420700. To make a reservation (essential Jun-Sep) send US$20 cheque to *Autoridad de Conservación y Desarrollo de Culebra*, attn Playa Flamenco, Apdo 217, Culebra, PR 00775 USA.

Eating There are several small restaurants in Dewey, offering local dishes and seafood. Takeaways
Prices range from available. *Dinghy Dock Restaurant* on the water in the lagoon, breakfast, lunch and dinner,
US$10-25 for a meal American and Caribbean food. *El Pesquerito*, breakfast and lunch, Puerto Rican and seafood, US$3-8. *Wai-Nam*, Chinese, lunch and dinner, cheap. Also restaurants at the hotels, *Mamacitas*, *Seabourne*, *Tamarindo*. For those who are self-catering, there are 7 grocery stores, *Culebra Deli*, a fish market and a liquor store. Everything is imported so prices are high.

Tour operators Scuba diving is spectacular in the waters around Culebra, where the sea is clear and the pristine
& watersports reefs provide lots to see. Dive shops are small and friendly, with flexible programmes and other
There are good, sandy watersports and boat trips on offer. *Culebra Divers* is opposite the ferry dock, run by Walter
beaches, clear water Rieder (Swiss) and Monika Frei (both instructors), T7420803, www.culebradivers.com *Culebra*
and a coral reef *Dive Shop*, T7420566. Kayak rental from *Ocean Safari*, Jim and Barbara Peters, T3791973, US$25 half day, guided expeditions US$45 half day, US$70 full day. Several people offer boat trips or water taxi, some of whom can also do fishing. *Pat's Water Taxi* and glass-bottom boat trips, from the dock by *Dinghy Dock Restaurant*, T5010011, to Culebrita US$40, Luís Peña US$20, glass-bottom tours US$15, snorkelling tours US$20-40. *Culebra Boat Rental*, T7873559,

hires 6-person skiffs for exploring and transport. *Jack's*, T3977494, offers boat trips for snorkelling or water taxi service to the cays offshore, as do *Tanama Glass-Bottom Boat*, T5010011, *Culebra Divers*, T7420803, *Guilins Water Taxi*, T7420575.

Local Road Public transport consists of vans. If they're not at the airport, walk into town. **Transport**
They also run from town to Flamenco Beach, but for access to other beaches, cars and bicycles can be hired and there is also a taxi service. **Bicycle hire** is US$12 per day from *Culebra Bike and Beach*(T7420434), Richard (T7420062) or Wille (T7420563); cars and jeeps from *Prestige* (7423242), *Richard and Kathy's Rentals*(T7420062), *Willy Solis*(T7423537), *R & W* (T7420563) and *Jerry's Jeeps* (T7420587). Taxi service with Marcelino (T7420292) or Cito (T7422787).

    Air Flights from San Juan International Airport take 30 mins, from Isla Grande Airport 30   *No direct flights*
mins and from Fajardo 15 mins. *Isla Nena*, at San Juan International Airport, T(888)2636213,   *Vieques-Culebra*
7411577, in CulebraT7420972, flies 4 times a day San Juan-Culebra, US$60 one way, US$115 return, also 3 times a day Culebra-Fajardo, US$25 one way, and Culebra-St Thomas US$50 on the mail flight Tue and Thu. *Vieques Air Link*, T7420254 in Culebra, T8633020 in Fajardo, T7223736 in San Juan, San Juan Isla Grande-Culebra twice a day, US$50 one way, US$95 round trip, and 3 times a day Fajardo-Culebra, US$25. *Air Culebra* is a charter company, T2686951, 7420446, US$300 one way for up to 5 people.

    Sea The ferry from Fajardo to Culebra takes about 1½ hrs, and costs US$2.25 per person   *At weekends the*
each way, cars about US$26 return. Fajardo-Culebra, Mon-Fri 0930, 1500, 1600 (cars), Wed,   *ferries are usually*
Fri 1000 (cars), Sat, Sun 0430 (cars, every other Sat), 0900, 1600. Return Culebra-Fajardo   *full, best to*
Mon-Fri 0700 (cars), 1100, 1630, Wed, Fri 1300 (cars), Sat, Sun 0700, 1400, 1730, 1800 (cars,   *reserve a ticket*
every other Sat). Reservations 3-4 weeks in advance needed for cars. Fajardo ticket and information office is open 0800-1100, 1300-1500, T8630705, 1-800-9812005 (Culebra T7423161). Ferries which take cars are slower and rougher and passengers tend to get seasick.

Background

History

Columbus, accompanied by a young nobleman, Juan Ponce de León, arrived in Puerto Rico on 19 November 1493. Attracted by tales of gold, Ponce obtained permission to colonize Boriquén (or Boriken), as it was called by the natives. Boriquén (later altered to Borinquén in poetry) meant 'land of the great lord' and was called that because of the belief that the god, Juracan, lived on the highest peak and controlled the weather from there. The word 'hurricane' is derived from this god's name.

    Because of Puerto Rico's excellent location at the gateway to Latin America, it played an important part in defending the Spanish Empire against attacks from French, English and Dutch. After the Spanish-American war, Spain ceded the island to the United States in 1898. The inhabitants became US citizens in 1917, and in 1948 they elected their own Governor, who is authorized to appoint his Cabinet and members of the island's Supreme Court. In 1952 Puerto Rico became a Commonwealth voluntarily associated with the United States.

    The island's status is constantly debated for both political and economic reasons as Puerto Rico is heavily dependent on US funding. The New Progressive Party (NPP) favours Puerto Rico's full accession to the USA as the 51st state. The Popular Democratic Party (PDP) favours enhancement of the existing Commonwealth status. Pro-independence groups receive less support, the Puerto Rican Independence Party (PIP) struggles to gain seats in Congress. A referendum on Puerto Rico's future status was held in 1991 and 1993.

    In December 1998 Puerto Ricans voted again in a referendum on the island's status. 46.5% was in favour of statehood, but 50.2% voted for 'none of the above' options, which were to continue the present Commonwealth status, enter the USA as a state of the union, free association, or become independent, with a 10-year transitional period for any change in status. 'None of the above' was included at the request of the PDP, which supports the present Commonwealth status but objected to the wording.

Puerto Rico

The presence of the US Navy on Vieques became an issue after a civilian was killed in 1999 during bombing practice. Local people on Vieques and Puerto Rico protested and called for a ban on live ammunition and the return of the land to the people of Vieques. Exercises using live ammunition were suspended in May 1999. Governor Rosselló rejected a US presidential panel's recommendation that exercises should continue for another five years. President Clinton offered to limit operations to 90 days a year instead of the previous 180, and then conceded that live ammunition would no longer be used, while offering US$40 mn in development aid for the island if residents accepted the five-year continuation. His proposals were rejected. A revised proposal from the Pentagon was also rejected and civil disobedience intensified during 2000. In May 2000 US Navy aircraft resumed bombing practice. Dummy ammunition was used.

In November 2000, Sila Calderón, of the PDP, a business executive and former Secretary of State in the previous PDP administration in the 1980s, was elected Governor on an anti-statehood platform. The PDP won the majority of seats in both houses, giving it a clear mandate not to become the 51st state of the union. The victory was also seen as a popular rejection of the agreement with the US administration to delay until 2003 the withdrawal of the Navy from its bombing range on Vieques. The Navy refused to transfer 8,000 acres of land on Vieques to the government, planned for 31 December, until Ms Calderón promised to stand by the agreement. In May 2003, amid general rejoicing, the Navy finally pulled out of Vieques and the land became a National Park.

Geography

Puerto Rico is the smallest of the Greater Antilles. Old volcanic mountains, long inactive, occupy a large part of the interior, with the highest peak, Cerro de Punta, at 1,338 m in the Cordillera Central. North of the Cordillera is the karst country where the limestone has been acted upon by water to produce a series of small steep hills (*mogotes*) and deep holes, both conical in shape. There is an extensive cave system, much of which is open to the public or can be explored with expert guidance. The mountains are surrounded by a coastal plain with the Atlantic shore beaches cooled all the year round by trade winds. Offshore are the sister islands of Vieques, Culebra and the even smaller Mona Island, where facilities are limited to a camp site.

Government

Puerto Rico is a self-governing Commonwealth in association with the USA (Estado Libre Asociado de Puerto Rico). The chief of state is the President of the United States of America. The head of government is an elected Governor. There are two legislative chambers: the House of Representatives, 51 seats, and the Senate, 27 seats. Two extra seats are granted in each house to the opposition if necessary to limit any party's control to two thirds. Puerto Ricans do not vote in US federal elections, nor do they pay federal taxes, when resident on the island.

Economy

The 'Operation Bootstrap' industrialization programme, supported by the US and Puerto Rican governments, began in 1948, and manufacturing for export subsequently became the most important sector of the economy. Until 1976, US Corporations were given tax incentives to set up in Puerto Rico and their profits were taxed only if repatriated. Industrial parks were built based on labour intensive industries to take advantage of Puerto Rico's low wages. In the mid-1970s, however, the strategy changed to attract capital intensive companies with the aim of avoiding the low wage trap. The agreement between the USA, Canada and Mexico for the North American Free Trade Agreement (NAFTA) also has implications for Puerto Rico because of competition for jobs and investment. Although wage levels are lower in Mexico, Section 936 gives companies in Puerto Rico an advantage in pharmaceuticals and hi-tec industries. In low-skill labour-intensive manufacturing, Mexico has the advantage. Puerto Rico currently employs 30,000 in the clothing industry. Dairy and livestock production is one of the leading agricultural activities; others are the cultivation of sugar, tobacco, coffee, pineapples and coconut. Rum has been a major export since the 19th century and the island supplies 83% of all the rum drunk in mainland USA. Tourism is another key element in the economy although it contributes only about 7% to gdp. Over 4 mn people visit Puerto Rico each year and spend about US$1.9 bn. Large construction projects are underway to boost tourism still further, with several 5-star hotels being built around the country and a massive Convention Center with adjacent 850-room hotel to open in 2005 at Isla Grande. Total investment in present and planned projects is over US$2.2 bn, which will increase hotel capacity by 8,627 rooms, or 56%.

Despite the progress made to industrialize the country, the economy has suffered from US budget cuts. Some 30% of all spending on gnp originates in Washington and high unemployment is possible because of food stamps and other US transfers. Migration is a safety valve, and there are more Puerto Ricans living in New York than San Juan. The economy depends heavily on tax incentives given to US mainland companies and on federal transfers.

Culture

One of the oldest musical traditions is that of the 19th-century Danza, associated particularly with the name of Juan Morel Campos and his phenomenal output of 549 compositions. This is European-derived salon music for ballroom dancing, slow, romantic and sentimental. The Institute of Puerto Rican Culture sponsors an annual competition for writers of danzas for the piano during the Puerto Rican Danza Week in May. The peasants of the interior, the Jíbaros, sing and dance the Seis, of Spanish origin, in its many varied forms, such as the Seis Chorreao, Seis Zapateao, Seis Corrido and Seis Bombeao. Other variants are named after places, like the Seis Cagueño and Seis Fajardeño. Favoured instruments are the *cuatro* and other varieties of the guitar, the *bordonúa*, *tiple*, *tres* and *quintillo*, backed by *güiro* (scraper), *maracas*, *pandereta* (tambourine) and *bomba* (drum) to provide rhythm. One uniquely Puerto Rican phenomenon is the singer's 'La-Le-Lo-Lai' introduction to the verses, which are in Spanish 10-line *décimas*. The beautiful Aguinaldos are sung at Christmastime, while the words of the Mapeyé express the Jíbaro's somewhat tragic view of life. Many artists have recorded the mountain music, notably El Gallito de Manatí, Ramito, Chuito el de Bayamón, Baltazar Carrero and El Jibarito de Lares.

Puerto Rico's best-known musical genre is the Plena, ironically developed by a black couple from Barbados, John Clark and Catherine George, known as 'Los Ingleses', who lived in the La Joya del Castillo neighbourhood of Ponce during the years of the First World War. With a four-line stanza and refrain in call-and-response between the 'Inspirador' (soloist) and chorus, the rhythm is distinctly African and the words embody calypso-style commentaries on social affairs and true-life incidents. Accompanying instruments were originally tambourines, then accordions and *güiros*, but nowadays include guitars, trumpets and clarinets. The Plena's most celebrated composer and performer was Manuel A Jiménez, known as 'Canario'.

There are few pure black people in Puerto Rico, although the majority have African blood, and the only black music is the Bomba, sung by the 'Cantaor' and chorus, accompanied by the drums called *buleadores* and *subidores*. The Bomba can be seen and heard at its best in the island's only black town of Loiza Aldea at the Feast of Santiago in late July. Rafael Cepeda and his family are the best known exponents.

The Jíbaro, mentioned above, is a common figure in Puerto Rican literature. It refers to the *campesino del interior*, a sort of Puerto Rican equivalent to the gaucho, native, but with predominantly hispanic features. The literary Jíbaro first appeared in the 19th century, with Manuel Alonso Pacheco's *El gíbaro* emerging as a cornerstone of the island's literature. Alonso attempted to describe and to interpret Puerto Rican life; he showed a form of rural life about to disappear in the face of bourgeois progress. The book also appeared at a time (1849) when romanticism was gaining popularity. Before this, there had been a definite gulf between the educated letters, chronicles and memoires of the 16th to 18th centuries and the oral traditions of the people. These included *coplas*, *décimas*, *aguinaldas* and folk tales.

Music & dance
There are several music festivals each year, celebrating different styles and forms, including a Jazzfest in May and the Casals Music Festival in June

Literature

Puerto Rico

The Jíbaro has survived the various literary trends, from 19th-century romanticism and *realismo costumbrista* (writing about manners and customs), through the change from Spanish to US influence, well into the 20th century.

One reason for this tenacity is the continual search for a Puerto Rican identity. When, in 1898, Spain relinquished power to the USA, many Puerto Ricans sought full independence. Among the writers of this time were José de Diego and Manuel Zeno Gandía. The latter's series of four novels, *Crónicas de un mundo enfermo* (*Garduña* – 1896, *La charca* – 1898, *El negocio* – 1922, *Redentores* – 1925), contain a strong element of social protest. For a variety of domestic reasons, many fled the island to seek adventures, happiness and wealth in the United States. While some writers and artists in the 1930s and 1940s tried to build a kind of nationalism around a mythical, rural past, others still favoured a separation from the colonialism which had characterized Puerto Rico's history. For a while, the former trend dominated, but by the 1960s the emigré culture had created a different set of themes against the search for the Puerto Rican secure in his/her national identity. These included the social problems of the islander in New York, shown in some of the novels of Enrique A Laguerre, *Trópico en Manhattan* by Guillermo Cotto Thorner, or stories such as *Spiks* by Pedro Juan Soto, or plays like René Marqués' *La carreta*. There is also the Americanization of the island, the figure of the 'piti-yanqui' (the native Puerto Rican who admires his North American neighbour) and the subordination of the agricultural to a US-based, industrial economy. Writers after 1965 who have documented this change include Rosario Ferré and the novelist and playwright, Luis Rafael Sánchez. The latter's *La guaracha del Macho Camacho* (1976) revolves around a traffic jam in a San Juan taken over by a popular song, *La vida es una cosa fenomenal*, a far cry from the Jíbaro's world.

US Virgin Islands

Introducing the US Virgin Islands

The three US Virgin Islands may be very different from each other, but all are very American. St Thomas attracts cruise ships and, when several are in port, the streets of town are heavily congested with shoppers. St John is dominated by the Virgin Islands National Park, which has been in existence since 1956 and has some excellent trails for walkers. St Croix is the poorest of the three but nevertheless still has a great deal to offer. All three have good hotels and are popular with the sailing fraternity.

Essentials

Climate The climate in the Virgin Islands is very pleasant, with the trade winds keeping the humidity down. The average temperature varies little between winter (77°F) and summer (82°F). Average annual rainfall is 40 ins. In recent years the islands have been badly hit by Hurricanes Hugo (1989), Luis (1995) and Lenny (1999), causing deaths and huge amounts of destruction, although this is now no longer evident.

Getting there

From the USA There are scheduled flights to St Croix and/or St Thomas with *American Airlines* (Baltimore, Boston, Miami, New York), *Delta* (Atlanta, Detroit, Washington DC), *United Airlines* (Chicago, Washington DC), *Continental* (New York), *US Air* (Philadelphia, Charlotte). **From Europe** No direct flights, connections can be made via Miami or Puerto Rico, St Maarten and Antigua. Regional airlines link the USVI with other Caribbean islands and there are flights to Anguilla, Antigua, St Barthélemy, Puerto Rico (San Juan and Fajardo), St Kitts, Nevis, St Maarten and the BVI. *Bohlke International Airways*, T7789177, has a charter service between St Thomas and St Croix and day trips to Virgin Gorda and Anegada in the BVI with lunch, swimming and sightseeing. *American Eagle*, *Gulfstream International*, *Cape Air* (T800 3520714, www.flycapeair.com) and *Seaborne Aviation* (seaplane, T7736442 in St Croix, T7771227 in St Thomas) all run services several times daily between Puerto Rico, St Thomas and St Croix.

Air *During the winter season there are many charter flights from the USA (Midwest, Northeast), Canada, UK and Denmark*

Ocean-going ships can be accommodated at **Charlotte Amalie** in St Thomas and **Frederiksted** and the **South Shore** cargo port in St Croix. There are regular services between the USVI and the BVI (passport or birth certificate needed). *Native Son* (T7748685) and *Smith's Ferry* (T7772922) alternate services from Charlotte Amalie to West End, Tortola (45 mins, US$40 return) and on to Road Town, Tortola (90 mins, US$40 return), several daily, some stop in Red Hook. *Smith's Ferry* also to Virgin Gorda. *Inter Island Boat Services* (T7766597) several daily between Cruz Bay, St John and West End, Tortola; three times a week, Red Hook and Cruz Bay to Jost Van Dyke, BVI; twice a week Red Hook-Cruz-Virgin Gorda.   **Ports of entry** Charlotte Amalie, St Thomas; Christiansted and Frederiksted, St Croix; Cruz Bay, St John. **Documents** The USVI are a territory of the USA but constitute a separate customs district. US boats with US citizens have to clear in here when coming from Puerto Rico (can be done by phone on St Croix) and all other islands. For more about custom fees, call Mr Harrigan on T7742510, ext 223. St Croix customs T7731011. When arriving by boat ensure that you have the correct visas for immigration purposes. All vessels must clear in upon arrival from a foreign port and all crew members aboard must go ashore with the captain to obtain entry into the USVI. Clearing customs and immigration on St John is a pain due to the crowded harbour. Anchor if you can find room, try northwest end of island or just outside harbour. On St Croix, foreign boats or boats with foreign passengers clear customs at Gallows Bay Dock.

Boat

Where to stay

There is an 8% tax on all forms of accommodation in the US Virgin Islands. Hotels may also charge 10-15% service, but most leave tipping to the individual. High season is mid-Dec to mid-Apr, but higher prices sometimes last into May, depending on carnival dates, despite lower hotel occupancy.

See individual towns for further information

Getting around

There are lots of flights between St Croix and St Thomas. *American Eagle*, *Cape Air* and other flights are available. *Seaborne Airlines* (seaplanes) (T7736442, www.seaborneairlines.com) has many flights a day between Frederiksted or Christiansted Harbour and Charlotte Amalie, 18 mins, US$75 one way for non-VI residents. Spectacular view arriving into St Croix and seeing the coral reef from the seaplanes. There is a strictly enforced 25-lb baggage weight (US$0.50 per lb overweight but excess baggage may not travel until later).

Air

US Virgin Islands

► ## Tourist offices overseas

Canada 703 Evans Av, Suite 106, Toronto, Ontario, M9C 5E9, T416-6227600, jsintzel@travmarkgroup.com
Denmark Park Allé 5, DK-8000, Aarhus Center, T(45)86-181933, usvi@danskvestindiskturist.dk
Italy Via Gherardini 2, 20145, Milan, T(39)02-33105841,
UK Power Road Studios, Chiswick, London W4 5PY, T020-79785222,
usvi@destination-marketing.co.uk
USA Chicago, IL, T312-6708784, usvichgo@earthlink.net; **Coral Gables**, FL, T305-4427200, usvimia@aol.com; **New York**, NY, T212-3322222, usviny@aol.com;
Washington DC, T202-6243590, usvidc@sso.org; **Atlanta**, GA, T404-6880906, usviatl@aol.com; **Los Angeles**, CA, T213-7390138, usvi_la@msn.com

Car The country speed limit is 35 mph and in towns it is 20 mph, although the traffic is so heavy you will be lucky if you can go that fast. On St John the speed limit is 20 mph everywhere. Driving is on the left, even though the cars are left-hand drive. Be sure to buckle up as there is a seatbelt law for the driver and front seat passenger that the police enforce with a vengeance (US$25 fine).

Sea Ferry St Thomas-St John, 20 mins from Red Hook (US$3 adult, US$1 child), 45 mins from Charlotte Amalie (US$7 adult, US$3 child), Cruz Bay-Red Hook hourly, Cruz Bay-Charlotte Amalie 7 a day, Transportation Services T7766282. This can be a bit bumpy. Car ferry St Thomas-St John, Boysons Inc, T7766294, Republic Barge T7794000. *The VI Fast Ferry*, T7190099, www.virginislandsfastferry.com, is a 600-passenger catamaran which operates between St Thomas and St Croix mid-Nov to mid-May, there are 3 a day, 75 mins, US$60 return. Private boats can be hired: *Dohm's Catamaran*, T7756501, will take you anywhere in a power boat.

Keeping in touch

Telephone
IDD code: 340

Local telephone calls within the USVI from pay phones are US$0.25-0.35 for each five minutes. Privately owned payphones charge for local calls, even 800 numbers. Innovative and Vitelcellular do not make extra charges. Radio Shack offers pre-paid cellular service, T7775644, 7741314, so does Cingular, bring your own phone or buy one of theirs, US$0.52 per minute in USVI and Puerto Rico. GSM is being introduced, T800-3310500.

Media The Thu edition of *The Daily News*, US$0.75, includes the weekend section listing restaurants, nightclubs, music and special events, for all three islands.

Shopping

See individual towns for further information

The USVI are a free port and tourist-related items are duty-free. Shops are usually shut on Sun unless there is a cruise ship in harbour. There are several rums available in white or gold, and some interesting fruit-flavoured ones as well. Cruzan gives guided tours of the distillery on St Croix, Mon-Fri 0900-1130, 1300-1615, but phone in advance, T6922280; US$3 adults, US$1 children. Locally woven crafts (hats, baskets, brooms, fish traps, bookmarks, Christmas tree ornaments) are made from coconut palms, sabal and wild teyer palm. Baskets are made from wiss and hoop vines. Handmade moco jumbi dolls are works of art.

Flora and fauna

The Virgin Islands' national bird is the yellow breast (*Coereba flaveola*); the national flower is the yellow cedar (*Tecoma stans*). The mongoose was brought to the islands during the plantation days to kill rats that ate the crops. Unfortunately rats are nocturnal and mongooses are not and they succeeded only in eliminating most of the parrots and snakes. Now you see them all over the islands, especially near the rubbish dumps. There are many small lizards and some iguanas of up to 4 ft long. The iguanas sleep in the trees and you can see them and

US Virgin Islands

Touching down

Boat information St Thomas Most moorings are privately owned. It is illegal to use a private mooring without permission from the DPNR. The dive companies have placed moorings near some dive locations on Buck Island, Saba Island, Little St James Island and a few others. There are dinghy docks at Yacht Haven Marina, along the waterfront near Coast Guard Dock, Frenchtown Marina, Crown Bay Marina, Water Island Ferry Dock (privately owned). **St John** The US Park Service has placed moorings to protect reefs and seagrass. A yacht may anchor in the park for no more than 14 days a year. Park moorings on north shore: Caneel Bay, Hawksnest, Cinnamon Bay, Maho, Francis Bay; on south shore: Salt Pond, Little Lameshur and Great Lameshur. Forbidden to anchor on south shore, moorings must be used. There are some private moorings for day charter boats in Maho Bay, Cruz Bay. Great Cruz Bay and Coral Bay are not within the Park territory and have privately owned moorings. **St Croix** Divers have placed mooring buoys at all dive locations to prevent damage to the reefs while anchoring. Stays are limited to 4 hrs. All moorings in the harbour are privately owned. Buck Island has moorings placed within the snorkelling area for day use only. Overnight anchoring is not allowed and boats must anchor in sand at southwest end of island. Marinas at St Croix Marine, Jones Maritime, St Croix Yachting Club, Green Cay Marina, Salt River Marina. Anchorages at Christiansted, Frederiksted (deep, so very difficult), Green Cay, Teague Bay by St Croix Yacht Club (reciprocates with members of other yacht clubs).

Business hours Banks: Mon-Fri 0830-1500; **Government offices:** Mon-Thu 0900-1700 (banks, filling stations and government offices close for local holidays).

Clothing Bathing suits are considered offensive when worn away from the beach, so cover up. There is a law against it, and you can even be fined for having your belly showing. It is illegal to go topless on Magens Beach.

Currency US dollar. Credit cards are widely accepted.

Departure tax No departure tax at the airport (charge of US$5 is included in the ticket).

Documents US citizens do not require passports but they do need proof of citizenship to return to the USA. Visitors of other nationalities will need passports, visas (or waiver for participating countries) and return/onward tickets, as they would for the mainland USA.

Emergency numbers T911.

Finding out more www.usvi.net, www.usvitourism.vi and www.usvichamber.com The following publications all have regularly updated tourist information: Explore St Thomas & St John, The St John Guidebook, Boutique Shopping Guide, St Croix This Week, Virgin Island Playground, What To Do St Thomas and St John, St John Tradewinds and St Thomas This Week. The free weekly Island Trader is aslo a good source of events and activities.

Official time Atlantic Standard Time, four hours behind GMT, one hour ahead of EST.

Public holidays New Year's Day, Three Kings Day (6 Jan), Martin Luther King Day (15 Jan), Presidents' Day (19 Feb), Holy Thu, Good Fri, Easter Mon, Memorial Day (28 May), Organic Act Day (18 Jun), Emancipation Day (3 Jul), Independence Day (4 Jul), Labour Day (beginning of Sep), Puerto Rico/Virgin Islands Friendship Day (mid-Oct), Liberty Day (1 Nov), Veterans' Day (11 Nov), Thanksgiving Day (mid-Nov), Christmas (25 and 26 Dec).

Safety Take the usual precautions against crime: lock your car, leave valuable jewellery at home and be careful walking around at night. Do not go to deserted beaches on your own. Couples have been held up at gunpoint and robbed and/or raped on the beach after dark. Youth unemployment is a problem. St John is generally safer than St Thomas, but take the usual precautions, there have been reports of attacks on Cinnamon Bay Beach, while crack cocaine is sold fairly openly on the streets in Cruz Bay.

Tipping As in mainland USA, tipping is 15%; hotels often add 10-15%.

Useful addresses Air Ambulance: Bohlke International Airways, T7789177 (day), 7721629 (night); recompression chamber 7762686.

Voltage 120 volts 60 cycles.

Weights and measures Imperial.

See also Directories of individual islands

US Virgin Islands

> ### Things to do in the US Virgin Islands
>
> - Try a **coquito**, a local rum concoction of Cruzan rum, coconut and sugar, sold on the street.
> - Dance to live music on the sand in the moonlight at **Miss Lucy's** restaurant on St John, where a pig roast is served every full moon.
> - Avoid the crowds on St Thomas and take a boat to one of the **uninhabited islets** offshore.
> - Take a tour of the restored **historic estates** on St Croix, sponsored by the St Croix Landmark Society several times a year.
> - Find a **rock pool** on a beach on St Croix and soak in nature's own hot tub where tidal water is warmed by the sun.

feed them (favourite food hibiscus flowers) at the Limetree Beach, at *Bluebeards Beach Club and Villas*, at Coral World and Frenchmans Reef. St John has a large population of wild donkeys on the upper hills which are pests.

The headquarters of the National Parks Service is on St John, T7166201, with lots of information, reference books and interpretative programmes

Most of St John is a national park. Hassel Island, off Charlotte Amalie, is also a park. *Virgin Islands Birdlife*, published by the USVI Co-operative Extension Service, with the US National Park Service, is available for birdwatchers. On St Croix, the National Parks Service office is in the Old Customs Building on the waterfront. Buck Island is listed as an underwater monument. In Christiansted, the *Environmental Association*, T7731989, office in Apothecary Hall Courtyard, Company St, runs hikes, boat trips and walks, and in Mar-May, in conjunction with Earthwatch and the US Fish and Wildlife Department, you can see the leatherback turtles at Sandy Point, one of 13 significant nesting sites worldwide (T7737545). The association has made Salt River (see page 419) a park for wildlife, reef and mangroves.

St Thomas

IDD code: 340
Colour map 2, grid B6
Population: 51,000

St Thomas is on practically every Caribbean cruise itinerary, and thousands of cruise ship passengers descend daily on Charlotte Amalie, the capital, for the ultimate shopping experience. Traffic grinds to a halt as congestion of roads and pavements becomes uncontrollable. Avoid the town when the cruise ships are in port and explore the island. St Thomas rises out of the sea to a range of hills that runs down its spine. The highest peak, Crown Mountain, is 1,550 ft. On St Peter Mountain, 1,500 ft, is a viewpoint at Mountain Top. There are various scenic roads to drive along, such as Skyline Drive (Route 40), from which both sides of the island can be seen simultaneously, and Mafolie Road (Route 35), which leaves Charlotte Amalie, heading north to cross the Skyline Drive becoming Magens Bay Road, and descends to the beautiful bay.

Ins and outs

Getting there
See Transport, page 414, for further details

The **Cyril E King** Airport (STT); the taxi stand is at the far left end of the terminal, a long way from the commuter flights from Puerto Rico and other islands. Taxi to town US$5 per person (US$1 for each bag). There are sporadic public buses 0600-1900 from the terminal to the town, US$1. Boats come in to Charlotte Amalie or Red Hook in the east.

Getting around

There is a bus service running west from Charlotte Amalie to the university and east to Red Hook. If you wish to drive yourself, rental firms are plentiful.

Tourist information
For safety, see page 405

The Visitors' Bureau at the town waterfront (a/c lounge, TV, public toilets, luggage storage US$1-2) and at the Havensight Welcome Center at the West Indian Company dock, are open Mon-Fri 0800-1700, Sat 0900-1300 (Department of Tourism, PO Box 6400, Charlotte Amalie, USVI 00804, T7748784, F7744390).

US Virgin Islands

Diving and marine life

Divers will enjoy over 200 dive sites, caves, coral reefs, drop-offs and lots of colourful fish. With such crystal clear waters, snorkelling is extremely popular. There are several shipwrecks, and even a wrecked plane to explore. *At-a-glance Snorkeller's Guide to St Thomas* by Nick Aquilar describes 15 snorkel spots in detail. Spearfishing or removing any living things from underwater such as coral, live shells or sea fans, is not permitted.

Dive sites

Many of the resorts offer diving packages or courses and there are many dive companies. Complete lists are available from the Tourist Board (*USVI Dive Guide*). Equipment and instruction for underwater photography are available. There are also several liveaboard sail/dive charters. *Coki Beach Dive Centre*, T7754220, www.cokidive.com, offers an introductory dive for US$40, cruise ships bring their guests here. *Chris Sawyer Diving Centre*, Red Hook, T7759495, www.sawyerdive.vi, specializes in quality service to small groups, great all-day wreck of the *Rhone* trip once a week (dives for locals on Sunday), certification classes every two weeks. There are other operators in island and at major hotels.

Dive centres
A one-tank dive costs around US$50 while a two-tank dive starts from US$70

The *Atlantis* **submarine** dives to 90 ft for those who cannot scuba dive but want to see the exotic fish, coral, sponges and other underwater life. Building VI, Bay L, Havensight Mall, St Thomas, T7765650 for reservations, or 7760288 for information (also kiosk on waterfront, usually 6 dives daily), www.GoAtlantis.com You have to take a 4-mile launch ride on the *Yukon III* to join the submarine at Buck Island. 1-hr day dives US$79, children 4-17 US$36.

The Environmental Association of St Thomas-St John (EAST) organizes whale watching during the migration season at the beginning of the year. Humpbacks are the most commonly sighted. Trips leave from the dock in Red Hook on a 77-ft catamaran, US$55 for non-members, US$45 for EAST members, for information T7761976.

Whale watching

Beaches and watersports

There are 44 beaches on St Thomas. Few are deserted though out of season they are less crowded. The most inaccessible, and therefore more likely to be empty, are those along the northwest coast, which need 4WD to get there. For solitude, take a boat to one of the uninhabited islets offshore. **Magens Bay** on the north coast is considered to be the finest on the island and wonderfully safe for small children. You can rent snorkelling equipment (not the best snorkelling on the island) and loungers. ■ *US$3 and a charge for cars. Changing facilities.* Other good beaches are at **Lindbergh Bay** (southwest, close to the airport runway, good for plane spotters), **Morningstar Bay** (south coast near *Marriott Frenchman's Reef Beach Resort*, beach and watersports equipment for hire), **Bolongo Bay** (south coast with a beach resort), **Sapphire Bay** (east coast, beach gear for rent, good snorkelling), **Brewer's Bay** (can be reached by bus from Charlotte Amalie, get off just beyond the airport), **Hull Bay** (north coast, good for surfing and snorkelling), **Coki Beach** (northeast, showers, lockers, waterskiing, jet skis, snorkelling equipment, good snorkelling just off the beach). The **Coral World Marine Park and Undersea Observatory** is at Coki Beach, giving you a first-hand view of marine life, from sharks and sting rays to more docile creatures. *Sea Trekkin* is here, for an undersea walk wearing breathing apparatus helmets, US$50. ■ *0900-1700. US$18. T7751555, coralworldvi.com*

Be careful of your possessions on the beach, particularly Coki Beach, and never leave anything unattended

US Virgin Islands

Windsurfing lessons and rentals at Morningstar, Magens Bay, Sapphire Beach, Secret Harbour and the *Renaissance Grand*. *West Indies Windsurfing*, T7756530, will deliver windsurfing boards, sunfish and kayaks to wherever you are staying. Snorkelling gear can be rented at all major hotels and the dive shops. Sunfish sailboats for rent at Morningstar, Magens Bay and the *Renaissance Grand*. Parasailing at some hotels or call *Caribbean Parasail and Watersports*, T7759360, www.viwatersports.com, who have a variety of jet skis, etc, to go fast and make a noise, or pedalos to go slowly and peacefully. *VI Ecotours*, T7792155, offer **kayaking** and **snorkelling** in the marine sanctuary in the last mangrove lagoon left on the

Watersports

south side of St Thomas. No experience necessary. If there is enough demand they run a night trip, recommended. For **rafting** there is *Caribbean Rafting Adventures*, T7759360, www.viwatersports.com

Day sails

Check the VI Charter League, T800-5242061, www.vicl.org

Day sailing of all types is available. Half-day sails from US$50, full day from US$100 and sunset cruises from US$40 are offered by many boats. Before taking a day trip on any boat, ask about size, any shade awning and the number of passengers. Many day sail boats limit their guests to 6 passengers, take a stop for snorkelling and provide drinks; however, it is often cheaper to take a tourist boat. You can explore on your own by renting a small power boat from Limnos Style, T7753203, www.limnoscharters.com; *Nauti Nymph*, T7755066, www.st- thomas.com/nauti nymph, 25-29-ft Fountain Power Boats; *See An Ski*, T7756265, 22/24/28-ft makos single/double engines. *Virgin Islands Power* (VIP), T7761510, 800-5242015, has the largest power yacht charter fleet and sportfishing fleet in the Caribbean, bareboat or crewed. Charter yachts available in a variety of luxury and size, with or without crew, cost the same as a good hotel.

Regattas

The annual Rolex Cup Regatta, www.rolexcupregatta.com, is held the last weekend inMar at St Thomas Yacht Club, T7756320, www.styc.net, and there are others in the first half of the year.

Fishing

There is deep-sea fishing, with the next world record in every class lurking just under the boat

The *USVI Fishing Club Tournament* is in **Jun**, the *Bastille Day Kingfish Tournament* is in **Jul** and the *USVI Open Atlantic Blue Marlin* tournament is held in **Aug** every year (T7742752); other game fish include white marlin, kingfish, sailfish, tarpon, Alison tuna and wahoo. No fishing licence is required for shoreline fishing; government pamphlets list 100 good spots (T7756762). For sportfishing charters and information contact *Charterboat Centre*, T800-8665714, also

St Thomas

	Sleeping	3 Bluebeard's Castle
1	Best Western Carib Beach Resort	4 Bolongo Bay Beach Club & Villas
2	Best Western Emerald Beach Resort	5 Elysian Beach Resort

known as *St Thomas Sports Fishing*, T7757990; *Doubleheader Sportfishing*, T7777317, www.dhsportfishing.com; Marlin Prince, T6935929, www.marlinprince.com

Charlotte Amalie

The harbour at Charlotte Amalie, capital of St Thomas and also of the entire USVI, still bustles with colour and excitement. As the Fort Christian Museum puts it, "Oversized, architecturally inappropriate buildings have marred the scenic beauty of the harbour. Harbour congestion has become a major problem." One could add that by day the streets are congested too. At night visitors tend to stay within their resorts. But, as the museum also points out, there are still a number of historical buildings.

Harbour
IDD code: 340
Population: 12,331

The town was built by the Danes, who named it after their King's consort, but to most visitors it remains 'St Thomas'. Beautiful old Danish houses painted in a variety of pastel colours are a reminder of the island's history. One recently opened to the public is **Haagensen House**, the home of a former Danish banker, with a courtyard, gardens and antique furniture. ■ *Daily 0900-1600. US$6. T7749605. Free shuttle service from Emancipation Garden.* Government House, off Kongens Gade, was built in 1865-87. The Enid M Baa Library and Archive is on Main Street, in another early 19th-century edifice. The former house of the French painter, Camille Pissaro, off Main Street, now houses shops and also displays and sells his paintings. One historical building which cannot be visited is the former Danish Consulate, on Denmark Hill, now the Governor's residence. For a good view of the town and the

Sights

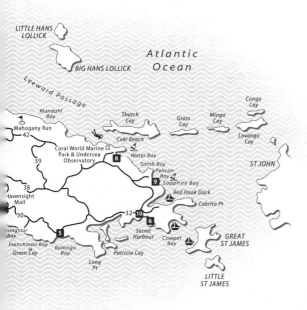

US Virgin Islands

6 Island Beachcomber   9 Secret Harbour Beach Resort
7 Point Pleasant Resort
8 Sapphire Beach Resort & Marina

surrounding area, take the **Paradise Point Tramway**, across the street from the cruise ship dock and Havensight Mall, actually a cable car which takes you on a seven-minute ride up 700 ft to **Paradise Point** where there is an observation deck and a bar, a parrot show, nature walks and shopping. The view of the harbour and lots of neighbouring islands gives some great photo opportunities. ■ *Daily 0900-1700. US$15 round trip. T7749809, www.paradisepointtramway.com.*

Churches
Be careful if walking to the Crystal Gade Synagogue and never walk there at night

There are over 14 historic churches in the USVI dating back to 1737. The Dutch Reformed Church is the oldest established church, having had a congregation since 1660, although the present building dates from 1846. The Frederick Lutheran Church dates from 1820 and its parish hall was once the residence of Jacob H S Lind (1806-27). On Crystal Gade is one of the oldest synagogues in the western hemisphere, an airy, domed building, with a sand floor and hurricane-proof walls; it has books for sale in the office, iced springwater and visitors are given a 10-minute introduction for free. It is worth a visit. The Hebrew Congregation of St Thomas was founded in 1796.

Fortifications

There are many old fortifications within the town. **Bluebeard's Castle Tower** and **Blackbeard's Castle**, the latter allegedly built in 1679 and lived in by the pirate and his 14 wives, is now a restaurant. The **Virgin Islands Museum** is in the former dungeon

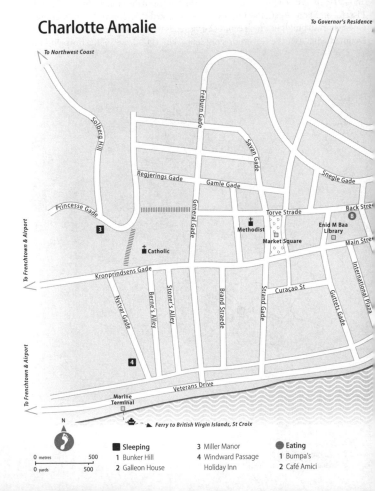

Charlotte Amalie

To Governor's Residence

To Northwest Coast

Solberg Hill

Freburn Gade

Savan Gade

Snegle Gade

Regjerings Gade

Gamle Gade

Princesse Gade

General Gade

Torve Strade

Back Street

3

Methodist

Enid M Baa Library

8

✝ Catholic

Market Square

Main Street

Kronprindsens Gade

Nytvar Gade

Berne's Alley

Stone's Alley

Brand Straede

Strand Gade

Curaçao St

Guttets Gade

International Plaza

To Frenchtown & Airport

4

Veterans Drive

To Frenchtown & Airport

Marine Terminal

⚓ *Ferry to British Virgin Islands, St Croix*

N

0 metres 500
0 yards 500

■ **Sleeping**
1 Bunker Hill
2 Galleon House
3 Miller Manor
4 Windward Passage Holiday Inn

● **Eating**
1 Bumpa's
2 Café Amici

US Virgin Islands

at **Fort Christian** (1666-80). There are historical and natural history sections and an art gallery. ■ *Mon-Fri 0830-1630. Free, but donations welcome as much restoration work remains to be done. T7764566.* In contrast to the red-painted fort is the green **Legislative Building**, originally the Danish police barracks (1874). ■ *Mon-Fri.*

Outside town

The **Old Mill**, up Crown Mountain Road from Sub Base traffic light is an old sugar mill open to the public. **Estate St Peter Greathouse and Botanical Gardens** has 500 varieties of plants, a stunning view and an art gallery for local artists.

Water Island

Its name comes from the once plentiful freshwater ponds, now salt ponds,

Water Island, at the west end of St Thomas' main harbour, is the smallest inhabited island. It is now known as the fourth USVI. It was purchased from Denmark by the USA in 1944 to use as a military base during the Second World War. **Fort Segarra** was built as an underground fort and later the island was used to test weapons. It was transferred to the Department of the Interior from Defense in 1952. A year later a 40-year lease of the entire island was given to a developer for construction of a hotel and homes. The hotel closed after Hurricane Hugo in 1989. The island's ownership was turned over to the VI Government and private island homeowners in December 1996. Open-air buildings on the beach are available for public use. At weekends the beach is busy with local residents and charter-boat guests.

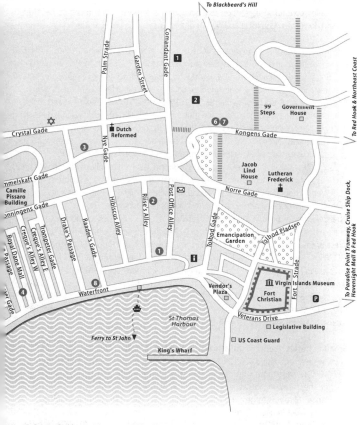

US Virgin Islands

Transport During the week, the **Kontiki** floating booze cruise makes daily stops; other day-charter boats may also stop when weather is rough. **Water Island Ferry**, www.nerc.com/~vacation/ferry.html, runs frequently Mon-Sat 0645-1800, US$7 round trip, with night runs Tue, Fri, Sat, US$5 one way, and a reduced service Sun and holidays. Weekly and monthly passes are available and special runs can be arranged with the Captain.

Hassel Island Hassel Island is part of US National Parks. There are ruins on the shore but no development has yet been carried out. There is a dilapidated dock where you can tie up a dinghy. Walk towards the ocean for a picnic and a great view of Frenchman's Reef and watch the ships entering the harbour; then hike on a trail to an old building; climb the wall at the back of the building to get an outstanding view of the area from Frenchman's Reef to Green Cay and see the surf breaking on three sets of rocks. Around the other end of the island is a small liveaboard boating community.

Essentials

There are many hotels, guesthouses, apartments, villas and cottages on St Thomas with a cluster around the east end. The cheaper places to stay are in town or up in the hills. The newer, top-of-the-range chain hotels are on the beach and include the huge *Marriott*, www.marriott.com, and *Renaissance*, www.renaissancehotels.com, hotels with all sporting and conference facilities. Summer rates are about 20% cheaper than winter. There is a Hotel Association counter at the airport to help you with reservations. You should be cautious around downtown Charlotte Amalie at night.

Sleeping
www.usvitourism.com, the Department of Tourism website, is very comprehensive and contains many more hotels than we have space for

Charlotte Amalie **LL** *Bluebeard's Castle*, on hillside overlooking town, T7741600, F7745134. 183 rooms, sports, pool, free shuttle to Magens Bay Beach and to Veterans' Drive. Heading towards the airport is **LL-L** *Windward Passage Holiday Inn*, T7745200, F7741231. Pool, restaurant, 151 rooms, walking distance from shops and ferries, shuttle to beach. The **LL** *Elysian Beach Resort* on Cowpet Bay, T7751000, F7760910, has 180 rooms and suites, fitness centre, tennis, pool, jacuzzi, watersports centre offering diving, kayaking, parasailing, use of facilities at *Bluebeard's*. **LL-L** *Point Pleasant Resort*, 6600 Estate Smith Bay, T7757200, www.pointpleasantresort.com Under 21s sharing parents' room free, 95 suites in 15 acres of tropical gardens, pool, tennis, watersports. **LL** *Sapphire Beach Resort & Marina*, T7756100, www.usvi.net/hotel/sapphire 171 rooms, pool, suites, villas, watersports, tennis, kitchens, restaurant, anyone under 19 free when sharing parents' room, children's activities. **LL** *Secret Harbour Beach Resort*, T7756550, www.st-thomas.com/shb.vi 64 suites, popular with honeymooners, watersports, tennis, kitchens, restaurant. On the south coast is **LL-L** *Bolongo Bay Beach Club & Villas*, 7150 Bolongo, T7751800, www.bolongo.com EP, CP or all-inclusive family resort, kids' offers, pool, beach, tennis, kitchen facilities, 2 restaurants. **West of Charlotte Amalie** **LL** *Best Western Emerald Beach Resort*, 8070 Lindbergh Bay, T7778800, www.emeraldbeach.com 90 rooms, pool, bar, restaurant, 'The Palms' rooms have ocean and airport view, tennis, watersports. Its sister resort is **L-AL** *Best Western Carib Beach Resort*, T7742525, same website. Smaller at 60 rooms, pool, casual, both on Lindbergh Bay, sheltered beach at end of airport runway, only drawback is aircraft noise. On the same bay, **AL** *Island Beachcomber*, T7745250, www.st-thomas.com/islandbeachcomber 47 rooms, on beach, by airport, free shuttle to town.

Small hotels and guesthouses **AL-A** *Danish Chalet Inn*, T7745764, www.wininn.com Good value, 10 rooms, friendly owners. **A-B** *Island View Guest House*, T7744270, www.st-thomas.com/islandviewguesthouse Great place to stay before or after a charter, near airport, great view. **AL** *Villa Blanca*, T7760749, www.st-thomas.com/villablanca 14 rooms, large gardens, on hillside, view of town and harbour, pool, quiet, family-run. **AL-A** *Bunker Hill Hotel*, 7A Commandant Gade, T7748056, www.bunkerhillhotel.com 15 rooms, a/c, TV, pool, airport transfers. **AL-B** *Galleon House*, T/F7746952, www.st-thomas.com/galleonhouse Swimming pool, veranda, gourmet breakfast, snorkel gear provided, discounts for senior citizens. **B-C** *Miller Manor*, on the hill behind the Catholic Cathedral, T7741535, millermanor-aida-leo@worldnet.attnet Clean, very friendly, a/c, 5 mins' walk to town, microwave and fridge in each room.

Charlotte Amalie   Expensive   For great French cuisine, *Banana Tree Grill* at Bluebeard's Castle, T7764050. Expensive, open for dinner Mon-Sat. *Hotel 1829*, on Government Hill, T7761829. Superb food and service, expensive, if you can't afford it go and have a look anyway, lovely old building and great view, happy hour 1700-2000, dinner daily. **Mid-range**   *Café Amici*, in A H Riise's Mall, T7765670. Open Mon-Sat 1030-1530, Sun 1030-1500, Italian and Mediterranean food, moderate prices.   *Green House*, on harbour front, Veterans Drive, T7747998. Excellent restaurant at reasonable prices, attracts younger crowd, steak, ribs, burgers, open 0800-2200, serves drinks, bar open until 0200, happy hour 1630-1900. *Hervé Restaurant & Wine Bar*, down town, T7779703. Open Mon-Sat, good variety of specials during happy hour at the bar, 1700-1900, patio bar on first floor. *Virgilio's*, between Main and Back streets, up from Storetvaer Gade, T7764920. Italian, good food and service, not cheap, lunch 1130-1500, dinner 1700-2200 Mon-Sat. The area west of the Market Square is more local, with restaurants and bars. **Cheap**   Award-winning ribs from *Bill's Texas Pit BBQ*, a mobile truck which shows up Tue-Sat in the Waterfront and Red Hook, also for lunch at Sub Base, the best on the island. *Bumpa's*, waterfront, T7765674. Upstairs, outdoors, small breakfast and lunch spot overlooking harbour, locally popular and inexpensive, no credit cards. *Cuzzins Caribbean Restaurant & Bar*, Back St, T7774711. Open for lunch Mon-Sat, dinner Tue-Sat, good, large, local meals, lunch can be dinner! West Indian cuisine, conch, fish, also drinks such as sea moss and maubi, vegetarian plates available. *Glady's Café*, in *Historic Royal Dane Mall*, T7746604. Open 0700-1530, Mon-Sat, local dishes such as salt fish and dumplings, mutton stew.

Frenchtown   *Alexander's Café*, T7744349. Grills, ribs, chilli and Italian, open Mon-Sat for lunch and dinner. *Craig and Sally's*, T7779949. International influences, new wave of American cuisine, very popular, open for lunch Tue-Sat, dinner Tue-Sun. *Hook, Line and Sinker*, T7769708. American, steak and seafood, vegetarian options, daily specials, open breakfast, lunch and dinner Mon-Sat. *The Point at Villa Olga*, at Villa Olga, T7744262. Not cheap, but excellent food.

Sub Base/Crown Bay   *Tickle's Dockside Pub*, T7761595 at Crown Bay Marina, T7759425 at American Yacht Harbour. American, burgers, chicken and ribs, open daily for breakfast, lunch and dinner. *Molly Malone's*, above *Tickle's*, overlooking water, open Tue-Sun.

East End/Red Hook   *Duffy's Love Shack*, Red Hook Plaza, T7792080. Good lunches, some unusual meals plus burgers, American, hotspot, very busy weekends, open daily. *Sopchoppy's*, waterfront, on upper level of American Yacht Harbour. *Latitude 18*, across the water from Red Hook Harbour, T7792495. Dinghy dock. Live entertainment occasionally, good food, varied, steak, seafood and pasta. *Romano's*, Smith Bay, T7750045. Italian and continental, lamb, seafood and pasta, open from 1800 Mon-Sat.

Bands and combos play nightly at most hotels. Several of the hotels offer limbo dancing 3 or 4 nights a week and the ubiquitous steel bands remain a great favourite with both visitors and residents.   *Coco Jo's*, at the *Marriott Beach Resorts*, T7768500, live entertainment and dancing, Crucian rum special 2000-2200, any rum-based drink US$2. *SIBS* on the mountain, Charlotte Amalie, offers happy hour, bar, late-night crowds, pool tables. *Room With A View* at *Bluebeard's Castle* offers free champagne to ladies 2200-0100. *Happy Buzzard*, downtown Charlotte Amalie, has happy hour all night and famous daiquirís. *Club Ryno*, Palm Passage, T7771059, has live jazz Fri nights. Some restaurants in **Frenchtown** offer live music. The *Reichhold Centre for the Arts*, part of the University of the Virgin Islands, has programmes with local or international performers. Concerts and other live music are held in *Tillett Gardens*, T7751929.

The **carnival** in *Apr* (T7763112 for precise date and events, www.vicarnival.com) is most spectacular. Dating back to the arrival of African slaves who danced bamboulas it was

Eating
The waterfront is safe in the early evening, but elsewhere you should take a taxi. There are many very good restaurants on the island, most of which are listed in tourist brochures, see page 405

Nightlife
St Thomas offers the greatest variety of nightlife in the Virgin Islands

Festivals

US Virgin Islands

originally based on ritual worship of the gods of Dahomey. The festivities have since been redirected towards Christianity with a marked US influence. Parades with costumed bands include the J'Ouvert Morning Tramp, the Children's Parade, Mocko Jumbis on stilts and steel bands. There are beauty queens and at least 4 groups of baton-twirling majorettes.

Shopping
Charlotte Amalie is packed with duty-free shops and shoppers of all description

If you want to shop seriously, St Thomas is the cheapest island of the 3 and has the largest selection. Nevertheless it is a good idea to have done your research at home and know what you want to buy. *Havensight Shopping Mall* is recommended for people who want to get away from crowds and parking problems, smaller selection than in town, but same shops. The *Dockside Bookshop* in Havensight Mall has books and other publications on the Virgin Islands and the Caribbean in general. Good **arts and crafts** centre at *Tillett Gardens*, opposite Four Winds Plaza. You can watch the craftsmen at work. *The Native Arts Coop* is a showcase for locally made goods and souvenirs opposite the Vendors Plaza.

Food *Gourmet Gallery* at Crown Bay Marina, *Plaza Extra* in Tutu Park Mall and *Havensight Deli* in Havensight Mall. Local produce can be bought in the Market Square (most produce brought in by farmers on Sat 0530) and there are some small supermarkets and grocery stores. *Solberg Supermart* on Solberg Hill has a launderette. *Marina Market* in Red Hook is a good gourmet-type deli, opposite St John Ferry Dock. *Pueblo Supermarket*, near Safe Haven Marina, Crown Bay Marina, *K-Mart* and *Cost U Less*.

Sports
For diving and watersports, see page 407 and 407

There are a few public **tennis** courts (2 at Sub Base), operating on a first-come first-served basis, but the hotel courts at the major resorts are mostly lit for night-time play and open for non-residents if you book. There is an 18-hole, 6,022-yd **golf** course at Mahogany Run, T800-2537103, green fee US$100, cheaper after 1400.

Tour operators

There are group tours by surrey, bus or taxi. *Island tours* in an open bus cost US$20 per person, many leave from Main St at about 1200; complete tours only are sold. **Helicopter**: contact *Air Center Helicopters*, T7757335.

Transport

Air Cyril E King International Airport is 2 miles, 12 mins, from Charlotte Amalie. Seaplanes come in at the Seaplane base (SPB) in the capital's harbour.

Road Bus: Vitran bus services (US$0.75 city fare, US$1 country fare, exact change) have 34 a/c buses that run from town to the university (passing near Yacht Haven Marina), to Four Winds Plaza and to Red Hook (past the hospital, K-Mart, Cost U Less). **Taxis**: Cabs are not metered but a list of fares is published in *St Thomas This Week* and *What To Do*; a fares list must be carried by each driver. Rates quoted are for 1 passenger and additional passengers are charged extra; drivers are notorious for trying to charge each passenger the single passenger rate. Airport to Red Hook is US$13 for 1, US$9 each additional passenger, town to Magens Bay is US$8.50 for 1, US$6 for extra person. When travelling on routes not covered by the official list, try to agree the fare in advance. There are extra charges between 2400 and 0600 and charges for luggage. A 2-hr taxi tour for 2 people costs US$30, additional passengers US$12 each. *VI Taxi Association* T7747457, *Wheatley Taxi Service and Tours*, T7751959. **Gypsy cabs**, unlicensed taxis, operating outside Charlotte Amalie, are cheaper but try to agree fare and route before getting in. **Car hire**: Rental agencies include *Budget*, T7765774, *Cowpet*, 7757376, *Avis*, 7741468, *Sun Island*, 7743333, *Discount*, 7764858, *VI Auto Rental*, 7763616 (Sub Base). Most have an office by the airport. Rates range from US$40-80 per day, unlimited mileage, vehicles from small cars to jeeps. Scooters from *Island Scooters*, opposite Havensight Mall, T7147408, US$55 per day.

Ferry There are many ferry boats to various destinations, including one from Red Hook to nearby St John (every hr from 0800 to 2400 plus 0630 and 0730 Mon-Fri, takes 20 mins, US$3 each way). Charlotte Amalie to St John, US$7, 45 mins; there is also a ferry from downtown to *Marriott Frenchman's Reef Beach Resort* and Morningstar beach, free for hotel guests, US$3 each way, leaving every hr 0900-1700, 15 mins. Ferry to Water Island runs frequently, see page 411.

Directory

Banks *Banco Popular de Puerto Rico*, T7767800. *Bank of Nova Scotia*, T7740037. *First Bank*, T7744800. **Communications** Internet: *Little Switzerland Internet Café*, Main St, upstairs, T7762010, www.littleswitzerland.com *Jascom*, Havensight Mall, building III, upper level, internet access and other services. **Post**: The postal system is the same as in the USA. **Telephone**: AT&T calling centre at Havensight and St Thomas Communications in Crown Bay Marina at Sub Base. Local and overseas calls, faxes, internet US$3 per 15 mins. **Embassies and consulates** On St Thomas: **Denmark**, T7760656. **Sweden**, T7746845. **Medical services** St Thomas has a 225-bed **hospital**, T7768311, and a 24-hr emergency services. Mobile medical units provide health services to outlying areas. *Red Hook Family Practice* is open Mon-Fri 1000-1600, walk in.

St John

Much of St John is a national park and it is its protected status that draws visitors. The island is covered with steep hills and is hot. The roads are steep and rocky and 4WD is required to get to many places. The population is mainly concentrated in the little town of Cruz Bay and the village of Coral Bay. A drive from Cruz Bay across to Coral Bay is a worthwhile experience and allows you to appreciate how much land is owned by the park, though there is not much in Coral Bay. Only 21 sq miles, St John is about 5 miles east of St Thomas and 35 miles north of St Croix.

IDD code: 340
Colour map 2, grid B6
Population: 4,197

Ins and outs

There is no airport on St John. Visitors arrive by ferry, see page 403 or by private yacht, see page 418.
There are 3 main roads though government maps show more roads that are 4WD dirt tracks. The road from Cruz Bay to Coral Bay is 7 miles but it takes 40 mins to drive it. Hiking is hot and hilly. You can always start walking and then catch a taxibus. Hitchhiking is easy.

Getting there & around
See Transport, page 418, for further details

The St John newspaper, *Tradewinds*, is published bi-weekly, US$0.50. Funny, informative and free, the *St John Guidebook* and map is available in shops and also at the ticket booth at the ferry dock.

Tourist information
For safety, see page 405

Beaches and watersports

North shore beaches can go from calm to a surfer's delight in winter when northerly swells roll in from the Atlantic, making the sea rough and dangerous. Go to the south for calm beaches and anchorages. In the National Park there are snack bars at Cinnamon Bay and Trunk Bay only. Bring water and lunch if you are hiking or going to other beaches which will not be so crowded.

Day trippers off cruise ships head for Hawk's Nest, Cinnamon and Trunk Bays, so avoid these areas if you want some space

Off **Trunk Bay**, the island's best beach, is an underwater snorkelling trail maintained by the National Parks Service. Not surprisingly, the beach tends to get rather crowded (especially when tour groups come in); lockers for hire, US$2 (deposit US$5), snorkelling equipment US$6 (deposit US$40) return by 1600. Other good beaches include **Hawk's Nest Bay**, **Caneel Bay**, **Cinnamon Bay** (there is a small museum of historical photographs and pictures here), **Salt Pond** (reached by Vitran bus, US$1 every two hours or so, when it's running, excellent beach with good snorkelling and a spectacular hike to Ram's Head), **Lameshur Bay** (difficult road but worth it), **Maho Bay** (beach is 5 ft from the road, lots of turtles, sometimes tarpon, nice and calm) and **Solomon Bay** (unofficial nudist beach about 30 minutes' walk from the road). **Reef Bay** has excellent snorkelling. Frett's Maho Bay Shuttle goes around the north shore coast to any of the beaches, which is easier than trying to reach them by road. **Jumbie Bay** has very good snorkelling, as does the north shore of **Francis Bay**, but if it is choppy, try **Mary Creek** instead, where you can snorkel among the mangroves or out to the coral reef at Anna Point.

Watersports **Windsurfers** can be rented at Cinnamon Bay and Maho Camps, sunfishes at Maho Camp. *Coral Bay Watersports*, T7766850, next to *Serafina*, rents power boats, sport fishing and tackle, and also offers diving, snorkelling, kayaking and windsurfing. Half-and full-day sails and fishing trips can be arranged by *Connections*, T7766922, *Noah's Little Arks* (Zodiacs), T6939030, *Proper Yachts*, T7766256. A recommended sailing and snorkelling trip is with Captain Phil on the *Wayward Sailor*, T6938555, US$85 for the day with a most knowledgeable host, who takes you out to the St James islands between St John and St Thomas. *Sadie Sea*, T7766421, is also good, offering a snorkelling tour around St John. You can rent a power boat with *Ocean Runner Powerboats*, T6938809. For 1- and 2-tank **scuba dives**, wreck dives and night dives: *Low Key Watersports* at Wharfside Village, specializes in personal attention, also **kayaking**, T800-8357718, 6938999; *Cruz Bay Watersports*, 3 locations, T7766234, offers a free snorkel map. Other dive operators are *Cinnamon Bay Watersports*, T7766330 (also kayaking and windsurfing), *East End Divers*, T7794994 or 6937519, Coral Bay. You can **snuba** (air in the boat, not on your back) at Trunk Bay, T6938063. *St John Snorkel Tours* have day and night tours, guided Reef Bay hikes, T7766922.

Regattas Yacht races include *St John Yacht Club Island Hopper Race* (Jan); *Coral Bay Yacht Club* (meets at *Skinny Legs*) *CATS* (programme for children), *ANTS* (adults) and *Thanksgiving Day Regatta*.

Virgin Islands National Park

There are 22 hikes in all, 14 on the north shore, eight on the south shore

The population of St John fell to less than a thousand people in 1950 when 85% of the land had reverted to bush and second-growth tropical forest. In the 1950s Laurance Rockefeller bought about half of the island but later donated his holdings to establish a national park which was to take up about two-thirds of the predominantly mountainous terrain. The Virgin Islands National Park was opened in 1956 and is covered by an extensive network of trails (some land in the park is still privately owned and not open to visitors). Several times a week a park ranger leads the Reef Bay hike, which passes through a variety of vegetation zones, visits an old sugar mill (**Annaberg**) and some unexplained petroglyphs, and ends with a ferry ride back to Cruz Bay. The trail can be hiked without the ranger, but the National Park trip provides a boat at the bottom of the trail so you do not need to walk back up the three-mile hill. You should reserve a place on the guided hike at the **Park Service Visitors' Centre**, Cruz Bay (on north side of harbour). Here you'll get park

St John

Sleeping
1 Caneel Bay Resort
2 Caribbean Villas
3 Cinnamon Bay Campgrounds
4 Estate Concordia Studios
5 Gallows Point Resort
6 Harmony Studios
7 Inn at Tamarind Court
8 Maho Bay Camps Inc
9 Suite St John

information, including informative displays, topographical and hiking trail maps, books on shells, birds, fish, plants, flowers and local history, and you can sign up for activities. ■ *Daily 0800-1630. T7766201.* The trails are well maintained and clearly signed with interpretative information along the way. Insect repellent is essential. A seashore walk in shallow water, using a glass-bottomed bucket to discover sea life, is recommended. A snorkel boat trip around St John, taking you to five or six reefs not accessible from land (and therefore less damaged), is a good way to see the island even if you do not snorkel. An informative, historical bus tour goes to the remote East End. There are evening programmes at Cinnamon Bay and Maho Bay camps, where rangers show slides and movies and hold informal talks.

■ *US$4 to enter the park at Trunk Bay and to view the Annaberg ruins.*

Essentials

Sleeping
Rates are published by the Department of Tourism at st-john.com/rates

LL *Caneel Bay Resort*, T7766111, www.caneelbay.com Lots of packages available in a variety of rooms or cottages, 166-room resort built in the late 1950s by Laurance Rockefeller, since 1993 managed by Rosewood Hotels and Resorts, several restaurants, bars, dress smartly after sunset, 11 all-weather tennis courts, complimentary watersports for guests including sunfish, windsurfers, also boat rentals, fishing and diving available, kids' club and exercise club, ferry service between Caneel Bay and downtown St Thomas, also to sister resort of *Little Dix Bay* on Virgin Gorda, BVI. **LL-L** *Gallows Point Resort*, T7766434, www.gallowspointresort.com 52 suites, fans, pool, watersports, kitchen facilities. **LL** *Suite St John* at Gallows Point, T7766969, www.gallowspoint.com 8 1-bedroom condos, sleep 4, luxury, full kitchens, every convenience, pool, beach. Within walking distance of town are **LL** *Caribbean Villas*, T7766152, www.caribbeanvilla.com 2-bedroom villas, pool, personal service, attentive management. **AL-C** *The Inn at Tamarind Court*, in Cruz Bay, T7766378, www.tamarindcourt.com Nothing special, adequate, inexpensive breakfast and dinner, bar, music and movies some nights.

At Cinnamon Bay (frequent taxi-buses from Cruz Bay) there is a **AL-A** campground and chalet site run by the National Park Service, usually full so book in advance, maximum stay 2 weeks; bare site **E**, a few shared showers, food reasonably priced in both the cafeteria and grocery store. Contact *Cinnamon Bay Campgrounds*, T7766330, F7766458. At Maho Bay (8 miles from Cruz Bay, regular bus service) there is a privately run campground, **AL** *Maho Bay Camps Inc*, Cruz Bay, T7766240, www.maho.org 'Tent cottages' are connected by a raised boardwalk to protect the environment, lots of steps, magnificent view from restaurant, lots of planned activities, attracts socially conscious, environmentally aware guests and staff, guests come back year after year, possible to work in return for your board. They also own **L** *Harmony Studios* (same phones, www.harmony-studios.com). Largely built from recycled materials, solar energy, 12 rooms, handicap access and **L-AL** *Estate Concordia Studios*, T6935855, www.concordia-studios.com 9 luxury condos overlooking Salt Pond Bay and **AL** 5 eco-tents, multi-level tent cottages with kitchen and bathroom. Other apartments/condos include **LL-L** *Battery Hill*, T/F6938261, www.batteryhill.com 9 units, good view, breezy, walk to beach or town. **LL** *Coconut Coast Villas*, T6939100, www.coconutcoast.com 10 studios, 6 m from water, kitchens, snorkelling. **LL** *Suite St John at Lavender Hill Estates*, T7766969, www.lavenderhill.com 11 waterfront condos, private balconies, some have computers, pool. **LL-L** *Villa Bougainvilla*, T7766420, www.DonaldSchnell.com Artist owned and maintained. **LL-L** *Villa Serenity*, T7766342, TerryRoberts@worldnet.att.net Owned and run by Terry Witham, lunchtime cook at *Miss Lucy's*, price depends on occupancy level, 4 bedrooms, 3 bathrooms, large deck with hammock and lounge chairs, great view but very private, no clothes necessary, convenient location close to *Maho Bay Campground* and its transport and other facilities. To rent a villa through an agency, contact *Vacation Vistas*, T7766462, www.vacationvistas.com 9 houses to rent all round the island, some with pools. *Catered To*, T7766641, www.cateredto.com, has rental homes and luxury villas. Others include *Vacation Homes*, T7766094, and *Windspree Vacation Homes*, T6935423, www.windspree com, which has homes and villas in Coral Bay.

US Virgin Islands

Eating

St John is known for fine dining

At the highest viewpoint on the island on Centerline Rd, Bordeaux Mountain, is *Chateau Bordeaux*, T7766611. Fine dining, expensive, dinner only, reservations advised. **In Cruz Bay** *Asolare*, Northshore Rd, T7794747. Expensive, Euro-Asian cuisine, lovely setting, dinner only, reservations recommended. *Café Roma*, T7766524. Italian food and good pizza, open evenings, also vegetarian dishes. *Chilly Billy's* upstairs at the Lumber Yard, T6938708. Serves great Bloody Marys for breakfast or any time, open 0800-1400 daily, breakfast all day on Sat and Sun. *Ellington's* at Gallow's Point, T6938490. Continental and seafood, lunch and dinner, closed Mon. *Hatsumana*, T6262076. Asian dishes, from satay and spring rolls to sushi and sashimi, open daily, lunch 1100-1500, dinner 1730-2130. *JJ's Tex Mex*, at the ferry dock in Cruz Bay. Great for breakfast or at any time. *KatiLady Deli*, T6938500, www.katilady.com   A vegetarian grocery and deli with a variety of foods to take away, including a salad bar, sandwiches, patties, juices and smoothies, as well as a catering service for villas. *Miss Lucy's*, on the way to Salt Pond, T6935244. Locally famous, worth the trip just for the conch chowder, full-moon parties are a tradition, with a pig roast (1800-2100, US$10) and a live band, ferries available from St Thomas. *Maho Bay Campground* run trips for the occasion, also Fri night steel band, Sat jazz night, Sun brunch with live jazz, closed Sep-Oct. *Morgan's Mango*, T6938141. Excellent seafood and steak, also vegetarian, open-air dining, great sauces, open evenings only, 1730-2200, reservations recommended. *Paradiso*, at Mongoose Junction, T6938899. American food, has children's menu, eat indoors or on balcony, open Mon-Sat 1100-1500, quite expensive. *Café Wahoo*, overlooking Cruz Bay, T6938489. On 3 floors, Crow's Nest, Oyster Bar and Beach Bar, American-influenced West Indian food, seafood, open 1100-2200. *Panini Beach*, T6937030. Pricey, seafood/Caribbean, dinner from 1800. *The Lime Inn*, T7766425. Seafood, steak, excellent lobster and pasta, all you can eat night on Wed, very popular with locals and visitors. *Uncle Joe's*, opposite the Post Office in Cruz Bay, no sign outside, just the barbecue grill. Great barbecued ribs. **At Coral Bay** *Skinny Legs* (named for owners), T7794982. Local hang-out, soup, sandwiches, grills and fish, open daily 1100-2100. *Shipwreck Landing*, T6935640. American cuisine, frozen drinks, nightly specials, open-air dining, live music every weekend.

Nightlife

Up-to-date information on events is posted on the trees around town or on the bulletin board in front of *Connections*. In Cruz Bay, the place to go and dance is *Fred's*, calypso and reggae Wed and Fri. Popular places to 'lime' (relax) are *Café Wahoo*, *JJ's*, and sitting in Cruz Bay Park, watching the world go by. See *Lucy's*, above for full-moon hog roast and music.

Festivals

Carnival is in the week of *4 Jul*, with lots of events in the 2 preceding weeks.

Shopping

Food is expensive (rum is cheaper than water) and the selection is limited

Scattered around Cruz Bay, Wharfside Village and Mongoose Junction are shops selling souvenirs, arts and crafts. Right in the Park is *Sparkey's*, selling newspapers, film, cold drinks, gifts. The *St John Drug Center Inc*, open daily. For groceries: *Starfish Market* (the largest) and *Marina Market* in Cruz Bay, *Joe's Discount* near *Shipwreck Landing* in Coral Bay. *Maiden Apple*, health food store, 1st floor of Boulton Centre, T6938781. Liquor and drinks at *Cases by the Sea*, near Coral Bay Watersports, grocery near *Shipwreck Tavern*, *Joe's Discount* and *Pickles Deli*. If you are camping it's a good idea to shop at the supermarkets on St Thomas. Fish and produce is sold from boats twice a week at the freight dock. *Love City Videos* at the Boulton Centre rents films. *Laundromat* next to *Raintree Inn*, Cruz Bay, Mon-Fri 0830-1730, Sat 0830-1200.

Sports

There is **tennis** at the large resorts and also 2 public courts available on a first-come-first-served basis. You can go **rock climbing** with *Adventures Unlimited*, T6935763. **Horse riding**, *Carolina Corral*, T6935778, beach rides, sunset and full-moon rides.

Tour operators

As well as the National Parks service (see above), *Thunderhawk Trail Guides*, T7741112, offers hikes through the national park.

Transport

Bus There are 2 Vitran buses, US$1 exact change only, from Cruz Bay to Coral Bay and Salt Pond about every hr. If one breaks down you have to wait for the next, a/c turned off going up hill, turned on for descent. **Car** Vehicles may be rented, but parking is difficult. There are 3 fuel stations, open 0800-1900, in Cruz Bay and Coral Bay, may be closed on holidays. Rental agencies include: *Hertz*, T7766695; *Delbert Hill's Jeep Rental*, T7766637; *Budget*, T7767575; *Avis*, T7766374; *Cool Breeze*, T7766588, *St John Car Rental*, T7766103; rates start from US$50 per day. **Taxi** Official taxi rates can be obtained from St John Police Department or by asking the taxi driver to show the official rate card (see page 414 for details). A 2-hr island tour costs US$30 for 1 or 2 passengers, or US$12 per person if there are 3 or more. Taxi from Cruz Bay to Trunk Bay, US$5.50; to Cinnamon Bay US$7. It is almost impossible to persuade a taxi to take you to Coral Bay, so hitchhike by waiting at the intersection by the supermarket deli.

Ferry To St Thomas: hourly 0700 to 2200 and 2315 to Red Hook, every 2 hrs 0715 to 1315, 1545 and 1715 to Charlotte Amalie (see page 414).

Banks *Banco Popular de Puerto Rico*, T6932777. *Bank of Novia Scotia*, T6939932. St John's banking hours are 0830-1500 Mon-Fri. **Communications** Internet: *Cyber Celtic Café/Quiet Mon Pub*, Cruz Bay town above *La Tapa*, T7794799, www.quietmon.com *Connections West* (Cruz Bay, T7766922), as well as arranging sailing trips and villa rentals, is the place for business services, local and international telephone calls, faxes, Western Union money transfers, photocopying, word-processing, notary, VHF radio calls and tourist information (they know everything that is happening). *Connections East*, T7794994. Does the same thing in Coral Bay. *Coral Bay Marine Services* for mail drop, message centre, if you have your own computer you can use their phonepoint to access email. **Medical services** St John has a 7-bed clinic, T7766400 and a 24-hr emergency service.

Directory

St Croix

St Croix (pronounced to rhyme with 'boy') is perceived as the poor relation of the main group of islands, but its lack of development is part of its charm and there is more to see here than on St Thomas. Columbus thought that St Croix looked like a lush garden when he first saw it during his second voyage in 1493. He landed at Salt River on the north coast, now a national park encompassing the landing site as well as the rich underwater Salt River drop off and canyon. It had been cultivated by the Carib Indians, who called it Ay-Ay, and the land still lies green and fertile between the rolling hills. Today agriculture has been surpassed by tourism and industry, including the huge Hovensa oil refinery on the south coast. The east of the island is rocky and arid terrain; the west is higher, wetter and forested. St Croix is the largest of the group with 84 sq miles, lying 40 miles south of St Thomas. People born on the island are called Crucians, while North Americans who move there are known as Continentals.

IDD code: 340
Colour map 2, grid C6
Population: 63,000

St Croix has it all: swimming, sailing, fishing, excellent restaurants, good shopping and, above all, great scuba diving

Ins and outs

See page 403 for details of flights to **Henry Rohlson** international airport. Taxis from the airport to Christiansted are US$5, to Frederiksted, US$4. A taxi dispatcher's booth is at the airport exit. Rates are listed in many publications.

Getting there
See Transport, page 426 for further details

A bus service runs between Christiansted and Frederiksted and between the airport and Christiansted every 1½ hrs, change buses at La Reine terminal. Public taxis link the 2 towns and there are taxis from the airport to Frederiksted. The major car rental agencies are represented at the airport, hotels and both cities. A 4WD car (US$50-60 a day) is ideal to drive along the scenic roads, for example to Ham's Bay or Point Udall. There is a distinct lack of road signs on St Croix, so if you use a car, take a good map.

Getting around

There is a Tourism Booth at the airport in the baggage claim area and next to it the First Stop Information Booth. In Christiansted there is a Visitors' Bureau on Queen St on the corner with King Cross St, open Mon-Fri 0800-1700 (Department of Tourism, PO Box 4536, Christiansted, USVI 00822-4538, T7730495, F7735074). In Frederiksted the Visitors' Centre is in the Old Custom House Building, Strand St, USVI 00840, T7720357. There is also an office next to the post office in Cruz Bay, St John (Department of Tourism, PO Box 200, Cruz Bay, USVI 00830, T7766450, F7779695.

Tourist information

US Virgin Islands

Diving and marine life

Dive sites   Scuba diving is very good around St Croix, with forests of elkhorn coral, black coral, brain coral, sea fans, a multitude of tropical fish, sea horses under the Frederiksted pier (great day or night dive for novices, an easy shore dive and one of the best in the USVI), walls and drop offs, reefs and wrecks. The wrecks are varied, some 40 years old and some recent, with marine life slowly growing on the structures and schools of fish taking up residence. They range from 75-300 ft in length and 15-110 ft deep, providing something for everyone, from the beginner to the experienced. Butler Bay off Frederiksted is home for six shipwrecks. Nearby in Truck Lagoon there are the remains of around 25 old truck chassis that were sunk by *Hess Oil* to promote marine growth and create an artificial reef. The wrecks of the *North Wind*, *The Virgin Islander Barge* and *Suffolk Maid* are close together, but usually done as two separate leisurely dives otherwise you have to swim rather briskly to get round them all. There are also the *Rosaomaira*, the deepest of the wrecks, and the *Coakly Bay*, the newest, while to the south is the *Sondra*, a shallow dive which can even be snorkelled, although there is not a great deal remaining on the site. Just behind the *Sondra* is the wreck of a motor boat.

Anchorage is crowded 1000-1600 with day charters; watch the charter boat's race for the best spots at 1000 and 1600   At **Buck Island** there are underwater snorkelling trails, the two main ones being Turtle Bay Trail and East End Trail. The fish are superb. The reef is an underwater national park covering over 850 acres, including the island. Hawksbill turtles nest on Buck Island and, during a 1993 Buck Island National Monument Sea Turtle Research Programme, Sandy Point leatherbacks were also observed nesting there. Half-day tours to Buck Island, including 1¼ hours snorkelling and 30 minutes at the beach, can be arranged through hotels or boat owners on the waterfront at Christiansted. Only six operators are licensed to take day charters to the island, which means that they are often crowded. Another attraction is the **Salt River coral canyon**.

St Croix

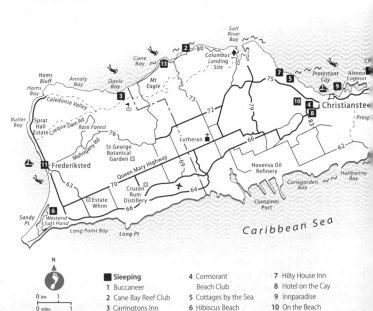

■ Sleeping	4 Cormorant	7 Hilty House Inn
1 Buccaneer	Beach Club	8 Hotel on the Cay
2 Cane Bay Reef Club	5 Cottages by the Sea	9 Innparadise
3 Carringtons Inn	6 Hibiscus Beach	10 On the Beach

Diving trips are arranged by several companies all round the island, many of which also charter boats out and offer sailing lessons. Dive companies include: *Dive Experience*, Christiansted, T7733307, 800-2359047, www.st-croix.com/diveexperience, who will dive even if only 2 people sign up, good offers on prices and good equipment, including masks with prescription lenses; *Anchor Dive Centre*, Salt River National Park, T/F7781522; *Cane Bay Dive Shop*, T7739913, F7785442, www.canebayscuba.com, great bay for snorkelling and wall diving, beach or boat dive; *Scubawest*, Frederiksted, T7723701, F7721852, www.divescubawest.com, specializes in pier night dives and wrecks; *N2 The Blue*, Cane Bay, T866-4514604, www.n2blue.com; *Scuba Shack*, Frederiksted, T772-DIVE, www.stcroixscubashack.com; *St Croix Ultimate Blue Water Adventures* (SCUBA), T7735994, www.stcroixscuba.com If you don't want to get wet, there is the semi-submersible *Oceanique*, T7737060, with day and night excursions in Christiansted harbour and around Protestant Cay.

Dive centres
During February, March and April you are likely to see humpback whales near the islands and dive boats sometimes go out to watch them

Beaches and watersports

Good beaches can be found at **Davis Bay**, **Protestant Cay**, **Buccaneer**, **the Reef**, **Cane Bay** (good snorkelling), **Grapetree Beach** and **Cormorant Beach**. Cramer Park on the east shore and Frederiksted beach to the north of the town both have changing facilities and showers. *Rainbow Beach Club*, 1½ km north of Frederiksted, has a spectacular sandy beach, restaurant and beach bar. All beaches are open to the public, but on those where there is a hotel (*Buccaneer* – good snorkelling) that maintains the beach, you may have to pay for the use of facilities. Try the isolated beach to the east of the *Buccaneer Hotel* (walk across the golf course), at *The Waves* restaurant at Cane Bay, or explore and find your own. Generally the north coast is best for surfing because there are no reefs to protect the beaches. On the northwest coast, the stretch from Northside Beach to Ham's Bay is easily accessible for shell collecting (but watch out for sea urchins at Ham's Bay beach); the road is alongside the beach. The road ends at the General Offshore Sonorbuoy Area (a naval installation at Ham's Bluff), which is a good place to see booby birds and frigate birds leaving at dawn and coming home to roost at dusk. Shells can also be found on Sprat Hall beach (ask at *Sprat Hall Plantation* for details).

There are some nice rock pools on various beaches, where the sun warms tidal waters and creates nature's own hot tub, great for a soak

Buck Island Reef
National Park BUCK ISLAND

Buck Island Channel

een Cay

Teague
Bay

Cramer
Park
Beach Point
Udall

Cramer
Park

East
End
Bay

Seven
Hills

Grapetree
Beach
Turner Hole

Great
Pond

Grass
Pt

Robin
Bay

Great
Pond Bay

ng Bay

St Croix Watersports, T7737060. Waterskiing, jet skiing, windsurfing, kayaking and parasailing are all on offer. *Virgin Kayak Co*, in Cane Bay, T7780071, explores the north shore from Annaly Bay to Salt River. *Caribbean Adventure Tours*, in Salt River, T7781522, offers historical, ecological and moonlight kayak tours. There are several companies offering day sails on crewed yachts. Jones Maritime has a dock with a few moorings, teaches sailing and may rent boats for day sailing to qualified individuals. There is an annual **Coral Reef Swim** towards the end of Oct, T7732100.

Watersports

The **St Croix International Cup Regatta** is held in Feb, with 3 days of ocean racing off the east coast, **Hookanson Memorial Race** in Jan and the **John Stuart Jervis Memorial** in Dec. Contact the *St Croix Yacht Club* for details, T7739531.

Regattas

US Virgin Islands

11 Sunterra Resorts
   Carambola Beach
12 Tamarind Reef
13 Waves at Cane Bay

US Virgin Islands

Christiansted

The old town   The old town square and waterfront area of Christiansted, the old Danish capital, still retain the colourful character of the early days. Red-roofed pastel houses built by early settlers climb the hills overlooking Kings Wharf and there is an old outdoor market. Many of the buildings are being restored and the dock is being improved to take small cruise ships (the reef prevents large ships entering the harbour), but it is unlikely to be overrun with cruise ship tourism like St Thomas. Old Christiansted is compact and easy to stroll. The best place to start is the Visitors' Bureau, on the corner of King Cross Street and Queen Street, where you can pick up brochures. Starting in February for six weeks the St Croix Landmarks Society runs house tours every Wednesday, T7720598.

Fortifications   **Fort Christiansvaern** was built by the Danes in 1749 on the foundations of a French fort dating from 1645. See the punishment cells, dungeons, barracks room, officers' kitchen, powder magazine, an exhibit of how to fire a cannon, and the battery, the best vantage point for photographing the old town and harbour. The fort and the surrounding historic buildings are run by the National Parks Service. ■ *0800-1645, US$2.* The old customs house in front of the fort is now its office.

Sights   The **Steeple Building** was built as a church by the Danes in 1734, then converted into a military bakery, storehouse and later a hospital. It is now a history museum. ■ *0930-1200, 1300-1500. US$2.* The area here is full of old Danish architecture, and many of the original buildings are still used. The West India and Guinea Co, which bought St Croix from the French and settled the island, built a warehouse on the corner of Church and Company Streets which is now a post office and Customs House.

On King Street is the building where the young Alexander Hamilton, who was to become one of the founding fathers of the USA, worked as a clerk in Nicolas Cruger's counting-house. Today the building houses the Little Switzerland shop.

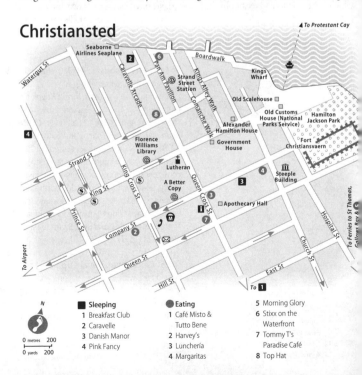

Christiansted

Sleeping	**Eating**	5 Morning Glory
1 Breakfast Club	1 Café Misto &	6 Stixx on the
2 Caravelle	Tutto Bene	Waterfront
3 Danish Manor	2 Harvey's	7 Tommy T's
4 Pink Fancy	3 Lunchería	Paradise Café
	4 Margaritas	8 Top Hat

0 metres 200
0 yards 200

Government House has all the hallmarks of the elegant and luxurious life of the merchants and planters in the days when 'sugar was king'. The centre section, built in 1742 as a merchant's residence, was bought by the Secret Council of St Croix in 1771 as a government office. It was later joined to another merchant's town house on the corner of Queen Cross Street and a handsome ballroom was added. The Governor stays here when he works away from Charlotte Amalie.

A **boardwalk** spans the entire waterfront of Christiansted, affording a wonderful stroll with lively restaurants, cafés and bars along the way. The boardwalk is well lit and security is tight with policemen on duty and security cameras. The seaplane lands alongside the boardwalk and park benches provide vantage points to enjoy the view. Between the waterfront and Strand Street there is a fascinating maze of arcades and alleys lined with boutiques, handicrafts and jewellery shops. Just offshore is **Protestant Cay** (just called The Cay), reached by ferry for US$3 return. It has a pleasant beach, and the *Hotel on the Cay* with restaurants, pool, tennis, watersports.

Around the island

Agriculture was long the staple of the economy, cattle and sugar the main activities, and ruins of sugar plantations with their Great Houses and windmills still remain. You can tour the restored estates several times a year. The **St Croix Heritage Trail** promotes culture, heritage and communities and was designated one of 50 Millennium Legacy Trails by the White House Millennium Council. There are many attractions to be toured. A good guide is available at www.millenniumtrails.org

Estate Whim has been restored to the way it was under Danish rule in the 1700s. There's a gift shop and candlelight concerts and other functions are held here, including an annual antiques auction, usually in March, which is considered one of the best places to find antique West Indian furniture. ■ *Mon-Sat 1000-1600. US$5, children under 12 US$1. T7720598, www.stcroixlandmarks.com The St Croix Landmark Society can be contacted here.* **St George Botanical Garden,** just off Centreline Road, in an old estate, has gardens amid the ruined buildings. ■ *Mon-Sat 0800-1600. US$5 for non-members.*

Frederiksted, 17 miles from Christiansted, is the only other town on St Croix. Historic buildings such as **Victoria House**, 7-8 Strand Street, and the Customs House, have been repaired following hurricane damage. **Fort Frederik** (1752) is a museum. This is the place where the proclamation freeing all Danish slaves was read, in 1848. An exhibition of old photos and newspaper articles and other display items shows the destruction caused by hurricanes. ■ *Mon-Fri 0830-1600. Free.* A **pier**, to accommodate at least two cruise ships, was built in 1993.

Frederiksted

The rainforest to the north of town is worth a visit. Two roads, the paved Mahogany Road (Route 76) and the unpaved Creque Dam Road (Road 58) traverse it.

Essentials

Best resorts LL *Buccaneer*, on Gallows Bay, north coast, T7732100, www.thebuccaneer.com 132 luxury rooms, 340 acres, 3 beaches, sports including golf (see page 425), tennis, fitness centre, watersports centre, restaurants, packages available, and **LL-L** *Sunterra Resorts Carambola Beach*, on Davis Bay, north coast, T7783800, www.sun terra.com 146 rooms in 25 2-storey villas, tennis, golf , pool, jacuzzis, snorkelling, scuba.

Sleeping
For hotel rates consult www.st-croix.com/ rates For small, intimate places to stay, check out www.smallinns stcroix.com, www.gotost croix.com or www.visitstcroix.com

Christiansted L *Hotel on the Cay*, on Protestant Cay, see page 423, in Christiansted harbour, T7732035, F7737046. Free ferry service, 55 rooms, also timeshare with kitchenettes, snorkelling, pool, beach, watersports, tennis, restaurants. **AL** *Caravelle*, 44A Queen Cross St, T7730687, www.hotelcaravelle.com 44 rooms, also good, with good restaurant, *Rumrunners*, pool, diving, transport to other sports facilities, diving packages available. **AL** *Danish Manor*, 2 Company St, T7731377, www.danishmanor.com Pool in old courtyard, renovated rooms.

US Virgin Islands

AL-B *Pink Fancy*, 27 Prince St, near shopping centre and waterfront, T7738460, www.pink fancy.com 18th-century townhouse, a National Historic Trust property, 13 rooms, honeymoon packages, bar, pool. **AL** *Hilty House Inn*, T/F7732594, hiltyhouse@worldnet.att.net House or cottage, breakfast, pool. **C** *The Breakfast Club*, 18 Queen Cross St, T7737383, www.the-breakfast-club.christiansted.vi.us 9 rooms with bath and kitchenette, breakfast, hot tub on deck. **Near Christiansted: LL-L** *Cormorant Beach Club and Hotel*, T7788920, www.cormorant-stcroix.com 1st class, beach, tennis, pool, deluxe, gay friendly. **West of Christiansted: L** *Hibiscus Beach Hotel*, T7734042, www.1hibiscus.com 37 beachfront rooms, hammocks on the beach, access for handicapped to beach, pool, restaurant, watersports in all-inclusive packages, special deals. **L-AL** *Innparadise*, Estate Golden Rock on Little Princess Hill overlooking Christiansted, T7139803, www.innparadisestcroix.com 5 small rooms, CP, private or shared bath, min stay 3 days, no smoking, pets or children under 12, 10% discount for over-50's. **L-A** *Carringtons Inn*, 4001 Estate Hermon Hill, T7130508, www.carringtonsinn.com 5 rooms, private bathrooms, CP, pool.

Northeast coast L *Tamarind Reef Hotel*, T7734455, www.usvi.net/hotel /tamarind 46 rooms, half have kitchenettes, a/c, fan, TV, balcony, all with seaview, 2 beaches, pool, snorkelling, boardsailing, kayaking at hotel, or diving, fishing, sailing from adjacent Green Cay Marina, croquet and tennis lawn, packages available.

Frederiksted Half a mile from town, **LL-A** *On The Beach*, T7721205, www. gaytraveling.com/onthebeach Pool, 20 rooms, suites, villas, kitchenettes, restaurants, serves gay community. **A** *The Frederiksted*, 442 Strand St, T7720500, www.frederikstedhotel.com Modern, fridge, TV, phones, pool, restaurant, bar, good, dive shop. **North of Frederiksted: LL-L** *Cane Bay Reef Club*, T/F7782966, www.canebay.com 9 suites with balconies over the sea, pool, restaurant, bar, weekly rates cheaper. **LL-L** *Waves At Cane Bay*, Kingshill, T7781805, www.thewavesatcanebay.com 12 ocean-front studios with balconies, cable TV, natural grotto pool, beach, good snorkelling and scuba. **South of Frederiksted: AL-A** *Cottages by the Sea*, T7720495, www.travelfacts.com/ Beach, watersports, Maid service.

There are several rental agents for villas and condominiums: *American Rentals*, 2001 Old Hospital St, Christiansted, T7738470, F7738472; *Island Villas*, 6 Company St, Christiansted, T7738821, www.ecani.com/island.villas; *Richards and Ayer Associates Realtors*, 340 Strand St, Frederiksted, T7720420, www.ayervirginislands.com All with a wide price range.

Eating
St Croix 'This Week' has a full listing of the many places to eat, from budget to elegant dining

Restaurant life on St Croix includes charcoal-broiled steaks and lobsters, West Indian Creole dishes and Danish and French specialities. Do not miss the open-air Crucian picnics. Local dishes include stewed or roast goat, red pea soup (a sweet soup of kidney beans and pork), callalou (dasheen soup); snacks, Johnny cakes (unleavened fried bread) and pate (pastry filled with spiced beef, chicken or salt fish); drinks, ginger beer, *mavi* (from the bark of a tree).

Christiansted *Café Misto*, Company St, T7736911. Salads, soup and sandwich bistro at lunchtime, 1100-1600, great variety, good quality, becomes lounge bar for *Tutto Bene* next door (same ownership) at night, 1700-2400, with Martini specials. *Harvey's Bar and Restaurant*, Company St, T7733433, local cuisine, conch, callaloo, goat stew; *Indies*, Company St, T6929440. Seafood and West Indian restaurant, also sushi on Wed and Fri nights at the bar. *Lunchería*, on Company St, in the courtyard of Apothecary Hall, T7734247. Mexican food, cheap margaritas, live music, open Mon-Sat lunch and dinner. Also on Company St are *Margaritas*, inexpensive Tex-Mex food, open Mon-Sat for lunch and dinner. *Morning Glory*, Gallows Bay Market Pl, T7236620. 26 blended coffees, also tea, New Orleans-style beignets. *Rumrunners*, on the waterfront at *Hotel Caravelle*, serves breakfast, lunch and dinner. *Stixx on the Waterfront*, Pan Am Pavilion, T7735157. Informal, lunch and dinner, pasta, pizza, seafood, daily specials, popular bar; watch the seaplanes from Kings Alley Yacht Club. *Tommy T's Paradise Café*, Queen Cross St, T7732985. Small local bar/restaurant, breakfast, lunch and dinner, sandwiches and daily specials, claustrophobic, no credit cards. *Top Hat*, Strand St, T7732346. Often mentioned in gourmet magazines, excellent and spotlessly clean but pricey

US Virgin Islands

at US$20-28 for entrées, Scandinavian food, Smorgaasbord, steaks and seafood, open Mon-Sat dinner only. *Tutto Bene*, Company St, T7735229. Italian bistro, fast service, wonderful food, daily specials, generous portions, reservations preferred as very popular.

Frederiksted *The Blue Moon*, 17 Strand St, T7722222. Seafood and native dishes plus music, dinner Tue-Sat, daily specials, great Sun brunch with jazz. *Motown Bar and Restaurant*, Strand St, T7729882. Goat stew, conch, shrimp, open for breakfast, lunch and dinner daily, cheap. *Café du Soleil*, Princess Passage, Strand St, T7725400. Tapas bar and Sun brunch 1000-1400.

Out of town The restaurant at *Paradise Sunset Beach Hotel,* Ham's Bluff, has been recommended, seafood and local food, open Mon-Thu for lunch and dinner. *Baggy's Wrinkle* and *Golden Rail* at St Croix Marina, Gallows Bay. Inexpensive daily specials, American food and barbecue, open Tue-Sun all day, no credit cards. *Cheeseburgers in Paradise*, on East End Rd, T7731119. Very popular, always crowded, open for lunch and dinner, inexpensive. *Columbus Cove*, Salt River National Park, near Columbus Landing. Open daily for breakfast, lunch and dinner, meat, fish and chicken platters, large portions, most dinners under US$15. *The Waves at Cane Bay*, T7781805. Expensive, good food, open for dinner Tue-Sat.

Nightlife Most hotels provide evening entertainment on a rotating basis, so it may be best to stay put and let the fun come to you. The *Hibiscus Beach Hotel* hosts the *Caribbean Dance Company* on Fri at 2030, and a steel pan band on Wed at 1830, also mandolin on Thu and a jazz trio on Sat at 2000. Some restaurants also provide entertainment, eg *Tivoli Gardens* (Queen Cross and Strand Streets) and *The Galleon* (Green Cay Marina, piano bar). *Club 9*, Hospital St. Crab races on Mon and Fri on the boardwalk, folk guitar on Wed, Green Flash rock Thu-Sat. *The Blue Moon*, 17 Strand St. Live jazz every Fri and on full moons. *Kings Alley Yacht Club* has open-air bandstand with music. Live music at *Deep End Bar* at Green Cay Marina. *Two plus Two Disco*, Northside Rd, west of Christiansted (closed Mon). Live entertainment Fri and Sat, US$5 cover charge; snack bar from 1200 till 1800. Cultural events take place at the *Island Centre*, a 600-seat theatre with an open-air amphitheatre seating another 1,600. Gambling at the *Divi Carina Bay Resort* casino on southeast coast, T7739700.

Festivals The *St Croix's Festival* lasts from early **Dec** right through Christmas to 6 Jan. There is another festival on the Sat nearest to **17 Mar**, St Patrick's Day, when there is a splendid parade with floats and music, T7731139. Mocko Jumbi dancing takes place at festivals and on other occasions; for information, contact Willard S John, PO Box 3162, Frederiksted, St Croix, USVI 00840, T7738909 (day), 7720225 (evening). *A Taste of St Croix* showcases the island's best chefs in early **Apr**, with over 40 hotels taking part, T6929922. In **Nov** there is a *Thanksgiving Jump-Up* (also Feb, May and Jul jump-ups), T7138012.

Shopping **Local art**: *Memories of St Croix* and *Kallaloo* in Christiansted, also the gift shop at the Whim Plantation. *St Croix Leap* (Life and Environmental Arts Project, Frederiksted, T7720421), on Route 76, the Paved Rain Forest Rd, is a woodworking centre. It is possible to buy the artefacts directly from here. They take orders for work and will ship to you. *Many Hands*, Pan Am Pavilion, sells arts and crafts from the Virgin Islands. For special **jewellery** go to *Sonya's*, in Christiansted. *The Natural Jewel*, King St, for pearl and larimar. *St Croix Landmarks*, museum store, teak, antique furniture, works by island artists. The **market** in Christiansted is on Company St. *Quin House* on Company St has galleries, Caribbean maps and prints, museum replica jewellery, mahogany furniture. For groceries, there is *K-Mart*, *Cost U Less* at Sunshine Mall and *Plaza Extras*, and several *Pueblo* stores along on the bus route. Gallows Bay has *Gallows Bay Market*, PO, bank, bookstore, hardware store, marine store.

Sports
For diving and watersports, see pages 420 and 421

Most of the large hotels have **tennis** courts for residents, but you can also play at the *Buccaneer Hotel*, the *Carambola*, Chenay Bay, Club St Croix, The Reef Club, the *Tamarind Reef Hotel* and others. There are 4 public courts at Canegata Park in Christiansted and 2 public courts near the fort in Frederiksted which can be used free of charge on a first come first served basis. 2 18-hole **golf** courses, one at the *Carambola*, T7785638, with pro shop, putting green

US Virgin Islands

and driving range, and the other at the *Buccaneer Hotel*, T7732100, also with putting green and pro shop. There is also a 9-hole course at *The Reef*, T7738844, green fee US$12.50. **Horse riding**: *Paul and Jill's Equestrian Stables*, T7722880 or 7722627, at Sprat Hall Plantation, 1½ miles north of Frederiksted, on Route 58, reserve 3 days in advance if possible for rides through the rainforest, past Danish ruins, for all levels of ability, English or Western styles, US$50 for 2 hours, no credit cards. You can play **croquet** at the *Tamarind Reef Hotel*. Rent a **mountain bike** and join *St Croix Bikes and Tours* for a tour of the rainforest or beach areas of west end of island, T7722343, www.stcroixbike.com *VI Cycling* organizes regular weekly rides and races for which there is a US$5 fee per participant, Mike Mcqueston T7730079.

In May a week of sports-related events culminate in the **St Croix International Triathlon**, with over 1,000 participants, www.stcroixtriathlon.com Phone Tom Guthrie or Miles Sperber, T7734470, for details of running courses and tours.

Transport **Bus** The bus service runs between Christiansted and Frederiksted, 0530-2130 every 30 mins (every hr on Sun), US$1. **Taxi** A taxi tour costs US$25, less for groups; contact *St Croix Taxi and Tours Association*, Henry E Rohlsen Airport, T7781088, F7786887; *Combined Tours*, T7722888. Taxi vans run between Christiansted and Frederiksted, US$2. For a limo service, try *Evans Limo Service*, T7734845. **Car hire** Rental agencies include *Avis*, at airport, T7789355/9365; *Budget* at airport, T7789636, or Christiansted (*King Christian Hotel* T7732285); *Hertz*, T7781402, or *Buccaneer Hotel*, T7732100 Ext 737; *Olympic*, just west of Christiansted, T7738000, free delivery and pick up; *Caribbean Jeep and Car Rental*, 6 Hospital St, Christiansted, T7734399; *Green Cay Jeep and Car Rental*, T7737227; *Berton*, 1 mile west of Christiansted, T7731516.

Directory **Communications** Internet: *A Better Copy*, on Company St between King Cross St and Queen Cross St, open Mon-Fri 0900-1700, also fax and photocopying; at the Florence Williams Library; *Strand Street Station*, in the Pan Am Pavilion, Christiansted, internet café, mail boxes, photocopies, faxes, pay phones, film processing, open 0900-1900; at *St Croix Bike & Tours*, Custom St, near the pier in Frederiksted, cybercafé, *Ben & Jerry's* ice cream, bike rental and tours, www.stcroixbike.com **Embassies and consulates** *Dutch*, T7737100. *Norwegian*, T7737100. **Medical services** St Croix has a 130-bed hospital, T7786311, and a 24-hr emergency service.

Background

History

The islands were 'discovered' by Columbus on his second voyage in 1493. He named them 'Las Once Mil Vírgenes' in honour of the legend of St Ursula and her 11,000 martyred virgins. There were Indian settlements in all the major islands of the group and the first hostile action with the Caribs took place during Columbus' visit. Spain asserted its exclusive right to settle the islands but did not colonize them, being more interested the Greater Antilles. European settlement did not begin until the 17th century, when few Indians were to be found. St Croix (Santa Cruz) was settled by the Dutch and the English around 1625, and later by the French. In 1645 the Dutch abandoned the island and went to St Eustatius and St Maarten. In 1650 the Spanish repossessed the island and drove off the English, but the French, under Philippe de Loinvilliers de Poincy of the Knights of Malta, persuaded the Spanish to sail for Puerto Rico. Three years later de Poincy formally deeded his islands to the Knights of Malta although the King of France retained sovereignty. St Croix prospered and planters gradually converted their coffee, ginger and tobacco plantations to sugar, and African slavery was introduced. Wars, illegal trading, privateering, piracy and religious conflicts finally persuaded the French Crown that a colony on St Croix was not militarily or economically feasible and in 1695 or 96 the colony was evacuated to St Domingue.

A plan for colonizing St Thomas was approved by Frederik III of Denmark in 1665 but the first settlement failed. The Danes asserted authority over St John in 1684, but the hostility of the English in Tortola prevented them from settling until 1717. In 1733 France sold St Croix to the Danish West India & Guinea Company and in 1754 the Danish West Indies became a royal colony. After the end of Company rule , St Thomas turned towards commerce while in St Croix plantation agriculture flourished. St Thomas became an important shipping centre with reliance on the slave trade. Denmark was the first European nation to end its participation in the slave trade, in 1802. Illegal trade continued, however, and British occupation of the Virgin Islands in the early 1800's prevented enforcement of the ban.

The Danish Virgin Islands reached a peak population of 43,178 in 1835. Sailing ships were replaced by steamships which found it less necessary to transship in St Thomas. Prosperity declined with a fall in sugar prices, a heavy debt burden, soil exhaustion, development of sugar beet in Europe, hurricanes and droughts and the abolition of slavery. In 1847 a Royal decree provided that all slaves would be free after 1859 but the impatient slaves rebelled in July 1848. By the late 19th century economic decline became pronounced. The sugar factory on St Croix was inefficient and in the 20th century the First World War meant less shipping for St Thomas, more inflation, unemployment and labour unrest. The Virgin Islands became a liability for Denmark and the economic benefits of colonialism no longer existed. Negotiations with the USA had taken place intermittently ever since the 1860s for cession of the Virgin Islands to the USA. The USA wanted a Caribbean naval base and, after the 1914 opening of the Panama Canal, was particularly concerned to guard against German acquisition of Caribbean territory. In 1917, the islands were sold for US$25mn but no progress was made for several years. The islands were under naval rule during and after the War and it was not until 1932 that US citizenship was granted to all natives of the Virgin Islands.

A devastating hurricane in 1928, followed by the stock market crash of 1929, brought US awareness of the need for economic and political modernization. Several years of drought, the financial collapse of the sugar refineries, high unemployment and low wages characterized these years. In 1931 naval rule was replaced by a civil government. In 1934, the Virgin Islands Company (VICO) was set up as a 'partnership programme'. The sugar and rum industry benefited from demand in the Second World War. VICO improved housing, land and social conditions, but the end of the wartime construction boom, wartime demand for rum, and the closing of the submarine base brought further economic recession. However, the severance of diplomatic relations between the USA and Cuba shifted tourism towards the islands. Construction boomed and there was even a labour shortage. VICO was disbanded in 1966, along with the production of sugar cane. Various tax incentives promoted the arrival of heavy industry, and during the 1960s the Harvey Alumina Company and the Hess Oil Company began operating on St Croix. By 1970, the economy was dominated by mainland investment and marked by managed enterprises based on imported labour from other Caribbean islands.

In September 1989, St Croix was hit by Hurricane Hugo, which tore through 90% of buildings and left 22,500 people homeless. The disaster was followed by civil unrest, with rioting, and US army troops were sent in to restore order. The territorial government, located on St Thomas, was slow to react to the disaster on St Croix and and criticized. St Croix's feeling of neglect led to attempts to balance the division of power between the islands, but calls for greater autonomy grew. After some delay, a referendum was held in October 1993, which presented voters with seven options on the island's status, grouped into three choices: continued or enhanced status, integration into the USA, or independence. However, the vote was inconclusive, with only 27% of the registered voters turning out; 50% were needed for a binding decision. Of those who did vote, 90% preferred the first option, leaving the process of constitutional change in some disarray.

Geography and people

The US Virgin Islands, in which the legacies of Danish ownership remain very apparent, comprise four main islands: St Thomas, St John, St Croix and Water Island. There are 68 islands in all, lying about 40 miles east of Puerto Rico. They have long been developed as holiday centres for US citizens and are distinct from the British Virgin Islands. The population has always been English-speaking, despite the long period of Danish control. Some Spanish is used on St Croix. The West Indian dialect is mostly English, with inflections from Dutch, Danish, French, Spanish, African languages and Creole.

US Virgin Islands

Government

In 1936 the Organic Act of the Virgin Islands of the United States provided for two municipal councils and a Legislative Assembly in the islands. Discrimination on the grounds of race, colour, sex or religious belief was forbidden. In 1946, the first black governor was appointed to the Virgin Islands and in 1950 the first native governor was appointed. In 1968 the Elective Governor Act was passed, to become effective in 1970 when, for the first time, Virgin Islanders would elect their own Governor and Lieutenant Governor. The Act also abolished the presidential veto of territorial legislation and authorized the legislature to override the Governor's veto by a two-thirds majority vote. The USVI is an unincorporated Territory under the US Department of Interior with a Delegate in the House of Representatives who has a vote in sittings of the whole House. The Governor is elected every four years. All persons born in the USVI are US citizens, but do not vote in presidential elections while on the islands.

Economy

USVI residents enjoy a comparatively high standard of living. Unemployment is low, but the working population is young and there is constant pressure for new jobs. The islands used to rely on the alumina plant, and the Hess oil refinery, for employment, but now the major economic activity is tourism.

Industry is better developed than in many Caribbean islands. In 1998 Hess Oil Co and Petróleos de Venezuela signed an agreement to create a company called Hovensa to operate the refinery on St Croix. Industrial incentives and tax concessions equivalent to those enjoyed by Puerto Rico attract new investors with US markets to the islands. Many US corporations have manufacturing operations in the USVI. The islands' lack of natural resources makes them heavily dependent on imports.

US Virgin Islands

British Virgin Islands

Introducing the British Virgin Islands

The British Virgin Islands have a reputation for excellent sailing between the islands and there are many charter companies offering crewed or bareboat yachts. Windsurfing is also top quality and both sports organize races and regattas which attract competitors of international standard. Races are accompanied by lots of parties and related activities typical of the yachtie fraternity. There are plenty of hotels, and a few really special places in isolated spots – popular with newly weds or the seriously rich. While there are some luxury, sizable resorts in the BVI, there are no high-rise hotels or casinos, and very few nightclubs. In fact, there is very little to do at all on land and nearly everything happens in the beautiful water which surrounds the islands. If you are keen on watersports and sailing and have adequate finances (the Virgin Islands are not cheap), you will enjoy island hopping around Sir Francis Drake Channel.

British Virgin Islands

Essentials

Before you travel

An authenticated birth or citizenship certificate or voter's registration with current picture ID **Documents**
may suffice for US or Canadian citizens, although a passport is recommended. All other nationalities need a valid **passport.** All visitors require a return or **onward ticket** and should be able
to prove their ability to fund their visit. Visitors from some countries, such as Guyana, require a
visa. The Chief Immigration Officer is in Road Town, T4943701 ext 2538, or T4944371.

Currency The US dollar is the legal tender. There are no restrictions on exchange. Try to **Money**
avoid large-denomination TCs. Cheques are rarely accepted; cash is king. There is a US$0.10
stamp duty on all cheques and TCs. **Credit cards** are all right for most hotels and the larger
restaurants, but not for the majority of bars/restaurants and they are not accepted on
Anegada except at the *Anegada Reef Hotel*.

The temperature averages 84°F in summer and 80°F in winter. At night temperatures may **Climate**
drop about 50°F. Average annual rainfall is 40 ins.

Getting there

There are international airports on Beef Island for Tortola (connecting bridge), and on Virgin **Air**
Gorda, with a domestic airport on Anegada. There are no direct flights from Europe or from *The main airport,*
the USA. **From Europe** Same-day connections can be made through Puerto Rico or *on Beef Island, was*
Antigua. **From the USA** Connecting flights can be arranged through Puerto Rico or the *expanded in 2002*
USVI. **From the Caribbean** *American Eagle*, T4952559, *Air Sunshine*, T4958900, *M & N Avi-* *with a new terminal*
ation, T4955553, *Cape Air* and *LIAT*, T4951187, fly several times a day from San Juan. *LIAT*, *Air*
Sunshine and *Cape Air* from St Thomas. *LIAT*, *American Eagle* and *Winair*, T4952577, from St
Maarten. *LIAT* and/or *Caribbean Star* from Anguilla, Antigua, Barbados, Dominica, Grenada,
Port of Spain, St Kitts, St Vincent. Virgin Gorda's air links are not especially good. *Air St*
Thomas and *Air Sunshine* fly from St Thomas and San Juan, while *M & N Aviation* also flies
from San Juan. Charter flights with *Fly BVI*, T4951747, *Clair Aero Services*, T4952271, *Air St*
Thomas, T4955935, *Caribbean Wings*, T4952309, and *Air Sunshine*.

There are frequent connections with the USVI, see page 403, and within the BVI, *Inter-Island* **Boat**
Boat Services, T4954166; also water taxi available, T7766501. *Native Son Inc*, T4954617,
Smiths Ferry Services, T4942355, *Speedy's*, T4955240.
    Ports of entry (British flag) Port Purcell at Road Town is the principal port of entry with
an 800-ft, deep water berth and a 500-ft pier for cargo ships; cruise ships dock at Wickham's
Cay, Road Town. There are others at West End (Soper's Hole), Tortola; St Thomas Bay, Virgin
Gorda; Anegada (customs and immigration 0715-1715 Mon-Fri, 0800-1530 Sat-Sun) and
Great Harbour, Jost Van Dyke. Small cruise ships can be seen off many of the islands.

Boat documents Customs clearance fee US$0.75, harbour dues US$7, US$10.50 for a boat *Jet skis must be*
registered under the name of a corporation. The captain may clear the crew, taking passports *declared on entry*
and boat documentation ashore. You may clear in and out at the same time if staying less *to the BVI, private*
than 72 hrs. Weekends incur overtime charges. A cruising permit is required by everyone *use is illegal*
cruising in the BVI: 1 Dec-30 Apr, all recorded charter boats US$2 per person per day, all
non-recorded charter boats US$4 per person per day; 1 May-30 Nov, US$0.75 and US$4
respectively. All privately owned yachts cruising in the BVI are charged nominal cruising fees.

Anchorages The BVI National Parks Trust, T4943904, has placed moorings at many dive
sites, available on a first come, first served basis. Purchase mooring use sticker from customs,
fee US$2 per person per day or US$25 per week. Buoys are colour coded: yellow for commercial dive boats, white for a boat with divers, orange for snorkelling and day use, and blue for
dinghy docks. Moorings have been placed and are maintained by Moor Seacure at *Cooper*

British Virgin Islands

▶ ## Tourist offices overseas

Germany *Wallstrasse 56, D-40878, Dusseldorf/Ratingin, T49-2102-711183, g.romberg@travelmarketing.de*
Italy *Piazza Caiazzo 3, 20124 Milan, T (39) 0266714374, staff@aigo.it*
UK *15 Upper Grosvenor St, London, W1K 7PJ, T020-73559585, infouk@bvitouristboard.com*
USA *370 Lexington Av, Suite 1605, New York,*

NY 10017, T212-6960400, bvitouristboard@worldnet.att.net; 3390 Peachtree Road NE, Suite 1000, Lenox Towers, Atlanta, GA 30326, T404-2408018, bviatlanta@worldnet.att.net; 3450 Wilshire Boulevard, Suite 1202, Los Angeles, CA 90010, T213-7368931, bvitb@pacbell.net

Island Beach Club, Marina Cay, *Drake's Anchorage, Abe's* (Jost Van Dyke), Penn's Landing, Leverick Bay, *Rhymer's*, Cane Garden Bay, *Anegada Reef Hotel*, Soper's Hole Marina, *Harris' Place*, Vixen Point (Prickly Pear Island, Gorda Sound), *Last Resort* (Trellis Bay), at US$20 per night. In winter months, northerly swells and high surf can make northern anchorages (and landing at the Baths) untenable. Listen to ZBVI 780AM for weather reports. There are 12 marinas on Tortola, 3 on Virgin Gorda, one on Peter Island and one on Marina Cay.

Touching down

Tourist information **Local tourist office** BVI Tourist Board, 2nd floor, AKARA Building, Wickhams Cay 1, Road Town, T4943134, F4943866, www.bvitouristboard.com; Also an office at Virgin Gorda Yacht Harbour, T4955181, F4956517; some offices overseas can help with reservations. The *BVI Welcome* is a bimonthly colour tourist guide, www.bviwelcome.com To find out what's on, weekly, monthly or annually, get the *Limin' Times,* updated every Thu, T4942413, www.limin-times.com The *Tourism Directory* is published annually and is a detailed listing of services. The tourist board has these and many other brochures.

Maps The Ordnance Survey publishes a map of the BVI in its World Maps series, with inset maps of Road Town and East End, Tortola, tourist information and some text; Ordnance Survey, Romsey Road, Southampton, SO9 4DH, T01703-792792. The tourist office distributes a road map, updated annually with some tourist information on resorts, restaurants and what to do.

Where to stay

Hotels There is a 7% hotel tax and a 10% service charge in the BVI. Rates apply to double rooms, EP, winter-summer. Hotels are mostly small, intimate and low-rise but few are cheap. **Villas** There are some truly luxurious houses for rent, with the most famous, or infamous, being Richard Branson's house on Necker Island. A wide choice of stylish properties is on offer. **Camping** Allowed only on authorized sites.

Getting around

Air *Clair Aero* flies from Tortola to Anegada Mon, Wed, Fri and Sun, US$60 round trip, also from St Thomas via Tortola, Mon, Wed, Fri, US$140 round trip, plus US$20 tax, T4952271. *Fly BVI* is another small charter airline with trips to Anegada US$155-600 one-way, depending on the size of the aircraft, also to Virgin Gorda, T4951747, www.fly-bvi.com Pack light, there is limited luggage space on the small aircraft. Or take a day trip to Anegada, US$125 per person from Tortola, US$175 from Virgin Gorda (min 2 people), including taxi, air fare, lobster lunch at the *Big Bamboo*, contact Fly BVI. If you can fill the aircraft, charters often work out cheaper.

Road
See also Transport, pages 445, 449 and 453

Car There are only about 50 miles of roads suitable for cars. Drive on the left. Maximum speed limit 40 mph, in residential areas 20 mph. Jeeps may be more useful than cars for exploring secluded beach areas. They can be hired on Tortola, Virgin Gorda and Anegada. Car rental offices (or the Traffic and Licensing Department) provide the necessary temporary BV

British Virgin Islands

◀

Touching down

Departure tax *US$10 , if you leave by air, and US$5 departure tax by sea. There is a cruise ship passenger tax of US$7.*
Emergency *Police, Fire or Ambulance, T999. The Virgin Islands Search and Rescue (VISAR) is a voluntary 24-hr marine service, T999 or Ch 16.*
Hours of business *Banks: Mon- Fri*

0900-1400 (FirstCaribbean 0900-1500; Chase Manhattan 0900- 1600; Chase opens Sat 0900-1200; **Government offices:** *Mon-Fri 0830-1630;* **Shops:** *Mon-Fri 0900-1700.*
Official time *Atlantic Standard Time, 4 hrs behind GMT, 1 hr ahead of EST.*
Voltage *110 volts, 60 cycles.*

driving licence (US$10) but you must also have a valid licence from your home country. **Car hire** It is advisable to book in advance in the peak season. Rates range from US$40-45 per day for a small car, US$45-70 per day for jeeps. Credit card needed with US$500 deposit. **Taxi** *BVI decor Association*, T4942875, island tours arranged.

Sea The ferry fares between Tortola and Virgin Gorda are about US$25 return and from Tortola to Jost Van Dyke US$15. Always check availability and departure times in advance. The **North Sound Express**, T4952138 has 6 daily crossings Beef Island-Spanish Town-Bitter End, 30 mins, reservations essential. To Leverick Bay (for Mosquito Island), 25 mins, US$20 one way, 1300, 1545, 1730. Return 0645, 0845, 1145, 1445, 1615. Bus service (not included in fare) to and from Road Town waterfront (Pussers) and Beef Island ferry dock. **Speedy's** , T4955240, has 4 crossings Mon, Wed, Fri and Sat between Virgin Gorda and Road Town, 6 on Tue and Thu, and 2 on Sun, also a service continuing to St Thomas, Tue, Thu and Sat. **Smiths Ferry Services**, T4942355, 4954495, cross from Virgin Gorda to Road Town then West End on their way to St John and St Thomas 4 times a day Mon-Sat, 3 times on Sun. **Peter Island Ferry**, T4952000, has 8 daily crossings from the Peter Island Ferry Dock, Road Town, to Peter Island, US$15 round trip. **Jost Van Dyke Ferry Service**, T4942997, 4 crossings a day between West End and Jost Van Dyke Mon-Sat, 3 on Sun. **Marina Cay Ferry**, T4942174, runs between Beef Island and *Pusser's Marina Cay* 8 times a day.

Keeping in touch

Post There is a post office in Road Town, branches in Tortola and Virgin Gorda and sub-branches in other islands. Postal rates for postcards are US$0.30 to the USA, US$0.35 to Europe and US$0,45 to the rest of the world; for aerogrammes US$0.35; for letters to the USA US$0.45, to Europe US$0.50, to the rest of the world US$0.75.

Telephone All telecommunications are operated by *Cable & Wireless*. Phone cards are available, US$5,
IDD code: 284 US$10, US$15 and US$20, discount rates in evenings at weekends. To make a credit card call, dial 111 and quote your card number. Dial 119 for the operator or 110 for the international operator. *Cable & Wireless* is at the centre of Road Town at Wickhams Cay I, open 0700-1900 Mon-Fri, 0700-1600 Sat, 0900-1400 Sun and public holidays, T4944444, also in The Valley, Virgin Gorda, T4955444. They also operate Tortola Marine Radio, call on VHF Ch 16, talk on 27 or 84. The **CCT Boatphone** company in Road Town offers cellular telephone services throughout the Virgin Islands for yachts, US$5 per day for service, US$4 per min; there is also a prepaid cellular service, **CCT Flexphone**, T4943825. To call VHF stations from a land phone, call Tortola Radio, T116. **Caribbean Connections** at *Village Cay Marina*, T4943623, has phone, fax, email, courier service. *Moorings* allows use of phone for collecting email. *Village Cay Marina* has a computer room. *Jolly Roger* has fax and email services.

Media **Newspapers** *The Island Sun*, www.islandsun.com is published on Fri, while the *BVI Beacon* comes out on Thu. *The Limin' Times*, printed weekly, is a free magazine giving entertainment news: nightlife, sports, music etc. *Standpoint* on Tue, is popular with young islanders, with lots of advertising. *All At Sea* is a local monthly lively tabloid for yachties, T4951090, editor@allatsea.net **Radio** *Radio ZBVI* broadcasts on 780AM. Weather reports for sailors are

British Virgin Islands

broadcast hourly from 0730 to 1830 every day. There are 4 FM stations: *Reggae* at 97.3, *Country* at 94.3, *Z Gold* at 91.7and *ZROD* at 103.7. **Television** *VITV*, Channel 5, is a locally owned station showing news, sports and entertainment programmes. Cable TV is widely available.

Food and drink

There are lots of good restaurants across the islands

Most things are imported and will cost at least the same as in Florida. Try local produce which is cheaper, yams and sweet potatoes rather than potatoes, for example. Fish dishes are often excellent, try snapper, dolphin (mahi mahi, fish, not the mammal), grouper, tuna and sword-fish, and don't miss the lobster. Once a rum producer for the Royal Navy 'Pussers' (Pursers), rum is available from *Pusser's* or supermarkets. Other local rums of varying quality are also sold by hotels and restaurants.

Shopping

The BVI are not duty-free

There are gift shops and boutiques in Road Town, Tortola and in Spanish Town, Virgin Gorda. The BVI Philatelic Bureau or Post Offices sell stamps for collectors. You can also buy BVI coins, but they are not used as a currency. *Samarkand*, on Main St, Tortola, sells gold and silver jewellery created by the local Bibby family with nautical themes; you can buy earrings of yachts, pelicans, etc and they will make anything to order, samarkand@caribwave.com, also a branch at Soper's Hole Wharf, West End: *Caribbean Jewellers*. *Sunny Caribbee Herb and Spice Co* , is on Main St with *Sunny Caribbee Gallery* next door, also at *Skyworld Restaurant* and *Long Bay Hotel*, selling spices, herbs, preserves and handicrafts, mail order and shipping services available. *Pusser's Co Store* in Road Town and West End, Tortola, and Leverick Bay, Virgin Gorda, sells nautical clothing, luggage and accessories as well as Pusser's Rum. *Turtle Dove Boutique*, in Road Town, has a good selection of gifts and home furnishings and a limited selection of books . *Caribbean Handprints*, Main St, has a silkscreen studio and shop with local designs and clothing made on site. *Crafts Alive*, Road Town, is a government funded crafts village where local artisans sell their work in a replica of a traditional village of wooden houses. Aragorn Dick Read has a working studio as part of his Caribbean arts and crafts shop, giving lessons in pottery, woodcarving and basketry. *Bamboushay* is a pottery studio in Nanny Cay where you can buy the work of Val Anderson, who specializes in blue and green glazes, the colour of the sea. *Pat's Pottery* is a roadside shop and studio run by Pat Faulkner on Anegada. She has a second outlet at Soper's Hole, West End, Tortola, where you can buy her bowls and domestic ware decorated with designs influenced by the sea.

Flora and fauna

There are 20 national parks, on land and underwater, protecting a variety of species of plant and wildlife. The BVI is home to the smallest lizard in the world, the cotton ginner, or dwarf gecko, while Anegada supports the last remaining population of the endangered indigenous *Cyclua pingui*, or Anegada rock iguana, which can grow up to 5 ft long (see page 452). Most of the land was cleared years ago for its timber or to grow crops, and it is now largely covered by secondary forest and scrub. In the areas with greatest rainfall there are mangoes and palm trees, while mangrove and sea grape can be found in some areas along the shore. There are a number of trees found only in the BVI. There are few large animals, but over 150 species of birds are found and there are lots of butterflies and other insects.

Diving and marine life

Considerable work is being done to establish marine parks and conserve the reefs. The Department of Conservation and Fisheries is in charge of the BVI's natural resources and fisheries management plan. The 11-mile **Horseshoe Reef** off the south shore of Anegada is one of the largest reefs in the world and is now a Protected Area. There are 80 visible wrecks around Anegada and many more covered by coral; about 300 ships are believed to have foundered on the reef.

Humpback whales migrate to the islands every year and the Department of Conservation and Fisheries is trying to estimate their numbers with the aim of designating the BVI waters as a marine mammal sanctuary. If you see any (mostly north of Tortola), let them know. Similarly, turtles are being counted with the help of volunteers in order to draw up protective legislation. Leatherback turtles travel to north shore beaches to nest, but their numbers have been declining fast. Hawksbill and green turtles are more common but still endangered. For several months of the year the killing of turtles or taking their eggs is prohibited and the export of turtle products is illegal. Despite the government's conservation policies, approval was granted for a captive dolphin programme, which started in 2001. Dolphins caught in the wild are now in the lagoon at Prospect Reef and tourists can swim with them.

Don't buy turtle-shell products or dishes containing turtle meat

There are over 60 charted dive sites, many of which are in underwater national parks. They include walls, pinnacles, coral reefs, caverns and wrecks. The most visited wreck is that of the *Rhone*, sunk in 1867 in a storm and broken in two. The bow section is in about 80 ft of water and you can swim through the hull. The stern is shallower and you can see the prop shaft and the propeller (and an octopus). Another wreck is the 246-ft *Chikuzen* sunk in 1981 about 6 miles north of Tortola, where you will see bigger fish such as barracuda and rays. Most Caribbean and Atlantic species of tropical fish and marine invertebrates can be found in BVI waters, with hard and soft corals, gorgonians and sea fans. Visibility ranges from 60-200 ft and the water temperature varies from 76°F in winter to 86°F in summer.

Watch out for fire coral, sea urchins and the occasional bristle worm

All users of moorings must have a national parks permit. These are available through dive operators, charter companies, government offices and the National Parks Trust, T4943904. National Parks Trust moorings are located at The Caves, The Indians, The Baths, Pelican Island, Carrot Shoal, dive sites at Peter Island, Cooper Island, Ginger Island and Norman Island, the *Rhone's* anchor, the wreck of the *Rhone*, the wreck of the *Fearless*, Deadchest Island, Blonde Rock, Guana Island, The Dogs and other popular diving and recreational sites.

There are several dive shops around the islands which offer individual tours, package deals with hotels or rendezvous with charter boats. Award-winning *Baskin in the Sun*, established in 1969 and a PADI 5-star dive centre, Is at Prospect Reef, Peter Island and Soper's Hole. They are often full with package business so book individual diving in good time, T4942858, 800-6502084, www.dive-baskin.com *Dive BVI*, another PADI 5-star operation (also NAUI courses) is at Virgin Gorda Yacht Harbour, Leverick Bay and Marina Cay, Virgin Gorda, T4955513, www.divebvi.com *Blue Water Divers* is at Nanny Cay and at Hodges Creek Marina/Maya Cove, Road Town, T4942847, bwdbvi@surfbvi.com *Kilbride's Sunchaser Scuba* is at the *Bitter End Yacht Club*, North Sound, Virgin Gorda, T4959638, F4957549. *Underwater Safaris*, a PADI 5-star, NAUI and SSI facility, is at *The Moorings*, Road Town (T4943965, F4945322), and has a small shop on Cooper Island which is used as a surface interval between dives in the area, for example the *Rhone*. If you want your own dive boat for the day with your own instructor, contact *Underwater Boat Services*, T4940024, www.scubabvi.com VHF 16, minimum fee per boat US$250 or US$90. Diving and watersports cruises can be booked with *Promenade Cruises* at *Village Cay Marina*, T4946020, www.yacht promenade.com They take a maximum of 10 guests on a 65-ft trimaran with 5 crew including 2 dive instructors, with windsurfers, waterskiing and tubing for when you are not underwater. Another trimaran is the 105-ft *Cuan Law*, the world's largest, which has 10 state rooms, 7 crew including dive instructors, kayaks, waterskis, hobie cats and underwater photography, T4942490, www.diveguideint.com/cuanlaw Underwater photography, camera rental, and film processing is offered by *Rainbow Visions Photo Center*, Prospect Reef, T4942749. They often join dive boats and take video film of you underwater.

Dive centres
A two-tank dive with equipment hire is US$80-90, a resort course US$95

Beaches and watersports

There are lovely sandy beaches on all the islands and many of them are remote, accessible only from the sea. The clean, crystal-clear waters around the islands provide excellent snorkelling, diving, cruising and fishing. Most of the hotels offer a wide variety of watersports, including windsurfing, sunfish, scuba, snorkelling and small boats.

Jet skis are banned; the only licensed operator is at the Sand Box on Prickly Pear Island

British Virgin Islands

Sailing

Navigation is not difficult, the water and weather are generally clear and there are many excellent cruising guides and charts for reference

'Bareboating' (self-crew yacht chartering) is extremely popular and the way most visitors see the islands. The BVI are one of the most popular destinations in the world for bareboaters. If you do not feel confident in handling a yacht, there are various options from fully-crewed luxury yachts to hiring a skipper to take you and your bareboat out for as long as you need. You can also rent a cabin on a private charter yacht, several charter companies find this a useful way of filling a boat. Most of the islands offer at least one beautiful bay and it is possible even at the height of the season to find deserted beaches and calm anchorages. Bareboaters are warned not to sail to Anegada because of the hazardous, unmarked route through the reef. The exception is the *Moorings* fleet, which organizes a special flotilla once a week from the *Bitter End Resort & Yacht Club* for its clients. If you are sailing independently, check the charts, ensure you approach in clear daylight when the sun is high, or call the *Anegada Reef Hotel* at Setting Point when you are within sight and they will direct you over the radio.

British Virgin Islands & national parks

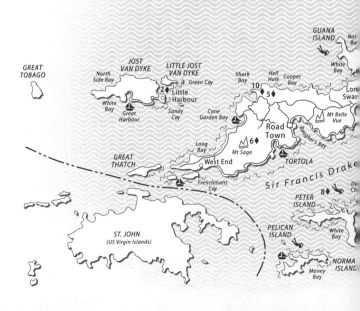

Charter companies are too numerous to list here, there are many on Tortola and several more on Virgin Gorda. Contact the tourist office for a list of bareboats with prices. **Sunsail**, the largest charter in the Caribbean, is at Hodges Creek, Maya Cove, halfway between Road Town and Beef Island Airport, where it has some 150 yachts, restaurants, shops and provisioning. For crewed yachts, try **The Moorings**, T4942332, **Yacht Connections**, T4945273, www.yacht-connections.com **Sail Vacations** (operates the 72-ft luxury ketch *Endless Summer II*), T4943656, www.EndlessSummer.com; **Regency Yacht Vacations,** at the Inner Harbour Marina, Wickham's Cay I, T4951970, www.regencyvacations.com (luxury 45-200 ft yachts for 2-20 people, gourmet cuisine, watersports); **BVI Yacht Charters,** T4944289, **Catamaran Charters**, T4946661; **Wanderlust Yacht Vacations,** T/F4942405, www.wanderlustcharters.com, and several others, will be able to match your needs with the hundreds of charter yachts available. Marinas are plentiful with yard services, haul out, fuel

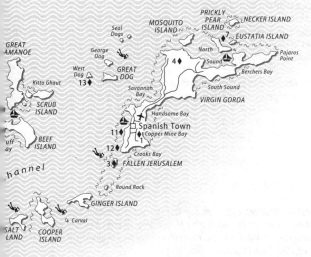

British Virgin Islands

◆ **National Parks**	7 Prickly Pear
1 Copper Mine	8 Rhone's Anchor
2 Diamond Cay	9 Rhone Marine Park
3 Fallen Jerusalem	10 Shark Bay
4 Gorda Peak Park	11 Spring Bay & The Crawl
5 Mt Healthy & Windmill Ruin	12 The Baths & Devil's Bay
6 Mt Sage	13 West Dog

N

0 km   3

0 miles   3

docks, water and showers. You can even tour the islands on a hobie cat: the *Stickl Sportcamp* organizes special sailing trips around the BVI, called 'Island Hopping on Hobiecats', where you sail during the day in a group and stay overnight on different islands, www.stickl.com

Sailing and boardsailing schools offer 3-hr to 1-week courses. The *Nick Trotter Sailing School* at the *Bitter End Resort & Yacht Club*, North Sound, T4942745, F4944756, has sailing and windsurfing courses for all ages with a wide variety of craft, very popular, principally for guests because of its isolated location. *Offshore Sailing School Ltd*, at *Prospect Reef*, T800-2214326, www.offshore-sailing.com, has courses on live-aboard cruising as well as learn-to-sail on dinghies. *Full Sail Sailing School* offers day sail and liveaboard courses with ASA certification at Seabreeze Marina, East End, T4940512, fullsail@surfbvi.com For private instruction with ASA certification, call Linda Hall, Tortola Marine Management Bareboat Vacations, T800-6330155.

Regattas

There are races of one sort or another going on all year round; check The BVI Welcome, or www.bviwelcome. com, for what is coming up, or contact the Royal BVI Yacht Club

The annual *Spring Regatta* (hosted by Nanny Cay) is held in Sir Francis Drake's Channel, considered one of the best sailing venues in the world. It is one third of the Caribbean Ocean Racing Triangle (CORT) series of regattas, www.bvispringregatta.org Contact the *Royal BVI Yacht Club*, T4943286, bviyc@surfbvi.com Ask for regatta discounts on rooms or slips. The annual *Dark and Stormy Race* is from Tortola to Anegada. Fireworks, dancing, food, drink and entertainment greet sailors on arrival in Anegada, where they take a day off before racing back to the *West End Yacht Club* (sponsored by the *Royal BVI Yacht Club*, T4943286 for information). The *Annual Anegada Yacht Race* is in **Aug**, with a route from Road Town to Anegada, *Foxy's Wooden Boat Regatta* is in **Sep** and in **Nov** *Pusser's* sponsor a *Round-Tortola* race.

Day Sails

Lots of yachts offer day-sails to all the little islands at around US$70-90 with snorkelling, beverages and sometimes lunch. When the cruise ships are in town they are often packed out. All day sail boats should carry the symbol of the Daycharter Association of the British Virgin Islands to prove they are properly licensed and have had safety checks.

Windsurfing

Windsurfing is popular in the islands and there is an annual Bacardi Hi-Ho (hook in and hold on) race which attracts windsurfers from all over the world, www.hiho- bvi.com *Boardsailing BVI* is at Trellis Bay, Beef Island, T4952447, and at Nanny Cay (a BiC Centre), T4940422, www.wind-surfing.vi, with schools and shops. As well as windsurfing they offer kayaks, surf boards and sail dinghies. *Hi Ho* at *Prospect Reef*, T4948304, has sales, rentals and instruction, also with kayaks and surfboards. Both schools have good equipment for beginners and advanced sailors. *Last Stop Sports*, at Nanny Cay, T4940564, lssbikes@surfbvi.com, has rental windsurfers, single and double kayaks, surfboards and bodyboards, lessons available.

Fishing

There are areas known to house ciguatera (fish poisoning) around the reefs, so contact the Fisheries Division before fishing

Sport fishing day trips are popular: *Anegada Reef Hotel*, Anegada, US$500-900, T4958002, offers sport fishing on a 46-ft Hatteras, inshore and bonefishing and has a tackle shop; *Pelican Charters*, Prospect Reef, T4967386, has a 46-ft Chris craft sportfisherman, US$600-950 for sportfishing, US$1,200 for marlin, full facilities. *Persistent Charters*, West End, T4954122, charge US$350 half day, US$650 full day on a 31-ft Tiara, everything included. A local permit is required for fishing, call the Fisheries Division for information, T4945682; spearfishing is not allowed, hunting on land is also banned and no firearms are allowed.

Holidays and festivals

Public holidays

New Year's Day, *H Lavity Stoutt's birthday* (first Mon in **Mar**), *Commonwealth Day* (second Mon in **Mar**), *Good Fri*, *Easter Mon*, *Whit Mon in May*, *Queen's Birthday* (second Mon in **Jun**), *Territory Day* (**1 Jul**), *Emancipation Festival* Mon-Wed beginning of **Aug**, *St Ursula's Day* (**21 Oct**), *Christmas Day*, *Boxing Day*.

Festivals

The *BVI Music festival*, started 2001, is held annually in the last week of **May** on Cane Garden Bay. The *BVI Emancipation* or Aug Festival is held beginning of *Aug*, celebrating the abolition of slavery. There is entertainment every night with steel bands, fungi and calypso music, a Prince and Princess show and a calypso show.

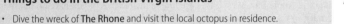

Things to do in the British Virgin Islands

- Dive the wreck of **The Rhone** and visit the local octopus in residence.
- A Painkiller is the local **rum**-based liquid anaesthetic, try it and see, preferably at sunset.
- Swim from your boat to the **Soggy Dollar Bar** on Jost Van Dyke, a yachtie favourite hangout.
- Walk for miles along the sandy beach or snorkel the reef off the north coast of Anegada, taking a break for a **lobster lunch** at Loblolly Bay.
- Sail to a deserted beach and just take it easy.

Tortola

Tortola, the main island, is where 81% of the total population live. Mount Sage, the highest point in the archipelago, rises to 1,780 ft, and traces of a primeval rainforest can still be found on its slopes. Walking trails have been marked through Mount Sage National Park. The south part of the island is mountainous and rocky, covered with scrub, frangipani and ginger thomas. The north has groves of bananas, mangoes and palm trees, and long sandy beaches.

IDD code: 284
Colour map 2, grid B6
Population: 16,000

Road Town

On the south shore, is the capital and business centre of the territory, dominated by marinas and financial companies which line the harbour. There are many gift shops, hotels and restaurants catering for the tourist market. Main Street, the most picturesque street, houses some of the oldest buildings and churches and the colonial prison (replaced by a modern prison in 1997 for 120 inmates). Until the 1960s, Main Street was the waterfront road, but land infill has allowed a dual carriageway, Waterfront Drive and Wickhams Cay, to be built between it and the sea. Wickhams Cay has very grand and imposing government offices on the waterfront overlooking the harbour entrance. Banks, offices, Cable & Wireless, the tourist office and a small craft village are also in this area. Small cruise ships call frequently.

The Governor resides in **Government House** above Waterfront Drive overlooking the harbour (T4942345). The old house is is being restored and new building is going on so there is no access at present. There is a fine display of flamboyant trees.

The 4-acre **Joseph Reynold O'Neal Botanic Gardens** near the police station in Road Town has a good selection of tropical and subtropical plants such as palm trees, succulents, ferns and orchids. There is a good booklet which gives a suggested route round the garden, pond, orchid house, fern house and medicinal herb garden. It is peaceful, luxuriant, with magnificent pergolas, recommended. ■ *Free admission, donations welcome.* The small **BVI Folk Museum** in a lovely old wooden building on Main Street, containing salvaged artefacts from the *Rhone*. ■ *Opened on request.* The **BVI Tourist Board** is at 2nd floor, AKARA Building, Wickhams Cay 1, Road Town, T4943134, F4943866, www.bvitouristboard.com

Around the island

There are also communities at East End and West End. **West End** has more facilities for visitors. *Soper's Hole* is a busy port of entry (ferries to St Thomas, St John and Jost Van Dyke leave from here) and popular meeting place for people on yachts, with bars, restaurants, boutiques and a dive shop. All the buildings are painted in bright pinks and blues. It is relaxing to sip cocktails on the dock and watch the yachts come and go. The *Jolly Roger*, on the opposite side of the bay is a popular yachtie hangout. The area is famous for being the former home of Edward Teach (Blackbeard the pirate).

British Virgin Islands

Watch out for strong rip currents at some of the north shore beaches, and seek local advice before swimming, especially if the surfers are out

The best beaches are along the northwest and north coasts. **Smugglers Cove**, **Long Bay** and **Apple Bay**, West End, have fine sandy beaches. If you have no transport, Smugglers Cove is an hour's walk on a dirt road over a steep hill from West End. The beach is usually deserted. Apple Bay is popular with surfers from November for a few months, as is the east end of Cane Garden Bay and Josiah's Bay. **Carrot Bay** is stony, there is no sand, but there are lots of pelicans and the village is pleasant, having a very Caribbean feel with several bars, palm trees and banana plants. **Cane Garden Bay** is the best beach and yachts can anchor there. There are two reefs with a marked gap in between. The **Callwood Rum Distillery** at Cane Garden Bay still produces rum with copper boiling vats and an old still and cane crusher in much the same way as it did in the 18th century. **Brewers Bay** is long and curving with plenty of shade and a small campsite in the trees by the beach. **Shark Bay** is a mixture of sand and rock, while on the hillside, in the Gaby Nitkin Nature Reserve, there are large volcanic boulders forming a 'Bat Cave' where wild orchids grow. Park on the main road and hike along the private road. **Elizabeth Bay** and **Long Bay**, East End, are also pleasant beaches.

Tortola is superb, but the full flavour of the BVI can only be discovered by cruising round the other islands. You can also take day trips on the regular ferry to Virgin Gorda, with lunch and a visit to The Baths included if you wish.

Essentials

Sleeping   **Road Town   LL-AL** *Treasure Isle*, on hillside overlooking the marina and Sir Francis Drake Channel, T4942501, www.treasureislehotel.com   40 rooms and 3 suites, pool, tennis, restaurant, a/c, TV, convenient for business travellers, used by people on crewed yacht charters for first and last night, helpful staff at front desk. Under same ownership and used by *Treasure Isle* for all watersports is the **LL-AL** *Moorings/Mariner Inn*, at the dockside for bareboat charters,

Tortola

Caribbean Sea

Sleeping
1 Cane Garden Bay & Callwood Distillery
2 Fort Recovery Estate
3 Frenchman's Cay
4 Josiah's Bay Inn
5 Long Bay

T4942332. 36 rooms with kitchenette, 4 suites, fan, tennis, small pool by bar, briefing room for those setting out on yachts. **LL-AL** *Village Cay Resort and Marina*, directly opposite on the other side of the harbour, T4942771, www. villagecay.com 18 clean, bright rooms, well-furnished although a bit sterile, TV, phone, cheaper rooms face inland, restaurant and bar overlooking yachts, good food, buffet with entertainment Fri 1800-2300, also showers, toilets and launderette for sailors. **LL-A** *Maria's By The Sea*, T4942595, F4942420. By new government buildings, overlooks sea but no beach, older part is simple, all have kitchenette, a/c, TV, phone, double beds, new wing has bigger rooms, balconies, conference room, friendly, Maria's cooking recommended, specials include lobster, conch, steak, light and airy entrance with bar, pool. **LL-AL** *Pussers Fort Burt*, on hillside opposite Marina, T4942587, fortburt@surfbvi.com On remains of Dutch fort, first hotel on island built 1953, now part of the *Pussers* chain, 12 rooms, 6 suites, 2 of which have plunge pool, all have phone, fax and PC data ports, restaurant and bar, convenient location, good views.

AL-B *Hotel Castle Maria*, up the hill overlooking Road Town, T4942553, hotelcastlemaria@ surfbvi.com 30 rooms, some triple and quads, kitchenette, a/c, cable TV, pool, restaurant, bar, car rentals, popular with local business travellers. **B** *A & L Inn*, 3 Fleming St, T4946343, alguesthouse@hotmail.com. 14 rooms with 2 double beds, a/c, TV, phone, café. About the cheapest on the island is **C-D** *Wayside Inn Guest House*, Road Town, near library, T4943606. 20 rooms, with fan, adequate but basic, shared bathrooms but not very clean.

South coast Heading west from Road Town you come to **LL-A** *Prospect Reef Resort*, T4943311, www.prospectreef.com A 15-acre resort specializing in package holidays, wide variety of rooms, studios, town houses and villas, some with sea view, comfortable, lots of sports and facilities, marina. **LL-B** *Nanny Cay Resort and Marina*, T4942512, nanrevs@surfbvi.com. 42 rooms, a/c, TV, VCRs, kitchenette, phone, deluxe rooms have 2 queen-size beds, standard rooms are darker, smaller, used by short stay people going out on bareboat charters, the marina was expanded and remodelled 2001-2002 and now hosts the

British Virgin Islands

Spring Regatta with a Regatta Village and lots of yacht facilities. **LL-L** *Villas at Fort Recovery Estate*, T4954354, www.fortrecovery.com 17 spacious and nicely furnished a/c villas of different sizes on small beach, CP, built around 17th-century Dutch fort, commissary, no restaurant, but à la carte room service available including complimentary dinner and snorkel trip for stays of over 7 nights, yoga, massage, good snorkelling offshore, pool, car essential. **LL-AL** *Frenchman's Cay Hotel*, West End, T4954844, www.frenchmans.com Beautiful hillside location on the cay overlooking the south coast of Tortola, 9 villas, all with view, fans, phone, a quiet resort with lots of repeat business, small sandy beach with reef for snorkelling, hammocks, tennis (fee for non-guests), pool, library, games, short trail out to point, Sun beach barbecue, bar, restaurant, TV in clubhouse. **A-C** *Jolly Roger Inn*, T4954559,

Road Town

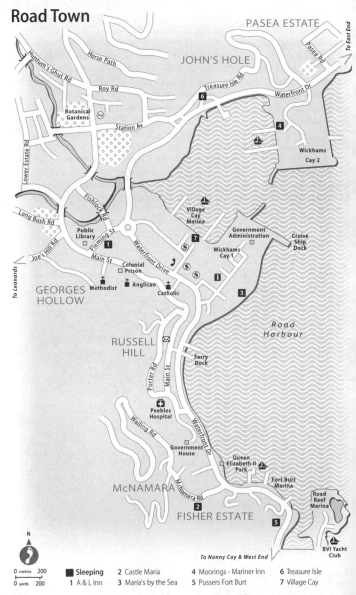

Sleeping	2 Castle Maria	4 Moorings - Mariner Inn	6 Treasure Isle
1 A & L Inn	3 Maria's by the Sea	5 Pussers Fort Burt	7 Village Cay

www.jollyrogerbvi.com A small inn and bar on waterfront at Soper's Hole. Live music at weekends so do not stay here if you want peace and quiet, convenient for ferries (see above), 6 brightly decorated, clean rooms, some with shared bathroom, fans, screens, singles, doubles, triples available, good breakfasts, busy restaurant and bar, meeting place, overnight mooring US$15/night for boats up to 60 ft, fax, email and ice services.

West coast Heading northeast, **LL-A** *Long Bay Beach Resort*, T4954252, www.longbay.com 80 rooms, studios and villas spread along the beach and up the hillside, a/c, TV, phone, fridge, 130-ft pool, the biggest in the BVI, tennis, pitch and put, spa and gym, car rental, 2 restaurants with vegetarian options, bars, surfboards, snorkelling equipment, nice beach, sandy with some rocks, level of sand can shift depending on season. **LL-B** *Sebastian's On The Beach*, Apple Bay, T4954212, www. sebastiansbvi.com Located either side of road, informal and popular surfers' hangout, the beachfront building was upgraded and expanded in 2002, now quite luxurious with large balconies, glass block showers, new tiled floors, also *Seaside Villas*, 9 luxury 2-bedroomed suites with huge balconies and views to Jost Van Dyke, fully equipped and every comfort, grocery 0800-2200, restaurant/bar overlooking sandy beach, happy hr 1600-1800, blend own rum, surfboards and boogieboards for rent. **B-C** *Cane Garden Bay (Rhymer's) Beach Hotel*, Cane Garden Bay, T4954639, F4954820. 27 basic but clean rooms, most with double bed and single bed, right on sandy beach, beach towels provided, store and shop, laundromat, restaurant/bar on beach, watersports companies on either side of hotel. **LL-B** *Ole Works Inn*, Cane Garden Bay, T4954837, oleworks@candwbvi.net Built around 300-year-old sugar factory, on beach, 18 rooms, honeymoon tower, bar, restaurant, gift shop.

North coast LL-B *Lambert Beach Resort*, East End, T4952877, lambert@caribsurf.com On a beautiful cove, 38 rooms and suites in villas which can sleep 8, beach-front dining, pool, tennis, watersports, boat trips, diving and other excursions can be arranged, library, videos, Italian-owned, Italian decor. **A-B** *Josiah's Bay Inn*, Josiah's Bay, T/F4952812, cindyclayton@yahoo.com Short walk to 4 beaches, 1-4 bedroom apartments, kitchens, TV, balconies with sea view, weekly rates, maid service twice a week, popular with surfers, take insect repellent. **LL-AL** *Josiah's Bay Cottages*, Road Town, T4946186, bestvac@surfbvi.com 9 1-bedroom cottages in garden, 5-min walk to beach, pool.

Self catering There is lots of self-catering accommodation in what are variously known as houses, villas, apartments, guesthouses, 'efficiencies' or 'housekeeping units'. Prices are usually set on a weekly basis according to size and standard of luxury, and there is often a 30-40% discount in the summer. Contact the tourist office for a full list and individual brochures. Many are also listed on www.bviwelcome.com **Camping** *Brewer's Bay Campground* on north coast, T4943463. Bare site US$10, tent hire US$35 for 2 people, babysitters available, beach bar and simple restaurant.

Road Town Restaurants serving West Indian specialities include *C & F Restaurant*, Purcell Estate, T4944941. Very popular with visitors and locals, excellent local food, slow but friendly service, dinner 1830-2300. *Mario's*, Palm Grove Shopping Centre, T4943883. Clean, a/c, good service, generous portions, open daily 0700-2300, happy hr 1700-1900. *Happy Lion*, next to Botanic Gardens, T4942574. Mon-Sat from 0700, noted for fresh fish and local dishes, also apartments to rent. *Beach Club Terrace*, at Baughers Bay, T4942272. Open 0800-2200, fish, mutton, conch, etc. *Aries Club*, Baughers Bay, T4941537. 0700-2200 Mon-Sat, West Indian and seafood. *Roti Palace*, Russel Hill, T4944196. Huge rotis (curry in a wrap). *The Fish Trap*, at the Columbus Centre, behind Village Cay Marina, T4943626. Open for lunch 1130-1500 Mon-Fri, 1130-1400 Sat and dinner daily 1830-2300, open-air, reservations recommended, inside is a popular yachtie bar open 1630-late serving good lower-priced bar meals. *The Captain's Table*, on the waterfront at Inner Harbour, T4943885. A French restaurant serving escargots, lobster, fish, lunch Mon-Fri, dinner daily from 1800, closed Sun out of season. *Pusser's Co Store & Pub* on Main St, Road Town, T4942467. Yachties' meeting place, good pub atmosphere, open 1100-2200, on ground floor bar, store and restaurant for simple dishes such as English pies and New York deli sandwiches, nickel beer on Thu, really is US$0.05 but not recommended, Tue is Ladies' Night', 'Pain Killer' cocktails recommended, strongest is 'Brain Killer', *Pusser's* also at Soper's Hole, Marina Cay and Leverick Bay.

Along this stretch of coast there are lots of rental villas, many of which are advertised simply with a notice outside, usually about US$100 per day

Eating

British Virgin Islands

Tavern in the Town, Road Town, next to *Pusser's*, T4942790. Traditional English pub food and atmosphere, sells Newcastle Brown Ale, garden looks out across harbour, open 1100-2300, closed Sat. *Mac's*, in the Clarence M Christian Building, T4946364. Local dishes, salads, pizza and pastries, open 0700-2000. *Midtown Restaurant*, Main St, T4942764. Curried conch, baked chicken, beef, whelk, saltfish, Mon-Sat 0700-2300. *Mr Fritz Oriental Restaurant*, in the Little Denmark building, T4945592. Classic Chinese dishes, lunch 1130-1530, dinner 1730 onwards. *Capriccio di Mare*, Waterfront Drive by ferry dock, overlooking water, T4945369. Italian café serving excellent coffee and delicious, if overpriced, snacks and continental lunches, open 0800-2100 Mon-Sat. *Spaghetti Junction*, www.spaghettijunction.net Italian restaurant run by John and April, long-established and popular with locals, yachties and ex-pats, appetizers US$4-10, main courses US$10-24, bar and nightclub alongside, see below. *Café Sito*, in Romasco building, T4947413.West Indian and international food, daily specials, 1100-2300. *Crandall's Pastry Plus*, T4945156. West Indian bakery across from Road Reef Marina, also rotis and main meals, 0800-1700. *Scato's Snack Bar*, T4942230. Above Sylvia's laundromat on Flemming St, open daily 1200-2200, local dishes. *Road Town Bakery*, Main St. Bakery and small café.

Nanny Cay *The Struggling Man*, Sea Cows Bay, between Road Town and Nanny Cay, T4944163. West Indian, breakfast, lunch and dinner. *Marina Plaza Café*, Nanny Cay Marina, T4944895. 0700-2100, Caribbean specials and international dishes. *Peg Leg Landing*, water's edge at Nanny Cay. From 1600, happy hr 1630-1830, bar meals from 1630, dinners from 1900.

West End *Pusser's Landing*, T4954554 and *Jolly Roger*, T4954559, fun, yachtie hangout, good pizza and burgers, good cheap breakfast, dinner US$7-15, open 0700-2300, and many more excellent restaurants in the hotels and yacht clubs.

Apple Bay *The Sugar Mill*, in an old mill, T4954355, www.sugarmillhotel.com, run by Californians, Jinx and Jefferson Morgan. Gourmet and elegant, 4-course dinner 1900, reservations, their cookbook is on-line, with some 250 recipes, 24-room hotel attached (no children in season), breakfast and lunch at beach bar. *The Apple*, Little Apple Bay, T4954437. Specializes in local seafood dishes, happy hr 1700-1900 with coconut chips and conch fritters. *Sebastian's On The Beach*, T4954212. Breakfast, lunch, dinner, international, happy hr 1600-1800.

Carrot Bay *Mrs Scatliffe's*, T4954556. Upstairs in a yellow and white building opposite the Primary School, local cuisine, home-grown fruit and vegetables, family fungi performance some evenings after dinner, lunch Mon-Fri 1200-1400, dinner daily 1900-2100, reservations essential. *Palm's Delight*, on the water, T4954863. Restaurant and snack bar, delicious barbecue and local cuisine, rotis and shrimp creole, open 1800-2200. *North Shore Shell Museum*, T4954714. Cracked conch, lobster, West Indian cooking, breakfast, lunch and dinner, happy hr 1600-1800. *Clem's By The Sea*, T4954350. West Indian specialities, goat stew, boiled fish and fungi, steel band, Mon, Sat, open 0900 until late.

Cane Garden Bay You can 'Jump Up' (Caribbean music), almost every night at *Rhymers*, T4954639. Serves breakfast, lunch and dinner, lobster special Thu night. Folk music and reggae at *Quito's Gazebo*, T4954837. Restaurant and beach bar at north end of Cane Garden Bay, lunch 1130-1500, rotis and burgers, dinner 1830-2130, fish fry Fri, closed Mon, local art work for sale. *Round Hill Catering*, T4959353. Open Mon, Tue, Thu, Fri, Sat 1830-2130, reservations needed, home-cooked local dishes served on balcony. There are a number of small restaurants serving excellent food along the road going towards the rum distillery ruins; check in the late afternoon to make reservations and find out what the menu will be.

Inland 10 mins' drive from Road Town or Cane Garden Bay is the *Skyworld Restaurant*, T4943567. With a panoramic view of all the Virgin Islands, food and prices reasonable, open from 1000, lunch 1130-1430, dinner 1700-1945, recommended for view. *Mario's Mountain View*, at the foot of Sage Mountain National Park, T4959536. Continental and local dishes, lunch 1100-1500, dinner 1830-2200.

East End *Brandywine Bay Restaurant*, run by Cele and Davide Pugliese, T4952301, brandywn@surfbvi.com Just 10 mins' drive from Road Town, one of the most exclusive restaurants on Tortola, indoor and outdoor dining, grills and Florentine food, cocktails 1730, dinner 1830-2100, full meal without wine about US$35-40 per person, closed Sun, reservations, Channel 16, anchorage 15-ft draft. *De Cal*, T4951429, on Blackburn Highway at Fat Hog's Bay, T4952627. Local style, rotis, pizza, breakfast, lunch, dinner, 0700-2200. Home-cooked dinners, excellent conch fritters, also after hrs dance spot.

If you are self-catering, you can get reasonably priced food from *K Mart's* and other super-markets at Port Purcell or at the *Rite Way* supermarkets a little closer to town. At the entrance to the *Moorings*, Wickhams Cay II, is the *Bon Appetit Deli*, T4945199. Cheese and wine as well as regular provisions; they also do sandwiches and lunch specials and party services. In Road Town is *Fort Wines Gourmet Shop*, T4942388, a wine shop with a high-class image but reasonable prices; you can also eat there, excellent light snacks (eg quiche) and wine by the glass.

Road Town *The Pub*, at Fort Burt Marina, T4942608. Dancing Fri-Sat, they also serve lunches and dinners, happy hr 1700-1900 daily and all day Fri with free hot wings 1700-1900 and music 1800-2200. *Bat Cave*, attached to *Spaghetti Junction*. Bar and nightclub, DJ music, happy hours 1700-1900 with wings for US$0.25, stay inside, a/c, no smoking, or go outside on the 'Bat Decks'. *Stone's Nest* is a weekend disco in Road Town, T4945182. The hotels organize live bands and movie nights. For more classical music, concerts by visiting artistes and chamber orchestras are often held at the H Lavity Stoutt Community College, T4944994. **East End** *Bing's Drop Inn Bar*. **Frenchman's Cay** *Pusser's Landing*, T4954554. Bands on Fri and Sat. **West End** *Jolly Roger*, T4954559, has live music and barbecue Tue, Fri, Sat in season, and often has bands. **Apple Bay** *The Bomba Shack*, on the beach in , T4954148. Music Wed and Sun, full-moon all-night party every month. *Romeo's*, T4954307. Thu barbecue and music, Sat fish fry and music. **Cane Garden Bay** *Quito's Gazebo*, T4954837. Live music nightly and the beat is quickened at weekends and holidays. **Maya Cove** *Calamaya*, on the dock side at Hodge's Creek Marina, T4952126. Breakfast, lunch, dinner, Fri live music, happy hr with tapas 1600-1800, bar menu.

Nightlife
See The Limin' Times for what's on

There is a **tennis** club on Tortola and many hotels have their own courts. **Horse riding** can be arranged through the hotels, or T4942262, *Shadow's Stables*, or T4940704, Ellis Thomas, for riding through Mount Sage National Park or down to Cane Garden Bay, Tortola. **Walking** and **birdwatching** are quite popular and trails have been laid out in some places. Sage Mountain on Tortola is a popular hike. Spectator sports include **cricket** and soft ball. **Gyms** include *Bodyworks*, T4942705, and *Cutting Edge*, T4959570. *Prospect Reef* has a healthclub where you can do aerobics, yoga, also tennis and 9-hole pitch and putt, T4943311 ext 245

Sports
For diving and watersports, see pages 434 and 435

Bicycle: All bicycles must be registered at the Traffic Licensing Office in Road Town and the licence plate must be fixed to the bicycle, cost US$5. *Last Stop Sports* at *The Moorings* on Wickham's Cay II rents and repairs mountain bikes, rental US$20 per day, T4940564, lssbikes@surfbvi.com **Bus**: There is a private local bus service on Tortola with cheap fares (US$2-4) but erratic timetable. Call *Scatos Bus Service* for information, T4945873. They go to few tourist destinations. **Car**: *Alphonso Car Rentals*, Fish Bay, T4948746, F4948735, cars US$40-45 per day, jeeps US$50-70, 20% less in summer; *Avis Rent-a-Car*, opposite Botanic Gardens, Road Town, T4942193, or West End, T4954973, US$35-50 per day winter, US$30-40 summer, cheaper weekly rates; *Denzil Clyne Car Rentals*, West End, T4954900, jeeps US$45-85 in winter, US$40-60 in summer; *International Car Rentals*, Road Town, I4942516, intercar@candwbvi.net, US$30-70; *National Car Rental*, Duff's Bottom and Long Bay, T4943197, US$45-75. **Taxi stands**: in Road Town, T4942322; on Beef Island, T4952378. Taxis are easy to come by on Tortola and fares are fixed, ask for a list or get one from the tourist office. The fare from Beef Island Airport to Road Town, Tortola is US$15 or US$8 if shared.

Transport
See also Getting around, page 432

Banks *Bank of Nova Scotia*, Road Town, T4942526. *FirstCaribbean International Bank* (formerly Barclays), Road Town, T4942173, F4944315, with agency at East End, Tortola. *Chase Manhattan Bank*, Road Town, T4942662, F4945106. *Development Bank of the Virgin Islands*, T4943737. *Banco Popular de Puerto Rico*, Road Town, T4942117, F4945294. *VP Bank (BVI) Ltd*, 65 Main St, Road Town, T4941100, F4941199. ATM machines at all banks, at Beef Island Airport, *Rite Way Supermarket* (Pasea), Soper's Hole, HL Stoutt Community College (Paraquita Bay) and *K-Mark's Supermarket* (Purcell Estate). **Medical services** *Peebles Hospital*, Road Town, T4943497, is a public hospital with X-ray and surgical facilities. Private X-ray and laboratory facilities are offered by B&F Medical Complex and Medicure Ltd. There are 12 doctors on Tortola. The closest Decompression Chamber is in nearby St Thomas, about 45 mins away. *Island Helicopters International*, 4992663, offers helicopter transfers for emergencies.

Directory

British Virgin Islands

Beef Island

During the buccaneering days this island was famed as a hunting ground for beef cattle

The main airport for the BVI is here. For many years the island was linked to Tortola by the Queen Elizabeth bridge, opened in 1966, but in 2003 it was dismantled and a new bridge was built (taxi to Road Town, US$15). Long Bay beach is on the north shore, as is Trellis Bay which has an excellent harbour and bars.

Sleeping, eating and bars LL-A *Beef Island Guest House*, T4952303, F4951611. 4 rooms on the beach, food available at its *De Loose Mongoose Bar*, VHF Ch 16, 0800-1600, 1800-2100, mostly burgers and sandwiches. *The Last Resort*, a bar run by Englishman Tony Snell and based on Bellamy Cay, provides a buffet menu plus one-man show cabaret, US$26, bar open all day, happy hr 1700-1900, dinner 1930, cabaret 2130, ferry service available, reservations required, T4952520 or channel 16. *Airport Restaurant*, T4952323, West Indian, open from 0730, dinner by reservation. Also *Boardsailing BVI*, the *Conch Shell Point Restaurant*, T4952285, VHF Ch 16, and a painting and jewellery shop.

Marina Cay

If sailing, enter from the north

This tiny private island of 6 acres just north of Beef Island was where Robb White wrote his book *Our Virgin Isle*, later made into a film starring Sidney Poitier and John Cassavetes. A reef encircles the island, offering some of the best snorkelling in the BVI.

Sleeping and eating A charming cottage hotel, **LL-A** *Pusser's Marina Cay*, comprises most of the island, T4942174, marinacy@surfbvi.com, or VHF Ch 16. Marina facilities (boats use mooring buoys and a dinghy dock), laundry, showers, diving, kayaking, sailing, snorkelling, etc, 4 rooms and 2 villas available, MAP. Bar, restaurant, beach barbecue on Fri, *Pussers Co Store* selling clothes and travel accessories. Ferry service from Trellis Bay jetty, 8 daily, ferries after 1900 on request for restaurant guests only.

Guana Island

North of Tortola, Guana Island is an 850-acre private island and wildlife sanctuary as well as having a very expensive hotel. The owners discourage visitors apart from hotel guests, in order to keep the island a sanctuary for wildlife. A few flamingos have been introduced to the island. They live in a small pond where the salinity fluctuates widely so their diets are supplemented with food and water if they need it. The birds used to live in a zoo, so they are fairly tame.

Sleeping LL *Guana Island*, T4942354, www.guana.com 15 rooms in stone cottages, 1 secluded beach house, tennis, restaurant, watersports, US$35 for airport transfers, no credit cards. The island is available for rent for up to 30 guests.

The Dogs

Northeast of Tortola are The Dogs, a group of small, uninhabited islands. West Dog is a national park. On Great Dog you can see frigate birds nesting. The islands are often used as a stopping-off point when sailing from North Sound to Jost Van Dyke, and are popular with divers coming from North Sound for the interesting rock formations, with canyons and bridges underwater. The best anchorages are on George Dog to the west of Kitchen Point and on the south side of Great Dog.

Virgin Gorda

IDD code: 284
Colour map 2, grid B6
Population: 5,000

Over a century ago, Virgin Gorda was the centre of population and commerce. It is now better known as the site of the geological curiosity called The Baths, where enormous smooth boulders form a natural swimming pool and underwater caves. The island is 7 miles long and the north half is mountainous, with a peak 1,370 ft high, while the south half is relatively flat.

Around the island

All land on Virgin Gorda over 1,000 ft is now a national park, with walking trails

There is a 3,000-ft airstrip near the main settlement, **Spanish Town**. The Virgin Gorda Yacht Harbour is here and besides the marina facilities with full yachting chandlery, there is a good supermarket, dive centre, bar/restaurant, a craft shop selling stamps, souvenir and clothes shops and phones, post box and taxis. There are some 20 secluded beaches, the most frequented being **Devil's Bay**, **Spring Bay**, and **Trunk**

Bay on the west coast. Between Devil's Bay and Spring Bay in the southwest are **The Baths**. The snorkelling here is good, especially going left from the beach. Unfortunately the popularity of The Baths with tour companies and cruise ships can lead to overcrowding. There are many day trips from Tortola and when a cruise ship is in port you cannot move on the beach. Just off the southwest tip of the island is **Fallen Jerusalem National Park**, an islet named for its spectacular tumble-down rock formation. On the southeast tip is **Copper Mine Point**, where the Spaniards allegedly mined copper, gold and silver some 400 years ago; the remains of a mine begun by Cornish miners in 1838 can be seen with the typical Engine House and other ruins, and you can find stones such as malachite and crystals embedded in quartz.

North of the island is **North Sound**, formed to the south and east by Virgin Gorda, to the north by Prickly Pear Island, and to the west by Mosquito Island. **Bitter End** and **Biras Creek** are good anchorages and both have a hotel and restaurant. *Biras Creek* charges US$15 for moorings; yachtsmen may use Deep Bay beach but others are reserved for hotel guests. *Bitter End* charges US$20 including water taxi to shore in the evenings. There is no road to either resort, you have to get a hotel launch from Gun Creek or the North Sound Express from Beef Island to *Bitter End Resort & Yacht Club*. Saba Rock is just off *Bitter End*; with food at the *Saba Rock Resort*. The **BVI Tourist Board** office is at Virgin Gorda Yacht Harbour, T4955181, F4956517, www.bvitouristboard.com

Essentials

South LL *Little Dix Bay*, T4955555, www.littledixbay.com Luxury 98-roomed chalet hotel, with 4 1-bedroom suites, on ½-mile beach, watersports, tennis, health and fitness centre, hiking trails in surrounding hills, lovely gardens, no TV or pool, strict dress code after sunset, 70% repeat guests in winter, honeymooners in summer, also owns and operates the airport and the Virgin Gorda Yacht Harbour. **LL-L** *Toad Hall*, contact Stephen Green, T4955397, www.toadhallvg.com Luxury rental home, sleeps 7, 3 bedrooms with garden showers, private access to The Baths beach, pool among the boulders, caves, great for children, US$3,500-5,500 per week. **LL-AL** *Fischer's Cove Beach Hotel*, St Thomas Bay, T4955252, F4955820. 12 studio

Sleeping

Virgin Gorda

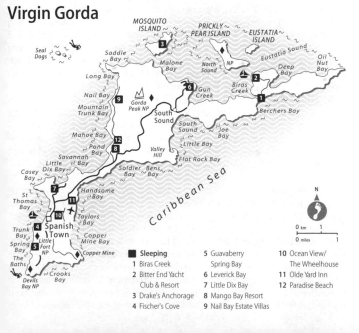

Sleeping
1 Biras Creek
2 Bitter End Yacht Club & Resort
3 Drake's Anchorage
4 Fischer's Cove
5 Guavaberry Spring Bay
6 Leverick Bay
7 Little Dix Bay
8 Mango Bay Resort
9 Nail Bay Estate Villas
10 Ocean View/ The Wheelhouse
11 Olde Yard Inn
12 Paradise Beach

British Virgin Islands

rooms, some with fan, some a/c, or 8 cottages with kitchenette, less space, some beachfront, balcony restaurant overlooking sea open 0730-2200, beach barbecue when calm. **LL-AL** *Guavaberry Spring Bay*, run by Tina and Ludwig Goschler, T4955227, www.guavaberryspringbay.com Well-equipped wooden cottages, beautiful location, sandy beach with shade 5 mins' walk through grounds, to the south are The Baths, to the north The Crawl, a National Park enclosing a natural swimming pool and more boulders. They also manage some rental villas. **LL-C** *Ocean View/The Wheelhouse*, T4955230. 12 rooms, close to ferry and harbour, pink building, small rooms but adequately furnished, TV, fan, a/c, restaurant, bar. **L-AL** *Olde Yard Inn*, T4955544, www.oldeyardinn.com Convenient for airport, 14 rooms, 1 suite, a/c available, downstairs rooms wood panelled and rather dark, pool, jacuzzi, health spa, poolside restaurant, good food, gardens, library with piano, games room, croquet, hammocks, small shop, complimentary shuttle or 10-15 mins on trail to beach, family-run.

Villas   There are several villas to rent around The Valley and Spring Bay and a few agencies, eg *Virgin Gorda Villa Rentals*, T4957421, leverick@surfbvi.com

North   Up the west coast, north of the Valley are 2 resorts which were built as one, so the villas are the same, **LL-A** *Mango Bay*, T4955672, www.mangobayresort.com 5 villas which can make 1-bedroomed units or the apartments can be connected to provide 2 or 3 bedrooms, very clean, light and airy, a/c, phone. **LL** *Katiche Point Greathouse*, www.katichepoint.com reservations through *Mango Bay*.High up on a point looking over the bay to other islands in the distance, with its own horizon swimming pool, sunken bath made out of Virgin Gorda boulders in the master bedroom and hammocks in the Crow's Nest for great views, narrow sandy beach, 4 suites and master suite sleep up to 13. **LL-AL** *Paradise Beach*, T4955871, www.paradise beachresort.com 7 units in 3 houses, snorkelling and fishing gear available, dinghy, rental car included. Further north at Nail Bay is a new development of villas, apartments and hotel, **LL-L** *Nail Bay Estate Villas*, T4948000, www.nailbay.com They manage *Diamond Beach Villas, Flame Trees, Sunset Watch* and *Turtle Bay Villa*, summer packages include car hire and you can also book dive packages. On the north coast is **L-A** *Leverick Bay Hotel and Vacation Villas*, T4957421, www.leverickbay.com Wide variety of spacious accommodation from hotel rooms to villas and condominiums built up a hillside with a great view of the jetty and the bay, *Pussers* is on site and all the buildings are painted the bright multi-colours which are *Pussers'* emblem, restaurant, tennis, pool, watersports, food store, laundry, shops, beauty therapy and massage at *The Spa*, T4957375. Perhaps the most exclusive resort on the island is **LL** *Biras Creek*, T4943555, www.biras.com Reached by launch from Gun Creek, or on the North Sound Express from Beef Island, on a spit of land overlooking both North Sound and Berchers Bay, helipad for transfers and daytrips. Luxury, cottages and suites spread along the Atlantic coast, restrictions on children, no phones or a/c, 2 tennis courts with pro, sailing trips, free watersports instruction, small pool overlooking ocean, nice little beach in sheltered bay with mangroves, very private, beach barbecues, good menu and view from the split level restaurant, popular with honeymooners. **LL** *The Bitter End Yacht Club and Resort*, North Sound, T4942746, www.beyc.com Reached by launch from Gun Creek or the North Sound Express from Beef Island or by yacht. Good for water lovers with a marina, sailing in all sizes of boats for all ages, yacht charters, facilities for visiting yachts, fishing (reef and bone), windsurfing, diving, plus instruction, stay on your boat, charter one of the 8 liveaboard yachts, or use the 100 rooms and chalets, spread out along coastal hillside (used to be 2 resorts), can be a long walk from your room to the clubhouse but taxi service available, 3 restaurants, shops and food stores.

Eating   *Giorgio's Table*, Mahoe Bay, T4955684. Next to *Mango Bay* resort at the foot of the point on which *Katiche Point* is built, authentic Italian food, 80% of ingredients imported from Italy, open 0900-2200. Restaurants serving West Indian recipes include *Anything Goes*, The Valley, T4955062, VHF Ch16. Curries and seafood, 1100-2200, takeaway and delivery locally. Also *Crab Hole*, South Valley, T4955307. Locals eat here, cheap West Indian food, curries, roti, conch, entertainment on Fri 0930-2400. *Lobster Pot*, at *Andy's Chateau de Pirate*, T4955252, VHF 16. Beach pig roast on Mon, seafood buffet on Thu, barbecue on Sat, all boat captains receive cocktail and 30% off main course with ID. *The Bath and Turtle*, Virgin Gorda Yacht Harbour, T4955239. Standard pub fare, open 0730-2200 daily, live entertainment Wed, good place to wait for the ferry. *Mine Shaft Café & Pub*, Coppermine Rd, T4955260, www.islands

online.com/mineshaft Bar open from 1000, restaurant from 1100, decorated as a mine shaft, lots of evening entertainment and miniature golf, adults US$5, kids US$3, West Indian barbecue Tue 1700-2200, try their drink, 'cave-in'. *Pusser's* Leverick Bay, T4957369. Breakfast and lunch 0800-1800 at beach bar, dinner 1800-2200, steaks, seafood. *Rock Café & Sports Bar*, T4945482. Open daily, mix of Italian and Caribbean dishes, moonlight parties and sports. *Mad Dog*, next to the parking lot at The Baths, T4955830. Drinks, sandwiches, T-shirts and friendly conversation, open 1000-1900. *Poor Man's Bar*, on the beach at The Baths. Also selling T-shirts, open 0930-1800, bring a bottle of water, toilets round the back. *Top of the Baths*, T4955497. Indoor and outdoor dining, breakfast, lunch and dinner. *Saba Rock Resort*, opposite *Bitter End Yacht Club*, T4957711. Bar with deck over the water, pub grub at lunchtime, buffet carvery and salad bar for dinner, also 5 rooms, water taxi service around North Sound.

Nightlife Live music at *The Bath and Turtle* and *Little Dix Bay*, live music and/or DJ at *Pirate's Pub*, *Pussers*, *Bitter End*, *Andy's Chateau*, *Chez Bamboo* and *Copper Mine*. *Mine Shaft* (also a fun place to eat, see above), has sunset copper hr daily 1600-1800, monthly full-moon parties, live band on Fri, Ladies' Night. Check the bulletin board at the Virgin Gorda Yacht Harbour for special events and concerts.

Transport **Car hire**: *Andy's Taxi and Jeep Rental*, The Valley, T4955511, fischers@candwbvi.net, VHF16, US$50-55, guided tours US$30; *L & S Jeep Rentals*, South Valley, T4955297, F4955342, small or large jeeps, US$45-70, US$280-455 per week, free pick-up in Spanish Town; *Speedy's Car Rentals*, The Valley, T4955235 and Leverick Bay, T4955240 discount with return ferry ticket, US$40-80 per day. **Taxi stands**: *Mahogany Taxi Service*, The Valley, T4955469, F4955072, offers tours and day trips, as well as car and jeep rental.

Directory **Banks** *FirstCaribbean International Bank* (formerly *Barclays*), The Valley, Virgin Gorda, T4955217, F4955163. ATM machines at bank and Virgin Gorda Yacht Harbour.

Mosquito Island Mosquito Island is privately owned and enjoys beautiful views over North Sound to Virgin Gorda and Prickly Pear Island. This 125-acre island is just northwest of Leverick Bay (complimentary five-minute boat trip to hotel from Leverick Bay). There is a lovely beach at South Bay, sandy with boulders, and there are trails leading from the hotel to this and other quiet, sandy coves but they are for hotel guests only. **Sleeping LL** *Drake's Anchorage Resort*, T4942254, www.drakesanchorage.com The island can be rented in its entirety, or you can just use the hotel, which has 3 villas, 4 suites and 4 rooms, all ocean front, only 24 guests, very expensive, rates AP, moorings, windsurfing, very quiet and relaxed atmosphere, bars, restaurant open to outside diners 0730-1000, 1200-1400, candlelit dinner seating time 1900, French-style menu, reservations essential for dinner before 1500. Closed Jul-Sep.

Prickly Pear Island Prickly Pear Island forms the northeast edge of North Sound. It has a lovely beach at Vixen Point with a small beach bar and a watersports centre. This is a great spot for volley ball, with a net permanently on the beach. Moorings near the *Sand Box* beach bar, with showers and ice, T4959122, VHF 16. The only legal jet-ski rental operation in the BVI is here. The island gets crowded when cruise ships come in.

Necker Island This 74-acre, private island northeast of Virgin Gorda is owned by Sir Richard Branson, who wanted a Virgin island to add to his Virgin enterprise. It is available for rent. The house and two cottages, all in Balinese style, sleep 26, fully staffed and cost an arm and a leg. The Bali Cliff open-sided bedroom and bathroom was made in Indonesia and re-assembled on the island. There is also a Balinese beach pool and dining pavilion. Lovely beaches, protected by a coral reef, tennis and watersports provided, private. Powerboats take 40 minutes from Beef Island, expect to get soaked, or go by helicopter or boat from Virgin Gorda. ■ *Contact Carolyn Wincer, 62 Buckingham Gate, London SW1E 6AT, T020-72276969, carolyn.wincer@limitededition.virgin.co.uk or* Virgin Travel Store, *T0870-4427218, Mon-Fri 0830-1830, www.virgintravelstore.com*

British Virgin Islands

Cooper Island In the chain of islands running southwest from Virgin Gorda is Cooper Island, which has a beach and harbour at Manchioneel Bay with palm trees and coral reefs. The island is only 1½ miles long and ½ mile wide, there are no roads, cars, TVs or nightlife. It is a place to relax and escape the rest of the world. The supply boat leaves Road Town Monday, Wednesday and Saturday; other days use *Underwater Safaris'* dive boat from *The Moorings*, Road Town; they have a dive shop on the island and use the beach club for surface intervals or to pick up divers from yachts anchored in the bay.

Sleeping L-A *Cooper Island Beach Club*, T4943721, info@Cooper-Island.com British owned and managed, there are 11 guest rooms with kitchen and bathroom, breakfast on request, lunch 1130-1430, dinner from 1830, reservations preferred, bar all day from 1000, do your grocery shopping on Tortola, shuttle service 3 times a week, electricity generator evenings only. **LL-AL** *Cooper Island Hideaways*, 2 beach-front cottages, contact Ginny Evans, 1920 Barg Lane, Cincinnati, OH 45230-1702, T513-2324126, ginnyevans@aol.com

Salt Island Very few people visit this lovely island, there are no ferries and access is only by private boat. There are two salt ponds from which salt is gathered by two ageing residents. A bag of salt is still sent to the British monarch every year as rent for the island, the remainder is sold to visitors and local restaurants. The two old men who live there welcome visitors and will show you the salt forming and packing process. They have a hut from which they sell conch shells and shell necklaces. There is a small settlement on the north side as well as a reef-protected lagoon on the east shore. The main reason people come here is for a rest stop between dives. The British mail ship *Rhone*, a 310-ft steamer, sank off Salt Island in a hurricane in 1867 and the site was used in the film *The Deep*. Those who perished were buried on Salt Island. The wreck is still almost intact in 20-80 ft of water and is very impressive. The dive is usually divided between the bow section and the stern section; in the former you can swim through the hull at a depth of about 70 ft, be prepared for darkness. In calm weather it is possible to snorkel part of it.

Dead Chest A tiny island in Salt Island Passage, between Salt Island and Peter Island, this is reputedly the island where the pirate Blackbeard abandoned sailors: "15 men on a Dead Man's Chest – Yo Ho Ho and a bottle of rum!".

Peter Island This 1,000-acre island has a tiny population and offers isolated, palm-fringed beaches, good anchorage and picnic spots. The exclusive, luxury. Eight daily ferry departures from Tortola, private guest launch from Tortola or St Thomas, helicopter from St Thomas or San Juan. The marina by the dive shop has a commissary selling basic foods, snacks and ice creams, and there are shower facilities for visiting sailors.

Sleeping LL *Peter Island Resort and Yacht Harbour* is built on reclaimed land jutting out into Sir Francis Drake Channel, forming a sheltered harbour with marine facilities, T4952000, www.peterisland.com Built by Norwegians, there are chalet-type cottages, harbour rooms, or beach rooms, a pool, tennis, horse riding, watersports, fitness centre, massage room, dress formally in evening.

Norman Island The island is reputed to be the 'Treasure Island' of Robert Louis Stevenson fame.
Be careful with the wild cattle: their tempers are unpredictable The floating bar/restaurant *William Thornton II*, T4940183 or VHF Ch 16, is anchored in the Bight of Norman to the north of the island. The first *William Thornton*, a converted 1910 Baltic Trader sank in 1995. There is also the *Billy Bones* beach bar, open for lunch and dinner, but otherwise the island is uninhabited. Launch service from Fort Burt Marina, Road Town, daily at 1715. On its rocky west coast are caves where treasure is said to have been discovered many years ago. These can be reached by small boats and there are several day trips on offer. There is excellent snorkelling around the caves and the reef in front slopes downward to a depth of 40 ft. **The Indians** off the northwest of Norman Island are pinnacles of rock sticking out of the sea with their neighbour, the gently rounded **Pelican Island**. Together they offer the diver and snorkeller a labyrinth of underwater reefs and caves. There are moorings, US$20, and tie-up for dinghies.

Jost Van Dyke

Lying to the west of Tortola, the island was named after a Dutch pirate. Dr William *Population: 300* Thornton, who designed the US Capitol in Washington DC, was born here. It is mountainous, with beaches at White Bay and Great Harbour Bay on the south coast. Great Harbour looks like the fantasy tropical island, a long horseshoe-shaped, white sandy beach, fringed with palm trees and dotted with beach bar/restaurants. Jost Van Dyke is a point of entry and has a Customs House at the end of the dock at Great Harbour. Electricity and a paved road came for the first time in 1991. There are moorings in Little Harbour where a marina is slowly being built and anchorages at Great Harbour, Sandy Cay and Green Cay. It is surrounded by some smaller islands, one of which is **Little Jost Van Dyke**, the birthplace in 1744 of Dr John Coakley Lettsom, the founder of the British Medical Society.

LL-AL *Sandcastle*, at White Bay, T4959888, www.sandcastle-bvi.com Owned by Debby **Sleeping** Pearse and Bruce Donath, 4 wooden cottages, basic amenities but great for total relaxation, hammocks between palm trees on the beach, snorkelling, windsurfing. *The Soggy Dollar Bar* is popular at weekends, most people arrive by boat and swim or wade ashore, aspires to be the birthplace of the infamous 'Pain killer'. **LL-B** *Rudy's Mariner Inn*, Great Harbour. T4959282. 5 rooms, beach bar and restaurant, kitchenettes, grocery, water taxi. Also *Rudy's Villa*, 2 rooms, bathroom. **LL-AL** *Sandy Ground Estates*, T4943391, sandygroundjvd@candwbvi.net 8 luxury villas, provisioning, free water taxi from/to Tortola. **LL** *White Bay Villas*, T410-5716692, www.jostvandyke.com 1, 2 and 3-bedroomed villas, luxury, cheaper in summer, great views, whales can sometimes be seen from the balcony. *White Bay Campground*, T4959312. Nice site, right on beautiful, sandy, White Bay, tents US$35, or bare sites US$15 (3 people).

Little Harbour *Harris' Place*, T4959302. Open daily, bar, restaurant, grocery, water taxi, live **Eating** music, Harris calls his place the friendliest spot in the BVIs, breakfast, lunch and dinner, happy hr 1100-1500, live music, all-you-can-eat lobster night on Mon, ferries from Tortola and St Thomas/St John arranged for these feasts. *Sidney's Peace and Love*, T4959271 or VHF Ch 16. Open from 0900, happy hr 1700-1830, pig roast Mon and Sat 1900, US$20, or all-you-can-eat pig and ribs, US$20, barbecue rib and chicken Sun, Tue and Thu, US$15, otherwise lunch and dinner usual steak, fish, shrimp or lobster. *Abe's By The Sea*, T4959329, abes@bvimail.com Breakfast, lunch and dinner, grocery store, happy hr 1700-1800, pig roast on Wed, US$18, call VHF Ch 16 for reservations, also has 3 rooms overlooking harbour, can be 1 apartment, **B**, friendly family.

    Great Harbour *Sandcastle* (see above), White Bay. For breakfast, lunch and gourmet, *Restaurants take turns* candle-lit dinner (must reserve dinner and order in advance to your specifications). *Ali* *in sponsoring a pig* *Baba's*, T4959280. Run by Baba Hatchett, west of the Customs House. Breakfast, lunch and *roast nightly in season* dinner, happy hr 1600-1800. *Rudy's Mariner's Rendezvous*, reservations T4959282 or VHF Ch 16. Open for dinner until 0100, US$12.50-22.50. *Club Paradise*, T4959267 or VHF Ch 16. Open daily, Mon lobster special US$20, Wed pig roast US$15, live entertainment regularly, lunch 1030-1600, dinner 1800-2100. *Foxy's Bar*, T4959258. Friendly and cheap, lunch Mon-Fri rotis and burgers, dinner daily, reservations by 1700, spontaneous calypso by Foxy, master story-teller and musician, in afternoon until end of happy hr, big parties on New Year's Eve and other holidays, hundreds of yachts arrive, wooden boat regatta on Labour Day draws boats from all over the Caribbean for a 3-day beach party, very easy to get invited on board to watch or race, special ferry service to USVI and Tortola. *Happy Laury*, T4959259. Very good value for breakfast, happy hr is 1500-1700, try the Happy Laury Pain Killer.

This small uninhabited islet just east of Jost Van Dyke is owned by Laurance **Sandy Cay** Rockefeller. It is covered with scrub but there is a pleasant trail set out around the whole island, which makes a good walk. Bright white beaches surround the island and provide excellent swimming. Offshore is a coral reef.

British Virgin Islands

Anegada

IDD code: 284
Colour map 2, grid B6
Population: 153

*The island is very
quiet and relaxed*

Unique among this group of islands because of its coral and limestone formation, the highest point is only 28 ft above sea level. There are still a few large iguanas, which are indigenous to the island. The Anegada rock iguana is part of a national parks' trust breeding programme after numbers declined to only 100, largely because juveniles fell prey to wild cats. Contact Rondel Smith, the national parks trust warden on Anegada (also a taxi driver), who can take you to see their burrows in the wild and the hatchlings in pens outside the Administration Building in the Settlement. Young adult rock iguanas will be released into the wild when they are big enough, but there are about 50 youngsters in captivity. Flamingos also used to be numerous on the island but were decimated by hunters. Twenty flamingos were released in 1992 in the ponds and four wild ones joined them two years later. In 1995 they bred five chicks, something of a record with flamingos reintroduced into the wild and now there are over 40 birds. They are best seen from the little bridge over The Creek on the road from the *Anegada Reef Hotel* to the airport turn-off. Hawksbill and Green Turtles nest all along the north shore; the Government has drawn up a conservation policy and the waters around the island are protected. The waters abound with fish and lobster, and the extensive reefs are popular with snorkellers and scuba divers who also explore wrecks of ships which foundered in years past. Some were said to hold treasure, but to date only a few doubloons have been discovered. Anegada has excellent fishing and is one of the top bone-fishing spots in the world. From the wharf on the south shore, all the way round to the west end, across the entire north shore (about 11 miles) is perfect, uninterrupted, white sandy beach. Any fences on the beach are to keep out cattle, not people. Loblolly Bay is popular with day trippers, partly because it has a beach bar at either end *The Big Bamboo* at the west end is busier and more accessible than *Flash of Beauty* at the east end, the only places where there is shade, partly because of the reef just offshore where snorkellers can explore caverns and ledges and see coral, nurse sharks, rays, turtles, barracuda and shoals of colourful fish. The beach is generally deserted. Bring water and sun screen.

The Settlement is a collection of wooden homes and some newer houses, a smart new government building, a few bars, little shops, a bakery, jeep hire and church.

Sleeping
Credit cards are not accepted on Anegada except at the Anegada Reef Hotel

LL-L *Anegada Reef Hotel*, T4958002, www.anagadareef.com or by VHF Ch 16. 18 rooms, FAP, where there is an anchorage, fishing packages, dive equipment, beach bar, restaurant, great service, famous lobster barbecue and infamous Nubian goat, Charlie, if arriving by yacht radio in advance for directions through the reef, car, minibus and bicycle hire, taxi service, beach shuttle, boutique, closed Sep-Oct. Also under same management, **AL-B** *Anegada Reef Cottages & Villa*, at Setting Point. 2-bedrooms, 2 bathrooms.

Anegada

■ Sleeping
1 Anegada Beach Cottages
2 Anegada Reef
3 Anegada Reef Cottages
4 Anegada Seaside Villas
5 Bonefish Villa
6 Ocean Range

0 km 1
0 miles 1

LL-L *Anegada Seaside Villas*, T4954966, www.anagadavillas.com 1-bedroom villas on the sand with sofa bed in living room, fans, CD player, well-equipped kitchen, large porch, barbecue. **A-B** *Ocean Range*, in the Settlement, T4959023. Single and adjoining rooms, kitchenettes available, sea view. **L-AL** *Anegada Beach Cottages*, Pomato Point, T4959466, www.anegadabeachcottages.com Suites in cottages, 1 or 2 bedrooms, close to water, well-spaced out from each other, simple accommodation with full amenities, snorkelling, fishing. **L** *Bonefish Villa*, Nutmeg Point on beach, close to restaurant, T4958045, smgeorge@worldnet.att.net Includes service and taxes.

Camping *Anegada Beach Campground*, T4959466. US$20-36 prepared site, bare site US$7 per day, plus 10% service, no credit cards, beach bar, restaurant, snorkelling. *Neptune's Treasure*, T4959439. Campsite and tents available US$15-25 per night, US$90-150 per week, US$7 bare site, no cooking, restaurant on site. *Mac's Place* campsite, T4958020. 8 ft by 10 ft tent US$38, prepared sites US$15-35, showers, toilets, grills, eating area.

Pomato Point Beach Restaurant, T4958038, VHF Ch 16, barbecue dinners, reserve by 1600, *ABC Car Rentals* is here, T4959466. *Neptune's Treasure*, T4959439. Breakfast, lunch, dinner, camping available, delicious breads and chutneys, make sure you take some home. *The Big Bamboo*, T4952019 (see above). Aubrey and his wife serve delicious lobster and conch on the beach at Loblolly Bay, VHF Ch 16. *Lobster Trap*, T4959466, VHF 16. Garden setting, on waterfront, open alternately with *Pomato Point*, breakfast, lunch and dinner (reservations required for dinner), barbecue lobster. *Anegada Reef Hotel*, T4958002. Breakfast, lunch and dinner but reserve by 1600 for dinner. *Cow Wreck Bar and Grill*, T4959461, on the beach. Open for lunch and dinner, lobster, conch and ribs. *Dotsy's Bakery and Sandwich Shop*, in The Settlement, T4959667. Open 0900-1900 for breakfast, lunch and dinner, fish and chips, burgers, pizza as well as breads and desserts. *Flash of Beauty*, at east end of Loblolly Bay, T4958104, VHF 16. Drinks, snacks and seafood, including lobster, open 1000-2100. Ask around in The Settlement for restaurants serving native dishes.

Eating
Make dinner reservations before 1600

A short stretch of concrete road leads from The Settlement to the airport turn-off; all other roads on the island are sand. There is no public transport except taxis and the best way to get around is to hire a jeep, bicycle or walk (take an umbrella for the sun or walk in the early evening). There is an airstrip 2,500 ft long and 60 ft wide, which can handle light aircraft. Day trips by boat from Tortola are available. There is no regular ferry service. Car, minibus and bicycle rentals are possible at the *Anegada Reef Hotel*, T4958002; *DW Jeep Rentals*, The Settlement, T4959677, 2-door jeeps and Subaru vans, US$40-55, US$240-300 per week, free drop-off and pick-up at airport; *ABC Car Rentals* is at Pomato Point, T4959466.

Transport

Background

Although discovered by the Spanish in 1493, the islands were first settled by Dutch buccaneers before being driven out by British buccaneers in 1666. In 1672 Britain formally claimed the islands when Tortola was annexed to the Leeward Islands, and in 1680 planters from Anguilla moved into Anegada and Virgin Gorda. Civil government was introduced in 1773 with an elected House of Assembly (white planters only) and a part-elected and part-nominated Legislative Council. Between 1872 and 1956 the islands were part of the Leeward Islands Federation (a British Colony), but then became a separately administered entity, in preference to joining the West Indies Federation of British territories. In 1960 direct responsibility was assumed by an appointed Administrator, later to become Governor. The Constitution became effective in 1967 with a ministerial system of government, but was later amended in 1977 to allow the islands greater autonomy in domestic affairs. In 1994, the British Government accepted a proposal from a constitutional review commission for the Legislative Council to be enlarged from nine to 13 seats. The four new members represent the territory as a single constituency. This plan created the first mixed electoral system in British parliamentary history, with voters having one vote for their constituency member as usual, plus four votes for the new territory-wide representatives. The British government pushed it into effect before 6 December 1994, the last

History
See page 550 for related background on the US Virgin Islands

British Virgin Islands

date for the dissolution of the legislature. There was considerable disquiet in the BVI and in the UK at the way in which it was rushed through without prior consultation and without the support of Chief Minister Lavity Stoutt's government.

Mr H Lavity Stoutt, of the Virgin Islands Party (VIP), became Chief Minister in 1967-71 and again in 1979-83 and in 1986. At the elections in February 1995 the Virgin Islands Party, still led by Mr Lavity Stoutt, won a third consecutive term in office. However, Mr Stoutt died in May 1995 and the Deputy Chief Minister Ralph O'Neal took over as Chief Minister. The VIP won the by-election after Mr Stoutt's death.

In the May 1999 elections the VIP retained power, winning seven seats, but it faced a less divided opposition. The newly formed National Democratic Party (NDP), led by Orlando Smith, attracted support from young professionals, winning five seats, while the Concerned Citizens' Movement (CCM) won one and the United Party (UP) failed to win any. In June 2003 the VIP was swept aside after 17 years in power when the NDP captured eight of the 13 seats in the general elections. The new Chief Minister is Orlando Smith, who campaigned with promises to spend more on social services and less on large construction projects. Demand for change was evident in the large voter turnout, which exceeded 72%, compared with 65% in 1999.

Geography & people The British Virgin Islands (BVI), grouped around Sir Francis Drake Channel, are less developed than the US group, and number some 60 islands, islets, rocks, and cays, of which only 16 or so are inhabited. They are all of volcanic origin except one, Anegada, which is coral and limestone.

The two major islands, Tortola and Virgin Gorda, along with the groups of Anegada and Jost Van Dyke, contain most of the total population of about 20,000, mainly of African descent. The resident population was only 10,985 in 1980 and most of the increase has come from inward migration of workers from the English-speaking Eastern Caribbean for the construction and tourist industries. About half the present population is of non-BVI origin. There has recently been a return flow of people from the Dominican Republic, whose parents and grandparents were originally from Tortola, seeking a higher standard of living. Everyone speaks English.

Government A nearly self-contained community, the islands are a British Overseas Territory with a Governor appointed by London, although to a large extent they are internally self-governing. The Governor presides over the Executive Council, made up of the Chief Minister, the Attorney-General and three other ministers. A Legislative Council comprises 13 members elected by universal adult suffrage (of which nine represent district constituencies and four represent the whole territory), one member appointed by the Governor, a Speaker elected from outside by members of the Council, and the Attorney-General as an ex-officio member.

Economy The economy is based predominantly on up-market tourism and earnings are around US$150 mn a year. There are approximately 1,300 hotel rooms, half of which are on Tortola and a third on Virgin Gorda, the rest being scattered around the other islands, but nearly half of those visitors who stay on the islands charter yachts and only sleep on land for their arrival and departure nights. Crewed yachts have been pushed rather than increasing bare boat charters. The *British Virgin Islands Film Commission* encourages film production in the islands and film crews bring considerable economic benefit through their use of local services and labour. A 550-ft cruise ship pier at Road Town, Tortola, can accommodate two medium-size cruise liners. The Government aims to attract the upper end of the cruise market and not to encourage the large ships.

A growth industry is the offshore company business, shipping, captive insurance and reinsurance, with little currency risk as the US dollar is the national currency; currently over one third of government revenue comes from this sector. Although the budget is in surplus, the Government is still receiving British capital assistance, and funding from the EC, the *Caribbean Development Bank* and the *Commonwealth Development Corporation*. The British government is now curtailing its capital funding and other sources of foreign finance are being explored.

Industry on the islands is limited to small scale operations such as rum, sand or gravel. Farming is limited to fruit, vegetables and some livestock, some of which are shipped to the USVI. Fishing is expanding both for export, sport and domestic consumption. However, nearly all the islands' needs are imported.

Leeward Islands

Introducing the Leeward Islands

The Leeward Islands are a geographical grouping of small, mostly volcanic islands in the northeastern Caribbean. The islands are a mixture of French, Dutch and British colonies and ex-colonies and combine within a small area very varied and rich cultures. Whereas in colonial times they were nearly all sugar producers, today they rely on tourism for a large part of their foreign exchange earnings and jobs. From luxury resorts to intimate guesthouses, gourmet restaurants to barefoot beach bars, there is a wide range of attractions on offer. Sailing, diving and other watersports are also well developed and highly rewarding.

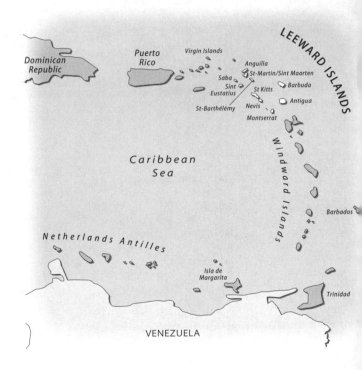

★

Things to do in Anguilla

- Plan your visit to coincide with **Moonsplash**, a music festival in March organized by Bankie Banx at the Dune Preserve on fabulous Rendezvous Bay.
- Take a **lobster lunch** at Island Harbour followed by some gentle snorkelling.
- **Sail** to one of the cays and spend a few hours exploring, snorkelling among the turtles and relaxing.
- Do a spot of **birdwatching** in the ponds and wetlands.

Anguilla

Anguilla is known for its luxury hotels and extensive sandy beaches. Its high standard of living makes it one of the safest islands and consequently one of the most relaxing. Visitors amuse themselves in the water during the day and eat at excellent restaurants and bars at night, taking in a weekend beach party with live music. There's not much else to do on this low-lying coral island, but that's why people come here.

IDD code: 264
Colour map 3, grid A1
Population: 8,960
(1992 census)

Ins and outs

International access points for Anguilla are Antigua, St Maarten or San Juan, Puerto Rico. From there you get a small plane to Wallblake Airport, or a boat from St-Martin to Blowing Point ferry terminal. Hotel transfers are not allowed, so you have to take a taxi on arrival.

Getting there
See Transport, page 465, for further details

There is no bus service but there are several **car hire** companies. Hired cars cannot be picked up from the airport because of local regulations, they have to be delivered to your hotel, but they can be dropped off at the airport. Watch out for loose goats and sheep on the roads. It is also possible to hire **bicycles** and **mopeds**.

Getting around
Driving is on the left. Speed limit 30 mph

The climate is subtropical with an average temperature of 80°F and a mean annual rainfall of 36 ins, falling mostly between Sep and Dec. Early cloud and rain usually clears by mid-morning.

Climate

Anguilla Department of Tourism, PO Box 1388, Old Factory Plaza, The Valley, T4972759, F4972710, www.anguilla-vacation.com Open weekdays 0800-1700, moving in 2003 to Coronation Av, near the roundabout. The office at the airport is closed at lunchtime, but the customs officers will often phone for a hotel reservation for you. The *Anguilla National Trust* welcomes members, office in the Museum Building, The Valley, T4975297, F4975571, axanat@anguillanet.com They have a map of archaeological and historical sites of Anguilla, worth getting if you want to explore caves, Amerindian sites or sugar mill rounds. Contact them or the *Anguilla Archaeological and Historical Society* for further information.

Tourist information

Flora and fauna

Although you will see colourful gardens, the island appears mostly covered with scrub. Nevertheless, there are 523 recorded species of flora, of which around 60% are native and the rest naturalized but introduced. The **north coast** has the most unspoilt open areas which have not been cultivated or built on. There are steep cliffs of over 100 ft high, with caves and sink holes, and inland are areas of dense vegetation. The most common plants are the white cedar, pigeonwood, manchineel, frangipani, five-finger trees, bromeliads and cacti. In this area you can find lizards, iguanas, snakes, bats and birds. The tiny ground lizard (*Ameiva pleei*) is endemic to Anguilla and you can often see their ribbon-like trails in the sand on the dunes and along the pond shores. **Katouche Valley** has a beach, a mangrove pond and a forest where you can find orchids and bromeliads and some patches of bamboo among the

A tree planting programme has been organized by the Anguilla Beautification Club (ABC); donations are welcome and you can 'adopt a tree'. Contact ABC Trees, PO Box 274, Anguilla

Leeward Islands

Touching down

See also Directory, page 466

Boat information *(own flag) In Road Bay get a cruising permit for other anchorages. Customs and Immigration at Blowing Point ferry port and Road Bay at Sandy Ground (at police station next to Johnno's on north side, near small pier). Free* **anchorage** *in Road Bay and Blowing Point. Fees are based on official tonnage. Charter boats pay additional anchoring fees. Bring your crew lists. Little Bay, Sandy Island and Prickly Pear have permanent moorings, other places have designated anchoring sites. Boats may not anchor in Rendezvous Bay or Little Bay. Every boat visiting a marine park must get a permit to tie up or anchor, fee US$15 for private vessels, US$23 for charter boats. If you want to scuba dive you pay a fee of US$4 per tank.*
Business hours *Banks Mon-Thu*

0800-1500, 0800-1700 Fri; **Government offices** *Mon-Fri 0800-1600;* **Shops** *0800-1700 or 1800, some grocery stores are open until 2100, a few on Sun;* **gas stations** *in The Valley, Mon-Sat 0700-2100, Sun 0900-1300, and at Blowing Point, Mon-Sun 0700-2400.*
Clothing *Bathing costumes are not worn in public places. Nude bathing and nude sunbathing are not allowed.*
Currency *The East Caribbean dollar, EC$. US dollars always accepted. EC$2.67-US$1.*
Departure tax *US$15 by air and US$3 by sea.*
Documents *All visitors need an onward ticket and a valid* **passport**, *except US citizens who need only show proof of identity with a photograph.* **Visas** *are not required by anyone. Proof of adequate funds is required if*

pepper cinnamon, mawby, sherry and turpentine trees. The valley ends at Cavannagh Cave, which was mined for phosphorous in the 19th century, but now is home to bats, birds, crabs and lizards. Birdwatching is good at **Little Bay**, Crocus Bay's north point and at the many ponds and coves, T4972759 for information. Anguilla has 136 recorded species of bird, including the blue-faced booby, kingfisher and the great blue heron. The national bird is the turtle dove.

Diving and marine life

Dive sites The Government is introducing a marine parks system, installing permanent moorings in certain areas to eliminate anchor damage. Designated marine parks include Dog Island, Island Harbour, Little Bay, Prickly Pear, Sandy Island, Seal Island and Shoal Bay. Mooring permits are required. Do not remove any marine life such as coral or shells from underwater. Spear fishing is prohibited. **Stoney Bay Marine Park Underwater Archaeological Preserve** was opened in March 1999. The park is protecting the wreck of a Spanish ship, *El Buen Consejo*, which ran aground on 8 July 1772 off the northern tip of Anguilla while on its way to Mexico with 50 Franciscan missionaries bound for the Philippines. It now lies about 100 yd offshore at a depth of 30 ft, with cannon, anchors and historical artefacts. Dives are fully guided and can only be done with *Shoal Bay Scuba and Watersports*. You are shown a video and given an overview of the ship's history.

There are good dives just off the coast, particularly for novices or for night dives, while the others are generally in a line due west of Sandy Island, northwest of Sandy Ground, and along the reef formed by **Prickly Pear Cays** and Sail Island. Off **Sandy Island**, there are lots of soft corals and sea-fans, while at Sandy Deep there is a wall which falls from 15-60 ft. There are also several wrecks, nine of which have been deliberately sunk as dive sites around the island, the most recent in 1993.

Further west, **Paintcan Reef** at a depth of 80 ft contains several acres of coral and you can sometimes find large turtles there. Nearby, **Authors Deep**, at 110 ft, has black coral, turtles and a host of small fish, but this is more for the experienced diver. On the north side of the Prickly Pear Cays you can find a beautiful underwater canyon with ledges and caves where nurse sharks often go to rest. Most of the reefs around Anguilla have some red coral; be careful not to touch it as it burns.

the Immigration Officer feels so inclined.
Emergency numbers *T911/999.*
Media Newspapers *Chronicle,* The Daily
Herald, The Light, *a local weekly. What We
Do In Anguilla is an annual tourist magazine.
Anguilla Life is a quarterly magazine.*
Radio *Radio Anguilla (T2218) is on medium
wave 1505 kHz and ZJF on FM 105 Mhz.*
Official time *GMT minus 4 hrs;
EST plus 1 hr.*
Public holidays *New Year's Day, Good Fri,
Easter Mon, Labour Day, Whit Mon, end of
May (Anguilla Day, commemorates Anguilla
Revolution which began 30 May 1967), the
Queen's official birthday in Jun, the first Mon
(Aug Mon) and the first Thu (Aug Thu) and Fri
(Constitution Day) in Aug, 19 Dec (Separation
Day), Christmas Day, Boxing Day.*

Tourist offices overseas *Germany, c/o
Sergat Deutschland, IM Guldenen Wingert
8-C, D-64342, Seeheim, T49-6257-962920,
F49-6257-962919,
r.morozow@t-online-de Italy, Piazza
Bertarelli 1, 20122 Milan, T39-02-72022466,
F39-02-72020162,
anguilla@bdp-comunicazione.com UK, River
Communications, PO Box 2119, Woodford
Green, London, 1G8 0GZ, T020-850666140,
F020-85058974,
anguilla4info@aol.com USA, KV Tourism
Marketing, 111 Decatur St, Doyleston County,
PA 18901, T264-8803511, F264-8803507,
enterprisefx@aol.com*
Voltage *110 volts AC, 60 cycles.*
Weights and measures *Metric, but some
imperial weights and measures are still used.*

Anguilla Divers, based at *La Sirena*, Mead's Bay and Island Harbour, dive the east end of the   **Dive centres**
island and offer PADI courses, in English, French, German or Spanish, T4974750, F4974632,
axadiver@anguillanet.com *Shoal Bay Scuba & Watersports*, T4974371. Dive master, Douglas
Carty, has his own boat, *Desha*, and offers diving, boat trips and charters, US$50 for a single
tank, US$90 for 2-tank dives and packages available, T4974567, dcarty@anguillanet.com

Beaches and watersports

There are 12 miles, 35 beaches, of fine white coral sand and crystal-clear water. Most of   *The beaches are*
them are protected by a ring of coral reefs and offshore islands. Beautiful **Shoal Bay** is   *clean, and many*
the most popular beach and very busy at weekends: island bands play here on Sundays   *are relatively*
until the evening. There are villas, guesthouses, casual restaurants and beach bars   *unpopulated, but*
(*Uncle Ernie's* has the cheapest drinks) for lunch and dinner. The snorkelling is good,   *nude (or topless)*
with the closer of two reefs only 10 yards from the shore, and you can rent snorkelling   *swimming*
and other watersports equipment. You can also rent lockers, beach umbrellas, loun-   *or sunbathing*
gers, rafts and towels. There may even be someone to sell you live lobster. **Mead's Bay**   *is not allowed*
is also popular, with a couple of small bars, top-class hotels and watersports. A controversial dolphin lagoon has been built here, stocked with dolphins from Cuba, allegedly
caught in the wild, which have been trained and are giving performances. Conservationists have protested against keeping the dolphins in captivity for the amusement of
tourists. For further information, contact the *Whale and Dolphin Conservation Society*, see page 60. The same company, *Dolphin Fantaseas*, has a dolphinarium on
Antigua, all in the name of 'conservation and education'. **Road Bay/Sandy Ground** is
known for its nightlife and restaurants and is the starting point for most day trips, dive
tours and a popular anchorage for visiting yachts. Watersports equipment rentals can
be organized here. **Scilly Cay** is a small cay off Island Harbour with good snorkelling.
A free ferry takes you to the bar on a palm-fringed beach where walls are made from
conch shells. Live music on Wednesday, Friday and Sunday. *Smitty's Bar*, across the
water at **Island Harbour**, is less sophisticated, tables made from old cable barrels, TV,
pool room, popular with the locals. Seafood comes straight off the boats. Beach chairs
and umbrellas are complimentary and snorkelling is good just off the beach. **Captain's Bay** is rougher but the scenery is dramatic and not many people go there. The
dirt road is full of potholes and goats, and may be impassable with a low car. At **Crocus
Bay** the rocks on both sides have attractive underwater scenery. There is a bar/

Leeward Islands

restaurant and toilets. At the end of **Limestone Bay** is a small beach with excellent snorkelling, but be careful, the sea can be rough here. **Little Bay**, with crystal-clear water and dramatic cliffs, is very difficult to reach but eagle rays, turtles and lots of fish can be seen, and as well as excellent snorkelling it is a birdwatcher's and photographer's dream; turn right in front of the old cottage hospital in The Valley, after about half a mile there are some trails leading down the cliff to the water, fishermen have put up a rope for the last bit down the rock face. Glass-bottom boats and cruise boats also come here or you can get a boat ride from Crocus Bay.

Watersports **Windsurfing** and **sailing** are readily available and some hotels offer waterskiing, paddle boats, snorkelling, fishing and sunfish sailing. Parasailing can be arranged at Shoal Bay. *Anguilla Watersports* offer waterskiing, T4975821. Jet skiing is prohibited. There are glass-bottom boats which can be hired for 1 or 2 people to operate themselves or crewed for groups. **Sport fishing** is available, contact *Gotcha*, T4972956; *Johnno's*, T4972728; *Rampoosin*, T4978868; *Sandy Island Enterprises*, T4975643; *No Mercy*, T4976383. Yacht or motorboat charters are offered with beach and snorkelling cruises around the island or trips to Philipsburg, St Maarten, charters to Saba, Statia, St-Barts on request. Operators change frequently. **Boat racing** is the national sport, the boats being a wooden sloop made in Anguilla. There are frequent races, but the most important are on **Anguilla Day** (30 May) and during **Carnival Week** in Aug.

Around the island

The island is low lying and, unlike its neighbours, it is not volcanic but of coral formation

Anguilla is a small island, about 35 miles square, and the most northerly of the Leeward Islands. It is arid, covered with low scrub and has few natural resources. The island's name comes from the Spanish word for 'eel', a reference to its long, narrow shape, 16 miles long but only an average of 3 miles wide. Its Carib name was Malliouhana, the sea serpent. The people of Anguilla, predominantly of African descent but with some traces of Irish blood, are very friendly and helpful. It is one of the safest islands in the Caribbean.

Anguilla

■ Sleeping	5 Carimar	10 Inter Island	14 Paradise Cove
1 Anguilla Great House	6 Cove Castles	Guest House	15 Rendezvous Bay
2 Arawak	7 CuisinArt	11 Lloyd's Guest House	16 Shoal Bay Villas
3 Blue Waters	8 Ferry Boat Inn	12 Malliouhana	17 Syd Ans, Sea
4 Cap Juluca	9 Frangipani	13 Milly's Inn	View & La Palma

Near **The Valley**, the island's administrative centre, with a population of 500, **Wallblake House** is a restored, 18th-century plantation house where the priest from **St Gerard's Roman Catholic Church** lives. The church itself is worth a visit to see the unusual ventilation. Several resident artists exhibit their work on Saturday mornings during the winter season in the grounds of Wallblake House. ■ *1000-1200 Tue-Fri. US$5 tour. T4972759.* The **Methodist church** is the oldest church, dating from 1830, a pretty building of stone and timber. **Anguilla National Museum** contains a collection of artefacts in a restored Anguillian cottage just west of the Public Library. It holds cultural and environmental exhibitions, and there is information on hiking trails and historical sites. ■ *T4975297.*

Local deposits of clay have been found and pottery is now made on the island. The work of Barbadian potter and sculptor, Courtney Devonish, his students and other artists, is on display at the **Devonish Art Gallery**, West End Road, T4972949, www.devonish.ai. On the other side of the road is **Cheddie's Carving Studio**, displaying Cheddie's skills with driftwood. He highlights a feature of the wood to carve and polish animals, birds, fish and people, leaving the rest of the wood untouched. At **Sandy Ground Village**, you can see the salt pond, around Great Road Pond, although it is not currently in operation. There is a mini museum at the *Pump House* bar, Sandy Ground. The building was once part of the salt factory and equipment used in the salt-making process is on display. ■ *T4975154.*

A local historian, Mr Colville Petty OBE, collects traditional household artefacts and nostalgic old photos, displayed in what is known as the **Heritage Collection Museum**. ■ *Mon-Sat 1000-1700, Sun 1300-1800. US$5, children under 12 US$3. South Hill Plaza on the main road, T4978737, petty@anguillanet.com*

Northeast of The Valley, by Shoal Village, is **The Fountain** national park, closed at present. Its focus is a cave which has constant fresh water and Amerindian petroglyphs. Artefacts have been found and it is hoped they will be housed in a museum at the site. Anguilla awaits detailed archaeological investigation, but it is thought that the island had several settlements and a social structure of some importance, judging by the ceremonial items which have been found. **Big Spring Cave** is an old Amerindian ceremonial centre where you can see petroglyphs. It is near **Island Harbour**, a fishing village with Irish ancestry.

Day trips can be arranged to some of the neighbouring islands or to the offshore islands and cays. **Sandy Island** is only 15 minutes from Sandy Ground Harbour and is a pleasant desert island for swimming or snorkelling. ■ *Motorboats or sailboats cross over hourly 1000-1500, US$8 per person. Lunch or drinks available from a beach bar under coconut palms, T4976395.* There are trips to **Prickly Pear**, six miles from Road Bay, worth a visit, where you can snorkel if you are not a scuba diver, or to some of the other cays where you can fish or just have a picnic. **Scrub Island**, two miles long and one mile wide, off the northeast tip of Anguilla, is an interesting mix of coral, scrub and other vegetation. It is uninhabited, except by goats. There is a lovely sandy beach on the west side and ruins of an abandoned tourist resort and airstrip. There can be quite a swell in the anchorage, so anchor well. Boats go from Road Bay, Shoal Bay or Island Harbour. Chartered yachts and motorboats leave from Road Bay or from Island Harbour for Scilly Cay, privately owned by Eudoxie and Sandra Wallace and also named **Gorgeous Scilly Cay**. They have their own boat with a free ferry service. ■ *1000-1700, lunch only, live music Wed, Fri, closed Sun.*

Islands offshore

Essentials

Anguilla has the reputation of catering for upmarket, independent travellers. This is reflected in the number of relatively small, chic and expensive hotels and beach clubs. Bargains can be found in the summer months, with discounts of over 50%. The Anguilla Department of Tourism has a list of all types of accommodation.

Sleeping

A 10% tax and 10-15% service charge will be added to the bill

Leeward Islands

Hotels **LL** *Cap Juluca* at Maundays Bay, T4976666, www.capjuluca.com Moorish design, bright white, luxury resort, 98 rooms, suites and 3-5 bedroom villas, CP, no keys, every facility here, massage, scrubs in your room, 2 beaches, chilled towels twice daily and sorbet brought to your sunbed in the afternoon, pool, watersports, tennis, croquet, full children's activity programmes, 3 restaurants or 24-hr room service, 179-acre estate, nature trail. **LL** *Cove Castles Villa Resort*, Shoal Bay West, T4976801, www.covecastles.com Futuristic architecture, 4 3-bedroom villas, 8 2-bedroom beach houses, very expensive, housekeeper, phone, TV, beach, tennis, sunfish, bicycles included, watersports available. **LL** *CuisinArt Resort & Spa*, Rendezvous Bay, T4982000, www.cuisinartresort.com Spa resort with lots of health treatments and wellness programme, cooking classes, 3 restaurants, grows fruit and vegetables hydroponically, excellent food, 93 luxury rooms, of which 60 are suites, huge marble bathrooms, blue and yellow colour scheme, walk-in wardrobes, patio with sun beds, doors sturdy enough to withstand 200 mph winds, children's playground, popular with guests who like to feel cosseted and eat well. **LL** *Frangipani Beach Club*, luxury resort on Mead's Bay beach, T4976442, www.frangipani.ai 15 deluxe units, 1-3 bedrooms, Spanish-style tiled roofs, multilevel, tiled floors, fans, cool, comfortable, large pool, substantial discounts in low season, meal plans available. **LL** *Malliouhana Hotel & Spa*, Mead's Bay, T4976111, www.malliouhana.com 55 large rooms with huge marble bathrooms and lots of cupboards, fridge and mini bar, no credit cards, vastly expensive, every luxury, very posh, attentive service, award-winning restaurant (lots of steps), more casual bistro on beach, new spa with treatment rooms rented by the half day, watersports (most complimentary), tennis, 2 pools, children welcome, playground and pool by the beach (hotel is closed Sep and Oct each year for refurbishment). **LL-L** *Anguilla Great House*, Rendezvous Bay, T4976061, www.anguillagreathouse.com Low-rise, low-key, family-run small hotel on wonderful beach, great location looking across to St-Martin, 27 simple but spacious interconnecting rooms, a/c, TV, fan, phone, good open-air restaurant and bar on beach, often live music in evenings, pool. **LL-AL** *Arawak Beach Resort*, T4974888, www.arawak beach.com Octagonal villas on the northeast coast near Big Spring ceremonial centre, overlooking Scilly Cay, health bar and restaurant. **LL-AL** *Rendezvous Bay Hotel*, T4976549, www.rendezvousbay.com The first beach hotel on the island and still owned by the Gumbs family, relaxing and friendly, 45 rooms, villas, well spread out on 60-acre property, rooms with veranda only a few metres from the sea, moderately good snorkelling, tennis, lovely empty beach, art gallery, games room, TV, piano, library, pool, internet access free for guests in office.

Inns of Anguilla is an association of over 20 villas or small hotels at moderate prices

Villas and apartments **LL-L** *Carimar Beach Club*, Mead's Bay, T4976881, www.carimar.com Colourful bougainvillea climbs over the arches of the patios and verandas, 24 comfortable 1-3-bedroom apartments, each privately owned so decor varies, full kitchens, fans, on beach, tennis, no pool, no restaurant but several within walking distance, also grocery store nearby, internet access in lobby, closed end-Aug-mid-Oct. **LL-L** *Paradise Cove*, Lower South Hill, T4976603, http://paradise.ai 5-min walk to beach at Cove Bay, but right by new golf course, 4 categories of spacious, comfortable suites, all with full kitchen, patio, a/c, TV, fan, also studios with kitchenette, connecting doors to make family apartments, laundry facilities on each floor, meeting rooms, fitness centre, pool, jacuzzi, kids' pool and pool bar, café for breakfast and lunch, dinner can be brought in, all tastefully decorated. **LL-L** *Shoal Bay Villas*, T4972051, www.sbvillas.ai 13 spacious 1-2-bedroom suites and studios with kitchen, near *Le Beach* restaurant, open 0700-2200, pool, watersports. **LL-AL** *Blue Waters Beach Apartments*, Shoal Bay West, T4976292, F4976982. 9 1-2-bedroom, self-catering apartments in brilliant white buildings on the beach, fans, restaurant, babysitting and maid service. **LL-A** *Ferry Boat Inn*, Cul de Sac, Blowing Point, T4976613, http://ai/ferryboatinn/ Right by the ferries but with reasonable beach and view of St-Martin, 4 large suites and 2 smaller ones, spacious living area light and cool, large balcony with great view and lots of breeze, a/c, fans, restaurant for lunch and dinner on seafront, daily maid service. **LL-A** *Harbour Villas*, T4974393 www.harbourvillas.ai Overlooking Gorgeous Scilly Cay, 7 apartments, 1-3 bedrooms, kitchens, laundry facilities, balcony, gardens lead down to beach.

L *Milly's Inn*, Shoal Bay, T4972465, www.millysinn.ai 4 apartments, living area, bedroom, bathroom and fully equipped kitchen, gleaming white tiles throughout, terrace or balcony with sea view, 3-min walk to beach, quiet, maid service, very good. **A-B** *Syd Ans Apartments*, Sandy Ground, T4973180, www.inns.ai/sydans 1-bedroom apartments,

Mexican restaurant, close to *Pump House* and *Johnno's*, convenient for nightlife. **AL-B** *Sea View*, Sandy Ground, T4972427, www.inns.ai/seaview 1-3 bedrooms, ceiling fans, kitchen facilities, beach across the road, salt ponds behind, clean, comfortable, always lots going on in this area. **B** *La Palma*, Sandy Ground, T4973260, www.inns.ai/lapalma 3 studios, on beach, restaurant, ceiling fans.

Guesthouses **A-B** *Inter Island Guest House*, Lower South Hill, T4976259, F4978207. 14 good-sized rooms with fridge, apartments, a/c, fans, kitchens, restaurant, huge conference room/banqueting hall, *Chandeliers* seats up to 400 for local functions. **A-B** *Lloyd's Guesthouse*, Crocus Hill, The Valley, T4972351, www.lloyds.ai On the highest point at 213 ft, good view over The Valley, smartly painted in yellow and white, this is the oldest guesthouse, opened in 1959. Run by Vida, David and Christine Lloyd, CP, 14 rooms, all with bathroom, TV, fan, old-fashioned charm, optional meal plan, family-style dining with other guests, mostly from other Caribbean islands, local dishes, drinks served but no bar. **E** *Casa Nadine*, The Valley, T4972358. 11 clean rooms, EP, with shower, kitchen facilities, basic, but very friendly and helpful, price reductions for longer stays, good views over The Valley from the roof.

Travellers on a lower budget or those wanting to avoid hotels can find accommodation in one of about 10 guesthouses

There are many excellent places to eat on the island for all palates and all budgets, from the elegant to beach barbecues. Beach bars and casual waterfront places provide a good lunch, for example *Uncle Ernie's*, Shoal Bay. The tourist guide *What We Do In Anguilla* has a listing. Most of the restaurants are small and reservations are needed, particularly in high season. There is a smooth Anguillian Rum, a blend from other islands matured in oak barrels, designed to be drunk on the rocks rather than in a punch. Visit the rum-tasting room at PYRAT Rums' factory on Sandy Ground Rd, open Mon-Fri 0800-1700, T4975003.

Eating
'Relish' is the local word for meat, not the accompaniment to it

Sandy Ground: *Le Saint Clair*, T4972833, VHF 16. French/Caribbean restaurant on beachfront, some Japanese dishes, open lunch and dinner, Sun brunch with live music 1000-1600, US$15, live jazz Mon, Thu, Sat, closed Sun night. *Ripples*, T4973380. Award-winning chef, try his lobster fritters, varied menu including vegetarian, open daily 1830-2300. *Ship's Galley*, 149/2040. Breakfast, lunch and dinner, West Indian cooking, closed Wed. *Barrel Stay*, T4972831. Mid-priced, French/Creole, fish soup, lobster, steak, open for lunch and dinner. **South Hill**: *Deon's Overlook*, Back St, T4974488. Tremendous view over Sandy Ground from top of cliff, open for lunch, dinner and cocktails, great food island-style served up by Chef Deon Thomas, who has done the rounds of hotel restaurants before opening his own, very popular place. *E's Oven*, T4988288. Nothing on menu over US$15, ranging from blue fish in basil cream sauce to sandwiches, owned by award-winning chef. *Flavours*, Back St. T4970629. Upstairs with view over Road Bay, run by Anguillian chef Rexie Fleming, Caribbean ingredients with international flavours such as roasted rack of goat in red wine sauce, as well as staples like fried plantain and breadfruit chips, open Mon-Sat, lunch and dinner (1830-2200), appetizers US$6-12, main courses US$13-17. *Tasty's*, T4972737, chefcarty@anguillanet.com. One of the best independent restaurants on the island, mainly seafood but also chicken, meat and vegetarian options, main dishes around US$14-24 for dinner, cheaper for lunch, try fried fish and johnny cakes for breakfast, great salads for lunch, varied menu, includes local goat curry, open 0800-2200, closed Thu. **The Valley**: *Pepperpot*, opposite high school, T4972328. Open 0700-2200, local food, local customers, especially after work, rotis, salt fish, curried goat, patties, takeaway available. **George Hill**: *Old House*, T4972228. Overlooking airport, watch flights from an old concrete home, happy hour 1700-1900, hot appetizers, open daily for breakfast, lunch and dinner, local food, seafood and grills. For breakfast, lunch and dinner, *The Landing Strip*, T4972268. View of airport, eat in or takeaway, Clarita Mason Mall on George Hill Rd, open daily. *Flight Deck*, on hill next to airport, T4972835. Bar and restaurant, local cuisine, breakfast, lunch and dinner, live music Fri, Sat nights. **Blowing Point**: *The Ferry Boat Inn*, on beach near ferry terminal, see Sleeping. View of St- Martin, European and West Indian food, lunch and dinner except Sun. **Mead's Bay**: *Blanchard's*, run by Bob and Melinda Blanchard, elegant wine list and fine dining with Oriental influences. 2 doors west, on the beach, is *Cocoplums*, T4976072. Good fish and seafood with local dishes such as plantains, rice and peas, vegetarian options, main dishes US$14-30. **Crocus Bay**: *Roy's Place*, beachfront, T4972470. Draught beer, fresh seafood, happy

Leeward Islands

hour 1700-1900, Sun brunch of roast beef and Yorkshire pudding, open 1200-1400, 1800-2100, closed Mon. **Shoal Bay**: *Le Beach Bar & Restaurant*, oldest restaurant on Shoal Bay East, T4975598. Steakhouse, surf'n'turf, salad bar, pizza, open daily for breakfast, lunch and dinner, happy hour 1700-1830, near *Shoal Bay Villas*. *Trattoria Tramonto & Oasis Beach Bar*, Shoal Bay West, next to *Blue Waters*, T4978819. Northern Italian chef, serious Italian cuisine, lunch casual 1200-1500, sunset champagne cocktails 1700-1800, dinner 1900-2130, only 10 tables so reservations essential, closed Mon. *Altamer*, Shoal Bay West, T4984040, www.altamer.com/restaurant Presided over by executive chef Maurice Leduc, on the beach, stainless steel kitchen behind glass so you can see what is going on, fabulous food, expensive, open breakfast, lunch and dinner, nightly entertainment in season. *Madeariman Reef*, Shoal Bay East, T4973833, www.madeariman.com Breakfast, lunch and dinner, casual, relaxed. **Island Harbour**: *Hibernia*, T4974290. Run by French and Irish couple, international menu with influences from their travelling experiences, closed low season.

For those who are self-catering, *Fat Cat*, Main Rd, George Hill, T4972307. Meals to go from the freezer, picnic meals, pies and cakes, open 1000-1800, closed Sun. *Gee Wee's Bakery & Catering*, on West End main road, between Shell station and *La Sirena* hotel, T4976462. Breads, cakes, pastries, sandwiches, Jamaican jerk chicken and pork, parties catered for, eat in, takeaway or delivery service. *Shalack's Café*, opposite *Albert's Supermarket*, T4973272. Cafeteria-style restaurant has variety of ready prepared meals, come in or order. *Vista Food Market*, South Hill Roundabout, T4972804. Good selection, cheeses, meats, pâtés, wines, beer, Cuban cigars, etc, open Mon-Sat 0800-1800. *Ashleys Supermarket*, South Valley. Open Mon-Fri 0700-2030, Sat 0700-2200, has a good range including produce from other islands. *Le Bon Pain*, Island Harbour, T4974090. French bakery, big choice, dishes made to order, good coffee. Fresh fish is brought to the fish market (*The Fishery*) on George Hill Mon-Sat between 1730-1900, call T4973170 to check what time the boats are coming in.

Nightlife

Out of season there is not much to do during the week. On Fri the whole island changes, several bars have live music; check the local papers

On Fri go to *Johnno's Place*, Sandy Ground; on Sun to brunch at *Roy's Place*, Crocus Bay, then around 1500 to *Johnno's Place* for a beach party. When the music dies people go to the neighbouring bar, *Ship's Galley*, for the night shift. *Uncle Ernie's Beach Bar* on Shoal Bay has a live band playing on Sun pm. *Madeariman Reef*, Shoal Bay, soca, calypso, reggae on Fri, Sat, Caribbean night with Spraka Wed. *Gorgeous Scilly Cay* has live daytime music on Wed, Fri and Sun, T4975123. At the weekend the *Dragon Disco* opens around midnight. *Mirrors Night Club and Bar*, at Swing High, above *Vista Food Market*, juke box with music from 1960s to now, happy hour nightly at 1900-2000, live entertainment at weekends. *Dune Preserve*, reggae and folk music from the Caribbean, run by *Bankie Banx*, at Rendezvous Bay on the beach next to *CuisinArt*, built out of bits of boats with a boat in the middle, great location. *The Pump House*, in the historic Anguilla Rd Salt Co Factory, Mon-Sat 1900-0200, eat, drink, dance or relax, great reggae on Sat, T4975154.

In high season the resort hotels have live music, steel bands, etc, check in the tourist *What We Do in Anguilla* monthly magazine. Look for shows with *North Sound*, *Mussington Brothers*, *Happy Hits* the most popular bands. *Dumpa and the Anvibes* is led by Pan Man Michael (Dumpa) Martin. *Xtreme Band*, formed in 2001 by several musicians who had been involved with the *Mussington Brothers*, plays a blend of Caribbean, French and Latin rhythms. There is no theatre, but plays are sometimes put on at the Ruthwill Auditorium. The Anguilla National Creative Arts Association (ANCAA) has a performing arts section, the National Theatre Group, which has training workshops and performs at hotels during high season. Visitors with theatre expertise are welcome to participate. Contact the theatre co-ordinator, Ray Tabor T4976685, rbtabor@anguillanet.com. The Mayoumba Folkloric Theatre puts on a song, dance and drama show at *La Sirena*, Mead's Bay, on Thu nights, T4976827.

Festivals

The annual *Moonsplash Music Festival* is a 3-day event held in **Mar** at *Dune Preserve* on Rendezvous Bay, organized principally by *Bankie Banx*, coinciding with the *Jazz and Arts Festival* T4972949, www.artfestival.ai There are international and local artists, including *Bankie Banx and the Dune People*, www.dunepreserve.com *Easter Monday Boat Racing* is a fund day, with lots of activities and picnics. In the last week of **May** there is the *Festival del Mar*, a sea festival with fishing tournaments, regattas and lots of seafood and *Anguilla Day* on 30 May commemorates the beginning of the Anguillian Revolution in 1967, with parades, boat races and sporting competitions. *Carnival/Anguilla Summer Festival* is at the beginning of **Aug** (the Fri before the first Mon), when the island comes to life with street dancing, Calypso competitions, the *Carnival Queen Coronation*, the *Prince and Princess Show*, nightly entertainment in The Valley and beach barbecues. The first week in **Nov** is *Tourism Week*.

Art galleries *Devonish Art Gallery*, West End Rd, T4972949, F4972735, http://devonish.ai, with works by Courtney Devonish and other local and international sculptors, painters, potters, etc. On the road from The Valley to Crocus Hill is *Loblolly Gallery*, T4972263, www.loblollygallery.com Open Tue-Sat 0900-1700, features 8 local artists working in oil and acrylic. *Savannah Gallery*, next to *Loblolly Gallery*, T4972263, F4974017. Paintings, prints and crafts from all over the Caribbean, a lot of Haitian art, several local artists too. *L'Atelier*, Michèle Lavalette, a French artist and photographer who specializes in flowers, in oil, acrylic and pastels, has her studio in North Hill, T4975668. Open daily 1000-1730, she has designed postage stamps. **Mother Weme** (Weme Caster) sells originals and limited edition prints of her paintings of local scenes from her home on the Sea Rocks, near Island Harbour, T4974504 for an appointment, prices for prints start from US$75 and for her acrylic and oil paintings from US$300. *The Arts and Crafts Centre*, next to the Public Library, T4972949. Pottery, lace, locally made dolls, shell art, paintings and prints. *Cheddie's Carving Studio*, opposite *Devonish Art Gallery*, T4976027. Cheddie Richardson is a wood sculptor who uses the roseberry roots found among the rocks on the shore, some of his pieces have been cast in bronze. Jo-Anne Mason has produced a map of all the art galleries with a brief description of each, available in hotels and galleries, www.anguillaart.com **Bookshop** *National Bookstore*, in the Social Security Complex next to Cable and Wireless, The Valley. Open Mon-Sat 0800-1700, wide selection of novels, magazines, non-fiction, children's books, tourist guides, Caribbean history and literature, managed by Mrs Kelly. A *Dictionary of Anguillian Language* is a 34-page booklet, published by the Adult and Continuing Education Unit. **Gifts** *Caribbean Fancy* boutique and gift shop is at George Hill at the traffic lights, T4973133, F4973513. **Music** *Ellie's Record Shop* sells Caribbean and international music, T4975073, F4975317. Open 1000-1800 at Fairplay Commercial Complex.

Shopping

There are public **tennis** courts at Ronald Webster Park. Several hotels have tennis courts but some are for guests only; *Cinnamon Reef* has 2 at a cost of US$25 per hr for non-residents; *Carimar Beach Club*, US$20 per hr; *Masara Resort*, US$10 per hr; *Rendezvous Bay*, US$5 per hour; *Spindrift Apartments*, US$5-10 per hr. For spectator sports, call the **Sports Officer**, T4972317, for information on fixtures. There is **cricket**, **basketball**, **soccer**, **volleyball**, **softball**, **cycling** and **track and field**. Cricket is played at the Ronald Webster Park, including international matches. **Horse riding**, with beach and trail rides, is offered by *Cliffside Riding Stables*, T2353667, 0930, 90 mins, US$50, 1100 and 1415, 1 hr, US$40, 1630, sunset ride US$50, private rides for experienced riders (English or Western saddles), US$60. The **Optimist Triathlon** is held at the beginning of Oct, with teams of 3 competing in fun or serious categories: bicycle, road run and swimming.

Sports
For diving and watersports, see pages 458 and 459

Malliouhana Travel and Tours, The Quarter, T4972431, mtt@anguillanet.com *Bennie's Travel and Tours*, Caribbean Commercial Centre, transfers, car rental, island tours, day trips, T4972788, bennies@anguillanet.com *J N Gumbs' Travel Agency* is the local LIAT and Winair agent, T4972238/9, F4973351.

Tour operators

Air **Wallblake Airport** is just outside The Valley, T4972514. *American Eagle*, T4973500, has a daily air link with Puerto Rico which connects with their other US flights. *LIAT* (at *Gumbs Travel Agency*), T4972238, and *Caribbean Star*, T4978698, have daily flights from Antigua. *Winair*, T4972238, F4973351, provides several daily flights from St Maarten (7 mins). Other routes served by *LIAT*, *Caribbean Star* and/or *Winair* are from Barbados, Dominica, Guyana, Nevis, St-Barts, St Kitts, St Thomas and Tortola. *Coastal Air Transport*, T4972431, flies from St Croix, US Virgin Islands. *Tyden Air*, T4972719, F4973079, operate charters and air taxi services

Transport

Leeward Islands

to the British and USVI, St Maarten and St Kitts. In St Maarten, you can get bookings for Anguilla on the spot. *Transanguilla*, another air taxi service, offers the flight for US$35 each way. *Carib Aviation*, T268-4623147, charter flights will meet any incoming flight in Antigua and fly you to Anguilla without you having to clear Antiguan customs.

Boat The principal port is **Sandy Ground**, T4976403. The service for the 20-min ferry between Blowing Point and Marigot starts at 0730 from Anguilla and 0800 from Marigot, and continues every 30-40 mins. 1-way fare US$10, children under 12 US$5, pay on board. The last ferry from Anguilla at 1815 and from Marigot at 1900 costs US$12. Put your name and passport number on the manifest before boarding (at booth at head of pier in Marigot or in the terminal at Blowing Point) and pay departure tax of US$3/EC$8 leaving Anguilla, US$2/€2 leaving Marigot. *Link Ferries* run a high speed catamaran charter service anytime, T4972231, www.ai/link/ On Tue, the *MV Deluxe* does a day trip to St-Barts, T4976289, F4976322, leaves 0915, returns 1700, US$65 return.

Car hire A local driving permit is issued on presentation of a valid driver's licence from your home country and can be bought at car rental offices; US$20 per month. There are several car hire companies, including *Apex (Avis)*, The Quarter , T4972642, F4975032; *Thrifty*, The Valley, T4972656; *Island Car Rentals*, T4972723, islandcar@anguillanet.com *Summer Set Car Rental*, T4975278, summerset@anguillanet.com *Highway Rent-a-Car*, George Hill, by the traffic lights, T4972183, www.rentalcars.ai, *Rodco*, T4972773, www.mrat.com/rodco Rates are from US$25 per day off season, US$40 per day high season, plus insurance, jeeps from US$45. You can normally bargain for a good rate if you rent for more than 3 days, 7th day is usually free, some offer discounts on internet bookings. Fuel costs US$1.84 per gallon for regular, US$1.86 unleaded. **Bicycle hire** Anguilla is flat so cycling is popular. Bikes are available from about US$10 per day, from hotels or about 6 rental companies.

Taxi Expensive and the driver usually quotes in US dollars, not EC dollars; rates are set by the Government: from Wallblake Airport to The Valley costs about US$6; from The Valley to Blowing Point (ferry) US$12; from the airport to *Cove Castles* or *Blue Waters* is US$22. Between 1800-0600 you pay US$2 extra. To hire a taxi for a 2-hr tour of the island is US$40 for 2 people, US$5 for additional passengers. Dispatchers are at the airport (T4975054) and ferry (T4976089); there is no central office.

Directory **Banks** In The Valley, *FirstCaribbean International Bank*, T4972301, F4972980, Box 140. *National Bank of Anguilla*, T4972101, www.nba.ai *Scotiabank*, Fairplay Commercial Centre, The Valley, T4973333, F4973344, ATM linked to Plus, Visa and Mastercard, maximum withdrawal US$600. **Communications Internet**: Most hotels offer internet access to their guests. *Internet Café Voyage*, Caribbean Commercial Centre, The Valley, T4985551, benjc@hotmail.com Mon-Sat 0900-1800, Sun 1400-1800, US$2 for 15 mins, US$7 for 1 hr, printing US$1 per page. *Bits & Bites*, Sandy Ground, next to *Johnno's*, is a breakfast and internet café, also rooms to rent. **Post**: The main post office is in The Valley, T4972528, F4975455. Open Mon-Fri 0800-1530. Commemorative stamps and other collections sold. **Telephone**: *Cable and Wireless*, T4973100, open Mon-Fri 0800-1700, Sat, Sun, holidays 0900-1300. Caribbean phone cards are available throughout the islands. There are 2 AT&T USA direct telephones by Cable and Wireless office in The Valley and by the airport. For credit card calls overseas T1800-8778000. **Embassies and consulates** As a British dependent territory, all are in the UK. **Medical services** The *Princess Alexandra Hospital*, T4972551/2. **Emergency**: T911/999. **Pharmacy**: T4972366/4973836. Most people drink bottled water, but there is also rainwater or desalinated water for household use.

Background

History The earliest known Amerindian site on Anguilla is at the northeast tip of the island, where tools and artefacts made from conch shells have been recovered and dated at around 1300 BC. Saladoid Amerindians settled on the island in the fourth century AD and brought their knowledge of agriculture, ceramics and their religious culture based on the god of cassava. By the sixth century large villages had been built at Rendezvous Bay and Sandy Ground with smaller ones at Shoal Bay and Island Harbour. Post Saladoid Amerindians from the

Greater Antilles arrived in the tenth century, building villages and setting up a chiefdom with a religious hierarchy. Several ceremonial items have been found and debris related to the manufacture of the three-pointed zemis, or spirit stones, associated with fertility rites. By the 17th century, Amerindians had disappeared from Anguilla: wiped out by enslavement and European diseases.

Anguilla was mentioned in 1564 when a French expedition passed en route from Dominica to Florida, but it was not until 1650 that it was colonized by the British. Despite several attempted invasions, by Caribs in 1656 and by the French in 1745 and 1796, it remained a British colony. From 1825 it became more closely associated with St Kitts for administrative purposes and was ultimately incorporated in the colony. In 1967 St Kitts-Nevis-Anguilla became a State in Association with the UK and gained internal independence. However, Anguilla opposed this development and almost immediately repudiated government from St Kitts. A breakaway movement was led by Ronald Webster of the People's Progressive Party (PPP). In 1969 British forces invaded the island to install a British Commissioner after negotiations had broken down. The episode is remembered locally for the unusual presence of the London Metropolitan Police, who remained on the island until 1972 when the Anguilla Police Force was established.

The post of Chief Minister alternated for two decades between the rival politicians, Ronald Webster and Emile Gumbs, leader of the Anguilla National Alliance (ANA), the latter holding office in 1977-80 and 1984-94. Mr Gumbs (now Sir Emile) retired from politics at the general elections held in March 1994. The main political parties are the ANA, the Anguilla United Party (AUP) and the Anguilla Democratic Party (ADP).

The March 1999 general elections were won by the governing coalition: the AUP and the ADP won two seats each while the ANA won three. Hubert Hughes (AUP) was sworn in as Chief Minister. His period of office was short-lived, however. The House of Assembly was paralysed after Mr Hughes lost a legal case against the Speaker and the ruling coalition fell apart when the ADP leader, Victor Banks, resigned from the administration and allied his party with the ANA. New elections were held in March 2000. The ANA again won three seats, the AUP two, ADP one and an independent one. Osbourne Fleming, leader of the ANA, became Chief Minister.

Government

Anguilla is a British Overseas Territory and Anguillians are British citizens with the right of abode in the UK. A Governor represents the Crown and has responsibility for international financial affairs. An Executive Council comprises four elected Ministers and two ex-officio members, and an 11-member legislative House of Assembly is presided over by a Speaker.

Economy

The main economic activities used to be livestock raising, lobster fishing, salt production and boat building, but tourism is now the major generator of foreign exchange and employment. There are some 1,000 rooms available in guesthouses, villas and apartments and hotels. Growth has been led by tourism, construction, communications and financial services.

There is some offshore banking and the Government aims to establish a reputable offshore financial services industry. 30 out of the 43 offshore banks, who pay an annual licence fee to the Government, had their licences cancelled in 1990 following a review of the sector. At the end of 1991 the House of Assembly approved legislation to tighten control of offshore finance, giving the Governor complete and final authority over the granting of licences. New financial services legislation enacted in late 1994 led to an increase in the number of registered offshore financial companies.

Previously, high levels of unemployment led to migration to other Caribbean islands and further afield, but the unemployment rate has fallen from 26% in 1985 to almost nil, and shortages of labour have delayed expansion programmes, as well as putting pressure on prices and wages. Work permits have been granted to more than 1,000 non-Anguillians, but many people have two jobs. Workers' remittances are crucial, particularly since the 1984 suspension of budgetary support in the form of UK grants-in-aid, although the British Government does still provide aid for the development programme, along with other donors such as the EU and the Caribbean Development Bank. There is no income tax and the Government gets its revenues from customs duties, bank licences, property and stamps.

Things to do in Saint-Martin/Sint Maarten

- Celebrate **Bastille Day** the Caribbean way with boat races and jump-ups.
- For a morning away from the beach visit the **butterfly farm** where there is a lovely collection of colourful specimens.
- Visit Philipsburg for a duty-free **shopping** spree and Marigot for French designer wear.
- You'll be spoilt for choice when it comes to wining and dining, but Grand Case specializes in open-air **waterfront bistros** and bars offering French gourmet food in the tropics.

Saint-Martin/Sint Maarten

IDD code:
St-Martin 590;
Sint Maarten 599-5
Colour map 3, grid B1
Population: St-Martin
28,518;
Sint Maarten 33,459

Shared amicably between Holland and France, this island is the smallest in the world to be divided by two nations and offers you two cultures within easy reach of each other. Good international air links have encouraged the construction of large resort hotels with casinos and duty-free shopping in the Dutch part. The French part, although increasingly Americanized, is considered more 'chic' and packed with restaurants, dedicated to the serious business of eating well. There are no border formalities, only a modest monument erected in 1948, which commemorates the division of the island three centuries earlier. Both sides have good harbours and marinas and are popular with the sailing crowd. Heavily populated, there are not many places on the island where houses have not been built, this is not somewhere to come to get away from it all, but it is ideal for a fun beach holiday perhaps in combination with a quieter island nearby. Island hopping is easy.

Ins and outs

Getting there   **Air**   International flights arrive at the **Juliana Airport** on the Dutch side. Sint Maarten has good long distance air connections, with charter and scheduled flights from Europe, the USA and the Caribbean. It is used as a jumping off point for many of the smaller islands in the area which do not have the capacity to receive large aircraft, such as Saba or Anguilla. A taxi to Marigot will cost about US$15. On the French side is the **Espérance Airport** which can only take 20-seater light planes for short hops to neighbouring islands. **Ferry**   There are good connections by sea with both Anguilla and St-Barthélemy most days. Can be an unpleasant trip to the latter. If rough, take the plane.

Getting around   There are **buses** between Philipsburg on the Dutch side and Marigot on the French side as well as to the main towns on the French side. There is no regular bus service between Philipsburg and the airport. However, occasional buses run from Philipsburg to Mullet Bay, past the airport, US$1.50. **Taxis** are available for short journeys and island tours. There can be a shortage of **cars** or jeeps for hire in high season. It is advisable to request one from your hotel when you book the room. Out of season car rental is inexpensive. Traffic is very heavy, not just at rush hour, and there are frequently traffic jams, so allow plenty of time for a journey.

Climate   Average temperature is 26.5° C, and average annual rainfall is 114 cm.

Tourist information   **Local tourist office**: Route de Sandy Ground, 97150 Saint-Martin, T875721, F875643, www.st-martin.org, open Mon-Fri 0830-1300, 1430-1730. Vineyard Office Park, 33 WG Buncamper Rd, Philipsburg, T5422337, F5422734, www.st-maarten.com Well supplied with brochures and guides. Also information desks on Front St.

Flora and fauna

In 1997 the *Nature Foundation Sint Maarten* (T5420267, F5420268, www.naturefoundationsxm.org) was set up, with assistance from the WWF, to protect and manage natural parks and provide education on their significance. Two parks form the initial programme, a marine park covering all the coastal waters of the Dutch side from Oyster Bay to Cupecoy Beach and some adjacent coastline, and a hillside park in the Cul de Sac area. A Nature Reserve (T0590-290272) was set up in the French part in 1998, with over 2,900 ha underwater and 170 ha on land in a strip along the coast in the northeast. Three large ecosystems included in the reserve are mangrove swamp, sea grass beds and coral cliffs, with the aim of maintaining biodiversity, flora and fauna and water quality.

Diving and marine life

Water visibility is usually 23-38 m and the water temperature averages over 21° C, which makes good snorkelling and scuba diving. Reefs surround the island providing habitats for a variety of fish while marine turtles nest on the beaches. **Wreck Alley** on Proselyte Reef, has several wrecks which can be explored on one dive. *HMS Proselyte* is a 200-year-old British frigate (mostly broken up and covered in coral, although cannon and anchors are visible), while *The Minnow* and *SS Lucy* are modern ships deliberately sunk as dive sites. Diving the east side is recommended in good weather, either from the shore or drift diving from a boat. The coral barrier reef is undamaged by silt run off and there are lots of fish, fed by Atlantic currents.

Dive sites

There are a dozen dive operators on the island offering a full range of courses. *Blue Ocean*, Baie Nettlé, T0590-878973, www.blueocean.ws; *Club Neptune*, Orient Bay Beach, T0590-509851,

Dive centres

Saint-Martin/Sint Maarten

Leeward Islands

Sleeping
1 Captain Oliver's
2 Carl's Unique Inn
3 Chez Martine, Hévèa, Les Alizés & Morning Star
4 Club Orient
5 Delfina
6 Fantastic
7 George's Guesthouse
8 Grand Case Beach Club
9 Holland House
10 Horny Toad
11 L'Espérance
12 La Samanna
13 Le Meridien
14 Mary's Boon
15 Nettle Bay Beach Club
16 Oyster Bay Beach
17 Pasanggrahan
18 Paula's Country Inn
19 Pavillon Beach
20 Royal Beach
21 Sea Breeze
22 Summit
23 Tamarind
24 White Sands

▶ ## Touching down

Boat information *(Dutch/French flag)*
Ports of entry Philipsburg and Marigot.
Yacht clearance is done at the port, both in
and out. Off-season hours 0900-1200,
1300-1600 Mon-Fri, 0900-1200 Sat, longer
hours in season, page Port Authority for
Sunday clearance.
Anchorages and marinas St Maarten
Great Bay Marina, Bobby's Marina, in
Simpson Bay Lagoon: Simpson Bay Yacht
Club, Island Water World, Port de Plaisance
Marina, Palapa Marina. No fee yet for
Simpson Bay Lagoon bridge. Dutch bridge
openings 0900, 1130, and 1730, outbound
boats first. This changes during the low
season. The French side opens Mon-Sat
0900, 1400, 1730, Sun 0900, 1730. Good
groceries and laundry in Lagoon. Radio net
VHF 78 at 0730. duty-free Caribbean
headquarters for boat parts, outboard
motors, beer. Saint-Martin Captain Oliver's
Marina, Oyster Pond, T0590-873347; Marina
Port La Royale, Marigot, T0590-872043;
Marina Fort-Louis, Marigot Waterfront,
T0590-511111,
marinafortlouis@wanadoo.fr Port de
Lonvilliers, Anse Marcel, T0590-873194;
Régie du Port de Marigot, T0590-875906

Business hours *Banks: 0900-1530;*
Offices: 0900-1600; Shops: 0900-1800.
Currency *On Sint Maarten the currency is*
the florin or Antillean guilder, while on
Saint-Martin the official currency is the euro,
but US dollars are accepted everywhere.
Travellers' cheques and credit cards are
widely accepted. ATMs on the French side
issue euros, but a few also dispense US
dollars.
Departure tax *Departure tax from*
Juliana *airport is US$6 to the Netherlands*
Antilles, and US$20 to international
destinations. Espérance airport taxes are
included in the airfare. Ferry departure tax to
Anguilla is US$2. Passengers staying less
than 24 hours are exempt, as are French
visitors returning to Guadeloupe or France
from Juliana Airport.
Documents *See page 829. Under a 1994*
Franco-Dutch immigration accord, visitors
to Dutch Sint Maarten have to meet French
immigration criteria, even if not visiting the
French side. Therefore, many nationalities
now have to obtain a French visa before
embarking on a shopping trip to
Philipsburg. The local immigration officials
are particularly concerned that you fill in

neptune-dive@wanadoo.fr; *Dive Adventures*, Pelican Marina at Simpson Bay, T5442640; *Ocean Explorer*, Simpson Bay Beach, T5445252, www.stmaartendiving.com; *Octoplus*, 15 Blvd de Grand Case, T0590-872062, www.octoplus-dive.com; *Trisport*, Simpson Bay, T5454384, www.stmartinstmaarten.com/trisport   Boats are often small with no shade.

Beaches and watersports

Topless bathing is accepted at beaches on the French side, but not on the Dutch

The bays on the south and west shores are excellent for swimming, diving and fishing, and the beaches are of fine white sand. **Great Bay** is home to Philipsburg and visiting cruise ships with a lovely clean beach lined with restaurants and bars. The peninsula of Fort Amsterdam protects **Little Bay**, the next bay west, which has the only shore dive site. **Cay Bay** is isolated and generally visited only by horse riders and mountain bikers because of its inaccessibility. **Simpson Bay** beach is a large sweep of sand with very few hotels on it, partly because of its proximity to the airport, sandwiched between the sea and the lagoon. **Maho Beach**, at the end of the runway, has regular Sunday beach parties with live music competitions; don't forget to duck when planes arrive and hang on to your towel before it is blown into the sea. The most popular beach is **Mullet Bay**, where you can rent umbrellas, beach chairs, etc. It can get crowded in season and at weekends. It is good for surfing when the swell comes from the north. The most westerly beach on the Dutch side of the island is **Cupecoy**, where rugged sandstone cliffs lead down to a narrow sandy beach, providing morning shade and a natural windbreak. This beach changes according to the seasons and is the only beach on the Dutch side where nudity is more or less

Leeward Islands

your tourist card with a hotel address, even if you do not know whether you'll be staying there.

Emergency numbers *Police T542212, 0590-875010, *Fire* T5426001, 0590-875008, *Ambulance* T911 (Dutch side), T0590-292934 (French side).*

Media **St Maarten** *Newspapers:* The Daily Herald *and* Today *come out six times a week. After 1500 in the shops on Front Street or at the airport you can find US newspapers (*New York Times, Miami Herald *and* San Juan Star*). *Radio:* PJD2 Radio is on medium wave 1300 kHz and FM 102.7 mHz. **St-Martin** *Newspapers:* Le Monde, France Soir *and* Le Figaro *from France are available 1-3 days after publication.* France Antilles, *same day. A few German and Italian magazines are sold at Maison de la Presse (opposite post office) and other locations.*

Official time *Atlantic Standard Time, 4 hrs behind GMT, 1 hr ahead of EST.*

Public holidays **Sint Maarten:** *New Year's Day, Carnival Mon (April), Good Fri, Easter Mon, Queen's Day 30 Apr, Labour Day (1 May), Ascension Day, St Maarten Day (11 Nov), Christmas Day, Boxing Day.*

Saint-Martin *See page 563 for French holidays.*

Tourist offices overseas *Minister Plenipotentiary of the Netherlands Antilles, Antillenhuis, Badhuisweg 175 , 2597 JP Den Haag, The Netherlands, T31-70-3066111, F31-70-3066110.* **St Maarten** *Canada* *3300 Bloor St West, Suite 3120-Centre Tower, Toronto, Ontario M8X 2X3, T1-514-416-2334348, F1-514-416-2339376.* **USA** *St Maarten Tourist Bureau, 675 Third Av, Suite 1806, New York, NY 10017, T1-212-9532084, F1-212-9532145; Yesawich, Pepperdine and Brown, Public Relations Division, 1900 Summit Tower Boulevard, Suite 600, Orlando, FL32810, T1-407-8751111, F1-407-8751115.* **St-Martin** *France Office du Tourisme de St-Martin, 30 rue St Marc, 75002 Paris, T/FT53-299999, otsxmparis@aol.com;* **USA** *St-Martin Tourist Board, 675 3rd Av Suite 1807, New York, NY 10017, T212-4758970, sxmtony@msn.com*

Voltage *220 volts 60 cycles on the French side. 110 volts AC, 60 cycles on the Dutch side.*

Weights and measures *Metric.*

---

tolerated. **Baie Longue** lives up to its name as the longest beach on the island, stretching away from the luxury hotel, *La Samanna*, on the cliff at the east end to Pointe du Canonnier, the most western point on the island. Round the point is **Plum Beach**, popular with surfers but also good for snorkelling around the points at each end. **Baie Rouge** is popular with cliffs at the eastern end to add interest. **Baie Nettlé** is a long strip of sand within easy reach of Marigot, but a number of hotels have made access to the whole length of it difficult. North of Marigot is **Friar's Bay**, a sheltered bay with a couple of restaurants, from where you can walk along a path to **Happy Bay** (new resort opening 2003). **Grand Case** beach has been eroded by storms but the sand is gradually coming back with each new swell. It is difficult to walk the length of it because the sea now reaches the foot of the buildings lining the shore in places. **Little Beach**, at the end of Grand Case beach has no shortage of sand but is dominated by the *Grand Case Beach Club* hotel. **Anse Marcel**, north of Grand Case, is a shallow beach, ideal for small children, but packed with guests from *Le Meridien* hotel. On the extreme north of the island is **Petites Cayes**, a narrow strip of sand fringed by reefs, a 25-minute walk along the coast from Cul de Sac.

On the east side, **Grandes Cayes** is popular for family picnics. **Cul-de-Sac** is a traditional village, and departure point for boats to the **Île de Tintamarre** (take all food and water with you) and **Pinel Island** (US$5 per person return) just offshore. The sea is calm and fishing boats come in here. **Baie Orientale** (Orient Bay) is beautiful but rough (beware of its undertow). There are several new developments along the beach and the area is often overrun with day visitors. At the southern end is a clothes-optional resort. Windsurfers and kitesurfers can be hired, with both a good

Leeward Islands

▶ ### Hurricanes Luis and Lenny

St Maarten was one of the islands worst hit by Hurricane Luis in September 1995. Six people were killed, damage of US$1bn was reported and at least 2,000 people lost their jobs in the tourist industry when hotels and about 300 yachts were smashed. The shanty towns housing Haitians and Dominicans were flattened and the government moved quickly to bulldoze the remains, offering jobs and a tent camp for those with papers and deportation for those without. Rebuilding of public buildings, including the hospital, started quickly; cruise ships returned in October but the airport was closed to commercial traffic until November. Only a third of all the private homes were insured, while others (including the Dawn Beach Resort) were victims of a crooked insurance broker who disappeared with their

premiums. Only half the island's hotel rooms were open for the winter season and several resorts remained closed. The hurricane highlighted low building standards and dodgy construction practices, particularly with newer houses. As soon as Philipsburg got back to normal, it was hit by another hurricane, and then another, until it had been hit by a total of six in 1996-99. In November 1999, Lenny struck from the Caribbean side, bringing winds and floods and more death and damage. Most hotels closed for repairs, flights were cancelled and cruise ships stayed away until December. Many insurance companies have decided to cease providing cover for Sint Maarten, and many businesses now shut at the beginning of the hurricane season in June, boarding up their property until the coast is clear again.

protected area for beginners and more open waters. *Club Nathalie Simon*, T0590-294157, www.wind-adventures.com, *Kontiki Watersport*, T0590-874689, www.sxm-game.com From here you can find boats to **Caye Verte**, just offshore. Round the point is **Le Galion**, good for families with protected water, and then **Baie de l'Embouchure**, a long strip of sand separating the Étang aux Poissons from the sea, great for windsurfing and kitesurfing. The next bay, **Baie Lucas** is good for snorkelling. **Oyster Pond** is a land-locked harbour which is difficult to enter because of the outlying reefs, but which is now home to a yacht club and bare boat charter. **Dawn Beach** nearby is popular with body surfers and snorkelling is good because of the reefs just offshore. **Guana Bay**, next to Dawn Beach, is the bodysurfers' best beach.

Day sails There are boat charter companies with sailing boats and motor boats, with or without a crew. You find most of them around Bobby's Marina, Philipsburg, from US$200 a day for bare boat, or around *Marina Port La Royale*, about US$360 per day for four people on a yacht with crew, or US$200-1,500 for a motor boat. There are some 40 boats offering different trips around the islands, some just going out for snorkelling on the reefs or taking cruise ship passengers around. Sailing trips with lunch and snorkelling to beaches around the island or smaller islands such as Tintamarre, Sandy Island or Prickly Pear (see Anguilla), cost about US$70 each. The *Swaliga*, a motor catamaran (US$50 per person plus US$7 port charge) sails daily to St-Barts from Philipsburg. Also the 70-ft motor catamaran, *Quicksilver*, and others which can be booked through Dockside Management (T5423436-7, F5422858) or hotels. On certain days there are sailings from Pelican Marina at Simpson Bay, or from Marigot. The trip to St-Barts is normally quite rough and unpleasant on the way there but better on the return journey. Check the weather, the swell and the waves can be up to 3½ m even on a nice day. The *Golden Eagle*, a new wing mast 76-ft catamaran, sails to Tintamarre from Great Bay Marina, four hours, US$45 per person, breakfast on board, snorkelling gear, T575828/5430068. Most boats offer some snacks, sodas and rum punch. Trips cost from US$50-75, plus departure tax. Check what is available from Marigot too.

Fishing For fishing there are numerous boats available for a whole (US$500-750) or half (US$280-375) day from Bobby's Marina, Pelican Marina, Great Bay Marina, the Marina Port Royale, Marina Anse Marcel or Marina Oyster Pond. Arrangements can be made through the hotels or contact the tourist offices for a current list of operators, including *Lee's Seafish Tours*, Simpson Bay, T5444233, and *Rudy's Fishing*, Beacon Hill, T5452177. Marlin, barracuda, dolphin fish and tuna are the best catches. Game fishing tournaments are held all year round. The St-Martin Bill-fish Tournament is in June, attracting competitors from other islands and a lot of activity around Marigot waterfront.

The largest annual regatta, the **Heineken Regatta**, www.heinekenregatta.com, **Regattas** takes place the first weekend in March and lasts for three days with a round-the-island race on the Friday. It is well attended with nearly 250 boats in 18 classes. A race to Nevis and back is held in mid-June with a day for resting/parties. Other regattas held are for catamarans, match racing with charter boats, windsurf-ing, etc. For information contact Mirian Leffers, St Maarten Yacht Club, Simpson Bay, T5442079, or ask Robbie Ferron at Budget Marina in Cole Bay, T5443134. A popular excursion is match racing on *Canada II*, *True North*, *True North IV* or *Stars and Stripes*, boats from the Americas Cup, US$70, races daily, 3 hours (call ahead, T5422366, Bobby's Marina).

Philipsburg

Philipsburg, the capital of Dutch Sint Maarten, is built on a narrow strip of sandy land between the sea and a shallow lake which was once a salt pond. It has two main streets, Front and Back, and a ringroad built on land reclaimed from the salt pond, which all run parallel to beautiful Great Bay Beach, perhaps the safest and cleanest 20-m wide city beach anywhere. Front Street is full of shops offering duty-free goods. Back Street contains low-cost clothes shops and low-budget Chinese restaurants.

The **St Maarten Museum** at Museum Arcade on 7 Front Street, is a restored 19th-century house, exhibiting the history and culture of the island. There is a museum shop. ■ *1000-1600 Mon-Fri, 0900-1200 Sat, closed Sun.* The historic **Courthouse** dating from 1793, on De Ruyterplein, better known as Wathey Square, faces the pier. In the past it has been used as a Council Hall, a weigh station, jail and until 1992, a post office. Now renovated, it is used exclusively as a courthouse.

The **harbour** is frequented by cruise ships and a host of smaller craft. Captain Hodge's Wharf can handle 1,800 passengers per hour and has a tourist information desk, telephones, toilets, taxis and live entertainment, but in January 2001 a new cruise ship harbour was opened outside Philipsburg. For information on outdoor concerts, choirs, theatre and art exhibitions, ask at the Cultural Centre of Philipsburg on Back Street (T5422056).

A large part of the island is occupied by **Simpson Bay Lagoon** which straddles the international boundary and is fringed by a narrow strip of land round its south-ern, western and northern shores. There are two bridges allowing an outlet to the sea. The main one, just east of Juliana Airport, on Simpson Bay, opens for a maxi-mum of 20 minutes at 0900, 1130 and 1730, to allow large boats to enter the lagoon. Just inside the lagoon by the bridge is a new harbour for mega yachts, an amazing sight. Allow extra time to get to the airport if coming from the east of the island at these times. The other bridge is a much smaller affair on the north side at Sandy Ground, just west of Marigot, used by fishing vessels and small craft.

Marigot

The capital of French Saint-Martin lies between Simpson Bay Lagoon and the Carib-bean sea. ('Marigot' is a French West Indian word meaning a spot from which rain water does not drain off, and forms marshy pools.) Despite lots of new building works, Marigot still has charm and the modern architecture is in keeping with the traditional style. Rue de la République has 19th-century Creole houses with ginger-bread fretwork and rue du Général-de-Gaulle is in the same style, though it dates only from the 1980s. Recent development includes the new, upscale Marina Fort-Louis in the bay in the shadow of the 18th-century fort on the hill, and the West Indies Shopping Mall overlooking the marina and the ferry.

Fruit market every morning in market place next to Marigot harbour, best on Wednesday and Saturday

Shopping is good. Boutiques offer French prêt-à-porter fashions and St-Barts batiks, and gift shops sell liqueurs, perfumes, and cosmetics at better duty-free prices than the Dutch side. At the *Marina Port La Royale* complex there are chic shops, cafés and bistros where you can sit and watch the boats. Rue de la République and rue de la Liberté also have good shopping with fashion names at prices below those of Europe or the USA. The market on the waterfront is a colourful affair with clothing and souvenirs available every day as well as the usual fruit and vegetables. On the right-hand side of the market (as you face the sea) is the taxi stand and the ferry departures to Anguilla and St-Barts. Public rest rooms are on the left next to *KFC*.

Beside the Tourist Office, on the Route de Sandy-Ground, the historical and archaeological **museum** 'On the trail of the Arawaks', has an exhibition from the first settlers of Saint-Martin around 3500 BC to 1960. There are sections on pre-Columbian, colonial and 20th-century history and geology, with lots of information on the salt industry, photos and a gift shop. Most of the archaeological exhibits came from the Hope Estate Plantation, which grew sugar cane and cotton in 1750-1850. ■ *0900-1600, Mon-Fri, T0590-292284. US$5 (US$2 children). Christophe Henocq, curator and president, leads tours to Hope Estate archaeological dig, 3 hrs, US$30.*

Around the island

Grand Case boasts it is the gastronomic centre of the island and the main street is lined with restaurants

Grand Case (locally pronounced *grand cars* in English), 13 km east of Marigot, is a quaint town by an old salt pond (which has been partially filled in to provide the Espérance airstrip) with a long sandy beach, partly eroded at the north end by hurricane damage. At the far northeast end is another beach, Petite Plage, delightfully *petite* in a calm bay. **Pic Paradise** (424 m) is a good lookout point from where, on a fine day, you can see Anguilla, Saba, St Eustatius, St Kitts, Nevis and St-Barts. By 4WD you can reach the top on the track used for access to the radio-television transmitting tower at the top; take a turn-off at Rambaud on the Marigot-Grand Case road. There are also footpaths from **Colombier** (1½ km) and **Orléans** (1 km). Colombier is a small, sleepy village with some wonderful gardens, well worth a visit. In Orléans you can visit the home of Roland Richardson, the only well-known native artist on St-Martin.

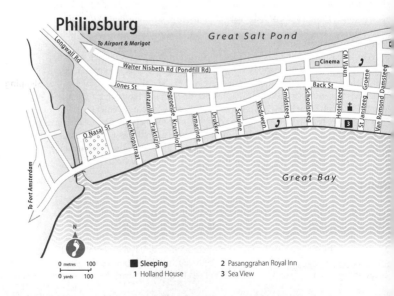

Philipsburg

Leeward Islands

		Sleeping		2 Pasanggrahan Royal Inn
0 metres 100		1 Holland House		3 Sea View
0 yards 100				

■ *1000-1800 on Thu, T590-873224*. **Loterie Farm** is a 150-acre farm at the foot of Pic Paradise, now a private nature reserve of humid forest. It is being restored by BJ Welch, who discovered it after damage caused by Hurricane Luis revealed a farmhouse (believed haunted by ghosts originating from a dispute and murder between the Gumbs and Fleming families) and stone walls. Trails once used by slaves have been marked in the forest up the mountain and in the fields for serious hiking or a gentle stroll. This is one of the few places left on the island where mature forest remains and it is a delight. ■ *Daily, sunrise to sunset. US$5, children under 5 free. Bar open all day, restaurant 0930-1500, 1800-2100, Tue-Sat, 0930-1800 Sun, Canadian chef, local and foreign flavours, great menu all under US$17, kids menu US$5 includes cluck cluck on stick with peanut sauce and moo cow burger, T0590-878616, loteriefarm@powerantilles.com.*

At **Baie L'Embouchure**, there is a butterfly farm on Le Galion Beach Road just before you get to the riding centre and animal rescue. It was opened in 1994 but has been rebuilt five times because of hurricanes. Best in the morning and in full sun when the butterflies are most active. ■ *0900-1530 daily. US$10 adults, US$5 children, reusable ticket. T590-873121, www.thebutterflyfarm.com*

There is a **zoo** on Arch Road in Madam Estate, close to New Amsterdam shopping centre, with a small exhibition of the fauna and flora from the islands. ■ *0900-1700 daily. US$10, children 3-12 years US$5, including a drink and a pass to visit any time during your stay. T5432030 .*

There are several ruined forts, but not a lot remains of them. It is a 10-minute climb to **Fort-Louis** (built 1767-89) overlooking Marigot Bay and Marigot. It was built in 1767-89 by Chavalier de Durat, who also oversaw the construction of a prison (now the fire brigade) and a bridge, known as the Pont de Durat, which opened up the village of Marigot to the north of the island. The fort was used to defend the settlement and its cotton, indigo and tobacco from pirates but fell into disuse after 1820. **Fort Amsterdam** was the first Dutch fort in the Caribbean, built in 1631 but captured by the Spanish in 1633 and partly pulled down before they left the island in 1648. It was still used for military purposes until the 19th century and as a signalling and communications station until the 1950s. Fort Amsterdam can be reached through the grounds of a private timeshare development. The guard allows visitors to park outside and walk to the fort. **Fort Willem** has a television transmitting tower and there is a good view from the top. Construction was started by the British, who called it Fort Trigge, at the beginning of the 19th century, but the Dutch renamed it in 1816. Fort Bel-Air and Sint Peter's Battery gave way to modern development although a few ruins are still visible near Great Bay Marina.

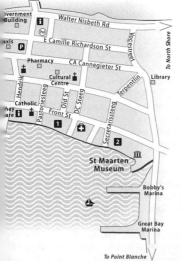

Essentials

Sleeping

There are several large resort hotels not listed here, offering lots of services and activities with all-inclusive packages available, most on the Dutch side but a few on the French side. Hotel prices are high but summer package deals can be good value if you shop around. For low budget accommodation the Dutch half is better than the French. The best way of finding an apartment is to look in the newspaper. A studio will cost about US$400-500 per month in a good residential location. Apartments at Simpson Bay Beach cost US$350-500 per week. On the Dutch side there is a 5-8% government tax on all hotel bills and a 10-15% service charge; the French side has a 5% tax.

Hotels LL *La Samanna*, Baie Longue, T0590-876400, www.lasamanna.com One of the most exclusive resorts in the Caribbean, now run by Orient Express, 81 rooms, suites and villas with huge bathrooms, Mediterranean-style hotel overlooks spectacular beaches, set in 55 acres with lush gardens, excellent dining and wine list, fitness centre, luxury spa, pool, all watersports, tennis, closed Sep-Oct. **LL** *Le Meridien*, Anse Marcel, T0590-876700, www.lemeridien.com In 2 parts occupying the whole of the bay, CP or all-inclusive: **LL** *L'Habitation*, 251 rooms including 12 suites and *Le Domaine*, 145 rooms including 20 suites, the former are larger and better, but both 4-star. Marina alongside for boat trips, surrounded by 150-acre nature reserve, 2 pools, health club, kids club, tennis, squash, racquet ball courts, archery, shuttle to towns and casino, 4 restaurants, bars, popular with Americans.

LL-AL *Grand Case Beach Club*, T0590-875187, www.gcbc.com On headland at north end of Grand Case beach with Petit Plage on other side. 75 studios and suites with kitchenettes, a/c, TV, large rooms, light and airy, very casual, tennis, non-motorized watersports, dive shop on site, video security, room service, car rental. **LL-AL** *Holland House Beach Hotel*, Front St, Philipsburg, T5422572, hollandhousehotel@megatropic.com 54 pleasant rooms downtown, most with kitchenettes, good sized bathrooms, free internet access in lobby, open-air bar and restaurant, on the beach, convenient. **LL-AL** *Summit Resort Hotel*, on hill overlooking lagoon with view of Marigot, T5452150, www.thesummitresort.com 56 EP rooms available plus 20% service and tax, the rest are timeshare, standard rooms have fridge, small sitting area, TV, a/c, deluxe are more spacious with kitchenette and washing machine, pool with view from sundeck, tennis, beach shuttle, outdoor café, internet access for guests.

LL-A *Club Orient* (naturist), Baie Orientale, T0590-873385, www.cluborient.com. Tennis, volleyball, watersports, massage, 136 beach or garden suites or chalets with kitchens for 3-4 people in extensive grounds, being upgraded to dispel former camping atmosphere, mature, relaxed clientele, mostly US, younger families in low season, restaurant, internet, grocery and shop. **LL-A** *Le Pavillon Beach*, Plage de Grand Case, T0590-879646, pavillon.beach@ wanadoo.fr New, elegant hotel on lagoon, walking distance from Grand Case, 6 studios, 17 suites and one honeymoon suite, CP, kitchenettes, phones, beach, watersports and land sports can be arranged. **LL-A** *Mary's Boon Beach Plantation*, 117 Simpson Bay Rd, T5454235, www.marysboon.com 24 rooms and studios with kitchenettes, right on the beach between the airport and the sea, EP plus 20% tax and service, traditional style decor, heavy wooden beds, good bathrooms, lower lobby rooms have no view and are dark, lots of books, restaurant open for breakfast, lunch and 1 sitting at dinner, US$30-40 for 3-course set menu with second helpings, excellent food. **LL-B** *Nettle Bay Beach Club*, Baie Nettlé, T0590-876868, www.hotelnettlebay.com Rooms and suites in 4 bays of 1-2 bedroom villas sleeping up to 6. 3-star, price includes breakfast and tax, a/c, TV, kitchenette, spiral staircase, all have beach view, 4 pools, 2 restaurants, tennis, jet skis,parking, close to shops. **LL-C** *White Sands Beach Club*, White Sands Rd 34, Beacon Hill, T5454370, F5452245. 11 rooms, couples only, private retreat, discounts for cash, all rooms have ocean view, parallel to airport runway.

L-AL *Captain Oliver's*, Oyster Pond, T0590-874026, www.captainolivers.com Right on the border, 50 rooms in bungalows with marina or ocean view to St-Barts, high wooden ceilings, fridge minibar, a/c, fan, TV, separate WC, breakfast and tax included, pool, boat shuttle to Dawn Beach, restaurant built over the water and therefore in Dutch territory, popular sushi bar, evening entertainment, internet access in lobby. Lots going on here at Captain Oliver's Marina, 150 slips, *Moorings*, www.moorings.com, *Sun Yachts*, www.sunyachts.com on site for yacht charters and other watersports on offer. The only drawback is the mini-zoo, with a sad monkey, crocodile and parrots in cages while tarpon, turtles and nurse sharks are in an aquarium. **L-AL** *The Horny Toad*, 2 Viaun Drive, Simpson Bay, T5454323, www.thehornytoadguesthouse.com 8 different apartments with full kitchens, some with a/c, beachfront have fans, no children under 7, between beach and airport in residential area, not seriously troubled by aircraft noise, well cared for, barbecue area, lots of repeat guests, run by Betty Vaughan. **L-AL** *Oyster Bay Beach Hotel*, on peninsula, T5436040, oyster@sintmaarten.net 40 rooms, next to Dawn Beach in large grounds, pool, watersports, boat rental. **L-A** *Pasanggrahan Royal Inn*, in Philipsburg, T5423588, F5422885. Formerly the Governor's home, the oldest inn and where the Dutch royal family would stay when visiting Sint Maarten, 30 rooms, pool, no children under 12, nice atmosphere.

AL *Chez Martine*, T0590-875159, chezmartine@powerantilles.com 7 rooms, kitchenettes, restaurant, overlooks Grand Case Bay. **AL-B** *Carl's Unique Inn*, Orange Grove, Cole Bay, T5442812, www.carlsinn.com 16 a/c studios and rooms of different sizes, some with kitchenette, CP, 15% service, 7% tax, meeting facilities, internet, popular with local business travellers, bakery and grocery downstairs, call in at airport pastry shop for free pick up. **AL-B** *Delfina*, 14-16 Tigris Rd, Dutch Lowlands/Cupecoy, T/F5453300, www.delfinahotel.com 12 rooms, CP plus 20% tax and service, in traditional-style wooden painted buildings, a/c, fan, fridge, German run by Boris and Michael, gay friendly, bar and breakfast room, pool, gardens, dog and cats, beach in walking distance, cell phones with prepaid cards for national and international calls, no fee. **AL-B** *L'Espérance*, 4 Tiger Rd, Cay Hill, T5425355, www.lesperance hotel.com In residential area, 22 good value suites, 1-bedroom suites have sitting room, TV, kitchenette, bedroom and bathroom, 2-bedroom suites have kitchen but only 1 bathroom, good sized rooms, being upgraded in 2003, glass doors open onto garden and pool, internet access in lobby, 5-min walk to main street and buses. **AL-B** *Tamarind*, Goldfinch Rd, Pointe Blanche, near Philipsburg, T542359, tamarind@sintmaarten.net 48 apartments with kitchenettes, semi-residential, swimming pool, deli, public laundry service, good for business travellers.

A-B *Hévèa*, 163 Blvd de Grand Case, T0590-875685, hevea@outremer.com Small colonial-style hotel, 8 rooms, suites and studios, kitchenettes, gourmet restaurant, beach across the street. **A-B** *Les Alizés*, Passage des Escargots, Grand Case, T590-879538, alizes1@hotmail.com 12 small rooms with basic kitchenette, tiny bathroom, a/c, no parking, but great location right on the beach, good for sunset watching from the balcony with view over yachts to Anguilla, short walk to restaurants and lolos. **A-B** *Morning Star*, Grand Case, T0590-879385. 9 rooms, a/c, kitchenette, pool, TV. **A-B** *Paula's Country Inn*, 6 Peach Rd, South Reward (ask taxi to go in direction of St Johns), T5483531, F5484868. 10 studios and apartments, all with kitchen, a/c, pool, garden, internet access, no restaurant. **A-C** *Sea View Hotel*, on Great Bay Beach, Philipsburg, T5422323, F5424356. 45 rooms, some with showers, casino, a/c, TV, children under 12 free.

B-C *Fantastic*, rue Low Town, St James, T0590-877109, F0590-877351. 20 rooms and apartments, kitchenette, TV, a/c. **B-C** *George's Guesthouse I & II*, T5422126, T/F5445363. 10 rooms in Cole Bay, 10 rooms in Philipsburg, a/c, kitchen. **B-C** *Lucy's*, Back St, T5422995. 9 rooms, clean and adequate, friendly and helpful, but overpriced, no children under 6. **B-C** *Royal Beach*, Baie Nettlé, T0590-291212, F0590-291204. 2 blocks at right angles to beach, one 2-star, the other 3-star with some suites, don't be put off by hurricane damage to outside, the rooms are spotless and excellent value, price includes great buffet breakfast and taxes, a/c, TV, large pool, shopping arcade alongside with grocery, post office, bars and restaurants, internet access, convenient. **B-C** *Sea Breeze*, 8 Welgelegen Rd, Cay Hill, T5426054, fortuno@sintmaarten.net 5 mins from Little Bay Beach, 30 simple rooms, most with kitchenette, some with only a fridge, small bathroom, a/c, TV, pool on top floor, residential area, parking, small restaurant on ground floor 0700-2300.

C-E *Marcus*, Front St, 7 rooms, T5422419. **C-E** *Jose's*, Back St, 15422231. Prepay for 6 nights, get 7th free, 11 rooms, very basic, mosquitoes and cockroaches.

Apartments and villas There are several agencies for short- or long-term lets: *Carimo*, rue du Général de Gaulle, Marigot, T0590-875758, carimo@powerantilles.com *IMAGE*, T0590-877804, image@powerantilles.com *IMMO-DOM*, 34 Les Bosquets, Concordia, T0590-870038, immo.dom@wanadoo.fr *Immobilière Antillaise*, T0590-870095, www.immob iliereantillaise.com *Impact*, T0590-872061. *Investimmo*, T0590-877520. *Sprimbarth*, Coin de la Mairie, rue Victor Maurasse, T0590-875865, sprimbarth@powerantilles.com *Cap Caraibes*, Place du Village d'Orient, T0590-520712, www.cap-caraibes.com Lots of properties in Orient Bay, beachfront studios to hillside villas, from US$700-9,000 a week. *Jennifer's Vacation Villas*, Plaza del Lago, Simpson Bay Yacht Club, T5443107, www.jennifersvacationvillas.com

Meals cost from around US$6 for a simple pasta dish or fresh tuna burger, but a restaurant meal will start at about US$12. On the French side, for simplicity €1=US$1, but ask for your bill to be made out in whichever currency is the stronger to avoid overcharging. The absence of tax on alcohol makes retail purchases inexpensive. The traditional Sint Maarten liqueur is *guavaberry*.

Eating
Many restaurants are closed September to October

Leeward Islands

Unrelated to guavas (botanical name *Eugenia Floribunda)*, it is made from rum and the local berries. The berries, found on the hills, ripen just before Christmas and are used in cocktails.

Marigot The *Claude Mini-Club*, T0590-875069, with its bar and dining arbour, French and Creole, serves a Caribbean buffet Wed and Sat, closed Aug and Sep. *Le Bar de la Mer*, Blvd de France, T0590-878179, serves lunch and dinner, good place to go before a disco. Many bars on the waterfront serving barbecue lunch and dinner. For travellers on a small budget try the snackbars and cafés on rue de Hollande. There are also lots of restaurants overlooking the boats at Marina Port Royale, many with open-air dining. *Brasserie de la Gare*, T0590-872064, a brasserie and pizzeria, open daily 1130-2230. More upmarket and expensive is *Jean Dupont*, at Marina Royale, T0590-877113. French gourmet with some Vietnamese and Thai specialities, open 1130-1530 (except Sun in low season), 1730-2300. *La Belle Epoque*, T0590-878770, French, Italian (lunchtime pizzas) and Creole. *Thai Garden*, on road to Sandy Ground, T0590-878844. Sushi, sashimi, weekends. *L'Arhawak*, T0590-879967, international, music, US$10-25. Browse around, see what takes your fancy. Food at these restaurants is usually around US$20-30 per person. *The Bridge*, Sandy Ground, T0590-296357. Grill, café and bar overlooking the lagoon, at night you can see huge fish feeding on shrimp and small fish, good local and Creole food, seafood, goat curry and delicious coconut tart, starters US$6-11, main courses US$11-20 (more for lobster), open Wed-Mon 1830-2230, closed Sep.

Grand Case has a reputation of having more restaurants than inhabitants. Most are open only for dinner and are on the street next to the beach, but these are generally more expensive than those on the other side of the boulevard and not recommended on a windy night. *Fish Pot*, 82 Blvd de Grand Case, T0590-875088, fish-pot@wanadoo.fr Romantic location overlooking the sea, ask for a table away from the lobster tank if you don't want to see the chef arguing with the occupants, excellent sea food and formal service but at a price, starters from €8, main courses from €22, desserts from €7 and wine from €25, open 1130-1500 in high season, dinner 1800-2230. *Rainbow*, 176 Blvd de Grand Case, T0590-875580, www.rainbow-café.com Traditional French cuisine, good service, seafront, with open-air terrace and bar on 2nd floor. *Le Tastevin*, 86 Blvd de Grand Case, T0590-875545 (open for lunch, beachside) and *L'Auberge Gourmande*, opposite, T0590-877337, are both owned by Martine and Daniel Passeri, local wine merchants, with a cellar of 1,300,000 bottles. *Le Ti Coin Créole*, T0590-879209. New, reasonable prices, local food in gingerbread traditional house. *L'Alabama*, 93 Blvd de Grand Case, T0590-878166. Owners Pascal and Kristin are most welcoming, traditional French food in garden away from traffic noise, US$30-50 per person. *L'Amandier*, T0590-872433, French cuisine, bar, pool, sea view, US$25-40 per person. From the small snackbars, *lolos*, near the little pier come savoury smells of barbecue fish, chicken, ribs and lobster as well as other local snacks, good value, meals for less than US$12, recommended. At weekends there is usually music in one of the bars/restaurants along the beach. **Baie Orientale** *Bikini Beach*, T0590-874325, for Spanish *tapas*, *paella* and *sangria*, as well as Angus beef and seafood, helped along with Brazilian music some nights, open for 3 meals daily. *Paradise View*, Hope Hill, T0590-294537, paradiseview4@yahoo.com Up on hill, tremendous panoramic view over Orient Bay and beyond, breezy, run by Claudette Davis, who has written a cookbook of local recipes, open 0900-1800 for burgers, sandwiches, soups and salads, all under US$10, main courses such as conch and dumplings US$15, closed Sat, coach stop, gift stalls outside. On the French-Dutch border, *Captain Oliver's*, Oyster Pond, T0590-873000, has wonderful food in a perfect atmosphere with fish swimming under your table, sushi and sashimi bar, live music and buffet on Sat nights. Next door is *Dinghy Dock*, a small bar where you can choose the size of your drinks and have a nice pub meal for US$10.

For the budget-minded try Back Street, where you mostly find Chinese and roti places

Philipsburg Expensive *Antoine*, 119 Front St, T5422964. French cuisine, great for lunch on the beach or dinner on the deck overlooking the sand. *Da Livio*, 189 Front St, T5422690, dalivio@megatropic.com High-class Italian restaurant on waterfront, run by Livio Bergamasco and his British wife, excellent seafood and pasta, not cheap at around US$60 per person for a full meal, excellent service, best waiters. Americanized French at *L'Escargot*, 96 Front St, T5422483, www.lescargotrestaurant.com Prices around US$50 per person, 8 different recipes for snails, 50 bottles of hot sauce, owners do a cabaret Fri night, book 2 days in advance. **Mid-range** *Mark's Place*, at Bush Rd 70, next to the Food Centre supermarket, has European food for US$20-30 per person. *Old Captain*, Front St 121,

T5426988, www.old-captain.com   Chinese and Indonesian buffet for US$30-40 per person, great sushi, sushi platter US$30, 10% discount for takeaway, waterfront restaurant open Mon-Sat 1100-2400, Sun 1100-1800. *Shiv Sagar*, 20 Front St, T5422299, shivsagar@sintmaarten.net   Indian food, large portions, Tandoori specialities, open for lunch and dinner. *The Greenhouse Bar and Restaurant*, next to Bobby's Marina, T5422941. American food with a Caribbean touch, US$10-40, great cocktails, happy hour 1630-1900 with half-price appetizers, enough for a meal, potato skins are two whole baked potatoes, DJ on Tue and Fri with dancing from 2100. *The Wajang Doll*, Front St 167, T5422687. Indonesian rijsttafel on waterfront, excellent food, Indonesian chef, UD$20-40 per person, pleasant place but uninspiring management and service. **Cheap** *Anand*, Hotelsteeg 5, T5425706, in the alley next to *L'Escargot*. Indian restaurant, cheap, popular with tourists and locals alike, US$15 per person. *Harbour View*, Front St 89, T5425200, right by the sea. Very popular, European and local food at about US$15 per person. *Kan Kantrie*, Front St 5, right on the beach. Authentic Surinamese and local cuisine, wonderful food for less than US$10. *The Jerk Grill and Bar*, EC Richardson St 29, opposite the police station. Local and Jamaican food, very popular with tourists and locals, US$10 per person. *Grill and Ribs*, Simpson Bay Rd, T5454498. The best ribs on the island, all you can eat for US$12.95, reservations essential. *Kangaroo Court Café*, next to Courthouse. Popular for lunch, nice inner porch, sandwiches, all kinds of coffee and tea, freshly baked bread and cakes every morning. *Vermeer Café*, New Amsterdam Shopping Centre. Dutch bar and restaurant, typical Dutch food, US$15-20, very popular on Fri.

Simpson Bay area   *Turtle Pier*, Airport Rd 116, T5452562. Reasonably priced at US$10 maximum per dish with an interesting setting built over the lagoon, live music 2 or 3 times a week, open for 3 meals daily, pity about the caged animals and birds at the entrance. *Tequila Tex Mex*, above *Rancho Restaurant*, Simpson Bay Rd, T5452495. Tasty Mexican food, à la carte and Mexican buffet Thu, US$12.95, all you can eat. *The Boathouse*, T5445409. For drinks and food, live music Fri night, reservations essential. *Jade's Atlantis Casino*, Cupecoy. Sushi bar and restaurant. *Top Carrot*, Simpson Bay Yacht Club, T5443381. Great-tasting health food. *Subway* is the place to find a healthy sandwich for under US$10, at Front St, T5420690, WJA Nisbeth Rd, 1542067/9, and Airport Rd, T5453355. If you need to eat while waiting for a plane, the best place is at *Yummie's Terrace*, bar and restaurant (best sushi on the island) across the street with a supermarket, *Stop & Shop*. Next door is *Lal's*, for Indian food. Alternatively go to *Carl's Bakery*, in the airport for wonderful pastries and snacks. Their main outlet is at *Carl's Unique Inn*, see above, excellent bread and cakes.

The most popular bars with nice sunsets are *Sunset Beach Bar*, 2 Beacon Hill Rd, Maho Beach at the end of the runway (see planes at close range), T5453998, *The Greenhouse* (see above) and *Chesterfield*, Great Bay, T5423484, where you can find yachtsmen if you want to hitchhike by boat. Casinos are a major attraction, most opening from noon to 0300. There are currently 12, all on the Dutch side and half of them in Philipsburg. The largest casino is *Casino Royale* at the *Maho Beach Hotel*, open 1300-0400 daily. At the Marina Port La Royale are *L'Alibi* nightclub, T0590-870839, *The In's* nightclub and the *Bodeguita del Medio* modelled on the famous bar of the same name in Havana. On Marigot Waterfront are *Havana Too* and *Planète* (Wed-Sun from 2200, techno on Tue from 2230, T0590-877261) clubs, *Follow Me* piano bar and *Le Bar de la Mer*, T0590-878179, bardelamer@wanadoo.fr, open 0800-0100 daily, restaurant, bar, ice cream shop, boutique and *Tito Salsa Café Latino* with dance lessons for salsa, merengue, bachata, zouk, rumba. In Grand Case are *Calmos Café* for live music and *The Pub*, a cocktail bar which holds a champagne party on Sun with a free glass to females after 2200. Grand Case normally has live music Fri-Sun in high season with beach party style entertainment in one of the many bars. The *Q Club* disco at Maho is the most popular on the island. *Bliss*, *Caravanserai Resort*, next to the *Sunset Beach Bar* (Beacon Hill), is a restaurant and nightclub, open-air dining and dancing. *The Castle*, at the Sunset Theatre Building, Simpson Bay, has a lounge, tapas, club, with different theme nights and DJs. Look out for *Jack* (Irish folk songs, etc), *Pandora's Box* (classic rock and roll), *King Beau Beau*, the most popular bands of the last few years. Every full moon there is a beach party at Friar's Bay starting around 2100-2200, barbecues on the beach every Fri and Sat. Fri evenings and Sun afternoons (popular with all the family) locals like *Boo Boo Jam*, at Baie Orientale, where there is lots of merengue, salsa and zouk.

Nightlife
St Martin's Week lists what's on where and when for the coming week

Leeward Islands

Entertainment　**Cinemas** *Le Cinéma MJC*, Sandy Ground, T0590-871844. *The Sunset Theatre*, in Simpson Bay, T5443630, has recent films, US$6. Opposite the New Amsterdam Shopping Centre there is a **bowling** centre, *FX Bowling*, T5428963, a cyberpub, restaurants and play areas for the kids.

Festivals　*Carnival* in Sint Maarten starts in **mid-Apr** and lasts for 3 weeks, culminating in the burning of King Mo-Mo. It is one of the biggest in the area, with up to 100,000 people taking part. Most events are held at the Carnival Village, next to the university. In Saint-Martin it is held pre-Lent in **Feb** and most of the events are at the Carnival Village in Marigot. It is not as big and grandiose as on the Dutch side, but it is growing and there are calypso and beauty contests and a Grand Parade. The *Heineken Regatta* in **Mar** is a big party on both sides of the island with lots of events organized around the yacht racing. *Bastille Day,*14 Jul, has live music, jump-ups and boat races; the celebrations move to Grand Case the weekend after (more fun) for *Schoelcher Day* on 21 Jul. On 11 Nov both sides of the island celebrate *Discovery Day* of St-Martin/St Maarten, the *Armistice* and there are celebrations in French Quarter. In Grand Case parades are held with costumes and music at *Christmas*, *New Year* and *Easter*.

Shopping　**Duty-free** shopping in Philipsburg is a tourist attraction, but it helps if you have an idea of
Check your duty-free　prices at home to compare, and shop around as prices vary. In the electronics and camera
allowance when　shops many outdated models are on display. European visitors planning to take home hi-fi or
returning home　domestic appliances should make sure that they can be switched to 220 volts. Most of the shops are along Front St. Open 0900-1800. *Guavaberry Emporium*, 8-10 Front St, is the best place to taste and buy the local liqueur, neat or in cocktail mixes. *Barrel Liquor*, 114 Old St (a mini mall), sells the cheapest **liquor** in town. Many liquor stores will deliver to your hotel or boat. *The Shipwreck Shop*, Front St, Philipsburg, T5422962, sells some **books** and magazines as well as gifts and T-shirts. Marigot has a large crop of **art galleries**, including *Camaïeu*, rue Kennedy, T0590-872578, *Galerie Valentin*, 112 Les Amandiers, T0590-870894, *Galeries Gingerbread*, Arrière Port de Galisbay, T0590-877321, *Graffiti's* at Les Amandiers, T0590-879533, and *Roland Richardson*, rue de la République, T0590-873221. The large **food** stores have imported foods from Holland, France and the USA (good prices for wine, beer and spirits).

Sports　All the large hotels have **tennis** courts, but check availability. There is an 18-hole championship
For diving and　**golf** course at *Mullet Bay Resort*, which stretches along the shores of Mullet Pond and Simpson
watersports, see　Bay Lagoon. The *Road Runners Club*, St Maarten, has a fun run of 5-10 km every Wed at 1730
pages 469 and 470　and Sun at 1830, starting from the *Pelican Resort & Casino* car park. On Sunday at 0700 there are two 20-km runs. There are monthly races with prizes and an annual relay race around the island to relive the legendary race between the Dutch and the French when they divided the island. Contact Rose, T5567815. **Horse riding** is available for all levels, whether you just want a beach ride, a swim with your horse, or flat work and show jumping lessons. *Lucky Stables* at 2 Tray Bay Drive, in Cape Bay, T5445255, F5442371, takes groups on a 2-hr trail and beach ride, 3 rides a day at 0930, 1500 and 2030, US$50 per person, children under 12 US$30. Beach rides, pony rides and riding lessons with *Bayside Riding Club*, Route du Galion, Orient Bay, T0590-873664 (Dutch side T5576822), bayside-riding-club@wanadoo.fr There are 40 km of trails for **hiking**, most of which are old paths used by settlers and slaves. They vary in length from 1 km to 6.5 km through inland or coastal scenery. For information contact *Association Action Nature*, T0590-879787, which has an information booth at the top of Pic Paradise, or the Dutch Hiking Club, T5424917. **Mountain bike** tours or just rental can be arranged with *Authentic French Tours*, Marigot, T0590-870511, www.authenticfrenchtours.com, *L2R Location 2 roues*, Galerie Commerciale Baie Nettlé, T0590-872059, contact@L2R-rentascoot.com, or *Tri-Sport*, Simpson Bay, T5454384, www.stmartinstmaarten.com/trisport

Transport　**Long distance　Air**　The international airport is Juliana, at Simpson Bay. Flight information T5455757. A taxi into Philipsburg costs US$10-15 and to Marigot US$15. **Air From Europe** *KLM* from Amsterdam, *Air France* from Paris. **From North America** Charlotte (*US Air*), Fort Lauderdale (*American Airlines*), Hartford (*US Air*), Los Angeles (*American Airlines*), Miami (*American Airlines*), New York (*American Airlines*, *Continental*), Philadelphia (*US Air*). **From the Caribbean** There are many from: Anguilla, Antigua, Barbados, Curaçao,

Dominica, Fort-de-France, Jamaica, Nevis, Pointe-à-Pitre, Port of Spain, Saba, St-Barthélemy, USVI (St Croix and St Thomas), St Eustatius, St Kitts, Puerto Rico, Santo Domingo and the British Virgin Islands (Tortola), with a variety of regional and international carriers. Espérance airport information, T875303. *Air Caraïbes* from Fort-de-France and Pointe-à-Pitre. *St Barth Commuter* from St-Barts. *Héliocéan*, for helicopter links and tours, Daniel Hazard, T871192.

Sea   There are no long distance sea communications except cruise ships which usually stay 5-9 hrs. Boats to Anguilla, Saba and St-Barts, leave from the French side. *Voyager*, T0590-871068, www.voyager-st-barths.com, high-speed ferries leave from the French side to Saba and St-Barts. St-Martin to St-Barts departs Marigot waterfront daily 0900 and 1815, 1½ hrs, depart Gustavia 0715, 1630, US$50 return plus US$7 port fees. On Wed there is also a ferry from *Captain Oliver's*, Oyster Pond, at 0845 (45 mins), returning 1645. The ferry to Saba departs Marigot Thu 0845, returning 1615, US$50 return plus US$7 port fees. Reservations required. Credit cards accepted. Look out for special deals taking in both islands with reduced rates to the second. Ferries from Marigot Waterfront to Anguilla leave every 30 mins (or more frequently) 0800-1740 with a later crossing at 1900, US$10 one way, late crossing US$12, children under 12 US$5, departure tax US$2 from Marigot, US$3 from Anguilla. Dockside management, T5424096 on Sint Maarten has details of boat transport.

Local Bicycle/scooter/motor bike hire from *Super Honda*, Bush Rd Cul-de-Sac, T5425712; *Moped Cruising*, Front St, T5422330; *OK Scooter Rental*, at *Maho Beach Hotel* and *Cupecoy Resort*, T5442115, 5444334; *Concordia*, T871424, from US$20 per day including helmets and insurance. Mountain bike hire, repair and sale from *Tri-Sport*, Airport Rd, T5454384, www.stmartinstmaarten.con/trisport, US$20 per day, delivery and pick up available, guided tours. If you have a heavyweight motorcycle licence, you can rent a Harley Davidson for US$112 a day at *Super Bikes*, 71 Union Rd, Cole Bay. **Bus** There is a fairly regular bus service from 0700 until 2400 between Philipsburg and Marigot (US$1.50), French Quarters and St Peters, and from Marigot to Grand Case on the French side. After 2000 there are few buses. The best place to catch a bus is on Back St. Buses run along Back St and Pondfill and only stop at bus stops. Outside towns, however, just wave to stop a bus. Fare is usually US$1 in town, US$1 for short trips, US$2 for long trips. There is no regular bus service between Philipsburg and the airport although the route to *Mullet Bay Resort* passes the airport. Buses on this route run mostly at the beginning and the end of the working day (although there are a few during the day) and drivers may refuse to take you, or charge extra, if you have a lot of luggage.   **Car hire** Foreign and international driving licences are accepted. Drive on the right. The speed limit is 40 kmph in urban areas, 60 kmph outside town, unless there are other signs. Many car hire companies have offices at the airport or in the hotels; free pick-up and delivery are standard and you can leave the car at the airport on departure. Prices range from US$35-55 per day. Car hire companies include: *Avis*, Airport Rd, T5452847, at the airport, T5453959, and St Jeans, Bellevue, T0590-875060; *Hertz*, Airport Rd, T5454541 and several locations around the island, hertzstmaarten@megatropic.com; *Budget*, Airport Rd, T5454030 and Cul de Sac, T0590-873822; *Cannegie Car Rental*, Front St, T5422397, airport, T5454329 and at Simpson Bay, T/F5453465; *Empress Rent-a-Car* T5443637 and at hotels; *Thrifty Car Rental*, at the airport, T5454231; *Safari Rentals*, Airport Rd, Simpson Bay, T5453185, safari@sintmaarten.net; *Alamo*, Airport Rd, Simpson Bay, T5455546; *National*, 17 Airport Rd, T5452488, F5452489; *Paradise*, 108 Airport Rd, T5453737, at the airport, T5452361, F5454378. Both tourist offices have full lists.   **Taxi** There are plenty of taxis, which are not metered so first check the fare, which is fixed according to your destination (the island is divided into zones) and number of people. Tip 10-15%. Trips to beaches or tours of the island can be arranged with taxi drivers. From Philipsburg (or Marigot) to Juliana Airport US$12, to Dawn Beach US$18, Mullet Bay US$16, Marigot to Grand Case US$10, Marigot to Oyster Pond, US$25, all for 2 passengers, additional passengers US$4, luggage extra, children under 12 half price. Night tariffs are an extra 25% 2200-2400, an extra 50% 2400-0600. Pick up taxi at the square next to the Courthouse in Philipsburg, T5422359, Juliana Airport, T5454317, or T147, in Marigot, T0590-875654, in Grand Case, T0590-877579.

Leeward Islands

Directory

Airline offices *American Airlines*, T5452040, 800-4337300. *Air France*, T5454212, 800-2372747, 0590-510202. *ALM*, T5454240, 800-3277230. *BWIA*, T5454646. *Continental*, T5453444, 800-2310856. *KLM*, T5454747, 800-3747747. *LIAT*, T5455428, 800-4680482. *US Airways*, T5454344, 800-6221015. *Winair*, T5454230, 800-6344907, F5454229. *Dutch Caribbean Airline* ticket office at Cannegieter St 93, Philipsburg, T5421564, www.flydce.com, Mon-Fri. **Banks** Banks include *Banque des Antilles Françaises (BDAF)*, rue de la République, Marigot, T0590-291330. *Banque Française Commerciale (BFC)*, Bellevue, Marigot, T0590-875380. *Banque Inchauspe*, Bellevue les Portes de St-Martin, T0590-872121. There are exchange houses for changing from euros to dollars, in rue du Kennedy and in the Marina Royale complex. *Scotiabank*, Back St, Philipsburg, T5422262/5423317, 1% commission on TCs. *Windward Islands Bank*, T5422313. Charges US$5 per TCs cashed. *Barclays Bank*, 29 Front St, T5423511. *RBTT Bank*, Emmaplein, T5423505. *Antilles Banking Corporation*, CA Cannegieter St 24, T5425908, other branches at Airport Rd and *Mullet Bay Resort*. There are lots of ATMs. **Communications** Internet: *Tel Net*, Front St, Philipsburg, 0730-1200, internet US$3 per hr, also phones and phone cards. *Cyberzone*, Emmaplein, Philipsburg, opposite Jump Up casino, internet café upstairs, lots of computers, good comfy seats, US$2.50 per hr. *Notions*, *The Mailbox* on the airport road near Simpson Bay. *St Maarten Yacht Club Marina Business Centre* and *Simpson Bay Marina Business Centre* have computers and email service. *Starbucks* coffee shop in the Maho area has a cybercafé. Post: The French post office, 25 rue de la Liberté, will hold mail, but only for 2 weeks. Letters sent c/o Capitainerie Marina Port La Royale, Marigot, will be kept 4-6 weeks. 2 safe places for holding mail are *Bobby's Marina*, PO Box 383, *Philipsburg and Island Water World*, PO Box 234, Cole Bay. It is not possible to send a parcel by sea, only airmail which is expensive. **Telephone**: To call the Dutch side from the French use the international code 00599 followed by the 7-digit number. To call the French side from the Dutch use the international code 00590-590 followed by a 6-digit number. Calls from one side of the island to the other are expensive. When calling within the Netherlands Antilles, dial 0 before the 7-digit number. There are several telephone booths on the French side but they only take telephone cards. 120 units for e13.7, sold at the post office and at the bookshop opposite. There are 8 telephones on the square in *Marigot* and 2 in *Grand Case* in front of the little pier. Telephone cards for the Dutch side of the island can be bought at Landsradio (Tel em) telecommunications office in Cannegieter St, open 0700 until midnight, or at Landsradio's offices at Simpson Bay, Cole Bay and St Peter's. Note that card phones at Juliana Airport, although marked as 'téléphone' and displaying instructions in French, do not work with French phone cards. The GSM network covers both the Dutch and French sides. **Medical services** Hospital: T0590-295757 on the French side. There is a hospital on Cay Hill, Sint Maarten, with 60 beds, all basic specialism, a haemodialysis department and 24-hr emergency services, T140. **Ambulance**: French side, T0590-292934; Dutch side T911. A helicopter airlift to Puerto Rico is available for extreme medical emergencies. **Useful numbers** Police: T5422112, 0590-875010. **Fire**: T5426001, 0590-875008.

Background

History

See also backgrounds to the Netherlands Antilles, the ABC Islands and the French Antilles

The Amerindians who originally settled on the island named it Sualiga, meaning land of salt. The belief that Columbus discovered the island on his second voyage in 1493 is disputed, with historians now claiming it was Nevis he named St Martin of Tours, and that later Spanish explorers misinterpreted his maps. The Spanish were not interested in settling the island and it wasn't until 1629 that French colonists finally arrived in the north, and 1631 that the Dutch were attracted to the salt ponds of the south. In the absence of the departed Caribs, the two nationalities lived amicably together. Spain then reconsidered and occupied Sint Maarten from 1633-48, fending off an attack by Peter Stuyvesant in 1644 which cost him his leg.

When the Spanish left, the Dutch and French settlers returned and after a few territorial skirmishes, they divided the island between them with the signing of the 23 March 1648 Treaty of Mount Concordia. Popular legend has it that the division of the island was settled with a race starting from Oyster Pond; The Frenchman went north and the Dutchman went south, but the Frenchman walked faster because he drank only wine while the Dutchman's penchant for genever (a drink similar to gin) slowed him down. Since 1648, however, St Maarten has changed hands 16 times, including brief occupations by the British, but the Dutch-French accord has been peaceably honoured at least since it was last revised in 1839.

At the height of its colonial period, sugar cane and livestock were the main agricultural activities, although the poor soil and lack of rain meant they were not very profitable. The abolition of slavery in 1863 broke up the plantation system and the population began to decline as ex-slaves left to look for work elsewhere. Most of the salt produced from the Great Salt Pond behind Philipsburg was exported to the USA and neighbouring islands, but by 1949 this industry had also ended and a further exodus to other islands took place. The remaining population survived on subsistence farming, fishing and remittances from relatives abroad.

However, in 50 years the island has become unrecognizable; hotels, resorts, villas and guesthouses now line the shore and there is no bay untouched by tourism. Cruise ship passengers, day trippers and stayover visitors are attracted by the duty-free shopping, casinos and a wide range of accommodation, as well as the beaches and watersports. Little of historical interest remains, but this has not hindered the tourist industry, which is among the most successful in the region. For those who want more than sun, sand and sea, the island's well-developed transport links make it an excellent jumping-off place for visiting other islands.

France and the Netherlands jointly monitor air and sea traffic around the island

In 1994 the electorate on the Dutch side were asked whether they wished to remain part of the Netherlands Antilles, have separate status within the kingdom (like Aruba), have complete integration with the Netherlands, or be independent. At the referendum, 59.8% voted for the status quo, while about 30% wanted separate status. This was the lowest vote in favour of remaining in the Federation, compared with 90.6% in St Eustatius, 86.3% in Saba, 88% in Bonaire and 73.6% (in 1993) in Curaçao. In April 2000 the electorate once again was asked whether they wished to remain part of the Netherlands Antilles or become independent. A majority of approximately 60% voted for 'status aparte' like Aruba. However, so far the Netherlands have not agreed to this.

The island is shared amicably by the Dutch, who have the southern 37 sq km of the island, and the French, calling their half Saint-Martin, who own the northern 52 sq km, an arrangement settled by the 1648 Treaty of Mount Concordia. The salt ponds in the south of the island attracted the Dutch and during the early 19th century the island enjoyed modest prosperity. The Dutch side of the island has the main airport and seaport and the majority of tourists. The west part of the island is low-lying and mostly taken up by the Simpson Bay Lagoon, which provides a safe anchorage for small craft. The lagoon is separated from the sea by a narrow strip of land on which the airport has been built. The rest of the Dutch part is hilly and dry and covered with scrub, although it can quickly turn green after rain.

Geography

The population of at least 62,000 (33,459 in St Maarten and 28,518 in St-Martin) has mushroomed with the tourist boom: the 1950 St Maarten census gave the total population at 1,484. While many of the residents were formerly ex-patriates who returned to their island, there is a large proportion who have come from other Caribbean islands to seek work. Few people speak Dutch, the official language of Sint Maarten, although Papiamento has increased with the migration of people from the ABC Dutch islands. Nearly everybody speaks English and there is a large Spanish-speaking contingent of guest workers from the Dominican Republic. The French side is noticeably Gallic and fewer speak English.

People

Saba

This tiny Dutch island Saba, pronounced 'Say-bah', rises out of the sea, green and lush. It is the smallest of the three Netherlands Antilles in the Leewards group, and despite some development it is still deserving of its official title, the 'Unspoiled Queen'. An extinct volcano, its peak is aptly named Mount Scenery. Underwater, the landscape is equally spectacular and divers treasure the marine park, noted for its 'virginity'. When not under water, visitors find walking rewarding. Ancient trails weave their way around the island, the most stunning being the 1,064 irregular steps up Mount Scenery through different types of tropical vegetation according to altitude. Lodging is expensive, in small, friendly hotels, guesthouses and cottages, where you won't need a key – there is no crime.

*IDD code: 599-4
Colour map 3, grid B1
Population: 1,349*

Ins and outs

By air (20 mins) or by sea (1½ hrs) from Sint Maarten. Saba claims to have the world's shortest commercial airport runway (400 m). Large aircraft cannot be accommodated. Planes do not

Getting there

Leeward Islands

Things to do in Saba

- When 2-3-m **tarpon** and 1-1.5-m **barracuda** are just around that rock and colourful fish and coral abound, what else should you do but dive, dive, dive?
- When you've done with diving, try walking the 1,064 irregular steps up **Mount Scenery** to get your heart and lungs pumping and enjoy the view of neighbouring islands across the sea.
- Don't miss the highest hotel in the Kingdom of the Netherlands! *Willards of Saba* offers peace and quiet with glorious views, but it's quite a hike to get up there.

land in bad weather in case they skid off the end. Sit up front behind the pilots for an excellent view of Saba when landing. On windy days the boat crossing can be very rough.

Getting around
Hitchhiking is safe, very easy and a common means of getting about

There are no buses on the island but you can hire a jeep or car. It is about 1½ hrs hike from the airport to Windwardside, through different scenery, vegetation and climate. There are taxis at the airport and a few others around the island. They can be hired for tours (US$40) and the drivers are knowledgeable guides.

Climate
The average temperature is 25-28°C during the day, but at night it can fall to 16-18°C. The higher up you get, the cooler it will be; so take a jersey, if hiking up the mountain. Average annual rainfall is 107 cm.

Tourist office
The Saba Tourist Board (Glenn Holm, Zuleyka and Angelique) is at Lambee's Pl in Windwardside, open Mon-Fri, 0800-1200, 1300-1700, PO Box 527, T4162231-2, www.sabatourism.com Plenty of leaflets and maps and the staff are friendly and helpful.

Flora and fauna

In September 1998, Hurricane Georges passed just a few kilometres south of Saba, with wind speeds of 290 kmph high up in the hills. Many of the bigger trees were blown down, but the island quickly recovered and the lower mountain slopes became green and lush after the rain. However, in 1999 Hurricane Lenny attacked from the west, the Caribbean side of the island, and almost totally destroyed the rainforest. Most of the trees were blown down or snapped off so that the mosses and rainforest undergrowth did not grow. Since the hurricane local people have worked very hard to restore the forest and it is getting back to its old shape.

Vegetation on Saba changes according to altitude, and a walk up Mount Scenery is a sightseeing highlight for the many different types of tropical vegetation. At an altitude of 490-610 m there is secondary rainforest with trees of between 5 and 10 m tall. Further up there are tree ferns of 4-5 m, then palm trees, then at 825 m the cloud forest begins (known as Elfin forest), where you find the mountain mahogany tree (*Freziera undulata*). Since Hurricane Lenny, however, the forest remains only in protected pockets. Wildlife on the island is limited to the endemic anole lizard (*Aanolis sabanus*, widespread), iguanas (the green iguana, *Iguana iguana*, the island's largest, can be seen sunbathing on Old Booby Hill in the afternoon), a harmless red-bellied racer snake (*Alsophis rufiventris*, can be seen on the Sandy Cruz and Mary's Point trails if you are quiet), and over 60 species of bird have been recorded, with many migratory birds coming to nest here. The trembler and the purple-throated hummingbird can be seen in the Elfin forest and the Sandy Cruz rainforest, where you can also find the wood hen.

The Saba Conservation Foundation (SCF), PO Box 501, Windwardside, Saba, T/F4162709, preserves the environment on land and underwater, developing protected areas, maintaining trails and promoting nature conservation. The Foundation can be contacted through the tourist office. Janine le Sueur, executive director

Touching down

Boat information *(Dutch flag) Go ashore to clear immigration with the Harbourmaster at Fort Bay or with the Police in The Bottom. Fort Bay has 3 free moorings but it is rolly with southeast winds. The Ladder and Well's Bay moorings (yellow buoys) are available for use by yachts for US$2 per person for anchoring and snorkelling, and US$3 per person for each dive you take on your own. Use a strong line and plenty of scope. Marine patrol will collect fees and explain the rules and regulations. The marine park has a leaflet with map of anchorages and dive sites.*

Business hours *Banks 0900-1530;* **Offices** *0900-1200, 1400-1800;* **Shops** *0900-1700.*

Currency *The florin or Antillean guilder is the local currency, but US dollars are accepted. Hotels and dive shops accept (Visa and Mastercard) credit cards, but no one else does. You may be charged extra for using credit cards because of the slow processing arrangements.*

Departure tax *Airport departure tax is US$5 to Netherlands Antilles, US$10 elsewhere.*

Documents *Saba is a free port so there are no customs formalities.*

Emergency numbers *Hospital T4163288.*

Official time *Atlantic Standard Time, 4 hrs behind GMT, 1 hr ahead of EST.*

Public holidays *New Year's Day, Good Fri, Easter Sun and Mon, Queen's Day (30 Apr), Labour Day (1 May), Ascension Day (Thu), Saba Day (Dec 7), Christmas Day, Boxing Day.*

Tourist office overseas *Antillenhuis, Badhuisweg 175, 2597JP Den Haag, The Netherlands, T31-70-3066111, F31-70-3512722.* **Dutch Caribbean Travel Center,** *Karlstrasse 12, 60329 Frankfurt/Main, Germany, T49-69-24001830, F49-69-24271521.*

Voltage *110 volts AC, 60 cycles.*

Weights and measures *Metric.*

See also Directory, page 491

---

of the SCF, can be contacted for information on hiking and rates. The trail manager and hiking guide of the SCF is James Johnson, appointments are made through the *Saba Trail Shop*, T4162630.

Diving and marine life

The waters around Saba became a marine park in 1987 and 30 permanent mooring buoys have been provided for dive boats (less than half of which are for big boats). The park includes waters from the highwater mark down to 60 m all the way around the island. Spearfishing is prohibited (except by Sabans, free diving in certain areas), as is the removal of coral or shells (Sabans are limited to 20 conches per person a year without the use of scuba). Saba has no permanent beaches so diving and snorkelling are from boats, mostly along the calmer south and west coasts.

Diving tourism is popular in the marine park, which is noted for its 'virginity'

The west coast from **Tent Bay** to **Ladder Bay**, together with **Man of War shoals**, **Diamond Rock** and the sea offshore comprise the main dive sites, where anchoring and fishing are prohibited. From Ladder Bay to Torrens Point is an all-purpose recreational zone which includes Saba's only beach at **Well's Bay**, a pebbly stretch of coast with shallow water for swimming and areas for diving, fishing, and boat anchorage. The beach comes and goes with the seasons and ocean currents but when it is there it is scenic and good for snorkelling. The concrete road ends here but there are no facilities, so take your own refreshments and arrange for a taxi to pick you up later. Another anchorage is west of Fort Bay. East of Fort Bay along the south, east and north coast all the way to Torrens Point is a multiple-use zone where fishing and diving are permitted. Torrens Point is a snorkeller's favorite with an alley through the rocks and a tunnel for divers. Some of the most visited dive sites are **Third Encounter**, **Outer Limits**, Diamond Rock and Man of War. **Tent Reef** is also a favourite. **Ladder Labyrinth** is a dive site which is good for snorkelling.

Saba's rugged, volcanic terrain is replicated underwater where there are mountains, swim throughs, lava flows, overhangs, reefs, walls, pinnacles and elkhorn coral forests

Dive operators collect the mandatory visitor fees to help maintain the park which is now self-financing. The marine park office is at Fort Bay, PO Box 18, The Bottom, T/F4163295, www.sabapark.com It is managed by a Dutchman, David Kooistra, and a Saban, Percy Tenholt, who are very helpful and keen to talk about conservation. The

Leeward Islands

Guide to the Saba Marine Park, by Tom Van't Hof, published by the Saba Conservation Foundation, is highly recommended, available at dive shops, the museum and souvenir shops, US$15. Saba now has a four-person recompression chamber at Fort Bay, operated by medical school people. There are many dive sites of 27-30 m; if you are doing three dives a day you must follow your dive tables and stay within your limit. It is recommended that you take every fourth day off and rest or go hiking. Summer visibility is 23-30 m with water temperatures of about 30°C, while winter visibility increases to 38 m and water temperatures fall to 24°C.

Not much fishing is done in these waters, so there is a wide range of sizes and varieties of fish to be seen. Tarpon and barracuda of up to 2½ m are common, as are giant sea turtles. From January to April humpback whales pass by on their migration south and can be encountered by divers, while in the winter dive boats are often accompanied by schools of porpoises. Smaller, tropical fish are not in short supply, and, together with bright red, orange, yellow and purple giant tube sponges and different coloured coral, are a photographer's delight. Divers are not allowed to feed the fish as it has been proved to alter fish behaviour and encourage the aggressive species.

Dive centres
The marine park fee is US$3 per person per dive, collected by the dive shops

There are 3 dive shops on Saba. *Saba Deep* in the Fort Bay harbour, T4163347, www.sabadeep.com, has NAUI, PADI, SSI, TDI and IANTD instructors and is a full-service dive centre with Nitrox and Drager Rebreathers. They have two 25-ft and one 30-ft fibreglass boats for small groups. 3 dives daily and return to the harbour between dives for the surface interval. All your gear is washed and taken care of during your stay and loaded on the boat for you, or there is well-maintained rental equipment (short wet suit US$10). Dive rates are US$56 single

Saba

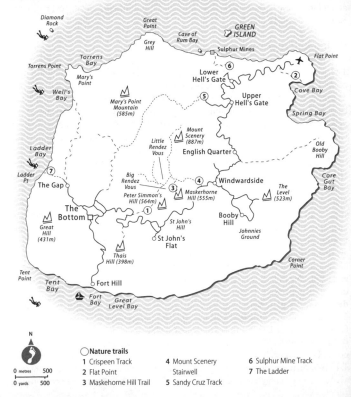

N

0 metres 500
0 yards 500

○ **Nature trails**

1 Crispeen Track	4 Mount Scenery Stairwell	6 Sulphur Mine Track
2 Flat Point	5 Sandy Cruz Track	7 The Ladder
3 Maskerhorne Hill Trail		

Leeward Islands

dive, US$101 double, US$141 triple, US$82 night, all including equipment, Marine Park fees and taxes. Dive packages, also including accommodation and transfers, are available.

Sea Saba Dive Centre has 2 locations: office and extensive retail shop at Lambee's Place, Windwardside, T4162246, www.seasaba.com; Fort Bay harbour depot for all rental equipment and compressors as well as a fabrication shop. They offer PADI and NAUI courses from beginner to divemaster and also Nitrox diving at US$59 a week, unlimited. *Sea Saba* has 2 large, 40-ft boats, but limits groups to 10 divers. 2 dives between 0930 and 1330 with the surface interval spent at Well's Bay for sunbathing, snorkelling or ocean kayaking. Drinks are available on board, some people take snacks. US$90 for 2 dives, including tax and equipment. Night dives on request.

Saba Divers at *Scout's Place*, Windwardside, T4162740, www.sabadivers.com Run by Wolfgang Tooten and Barbara Schäfer, of Germany. PADI, SSI, DAN, CMAS courses offered in several languages, diving and accommodation packages available. The dive shop is at *Scout's Place* and is under the same management. You don't have to stay there to dive with them, but if you do you will get a 10% discount on diving. They normally do a 2-tank dive in the morning, 0930-1330, and afternoon and night dives are available on request, US$41 per dive. Equipment, tanks and weights US$10 a day. Special prices for yachties, who can be picked up from their boat, contact the office or the boat, *Big Blue*, on VHF Ch 16.

Walking

Before the road was built people got about Saba by donkey or on foot, and there are still numerous steep trails and stone steps linking villages which make strenuous, yet satisfying, walking. The Saba Conservation Foundation (see Flora and fauna above) preserves and marks trails for those who like a challenge and for those who prefer a gentle stroll. All of them are accessible from the road and many can be done without a guide. However, they are all on private land and you are requested not to stray off the tracks. Named trails include: The Ladder, Crispeen Track, Maskerhorne Hill Trail, Mt Scenery Stairwell, Sandy Cruz Track, Sulphur Mine Track and Flat Point.

The most spectacular hike is probably the one from Windwardside up 1,064 steps of varying sizes and intervals to the crest of **Mount Scenery**, best done on a clear day otherwise you end up in the clouds. It is a hard slog, 1½ hours each way, but a road goes part of the way up. The summit has now been cleared (*Cable & Wireless* have built a telecommunications tower there by helicopter drops) and there is a spectacular view down to Windwardside and the surrounding isles if it is not cloudy. Take a sweater and waterproof jacket, it can be very rough and slippery after rain. There are lots of birds, lizards, snakes and land crabs, and the botanical changes are noticeable as you climb. There is also a five-hour walk through a variety of ecosystems circling Mount Scenery. Starting from Windwardside, walk up the road to Upper Hell's Gate, then take the Sandy Cruz trail to the banana plantation. Proceed on the Sandy Cruz trail extension to Troy Hill, where you meet the road which takes you to The Bottom. A short walk up the road out of The Bottom towards Windwardside brings you to the start of the Crispeen Track, which is followed back to Windwardside.

The Ladder is a long path of stone steps from the shore up to The Bottom, up which all provisions used to be hauled from boats before the road was built. For the **Sulphur Mine** take the turning at **Hell's Gate** (church has a big sign saying Hell's Gate outside it!), past *The Gate House* and keep on to the end of the houses. After some steps the trail begins. Walk for about 20 minutes until you get to a sign for a turning to the right leading down to the remains of the old mines and the cliffs of the north coast, with splendid scenery. It is also possible to carry on along the island, through forests less damaged by the hurricanes, towards **Mary's Point**. However, the Conservation Foundation does not recommend you go far along this old path as several people have got lost. Best to take a guide. There are magnificent views of the northern coastal cliffs, but there is a danger of rock falls set off by feral goats which may be above you. A very nice lookout point is from **Booby Hill**, up the 66 terraced steps to the Booby Hill Peak.

There is a picnic place overlooking Ladder Bay

Leeward Islands

The tourist office has leaflets on the nature trails and hiking on Saba, but in many places a guide is recommended. Interpretative and directional signs are variable because of weather damage. *Saban Trails… A Walking & Hiking Guide* published by the Saba Conservation Foundation, gives information on 11 trails and the flora, fauna and historical remains. However, it was published in 1998 before Hurricane Lenny. James Johnson, T4162630, a local man and the trails manager, does guided tours after 1500 weekdays and all day at weekends, US$40-50 per group, maximum eight people. He knows the island intimately and although he only knows local plant and animal names, he makes up for this with stories about past inhabitants.

Around the island

There are four picture book villages on Saba, connected by a single spectacular 10.5-km road which begins at the airport and ends at the pier. The road itself is a feat of engineering, designed and built in the 1940s by Josephus Lambert Hassell (1906-83), who studied road construction by correspondence course after Dutch engineers said it was impossible to build a road on Saba. From the airport, the road rises to **Hell's Gate** and then on through banana plantations to **Windwardside**, where most of the hotels and shops are situated. There is a small museum, a bank and post office. **Lambee's Place**, originally the home of Josephus Lambert Hassell, now houses the tourist office, *Sea Saba Dive Shop*, *Bread fruit Gallery*, *El Momo Folk Art* and *Y2K Café* (bakery, bar and grill). The **Harry L Johnson Museum** was once a sea captain's house, built in 1840 and a typical, tiny, four-room Saban house on one floor. It is now filled with antique furniture and family memorabilia. The kitchen is in its original state. Croquet is played on Sunday afternoon in the museum grounds. ■ *1000-1200, 1400-1600 Mon-Fri. US$2.*

Windwardside

To Hell's Gate

Roman Catholic
Church of St Paul's
Conversion

Carmel Shop

El Momo Folk Art

3

Sea Saba Dive Shop

Breadfruit Gallery

Barclays (S)

Lambee's Place

To St John's

Holy Trinity Anglican

Harry L Johnson Museum 🏛

The Level

Antilles (S)

1

4

✉ Library

Guido's

3

Booby Hill

2

N

| 0 metres | 50 |
| 0 yards | 50 |

■ **Sleeping**
1 Cottage Club
2 El Momo Cottages
3 Juliana's/Tropics Café/ Johnson's Rent a Car
4 Scout's Place & Saba Divers

● **Eating**
1 Brigadoon
2 Saba Chinese
3 Y2K Café

The road goes on past Kate's Hill, Peter Simon's Hill and Big Rendezvous to **St John's**, where the schools are, and which has a wonderful view of St Eustatius, then climbs over the mountain and drops sharply down to **The Bottom**, the island's seat of government, with a population of 350. The Bottom is on a plateau, 245 m above the sea. It can be hot, as there is little breeze. Leaving The Bottom, the road makes its final descent to **Fort Bay**, where small cruise ships, yachts and the ferry from St Maarten arrive at the 85-m pier. Most of the houses on the island are painted white with red roofs and some have green shutters. Heleen Cornet's book, *Saban Cottages*, gives background information on some interesting houses.

Essentials

There are no resort hotels yet on Saba and even the most expensive are small and friendly. Dec-Apr is the busiest and most expensive season, although divers come throughout the year. Jul is also busy because of Carnival and students return from foreign universities. All the hotels offer dive packages. There is a 5% room tax, sometimes a 3% turnover tax (TOT) and usually a 10-15% service charge. The tourist office has a list of 1-3-bedroom **cottages** and **apartments** for rent from US$50 a night, which can be let on a weekly or monthly basis.

Sleeping
Hotels do not usually give you a room key; there is no crime. The four policemen on the island boast that the cells are only used as overspill when the hotels are full!

Windwardside AL *The Cottage Club*, outside Windwardside, on hill with wonderful views of Mount Scenery, English Quarter and the sea, T4162486, cottageclub@unspoiledqueen.com Owned by Johnson family who also own supermarket, 10 white cottages with red roofs in local style, kitchen, TV, phone, natural stone swimming pool. **AL-A** *Juliana's*, further up the hill, T4162269, www.julianas-hotel.com Owned by Juliana and Franklin Johnson, descendants of original settlers, 9 rooms, cable TV, balcony or patio, also 1-bedroom apartment and 2 renovated Saban cottages with 2 bedrooms, mountain and ocean views, pool, café, bar. **AL-B** *Scout's Place*, T4162205, sabadivers@unspoiledqueen.com Redeveloped by a German couple in 2001 as a dive resort, packages available, beautiful views, CP, 4 basic but comfortable rooms in former government guesthouse, 10 rooms in new wing, most with cable TV, fan and fridge, simple, relaxed, slow service, pool, restaurant, bar and boutique.

A-B *Ecolodge Rendez-Vous*, 20 mins' walk from Windwardside, T4163348, www.ecolodge-saba.com 12 Saba-style simple cabins sleeping 2-4 (2 downstairs, 2 in the loft), restaurant, sun deck, solar-powered hot tub, solar showers, composting toilets, home grown fruit and vegetables, 5-min hike from nearest road but donkey, Eco, will carry your bags, family-run by artist Heleen Cornet, conservationist Tom Van't Hof, their son, Bernt, who is a chef, his partner Angelique and his cousin JJ.

On Booby Hill LL *Willard's of Saba*, T4162498, willard@sintmaarten.net The highest hotel in the Kingdom of the Netherlands! 7 luxury or VIP suites in main building or bungalows further up the hill, all with incredible views, tennis, jacuzzi, solar-heated pool, restaurant with fireplace, long walk out of town up a slope so steep some taxi drivers refuse to go up it, jeep therefore recommended, good for those who want peace and quiet and are prepared to pay for it, no children under 14. **C** *El Momo Cottages*, halfway up Jimmy's Hill, 5 mins from Windwardside, T/F4162265, www.elmomo.com Up 60 steps, superb view, beautiful garden, 6 rooms, built in gingerbread style, separate bathroom building, also an *Eco Cottage* in the sky, the highest, with the best view and the most privacy, simple but clean, friendly, great breakfast US$5.95, snacks available, pool, the only place for budget travellers, so book ahead.

The Bottom AL *Cranston's Antique Inn*, T4163203, F4163469. 130-year-old inn, 5 rooms, 4-poster beds, pool. **LL-L** *Queen's Garden Resort*, T4163494, www.queensaba.com Troy Hill, overlooking The Bottom. 12 1- or 2-bedroom apartments, fully equipped, spectacular view, garden, discounts for weekly rates, *Mango Royale* restaurant. **Hell's Gate AL-A** *The Gate House*, T4162416, www.sabagatehouse.com Reopened 2001, 6 rooms, CP, 2 with kitchenettes, cottage sleeps 3, luxury villa for 10, 2 pools, restaurant.

Eating **Windwardside** At *Scout's Place*, T4162205. Breakfast 0700-1000, lunch, sandwiches and
Many restaurants salads. *Saba Chinese Restaurant*, T4162353. Cantonese food, salads, steaks, good food,
close by 2130, great view, open Tue-Sun 1730-2300, also lunch on Sun 1100-1500, from US$8, best bet for a
so eat early late meal, no reservations. *Tropics Café* at *Juliana's*, Windwardside, T4162469. Does daily
breakfast, burgers and snacks at lunchtime, sandwiches with home-made bread, full dinner
daily except Mon US$9-16, go early, poolside with sea view, takeaway available. *Brigadoon*,
T4162380. In old Saban house close to centre, good reputation with locals, open daily
1800-2100, dinner from US$10, lunch for groups by reservation only, international, creole
and Caribbean food, fresh seafood, lobster tank. *Y2K Café*, Lambee's Pl. Bakery, bar and grill,
pastries and pizzas, kids' menu, great restaurant, lunch and dinner, a few steps away from the
foot of the Mount Scenery trail, closed Sun.

Rest of the island *Mango Royale*, at *Queen's Garden Resort*, The Bottom (see above). Run by
French chef and his wife, French cuisine with Caribbean flair using local fresh ingredients,
excellent pastries, interesting wines, check for theme nights, poolside barbecues, dinner and
dance, Sun brunches, etc. *Lollipop*, T4163330. A small restaurant on the mountainside overlooking The Bottom on the way to St John's, free taxi pick-up (waiter is also the driver), excellent
3-course meal for about US$20, fresh lobster, conch melts in the mouth, local cuisine including
goat and land crab, open breakfast, lunch or dinner, recommended for lunch, walk it off afterwards. *Sea View*, The Bottom, under Thais Hill. Great view over Tent Bay, new, looks like Swiss
chalet, private room for 8, restaurant seats 40, only grilled food, open for lunch and dinner. *In
Two Deep*, Fort Bay, T4163438. Used by divers, open 0800-1800, New England-style food, overlooks water, lunch US$10-12. *Gate House Café*, Hell's Gate, T4162416. Limited menu for lunch,
dinner from 1830, Mon-Sat, Saban and French cuisine (chef Michel), duck, creole fish , curried
lobster and home-made ice cream recommended, excellent wine list.

Nightlife Most of the nightlife takes place at the restaurants. At weekends there are sometimes barbecues, steel bands and dances. Generally, though, the island is quiet at night. In
Windwardside, *Guido's* on Fri, Sat, pool room makes way for a disco, popular with all sections
of the community, soca, reggae, rap and disco, loud.

Festivals Queen's Birthday is *30 Apr*, when there are ceremonies commemorating the coronation
of Queen Beatrix and the Queen Mother's birthday. **Carnival** (Saba Summer Festival) is a
week near the end of *Jul* and is celebrated with jump-ups, music and costumed dancing,
shows, food, games and contests including the Saba Hill Climb. There are parades on the
last weekend and Carnival Mon at the end is a public holiday. **Saba Days** are a mini-carnival at the first weekend in *Dec*, when donkey races are held, with dancing, steel bands, barbecues and other festivities.

Shopping **Local crafts** have been developed by the *Saba Artisan Foundation* in The Bottom and
include dolls, books and silk-screened textiles and clothing. The typical local, drawn-thread
work 'Saba lace' (also known as 'Spanish work' because it was learned by a Saban woman in a
Spanish convent in Venezuela at the end of the last century) is sold at several shops on the
island. Taxi drivers may make unofficial stops at the houses where Saba lace, dolls, pillows,
etc, are made. Boutiques in Windwardside sell a variety of gifts. There are several **art galleries** in Windwardside where local artists have their studios and sell their watercolours, oil
paintings, prints and sculptures. Ask the tourist office for a leaflet. **Saba Spice** is the local
rum, very strong (150° proof) and mixed with spices, particularly cloves, and sugar.

Transport **Long distance** **Air** *Winair*, the only scheduled airline, has 5-6 daily 20-seater flights from
St Maarten (15 mins, US$97-120 return) some of which come via St Eustatius. It is essential to
reconfirm your return flight. Reservations in St Maarten, T5454230, flight information
T5454210. **Sea** *The Voyager*, a monohull boat carrying 150 passengers, leaves the main pier,
Marigot, St-Martin, Thu 0845, returns 1615, leaves **Bobby's Marina**, Philipsburg, Sint
Maarten, Thu 0900, returns 1615, one way US$40 (children half price), return US$60. Island
tour of Saba with lunch, US$30, reservations recommended. Dockside Management, Sint

Maarten, T5424096, voyager-st-barths.com *The Edge* sails Wed, Thu, Fri, Sat and Sun at 0900, 1 hr, from Simpson Bay/Pelican Marina, St Maarten, T5444505, returns 1700, US$40 one way, US$60 return. A deep-water pier at Fort Bay allows cruise ships to call.

Local Car hire Drive on the right. *Caja's Enterprises NV*, at The Bottom, T4163460, F4163463; *Mike's and Son Car Rental*, The Bottom, T/F4163259. Doing it through a hotel can cost you US$10 more. **Taxi** *Eddie*, T/F4162640; *Wilfred*, T4162238; *Garvis*, T4162358; *Billy*, T4162262; *Evelyn*, T4163292; *Anthony*, T4162378; *Manny*, T4163328; *Wayne*, T4162277.

Banks *Barclays Bank*, Windwardside, T4162216. Open 0830-1530, Mon-Fri, currency exchange, advances, transfers, TCs. *Antilles Banking*, Windwardside, T4162631. Open Mon-Wed 0830-1500, Thu-Fri 0830-1600. *The Windward Island Bank*, Windwardside, T4162274. **Communications** Post: airmail takes about 2 weeks to the USA or Europe. *Federal Express* is available. The post office in Windwardside is open 0800-1200, 1300-1700. **Telephones**: most hotels have direct dialling worldwide, otherwise overseas calls can be made from Landsradio phone booths in Windwardside or The Bottom. When calling within the Netherlands Antilles, dial 0 before the 7-digit number. **Medical services** Hospital: T4163288.

Directory

Background

Saba, pronounced 'Say-bah', was first discovered by Columbus on his second voyage in 1493 but was not colonized. Sir Francis Drake sighted it in 1595, as did the Dutchmen Pieter Schouten in 1624 and Piet Heyn in 1626. Some shipwrecked Englishmen landed in 1632, finding it uninhabited. In 1635 the French claimed it but in the 1640s the Dutch settled it, building communities at Tent Bay and The Bottom. However, it was not until 1816 that the island became definitively Dutch, the interregnum being marked by 12 changes in sovereignty, with the English, Dutch, French and Spanish all claiming possession.

History
See also background to the Netherlands Antilles, page 859

The island is an extinct volcano which shoots out of the sea, green with lush vegetation but without beaches. In fact there is only one inlet amidst the sheer cliffs where boats can come in to dock. The highest peak of this rugged island, Mount Scenery (887 m), also known as 'the Mountain', is also the highest point in all the Netherlands. Because of the difficult terrain there were no roads on Saba until 1943, only hand-carved steps in the volcanic rock. The main road has concrete barriers, partly to prevent cars driving over the edge and partly because of landslides, which can be frequent after rain. Only 13 sq km, Saba lies 45 km south of St Maarten and 27 km northwest of Sint Eustatius.

Geography

Although the island was once inhabited by Caribs, relics of whom have been found, there is no trace of their ancestry in the local inhabitants. The population is half white (descendants of Dutch, English and Scots settlers) and half black. Their physical isolation and the difficult terrain has enabled them to develop their ingenuity for self sufficiency and to live in harmony with their environment. Originally farmers and seafarers, the construction in 1963 of the Juancho E Yrausquin Airport on the only flat part of the island, and the serpentine road which connects it tenuously to the rest of the island, brought a new and more lucrative source of income: tourism.

People

The island's geographical limitations have meant that tourism has evolved in a small, intimate way. About 24,000 tourists visit each year, most of whom are day trippers. There are only 100 beds available in the hotels and guesthouses, as well as a few cottages to rent. Those who stay are few enough to get to know the friendliness and hospitality of their hosts, who all speak English, even though Dutch is the official language. Currently, the major source of income is the US Medical School, opened in 1993, which attracts over 250 (mainly US) students from overseas, who spend about US$1,000 a month. Development is small scale; the island still merits its unofficial title, 'the Unspoiled Queen'. There is no unemployment among the workforce of 600. The island is spotlessly clean; the streets are swept by hand every day.

Leeward Islands

Things to do in Sint Eustatius

- Hike up **The Quill**, a dormant volcano with lush rainforest in its crater: tree ferns, bromeliads, mahogany and begonias, where locals hunt for land crabs by flashlight at night.
- Dive the wrecks and reefs in the **marine park** where there are lots of big fish to bump into but very few other divers.
- Visit the ruins of the 18th-century **synagogue** and the **Jewish cemetery** to get an idea of Statia's colonial and prosperous past.
- Go beachcombing at **Zeelandia Beach**, a 3-km stretch on the windward side of the island. Great after a storm to see what has been washed up from Africa.

Sint Eustatius

IDD code: 599-3
Colour map 3, grid B1
Population: 2,100

Very few tourists make the effort to visit this Dutch outpost, but Sint Eustatius has a rich colonial history and a prosperous past. Having made its fortune in the 18th century out of the slave trade and commerce in plantation crops, it lost it in the 19th century with the abolition of slavery and has never really recovered. The main town, Oranjestad, still has the fortifications and remains of warehouses from its heyday, parts of which are being restored as hotels and restaurants. A lot of renovation has already taken place, tourism is picking up and this is an off-the-beaten-track destination worthy of investigation, particularly by divers. There are walking trails up into the rainforest of the extinct volcano, The Quill, and diving is good in the marine park. The name 'Statia' comes from St Anastasia, as it was named by Columbus, but the Dutch later changed it to Sint Eustatius. Unofficially it is known as 'the historic gem'.

Ins and outs

Getting there
When you come in to land, the view of The Quill is impressive

It is possible to get to Statia in a day from many US cities, but you will have to change planes in Sint Maarten. All flights are in small planes, although the airport has been extended to 1,600 m to allow larger jets to land. There are currently no ferries.

Getting around
See Transport, page 498, for further details

There is no public transport on the island but cars and taxis can be hired. Driving is on the right, but some roads are so narrow you have to pass where you can. Watch out for cows, donkeys, goats and sheep roaming around freely. They are a traffic hazard. Taxi drivers are well-informed guides and can arrange excursions, although most places are within walking distance if you are energetic (less than 30 mins' walk from the airport to town).

Climate

Average temperature is around 31°C in the daytime and 27°C at night. Average rainfall is 114 cm in a year. Water temperature in the sea is 26-29°C depending on the time of year.

Tourist information

The St Eustatius Tourism Development Foundation (Mr Francis), Fort Oranjestraat, Mon-Fri 0800-1700, T/F3182433, Tourism Information booth at the airport, T3182620; at the Harbour Office, T3182205, www.statiatourism.com *The St Eustatius Historical Foundation*, Wilhelminaweg 3, PO Box 71, Oranjestad A255, T3182288, F3182202 c/o Eutel. The Foundation publishes a newsletter 4 times a year and runs the Museum (see above) and the Tourist Information Centre and Gallery, 'Little House on the Bay', a replica gingerbread house, open Mon-Sat 0930-1200, Sun 1500-1700, but staffed seasonally by volunteers so opening times are approximate. Local artists and artisans sell their work here. *STENAPA*, Jan Faber, President, White Wall Rd, St Eustatius, Netherlands Antilles, T/F3182661. Good information on walks, trails and conservation at the office by the dock.

Touching down

Boat information The Harbour Office is open 0800-1700, after hours sailors should see guard at the gate who will give directions to the local police station. If not leaving before 0800 clear customs in the morning, T3182888, F3182205, VHF Channel 14. The Harbour Master, Murvin Gittens, works Mon-Fri, 0800-1600. Fly an Antillean flag. Oranje Baai is the only anchorage, prices are based on tonnage, 0-5 tons US$5; 6-15 tons US$10; +16 tons US$15. These rates are valid for three days. After three days, sailors pay an extra fee of US$5 per day. The long pier accommodates ships with draft not exceeding 14ft, the short pier has vessels with draft of up to 10 ft. Marine weather is on VHF 1 or 162.550 MHz continual broadcast. Blue Bead Restaurant sells ice.

Business hours Offices: 0900-1600; **Shops**: 0900-1700; **Banks**: 0900-1530.

Clothing No topless bathing anywhere on the island and men are not allowed to walk without shirts on in public streets.

Currency The currency is the florin or Antillean guilder, but US dollars are accepted everywhere. Credit cards are not widely used (Amex hardly ever accepted, Visa and Mastercard better). Check at hotels and restaurants. US$100 bills often not accepted.

Departure tax Airport departure tax is US$5 for Antilles, US$10 international. If you visit for the day and pay departure tax on St Maarten, you do not have to pay the tax when you leave Statia. If you pay the tax on Statia and are in-transit on St Maarten you do not have to pay tax on St Maarten. You will need to show your tickets and boarding pass for your next flight at the tax window.

Documents There are no customs regulations as Statia is a free port.

Official time Atlantic Standard Time, 4 hrs behind GMT, 1 hr ahead of EST, all year.

Public holidays New Year's Day (fireworks at midnight), Good Fri, Easter Sun, Easter Mon, Queens Day (30 Apr), Labour Day (1 May), Ascension Day, Statia/America Day (16 Nov), Christmas Day, Boxing Day.

Tourist office overseas In USA/Canada: Gail Knopfler, Classic Communications International, PO Box 6322, Boca Raton, FL33427, T561-3948580, F561-4884294. **In Europe**: Antillenhuis, Badhuisweg 175 , 2597JP Den Haag, The Netherlands, T70-3066111, F70-3066110.

Voltage 110 volts A/C 60 cycles.

Weights and measures Metric.

See also Directory, page 499

Flora and fauna

Despite the small size of the island, in the 17th and 18th centuries there were more than 70 plantations, worked intensively by slaves. As a result, most of the original forest has disappeared except on the most inhospitable parts of the volcano. Nevertheless there are 17 different kinds of orchid and 58 species of bird, of which 25 are resident and breeding, 21 migrants from North America and 12 seabirds. There are iguanas, land crabs, tree frogs and lots of butterflies. Unfortunately there are lots of goats too, which eat everything in sight. The Antilles iguana *(Iguana delicatissima)* is rare and threatened and has now been protected by law. The young and females vary from bright green to dull grey, while the large males can be nearly black. The population is stronger on St Eustatius than on neighbouring islands because the mongoose was never introduced here. Neither was the green iguana, with which it has interbred on some islands. The red-bellied racer (*Alsophis rufiventris*) is a small snake found only on Statia and Saba. It is brown with black markings on its back and a pink belly. It is not poisonous and kills its prey (small reptiles and baby rats) by strangulation.

STENAPA, the St Eustatius National Parks Foundation, was founded in 1996. This organization is responsible for the marine park, The Quill, Boven, Gilboa Hill, Signal Hill and Little Mountain. In 1998 **The Quill** was declared a national park, consisting of the volcano and the limestone White Wall to its south. The Quill is protected above 250 m, but the White Wall is protected down to the high water line. At the crater of The Quill there are many species usually found in tropical rainforest: huge tree ferns, mahogany, giant elephant ears, begonias, figs, plantains, bromeliads, the balsam tree and many more. The southern slope of the mountain has not

Leeward Islands

been fully explored by botanists. STENAPA has developed the 5.6-ha **Miriam C Schmidt Botanical Garden** on the southeast side of The Quill in the area called 'Behind the Mountain'. There are barbecue areas, a picnic pavilion, marked trails, a bee yard and orchid gardens.

Diving and marine life

Water visibility can be over 30 m and diving and snorkelling are very good

Statia's waters offer a wonderful combination of coral reefs, marine life and historic shipwrecks. Diving is excellent, with plenty of corals, sea fans, hydroids and big fish such as groupers and barracudas, as well as rays, turtles and the occasional dolphin, but unlike some other Caribbean diving destinations, you will not bump into any other divers underwater. St Eustatius Marine Park was established in 1996 and became operational in 1998. STENAPA has identified four protected areas: the southern part from Crooks Castle to White Wall is a restricted fishing zone; the wreck sites in Oranje Bay, STENAPA Reef (a modern wreck site) and the northern

Sint Eustatius

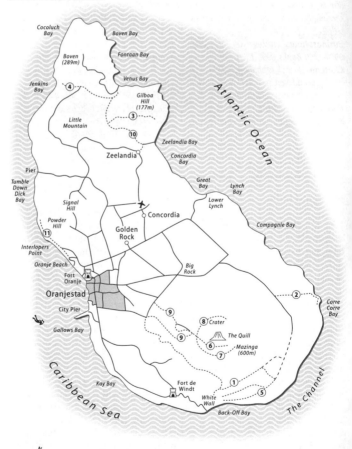

Nature trails
1 Around the mountain
2 Corre Corre Bay
3 Gilboa Hill
4 Jenkins Bay
5 Soldier Gut
6 The Crater
7 The Mazinga
8 The Panorama
9 The Quill
10 Venus Bay
11 White Bird

Leeward Islands

marine park are open for fishing and diving. Marine park fees are US$3 per dive, US$3 per snorkelling trip when using the park buoys, US$35 for a non-resident annual pass. You may not anchor anywhere in the park, spear guns and spear fishing are prohibited in all waters around Statia, nothing may be removed, whether animals, plants or historical artefacts, you may not touch or feed marine life. The marine park office is at Lower Town, close to the harbour.

Dive Statia is run by Rudy and Rinda Hees, T3182435, F3182539, www.divestatia. com They have a comfortable, purpose-built, 26-ft catamaran for diving, on which they take up to 10 divers and 2 dive masters/instructors. They also have a 14-ft rigid boat for training or special dives. A full range of courses is offered at this Gold Palm 5-star PADI operation, including Nitrox certification, and families with children of 12 and above are welcome. 3 dives a day with night dives on request, all dives are fully guided. A package of dives is the best value; a single tank dive costs US$35. Equipment rental is available, PADI open water 4-day course US$350, snorkel trips US$25 with equipment, accommodation and diving packages available with most hotels.

Dive centres
You must by law dive with a local company

    Golden Rock Dive Centre, opposite the *Blue Bead Restaurant*, is owned by Glen Fairs, T/F3182964, www.goldenrockdive.net US$45 per dive, hotel/dive packages, PADI open water course US$350. *Golden Rock* also offers charter fishing and boat trips to Saba. *Scubaqua* (PADI, SSI, CMAS) is at the *Golden Era Hotel*, T/F3182160, scubaqua@goldenrock.net, with their own pier. They have 1 boat, taking 12 divers, and an inflatable for dive courses. Groups per instructor are no more than 6 and the captain stays on board the boat. Drift diving for whale watching is organized between end-Jan and Apr, and they also offer waterskiing, wakeboards and fishing trips. A single dive costs US$29, equipment rental US$20, snorkelling trips with lunch on the beach US$25, full open-water certification course with equipment is US$350.

On leaving Statia Customs officials may give you and your luggage a rigorous search if they discover you are a diver. They are looking for treasure, or artefacts – beware

Beaches and watersports

Oranje Beach stretches for 1.5 km along the coast away from Lower Town. The length and width of the beach varies according to the season and the weather, but being on the Leeward side it is safe for swimming and other watersports. On the Windward side are two fine beaches, but there is a strong undertow and they are not considered safe for swimming. **Zeelandia Beach** is 3 km of off-white sand with heavy surf and interesting beachcombing, particularly after a storm. It is safe to wade and splash about in the surf but not to swim. There is a short dirt road down to the beach; do not drive too close to the beach or you will get stuck in the sand. Avoid the rocks at the end of the beach as they are very dangerous. **Lynch Beach**, also on the Atlantic side, is small and safer for children in parts, but ask local advice.

Walking

The tourist office has a guide leaflet describing 11 trails. **Quill** hikes with local guides are available with a voucher system from the tourist office or participating hotels. Some of these trails are in bad condition, overgrown and sometimes difficult to follow. STENAPA is in the process of restoring and extending Statia's trail system. They plan to make a trail from town to the botanical garden which will wind around the south side of The Quill. STENAPA also plans to restore the path around the rim of The Quill (damaged in 1989 by Hurricane Hugo). The foundation has built a new, clearly marked, trail from Rosemary Lane to the rainforest crater at the top of The Quill, which is remarkable for its contrast with the dry scrub of the rest of the island. After about 20 minutes' walk there is a left turn to The Quill. Carry on if you want to overlook the White Wall. The walk up to the lip of the crater is easy. You will see butterflies, all sizes of lizard, hundreds of land crabs and, if you go quietly, the red-bellied racer snake. At the top in one direction is the panorama trail. The other direction leads to the highest point, called **Mazinga**, which affords a magnificent view. The first 10 minutes of the walk to the Mazinga is easy, then there is a turn to the left marked where it becomes a scramble because of hurricane damage. The last 20 m up to the summit is only for the very experienced. The plant life includes mahogany and bread fruit trees, arums, bromeliads, lianas and orchids. Although it is still quite a hike (about 45 minutes), the new path is in much better shape. From the rim, hikers can walk down a path to the centre. The vegetation in the crater is dense, forming the breeding ground for land crabs, which Statians catch at night. A local guide is recommended. Professional hiking guide Charley Lopes (brother of Roland at the tourist office) arrives at dawn in full combats and beret like Rambo, but tends to go quickly without much explanation, fine for The Quill crater walk, better to go alone if birdwatching.

A road, and then a track, leads round the lower slopes of The Quill to the **White Wall**, a massive slab of limestone which was once pushed out of the sea by volcanic forces and is now clearly visible from miles away across the sea. You can also see it from **Fort de Windt**, built in 1753, the ruins of which are open to the public, at the end of the road south from Lower Town. St Kitts can also be seen clearly from here. About 14 forts or batteries were built around the island by the end of the 18th century, but the ruins of few of them are accessible or even visible nowadays. STENAPA has made a new trail to the **Boven**, the highest peak on the north side of the island. This is a strenuous, steep, four-hour hike (round trip) but well worth it for the view.

Oranjestad

Oranjestad is the capital, set on a cliff overlooking the long beach below and divided between Upper Town and Lower Town. The town used to be defended by **Fort Oranje** (pronounced Orahn'ya) perched on a rocky bluff. Built in 1636 on the site of a 1629 French fortification, the preserved ruins of the fort have now been restored following a fire in 1990, and large black cannon still point out to sea. The administrative buildings of the island's Government are here. Other places of historical interest include the ruins of the **Honen Dalim Synagogue** built in 1739 and the nearby cemetery. Statia once had a flourishing Jewish community and was a refuge for Sephardic and Ashkenazic Jews, but with the economic decline after the sacking of Oranjestad by Admiral Rodney, most of the Jewish congregation left. The **Dutch Reformed Church**, consecrated in 1755, suffered a similar fate when its congregation fled. The square tower has been restored but the walls are open to the elements. Legend has it that Admiral Rodney found most of his booty here after noticing that there were a surprising number of funerals for such a small population. A coffin, which he ordered to be opened, was found to be full of valuables and further digging revealed much more.

It is possible to walk round the village and see the sights in a morning. The museum or tourist office will provide you with a Walking Tour brochure listing the historical sites

On Wilhelminaweg in the centre, the 18th-century Doncker/De Graaff House, once a private merchant's house and also where Admiral Rodney lived, has been restored and is now the **Museum of the St Eustatius Historical Foundation**. There is a pre-Columbian section which includes an Amerindian skeleton and a reconstruction of 18th-century rooms at the height of Statia's prosperity. It is worth a visit for the graphic descriptions of the slave trade. Archaeological excavations at Golden Rock near the airport have uncovered a large Amerindian village with the only complete floor plan of Indian houses found in the Caribbean. All the houses are round or slightly oval, vary in size and accommodate up to 30 people. Large timbers up to 8 m high were set in deep holes for the framework of the biggest houses. The museum contains pottery buried in the ceremonial area of the village next to a grave. The curator normally explains the history of the exhibits. ■ *Mon-Fri 0900-1700, Sat, Sun and holidays 0900-1200. US$2, children US$1. T3182288.*

In its heyday Lower Town stretched for 3 km along the bay, with warehouses, taverns and slave markets attracting commercial traffic. Parts are now being restored as hotels or restaurants. Seven privately owned houses have been renovated as part of the Historic Core Development Plan. If you like beachcombing, blue, five-sided slave beads over 200 years old can be found along the shore.

Berkels family museum, with a collection of household utensils and antiques, is on the Lynch Plantation, on the northeast side of the island. ■ *T3182338.*

Essentials

LL-AL *Old Gin House*, T3182319, www.oldginhouse.com   Now owned by *Holland House Hotel* on Sint Maarten and upgraded into a luxury place to stay. Built with old bricks of 18th-century cotton gin house, 2 fancy suites, 14 rooms, large beds, a/c, TV, phones, CP, the nicest place to stay, English manager, William, will ensure you have a wonderful time, the Belgian chef creates fabulous dinners, credit cards accepted. **AL-B** *King's Well*, between Upper and Lower Town in King's Well, north end of beach by *Smoke Alley*, T/F3182538. Run by Win and Laura, popular with divers and sailors, rooms sparsely furnished but large, CP, ceiling fans, not always very clean, some rooms overlook bar, more expensive have spectacular sea view, accepts Visa/Mastercard. **A** *Golden Era Hotel*, Lower Town, T3182345, goldera@sintmaarten.net   On the beach, modern, 20 rooms, not much charm but convenient and dive shop on premises, manager Roy Hooker is also the cook, friendly but extremely slow service, snack bar/restaurant good, credit cards. **C** *Henriquez Guesthouse* at Prinsesweg, T3182424. On road to airport, 3 mins' walk, 9 apartments, 1 or 2 bedrooms, a/c, TV, mini-fridge, bar and restaurant, barbecue, weekly and monthly rates negotiable. Off the road towards The Quill, **D** *Daniel's Guest House*, on Rosemary Laan, T3182358. Unmarked, ask in Brown's supermarket at bottom of road, Miz Brown is very helpful, no hot water but use of kitchen, taxi available.

Sleeping
Expect a 7% government tax, a 15% service charge and sometimes a 5% surcharge on top of quoted rates. The tourist office has a list of home rentals

Creole and international food at the *Golden Era Hotel*, service can be slow. *The King's Well*, good lobster, steak, German food, Jaeger- and Wienerschnitzels, cocktails, friendly atmosphere, owners like to chat and play cards with guests, lunch is served 1200-1400, dinner from 1800-2100, reservations requested. *Smoke Alley*, Austrian-owned, open-air restaurant

Eating
Tap water is usually rainwater and not for drinking

Oranjestad (St Eustatius)

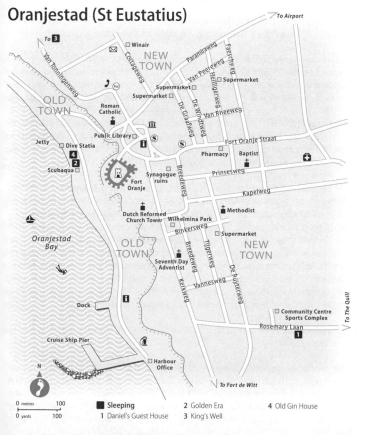

	Sleeping	2 Golden Era	4 Old Gin House
	1 Daniel's Guest House	3 King's Well	

Leeward Islands

overlooking the water, varied menu, Mexican, burgers, etc, and a fun place to be, very popular, occasional live music, lovely place to watch the sunset, closed Tue. *The Old Gin House*, recently renovated, gourmet dining, Belgian chef used to have a Michelin star in Belgium.

Cheaper meals at *Chinese Restaurant*, Prinsesweg 9, T3182389. Shut Sun, tell cook not to put in MSG, no credit cards. *Happy City Chinese Restaurant*, around the corner from Duggins Supermarket, T3182540. Open 1130-2300, a/c, no smoking, closed Wed. *Ocean View Terrace*, just by tourist office and Governor's House, T3182733. An ideal place to watch the sunset. The menu has improved considerably, seafood specials and shrimp creole recommended, daily specials are reasonably priced, occasional live music, happy hour and BBQ on Fri, good place to meet locals, although service could be friendlier, closed Tue. *Blue Bead Bar and Restaurant*, right on beach, T3182873. West Indian, American, Indonesian and international food, reasonably priced daily specials, lunch Mon-Sat 1130-1430, Sun brunch 1100-1430, dinner 1800-2100, bar hrs 1000-2200, occasionally stays open later. *Cool Corner*, on the square opposite museum, T3182523. A popular bar, run by Chucky, who manages to serve drinks, talk to customers and prepare decent Chinese food. *Sonny's Place*, next to *Mazinga Gift Shop*, T3182609. Popular hangout for locals and terminal employees, pool and football tables, music is good, Sonny serves good creole and Chinese food at reasonable prices, lunch and dinner, chicken, fish and daily specials recommended, service can be slow.

For fresh **fish**, go to the fish processing plant (Statia Fish Handling) at Lower Town opposite short pier, Mon-Fri, usually 0800-1300, depending on the catch, they will clean the fish for you. If it is not available at the fish plant approach the local fishermen at the harbour. Grocers sell frozen fish. Lobster is available fresh Nov-Mar. Fresh **bread** is baked daily and best bought at 'fresh bread time', which varies according to who makes it. Bake sales are announced by the town crier: open-air **takeaway** meals of local dishes some Fri and Sat, from 1100, usually at *Charlie's Place*, just below *Mazinga Gift Shop* and Africa Crossroads Park opposite museum. Hotels serve purified water. Bottled water is sold at groceries.

Nightlife Statians like partying and every weekend something is always going on. Quite often you will hear a 'road block' from far away: cars stopped with huge stereos blaring and everyone jumping up in the street. Ask anybody what is going on next weekend, or just wait for the music to start in the evening. The only nightclub is *Peace and Love Night Club*, Paramiraweg.

Shopping *Mazinga Gift Shop* sells local books and a wide range of gifts and duty-free liquor, T3182245, F3182230. Some local crafts, mostly woodworking, are sold at *Paper Corner*, *Dive Statia* and *Under the Tree* next to *Allrun Supermarket*. Arts and crafts also sold at the **Little House on the Bay**, run by the St Eustatius Historical Foundation.

Festivals On **Easter Mon** there are beach picnics with music and drinking. *Queen Mother Juliana's birthday* is celebrated on **30 Apr** with cultural events, sports, food and music. *Emancipation Day* on **1 Jul** has celebrations of the abolition of slavery. The *Antillian Games* are held in the 2nd week of **Jul** with sporting competitions between all the islands of the Netherlands Antilles. *Carnival*, the main event of the year is held over 10 days in **Jul-Aug**, and is celebrated with steel bands, sports and contests and also including a Grand Parade on the last Sun of the month. *Antillian Day* is on **21 Oct**, with flag ceremonies, games and fetes. *Statia/America Day* is on 16 Nov, with lots of cultural festivities and activities commemorating the First Salute to the American Flag by a foreign government in 1776. On **Boxing Day** actors parade through the streets depicting the social, cultural or political group of the year.

Tour operators For a 2-hr historical tour by minibus around the island, ask for Mr Danial at the tourist office in Fort Oranje, US$40.

Transport **Air** *Winair* has several daily 20-min flights from St Maarten (US$110 return) connecting with flights from the USA, Europe and other islands. There are other connecting *Winair* flights from Saba (10 mins). Reservations T5454230, flight information T5454210. *Golden Rock Airways* can arrange charters. **Local Car hire** To hire a car you need a driving licence from your own country or an international driver's licence. The speed limit is 50 kmph and 30 kmph in residential areas. Companies include *Brown's*, T/F3182266, US$45 per day including tax and insurance, weekend deals; *Rainbow*, T3182811, F3182586, US$35 plus US$5 CDW; *ARC*, T3182595, F3182594, US$35 plus tax and insurance, near airport; *Lady Ama's Services*, T3182712, F3182572, US$30-45, 5% surcharge on day rates; *Avis Rent-A-Car*, T3182303, F3182285, US$40 per day, US$35 second day (CDW is US$7.50 per day, US$50 per week).

Banks *Barclays Bank*, Emmaweg, T3182392, F3182734. Open Mon-Fri 0830-1530. *Centrale* **Directory**
Hypotheek Bank, W Flemming, Princess Garden, T3182107. The *Windward Islands Bank* is by *Mazinga Gift Shop*, open Mon-Fri 0830-1200, 1330-1530, T3182846, F3182850. **Communications** Post: the post office is at Fiscal Rd, T3182207, F3182457. Open Mon-Fri 0730-1600. Airmail letters to the USA, Canada, Holland, US$1.25 1st 10 gm, to the Caribbean US$1, postcards US$0.62 and US$0.51, aerograms US$0.71. Express mail is available. Limited banking services also available. There are special stamp issues and First Day Covers for collectors. *UPS* agent is Arlene Cuvalay, Golden Rock, T3182595, F3182594. *Lady Ama's Services* is agent for *Federal Express*, Fort Oranjestraat, T3182712, F3182572. **Telephone**: Telephone cards of US$10 and US$17 can be used at phone booth outside near police station and at the corner of Korthalsweg, at the airport, at the harbour and the road to the airport, for local or international calls. When calling within the Netherlands Antilles, dial 0 before the 7-digit number. **Medical services** The *Queen Beatrix Medical Centre* is on Prinsesweg, T3182371 for Nurses Station, an ambulance, or T3182211 for a doctor. Doctors are on 24-hr call.

Background

Sint Eustatius, or Statia, was originally settled by Caribs. The island was sighted by Columbus on **History**
his second voyage but never settled by the Spanish. The Dutch first colonized it in 1636 and *See also background*
built Fort Oranje. The island reached a peak of prosperity in the 18th century, when the devel- *to the Netherlands*
opment of commerce brought about 8,000 people to the tiny island, over half of whom were *Antilles, the ABC*
slaves, and the number of ships visiting the port was around 3,500 a year. Trading in sugar, *chapter, page 859*
tobacco and cotton proved more profitable than trying to grow them and the slave trade was particularly lucrative, gaining the island the nickname of 'The Golden Rock'.

   The island still celebrates 16 November 1776 when the cannon of Fort Oranje unknowingly fired the first official salute by a foreign nation to the American colours. At that time, Statia was a major trans-shipment point for arms and supplies to George Washington's troops. The arms were stored in the yellow ballast brick warehouses built all along the Bay and then taken by blockade runners to Boston, New York and Charleston. However, the salute brought retaliatory action from the English, and in 1781 the port was taken without a shot being fired by troops under Admiral George Brydges Rodney, who captured 150 merchant ships and £5 million of booty before being expelled by the French the following year.

   With continuing transfers of power, the economy never recovered, many merchants were banished and the population began to decline. The emancipation of slaves in 1863 brought an end to any surviving plantation agriculture and the remaining inhabitants were reduced to subsistence farming and dependency upon remittances from relatives abroad. Prosperity has returned recently with the advent of tourism and the island is still relatively underdeveloped.

The island of Sint Eustatius, 56 km south of St Maarten and 27 km southeast of Saba, is domi- **Geography**
nated by the long-extinct volcano called 'The Quill' at the south end, inside which is a lush rain-forest. The north part of the island is hilly and uninhabited except for Statia Terminals, a fuel depot; most people live in the central plain where the airport is.

Statia is quiet and friendly and the poorest of the three Dutch islands, with only 2,100 people **People**
living on the 30.6 sq km island. A variety of nationalities are represented, the island having changed hands 22 times in the past, but the majority are of black African descent. Everybody speaks English, although Dutch is the official language and is taught in schools.

The traditional economic activities of fishing, farming and trading have been aug- **Economy**
mented by an oil storage and refuelling facility, but tourism has had a slow start. The island is popular with divers looking for something a bit different and off the beaten track. It is the sort of place where you will be greeted by passers by and there is no crime.

Leeward Islands

Things to do in Saint-Barts

- Stir yourself and hike to **Colombier Beach**, the most beautiful on the island. You'll appreciate it far more after a walk than if you take a boat ride.
- Treat yourself to some very fine dining, from coffee and croissants for breakfast at a harbour front café, to a **gourmet evening meal** with excellent French wine, St-Barts is not short of skilful French chefs.
- See and be seen. **Spot the celebrities** in their faded jeans and French T-shirts. St-Barts is chic and the international in-crowd holidays here.

Saint-Barthélemy

IDD code: 590
Colour map 3, grid B1
Population: 5,038

Saint-Barthélemy (also known as St-Barts), in the Leewards, has lush volcanic hillsides and 22 splendid white sandy beaches, most of which are protected by both cliff and reef. It has gained a reputation as the place to go for the rich and famous. It is chic and expensive and its many beautiful beaches are dotted with luxury hotels and villas, designed for those who appreciate privacy. Gourmet French restaurants and Creole bistros can be found all over the island. This is a place to indulge yourself.

Ins and outs

Getting there
Only small planes carrying a maximum of 20 passengers can land on the short runway

St-Barts is only a short hop from St Maarten/St-Martin and there are dozens of daily flights from both the French and Dutch sides from 0700-1700 in small planes. There are also good links with other neighbouring islands. It is difficult to get there in a day from Europe, although it is possible from Paris via St Maarten. From the USA the best connections are via San Juan. You can also get there by boat from St-Martin.

Getting around
See page 505 for further details

Taxi tours are available for a quick tour of the island, but if you are renting a villa you will need car or mini moke hire for visiting different beaches or for shopping.

Tourist information

Quai de Gaulle, Gustavia, T0590-278727, www.st.barths.com Open Mon-Thu 0830-1230, 1400-1730, Fri 0830-1230, 1400-1700.

Diving and marine life

There is excellent diving all round St-Barts, especially out round the offshore rocks, like the Groupers, and islands like Île Fourche. Sometimes in May the migrating sperm whales pass close by. From April to August female sea turtles come to Colombier, Flamands and Corossol to lay their eggs.

Dive centres

There are dive shops in Gustavia: *La Bulle*, T276225; *St Barth Plongée*, T0590-275444, www.st-barthplongee.com; *Marine Service*, T0590-277031, *West Indies Dive*, T0590-277034, *Mair Maid*, T0690-587929 and *Plongée Caraïbes*, T0690-546614. A single dive is about US$50, or there are packages of 5 or 10 dives for US$220 or US$400. PADI open-water certification costs US$480.

Fishing

Deep-sea fishing can be arranged with *Océan Must Marina* at La Pointe, Gustavia, T0590-276225, F0590-279517, VHF 10, who also charter boats for cruising, diving, waterskiing and offer a full service marina. *Marine Service* at Quai du Yacht Club, Gustavia, T0590-277034 F0590-277036, VHF 74, also do deep-sea fishing trips and the same watersports and boat rentals. The price depends on the type of boat (4-8 people) and ranges from US$470-640 for a half day to US$780-1,100 for a full day with open bar and picnic lunch.

Leeward Islands

Touching down

Boat information *(French flag) Outside the inner harbour of Gustavia, daily anchorage fee of US$2.50-5, depending on location. Inside the main harbour, stern to or on double moorings, fees are based on length of boat. Water, waste disposal, showers and toilets are available at the dock. Other anchorages around the island are free. Provisioning and some marine supplies.*

Business hours *0800-1200, 1430-1700, morning only on Wed-Sat.*

Currency *As on Saint-Martin, the euro, but dollars are widely accepted and often interchangeable.*

Embassies and consulates *None as it is a French département.*

Emergency numbers *Gendarmerie T0590-276012,* **Police** *T0590-276666,* **Fire** *T0590-276231.*

Official time *GMT minus 4 hrs.*

Public holidays *See Guadeloupe, page 563.*

Useful addresses *Sub Prefect: T0590-276328. Radio St-Barts: T0590-277474, broadcasting on FM 98 mHz.*

Voltage *220 volts AC, 50 cycles.*

Weights and measures *Metric.*

Beaches and watersports

The main resort area is **Baie de Saint-Jean**, which is two beaches divided by *Eden Rock*, with several bars and restaurants open for lunch or a snack, watersports, but no waterskiing, ideal for families, good windsurfing, safe swimming, some snorkelling. Motorized watersports are only allowed 150 m off the beach. Others are **Lorient**, **Marigot**, **Grand Cul de Sac** on the north coast, **Grande Saline**, **Gouverneur** on the south, and **Colombier** and **Flamands** at the northwest tip.

Some beaches are more accessible than others, most are uncrowded

Saint-Barthélemy

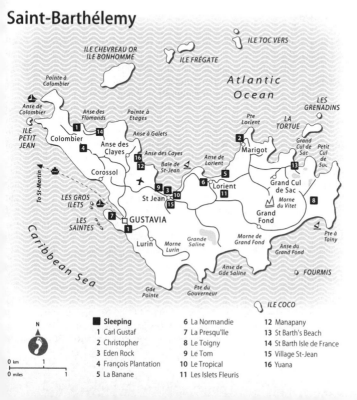

Sleeping
1 Carl Gustaf
2 Christopher
3 Eden Rock
4 François Plantation
5 La Banane

6 La Normandie
7 La Presqu'île
8 Le Toigny
9 Le Tom
10 Le Tropical
11 Les Islets Fleuris

12 Manapany
13 St Barth's Beach
14 St Barth Isle de France
15 Village St-Jean
16 Yuana

Leeward Islands

To get to **Gouverneur** from Gustavia take the road to Lurin. A sign will direct you to the dirt road leading down to the beach, lovely panoramic view over to the neighbouring islands, where there is white sand with palm trees for shade. A legend says that the 17th-century pirate, Montbars the Exterminator, hid his treasures in a cove here and they have never been found. Also a very good spot for snorkelling. **Colombier Beach** is the most beautiful on St-Barts. It cannot be reached by car but is well worth the 20-30 minutes' walk for the majestic views of the island. Park the car at Colombier, there are two trails going down to the beach. There are also several day tours by boat from Gustavia. **Flamands** beach is of very clean white sand. The surf can be rough, watersports available. In Corossol is the **Inter Oceans Museum**, an absorbing, private collection of 9,000 seashells, corals and stuffed fish from all around the world. ■ *Tue-Sun 0900-1230, 1400-1700 (Mon groups only). T0590-276297.* **Petite Anse de Galet**, in Gustavia, three or four minutes' walk from Fort Karl, is also known as Shell Beach. Trees give shade and swimming is safe, shelling is of course extremely good.

St-Barts is a popular midway staging post on the yachting route between Antigua and the Virgin Islands. Boat charters are available, also courses in, or facilities for, windsurfing (**Toiny** is a windsurfers' favourite beach, watch out for strong currents), snorkelling (very good, particularly at Marigot), waterskiing and sailing.

Watersports *St-Barth Water Play*, Baie de Saint-Jean, T0590-277122, is a BiC Centre, offering lessons and equipment rental. *Eden Rock Sea Sport Club*, also at Baie de Saint-Jean, T0590-297993, has *Fanatic* equipment for rent. At the *Saint-Barth Beach Hotel*, Grand Cul-de-Sac, **Wind Wave Power** has Mistral gear at their windsurf school. Surfboard rental (not windsurfing) at **Hookipa**, T0590-278257. Sailing and snorkelling cruises are offered by several catamarans. They go to Colombier Beach, Fourche Island, Tintamarre, Anguilla or St-Martin. Half-day cruises cost US$55-60, whole day with lunch US$90-95, sunset cruises US$46.

Gustavia

In Gustavia, the capital, there are branches of several well known French shops (such as Cartier). The small crowd of town habitués is mostly young, chic and French. The food, wine and aromas are equally Gallic, St-Tropez style. The harbour or Carénage was renamed Gustavia after the 18th-century Swedish king, Gustavus III, and became a free port, marking the beginning of the island's greatest prosperity.

In 1852 a fire severely damaged the capital, although the Swedish influence is still evidenced in the city hall, the belfries, the forts (Karl, Oscar and Gustave), the street names and the trim stone houses which line the harbour. In the southeast corner in front of the Anglican church is a truly massive anchor. Probably from a British Royal Navy frigate, and dating from the late 18th century, it weighs 10 tons. Marked "Liverpool...Wood...London", it came to Gustavia by curious means in 1981. The cable of a tug towing a barge across from St Thomas fouled on something at the entrance of the harbour. A man dived down to have a look and found the anchor. It is thought that the cable dragged it up as the tug left St Thomas and, suspended below water, it got carried across. **St-Barts Municipal Museum** with an exhibition of the history, traditions and local crafts of the island, is at La Pointe, near the *Wall House*. ■ *Mon 1430-1800, Tue-Fri 0830-1230, 1430-1800, Sat 0900-1300. €1.50, T0590-237900.*

Essentials

Sleeping **Gustavia LL** *Carl Gustaf*, rue des Normands, Gustavia 97133, T0590-277900 carlgustaf@compuserve.com, overlooking harbour, 14 1- or 2-bedroom suites, luxury, with high prices to match, breakfast and airport transfers, kitchenette, private mini pool and sun deck, stereos, gym-sauna, poolside restaurant, short walk to beach. **C** *La Presqu'île* T0590-276460, F0590-277230. 10 rooms.

North coast At Colombier, overlooking Flamands Beach is **LL** *François Plantation*, T0590-298022, info@francois-plantation.com Elegant hotel with 12 bungalows, pool, restaurant, breakfast. **LL** *St Barth Isle de France*, Baie des Flamands 97098, T0590-276181, isledefr@saint-barths.com Luxury hotel, 31 rooms, bungalows and suites, tennis, pool, squash, fitness centre, restaurant, can arrange watersports and horse riding, closed Sep-Oct. The luxury, 4-star **LL** *Manapany Cottages*, T0590-276655, manapany@saint_barth.com Cottages, suites, apartments and rooms on hillside, descending to beach, 56 beds in all, pool, tennis, jacuzzi, some villas have private pools, 2 gourmet restaurants. **LL** *Le Tom Beach Hotel*, Plage de St-Jean, T0590-275313, F0590-275315. 12 rooms on beach, luxury 4-poster beds, a/c, fans, private terraces, restaurant with good view and fresh lobster specialities, multilingual staff. **LL** *Eden Rock*, T0590-277294, info@edenrockhotel.com On a promontory in St-Jean Bay. Long a celebrity favourite, Greta Garbo slept here, 2 beaches, watersports centre and 27-ft boat for fishing, short walk along beach to airstrip, 2 fine restaurants, lobster tank, exceptional wine cellar, 12 rooms, all luxuries, multilingual staff, British-owned. A few hundred metres from Lorient Beach is **LL** *La Banane*, T0590-276825, labanane@wanadoo.fr Pastel-painted bungalows, all different, 9 rooms, 2 pools, lots of bananas, fine dining, breakfast, airport transfers and tax and service included in rate. **LL** *The Christopher Hotel*, Pointe Milou, T0590-276363, christopherhotel@compuserve.com A Sofitel Coralia hotel with 4 stars, stunning sea views. 41 rooms, a/c with sitting room and bathroom, terrace, balcony or patio, 3 rooms with facilities for the disabled, shuttle service to beaches, large pool, Total Fitness Club, watersports arranged, closed Sep. **LL** *St-Barts Beach Hotel*, T0590-276070, www.saintbarthbeachhotel.com 36 rooms and 8 luxury villas, pool, gym, tennis, windsurfing school, built on strip of land between sea and lagoon, conference facilities. In the east, at Anse de Toiny, **LL** *Le Toiny*, T0590-278888, www.letoiny.com 4-star hotel, CP, service, tax and airport transfers included, 13 villa suites, plunge pools, restaurant, bar, room service, high luxury, closed Sep-Oct. In the hills above Lorient, **LL-L** *Les Islets Fleuris*, Hauts de Lorient 97133, T0590-276422, caraibes@saint-barths.com 7 studios, pool, kitchenettes, lovely views over coastline, maid service, car rental available with room package. 5 mins from Baie de St-Jean is **LL-L** *Yuana*, Anse des Cayes, T0590-278084, www.yuana.com On hillside in gardens overlooking coastline, 12 rooms, kitchenette, balcony, TV, video, pool, breakfast, laundry, own boat, *Le Yuana*, for deep-sea fishing and excursions. **LL-AL** *Le Tropical*, St-Jean Beach, T0590-276487, tropicalhotel@ compuserve.com 20 seaview and garden view rooms, overlooking beach, in lush garden, pool with panoramic sea view, short walk to beach, excursions arranged, closed 1 Jun-15 Jul. **LL-AL** *Village St-Jean*, T0590- 276139, vsjhotel@compuserve.com on hillside overlooking Baie de St-Jean. 20 1-2 bedroom cottages with kitchenettes, 4 rooms with fridge, special packages available, pool, jacuzzi, restaurant, watersports facilities. **B-C** *La Normandie*, Lorient, T0590- 276166, www.st-barts.net/lanormandie 8 large or small a/c rooms, fridge, breakfast US$6.50.

Gustavia

Quai Jeanne d'Arc

Fort Gustav

To Airport

Caribbean Sea

Fort Oscar

Municipal Museum

Pharmacy

To Saint Jean

Rue Duquesne

Rue Chanzy

Rue Avatel

Rue de la République

Quai de la République

Town Hall

R du Port

R de la France

Rue du Roi Oscar

Rue Schoelcher

Rue Jean Bart

Boats to/from St-Martin

Rue du Général

Rue Bord du Mer

Rue Dugomier

Rue Jeanne d'Arc

de Gaulle

Anchor

Rue du Centenaire

Rue Irénée de Bruyn

Rue Gambetta

Rue Courbet

Rue de l'Eglise

Fort Karl

Rue Victor Hugo

Plage de Grands Galets (Shell Beach)

100 metres
100 yards

● Eating
1 Wall House

Leeward Islands

Apartments and villas In the USA contact *French Caribbean International*, T800-3222223, www.frenchcaribbean.com On St-Barts contact the following agencies: *Sibarth Real Estate*, BP 55, Gustavia, 97133 St-Barts, T0590-276238, F0590-276052. *New Agency*, Quai de la République, Gustavia, T0590-278114, F0590-278767. *Claudine Mora Immobilier* (CMI), Galeries du Commerce, Saint-Jean, T0590-278088, F0590-278085. *Immo-Antilles*, Gustavia, T0590-279046, F0590-276795. *Ici et Là*, Quai de la République, T0590-277878, F0590-277828.

Eating
Food in St-Barts is expensive. Expect to pay minimum US$25 for dinner

There are many excellent restaurants, mostly French but some Creole and Italian, even Indonesian, a few vegetarian options and lots of seafood. See *Ti Gourmet Saint-Barth*, a free pocket booklet, for a listing, the *Ti Creux* section lists snacks and takeaways.

Gustavia *Wall House*, T0590-277183 for reservations, for French cuisine on the waterfront with harbour view, *plat du jour* at lunch US$7.50, wine from US$12.50 a bottle, dinner good 5-course *menu* US$22, wines from US$20.50; *Au Port* also offers fine dining overlooking the harbour, T0590-276236. One of the most expensive restaurants on the island. *Le Repaire*, rue de la République, is a good restaurant at the *Yacht Club*, in the public part of the Sailing School, overlooking the harbour, open 0600-0100, closed Sun, few but well-prepared French dishes (also has a few rooms to let, T0590-277248); *Bar Le Select* is a central meeting spot, an informal bar for lunch with hamburger menu, but also one of the most popular night-time bars and sort of general store. *L'Escale*, across the harbour, a pizza, pasta place with low prices for St-Barts but still expensive, closed Oct, T0590-278106. A local place serving Creole food is *Eddy's*, T275417, closed Sun. Try the bakery on rue du Roi Oscar II, they open 0600, closed Mon. *La Crêperie* on the same street is open 0700-2300, closed Sun, and does American and Continental breakfast as well as sweet and savoury *crêpes*, salads and ice creams. *La Gloriette*, on the beach at Grand Cul de Sac, T0590-277566, serves superb, authentic Creole cuisine.

Festivals *Carnival* is held before Lent, on Mardi Gras and Ash Wed. The *Festival of Gustavia* is 20 Aug, with dragnet fishing contests, dances and parties, while **24 Aug** is the day of the island's patron saint, *St Barthélemy*, when the church bells ring, boats are blessed and there are regattas, fireworks and a public ball. On **25 Aug** the *Feast of St Louis* is celebrated in the village of Corossol, with a fishing festival, *pétanque, belote*, dancing and fireworks. *Fête du Vent* held in Lorient on **26-27 Aug** is similar. The *St-Barts Regatta* in **Feb** is the main event for sailors (St-Barts Yacht Club, T0590-277041). Other regattas should be checked at *Lou Lou's Marine Shop*, Gustavia, because none is fixed annually. Every other year in **May** there is a *Transatlantic Sailboat Race* from Brittany in France to St-Barts. The traditional sailboats participate in all public events like *Bastille Day*, *Gustavia Day* with their own regattas and also hold 1 regatta a month. A *music festival* is held annually in **Jan** with 2 weeks of classical, folk, jazz music and ballet performed by both school children and guest artists and musicians from abroad in Gustavia and Lorient churches. A *Gourmet Festival* is held in **Apr**, and an *International Art Exhibition* in **Dec**. On the last weekend in **Apr** is the *St-Barth Festival of Caribbean Cinema*, a festival for filmmakers throughout the Caribbean. Films are shown in their original language (with French subtitles).

Nightlife
Most of the nightlife starts around the bars at Baie de St-Jean

In Gustavia at *Bar Le Select* (closed Sun). In Lurin try *New Feeling* (open from 2200, disco, billiards, T0590-278867), *La Banane Cabaret Show* plays at *El Sereno Beach Hotel*. There are discos at *Le Petit Club* in Gustavia, T0590-276633, lepetitclub@saint-barths.com open from 2200. *La Licorne*, T0590-278394, more local, Sat only. Contact the tourist office for details of concerts and ballets held in the Jan music festival, see above.

Shopping A wide range of goods is available from T-shirts to duty-free luxury goods and fine wines There are 5 small shopping centres in Saint-Jean: La Savane, Les Galeries du Commerce, La Villa Créole, Centre Commercial de St-Jean and Centre Commercial de Neptune. St-Barts is the place to find designer labels such as Gianni Versace, Hermès and Ralph Lauren.

Sports
For watersports, see pages 500 and 502

Tennis at several hotels, guests take priority. Also at ASCCO in Colombier, 2 lit courts T0590-276107, AJOE in Lorient, 2 courts, 1 lit court, T0590-276763. **Horse riding** at Flamands, Coralie Fournier, T0690-629930.

Leeward Islands

Air Scheduled flights from Anguilla (*Coastal Air Transport*), Pointe-à-Pitre (*Air Caraïbes*), St   **Transport**
Croix (*Coastal Air Transport*), Sint Maarten (*Winair, Air Caraïbes, Saint Barth Commuter*),
St-Martin (*Saint Barth Commuter*), St Thomas (*Air St Thomas*), San Juan (*Air St Thomas*).
Charters available locally with *St Barth Commuter*, T0590-275454 and *Air Caraïbes*,
T0590-276190, *Winair* T0590-276101, *Air St Thomas* T0590-277176. **Sea**   *Voyager* have
scheduled services between St Maarten/St Martin, St-Barts and Saba, contact *St-Barth Ship
Service* for details, Quai de la République, T0590-275410, 871068. Several catamarans go to
St-Barts from Sint Maarten, leaving in the morning and returning in the afternoon so you can
do a day trip. **Car hire** Many agencies at the airport. *Aubin* T0590-277303, *Avis*
T0590-277143, *Budget* T0590-276630, *Europcar* T0590-277333, *Gumbs Rental*
T0590-277532, *Hertz* T0590-277114, *Island Car Rental* T0590-277001, *Questel*
T0590-277322, *Soleil Caraïbes* T0590-276718, *Turbe* T0590-277142. It is not easy to hire a
car for only one day, except out of season, mini mokes from US$35 per day: ask your hotel to
obtain a car if required. **Scooters** can be rented from *Rent Some Fun* T0590-277059, *Chez
Beranger* T0590-278900, *Saint Barth Moto Bike* T0590-276789. *Denis Dufau*, Saint-Jean,
T0590-275483, is a Harley Davidson shop. There are 2 gas stations, one near the airport terminal, open Mon-Sat 0730-1700, the other in Lorient open Mon-Wed, Fri 0730-1700, Sat
morning. There is a **taxi** stand at the airport T0590-277581, and in Gustavia T0590-276631.
Minibuses (and ordinary taxis) do island tours, US$45/45 mins, US$50/1hr, or US$65/1½ hrs.

Banks *Banque Nationale de Paris* (0745-1200, 1405-1530) with an ATM that is supposed to work 24 hrs   **Directory**
with US and European credit cards, Visa, Mastercard and Eurocard, but is reported to work only with the
French 'carte bleue', T0590-276370, F0590-278570. *Banque Française Commerciale* (0745-1215,
1400-1630, Mon, Tue, Thu, Fri), withdrawals at counter with Visa, Mastercard and Eurocard,
T0590-276262, F0590-278775, both in Gustavia. BFC head office is at Saint-Jean, Galeries du Commerce
(open Tue-Fri 0815-1215, 1400-1700, Sat 0800-1300) where there is an ATM open 24 hrs for withdrawals
in US$ or €, T0590-276588, F0590-278148. *Crédit Martiniquais*, at Le Carré d'Or in the centre of Gustavia
(open Mon-Fri 0815-1215, 1400-1615), T0590-278657, F0590-278279. *Crédit Agricole*, rue Bord de Mer,
Gustavia, ATM accepts nearly all cards including eurocheque cards (cheaper than cash advance with
credit card), also automatic bank note exchange machine (open Tue-Fri 0800-1300, 1430-1700, Sat
0800-1300), T0590-278990, F0590-276461. *Crédit Lyonnais West Indies*, rue Auguste Nyman, Gustavia
(open Mon-Fri 0900-1200, 1400-1700), T279200, F279191. **Communications** Post: In Gustavia there
are 3 post offices: open 0730-1500 Mon, Tue, Thu, Fri, 0730-1200 Wed, Sat, T0590-276200,
F0590-278203; in Saint-Jean: open 0800-1400 Mon, Tue, Thu, Fri, 0730-1100 Wed, Sat, T0590-276402. In
Lorient: open 0700-1100 Mon-Fri, 0800-1000 Sat, T0590-276135. **Telephone**: The SiBarth agency on
General de Gaulle in Gustavia, T0590-276238, F0590-276052, has a fax service and a mail holding service.
There are phone booths on the Quai de Gaulle, at the airport, Galeries du Commerce and Flamands,
among other places. There are some phones which take coins but most take phone cards. There is a USA
Direct phone at the airport; you can phone the USA using a phone card and have the recipient return the
call to the payphone. **Medical services** T0590-276035. **Doctor** on call: T0590-277304.

Background

Although called Ouanalao by the Caribs, the island was renamed after Christopher Colum-   **History**
bus' brother, when discovered in November 1496. It was first settled by French colonists
from Dieppe in 1645. After a brief possession by the Order of the Knights of Malta, and ravag-
ing by the Caribs, it was bought by the Compagnie des Îles and added to the French royal
domain in 1672. In 1784, France ceded the island to Sweden in exchange for trading rights in
the port of Göteborg. In 1801, St-Barts was attacked by the British, but for most of this period
it was peaceful and commercially successful. The island was handed back to France after a
referendum in 1878.

St-Barts is administered by the sub-prefect in Saint-Martin and is attached administratively   **Government**
to the département of Guadeloupe. The island has its own elected mayor, who holds office   **& economy**
for six years. St-Barts relies on its free port status and tourism for the bulk of its revenue. It is
only 24 sq km, 230 km north of Guadeloupe, 240 km east of the Virgin Islands, and 35 km
southeast of Saint-Martin.

Leeward Islands

People

Twice as many tourists as the island's population pass through each month

St-Barts is inhabited mostly by people of Breton, Norman, and Poitevin descent who live in quiet harmony with the small percentage of blacks. Norman dialect is still widely spoken, while many islanders also speak English, but French is the dominant language. A few elderly women still wear traditional costumes (with their characteristic starched white bonnets called *kichnottes*); they cultivate sweet potato patches despite the dry, rocky soil, also weaving palm fronds into hats and bags which they sell in the village of Corossol. The men traditionally smuggled rum among neighbouring islands and now import liqueurs and perfumes, raise cattle, and fish for lobsters offshore. Immigrants from France have taken the best jobs in hotels and restaurants though and relations there are sometimes strained. St-Barts has become a very 'chic' and expensive holiday destination; the Rockefellers and Rothschilds own property on the island, while the rich, royal and famous stay in the luxury villas dotted around the island.

Antigua

IDD code: 268
Colour map 3,
grid B/C3
Population: 75,741

A family holiday destination with great beaches, watersports and safe swimming. Direct, non-stop flights from Europe and North America make this island ideal for introducing children to the Caribbean. Good transport links with other islands facilitate two-centre holidays or more extensive island hopping. English Harbour is particularly picturesque, with yachts filling a historic bay that has been a popular staging post for centuries. Nelson's Dockyard and ruined forts are overlooked by the old battery on Shirley Heights, now better known for Sunday jump-ups, reggae and steel bands. Some 30 miles to the north of Antigua, the coral island of Barbuda is attractive for hikers, nature lovers, cyclists and beachcombers

Antigua

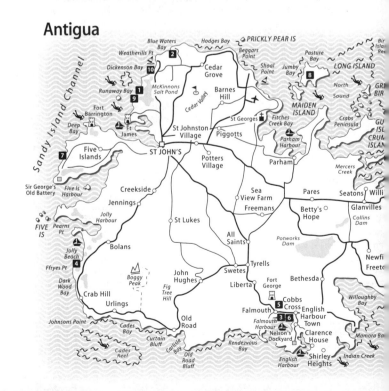

Leeward Islands

Things to do in Antigua and Barbuda

- Visit **Nelson's Dockyard** and the forts of **English Harbour** and **Shirley Heights**, for a reminder of colonial maritime history.
- **Kayak** through the mangroves and round the cays off the northeast coast.
- Go birdwatching at the **Frigate Bird Sanctuary** on Barbuda, a spectacular breeding colony on the lagoon.
- Watch the sunrise on beautiful **Half Moon Bay Beach**.

Ins and outs

Antigua has excellent communications by air with Europe and North America as well as with neighbouring islands, making it ideal for a 2-centre holiday or the starting point for more protracted island hopping. It is not so easy to get there by sea, other than on a cruise ship or cargo boat, as there are no formal ferry links except to Montserrat.

Getting there
See Transport, page 519, for further information

Renting a **car** is probably the best way to see the islands' sights, as the bus service is inadequate, but be aware that roads are very bumpy and narrow and speed bumps are poorly marked. **Cycling** is not very interesting, the roads are generally flat and traffic is moderate. There are car hire companies in St John's and some at the airport, most will pick you up. Be careful with one way streets in St John's. At night people do not always dim their headlights. Watch out for pedestrians at night. **Minivans** (shared taxis) go to some parts of the island (for example Old Road) from the West End bus terminal by the market in St John's. **Buses** serve the southern part of the island but not the north, so there are no buses to the airport.

Getting around
Drive on the left, watch out for pot holes, narrow streets and animals straying across the street in the dark

Antigua is a dry island with average rainfall of about 45 ins a year, and although Sep Nov is rainy season, the showers are usually short. This is a hurricane season and storms can cause costly damage. Temperatures range from 73°F to 85°F between winter and summer and the trade winds blow constantly.

Climate

Antigua Tourist Office, Nevis St/Friendly Alley. T4620480, www.antigua-barbuda.org Mon-Fri 0830-1600, Sat 0830-1200. Gives list of official taxi charges and hotel information. **Barbuda** has a Tourism Department here, too. The *Antigua Tourist Office* at the airport helps book accommodation mainly at the more expensive resorts. The *Antigua Hotels and Tourist Association*, Lower Newgate St, St John's, T4620374,, www.antiguahotels.org

Tourist information

■ **Sleeping**
1 Barrymore Beach Club
2 Blue Waters
3 Catamaran
4 Coco's Antigua
5 Country Inn
6 Falmouth Harbour Hillside Apartments
7 Hawksbill
8 Jumby Bay
9 Lashings
10 Siboney Beach Club
11 Tree Tops

Flora and fauna

Around 150 different birds have been observed in Antigua and Barbuda, of which a third are year-round residents and the rest seasonal or migrants. Good spots for birdwatching include **Potworks Dam**, noted for the great blue heron in spring and many water fowl. **Great Bird Island** is home to the red-billed tropic

Leeward Islands

▶ ## Touching down

Boat information (Own flag). All yachts must clear in and obtain a cruising permit in Antigua but may clear out of either Antigua or at the C & I office in Barbuda. Customs and Immigration offices are at English Harbour (no overtime charges), Crabbs Marina, St John's and Jolly Harbour (boats must be brought inside the marina for exit clearance). Entry fees and monthly cruising permits are on a sliding scale depending on the size of boat. There are additional fees for anchoring or stern to dockage in English Harbour and Falmouth, an EC$5 charge per person plus electricity and water used. Dinghies must show lights at night and barbecues are prohibited in the harbour. The Antigua and Barbuda Marine Guide is distributed free by the Department of Tourism and contains lots of information on anchorages and marine supplies, www.antiguamarineguide.com There are marinas at English Harbour, Falmouth Harbour (Antigua Slipway, Falmouth Harbour Marina, Catamaran Marina, Antigua Yacht Club), Parham Harbour (Crabbs Slipway), Jolly Harbour, St James's Club, and anchorages at Cades Reef, Carlisle Bay, Morris Bay (Curtain Bluff), Ffryes Bay, Crab Hill Bay, Five Islands Bay, Deep Bay, Morris Bay (Jolly Beach), Dickenson Bay, Parham Harbour and at several of the small islands if you can negotiate the reefs, for example Long Island, Guiana Bay, Green Island and Nonsuch Bay.
Business hours Banks:

Mon-Thu 0800-1400; Fri 0800-1200, 1400-1600. Bank of Antigua opens Sat 0800-1200. **Shops**: Mon-Wed and Fri 0800-1200, 1300-1600. Thu and Sat are early closing days for most non-tourist shops. On Sun everything closes except King's Casino, although KFC and Epicurean open in the afternoon.
Currency Eastern Caribbean dollars are used, at a rate of EC$2.70=US$1.
Exchange US dollars are accepted in most places, but no one will know the exchange rate of other currencies. The conventional rate of exchange if you want to pay in US dollars is EC$2.50=US$1, so it is worth changing money in a bank. **Credit cards** are accepted, especially Visa and American Express, but small restaurants will take only cash or TCs. Always verify whether hotels, taxis, etc are quoting you US or EC dollars, you can be cheated. Take care not to get left with excess EC$ on departure. The airport **bank** is open Mon-Thu 0900-1500, 0900-1330 Fri, so closed when most long-haul flights come in.
Departure tax Airport departure charges amount to US$30 per person. Children under 12 pay half. Cash only.
Documents A **valid onward ticket** is necessary. American, Canadian and British nationals need only photo ID and proof of citizenship. **Passports** but not **visas** are required by nationals of other Commonwealth countries, British Dependent

---

bird and on **Man of War Island**, Barbuda, frigate birds breed. The Antiguan Racer Conservation Project was set up in 1995 to save the harmless Antiguan racer snake (*Alsophis antiguae*) which had been devastated by mongooses and black rats. The 60 remaining snakes were all on Great Bird Island and a campaign to eliminate the rats here and on other offshore islands helped their numbers to increase, together with other rare wildlife. Racers have now been reintroduced to other islands.

Diving and marine life

Dive sites
There are barrier reefs around most of Antigua which are host to lots of colourful fish and underwater plant life

Diving is mostly shallow, up to 60 ft, except below **Shirley Heights**, where dives are up to 110 ft, or **Sunken Rock**, with a depth of 122 ft where the cleft rock formation gives the impression of a cave dive. Popular sites are **Cades Reef**, which runs for 2½ miles along the leeward side of the island and is an underwater park; **Sandy Island Reef**, covered with several types of coral and only 30-50 ft deep; **Horseshoe Reef**, **Barracuda Alley** and **Little Bird Island**. There are also some wrecks to explore including the *Andes*, in 20 ft of water in Deep Bay, but others have disappeared in the recent hurricanes. Diving off Barbuda is for certified divers only with wrecks to explore as well as reefs. The water is fairly shallow, so snorkelling can be enjoyable

Territories, and many other countries if their stay does not exceed 6 months. The following countries need valid passports but not visas: Argentina, Austria, Belgium, Brazil, Chile, Denmark, Finland, France, Germany, Greece, Ireland, Italy, Japan, Liechtenstein, Luxembourg, Malta, Mexico, Monaco, Netherlands, Norway, Peru, Portugal, Spain, Suriname, Sweden, Switzerland, Turkey and Venezuela. Nationals of all other countries require visas, unless they are in transit for less than 24 hours. Visitors must satisfy immigration officials that they have enough money for their stay. You will not be allowed through Immigration without somewhere to stay. The Tourist Office can help you and you can always change your mind later.

Emergency numbers *Police T4620125, Hospital T4620251.*

Health *Tiny sandflies, known locally as 'noseeums' often appear on the beaches in the late afternoon and can give nasty stings. Keep a good supply of repellent and make sure you wash off all sand to avoid taking them with you from the beach. Do not eat the little green apples of the manchineel tree, as they are poisonous, and don't sit under the tree in the rain as the dripping oil from the leaves causes blisters. Some beaches, particularly those on the west coast, get jellyfish at certain times of the year, for example Jul/Aug.*

Official time *Atlantic standard time, 4 hrs behind GMT, 1 hr ahead of EST.*

Public holidays *New Year's Day, Good Fri, Easter Mon, Labour Day (first Mon in May), Whit Mon (end-May), Queen's Birthday (second Sat in Jun), Caricom Day, beginning of Jul (whole island closes down), Carnival (first Mon and Tue in Aug), Independence Day (1 Nov), Christmas Day and Boxing Day.*

Safety *Travel in Antigua is generally hassle free, but normal precautions against theft should be taken. There have been some serious incidents on isolated beaches, so caution should be taken in these areas.*

Tourist offices overseas *Canada: 60 St Clair Av East, Suite 601, Toronto, Ontario, M4T IN5, T416-9613085, info@antigua-barbuda-ca.com France: 43 Av de Friedland, 75008 Paris, T33-1-53751571, ot.antigua-barbuda@wanadoo.fr Germany: Thomas Str 11, D-61348, Bad Homburg, T49-617221504, antigua-barbuda@karibik.org Italy: Via Santa Maria alla Porta 9, I-20123 Milan, T/F39-2877983, infoantigua@antigua-barbuda.it UK: Antigua House, 15 Thayer St, London W1M 5LD, T020-74867073/5, antbar@msn.com USA: 610 Fifth Av, Suite 311, New York, NY 10020, T212-5414117, info@antigua-barbuda.org; 25 SE 2nd Av, Suite 300, Miami, FL 33131, T305-3816762.*

Voltage *220 volts usually, but 110 volts in some areas, check before using your own appliances. Many hotels have transformers.*

Weights and measures *Imperial.*

At **Pasture Bay**, on Long Island, the hawksbill turtle lays its eggs from late May to December. The Environmental Awareness Group (EAG) organizes turtle watches. Huge controversy surrounds the Government's approval in 2001of a captive dolphin programme (the company involved is being investigated in the USA for illegal purchase of dolphins from Cuba) and legal action is pending from conservation groups. Dolphins are being caught in the wild and taught to perform tricks, in the name of education and conservation, in return for frozen fish and antibiotics. The Prime Minister stated that Antigua's tourist industry had to keep up with the competition in the attractions it offered to cruise ship visitors.

Dive centres Dive shops are located nearly all round the island and include: *Aquanaut Diving Centre*, at *St James's Club*, T4605000; *Dive Antigua*, Rex Halcyon Hotel, T4623483, F4627787, www.diveantigua.com; *Curtain Bluff Dive Shop*, Curtain Bluff Hotel, T4628400 (certified hotel guests only); *Deep Bay Divers* in St John's at Redcliff Quay, T4638000, www.deepbaydivers.com; *Dockyard Divers* at Nelson's Dockyard, T4601178, F4601179; www.dockyarddivers.com; *Octopus Divers* at English Harbour, T4606286, F4638528, octopusdivers@candw.ag; *Jolly Dive* at Jolly Beach Resort, T4628305, www.kokomocat.com/jollyd.htm

Leeward Islands

Beaches and watersports

Tourist brochures will never tire of telling you that there are 365 beaches on Antigua, one for every day of the year, some of which are deserted

The nearest beach to St John's is **Fort James** which can be pleasant, with its palm trees and a few boulders. However, it gets crowded at weekends, and at times it becomes rough and so has a milky appearance, lots of weed and is not good for swimming. It is also rather secluded and confrontations with drug-users have been recorded there, so do not go alone. Further away, but better, is **Dickenson Bay** but there are hotels all along the beach which fence off their property and some pump sewage into the sea which can be smelly. **Soldier's Bay**, next to the *Blue Waters Hotel*, is shallow and picturesque. Instead of following the sign, park your car in the hotel car park, which has shade, walk left across the property, climb through the hole in the fence and in about three minutes you are there. Also good is **Deep Bay** which, like most beaches, can only be reached by taxi or car. There are several nice beaches on the peninsula west of St John's. On **Trafalgar Beach** condominiums have been built on the rocks overlooking the small, sheltered bay. If you go through Five Islands village you come to **Galley Bay**, a secluded and unspoilt hotel beach which is popular with locals and joggers at sunset. The four **Hawksbill** beaches at the end of the peninsula are crescent shaped, very scenic and unspoilt. Hotel guests tend to use the second beach, leaving the other three empty. Take drinks to the furthest one (clothes optional, secluded, pleasant) as there are no facilities and you may have the place to yourself. At **Half Moon Bay**, in the east there is plenty of room on a lovely long, white-sand beach; the waves can be rough in the centre of the bay, but the water is calm at the north end. There are no facilities here. Near English Harbour is **Galleon Beach**, which is splendid, water taxi from English Harbour, EC$2. It has an excellent hotel and restaurant. There is a cave on **Windward Beach**, near English Harbour, which is good for a moonlight bonfire (go in a group, not just as a couple). Follow the road past the Antigua Yacht Club leading to Pigeon Beach and turn left to Windward Beach on a bumpy track, best with a 4WD. Also excellent is **Pigeon Point**, reached by turning left at the *Last Lemming* restaurant and following the path up and over the hill. **Dark Wood Beach**, on the road from St John's to Old Road round the southwest coast has a bar and restaurant.

Watersports Antigua offers waterskiing, windsurfing, parasailing, snorkelling, kayaking, kite surfing and swimming with stingrays. **Dickenson Bay** is the only beach with public hire of watersports equipment, but some hotels will hire to the public, especially out of season. The *Sandals* all-inclusive resort on Dickenson Bay will admit outsiders, at US$150 per couple 1000-1800 or US$130 for the evening, giving you the use of all sports facilities, meals, bar, etc. *Patrick's Windsurfing School*, T4619463, windsurfingantigua@hotmail.com, at Dutchman's Bay north of the airport, offers instruction to beginners (guarantee to achieve in 2 hrs or no charge), intermediate and advanced windsurfers. Patrick will travel to any hotel requested. Kite surfing lessons, rentals and sales are offered by an IKO-approved school, *Kite Antigua*. Try a 30-min orientation class on land for US$30 and move on from there, T7273983, 0900-1700 on the beach, T/F 4603414 after 1800, www.kiteantigua.com *Paddles* offers an excellent half-day eco tour of the mangroves and islands off the northeast shore with snorkelling and hiking, T4631944, www.antiguapaddles.com, while *Kayak Antigua* also takes you through the mangroves in the northeast, T4801225, tropad@candw.ag *Sting Ray City*, T5627297, stingray@candw.ag, is modelled on the Grand Cayman experience of snorkellers interacting with stingrays. At present the rays are confined in a spacious pen on a sand bank in the sea while they become accustomed to feeding in the area, but once they have become territorial the pen will be dismantled. The operation is well run and visitors are limited, but it is encouraging the concentration of a single species dependent on human handouts. *Adventure Antigua*, T7273261, www.adventureantigua.com, offers an eco tour by boat around the North Sound islands exploring those less visited, snorkelling, lunch and drinks for US$90.

Sailing The *Antigua Yacht Club* holds races every Thu and anyone wishing to crew should listen to
Races are held throughout the year English Harbour Radio at 0900 on VHF 68/06 that morning. *Jolly Harbour Yacht Club* holds races as well as the **Red Stripe Regatta** in Feb and **Jolly Harbour Regatta** in Sep. The **Classic**

Regatta in the second half of Apr is spectacular, with yawls, ketches, schooners and square-masted vessels displaying their sails. During Classic Week you can ride on a Classic yacht in the regatta by donating US$100 to charity (*The Hourglass Foundation*), contact Hans Smit at the *Gold Smitty* in Redcliff Quay, T4622601. **Antigua Sailing Week** begins at the end of Apr with 5 days of races, T5623276, F5623277, www.sailingweek.com

A full-service marina was built at Jolly Harbour in 1992, just south of Ffryes Point, T4626042, www.jollyharbour-marina.com There are 159 slips (103 fully serviced) for yachts of up to 260 ft and 12 ft draft, with a mega yacht facility. Several day charter boats have moved there. For cruisers or bare boat charters Antigua offers good provisioning, and marine supplies abound, with facilities to haul out boats as well. Haulout can be done at Antigua Slipway or Jolly Harbour; there are several other marinas as well. **Charter fleets** include *Sun Yacht Charter Services*, T5622893, charterservices@candw.ag, and *Nicholson's Yacht Charters*, T4601093, nicholsoncy@ candw.ag. There are too many anchorages to list.

Shorty's Glass-Bottom Boat at Dickenson Bay, takes people out to the coral reefs; there are also excursions to Bird Island, food and drink provided. Trips round the island with stops at smaller islands such as Bird Island, Prickly Pear Island, or even Barbuda or Montserrat, can be arranged for US$60-90 on the catamarans run by *Kokomo Cat*, T4627245, www.kokomocat.com, and *Wadadli Cats*, T4624792, www.wadadli cats.com. *Sentio*, T4647127, is a luxury 50-ft sailing yacht (operating from *Curtain Bluff* in winter and English Harbour in summer) for small groups, honeymooners, families, for special trips, beach exploring, overnight to Barbuda or sailing instruction. The *Caribbean Queen*, T4618675, www.ticruises.com, is a 69-ft catamaran which sails the Antiguan waters with a live steel band, barbecue, snorkelling and more. There is also, of course, the *Jolly Roger*, T4622064, a wooden sailing ship used for entertaining would-be pirates, with Wed and Fri lunchtime cruises, Thu cocktail cruises and Sat night barbecue and dancing cruise, helped along with rum punch.

Day sails
Cocktail and barbecue cruises are reasonably priced

For fishing charters, *Nightwing*, T4605337, www.fishantigua.com, a 35-ft Bertrum, leaves from Falmouth Harbour, US$550 for 4 hrs, US$850 for 8 hrs, plus tip. *Overdraft*, T4644954, www.antiguafishing.com, a 40-ft fishing boat leaves from Nelsons Dockyard, US$400 for 4 hrs, US$500 for 6 hrs, or US$600 for 8 hrs. *Obsession*, T4623174, www.charternet.com/charters/obsession, is a 45-ft Hatteras which leaves from Falmouth Harbour.

Fishing
There is a sport fishing tournament over the Whit weekend at the end of May

St John's

Built around the largest of the natural harbours is St John's, the capital. Although poor, slum areas remain, the area around the cruise ship docks has been developed for tourism and the town is a mixture of the old and the new. New boutiques, duty-free shops and restaurants are vying for custom. **Redcliff Quay** is a picturesque area of restored historical buildings now full of souvenir shops. **Heritage Quay** is a duty-free shopping complex with a casino, strategically placed to catch cruise ship visitors. When a cruise ship is in dock many passengers come ashore and it becomes very crowded. There is a vendors' mall next to Heritage Quay, selling souvenirs.

Population: 30,000

Most activity now takes place around the two quay developments

However, St John's does have interesting historical associations. Nelson served in Antigua as a young man for almost three years, and visited it again in 1805, during his long chase of Villeneuve which was to end with the Battle of Trafalgar. Some of the old buildings in St John's, including the Anglican cathedral, have been damaged several times by earthquakes, the last one in 1974. A cathedral in St John's was first built in 1683, but replaced in 1745 and then again in 1843 after an earthquake, at which time it was built of stone. Its twin towers can be seen from all over St John's. It has a wonderfully cool interior lined with pitch pine timber. Donations requested.

The **Museum of Antigua and Barbuda** at the former courthouse in Long Street is worth a visit, both to see the exhibition of pre-Columbian and colonial archaeology and anthropology of Antigua, and for the courthouse building itself, first built in 1750, damaged by earthquakes in 1843 and 1974, but now restored. There is also Viv

Museum

Richards' cricket bat, with which he scored the fastest century. The *Historical and Archaeological Society (HAS)* based at the museum publishes a useful and interesting newsletter. They also organize field trips. ■ *Mon-Fri 0830-1600, Sat 1000-1400. Free, although donations requested; interesting gift shop with locally made items. T/F4624930/1469, museum@candw.ag*

Fortifications   West of St John's are the ruins of **Fort Barrington**, on a promontory at Goat Hill overlooking Deep Bay and the entrance to St John's Harbour. It was erected by Governor Burt, who gave up active duty in 1780 suffering from psychiatric disorders; a stone placed in one of the walls at the fort describes him grandly as 'Imperator and Gubernator' of the Carib Islands. The previous fortifications saw the most action in Antigua's history, with the French and English battling for possession in the 17th century. At the other side of the harbour are the ruins of **Fort James**, from where you can get a good view of St John's. There was originally a fort on this site dating from 1675, but most now dates from 1749. To get there, head north out of St John's, turn west by *Barrymore Hotel* to the sea, then follow the road parallel to the beach to the end.

Around the island

Finding your way around is not easy, there are no road signs and street names are rarely in evidence

Antigua, with about 108 sq miles, is the largest of the Leewards, and also one of the most popular. Its dependencies are nearby Barbuda and Redonda. The island is low-lying and composed of volcanic rock, coral and limestone. **Boggy Peak**, its highest elevation, rises to 1,330 ft. There is nothing spectacular about its landscape, although the rolling hills and flowering trees are picturesque. Its coastline however,

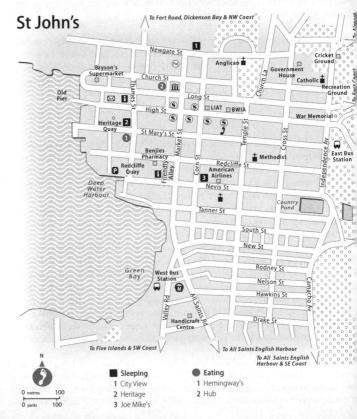

St John's

Sleeping
1 City View
2 Heritage
3 Joe Mike's

Eating
1 Hemingway's
2 Hub

curving into coves and graceful harbours with 365 soft white-sand beaches fringed with palm trees, is among the most attractive in the West Indies.

On the other side of the island from St John's is **English Harbour**, which has become one of the world's most attractive yachting centres and is now a 'hot spot' at night for tourists. Here Nelson's Dockyard, the hub of English maritime power in the region, has been restored and is one of the most interesting historical monuments in the West Indies. It was designated a national park in 1985. The TV film *Longitude*, starring Jeremy Irons, was filmed here, standing in for Jamaica and Barbados. ■ *US$1.60, children under 12 free. Souvenirs and T-shirts are on sale at the entrance. Parks Commissioner, T4601379.* The **Nelson's Dockyard Museum** has been renovated to give the complete history of this famous Georgian Naval Yard and the story of famous English Harbour. See *Admiral's Inn*, with its boat and mast yard, slipway and pillars still standing, but which suffered earthquake damage in the 19th century. The *Copper and Lumber Store* is now a hotel, bar and restaurant. On the quay are three large capstans, showing signs of wear and tear. Boat charters can be arranged from here; also a 20-30-minute cruise round the historic dockyard for US$6 on *Horatio*, from outside the *Copper and Lumber Store*, depending on seasonal demand. A footpath leads round the bay to **Fort Berkeley** at the harbour mouth, well grazed by goats, and wonderful views. Near the dockyard, **Clarence House** still stands where the future King of England, William IV, stayed when he served as a midshipman.

On the left of the road from English Harbour to Shirley Heights are the remains of the British Navy's magazines and a small branch road to the Dow Hill Interpretation Centre, which offers an interesting 15-minute multimedia show every 15 minutes on the history of the island. There is a gift shop, restaurant and small museum with shell display. Local guides are also available.

At **Shirley Heights**, overlooking English Harbour, are the ruins of fortifications built in the 18th century, with a wonderful view. Some buildings, like officers' quarters, are still standing, restored but roofless, which give an idea of their former grandeur. At the lookout point, or Battery, at the south end is a bar and restaurant. On Sunday at the dockyard below you can hear a steel band 1600-1900, followed by reggae 1900-2200, very loud and popular. Barbecued burgers, chicken, ribs and salad. There is often some activity on Thursday too. It is usually full of tourists, often packed, and later on the crowd can be drunk and rowdy. **Great George Fort**, on Monk's Hill, above Falmouth Harbour (a 30-minute walk from the village of Liberta, and from Cobb's Cross near English Harbour) has been less well preserved.

Watch the sun set over the west coast with a sundowner and maybe you'll see the green flash

Fig Tree Drive between Old Road and the Catholic church on the road going north from Liberta, is a steep, winding road, through mountainous rainforest. It is greener and more scenic than most of the island, but the rainforest is scanty and incomparable with islands like Dominica. If travelling by bicycle make sure you go *down* Fig Tree Drive from the All Saints to Liberta road, heading towards Old Road; the hill is very steep.

Boggy Peak, in the southwest, is the highest point on the island and from the top you can get wonderful views over to Guadeloupe, St Kitts, Nevis and Montserrat. It is a good walk up, or you can take a car. From Urlings walk (or take minibus) about ½-¾ mile in the direction of Old Town. There is a clear track on the left (ask the bus driver to drop you off there) which is very straight then ascends quite steeply. When you get to the top, walk round the fence surrounding the Cable and Wireless buildings to get a good view in all directions. It takes over an hour to walk up (signs say it is a private road) and you are advised not to wander around alone.

If you have a car, try taking the road out to the airport from St John's. Do not enter the airport, but take the right fork which runs alongside it. After about 1½ miles take a right turn down a small road to **St George's Church**, on Fitches Creek Bay, built in 1687 in a beautiful location, and with interesting gravestones. From there, follow the rough road round the coast to **Parham**, which was the first British settlement on the island and has an attractive and unusual octagonal church, **St Peter's**, which dates from the 1840s, surrounded by flamboyant trees. From Parham go due south and

Leeward Islands

then east at the petrol station through Pares to Willikies. On this road, just past Pares village, is a sign to **Betty's Hope**, a ruined sugar estate built in 1650 and owned by the Codrington family from 1674 to 1944. Restoration was carried out by the Antigua Museum in St John's and it was officially opened in 1995. One of the twin windmills can sometimes be seen working. ■ *Visitors' centre, 0830-1600 (except Tue and Sun), tells the story of life on a sugar plantation. Well worth a visit. For a guided tour contact the Antigua Museum, T4624930 or Lionel George, T4601356.*

After Willikies the road is signed to the *Pineapple Beach Club* at Long Bay, but before you get there, take a right turn down a small road, which deteriorates to a bumpy track, to **Devil's Bridge** at Indian Town Point. The area on the Atlantic coast is a national park where rough waves have carved out the bridge and made blow-holes, not easily visible at first, but quite impressive when the spray breaks through. Good view of Long Bay and the headland.

Essentials

Sleeping
There is a 10% service charge and 8.5% government tax at all hotels. Porters expect a tip of US$1-2 per bag

There are hotels, resorts and apartments all round the island. The greatest concentration of developments is in the area around St John's, along the coast to the west and also to the north in a clockwise direction to the airport. A second cluster is around English Harbour and Falmouth Harbour in the southeast of the island. Many may be closed Sep-Oct. There are lots of self-catering apartments, but a common complaint is that sufficient provisions are not available locally and you have to go into St John's for shopping. **Camping** is illegal.

St John's L-A *Heritage Hotel*, Heritage Quay, St John's, T4621247/8, heritagehotel@candw.ag Right by cruise ships, caters for business travellers, discounts available. In same management group is **AL** *City View*, Newgate St, T5620256-9, cityviewhotel@candw.ag 38 rooms with patios, a/c, kitchen, fridge, cable TV, phone, restaurant and room service, conference room. **C** *Joe Mike's Hotel*, in Corn Alley and Nevis St, T4621142, joemikes@candw.ag Special rates can be negotiated but not by phone, rooms OK, no balconies, weak a/c, no food but downstairs are fast food, restaurant and bar, casino, ice cream parlour, cocktail lounge, beauty salon and mini-mart. **C** *Murphy's Apartments*, All Saints Rd, T4611183. Run by Elaine Murphy, apartments modernized, every amenity, breakfast US$5, also longer-term lets, lovely garden. **E** *Pigottsville Guest House*, at Clare Hall, T4620592. No signs, about 2 miles from the airport and within easy walking distance of St

English Harbour & Shirley Heights

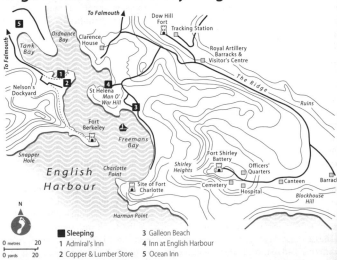

■ Sleeping
1 Admiral's Inn
2 Copper & Lumber Store
3 Galleon Beach
4 Inn at English Harbour
5 Ocean Inn

N

0 metres   20
0 yards   20

John's, 20 rooms. **E-F** *Montgomery Hotel*, Tindale Rd, T4621164. Usually plenty of room except during carnival and cricket matches, central but not a very nice part of town, noisy roosters across the street, scruffy and basic, 24 small rooms, 8 with private bath, rest with shared bath, rats in downstairs rooms, no water after midnight, cable TV, the owner also has some apartments north of St John's.

West of St John's **LL** *Hawksbill Beach Resort*, 4 miles from St John's (a US$12 taxi ride), T4620301, www.hawksbill.com 39 acres and 4 lovely beaches, good food, meal plans available, friendly staff, tennis, table tennis, pool, watersports, pleasant rooms in 2-storey blocks or cottages with ceiling fans and a/c, some redecorated 2003.

Runaway Bay **LL-AL** *Barrymore Beach Club*, on Runaway Bay, 2 miles from St John's, T4624101, www.antigua.wheretostay.com/property/437.html Rooms and apartments, clean, comfortable, on white-sand beach. **AL-A** *Lashings*, T4624491, www.lashings.com On clean, sandy beach with shade from palm trees and sea grape, 16 double or family rooms includes breakfast, special deals for visiting cricket teams, 5-10 min beach walk from *Barrymore Beach Apartments*, vehicle hire needed.

Dickenson Bay LL-AL *Siboney Beach Club*, T4620806, siboney@candw.ag 12 a/c suites in gardens by beach, good restaurant, watersports available nearby. *Several large resorts here including Sandals*

North coast **LL-AL** *Blue Waters*, T4620290, www.blue waters.net 77 rooms and villas on beach, room only or all inclusive, pool, watersports.

Southwest **L-AL per person** *Coco's Antigua*, T4602626, www.cocoshotel.com 14 rooms in chattel-style cottages, view of Jolly Beach and Five Islands, lovely location built on a bluff with gorgeous balconies and pleasant breeze, very romantic, fan, fridge, restaurant, pool, all-inclusive rate. *There are several luxury all-inclusives, not included here*

Falmouth Harbour **L-A** *Catamaran Hotel and Marina*, T4601036, www.catamaran-antigua.com On narrow man-made beach by yachts, on bus route or 30-min walk to Nelson's Dockyard, 14 rooms and suites, a/c, fans, some with TV, single or double beds, cribs for kids, internet across the road, *Jimmie's* restaurant around the corner. **L-A** *Country Inn*, Monk's Hill Rd, Cobb's Cross, on hillside overlooking harbour, T/F4601469, www.countryinnantigua.com Main house and self-catering cottages in traditional gingerbread style, breezy, fabulous view, balconies, hammocks, open-plan accommodation, small pool on hill top, access up poor road and steep hill, 4WD essential, manager Danny will take you hiking or partying, eco-conscious owners. **AL-A** *Falmouth Harbour Hillside Apartments* (same management as *Admiral's Inn*), T4601027, F4601534. Good value, 4 hillside studio apartments near beach, very clean, friendly staff, boats and other watersports equipment, all apartments have lovely view of harbour, but guests on massive yachts can be noisy at night.

English Harbour **LL-AL** *Copper and Lumber Store* (restored dockyard building), T4601058, F4629215. Studios and suites available, boat transport to nearby beaches. **LL-AL** *Galleon Beach*, T4601024, www.galleonbeach.com 1-, 2- or 3-bedroom comfortable and tasteful villas with additional sofa bed, on beach at Freemans Bay, spacious grounds, glorious views, fully equipped, tennis, sunfish, windsurfing, beach bar and restaurant, ferry to Nelson's Dockyard. **LL-AL** *The Inn at English Harbour*, St John's, T4601014, www.theinn.ag Set in 12 acres with lovely white-sand beach, old style, stone main house with dining room, bar and library, 6 hillside rooms with view of bay, 28 luxury beachfront rooms and junior suites newly built back from the sea after hurricane damage, heavy hardwood furniture and vaulted ceilings, fan, TV, minibar, internet access, well-equipped bathrooms, beach bar or terrace restaurant, watersports, tennis, fitness centre. **AL-A** *Admiral's Inn*, T4601027, www.antiguanice.com/admirals/index.html 14 rooms of varying sizes in restored 17th-century building, very pleasant, transport to the beach, complimentary sunfish and snorkelling equipment, excellent location, good food. **AL-C** *Ocean Inn*, T4601263, www.theoceaninn.com On hillside overlooking English Harbour, spectacular view of yachts and old buildings, breezy, small pool, CP, small basic rooms and small bathrooms, TV, a/c, fridge, carpet or tiles, some rooms share bathroom, meals on request. **D-E** *The Sleep Inn*, just outside the gates of Nelson's Dockyard, T5623082. 14 rooms, very simple but tidy inn, good value, private bath, ceiling fans, shared kitchen, meals on request, very local.

East **LL** *Harmony Hall*, T4604120, www.harmonyhall.com CP, simple cottages, use of boat, meal plans available, excellent restaurant, pool, dock for visiting yachts, beach, very popular. **LL-L** *Tree Tops Cottage*, T4604423, www.caribbeanavenue.com/tree-tops/index.html Charming 2-bedroom, 2-bathroom villa on hillside 5 mins from Half Moon Beach, well-equipped, comfortable, breezy, lovely deck for relaxing, quiet, car needed.

Long Island **LL** *Jumby Bay*, taken over by Rosewood in 2002, US$6.5 mn refurbishment and expansion continue at the 300-acre property, 39 rooms, 18 2-3-bedroom villas and private cottage, with an infinity swimming pool, spa and tennis.

Near airport If you are changing planes and have to stop over, **A-D** *Amarylis*, on Airport Rd, T4628690, F5620375. 22 rooms, comfortable, with *Calypso Café*, good West Indian and seafood in a nice atmosphere. **B** *The Airport Hotel*, T4621191, F4621534. Where some airlines dump you if a missed connection is their fault, rather basic but adequate for a night stop, restaurant and bar with outdoor patio, reasonably priced food, happy hour drinks Mon-Fri.

Eating

Oranges are green, while the native pineapple is called the Antigua black

In addition to a wide selection of imported delicacies served in the larger hotels, local specialities, found in smaller restaurants in St John's, often very reasonable, should never be missed: saltfish (traditionally eaten at breakfast in a tomato and onion sauce), pepper-pot with fungi (a kind of cornmeal dumpling), goat water (hot goat stew), shellfish (the local name for trunk fish), conch stew and the local staple, chicken and rice. *Ducana* is made from grated sweet potato and coconut, mixed with pumpkin, sugar and spices and boiled in a banana leaf. Tropical fruits and vegetables found on other Caribbean islands are also found here: bread fruit, cristophine, dasheen, eddo, mango, guava and pawpaw (papaya). Locally made *Sunshine* ice cream, American-style, is available in most supermarkets. Imported wines and spirits are reasonably priced but local drinks (fruit and sugar cane juice, coconut milk, and Antiguan rum punches and swizzles, ice cold) must be experienced. The local Cavalier rum is a light golden colour, usually used for mixes. Beer can be bought at good prices from most supermarkets and the Wadadli Brewery on Crabbs peninsula. There are no licensing restrictions. Tap water is safe all over the island. If you are planning to eat out in hotels, you need to allow at least US$300 per person per week, but it is possible to eat much more cheaply in the local restaurants in St John's.

A 7¾% tax on all meals and drinks is added to your bill. Restaurants tend to move, close down or change names frequently

St John's *Hemingway's*, T4622763. Drink, lunch or dinner West Indian style upstairs on cool veranda overlooking Lower St Mary's St at entrance to Heritage Quay, open Mon-Sat from 0830, main course US$9-22. *Home*, Gambles Terr, T4617651, 20-min walk from tourist area but worth it. Caribbean haute cuisine, Italian pasta dishes, exotic desserts, about US$30-37 per person, very elegant but no stiff formality, friendly atmosphere, service excellent, welcoming to families, run by Antiguan Carl Thomas and his German wife Rita, open from 1800-2300. *Mama Lolo's*, in Redcliffe Quay, T5621552, mamalol@candw.ag Best vegetarian lunch, choice of 2, 3, or 4 cooked dishes plus a salad for US$6.50, US$9.25 or US$10.75, great mixed fruit and vegetable juices. *O'Grady's*, Nevis St. Good for pub grub, US$9-10, darts and pool. *Pizzas in Paradise*, at Redcliffe Quay, T4622621. Very popular at lunchtime, salads and sandwiches as well as pizzas, around US$9-10, open Mon-Sat 0830-2300. *Smoking Joe's*, opposite the cricket ground. For barbecued ribs, chicken, etc, Joe is a local calypsonian. *The Hub*, Long St and Soul Alley, opposite the Museum, T4620616. Open daily from 0730 until 2200 (or later for drinks), good meals, live jazz on Sat night, local cuisine, friendly, pleasant atmosphere. For fast food lovers there is *Kentucky Fried Chicken* on High and Thames Sts, and a 2nd branch on Fort Rd, T4621973. *Charlie's Outdoor Café*, at Jasmine Court Mall on Friars Hill Rd, T5622233. Open for breakfast, lunch and afternoon tea, in tropical garden setting in West Indian colonial style mini shopping mall, salads, soups and sandwiches, around US$9.

In **Hodges Bay** area, near the airport, *Le Bistro*, T4623881. Excellent French food, dinner only, closed Mon. At the airport, *Big Banana* is surprisingly good, clean and efficient, closed Sun. At the airport, *The Sticky Wicket*, T4817000. Restaurant and bar, overlooks the cricket ground and has TVs for watching sporting events, convenient if you have a long wait for your plane, much more comfortable than the airport but expensive, lunch and dinner daily.

Runaway Bay Cricketing friends Richie Richardson and David Folb (Chairman of Lashings Cricket Club in Maidstone, Kent), run *Lashings Beach Café* bar and restaurant, from chilli to lobster, special deals at hotel for visiting cricket teams, if you beat the Lashings team you get free food and drinks. Late night hot spot with loud music and dancing. *The Beach*, T4624158. Same owners as the *Big Banana*, open daily for breakfast, lunch and dinner, East meets West theme with smoked sushi, Middle Eastern dishes and salads, pastas and seafoods, main dishes around

US$18-20, credit cards accepted, reservations suggested. On Wed and Fri nights, 1630-2100, an Englishman serves fish and chips (and shrimp and Pot Pies; great Indian curry on Wed) for around US$5-10 from a truck on the road outside *Buccaneer Cove* at Dickenson Bay, T5602334, just past the *Siboney* driveway, very busy, lots of locals, not to be missed.

Galley Bay *Chez Pascal*, overlooking Galley Bay, T4623232. Gourmet, authentic French food from French chef Pascal, expect to pay over US$55 per person.

Jolly Harbour At Jolly Harbour marine complex there is an Italian *trattoria*, *Al Porto*, T4627695. Pasta, pizzas, seafood in al fresco setting, poor service, meals from US$10, open daily lunch and dinner, closed 1500-1900. *Peter's* next door. Excellent, barbecued fresh fish and lobster, prices from US$6. *OJ's Beach Bar & Restaurant*, Crab Hill, T4600184, on beach. Excellent setting, simple menu but good food and service, economical prices, no credit cards.

English Harbour *Abracadabra* just outside Nelson's Dockyard, T4602701. Lively video bar, live music some evenings, Italian and Continental dishes, open every evening, closed Sep-Oct. *Admiral's Inn*, Nelson's Dockyard, T4601027. Breakfast (slow but good value, recommended), lunch and dinner (limited selection but good, slightly overpriced), yachtsman's dinner EC$40, closed Sep. Near St James's Club *Alberto's*, T4603007. Choice dining spot frequented by ex-pat 'locals' plus celebrities like Eric Clapton, Timothy Dalton, Italian-run, open-air tropical setting, fresh seafood and pasta always available, expect to pay over US$55, reservations essential. *Catherine's Café* at the Antigua Slipway in Nelson's Dockyard, T4605050. French chef, divine crêpes, quiches, assorted salads, lovely setting right on water, open daily, breakfast and lunch only, average price US$18-20. *Eden Café* is next to *Abracadabra*, in a 300-year-old building. Breakfast specials are 100% fruit smoothies and fresh French pastry, excellent Mediterranean salad specialities at lunch, around US$9-10, Fri-Sat open midnight till 0400 for late night sandwiches and coffee for the dancing crowd, credit cards accepted. *HQ*, upstairs in the historic Headquarters Building inside English Harbour, T5622562. Open daily for all 3 meals, dinner reservations suggested, credit cards accepted. *Grace Before Meals*, between English Harbour and Falmouth Harbour. A cheaper alternative to the many expensive restaurants, rotis, pizzas and other good value meals to eat in or take away. Between English and Falmouth Harbours, *Le Cap Horn*, T4601194. Pizzeria, Argentine Churrasco steak, lobster, some French dishes, great food, open 1830-2300 Mon-Sat. *Life*, just before entrance to Nelson's Dockyard, no phone, restaurant and disco, evenings only, open-air with lively crowd and good value meals for US$15. *Mario's Pizzeria*, T4601318. Delicious pizza baked in stone ovens, around US$7-8, also famous for fresh bread. *Southern Cross*, expensive Italian restaurant, over US$55 per person, upstairs on jetty off Antigua Yacht Club, delicious food, closed in summer. *The Dry Dock*, at the entrance to the Antigua Yacht Club Marina. Open every day, restaurant and bar, prices around US$15, with big screen TVs for sport and Antigua Race Week events.

East *Eastern Parkway*, also known as *Harry's Bar* is at Half Moon Bay Beach, T4604402. Open-air covered beach bar, snacks, cold drinks, burgers and very local specialities like bread and saltfish, goat curry, very casual dining on premises or takeaway, good value at around US$5-6, open daily. *Harmony Hall*, T4604120, www.harmonyhall.com Excellent Italian restaurant written up in many gourmet magazines, although management changed 2003, considered one of the best on the island, lunch daily, from US$22, dinner Fri-Sat, reservations essential, art gallery, panoramic view of Green Island.

Antigua Carnival is at the end of *Jul* and lasts until the 1st Tue in *Aug*. The main event is 'J'ouvert', or 'Juvé' morning when from 0400 people come into town dancing behind steel and brass bands. Hotels and airlines tend to be booked up well in advance. For information contact the Carnival Committee, High St, St John's, T4620194. **Barbuda** has a smaller carnival in *May*, known as 'Caribana '. An annual **jazz festival** is held, usually in late *May*, with concerts at Fort James, the *Sandpiper Reef Hotel*, King's Casino and on the *Jolly Roger*. Contact the Tourist Office for a programme. A **hot air balloon festival** is held at the end of *Oct*.

Festivals

The largest hotels provide dancing, calypso, steel bands, limbo dancers and moonlight barbecues. At the entrance to the Dockyard, *Life*, all music, see Eating, above. In the Dockyard, Fri night *Copper and Lumber* have 2 for the price of 1, Wed jazz, Thu karaoke. *Galley Bar* is popular with occasional entertainment. *Mad Mongoose*, *The Dry Dock* and *Abracadabra* nearly always

Nightlife

English Harbour area has become the hot spot for tourists

lively, with dancing. Elsewhere, *Putters*, Dickenson Bay, has mini golf course. The *King's Casino* in Heritage Quay awaits cruise ship passengers. Be warned that casino employees entice you off the street with the lure of winning easy money. After an initial spell of amazing luck, one reader (not a gambler) lost US$3,500 in 20 mins. Casinos at *Royal Antiguan* (only slot machines) and *St James's Club*. At *Dubarry's* bar there is jazz on Sun night, rum punch party on Tue, barbecue on Thu, take swimsuit, parties tend to end up in, not just by, the pool. *Miller's*, at Fort James. Serves lunch, dinner or just drinks, often has live music, for example reggae bands, especially on Sun after Shirley Heights, owned by a local jazz hero. A free newspaper, *It's Happening, You're Welcome*, contains lots of information on forthcoming events.

Shopping

Market day in St John's is Sat

The market building is at the south end of Market St but there are goods on sale all around. In season, there is a good supply of fruit and vegetables, which are easy to obtain on the island. The main supermarket in St John's is *Food Emporium*, on Long St. *Woods Center* is a modern shopping mall with a wide variety of shops including *The Epicurean Supermarket*, the most modern, well-stocked supermarket on the island, a drugstore, post office, dental clinic, dry cleaners and numerous other shops. *Gourmet Basket* on Airport Rd in the Island Provision Compound, near *Best Cellars Wines*, has gourmet items and a deli. Most grocery stores open 0800-2200, although many close at 1300 on Thu. You can buy fish from the fishing boats at the back of the Casino or from *Caribbean Seafoods* in Cassada Gardens near the horse racetrack (T4626113), large selection of cleaned and ready-to-cook seafood, freshly caught (by their own fishing boat), vacuum packed and quick frozen. Heritage Quay (has public toilets) and Redcliffe Quay are shopping complexes with expensive duty-free shops in the former, and boutiques. The latter has bars and restaurants and a parking lot, free if you are shopping there. There are 2 grocery and liquor stores at *Antigua Yacht Club* dock. Some tourist shops offer 10% reductions to locals; they compensate by overcharging tourists. Duty-free shops at the airport are more expensive than normal shops in town. *The Best of Books*, Benjies Ball upstairs, Redcliffe St, T5623198, bestofbooks@yahoo.com, really does have the best selection of Caribbean and international books, newspapers and magazines in all the Leeward Islands. *The Map Shop*, St Mary St, T4623993, carries a reasonable selection of Caribbean literature plus reference books and guides to history, culture, fauna and flora of the Caribbean. The public library on Market St has a good Caribbean section, particularly non-fiction, for those who want to read but not buy. *Harmony Hall*, Brown's Bay Mill, near Freetown, T4604120. An art gallery and gift shop, open daily 1000-1800, exhibiting and selling paintings, sculpture and crafts from leading Caribbean artists, popular for a lunch stop at the restaurant while touring by car or yacht, closed May-Oct.

Sports

For watersports, sailing and fishing, see pages 510 and 511

Cricket is the national sport and Antigua has produced many famous cricketers, including captains of the West Indies team: Sir Viv Richards and Richie Richardson, fast bowlers: Andy Roberts and Curtly Ambrose, Kenneth Benjamin, Eldine Baptiste and Winston Benjamin. Test matches are played at the Antigua Recreation Ground, ARG to locals. Matches are helped along by DJ Chickie's Hi Fi and characters like Gravy, the cross-dressing cheerleader who entertains during intervals. Brian Lara scored his world record 375 here in 1994. There are also good cricket pitches at the Sticky Wicket by the airport and at the *Jolly Beach Hotel* (where the teams usually stay), which are used as practice grounds during an international match, team training for the West Indies and for touring teams. There are matches between Antiguan teams and against teams from other islands, and local matches can be seen in St John's near the market and all over the island in the evenings and at weekends. The West Indies Cricket Board has information on Test Matches, T4605462. The cricket season runs from Jan to Jul. Seasons for other spectator sports are: **netball** Jan-Jul, **basketball** Feb-Jul, **volleyball** Dec-Jul, **football** Aug-Feb.

Golf There are 2 18-hole golf courses: a professional (but rather dried out) one at *Cedar Valley*, near St John's, T4620161 and a par 71 championship course at *Jolly Harbour*, T4623085. The Antigua Open is played at Cedar Valley in Nov. Rental equipment available at both courses, but not very good at Cedar Valley. Miniature golf can be played at *Putters Bar & Grill*, also known as the *Dickenson Park Leisure Centre*, Dickenson Bay, T4634653, where there is an 18-hole, floodlit course. At the Centre there is also a **squash** court, a floodlit **skateboard** park (equipment for hire), **pool** tables, video store and video arcade, open 0800 onwards.

Hiking Organized hikes are arranged frequently to historical and natural attractions and can be a good way of seeing the island. Once a month the *Historical and Archaeological Society* organize hikes free of charge. *Hash House Harriers* arrange hikes off the beaten track every other Sat at 1600, free of charge, contact Bunnie Butler T4610643 or David Crump T4610686. The *Environmental Awareness Group* offers monthly excursions, T4626236. *The Hiking Company*, T4601151, run by Peter Todd, takes groups of 6 minimum, 0900-1700, for moderate hikes in the southwest, with lunch on a beach for swimming afterwards. *Tropikelly Trails*, T4610380, has escorted hiking 0800 and 1500, also starting at Wallings Reservoir and going down Fig Tree Drive, water and walking sticks provided.

Tennis Many of the large hotels have courts: *Royal Antiguan Hotel*, T4623733, Deep Bay; *Temo Sports*, a tennis and squash club open to the public in English Harbour (sports complex with floodlit tennis courts, glass-backed squash courts, bar/bistro, equipment rental, open Mon-Sat 0700-2200, no credit cards, T4601781, VHF 68). The *Jolly Harbour* development includes BBR Sportive, with lit tennis and squash courts (US$20 per 30 mins) and a 25 m swimming pool, open 0800-2100, food and drink available, T4626260, VHF Channel 68.

Riding is available through some of the hotels. *Spring Hill Riding Club*, on the road to Rendezvous Bay, offers fully insured tuition from BHS qualified instructors, English style, show jumping, dressage, horses and ponies, beach rides, swimming on horseback, forest rides, open daily from 0730, T4607787, 7733139. **Horse racing** takes place on public holidays at Cassada Gardens Race Track and also on Barbuda.

Tour operators

Mac's Tracks, run by Brian MacMillan, St John's (home T4627376), F4611187, 2-4-hr hikes on special request, from US$10 per person, exploring the countryside, lunch and transport to start of hike can be arranged, to Boggy Peak, Mt McNish, Monterose Hill, Signal Hill and Green Castle Hill. *Tropikelly Trails*, St John's, T4610383, www.tropikellytrails.com US$65 per person, Mon-Fri tours include drinks, lunch, hotel pick-up, 5-6 hrs to Body Pond, Monk's Hill, the government pineapple farm, Boggy Peak and the silk cotton tree at Cades Bay, where 10 people can stand inside the trunk.

Transport

Long distance Air V C Bird Airport, some 4½ miles from St John's, is the centre for air traffic in the area. *British Airways* (T4620876, from London Gatwick, connections with Barbados, Port of Spain and St Lucia), *BWIA* (from London Heathrow) and *Virgin Atlantic* (from Gatwick). *American Airlines* (from Miami, Baltimore, Boston, Philadelphia and Washington via San Juan, New York via St Maarten, Raleigh/Durham direct), *Continental* (from Newark, NJ), *BWIA* (from New York JFK, Miami), *Air Jamaica* (from New York JFK), *BWIA* and *Air Canada*, T4621147 (from Toronto). There are frequent air services to neighbouring islands (Anguilla, Barbados, Barbuda, Dominica, Grenada, Guyana, Jamaica, Nevis, Guadeloupe, Trinidad, St Croix, St Kitts, St Lucia, St Maarten, St Thomas, St Vincent, Puerto Rico, Tortola) operated by *LIAT* (T4620700), *Caribbean Star* (T4802550), *BWIA* (T4620260), *Winair* , *Continental*, *American Eagle*. *Carib Aviation* arranges charters to neighbouring islands in planes carrying 5, 6 or 9 passengers and can often work out cheaper and more convenient. The office is at the airport, T4623147, F4623125, 0800-1700, after office hrs T4611650. They will meet incoming flights if you are transferring to another island, and make sure you make your return connection. Also day tours. **Helicopter** *Carib Aviation* operates the helicopter service from the airport to Montserrat, daily except Wed, 0730, 1030 (not Sat, Sun), 1500 (Sun only), 1630, returning 0800, 1530 (not Sat), 1700, US$112 return plus departure tax. *Caribbean Helicopters*, helitours, custom charters and day trips, daily, 15-min island tour, US$75 per person, 30-min tour US$130, 45-min Montserrat Volcano tour, US$190, T4605900, F4605901, www.caribbeanhighlights.com/helicopter/default.htm **Ferry** to Montserrat leaves Heritage Quay (if there are no cruise ships, otherwise from the port) Mon, Wed, Fri 0630, 1600, returning from Little Bay 0800, 1730, 1 hr, Tue, Thu 0900, 1600, returning 1030, 1710, US$45 day return on Sat, plus departure tax, no service Sun. Be at the dock at least 1 hr beforehand to clear immigration, which stops 30 mins before departure. At weekends and holiday times get there even earlier. Contact *Carib World Travel*, T4606101, F4802995. There are occasional boat services to St Kitts and Dominica; see boat captains at Fisherman's Wharf. There is a cargo boat to Dominica once a week and you can arrange a passage through Vernon Edwards Shipping Company on Thames St.

Leeward Islands

Local Bicycle Bicycle hire from *Cycle Krazy* on Pope's Head St, T4629253. Hire of mountain bike, helmet, lock, cheaper for over 3 days, Mon-Sat, races organized, contact for cycling clubs and Antigua & Barbuda Amateur Cycling Association. *Bikes Plus*, Independence Drive, T4622453, only rent by the day. **Bus** Buses are banned from north of the line from the airport to St John's, but run frequently between St John's and English Harbour, EC$2.50. There are also buses from the east terminal by the war memorial to Willikies, whence a 20-min walk to Long Bay Beach and to Parham. There are no buses to the airport and very few to beaches though 2 good swimming beaches on the way to Old Road can be reached by bus. Bus frequency can be variable, and there are very few after dark or on Sun. Buses usually go when they are full, ask the driver where he is going. They are numbered and destinations are on display boards at the West Bus Station. Buses to Old Road are half hourly on average, though more frequent around 0800 and 1600. **Car hire** A local driving licence, US$20, valid for 3 months, must be purchased on presentation of a foreign (not international) licence. There is a 24-hr petrol station on Old Parham Rd outside St John's. Petrol costs US$2.25 per gallon everywhere. A complete list of car hire companies is available on the Board of Tourism website. *Hertz*, T4624114/5; *Avis*, T4622840, *Dollar Rental*, T4620362 (Factory Rd); *National*, T4622113; at *Oakland Rent-A-Car*, T4623021. Rates are from US$45 per day, US$225 a week (no mileage charge), including insurance charges, in summer, more in winter. **Hitchhiking** is easy in daylight, but at night you might fall prey to a taxi driver. **Taxi** Taxis have TX registration plates. In St John's there is a taxi rank on St Mary St, or outside the supermarket. They are not metered and frequently try to overcharge, or else have no change, so agree a price first, they should have a EC$ price list so ask to see it. There is a list of government-approved taxi rates posted in EC$ and US$ at the airport just after customs. From St John's to Runaway Bay, 10 mins, is US$6. From the airport to *Admiral's Inn*, *St James's Club*, *Falmouth Beach Apartments*, *Curtain Bluff*, *Harmony Hall*, Darkwood Beach, etc, is US$24/EC$64; to *Sandals*, *Antigua Village* and Dickenson Bay area US$13/EC$34; to *Blue Waters* US$10/EC$27; *Hawksbill* and Five Islands US$16/EC$42. From the airport to town EC$21 per person. If going to the airport early in the morning, book a taxi the night before as there are not many around. A day tour normally costs about US$70 for 1-4 people, US$76 for 5-7 people. Taxi excursions advertised in the hotels are generally overpriced. Tips for taxi drivers are usually 10%.

Directory **Banks** *Scotia Bank*, *FirstCaribbean Intrernational Bank*, *Royal Bank of Canada*, *Canadian Imperial Bank of Commerce*, *Antigua and Barbuda Investment Bank*, *Antigua Commercial Bank*, all in the centre of St John's. Mosts banks take Mastercard and Visa. A tax of 1% is levied on all foreign exchange transactions but there may be additional charges on TCs. Casinos will change TCs without a fee. *American Express* is at Antours near Heritage Quay, staff helpful and friendly. **Communications** Internet: You can set up internet access for your own computer before arriving through www.cwantigua.com with charges billed to a credit card. Cable and Wireless Cybercafé at Antigua Yacht Club (bring your own computer, or use theirs). Also email, messages, etc, at *International Connections* at AYC dock; *Internet Café*, Upper Church St, St John's; *Cyber Stop II*, Falmouth Harbour, T4603575, Mon-Fri 1000-1800, Sat 1000-1400, EC$20 for 35 mins, EC$30 for 1 hr, EC$10 each subsequent 30 mins; *Comnett Ltd*, upstairs above Fedex in Redcliffe Quay, St John's, T4621040, www.comnett-online.com good machines, US$3 for 15 mins. **Post**: Post office at the end of Long St, St John's, opposite the supermarket. Open Mon-Thu, 0815-1200, 1300-1600, until 1700 on Fri; also a post office at the Woods Shopping Centre, the airport and at English Harbour. A postcard to the USA costs EC$0.75. *Federal Express* is on Church St. *DHL* is in the Vernon Edwards building on Thames St. **Telephone**: *Cable and Wireless Ltd*, Long St, St John's, the Woods Mall and at English Harbour. Prepaid cards are available for overseas calls and for cell phones. GSM tri-band handsets can be used by purchase of a SIM card from Apua T7272782, www.apuanet.com **Embassies and consulates** The *British High Commission* is at the Price Waterhouse Centre (PO Box 483), 11 Old Parham Rd, St John's, T4620008/9, F4622806.

Barbuda

IDD code: 268
Colour map 3, grid B3
Population: 1,500

Some 30 miles to the north of Antigua is Barbuda, a flat coral island some 68 miles square, one of the two island dependencies of Antigua. Most residents live in the only village on the island, **Codrington**, which stands on the edge of a large lagoon. Barbuda has a fascinating history, having been privately owned in colonial times by the Codrington family, who used it to supply their sugar estates on Antigua with food and slaves. This caused problems after emancipation as all property belonged to the Codringtons and the freed slaves were trapped with no jobs, no land and no laws. After many years and court cases, Antiguan law was applied to the island, but while Barbudans may own their own houses, all other land is generally held by the Government. In places you can see the remains of the stone wall used to demarcate the limit of the village within which everybody had to live until 1976, when the creation of a local government inspired people to move further afield. You can also see the village well which was used to draw water until the 1980s. A visit to Barbuda is like stepping back in time: there are few paved roads, life is slow and simple, there is no crime and the people are friendly.

This is one of the few islands in the area where there is still abundant wildlife, although much of it has been introduced by man: duck, guinea fowl, plover, pigeon, wild deer, pigs, goats, sheep, horses and donkeys, left over from the Codrington era. There is an impressive **Frigate Bird Sanctuary** (the largest colony in the world) in the mangroves in Codrington Lagoon, particularly on Man of War Island where thousands of birds mate and breed between August and February. The sanctuary is definitely worth a visit and the sight of some 10,000 frigates raising their young is stunning (see box, page 522). Visitors are taken to only one or two spots to view the birds, and ropes keep the boats from getting too close. The rest of the birds are left entirely at peace. There are also brown boobies nesting alongside the frigates and pelicans can be seen in the lagoon. An endemic warbler (*Dendroica subita*) lives on Barbuda and although DNA studies have been carried out, numbers and habitat requirements are so far unknown.

Palaster Reef is a marine reserve to protect the reef and the shipwrecks (there are around 60 ships documented and the Codringtons made a healthy income from wrecking). The seas are rich with impressive formations of elkhorn and staghorn coral, all types of crustacean and tropical fish. Lobster is plentiful and a mainstay of nearly every meal. Diving is extremely rewarding, particularly if you like exploring wrecks, but you will need to take a guide. You can take your own scuba gear or hire it from Byron Askie (certified divers only), T5623234. For two to four people he charges US$80 per person (US$150 for a single diver), including gear, boat and three dives. Snorkelling equipment is available but is more expensive than on Antigua.

Detailed maps are available locally from the Codrington post office, otherwise from the map shop in Jardine Court, St Mary's, St John's, or the Barbuda Board of Tourism in Antigua see page 507

The **beaches** are an outstanding feature of Barbuda and are arguably the most magnificent in the whole Caribbean. The longest beach is a swathe of white sand stretching for 17 miles down the west side, while the most spectacular is the pink sand beach at Palmetto Point, made up of zillions of tiny pink shells. There are no beach bars or vendors, you will probably be the only person for miles. There is no shade except around Palm Beach where a few palm trees survived past hurricane damage.

The **Gunchup Caves** near Two Foot Bay are interesting to explore. Men have used them for shelter since the days of the Amerindians. Dark Cave is home to a blind shrimp (*Typhlatya monae*) found only in these pools and in the Mona Island off Puerto Rico, but access is difficult. A road is planned. The island has a Martello tower and fort, the most complete historical site on the island.

Barbuda

2	Coco Point Lodge
3	Island Chalet
4	K-Club
5	Nedd's Guest House
6	Palmetto Beach
7	Telly's Guest House

Sleeping
1 Bus Stop

Leeward Islands

▶ **Frigate birds**

Fregata magnificens *are indeed magnificent when seen soaring high in the air, using the thermals to suspend themselves on their huge wings for days at a time, and travel great distances. Frigates are one of the oldest known birds, with a history spanning 50 million years, and during that time they've picked up a trick or two. One of them, piracy, has earned them the nickname of Man-O'-War bird. Their fishing technique relies on finding fish or squid close to the surface which they can just skim off, but failing that they have developed a method of hassling other seabirds, encouraging them to regurgitate whatever they have just caught. In an amazing display of aerobatics, the frigate birds manage to catch the food before it hits the water and get a free meal.*

The breeding colony on Barbuda is believed to be the largest in the world, larger even than that of the Galapagos. Locals will tell you that there are some 10,000 birds, having recovered from the effects of Hurricane Luis in 1995, but numbers are anyone's guess. The breeding season is roughly September-January, although even later you can still see males displaying their bright red pouches, blowing them up like balloons to attract a mate. It is the male who chooses a nest site, and when he is sure he has found a long-term partner, he builds a precarious nest of twigs in the mangroves alongside all the other males. The female lays a single egg, which the male incubates and initially cares for once it is hatched. The chick is born white and fluffy and sits on the twiggy nest, suspended above the water, for 8-10 months until it is fully fledged. It takes a lot longer to be fully proficient at flying and feeding itself.

The tower is 56ft high and once had nine guns to defend the southwest approach. From Codrington, River Road runs three miles to **Palmetto Point**, past Cocoa Point and on to Spanish Point, a half-mile finger of land that divides the Atlantic from the Caribbean Sea. There is a small ruin of a lookout post here and the most important Arawak settlements found in Barbuda. Horse racing takes place on a dirt track south of Codrington. You can sometimes see the horses being exercised around the island and taken for a swim behind a boat in the lagoon.

Sleeping
Accommodation is either expensive and exclusive or basic, with little in between

LL *Coco Point Lodge*, T4623816, F4625340. The ultimate in exclusivity, islanders and non-guests are not admitted, you have to be 'someone' to stay here, price includes all meals and drinks and airfare from Antigua. **LL** *K-Club*, T4600300, www.kclubbarbuda.com Owned and designed by Italian designer, 45 rooms, everywhere painted turquoise and white, with its own 9-hole golf course as well as watersports and a pool, welcomes islanders and non-residents, excellent food, fabulous beach, open mid-Nov to end-Aug, no under 12s. **LL-L** *Palmetto Beach Hotel*, T4600442, www.palmettohotel.com A more informal beachfront hotel on 11-mile beach at Palmetto Point. 22 junior suites and a villa with 2 more suites, FAP, tennis, pool, water sports, diving (www.enjoyscuba.com) bikes, volleyball, library, closed Sep- Nov, changes in management in 2003 may lead to a renovation. **A-B** *The Island Chalet*, in the heart of Codrington, T7730066, Mrs Myra Askie. 4 rooms with small double bed and rollaway can sleep 3 at a pinch, shared kitchen and living room facilities of a good standard, grocery across the square, price comes down at weekends when noise levels rise at night. **C** *Telly's Guest House* in Codrington, T4600021, ask for Amanda. Sleeps 6, screens, fans, TV with local channel only, no phone, kitchen available, basic grocery shopping nearby. **C** *Nedd's Guest House*, T4600021. Simple. **C** *The Bus Stop*, T4600081. Guesthouse with TV in rooms and private bathroom. Several private homes offer accommodation, although these change if a long-term rental is taken. Take mosquito repellent and earplugs if you are in the centre of Codrington at weekends.

Eating

There are not many restaurants and they tend to close in the evening, so check beforehand. You can ask local people to cook for you but be prepared to fend for yourself sometimes. The *Palm Tree* has local food. For home cooking try *Claudia Hopkins*, T4600022, or the *Block Boys*, T4600012, at weekends. *The Green Door*, in the centre of town, is the island's first bar, open daily for bingo and entertainment in the evenings, food on request. *The Lyme*, by the lagoon, is another bar with nightlife.

The *ArtCafé* in Codrington, T4600434, artcafe@candw.ag, has a detailed hand-drawn map, useful information and hand-made crafts. Owner Claire Frank is happy to share her detailed knowledge of the island. Internet use for a small fee if her computer is available.

Shopping

Day tours include the Bird Sanctuary, Highland House, the caves and the Martello tower, anything can be arranged, eg bicycles, horse riding, hiking, contact *Red Fox*, T4600065, *George Burton*, T4600103, *Linton Thomas*, T7279957, *Barbuda Vacations*, Kenroy Walcott, T7737660, *Claire Frank*, T4600434, artcafe@candw.ag Bicycle tours are available from *Jonathan Pierra*, T7739599, on the island 4 months of the year. *Excellance* catamaran, T4801225, tropad@candw.ag, does a day trip from Antigua Wed, Sun 0900-1600, lunch, drinks, snorkelling. Barbuda tours available on arrival to the Bird Sanctuary. The *Barbuda Taxi Association* will do tours, T7279957. The tourist board is attempting to implement safety standards for boats operating in the lagoon; before booking, ask whether the boat has lifejackets, communication equipment and insurance in the event of an accident.

Tour operators

Air There are 2 airports; the main one is just south of Codrington. Flights take 10 mins from St John's. *Carib Aviation* will arrange charters and day trips. Return ticket costs US$74. The 2nd airport only serves *Coco Point*. **Road** It is possible to hire jeeps: *Linton Thomas*, T4600081, has a pick-up truck for US$50 per day or US$65 overnight; *Byron Askie* rents jeeps for US$60 a day or negotiate longer rental rate, T5623134, 7736082; *Junie Walker*, T4600619. **Horses** can be hired in Codrington, otherwise everywhere is a long hot walk, so take drinks with you.

Transport

Redonda

Antigua's second dependency, 35 miles to the southwest and half a mile square, is little more than a rocky volcanic islet and is uninhabited. Columbus sighted the island on 12 November 1493 and named it after a church in Cadiz called Santa María la Redonda. He did not land, however, and thus did not formally claim the island. Neither did anyone else until 1865 when Matthew Dowdy Shiell, an Irish sea trader from Montserrat, celebrated the birth of a long-awaited son by leading an expedition of friends to Redonda and claiming it as his kingdom. In 1872, the island was annexed by Britain and came under the jurisdiction of the colony of Antigua, despite protests from the Shiells. The title of King was not disputed, however, and has survived to this day. The island was never inhabited, although for some years guano was extracted by the *Redonda Phosphate Company* until the works were blown away by a hurricane.

Colour map 3, grid C2

In 1880 MD Shiell abdicated in favour of his son, Matthew Phipps Shiell, who became King Felipe of Redonda, but emigrated to the UK where he was educated and became a prolific and popular novelist. His best known novel was *The Purple Cloud* (1901), which was later made into a film, *The World, the Flesh and the Devil*, starring Harry Belafonte. On his death in 1947, he appointed as his literary executor and successor to the throne his friend John Gawsworth, the poet, who became Juan, the third King of Redonda, but continued to live in London. His reign was notable for his idea of an 'intellectual aristocracy' of the realm of Redonda and he conferred titles on his literary friends, including Victor Gollancz, the publisher, JB Priestley, Dorothy L Sayers and Lawrence Durrell. This eccentric pastime hit a crisis when declining fortunes and increasing time spent in the pub sparked a rash of new titles to all and sundry, and a number of abdications in different pubs. The succession was, and still is, disputed.

The *Redondan Cultural Foundation* is an independent association of people interested in Redonda, its history and its monarchs, which tries to steer through the minefield of Redondan politics. It was established in 1988 by the late Reverend Paul de Fortis and exists to promote the writings of MP Shiell, John Gawsworth and other authors of the realm's 'intellectual aristocracy'. It celebrates Redonda as 'the last outpost of Bohemia'. The foundation published *The Kingdom of Redonda 1865- 1990* in association with the Aylesford Press (1991), and also publishes a regular newsletter.

Leeward Islands

Meanwhile, on Redonda, all is much the same for the goats, lizards and seabirds, who live an undisturbed life apart from the occasional birdwatcher who might come to find the burrowing owl, now extinct on Antigua.

Background

History Antigua (pronounced Anteega) was first inhabited by the Siboney (stone people), whose settlements date back to at least 2400 BC. The Arawaks lived on the island between about AD 35 and 1100. Columbus landed on his second voyage in 1493 and named the island Santa María de la Antigua. Spanish and French colonists attempted to settle there, but were discouraged by the absence of freshwater springs and attacks by the Caribs. In 1632 the English successfully colonized the island and, apart from a brief interlude in 1666 when held by the French, the island and its dependencies, Barbuda and uninhabited Redonda, remained British. Sir Christopher Codrington established the first large sugar estate in Antigua in 1674, and leased Barbuda to raise provisions for his plantations. Barbuda's only village is named after him. Forests were cleared for sugarcane production and African slave labour was imported. Today, many Antiguans blame frequent droughts on the island's lack of trees to attract rainfall, and ruined towers of sugar plantations stand as testament to the destruction and consequent barrenness of the landscape. In the 17th and 18th centuries, Antigua was important for its natural harbours, where British ships could be refitted safe from hurricanes and from attack. The Dockyard and the many fortifications date from this period. *Shirley Heights, The Story of the Red Coats in Antigua*, by Charles W E Jane, published by the Reference Library of Nelson's Dockyard National Park Foundation at English Harbour, Antigua, in 1982, gives a detailed account of the military history of the island and the building of the fortifications.

The slaves were emancipated in 1834 but economic opportunities for the freed labourers were limited by a lack of surplus farming land, no access to credit, and an economy built on agriculture rather than manufacturing. Conditions for black people were little better than under slavery and in many cases the planters treated them worse. Poor labour conditions persisted and violence erupted in the first part of the 20th century as workers protested against low wages, food shortages and poor living conditions. In 1939, to alleviate the seething discontent, the first labour movement was formed: the Antigua Trades and Labour Union. Vere Cornwall Bird became the union's president in 1943 and with other trade unionists formed the Antigua Labour Party (ALP). In 1946 the ALP won the first of a long series of electoral victories, being voted out of office only in 1971-76 when the Progressive Labour Movement won the general election. For a graphic account of the terrible conditions in which black people lived and worked during slavery and its aftermath, read *To Shoot Hard Labour (The Life and Times of Samuel Smith, an Antiguan Workingman 1877-1982)*, by Keithlyn B Smith and Fernando C Smith, published by Karia Press, London, and Edan's Publishers, Toronto.

Antigua was administered as part of the Leeward Islands until 1959 and attained associated status, with full internal self-government in 1967. Antigua and Barbuda, as a single territory, became independent in November 1981, despite a strong campaign for separate independence by Barbuda. Vere C Bird became the first Prime Minister and in 1989, at the age of 79, he took office for the fourth consecutive time. The general elections were marked by some irregularities and allegations of bribery, but the ALP won 15 of the 16 seats for Antigua in the 17-seat House of Representatives, the remaining seats being taken by the United National Democratic Party and the Barbuda People's Movement, for Barbuda. Mr Bird appointed a largely unchanged cabinet which included several members of his family.

In 1990 the Government was rocked by an arms smuggling scandal, which exposed corruption at an international level when allegations were made that Antigua had been used as a transit point for shipments of arms from Israel to the Medellín cocaine cartel in Colombia. Communications and Works Minister, Vere Bird Jr, the Prime Minister's son, became the subject of a judicial inquiry, following a complaint from the Colombian Government, for having signed authorization documents. His Cabinet appointment was revoked but he remained an MP. The Blom-Cooper report recommended no prosecutions, although it undermined the credibility of the Government and highlighted the rivalry between the two sons, Vere Jr and Lester Bird. The report also recommended that Vere Bird Jr be banned from holding public office.

Repeated calls for the resignation of Prime Minister Vere Bird were ignored although several ministers resigned from his Government. Demonstrations were organized in 1992 by the newly-formed three-party United Opposition Front, seeking the resignation of the Prime Minister amid allegations of his theft and corruption. Fresh allegations of corruption were published in 1993 by the weekly opposition newspaper, *Outlet*, concerning property development contracts and misuse of public funds, resulting in a libel action issued by Lester Bird. *Outlet*, for many years edited by Tim Hector, who died in 2002, has been the most outspoken critic of the Bird administration, frequently exposing corruption and fraud.

Vere Bird finally retired as Prime Minister in February 1994 at the age of 84. He was succeeded by his son, Lester, who led the ALP into the general elections held in March, winning its ninth out of 10 elections held since 1951 but with a reduced majority. The United Progressive Party (formerly the United Opposition Front), led by Baldwin Spencer, won five seats, the largest number for any opposition party in the country's history.

The new government was not free of allegations of corruption scandals (Ivor Bird, a younger Bird brother and general manager of the ZDK radio station was arrested and fined for taking possession of 12kg of cocaine at the airport) although Prime Minister Bird made efforts to portray a more professional administration. Economic adjustment was given priority and new tax policies sparked protest demonstrations and strikes. Efforts were made to clean up Antigua's poor reputation with the appointment in 1996 of a special advisor on control of illicit drugs and money laundering. 11 offshore banks were closed by the end of 1997 and new legislation was approved in 1998 to close loopholes taken advantage of by international criminal organizations. However, this did not go far enough to satisfy US and UK regulators, who believed money laundering was still taking place. The Government bowed to the criticism and set up a committee in 1999 to study the areas of concern in its offshore financial services legislation.

In March 1999 the ALP won its sixth successive general election, increasing its representation in parliament to 12 seats, while the UPP won four and the BPM retained the Barbuda seat. The new cabinet was notable for the appointment of Vere Bird Jr as Minister of Agriculture, Lands and Fisheries. Corruption is still endemic, with a scandal in 2002-03 surrounding fraud in the state health insurance fund, where over US$230 million was unaccounted for.

Government

Antigua and Barbuda is a constitutional monarchy within the Commonwealth, and the British Crown is represented by a Governor General. The head of government is the Prime Minister. There are two legislative houses: a directly elected 17-member House of Representatives and a 17-member Upper House, or Senate, appointed by the Governor General, mainly on the advice of the Prime Minister and the Leader of the Opposition. Antigua is divided into six parishes: St George, St John's, St Mary, St Paul, St Peter and St Phillip. Community councils on Antigua and the local government council on Barbuda are the organs of local government. The Barbuda Council has nine seats, with partial elections held every two years.

Economy

The economy was long dominated by the cultivation of sugar, the major export earner until 1960 when prices fell dramatically and crippled the industry. By 1972 sugar had largely disappeared and farming had shifted towards fruit, vegetables, cotton and livestock. The economy is now based on services, principally tourism and offshore banking, where improvements in legislation were made in 1999-2000 to prevent money laundering. Hotels and restaurants contribute about 25% of gross domestic product and employ about one-third of the work force. Tourism receipts make up about 60% of total foreign exchange earnings and there are about 5,000 hotel rooms. Tourist numbers are highly susceptible to disasters such as hurricanes, the 11 September terrorist attacks in the USA, and the vagaries of the airline industry.

There is some light industry which has been encouraged by tax and other incentives, but manufacturing for export is hampered by high wages and energy costs. A major expansion of tourist infrastructure has taken place, with development of harbour, airport, road and hotel facilities. This investment has not yet touched the bulk of the population, and in rural areas small wooden shacks still constitute the most common form of dwelling, often alongside resorts and villa developments.

Leeward Islands

> **Things to do in St Kitts and Nevis**
>
> - Take a ride on the **Sugar Train** round St Kitts, for the best view and perspective on the importance of sugar through the ages.
> - Visit the **aquarium** at Under the Sea, Oualie Beach, Nevis, for an exciting but educational view on life under the waves.
> - Try a **saltfish and johnny cake sandwich** sold on the Circus in Basseterre and wash it down with coconut water from the nearby vendor – a bellyful.
> - Go **mountain biking** on Nevis along the goat trails and donkey paths around Nevis Peak for an exhilarating view of other islands and a look at monkeys and other wildlife.

St Kitts and Nevis

IDD code: 869
Colour map 3, grid B2

The islands of St Kitts (officially named St Christopher) and Nevis are in the north part of the Leeward Islands in the Eastern Caribbean. Slightly off the beaten track, neither island is overrun with tourists; St Kitts is developing its southern peninsula where there are sandy beaches, but most of the island is untouched. Rugged volcanic peaks, forests and old fortresses produce spectacular views, and hiking is very rewarding. Two miles away, the conical island of Nevis is smaller, quieter and very desirable. Plantation houses have been converted into some of the most romantic hotels in the Caribbean, very popular with honeymooners. While one federation, the sister islands are quite different. St Kitts, the larger, is more cosmopolitan and livelier, while Nevis is quieter and more sedate. Wherever you go on these two small islands there are breathtaking, panoramic views of the sea, mountains, cultivated fields and small villages.

Ins and outs

Getting there
See Transport, page 546, for further details

There are charter flights, such as *Monarch*, which flies direct from Gatwick to St Kitts, but no direct scheduled flights to St Kitts and Nevis from Europe or North America. You have to fly to a neighbouring island and change planes. Cruise ships call at St Kitts, but otherwise there are few links by boat with other islands and they tend to be informal.

Getting around
Driving is on the left

Buses on both islands are cheap and speedy. Drivers are generally very obliging and, if asked, may even divert their route to accommodate you. They run from very early in the morning until 2300 on St Kitts, but on Nevis there is a reduced service after 1600 and very few after 1800. Buses are identified by their green H registration plate, flag them down with a wave. **Cars**, jeeps and mini mokes can be hired from a variety of agencies on both islands. The main road on St Kitts is, for the most part, very good and motorists, especially bus drivers, can be very fast. On Nevis the paved road round the island is good except in the northeast, but storm ditches frequently cross it, so drive slowly and carefully. Parking in both Basseterre and Charlestown is difficult. Several passenger **ferries** including the *Caribe Queen*, *Carib Breeze* and *MV Sea Hustler* operate on a regular schedule between St Kitts and Nevis.

Climate

The weather is pleasant all year round, but the best time to visit is during the drier months from Nov-May. The temperature varies between 62°F and 91°F, tempered by sea winds and with an average annual rainfall of 55 ins on St Kitts and 48 ins on Nevis.

Tourist information

The **St Kitts Department of Tourism**, Pelican Mall, Basseterre, T4652620, F4658794, mintitcc@stkittstourism.kn, and the **Nevis Tourist Office**, Old Treasury Building, Main St, Charlestown, T4697550, F4697551, nta2001@caribsurf.com, are both extremely helpful, with plenty of information available, open Mon-Fri 0800-1600, with the Nevis office also open Sat 0900-1200. www.stkitts-tourism.com and www.nevisisland.com

Flora and fauna

Both islands are home to the green vervet monkey, introduced by the French some 300 years ago. They can be seen in many areas including Brimstone Hill but can be a pest to farmers. To keep down numbers, many have been exported for medical research. The monkey is the same animal as on Barbados but the Kittitians used to eat them. Another animal, the mongoose, imported to kill rats and snakes in the sugar estates, never achieved its original purpose (rats being nocturnal whereas the mongoose is active by day). It has contributed to the extinction of many species of lizard, ground-nesting birds, green iguanas, brown snakes and red-legged tortoises. There are some wild deer on the southeast peninsula, imported originally from Puerto Rico by Philip Todd in the 1930s. In common with other West Indian islands, there are highly vocal frogs, lizards (the anole is the most common), fruit bats, insect bats and butterflies, although nothing particularly rare. Birds are typical of the region, with brown pelicans and frigate birds to be seen, as well as three species of hummingbird.

St Kitts and Nevis have the earliest documented evidence of honeybees in the Caribbean

St Kitts and Nevis are small islands, yet have a wide variety of habitats, with rainforest, dry woodland, wetland, grassland and salt ponds. The forests on the sister islands are restricted in scale, but St Kitts is one of the few areas of the world where the forest is expanding. It provides a habitat for wild orchids, candlewoods and exotic vines. Fruits and flowers, both wild and cultivated, are in abundance, particularly in the gorgeous gardens of Nevis. Trees include several varieties of the stately royal palm, the spiny-trunked sandbox tree, silk-cotton tree, and the turpentine or gum tree. Visitors can explore the rainforests on foot with guides and gentle hikes through trails and estates also reap many rewards. Several trails are clear and do not need a guide, although note that there are no marked trails; care should be taken and advice sought. Comparatively clear trails include Old Road to Philips, the old British military road, which connected the British settlements on the northeast and southwest coasts of St Kitts without going through French territory when the island was partitioned. There are also trails from Belmont to the crater of Mount Liamuiga, from Saddlers to the Peak, from Lamberts or the top of Wingfield Heights to Dos d'Ane lake (known locally as Dos d'Ane pond).

Diving and marine life

There is very good snorkelling and scuba diving. Most dive sites are on the Caribbean side of the islands, where the reef starts in shallow water and falls off to 100 ft or more. Between the two islands there is a shelf in only 25 ft of water which attracts lots of fish, including angelfish, to the corals, sea fans and sponges. There is black coral off the southeast peninsula, coral caves, reefs and wrecks with abundant fish and other sea creatures of all sizes and colours. Off St Kitts good reefs to dive include **Turtle Reef** (off Shitten Bay) which is good for beginners and snorkelling, **Coconut Reef** in Basseterre Bay and **Pump Bay** by Sandy Point. Much of the diving is suitable for novices and few of the major sites are deeper than 70 ft.

Dive sites

The waters around St Kitts are the resting place of several ship wrecks. The Anglo-Danish Maritime Archaeological Team (ADMAT) set up a field school in 2003, the largest of this sort ever carried out in the Caribbean. The aim is to record two pre-1760s ship wrecks uncovered by recent hurricanes in White House Bay. Diving around St Kitts can be an exciting adventure as you are taken back in history to a time when the Caribbean was a battleground and a burial ground. Several wrecks and some other sites are actually shallow enough for very rewarding snorkelling although the very best snorkelling around St Kitts is only accessible by boat.

In Nevis, snorkelling off **Oualie Beach** is excellent and is also good at Nisbett Beach and Tamarind Bay. Good dive sites include Monkey Shoal, where you can find angel fish, black durgons, octopus, flying gurnard and maybe nurse sharks in the overhangs, crevices and grottos of this densely covered reef. Devil's Caves are another series of grottos, where you can see lobster and squirrelfish and often turtles

Touching down

Boat information *(own flag) List all anchorage stops on cruising permit at the Port Authority in Basseterre and clear with immigration in Nevis. Port dues start at EC$6 based on size. There is no additional charge in Nevis once you have cleared in St Kitts.*

Anchorages *Port Zante Marina in Basseterre, White House and Ballast Bay are the best on St Kitts, Oualie Beach on Nevis is beautiful. Groceries, alcohol, laundry, propane. Can have fuel delivered to dock and buy water by the cubic ton. Marina charges including water: under 40 ft, US$0.40 per ft; 40-70 ft, US$0.60; over 70 ft, US$1.20. For information, Port Authority, T4658121, Port Zante, T4665021.*

Business hours *Offices: 0900-1600; **Shops:** Mon-Sat 0800-1600, some open on Sun if a cruise ship is in port. Early closing Thu and also Sat for some shops.*

Currency *East Caribbean dollar, EC$. US dollars accepted. EC$2.70=US$1. When prices are quoted in both currencies, for example for departure tax, taxi fares, a notional rate of EC$2.50=US$1 is used. There are no restrictions on the amount of foreign currency that can be imported or exported, but the amount of local currency exported is limited to the amount you imported and declared. Visa and Mastercard are the most widely used credit cards.*

Departure tax *There is an airport departure tax of US$15 per person, not payable for stays of less than 24 hrs (or when you leave on the same flight number as you arrived the previous day, that is slightly more than 24 hrs), and an environmental levy of US$1.50.*

Documents *US and Canadian visitors need only produce proof of citizenship to stay up to six months. OECS nationals need a driver's licence or birth certificate. Other nationalities need **passports** and a **return ticket**, but for up to six months **visas** are not required for Commonwealth and EU countries, Finland, Iceland, Liechtenstein, Norway, San Marino, Sweden, Switzerland, Turkey, Uruguay, Venezuela and nationals of other member countries of the OAS, with the exception of the Dominican Republic and Haiti who do require visas. Visas can be extended for US$20 per*

riding the surge. Nag's Head, just off Oualie Beach, is a schooling ground for big fish such as king mackerel, barracuda, jacks and yellowtail snappers. Some dive operators will take you as far as Redonda, where diving is superb and untouched.

Dive centres **St Kitts** *Kenneth's Dive Centre* based in Basseterre (Bay Rd, T4652670); Kenneth Samuel, a PADI-certified Dive Master (friendly and helpful), offers courses, dive packages (single-tank dive US$50, US$75 2-tank dive, 4-day package US$245) and all equipment. There are facilities for people with disabilities. *Pro-Divers* at *Ocean Terrace Inn*, has a large boat and takes large parties diving, PADI instruction, T4663483, prodiver@caribsurf.com Dive gear available for rent, dive packages available, single-tank dive US$45, 2-tank dive US$70, 3-hr snorkelling US$35. Ocean kayaks available for hire. *Dive St Kitts* is at *Birdrock Beach Hotel,* offering PADI instruction, T4651189, F4653696, 2-tank dive US$70, PADI Open Water certification US$350. A water taxi to Nevis is US$25 per person, minimum 6 passengers.

Nevis *Scuba Safaris*, a 5-star operation run by Ellis Chaderton, is based at Oualie Beach, T4699518, F4699619, scubanev@caribsurf.com:diving (US$45 for a single-tank dive, US$80 for 2 tanks), PADI and NAUI instruction and equipment rental. Trips to see dolphins and humpback whales can be arranged.

Beaches and watersports

St Kitts
Swimming is not safe on the Atlantic side of the island because of strong currents

Most of the beaches are of black, volcanic sand, but several of those fringing the southeast peninsula have lighter coloured sand. Swimming is very good in the Frigate Bay area where all watersports are available. The southeast peninsula itself has white-sand beaches. **Banana Bay, Cockleshell Bay** and **Mosquito Bay** all have sandy beaches, calm water and picturesque views of Nevis just across the straits. There has been little development here so far, but there is the *Turtle Beach Bar and Grill* at Mosquito Bay with watersports on offer. The beach is cleaned regularly because lots of weed comes in if the wind is in the wrong direction. On Cockleshell Beach there is a bar at weekends

Leeward Islands

month for the first three months and then US$30 for the following three months up to a maximum of six months.

Embassies and consulates None.

Emergency numbers T911.

Media *Newspapers* The Observer, The Democrat, *the* Leeward Times *(weekly) or* The Labour Spokesman *(twice weekly).* **Radio and TV** AM/FM ZIZ Radio medium wave 555 kHz and 96 FM; Choice 105.3 FM; Sugar City Rock 90.3 FM; Goodwill Radio 104.5 FM; WINN 98.9 FM; Big Wave 96.7 FM. VON Radio in Nevis 895 kHz medium wave and Radio Paradise 825 kHz. Two TV stations: the state run ZIZ and Nevis-based Christian station Trinity Broadcasting.

Official time Atlantic Standard Time, 4 hrs behind GMT, 1 hr ahead of EST.

Public holidays New Year's Day (1 Jan), Carnival Day/Las' Lap (2 Jan), Good Fri, Easter Mon, May Day (1st Mon in May), Whit Mon (end of May), the Queen's birthday (Jun), Aug Mon/Emancipation Day (beginning of the month), National Heroes Day (16 Sep), Independence Day (19 Sep), Christmas Day (25 Dec), Boxing Day (26 Dec).

Safety Note that the penalties for possession of narcotics are very severe and no mercy is shown towards tourists. Theft has increased, do not leave your things unattended in a car or on the beach. **Health** Mains water is chlorinated, but bottled water is available if preferred for drinking, particularly outside the main towns. A yellow fever or cholera vaccination certificate is required if you are arriving from an infected area.

Tourist offices overseas Canada 133 Richmond St West, Suite 311, Toronto, T416-3686707, Canada_office@st.kittstourism.kn **UK**: 10 Kensington Court, London W8 5DL, T020-73760881, uk-europe.office@stkittstourism.kn **USA** 414 East 75th St, New York NY 10021, T212-5351234, info@stkittstourism.kn

Voltage 230 volts AC/60 cycles (some hotels have 110 volts).

Weights and measures Imperial.

---

with local food. The water here is calm and shallow, great for families. Major's Bay has been messed up by hurricanes and storms. **Sand Bank** is a lovely curved bay with good sand, and protected despite being on the Atlantic. Kite flying is good but you can also potter about in the shallow water. It is easily reached from the road a short distance down a dirt track. **North Friars Bay** is a broad sweep of sand, but it is on the Atlantic and not protected. **South Friars Bay** on the Caribbean coast is lovely and the most popular beach for cruise ship passengers, with lots of beach bars, and it can get very busy at weekends. **White House Bay** is on the Caribbean and popular as an anchorage for yachts, as well as a great dive site for wrecks.

Nevis

The beautiful four mile **Pinney's Beach** is only a few minutes' walk from Charlestown and is never crowded. The entire middle stretch of Pinney's Beach has been given over to a 218-room *Four Seasons Hotel*. The sun loungers are for guests only, but the public has access to the beach and there are watersports available. Huge amounts of sand were imported after Hurricane Lenny and breakwaters were built to protect the beach by the hotel, but much of the beach has remained stony since the hurricane. **Tamarind Bay** is now popular, with plenty of sand. On the Atlantic side of Nevis, the beaches tend to be rocky and the swimming treacherous; there is, though, an excellent beach at White Bay in the southwest.

Watersports

St Kitts *Leeward Island Charters' Caona II*, a 47-ft catamaran, 67-ft *Eagle*, or *Spirit of St Kitts*, a 70-ft catamaran, T4657474, F4657070, office next to the *Ballahoo* restaurant above the Circus for bookings and private charters, take visitors on a sail, snorkel and beach barbecue. Sailing is popular. The *St Kitts-Nevis Boating Club*, T4658766, organizes sunfish races, check the bulletin board for details at *PJ's Pizza Bar* (T4658373), Frigate Bay, the *Ballahoo* (T4654197) in Basseterre, or Dougie Brookes who manages the boatyard *Caribee Yachts* (T4658411). *Blue Water Safaris*, T4664933, waterfun@caribsurf.com, has 1 boat, *Caretaker* (38 ft) and 2 catamarans, *Falcon* (55 ft) and *Irie Lime* (65 ft), offering fishing (US$60 per person), moonlight cruises (US$25), party

Leeward Islands

cruises (US$25), Nevis day tours (US$60), sunset cruises (US$35) and snorkelling trips (US$35), private snorkelling, sailing and fishing charters (US$360 half day). *Mr X Watersports*, located next to *Monkey Bar* in Frigate Bay, T4654995, rents windsurfing and snorkelling equipment, and offers fishing trips and weekly all-inclusive packages.

There is a wide range of other water-based activities, such as jet-skis, waterskiing, windsurfing, etc. *Fantasy Parasailing*, T4668930, bentels@caribsurf.com, takes up to 6 up in the air with optional dips in the sea. Deep-sea fishing can be arranged. *Oliver Spencer*, T4656314, a fisherman based in Old Road, is happy to take visitors. In summer there is a race for windsurfers and sunfish to Nevis.

Nevis Watersports facilities are available at *Oualie Beach Club*. Sea kayaks can be rented for US$15 per hr single, US$20 for a double, hobie cates are US$45-95 an hr, no credit cards. *Windsurf'n'Mountainbike Nevis*, *Wheel World* cycling shop, T4699682, www.mountain bikenevis.com, for windsurfing (www.windsurfingnevis.com), rentals and lessons: beginners US$50 for 2 hrs, intermediate and advanced US$30 for 1 hr, rentals US$65-95 a day, US$20-30 an hr. The *Sea Brat* and *Sea Troll* can be chartered from *Nevis Water Sports* at Oualie Beach for fishing or leisure tours, T4699060, www.fishnevis.com *Under the Sea* is a small aquarium run by Barbara Whitman as an educational venture. She takes groups snorkelling after a hands-on talk about the contents of her aquarium and you learn to look out for the smaller creatures underwater. Entrance US$5, with snorkelling US$40 (US$30 children 5-12), snorkel gear US$5, T4691291, www.undertheseanevis.com Watersports also at *Newcastle Bay Marina*, T4699395, or information from *Mount Nevis Hotel and Beach Club*, T4699373, F4699375.

St Kitts

IDD code: 869
Colour map 3, grid B2
Population: 35,340

St Kitts is made up of three groups of rugged volcano peaks split by deep ravines and a low-lying peninsula in the southeast where there are salt ponds and fine beaches. The dormant volcano, Mount Liamuiga (3,792 ft, pronounced Lie-a-mee-ga) occupies the central part of the island. The mountain was previously named Mount Misery by the British, but has now reverted to its Carib name, meaning 'fertile land'. The foothills of the mountains, particularly in the north, are covered with sugar cane plantations and grassland, while the uncultivated lowland slopes are covered with forest and fruit trees.

Basseterre

Population: 15,000

The port of Basseterre is the capital and largest town. By West Indian standards, it is quite big and as such has a quite different feel from its close neighbour, Charlestown. It was founded some 70 years later in 1727. Earthquakes, hurricanes and finally a disastrous fire destroyed the town in 1867 and consequently its buildings are comparatively modern. There is a complete mishmash of architectural styles from elegant Georgian buildings with arcades, verandas and jalousies, mostly in good condition, to hideous 20th-century concrete block houses. In recent years, the development of tourism has meant a certain amount of redevelopment in the centre. An old warehouse on the waterfront has been converted into the Pelican Mall, a duty-free shopping and recreational complex. It also houses the Ministry of Tourism and a lounge for guests of the *Four Seasons Hotel* in Nevis awaiting transport. A new cruise ship berth has been built on the waterfront between Bramble Street and College Street in the heart of Basseterre, capable of accommodating the largest ships afloat, together with a sailing and power boat marina, and berthing facilities for the inter-island ferry, the *Caribe Queen*.

At the south end of Fort Street on Bay Road is the imposing façade of the **Old Treasury Building**, with a dome covering an arched gateway. It has been converted into a museum of national culture and arts, and also houses the **St Christopher Heritage Society**, which has a small, interesting display of old photographs and artefacts. They work on conservation projects and are grateful for donations. ■ *Mon-Tue, Thu-Fri 0830-1300, 1400-1600, Wed, Sat, 0830-1300*, T4655584 **The Circus**, styled after

London's Piccadilly Circus (but looking nothing like it), is the centre of the town. It is busiest on Friday afternoon and comes alive with locals 'liming' (relaxing). The clock tower is a memorial to Thomas Berkely, former president of the General Legislative Council. Head north up Fort Street, turn left at the main thoroughfare (Cayon Street) and you will come to **St George's** church, set in its own large garden, with a massive, square buttressed tower. The site was originally a Jesuit church, Notre Dame, which was razed to the ground by the English in 1706. Rebuilt four years later and renamed St George's, it suffered damage from hurricanes and earthquakes on several occasions. It, too, was a victim of the 1867 fire. It was rebuilt in 1869 and contains some nice stained-glass windows. There is a fine view of the town from the tower.

Independence Square was built in 1790 and is surrounded now by a low white fence; eight gates let paths converge on a fountain in the middle of the square (it looks like the Union Jack when seen from the air). There are gaily painted muses on top of the fountain. Originally designed for slave auctions and council meetings, it now contains many plants, spacious lawns and lovely old trees. It is surrounded by 18th-century houses and, at its east end, the Roman Catholic cathedral with its twin towers. Built in 1927, the Immaculate Conception is surprisingly plain inside. At 10 North Square Street you can visit the very attractive building housing the **Spencer Cameron Art Gallery**. See Rosey Cameron-Smith's paintings and prints of local views and customs, as well as an impressive selection of the work of other artists, T/F4651617. On West Independence Square, the Courthouse reflects the old one

St Kitts

■ Sleeping

1 Bird Rock Beach
2 Fairview Inn
3 Frigate Bay Resort
4 Gateway Inn

5 Golden Lemon
6 Inner Circle Guest House
7 Morgan Heights Condos
8 Ocean Terrace Inn

9 Ottleys Plantation Inn
10 Rawlins Plantation
11 Rex Papillon St Kitts
12 Timothy Beach Resort
13 Trinity Inn Apartments

Leeward Islands

which burnt down in 1867. It is an impressive building in the colonial style. The **Bank of Nova Scotia** houses some interesting paintings of Brimstone Hill by Lt Lees of the Royal Engineers, circa 1783.

The **International House Museum** on Central Street was designed by Winston Zack Nisbett, a cultural preservationist and friend of the previous owner of the property, Edgar Challenger, a well-known trade unionist and historian, who died in January 2001. Challenger's residence was a gold mine of traditional utensils and equipment used in 1920-40, as well as books on the history of the Federation. ■ *Mon-Fri 1000-1700, Sat 1000-1300, Sun 1300-1700. US$5 for visitors, EC$5 for locals. T4650542.*

Around the island

A clockwise route around the island will enable you to see most of the historical sites

A cheap way of touring the island is to take a minibus from Basseterre (Bay Road) to Dieppe Bay Town, then walk to Saddlers (there might be a minibus if you are lucky, but it is only half a mile up the road) where you can get another minibus back to Basseterre along the Atlantic coast. Evidence of sugar cane is everywhere on the comparatively flat, fertile coastal plain. You will drive through large fields of cane and glimpse the narrow gauge railway which is now used to transport it from the fields. Disused sugar mills are also often seen. Around the island are the **Great Houses**: Fairview, Romney Manor (destroyed by fire in 1995), *Golden Lemon*, the White House, *Rawlins* and perhaps most famous for its colonial splendour, *Ottley's*. They have nearly all been converted into hotels and have excellent restaurants.

Basseterre

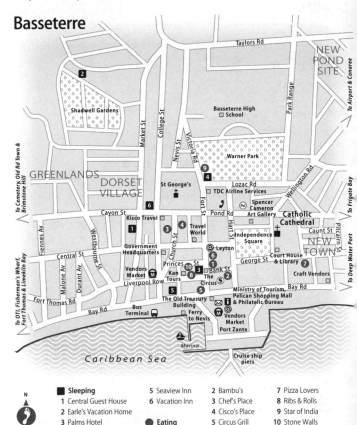

Sleeping ■	5 Seaview Inn	2 Bambu's	7 Pizza Lovers
1 Central Guest House	6 Vacation Inn	3 Chef's Place	8 Ribs & Rolls
2 Earle's Vacation Home		4 Cisco's Place	9 Star of India
3 Palms Hotel	Eating ●	5 Circus Grill	10 Stone Walls
4 Park View Inn	1 Ballahoo	6 Oasis Café	

The Sugar Train

The sugar industry was revolutionized in St Kitts when first the estates moved from wind to steam power in 1870 and then a central sugar factory was built in Basseterre in 1912. A narrow-gauge railway was built in 1912-26 to deliver cane from the fields to the central sugar mill and it was the beginning of the end for all the small estate-based sugar mills dotted around the island. Many sail-less windmills still stand as relics of the old ways. Although the track initially ran as two spurs either side of the island, planters soon saw the sense of abandoning other delivery systems and it was extended to be a circular route all round the coast. With the decline in the sugar industry at the end of the 20th century, the track fell into disrepair but has now been renovated with new rails and bridges by the company running the tourist train, for the added benefit of the sugar company. The St Kitts Scenic Railway, which opened in 2003, is the perfect way to see the whole island, far better than touring by car as you get a much better view. The railway is mostly uphill from the road, although in many places it runs along the coast, and with the double decker carriages you are above the sugar cane which blocks your view from a car. Around the north of the island you pass several primary schools where crowds of children come out to wave and shout hello to their popular new train. The locomotive originated in Romania but was sold to Poland for sugar beet transport before coming to St Kitts for sugar cane. The power car was built in Colorado, USA, while the 'island series' carriages, the first of their kind, were built in Seattle, Washington, USA. The rails were brought from the UK, Belgium, the USA and abandoned sugar track in Cuba, the sleepers are hard wood from Guyana. An Alaskan engineer is always on board to answer questions and a Kittitian choir will serenade you.

St Kitts Scenic Railway departs 0820 and 1310 from Needsmust station near the airport, 3 hours 10 minutes. It is expensive, at US$89 per adult, US$44.50 per child, or break your journey with a tour of Brimstone Hill Fortress for US$123, returning to the starting point by bus. A maximum of 28 guests per carriage have a seat on both levels, the upper open-air deck and the lower, enclosed, a/c carriage. Reservations essential, T4657263, F4664815, www.stkittsscenicrailway.com

---

The island is dominated by the southeast range of mountains (1,159 ft) and the higher northwest range which contains **Mount Verchilds** (2,931 ft) and the crater of **Mount Liamuiga** (3,792 ft). To climb **Mount Liamuiga** independently, get a bus to St Paul's. Just after the village entrance sign there is a track leading through farm buildings which you follow through the canefields. After 20 minutes take a left fork, ask people working in the fields if you are unsure. At the edge of the forest, the track becomes a path, which is easy to follow and leads through wonderful trees. At 2,600 ft is the crater into which you can climb, holding on to vines and roots; on the steady climb from the end of the road note the wild orchids in the forest. A full day is required for this climb which is really only for experienced hikers. To get beyond the crater to the summit you need a guide. You can reach the attractive, but secluded, Dos d'Ane pond near **Mount Verchilds** from the Wingfield Estate, a guide is recommended.

Mountain treks

If you hear something in the upper branches, look up before the monkeys disappear

The west coast is guarded by no less than nine **forts** and the magnificent Brimstone Hill Fortress. Taking the road out of Basseterre, you will pass the sites of seven of them: Fort Thomas, Palmetto Point Fort, Stone Fort, Fort Charles, Charles Fort, Sandy Point Fort and Fig Tree Fort. The remaining two are to the south of Basseterre: Fort Smith and Fort Tyson. Little remains of any of them. A peaceful spot to admire some of Stone Fort's ruins is a swing for two built by local Rastaman, Jahbalo. At Trinity Church, turn right, up the dirt path. At the sugar mill there are some ruins to your right. Climb the small mound to find the swing with a view towards cane fields and the Caribbean.

The west coast

The first point of interest is situated just before Old Road Town. Sir Thomas Warner landed at Old Road Bay in 1623 and was joined in 1625 by the crew of a French ship badly mauled by the Spanish. They were initially befriended by the local chief

Leeward Islands

Tegreman, but the Caribs became alarmed at the rapid colonization of the island. 3,000 Caribs tried to mount an attack in 1626. 2,000 of them were massacred by the combined French and English forces in the deep ravine at **Bloody Point** (the site of Stone Fort). An amicable settlement meant that the English held the central portion of the island roughly in line from Sandy Point to Saddlers in the north to Bloody Point across to Cayon in the south. French names can be traced in both of their areas of influence (Dieppe Bay Town in the north, the parishes are called Capisterre and Basseterre in the south). The southeast peninsula was neutral. This rapprochement did not last long as, following the colonization of Martinique and Guadeloupe, the French wished to increase their sphere of influence. St Kitts became a target and in 1664 they squeezed the English from the island. For 200 years the coast was defended by troops from one nation or another.

At Old Road Town you turn right to visit **Wingfield Estate**, home to *Caribelle Batik*. You drive through a sugar mill and the edge of rainforest. Unfortunately, Romney Manor was destroyed by fire in 1995, but the gardens remain with views over the coast and a 350-year old saman tree. ■ *Mon-Fri, 0830-1600. T4656253, F4653629.* Apart from a well-stocked shop you can watch the artists producing the colourful and highly attractive material. A guide will explain the process. Also near here the remains of the island's Amerindian civilization can be seen on large stones with drawings and petroglyphs. If you keep driving to the left of Romney Manor and *Caribelle Batik*, you will find one of the highest paved roads on the island. It is a tough climb so be sure to have a sturdy car or legs. A large flat rock at the top is perfect to admire the spectacular view of the mountains. To the right is a smaller path that leads to an incredible over-view of Bat Hole Ghaut. Magnificent views of tropical rainforest in myriad greens.

At the village of **Middle Island**, you will see, on your right and slightly up the hill, the church of St Thomas at the head of an avenue of dead or dying royal palms. Here is buried Sir Thomas Warner who died on 10 March 1648. The raised tomb under a can-opy is inscribed 'General of y Caribee'. There is also a bronze plaque with a copy of the inscription inside the church. Other early tombs are of Captain John Pogson (1656) and Sir Charles Payne, 'Major General of Leeward Carribee Islands', who was buried in 1744. The tower, built in 1880, fell during earth tremors in 1974.

Brimstone Hill

Brimstone Hill Fortress was inaugurated as a national park by the Queen in October 1985 and made a UNESCO World Heritage Site in October 2000

The **Brimstone Hill Fortress National Park**, one of the 'Gibraltars of the West Indies' (a title it shares with Les Saintes, off Guadeloupe), sprawls over 38 acres on the slopes of a hill 800 ft above the sea. It commands an incredible view of St Kitts and Nevis and on clear days, Anguilla (67 miles), Montserrat (40 miles), Saba (20 miles), St Eustatius (5 miles), St-Barts (40 miles) and St-Martin (45 miles) can be seen. The English mounted the first cannon on Brimstone Hill in 1690 in an attempt to force the French from Fort Charles below and the fortress was not aban-doned until 1852. It has been constructed mainly out of local volcanic stones and was designed along classic defensive lines. The five bastions overlook each other and also guard the only road as it zig zags up to the parade ground. The entrance is at the Barrier Redan where payment is made. Pass the Magazine Bastion but stop at the Orillon Bastion which contains the massive ordnance store (165 ft long with walls at least 6 ft thick). The hospital was located here and under the south wall is a small cemetery. You then arrive at the Prince of Wales Bastion (note the name of J Sutherland, 93rd Highlanders 24 October 1822 carved in the wall next to one of the cannon) from where there are good views over to the parade ground. Park at the parade ground, there is a small snack bar and good gift shop near the warrant offi-cer's quarters with barrels of pork outside it. Stop for a good video introduction at the DL Matheson Visitor Centre. A narrow and quite steep path leads to Fort George, the Citadel and the highest defensive position. Restoration is continuing and several areas have been converted to form a most interesting museum. Bar-rack rooms now hold well-presented and informative displays (pre-Columbian, American, English, French and Garrison). Guides are on hand to give more detailed explanations of the fortifications. ■ *Daily 0930-1730 daily. Entrance*

EC$13 or US$5 for foreigners, EC$2 for nationals, children half price. Allow up to 2 hrs. Turn right off the coastal road just before J's Place (drink and local food, open from 1100, T4656264, the caged green vervet monkeys are very aggressive). The local minibus to Brimstone Hill is EC$2.25, then walk up to the fortress, less than 30 mins but extremely steep. For fit climbers only. www.brimstonehillfortress.org

Rawlins Plantation, reached up a long drive through canefields, has magnificent gardens full of tropical plants and flowers and is an excellent place to stop for lunch on a tour of the island. Alternatively, there is a black sand beach at **Dieppe Bay** with the excellent *Golden Lemon*. Pass through Saddlers to the **Black Rocks**. Here lava has flowed into the sea, providing interesting rock formations. *Ottley's Plantation's* grounds are not as magnificent as at *Rawlins*, but there are easy, well-marked short walks through the rainforest. The main road continues through Cayon (turn right uphill to Spooners for a look at the abandoned Cotton Ginnery) back to Basseterre via the RL Bradshaw Airport. With advance notice, during harvest season you can tour the sugar factory near the airport, very interesting and informative. ■ *Feb-Aug. T4658157.*

The north coast

To visit the southeast peninsula, turn off the roundabout at the end of Wellington Road (opposite turning to the airport) and at the end of this new road turn left. This leads to the narrow spit of land sandwiched between North and South Frigate Bays. This area is being heavily developed with large hotels and condominiums, the natural lagoons providing an additional attraction. The six-mile Dr Kennedy A Simmonds Highway runs from Frigate Bay to Major's Bay along the backbone of the peninsula and overlooks North and South Friars Bays where you may see green vervet monkeys before descending to White House Bay. Skirt the Great Salt Pond. Half way round turn left to reach Sand Bank Bay, a lovely secluded bay (unmarked left turn down dirt road). Continue on the main highway and turn left for Cockleshell Bay and Turtle Beach (good for watersports and stunning views across to Nevis). The main road leads to Major's Bay.

The southeast peninsula

Nevis

Across the two-mile Narrows Channel from St Kitts is the beautiful little island of Nevis. The islands covers an area of 36 sq miles and the central peak, 3,232 ft, is usually shrouded in white clouds and mist. It reminded Columbus of Spanish snow-capped mountains and so he called the island 'Las Nieves'. For the Caribs, it was Oualie, the land of beautiful water. Smaller than St Kitts, it is also quieter. The atmosphere is low-key and easy-going; all the same, it is an expensive island. Agricultural workers have left their smallholdings for jobs in hotels or driving taxis as numbers of tourists, particularly from North America, have risen.

IDD code: 869
Colour map 3, grid B2
Population: 9,000

Charlestown

The main town is Charlestown, one of the best preserved old towns in the Caribbean, with several interesting buildings dating from the 18th century. It is small and compact, on Gallows Bay, guarded by Fort Charles to the south and the long sweep of Pinney's Beach to the north. Nevis had the only court in the West Indies to try and hang pirates. Prisoners were taken from the courthouse across the swamp to where the gallows were set up, hence the name, Gallows Bay. There are plans for a national park to protect the swamp, which is a habitat for many birds, animals and plants.

D R Walwyn's Plaza is dominated by the balconied Customs House built in 1837.The Tourist Office is in the newly restored Old Treasury Building. **Memorial Square** is larger and more impressive than D R Walwyn's Plaza, the War Memorial is in a small garden. The courthouse and library were built in 1825 and used as the

Leeward Islands

Nevis Government Headquarters, but largely destroyed by fire in 1873. The little square tower was erected in 1909-10. It contains a clock which keeps accurate time with an elaborate pulley and chain system. In the library you can see it, together with the weights, among the elaborate roof trusses. *Mon-Fri 0900-1800, Sat 0900-1700. The courthouse is closed to the public, look in through the open windows.*

Along Government Road is the well-preserved **Jewish Cemetery**. The earliest evidence of a Jewish community on the island dates from 1677-78, when there were four families. By the end of the century there were 17 households, a thriving synagogue and part of the main street was known as Jew Street, but invasion by the French in 1706 and 1783, hurricanes and the decline of the sugar industry in the 18th century led to an economic downturn and emigration. By the end of the 18th century only three Jewish households remained, and now there is no evidence of their presence except for the cemetery where 19 stones date from 1679-1730. At the small **market** a wide range of island produce is on sale. ■ *Markets on Tue, Thu and Sat mornings, best on Sat.* Market Street to the right houses the **Philatelic Bureau**. ■ *0800-1600 Mon-Fri, a/c.* The **Cotton Ginnery** was, until 1994, in use

Nevis

Leeward Islands

N

0 km   1
0 miles   1

■ **Sleeping**
1 Banyan Tree
2 Golden Rock Plantation Inn
3 Hermitage Plantation Inn
4 Hurricane Cove Bungalows
5 Montpelier Plantation Inn
6 Mount Nevis
7 Nisbet Plantation Beach Club
8 Old Manor
9 Oualie Beach
10 Philsha's
11 Yamseed Inn

● **Eating**
1 Bananas
2 Cla Cha Del
3 Jade Garden
4 Martha's Tea House
5 Miss June's
6 Seafood Madness
7 Sunshines by the Sea
8 Tequila Sheila's

● **Bars & clubs**
9 Sand Dollar Bar & Grill

during the cotton-picking season (February-July). In 1995 it was moved out to the New River Estate, Gingerland, where it is in a renovated building next to the sugar mill ruins there. As part of the Nevis Port upgrade, another Cotton Ginnery building now houses 10 gift shops and a restaurant. On Chapel Street the **Wesleyan Holiness Manse**, built in 1812, is one of the oldest stone buildings surviving on the island, while the **Methodist Manse** (next to the prominent church) has the oldest wooden structure, the second floor was built in 1802.

The **Museum of Nevis History** at the Birthplace of Alexander Hamilton is next to the sea and set in an attractive garden. The original house was built around 1680 but destroyed in the 1840s, probably by an earthquake. This house was rebuilt in 1983 and dedicated during the Islands' Independence celebration in September of that year. The Nevis House of Assembly meets in the rooms upstairs, while the rather cramped museum occupies the ground floor. Alexander Hamilton, Nevis' most famous son, was born in Charlestown on 11 January 1757. He lived on Nevis for only five years before leaving for St Croix with his family. About half of the display is given over to various memorabilia and pictures of his life. The rest contains examples of Amerindian pottery, African culture imported by the slaves, cooking implements and recipes, a rum still, a model of a Nevis lighter, the ceremonial clothes of the Warden which were worn on the Queen's birthday and Remembrance Day and a section on nature conservation. There is a small shop which sells local produce and some interesting books. All proceeds go to the upkeep of the museum.
■ *Mon-Fri 0900-1600, Sat 0900-1200. US$2. T4695786.*

Around the island

Nevis is divided into five parishes, each with its own Anglican church, but these make up a tiny fraction of the total of 80 churches for other denominations on the island. On Sunday church bells start ringing from 0600, calling the faithful to services lasting three hours or more, and it is a quiet day everywhere.

Charlestown

To Airport, Pinney's Beach & Newcastle

Museum of Nevis History
Crosses Alley
Methodist
Chapel St
Wesleyan Holiness Manse
Main St
Customs
DR Walwyn Plaza
Happy Hill Dr
Cotton Ginnery
Memorial Sq
Prince William St
War Memorial Square
Jewish Cemetery
Courthouse & Public Library
Philatelic Bureau
Main St
Gallows Bay
Parkville Plaza
Park Rd
Horatio Nelson Museum
Spring House
To Fort Charles
Bath Hotel (Ruined)

To St John's Fig Tree Anglican Church, Montpelier Great House & Gingerland

N
not to scale

Eating
1 Café des Arts
2 Calypso Bistro
3 Eddy's
4 Unella's By the Sea

Taking the road south out of Charlestown, you can visit the rather unkempt **Fort Charles**. Fork right at the Shell station and again at the mini roundabout, keep right along the sea shore (rough track), past the wine company building and through gates at the end of the track. The fort was built before 1690 and altered many times before being completed in 1783-90. Nothing much remains apart from the circular well and a small building (possibly the magazine). The gun emplacements looking across to St Kitts are being badly eroded by the sea, some cannon have been moved to hotels. The Nevis Council surrendered to the French here in 1782 during the siege of Brimstone Hill on St Kitts.

Back on the main road and only about half a mile outside Charlestown lies the largely ruined **Bath Hotel** and **Spring House**. Built by the Huggins family in 1778, it is reputed to be one of the oldest hotels in the Caribbean and is to be renovated as a cultural centre. The Spring House lies over a fault which supplies constant hot water at 108°F. There are no

Leeward Islands

facilities but you can bathe at your own risk. Most locals bathe further downstream, often stark naked. A new building has been erected to house the **Horatio Nelson Museum**, dedicated in 1992 to commemorate the 205th anniversary of the wedding of Admiral Nelson to Fanny Nisbett. Based on a collection donated by Mr Robert Abrahams, an American, the museum contains memorabilia including letters, china, pictures, furniture and books (request to see the excellent collection of historical documents and display of 17th-century clay pipes). A replica of Nelson's military uniform was unveiled at the museum and presented to the local government by the British High Commissioner in January 2001. Nelson was not always popular, having come to the island to enforce the Navigation Acts which forbade the newly independent American states trading with British colonies. In his ship *HMS Boreas,* he impounded four American ships and their cargoes. The Nevis merchants immediately claimed £40,000 losses against Nelson, who had to remain on board his ship for eight weeks to escape being put into gaol. It was only after Prince William, captain of *HMS Pegasus,* arrived in Antigua that Nelson gained social acceptability and married the widow, Fanny Woodward Nisbett (reputedly for her uncle's money; this proved a disappointment as her uncle left the island and spent his wealth in London). The museum also contains some pre-Columbian artefacts and displays on local history, including sugar and slavery. Outside, behind the museum rests the *Pioneer*, a Nevis lighter and the last sugar boat sailing to St Kitts. There are plans to renovate it, but to get a better idea of what it looked like, there is a model in the museum. ■ *Mon-Fri 0900-1600, Sat 0900-1200. US$2. Gift shop.*

More evidence of the Nelson connection is found at the **St John's Fig Tree Anglican Church** about two miles on from the Bath House. Originally built in 1680, the church was rebuilt in 1838 and again in 1895. The marriage certificate of Nelson and Fanny Nisbett is displayed here. There are interesting memorials to Fanny's father William Woodward and also to her first husband Dr Josiah Nisbett. Many died of the fever during this period and if you lift the red carpet in the central aisles you can see old tombstones, many connected with the then leading family, the Herberts. The graveyard has many examples of tombstones in family groups dating from the 1780s.

Slightly off the main road to the south lies **Montpelier Great House** where the marriage of Nelson and Mrs Nisbett actually took place; a plaque is set in the gatepost. The plantation is now a hotel with pleasant gardens. Enormous toads live in the lily ponds formed out of old sugar pans. A very pleasant place for lunch or a drink. Beyond the house lies **Saddle Hill** (1,250 ft). It has the remains of a small fort, **Saddle Hill Battery**, and it is reputedly where Nelson would look out for illegal shipping. Nevisians had a grandstand view from here of the siege of Brimstone Hill by the French in 1782. You can follow several goat/nature trails on the hill, giant aloes abound, a track starts at Clay Ghaut, but most trails beyond the fort are dense and overgrown. Near Montpelier is the **Botanical Garden**, 7 acres of nicely laid out plants from around the world: cactus, bamboo, orchids, flowering trees and shrubs, heliconias and rose gardens, a mermaid fountain, a greenhouse with bridges, ponds, waterfall and tea house with English high tea and gift shop. The landscaping is beautiful and it is the perfect spot for relaxation, picnics, small gatherings, weddings, but it is not wheelchair friendly. ■ *Gardens open Nov-Mar Mon-Sat 1000-1630, other months phone ahead. EC$20, children half price. Tea house 1000-1700. T4693399.*

The small parish of **Gingerland** is reached after about three miles. Its rich soils made it the centre of the island's ginger root production (also cinnamon and nutmeg), but it is noteworthy for the very unusual octagonal Methodist church built in 1830. You turn right here along Hanleys Road to reach **White Bay Beach**. Go all the way down to the bottom and turn left at the Indian Castle experimental farm, past the race course (on Black Bay) and Red Cliff. There is a small shelter but no general shade. Beware, this is the Atlantic coast, the sea can be very rough and dangerous. On quieter days, the surf is fun and there are good views across to Montserrat. On the way back beware of the deep storm drain crossing the road near the church. At Clay Ghaut, Gingerland, is the **Eva Wilkin Gallery** in an old windmill. Started by Howard and

Marlene Paine, it has a permanent exhibition of paintings and drawings by Nevisian Eva Wilkin MBE (whose studio it was until her death in 1989), prints of which are available, also antique maps, etc. ■ *Mon-Fri 1000-1500, or by appointment, T4692673.*

After Gingerland the land becomes more barren and this side of the island is much drier. Several sugar mills were built here because of the wind, notably **Coconut Walk Estate**, **New River Estate** (fairly intact) and the **Eden Brown Estate**, built around 1740. A duel took place between the groom and the bride's brother at the wedding of Julia Huggins. The brother was killed and the fiancé fled the island to escape trial and execution. Julia became a recluse and the great house was abandoned. It has the reputation of being haunted. Although government owned and open to the public, the ruins are in a poor condition and care should be taken.

The island road continues north through Butlers and Brick Kiln (known locally as Brick Lyn), past St James' Church (Hick's village), Long Haul and Newcastle Bays (with the *Nisbet Plantation Inn*) to the small fishing community of **Newcastle**. You can visit the Newcastle Pottery where distinctive red clay is used to make, among other things, the traditional Nevis cooking pot. The Newcastle **Redoubt** can be seen from the road. Built in the early 17th century, it was used as a refuge from Carib attack and may have been the site of a Carib attack in 1656. The airport is situated here.

The road continues through an increasingly fertile landscape, and there are fine views across the Narrows to the southeast peninsula of St Kitts, with **Booby Island** in the middle of the channel, the latter being mostly inhabited by pelicans (all birds are referred to as boobies by the local population). It offers good diving. The small hill on your left is **Round Hill** (1,014 ft). It can be reached on the road between Cades Bay and Camps Village. Turn off the road at Fountain village by the Methodist church. There are good views from the radio station at the top over Charlestown, across to St Kitts and beyond to Antigua. There is a small beach at **Mosquito Bay** and some good snorkelling can be had under the cliffs of Hurricane Hill. The *Oualie Beach Hotel* offers a range of watersport facilities including scuba diving and snorkelling equipment. On Sunday afternoons there is often live music and a barbecue at Mosquito Bay. Sailing trips can be negotiated with locals.

Under Round Hill lies **Cottle Chapel** (1824). It was the first Anglican place on Nevis where slaves could be taught and worship with their masters. Under restoration, its beautiful little font can be seen in the Museum of Nevis History. Nearby, just off the island road, lies **Fort Ashby**. Nothing remains of the Fort (it is now a restaurant on Cades Bay although the cannon are in their original positions). It protected Jamestown, the original settlement and former capital, which was supposedly destroyed by an earthquake and tidal wave in 1690, and was originally called St James's Fort. Drive past the Nelson springs (where the barrels from *HMS Boreas* were filled) and **St Thomas's Church** (built in 1643, one of the oldest surviving in the Caribbean) to Pinney's Beach. There are many tracks leading down to the beach, often with a small hut or beach bar at the end of them. The *Four Seasons Hotel* lies in the middle of the beach. Behind the resort is the Robert Trent Jones II golf course which straddles the island road. The manicured fairways and greens are in marked contrast with the quiet beauty of the rest of the island but the hotel's considerable efforts at landscaping have lessened its impact.

Essentials

There is a wide variety of accommodation ranging from first-class hotels to rented cottages, but it is advisable to book in advance. Reductions are available in summer. The *St Kitts/Nevis Hotel Association* can be reached at PO Box 438, Basseterre, St Kitts, T4655304, F4657746.

Basseterre LL-L *Ocean Terrace Inn* (*OTI*), T4652754, www.oceanterraceinn.net Nondescript architecture, apartments, suites and rooms, a/c, TV, fan, 3 pools, hot tub, fitness centre, beach shuttle, Pro-Divers and Fisherman's Wharf across the road on water front, business centre, fairly expensive but nice restaurant with views over Basseterre harbour, good service

Sleeping on St Kitts
There is a 9% occupancy tax and 10% service charge. In restaurants about 10-15% is expected

Leeward Islands

throughout. **L-A** *Palms Hotel*, T4650800, www.palmshotel.com, central, on The Circus. 12 pleasant junior, 1- and 2-bedroom suites, mini bar, tea and coffee machine. **B-D** *Vacation Inn*, corner of Cayon and College St, T4654628. Convenient for town, noisy but clean. Reductions for children under 8, a/c, fans, restaurant, pool. **C** *Earle's Vacation Home*, T4657546, www.geocities.com/earlesvh Fully furnished, simple, self-contained 1-2-bedroom apartments, walking distance from the centre, long-term rental available. **C-E** *Central Guest House and Apartments*, T4652278, ideally located in the heart of town. Rooms with or without kitchenette. **C-E** *Parkview Inn*, Victoria Rd, next to *Parkview Amusements*, T4652100. Basic. **C-E** *Sea View Inn*, Bay Rd, T4652278, opposite buses. 10 double rooms, 6 suites, a/c, good restaurant.

Outside Basseterre **LL** *Golden Lemon*, Dieppe Bay, T4657260, www.goldenlemon.com, on beach about 15 miles from Basseterre with view of Saba and Statia. Opened in 1963 and run by elderly male couple, 34 rooms, CP, in charming old plantation house with wooden floors, high beds reached by step ladder, or 1-2-bedroom new, spacious cottages with pools, pool, tennis, watersports, good snorkelling on reef, restaurant, lovely atmosphere, no children under 18. **LL** *Ottley's Plantation Inn*, 520 ft above sea level in 35 acres with view to the sea, T4657234, www.ottleys.com Rooms in the 1832 great house or in luxury cottages in the beautiful tropical gardens, spacious, elegantly furnished, large bathrooms, a/c, fans, plunge pools, full size pool in ruins of sugar factory. Run by US family, very hospitable and knowledgeable, nice walks, beach shuttle, packages available, excellent restaurant catering for all diets. **LL** *Rawlins Plantation*, 16 miles from Basseterre in the northwest of the island, T4656221, Rawplant@caribsurf. com 350 ft above sea level looking out over sugar plantation. Tranquil and delightful, British colonial style, offers grass tennis, swimming pool, croquet, great walking opportunities, no credit cards accepted, 10 rooms in cottages in garden of main house built on remains of boiling house, honeymoon suite in sugar mill, bright cotton fabrics, wooden floors, no TV or mini-bar, MAP, excellent food, set menus, produce from kitchen garden. **LL-A** *Bird Rock Beach Hotel*, T4658914, www.birdrockbeach.com 38 connecting rooms/suites, redecorated a cheerful yellow in 2003, a/c, TV, small bathrooms, up on the cliffs, all with sea view, small beach and beach bar below, pool, tennis, volleyball, watersports, *Dive St Kitts* on site, restaurant, a pleasant beach hotel also convenient for Basseterre. **AL-B** *Morgan Heights Condominiums*, T4658633, www.skbee.com/morganheights Beautiful views of Atlantic Coast and southeast peninsula, restaurant. **AL-B** *Fairview Inn*, close to Basseterre is a cottage complex situated around an 18th-century French house, T4652472, wall@caribsurf.com West of Basseterre, **C** *Trinity Inn Apartments*, Palmetto Point, T4653226, www.islandimages.com-trinity A/c, pool, restaurant, riding stables, convenient for buses, no gardens, you get what you pay for. **C-D** *Inner Circle Guest House*, in the village of St Paul's, 14 miles from Basseterre, reached by minibus, T4665857. Newly built, clean, village experience.

Dominating Frigate Bay is the monstrous new five-star St Kitts Marriott Royal Beach, with 900 rooms, the largest casino in the Caribbean, a golf course, amphitheatre, state-of-the-art gym and spa, restaurants, etc

Frigate Bay area **LL-AL** *Rex Papillon St Kitts*, T4658037/8, www.rexresorts.com EP or all-inclusive, 100 rooms and suites, cool colours, 2 pools, 3 restaurants, tennis, pleasantly laid out opposite the golf course, on windswept Atlantic beach only good for sunbathing, no swimming. **LL-A** *Frigate Bay Resort*, T4658935, www.frigatebay.com Not directly on beach, 5-min walk round hillside, colourful yellow, white, blue decor, 64 rooms, studios and suites in 4 blocks, pool or hillside views, a/c, fan, TV, fridge, studios have kitchen, pleasant medium-sized hotel, casual restaurant by pool, friendly management. **LL-A** *Timothy Beach Resort*, T4658597, www.timothybeachresort.com The only hotel in this area on the Caribbean, 3-star, good value, connecting rooms and studios with kitchens, versatile arrangements to make apartments or town house to sleep 2-10, mountain or sea view, *Mr X Watersports* on beach, internet access, *Sunset Café* for local food and priced in EC$, pool, steps down to sea. **B** *Gateway Inn*, T4657155, gateway@caribsurf.com 10 self-catering apartments, a/c, phone, TV, laundry, 10 mins from beach or golf course. **C** *Rock Haven Bed & Breakfast*, T/F4655503. Suite with kitchen facilities, TV, laundry facilities, views of both coasts.

Sleeping on Nevis Accommodation on Nevis tends to be upmarket, in reconstructions of old plantation Great Houses, tastefully decorated in an English style (collectively called *The Inns of Nevis*). They are small and intimate in contrast to the 218-room *Four Seasons Resort Nevis* which dominates Pinney's Beach with its US-style resort, luxury spa (15 masseurs) and golf course. **LL** *Montpelier Plantation Inn and Beach Club*, also St John's, T4693462, www.montpeliernevis.com The Hoffman family took over and redecorated this beautiful old property in 2002, on 30 acres, 750 ft above sea level, a favourite with British tourists. Luxury touches include a welcome with cold towels and rum punch, being taken straight to your room, registering later. Delightful, friendly and helpful, long-serving staff, pool, tennis, lovely gardens, beach shuttle, child reductions, 17 rooms painted white with cool green or white flourishes, fresh fruit daily, lounge, library, excellent restaurant with view over island, fruit, vegetables and sugar grown on site. The **LL** *Nisbet Plantation Beach Club*, St James, on ½-mile beach close to airport, T4699325, www.nisbetplantation.com The only plantation inn on the beach, 38 comfortable rooms in hexagonal cottages/suites in the gardens of the 1776 Great House, spread out down the hill to the sea, a/c, fans, tennis, pool, croquet, beach bar for lunch, restaurant, bar and TV lounge in the traditional plantation-style Great House, huge breakfasts, delicious afternoon tea and excellent dinner, MAP, lots of repeat guests.

LL-L *Hermitage Plantation Inn*, St John's Parish, T4693477, www.hermitagenevis.com Run by Richard and Maureen Lupinacci, very friendly, beautiful wooden cottages, all different, some rather small, 4-poster beds, the Planter's House dates from 1680-1740 and is believed to be the oldest wooden house in the Caribbean, old furniture, and prints on the walls, chintz furnishings, tennis, pool, stunning rural setting with view down to sea, many guests extend their stay, romance/equestrian/adventure/diving packages offered, stables on site. **LL-L** *Mount Nevis Hotel and Beach Club*, T4699373, www.mountnevishotel.com Built 1989 on site of old lime factory, family-owned, 32 modern rooms, studios and apartments, CP, a/c, kitchens, TV, VCR, phone, pool, fitness centre, massage, conference centre, great view of St Kitts, Cat Ghaut golf course by the entrance, beach club on small beach near airport runway. **LL-L** *Old Manor*, T4693445, www.oldmanornevis.com In restored 1690 sugar plantation has 12 spacious rooms and suites which incorporate the stone walls of the old mill buildings, with wooden walls, shutters and louvred windows, 800 ft above sea level, delightfully breezy and cool, no a/c needed, old furnishings, and prints of old maps and pictures on the walls, good restaurant with view to Montserrat, tropical gardens, beach shuttle, pool.

LL-AL *Golden Rock Plantation Inn*, St George's Parish, T4693346, www.golden-rock.com 7 cottages, 14 simple but comfortable rooms around 18th century plantation house, 2-storey suite in old windmill for honeymooners/families, antique furniture, 4-poster beds, plenty of breeze up on the hill, no a/c needed, ocean view all the way to Montserrat, family plan available, pool (formerly the sugar mill cistern), tennis, beach shuttle, specialist interest tours, principally of ecological content, excellent hiking excursions, enjoy afternoon tea and watch the monkeys. **LL-AL** *Hurricane Cove Bungalows*, T/F4699462, www.hurricanecove.com, on hillside with wonderful seaview. 11 1 to 3-bedroom, well-equipped wooden bungalows of Finnish design, some with private pools, swimming pool, above Oualie Beach, path down to beach, good snorkelling. Sports facilities nearby, 3-night minimum stay in winter, long-term discounts. **LL-AL** *Oualie Beach Hotel*, T4699735, F4699176, www.oualiebeach.com Safe for children, comfortable, 32 well-equipped rooms, studios, in cottages with view of bay, deluxe rooms on beach, a/c, fans, TV, non-smoking, massage room, email for guests, meal plans available, bar and restaurant on the sand, very casual and relaxed, string band on Sat (traditional instruments), Oualie Beach Boy Band on Tue, mountain bikes, diving, kayaking and other watersports.

There are also many guesthouses, apartments and cottages: **L-AL** *The Banyan Tree Bed & Breakfast*, T800-6396109, www.banyantreebandb.com 2 rooms in the guesthouse and 1-bedroom suite with kitchenette in *Bamboo House*, 700 ft above sea level near Morning Star village on 6-acre farm growing flowers, spices and raising Barbados black-belly sheep, lots of fruit trees and a 300-year-old banyan tree. **L-A** *Yamseed Inn*, right by the airport on the beach, T4699361. 2 guest rooms and 2 beach cottages, including delicious breakfast, lovely view of St Kitts, beautiful gardens, excellent value. Friendly, helpful owner Sybil Siegfried can arrange crossings from St Kitts and car hire. **L-B** *Philsha's*, Pinney's Rd, a few mins from Charlestown, T4695253, F4697315, www.geocities.com/philshas Family-run, close to beach, single and double rooms, a/c, some self-catering, TV, laundry facilities, phone, large rooms, tiled floors, Nevisian-style decor, clean and new. **C** *JP's*, in town near pier and market, T4690287, jpwalters@caribsurf.com Popular with yachties wanting terra firma, simple rooms, a/c, fans, fridge, lounge with TV, restaurant on site.

Leeward Islands

Eating on St Kitts

There are many places offering snacks, light meals, ice creams and drinks in Basseterre and in the Frigate Bay area. Look out for places selling excellent local patties and fruit juices

Food on the whole is good. Apart from almost every kind of imported food and drink, there is a wide variety of fresh seafood (red snapper, lobster, kingfish, blue parrot), and local vegetables. There are certain dishes that you certainly must try. Some of them are: conkey (usually available during Easter), ital which the local rastas make (food seasoned with all natural spices, no salt but very delicious), also try black pudding, goat water, saltfish and johnny cakes and souse. They are all foods which Kittitians love to eat, especially on Saturdays when no one wants to eat at home. The excellent local spirit is CSR – Cane Spirit Rothschild – produced in St Kitts by Baron de Rothschild (now in a joint venture with *Demerara Distillers Ltd of Guyana*). It is drunk neat, with ice or water, or with 'Ting', the local grapefruit soft drink (also highly recommended). Tours of the CSR factory are possible. The hotels have restaurants, usually serving local specialities. Most of the *Plantation Inns* on both islands offer Sun brunch, usually a 3-course meal and excellent value at around US$25 per person.

Most places close on Sunday; it can be difficult to get a meal in town that day

Basseterre Expensive *Fisherman's Wharf*, T4652754, beside *OTI* offers tasty fresh fish, barbecued chicken, etc and help yourself to vegetables for US$25-35, conch chowder recommended. **Mid-range** *Star of India*, Victoria Rd, T4661537. Chef from Bombay, authentic Indian food, open 0900-2200, closed Sun. *Ballahoo* on the corner of Bank St and Fort St, T4654197, www.ballahoo.com Great central meeting place, lovely view of The Circus, excellent local food at reasonable prices, open Mon-Sat 0800-2200. *Bambu's*, Bank St, T4665280. Good snacks, salads, burgers, wings, nachos, etc, happy hour Fri 1700-1900, wide range of drinks, 1000-2200, later on Sat. *Circus Grill*, T4650143. Good well-presented food, a bit more expensive than *Ballahoo*, open Mon-Sat 1130-2200. *Stone Walls*, Princes St, T4655248. Excellent food, special theme nights, open Mon-Sat 1700-2300, in pleasant garden. Good, predictable Chinese food is at *Kim Sha*, Bay Rd, T4660022, open 1030-2130 and *Kim Xing*, Cayon St, T4666692. Generous portions, fast service, reasonable prices. *Rank's Eat Rite Specialities*, corner Johnston Av and Union St, T4658190. Fresh, low-fat meals, quaint, clean, friendly, veggie/fish burgers, tuna melt, fish meals, local drinks. **Cheap** *Cisco's Place*, Church St, T4659009. Inexpensive lunches. *Leyton Internet Café*, Amory Mall, T4667873. Sending emails home is a bit expensive (see below), but good freshly baked cakes, pastries, sandwiches, coffee and tea. Open 0900-1900. *Oasis Café*, TDC Mall, Basseterre, T4657065. Open Mon-Sat. *Victor's Hideaway*, Stainforth St, New Town, Basseterre, T4652518. Open 0900-1500, 1830-late. *Chef's Place*, Church St, T465176. Good breakfasts and West Indian food at reasonable price, 0900-2100 Mon-Sat. *Pizza Lovers*, George St, New Town, T4656870. Filling, tasty, cheap, open 1800-2300. For a very local experience try *Razba's Veggie Pizza Parlour*, on Johnston Av, T4656738. Most of the clientele are Rastafarian vegetarians who come for a good 'lime' and are friendly to new faces. Similar atmosphere 2 blocks away at *Rasco-Tec*, look for the Bob Marley mural, open 1000-2100. T4668843. *The Family Snackette*, Liverpool Row, T4652601. Quaint setting, local food and drinks. *Central Delight Refreshment Bar*, Central St, T4651142. A place to relax, ice cream, hamburgers, hot dogs, sandwiches. *Ribs and Rolls*, Princes St, T4663474. Ribs and pastries, 0900-1700 daily. *Lamby's Weekends*, just outside Basseterre heading east at entrance to Keys village. Fri-Sun 1700-2300, tasty, fresh, delicious local food, specializes in black pudding and souse, family atmosphere.

Popular and cheaper than the international fast-food chains is the local equivalent *Redi-Fried Chicken*, on the ground floor of the cinema on Bay Rd, T4651301. Tasty chicken and chips, moderate prices. Local bakeries have a variety of savoury and sweet baked goods at affordable prices. Most now have dining sections as the competitive bakery business heats up. The main bakeries are *Fancy Loaf*, T4655415, *American Bakery*, T4652136, *Island Bakeries Ltd*, T4658034, *Browne & Sons*, T4652776, *Fraites & Sons*, T4654629 and *Fulton's*, T4659538.

Frigate Bay Expensive *Marshall's*, at *Horizons Villa Resort*, T4668245. Romantic poolside dining with ocean view, exquisite food, not to be missed. *Breezes*, at *Papillon St Kitts*, T4658037. Breezy with excellent ocean view, pricey menu with tasty, but small, portions. **Mid-range** *Sunset Café*, Timothy Beach Resort, T4657085. Serves local seafood, burgers, open daily, 0700-2300, good. *Cisco's Atlantic Bistro*, T4667007. Big portions, open daily, 1900-2200, bar 1730-2230, reservations before opening time T4669009, ask for Shanta. *Doo Wop Days*, an Italian café and bar, T4651960, F4658506. Owned by Joe and Linda Pozzolo who have 50s, 60s and 70s entertainment and karaoke on weekends, open 1800-2300,

Leeward Islands

closed Tue. *PJ's Pizza*, T4658373. Open from 1000 Tue-Sat. At the end of the peninsula, *Turtle Beach Bar and Grill*, T4699086, F4667771. Good food, vegetarian options, friendly, but expensive, US$8 for a Carib beer, check your bill, open daily 0945-1800 and Thu-Sat 1900-2100, live steel band on Sun and lunchtime.

Around the island Expensive For elegant dining in a cool, natural environment, try the *Royal Palm* at *Ottley's Plantation Inn*, away from the hustle and bustle. **Mid-range** Small restaurants around the island serving West Indian food include *Manhattan Gardens*, Old Road Town, T4659121. Open 1100-1500, reservations. Across the street, try *Sprat Net*, by the sea, T4656314. Run by Spencer family, serves fresh fish and goat water, busy at weekends. Highly recommended for good atmosphere and reasonably priced food, one of the places to be at weekends, open Thu-Sun. **Cheap** In Cayon in the east, *Penny's*, T4669821. Caters mostly for locals, local food, burgers, drinks, spacious and clean in village setting.

The best restaurants are in the hotels and it is usually necessary to reserve a table; exceptional cuisine as well as barbecues and entertainment on certain nights of the week. **Charlestown** There are very few eating places and none of them is expensive. *Eddy's* on Main St opposite Memorial Sq and the handicraft cooperative, is a tourist favourite for local food, T4695958. Drinks and music with string bands, bush bands or steel bands Sat 2000-2300, happy hour Wed 1700-2000. *Calypso Bistro*, Chapel St, T4695110. Bar and grill. *Unella's by the Sea*, T4695574, on the waterfront offers great views although the service is slow. *Café des Arts*, between the museum and *Unella's*, on the waterfront. Open for breakfast and lunch, closes around 1600, tables outside for salads, sandwiches, quiche, US$7.50-10, upstairs and at the back of the house is an art gallery exhibiting and selling work of local artists from St Kitts and Nevis.

Around the island Expensive The *Oualie Beach Club* does local lunches and dinners, T4699735, 0700-2100. *Oualie Beach* has a Caribbean buffet on Sat with live music and masquerade dance, and surf and turf beach barbecue on Tue. *Sunshines by the Sea*, T4695817. Seafood and Sun bonfire on Pinney's Beach. *Miss June's*, Jones Bay, T4695330, www.missjunes.com Open on request when there is enough demand. Miss June, originally from Trinidad, serves a Caribbean 5-course dinner party, preceded by cocktails and *hors d'oeuvres* on the veranda at 1930, wine, coffee and liqueurs included in price, US$65 including tax but not service, credit cards accepted, reservations essential. *Seafood Madness*, T4690558. Great for takeaway orders, all sorts of seafood, also chicken and ribs, open 0730-2100. *Jade Garden*, T4699762, Newcastle. Healthy cuisine, salads, pizza, deli. *Newcastle Bay Marina*, T4699395. Italian and Spanish dinners. *Bananas*, T4698262, F4655195, on Tamarind Bay offers spectacular views of St Kitts. Perched up on the cliff top, you take a cable car up to the bistro. Good food, different menu nightly, mix of Thai, European and Caribbean dishes, salads, ribs, seafood, chicken, etc, appetizers and desserts US$7-12, main courses US$16-30, live music Sat from 2100 until about 0200 depending on demand. *What's New Under the Sea*, Tamarind Bay, T4691291. Dine on an aquarium table, try 'wings and stings', open daily for lunch 1200-1600, Fri happy hour 1730-1830. **Mid-range** *Gallipot*, on the beach north of Oualie, T4698230. Lovely location on little bay, perfect for yachts, showers, laundry and cottages available as well as food, great fresh fish, family-run, can spend all day here, towels, soap and shampoo if you ask. Open 1200-2200 Thu-Sat (kitchen open 1200-1500, 1800-2100), 1200-1730 Sun, when there is a special roast beef lunch, very popular, reservations essential.*Mem's Pizzería*, Prospect Garden, T4691390. Excellent lobster pizza, seafood recommended. *Sand Dollar Bar and Grill*, T4695319, F4690614, next to the *Four Seasons Hotel*. Offers entertainment and happy hour Tue-Fri, closed Mon, party night is Fri, very popular. For excellent local food try *Cla Cha Del Restaurant and Bar*, T4691841, completely out of the way in Newcastle (close to the airport) with good atmosphere at weekends. *Tequila Sheilas*, T4698633, F4690129, on Cades Bay. *The* place to be at weekends with dancing until late, on the beach, open Thu-Sun or daily when busy, popular for Sun brunch. **Cheap** *Culturama Bar*, Jessups, T4695206. Seafood specialities. At the Botanical Gardens *Martha's Tea House* serves sandwiches, scones with Devonshire cream and tapas, panoramic views, T4693680. *Sea King*, Shaws Rd, Newcastle. Full selection of Chinese food, open daily 1130-2300.

Eating on Nevis
Most restaurants only open in the evenings in the off season or even shut completely

Leeward Islands

Nightlife

The club scene has no set hours; doors open around 2200 with people arriving at around 2300 - 2400

St Kitts Steel pan on Fri nights at *OTI*. A good place for a drink in Basseterre is *TOTTs*, opposite post office on the Bay Rd. *Malloy's Irish Pub*, next to Bird Rock Beach and a second location at Baker's Corner, Basseterre, close to the bus stop for buses going up the west side, not as picturesque, but easy to find. One-of-a-kind alternative to other forms of nightlife on St Kitts, friendly atmosphere. *Bobsy's Bar & Grill*, upper end of Cayon St, T4666133. Popular hang out with locals and visitors, Tue-Thu 1600-2300, later at weekends. *Flamingo Restaurant and Bar*, T4650898, on Monkey Hill. Pool tables and a small dance floor. Most dance floors provide a wide variety of music and entrance costs US$3.50-18.50, depending on the occasion, with overseas performers commanding the upper limit. Nightclubs have a great mix of calypso, soca, salsa, hip-hop, reggae, dance hall, R&B, house, techno and other types of music. Recommended is the salsa class 2000 on Wed at the *Community Centre* on Victoria Rd. You will leave after your first class well on the way to salsa greatness. There are many residents of Latin American origin and their influence has generated a great deal of interest in salsa. Friendly and lively atmosphere. The *Lighthouse Disco* is very popular with locals on Sat and Sun nights, a club scene, gets going after midnight. For the real local experience you may want to visit another of the dance clubs or dance spots out in the country area: *BCA*, T4657606/7, at Saddlers; *Manhattan Gardens*, T4659121, and *Sprat Net*, in Old Road, *Off Limit*, in Cayon, T4669821, and the *Inner Circle Club*, at St Paul's, where action takes place by announcement. *Club Atmosphere* is a newly opened club just outside Basseterre in the Canada Estate area. These venues are frequented by some of the region's top DJs as well as local bands playing local music. Nightclubs include *Lions Den Club*, T4652582, in Bird Rock and *The Pumpkin*, Newton Ground. Lots of fun and dancing with the local crowd, hot on Fri and Sat, DJs and occasionally local bands perform. On Sun *Turtle Beach* at the end of the southeast peninsula usually has sunset dancing until midnight.

Dance spots on **Nevis** include *Under the Sea* at Tamarind Bay, T4691291, where anything goes; *Tequila Sheilas* at the end of Pinney's Beach, T4698633; *Sand Dollar Bar & Grill*, next to *Four Seasons*, T4695319. *Dick's Bar*, in Brick Kiln village, nightclub and bar, local string bands and seasonal entertainment. *Blackie's*, in Gingerland, nightclub with disco, visiting bands, Fri-Sun from 2200. *Waves*, Bath village, nightclub and bingo Thu-Sun, entertainment, bands from St Kitts. Look for posters, radio announcements or ask what's on at the tourist office.

Festivals

St Kitts and Nevis are very proud of their masquerade traditions

The liveliest time to visit **St Kitts** is for the *Carnival* held over **Christmas** and the **New Year**, with parades, calypso competitions and street dancing. It is a favourite time of year for many Kittitians and Nevisians. Spirits are high and there is never a dull moment. For details, contact the Ministry of Culture, www.stkittscarnival.com St Kitts also holds a *music festival* at the end of **Jun**; 4 nights of calypso, reggae, R&B, jazz, street-style, gospel, country and western and rap, with local and famous overseas artists. On **Nevis**, the annual equivalent of carnival is *Culturama*, held in end-**Jul** and **Aug**, finishing on the first Mon in Aug. There is a Queen show, calypso competition, local bands and guest bands and many 'street jams'. The Nevis Tourist Office has full details or contact the Department of Culture, T4695521, Mon-Fri 0800-1600.

Shopping

The shopper has plenty of choice and is not swamped by US or British merchandise. Shops are well stocked. Local Sea Island cotton wear and cane and basketwork are attractive and reasonable. There are vendors' markets at the Craft House on the Bay Rd and on Lower College St Ghaut and Liverpool Row. *Walls Deluxe Record and Bookshop* on Fort St has a good selection of music and Caribbean books, maps, cards, games, open Mon-Thu 0800-1700, Fri 0800-1800, Sat 0800-1630. *Brown Sugar* clothing line, Upper Central St, T4664664, is owned by Judith Rawlins, a young local designer. Her clothing is very attractive, Caribbean style without the bright colours, all designed and sewn by Judith herself. *The Island Hopper Boutique* at The Circus, underneath the *Ballahoo* restaurant, stocks the *Caribelle Batik* range of cotton fashions and also carries clothes from Trinidad, St Lucia, Barbados and Haiti; open 0800-1600 Mon-Fri, 0800-1300 Sat, T4652905; also at The Arcade, Charlestown, Nevis, T4691491. Just across from the *Island Hopper* is *Island Fever*, Palms Arcade, T4652599, www.islandfever.biz, open Mon-Fri 0830-1630, Sat 0830-1500, another shop specializing in souvenirs and island-style clothing, bags and watches. There is also a branch at Henville's Plaza, Charlestown, open Mon-Sat 0900-1700, T4690867. *The Stonewall Boutique* on Princes St sells quality local crafts and imports. *The Plantation Picture House*, at *Ralwlins* Plantation is Kate Spencer's studio and gallery of portraits, still life and landscapes in oils and watercolours, her designs are also on silk, open 1100-1700, T4657740. She also has a shop in Basseterre, on Bank St, just off The Circus, called *Kate*, with paintings, prints, silk sarongs, hats by Dale Isaac, and another shop in Main St, Charlestown. *Glass Island*, 4 Princes St, T/F4666771, www.glassisland.com, is a working glass shop which produces glass tiles, platters, jewellery and gifts. There are several local craft shops in Charlestown. Next to the tourist office is *Nevis Handicraft Co-operative*, Main St, T4691746. In Newcastle there is a pottery, with red clay artefacts including bowls and candleholders. You can watch potters at work. The kilns are fired by burning coconut husks.

The public **markets** in Basseterre and Charlestown are busiest Sat morning, good for fruit and vegetables, also fish stalls and butchers. Supermarkets in Basseterre include *B & K Superfood* on the south side of Independence Sq and George St, *Horsfords Valumart* on Wellington Rd, and *Rams* on Bay Rd and at Bird Rock. On Nevis, there are well-stocked supermarkets: *Nisbets* in Newcastle and *Superfood*, Parkville Plaza, Charlestown.

There are philatelic bureaux on both St Kitts and Nevis which are famous (the latter more so) for their first-day covers of the islands' fauna and flora, undersea life, history and carnival. The St Kitts' bureau is in *Pelican Shopping Mall*, open Mon-Wed, Fri-Sat 0800-1200, 1300-1500, Thu 0800-1100. The Nevis bureau is open Mon-Fri 0800-1600.

Sports

For diving and watersports, see pages 527 and 528

Nevis horses are thoroughbred/Creole crosses, mostly retired from racing on Nevis, where it is the second most popular sport after cricket

Horse riding On **St Kitts** there are *Trinity Stables*, T4653226, beach tours US$25 per hr, rainforest tour US$40, and *Royal Stables* at West Farm, T4652222, F4654444. On **Nevis** at the *Hermitage Plantation, T4693477, F4692481, they have horse-drawn carriage tours, US$50 per 30 mins, and horse riding US$45 for 1½ hrs. There is also the Nevis Equestrian Centre*, Main Rd, Clifton Estate, Cotton Ground, T4698118, guilbert@caribsurf.com, run by John and Ali Jordan Guilbert and Erika Guilbert-Walters. They offer 10 different rides from US$50 with a combination of trail and beach, English or Western saddles, for novice or experienced riders, and have an arena for lessons, US$20-30. They even have a 6-hr cross island ride, but don't try that if you're not used to sitting in a saddle. **Horse racing** The *Nevis Turf and Jockey Club* meets at least 6 times a year to race island thoroughbreds: New Year's Day, Tourism Week (Feb), Easter, May Day, Aug during *Culturama*, Independence Day and Boxing Day. Facilities past Market Shop and down Hanley's Rd include a grandstand seating 200, washrooms, a pari-mutuel booth, good food and dancing well into the night; this is part folk festival, part carnival, with no social barriers. There is a minimum of 5 races on the seaside track, where you can see Redonda, Montserrat and Antigua in the distance and often whales spouting or breaching. Races start mid-afternoon and end at dusk. There is an average of 4 horses in each race, run clockwise over a distance of 5.5 to 8 furlongs (1 mile), with a hill up to the home stretch. Contact Richard Lupinacci, who resurrected racing in the 1980s, at the *Hermitage Inn* for details, T4693477, F4692481. Look out for the more amusing **donkey races**. Nevis is known for its large number of donkeys. A donkey ride is an unusual and exciting way to see the sights. Make sure you're wearing jeans. Some donkey rides are organized through hotels and tour agents. **Cycling** *Blue Water Safaris*, T4664933, F4666740, waterfun@caribsurf.com, now offer mountain biking tours (US$15), island biking tours and beach outings. *Wheel World* (or *Windsurf'n'Mountainbike Nevis*) at the *Oualie Beach Club*, Nevis, organizes races, triathlons, tours, bike hire (US$20-35 a day, US$120-195 a week) and a cycle club, *The Trailblazers*; there are always competitions going on. Contact Winston Crooke, T4699682, www.mountainbikenevis.com Nevis is great for off-road cycling and even some of the roads are no more than tracks. *Fun Bikes St Kitts*, T4663202, have all-terrain quad bikes, fully guided tours, riding through cane fields, rainforest, villages and plantations with spectacular views of St Kitts, 3 excursions daily at 0830, 1130 and 1400, for about 3-4 hrs. **Golf** *Royal St Kitts Golf Course*, T4658339 is an 18-hole international championship golf course at Frigate Bay (use and hire of buggies compulsory) and there is a 9-hole golf course at *Golden Rock*, St Kitts, T4658103, where a fun day is held on the last Sun of the month. On Nevis, the *Four Seasons*, T4691111, F4691112, has an 18-hole golf course. **Triathlon** *The St Kitts Triathlon*, an ITU international race, is held on the second Sun in May, www.stkittstriathlon.com Professional triathletes compete to gain official points to qualify for the Olympic games; this is preceded by an amateur race. The grandstand is at *Timothy Beach Hotel*.

Leeward Islands

Tour operators There are several good island tours, including excellent hiking tours to the volcano and through the rainforest on St Kitts, and over old sugar plantations and through the forested hill of Nevis. **St Kitts**: *Kriss Tours*, T4654042, US$50 per full day, overnight camping US$90. *Greg's Safaris*, T4654121, F4650707, www.skbee.com/safaris, pleasant and informative, US$40-80. *Periwinkle Tours*, T4656314, F4657210, offers guided walks, US$30-35. **Nevis**: *Sunrise Tours*, T4692758, trips to Nevis Peak (4 hrs round trip, US$35 per person), Saddle Hill (1½ hrs, US$30) or the Water Source (3 hrs, US$40). *Heb's Nature Tours* is run by Michael Herbert, Rawlins village, Gingerland, T4692501, offering similar tours: Mount Nevis (5 hrs, US$35-40), rainforest hike (4 hrs, US$25-30), Saddle Hill hike (3 hrs, US$20-25), medicinal plants (2 hrs, US$15) and Camp Spring (2½ hrs, US$15-20), price depends on numbers. *Top to Bottom*, T4699080, is run by biologists Jim and Nikki Johnson, who are very flexible and organize walks to suit you, also a night-time, star-gazing walk, mostly 2-3 hrs, US$25 per person, children half price, snacks of fruit and coconut included. David Rollinson of *Eco-Tours*, T4692091, droll@caribsurf.com is very knowledgeable; he offers 'eco rambles' over the 18th-century Coconut Walk and New River Estates and a 'Sugar trail' Mountravers hike over the old Pinney Estate (US$25 per person) as well as Sun morning strolls round historic Charlestown (US$10 per person).

Transport

In season there are weekly charter flights from North America and Europe, but these change frequently

Air *Monarch* flies weekly (Sat) from London Gatwick to St Kitts and on to Tobago, returning from there to London. *Air Transat* offers a weekly flight directly into St Kitts from Toronto. Connections with the USA and Europe can be made through San Juan (*American Eagle*), St Maarten (*LIAT* and *Winair*), Barbados (*Caribbean Star*) and Antigua (*LIAT*, *Caribbean Star*). There are good connections with other Caribbean Islands (Anguilla, Dominica, St Croix, St Eustatius, St Thomas and Tortola) with *LIAT*, *Caribbean Star* and *Windward Islands Airways* (*Winair*). Flights to Nevis from Anguilla (*Coastal Air Transport*), Antigua (*Winair*), St-Barts (*Coastal Air Transport*), St Croix (*Coastal Air Transport*), St Eustatius (*Winair*), St Kitts (*Nevis Express*, *Winair*,) and St Maarten (*LIAT* and *Winair*), San Juan (*Nevis Express*). *Nevis Express* has daily flights between St Kitts and Nevis, US$35, 6 mins, also charter service. The grander hotels on Nevis will arrange chartered air transfers from Antigua or St Kitts for their guests (for instance, *Carib Aviation* from Antigua), highly recommended to avoid the crush.

Airports RL Bradshaw International, St Kitts' Airport, is 2 miles from Basseterre. Get a bus from the bus stop at the roundabout northeast of Independence Sq, EC$1.25, to the airport and walk the last 5 mins from the main road; some buses might go up to the terminal. If you have not much luggage, it is easy to walk from Basseterre to the airport. There are duty-free and gift shops and a café, but they tend to open for long-haul flights only. Even the bar in the departure lounge is often shut. On Nevis, the **Vance Amory Airport** is at Newcastle, 7 miles from Charlestown (on the main road, bus to Charlestown EC$3.50). The terminal is new and smart and there is a Visa ATM. Expect to have your baggage searched on your way in to either island.

Sea The new port in Basseterre is Port Zante, which can accommodate 2 of the largest cruise ships. **Ferry** The crossing between St Kitts and Nevis takes 45-60 mins and costs US$6-8 one way plus EC$1 tax (*Caribe Queen*, *Sea Hustler*, *Caribe Breeze*). Several daily departures from 0700, depending on the boat. Confirm sailing times with Ministry of Communications, T4652521, Mon-Fri 0800-1600. Tickets can only be purchased from the quay just prior to departure, so turn up about 1 hr in advance to avoid disappointment. Island tours operate from St Kitts and there is also a water taxi service between the 2 islands: US$25 return, minimum 4 passengers, 20 mins, operated by *Kenneth's Dive Centre*, T4652670 in advance, or Pro-Divers, US$20, 10 mins, T4653223, 4699086. The *Four Seasons Hotel* has ferry boats running exclusively for guests' flights, US$57 round trip. *Oualie Beach* also arranges transfers for guests from St Kitts Airport via Turtle Beach (day) or Port Zante (night) with a water taxi.

Local Bus Minibuses do not run on a scheduled basis, but follow a set route (more or less), EC$1-3 on most routes, EC$3 from Basseterre to the north of the island, frequent service from the bus terminal close to the market area on the Bay Rd from where buses go west to Sandy Point. To catch a bus east, wait off Bakers Corner at the east end of Cayon St. There are no minibuses from Frigate Bay and the southeast peninsula. On Nevis buses start outside *Foodworld Cash & Carry* and go to all points, but are not very regular, EC$1-3.50; an island tour is possible, if time consuming.

Car hire Fuel is US$2 per gallon. Most rental companies will help you obtain the oblig-atory temporary driving licence, EC$50, valid for a year, from the Traffic Department. If you rent for 3-day minimum you can arrange for a car on the sister island if you do a day trip to St Kitts or Nevis. Hire companies include: *Thrifty/TDC Rentals*, West Independence Square St, Basseterre, T4652991, F4668855, or Bay Rd, Charlestown, T4695690, F4691329, also at *Four Seasons*, T4691111, tdcrent@caribsurf.com; *Caines Rent-A-Car*, Princes St, Basseterre, T4652366, F4656172; *Sunshine Car Rental*, Cayon St, Basseterre, T4652193, Hondas and Korando jeeps. Others include *A & T Car*, T4654030; *Delisle Walwyn*, T4658449; *Huggins*, T4658080; *Courtesy Car Rentals*, Wigley Av, Basseterre, T4657804; *G & L*, CAP Southwell Industrial Site, T4668040/1, www.gandlcarrentals.com If you are arriving in St Kitts from Nevis, there are several car hire companies on Independence Sq, some 3 mins' walk from the ferry pier. One of the most convenient is *Avis Car Rental*, South Independence Square St, T4651043, F4666846 (Suzuki jeeps, Nissan automatics, efficient). *Nisbett Rentals Ltd*, 100 yds from Newcastle Airport, mini moke US$40 per day, collision damage waiver US$8 per day, recommended, particularly if you are flying in/out of Nevis, T4699211, open 0700-1900. *Avis*, T4691240, and *Discount*, T4690343. On Nevis, *Striker's*, Hermitage, T4692654, *Nevis Car Rental*, Newcastle, T4699837, *Avis*, Stoney Grove, T4691241 and oth-ers. The Tourist Office has a list. Companies insist on you having collision damage waiver, which adds another US$5-10 to quoted rates. There is a 5% tax on car rentals. **Bicycle rental** on Craddock Rd, T4695235.

If visiting at carnival time you should book car hire a long time in advance

Taxi Taxis have a yellow T registration plate. Maximum taxi fares are set, for example: On **St Kitts**, from airport to Basseterre US$7, to Frigate Bay US$11, to Sandy Point US$15. Round trip from Basseterre to Romney Manor US$26, to Brimstone Hill US$32. Taxis within Basseterre cost EC$10, with additional charges for waiting or for more than 2 pieces of lug-gage. A southeast peninsula tour is US$40, an island tour US$60. On **Nevis** a taxi from the airport to Charlestown costs US$14, to *Oualie Beach*, US$9. A 50% extra charge is made on both islands between 2200 and 0600. Tours of Nevis cost US$20 per hr and a whole-island tour costs US$50. Recommended is *TC Taxis* T4692911, 07836628301, tctaxi@caribsurf.com, TC is fun, very knowledgeable about the island and works with other good drivers.

The Visitor magazine and airports have a list of recommended fares. There is no need to tip

Airlines *Caribbean Star Airlines* has its regional headquarters at the airport, T4655929. *USAir*, Kisco Travel, Central St, Basseterre, T4654167. *LIAT*, *TDC Airline Services*, Basseterre, T465-2511/2286, and *Evelyn's Travel*, on Main St, Charlestown, general sales agent for *BWIA*, *LIAT*, *American Airlines* and *British Airways*, Charlestown, T469-5302/5238; *BWIA*, T4652286 on St Kitts, T4695238 on Nevis; *American Eagle*, T4658490 (St Kitts); *Winair*, Sprott St, Basseterre, T4652186 on St Kitts, 4695583 on Nevis; *Carib Aviation*, T4653055 (The Circus, Basseterre and R L Bradshaw Airport, St Kitts), F4653168, T4699295 (Newcastle Airport, Nevis). *Nevis Express*, T4699755/6, F4699751, www.nevisexpress.com *Air St Kitts Nevis*, Basseterre, T4658571, F4699018, a charter company specializing in day excursions and other services to neighbouring islands. Also air ambulance with medical staff.

Directory

Banks On St Kitts: *Eastern Caribbean Central Bank (ECCB)* is based in Basseterre, and is responsible for the issue of currency in Antigua and Barbuda, Dominica, Grenada, Montserrat, St Kitts and Nevis, St Lucia and St Vincent and the Grenadines. There is a local bank on St Kitts: *St Kitts-Nevis-Anguilla National Bank*, 5 branches: on the corner of Central St and West Independence Square St; Pelican Mall; Sandy Point, T4652204, open 0830-1500 except Thu 0830-1200, Sat 0830-1100; a branch at Saddlers village, T4657362, opens 0830-1300 except Thu 0830-1200 and Sat 0830-1100. *FirstCaribbean Central Bank*, 1 on The Circus, Basseterre, T4652519, open Mon-Thu 0800-1500, Fri 0800-1700, the other at Frigate Bay, T4652264, open Mon-Thu 0800-1300, Fri 0800-1300, 1500-1700. *Royal Bank of Canada*, on The Circus, Basseterre, T4652519, open Mon-Thu 0800-1500, Fri 0800-1700. *Bank of Nova Scotia*, Fort St, T4654141, open Mon-Thu 0800-1500, Fri 0800-1700. On Nevis: all banks are in Charlestown: the *Bank of Nevis*, Main St, T4695564; *FirstCaribbean*, Main St, T4691988; *Bank of Nova Scotia*, Main St, T4695411. Open 0800-1400 Mon-Fri, except last Fri in month 0800-1600. Avoid lunchtimes (1200-1300) as banks are busy with local workers. Visa and MasterCard accepted.

If you are in a hurry, choose a foreign bank as their queues are often shorter. ATMs are available at all banks but dispense local currency only

Communications Internet: At the Pelican Mall on the Bay Rd in Basseterre, where Cable & Wireless has a public internet machine. *Leyton's Internet Café*, at the Amory Mall, T4667873, EC$0.25 per min or EC$15 per hr. *Dot Com* internet café on The Circus, Basseterre, Mon-Fri 0900-1630, Sat 0900-1300. On Nevis, *Connexions Internet Café* on Main St, T4699675, EC$0.50 per min, or EC$50 a

Leeward Islands

day, 0900-2100 Mon-Sat, occasionally Sun if cruise ship in port. **Post**: Post office in Basseterre is on Bay Rd, open Mon-Sat 0800-1500 except Thu when it closes at 1100 and Sat at 1200; in Charlestown on Main St, open from 0800-1500 except Thu, closes at 1100, and Sat at 1130. Courier services including *DHL*, *Fed Ex*, on both islands. **Telephone**: *Cable & Wireless* has digital telecommunications systems for the 2 islands. Telemessages and faxes can be sent from the main office on Cayon St, Basseterre. Credit card calls T1-800-8778000. USA direct public phones available at C & W office. Phone cards are sold in denominations of EC$10, 20 and 40. Coin boxes take EC quarters minimum and EC dollars. Call charges are from US$5 for 3 mins to the USA, Canada or the UK. *The Boat Phone Company* on the Victoria Rd, T/F4663003, F4653033, offers cellular phone service for yachts.

Background

History Before Columbus's arrival in 1493, there were Amerindians living on both islands, whose relics can still be seen in some areas. As in most of the other islands, however, they were slaughtered by European immigrants, although the Caribs fought off the British and the French for many years and their battle scenes are celebrated locally. St Kitts became the first British settlement in the West Indies in 1623 and soon became an important colony for its sugar industry, with the importation of large numbers of African slaves. In April 1690 a severe earthquake struck, causing heavy damage to St Kitts, Nevis and Redonda. It was followed by a tidal wave which compounded the damage and, it is believed, destroyed Nevis' first capital, Jamestown.

For a time St Kitts was shared by France and England; partition was ended by the Peace of Utrecht in 1713 and it finally became a British colony in 1783. From 1816, St Christopher, Nevis, Anguilla and the British Virgin Islands were administered as a single colony until the Leeward Islands Federation was formed in 1871. (For a detailed history of Nevis during this period, read *Swords, Ships and Sugar–A History of Nevis to 1900*, by Vincent Hubbard, available in St Kitts and Nevis bookshops.)

From 1958, St Kitts-Nevis and Anguilla belonged to the West Indies Federation until its dissolution in 1962. In 1967 their constitutional status was changed from Crown Colony to a state in voluntary association with Britain, in a first step towards independence. Robert L Bradshaw was the first Premier of the Associated State. Local councils were set up in Anguilla and Nevis to give those islands more authority over local affairs. Anguilla broke away from the group and was re-established as a Crown Colony in 1971. During the 1970s independence was a burning issue but Nevis' local council was keen to follow Anguilla's lead rather than become independent with St Kitts. Negotiations were stalled because of British opposition to Nevis becoming a Crown Colony. Eventually, on 19 September 1983, St Kitts and Nevis became independent as a single nation.

The main political parties are the People's Action Movement (PAM), the St Kitts and Nevis Labour Party (SKNLP), the Nevis Reformation Party (NRP) and the Concerned Citizens Movement (CCM). Dr Kennedy Simmonds (PAM) was elected Prime Minister in 1980 and held office until July 1995. Elections in November 1993 were highly controversial when PAM and the SKNLP each won four seats, the CCM two and the NRP one. The CCM declined to join in a coalition government to form a majority with either major party. The Governor then asked Dr Kennedy Simmonds to form a minority government with the support of the NRP, PAM's previous coalition partner. This move was highly unpopular, given that the Labour Party had won 54.4% of votes cast in St Kitts compared with 41.7% for PAM. A state of emergency was declared for 10 days in December because of rioting and other disturbances, a curfew was imposed for five days and a detachment of soldiers from the Regional Security System joined the local police force for a week. Negotiations between Dr Denzil Douglas, the SKNLP leader, and Dr Simmonds for a caretaker government for six months, followed by fresh elections, failed. More clashes greeted the budget presentation in February 1994 with the SKNLP boycotting parliament (except to take the oath of allegiance in May) in support of fresh elections.

Also during 1994, St Kitts was rocked by a corruption scandal linked to senior political officials involving drugs trafficking, murder and prison riots. It was alleged that traffickers were exploiting St Kitts and Nevis and avoiding the better monitored, traditional routes

The crisis pushed the Government into calling a forum for national unity, at which it was decided that a general election should be held, three years ahead of schedule. In the meantime, all parties in the National Assembly participated in decisions on matters such as foreign investment and a code of conduct to regulate political activity. A Commonwealth observer team monitored the elections to prevent a recurrence of the 1993 disturbances.

In the months leading up to the 3 July elections, British police officers were brought in to assist the local police. The campaign was marred by political party rivalry which was often violent, but the result was an overwhelming victory for the SKNLP, which won seven seats. PAM was reduced to one, while the CCM and the NRP continued to hold two seats and one seat respectively. Dr Denzil Douglas became Prime Minister.

In 1992 Mr Simeon Daniel, the Premier of Nevis for 21 years, lost his assembly seat in elections which saw Mr Vance Amory (CCM) become the new leader. Mr Amory is in favour of the secession of Nevis from the federal state.

Nevis' assembly voted unanimously for secession in 1997. However, a referendum on seccession in July 1998 was unsuccessful when it failed to gain the approval of two-thirds of the electorate.

In September 1998 Hurricane Georges devastated the island of St Kitts. About 75% of homes were extensively damaged. A record clean up brought the island back to normal by the end of the year and most tourist facilities were open for business by the winter high season. In November 1999 the leeward side of both islands was hit by Hurricane Lenny, which brought high seas and flooding, wiping out many beaches and damaging hotels. *The Four Seasons Hotel* in Nevis remained closed for a year for repairs which included importing sand and constructing a breakwater to protect the beach by the hotel.

General elections were held in March 2000 and the SKNLP was returned to power, winning all eight seats in St Kitts. There was no change in Nevis, the CCM winning two seats and the NRP one. Dr Kennedy Simmonds, leader of PAM since 1976, announced his resignation in 2000. The new leader of the opposition is Mr Lindsey Grant, a lawyer. PAM had claimed massive fraud in the elections, in which it won 35.5% of the vote in St Kitts but no seats.

Government

St Christopher and Nevis is a constitutional monarchy within the Commonwealth. The British monarch is Head of State and is represented locally by a Governor General. The National Assembly has 11 seats, of which three are from Nevis constituencies and eight from St Kitts. There are also four nominated Senators. Under the Federal system, Nevis also has a separate legislature and its own premier. Under the constitution it may secede from the Government of the Federation.

Economy

Sugar, the traditional base of economic production, nowadays accounts for only about 2% of GDP, although it still occupies a dominant role within the agricultural sector and generates about a third of export revenues. Low prices for sugar in the world markets, hurricane damage, droughts, cane fires and the falling value of the euro, mean the industry runs at a loss. The Government has been encouraged to diversify away from sugar dependence and reduce food imports. More vegetables, sweet potatoes and yams are now being grown, while on Nevis, Sea Island cotton and coconuts are more common on smallholdings. Livestock farming and manufacturing are developing industries. There are enclave industries, such as electronic assembly, data processing and garment manufacturing (now over a quarter of total exports), which export to the USA and Caricom trading partners, while sales of sugar-based products such as pure cane spirit go mainly outside the region.

Tourism has become an important foreign exchange earner, and now contributes about 10% of GDP. The construction industry has benefited from the expansion of tourist infrastructure. The Government is increasing cruise ship arrivals with port improvement projects enabling several cruise liners to berth at the same time, while stopover arrivals will be encouraged by the large resort development projects on the southeast peninsula of St Kitts, and airport improvements.

Leeward Islands

> ### Things to do in Montserrat
>
> - Visit the **Volcano Visitors' Centre** for all you ever wanted to know or see about the volcanic eruptions.
> - Join a ranger for a **hike** in the hills along old trails and through unspoilt forest
> - Celebrate **St Patrick's Day** in the sun with Irish Montserratians.
> - Go dancing in **Little Bay** where nightlife is on the beach.

Montserrat

IDD code: 664
Colour map 3, grid C2
Population 4,500

Montserrat is incomparable. The Irish-influenced 'Emerald Isle' is totally unspoiled by tourism but its volcano has put it on the map. Here you can enjoy views of a glowing volcano, moonscape-type volcanic areas, deserted black sand beaches, a network of challenging mountain trails, historic sites and perhaps the friendliest people in the region. Only the northern third of the island is populated because of the volcano and the 4,500 inhabitants are developing the area in style.

Ins and outs

Getting there
See Transport, page 556, for further details

The airport on the east coast has long been closed because of volcanic activity. Air service is by helicopter to **Gerald's Heliport** from Antigua, although a new airport is being built for completion in mid-2004. You get a good view of the island and the volcano on the 15-min flight from Antigua. Alternatively, there is a **ferry** from Antigua which takes an hr.

Getting around
Driving is on the left

Roads are paved and fairly good, but narrow and twisty. There are many pebbles on the roads and you must be careful, especially when walking on inclines. Drivers travel fast, passing on blind corners with much use of their horns. There are several **car hire** companies. **Hitching** is safe and easy. The standard fare in minibuses is EC$2. Outside the fixed times and routes they operate as taxis and journeys can be arranged with drivers for an extra fee. **Taxis** are usually small buses, which can be shared. Fares are set and listed by the Tourist Board.

Climate

Although tropical, the humidity in Montserrat is low and there is often rain overnight which clears the atmosphere. The average temperature is 26-27°C with little variation from one season to another. The wettest months are Nov, Dec and Jan.

Tourist Information

Montserrat Tourist Board, Salem, T4912230, F4917430, www.visitmontserrat.com

Flora and fauna

A walk around the Silver Hills in the extreme north reveals a dramatic coastline where you can find lots of seabirds

Natural vegetation is confined mostly to the summits of hills, where elfin woodlands occur. At lower levels, fern groves are plentiful and lower still, cacti, sage bush and acacias. Flowers and fruit are typical of the Caribbean with many bay trees, from which bay oil (or rum) is distilled, the national tree, the mango and the national flower, *Heliconia caribaea* (a wild banana known locally as 'lobster claw'). There are 34 species of bird resident on the island and many more migrants. Unique to Montserrat is the Montserrat oriole, *Icterus oberi*, a black and gold oriole named the national bird. The British FCO is funding a project to study the effect of the volcano on the oriole. There are also the rare forest thrush, the bridled quail dove, mangrove cuckoo, trembler and purple-throated carib. Many of these can be seen along the Centre Hills trail in the middle of the island between the ash-covered Soufrière Hills and the Silver Hills. The vegetation here is biologically diverse and supports a variety of wildlife. Montserrat cannot boast many wild animals, although it shares the terrestrial frog, known as the mountain chicken, only with Dominica. Agoutis, bats and lizards, including iguanas which can grow to

Leeward Islands

Touching down

Boat information *Little Bay, 55-m jetty with a depth of 1.7 m-4.6 m. Contact the Montserrat Port Authority, channel 16, for mooring details.*

Business hours *Government offices: Mon-Fri 0800-1600;* **Shops**: *0800-1600, but early closing Wed and Sat afternoons.*

Currency *The currency is the East Caribbean dollar, EC\$. The exchange rate is fixed at EC\$2.70=US\$1, but there are variations depending on where you change your money. US and Canadian dollars are widely accepted. All major credit cards and TCs accepted.*

Departure tax *US\$10 for Caricom residents and US\$17 for visitors.*

Documents *A valid* **passport** *is required except for US, Canadian and British visitors, who must only show proof of citizenship for stays of up to six months. Citizens of Caricom countries may travel with their official ID card.* **Visas**, *which may be required for visitors from Haiti and Cuba, can be obtained from British consulate offices. An onward or* **return ticket** *is required.*

Duty-free allowance *200 cigarettes, 50 cigars, 40 ozs of alcoholic beverages, six ozs perfume. Little Bay (Main Office, Brades), open 0800-1600 Mon-Fri, for yachts and small craft, T4913816, 4912456, F4916909, customms@candw.ag*

Emergency numbers *Accident and emergency T4912802, Hospital T4912552/7404.*

Media **Newspapers** *Montserrat Reporter, published Fri, www.montserratreporter.org*

The Governor's Office in Montserrat produces a monthly free newsletter The Montserrat Newsletter, *www.montserrat-newsletter.com*

Radio *Radio Montserrat ZJB relays the BBC World Service news at 0700 daily. ZJB posts a daily, local, 10-min audio news broadcast on the internet at www.mratgov.com/newsradio.htm Gem Radio is an exclusive outlet for the Associated Press. Family FM has regional news twice a day.* **Television** *Satellite TV/Cable is operational in most areas, and stations broadcasting from nearby islands can be received.*

Official time *Atlantic Standard Time, 4 hrs behind GMT, 1 hr ahead of EST.*

Public holidays *New Year's Day, St Patrick's Day (17 Mar), Good Fri, Easter Mon, Labour Day (first Mon in May), Whit Mon (7th Mon after Easter), Queen's birthday (middle Mon in Jun) first Mon in Aug, Christmas Day, Boxing Day (26 Dec) and Festival Day (31 Dec).*

Tourist offices overseas *Germany, Montserrat Tourist Board/West India Committee, Lomer Strasse 28, D-22047 Hamburg 70, T4940-6958846, F4940-3800051.* **UK**, *c/o CTO, 42 Westminster Palace Gardens, Artillery Row, London SW1P 1RR, T020-72224325, F020-72224325, cto@carib-tourism.com* **USA**, *c/o CTO, 80 Broad St, 32nd floor, New York, NY 10004, T212-6359530, F212-6359511, get2cto@dorsai.org*

Voltage *220/110 volts, 60 cycles.*

Weights and measures *Imperial.*

---

over 4 ft in length (they used to take the balls on the golf course, mistaking them for eggs), can all be found and tree frogs contribute to the island's 'night-music'.

The Montserrat National Trust is in Olveston, on the North Main Road, with a Natural History Centre and a botanical garden. ■ *Mon-Fri 0830-1630, Sat 0900-1300. T4913086, F4913046, www.montserratnationaltrust.com*

Diving and marine life

The volcano has had an unexpected benefit for Montserrat's underwater life, as the 2-mile exclusion zone has created a marine reserve, with no one going in to the area for some years. The waters are teeming with fish, coral and sponges and their larvae have drifted with the currents to the reefs of the north where the best dive sites are. Shore diving is good from Lime Kiln Bay, where there are ledges with coral, sponges and lots of fish; Woodlands Bay, where there is a shallow reef at 25 to 30 ft; at Carr's Bay where there are some excellent coral and interesting fish about 400 yd from the shore; and at Little Bay. There are some shallow dives from

Montserrat has a modest reputation as an undiscovered destination with much virgin diving

Leeward Islands

boats, suitable for novices or a second dive, but also deep dives for experienced divers. Pinnacle is a deep dive, dropping from 65 to 300 ft, where you can see brain coral, sponges and lots of fish.

Dive centres Diving and kayaking are offered by *Sea Wolf Diving School*, Woodlands, T4917807, www.seawolfdivingschool.com A shore dive costs US$40, a single-tank boat dive US$60, 2 tanks US$80, scuba equipment hire US$30, snorkel gear rental US$10. They also offer kayak diving, US$60, PADI courses, snorkelling tours and boat trips. Wolf and Inge Krebs started the dive operation in 1992 and there is little they don't know about Montserrat underwater.

Montserrat

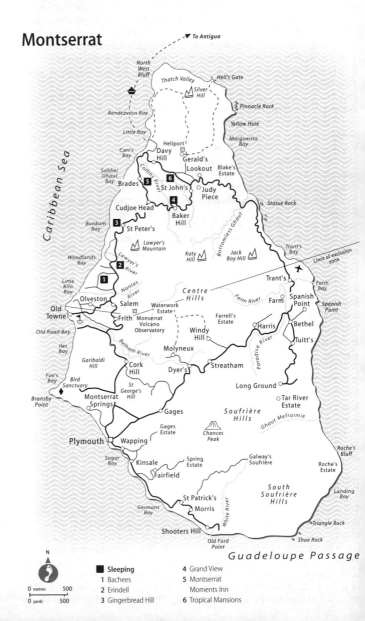

To Antigua

North West Bluff

Thatch Valley

Hell's Gate

Silver Hill

Pinnacle Rock

Rendezvous Bay

Yellow Hole

Little Bay

Marguerita Bay

Carr's Bay

Heliport

Davy Hill

Gerald's Lookout

Blake's Estate

Soldier Ghaut Bay

Brades

St John's

6

Judy Piece

Statue Rock

Cudjoe Head

4

Baker Hill

Bunkum Bay

3

St Peter's

Lawyer's Mountain

Katy Hill

Bottomless Ghaut

Jack Boy Hill

Trant's Bay

Limit of exclusion zone

Woodlands Bay

2

Lawyer's River

Nantes River

Centre Hills

Farm River

Trant's

Farm Bay

Lime Kiln Bay

1

Olveston

Salem

Waterwork Estate

Farm

Spanish Point

Spanish Point

Old Towne

Frith

Monserrat Volcano Observatory

Farrell's Estate

Harris

Bethel

Old Road Bay

Windy Hill

Tuitt's

Iles Bay

Belham River

Molyneux

Paradise River

Garibaldi Hill

Cork Hill

Dyer's

Streatham

Fox's Bay

Bird Sanctuary

St George's Hill

Long Ground

Bransby Point

Montserrat Springs

Gages

Tar River Estate

Ghaut Mefraimie

Soufrière Hills

Plymouth

Wapping

Gages Estate

Chances Peak

Roche's Bluff

Sugar Bay

Kinsale

Spring Estate

Galway's Soufrière

Roche's Estate

Landing Bay

Fairfield

South Soufrière Hills

Germans Bay

St Patrick's

Morris

White River

Shooters Hill

Old Ford Point

Triangle Rock

Shoe Rock

Guadeloupe Passage

N

0 metres 500
0 yards 500

■ **Sleeping**
1 Bachees
2 Erindell
3 Gingerbread Hill

4 Grand View
5 Montserrat
  Moments Inn
6 Tropical Mansions

Beaches and watersports

Montserrat's beaches are volcanic 'black' sand, which in reality means the sand may be a silvery grey or dark golden brown colour. The single white coral beach is at Rendezvous Bay in the north of the island. It is a stiff hike from Little Bay along a very steep mountainous trail (not suitable for small children). Take food and water, it is a long hot walk until you reach your refreshing swim. There is no shade on the beach, avoid the poisonous manchineel trees and the spiny sea urchins among the rocks at the north end. You can also take a boat, and it is quite a good idea to walk there and arrange for a boat to come and pick you up at an agreed time. The best of the rest of the beaches, all on the west of the island and black sand, are Woodlands (National Trust, beach house, washrooms), where you can safely swim through caves, Lime Kiln Bay, tiny Bunkum Bay, Carr's Bay and Little Bay in the north. Sports fishing can be arranged with Danny Sweeney, Olveston, T4915645, mwilson@candw.ag

Around the island

The **volcano** is now a tourist attraction and can best be viewed from the Montserrat Volcano Observatory, where visits are also possible on weekday afternoons when volcanic activity permits. Video shows of volcanic activity and a tour of the monitoring rooms and equipment are available, and an expert guide from the scientific community will be available to show you around. ■ *1530-1600 Mon-Fri. US$4 adults, US$2 children. T4915647, www.mvo.ms* Spectacular views of the volcano and its damage can also be viewed in safety from Jack Boy Hill in the east, close to the start of the Exclusion Zone. Do not attempt to enter the Exclusion Zone as it is very dangerous and hefty fines are levied on anyone caught in there. From here you can see the grey, ash-covered flanks of what is Chances Peak, in stark contrast with the Centre Hills, which are still green, forested and fertile.

If the volcano is dangerously active visitors are excluded

    Plymouth, the former capital, was flooded with ash up to the first floor of the colonial buildings and completely destroyed. Administrative offices have now moved to buildings in other villages in the north of the island and are rather scattered around. There are plans to develop the Little Bay area as a future capital. The port is here and a state-of-the-art performance centre/convention centre is being built, to open in 2004, with an adjacent open-air performing area to replace the Festival Village.

Essentials

L-A *Tropical Mansions*, Sweeneys, T4918273, www.tropicalmansion.com 18 rooms, CP, some with kitchenette, honeymoon suite, nicely furnished, pool, poor service in restaurant. **AL-B** *Grand View*, Baker Hill, looking towards Antigua, Nevis and Redonda, T4912284, www.mygrandview.com Twin beds, private or shared bathroom, or double bed, kitchenette and private bathroom, extra beds can be accommodated, TV, parking, CP, restaurant and bar, radio station downstairs, great for ham radio enthusiasts, internet access, run by Theresa Silcott. **A-C** *Montserrat Moments Inn*, Manjack Heights, T4917707, flogriff@candw.ag Rooms of different sizes with TV, fridge, a/c or fan, shared or private bathroom, CP, other meals by reservation, shared kitchenette, email, laundry facilities. **B-C** *Gingerbread Hill*, St Peter's, T4914582, www.volcano-island.com David and Clover Lea run a delightful guesthouse with incredible views and lovely 3-acre gardens, rooms or whole house available, veranda, or backpacker's special in basic room or charming room adjoining their own house, bathroom, deck, fridge, TV, phone, email, meals on request, tent and camping equipment available, bikes, rental car, family atmosphere, the Leas have 3 sons to enliven your stay. **B** *Erindell*, Gros Michel Drive, Woodlands, next to *Sea Wolf Diving*, T4913655, erindell@candw.ag Private entrance, twin beds, pleasant rooms, private bathroom, TV, phone, fans, full meal service except Sat night, pool, free laundry, discounts for Caricom residents, no credit cards, 1 min to bus route, 15-min walk to beach, snorkelling equipment, hiking and diving packages. **B** *Bachee's*, Olveston, T4917509. 3 rooms in pleasant house with gardens in a residential area.

Sleeping
Hotel tax is 10%, service is usually 10%

Leeward Islands

Rooms and apartments C *Egret House*, Woodlands, T/F4915316. Apartment overlooks Woodlands Beach, sleeps 2, no children, bedroom with large bed, sitting room, kitchen, bathroom, shower, stairs to sundeck and pool, TV, phones, fans. A *David and Maureen Hodd*, Olveston, T4915248, F4915016. Weekly and monthly rates, discounts for Caricom residents, apartment sleeps 2, views of sea and mountains, quiet, TV, phone, washing machine, kitchen, meals can be arranged. C *Levons and Camilla Watts*, Olveston, T4913179, amswt@email.com 1-bedroom apartment, phone, TV, kitchenette, laundry facilities. C *Bob and Beryl Chadwick*, Woodlands, T4919251. 1-bedroom apartment in pleasant gardens.

Villa rental Most villas have their own pools, terraces with sea views, gardens and maid service. Rental agencies include: *Kirwan's Secluded Hideaway*, Olveston, T4913405, F4912546; *Montserrat Enterprises Ltd*, Old Towne, T4912431, F4914660; *Neville Bradshaw Agencies*, Old Towne, T4915270, F4915069; *Jacquie Ryan Enterprises Ltd*, Olveston, T4912055, F4913257; *Tradewinds Real Estate*, Old Towne, T4912004, www.tradewindsmontserrat.com; *West Indies Real Estate*, Olveston, T4918666, www.wirealest.com

Eating

Several places do takeaway meals. Some places only open if you make a reservation in advance, so it is best to check

A large frog called mountain chicken, indigenous here and in Dominica, is the local delicacy. Goat water stew is another local dish commonly found on the menu. Most other foods, like steak and fish, are imported.

Working in a roughly south-north direction, **Olveston** *Jumping Jack's Bar*, T4915645. Danny and Margaret serve guests from their home where lunch and dinner are served on their balcony with lovely sea views. *The Attic* ,T4912008. Open for lunch except Sun for their special roti and fixed menu. **Salem** *Monica's Bar*, T4914182. Takeaway lunches. *Village Place*, for Jamaican jerk pork and chicken. **Runaway Point** *Etcetera Shoppe*, 540 Runaway Point Circle, T4915146. Call for reservations, only open for Wed lunch, Fri night dinner and Sun brunch. **Woodlands** *Ziggy's Restaurant*, T4918282, Mahogany Loop, second turning on the right from the main road. Dinner by reservation only, the island's leading restaurant, international cuisine, Ziggy has been serving great food since the early 1990s, lobster quadrille, jerk pork, chocolate sludge. **Fogarty Hill** *The People's Place*, T4917528. Lunches and takeaway meals, local food, great roti. **Cudjoe Head** *Fins & Wings*, T4918219. Lunch or takeaway, fish, chicken, local drinks. **Baker Hill** *Grand View*, a guesthouse with restaurant and bar open to non-residents for breakfast, lunch and dinner (by appointment). **Brades Main Road** *Tina's Restaurant*, T4913538. Local food, chicken and fish and local vegetables, prices from US$16.50-24 for a meal. *Tuitt's Pizzeria*, T4914606. Open Mon-Sat for pizza. *Economy Bakery*, T4916678. Fresh bread, sandwiches and snacks. **Carr's Bay** *Root's Man Beach Bar*, T4915957. Vegetarian meal, in rustic setting, orders only. **Little Bay** *Good Life Night Club & Restaurant*, T4914576. Newly built on a hillside overlooking the beach, great disco for weekend dancing, check for meal hrs, prices from about US$16.50. *Bitter End Beach Bar*, T4913146. Seafood and snacks on the beach, lunch from US$5.50-9.50, dinner from US$7.50. **Davy Hill Main Road** *Di's Snackette*, T4915450. Lunches and snacks. *Annie's Snackette*, T4915380. Snacks and takeaway. **Sweeney's** *Richard Samuel's*, T4912475. Fresh bread and snacks. *La Colage Bar & Restaurant*, T4914136. Creole cuisine, lunch from US$5.50, dinner from US$7.50, boutique for clothes and accessories attached. *Morgan's Spotlight Bar & Restaurant*, T4915419. Local food, large portions, goat water. *Peter's Bakery*, a whole range of tasty, freshly baked snacks. **Gerald's** *Cockpit Bar & Restaurant*, at Gerald's Heliport, T4914478. Montserrat version of the airport café, serves breakfast and lunch, popular for 'liming'. **St John's** *JJ's Cuisine*, Main Rd, T4919024. Breakfast, lunch and dinner, international cuisine, call ahead. *Howe's Flamboyant Bar*, T4913008. Pool table for entertainment after a meal.

Entertainment

Bars occasionally present live music featuring calypsonians; these are advertised on the radio

There are two nightclubs, *Club VIP* on Baker Hill and *The Good Life* at Little Bay, where disco music prevails. *The Bitter End Beach Bar*, occasionally presents live bands from Antigua and the wider Caribbean. *The Grand View Bar & Restaurant* on Baker Hill promotes live jazz featuring local and regional groups on the last Fri of each month to catch the after work crowd. *Tropical Mansions Hotel* has young musicians on parade most Fri evenings after work. *Festival Village*, at Little Bay, is open all year and has some music at weekends.

Leeward Islands

Hurricanes and volcanoes

In 1989, Montserrat was devastated by Hurricane Hugo, the first hurricane to strike the island for 61 years. No part of the island was untouched by the 150 mph winds as 400-year-old trees were uprooted, 95% of the housing stock was damaged or destroyed, agriculture was reduced to below subsistence level and even the 180-ft jetty at Plymouth harbour completely disappeared, causing problems for relief supplies. However, within a few months, all public utilities were restored and the remaining standing or injured trees were in leaf again.

In 1995 the lives of Montserratians were again disrupted, this time by volcanic activity. The residents of Plymouth and villages in the south were evacuated to the north as lava, rocks and ash belched from the Soufrière Hills for the first time since the 1930s. Activity increased in 1997; during March and April pyroclastic flows reached 2 miles down the south side of the volcano, the former tourist attractions of the Great Alps Waterfall and Galways Soufrière were covered, there was a partial collapse of Galways Wall and lava flowed down the Tar River Valley. In May the volcanic dome was growing at 3.7 cubic metres per second, and in June a huge explosion occurred when a sudden pyroclastic flow of hot rock, gas and ash poured down the volcano at 200 mph. It engulfed 19 people, destroyed seven villages and some 200 homes, including Farm and Trant's to the north of the volcano. The flow, which resulted from a partial collapse of the lava dome, came to within 50 yd of the sea, close to the airport runway, which had to be closed. The eruption sent an ash cloud 6 miles into the air and people were forced to wear ash masks. In August another bout of activity destroyed Plymouth, which caught fire under a shower of red hot lava. It now looks like a lunar landscape, completely covered by grey ash. In December 1997 there was a huge dome collapse which created a 600-yd amphitheatre around Galways Soufrière. The lava flows destroyed the deserted communities of St Patrick's, Gingoes and Morris and severely damaged Trials, Fairfield and Kinsale, south of Plymouth. The White River delta was increased to about 1 mile and the water level rose by about 3 ft. During 1998-99 dome collapses continued, with ash clouds at times up to 8 miles high, but scientists reported that the dome, while still hot, was gradually cooling and entering a quieter phase. In 2000 there was further activity and in July 2003 the dome of the volcano collapsed and a thick cloud of ash and rocks spread across the island. For daily scientific updates about the volcanic activity: www.mvp.ms

Festivals

Not surprisingly in the 'Emerald Isle', *St Patrick's Day* (a national holiday) is celebrated on **17 Mar** with concerts, masquerades and other festivities. The *Queen's Birthday* is celebrated on the 2nd Sat in **Jun** with parades, salutes and the raising of flags. Another national knees-up is *Aug Mon Weekend*, connected to *Emancipation Day* on **1 Aug**, commemorating the abolition of slavery in 1834. There are beach barbecues and picnics all weekend. Cudjoe Head Day on the Sat starts with a big breakfast and carries on late into the night, while St Peter's Anglican Fete is held in the village rectory grounds on the Mon. The island's main festival is the *Christmas* season, which starts around **12 Dec** and continues through New Year's Day. There are shows, concerts, calypso competitions, jump-ups and masquerades and of course lots of festivities and parties on *New Year's Eve*, helped down with lots of goat water.

Shopping

Montserrat's postage stamps have traditionally been collectors' items and you can buy them from the Montserrat Philatelic Bureau in Salem, T4912996, F4912042. It has 6 issues a year and a definitive issue every 4-5 years, having issued its own stamps since 1876. The volcanic eruption is featured, as is the eclipse of the sun. Also in Salem, the *Sea Island Cotton Shop* has the best in locally grown and manufactured cotton products and *Bennie's Jewelry Shop* sells locally made jewelry. For music, T-shirts and other clothing go to *Arrow's Manshop*, Salem, T4913852, or *Sweeneys*, T4916355. Photos of Montserrat and the volcano are sold at *Kevin's Photo Shop*, Cudjoe Head, T4916177, and

Leeward Islands

at *Woolcock's Craft & Photo Gallery*, BBC Building in Brades, T4912025, while *Sea Wolf*, Woodlands, T4917807, have postcards of underwater Montserrat and other crafts and gifts. Art and crafts and other souvenirs at *Oriole Gift Shop*, Salem, T4913086, next to the National Trust. *Kirnon's Products*, Cudjoe Head, T4916385, sells local pepper sauce, guava cheese, jellies, liqueurs and other local goodies. Leslie and Cynthia Williams sell honey in Brades, T4914014. *Howe's Enterprises*, in St John's, makes a wide range of rums, jellies, jams, sauces and seasonings, all in attractive packaging, good gifts.

Sports

For diving and watersports, see pages 553 and 551

There are some excellent mountain **walks** in the north of the island. Contact the Montserrat National Trust, T4913086, as they maintain the trails and can advise you on guides. Hiking with a forest ranger is usually US$20 per person depending on the size of the group. First class **cricket** is played at the Salem Cricket Ground, and each weekend in Jan-Jun you can see local and regional cricketers playing. There is a brand new **football** stadium, Phoenix Park, in the north and football is played at weekends Jul-Dec.

Tour operators

Sightseeing can be arranged with *Carib World Travel*, Sweeneys, T4912714, F4912713; *Double X Tours*, Olveston, T4915470, meader@candw.ag; *Grant Enterprises & Trading*, Olveston, T4919654, casselj@candw.ag; *Jenny's Tours*, St John's, Antigua, T268-4619361, burkeb@candw.ag; *Runaway Travel*, Sweeneys, T4912776, runaway@candw.ag; *Slim's Tours*, T4914479.

Transport

You can take only one piece of luggage on the helicopter, but unlimited amounts on the boat. Credit cards are not accepted on either the ferry or the helicopter

Air Helicopter seats available, several daily except Wed and Sat from Antigua, US$55 one way. Check with agent for times, which are always changing, and make sure you book well in advance otherwise it can be hard to get on. Agents in Antigua are *Carib Aviation*, VC Bird International Airport, T268-4623147, caribav@candw.ag Agents in Montserrat are *Montserrat Aviation Services*, Nixons, T4912533, F4917186. Charter helicopter service is offered by *Caribbean Helicopters*, Jolly Harbour, Antigua, T268-4605900, helicopters@candw.ag They also do a 45-min aerial Montserrat Volcano Tour from Jolly Harbour, Antigua, for US$190 per person, around and over the cone. **Boat** *Opal Express* ferry from Heritage Quay (or the main port when cruise ships are in), St John's, Antigua, to Little Bay, Montserrat, seats 300, a/c, leaves Antigua Mon-Sat 0630, 1600, returns from Little Bay 0800, 1730, 1 hr, US$40 one way, US$48 day return, Sat only. Agents in Antigua, *Carib World Travel*, Lower Redcliffe St, St John's, T268-4802980, F268-4802985; in Montserrat, *Montserrat Aviation Services* (see above). **Car hire** With a valid driving licence, you can obtain a local 3-month licence (EC$30/US$12) at the Police Station in Salem, open 24 hrs Mon-Fri, T4912555. *Be-Peep's Car Rentals*, Olveston, T4913787, for cars and jeeps; *Equipment & Supplies Ltd*, Olveston, T4912402, for cars and vans; *Ethelyne's Car Rental*, Olveston, T4912855; *Grant Enterprises & Trading*, Olveston, T4919654; *KC's Car Rentals*, Olveston, T4915756; *Montserrat Company Ltd*, Old Towne, T4912431; *Neville Bradshaw Agencies*, Olveston, T4915270; *Joe Oliver*, Barzey's, T4914276, for jeeps; *MS Osborne Ltd*, Brades, T4912494; *Pickett Van Rentals*, Salem, T4915470, for vans; *Zeekies Rentals*, Baker Hill, T4914515. **Taxi** Recommended taxi drivers for tours and taxi service: Joe Phillip, T4913432, phillipj@candw.ag

Directory

Banks *Bank of Montserrat*, St Peters, T4913843, F4913163, open Mon, Tue Thu 0800-1400, Wed 0800-1300, Fri 0800-1500. *Royal Bank of Canada*, Brades, T4912426-8, F4913391, open Mon-Thu 0900-1400, Fri 0900-1500. The American Express agent is *Carib World Travel*, at Davy Hill, T4912714, F4912713. **Communications** Internet: *CompuGET* cybercafé in Brades, T4919654, granten@candw.ag; *Jim Lee's Computer Services*, St Peter's, T4918499, leej@candw.ag **Post:** Post office open Mon-Fri 0815-1555, T4912457. **Telephone:** *Cable and Wireless* (West Indies) Ltd, at Sweeneys, T4912112, F4913599, Mon-Fri 0800-1600, with a digital telephone system, international dialling, telegraph, fax and data facilities. Phone cards are available, as are credit card service, toll free 800 service and cellular phones. **Medical services** The hospital is in St John's, for most routine and surgical emergencies, T4912802. Private doctors and a dentist are also available Serious medical cases are taken by helicopter to Antigua or Guadeloupe.

Background

Columbus sighted Montserrat on 11 November 1493, naming it after an abbey of the **History** same name in Spain, where the founder of the Jesuits, Ignacio de Loyola, experienced the vision which led to his forming that famous order of monks. At that time, a few Carib Indians lived on the island but by the middle of the 17th century they had disappeared. The Caribs named the island Alliouagana, which means 'land of the prickly bush'. Montserrat was eventually settled by the British Thomas Warner, who brought English and Irish Catholics from their uneasy base in the Protestant island of St Kitts. Once established as an Irish-Catholic colony, the only one in the Caribbean, Catholic refugees fled there from persecution in Virginia and, following his victory at Drogheda in 1649, Cromwell sent some of his Irish political prisoners to Montserrat. By 1648 there were 1,000 Irish families on the island. An Irishman brought some of the first slaves in 1651 and the economy became based on sugar. Slaves quickly outnumbered the original British indentured servants. A slave rebellion in 1768, appropriately enough on St Patrick's Day, led to all the rebels being executed, and today they are celebrated as freedom fighters. Montserrat was invaded several times by the French during the 17th and 18th centuries, sometimes with assistance from the resident Irish, but the island returned to British control under the Treaty of Versailles (1783) and has remained a colony to this day.

Political parties include the New People's Liberation Movement (New PLM), the National Development Party (NDP), the National Progressive Party (NPP), the Movement for National Reconstruction (MNR) and the People's Progressive Alliance (PPA). On 2 April 2001 General Elections saw the New PLM Party of John Osborne (a former Chief Minister) win seven of the nine seats in the Legislative Council. The NPP, led by Reuben T Meade, won the remaining two seats.

The main concern of the government since the eruption of the volcano in 1995 and thereafter is to replace the destroyed infrastructure of the south. With British funding there have been built new schools, housing, hospital, fuel terminal, power station, factory shells, offices, roads, water systems, port, heliport and airport. In all, in excess of £250 mn has been spent by the British Government to rebuild Montserrat. A few Montserratians are beginning to return home from overseas and there has been a big influx of workers from other Caricom countries to help the rebuilding process.

Montserrat, known as 'the Emerald Isle', is dominated by three mountain ranges. Mount **Geography** Chance, in the Soufrière Hills, rises to 3,000 ft above sea level. This active volcano had been erupting for two years before it exploded in August 1997, destroying some villages and the capital, Plymouth. As a result, the south, which like the rest of the island used to be all lushly green, is now grey with ash. Montserrat was off-limits for tourism for a few years, but the still-active volcano is now attracting visitors and facilities are being restored. The islands is about 11 miles long and 7 miles wide, although the volcano's eruptions have increased the land surface in the south.

A British Overseas Territory, Montserrat has a representative government with a ministe- **Government** rial system. Queen Elizabeth II is Head of State and is represented by a resident Governor. The Government consists of a Legislative and an Executive Council, with elections being held every five years for membership in the former. The head of Government is called the Chief Minister; a Speaker presides over the nine-member Legislative Council. As executive authority and head of the civil service, the Governor is responsible for defence, internal security, financial services and external affairs.

Tourism used to contribute about 30% of GDP, it was the largest supplier of foreign **Economy** exchange and the Government actively encouraged investment in tourism projects. The influx of foreign residents in the 1980s saw a sharp rise in real estate deals and building construction with a parallel dependence on imports of capital and consumer goods. Gross domestic product grew rapidly at the end of the 1980s, expanding by 12.8% in 1988, although a slower rate was recorded in 1989 because of the devastation wreaked

Leeward Islands

by Hurricane Hugo. 95% of the housing stock was totally or partially destroyed; production and exports were disrupted, infrastructure was severely damaged; public sector finances were hit by reduced income and greater expenditure demands; tourism slumped. Similar economic disruption occurred as a result of the volcanic eruption in 1995-1997 (see box) when the south had to be evacuated to the north. Most ex-pats left the island and tourists stayed away. The island now depends on aid from the UK but is beginning to recover, with new construction and hotels opening up again. A new airport is under construction with British and EU monies and is expected to open mid-2004.

People   The vast majority of the people are of African descent. Before the volcano erupted there was an influx of white Americans, Canadians and Britons who purchased retirement homes on the island. Montserratians are notable for their easy friendliness to visitors, speaking English flavoured by dialect and the odd Irish expression. There is virtually no crime and everyone leaves their doors unlocked. The population used to hover around 11,000, but emigration since the volcano started erupting in 1995 has reduced numbers to 4,500. Montserratians are British citizens with the right of abode in the UK.

Culture   The Irish influence can still be seen in national emblems. On arrival your passport is stamped

On Montserrat a with a green shamrock, the island's flag and crest show a woman, Erin of Irish legend, com-
'maroon' is not a plete with her harp. There are many Irish names, of both people and places, and the national
runaway slave but dish, goat water stew, is supposedly based on a traditional Irish recipe, although some histo-
the local equivalent rians claim it is of African origin. A popular local folk dance, the Bam-chick-a-lay resembles
of 'barn-raising', Irish step dances and musical bands may include a fife and a drum similar to the Irish
when everyone helps bodhran. The new Government House at Woodlands has a shamrock fixed to its roof.
to build a house,
lay a garden, etc   The African heritage dominates, however, whether it be in Caribbean musical forms like calypso (the veteran Arrow is now an international superstar and can still be found on the island, having moved his operation north out of the volcano evacuation zone), steel bands or the costumed masqueraders who parade during the Christmas season. Another element in the African cultural heritage are the Jumbie Dancers, who combine dancing and healing. Only those who are intimate with the island and its inhabitants will be able to witness their ceremonies, though. Local choirs, like the long-established Emerald Community Singers, mix calypso with traditional folk songs and spirituals in their repertoire, and the String Bands of the island play the African shak-shak, made from a calabash gourd, as well as the imported Hawaiian ukelele.

Sir George Martin's famed recording studios, the Air Studios, on the edge of Belham Valley, used to attract rock megastars such as Elton John, the Rolling Stones and Sting to the island, but the studios were closed after Hurricane Hugo. He is now building a Performing Arts/Cultural Centre at Little Bay (to replace the Festival Village). In 1997, Sir George Martin organized a gala fundraising concert for Montserrat at the Royal Albert Hall in London, which included (Sir) Paul McCartney, (Sir) Elton John, Eric Clapton, Sting, Mark Knopfler, Jimmy Buffet and Arrow, who had used Air Studios in the past. At the same time a show was put on at Gerald's Bottom on Montserrat by other musicians who had used the recording studios. *The Climax Blues Band* reformed for the occasion and Bankie Banks appeared, along with 18 local acts in what was optimistically called 'Many Happy Returns'. A second 'Many Happy Returns' concert was held in 1999 to coincide with St Patrick's Day festivities. Local and London-based bands, choirs and acts attracted a crowd of 3,000, or 75% of the population at that time, and the finale was provided by the king of soca, Arrow and his band. Lately, some of the touring calypso shows such as Shadow and Sparrow, that have played Antigua, have taken the ferry over to Montserrat and put on memorable shows at the *Bitter End Beach Bar* in Little Bay.

French Antilles

Introducing the French Antilles

The French Caribbean Islands form two Départements d'Outremer: one comprises Martinique, and the other Guadeloupe with its offshore group (Marie-Galante, Les Saintes and La Désirade). Two more distant islands, Saint-Barthélemy and Saint-Martin, are included in the Leeward Islands (see pages 468 and 500). Geographically, Guadeloupe and Martinique form the northern group of the Windward Islands, with the ex-British island of Dominica in the centre of them.

These larger islands both have mountains and forests where you can find rushing streams, waterfalls and pools for bathing in. The best beaches, however, are in the more arid parts, which are flatter. The smaller islands are fairly hilly but dry, particularly those in the Leewards. Some beautiful French colonial architecture remains, sometimes with iron balconies and intricate fretwork, but many modern buildings are concrete blocks and lack charm.

Visitors are often surprised by how French the islands are: the inhabitants are French citizens, the currency is the euro and the people eat croissants and baguettes. The African connection is strong too, dating back to slavery on the plantations. Most people speak Creole, there are African rhythms and instruments in the music and African influences in art and literature.

French Antilles

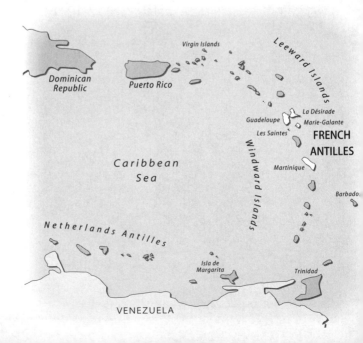

Essentials

Before you travel

The regulations are the same as for France. In most cases the only document required for entry is a **passport**, the exceptions being citizens of Australia, South Africa, Bolivia, Dominica, Barbados, Jamaica, Trinidad, Haiti, Honduras, El Salvador, Dominican Republic, Turkey, when a **visa** is required. St Lucians are allowed to enter without visas for visits of up to 15 days. Any non-EU citizen staying longer than 3 months needs an extended visa. Citizens of the USA and Canada staying less than 3 weeks do not need a passport, although some form of identification with a photo is required. An onward ticket is necessary but not always asked for. EU citizens need not fill in a landing card. They are entitled to use local medical services on production of a stamped E11 form, obtainable in their home country (eg UK Post Office).

Documents

With the abolition of EU frontiers, Europeans are able to bring back the same entitlements as from mainland France. However you could run into problems if returning via Antigua, with a long, uncomfortable wait in transit. Take a direct flight to France if buying in bulk.

Customs

Vaccination certificates are not required if you are French, an EU citizen, American or Canadian, but if you come from South America or some of the Caribbean Islands an international certificate for small pox and yellow fever vaccinations is compulsory.

Vaccination

Language

The cultural, social and educational systems of France are used and the official language is French. Creole is widely spoken on Guadeloupe and Martinique; it has West African grammatical structures and uses a mainly French-derived vocabulary. It is the everyday language of most Guadeloupean and Martiniquan people and can be heard on the radio; some stations use it almost exclusively. English is not widely spoken.

A knowledge of French is a great advantage

Money

There are money-changing offices in the big hotels and at airports. The euro is the legal tender although US$ are accepted except in post offices and on buses. There is no limit to travellers' cheques and letters of credit being imported, but a declaration of foreign bank notes in excess of €533.60 must be made.

Food and drink

Restaurants divide fairly neatly into French cuisine or more moderate Creole. There is often a *plat du jour* as there would be in France and very reasonable 2-3 course *menu touristique* meals. Children may find Creole food rather spicy.

Restaurants

A delightful blend of French, African, and Indian influences is found in Creole dishes, the cuisine is quite distinctive. Basic traditional French and African recipes using local ingredients; seafood, tropical fruits and vegetables are combined with exotic seasonings to give rich colour and flavour. These local specialities are not to be missed: *Ti-boudin*, a well seasoned sausage; *blaff* is red snapper or other fish, possibly sea urchins (*chadrons*) cooked with local spices and onions, somewhere between a soup and a stew; *ragout*, a spicy stew often made with squid (*chatrous*), or conch (*lambis*), or with meat; *colombo*, a recipe introduced by Hindu immigrants in the 19th century, is a thick curry; *poulet au coco*, chicken prepared with coconut; chunks of steakfish seasoned and grilled; *morue* (salt cod) made into sauces and *accras* (hot fishy fritters from Africa) or *chiquetaille* (grilled), or used in *feroce d'avocat*, a pulp of avocados, peppers and manioc flour; *langouste* (lobster), *crabe* (crab), *écrevisses*, *ouassous*, *z'habitants* (crayfish), *gambas* (prawns) and *vivaneau* (snapper) are often fricasseed, grilled or barbecued with hot pepper sauce. A good starter is *crabe farci* (stuffed land crab). Main

Local cuisine

French Antilles

▶ **Tourist offices overseas**

Belgium *Service Official Français du Tourisme: 21 Avenue de la Toison d'Or, 1060 Brussels, 25053810, info@francetourisme.be*
Canada *French Government Tourist Office, 1981 Avenue MacGill College, Suite 490, Montréal, Quebec, H 3A 2W9, T514-8448566, tourist.martiniquemontreal@qc.aira.com; 30 St Patrick Street, Suite 700, Toronto, T416-5934723.*
France *Office Inter-Régional du Tourisme des Antilles Françaises and Office du Tourisme de la Martinique, 2 rue des Moulins, 75001 Paris, T44778600, info@martiniquetourisme.com; Gîtes de France, 35 rue Godot de Mauroy, 75009 Paris, T47422543. Guadeloupe Tourist Office, 43 rue des Tilleuls, 92100 Boulogne, T46040088.*
Germany *Bureau du Tourisme de la Guadeloupe, Bethmannstrasse 58, 6000 Frankfurt AM Main 1, T0049-69283293, guadeloupe@karibik.org; Fremdenverkehrsamt Martinique, Westendstrasse 47-D, 60325 Frankfurt am Main, T49-6997-580131, franceprofi@mdlf.de*
Italy *Via Larga, 7, 20122 Milan, T392-58486655, info@turismofrancese.it*
Spain *Administration: Gran Via, 59-28013 Madrid, T5418808.*

Sweden/Denmark *Ny Ostergade 33, DK 1101 Copenhagen, T45-33114912; The Commercial Representative Office Nordic Countries, PO Box 4031 Fregativägen 14, South 181 04 Lidingo, T468-7655865.*
Switzerland *Rennweg 42, Postfach 7226, 8023 Zurich, T41-12174600, tourismefrance@bluewin.ch*
UK *178 Piccadilly, London, T020-76292869, info@mdlf.co.uk*
USA *French West Indies Tourist Office, 444 Madison Av, 16th floor, New York, NY 10020, T212-7571125; The Martinique Promotion Bureau, 444 Madison Av, 16th floor, New York, NY10022, T212-8386887, info@martinique@.org; French Government Tourist Office, 645 North Michigan Avenue, Suite 3360, Chicago, Illinois 60611, T312-7517800; French Government Tourist Office, 9454 Wilshire Blvd, Beverley Hills, CA 90212, T310-2716665; Guadeloupe Tourist Office, 161 Washington Valley Road, Warren, NJ 07059, T88-4-GUADELOUPE. French Government Tourist Office, Suite 205, 2305 Cedar Spring Road, Dallas, TX 75201, F214-7204010.*

dishes are usually accompanied by white rice, breadfruit, yams or *patate douce* (sweet potatoes) with plantains and red beans or lentils. *Christophine* (Creole: *chayotte*) *au gratin*; a large knobbly vegetable grilled with grated cheese and breadcrumbs, or fresh *crudités* are delicious, lighter side dishes. Fresh fruit often ends the meal; pineapples, papayas, soursops and bananas can be found all year round and mangoes, guavas and sugar apples in season. Ice cream (*glace*) is also a favourite dessert, particularly guava or soursop (*corossol*).

Drink
Tap water is drinkable

As in other Caribbean islands the main alcoholic drink is rum. It is nearly all made from the juice of the cane, *rhum agricole,* unlike elsewhere in the Caribbean where it is made from molasses. *Ti punch* is rum mixed with a little cane syrup or sugar syrup and a slice of lime and is a popular drink at any time of the day. *Shrub* is a delicious Christmas liqueur made from macerated rum and orange peel. *Planteur* is a rum and fruit juice punch. Martiniquan rum has a distinctive flavour and is famous for its strength, but rum from Guadeloupe and Marie Galante has been equally praised. There is a huge choice of Martiniquan rum, recommended brands being Trois Rivières, Mauny, St James and St Clément. On Guadeloupe try Damoiseau and especially on Marie Galante, Père Labat. French wines are everywhere and are not expensive in supermarkets or even small village shops. A good local beer is *Lorraine*, a clean-tasting beer which claims to be 'brewed for the tropics'. Locally-brewed Guinness, at 7% alcohol by volume, stronger than its Irish counterpart, is thick and rich. *Malta*, a non-alcoholic beverage similar to malt beer, is produced by most breweries and said to be full of minerals and vitamins. Thirst quenching non-alcoholic drinks to look out for are the fresh fruit juices served in most snackbars and cafés. Guava, soursop, passion fruit and sugar cane juice are commonly seen.

Touching down

Boat information *(French flag) Deshaies, Basse-Terre and Pointe-à-Pitre are ports of entry butÎles des Saintes is not. No charge for EU or US citizens. French forms to fill in. Pointe-à-Pitre has good groceries, marine supplies, fuel, water, free 220 V electricity, bus to town from marina. Free dinghy dock in marina. duty-free fuel when you clear out of the country. Charter companies include Moorings, Jet Sea, Stardust ATM.*

Business hours *Banks: Mon-Fri 0800-1200, 1400-1600.* **Government offices:** *Mon and Fri 0730-1300, 1500-1630, Tue-Thu 0730-1300.* **Shops:** *Mon-Fri 0800-1200, 1430-1700; Sat morning only.*

Currency *Euro. Exchange rates vary. Post offices change dollars but not all. Exchange facility at the airport. There is a 24-hour ATM at Bas-du-Fort marina which accepts euros,*

sterling, US, EC and Canadian dollars and yen. It can be difficult to change EC dollars.

Emergency numbers *Hospital T0590-891010/ 891120 in Pointe-à-Pitre.*

Official time *GMT muinus 4 hrs.*

Public holidays *New Year's Day; Easter Sun and Easter Mon; Labour Day on 1 May; Ascension Day; Whit Mon; 8 May VE Day; 27 May Slavery Abolition Day; National/Bastille Day on 14 Jul; Schoelcher Day on 21 Jul; Assumption Day in Aug; All Saints' Day on 1 Nov; All Souls' Day on 2 Nov; Armistice Day on 11 Nov and Christmas Day.*

Useful addresses *Gendarmerie: T0590-820059,* **Police:** *T0590-821317 in Pointe-à-Pitre, T0590-811155 in Basse-Terre;* **Nautical assistance:** *T0590-829108.*

Voltage *220 volts AC, 50 cycles.*

Weights and measures *Metric.*

See also Directory, page 579

Holidays and festivals

Another feature common to the two main islands is the pre-Lenten Carnival, less touristy than most. It ends with impressive Ash Wednesday ceremonies (especially in Martinique), when the population dresses in black and white, and processions take place that combine the seriousness of the first day of the Christian Lent with the funeral of the Carnival King (Vaval). **Carnival**

The spectacles of cockfighting and mongoose versus snake are popular throughout the French Islands. Betting shops are full of atmosphere (they are usually attached to a bar). Horse racing is held on Martinique, but not Guadeloupe, but on both islands gambling on all types of mainland France track events is very keen. **Sports**

Guadeloupe

This is France in the tropics, the islands having the same status as any French département on the mainland. They have the same morning smells too: coffee, warm croissants, baking baguettes. Guadeloupe is really two islands: the western Basse-Terre, which is mountainous and forested, 'green Guadeloupe', with a huge national park on and offshore; and Grande-Terre, to the east, which is smaller, flatter and more densely populated. Large areas of the island are used for growing sugar cane, particularly on Grande-Terre and bananas and other fruits and flowers thrive on the rich volcanic soil of Basse-Terre. The best beaches are of golden sand from the coral limestone of Grande-Terre. Tourists come mostly from France. The outer islands of Les Saintes, La Désirade and Marie Galante are easily reached from Guadeloupe but are quiet and untouched by mass tourism.

IDD code: 0590 (don't be confused, the local code is also 590) Colour map 4, grid A4 Population: 422,000

French Antilles

Ins and outs

All European connections are with Paris and there are daily flights with *Air France* and *Air Corsair*. There are also charter flights. Apart from *Air Canada*, which flies from Montréal, the only other scheduled services from North America are *Air France's* daily flights from Miami, although connections can be made with *American Eagle's* flight from San Juan, Puerto Rico. **Getting there**

See Transport, page 578, for further details

Things to do in Guadeloupe

- Indulge in some noisy spectator sport at the raucous **bullock cart racing** on Grande-Terre.
- Tour the **rum distilleries**, taste the wonderful *rhum agricole*, made from the pure juice of the cane, then sober up with a visit to an historic **coffee plantation** and lots of delicious coffee.
- Take a day trip to **Les Saintes**, Marie Galante, or little visited La Désirade. Better still, stay overnight to really unwind into a traditional way of life.
- Hike through the forests, climb the mountains and cool off in the streams and waterfalls of the **national park on Basse-Terre**.

Connections are good with neighbouring islands if you want to island hop. This is also possible by sea, as there are high-speed ferries between Guadeloupe, Les Saintes, Martinique, St Lucia and Dominica. Cruise ships call frequently and are increasingly using Guadeloupe as a useful stopover on their way to the Mediterranean for summer cruising.

Getting around
Buses play zouk music at top volume – exhilarating or deafening, depending on your mood

Bus There are 3 main bus terminals in Pointe-à-Pitre. It is possible to cover the whole island by bus in a day – cheap, interesting and easy, but exhausting. You can just stop the bus at the side of the road or wait at the bus stations in the villages. Buses are crowded at peak times; have your money ready when you get off.

Car Car hire is available mainly at the airport, but can also be arranged through the major hotels. A small, old Peugeot will cost about US$50 per day. International and local agencies are represented. Pointe-à-Pitre has a dual carriage ring road which runs from Gosier across the Rivière Salée to the industrial centre at Baie-Mahault and south towards Petit-Bourg. The metred taxis are expensive and some now accept credit cards. Fares increase at night. They are mainly found at the airports and outside the main hotels, although you can also phone for one. From the airport to Place de la Victoire, US$11-14, more at weekends. Bicycles can be rented.

Climate The temperature on the coasts varies between 22°C and 30°C, but is about 3°C lower in the interior. Jan-Apr is the dry season (called *carême*), Jul-Nov the wet season (*l'hivernage*), with most rain falling Sep-Nov. Trade winds moderate temperatures the year round.

Tourist information Tourist offices in Guadeloupe, www.lesilesdeguadeloupe.com: 5 Square de la Banque, BP 422-97163, Pointe- à-Pitre, T0590- 820930, F0590- 838922 (the *Gîtes* office next door is helpful); Maison du Port, Cours Nolivos, Basse- Terre, T0590- 812483; Av de l'Europe, Saint-François, T0590- 884874, and at airport. **Maps** The *Serie Bleu* maps (1:25,000, 7 maps of Guadeloupe, No 4601G-4607G) issued by the Institut Geógraphique National, Paris, which include all hiking trails, are available at the bigger book stores in the rue Frébault in Pointe-à-Pitre, and at *Le Joyeux* hotel in Trois Rivières/Le Faubourg for US$7.50. Also available from MapLink in the USA, T805-6926777.

Flora and fauna

The comparatively low-lying Grande-Terre is mainly given over to sugar cane, livestock raising and fruit trees (mango, coconut, papaya, guava, etc). Mostly a limestone plateau, it does have a hilly region, Les Grands-Fonds, and a marshy, mangrove coast extending as far north as Port-Louis. The vegetation of Basse-Terre ranges from tropical forest (40% of the land is forested: trees such as the mahogany and gommier, climbing plants, wild orchids) to the cultivated coasts: sugar cane on the windward side, bananas in the south and coffee and vanilla on the leeward. On both parts the flowers are a delight, especially the anthuriums and hibiscus.

The island's **national park**, known as the **Parc Naturel** (Habitation Beausoleil, BP 13 Montéran, 97120 Saint-Claude, T0590-802425, F0590-800546), the seventh largest in France, includes 30,000 ha of forest land in the centre of Basse-Terre, which is by far the more scenic part. As the island is volcanic there are a number of related places to visit. Do not pick flowers, fish, hunt, drop litter, play music or wash anything in the rivers. Dogs are banned. Trails have been marked out all over the park, including to the dome of Soufrière volcano with its fumaroles, cauldrons and sulphur fields (see below). The national park includes three protected land and sea reserves, open to the public: **Les Réserves Naturelles des Pitons du Nord et de Beaugendre, La Réserve Naturelle du Grand Cul-de-Sac Marin and La Réserve Naturelle de Pigeon**, or **Réserve Cousteau** (see below). The waters after which the Caribs named the island come hot (as at the Ravine Chaude springs on the Rivière à Goyaves), tumbling (the waterfalls of the Carbet River and the Cascade aux Écrevisses on the Corossol), and tranquil (the lakes of Grand Étang, As de Pique and Étang Zombi).

The park has no gates, no opening hours and no admission fee

A **Maison du Volcan** at Saint-Claude (open 1000-1800) and a **Maison de la Fôret** (1000-1700) on the Route de la Traversée give information on the volcano and its surrounding forest. From the Maison de la Forêt there are 10-, 20- and 60-minute forest walks which will take you deep among the towering trees. The **Cascade aux Écrevisses**, a waterfall and small pool, is about 2 km from the Maison (clearly marked) and is a popular place to swim and spend the day. The **Parc Zoologique et Botanique** above Mahaut, houses many of the species which exist in the Natural Park, such as mongoose, racoon, iguana and land turtle, unfortunately in very small cages. A hanging bridge, the *Canopée*, links the tree tops. ■ *0900-1700. €3.80, children, €2.30. T0590-988352. Fine panoramic views from the café (free drink included in entrance ticket) and the simple but excellent Ti-Racoon restaurant serves lunch daily except Mon.*

The national park's emblem is the *raton laveur* (racoon) which, although protected, is very rare. You are much more likely to see birds and insects in the park. On La Désirade a few agoutis survive, as well as iguana, which can also be found on Les Saintes. Much of the island's indigenous wildlife has vanished.

Diving and marine life

On the Leeward Coast (Côte-Sous-le-Vent, or the Golden Corniche), is the **Underwater Reserve** developed by Jacques Cousteau.

Nautilus, T0590-988908, F0590-988566, a glass-bottom boat, takes you round the marine park, departing from Malendure beach, south of Mahaut 1030, 1200, 1430 and 1600. US$11.50 adults, children 5-12 years half price. The boat anchors for about 15 mins off **Ilet Pigeon** for snorkelling, but it is rather deep to see much. In wet weather the water becomes too murky to see anything. The boat is often booked solid by cruise ship visitors. Diving trips can be arranged at *Les Heures Saines*, T0590-988663, at Rocher de Malendure, or *Chez Guy et Christian*, Plaisir Plongée Caraïbe, T0590-988243, F0590-988284, friendly, recommended for beginners' confidence, well equipped, packages with accommodation provided, at Pigeon, Bouillante.

Dive centres
Lots of dive companies along the Leeward coast and on Grande-Terre, with no shortage of dive sites

Beaches

Petit Havre is popular with its small coves and reefs offshore. Here are mostly fishermen and locals and a small shed selling fish meals and beer. The best is at **Sainte-Anne** where the fine white sand and crystal clear water of a constant depth of 1.5 m far from shore make idyllic bathing; the **Plage du Bourg** in town is ideal for young children, the Plage de la Caravelle west of town, is excellent; part is public and part with access only through the *Club Med*. About 2 km from the town is the Plage de Bois Jolan, reached down a track, where the water is shallow enough to walk to the protecting reef. Further east are good beaches at St-François and the 11-km road to Pointe des Colibris skirts the **Anse Kahouanne** with lots of tracks going down to the sea; sand is limited but there are snorkelling possibilities.

Guadeloupe has excellent beaches for swimming, mostly between Gosier and St-François on Grande-Terre. More deserted beaches can be found on the northeast of Grande-Terre

French Antilles

On the north coast of the peninsula is **Plage Tarare**, where there is a good restaurant by the car park. This is the only official nudist beach in Guadeloupe. **Plage de l'Anse à la Gourde** has good sand and is popular with campers at weekends.

On the leeward coast of Basse-Terre are some good beaches. South of Pointe Noire on the west coast is **Plage Caraïbe**, which is clean, calm and beautiful, with restaurant *Le Reflet* (helpful owners), picnic facilities, toilets and a shower. A small,

Guadeloupe & outer islands

Caribbean Sea

Pointe d'Antigues

Port Loui

ILET À KAHOUANNE

Pointe Allègre

Plage de Clugny

Underwater Reserve

ILET À FAJOU

10 Duzer

Grande Anse

D18

Ste-Rose

Grand Cul-de-Sac Marin

Pnte Granger

Deshaies **5** **16** **22** **6**

N2

Ferry

Lamentin

Baie-Mahault

R Salée

Trace des Contrabandiers

Belcourt

Pointe-à-Pitre

Pointe-Noire

Maison du Bois

R Goyaves

N10

Anse Caraïbe

parc

Ravine Chaude

D1

Petit Cul-de-Sac Marin

Mahaut

Parc Zoologique

2 D23

Tabanon

Petit-Bourg

Underwater Reserve

Les Mamelles

Maison de la Forêt

Cascade aux Ecrevisses

Vernou

N1

Plage de Viard

Bouillante **9**

Pitons de Bouillante (1,088m)

Naturel

Matéliane (1,298m)

Chutes du Moreau

Goyave

Morne Rouge

Forêt de Sainte-Marie

Marigot

Trace Victor Hugues

Ste-Marie

Basse-Terre

Pointe Constant

To Les Sainte & Marie Gale

Maison du Café

La Soufrière (1,467m)

Vieux-Habitants

Chutes du Carbet

Routhiers

Matouba

Maison du Volcan

Savane à Mulets

Bois Debout

Capesterre-Belle-Eau

25 **23**

St-Claude

Etang Zombi

Pointe du Carbet

La Citerne

As de Pique

Grand Etang

St-Sauveur

Baillif

N3

Gourbeyre

Bananier

N1

Basse-Terre

Fort Luis Delgrés

Monts Caraïbes

17

Anse Turlet

11 **18**

Grande Pointe

Trois-Rivières

Grande Anse

Vieux-Fort

Pointe à Launay

To Les Saintes

To Les Saintes

black-sand beach, La Grand Anse, just west of Trois Rivières, has a barbecue and drinks (expensive) on the beach and a shower and toilets (which do not always work). In the northwest, **La Grande Anse**, 30 minutes' walk north of Deshaies, is superb and undeveloped with no hotels, golden sand but no snorkelling except round a large rock where the current is quite strong. Body surfing is good when the waves are big. Beach restaurant at the south end with charcoal-grilled chicken. On

French Antilles

■ Sleeping	9 Domaine de Malendure	17 Le Jardin Malanga
1 Anse des Rochers Anchorage	10 Fort Royal	18 Le Joyeux
2 Auberge de la Distillerie	11 Grand' Anse	19 Les Flamboyants
3 Auberge de la Vieille Tour	12 Iguana Bay Villas	20 Novotel Coralia
4 Auberge le Grand Large/	13 La Cocoteraie/Kaye' la/	21 Plantation Ste-Marthe
Mini Beach/La Toubana	Chez Honore	22 Pointe Batterie
5 Chez Jean Memorin	14 La Créole Beach/Les	23 Relais de la Grand Soufrière
6 Chez M Eric Bernier	Résidences Yucca/Palmes	24 Serge's Guest House
7 Club Mediterranee	15 La Marie-Gaillarde	25 St-Georges
8 Corossol	16 La Vigie	

Sunday people sell hot Creole food quite cheaply. The beaches on the north coast of Basse-Terre can be dangerous and at **Plage de Clugny** there are warning signs as there have been drownings.

Watersports Most beach hotels offer windsurfing for guests and visitors, and some arrange waterskiing and diving courses. Windsurfers gather at the *UCPA Hotel Club* in St-François. The tradewinds are best Dec-May and the best places are St-François, Sainte-Anne and Gosier.

Courses and board rental are available at *Sport Away Ecole Nathalie Simon*, St-François, T/F0590-887204, *LCS*, Ste-Anne, T0590-881517, F0590-881521, and *UCPA*, St-François, T0590-886480, F0590-884350. Surfing is also now popular at Le Moule, Port-Louis, La Pointe des Châteaux, Ste-Anne and St-François. The *Comité Guadeloupéen de Surf* is at the *Karukera Surf Club*, Le Moule, T0590-231093. There is also the *Arawak Surf Club*, T0590-236068, F0590-237589.

Sailing Sailing boats can be chartered for any duration from Captain Lemaire, Carénage A, Route du Gosier, 97110 Pointe-à-Pitre. A crew of 3 works out at about US$75-100 per person per day, excluding food, or US$250-300 per boat. There are 2 marinas between Pointe-à-Pitre and Gosier, and good, shallow-draught anchorage at Gosier. The **Route du Rhum** race is held every 4 years, with multi-hull boats racing between St-Malo, France, and Pointe-à-Pitre. The record is 14 days, 10 hrs and 8 mins.

Day sails *King Papyrus* at Marina Bas du Fort, Gosier, T0590-909298, F0590-907171, takes you on an all day cruise to Ilet Caret with a visit to the mangroves. The mangroves can also be visited on water scooters, T887193 in St-François, or T850277 for excursions starting from Morne-à-l'Eau. *La Compagnie des Bateaux Verts*, Marina Bas-du-Fort, T0590-907717, F0590-907920, starts with the Aquarium and then takes you to the marine park on the 48-passenger glass-bottomed *Kio*, with scientists on board to explain the ecosystems. *Falling Star*, T0590-885396, F0590-887794, a 46-ft catamaran, offers all-day sails to the island of Petite- Terre. *Awak*, T0590-885353, F0590-886043, a 46-ft vedette with a glass bottom, also goes to Petite-Terre. From Pigeon Buillante there are several glass-bottomed boat excursions: *Aquarius* has 3 2-hr trips, at 1000, 1230 and 1500, T0590-988730, F0590-901185. *Nautilus* has 2 glass-bottomed boats and a submarine.

There are several excursions offered, ranging from the booze cruise or sunset cruise variety to more scientific and educational trips

Fishing Blue marlin, kingfish, barracuda, bonita can be fished all year round, but there are seasons for other species. There are lots of fishing contests organized throughout the year. Well-equipped boats go out for full- or half-day excursions from Bouillante: *Fishing Club Antilles*, T0590-987010, *Francis Ricard*, T0590-987377; and from Le Rocher de Malendure: *Franck Nouy*, T0590-987084, who also offers 5 and 8-day trips. Fishing boats also go out from Marina Bas du Fort and Gosier.

Deep-sea fishing is best off the Côte-sous-le-vent, where the fishing area is 20 minutes from Ilet Pigeon

Pointe-à-Pitre

Population: 141,000
Colour map 4, grid A4

On Grande-Terre at the south end of the Rivière Salée, Pointe-à-Pitre is the chief commercial centre of Guadeloupe. The ports for inter-island ferries, commercial and cruise shipping are at its heart while the airport, Pole Caraïbes, is nearby. The inhabitants call themselves 'Les Pointus'. The city lies to the south of the Route National N1 to Basse-Terre and any of the intercepts will take you to the old city centre. Its early colonial buildings were largely destroyed by an earthquake in 1843; nowadays it is an odd mixture of parts which could have been transplanted from provincial France and parts which are Caribbean, surrounded by low-cost housing blocks.

The central **Place de la Victoire** is where the French Revolutionary troops defeated the British invaders in 1794. Robespierre sent Victor Hugues from Paris with two aims: throw out the British and bring the Terror to the island. He brought a portable guillotine in his luggage, set it up here, and guillotined or shot over 700 whites, and even a few men of colour, for bearing arms on the British side. Most were from the plantocracy. Their estates were confiscated, and all slaves freed. The streets adjacent to the square contain the oldest buildings, mostly from the 19th and early 20th centuries, including the Sous-Préfecture, once a barracks. There are some flame trees at the north end and pleasant gardens. In the middle is a bust of Félix Eboue (1884-1944), the only black governor in colonial times, 1936-38. At the southwest corner is a war memorial dedicated to *La Guadeloupe et ses enfants, morts pour La France 1914-18*, flanked by two First World War guns. Behind it is the **tourist office**. On the east side of the square is the art deco Renaissance Cinema. At its south end is **La Darse**, where fishing boats come in. To the west is the new Port Authority development for inter-island ferries and cruise ships.

Pointe-à-Pitre

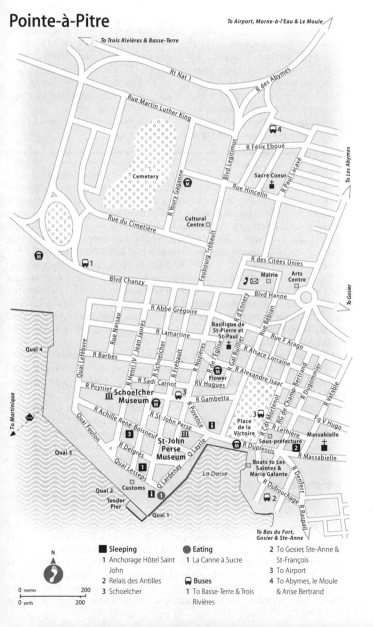

N		
0 metres	200	
0 yards	200	

● **Sleeping**
1 Anchorage Hôtel Saint John
2 Relais des Antilles
3 Schoelcher

● **Eating**
1 La Canne à Sucre

🚌 **Buses**
1 To Basse-Terre & Trois Rivières

2 To Gosier, Ste-Anne & St-François
3 To Airport
4 To Abymes, le Moule & Anse Bertrand

▶ ## Victor Hugues: Opportunist Revolutionary

A baker's son, from Marseille, Victor Hugues was determined to make his way in the world, and went to Saint-Domingue, then a French colony, now Haiti, where he found prosperity as the baker to the French army. However, the Haitians started their own revolution. Ruined, Hugues returned to France, and saw his chance by throwing himself in with the most extreme revolutionaries. Though he had seen his brother and uncle killed in Haiti, he posed as a friend of the blacks, and was rewarded by being sent as Commissioner for the National Convention to the Antilles, to free the slaves, use them as the instrument to force out the British (he started revolts in St Lucia, St Vincent and Grenada with his agents), and seize royalists' property. He became the master of Guadeloupe, digging up the body of the former British commander and exhibiting it. He seemed pitiless. He was also greedy: he soon married a rich planter's daughter, and put the 'freed' slaves to forced labour in the cane fields, at which they were made to sing revolutionary songs in praise of the Republic. The US government put pressure on Paris to remove him (he was interfering with US trade). French government officials invited him to a banquet on board a warship: at its end, he was arrested, and the vessel weighed anchor immediately for France. Later, he was sent as Governor to French Guiana, where slavery was again established, He returned to France and, after some years, went back to Guiana to run a plantation, of course with slave labour.

The **Place de l'Église** lies northwest of the Place de la Victoire behind the *Hôtel Normandie*. The 1840s ochre-coloured Basilique de St Pierre et St Paul is held up by unusual metal columns supporting a gallery around the top of the church with some elaborate gingerbread-style metal work. Outside there is a bubbling fountain and a bust of Admiral Gourbeyre, the governor who helped the people of Pointe-à-Pitre after the huge 1843 earthquake in which 5,000 lost their lives and most buildings were partially or completely destroyed (see also Fort Louis Delgrès, Basse-Terre). The square is flanked by the 1930s art deco Palais de Justice and flower stalls.

The red-roofed central **market** place (between rues Peynier, Fréboult, St-John Perse and Schoelcher) is the nearest thing to local hustling. Women (some wearing the traditional Madras cotton headties) try to sell you spices, fruit, vegetables or hats. There are other markets on the dockside in Place de la Victoire, between Blvd Chanzy and the docks and between Blvd Légitimus and the cemetery. Local handicrafts, and Madras cotton are good buys.

Musée Schoelcher celebrates a key figure in the liberation of the slaves. He gave some of his personal art collection in 1883 to Guadeloupe, which survives in its original, elaborately decorated, specially built, 'Belle Epoque' home. Other exhibits on his life and on the slave trade. ■ *0900-1230, 1400-1730, closed Wed, Sat pm and Sun. €1.50. 24 rue Peynier, T0590-821804.* **Musée Saint-John Perse**, in a lovely colonial-style house, is dedicated to the poet and diplomat born in Guadeloupe of planter stock. His real name was Alexis Saint-Léger. The collection gives a picture of the lifestyle of island whites, the 'békés'. ■ *0830-1230, 1430-1730, closed Sat pm and Sun. €1.50, children half price. 9 rue Nozières et A R Boisneuf, T0590-900192.*

Grande-Terre

Just outside Pointe-à-Pitre on the N4 towards Gosier is **Bas du Fort**, the site of a large marina, one of the biggest in the Caribbean. The **Aquarium** is here, at Place Creole. It has about 30 ponds with species only from the Caribbean Sea, including fish, turtles and nurse sharks. *Daily 0900-1900. €5.35, children under 12 €3. T0590-909238.* At the next turning off the main road to Gosier (follow the signs to the CORA hypermarket) are the ruins of the 18th-century fortress, **Fort Fleur d'Epée** which once guarded the east approaches to Pointe-à-Pitre. There are now pleasant, shady gardens within the ramparts. Art exhibitions are regularly held either in the officers' quarters or in the underground rooms. Also note the graffiti with pictures of old sailing ships. Excellent views of Pointe-à-Pitre and across Petit Cul-de-Sac Marin towards the mountains of Basse-Terre. ■ *Daily 0800-1800. Free.*

The corridor leading to Gosier from Pointe-à-Pitre is built up, extending up into the hills above the coast road. Nevertheless, Gosier is a pleasant place with plenty of atmosphere. There is a marvellous picnic spot overlooking a small beach (Plage de l'Anse Canot). Don't miss the little island about 100 m offshore (Ilet du Gosier) and lighthouse. You could swim to it, there is a channel marked by buoys, but watch out for speed boats. Fishermen provide a regular ferry service and locals picnic here at weekends. Old Gosier has one of the finest hotels in the island, the *Auberge de la Vieille Tour*, built around an 18th-century windmill tower, and has a great selection of restaurants, ranging from high cuisine at the *Auberge* and *La Mandarine* to take-aways on the main street, Blvd Charles-de-Gaulle. The modern part of the resort with three-star beach hotels is at the western side, between Pointe de la Verdure and under Fort Fleur de l'Épée. Built on reclaimed mangrove marshes, the beaches are quite acceptable with the usual watersports facilities.

Gosier
The original holiday centre of Guadeloupe, with hotels, restaurants, nightclubs

The south coast between Gosier and **Sainte-Anne** is hilly with cliffs, and on most headlands there are huge condominium developments looking across the sea to Marie-Galante as well as to the south tip of Basse-Terre. Sainte-Anne is a small, pleasant town and has a small church with a slightly crooked spire overlooking the square. Here you will find the **Plage de la Caravelle**, rated by some as the best on the island. The land gradually subsides towards St-François, originally a fishing village but now home to luxury hotels. There is a light aircraft landing strip and a golf course. You can catch the ferry to La Désirade from here.

South coast east of Gosier

The rugged **Pointe des Châteaux** at the easternmost tip of the island is part of the national park. From the car park, there is a small, self-guided walk to the cross (**Pointe des Colibris**) erected in 1951, on the point where there are two 'compass' tables showing distances to landmarks. The limestone outcrop is steep in places. The view over the island of **La Roche** (housing a colony of sooty terns, *Sterna fuscata*) to La Désirade is spectacular, especially on a windy day when the sea whips over the rocks. Take the slightly longer return path around the headland as you get good views of the completely flat Petite Terre with its lighthouse and on clear days Marie-Galante (30 km), Les Saintes (60 km) and Dominica (75 km). Note the **Grandes Salines** (salt lagoons) where flamingoes were once common. There are stalls selling handicrafts, spices and a local aphrodisiac, *Bois Bande*. A tree bark, this is also available as a liqueur ('gives strength to men, pleasure to women') and as an infusion in rum. The beach between the two points is dangerous.

Le Moule was the original capital of Guadeloupe and there are still some cannon from the fortifications against English attack. A pre-Columbian Arawak village, called **Morel**, has recently been uncovered on the beautiful sandy beaches north of the town. The **Musée d'Archéologie Précolombienne Edgar Clerc** is at La Rosette. It houses the collection of the researcher, Edgar Clerc, of artefacts found on Guadeloupe and also puts on temporary exhibitions. ■ *0900-1230, 1400-1730. Free.* On the Abymes road (D101) from Le Moule is the **Distillerie Bellevue**, makers of *Rhum Damoiseau*. ■ *Tours Mon-Fri 0800-1400.*

East coast
Take a good map as it is easy to get lost on the little roads in the sugar cane fields

Grande-Terre's leeward coast has beaches at Port-Louis and Petit-Canal which are the usual concrete towns with restaurant and filling station. North of Anse Bertrand there is a fine clean, sandy beach, **Anse Laborde**, which has plenty of shade, a restaurant, and a reef close to the beach, good for snorkelling. Inland, at **Morne-à-l'Eau**, there is a remarkable terraced cemetery built around a natural amphitheatre, very atmospheric on All Saints' Day when lit by thousands of candles.

Leeward coast

French Antilles

Basse-Terre

On the other wing of the island, the town of Basse-Terre is the administrative capital of Guadeloupe and the entire Départment. It is a charming port town of narrow streets, pretty colonial buildings and well laid-out squares with palm and tamarind trees in a lovely setting between the sea and the great volcano La Soufrière.

Sights
Market day is Saturday

There is a 17th-century cathedral and the well-preserved ruins of **Fort Louis Delgrès**. The British occupied the fort from 1759 to 1763 and again from 1810 to 1816. It was fought over and renamed many times, being given its present name in 1989 in memory of the black commander who died resisting the re-imposition of slavery. ■ *Daily 0700-1700. Free. T0590-813748.* The **Grande Caverne** is a museum, with an exhibition of clothes and photographs of the area. In the cemetery is a monument to Admiral Gourbeyre. The date is not that of his death (he disappeared at sea in 1845) but of 8 February 1843 when there was a huge earthquake; the Admiral worked tirelessly to help its victims.

Basse-Terre

To Vieux-Habitants & Côte-Sous-le-Vent

Rue Dumanoir
Rue Daniel Beauperthuy
des Corsaires
R Dr Pitat
Rue Baudet
R Peynier
R Schoelcher
Rue Toussaint Louverture
To Les Saintes
Port
Rue Maurice Marie Claire
BEAUVALLON
+ **Cathedral**
Rue Bebian
FG Casse
PETITE GUINEE
Allée des Lauriers
Rue Leonard
Rue de la République
Ali Capt Bebel
Rivaux des Herbes
Botanical Gardens
Jardin Pichon
Conseil Général
Blvd Gouverneur Félix Eboué
Rue Victor Hugues
RN 3
Blvd Général de Gaulle
□ Palais de Justice
Rue E Martini
Rue Luther King
VERSAILLES
To St-Claude Matouba Soufrière
Mt Carmel
R Rémy Naïnouta
F Eboué Stadium
□ **Préfecture**
Av Paul Lacavé
N
Fort Delgrès
To Trois Rivières, Pointe-à-Pitre

| 0 metres | 200 |
| 0 yards | 200 |

■ **Sleeping**
1 Basse-Terre-Charlery

Saint-Claude, a wealthy suburb and summer resort 6 km into the hills, is surrounded by coffee trees and tropical gardens. **La Bonifièrie**, an old coffee plantation still has its old wooden waterwheel, while **Mangofil** has a canopée: a wooden walkway through the tree tops. **Matouba**, above Saint-Claude, is an East Indian village in lovely surroundings (waterfall and springs, the mineral water is bottled here) with a good restaurant. On the outskirts of the village is a monument to Louis Delgrès on the spot where he and his companions were caught and killed by Napoléon's troops. There are hot springs a good walk above the village (1,281 m).

On Basse-Terre island one of the main sights is the volcano **La Soufrière**, reached through a primeval rainforest. A narrow, twisty road leads up from Basse-Terre town to a car park at **Savane à Mulets** (1,142 m) from where the crater, 300 m higher, is a 1½ hour climb up the Chemin des Dames, a fascinating trail with changing flora, but becoming eroded through overuse. Buses go to Saint-Claude from where it is a 6- km walk to Savane à Mulets. From the top there is a spectacular view, observe the mountain for a few days to see whether early morning or midday is clearest. The summit is quite flat; the main vent is to the south and there are discs in the ground to help you find it in the fog. You can come down along a forest path, the Trace Carmichael, to the Chutes de Carbet waterfalls.

There are three waterfalls 20 m, 110 m and 125 m. You can swim in the warm, sulphuric pools, but beware of flash floods after rain higher up. The path is rough and often muddy. There is a picnic place, Aire d'Arrivée, 15 minutes, where there are barbecue stalls (good chicken). The D4 road starts here and descends to St-Sauveur.

La Citerne, a neighbouring volcano, has a completely round crater. There is a trail but part requires climbing ladders straight up the wall. Also on this side are **Grand Étang** and **Étang Zombi**. You can drive, hitchhike or walk down the D4 road from the Chutes de Carbet to the edge of Grand Étang and walk around it, about 1 hour through lush vegetation. Do not swim in the lake because of bilharzia. There are also marked trails to **Étang de l'As de Pique**, high above Grand Étang to the south on the slope of La Madeleine (two hours) and the Trace de Moscou which leads southwest to the Plateau du Palmiste (two and a half hours), from where a road leads down to Gourbeyre. Walk down to St-Sauveur for fine views over banana plantations, the coast and Les Saintes.

You can walk the **Trace Victor Hugues**, along the main ridge of Basse-Terre (a 29-km hike), and a number of other Traces. A parallel route follows the River Moreau from Goyave up to the **Chutes du Moreau**. Turn off the N1 opposite the turning to Goyave and signposted to the falls. The made up road turns to gravel and then ends. From here the trail will take you about two hours with five river crossings, so take appropriate footwear. After the fifth crossing the trail rises steeply and there are steel ropes to help you up the slope. From here it is another 10 minutes to the falls. Also recommended is the River Quiock trail, three or four hours depending on conditions, but take the Serie Bleu map; despite being well marked originally, storm damage has made it difficult to find all the markers. It can be very muddy, wear good boots. You can start from the car park at the **Cascade aux Écrevisses** (see above) on the D23. Walk 300 m along the road and take a path to the right (follow the sign to the Pathfinders camp) to Piolet, near the entrance to the Bras-David-Tropical-Parc on the other side of the road. The trail leads down to where the River Quiock meets the larger river Bras-David, carefully cross the river, then the trail heads west along the Quiock until returning to the D23.

Capesterre-Belle-Eau is Guadeloupe's third largest town and is an important agricultural centre with a market. The Allée de Flamboyants, a spectacular avenue of flame trees which flower May-September lines the coast road heading north, while the **Allée Dumanoir**, is a magnificent 1-km avenue of royal palms heading south.

La Soufrière
Don't wear too much clothing for the climb, but take a sweater as it can get quite chilly

Allow at least five hours to walk from Capesterre to St-Sauveur via the waterfalls and Grand Étang and wear good hiking shoes

Parc Naturel
Other features of the natural park are described under Flora and fauna, above. For hiking guides, see Sports, page 578

East coast

French Antilles

▶ ## Louis Delgrès

Born in Martinique, Louis Delgrès, a mulatto, enlisted in the French colonial forces at 17 to fight against the English in the last year of the American War of Independence. As a professional soldier he was captured by the British in 1794, sent to England as a prisoner, exchanged by the revolutionary government for a British soldier, and sent to Guadeloupe as a lieutenant. He first fought against black rebels but, recognizing the justice of their cause, changed sides and took command. Entrenched in the fort at Basse-Terre (then called Fort

Saint-Charles) he defied General Richepance, who had been ordered by Napoléon to disarm the black troops and re-impose slavery. Faced with overwhelming force, Delgrès issued a letter to French public opinion and to "the entire universe, a last cry of innocence and despair". He claimed that because of racial prejudice, his troops, in spite of their loyalty, were to be hounded to death. This declaration, on 10 May 1802, is now to be seen in bronze on the walls of the fort. 18 days later, at Matouba, on the slopes of La Soufrière, all were killed.

At **Sainte-Marie**, a statue erected in 1916 commemorates the site of Columbus' landing in 1493. It has now been defaced by nationalists. South of Sainte-Marie, near Carangaise, there is a Hindu temple, built in 1974 by René Komla, richly decorated with statues of Vishnu and Ganesh outside.

The most northern town on this side of Basse-Terre is **Petit-Bourg**, on the opposite side of the bay from Pointe-à-Pitre and overlooking the little islands in the Petit Cul-de-Sac Marin. Inland from here, at Cabout, is **Le Domaine de Valombreuse**, **Parc Floral**, where over 1,000 species of flowers can be found and masses of birds enjoying the plant life. Flowers are for sale and can be packed for export and collected at the airport. ■ *0900-1700. Guided tours available for groups; restaurant by a river in the forest open for lunch, and for dinner for groups of 10 or more by reservation. T0590-955050, F0590-955090, valomb@outremer.com*

Southern Basse-Terre

The **Centre de Broderie**, Fort l'Olive, Vieux-Fort, showcases the work of some 40 lacemakers and embroiderers ■ *Daily 0830-1800. T0590-920414.* There are attractive gardens surrounding the lighthouse at **Vieux-Fort**, with good views.

Amerindian rock carvings dating from around AD 300-400, are at the **Parc Archéologique des Roches Gravées**, near Trois Rivières; the most important is a drawing of the head of a Carib chief inside a cave. The archipelago of Guadeloupe has a large concentration of inscribed stones. The site is now in a garden setting, with wardens (it's a good idea to consult the leaflet because some of the engravings on the stones are hard to decipher; many are badly eroded; the pamphlet also explains the garden's trees). ■ *0830-1700. US$0.60 entry, children free. T0590-929188. The park is a 10-min walk down from the church in Trois Rivières where the buses stop.* Five minutes further down the hill is the boat dock for Les Saintes (paying car park).

West coast

Between Basse-Terre town and the Route de la Traversée on the west coast are **Vieux-Habitants**, with a restored 17th-century church, the largest coffee museum on the island and the underwater reserve (see page 565). Contact the Syndicat d'Initiative de Bouillante, T0590-987348, for information on the Bouillante area, which considers itself the capital of diving.

A good three-hour hike is the Trace des Contrebandiers, from the Maison du Bois (when you leave the trail on the other side you will need to hitchhike)

North of the Traversée, on the N2, is **Pointe Noire**, a small fishing town. Just south of the town is the **Maison du Bois** at Bourg, a cabinet-making and woodworking centre with a permanent exhibition of furniture and other things made of wood. ■ *Daily, 0915-1700. US$0.70.* Also near here at Grand Plaine is the **Maison du Cacao**, with displays on the origin of cocoa, its cultivation and processing and you can taste it. ■ *Mon-Sat 0900-1700, Sun 0900-1300. T0590-982523, F0590-982123.* There are several coffee museums and plantations you can visit. The **Maison du Café** is the largest museum at **L'habitation La Grivelière,** Vallée de Grande Rivière, devoted to the celebrated Bonifieur coffee. ■ *Guided tours on the hour Dec-Apr, Jul-Aug from 1000-1600* *and at 1630, less frequent other months, closed Sep. T0590-983414.* At **Le Domaine de Vanibel**, near Vieux-Habitants, another coffee plantation offers tours and accommodation, part of the *Gîtes de France*. ■ *Mon-Sat 0900-1600, guided tours at 1400, 1500, 1600. T0590-984079.* At **Acomat** is **La Caféière Beauséjour** in a 17th-century house with coffee museum, restaurant and good cottage accommodation (**B**). ■ *Open Tue-Sun 1000-1700. Closed Sep-mid-Oct. T0590-981009, www.cafeiere beausejour.com* On the Côte-Sous-Le-Vent are the calm, clean beaches at Ferry and Grand-Anse and the rougher ones at Deshaies.

Round the north of Basse-Terre is the town of **Sainte-Rose** where you can visit the rum museum, **Musée du Rhum**, at the **Distillerie Reimonenq**, Bellevue Sainte-Rose. In addition, there is a display of butterflies and other insects in the **Galerie des Plus Beaux Insectes du Monde** and 30 model sailing ships from the earliest to the present day. ■ *Mon-Sat 0900-1700. US$6, children half price. T0590-287004.* The road continues south to Lamentin and the hot springs at Ravine Chaude (Thermal Station T0590-257829). Near Lamentin you can visit the **Domaine de Séverin** distillery at La Boucan, still using a paddle wheel. Guided tours twice a day on a miniature train. You can taste and buy rums and fruit punches. ■ *Mon-Sat 0800-1300, 1400-1800, Sun 0900-1200. Tours in the morning except Sun. T0590-289196. Restaurant open for lunch Tue-Sun, and dinner Thu, Fri, Sat, local specialities, accommodation available.*

Northern Basse-Terre

Essentials

Pointe-à-Pitre A *Anchorage Hôtel Saint John*, rue Quai Lesseps, T0590-825157, F0590-825261. A/c, TV, balcony, comfortable, very good. **C-D** *Schoelcher*, rue Schoelcher. Reasonably-priced restaurant. **C-D** *Relais des Antilles*, corner of rue Massabielle and rue Vatable, just off the Place de la Victoire. Basic, noisy but friendly. **C-D** *Pension Mme Rilsy*, T0590-918171, 34 Bis rue Peynier. CP, very friendly. Reported to take students only.

Sleeping: Grande-Terre
The tourist board has current hotel price lists (information desk at the airport but no reservations)

Bas du Fort Bay/Gosier (tourist area). **LL** *Auberge de la Vieille Tour* (Sofitel Coralia), Montauban, 97190 Gosier, T0590-842323, F0590-843343. Named after an 18th-century sugar tower incorporated into the main building. On a bluff over the sea, beach, pool, tennis, 182 rooms, 3 2-room bungalows and 8 rooms in French colonial style, gourmet restaurant, with the only Maître Cuisinier in the French Antilles. **LL-AL** *La Créole Beach*, Pointe de la Verdure, T904646, F904666. 156 rooms, good sized rooms, pool, bar and restaurant, watersports arranged, tennis, volley ball and putting green available. Also under same management are **LL-AL** *Novotel Coralia*, Bas du Fort, T0590-904000, H0458@accor-hotels.com Huge range of sporting activities and evening entertainment, child friendly. **LL-A** *Les Résidences Yucca*, 100 studios and **LL-AL** *Hôtel Palmes*, www.leadershotel.gp 63 rooms and suites, which share facilities of *La Créole Beach*. **B** *Les Flamboyants*, T0590-841411, F0590-845356. Pool, seaview, some kitchenettes, friendly, clean, a/c. **C** *Serge's Guest House*, on seafront, T0590-841025, F0590-843949. Very basic, not very clean, convenient for buses and beach, has nice garden and swimming pool. A smaller establishment is the **E-F** *Hotel Corossol*, Mathurin, T0590-843989. 8 rooms, friendly, good meals, 20 mins' walk to Gosier. Many places advertise rooms to let.

Sainte-Anne *Club Méditerranée* has a hotel-village: *La Caravelle*, on a spectacular white-sand beach, perhaps the best on Guadeloupe, surrounded by a 13-ha reserve, T0590-854950, F0590-854970. **AL** *Auberge le Grand Large*, T0590-854828, F0590-881669. Neither grand nor large, but friendly and with good restaurant on the beach. **AL** *Mini Beach*, T0590-882113, F0590-881929. 1 km from town, on the beach, relaxed, good location, many restaurants nearby, can fall to half price in summer, good restaurant. Between Gosier and Ste-Anne, at La Marie-Gaillarde, is **B-C** *La Marie-Gaillarde*, T0590-858429, overlooking Les Grands Fonds, 2 km from Petit Havre beach. 9 rooms can fit 3-4 people, with restaurant and bar. **LL-AL** *La Toubana*, T0590-882578, F0590-883890, toubana@leaderhotels.gp 32 cottages, a/c, kitchenettes, phones, terraces, pool, private beach, tennis, pocket billiards, *Club Med* and islands, *Toubana* is Arawak for 'little house', restaurant serves French and Creole cuisine.

French Antilles

Saint-François LL *La Cocoteraie*, Av de l'Europe, T0590-887981, cocoteraie@wanadoo.fr 50 deluxe suites, beach front, pool side, garden view or marina view, between lagoon and golf course, spectacular pool, tennis, beautiful architecture. **LL-L** *Plantation Ste-Marthe* (Euro Dom Hotels), T0590-931111, psm@netguacom.fr Former sugar plantation on hill away from sea, new colonial-style buildings, 120 magnificent rooms with large terrace, a/c, restaurant, bars, 900 sq m swimming pool, close to golf course, fully equipped conference centre. **LL-AL** *Anse des Rochers Anchorage*, T0590-939000, www.hôtels-anchorage.com 228 spacious rooms in 3 buildings plus 32 villas with 4 rooms each, a/c, kitchenettes, beautiful seaside resort, Creole architecture, in 25 acres of gardens, fine restaurants, huge pool, tennis, volleyball, excursions, watersports, golf nearby. **AL-A** *Hôtel Kaye'la*, T0590-887777, F0590-887467, on the marina. Built 1990, 75 rooms for up to 4 people, a/c, pool, bar, restaurant, walking distance to restaurants, convenient for boat trips from marina. **C** *Chez Honoré*, Place du Marché, T0590-884061, F0590-886073. Clean, simple, friendly, noisy because of the disco next door. Good seafood.

Pointe des Châteaux LL *Iguana Bay Villas*, T0590-884880, F0590-886719. 17 villas, 2-3 bedrooms, private pools, overlooking La Désirade, pretty beach, private.

Sleeping:
Basse-Terre
Accommodation is neither plentiful nor high class in Basse-Terre city

Basse-Terre E *Hotel Basse-Terre-Charlery*, 56 rue Maurice Marie Claire, T0590-811978. Central, basic, clean and cheap, good oriental restaurant next door. At **Saint-Claude AL-A** *St-Georges*, rue Gratien Parize, T0590-801010, F0590-803050. 40 rooms including 2 suites, fitness room, squash, pool, billiards, meeting rooms, bar, restaurant *Le Lamasure*, snack bar. **A-B** *Relais de la Grand Soufrière*, T0590-800127, F0590-801840, regular bus service to Basse-Terre, including Sun, an elegant but rather poorly converted old plantation mansion, a/c, attractive surroundings, old wooden furniture, friendly staff. **Bouillante LL-A** *Domaine de Malendure*, T0590-989212, F0590-989210. 50 loft suites with views of Ilet Pigeon, on hillside, 400 m from sea, good location for diving or walking, pool, restaurant, car rental, shuttle to Malendure beach or Grand Anse beach, car rental in advance recommended. **Deshaies LL-AL** *Pointe Batterie Villas*, T0590-285703, F0590-2805728. 24 1-2 bedroom villas, a/c, decks, pool, on the water, charming, some have private pools, excellent restaurant. **L** *Fort Royal*, T0590-255000, F0590-255001. Dramatically set on a promontory between 2 beautiful but rather rough beaches. **B** *La Vigie*, overlooking Deshaies bay, T0590-284252. Small studios with kitchenette, bathroom, terrace, fan, cleaned daily. **D** *Chez M Eric Bernier*, T0590-284004 or 0590-284270. Rooms on waterfront, opposite *Le Mouillage* restaurant more rooms are available. **E** *Chez Jean Memorin*, T0590-284090, just outside town on hill in direction of Grand Anse beach. 1 bedroom, TV. **AL-B** *Auberge de la Distillerie*, Route de Versailles, Tabanon, T0590-942591, F0590-941191. 16 rooms, pool, jacuzzi, pocket billiards, country inn at entrance to Parc Naturel surrounded by pineapple fields, Creole restaurant, *Le Bitaco* and small pizza café, the owner also designed **AL-A** *Créol'Inn*, Bel'Air Desrozières, T0590-942256, F0590-941928. 20 cabins in wooded area, kitchenette, hammocks, pool, barbecue, snack bar. **Trois Rivières C** *Le Joyeux*, a US$0.50 bus ride from the centre of the town (bus stop right outside) or short walk, in Le Faubourg, 100 m above the sea, T0590-927478, F0590-927707. 6 simple rooms, kitchenettes, Creole restaurant, bar, disco, closed Mon except for reservations, good views to Les Saintes, very friendly, transfers to the boat dock. **LL-AL** *Le Jardin Malanga*, T0590-926757, F0590-926758. Beautifully renovated 1927 Creole house and bungalows, hillside setting in banana plantation, lovely views, terraces, mini-bar, bath tubs, huge beds, pool, car rental in advance recommended. **AL** *Grand'Anse*, T0590-929047, F0590-929369. Bungalows, also has Creole restaurant.

Gîtes Throughout the island there are a large number of *gîtes* for rent on a daily, weekly or monthly basis. Weekly rates range from US$100 to US$450, but most are in the US$150-225 bracket. The tourist offices in both Pointe-à-Pitre and Basse-Terre have lists of the properties available and should be consulted in the first instance, or you can contact the *Association Guadeloupéenne des Gîtes Ruraux et du Tourisme Vert* (*Relais Guadeloupe des Gîtes de France*), at the Centre d'Échanges Ruddy Nuthila, T0590-916433, F0590-914540, www.itca.fr/GDF/971. *Gîtes* are arranged by the local Syndicat d'Initiative, who charge a 5%

rental fee. One recommended *gîte* in Trois Rivières is **E** *Chez Dampierre*, T0590-989869, a bungalow for 2 in a beautiful garden, convenient location.

Camping is not well organized and the tourist office does not therefore have much information. Ask mayors if you may camp on municipal land, or owners on private property. Camper vans can be arranged through *Découverts et Loisirs Créoles* in Abymes, T0590-205565.

Camping

Pointe-à-Pitre *La Canne à Sucre*, Quai No 1, Port Autonome. Faces the sea, mixes Creole and French, menu US$10, Creole buffet Sat 1200, also does teas, ice creams. *Relais des Antilles*, near the *Auberge Henri IV*, in a private house, good Creole cooking, cheap meals (ask Valentin at the *Auberge* for directions). *Krishna*, 47 rue A R Boisneuf, Indian. **Grande-Terre holiday coast** *La Case Créole*, Route de la Rivière, and *Chez Rosette*, Av Général-de-Gaulle, both Creole at **Gosier**. *Le Boukarou*, rue Montauban, T0590-841037. Good Italian, pizza made on charcoal grill, moderately priced. Lots of small restaurants in Gosier: pizzas, Vietnamese, Chinese and of course French. The local pizza house is near the park, good for takeaways. The *pâtisserie* is good for an early morning coffee while collecting the *baguettes*; *La Mandarine*, highly rated, funny staff, worth a stop; *Chez Gina*, in a little village cafétière, 2.5 km inland, up the hill, excellent food, order in advance in the morning for an evening meal, 4 courses and apéritif, served in a sort of garage with flowers, friendly, don't be put off by the untidy surroundings. *Côté Jardin*, at Bas du Fort marina. French. *La Plantation*, same location, same cuisine. **Saint-François** *Le Vieux Port*, T 0590-884660. Menu €10.50, seaside, in typical Creole house, wonderful lobster, fish. *Madame Jerco* has good food in a small creaking house. Close to the old harbour, *Kotesit*, T0590-884084, fresh langouste and other seafood, don't miss the 'marquise au chocolat'. On the way to Pointe des Chateaux, *Iguane Café* uses local ingredients, good service.

Eating: Grande-Terre

Look in the excellent free guides Ti Gourmet *Guadeloupe or Delices de la Guadeloupe for recipes, restaurants, cafés and pâtisseries. Many are closed in the evening*

Chez Paul in **Matouba**, T0590-802920, has been recommended for Creole and East Indian cuisine. At **Bouillante**, *Chez Loulouse*, Plage de Malendure, T0590-987034, beach restaurant, Creole fare. *Restaurant de la Phare*, **Vieux Fort**, good Creole cooking, excellent fresh fish, reasonable prices, dance hall attached. **Deshaies** *Karacoli*, beside Grand Anse Beach. Authentic Creole cooking at its best, the local Salcede brother and sister who run it have won many awards, fish and shellfish superb, menu US$11. Other reasonably priced restaurants include *Le Madras* and *Le Mouillage*, serving Creole food. For breakfast try the *boulangerie* opposite *Le Mouillage* for croissants, pain au chocolat, coffee, juice. The *Relais de la Grande Soufrière*, at Saint-Claude. Very good Creole meals at reasonable prices, T0590-800127. **At Petit Bourg**, *Domaine de Valombreuse*, Cabout. in the heart of the forest, T0590-955050. Watch the many-coloured birds while you eat, crayfish special, menus begin at US$8.50.

Eating: Basse-Terre

For a description of local cuisine, see page 561. Menus (3-course lunch) start at €8

Around the Marina Bas-du-Fort there are several bars with live music, such as *Velvet, Zoo Rock* and *La Mexicana*. There is also a disco, *La Citée Perdue*. Other discos can be found in Gosier: *Le 116* (the favourite of the younger crowd), *Le Caraïbe II, New Land,* and the most exclusive, *Le Zenith*. Salsa fans have fun at the *Lolapalooza* in the heart of Gosier. At Le Moule, there is *Shiva*. In the Basse-Terre area the *Plantation* is the most exclusive disco. There is a casino and cabaret in Gosier, Pointe de la Verdure, casino open from 2100, closed Sun, bring identification, T0590-841833, local and international artistes at the cabaret. Another casino at Av de l'Europe, St-François, T0590-884131, open from 2100, closed Mon, bring identification. **Cinemas**: Rex, with 4 screens, T0590-822020, in Pointe-à-Pitre; D'Arbaud, 2 screens, T0590-811835, in Basse-Terre; Cinéma L'Image, in Gosier.

Nightlife

Carnival warm-up starts on Epiphany with different events each Sun, until the climax on the last weekend, with the frenetic parading of *les jours gras* Sun, Mon, and *Mardi Gras*. On *Ash Wednesday* (*Mercredi des Cendres*) devils and she-devils dance and sing to tam-tams as the effigy of Valval, the spirit of Carnival, is taken off to be burned and thrown into the sea. The *Fish and Sea Festival* is in mid-Apr with beach parties, boat races, crab races, etc. *La Fête des Cuisinières* (Cooks' Festival) in the middle of **Aug** is a lot of fun with parades in Creole costumes and music as well as food and cooking. It is held on the feast of St Lawrence, the

Festivals

patron saint of women cooks, and the event starts with a Mass. Some 250 cordon bleu cooks from the Women's Cooking Association wear their typical colourful dresses with Madras scarves and lots of jewellery for the parade through Pointe-à-Pitre. Other festivals include the *Fête du Gwo Ka* (Festival of the Big Drums) in **Jul**, the *Old Créole Songs Festival* in **Oct**, *St Cecilia's Day* in **Nov**.

Shopping There are lots of hypermarkets just like in France, stocked with excellent cheese counters and massive wine departments. Generally open Mon-Sat 0800-2030. Most things are imported from France. In Gosier there is a supermarket on the road to Plage de l'Anse Canot, open on Sun, otherwise hypermarkets are better value and cleaner. Small minimarts, local corner shops, can also be found.

Sports **Hiking** in the Parc Naturel, contact the *Organisation des Guides de Montagne de la Caraïbe*
A guided hike to La (OGMC), Maison Forestière, 97120 Matouba, T0590-800579, or in St-Claude, T0590-802425,
Soufrière will cost or the *Bureau des Guides*, Basse Terre, T0590-991873. Guides certified by the French govern-
around US$45, make ment are available for hikes of 1-5 days. Approximate hiking times, mileage and description
sure the guide of terrain and flora are included in the booklet *Promenades et Randonnées*. **Horse riding** at
speaks a language Gosier, T0590-840486, *La Martingale*, La Jaille, T0590-262839 and *Ranch Caraïbes*,
you understand T0590-821154. Also *Horse Farm*, St-Claude, T0590-815221, F0590-819073, for groups of
For diving and 6-12 people riding in the forest. In August a **cycling** race takes place over 10 days, going to all
watersports, parts of the island. *Le Tour Cycliste de la Guadeloupe* draws local and international competi-
see page 565 tors and is an excuse for festivities and parties. The *Association Guadeloupéenne de VTT*
(mountain biking association) can be contacted at Pointe-à-Pitre, T0590-828267. For cycling tours of Guadeloupe, *Karucyclo*, T0590-822139, 0590-284659. There is an 18-hole, interna-tional **golf** course on the edge of the lagoon at Saint-François (T0590-884187, F0590-884220), designed by Robert Trent Jones.

Bullock cart racing is popular on the west coast of Grande-Terre and draws large crowds. They race along the flat, then turn sharply and charge up a steep hill. The wheels are then chocked and they have to see how far they can get, zig-zag fashion, with about 10 mins of very hard work. Much shouting, plenty of beer, food tents and an overloud PA system. **Cockfighting** is very popular and there are pits all over the place. The season runs from Nov-Jul and involves serious gambling. The only pit open all year is Bélair, Morne-à-l'Eau, Tue, Thu, Fri and Sun, T0590-242370.

Tour operators *Emeraude Guadeloupe*, St-Claude, T0590-819828, F0590-819812, offers hiking in forests and mountains, with cultural visits and contact with local families, also lodging in small hotels, mountain bike excursions and other activities. *Parfum d'Aventures*, St-François, T0590-884762, F0590-884791, has canoes and kayaks, 4WD excursions, hiking and water scooters. *Guadeloupe Découverte*, Jarry, T0590-252087, F0590-266665, canoes and kayaks, hiking, mountain biking and 4WD excursions. *Vert Intense*, T0590-993473, kayaks, canoes, hiking.

Transport **Air From Europe**: Like Martinique, Guadeloupe is on *Air France*'s daily direct route from Paris (about 8 hrs) from both Orly and Charles de Gaulle airports. *Air Corsair* also flies daily from Paris. **From North America** *Air Canada* has direct flights from Montréal. *Air France* flies from Miami. *American Eagle* has flights from San Juan, with connections from the USA. **From the Caribbean** *LIAT* offers inter-Caribbean connections via Antigua and Dominica. *Air Caraïbes* connects Pointe-à-Pitre with Fort-de-France (lots of flights every day), La Désirade, Marie- Galante, St Barts, St Lucia, Sint Maarten, St-Martin, Santo Domingo and Terre-de-Haut. *Air Antilles Express* flies to Fort-de-France and St-Martin. Other services include *Air France* from Cayenne, Fort-de-France and Port-au-Prince; *Cubana* from Havana.

Airport Le Raizet Airport is used for regional flights while the new, modern **Pole Caraïbes Airport** is for international ones. Information, T089689755. They are quite far apart, a taxi ride, and if you have a rental car (kept on the old airport side of the airfield) you will have to get the shuttle to the new terminal. There is no bus service to the new airport, but take the shuttle bus to Le Raizet and then bus into town from the other side of the car park, over roundabout and outside Cora (Mamouth) supermarket, US$0.80 to Place de la Victoire. No buses Sat afternoon or Sun. Taxi fares (T0590-207474) from the airport are approximately US$20 to Gosier, US$40 to Ste-Anne, US$60 to Saint-François and US$16 to Bas-du-Fort. Prices go up by 40% 2100-0700, all day Sun and on holidays.

Sea Numerous cruise lines sail from US and French ports. Pointe-à-Pitre has berths for 4 cruise ships and marinas for yachts. There are fast, scheduled **ferry** services from Pointe-à-Pitre to Marie-Galante, Les Saintes, Dominica, St Lucia and Martinique. *L'Express des Îles* has a car ferry daily from Pointe-à-Pitre to Fort-de-France at 0800 Mon-Sat, 1400 Sun and an additional service at 1200 on Fri, 3 hrs 45 mins. See St Lucia and Dominica chapters for details of services to those islands. *ATE/Trans Antilles Express* (*L'Express des Îles*) offers excursions with accommodation, day trips with lunch, or transport only, T0590-831245, F0590-911105, La Darse, Pointe-à-Pitre. Agents include *T-Maritimes Brudey Frères*, Centre St-John Perse, 97110 Pointe-à-Pitre, T0590-916087. You can get a small motor-sail vessel to Dominica from Pointe-à-Pitre for not much less than the flight, leaving at 1300, 3 days a week, 2 hrs.

Local Bus: there are 3 main bus terminals in Pointe-à-Pitre: from rue Dubouchage, La Darse (by Place de la Victoire), buses run to Gosier (US$0.70), Ste-Anne (US$2), Saint-François (US$2); for north Grande-Terre destinations, buses leave from the Morne Ferret and Mortenol station, off Blvd Légitimus. From Bergevin station, Blvd Chanzy (near the cemetery) they go to Trois Rivières (US$4) and Basse-Terre (US$4.25, 2 hrs). Pointe-à-Pitre to La Grande Anse, US$3, 1¾ hrs. Buses from Pointe-à-Pitre to Deshaies leave from Gare Routière, 1¼ hrs, US$3.50. Basse-Terre to Trois Rivières, 20 mins. The terminal in Basse-Terre is on Blvd Général-de-Gaulle, between the market and the sea. Buses run between 0530 and 1800, leaving for the main destinations every 15 mins or when full. After 1800 and after 1300 on Sat and Sun it is often impossible to get anywhere.

Car There can be major traffic holdups in the rush hour in and around Pointe-à-Pitre; expect to find slow moving traffic on the major routes for up to 20 km out of the capital. Bottlenecks include the roundabout at the university at Bas-du-Fort, the turning to Le Raizet and beyond to Abymes and the turnoff to Baie-Mahault. In the city, parking is bad in the daytime. There are no car parks, just meters. There are 2 zones, green (about US$0.70 for maximum 8 hrs) and orange (cheaper). The system doesn't operate 1230-1400. Most traffic is one way.

Car hire *Avis*, T0590-211354, F0590-211355; *Budget*, T0590-827250, F0590-917208; *Europcar*, T0590-266064, F0590-268373; *Hertz*, T0590-938945, F0590-916959, and there are offices at the airport. At Trois Rivières, Rosan Martin, *Location de Voitures*, is close to the dock, T0590-929424. *Tropic-Car*, 25 rue Schoelcher, T0590-918437, F0590-913194, evenings and weekends T0590-840725, has a variety of models for hire. Fully equipped camper vans can be hired from several agencies: *Antilles Local Soleil*, Gosier, T0590-957200; *Vert'Bleu Location*, T0590-285125, F0590-285295. There are also mopeds for hire in Pointe-à-Pitre, Gosier, Saint-François, or through hotels. Motorbikes from *Equateur Motos*, T0590-845994, F0590-845977. *Dom Location*, rue Saint-Aude Ferly, Saint-François, T/F0590-888481, hires scooters, motorbikes and cars half day to 1 week, scooters US$25 per day. Mokes and scooters can be rented at Ste-Anne. If you don't have a credit card you normally have to deposit up to US$700 for a car; US$430 for a scooter; and US$145 for moped or bicycle. Bicycle rental from *Rent- a-Bike*, *Kalenda Raut Hotel*, Saint-François, T0590-845100, *Atlantic*, Saint-François, around US$10 per day.

Airline offices *Air France*, Blvd Légitimus, Pointe-à-Pitre, T0590-825000; *Air Canada*, T0590-836249; *LIAT*, T0590-211393; *Air Antilles Express*, T0590-648648, www.airantilles.com; *American Eagle*, T0590-211180. **Banks** *Banque Nationale de Paris* (good for Visa cash advances), *Banque Populaire*, *Banque des Antilles Françaises*, *Crédit Maritime*, *Crédit Agricole* and *Société Générale de Banque aux Antilles*, all have branches throughout the island. Banks charge 1% commission and 4% *dessier* (filing fee). No commission charged on French traveller's cheques. Exchange is handled up to midday so go early to avoid the late morning pandemonium. *American Express* is at Petreluzzi Travel, 2 rue Henri IV, English spoken, helpful. Credit cards are widely accepted, including at the hypermarkets. **Communications** Post: Post office and telephone building in Pointe-à-Pitre is on Blvd Hanne, crowded, sweltering. Post and phones in Basse-Terre is on rue Dr Pitat, between Dumanoir and Ciceron, smaller but a bit more comfortable than the Pointe-à-Pitre office. Parcel post is a problem and you can usually send parcels of up to 2 kg only. In Pointe-à-Pitre there is an office near the stadium

Directory

French Antilles

where you can mail parcels of up to 7 kg by air but it is unreliable. Unlike in France, stamps are not sold in bars and tobacconists (although if you buy a postcard or envelope they will probably have a stamp). **Telephone**: For local calls you must buy phone cards (*télécartes*, US$6 or US$14, from a *tabac*); to call abroad, you must hand over identification at the desk (calls to the USA US$1.85 per min, Europe US$2.65 per min, Australia US$3.30 per min; hotels charge twice as much). You can not make a credit card or collect call abroad from a pay phone. You can not have a call returned to a pay phone either. **Consulates** (All embassies are in France) **Germany**, T0590-503839. **Holland**, T0590-733161. **Sweden**, T0590-735494. **Switzerland**, T0590-503650. **US**, T0590-631303. **Medical** services Hospital T0590- 891010/ 891120 in Pointe-à-Pitre. There are 9 hospitals and 15 clinics.

Les Saintes

IDD code:590
Colour map 4, grid A4
Population: 2,036

On Les Saintes, a string of small islands named 'Los Santos' by Columbus, only Terre-de-Haut and Terre-de-Bas are inhabited. The people are mostly descendants of poor Breton colonists who until recently intermarried little with other West Indian races. Sugar cane was never introduced here as a plantation crop and so large numbers of black slaves never came either. The population is predominantly light-skinned and many people have blue eyes. Some still wear the round bamboo and linen hat, the salako, which the locals call a chapeau annamite. A Saintois sailor brought one back from Indo-China (Annan) over a century ago, and everybody took to it. Fishing is still the main occupation on the islands, but tourism is increasingly important. The islands are a popular excursion from Guadeloupe and with a good, natural harbour, many small cruise ships spend the day here. Nevertheless, an overnight stay is recommended so that you can appreciate the islanders' traditional way of life, once the day trippers leave at 1600. Public holidays are particularly heavy days with hundreds of day trippers.

Terre-de-Haut & Les Saintes

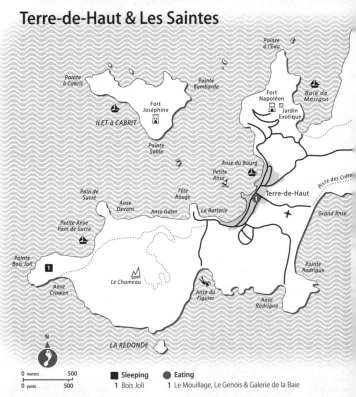

■ **Sleeping**	● **Eating**
1 Bois Joli	1 Le Mouillage, Le Genois & Galerie de la Baie

Terre-de-Haut is the main island visited by tourists (**Tourist office**, 39 rue de la Grande Anse, T0590-995860, www.omt-lessaintes.com). Irregularly shaped and surprisingly barren, it is about 6 km long and 2 km wide at its widest point. Most of the 1,500 inhabitants live around the Anse Mire, looking across to **Ilet à Cabrit** where there are the ruins of Fort Joséphine. There are some excellent beaches including Pont Pierre, or Pompierre, where snorkelling is good and camping is possible, Marigot, L'Anse du Figuier (good diving, no shade), L'Anse Crawen and Grand'Anse (white sand, rougher waters, swimming not allowed). The UCPA sailing school at Petit Anse offers sailing or windsurfing courses. Walking on the islands is good, either to the beaches, or to the top of **Le Chameau** (TV mast on top) on Terre-de-Haut's west end (spectacular views of Les Saintes, Marie-Galante, Guadeloupe and Dominica). Killer climb. It may be only 350 m or so, but it is steep.

Terre-de-Haut

An easy trail, Trace des Crêtes, starts at Terre-de-Haut. Turn right at the pier, follow the main street about 100 m, turn left at the chapel and follow the road up to Le Marigot (look out for the *sentier du morne morel* sign behind the restaurant on the south side of the bay) and on to the beach of Pont Pierre, a lovely golden beach with rocks, Roches Percées, in the bay. Boats and diving equipment can be rented at the landing stage. At the end of the beach the trail leads up the hill where you have a good view of the islands, if you keep left, one branch of the trail leads to Grand'Anse beach. The pretty 'white' cemetery, La **Cimétière Rose**, with paths bordered by shells, is worth visiting is close to the beach and from here you can walk back to Terre-de-Haut, about 1½ hours in total. Alternatively, you can walk along Grand'Anse and on to Pointe Rodriguez and the small cove Anse Rodriguez below it.

Goats can be a nuisance if you decide to picnic

Fort Napoléon is high up on Pointe à l'Eau, and the museum in the fort gives the French view of the decisive sea battle of Les Saintes (1782 – the English Admiral Rodney defeated and scattered the fleet of France's commander the Comte de Grasse, who was sailing to attack Jamaica). The fort itself dates only from the 1840s. The exhibitions are good with interesting models of the ships and battles. A guide will give you a 30-minute tour (in French) of the main building. There are exhibits also of local fishing (including a *saintois*, a boat, originally with a sail, but now diesel-powered) and crafts, a bookshop and drinks on sale. Around the ramparts is the Jardin Exotique which specializes in growing succulents and includes a wild area where plants native to Les Saintes are grown. ■ *0900-1230 except 1 Jan, 1 May, 15-16 Aug and 25 Dec. US$3, students with identity cards and children 6-12 half price.*

Les Saintes

Terre-de-Bas is home to about 1,500 people, mostly fishermen, but many have left for work in France. Boats land at Grande Baie which is a small inlet guarded by a fort and two small statues. You get good views of La Coche and Grand Ilet (two of the uninhabited islands) on the way across. There is a good little information centre at the dock. Buses will meet the ferry and you can go to the main settlement at **Petite Anse**

Terre-de-Bas

French Antilles

where there is a fishing port, secondary school for the islands and a pretty little church with a red roof (tour approximately 40 minutes US$4.25). The beach at Grand Anse is very pleasant and there are a few bars and restaurants nearby (*A La Belle Étoile* is actually on the beach). There is a track from Petite Anse to Grand Anse which is a good walk. It is very quiet compared with Terre-de-Haut. *Salakos* and wood carvings are made locally.

Sleeping

The telephone at the jetty only takes phone cards

Terre-de-Haut LL-A *Bois Joli*, reached by 10-min boat ride or 5-min scooter ride from town, at the west end of the island on hillside, T0590- 995038, F0590- 995505, gorgeous setting, hotel van transport to town or airport, 22 rooms, 8 bungalows, MAP, pool, bar, restaurant, 2 beaches, watersports. **AL** *Kanaoa*, Anse Mire, T0590- 995136, F0590- 995194. 8 rooms, 2 studios, 6 bungalows, a/c, but rather basic, fair restaurant used by tour groups, evening entertainment in season, English spoken, beautiful waterfront setting 10 mins' walk from landing jetty, very quiet. **B** *La Saintoise*, T0590- 995250, in town. 10 rooms, CP, a/c, restaurant. *Auberge Les Petits Saints aux Anacardiers*, La Savane, T0590- 995099, F0590-995451. Former mayor's house overlooking town and bay, furnished with French antiques, attractive, intimate, 10 rooms, 2 bungalows, 1 suite, a/c, clean, pool, sauna, art gallery, good restaurant. **B** *Jeanne d'Arc*, T0590- 995041, at Fond de Curé village on south coast, good, 10 rooms. **Terre-de-Bas** There is one hotel, *Le Poisson Volant*, 9 rooms, T0590- 998147.

On both Terre-de-Haut and Terre-de-Bas there are rooms and houses to rent; tourist office has list of phone numbers. Recommended are **Mme Bonbon**, T0590- 905052, on the road to the airfield, who has several rooms; **Mme Bernadette Cassin**, T0590- 995422, clean studio under her house on road to cemetery, cheaper without kitchen facilities, if she is full she has family and friends who offer rooms; and **Mme Maisonneuve**, T0590-995338, on the same road as the *Mairie*. Reservations are recommended in peak season, especially Christmas and New Year.

Eating

There is a shortage of water on the island

Terre-de-Haut Home-made coconut rum punches are recommended, particularly in the little bar on the right hand side of the *gendarmerie* in front of the jetty. Check beer prices before ordering, cheapest US$2. *Le Mouillage* restaurant, T0590-995057, recommended. *Le Genois*, T0590-995301, excellent and cheap pizza house on water's edge by harbour square, also does takeaways. *La Saladerie*, at top of steps on road to Fort Napoléon, T0590-995343, popular, not always open out of season. *Galerie de la Baie*, first floor overlooking harbour, snacks and very expensive ice cream. The *boulangerie* next to the *Mairie* is open from 0530, good. The supermarkets are expensive, double French prices. There are a couple of markets every morning on the road towards the post office, good for fresh produce. Terre-de-Bas There are 2 or 3 restaurants serving Creole food and snacks.

Transport

No public transport after dark

Air Daily flights from Pointe-à-Pitre, 15 mins, *Air Caraïbes*, US$26 one way, US$52 return, children US$40 return. **Ferry** *Deher CTM* (T995068, F995683) have 6 daily boats from Trois Rivières (Guadeloupe) to Terre-de-Haut, US$13.50 round trip. *Trans Antilles Express* from Pointe-à-Pitre to Terre-de-Haut daily 0800 all year, returning 1600; also from Marina Saint-François, Tue, Wed, Thu, 0800, Dec-May, returning 1600 same days, all US$23 round trip, children US$12. *Transport Maritimes Brudey Frères*, T0590-900448, from Marina Saint-François to Les Saintes Mon, Fri, 0800 Dec-May, and from Darse, Pointe-à-Pitre to Les Saintes and Marie Galante daily 0800, returning 1545, same prices as *Trans Antilles Express*. There are also day charters from Pointe-à-Pitre and Saint-François Marina in high season. The crossing takes about 45 mins. The ferry between Terre-de-Haut and Terre-de-Bas, *Navette L'Inter,* runs about 5 times a day, US$3.50, US$2 for children, return) passing the Pain de Sucre. **Road Bus**: mini-buses take day trippers all over Terre-de-Haut; tour of the island US$7.50, bus up to Fort Napoléon, US$1.50 (or 25 mins' walk). **Bike**: several central locations, US$11.50 per day. **Scooter** rental, US$30 per day.It is not necessary to hire a scooter, as you can walk to most places. Scooters are banned from the town 0900-1200, 1400-1600 and have to be pushed. At the Mairie (town hall) you can get basic information.

Marie-Galante

Marie-Galante, a small pancake-round, mostly flat island of 158 sq km, 22 km south of Grande-Terre, is simple and old-fashioned but surprisingly sophisticated when it comes to food and drink. It was named by Christopher Columbus after his own ship, the *Santa María La Galante*, and has three settlements. The largest is **Grand-Bourg** in the southwest with a population of around 8,000; **Capesterre** is in the southeast and **Saint-Louis** (sugar factory) in the northwest. By Grand-Bourg plage try the *batterie de sirop*, selling a treacle-like sugar cane syrup mixed with rum and lime or with water.

If you want an authentic (and proud of it) island, friendly, but determined to preserve its own way of life, this is it. Information is available from *Office de Tourisme de Marie Galante*, T0590-975651, www.ot-mariegalante.com There is only one medium-sized hotel. The islanders are resisting further hotel developments preferring *gîtes* and guesthouses. It's a traditional rural way of life, based on sugar cane. Peasant proprietors still take canes to the mill by ox-cart. This makes a good photo, which they don't mind a bit. The beaches, so far almost completely untouched by the tourist flood, are superb. By Capesterre, the **Plage de la Feuillère** has fine sand beaches and is protected by the coral reef offshore. Follow the path north to Les Galeries, which are large cliffs eroded by the sea to make a covered walkway over 15 m above sea level. There is a pleasant beach at **Anse de Vieux Fort**, the site of the first settlement on the island in 1648 and of a series of fierce skirmishes between the French and the Amerindians.

The **Trou à Diable** (off the D202) is a massive cave which runs deep into the earth. To visit it, it is essential to have strong shoes, a torch, and a guide. The descent requires

IDD code: 590
Colour map 4, grid A5
Population: 13,463

Marie Galante

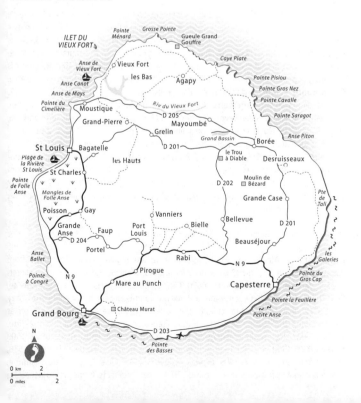

French Antilles

ropes and should not be unassisted. The D202 road meets the D201 at La Grande Barre, from where there are views of the north end of the island and to Guadeloupe. On the coast there are limestone cliffs which have been eroded in places to form arches. One is at Gueule Grand Gouffre and another is further east at Caye Plate.

In the 19th century the island boasted over 100 sugar mills; a few have been restored and may be visited: Basses, Grand-Pierre, Agapy and Murat. Only at Bézard, (around 7 km due north of Capesterre), can you appreciate the glory of a great windmill in full sail. The former plantation houses of **Château Murat** and **Brûle** are interesting. Murat gives a good impression of the great 18th-century plantations; below the sweeping lawn lies the old sugar mill with cane crushing machinery still intact. Behind the house is a walled herb garden. ■ *Museum open Mon-Thu 0900-1300, 1500-1800, Sat and Sun 0900-1200. Free.* The **Bellevue** rum distillery on the D202 is a cottage industry. The rum (*agricole*, made from sugar cane) is very powerful and you will be invited to taste and buy. You may also be offered bags of brown sugar and dessicated coconut, a surprisingly nice combination. At the **Distillerie Bielle** you can taste and buy rum as well as ceramic rum flasks made at the pottery *atelier*. ■ *1000-1200, Mon-Sat. T0590-979362.* The **Distillerie Poisson** in the west on the N9 makes the *Père Labat* rum and is open for visits (also small museum) with tastings of rum and liqueurs. Fascinating old 19th-century machinery, still in use. ■ *0700-1100, Mon-Sat. Free. T0590-970379.* On the road to Duclos, going north, is the *mare au Punch*, the 'sea of Punch'. The story is that when the revolution came, the slaves, to celebrate, gathered together all the rum they could find and, in this pond, made the biggest bowl of punch the Caribbean had ever seen. Alas, as the display boards indicate, this attractive tale is unlikely, but it's a good story, with underlying truth of the fight against oppression.

Sleeping

24-hour advance booking is necessary. For rooms (inquire at the tourist board) and gîtes, contact Gîtes de France Guadeloupe

St-Louis *Le Salut* is in the town centre south of the pier, T0590-970267. 15 rooms, a/c, restaurant and bar. North of St-Louis, 2 km from Vieux-Fort beach on a cliff, is *Au Village de Menard*, T0590-970945. 7 bungalows, pool, mountain bikes, English spoken. Near St Louis is **B** *Cohoba*, at Folle Anse, T805-9679850 in Europe. 100 rather small rooms, 30 with kitchenettes, some have sitting room with sofa bed sleeping one, a/c, TV, 2 restaurants, pool, large conference room, bar, white-sand beach, windsurfing. Other hotels are in **C-D** range. There is a family *pension*, **E** *La Coquillage*, room only or half-board available. **Grand-Bourg** *L'Auberge de l'Arbre à Pain*, rue Jeanne d'Arc, T0590-977369. 7 rooms, CP, a/c, restaurant and bar. **Capesterre** *Hotel Hajo*, Beaurenom, T0590-973276. 6 rooms, fan, restaurant and bar. *Le Soleil Levant*, 42 rue de la Marine, overlooking Capesterre and sea, T0590-973155, F0590-974165. 10 rooms and studios, pool, kitchenettes, restaurant for breakfast and dinner, evening entertainment, car rental. *Le Touloulou*, T0590-973263, F0590-973359. On the Grand Bourg road, 2 km from Capesterre. Clean, well-equipped bungalows backing directly on to the sea, disco and restaurant nearby. *Le Belvedere*, 4 km from Capesterre, 5 km from Grand-Bourg, 2 mins from the beach, T/F0590-973295. 7 rooms, 12 beds, restaurant open for lunch and dinner, Creole seafood, crayfish, bouillabaisse, evening entertainment, welcome cocktail.

Entertainment There is a cinema in Grand-Bourg, *El Rancho*.

Transport **Long distance Air** To get to the island there are regular flights (20 mins) from Pointe-à-Pitre, which is only 43 km away (*Air Caraïbes*, as above, US$52 round trip, children US$39). *Marie-Galante Aviation*, T0590-977702, offers charters and air taxi service. **Sea** There are **ferries** between Pointe-à-Pitre and Grand-Bourg and it is possible to do a day trip (US$12 1 way, US$23 return, children US$12, 1-1½ hrs, times are posted on the booth at the dockside): The *Maria* and *Trident* (Brudy Frères, Centre St-John Perse, Point-à-Pitre, T0590-916087) have daily crossings to Grand Bourg via Saint-Louis, 0545, 0800, 1500 Mon-Fri, 0800, 1300 Sat, 0800, 1645 Sun, returning 1300, 1630 Mon-Fri, 0930, 1630 Sat, 1530, 1800, 1900 Sun. *Trans Antilles Express*, T0590-831245, Quai Gatine Gare Maritime, Pointe-à-Pitre, has fast catamarans taking 300-450 passengers. To Grand-Bourg departing

French Antilles

0800, 1230, 1700 Mon-Sat, 0800, 1700, 1900 Sun, returning from Grand-Bourg 0600, 0900, 1545 Mon-Sat, 0600, 1545 1800 Sun. To Saint-Louis 1230 Mon, Sat, returning 0700 Mon and 1800 Fri. Saint-François to Saint-Louis departing Tue and Thu 0800, returning same days 1645. *Amanda Galante*, a car ferry, T0590-831989, crosses from Pointe-à-Pitre to Saint-Louis in 1½ hrs, US$80 car and driver return, US$7 for each passenger, takes 22 cars and 156 passengers. *Trans Antilles Express* offer full and half-day tours to Marie-Galante from Pointe-à-Pitre, includes boat trip, visits to beaches, the towns, sugar factories, rum distillery (plus tasting) and other sites (0800-1630 daily, except 0730 weekends, US$33, or US$26 for half day, meals US$10.50 extra). Generally you are better off hiring a car or scooter and doing it independently. You can also get a ferry Les Saintes-Marie Galante-Saint-Louis on Tue and Thu in high season.

Local Bus: on the island there are buses and taxis. **Car hire**: self-drive cars can be hired from the airport or in the towns. Rates for a full day US$36, for part of a day US$27 (US$285 deposit); scooters US$21 (US$145 deposit).

La Désirade

La Désirade is an attractive but rather arid island, 10 km east of the Pointe du Chateau on Grande-Terre, whose inhabitants make their living in fishing, sheep-rearing and cultivating cotton and maize. A 10-km road runs from the airport along the south coast to the east end of the island, where a giant cactus plantation can be seen. At the northeast end of the island is Pointe du Mombin where there is an outstanding view of the coastline. There are excellent beaches, such as at Grande Anse and Souffleur. Perhaps the nicest is in the east at a village called Baie-Mahault, enhanced by a good restaurant/bar, *Chez Céce*, where you can sample dozens of different rum punches. The northern part of the island is rugged, with cliffs against which the Atlantic waves crash, and ravines, savagely beautiful but inhospitable, no one lives here.

Colour map 4, grid A5
Population: 1,700

Columbus named the island as it was the first land he saw on his second voyage in 1493. Archaeological research has shown evidence of Amerindian settlement but it was uninhabited when Columbus passed by. La Désirade was occupied by the French for the first time in 1725, when all the lepers on Guadeloupe were sent there during an epidemic. In 1930 a leper hospital was built, but was closed in 1954.

Rainfall is very low here and the dry season lasts from January to August. The lack of fresh water has always hampered economic activity. In 1991, however, La Désirade was linked to Grande-Terre underwater with a fresh water supply. A plaque at l'Anse des Galets commemorates this. The dryness and few people have helped wildlife to survive: rare birds, the agouti (a very edible rodent, the size of a small rabbit), and the iguana (also edible).

D *L'Oasis du Désert*, Quartier Désert Saline, T0590-200212, 8 rooms, restaurant, reservations advisable. *Le Mirage*, T0590-200108, F0590-200745, 7 rooms, restaurant. *Le Kilibibi*, T0590-200097, local specialities. *La Payotte*, seafood, T0590-200194. *Chez Marraine*, T0590-200093, Creole.

Sleeping & eating

Air There are daily 10-min air services from Guadeloupe 0700, 1545 Mon, Thu, Fri, return 0730, 1615 (*Air Caraïbes*), US$51 round trip, children US$39. **Sea** Boat services from St-François, Guadeloupe, by Vedette Impériale, a rapid motorboat, T0590-885806, journey time 45 mins. Departs Mon-Fri and Sun 0800 and 1700, Sat 0800, 1400, 1700, return Mon-Fri 0615 and 1600, Sat 0615, 1100, 1600, Sun 0600, 1600, US$17 return, children half price. Some companies offer day trips with tours and meals for US$43. **Road** Taxi/minibuses normally meet incoming flights and boats. There are bicycles and scooters for hire.

Transport

French Antilles

Touching down

See also Directory, page 600

Boat information (French Flag) Fort-de-France, St-Pierre and Le Marin are ports of entry. No fees or visas for EU or US citizens. French forms to clear in and out. The facilities are among the best in the Caribbean. Anchorages at St-Pierre, Fort-de-France, Anse Mitan, Les Trois-Ilets, Anse Noir, Grand and Petit Anse d'Arlets, Ste-Anne, Cul-de-Sac Marin. Marinas at Fort-de-France, Les Trois-Ilets, Le Marin. The marina at Pointe du Bout is reported safe, but congested and hot. Major charter companies include Moorings Antilles at Club Nautique du Marin (T0596-747539), Sun Sail (Soleil et Voile, Capitainerie Marina Pointo du Bout, T0596-660914), and Stardust (Port de Plaisance du Marin, T0596-749817). Many other smaller companies. For those looking to hitch on a boat, look at noticeboards at the yacht clubs, especially the bar at the Public Jetty and refuelling at the west end of Blvd Alfassa on the Baie des Flamands.

Business hours Banks: Mon-Fri 0730-1800, Sat 0730-1300. Nearly everything closes from 1200-1500 and on Sun. **Shops:** 0900-1800.

Currency Euro.

Documents See page 561.

Emergency numbers Fire T18. **Police** T17. **Gendarmerie**, rue Victor Sévère, 97200 Fort-de-France, T0596-635151. **Hôtel de Police** T0596-553000. **Sea rescue** T0596-639205, 0596-632088, radio phone (international), T10.

Official time GMT minus four hours.

Public holidays The same as Guadeloupe, see page 563.

Voltage 220 volts AC.

Weights and measures Metric.

Martinique

IDD code: 596 (don't be confused, the local code is also 0590) Colour map 4, grid B5 Population: 399,000

Martinique at first glance is a piece of France transported to the tropics, where language and customs have adapted to the climate. There is something for everybody here: a variety of hotels; good beaches; watersports; historical attractions; beautiful scenery; hiking; birdwatching and countless other activities. Tourism is well developed in the south, but a large part of the more mountainous north is taken up by protected rainforest. The scenery is dramatic and very beautiful, with lush rainforest coating the slopes of the mountains and swathes of sugar cane grown on the plain. The volcano, Pelée, last erupted in 1902, when it destroyed the former capital, St-Pierre, killing all but one of its 26,000 inhabitants. It was on Martinique at the end of the 17th century that the Dominican friar, Père Labat, perfected the process of making rum.

Ins and outs

Getting there
See page 599 for further details
There are several daily flights from Paris, but no direct flights from any other European cities. The only direct flights from the USA are with **Air France** from Miami, so North American connections are best done there or go via San Juan, Puerto Rico. Links with neighbouring islands are good, both by air and by sea, so island hopping is easily done.

Getting around There are no buses to the airport (though the Sainte-Anne buses go close), a metered taxi is the only way of getting into town, costing US$10-17. Buses are best for short journeys while collective taxis, known as Taxicos, run all over the island. If you want to drive yourself, there are numerous car hire firms at the airport and around town, see page 599 for details.

Climate The lushness of Martinique's vegetation is evidence that it has a far higher rainfall than many of the islands, due to its mountainous relief. The wet season lasts from Jun to late Nov with frequent sudden heavy showers. The dry season lasts from Dec to May and the year round average temperature is 26°C although the highlands are quite cool.

Tourist information Lamentin Airport, T0596-421805; Bord de la Mer, Fort-de-France, T0596-637960, F0596-736693, www.martinique.org, www.touristmartinique.com www.martinique. cci.fr Office Départemental du Tourisme de la Martinique, BP 520, 97206

> ## Things to do in Martinique
>
> - Make the most of the **delicious Creole food**, eat out as much as you can and, after a night on the town, head for the mobile eateries on Blvd Chevalier de Sainte-Marthe next to the Savane.
> - Don't miss the atmospheric ruins of **St-Pierre**, the 'Petit Paris' which was crushed and burned in 1902 when the volcano exrupted and killed 26,000 people.
> - Lie on the 4-km beach at **Le Diamant**, admire Diamond Rock offshore and imagine the lives of the 20 British sailors stationed there for over a year in 1804.
> - Treat yourself to a night at the elegant **Plantation Leyritz**, a former plantation house in the extreme north.

Fort-de-France Cédex. There are local information bureaux (Syndicat d'Initiative) all round the island, many of which can be found through the town hall (Mairie).

Watersports

Yole (yawl) races (large sailing boats with coloured sails and teams of oarsmen) are an amazing sight at festivals all over the island from July to January. In Fort-de-France races take place in November and December from the little beach next to Desnambuc quay. Other major sailing occasions include the Schoelcher International Nautical Week in February, with sailing and windsurfing competitions; International Sailing Week in March (Yacht Club of Fort-de-France); the Aqua Festival, the Great Nautical Celebration at Robert in April; the Yawl Regatta Tour of Martinique in July or August, when over a period of eight days about 20 yawls race.

Diving is especially good along the coral reef between St-Pierre and Le Prêcheur, over the wrecks off St-Pierre and along the south coast.

Dive centres There are lots of dive operators, most of which are based at the large hotels. For those who do not dive, there are the *Kelennea*, T0596-660550, F0596-660552, glass-bottomed boat at Marina Pointe du Bout, Trois Ilets, and the *Aquabulle* at Marin, T0596-746969, which has a glass hull. To get even further under the water, there are two semi-submersibles: *Aquascope Seadom Explorer*, Marina Pointe du Bout, T0596-683609, and *Zemis Aquascope*, rue de Caritan, Ponton de la Mairie, T0596-748741.

Watersports Sailing and windsurfing at the *Club de la Voile de Fort-de-France*, Pointe de la Vièrge, T0596-614969, and Pointe des Carrières, T0596-633137; *Club Nautique de Marin*, Bassin la Tortue, Pointe du Marin, T0596-749248; *Club Nautique du François*, Route de la Jetée, T0596-543100; *Club Nautique du Vauclin*, Pointe Faula, T0596-745058; *Yacht Club de la Martinique*, Fort de France, T0596-702360; *Base de Plein Air et de Loisirs*, Anse Spoutourne, Tartane, T0596-582432. There are motor boats and sailing boats for hire. Windsurfing is available on hotel beaches where there are board rentals. Jet skiing, sea scooters and waterskiing at Pointe du Bout hotel beaches, *Marouba Club* (Carbet) and Pointe Marin beach in Ste-Anne.

Fishing Many hotels organize fishing trips for their guests. Deep-sea fishing can be arranged at *Bathy's Club* (*Meridien*), T0596-660000 or *Rayon Vert*, T0596-788056, around US\$575 per boat.

Fort-de-France

Fort-de-France was originally built around the Fort St-Louis in the 17th century. The settlement's first name was Fort-Royal and its inhabitants are still called Foyalais. The city of today consists of a crowded centre bordered by the waterfront and sprawling suburbs extending into the surrounding hills and plateaux. The bars, restaurants, and shops give a French atmosphere quite unlike that of other

French Antilles

Caribbean cities. Traffic is very dense and street parking is almost impossible. Most people live in the suburbs and even the discos are out of the old town centre, which is deserted at weekends after Saturday midday. The port is to the east of the town centre, where the Baie du Carenage houses the naval base, yacht club, cargo ships and luxury cruise liners.

Martinique

2 Anse Caritan	10 Framissima	18 Le Village de Tartane
3 Auberge de l'Anse Mitan	11 Habitation Lagrange	19 Le Village du Diamant
4 Aux Délices de la Mer	12 La Bonne Auberge	20 Madras
5 Calypso	13 La Frégate Bleu	21 Marouba Club
6 Chanteur Vacances	14 La Nouvelle Vague	22 Plantation de Leyritz
7 Chez Julot	15 Le Cristophe Colomb	23 Primerêve
8 Diamant les Bains	16 Le Nid Tropical	24 St Aubin
9 Domaine de Belleford	17 Les Brisants	

■ Sleeping
1 Amyris

The impressive **Fort St-Louis** still functions as a military base. Built in Vauban style, it dominates the waterfront. It is still an active military base and has been closed to the public after the 9/11 terrorist attack in New York. ■ *Les Amis du Fort-St- Louis, T0596-605459*. Adjacent to the fort is **La Savane**, the old parade ground, now a 5-ha park planted with palms, tamarinds, and other tropical trees and shrubs. The park contains statues of two famous figures: Pierre Belain d'Esnambuc, the leader of the first French settlers on Martinique, and Empress Josephine (now beheaded by *Independentistes*), first wife of Napoléon Bonaparte, who was born on the island.

The Bibliothèque Schoelcher is situated on the corner of rue Victor Sévère and rue de la Liberté, just across the road from the Savane. Schoelcher (1804-1893) devoted his life to the abolition of slavery. He gave much of his library to Martinique but most was burned in the fire of the town centre in 1890. The building to house the collection was commissioned, but not built, before the fire. It was designed by Henry Picq, a French architect married to a woman from Martinique. The Eiffel engineering company constructed it in iron, shipped it to the island and it opened in 1893. On the exterior you can see the names of freedom campaigners, including John Brown, of the USA, William Wilberforce, of the UK and Toussaint Louverture, of Haiti. Today it still functions as a library and regularly holds exhibitions. ■ *0830-1730 Mon-Thu, 0830-1200 Fri-Sat. T0596-702667*.

Just along the rue de la Liberté towards the seafront is the **Musée Départemental d'Archéologie Précolombienne**. It contains relics of the Arawak and Carib Indians: pottery, statuettes, bones, reconstructions of villages, maps, etc. Worth a visit. ■ *0900-1300, 1430-1700 Mon-Fri, 0900-1200 Sat. US$1.50. T0596-715705*. In the centre of town, in the Square of Père Labat, rue Schoelcher, there is a second chance to see the architecture of Henri Picq with the **Cathedral of St-Louis** which towers above the Fort-de-France skyline. This, too, is mainly of iron, in a romanesque-byzantine style. The arms of past bishops, in stained glass, give colour to the choir. In a beautiful Creole villa dating back to 1887, is the **Musée Régional d'Histoire et d'Ethnographie de la Martinique** on Blvd Générale de Gaulle, opposite the Atrium Theatre. It is a modern museum, opened in 1999, and strong on the origins, customs and traditions of the people of Martinique. ■ *€1.80. T0596-728187. F0596-637411*.

The **Parc Floral et Culturel** (also called **Galerie de Géologie et de Botanie** or **Exotarium**) is a shady park containing two galleries, one of which concentrates on the geology of the island, the other on the flora, and mid-19th-century wooden barracks now housing 11 workshops for local artisans. Almost 2,800 species of plants have been identified in Martinique and the Parc Floral has a very good selection. ■ *Mon-Fri 0900-1230, 1430-1730, closed Sat and Sun. US$1.75 adults, US$0.50 children. T0596-706841*. Next to the Parc Floral are a feature of Fort-de-France not to be missed, the **markets**. The fishmarket is by the Madame River, facing the Place José Martí, where fishermen unload from their small boats or *gommiers*. Close by is one of several markets selling fruit, vegetables and flowers as well as exotic spices. The markets hum with activity from 0500 to sunset, but are best on Friday and Saturday.

The coastal road heading north through Schoelcher from Fort-de-France hugs the coast, zigzagging north through **Case-Pilote** (named after a friendly Carib chief), where there is a 17th-century church. It then passes through several fishing villages and is flanked by beaches that gradually become blacker with volcanic sand. **Le Carbet** is where Columbus is presumed to have landed (monument). A *carbet* was the great meeting house of the Caribs. There are several good restaurants, mostly fish, on the beach. **Habitation Anse Latouche** is at the end of Carbet village on the coast. The ruins of a 17th-century sugar plantation are surrounded by a beautiful garden focusing on local flowers and shrubs and an exhibition of butterflies. There is not much left of the main house, having been destroyed by the 1902 volcanic eruption (see below), but there is a beautiful viaduct from a dam to a big waterwheel

The northwest coast

French Antilles

which used to drive the sugar mill. ■ *Mon-Sat 1000-1600. US$2, children 7-12 US$1.50, or US$5.80 and US$2 for joint entry to Balata Gardens. T0596-781919.* At the popular beach of **Anse Turin** just north of Le Carbet, is the small **Gauguin Museum**. The artist stayed at Anse Turin during 1887 before he went to Tahiti. The museum has copies (mostly photographic) of letters, sketches and some reproductions of his work. Nothing is original. Local artists' paintings and ceramics are sometimes on sale. There is an interesting section on the local traditional women's costume and its elements, *la grande robe, le madras,* and *le foulard*, the head-tie which was knotted to indicate how engaged the wearer's affections were. ■ *0900-1730 daily. US$3. T0596-782266.*

St-Pierre To the north of Carbet is the famous **St-Pierre**. The town is well worth a visit and is an eerie reminder of destructive natural forces in the Caribbean. The modern village is built on the ruins of the former capital of Martinique, which was destroyed by a cloud of molten volcanic ash when **La Montagne Pelée** erupted on 8 May 1902. As

Fort-de-France

N

0 metres   100
0 yards   100

■ **Sleeping**
1 Impératrice
2 La Malmaison
3 Un Coin de Paris

Island of three queens

◀

*Martinique was historically the aristocrat
of the French Antilles, looking down on
the more bourgeois Guadeloupais.
Josephine, the first wife of Napoléon I
was born at Trois-Ilets. Her cousin, Aimée
Dubuc de Rivery, was kidnapped on the
high seas, and sold to the Sultan of
Turkey, becoming one of his favourite
wives, and mother of his successor.
Madame de Maintenon spent much of
her youth in the island: later she secretly
married Louis XIV. Thus, to some,*

*Martinique was known as 'the island
of three queens'. Delgrès, who fought
Napoleon's troops seeking to re-impose
slavery in Guadeloupe, was a mulatto
from Martinique. The island has been the
birthplace of many black writers,
including Aimé Césaire (b 1913), the
doyen of* négritude *and of black cultural
awareness. The blood of Africa flowed, via
Martinique, through the veins of the
French writer, Colette, one of whose
ancestors came from the island.*

the cultural and economic capital, the town was known as the 'Petit Paris' of the West Indies. Out of 26,000 inhabitants (St-Pierrotains) there was only one survivor, Auguste Cyparis (also known as Sylbaris), a casual labourer who had been thrown drunk into a cell for the night. Today his small cell is one of the ruins that visitors can still see. The prison is beside the remains of the once splendid and celebrated theatre of St-Pierre on rue Victor Hugo. You can see the broad sweep of steps up to the entrance, the huge stage area, the first floor boxes and the rusting remains of the electric stage lighting. In the **Musée Volcanologique Franck-Perret** is an interesting collection of objects (mostly by Perret, an American) and documents evoking life before 1902 and remains from the disaster: household metal and glass objects charred and deformed by the extreme heat, photographs and volcanology displays. ■ *0900-1700 daily. US$1.50. T0596-781516.* The bridge over the Rivière Roxelane, built in 1766, leads to the oldest part of the town, the Quartier du Fort. The ruins of the church are among the most moving.

The next village on the coastal road is the picturesque fishing village of **Le Prêcheur**. Madame de Maintenon, who married Louis XIV lived here. The three bells outside the church date from that time. The road then continues towards the spectacular beach of **Anse Céron** where the sand seems to be at its blackest. A rock called the Pearl juts out from the sea which is roughish but swimming is possible. It is a wild and beautiful beach, a pleasant change from the calm, white-sand tourist beaches in the south. Turn inland to **Habitation Céron**, a plantation where the early sugar buildings are largely intact and there is an attractive botanic walk. There are huge ponds where succulent crayfish are raised. These, with homegrown fruit and vegetables make an excellent three-course lunch for US$25 including a rum punch. ■ *0930-1700 daily. T0596-529453.*

It is possible to follow a track 18 km through the rainforest around the northern coast, but a guide is essential. The first 20 minutes on a concrete road are discouraging, but once in the forest the path is cooler and the views beautiful. At the extreme north of the island is another small fishing village, **Grande Rivière** set in breathtaking scenery characteristic of this part of the island; plunging cliffs covered with the lush vegetation of the rainforest. The island of Dominica faces the village from across the sea. Winding roads lead through the mountains to the next village, Macouba, perched on top of a cliff.

*Watch out for
fer-de-lance snakes
and bilharzia in
the streams*

French Antilles

La Route de la Trace winds through the tropical rainforest on the slopes of the Pitons du Carbet from Fort-de-France to **Morne Rouge** on the southern slope of Montagne Pelée. The town was hit by a second eruption of Pelée on 20 August 1902. At **Le Jardin de la Pelée**, on the hill above the town, there is a fine display of local flora, well labelled, and information on the volcano (T0596-524251). The Parc Naturel forest itself is truly magnificent, covering the sides of the steep, inland

**The tropical
rainforest &
La Montagne
Pelée**

mountains (Les Pitons de Carbet and Pelée) with a bewildering array of lush, green vegetation that stretches for miles. Giant bamboo, mountain palms, chestnut and mahogany trees, over a thousand species of fern and many climbing and hanging parasitic plants and orchids are examples of rainforest vegetation.

At **Balata**, not far from the capital along the Route de la Trace is the bizarre sight of the **Sacré Coeur**, a smaller version of Paris's votive Sacré-Coeur de Montmartre, perched high up in the forest. A little further along the road is the **Le Jardin de Balata** with superb views across the Baie de Fort-de-France to Trois-Ilets. The gardens feature a collection of 3,000 species with magnificent anthuriums, numerous hummingbirds and brilliant green lizards. ■ *0900-1700 daily. US$5.80, children aged 7-12 US$2, includes entry to Habitation Anse Latouche. T0596-644873, F0596-647340. Signs are in French.*

La Montagne Pelée is reached via a track branching off the Route de la Trace, between Morne Rouge and Ajoupa-Bouillon, where there is a delightful garden-park, **Les Ombrages Botaniques**. ■ *0900-1700. US$3, children US$1.50.* From the car park at the foot of the volcano there is a view of the Atlantic Coast, Morne Rouge and the bay of St-Pierre. The mountain air is deliciously fresh and cool even at the foot of the volcano. Not far away are **Les Gorges de la Falaise**, a series of small gorges along 3 km of the Falaise River, wonderful for swimming in, accessible only by following the course of the river on foot. Much of the walk is actually wading in the water and you clamber over waterfalls. ■ *The local Syndicat d'Initiative in Ajoupa-Bouillon organizes guided tours up the river. T0596-533287. US$6.50 including waterproof pack and fruit juice.*

North coast The area of **Basse-Pointe** is the pineapple cultivation area of the island, where huge fields of spikey pineapple tops can be seen. Basse-Pointe is an old settlement with a late 17th-century church and a good view of the cliffs from the cemetery. Inland from here is **Plantation Leyritz**, a former plantation, complete with slave houses and machinery. The 18th-century owner's house is now an elegant hotel where the French government has entertained foreign presidents. You can walk round the gardens and eat in what was once the sugar boiling house. There is an exhibition of tiny tableaux featuring dolls made from plants and vegetables, exploiting the colours and textures of tropical leaves. ■ *1000-1830 daily, T0596-785392.*

From the N1 road along the northeast coast tempting beaches with crashing waves are visible, but the Atlantic Coast is too dangerous for swimming, except at **Anse Azérot**, just south of **Sainte-Marie**. To the north is **Fond St-Jacques**, a cultural centre which used to be a Dominican monastery and sugar plantation. Buildings date from 1689 and at its height the Dominicans utilized 1,000 slaves. It was here that Père Labat perfected the distilling of rum. His memoirs are a prime source of information on plantation life. Modern art exhibitions are also held at the centre. ■ *Mon-Fri 0800-1700. US$2 adults, US$0.75 children. T0596-691012.* Nearby, **Musée du Rhum Saint-James** in the St James Distillery, explains the process and history of rum production, and rum tasting. ■ *Mon-Fri 0900-1700 and Sat-Sun 0900-1200. Free. T0596-693002.*

Caravelle peninsula The seafront at **La Trinité** is a grand promenade with modern and 19th-century buildings and monuments, which looks out onto the **Presqu'ile de la Caravelle**, where the vegetation is scrubby but the scenery is gently interesting. The peninsula has beaches at **Tartane** (the only village on the Caravelle), Anse l'Étang (the best, surfing possible) and **Anse du Bout**. It is an area protected by the **Parc Naturel of Martinique**; several well-marked paths criss-cross the peninsula so that visitors can enjoy the varied flora and fauna. It is also possible to visit the historic ruins of the **Château Dubuc** and various buildings that belonged to the Dubuc family, including slave smugglers and privateers. ■ *0830-1730 daily. US$2, children US$1. T0596-474548.*

From the Caravelle peninsula the Atlantic coast is characterized by deep, protected, shallow, sandy bays, good for swimming, surfing and sailing and innumerable islets offshore. The road runs southeast through Le Robert and Le François to the more mountainous area around **Le Vauclin** where the main activity is fishing. There are some interesting art-deco buildings from the 1920s on its steep streets. **The Baignoire de Josephine** has sand-banks and is featured on local boat trips. **Pointe Faula** is a very safe beach here, with dazzling white sand and shallow water. To the south of Vauclin a road leads to Anse Macabou, a group of impressive white-sand beaches.

Southeast coast

The small village of **Les Trois-Ilets**, across the bay from Fort-de-France, has a charming main square and is surrounded by tourist attractions. Empress Josephine, born Marie Josèph Rose Tascher de la Pagerie, was baptized in the church on the square. Her mother is buried here and the church, restored by Napoléon III, is a shrine to the Napoleonic legend. Even more so is **Le domaine de la Pagerie**, the family's sugar plantation, about 4 km from the village. Josephine was probably born here in 1763, and lived here until she was 16. In 1766 a hurricane blew away the graceful plantation house and the family lived above the sugar boiling house. The ruins can be seen and, in the renovated kitchen, a stone building, there is an excellent collection of furniture, documents and portraits. ■ *Tue-Fri 0900-1730, Sat-Sun 0900-1300, 1430-1730. US$3, US$0.75 children. T0596-683455, F0596-683841*. At Pointe Vatable, 2 km east of Trois-Ilets, is the sugar cane museum (**La Maison de la Canne**) which uses documents, machinery and superb models of to illustrate the history of the Martiniquan sugar industry. Recommended. Guided tours are available. ■ *0900-1700 daily except Mon. US$2, children US$0.75. T0596-683204*.

South Martinique

A short bus ride from Trois-Ilets is the tourist complex of **Pointe du Bout**, directly opposite Fort-de-France. There is a marina, a Creole village, where some of the shops, cafés, bars, restaurants and souvenir stands can be found, discos, sports and a conglomeration of luxury hotels. The first beach after stepping off the ferry is a crowded strip of sand in front of the *Hotel Meridien*, almost completely covered with deckchairs for hire. Perhaps preferable is the beach at **Anse Mitan** (ferry from Fort-de-France), a 5-minute walk away, where there are numerous reasonably priced restaurants and bars. **Anse à l'Ane**, a little way along the coast to the west is quieter and has a pleasant atmosphere. **Grande Anse** is a magnificent beach, although it does get crowded at weekends. Just south of the nearby pretty village **Anse d'Arlets** (ferry from Fort-de-France) and around the **Pointe du Diamant** is **Le Diamant**. This is an idyllic golden sand beach stretching for 4 km along the south coast and dominated by the famous **Rocher du Diamant** (Diamond Rock). This huge 176-m rock, of volcanic origin, is about 4 km out to sea and was occupied by the English during the Napoleonic Wars. They stationed four cannons and about 20 sailors there in 1804 before the French reconquered it 1½ years later. Negotiate with a fisherman if you want to visit.

*Ferries – vedettes –
every 15 minutes
Fort-de-France to
Pointe du Bout, three
companies, US$5
return, tickets valid on
all ferries, bicycles at
no extra charge*

Inland and to the east of Diamant is the town of **Rivière-Pilote**, the largest settlement in the south of the island, with the **Mauny Rum** distillery. ■ *Mon-Fri 0930-1730, Sat 0900-1300. Free guided tours. T0596-626208*. The famous **Cléry cock-fighting pit** stages regular mongoose-snake fights. ■ *Sun afternoon. T0596-626169*. The largest marina on the island is at **Le Marin**, which boasts a very fine 18th-century Jesuit church. Southwards are long white-sand beaches lined with palm groves, and calm clear sea.

At **Sainte-Anne** an extensive *Club Méditerranée* complex has its own section of beach adjacent to the long public beach, T0596-767272 to buy an all-inclusive day pass. Sainte-Anne beach is picturesque and shady with trees that overhang the sea in some places. The water is calm, ideal for toddlers. There is a wide selection of lively bars and restaurants and all types of watersports equipment: windsurfers, catamarans, seedoos, kayaks, sunfish. The swimming area is marked off with yellow buoys. Ferries sail from Fort-de-France, 2½ to 3½ hours. There is a Jesuit church of 1766 opposite the jetty.

French Antilles

The road heading east from Marin leads to the beach at **Cap Chevalier**, a popular family beach at weekends. Among others along the barrier reef, the **Ilet Chevalier**, a bird sanctuary, is visible from here. At the southernmost tip of the island is the famous **Grande Anse des Salines** and the beaches of **Dunkerque**, **Baham** and **Anse Trabaud**, all of which are remarkably attractive. Inland from Anse Trabaud lies the salt marsh and the forest petrified by former lava flow. Birdwatching is good at the **Étang des Salines** and in the sandy marshes around the Baie des Anglais.

Essentials

Sleeping

Two useful websites are www.club-hoteliers-martinique.asso.fr and www.martinique-hotel.com

Information and reservations can be made through Centrale de Réservation, BP 823-97200 Fort-de- France Cédex, T0596-715611, F0596-736693. The tourist office at the airport is helpful and will help you get a room for your first night if you have not booked beforehand. Alternatively, for *gîtes* and country guesthouses, contact the *Fédération Martiniquaise des Offices de Tourisme et Syndicat D'Initiative*, Maison du Tourisme Vert, 9 Blvd du Géneral de Gaulle, BP 1122, 97248 Fort-de-France Cédex, T0596-631854, F0596-701716. Generally, prices are high, but there are some bargains at the best resort hotels, especially out of season, which can work out cheaper than other inferior hotels nearer Fort-de-France. The 5 Sofitel/Accor hotels often offer up to 40% off; book online at www.accorhotels.com Some hotels add 10% service charge and/or 5% government tax to the bill.

Several big resort hotels include Sofitel Bakoua and Novotel Coralia Carayou, Point du Bout

Pointe du Bout and Les Trois-Ilets **A-B** *Auberge de l'Anse Mitan*, T0596-660112, F0596-660105. A friendly, family-run hotel with apartments and rooms. **B-C** *Le Nid Tropical*, rents studios and has a lively beach bar and restaurant, T0596-683130, F0596-684743. Also camping, see below. **B** *La Bonne Auberge*, T0596-660155, F0596-660450. Again basic but clean, offering underwater fishing and watersports.

Fort-de-France LL-L *Framissima*, Schoelcher, on the outskirts of Fort-de-France, T0596-614949, F0596-617057. Pool, tennis courts, gym, disco, conference facilities, restaurant, bars, casino, very fine hotel. **AL-B** *Squash Hotel*, 3 Blvd de Verdun, T0596-630001, F0596-630074. 108 modern rooms, pool, 3 squash courts, gym, dancing room, saunas, jacuzzi, billards, conference facilities, impersonal, concrete ambience, but friendly staff. **A-B** *Impératrice*, T0596-630682, F0596-726630, rue de la Liberté. 1950s decor and architecture, apparently unchanged since it was built in 1957. **B** *La Malmaison*, rue de la Liberté, opposite the Savane, T0596-639085, F0596-600393. Good and clean, spacious. Both these hotels have lively bars and restaurants frequented by a young crowd. **B-C** *Le Gommier*, 3 rue Jacques Cazotte, T0596-718855, F0596-730696. One of the oldest buildings in town. Has clean spacious rooms and good continental breakfasts, friendly management. In the elegant suburbs of Didier is the **B-C** *Victoria*, Route de Didier, 97200 Fort-de-France, T0596-605678, F0596-600024, on hillside overlooking bay. Popular with businessmen as well as holiday makers, 37 rooms, good restaurant, a/c, TV, phone, fridge, buses into town every few mins, pool. **C** *Balisier*, 21 rue Victor Hugo, T/F0596-714654. Very centrally located with view over the port, good value. **C** *Carib*, 9 rue du Matouba, T0596-601985. A/c, wrought-iron beds, hardwood floors, very clean and appealing, good location. **C** *Un Coin de Paris*, rue Lazare Carnot, T0596-700852, F0596-630951. Small, friendly and cheap.

Novotel Coralia Diamant and Mercure Coralia Diamant are big at this resort

Diamant AL *Calypso*, Les Hauts du Diamant, T0596-764081, F0596-764084, 500 m from beach, walking distance to village. 60 rooms and suites in 11 buildings, superb views of Diamant Rock, pool, bar, restaurant, car rental. **AL-B** *Diamant les Bains*, T0596-764014, F0596-762700. Fine views over swimming pool and sea. **AL** *Le Village du Diamant*, T0596-764189, F0596-635332. Basic, beachside bungalows, rooms or apartments for rent.

Pierre et Vacances is such a large holiday village here it is familiarly called Village de Sainte-Luce

Sainte-Luce A *Amyris*, by the beach of Pointe Philippeau, T0596-621200, F0596-621210, amyris@cgit.com 3-star, in Karibéa chain, 110 rooms of which are wheelchair-accessible, all amenities, very nice. **B** *Aux Délices de la Mer*, T0596-625012. Offers fishing amongst other activities, only 5 rooms, Creole restaurant.

Outside Sainte-Anne Just south of Ste-Anne on sandy beach is **LL-AL** *Hôtel Anse Caritan*, T0596-767412, F0596-767259. 96 rooms with views across to Diamond Rock, a/c, terraces, kitchenettes, phone, pool, restaurant, watersports and excursions arranged. **L-AL** *Domaine de Belleford*, 97227 Ste-Anne, T0596-769232, F0596-769140. 186 rooms and suites in 5 sections, 500 m from beach, popular with Europeans, terraces, kitchenettes, 4 pools, 2 restaurants, bar, boutiques, car rental.

Atlantic coast **LL** *Habitation Lagrange*, Le Marigot, T0596-536060, F0596-535058. 16 rooms, one suite, 4-poster beds, terraces, luxury, in tropical gardens, 18th-century buildings, decorated in colonial style, private, romantic, beautiful pool, tennis, superb restaurant, in the rainforest, 20 mins from beach. **LL-B** *La Frégate Bleu*, T0596-545466, F0596-547848. 7 spacious, elegant seaview rooms decorated with antiques, Persian rugs, 4-poster beds, kitchenettes, terraces, charming hilltop site, gingerbread trimmings, helpful, English-speaking staff. **AL** *Le Village de Tartane* near Tartane, T0596-580633, F0596-635332. Bungalows with kitchenette around pool. **A-B** *Les Brisants*, T0596-543257, F0596-546913, at François, provides good Creole cuisine. On the old NI, near Trinité, within easy reach of the Caravelle peninsula, **A-B** *St Aubin*, T0596-693477, F0596-694114. A magnificent colonial-style hotel, once a plantation house, splendid location, views and exterior, but interior badly damaged by 1960s refurbishment, 15 a/c rooms. **A-C** *Hôtel Primerêve*, Anse Azérot, just south of Ste Marie, T0596-694040, F0596-690937. 20 rooms, 80 suites, new hotel on hillside, elegant, 5-min walk to superb beach, secluded cove, pool, good restaurant, tennis, snorkelling, easy access to rainforest. **B-C** *Chez Julot*, rue Gabriel Perí, Vauclin, T0596-744093. Modest but pleasant hotel, one street back from foreshore road, a/c, restaurant, bar. In Tartane, **B-C** *Madras*, T0596-583395, F0596-583363. On the beach, spotless rooms, seaview or road view,restaurant.

Basse Pointe **AL-A** *Plantation de Leyritz*, T0596-785392, F0596-789244. Former plantation house in beautiful grounds with lots of insects because of all the fruit trees and water, glamorous accommodation, excellent restaurant serving local specialities, efficient and friendly service, pool, tennis courts, health spa, disco. **D** *Chanteur Vacances*, Grand-Rivière, T0596-557373. Simple, clean hotel, 7 rooms, shared facilities, restaurant.

West coast **C** *La Nouvelle Vague*, within easy reach of the ruined town of St-Pierre, T0596-781434. 5 rooms over bar, overlooks beach. **C** *Le Cristophe Colomb*, Carbet, T0596-780538, F0596-780642. On beach, good value. **LL-AL** *Marouba Club*, Carbet, T0596-780021, F0596-780565. Apartments and bungalows, pool, disco, CP or MAP rates.

Ducos **C** *Airport*, T0596-560183. 6 rooms, basic a/c, hot water, no restaurant.

Youth hostels Fédération des Oeuvres Laïques (FOL), head office at 31 rue Perrinon, Fort de France, T0596-635022, F0596-638367, has a hostel (**C**) along the Route de Didier, rue de Prof Raymond Garcia, T0596-640410, 640017. It is several km from the town centre and difficult to find. No public transport in evenings, taxis can make staying here expensive. Rooms sleep 2 or 4 with shower and toilet, basic.

Camping The most convenient campsite for Fort-de-France is at Anse à l'Ane, *Le Nid Tropical* campsite, US$10 for 2 people if you have your own tent, US$14 if you rent one, also cabins and apartments with kitchenette, T0596-683130, F0596-684743. A small bakery/restaurant on the beach serves cheap meals, bread and pastries. On the south coast, Ste-Luce has a good campsite (no tents for hire) with adequate facilities in the *VVF Hotel*, T0596-625284. *Camping Municipal* at Ste-Anne is popular with a pleasant situation in a shady grove right on the cleanest and nicest beach, next to the *Club Med*, US$7, cheap food available.

You can rent tents from Chanteur Vacances, 65 rue Perrinon, Fort-de-France, T0596-716619, around US$5 per day

French Antilles

Sampling the French and Creole cuisine is one of the great pleasures of visiting Martinique. A meal at a decent restaurant without wine would be US$7-15, depending on the venue and the menu. For a description of local food, see page 561.

Fort-de-France *La Crêperie*, 4 rue Garnier Pagès, T0596-606209. For crêpes and salads, closed Sat midday, Sun. *Le Vieux Milan*, 60 Av des Caraïbes, T0596-603531. Italian atmosphere, excellent pizza US$7-11, closed Sat, Sun. There are several restaurants serving Vietnamese and Chinese food, including *Le Chinatown*, 20 rue Victor Hugo, T0596-718262. Mon-Fri lunch. *Indo*, 105 route de la Folie, T0596-716325. Vietnamese, closed Sun evening

Eating
The small booklet, Ti Gourmet Martinique, gives many restaurants, with details and prices.

and Mon. *Le Xuandre*, Voie No 2 Pointe des Nègres, T0596-615470. Vietnamese, evenings only, closed Mon. *Le Couscousser*, 1 rue Perrinon, looking out on to Bibliothèque Schoelcher. Excellent with choice of sauces and meats to accompany *couscous*, reasonably priced, Algerian red wine goes well with the food, open Mon-Fri 1200-1500, 1900-2300, Sat 1900-2300, T0596-600642. *Les Cèdres*, Lebanese, rue Redoute de Matouba. Kebabs and other Lebanese meze, owner speaks English, major credit cards accepted. *Le Salambo*, Patio de Cluny, T0596-704778. Tunisian, closed Sun, Mon, Tue. *Le Beyrouth*, 9 rue Redoute de Matouba, T0596-606745. Lebanese, lunch menu from US$11.50. *Le Méchoui*, Pte Simon, behind Bricogite, T0596-715812. Moroccan, reservations preferred, takeaway service, open 1200-1600, 1900-2400, closed Sun. *Las Tapas de Sevillas*, 7 rue Garnier Pagès, T0596-637123. Spanish.

Good snackbars and cafés serve various substantial sandwiches and *menus du jour*. The area around Place Clemenceau has lots of scope; *Le Clemenceau* is very good value and extremely friendly, try the *accras* or a fresh *crudité* salad. *Le Lem* on Blvd Général-de-Gaulle has superior fast food at low prices and a young crowd. It also stays open later (until 2100) than many restaurants that close in the evenings and on Sun. Behind the Parc Floral on rue de Royan is the *Kowossol*, a tiny vegetarian café which serves a cheap and healthy *menu du jour*. The pizzas and the fruit juice especially delicious – try *gingembre* (ginger) or *ananas* (pineapple). On François Arago *Los Amigos* and *Le Coq d'Or* are particularly good for substantial sandwiches for around US$2. Try *poisson* (steak fish) or *poulet* (chicken). *Le Renouveau* on Blvd Allègre offers delicious, filling *menus du jour* for US$6, again with a warm welcome. In the **market** at Fort-de-France are small kiosks selling Creole *menu du jour* for US$7 including dessert and drink, other meals also served, with tablecloths and flowers on table, Miriam enthusiastically greets customers at *Chez Louise* and explains menu in English. As in France, there are *Traiteurs* opening up, offering stylish takeaway meals which you select at the shop, helpful to vegetarians. Ask for the latest list at the tourist office.

The place to head for in the evening when these eateries close, is the Blvd Chevalier de Ste-Marthe next to the Savane. Here, every evening until late, vans and caravans serve delicious meals to take away, or to eat at tables under canvas awnings accompanied by loud Zouk music. The scene is bustling and lively, in contrast to the rest of the city at night-time and the air is filled with wonderful aromas. Try *lambis* (conch) in a sandwich (US$2) or on a *brochette* (like a kebab) with rice and salad (US$4). Paella and *Colombo* are good buys (US$6) and the crêpes whether sweet or savoury are delicious.

Anse Mitan Among the many restaurants across the Baie des Flamands is the charming *L'Amphore* where the fresh lobster is delicious, T0596-660309, closed Mon-Tue, lunchtime, open every evening 1900-0300. *Bambou* is a little further along the beach, specializes in fresh fish and offers an excellent *menu du jour*. *Chez Jojo* on the beach at Anse à l'Ane, T0596-683743, has a varied seafood menu. 2-star restaurants include *Auberge de l'Anse Mitan*, T0596-660112. Open every evening, reservations required. **Hemingway's** off Anse Mitan beach. Flat fee for Creole buffet, small or large plate, opens 1900, arrive early for first sitting, soon fills up. At **Diamant**, *La Case Créole*, Place de l'Église, T0596-660000. French and Creole, seafood and other specialities, open daily 1100-1600, 1900-2330. There are several restaurants in the town which front directly on to the beach, mostly offering Creole cooking and seafood. In **Pointe du Bout** marina, *La Marine Bar and Restaurant*, good pizza, drink wine, not beer, good seafood platter. *l'Embarquerie* snack bar by ferry dock has happy hour 3 times a day, 1030-1130, 1430-1530, 1700-1800, buy a local Corsaire beer, get one free. *Pizzeria* and snack bar at innermost corner of Pointe du Bout marina sells beer for €1.5. Reasonably priced salads and menu du jour at *Hibiscus Restaurant* with use of hotel pool for the afternoon. *Bakou Hotel* dock bar is a great place to meet yachties and watch the sunset.

West coast *Grain d'Or*, Carbet, T0596-780691. Spacious, airy restaurant, good spot to sample Martinique's seafood specialities, open daily. *La Cabane des Pêcheurs*, on the beach T0596-780572. Tasty seafood and exotic atmosphere, reservations advised as it is very popular, friendly staff. *Le Trou Crabe*, Le Coin, at beginning of village, T0596-780414, F0596-780514. Open daily except Sun evenings, beach restaurant, rather smart, French and Creole cuisine, offers Lyonnais specialities. *L'Imprévu*, on the beach, T0596-780102, F0596-780866. Open daily except Sun and Mon evenings, Creole musical entertainment Fr evening except during Lent, very local, excellent dinner of Creole specialities including shark, lobster, 3 courses and house wine from US$22. *Chez Ginette*, on the coast, north of St-Pierre, T0596-529028. Good food but overpriced, closed Thu.

North coast *Plantation Leyritz*, near Basse Pointe, T0596-785392. Restaurant in restored plantation house, waterfalls trickling down the walls giving a cool, peaceful feel to the place, elegant dining, good food and service, open daily. *Chez Tante Arlette*, rue Louis de Lucy de Fossarieu, Grand' Rivière, T0596-557575. Excellent Creole food in cool, pleasant surroundings, finished off with home made liqueurs.

South coast At **Ste-Anne**, dine in style at the *Manoir de Beauregard* or at *Les Filets Bleus*, on the beach and lighter on the pocket, T0596-767342, closed Sun evening, Mon. *Anthor* on front street and *L'Ouire Mer* serve reasonable Creole meals and pizza. *Les Tamariniers* chef decorates expensive dishes with flowers, closed Tue evenings, Wed. *Poi et Virginie*, overlooks bay with good seafood, closed Mon. *Chez Gracieuse*, Cap Chevalier, T0596-767231. Good, moderate-price Creole restaurant, choose the terrace and order the catch of the day, open daily.

The *Ballet Martiniquais* (T0596-634388) is one of the world's most prestigious folk ballet companies. Representing everyday scenes in their dance, they wear colourful local costume and are accompanied by traditional rhythms. Seek information from the tourist office about performances and venues, usually one of the large hotels (*Novotel, Caritan, Bakoua*). *CMAC* (Centre Martiniquais d'Action Culturelle, Av Franz Fanon, Fort-de-France, T0596-617676) organizes plays, concerts, the showing of films and documentaries all year round and an annual festival in Dec.

Entertainment
Even if your visit doesn't coincide with any festivals, you'll find plenty of other entertainment

Cinemas There are several comfortable, a/c cinemas in Fort-de-France and the communes. No film is in English; tickets cost US$4.25. A state-of-the-art multiscreen complex is in the Palais de Congres de Madiana, T0596-721515, at Schoelcher. Turn off the main highway just before Anse Madame, taking the road right, leading to the university. The road to the Palais is the first on the right. **Theatres** The main theatres are the *Théâtre Municipal* in the fine old Hôtel de Ville building and *Théâtre de la Soif Nouvelle* in the Place Clemenceau. The *Théâtre Atrium*, on the corner of rue de la Redoute du Marouba, opened in 1998, state of the art hall, shows every evening, operas, plays, concerts, dance, etc, T0596-607878, F0596-608820, atrium-info@cgste.mq

The main pre-lenten **carnival**, takes place in *Feb or Mar* when the whole of Martinique takes to the streets in fantastic costume. Sun is the day of disguises and masked revellers, Mon sees burlesque marriages of improbable couples, Tue **Mardi Gras** is the day of the horned red devils and themed floats. On **Ash Wed**, black and white clad 'devils' parade the streets of Fort-de-France lamenting loudly over the death of Vaval, a gigantic *bwabwa* (the figures carried in *Carnaval*), Both the symbol and the presiding 'god' of carnival, his guise differs from year to year. It is chosen secretly by the carnival committee and only revealed at the first parade on Tue. At **Easter** time, the children fly coloured kites which once had razors attached to their tails for kite fights in the wind. SERMAC (Parc Floral et Culturel and at the Théâtre Municipal) organizes a 2-week arts festival in Fort-de-France in *Jul* with local and foreign artistes performing plays and dance, T0596-716625. At **Toussaint** in *Nov*, the towns are lit by candlelight processions making their way to the cemeteries to sit with the dead. Every village celebrates its **Saint's Day** with games, shows and folk dancing, usually over the nearest weekend. The town of Saint-Marie holds a **cultural festival** in *Jul*, and Ajoupa-Bouillon has a **festival of the crayfish**, while in *Aug* the town of Marin holds its **cultural festival**. Among the many other festivities there is the **Martinique Food Show**, in *Apr*, a culinary fair with lots of competitions; **the May of St-Pierre**, in *May*, which commemorates the eruption of the volcano La Montagne Pelée; the biennial International **Jazz Festival**, or **World Crossroads** of the Guitar, in *Dec*.

Festivals

Nightclubs abound and tend to be expensive (US$10 to get in and the same price for a drink, whether orange juice or a large whisky). At *Le Coco Loco*, rue Ernest Deproge in Fort-de-France, a bar and restaurant with dinner shows, regular jazz sessions are held, T0596-636377. Along Blvd Allègre in Fort-de-France: *Bella Vitta* at No 4, *L'Exclusif, L'Extase*

Nightlife
Choubouloute, the local entertainments guide, is found in most bars and hotels

French Antilles

and *Le Club O Peyi* at No 20. *Le Cheyenne*, rue Joseph Compère, Fort-de-France. *Waïkiki* is a bar with entertainment at Pointe Simon, Fort-de-France. *La Feuille de Tôle*, is an entertainment bar in Schoelcher. There are several bars (*piano bar* or *café théâtre*) where you can listen to various types of music, some have karaoke or cabaret some nights. On rue E Deproge 28, is *Le Mayflower*, a bar and restaurant, pub style with karaoke, and at No 104 is *Le Terminal*, a bar/nightclub. *Latin's Club* is a piano bar at rue Lamartine, Fort-de-France. *Le Pub*, is a bar and restaurant open late down town at Pointe Simon, Fort-de-France. *Le Tribal*, 14 François Arago, Fort-de-France, has a bar, restaurant and disco. Others around the island include *L'Amphore*, a bar and restaurant with karaoke, on the beach of Anse Mitan at Trois Ilets; *Boule de Neige* is a bar and ice cream shop at the marina at Trois Ilets; *L'Endroit*, bar and restaurant at Pointe Marin, Ste Anne, T0596-767674. *Le Calebasse Café*, Marin, not far from the beach, T0596-746927, very lively at night with high quality performances by local musicians and artists, excellent café ambiance. Discos are plentiful and you can hear a wide range of music. In Fort-de-France: *Manhattan*, rue François Arago, also *Le Tribal*, see above, *Cheyenne*, at Parking Pilo, *Le Negresco*, at Pointe Simon, *Xénakis Club*, 6 rue Paul Nardal. Out of town, *L'Alibi*, on the outskirts at Morne Tartenson; *L'As*, at Quartier Lementin, Soudon; *La Baraka*, Pointe du Bout, Trois Ilets; *Chalet*, Quartier Rivière Salée, Laugier; *Crazy Night*, at Ste-Luce on the road to Diamant; *H' Club*, Quartier Ducos, Beauville; *L'Etoile de Choco*, Saint-Joseph; *Palatio*, on the outskirts of Fort-de-France at Village de Rivière Roche; *Starion*, also on the outskirts at 180 Av Maurice Bishop; *Top Night Club*, at Trinité in the northeast at Zone Artisanale Bac; *Zipp's Club*, Dumaine, François, T0596-546545. The new, main casino is at Schoelcher, the *Casino Batelière Plaza*, with tables and slot machines, open 1000-0300, at the entrance to the *Hôtel Framissima*. Casinos charge €9 entrance fee if you are not staying at the hotel, take passport or identification card.

Shopping Fort-de-France has an abundance of boutiques selling the latest Paris fashions, as well as items by local designers, and numerous street markets where local handicrafts are on sale. rue Victor Hugo and its 2 *galleries* (malls) have clothing and perfume. Jewellery shops are mostly in rue Isambert and rue Lamartine, selling crystal, china and silverware, and gold jewellery. At markets in the Savane and near the cathedral bamboo goods, wickerwork, shells, leather goods, T-shirts, silk scarves and the like are sold. Wines and spirits imported from France and local liqueurs made from exotic fruits are readily available, and Martiniquan rum is an excellent buy. There are large shopping centres at Cluny, Dillon, and Bellevue and the big La Galléria on the airport road. Annette supermarket at Le Marin has a free shuttle service from the Marina. St Anne has several small groceries open daily, catering to the tourist trade. US and Canadian dollars are accepted nearly everywhere and many tourist shops offer a 20% discount on goods bought with a credit card or TC's.

Sports **Tennis** courts are at many large hotels where visitors can play at night as well as during the
For watersports day. There are also about 40 clubs round the island where you can play by obtaining tempo-
and fishing, rary membership. For more information contact *La Ligue Regional de Tennis*, Petit Manoir,
see pages 587 Lamentin, T0596-510800.
and 587

Golf At Trois-Ilets is a magnificent, 18-hole championship golf course designed by Henry Trent Jones, with various facilities including 2 tennis courts, shops, snackbar, lessons and equipment hire. Green fees in high season are US$46 and in low season US$39, or you can book for a week (US$285, US$227) or a month (US$960, US$900). Electric carts and other equipment are available for rent. Contact *Golf Country Club de la Martinique*, 97229 Trois-Ilets, T0596-683281, F0596-683897. 2 mini-golf courses are at Madiana Plage à Schoelcher and Anse l'Étang à Tartane.

Riding is a good way to see Martinique's superb countryside; *Ranch Jack*, Morne Habitue-Quartier Espérance, T0596-683769; *Black Horse*, La Pagerie, Trois-Ilets, T0596-683780; *La Cavale*, Diamant, T0596-762294; and others offering schooling, hacking and other facilities. At *Plantation Leyritz* there are 2 horses for guests' use.

Cycling Touring the island by bike is one of the activities offered by the Parc Naturel Régional, T0596-731930. *VT Tilt*, Anse Mitan, Trois-Ilets, offers excursions by bike and cycle groups, T0596-660101, F0596-511400.

French Antilles

Spectator sports **Mongoose** and **snake** fights and **cockfights** are widespread from Dec-Aug at Pitt Quartier Bac, Ducos, T0596-560560; *Pitt Marceny* (the most popular), Le Lamentin, T0596-512847, *Pitt Cléry*, Rivière-Pilote, T0596-626169, and many others. **Horse racing** is at the *Carrière* racetrack at Lamentin, T0596-512509.

Guided tours: of the island by bus, trips on sailing boats and cruise ships around Martinique and to neighbouring islands, and excursions on glass-bottom boats are organized: *STT Voyages*, 23 rue Blénac, Fort-de-France, T0596-716812; *Carib Jet*, Lamentin Airport, T0596-519000; *Madinina Tours*, 89 rue Blénac, 97200 Fort-de-France, T0596-706525, F0596-730953; *Caribtours*, Marina Pointe du Bout, 97229 Trois-llets, T0596-660448, F0596-660706; *Colibri Tours*, Immeuble Laouchez-ZI, Cocotte 97224, Ducos, T0596-771300, F0596-771289; *AVS* Angle des rues F Arago et E Deproge, Fort-de-France, T0596-635555; *M Vacances*, 97290 Marin, T0596-748561, F0596-747107; *Biguine Voyages*, 51 rue Victor Hugo, Fort-de-France, T0596-718787, F0596-605596. Ms Mylene Richard, *Caribbean Spirit*, 23 rue Simón Bolívar, 97200 Fort-de-France, T0596-274651, F0596-724651, arranges tours and accommodation for the physically disadvantaged. **Hiking**: contact the **Parc Naturel Régional**, Blvd Général-de-Gaulle, T731930, for well-organized walks in the island's beauty spots such as the rainforest and the Caravelle Peninsula, €9.15-12.20 including the coach fare to the walk's starting point. Guides can be found through the tourist office, or at Morne Rouge for climbing Montagne Pelée and at Ajoupa-Bouillon for the Gorge de la Falaise walk.

Tour operators

Air Scheduled direct flights from **Europe** (Paris only) are with *Air France* and *Air Corsair*. **From North America**, *Air France* from Miami. *Air France* also has direct flights from Caracas, Cayenne, Pointe-à-Pitre, Port-au-Prince and Port of Spain. Ask *Air France* for youth fares if under 26, or for seasonal prices. **From the Caribbean**, *Air Caraïbes* flies from Canouan, Guadeloupe, St Lucia, St Maarten, St-Martin, Santo Domingo and Union Island. *Cubana* from Havana. **Airport** Lamentin Airport, T0596-421600. There is a tourist office for hotel reservations and information, T0596-421805, *Crédit Agricole* and *Change Caraïbes* for foreign currency exchange (see below), car rental offices and ground tour operators. To get to the airport at Lamentin, either take a taxi, or take a bus marked 'Ducos' and ask to be set down on the highway near the airport. The fare is US$1.25 and the buses take reasonable-sized luggage. Do not attempt to cycle to or from the airport, and Fort-de-France or Trois-llets, as the highway is 4 lanes each way, traffic is heavy and fast, and the shoulder is almost non-existent.

Sea *L'Express des Îles* hydrofoil ferry service to St Lucia, Dominica and Pointe-à-Pitre, Guadeloupe. Fares and schedules appear in the daily paper, *France-Antilles* or contact Terminal Interlles 97200 Fort-de-France, T0596-631211, F0596-633447. Overnight packages available with several hotels, also car hire. Agents are Brudey Frères, 108 rue Victor Hugo, 97200 Fort-de-France, T0596-700850 for timetable information. Martinique is on the route of most Caribbean cruises. Information on travelling by cargo boat can be obtained from the travel agency next door to the CGM office at the harbour, but if going to South America it is cheaper to fly.

Transport

Local Bus: There are plenty of buses running between Fort-de-France and the suburbs which can be caught at Blvd Général-de-Gaulle. The buses are all managed by *Mozaik*, and leave when they're full. Short journeys cost around €0.95 if paid for in advance at a company kiosk, €1.14 if paid on the bus, children €0.55; buses run from 0500-2000 approximately. To request a stop shout "Arrête"! To go further afield, eg to Balata, costs €1.68. The taxi collectif or *taxico* (estate cars or minibuses) run all over the island until about 1800. From Fort-de-France to Ste-Anne €6.14, Diamant €3.16, St-Pierre €3.49. **Car hire**: *Europcar Interent*, Aéroport Lamentin, T0596-421688, F0596-518115, Fort-de-France T0596-733313 and several hotels; *Hertz*, kiosk at the airport, T0596-421690, F0596-514626; *Avis* at the airport, T421692. Prices start from US$30 a day for a Citroën AX or Renault 5. It will normally be cheaper to have unlimited mileage. You can get a discount if you book your car from abroad at least 48 hrs in advance. An international driver's licence is required for those staying over 20 days. Car hire companies in Fort de France close at weekends. If you want to return a car you have to go to the airport, you can't even drop off the key in town. One look at Fort-de-France's congested streets will tell you it's well worth avoiding driving in the city centre. Parking in central Fort-de-France is only legal with a season ticket and the capital's

French Antilles

traffic wardens are very efficient; cars may be towed away. Park near la Savane (US$0.40 per hr). **Motorcycle**: Mopeds can be hired at *Funny*, in Fort-de-France, T0596-633305; *Discount*, Trois-Ilets, T0596-660534; and *Grabin's Car Rental*, Morne Calebasse, T0596-715161. Motorcycles of 125cc and over need a licence, those of 50cc do not. Rental for all is about US$25 per day. A **bicycle** can be hired for US$7 per day, US$36 per week, US$50 per fortnight, from *Funny*, T0596-633305; *Discount*, T0596-660437; *TS Location Sarl*, T634282, all in Fort-de-France. **Taxi**: There is a 40% surcharge on taxi fares between 1900 and 0600 and on Sun. Taxi stands are at the Savane, along Blvd Général-de-Gaulle and Place Clemenceau.

Ferry There are ferries running between Desnambuc quay on the seafront and Pointe du Bout, Anse Mitan and Anse à l'Ane. These run until about 2300 to Pointe du Bout and 1830 to Anse Mitan and Anse à l'Ane and apart from a few taxis are about the only form of transport on a Sun or after 2000. Make sure you get on the right one. The 20-min ferry from Fort-de-France to Trois-Ilets costs US$5 return, is punctual, pleasurable and saves a 45-min drive by road.There are also irregular ferries from Fort-de-France to Ste-Anne, 2½ -3½ hrs. For information about ferry timetables call T0596-730553 for Somatour and T0596-630646 for Madinina.

Directory **Airline offices** *Air France*, T0596-553300; *Air Corsair*, T0596-705970; *American Eagle*, T0596-421919,0596- 511229; *LIAT*, T0596-421602,0596- 512111. Charter companies include *Air Foyal*, T0596-511154; *Air Caraïbes*, T0596-511727; *Air St-Martin*, T0596-515703; *Jet Aviation Service*, T0596-515703; *Antilles Aero Service*, T0596-516688; *Envol*, T0596-684549 (sight seeing trips round the island). **Banks** *Change Caraïbes*, airport, open 0730-2130 Mon-Sat, 0800-1200, 1400-2100 Sun, T0596-421711, rue Ernest Deproge, 97200, Fort-de-France, open 0730-1800 Mon-Fri, 0800-1300 Sat, T0596-602840; *Crédit Agricole* also has an office at the airport for currency exchange, open 0730-1230, 1430-1800 Tue-Fri, 0800-1130 Sat, T0596-512599, also at rue Ernest Deproge, T0596-731706, closed Mon, open Sat morning. *Banque Française Commerciale*, 6/10 rue Ernest Deproge, T0596-638257. *Banque des Antilles Françaises*, 34 rue Lamartine, T0596-607272, *Société Générale de Banque aux Antilles*, 19 rue de la Liberté, T0596-597070. *Crédit Martiniquais*, 17 rue de la Liberté, T0596-599300. *BRED*, Place Monseigneur Romero, T0596-632267. *Martinique Change*, 137 rue Victor Hugo, T0596-638033 and in Trois-Ilets T0596-660444. *Banque National de Paris*, 72 Av des Caraïbes, T0596-594600 (the best for cash advances on Visa, no commission). Banks and exchange houses charge 5% commission on TCs. Not all banks accept US dollar TCs. Some banks charge US$2-4 for any size transaction, so change as much as you think you're going to need. Always go to the bank early; by mid-morning they are very crowded. Do not change US dollars at the Post Office in Fort-de-France, nor at restaurants, supermarkets and shops because you lose about 30% because of the poor exchange rate and commission. Check the rate when you pay for things with US dollars cash, credit card purchases are better. *American Express* at Roger Albert Voyages, 10 rue Victor Hugo, upstairs, efficient. **Communications** **Internet**: Le Web, 4 rue Blénac, T0596-735397, high-speed connection, scanner, web cam, printer, English, French and German spoken, € 3 per 15 mins, € 6 per 30 mins, half price for students, soldiers and unemployed, 0900-2400 Mon-Sat. **Post**: Post offices are open from 0700-1800 and Sat mornings. The main post office is on rue de la Liberté and always has long queues. Post card to USA US$0.50. **Telephone**: Nearly all public telephones are cardphones except a few in bars and hotels which take coins. At the PTT office in rue Antoine Siger, just off the Savane, there are numerous card and coin phones and *Télécartes* (phone cards) are sold. These can also be bought in most newsagents, cafés, and some shops for US$5 upwards. A 50-unit card (about US$8) lasts nearly 4 mins when phoning North America; a 120-unit card costs about US$16. Don't get caught out on arrival at the airport where there are only cardphones. Try the tourist office where they are very helpful and will phone round endless hotels to find the unprepared new arrival a room. You cannot have a call returned to a payphone. Directory enquiries, T12. To make a long distance credit card or collect phone call from a pay phone: buy the smallest card possible and insert in phone, dial 0800-990011 to get USA direct English speaking operator for credit card or collect or dial USA DIRECT calls. Other lines available for Sprint and MCI. Check in the phone book for other numbers. To dial non-French islands in Caribbean dial 00 plus 3-figure code and local number. **Consulates** See also Guadeloupe directory. **Belgium**, Dillon Valmenière, T0596-595052. **Denmark**, 13 rue Victor Sévère, Fort-de-France, T0596-713786, gdj@aquaform.net **Germany**, Acajou, Lamentin, T0596-505097. Italy, 28 Blvd Allègre, Fort-de-France, T0596-705475. **Netherlands**, 44 Av Maurice Bishop, T0596-733161. **Spain** Lot Haute Frégate, François, T0596-542779. **Switzerland**, La Trompeuse, Le Lamentin, T0596-501243. **UK**, Le Petit Pavois, 96 Route du Phare, T0596-615630. **Medical services** **Hospitals**: There are 18 hospitals and clinics which are well equipped and well staffed. EU citizens have reciprocal state health rights and hospitals are up to metropolitan France standards. In an emergency: *SAMU*, Pierre Zobda Quitman Hospital, 97232 Le Lamentin, T0596-751515. **Ambulance service**: T0596-715948.

Background

History

Both Guadeloupe and Martinique were sighted by Columbus on his second voyage in 1493, but no colonies were established by the Spanish because the islands were inhabited by the Caribs; it was not until 1635 that French settlers arrived. Because of their wealth from sugar, the islands became a bone of contention between Britain and France, but were not lost like some other islands. The important dates in the later history of the islands are 1848, when the slaves were freed (Victor Schoelcher guiding the legislation through parliament); 1946, when the islands ceased to be colonies and became Départments (Départements d'Outre Mer - DOM); and 1974, when they each also became economic Régions.

2004 is the 200th anniversary of the birth of Schoelcher, marked by celebrations and exhibitions

Guadeloupe

Christopher Columbus named Guadeloupe after the Virgin of Guadalupe, of Extremadura, Spain, in 1493. The Caribs, who had inhabited the island, called it Karukera, meaning 'island of beautiful waters'. As in most of the Lesser Antilles, the Spanish never settled, and Guadeloupe's history closely resembles that of Martinique, beginning with French colonization in 1635. The first slaves had been brought to the island by 1650. In the first half of the 17th century, Guadeloupe did not enjoy the same levels of prosperity, defence or peace as Martinique. After four years of English occupation, in 1763 Louis XV handed over Canada to Britain to regain his hold on the islands with the Treaty of Paris. The French Revolution brought a period of uncertainty, including a reign of terror under Victor Hugues. Those landowners who were not guillotined fled; slavery was abolished, only to be restored in 1802 by Napoléon. The slaves were finally freed in 1848, largely because of work by Victor Schoelcher. After 1848, the sugar plantations suffered from a lack of manpower, although indentured labour was brought in from East India.

Despite having equal status with Martinique, first as a Département then as a Région, Guadeloupe's image as the less sophisticated, poor relation persists. In common with Martinique, though, its main political voice is radical (unlike the more conservative Saint-Barthélemy and Saint-Martin), often in the past marked by a more violent pro-independence movement.

Martinique

When Christopher Columbus first sighted Martinique, it was also inhabited by the Carib Indians who had killed or absorbed the Arawaks, the previous settlers of the Lesser Antilles some 200-300 years previously. He did not land until 15 June 1502, when he put in at Le Carbet. Columbus named the island Martinica in honour of St Martin; the Caribs called it Madinina, or island of flowers. The Spanish never settled. In 1635 Martinique was colonized by the French under the leadership of Pierre Belain d'Esnambuc. His nephew, Jacques du Parquet, governed in 1637-58 and started to develop the island; when he died, his widow took over. The cultivation of sugar cane and the importation of slaves from West Africa commenced. Fierce battles took place between the Caribs and the French until 1660 when a treaty was signed under which the Caribs agreed to occupy only the Atlantic side of the island. Peace was shortlived, however, and the Indians were soon completely exterminated. Louis XIV bought many of the du Parquet land rights and appointed an administrating company, making Martinique the capital of France's Caribbean possessions. In 1762 England occupied Martinique for nine months, only to return it with Guadeloupe to the French in exchange for Canada, Senegal, the Grenadines, St Vincent, and Tobago. France was content to retain Martinique and Guadeloupe because of the importance of the sugar trade at the time.

More unrest followed when in 1789 the French Revolution inspired slaves to fight for their emancipation. White artisans, soldiers, small merchants and free people of mixed race also embraced its principles. In 1792 a royalist governor re-established control but he was expelled by a revolutionary force sent from France. The capital, Fort-Royal became République-Ville and Paris abolished slavery. Martinique was occupied by the English again from 1794 to 1815 (with one interruption), at the request of the plantation owners of the island who wanted to preserve slavery. Slavery was finally abolished in

French Antilles

602 MARTINIQUE: BACKGROUND

1848 in the French colonies and in the following years 25,000 immigrant workers from India and a few from Indo-China came to Martinique to supplement the remaining workforce on the plantations.

In 1946 Martinique became an overseas Département (DOM), with all the rights of any department in metropolitan France. The bill was steered through the National Assembly by Martinique's Deputy, Aimé Césaire (1913-), poet, mayor of Fort-de-France and a pioneer of *négritude* (see page 603). In 1974 Martinique also became a Région, giving it more economic advantages.

Geography

Guadeloupe Guadeloupe is really two islands, Basse-Terre and Grande-Terre, separated by the narrow bridged strait of the Rivière Salée. To the west is mountainous Basse-Terre, with the volcano Grande Soufrière (1,484 m) at its centre. It has an area of 848 sq km, a total of 150,000 inhabitants, and the administrative capital of the same name on its southwest coast. The commercial capital is Pointe-à-Pitre, situated in the flat half of the island, Grande-Terre. On the cliff-edged Caribbean coast, there was only one low-lying and hospitable shore (*terre* means shore in French, as well as land, hence, Basse-Terre). This was settled first, substantially from the 1640s, and became the capital. At that time, only the mountainous western island was called Guadeloupe. On its east coast was another settlement, Capesterre (which means that part of an island first sighted on the voyage from Europe). Grande-Terre came into its own around two or three decades later, when sugar cane cultivation took off. Grande also means wide in French, which it is. As it assumed the greater commercial importance the name 'Guadeloupe' came to mean both islands.

Martinique The island is 80 km from north to south and 32 km at its widest with mountains in the north and south and a low-lying 'waist' where most people live. The coastline is irregular in the southern half, with peninsulas and promontories protecting islets and sandy bays. Martinique's neighbouring islands are Dominica to the north and St Lucia to the south. Martinique is volcanic in origin and one active volcano still exists, La Montagne Pelée (1,397 m), situated to the northwest, which had its last major eruption in 1902. The rest of the island is also very mountainous; the Pitons de Carbet (maximum 1,196 m) are in the centre of the island and La Montagne du Vauclin (504 m) is in the south. Small hills or *mornes* link these mountains and there is a central plain, Le Lamentin, where sugar cane is planted. An extensive tropical rainforest covers parts of the north of the island, as well as pineapple and banana plantations. The coastline is varied: steep cliffs and volcanic, black and grey sand coves in the north and on the rugged Atlantic coast, and calmer seas with large white or gold sand beaches in the south and on the Caribbean coast.

Economy

Guadeloupe Agriculture and tourism are the principal activities. Bananas have displaced sugar as the single most important export earner accounting for 25% of all exports. Sugar and its by-products generate about 15% of exports. Melons and tropical flowers have been promoted for sale abroad, while many other fruits, vegetables and coffee are grown mainly for the domestic market. Wages and conditions similar to those in metropolitan France force the price of local products to levels viable only on the parent market; 66% of all exports go to France and 11% to Martinique (most exports are agricultural products). Unemployment is high. Infrastructural projects are funded by the French government and the EU's regional aid programmes.

Martinique Martinique is dependent upon France for government spending equivalent to about 70% of GNP, without which there would be no public services or social welfare. Fishing contributes to the local food supply but much of the domestic market is met by imports. Most manufactured goods are imported, adding to the cost of living. There is some light industry and the major industrial plants are an oil refinery, rum distilleries and a cement works, while there is also fruit canning, soft drinks manufacturing and polyethylene and fertilizer plants.

Tourism is the greatest area of economic expansion. Of total stopover visitors, 80% come from France and 3% from the USA, while of total cruise ship visitors, 72% come from the USA, 14% from the whole of Europe and 9% from Canada. Tourism income is now around US$300 mn a year.

Government

The people of Martinique and Guadeloupe are French citizens, and both Départements are officially and administratively part of France. The President of the French Republic is Head of State. Local government is run by a Prefect (appointed by the French Minister for the Interior), the General Council (directly elected) and the Regional Council (elected, proportional representation). There are two different legislative bodies: the General Council and the Regional Council. Each Département is represented by four directly elected Deputies to the National Assembly in Paris, by two indirectly elected Senators in the Senate and by one representative on the Economic and Social Council. The General Council votes on matters of interest to the Département, administers and manages local services and allocates funds to the local councils, or *communes*. The Regional Council concentrates on economic development.

Culture

Music & dance

African dances: the *calinda, laghia, bel-air, haut-taille, gragé* and others are still performed in remote villages. The famous biguine is a more sophisticated dance, and the mazurka can also be heard. French Antillean music is, like most other Caribbean styles, hybrid, a mixture of African (particularly percussion), European, Latin and, latterly, US and other Caribbean musical forms. Currently very popular, on the islands and in mainland France, is zouk, a hi-tech music which overlays electronics on more traditional rhythms. Guadeloupe has a more overt African culture than Martinique, and here, the *gros-ka*, now written as spoken in Creole, *gwo-ka* (Big Drum), has seven distinct rhythms, some, like the *Mendé*, directly attributable to African origins. Musicians such as Robert Oumaou in Guadeloupe work within this framework, outreaching via such styles as jazz to create new and vibrant music.

Customs

Traditional costume is commonly seen in the form of brightly coloured, chequered *Madras* cotton garments. The mixture of French and Creole language and culture gives Martinique and Guadeloupe an ambience quite different from that of the rest of the Caribbean. An extra dimension is added by the Hindu traditions and festivals celebrated by the descendants of the 19th-century indentured labourers.

Literature

The dominance of French educational and social regimes on its colonial possessions led, in the 1930s and 1940s, to a literary movement which had a profound influence on black writing the world over. This was *négritude*, which grew up in Paris among black students from the Caribbean and Africa. Drawing particularly on Haitian nationalism (1915-30), the *négritude* writers sought to restore black pride which had been completely denied by French education. The leaders in the field were Aimé Césaire (1913-) of Martinique, Léopold Senghor of Senegal and Léon Damas of Guyane. Césaire's first affirmation of this ideology was *Cahier d'un retour au pays natal* (1939); in subsequent works and in political life (he was mayor of Fort-de-France) he maintained his attack on the "white man's superiority complex" and worked, in common with another Martiniquan writer, Frantz Fanon, towards "the creation of a new system of essentially humane values" (Mazisi Kunene in his introduction to the Penguin edition of *Return to My Native Land*, 1969).

French Antilles

Windward Islands

Introducing the Windward Islands

The Windward Islands include four independent nations: Dominica, St Lucia, St Vincent and the Grenadines and Grenada as well as the French Antilles which are départements of France (see page 559). They are a series of volcanic peaks jutting out and forming a barrier between the Atlantic Ocean and the Caribbean Sea. Sulphur fumaroles and hot springs can be found on some islands where the volcanoes are dormant but not dead. There are large areas of lush rainforest with national parks protecting places of biodiversity or natural beauty on land or underwater.The islands are a haven for birds and the sea is teeming with fish and other marine life. Hikers and birdwatchers are spoilt for choice in the larger islands of the Windwards, while yachtsmen are similarly blessed when navigating among the smaller Grenadines, one of the world's most popular sailing destinations. Bananas are still an important source of income on the Windward Islands, but agriculture is diversifying with other tropical fruits and flowers now being exported. Tourism is the leading foreign-exchange earner, providing the jobs which have been lost in traditional activities.

Things to do in Dominica

- Dive at **Champagne** and swim through the bubbles of hot underwater springs.
- For adventurous hiking and superb views, try **Morne Anglais**. At 3,882 m its not Dominica's highest peak, but not as often shrouded in clouds as the others.
- **Morne Trois Pitons National Park**, the only UNESCO World Heritage Site in the Windward Islands, should not be missed by nature lovers.
- Spend time in **Calibishie**, a fishing village overlooking Guadeloupe.
- The **World Creole Music Festival** in late October is worth risking hurricane season for.

★

See also Directory, page 624

Windward Islands

Dominica

Known as the 'Nature Island' of the Caribbean, Dominica (pronounced Domineeca) is the place to come for dense forests, volcanic hills, rivers, waterfalls and the Boiling Lake. It is also a highly regarded diving destination, with a good marine park system, and for much of the year you can see whales and dolphins offshore. Hotels around the island are small, intimate and low-key, greater development being deterred by the lack of beaches. It is the only island where Caribs have survived and they still retain many of their traditions such as canoe carving. The island's culture and language are an amalgam of the native and immigrant peoples; Carib, French, English, African.

IDD code: 767
Colour map 4, grid A5
Population: 74,400

Ins and outs

There are no direct flights from **Europe** or **North America** to Dominica. Connections must be made in Puerto Rico, St Maarten, Antigua, St Lucia or the French Antilles. There are 2 reliable ferry services from St Lucia and the French Antilles, but it can be rough in the channel.

Getting there
See Transport, page 623, for further details

Road It is a good idea to rent a car or jeep as buses take a lot of planning. Dominicans drive fast so you may want to take a taxi to enjoy the views. Main roads are fairly good; the Portsmouth-Marigot road built in 1987 is excellent, but in towns and south of Roseau, roads are narrow and in poor condition. Apart from the Soufrière/ Scotts Head route, it is difficult to get anywhere on the island by **public transport**, and return to Roseau in one day, because buses leave Marigot, or wherever, to arrive in Roseau around 0700, then return at about 1300. It is just possible to get to Portsmouth and return in one day, the first bus is at 1000, returning at 1600.

Getting around
There are few road signs, but with a good map finding your way is not difficult

Daytime temperatures average between 70° F and 85° F, though the nights are much cooler in the mountains. The rainy season is from Jul to Oct though showers occur all through the year. Note that the mountains are much wetter and cooler than the coast. Roseau receives about 85 in of rain a year, while the mountains get over 340 in.

Climate

The **Dominica Division of Tourism** has its headquarters in the National Development Corporation, in a converted Rose's Lime Juice factory, Valley Rd, Roseau (T4482045, www.dominica.dm). There is a Dominica Information Desk in the arrival section of VC Bird International Airport, Antigua, open daily. A useful brochure is *Discover Dominica* available free from the tourist offices in the Old Market Square (open Mon-Fri 0800-1600, Sat 0900-1300) and at both airports (Canefield Airport open daily 0615-1115, 1415-1730 – or last flight; the Melville Hall one is only open at flight arrival times). Other useful guides and booklets are produced by the **Forestry Division** and are available from their offices in the Botanical Gardens, priced from EC$0.25-EC$15.

Tourist information

Windward Islands

Touching down

See also Directory, page 624

Boat information (own flag) Roseau, Portsmouth and Anse de Mai in the east are ports of entry. Obtain coast-wide permit. EC$1 to clear in. Customs main office is at the deep water harbour at Woodbridge Bay where all the large ships come in (T4484462). You can also clear at the Bayfront. Other offices are at Roseau, Anse de Mai, Portsmouth and at both airports. Anchor at Salisbury, Castaways Beach Hotel, Layou River, All One Bar in Loubiere. A marina is being built at the Coconut Beach Hotel near Portsmouth, with slips for 40 boats, full service. Do not anchor in Scotts Head/Soufrière Bay (marine reserve) or Douglas Bay or where fishing activities are underway. Waste disposal at the commercial docks in Portsmouth and Roseau.

Business hours Banks: Mon-Thu 0800- 1400, Fri 0800-1700. **Government offices:** Mon 0800-1300, 1400-1700, Tue-Fri 0800- 1300, 1400-1700. **Shops:** Mon-Fri 0800-1300, 1400-1600, Sat 0800-1300. Some supermarkets in Roseau stay open until 2000 and local shops may be open at 2200 even on Sun.

Clothing informal, though swimsuits are not worn on the streets. A sweater is recommended for the evenings. When hiking, take good walking shoes as well as a raincoat and/or a pullover; a dry T-shirt is also a good idea.

Currency East Caribbean dollar, EC$. EC$2.67=US$1.

Departure tax EC$50/US$18.50; day trippers pay EC$5; under 12s are free.

Documents All visitors entering Dominica must be in possession of an **outward ticket** and a valid **passport**. Proof of citizenship with photo is acceptable for US and Canadian citizens. A Carte d'Identité allows French nationals to visit for up to two weeks. Immigration normally grants stays of 21 days on arrival; extensions can be applied for and require an outward ticket.

Emergency numbers T999 for Police, Fire and Ambulance.

Language English is the official language but **patois** is spoken widely. It is very similar to that spoken on St Lucia and to the Creole of

Flora and fauna

Entrance to 'ecological' sites in Dominica is US$2; day-pass US$5; week-pass US$10, ticket should be bought in advance from agencies or at the sites

There are several national parks, including the **Morne Trois Pitons** (17,000 acres and a UNESCO World Heritage Site) in the south, the **Central Forest Reserve** and the **Northern Forest Reserve**, which together protect rainforest covering much of the island's mountainous interior. At the highest levels on the island is elfin woodland, characterized by dense vegetation and low-growing plants. Elfin woodland and high montane thicket give way to rainforest at altitudes between 1,000 and 2,500 ft, extending over about 60% of the island. The Morne Trois Pitons Reserve has the richest biodiversity in the Lesser Antilles. It contains five volcanoes, on the slopes of which there are 50 fumaroles and hot springs, freshwater lakes and a 'boiling lake'.

The **Cabrits Peninsula** in the northwest was declared a national park in 1986. Covering 1,313 acres, its twin hills covered by dry forest, it is separated from the island by marshland (a pier and cruise ship reception centre have been built) which is a nesting place for herons and doves and hosts a variety of migrant bird species. A walk through the woods and around the buildings of **Fort Shirley** (abandoned in 1854) will reveal much flora and wildlife. The scuttling hermit (or soldier) and black crabs, ground lizard (abòlò) and tree lizard are most visible.

Dominica is a botanist's and a birdwatcher's paradise

In addition to the huge variety of trees, many of which flower in March and April, there are orchids and wild gardens in the valleys. Bwa Kwaib or Carib wood (*Sabinea carinalis*) is the national flower; found mostly growing along parts of the west coast. Indigenous birds to the island are the imperial parrot, or sisserou (*Amazona imperialis*), which is critically endangered, and its marginally less threatened relative, the red-necked parrot, or Jacquot (*Amazona arausiaca*). The sisserou is the national bird. They can be seen in the **Syndicate** area in the northwest, which is now a protected reserve (accessible by 4WD only). There is a nature trail but signs are difficult to spot. The parrots are most evident during their courting season, in April and

Martinique and Haiti but people tend to speak more slowly (see page 626).
Media *DBS (State radio) broadcasts on AM 595 kHz and FM 88.1, 88.6. 89.5, 103.2 and 103.6 MHz. Kairi Fm has a more lively presentation style, on FM 93.1, 107.9 MHz. Q95 (95.1 FM) is new and popular. Vol is on AM 1060 KHz, FM 102.1, 90.6 MHz. There are two religious radio stations (one Protestant and one Catholic) as well as a repeater for St Lucian Radio Caribbean International on FM 98.1 Mhz.*
Official time *Atlantic Standard Time, four hours behind GMT, one ahead of EST.*
Public holidays *1 Jan; Carnival; Good Fri and Easter Mon; first Mon in May; Whit Mon; first Mon in Aug; 3-4 Nov (Independence); Christmas Day and Boxing Day. A merchant's holiday takes place on 2 Jan, when all shops and restaurants and most government offices are closed, although banks and hotels stay open.*
Safety *Crime is rising and there have been muggings on beaches at Castle Bruce in the east and Hampstead on the northeast coast.*

There are often robberies around Calibishie and you must never leave valuables unattended on the beaches in that area, even if you can see them. Grand Bay is an area to avoid at carnival time, which is celebrated with much 'enthusiasm', including guns and machetes. Theft is normally non-violent and is of cash and easily saleable items (for example jewellery) rather than credit cards. Always report theft to the police, they generally have a shrewd idea of where to look for stolen goods and sometimes recover them.
Tourist offices overseas *France KPMG Axe Consultants, 12 rue de Madrid, 75008 Paris, T53424100, F43-873285.* **UK Dominica High Commission**, *1 Collingham Gardens, Earls Court, London SW5 0HW, T020-78351937, F020-73738743, or the* **Caribbean Tourism Organization**, *Suite 3.15, Vigilant House, 120 Wilton Road, Victoria, London SW1V 1JZ, T020-72338382, F020-78738551.*
Voltage *220/240 volts AC, 50 cycles.*
Weights and measures *Imperial.*

early May. To get the best from a parrot-watching trip, it is worth taking a guide. Bertrand Jno Baptiste, of the Forestry Division, T4482401, and Homid Laurent, T4497147, have been recommended. While there are other rare species, such as the forest thrush and the blue-headed hummingbird, there are a great many others which are easily spotted (the purple-throated carib and Antillean-crested hummingbirds, for instance), or heard (the *siffleur montagne*). Waterfowl can be seen on the lakes, waders on the coastal wetlands (many are migrants).

There are fewer species of mammal (agouti, manicou-opossum, wild pig and bats in caves, most particularly at Thiband on the northeast coast), but there is a wealth of insect life (for example, over 55 species of butterfly) and reptiles. There is the rare iguana, the *crapaud* (a large frog, eaten under the name of mountain chicken) and five snakes, none poisonous (includes the boa constrictor, or *tête-chien*). Certain parts of the coast are used as nesting grounds by sea turtles (hawksbill, leatherback and green). As a result of over-hunting, the Forestry Division has extended the close season for hunting wildlife like *crapaud*.

The Forestry Division in the Botanical Gardens, Roseau, has a wide range of publications, trail maps, park guides, posters and leaflets (some free) on Dominica's wildlife and National Parks, T4482401, F4487999.

Diving and marine life

Dominica is highly regarded as a diving destination and has been featured in most diving magazines as 'undiscovered'. Features include wall dives, drop-offs, reefs, hot, freshwater springs under the sea, sponges, black coral, pinnacles and wrecks, all in unpolluted water. Due to steep drops the sediment falls away and visibility is excellent, at up to 30 m depending on the weather.

Windward Islands

Dominica

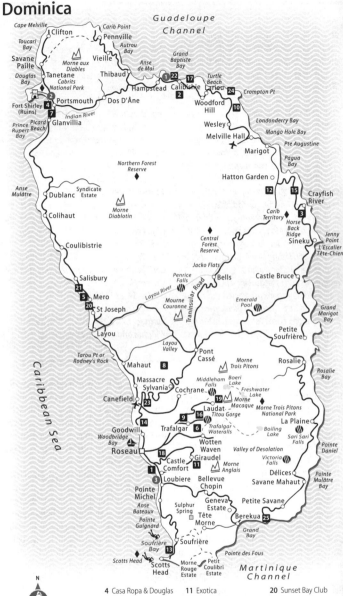

There is a marine park conservation area in **Toucari Bay** and part of **Douglas Bay**, north of the Cabrits, but the most popular scuba sites are south of Roseau, at **Pointe Guignard**, **Soufrière Bay** and **Scotts Head**. An unusual site is **Champagne**, with underwater hot springs where you swim through bubbles, good for snorkelling. This area in the southeast, **Soufrière-Scotts Head**, is now a marine park without moorings so that all diving is drift diving and boats pick up divers where they surface. Areas may be designated for diving and other areas for fishing. Along the south and southeast coast there are more dive sites but because of the Atlantic currents, these are for experienced, adventurous divers only. Note that the taking of conch, coral, lobster, sponge, turtle eggs, etc, is forbidden and you may not put down anchor in coral and on reefs; use the designated moorings. Snorkelling is good in the same general areas as diving, including Douglas Bay and the Scott's Head/Soufrière Bay Marine Reserve.

Dive sites
Many drop-offs are close to the beaches but access is poor and boats are essential

    Whale watching is extremely popular, and the success rate is the best in the eastern Caribbean. The female whales and their calves are in the Caribbean waters for much of the year, with only the mature males leaving to feed for any length of time. If your trip is successful, you could be treated to the sight of mothers and their young swimming close to the boat, or young males making enormous jumps before diving below the waves. Dolphin are abundant too, particularly in the Soufrière Bay area and even if you miss the whales your boat is accompanied by a school of playful dolphin. Several different types of whales have been spotted not far from the west shore where the deep, calm waters are ideal for these mammals. Sperm whales are regularly seen, especially during the winter months, as are large numbers of spinner and spotted dolphins. You can also sometimes see pilot whales, pseudorcas, pygmy sperm whales, bottlenose dolphins, Risso's dolphins and melon-headed whales. Whale-watching trips can be arranged with the *Anchorage Hotel* (Thursday, Sunday 1400-1800), *Dive Dominica* (Wednesday, Sunday 1400), or *Game Fishing Dominica*, T4496638. Whales and dolphins are frequently seen on half- or full-day cruises on the *Carmela*, see below.

Whale watching trips cost $US40-50 per person

Scuba diving is permitted only through one of the island's registered dive operators or with written permission from the Fisheries Division. Single-tank dives are from US$42 and 2-tank dives are from US$63. **Dive Dominica Ltd**, at the *Castle Comfort Lodge*, T4482188, www.castlecomfortdivelodge.com, offers full diving and accommodation packages, courses, single or multiple-day dives, night dives and equipment rental. Owned by Derek Perryman, this company is one of the most friendly and experienced operations, recommended for its professional service. **Anchorage Dive Centre**, T4482638, anchorage@cwdom.dm, is based at the *Anchorage Hotel*, Castle Comfort, with a sister operation at the *Portsmouth Beach Hotel*. This is another long-established operation with a good reputation, owned by Andrew Armour. **Dive Castaways** at the *Castaways Beach Hotel*, T4496244, www.castaways.dm, covers the northern dive sites. **Cabrits Dive Centre**, operate from Picard Estate, Portsmouth, T4453010, www.cabritsdive.com, diving and snorkelling in the less-visited north of the island; **East Carib Dive Centre**, Salisbury T4996575, www.eastcaribdive.dm, is based at the *Lauro Club*, contact Harald Zahn; and **Nature Island Dive** at Soufrière T4498181, www.natureislanddive.com, also snorkelling, kayaking and mountain biking, is run by a team of divers from around the world. Ask them about accommodation and dive packages; they have a bayside wooden cottage on stilts with porch for up to 4 divers, *Gallette*.

Dive centres
Snorkelling trips, around US$26, are particularly recommended for the Champagne area

Beaches

The Caribbean side of Dominica gains or loses sand according to swells and storms but the black coral sandy areas are few and far between. A small one exists just off Scotts Head (favoured as a teaching ground for divers, snorkellers and canoeists, so sometimes crowded), but further north you must travel to Mero beach or *Castaways Beach Hotel*. **Macousheri Bay** and **Coconut Beach** near Portsmouth are probably the best areas for Caribbean bathing. Don't be tempted to swim anywhere near Roseau or the larger villages because of effluent. For some really beautiful, unspoilt,

Compared with other Caribbean islands, Dominica has few good beaches, but the river bathing is excellent

white sandy beaches, hire a 4WD and investigate the bays of the northeast coast. **Turtle Beach**, **Pointe Baptiste**(impressive red cliffs) **Hampstead** and **Woodford Hill** are all beautiful but the Atlantic coast is dangerous. Look at the sea and swim in the rivers is the safest advice. Very strong swimmers may be exhilarated by **Titou Gorge**, near Laudat, where the water flows powerfully through a narrow canyon and emerges by a hot mineral cascade.

Watersports
Very few water-sports are on offer

Game Fishing Dominica is at the *Castaways Beach Hotel* (T4496638) with charters at US$400 half day or US$600 full day. The first Dominica International Sportfishing Tournament was held in 1996 and annually since then in May. **Sea kayaks** can be hired from *Nature Island Dive* (see above), rates are US$11 per hour, US$26 per half day and US$42 per full day, lifejackets and instruction in Soufrière Bay provided. Guided tours are available. *Wave Dancer* at Portsmouth, T4454580, offers kayaks, tubing and windsurfing.

Gusty winds coming down from the hills make **sailing** difficult and unreliable; conditions are rarely suitable for the beginner. The best harbour for yachts is Portsmouth (Prince Rupert Bay), but you should guard your possessions. Stealing from yachts is quite common. The jetty in Roseau (see below) is designed for small craft, such as yachts, clearing for port entry.

Some hotels have moorings: *Fort Young* charges US$5 per day, US$30 per week, US$100 per month; *Reigate Waterfront* and *Anchorage* have moorings and a pier, and yachtsmen and women are invited to use the hotels' facilities. *All One Bar* in Loubiere, www.allonebar.com, also offers moorings. Half-day and full-day cruises are offered by *Carmela*, a 30-m sailing vessel, www.avirtualcominica.com/carmela-charters, T4482282.

Roseau

Streets have been given signs but it is still tricky to find your way around Roseau; you may need to ask for directions

Roseau, the main town, is small, ramshackle and friendly, with a surprising number of pretty old buildings still intact. The houses look a bit tatty with rusting tin roofs and a general lack of paint, but there is still some attractive gingerbread fretwork in the traditional style on streets like Castle Street. Quite a lot of redevelopment has taken place over the last few years, improving access and making the waterfront more attractive. The Old Market Plaza is a pedestrian area, with shops in the middle. The old, red market cross has been retained, with 'keep the pavement dry' picked out in white paint. Between the Plaza and the sea is the old post office, now housing the **Dominican Museum**, which is well worth a visit. ■ *Mon-Fri 0900-1600, Sat 0900-1200. EC$2. T4482401.* The **market**, at the north end of Bay Street, is a fascinating sight on Saturday mornings from about 0600-1000; it is also lively on Friday morning, closed Sunday. The sea wall was completed in late 1993, which has greatly improved the waterfront area of town, known as the **Bay Front** or **Dame Eugenia Charles Blvd**, after the Prime Minister who promoted the development. The Roseau jetty, destroyed by Hurricane David in 1979, was rebuilt in the Seawall and Bay Front Development Project for the use of yachts and other small craft. A promenade with trees and benches, a road from the Old Jetty to Victoria Street, and parking bays take up most of the space. A new T-shaped cruise ship jetty, completed in 1995, where for several weeks in the winter season ships tower above the town pouring forth tourists.

The 40-acre **Botanical Gardens** dating from 1890 are principally an arboretum; they have a collection of plant species, including an orchid house. Several Jacquot and Sisserou parrots can be seen in the bird sanctuary in the park, thanks in part to the Jersey Wildlife Preservation Trust. Breeding programmes are underway; some of the offspring will be released to the wild.

Around the island

Trafalgar waterfalls

The Trafalgar waterfalls in the Roseau Valley, 8 km from the capital, have been the most popular tourist site for many years. Hot and cold water flowed in two spectacular cascades in the forest, but unfortunately the volume of the hot fall was sharply diminished by a hydroelectric scheme higher up and a landslide after the September 1995 hurricanes covered both the hot and cold water pools. The path to the falls is easy to follow, but if you want to go further than the viewing point, take a guide because there is a lot of scrambling over rocks and it can be difficult at times. Trying to cross over the falls at the top is very hazardous. Bathing is possible in pools in the river beneath the falls. There are always lots of guides. Some guides can be abusive if you insist on going alone. Agree the price before setting out, around EC$10 for two or more people in a group. The Trafalgar Falls are crowded because they are close to the road (bus from outside the Astaphan supermarket in Roseau or walk). A natural sulphur pool has been set up at *Papillote* restaurant by the falls, in lovely gardens. There is also a one-hour trail from the sulphur springs of the settlement of Wotten Waven through forest and banana plantations across the Trois Pitons River up to the Trafalgar Falls.

Much of the south part of the island (17,000 acres) has since 1975 been designated the Morne Trois Pitons National Park and in 1998 it became a World Heritage Site. Evidence of volcanic activity is manifested in hot springs, sulphur emissions and the occasional small eruption. Its attractions include the **Boiling Lake** (92°C), which may be the largest of its kind in the world (the other contender is in New Zealand) and reached after a 6-mile climb from Laudat, returning on the same path. An experienced guide is recommended as, although easy to follow, the trail can be treacherous, particularly

Morne Trois Pitons National Park
In 1999 a guide fell in the lake . He was burned up to his waist and spent three months in hospital

Roseau

when mist descends, (guides: EC$100 per couple, EC$180 for two couples; Lambert Charles, T4483365, knowledgeable; Kenrich Johnson, informative; Edison and Loftus Joseph, Wotten Waven, T4489192 at a telephone box).

In the valley below the Boiling Lake is a spectacular region known as the **Valley of Desolation**, where the forest has been destroyed by sulphuric emissions. A small volcanic eruption in 1997, not considered cause for alarm, caused ash to scatter over an area of about 50 sq ft. At the beginning of the trail to the Boiling Lake is the Titou Gorge, now considerably damaged by rock fall from the hydroelectric development in the area, where a hot and a cold stream mingle. However, there is nothing more refreshing or soothing after hiking to and from the Boiling Lake than swimming through the Titou Gorge. The Kent Gilbert Trail starts in La Plaine and is about 4½ miles long. It affords views of the Sari Sari and Bolive Falls, but avoids the Valley of Desolation. While this makes it a less strenuous route is less impressive.

Do not swim here, it is the drinking water reservoir for Roseau

Also in the park is the **Freshwater Lake**; east of **Morne Macaque** at 2,500 ft above sea level, two miles from Laudat. A 45-minute trail (follow the road where the river joins the lake, half a mile to the pipeline, take the left path through the forest) leads to the island's highest lake, **Boeri**, between Morne Macaque and **Morne Trois Pitons**.

The National Park Service has built a series of paths, the Middleham Trails, through the rainforest on the northwest border of the park. The trails are accessible from Sylvania on the Transinsular Road, or Cochrane, although the signs from Sylvania are not clear. The road to Cochrane is by the Old Mill Cultural Centre in Canefield, once through the village the trail is marked. About 1½-2 hours' walk from Cochrane are the **Middleham Falls**, about 250-ft high, falling into a beautiful blue pool in the middle of the forest. Once past the Middleham Falls the trail emerges on the Laudat road. Turn inland at *Sisserou Hotel* and then immediately right behind the Texaco garage (30-minute walk from Roseau) a steep road leads 2½ miles up to Giraudel (50-minute walk). From behind the school here a trail goes up through a succession of smallholdings to **Morne Anglais** (3,683 ft) (2-hour walk from Giraudel). This is the easiest of the high mountains to climb. The trail is fairly easy to follow but someone will need to show you the first part through the smallholdings. Ask in the village or go with a guide.

South of Roseau

In the far south are the villages of **Soufrière** and **Scotts Head**. Both are worth visiting for their stunning setting on the sea with the mountain backdrop and brightly painted fishing boats on the shore. There are plenty of buses to Scotts Head, over the mountain with excellent views all the way to Martinique. Ask around the fishing huts if you are hungry, and you will be directed to various buildings without signs where you can eat chicken pilau for EC$6 and watch dominoes being played. The *Sundowner* restaurant, just across from the fishing area boasts the only visitor lavatories

On the south coast is **Grand Bay**, where there is a large beach (dangerous for swimming), the 10 ft high Belle Croix and the **Geneva Estate**, founded in the 18th century by the Martinican Jesuit, Father Antoine La Valette, and at one time the home of the novelist Jean Rhys. From Grand Bay, it is a two-hour walk over the hill, past Sulphur Spring to Soufrière. The area has a reputation for violence related to the growing of marijuana, see Safety, page 608.

Leeward coast

The Leeward coastal road, north from Roseau, comes first to **Canefield**, passing the turning for the twisting Imperial Road to the centre of the island, and then the small airport. The coast road passes through **Massacre**, reputed to be the settlement where 80 Caribs were killed by British troops in 1674. Among those who died was Indian Warner, Deputy Governor of Dominica, illegitimate son of Sir Thomas Warner (Governor of St Kitts) and half-brother of the commander of the British troops, Colonel Philip Warner. From the church perched above the village there are good views of the coast. The next village is **Mahaut** and just north of here near DCP a newly paved road, called Warner Road, climbs steeply up towards Morne Couroune. It then levels out and joins the main Layou Valley road at the Layou

Valley Plaza, a few kilometres west of the Pont Cassé roundabout. The views are stunning and are best when coming down hill.

North of the Transinsular road are the **Central Forest Reserve** and **Northern Forest Reserve**. In the latter is **Morne Diablotin**. From Dublanc, walk 1½ hours on a minor road and you will see a sign. The trail to the summit is very rough, about 3 hours' steep walking and climbing up and 2½ hours down, not for the faint hearted, take a guide.

The coastal road continues to Portsmouth, the second town. Nearby are the ruins of the 18th-century **Fort Shirley** on the Cabrits, which has a museum in one of the restored buildings (site pass required, US$2 at the gate). It is very run down but there is an excellent plan of how the fort once was. Clearly marked paths lead to the Commander's Quarters, Douglas Battery and other outlying areas. The colonial fortifications, apart from the main buildings are strangled by ficus roots, and cannon, which used to point out to sea, now aim at the forest. The cruise ship jetty (small ships only) has a visitors' centre. Prince Rupert Bay has been much visited: Columbus landed here in 1504, and in 1535 the Spanish Council of the Indies declared the bay a station for its treasure ships. Sir Francis Drake, Prince Rupert and John Hawkins all traded with the Caribs. Construction of Fort Shirley began in 1774. It was abandoned in 1854 and restoration began in 1982.

Portsmouth

From the bridge just south of Portsmouth, boats make regular, trips up the **Indian River** (US$12 per person, 40 minutes), a peaceful trip through a tunnel of vegetation as long as you are not accompanied by boatloads of other tourists. There is a bar open at the final landing place on this lovely river which accommodates large numbers of cruise ship passengers and serves them the very potent spiced rum, aptly named *Dynamite*. You can then walk through fields and forest to the edge of a marsh where migrating birds come in the winter.

Indian River

Negotiate with the boatmen about price and insist they use oars rather than a motor. Competition for passengers is keen

Portsmouth

To Cape Melville
Toucari Bay
Toucari
Savane Paille
Douglas Point
Douglas Bay
Tanetane
Salt River
Manicou River
To Penville
Cabrits National Park
Bell Hall River
Prince Rupert Bluff Point
West Cabrit
East Cabrit
Jetty
Fort Shirley (Ruins)
Lagon River
North River
To Calibishie
Lagon
Portsmouth (Grand Anse)
Jetty
Prince Rupert Bay
Glanvillia
Indian River
Banana Loading Sheds
Jetties
Picard Beach
To Roseau
N
km 1
miles 1

From Portsmouth, a road carries on to the **Cabrits National Park** and the island's north tip at **Cape Melville**. A trail leads off this at Savanne Paille; it is a beautiful hike over the mountain, through a valley with sulphur springs, to Penville on the north coast, where you can pick up the road heading south. Allow several hours.

Another road from Portsmouth heads east, following the Indian River for much of the way, winding up and down to the bays and extensive coconut palm plantations of the northwest coast, Calibishie, Melville Hall Airport and Marigot. There are some beautiful sandy beaches at Hampstead and Larieu. **Calibishie** is a charming fishing village looking out towards Guadeloupe. There are hiking trails to the forest and wide, sandy beaches nearby; local guides are available. Transport to most areas in the north is good, as is accommodation. There are some grocery stores, restaurants, post office, petrol station and a health clinic.

The north

Windward Islands

Transinsular road

Watch for land crabs' holes; orange juveniles come out by day, white adults by night

The shortest route from Roseau to Marigot and Melville Hall is via the Transinsular Road. It climbs steeply with many bends from Canefield. Along this road you will see coconut and cocoa groves, banana plants all along the gorge, together with dasheen, tannia, oranges and grapefruit. At Pont Cassé, the road divides three ways at one of the island's few roundabouts.

Heading west from Pont Cassé the road affords some spectacular views. Layou River has some good spots for bathing, one of which is particularly good. Just over five miles from the roundabout there is a narrow foot path on the right, immediately before a sizeable road bridge. It passes through a banana field to the riverside. On the opposite bank a concrete bath has been built around a hot spring to create an open-air hot tub (Glo Cho) with room for four or five good friends.

Heading north from Pont Cassé, a 20-minute walk from *Spanny's Bar* on the main road leads you to **Penrice Falls**, two small waterfalls. There is great, but cold, swimming in the pool at the second fall. At Bells there is a fascinating and beautiful walk to **Jacko Flats**. Here a group of maroons (escaped slaves) led by Jacko had their encampment in the late 17th and early 18th centuries. Carved into the cliffs of the Layou River gorge, a flight of giant steps rises 300 ft up to a plateau on which the maroons had their camp. Ask at the *Paradise Bar* in Bells for a guide and dress for river walking since much of the trail is in the river itself.

Heading east from Pont Cassé, the path up the Trois Pitons is signed on the right just after the roundabout, 3 hours to the summit. The **Emerald Pool** is a small, but pretty waterfall in a grotto in the forest, 15 minutes by path from the Pont Cassé-Castle Bruce road. Avoid the area on days when cruise ships have docked. There is a reception area, with snack bar, interpretation centre, stalls and toilet facilities. There are no buses from Roseau but you can catch a minibus to Canefield and wait at the junction for a bus going to Castle Bruce.

The Atlantic coast

This coast is much more rugged than the Caribbean, with smaller trees, sandy or pebbly bays, palms and dramatic cliffs. **Castle Bruce** is a lovely bay and there are good views all around. After Castle Bruce the road enters the **Carib Territory**, although there is only a very small sign to indicate this; to appreciate it fully, a guide is essential. **Horseback Ridge** affords views of the sea, mountains, the Concord Valley and Bataka village. At **Crayfish River**, a waterfall tumbles directly into the sea by a beach of large stones.

Traditional methods of making canoes from tree trunks can be seen in the Carib Territory. In May 1997 11 Caribs paddled a 35-ft canoe, carved from a gommier tree, to Guyana, reversing the migratory journey of their ancestors

The Save the Children Fund assisted the Waitikubuli Karifuna Development Committee to construct two traditional buildings near **Salybia**: a large oval *carbet* (the nucleus of the extended Carib family group), and an A-frame *mouina*. The former is a community centre, the latter a library and office of the elected chief. The Carib chief is elected for five years and his main tasks are to organize the distribution of land and the preservation of Carib culture. The dilapidated Church of the Immaculate Conception at Salybia is being restored as a Carib Museum, its design is based on the traditional *mouina* and has a canoe for its altar, murals about Carib history both inside and out. Outside is a cemetery and a three-stone monument to the first three Carib chiefs after colonization: Jolly John, Auguiste and Corriett.

L'Escalier Tête-Chien, at Jenny Point in Sineku is a line of rock climbing out of the sea and up the headland. It is most obvious in the sea and shore, but on the point each rock bears the imprint of a scale, circle or line, like the markings on a snake. It is said that the Caribs used to follow the snake staircase (which was made by the Master Tête-Chien) up to its head in the mountains, thus gaining special powers.

Sea bathing here is very dangerous

In the southeast at La Plaine a fairly easy trail can be followed to the **Sari Sari Falls** (about 150 ft high). At Délices, you can see the **Victoria Falls** from the road. Take an experienced guide if you attempt the steep hike to either of these Falls and avoid in the rainy season. The White River falls in to the Atlantic at **Savane Mahaut**, reached by a steep road from Victoria Laroche down to the sea. There are delightful places to picnic, rest or swim in the river. At the weekend local families picnic and wash their cars here. Be wary of flash floods and do not cross the river after heavy rainfall.

A road has been cut between the village of **Petite Savanne** and the **White River** linking the south and east coasts. It is extremely steep but offers spectacular views of both the Victoria Falls and the steam rising from the Boiling Lake. A new eco-friendly 50-cottage resort and spa has been built close to the White River, to open end-2003, www.junglebaydominica.com

Essentials

Hotels LL-A *Fort Young Hotel*, within the old fort, T4485000, www.fortyounghotel.com Ocean front rooms and suites of an excellent standard and full conference facilities for the business traveller, lots of facilities, service brusque, food adequate, pool, exercise room, jetty, waterfront restaurant, the atmosphere is more relaxed on weekends, special events like concerts and barbecues and a popular Happy Hour every Fri, 1800-1900. **L-AL** *Garraway*, Place Heritage, 1 Bay Front, T4498800, www.garrawayhotel.com 31 rooms and suites, again of a good standard, conference facilities, restaurant, cocktail bar, senior citizen discounts and weekend deals available. **AL-B** *Sutton Place Hotel*, 25 Old St, T4498700, avirtualdominica.com/sutton.htm 8 rooms, beautiful decor, excellent service, self-catering suites available.

    Guesthouses C *Honychurch Apartment*, 5 Cross St, T4483346. Very central, discounts for a week, even nicer to stay at their D'Auchamps Apartments up in the Trafalgar Valley and hire a car, see below. **D-E** *Cherry Lodge*, 20 Kennedy Av, T4482366. Historic and quaint, some rooms with bath, rooms can be noisy and mosquitoes abundant, coils provided but no fans, good value meals available to order. **D-E** *Ma Bass Central Guest House*, 44 Fields Lane, T4482999. 7 rooms, fans, food available. **E** *Vena's Guesthouse*, 48 Cork St, T4483286. 15 rooms, prices higher during carnival, Jean Rhys' birth place, interesting, rather inefficient, rooms small and grim, rooms without bath more spacious and comfortable but noisy, *The World of Food* restaurant is next door.

Outside Roseau, up a steep and windy hill (King's Hill), is **L-C** *Reigate Hall*, T4484031, F4484034. A splendid location but laid back management, recommended for sunset rum punch to watch the Green Flash. 15 rooms and suites, a/c, service in restaurant sloppy and slow, bar, swimming pool, tennis courts, dive packages with Dive Dominica. Further up the Roseau Valley are **A-E** *Chez Ophelia Cottage Apartments*, T4483438, mariem@mail.cwdom.dm Your host is the famous singer Ophelia, Dominica's 'First Lady of Song', close to Trafalgar Falls. **C** *Cocoa Cottage*, T4480412. A neat, clean and homely B&B in the middle of Trafalgar Valley.

L-A *Evergreen*, T4483288, www.avirtualdominica.com/evergreen.htm 16 rooms, with breakfast, a/c, TV, bar, good restaurant overlooking the sea. **AL** *Exotica*, T4488839, www.exotica-cottages.com Nestled under the peaks of Morne Anglais close to Giraudel, ecotourism centre, run by Athie Martin, president of the Dominica Conservation Society, 8 wooden cottages, sympathetic design, good base for hiking, self-catering, with advance the *Sugar Apple Café* will prepare meals. **AL-A** *Castle Comfort Lodge*, T4482188, www.castlecomfortdivelodge.com Very friendly, professional, 15 rooms, excellent local food, good service. A 7-night 10-dive package available includes transfers, 1-night dive, unlimited shore diving, tax and service, US$990. **AL-B** *Anchorage*, on seafront, T4482638, www.anchoragehotel.dm Waterfront restaurant, rooms rather tatty, bar, friendly but slow service, food nothing special although Thu buffet very good and popular with locals, swimming pool and diving facilities, a 7-night, 10-dive package available, squash court. **AL-C** *Reigate Waterfront*, T4483111, F4484034. Under renovation 2003. A friendly, delightful place to stay, family-run, with good restaurant and excellent service, well-known barbecue Wed night, host to weekly shows in the month before carnival and noisy.

LL-A *The Wesleeann Hotel and Suites*, T4490419, F4492473, towers over 8th St in Canefield. Tastefully decorated apartments with kitchen, bathroom, balcony and daily maid service, for daily or longer rental. **AL-C** *The Hummingbird Inn*, Morne Daniel, Roseau, T/F4491042.

Sleeping
Roseau
There are some small, informal hotels, guesthouses and apartment facilities here.

Do verify whether tax (5%) is included in the quoted rate

Apartments are available to rent in & around Roseau, check at the Tourist Office, look in the New Chronicle, Tropical Star or ask a taxi driver

South of Roseau

Castle Comfort

Near Canefield

Windward Islands

Windward Islands

Rooms (small, luggage a problem) or a suite, run by Mrs Finucane who is knowledgeable on Dominica, peaceful, simple, comfortable, good food, slow service, stunning views down the hill over the sea, 5 mins north of Roseau, on bus route. **A** *Crescent Moon Cabins*, T/F4493449, www.avirtualcominica.com/crescentmooncabins/, high above Mahaut but reached from the main Transinsular Rd, about 30 mins from Roseau. Well-furnished wooden cabins in a delightful, secluded setting, double and single bed, run by Americans Ron (former chef) and Jean Viveralli, good home cooking, local style, fresh organic fruit and vegetables from on-site greenhouse and gardens, own roasted coffee, fresh spring water, cold water in cabins but hot shower by main house, breakfast US$8, lunch US$10, can be packed for picnic, dinner US$15, car hire recommended, *Island Car Rentals* will give a discount for guests.

Near Trafalgar Falls **AL-A** *Papillote Wilderness Retreat*, T4482287, www.papillote.dm 10 suites or cottage in beautiful botanical gardens landscaped by owner Anne Jean Baptiste, with hot mineral pool and geese, birdwatching house, food good but slightly limited for long stay; restaurant for non-residents near road, lunch and dinner, food well prepared and nicely presented, closed Sun (avoid days when cruise ship passengers invade, reservations required), arts and crafts boutique, take torch and umbrella, good road from the nearby village of Trafalgar all the way to the falls car park, spectacular setting. On the road to Trafalgar and Papillote, the Honychurch family rents self-contained cottages on their lovely estate, **C** *D'Auchamps*, T4483346, honychurchs@cwdom.dm Guests can enjoy the lush botanical gardens, the Garden Cabin sleeps maximum 3, no hot water, outside shower, the Small Cottage sleeps 4, hot water, fully equipped. **B-C** *Roxy's Mountain Lodge* in Laudat, T/F4484845, bruneyr@cwdom.dm 2,000 ft above sea level, established 1960, good breakfast and hearty supper, friendly owners, 17 basic rooms, good beds, hot showers, also apartment, 4-6 people, Boiling Lake, Boeri Lake, Middleham Falls, Trafalgar Falls and Freshwater Lake, all within walking distance, guides arranged if required, transport into Roseau 0700 except Sun, returning 1615, EC$3.

South coast **AL** *Zandoli Inn*, Roche Cassee near fishing village of Stowe, T4463161, www.zandoli.com Secluded, superb mountain and seaviews to Martinique, 5 rooms with balconies, includes continental breakfast, plunge pool, 6 acres of seaside tropical forest. **B-D** *Herche's Place*, Bay St, Scotts Head, T4487749, herches@cwdom.dm 10 rooms, fans, a/c, TV, Sundowner Café, watersports, diving, fishing arranged.

Leeward coast **AL-A** *Castaways*, Mero, T4496244, F4496246, just north of St Joseph. Convenient with hired car for visiting all parts of the island, on black sand beach, restaurant, beach barbecue on Sun, popular, watch out for beach cricket balls, staff slow but friendly, reasonable rooms all with balcony and seaview but in need of redecoration, ask for fan and mosquito net, good tennis court, sailing sometimes available, dive shop attached, German spoken, dive package available. **AL-A** *Sunset Bay Club*, Batalie Beach in the middle of the west coast, T4466522, www.sunsetbayclub.com. Run by Belgian family, all-inclusive or room only, bungalows, suites, pool, sauna. **B** *Tamarind Tree Hotel & Restaurant*, near Salisbury, T/F4497395, www.tamarindtreedominica.com On cliff between Macoucherie and Salisbury beaches, 8 rooms, wheelchair accessible, fan, fridge, pool, food recommended, Sun brunch all-you-can-eat buffet 1000-1500. **E** *Chez La Doudou Pension*, Salisbury, T4996575. Guesthouse, CP, run by Beatrice (French) and Harald (German), the owners of *East Carib Dive Centre* (see page 611), very nice, good breakfast.

Portsmouth **AL-B** *Picard Beach Cottage Resort*, T4455131, pbh@cwdom.dm An attractive open-sided restaurant and bar, self-catering cottages which, at a pinch, can sleep 4, good sea bathing with coral reef, 7-night, 10-dive, package available. On Picard Beach, **B** *Coconut Beach*, T4455393, F4455693. Beachfront bungalows, apartments, snorkelling, diving, windsurfing, volleyball, excursions, restaurant, marina planned. **C** *Sister Sea Lodge*, Prince Rupert's Bay Beach bar, T/F4455211, sangow@cwdom.dm Fresh fish and 6 apartments set in lovely gardens, spacious, self-contained, insect nets, 2 double beds, bathroom, run by Elka and Harta (German) Sango, yachts can moor in the bay, sandy outside beach bar. **D** *Casa Ropa*, on Bay

St, T4455492, F4455277. Rooms or apartments with bath, single downstairs, friendly, clean. **E** *Douglas Guest House*, Bay St, T4455253. Single, double or triple rooms, ask for fan, clean, next to noisy disco and cinema.

Calibishie LL-L *Pointe Baptiste* estate rents out the Main House, www.avirtualdo minica.com/pointeb.htm Sleeps 8, includes cook and maid, weekly rates available, spectacular view from the airy veranda, cool breezes, house built in 1932, wooden, perfect for children, cot, also B smaller house sleeping 2, self-catering, book locally through the manager Annick Giraud, guinguette@cwdom.dm **L-A** *Eden Estate House* is also available for rent, T4482638, F4485680. 3 bedrooms, in middle of coconut and fruit plantation, only 3 miles from Melville Hall Airport, maid service can be provided. **AL** *Wind Blow Estate*, Calibishie. Apartments, 1 or 2 bedrooms, fans, sun deck, great view of Guadeloupe and Marie Galante, parking, security guard, sisserou parrot nests on the estate. **AL** *Calibishie Lodges*, Main Rd, T4458537, www.calibishie-lodges.com Cottages sleep 4, 100 m from sea, above the village, TV, kitchen, shower or bath, pool, bar and restaurant, internet access, check price and extra charges. In Calibishie, **AL-C** *Veranda View*, T4458900, lawrence@cwdom.dm Run by Mrs Teddy Lawrence, facing beach, beautiful view of Guadeloupe, clean, 3 bright and large rooms, CP, light cooking facilities, hot showers. **A-B** *Sea Cliff Cottages*, 15 mins' walk from Calibishie, T/F4458998 Dec-May, T/F6137563116 Jun-Nov, www.dominica-cottages.com 3 cottages, 1-3 bedrooms, kitchens, veranda, fruit trees in the garden for seasonal use, path to beach, snorkelling good, river good for children to play in, small island within swimming distance. **C** *Windswept Guest House*, T4458982, between Calibishie and airport. Quiet, secluded, clean, close to excellent beach.

North coast

Windward Islands

A-B *Floral Gardens*, Concord Village, at the edge of the Carib Territory, T/F4457636. Comfortable rooms, CP, apartments, 10% discount for stays of 5 days and over, dinner, excellent food but expensive and service very slow, lovely gardens by the Pagua River where you can swim, 15 mins away from beaches of Woodford Hill, electrics basic, ask for a mosquito coil for your room, many minibuses in the morning, easy to get a pick-up, bus to Roseau EC$9, 1 hr, bus to airport and Woodford Hill Beach, lovely walks in the area, either into the Carib territory or around Atkinson further north. Charles Williams and his wife, Margaret, run the **C-E** *Carib Territory Guest House*, Crayfish River, on the main road, T4457256, www.avirtualdomi-nica.com/ctgh.htm She cooks if meals are ordered in advance but there are no restaurants nearby, so you may go hungry, water intermittent, good base, he also does island-wide tours but is better on his own patch. About a mile away, **F** *Olive's Guest House* at Atkinson, T4457521. Slightly set back off the road, bamboo huts, comfortable, friendly, meals extra.

Inland
Camping is not encouraged and, in the national parks, it is forbidden

On weekdays in the capital the lunch hour begins at 1300 and places fill up quickly. Dominicans eat their main meal at lunch. Generally, Dominicans eating out do so in restaurants at lunchtime and in hotels at night. **US$17 and above** At the Fort Young Hotel there are 2 restaurants: *Marquis de Bouille*, at the front of the hotel, serves international and Creole food with themed buffet lunches, barbecue with steel band Mon night, while *The Waterfront* has a charming, wooden-balconied seafront location with a more romantic and elegant style. *La Robe Créole*, 3 Victoria St, T4482896. Creole and European, vegetarian available, good but expensive, service inattentive, open Mon-Sat 1100-1500, 1830-2130. **US$13-17** *Restaurant Paiho*, 10 Church St, T4488999. Good Chinese food, delicious fruit punch, uncrowded, slightly pricey, open Mon-Sat 1100-1500, 1730-2230, Sun 1800-2200. **US$9-13** *Garden Chinese Restaurant*, 80 King George V St, opposite Astaphan's store, T4483389. Behind a slightly run-down exterior is an excellent a/c restaurant with a wide range of well-priced Chinese dishes. *The World of Food*, next to *Vena's Guesthouse*. Local dishes but unexciting, good breakfast about EC$10, lunch and dinners EC$20-30, drink your beer under a huge mango tree which belonged to writer Jean Rhys's family garden. *Taiwanese Delicacies*, between Newtown and Castle Comfort. New Chinese restaurant with a good atmosphere, open daily, good food and friendly hosts, see Nightlife, below for karaoke. **US$5-9** *Ti-Caz (Coco-Rico) Café*, Bayfront. French restaurant, bar, wine store and grocery, excellent range, good service, pleasant environment, sidewalk café. *Guiyave*, 15 Cork St. For midday snacks and juices, patisserie and salad bar, popular, crowded

Eating: Roseau
5% sales tax is added to meal charges

after 1300. *Syme Zees*, 2 locations, guesthouse in Laudat, and a bar/restaurant on King George St. Famous for Thu night jazz, also a good lunchtime spot for generous helpings, fried fish recommended. *Cornerhouse*, 6 King George V St, T4499000. Opposite Old Market, open Mon 0800-1530, Tue-Fri 0800-2200, Sat 1000-2200, breakfast, lunch and dinner, soups, salads, sandwiches, bagels, music, books, magazines, newspapers, internet access, popular pub quiz night Wed 2000. *Continental Inn*, 37 Queen Mary St, Roseau, T4482214/5. Open 0700-2130, Creole cuisine, mountain chicken, seafood, rotis, delivery in Roseau area, credit cards accepted. *Pearl's Cuisine*, 50 King George V St. Good range of inexpensive local food, with nice balcony. Under the same ownership as *La Robe Créole* is the *Mousehole Café*, underneath. Excellent for pies and local pasties. *Mousehole Too*, 10 Kennedy Av, near Whitchurch Centre, T4482896. Has seating, 0800-1500. *Créole Kitchen Ltd*, in Woodstone Shopping Mall on corner of George St and Cork St. Fried or barbecued chicken, snacks, cold drinks, Mon-Thu 0800-2300, Fri-Sat 0800-1200, Sun 1500-2300. *Cottage Restaurant*, Hillsborough St. Friendly, fish, rice, salad and provisions for EC$10. For vegetarian food try *Back-A-Yard*, on Castle St, just up the hill from the Garraway Hotel. Lots of 'snackettes', for example *Hope Café*, 17 Steber St. Good local dishes and snacks, lively, open late; *Celia's Snack*, on Great Marlborough St, EC$1.50 for delicious bread and codfish, good local ice cream, fruit juice. *Erick's Bakery* has a small patisserie on Old St for 'tasty island treats'.

Eating: around the island

Evergreen Hotel, at Castle Comfort, see above. Good reputation, pleasant seafront location, meals from US$13. On Thu night the *Ocean Terrace Restaurant* at the Anchorage has a good value barbecue buffet and reggae band. *Papillote* (see page 618), T4482287. Book before 1600, take swimming costume and towel to bathe in sulphur pool under the stars. *New Stop Café and Bar*, close to Trafalgar Falls. Overlooking river, just down the road from Papillotte, tiny, outdoors, seats 10-15 people, delicious food. Contact the proprietors in the morning (c/o Mayfield Denis) to arrange menu, also good for beer, conversation and reggae. *Reigate Hall Hotel* (see above), book ahead, slow service but ask to eat out on balcony overlooking valley of Roseau, catch the sunset for spectacular view. *George Chicken Shack*, on roadside between Emerald Pool and Pont Cassé. Small bar, cold beer and great fried chicken. *La Flambeau Restaurant* at Picard Beach Cottages, near Portsmouth. Comfortable, has an attractive beachside setting, takeaway food and drinks for the beach, but service criticized. *Purple Turtle*, Lagoon, Portsmouth, T4455296. On beach, open Mon-Fri 1000-2300, Sat-Sun 1000-0200, snacks and full meals, good roti, local and international food, karaoke at weekends. *Mango's Bar & Restaurant*, Bay St, Portsmouth, T4453099. Yellow and white house with tin roof, mural inside of island life, varied menu, open daily 0800-2300, credit cards accepted. The *DomCan's Café* is pleasantly located right on the beach at Calibishie, T4458769. Good service, open 0900-2200, lunch of sandwiches and burgers, dinner fish, chicken, mountain chicken. *Chez Wen*, Scott's Head, T4486668. Overlooking the bay serving shellfish and drinks, popular with divers, good prices. *Marilyn's*, by the Rosalie River in the east, about 1 mile from boxing plant, run by Americans, lovely setting on covered patio with river gushing over large rocks amid lush foliage, limited menu of local and American food.

Local food

Fried chicken, bakes (a fried dough patty filled with tuna, codfish or corned beef) and rotis (pancake-like parcel of curried chicken and veg) are the most popular snacks available in most bakeries. There is plenty of local fruit and vegetables, fish and 'mountain chicken (crapaud, or frog)' in season. Try the seedless golden grapefruit, US$1 for 6 in the market. The term 'provisions' on a menu refers to root vegetables: dasheen, yams, sweet potatoes tannia, pumpkins, etc. Try the sea-moss drink, rather like a vanilla milk shake (with a reputation as an aphrodisiac), also drunk on Grenada, see page 703. *The Shacks*, next to Ross Medical School on the Portsmouth-Roseau road in Portsmouth are food stalls serving cheap and good snack food, hot roti and fried chicken, bakes, pastries, fruit, fresh juices. On Portsmouth's Bay Rd there are several snackettes selling roti and bakes at lunchtime.

Nightlife

There is no place that only tourists go

Friday is *the* night out, with people (locals and tourists alike) moving from *Fort Young*'s Happy Hour across to *La Robe*'s Happy Hour or to *Garraway*'s, into town and *Cornerhouse*, then on to *Cellar's Bar* for karaoke night with a distinct Caribbean flavour. If you've still got energy, its on to

Ashma's Bar or to one of the discos such as *Magic* or *Warehouse* (see below), which never get going until after midnight. However, there are a growing number of places to eat and hang out south of Roseau, in the 2-mile stretch from the city centre to the village of Loubiere. They represent a good cross section of bars, places to eat and nightspots, ranging from down-to-earth to up-market. Heading from Roseau, *Taiwanese Delicacies*, between Newtown and Castle Comfort, start your evening with brazed shrimp or sweet and sour. If its happening, partake of some karaoke. *All One Bar*, in Castle Comfort, a nice casual spot with tables by the sea and a good range of drinks. Great place to watch the sun go down. *Spiders*, Loubiere, is guaranteed to be open when everywhere else has closed, it is a hole in the wall with great Caribbean music, some of the cheapest beers, fried chicken and the famous Spider Pies (they are actually fish and cost EC$1.25. *Palm Grove* is a new, popular nightspot, at Louisville in the Roseau Valley, about 2 miles from Roseau, T4485434. Particularly good around Carnival when it hosts Calypso shows, 'tents', EC$25, major shows EC$45. Open 1000-2300, Mon-Sat, food served.

For lovers of zouk music, look out for live performances by *WCK, Midnight Groovers* or *First Serenade*. Mid-week entertainment at *Anchorage* and *Sutton Place* hotels. Weekends at *Fort Young Hotel*, Fri night happy hour 1800-1900, live music, popular with ex-pats, tourists and locals alike, nightclub open Fri and Sat. *Symes-Zee* on King George V St is the spot to be on Thu night with live jazz and friendly atmosphere. *Cellars Bar*, downstairs at *Sutton Place Hotel*, Old St. Lively after-work bar, big screen TV, karaoke, jazz, a/c. *Warehouse* disco at Canefield on Sat, in converted sugar mill by the airport, gets going after 2400. Recommended. In Portsmouth, *Rivers International Nightclub and Bar*, opposite Ross University. Open Fri-Sun from 2200, a/c, local and international music T4454777. *The Arawak House of Culture*, Hillsborough St in Roseau, next to Government Headquarters, can seat 540 for plays, concerts, dance shows and recitals. Performances are also held at the *Old Mill Cultural Centre* in Canefield. *Carib Cinema*, Old St and Kennedy Av. A/c, 2 bars, 4 shows at weekends, 1 nightly on weekdays, T4481819.

Festivals

Carnival is on the Mon and Tue before *Ash Wed*; it lacks the sponsorship of a carnival like Trinidad's, but it is one of the most spontaneous and friendly. Sensay costume has returned to the streets: layer upon layer of banana or cloth is used for the costume, a scary mask is worn over the face, usually with horns, and large platform clog boots finish the effect. Large quantities of beer are required for anyone who can wear this costume and dance the streets for several hours in the midday sun. An annual *Divefest* is held in *Jul*, with lots of activities, races, underwater treasure hunts, cruises, etc. Funds are being raised for a recompression chamber, contact the Watersports Association, T4482188, dive@cwdom.dm The **Independence Folk Festival** starts in late *Sep* running up to **Independence Day** in *Nov*. Independence celebrations (3/4 Nov) feature local folk dances, competitions, storytelling, music and crafts. In *Oct* Dominica hosts the **World Creole Music Festival**, with Cadence, Zouk, Compas, Bouyou and Soukous. Artists come from other islands such as Haiti, Martinique and Cuba, or further afield from Africa, the UK and Louisiana, as well as from Dominica. A season ticket costs US$46, or US$22 on the gate. On **Creole Day**, the last Fri in *Oct*, the vast majority of girls and women wear the national dress, 'la wobe douillete', to work and school and most shop assistants, bank clerks, etc, speak only Creole to the public.

During Carnival, laws of libel & slander are suspended For information about any festivals contact the Dominica Festivals Commission, 23 Great Marlborough St, Roseau, T4484833, dfc@cwdom.dm

Around the island, villages hold their own festivals: *Isidore* in Grand Bay at Pentecost; *Fête Marin* (St Peter's) in Portsmouth in Jun-Jul, as well as in Soufrière/Scott's Head, Colihaut/Dublanc and Anse de Mai; *St Theresa* in Salisbury in Oct; *St Anne* in Mahaut on 26 Jul; *St Géraud in St Joseph* in Oct and *Feast of La Salette* in Point Michel in Sep.

Shopping

The *Craft Market*, at the Old Market, is a good place to start and get an idea of what is available. At *Tropicrafts*, Queen Mary St, you can see the women making the famous vetiver-grass mats. It takes 4 weeks to complete a 10 ft mat. Note 4% extra charged on VISA. Portsmouth has a sizeable craft shop at the Cruise Ship Berth on the Cabrits but prices are much higher than in Roseau. Other good buys are local Bay Rum (aftershave and body rub), coconut soap, tea, coffee, marmalade, hand cream, shampoo, spices, chocolate and candles. Bello 'Special' or 'Classic' pepper sauce is a good souvenir. The public market is lively and

Straw goods are among the best and cheapest in the Caribbean; they can be bought in the Carib Territory & Roseau

Windward Islands

friendly. Try a jelly coconut. *Paperbacks* at 6 King George V St. Caribbean and other English books and magazines. *Front Line Co-operative Services Ltd*, 78 Queen Mary St, T4488664. Books, CDs, cassettes, stationery, photography, etc. *Muzik Land*, 20 Fields Lane, Roseau, is good for local music. *Dominica Pottery* has a showroom on corner of Bayfront and Kennedy Av with plenty of original pieces made by inmates of the prison. Batiks are made locally and available from *Cotton House Batik*, 8 Kings Lane. Many local crafts available at the *NDFD Small Business Complex*, 9 Great Marlborough St.

If you are in a self-catering cottage anywhere on the island, local farmers may visit with their fresh produce for sale. At Portsmouth there is an excellent market twice a week where you can find fresh fruit, vegetables and spices locally grown. To buy fresh fish listen for the fishermen blowing their conch shells in the street; there is no fish shop in Roseau but fish can be bought at the Fisheries Complex or in the market on Fri and Sat, get there early, usually EC$7 per pound. Fishing villages such as Calibishie (north coast) or Fond St Jean (south coast) are good sources of fresh fish; go down to the bay side around 1630 when the boats come in and get some kingfish or snapper for your evening meal. *Whitchurch Supermarket*, Old St, Roseau, has good range at reasonable prices, open Mon-Thu 0800-1900, Fri-Sat 0800-2000. The largest supermarket is *Brizee's Mart*, 5 mins from Roseau centre, T4482087, Canefield. Open Mon-Thu 0900-2000, Fri-Sat 0900-2100. In Portsmouth is *James Supermarket*, opposite Ross Medical School, good selection of staples and imported foodstuffs, frozen meats, ham, etc, also prepaid phone cards.

Sports **Football** and **cricket** are among the most popular national sports; watch cricket in the beautiful setting of the **Botanical Gardens** or at the dramatic pitch at **Petit Savanne** where 2 sides of the boundary line run along a cliff overlooking the Atlantic. Hitting a 6 will mean the loss of a ball into the ocean. The next best pitch is at **Macoucherie**, close to the rum distillery. **Basketball** and **netball** are also enthusiastically played. There are hard **tennis** courts at the privately owned *Dominica Club* (T4482995), *Reigate Hall* and *Castaways*, rental for minimal fee, bring your own racket. **Cycling** is growing in popularity and the island's roads, although twisty, are good. Mountain bikes can be hired from *Nature Island Dive* at Soufrière, see Transport, below, where there are marked off-road trails. **Hiking** in the mountains is excellent, and hotels and tour companies arrange this type of excursion. **Mountain climbing** can be organized through the Forestry Division, T4482401. Guides are necessary for any forays into the mountains or forests, some areas of which are still uncharted. **Horse riding** can be arranged through Dave Winston at High Ride Stables, who operates from Bellevie Chopin on the road to Grand Bay (T4486296, highridestables@yahoo.com), US$25 per hr. He also offers **ATV** tours through the rainforest.

Tour operators Island tours can be arranged through many of the hotels. The most knowledgeable operators are *Ken's Hinterland Adventure Tours and Taxi Service (Khatts Ltd)*, *Fort Young Hotel*, Roseau, T4484850, khatts@cwdom.dm Ken and Clem recommended, lots of languages spoken. *Lambert Charles*, strong on conservation and hiking, no office but T4483365. *Nature Island Destinations*, T449 6233,helpfullyarranges everything from accommodation to car hire, scuba diving and whalewatching, for all budgets and tastes. Bobby Frederick of *Ras Tours*, T4480412, tailors tours to visitors needs and a half day tour costs US$40; *Alfred Rolle's Unique Tour Services*, Trafalgar Village, T4487198, or through Papillote, Alfred is recommended. *Escape*, T4485240, open Nov-Apr, offers river rafting, river hiking, tubing and other adventure activities, from US$70 per person (minimum US$140), includes equipment, transport, guide, insurance, canyoning and cascading offered. Check beforehand which tours are offered on a daily basis or once or twice a week. You may have to wait for the tour you want or be offered an alternative. German, French, Spanish and English are offered at different agencies. The *Whitchurch Travel Agency*, Old St, Roseau, T4482181, www.whitchurch.com, handles local tours as well as foreign travel and represents American Express Travel Related Services, several airlines and L'Express des Îles. **Guides:** You will need a guide for hiking in the mountains, which you can organize through the tour companies or independently. Guesthouses can be good sources of information and recommendations. **Maps:** The Ordnance Survey, Romsey Rd, Southampton, SO9 49H, UK, T01703-792792, publishes a 1:50,000 colourful map of Dominica, with a 1:10,000 street map insert of Roseau, includes roads, footpaths, contours, forests, reserves and National Parks. This can be bought at the Old Market tourist office in Roseau.

Air From Anguilla, Antigua, Barbados, Fort-de-France, Grenada, Pointe-à-Pitre, Port of Spain, St Kitts, St Lucia, Sint Maarten, St Vincent and Tortola/Beef Island (BVI) *LIAT*, *WINAIR*, and/or *Caribbean Star*; from San Juan, *American Eagle*. **Airport** Dominica has 2 airports, **Melville Hall** (DOM) in the northeast, which handles most planes (including *Liat*), and **Canefield** (DCF) near Roseau, which takes only very small aircraft. Check which your flight will be using. Melville Hall has no currency exchange facilities, so if you are arriving from Europe it is best to have US dollars to hand. Melville Hall is 36 miles from Roseau; shuttle taxis cost US$18 per person, whichever route the driver takes. From Melville Hall to Portsmouth by taxi is EC$30. These rates are per seat; find someone to share with, or it will be assumed you want the vehicle to yourself, which is much more expensive. Canefield is only a 10 mins drive from Roseau; taxi fare to town is US$8 per person for up to 4 passengers. Minibus (public transport) fare from Canefield to Roseau is EC$2. (You must flag one down on the highway passing the airport, frequent service weekdays, very few on Sun.)

Transport *Variable winds and short landing strips mean that planes do not land before 0600 or after 1800 in the dark*

Sea Ferries operate between Dominica and the French islands and on to St Lucia. Roseau to **Fort-de-France** Mon, Wed, Sat 1015, Fri 1415 and Sun 1615, 2½ hrs, US$102 return, to **Pointe-à-Pitre** Mon 1600, Wed, Fri 1700, Sat 1100, Sun 1730, 1 ¾ hrs, US$89 return, to **Castries** Fri 1415, Sun 1615, around 3-3 ¾ hrs, US$116 return. Day trips are only possible to Fort-de-France, Mon and Wed, all other routes require an overnight stay. Check timetables before planning a trip. The **L'Express desÎles** agency office is upstairs in the Whitchurch Centre, T4482181, www.express-des-iles.com.

Port tax on departure from Roseau is EC$7

Local Bicycle: Mountain bike rental: *Nature Island Dive*, T4498181, US$11 per hr, US$21 half day, US$32 per day. Biking excursions also arranged, US$84 per person with guide. Roads are good for cycling, traffic is generally light with the exception of the stretch from Roseau to Layou. Between Canefield and Pont Casse it is very steep, twisty and challenging.

Bus Minibuses run from point to point. Those from Roseau to the northwest and northeast leave from between the east and west bridges near the modern market; to **Trafalgar** and **Laudat** from Valley Rd, near the Police Headquarters; for the south and **Petite Savane** from Old Market Plaza. They are difficult to get on early morning unless you can get on a 0630 bus out to the villages to pick up schoolchildren. Many buses pass the hotels south of Roseau. Fares are fixed by the Government. Roseau to **Salisbury** is EC$4, to **Portsmouth** EC$8, to **Woodford Hill** EC$9.95, to **Marigot** EC$9.50, to **Castle Bruce** EC$7.50, **Canefield** EC$2, **Laudat** EC$3.50, **Trafalgar** EC$2.75, **Soufrière/ScottsHead** EC$4.

Car You must purchase a local driving permit, valid for 1 month, for US$11, for which a valid international or home driving licence is required. The permit may be bought from the police at airports, rental agencies, or at the Traffic Dept, High St, Roseau or Bay St, Portsmouth (Mon to Fri). **Car hire** Rates are about US$60 per day for a car, including CDW and 5% tax, and US$70 for a jeep; unlimited mileage for hiring for three days or more. A car rental phone can be found at the airport and several of the companies will pick you up from there and help to arrange the licence. *Island Car Rentals*, Goodwill Rd, Roseau, T448-2886/3425, F4480737. Offers packages with choice of accommodation at 23 hotels island-wide, for example 7 nights US$499 per person, 2 nights US$245, free delivery and pick up anywhere, 24-hr emergency service. *Garraway Rent-a-Car*, 17 Old St, Roseau, T4482891, a/c car US$50 per day; *Best Deal*, T4499204, www.avirtualdominica.com/bestdeal Popular and reliable; *Anselm's*, 3 Great Marlborough St, T4482730. *Budget*, Canefield Industrial Estate, opposite airport, T4492080, recommended as cheaper, more reliable and informative than some other companies, courteous and efficient, cars in good condition. Also recommended for service is *Courtesy Car Rental*, 10 Winston Lane, Goodwill, Roseau, T4487763, www.avirtualdominica.com/courtesycarrental Cars from US$39 per day, and jeeps up to US$66 per day, cheaper for longer, plus tax and CDW, free pick up and drop off from Canefield, ferry and hotels within 5 miles of office, but not from Melville Hall, which incurs extra charges. *Wide Range Car Rentals*, 79 Bath Rd, T4483181. Rents out old Lada cars for US$30 per day, not recommended for smaller roads, also Suzuki jeeps, US$60 per day including 80 miles and CDW free; *Valley*, T4483233,

Driving is on the left. The steering wheel may be on either side. The speed limit is 10 mph near schools, 20 mph in Roseau and villages. No limit elsewhere

Windward Islands

www.valleycarrentals.com On Goodwill Rd, next to *Dominican Banana Marketing Corporation*, or in Portsmouth, T4455252, free delivery to Canefield and within 5 miles of Roseau or Portsmouth offices, cars in need of maintenance but in the cheaper category; also on Goodwill Rd, *S T L*, US$387 per 10 days including EC$20 licence and insurance, T4482340, free deliveries as for *Valley*, but only in Roseau area. It is extremely difficult to hire a vehicle between Christmas and New Year without prior reservation.

Taxis and minivans have HA or H on the licence plate

Taxi A sightseeing tour by taxi will cost US$18 per hr per car (4 people), but it is wise to use experienced local tour operators for sightseeing, particularly if hiking is involved. Fares on set routes are fixed by the Government. Ask at your hotel for a taxi and if you want one after 1800 you should arrange it in advance. In Roseau, *Mally's Tour & Taxi Service*, 64 Cork St, T448-3360/3114, F4483689 (if planning a day trip out of town on public transport, you can sometimes arrange to be picked up and returned to Roseau by their airport taxi service), *Eddie*, 8 Hillsborough St, T4486003, and others.

Directory **Airline offices** *LIAT*, King George V St, Roseau, T4482421/2, Canefield Airport T4491421, Melville Hall T4457242. *American Eagle*, T4457204. **Banks** *Royal Bank of Canada*, Bay St, Roseau, T4482771. *FirstCaribbean International Bank Plc*, 2 Old St, T4482571 (branch in Portsmouth, T4455271). *National Commercial Bank of Dominica*, 64 Hillsborough St, T4484401. Opens lunchtime, branch at Portsmouth, T4455430, and at Canefield near the airport. *Banque Française Commerciale*, Queen Mary St, T4484040. *Scotia Bank*, 28 Hillsborough St, T4485800. Visa and Mastercard accepted with cash advances from all banks. **Communications** Post: Hillsborough St and Bay St, Roseau, 0800-1600 Mon-Fri. A mural depicts the development of the postal service in Dominica. It has a philately counter and list of other stamp sellers around the island. A postcard to the USA or Europe costs EC$0.55, letters EC$0.90. Parcels go airmail only. Post your mail at the main post office if possible, post boxes around the country are not all in operation and there is no indication of which ones are out of service. *DHL* is in the Whitchurch Centre, represented by Whitchurch Travel Agency, T4482181, F4485787. **Telephone**: telephone and fax services at *Cable & Wireless (Dominica)*, Mercury House, Hanover St, Roseau. Open 0700-2000, Mon-Sat. Phone cards are available for EC$10, 20 and 40. *Cable & Wireless* has cellular service, credit card calling and a cybercafé on Kennedy Av, Roseau, T4481000, www.cwdom.dm *Marpin Telecommunications*, Bay St, Roseau, is much cheaper for international calls and email. *Cornerhouse*, 6 King George St, T4499000. 3 computers for internet access, cornerhoused@hotmail.com, with food. **Embassies and consulates** Belgium, T4482168. France, T4482033. Netherlands, T4483841. Spain, T4482063. Sweden, T4482181. UK, T4481000. **Medical services** Hillborough St Clinic is quite large with pharmacy attached. Princess Margaret Hospital, T4482231, has a casualty department , good and efficient, but note that you have to pay in advance for everything (for example EC$80 for consultation, EC$160 for X-ray). Outside Roseau there are also hospitals in **Grand Bay**, T4463706; **Marigot**, T4457091 and **Portsmouth**, T4455237.

Background

History The Caribs, who supplanted the Arawaks on Dominica, called the island Waitikubuli, ('tall is her body'). Columbus sighted it on 3 November 1493, a Sunday (hence the current name), but the Spanish took no interest in the island. It was fought over by the French, British and Caribs. In 1660, the two European powers agreed to leave Dominica to the Caribs, but the arrangement lasted very few years; in 1686, the island was declared neutral, again with little success. As France and England renewed hostilities, the Caribs were divided between the opposed forces and suffered the heaviest losses in consequence. In 1763, Dominica was ceded to Britain, and in 1805, possession was finally settled. Nevertheless, its position between the French colonies of Guadeloupe and Martinique, and the strong French presence over the years, ensured that despite English institutions and language the French influence was never eliminated.

During the 19th century, Dominica was largely neglected and underdevelopment provoked social unrest. Henry Hesketh Bell, the colonial administrator from 1899 to 1905, made great improvements to infrastructure and the economy, but by the late 1930s the British Government's Moyne Commission discovered a return to a high level of poverty on the island. Assistance to the island was increased with some emphasis put on road building to open up the interior. This, together with agricultural expansion, house building and use of the abundant hydro resources for power, contributed to development in the 1950s and 1960s.

In 1939, Dominica was transferred from the Leeward to the Windward Islands Federation; it gained separate status and a new constitution in 1960, and full internal autonomy in 1967. The Commonwealth of Dominica became an independent republic within the Commonwealth in 1978. The Dominica Labour Party dominated island politics after 1961, ushering in all the constitutional changes. Following independence, however, internal divisions and public dissatisfaction with the administration led to its defeat by the Dominica Freedom Party in the 1980 elections. The DFP Prime Minister, Miss (now Dame) Mary Eugenia Charles, adopted a pro-business, pro-United States line to lessen the island's dependence on limited crops and markets. She was re-elected in 1985 and again in 1990, having survived an earlier attempted invasion by supporters of former DLP premier, Patrick John.

In 1995 Dame Eugenia retired at the age of 76, having led her party since 1968. The general elections won by the United Workers Party (UWP) and Mr Edison James was sworn in as Prime Minister. The most recent general elections in January 2000 gave the Dominica Labour Party (DLP) 42.9%, the UWP 43.4% and the DFP 13.6% of the vote. The DLP and DFP formed a coalition and on 3 February Mr Rosie Douglas was sworn in as Prime Minister. However, the country was stunned by his death, aged 58, in 2000. He was replaced by his deputy, Pierre Charles.

For a history of the island, see The Dominica Story, by Lennox Honychurch, ISBN 0-333-62776-8

Geography

Dominica is one of the largest and most mountainous of the anglophone Windward Islands. The highest peak, Morne Diablotin, rises to 4,747 ft and is often shrouded in mist. It is known as the Nature Island of the Caribbean with parks and reserves protecting vast areas of forest that cover most of the interior. In addition, the frequent rainfall and many rivers have led to some very dramatic seascapes with beautiful hard and soft coral. It is 29 miles long and 16 miles wide, with an area of 290 sq miles.

People

Materially, it is one of the poorest islands in the Caribbean. There are many small farmers, the island's mountainous terrain discourages the creation of large estates. In Dominica, over 2,000 descendants of the original inhabitants of the Caribbean, the once warlike Caribs, live in the Carib Territory, a 3,700-acre 'reservation' established in 1903 in the northeast. There are no surviving speakers of the Carib language on the island. The total population is otherwise almost entirely of African descent, of whom about 29% live in the parish of St George, around Roseau. Other parishes are more sparsely populated. The parish of St John, in which Portsmouth (the second largest town) is situated contains only about 5,000 people, or 7% of the population.

Like St Lucia, Dominica was once a French possession and although English is the official tongue, most of the inhabitants also speak Creole French (French-based patois). In the Marigot/Wesley area a type of English called *kokoy* is used; the original settlers of the area, freed slaves, came from Antigua and are mostly Methodists. Catholicism predominates, though there are some Protestant denominations and an increasing number of fundamentalist sects, imported from the USA.

Government

Dominica is a fully independent member of the British Commonwealth. The single chamber House of Assembly has 31 members: 21 elected by the constituencies, nine Senators appointed by the President on the advice of the Prime Minister and Leader of the Opposition, and the Attorney-General. The Prime Minister and Leader of the Opposition also nominate the President, who holds office for five years.

Economy

Owing to the difficulty of the terrain, only about a quarter of the island is cultivated. Nevertheless, it is self-sufficient in fruit and vegetables and agriculture contributes about 20% to gross domestic product. The main products are bananas (the principal export), coconuts (most of which are used in soap and cooking oil production), grapefruit, limes and other citrus fruits. The opening up of the European market in 1992 affected Dominica's banana industry. Together with the other Windward Islands producers it has to compete with the large exporters from the US dollar areas, mainly in Latin America. Other crops are under development; coffee, cocoa, mango, citrus and root crops such as dasheen, to diversify away from bananas.

Manufacturing industry is small but takes advantage of locally generated hydroelectricity. *Dominica Coconut Products (DCP)* is Dominica's largest business. Labour intensive electronic assembly plants, data processing and clothing manufacturing are being encouraged for

Windward Islands

their foreign exchange earnings potential. Tourism is being promoted with the emphasis officially on nature tourism. Total stayover visitor arrivals are around 74,000 a year. The aim is for the development of sustainable long-term tourism projects.

In 1997 the first offshore banks were registered in a bid to increase fee income from abroad. Legislation exists for international shipping registration, offshore trust companies and exempt insurance companies. Internet gambling companies have been granted operating licences. International Business Companies (IBC) can be formed over the internet. The Government also sells passports to investors. The first economic citizens came from Taiwan in 1992, but then there was a surge of interest from Eastern Europe, particularly Russia, which caused concern about money laundering and smuggling. Following the threat of being put on the OECD Financial Action Task Force blacklist, Dominica cleaned up its offshore sector. Few offshore banks exist now.

Culture

The World Creole Music Festival in October is a great insight into regional music trends, whether it's Cadence, Soukous, Compas, Zouk or Bouyou

Popular culture reflects the mixture of native and immigrant peoples. While most places on Dominica have a Carib, a French or an English name, the indigenous Carib traditions and way of life have been localized in the northeast, giving way to a dominant amalgam of Creole (French and African) tradition. Dominicans are proud of their local language, which is increasingly being used in print. A dictionary was published in 1991 by the *Konmité pou Etid Kwéyol* (Committee for Creole Studies). You can get hold of this at the Cultural Division, 30 Queen Mary Street on the corner of King George V Street in Roseau. There has recently been a great increase in the awareness of the arts and crafts. Wander the side streets of Roseau to find small shops and galleries. *Gallery Number 4*, at 4 Hanover Street near the Old Market, is home to a number of artists, including Ellingsworth Moses and Earle Etienne.

There is a thriving music scene, helped by the establishment recently of the WICE recording studio in Dominica. Popular local bands include *WCK, First Serenade* and *Midnight Groovers*, who you can often catch at discos and nightclubs. *Midnight Groovers* is led by Phillip 'Chubby' Mark, known as the 'King of Cadence-Lypso'. Anthony Gussie leads his band *Black Affairs Plus*, and sings in French, English, Creole and Kokoy.

Literature

The best known of Dominica's writers are the novelists Jean Rhys and Phyllis Shand Allfrey. Rhys (1894-1979), who spent much of her life in Europe, wrote mainly about that continent; only flashback scenes in *Voyage in the Dark* (1934), her superb last novel, *Wide Sargasso Sea* (1966), which was made into a film in 1991, her uncompleted autobiography, *Smile Please* and resonances in some of her short stories draw on her West Indian experiences. Allfrey published only one novel, *The Orchid House* (1953); *In the Cabinet* was left unfinished at her death in 1986. Allfrey was one of the founder members of the Dominica Labour Party, became a cabinet minister in the short-lived West Indian Federation, and was later editor of the *Dominica Herald* and *Dominica Star* newspapers. *The Orchid House* was filmed by Channel 4 (UK) in 1990 for international transmission as a four-part series.

St Lucia

IDD code: 758
Colour map 4, grid B5

Very popular as both a family holiday destination and a romantic paradise for honeymooners, St Lucia (pronounced 'Loosha') offers something for everyone. Its beaches are golden or black sand, some with the spectacular setting of the Pitons as a backdrop, and many are favoured by turtles as a nesting site. Offshore there is good diving and snorkelling, with a marine park along part of the west coast. Rodney Bay is one of the best marinas in the West Indies and windsurfing and other watersports are available. The mountainous interior is outstandingly beautiful and there are several forest reserves to protect the St Lucian parrot and other wildlife. Sightseeing opportunities include sulphur springs, colonial fortifications and plantation tours. St Lucia has a rich cultural heritage, having alternated between the French and English colonial powers, both of whom used African slaves, and has produced some of the finest writers and artists in the region. The island has the distinction of having produced two Nobel prize winners, the highest per capita number of Nobel Laureates ever, anywhere.

★

Things to do in St Lucia

- Take a walk on the wild side and explore the **Atlantic beaches** where the **leatherback turtles** lay their eggs.
- Put on your hiking boots, explore the rainforest trails and see if you can spot the St Lucia parrot.
- Treat yourself to a meal at the **Ladera Resort** overlooking the majestic Pitons.
- Snorkel or shore dive at the marine park at **Anse Chastenet**.
- The **Jazz Festival** gets better by the year, with great concerts and fringe events.

Ins and outs

St Lucia is well served with scheduled and charter flights from Europe and North America and you can often pick up quite cheap deals on package holidays. Connections with other islands are good and it is easy to arrange a multi-centre trip. Some flights come via Antigua, and some via Barbados. You can also get to St Lucia by sea from the French Antilles.

Getting there
See Transport, page 651, for more details

Bus is the cheapest means of getting around St Lucia. The service has been described as tiresome by some, but as reliable by others. St Lucia's buses are usually privately owned minibuses and have no fixed timetable. The north is better served than the south and buses around Castries and Gros Islet run until 2200, or later for the Fri night Jump-up at Gros Islet. There are several **car hire** companies on the island, some of which are open to negotiation, but it is cheaper and more reliable to hire in advance. Castries roads are very congested and there are more one-way streets than ever. However, it is possible to get on to the new Millennium highway which comes out in Cul de Sac without going into the heart of Castries. If you're **cycling**, the best way to get round the island is anti-clockwise, thus ensuring long but gradual uphills and steep, fast downhills.

Getting around
Driving is on the left

The dry season is roughly from Jan-May but with showers to keep things green. The rainy season starts in Jun lasting almost to the end of the year. The northeast trade winds are a cooling influence. Rainfall varies (according to altitude) in different parts of the island from 60 to 138 in. Tropical storms in Sep-Nov can cause flooding and mudslides.

Climate
The mean annual temperature is about 26°C

St Lucia Tourist Board, Sure Line Building, on main Castries-Gros Islet highway just north of the Vigie roundabout, Castries, St Lucia, T4524094, F4531121, www.stlucia.org Information centres at the *Pointe Seraphine Duty-Free Complex*; Jeremie St, opposite the Fire Dept; George F Charles Airport (most helpful but closed for lunch 1300-1500), T4522596; Hewanorra Airport (very helpful, particularly with hotel reservations, only open when flights are due or leave), T4546644 and Soufrière (very helpful, local phone calls free), T4597419. *The Tropical Traveller* is distributed free to hotels, shops, restaurants, etc every month and contains some extremely useful information, www.tropicaltravellers.com *The St Lucia Hotel and Tourism Association* publishes a tourist guide, *Visions of St Lucia*, T4525978, www.stluciatravel.com.lc, also of a high standard and widely available.

Tourist information

   Maps of the island may be obtained from the Land Survey in the last government building. At 1:50,000 they are the best but not 100% accurate. *Ordnance Survey*, Romsey Rd, Southampton, UK (T01703-792792), produce a map of St Lucia in their World Maps series which includes tourist information such as hotels, beaches, climbing and climate. The Tourist Board map is free.

Flora and fauna

The fauna and flora of St Lucia are very similar to that of Dominica, the Windwards chain of islands having been colonized by plants and animals originally from South and Central America, with some endemic species such as sisserou and jacquot.

▶ ## Touching down

See also Directory, page 653

Boat information (own flag) Rodney Bay (Customs open 0800-1800 but overtime charges from 1600), Marigot, Castries, Soufrière (clear in at police station) and Vieux Fort are ports of entry. Pratique EC$10 up to 100 tons. Clearance EC$5 for under 40 ft, EC$15 for over 40 ft. Navigational aids EC$15. Charter boats pay additional fees. Anchorages at Rodney Bay, Castries, Marigot Bay (managed by Moorings), Soufrière (see page 632) and Vieux Fort. Marinas at Rodney Bay, Marigot and Castries Yacht Centre.

Business hours Banks: Mon-Thu 0800-1500, Fri 0800-1700, in Rodney Bay banks open on Sat until 1200; **Government offices**: Mon-Fri 0830-1230, 1330-1600; **Shops**: Mon-Fri 0800-1230, 1330-1700, Sat 0800-1230), super- markets stay open later;

Clothing Lightweight clothing all year; a summer sweater for cooler evenings, a light mac and umbrella for the wet season. Short shorts and swimming costumes are not worn in town.

Currency East Caribbean dollar, EC$. EC$2.67=US$1. Banks offer better rates than hotels.

Departure tax At both airports there is a departure tax of EC$54, US$22, for anyone over 12, except for St Lucian nationals going anywhere and Caricom nationals travelling within Caricom, for whom it is EC$35, US$13. By ferry, departure tax is EC$25.

Documents Visitors must carry valid passports except citizens of the USA and Canada, who may enter with adequate proof of identity, as long as they do not stay longer than six months. Citizens of the Organization of Eastern Caribbean States (OECS) may enter with only a driving licence or identity card.

Visas are not required by nationals of all Commonwealth countries, all EC countries except Eire and Portugal, all Scandinavian countries, Switzerland, Liechtenstein, Turkey, Tunisia, Uruguay and Venezuela. Anyone else needs a visa, check requirements, etc, at an embassy or high commission. Without exception, visitors need a **return ticket**. You also need an onward **address**. **On arrival** you will be given a 42-day stamp in your passport. The immigration office at the central police station in Castries is bureaucratic about extensions; they cost EC$40 per period and it is worth getting one up to the date of your return ticket.

Emergency numbers T911.

Media Newspapers The Voice comes out Tue, Thu, Sat, The Mirror on Fri, One Caribbean on Sat, The Crusader on Sat and The Star on Wed and Sat.

Radio The commercial radio station, Radio Caribbean International (RCI), broadcasts daily in Kweyol and English, and the government-owned station, Radio St Lucia (RSL), broadcasts in Kweyol and English. It has some fine programmes such as Sports Zone

Rainforest would have covered most of the island prior to European colonization but the most dramatic loss has been in the last 20 years. Much of the remaining forest is protected, mainly for water supply, but also specifically for wildlife in places. To date, more than 1,500 different species of flowering plants have been documented, including imported exotica like the hibiscus and flamboyant, with nine endemic

and if you want to hear the concerns of St Lucians listen to Constitution Park *at 1400* (only the Thu broadcast is in Kweyol). RCI and RSL have 2 FM and an AM station each. Other stations are Radio 100 (Helen FM); the Wave (formerly GEM) has 2 FM, and broadcasts rhythm and soul.

Television Local stations: Government station NTV on Channel 3, HTS on Channel 4 and DBS on Channel 10. HTS has an occasional programme in Kweyol and speeches by government officials. There is much cable TV.

Official time Atlantic Standard Time, four hours behind GMT, one ahead of EST. In 'summer time', five hours behind GMT, on a par with EST.

Public holidays New Year's Day (1 and 2 Jan), Independence Day on 22 Feb, Good Fri, Easter Mon, Labour Day on 1 May, Whit Mon, Corpus Christi, Carnival, Emancipation Day (1 Aug), Thanksgiving Day (1st Mon in Oct), National Day on 13 Dec, Christmas Day and Boxing Day.

Safety When visiting the waterfalls and sulphur springs on Soufrière be prepared to say no firmly, 'guides' are sometimes persistent and bothersome. Visiting with a hired car (H reg) can be a hassle. The signs to Sulphur Springs are sometimes removed so you have to ask the way and are expected to give a tip. Unemployment and poverty have increased with the world economic downturn. Harassment and hostility towards tourists, drug abuse and crime is a problem, but not of a violent nature. People using organized tours generally have no problem. Be careful taking photographs, although everybody seems to be accustomed to cameras in the market. The use and sale of narcotics is illegal and penalties are severe. Most readily available is marijuana, which is frequently offered to tourists, but hard drugs can also be a problem. Never sleep at night on the beach; you will lose your belongings. Avoid going alone off the beaten track, do not wear expensive jewellery when shopping and stay in well-populated parts of the beach.

Tourist offices overseas France ANI, 53 rue François Ler, 7th floor, Paris 75008, T47-203966, F47-230695. **UK** 421a Finchley Rd, London NW3 6HJ, T020-74313675, stlucia@axissm.com **USA** 9th Floor, 800 2nd Av, New York, NY 10017, T800-4563984, stluciatourism@aol.com **Canada** 8 King St East, Suite 700, Toronto, Ontario M5 1B5, T416-3624242, sltbcanada@aol.com

Voltage 220 v, 50 cycles. A few hotels are 110 v, 60 cycles. Most sockets take three-pin square plugs (UK standard), but some take two-pin round plugs or flat US plugs. Adaptors generally available in hotels.

Weights and measures Imperial, though metric measurements are being introduced.

---

species. There are several endemic reptile species including St Lucia tree lizard, pygmy gecko, Maria Islands ground lizard and Maria Islands grass snake. The only snake which is dangerous is the fer de lance which is restricted to dry scrub woodland on the east coast near Grande Anse and Louvet and also near Anse La Raye and Canaries in the west. The forest dwelling agouti is rarely seen, but the manicou is present throughout the island, and is frequently seen on the road, a victim of the night time traffic. The mongoose, first introduced into Jamaica in 1872 to control the rats in the cane fields, is also present. Several species of bats have been recorded.

The national bird is the colourful St Lucian parrot (*Amazona versicolor*), seen in the dense rainforest around Quillesse and Barre de l'Isle. Other endemic birds are the St Lucia oriole (endangered), Semper's warbler (believed extinct) and the St Lucia black finch (endangered). In the north of the island birdwatching is good at Bois d'Orange swamp, Piton Flor Reserve and Grand Anse; in the east at Edmond Forest Reserve and in the south Eau Piquant Pond, also called Boriel's Pond.

The isolated east coast beaches are rarely visited and have exceptional wildlife. Leatherbacks and other **turtles** nest at Grand Anse and Anse Louvet. Turtle watching is organized during March to July when green, hawksbill and leatherback turtles come ashore on Grand Anse to lay eggs (see box). This area is also the main stronghold of the white-breasted thrasher and St Lucia wren; there are also iguanas (although you will be lucky to see one) and unfortunately the fer de lance snake, although attacks are rare.

The bite is not fatal but requires hospitalization. Avoid walking through the bush, especially at night, and wear shoes or boots and long trousers.

In the south, Cap Moule à Chique has spectacular views and good bird populations. The **Maria Islands**, just offshore, are home to two endemic reptiles, a colourful lizard and small, rare, harmless snake, the Kouwes snake (see page 55). The lizard,

St Lucia

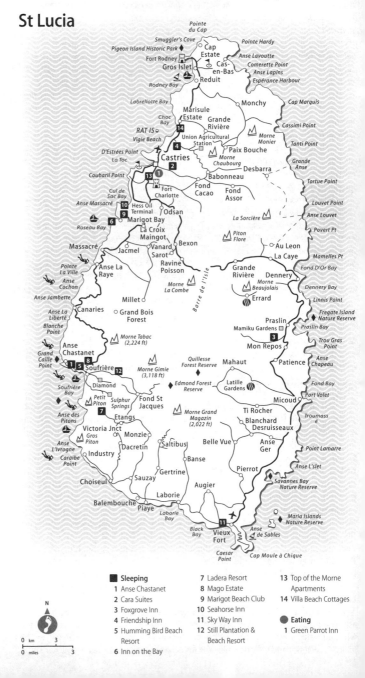

Sleeping	7 Ladera Resort	13 Top of the Morne
1 Anse Chastanet	8 Mago Estate	Apartments
2 Cara Suites	9 Marigot Beach Club	14 Villa Beach Cottages
3 Foxgrove Inn	10 Seahorse Inn	
4 Friendship Inn	11 Sky Way Inn	● **Eating**
5 Humming Bird Beach	12 Still Plantation &	1 Green Parrot Inn
Resort	Beach Resort	
6 Inn on the Bay		

◀

Windward Islands

Turtles at Grand Anse

A 1,000-pound turtle slips from the ocean waves and pauses on the edge of the surf. All is quiet. In the light of the moon, she hauls her heavy body further up the beach. A cluster of people stand motionless and nearly breathless, fearful that the giant sea turtle will sense them and return to the ocean without laying her eggs. The leatherback turtle (Demochelys coriacea) roams the open oceans, feeding on a diet of giant jellyfish. Only a mature female comes ashore and then only to make a nest and lay 60-120 eggs, perhaps several times in one season but only every two to three years.

All sea turtles are endangered. Sand mining, construction close to the water, human and other animal and bird predators, destroy habitats. Grand Anse beach in St Lucia is one of

the most important beaches in the Caribbean for the nesting leatherbacks. From honeymooners to retirees, tourists and St Lucians all hope for a memorable experience counting the leathery eggs as they drop when the sea turtle comes ashore, oblivious to all. Visits to Grand Anse to see the turtles can only be done in organized groups in March-July. Contact Heritage Tours, T4516058, heritagetours@candw.lc The Desbarras community conducts tours with 14 trained guides available. Hotel transfers and evening meal are part of the package: set off 1600, return around 0700, take food, drink, torch, insect repellent, good walking shoes, warm clothing, tents supplied, be prepared for wind, rain or perfect nights, children welcome.

Cnemidophorus vanzoi, is known as **zandoli te** in Creole. The males, about 18 cm long, sport the colours of the national flag. The National Trust (T4525005, natrust@candw.lc) runs day trips with a licensed guide. All participants must be capable swimmers. Interpretive facilities are on the mainland at Anse de Sables, where you can arrange boat transport. Unauthorized access is not allowed. Good beach, excellent snorkelling. From 15 May to 31 July public access is not permitted while the birds are nesting in their hundreds on the cliffs and on the ground. However, you can visit the **Fregate Islands Nature Reserve**, handed over to the National Trust by the Government in 1989. Frigate birds nest here and the dry forest also harbours the trembler, the St Lucian oriole and the ramier. The reserve includes a section of mangrove and is the natural habitat of the boa constrictor (tête chien). **Praslin Island** is one of only two islands where the St Lucian whiptail lives. They used to live only on Maria Major Island until being successfully introduced here to prevent annihilation by hurricanes or any other natural disaster. ■ *Entrance to Fregate Islands Nature Reserve US$5 (no tour guide), children 5-12 US$0.75, residents US$1.85. Eastern Nature Trail min 4 people US$12 per person, tour guide US$16. With transport, guide and lunch US$45, including boat ride to Praslin Island US$55. The same package for only 2 is US$60 and US$65. For the Maria Islands, US$35 for one person, US$30 for 2 and a group rate (min 8 people) is US$25 per person. The package of transport, tour, lunch for min 4 people is US$75 per person. Tours can also be arranged with Peter Ernest, of Eastern Tours, T4553099, a former area manager for the Trust.*

In the north of the island **Union** is the site of the **Forestry Department** headquarters, where there is a nature trail, open to the public, a medicinal garden and a small, well-run zoo. The Forestry Department organizes hiking across the island through rainforest and mature mahogany, Caribbean pine and blue mahoe plantations which will give you the best chance of seeing the St Lucia parrot, as well as other rainforest birds: thrashers, vireos, hummingbirds, flycatchers, etc. Contact Adams Toussaint, T4502231 ext 306 or 4502078, who is in charge of all Forestry Department tours. Donald Anthony, a senior Forestry Officer, is also available as a private guide for hikers and bird watchers, contact him at Forestry or T4521799. The **transinsular rainforest walk** from Mahaut to Soufrière via Fond St Jacques (about 2½ hrs Mahaut to Fond St Jacques) is good for birdwatching. You need a permit from the Forestry Department, US$10 (US$5 for children). Tours are franchised to tour operators and a guide is certainly useful but organized tours are often noisy and

Hiking
Wear good shoes and expect to get wet and muddy. Birdwatchers are advised to get a permit and organize a private trip in a small party

scare the parrots higher into the mountains. Get your own permit from the Forestry Department if you feel confident about finding your own way. There is a good chance of seeing the St Lucian parrot on the **Barre de l'Isle rainforest walk**, for which a permit is also needed. The 10-mile trail from Barre de l'Isle to Quillesse includes the climb all the way up to **Mount La Combe** (about two hours from the road). There is now an eco-lodge at the Quillesse end, where hikers can stay overnight (extra fee for this) or camp in a tent. Recommended only for the physically fit and experienced hikers. In the **Edmond Forest Reserve** is the **Enbas Saut Falls trail** (below the Falls), moderate to strenuous, at the foot of Mount Gimie, with a combination of rainforest, cloud forest and elfin woodlands. **La Sorcière** and **Piton Flore** are densely forested mountains in the north with excellent rainforest vegetation. Piton Flore can be walked up in 40 minutes although it is a strenuous climb and you will need to ask how to get to the top, from where there are spectacular views. It is the last recorded location of Semper's warbler.

In 1997 the Tourist Board announced the development of a series of nature trails as part of a nature/heritage tourism programme. There are gentle hikes and strenuous climbs, including a 2½-mile **Morne Tabac** climb, a ridge hike beginning at Malmaison; the **Anse Galet Nature Walk** and the 8-mile **Morne Gimie Climb** over four mountain peaks. New nature centres and national parks are being developed. One new trail is the **Millet Trail**, which meanders around the catchment area of the Roseau Dam. You can hike from one side of the island to the other, from Micoud to Soufrière, a 5-mile, 5-hour trek. The **St Lucia National Trust** (T4525005) has fairly regular field trips, usually the last Sunday of the month, popular with locals and tourists of all ages. The cost varies according to transport costs, membership US$10 a year.

Diving and marine life

Dive sites
Visitors must dive with a local company

There is some very good diving off the west coast, although this is somewhat dependent on the weather, as heavy rain tends to create high sediment loads in the rivers and sea. Diving off the east coast is not so good and can be risky unless you are a competent diver. One of the best beach entry dives in the Caribbean is directly off **Anse Chastanet**, where an underwater shelf drops off from about 10 ft down to 60 ft and there is a good dive over **Turtle Reef** in the bay, where there are over 25 different types of coral. Below the **Petit Piton** are impressive sponge and coral communities on a drop to 200 ft of spectacular wall. There are gorgonians, black coral trees, huge barrel sponges and plenty of other beautiful reef life. The area in front of the *Anse Chastanet Hotel* is a buoyed off Marine Reserve, stretching from the west point at **Grand Caille North** to **Chamin Cove**. Only the hotel boats and local fishermen's canoes are allowed in. By the jetty, a roped-off area is used by snorkellers and beginner divers. Other popular dive sites include **Anse L'Ivrogne**, **Anse La Raye Point** (good snorkelling also at **Anse La Raye**) and the **Pinnacles** (an impressive site where four pinnacles rise to within 10 ft of the surface), not forgetting the **wrecks**, such as the *Volga* (in 20 ft of water north of Castries harbour, well broken up, subject to swell, requires caution), the *Waiwinette* (several miles south of Vieux Fort, strong currents, competent divers only), and the 165-ft *Lesleen M* (deliberately sunk in 1986 off Anse Cochon Bay in 60 ft of water).

The Fisheries Department is pursuing an active marine protection programme

It is illegal take any coral or undersized shellfish. Corals and sponges should not even be touched. It is also illegal to buy or sell coral products on St Lucia. The *Soufrière Marine Management Association* preserves the environment between Anse Chastanet and Anse L'Ivrogne to the south. They have placed moorings in the reserve, which yachts are required to take, charges are on a sliding scale depending on the size of the boat. Collection of marine mammals (dead or alive) is prohibited, spearguns are illegal and anchoring is prohibited. Rangers come by at night to collect the fee and explain the programme. Dive moorings have been installed and are being financed with Marine Reserve Fees, US$4 daily, US$12 a year.

Scuba St Lucia (PADI 5-star, SSI and DAN) operates from Anse Chastanet, **Dive centres**
www.scubastlucia.com or contact them through the hotel, 3 dive boats with oxygen on
each, photographic hire and film processing, video filming and courses, day and night dives,
resort courses and full PADI certification, multilingual staff, pick-up service Mon-Sat from
hotels north of Castries, day packages for divers, snorkellers, beginners and others include
lunch and equipment. *Buddies Scuba* (PADI, BSAC) at Rodney Bay Marina, T/F4529086,
2-tank day dives, 1-tank night dives, camera rental, open water certification or resort course,
dive packages available. *Moorings Scuba Centre* at Marigot Bay, T4514357, *Dive Fair Helen*
at the *Ti Kaye Village*, T4517716, and *Frog's Diving* at the *Windjammer Resort* on Labrellotte
Bay, T4520913, all offer PADI courses. A single-tank dive costs around US$35-55, introduc-
tory resort courses are about US$65-90, a six-dive package US$175 and open water certification courses US$380-495, plus 10% service charge.

You can see the underwater world without getting wet by taking a ride on the semi-submersible, *Aquabulle*, operated by *Water Sport World* at Rodney Bay Marina, T4584292,
watersports@candw.lc Departures are at 0900 and 1500, 1½ hrs, US$30 adults, US$15
under 16, 1 child under 10 free if accompanied by 2 adults.

Whale and dolphin watching is now popular. Sightings have been good and interest is high. **Whale**
Nov-Jun is best, when sperm whales and humpbacks are seen. 2 branches of the Hackshaw **watching**
family offer tours as well as sport fishing (see below): *Captain Mike's*, T4527044,
www.captmikes.com, and *Hackshaw's Boat Charter and Sport Fishing*, T4530553,
hackshawc@candw.lc *The Soufrière Water Taxi Association*, T4597239, will also arrange trips.

Beaches and watersports

The Atlantic east coast has heavy surf, is dangerous and difficult to get to without *Swimming is not safe*
local knowledge or the Ordnance Survey map and 4WD. However, it is very spectac- *on the Atlantic,*
ular and isolated beaches make a pleasant change from the west coast. Many are *east side, there is a*
important habitats and nesting places for the island's wildlife. **Cas en Bas Beach** can *strong undertow*
be reached from Gros Islet (45 minutes' walk, or arrange taxi), it is sheltered, shady
but challenging for experienced windsurfers. *Marjorie's Beach Bar*, T4508637, can
organize hikes and horse riding finishing with a meal at the restaurant. A residential
development is under construction which should lead to road improvements. **Donkey Beach** can be reached from there by taking a track to the north (20 minutes'
walk), the scenery is wild and open and it is windy. To the south of Cas en Bas Beach
are **Anse Louvet**, **Anse Comerette** and **Anse Lapins**, follow the rocks, it is a
30-minute walk to the first and an hour to the last. Access is also possible from
Monchy and Dennery (but only over private property). They are deserted, windswept beaches and headlands. There are Indian stone carvings on **Dauphin Beach**,
which can be reached from Monchy (reasonable with jeep). Once on the beach,
wade across the river and walk back in the flat, clear area below the bush land. After
about 50 yd you'll find long stones with regular depressions. Another 20 yd and
you'll find a stone pillar about which Robert Devaux wrote: "The carving appears to
be a family of three – male, female and child. It is finely executed and must have
taken some prehistoric 'Michelangelo' a considerable time to complete the carving"
(*St Lucia Historic Sites*, St Lucia National Trust, 1975, highly recommended, in the
library at the Folk Research Centre). It is now used as the St Lucia National Trust's
logo. Unfortunately the stone pillar has been badly tampered with. A few metres further inland is the ruin of a colonial church tower, destroyed in 1795 during the
French Revolution of St Lucia together with the rest of the settlement. **Grande Anse**,
further south, is a long windy beach, currently not open to the general public
although turtle watching is organized, April-August (see box).

Anse Louvet is a sheltered beach in a stunning setting, three hours' walk but not *Louvet has a special,*
drivable from Desbarra, 2 hours' walk, or drive if possible, from Aux Leon; the steep *spooky atmosphere*
track is impassable on a wet day. Ask locally about the eratic state of the roads.
Walking takes as long as driving; take lots of water. La Sorcière mountain forms a

long wall which seems to separate Louvet from the rest of the world. Rugged cliffs are beaten by waves and there is a blow hole. A high waterfall in the forest can be reached by following the river from the ford in the main valley (little water flow).

All the west coast beaches have good swimming but many are dominated by resort hotels. Many lost sand during Hurricane Lenny in 1999 (see page 56)

The beaches on the west coast north of Castries can be reached by bus with a short walk down to the sea. **Vigie** (1½ miles from Castries) is a lovely strip of sand with plenty of shade, popular and cleaned regularly. Its only drawback is that it runs parallel to the airport runway but that is compensated by the lack of hotels (except *Rendezvous* at one end) and low levels of pollution. **Choc Bay** has good sand, shade and chairs provided by the restaurant, *Wharf* (get off the bus after *Sandals Halcyon*). Used mainly by cruise ship passengers and locals, there are kayaks, sea cycles and sunfish for hire 0900-1800 daily. **Marisule** is a small, rocky beach, good for local colour with fishing boats and nets. **Labrellotte Bay** is the location for the up-market *East Winds* and *Windjammer Landing*. **Trouya** is a small, usually deserted bay (except on public holidays), best reached on foot or 4WD. **Rodney Bay** has another excellent beach at **Reduit**, dominated by the *Papillon, Rex St Lucian* (parasailing) and *Royal St Lucian* hotels, where you can use their bars and sports hire facilities but it is crowded with guests. The northern part of the bay is cut off by the marina and is now a 45-minute walk or 5 to 10-minute bus ride to Gros Islet. There are more beaches on the way to **Pigeon Island**, with ample shade and two small beaches on Pigeon Island itself. Further north by *Club St Lucia* **Smugglers' Cove**, another good snorkelling spot.

Heading south from Castries, beaches at small towns are not generally used by tourists; lack of proper sanitation means they are often polluted. Beaches away from habitation are always a better bet. **Marigot Bay** is a popular tourist spot. **Anse Chastanet** is well used with great snorkelling, see page 651. **Anse Cochon** is also popular, visited by boats doing day trips, and guests at the *Ti Kaye Village*. The smell of motor boats can be unpleasant. The trade winds blow in to the south shore and sandy beach of **Anse de Sables** near Vieux Fort offers ideal **windsurfing**. The sea here is wild and invigorating and comes straight across the Atlantic.

Fishing

www.worldwide fishing.com/stlucia

Fishing trips for barracuda, mackerel, king fish and other varieties can be arranged. Several sport fishing boats sail from Rodney Bay Marina (see Whale watching, above). There is an annual billfish tournament, at which a Martiniquan recently landed a 707-lb blue marlin, putting the earlier record of 549 lbs in the shade.

Sailing

At Marigot Bay and Rodney Bay you can hire any size of craft, the larger ones coming complete with crew if you want. Many of these yachts sail down to the Grenadines. Rodney Bay has been developed to accommodate 1,000 yachts (with 232 berths in a full-service boatyard and additional moorings in the lagoon) and hosts the annual Atlantic Rally for Cruisers race, with about 250 yachts arriving there in Dec. Charters can be arranged to sail to neighbouring islands. At **Rodney Bay Marina** is: *Destination St Lucia* (DSL), T4528531, yachts from 38-52 ft, bareboat charters, multilingual staff. At **Marigot Bay**: *The Moorings*, T4514357, bareboat fleet of 38-50 ft Beneteaus and crewed fleet of 50-60 ft yachts, 45-room hotel for accommodation prior to departure or on return, watersports, diving, windsurfing. Soufrière has a good anchorage, but as the water is deep it is necessary to anchor close in. There is a pier for short term tie-ups.

Day sails

At the swimming stop local divers may try to sell you coral. It is illegal

As some of the best views are from the sea, it is recommended to take at least 1 boat trip. There are several boats which sail down the west coast to Soufrière, where you stop to visit the volcano, Diamond Falls and the Botanical Gardens, followed by lunch and return sail with a stop somewhere for swimming and snorkelling. The price usually includes all transport, lunch, drinks and snorkelling gear; the *Unicorn*, based at Vigie Marina, T4526811, is a 140-ft replica of a 19th-century brig which started life in 1947 as a Baltic trader (used in the filming of *Roots*). Sailings are 0930 Mon-Fri in high season, and have been recommended, US$90 per person, children under 12 US$40, including lunch and the inevitable rum punch. Champagne and sunset cruises available on Mon, 1700-1900, adults, US$40, children US$20. You can also book through hotel tour desks. Other excursions on catamarans (*Endless Summer I, Endless Summer II, Sun Kiss, Mango Tango, Tango II*) and private yachts can be booked with tour operators in Castries or through the hotels. The catamarans are usually very over-crowded and devoid of character but cost the same as the *Unicorn*. An alternative to the brig is to charter a yacht with skipper and mate. Motor boats can also be chartered for customized trips including fishing and snorkelling. A day charter costs US$400 for 1-4 people, with a capacity for up to 8 more at US$5 per person. A week's trip to the Grenadines, around US$2,700, low season, for up to 4 passengers. *St Lucian Wave Riders*, T4841410, do a day trip to Martinique on Fri, leaving Rodney Bay Marina at 0730, returning 1730, US$129 including food and drink. Lots of time for sightseeing, shopping, beach barbecue and snorkelling.

Windward Islands

Castries

The capital, Castries, is splendidly set on a natural harbour against a background of mountains. It used to be guarded by the great fortress of Morne Fortune (Fort Charlotte and Derrière Fort). There is a spectacular view from the road just below Morne Fortune where the town appears as a kaleidoscope of colour. The area close to the centre is thoroughly modern but the bustle of its safe streets more than compensates. The city centre is very crowded when cruise ships come in.

Population: 60,000

Largely rebuilt after being destroyed by four major fires, the last in 1948, the commercial centre and government offices are built of concrete. Only the buildings to the south of Derek Walcott Square and behind Brazil Street were saved. Here you will see late 19th- and early 20th-century wooden buildings built in French style with three storeys, their gingerbread fretwork balconies overhanging the pavement. The other area which survived was the market on the north side of Jeremie Street. Built entirely of iron in 1894, it was conceived by Mr Augier, member of the Town Board, to enhance the appearance of the town and also provide a sheltered place where fruit and produce could be sold hygienically. A new market has been built next door to house the many fruit sellers on the ground floor, while on the first floor and in an arcade opposite are vendors of T-shirts, crafts, spices, basket work, leeches and hot pepper sauce. On the eastern side of the old market there is a little arcade with small booths where vendors provide good vegetarian food, Creole meals and local juices. Further along Jeremie Street on the waterfront is a large new shopping centre with duty-free shops: La Place Carenage. The tallest building in the city is the seven-storey Financial Centre at the corner of Jeremie and Bridge Streets, with a joyous sculpture by local artist, Ricky George.

Sights
*Heritage Tours offer a walking tour of Castries,
www.heritagetours stlucia.com*

Derek Walcott Square was the site of the Place D'Armes in 1768 when the town transferred from Vigie. Renamed Promenade Square, it then became Columbus Square in 1893. In 1993 it was renamed in honour of poet Derek Walcott, see page 655, and contains busts of both Nobel Laureates. It was the original site of the courthouse and the market. The library is on its west side. The giant Saman tree is about 400 years old. On its east side lies the **Cathedral** which bursts into colour inside. Suffused with yellow light, the side altars are often covered with flowers while votive candles placed in red, green and yellow jars give a fairy tale effect. The ceiling, supported by delicate iron arches and braces is decorated with large panelled portraits of the apostles. Above the central altar with its four carved screens, the apse ceiling has paintings of five female saints with St Lucy in the centre. The walls have murals by Dunstan St Omer, one of St Lucia's better known artists (see page 656). They are of the stations of the cross and are unusual in that the people in the paintings are black.

On the outskirts of Castries is **Pointe Seraphine**, a duty-free complex, near the port. Take the John Compton Highway north towards Vigie Airport and branch off just past the fish market. ■ *Mon-Fri 0800-1630. Plenty of people who will 'mind your car' here. Ignore them. Ferry from La Place Carenage every 10 mins, $US1.* The unusual pyramid-shaped building is the Alliance Française cultural centre.

Windward Islands

Excursions Just south of Castries is Government House with its curious metalwork crown, at the top of Morne Fortune. There is a small **museum** ■ *Tue and Thu 1000-1200, 1400-1600. Donations welcome.* From here carry on to **Fort Charlotte**, the old Morne Fortune fortress (now Sir Arthur Lewis Community College). You will pass the Apostles' battery (1888) and Provost's redoubt (1782). Each has spectacular views, but the best is from the Inniskilling Monument at the far side of the college (just beyond the old Combermere barracks) where you get an excellent view of the town, coast, mountains and Martinique. It was here in 1796 that General Moore launched an attack on the French. The steep slopes give some idea of how fierce the two days of fighting must have been. As a rare honour, the 27th Inniskillings Regiment were allowed to fly their regimental flag for one hour after they took the fortress before the Union Jack was raised. Sir Arthur Lewis, Nobel Laureate in Economics, is buried in front of the Inniskilling Monument.

On returning to Castries, branch left at Government House to visit **La Toc** point with its luxury *Sandals* hotel. Take the road to the hotel through its beautiful gardens

Castries

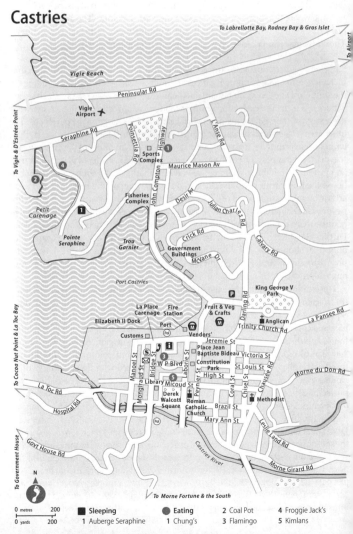

0 metres	200	■ **Sleeping**	● **Eating**	2 Coal Pot	4 Froggie Jack's
0 yards	200	1 Auberge Seraphine	1 Chung's	3 Flamingo	5 Kimlans

and take the path to the right of the security gate if you want to visit the beach. Further on is the road leading to Bagshaws studio. You can buy attractive silkscreen clothes and household linens and visit the printshop to watch the screen printing process. ■ *Mon-Fri 0830-1600, Sat 0830-1200. Carry your return ticket for a discount.* Close to Bagshaws is La Toc Battery, the best restored military fort, visited mostly by cruise ship visitors. For information or a tour call, Alice Bagshaw, T4526039, or enquire at the shop. The National Trust also do tours of the Morne Fortune Historic Area.

North to Pointe du Cap

The part of the island to the north of Castries is the principal resort area, it contains the best beaches and the hotels are largely self-contained. It is the driest part of the island. The John Compton highway leaves Castries past Vigie Airport and follows the curves of Vigie Beach and Choc Bay. Where the road leaves the bay and just before it crosses the Choc River, a right turn to Babonneau will take you past the **Union Agricultural station** (about one mile), see Flora and fauna above.

Rodney Bay was the site of the **US Naval Air Station of Reduit**. Built in 1941, the Americans made an attempt to reclaim the swamps and the bay was dredged. It was the first of a chain of bases established to protect the Panama Canal. Acting as a communications centre, it supported a squadron of sea planes. The base was eventually closed in 1947. It was not until much later when a causeway and marina were built that the wetlands vanished. The whole area now supports a mass of tourist facilities with a lovely beach. You can pass through the entrance gates of the old Naval Air Station or take the next left turn off the main road at the junction leading to *JQ's Mall*, to reach the hotels and restaurants. If you drive to the end of the road there is good access to the beach. Rodney Bay is an excellent base for watersports; it is ideal for windsurfing. At the back of the development is a large marina. Development is still taking place and at Rodney Heights a huge area has been set aside for big houses. The normally sleepy fishing village of **Gros Islet** holds a popular jump-up in the street each Friday night, from 2200, music, dancing, bars, cheap food, more tourists than locals but enjoyed by night owls. Try the grilled conch from one of the booths selling local dishes but stay away from anyone offering drugs.

Rodney Bay
Jerome's water taxi will get you around the bay, to Pigeon Island or further afield, T3841961

About ¾ mile after Elliot's Shell filling station on the outskirts of Gros Islet, turn left to Pigeon Island National Landmark, once an island, now joined to the mainland by a causeway on which a 300-room hotel (*Sandals Grande*) has been built with a bright blue roof. The park was opened by Princess Alexandra on 23 February 1979 as part of St Lucia's Independence celebrations. It has two peaks which are joined by a saddle. The higher rises to a height of about 360 ft. Managed by the National Trust, the island is of considerable archaeological and historical interest. Amerindian remains have been found, the French pirate François Leclerc (known as Jamb de Bois for his wooden leg) used the large cave on the north shore and the Duke of Montagu tried to colonize it in 1722 (but abandoned it after one afternoon). From here, Admiral Rodney set sail in 1782 to meet the French navy at the Battle of Les Saintes (see under Guadeloupe). It was captured by the Brigands (French slaves freed by the leaders of the French revolution) in 1795 but retaken in 1798 by the English. Used as a quarantine centre from 1842 it was abandoned in 1904 but became a US observation post during the Second World War. The island finally became the home of Josset Agnes Huchinson, a member of the D'Oyly Carte Theatre who leased the island from 1937 to 1976. The bay became a busy yacht haven and 'Joss' held large parties to entertain the crews. Her abandoned house can still be seen on the south shore of the island. On the lower of the two peaks lies **Fort Rodney**. The museum (located in the Officers' Mess and rebuilt to the original design) contains a display of the work of the National Trust. ■ *Daily 0900-1700; museum closed Sun. Entry to park and museum EC$10 visitors, EC$5 residents (free after 1700 but only to the restaurants).*

Pigeon Island

Windward Islands

North coast
*For more details
see Beaches
and watersports,
page 633*

The road north passes through the Cap Estate (golf course and the *Club St Lucia*) to **Pointe du Cap**, a viewpoint some 470 ft high with a splendid panorama along the coast. A good circular walk from Gros Islet can be done to Cas-en-Bas taking the road past *La Panache Guesthouse* (ask the owner, Henry Augustin for directions if necessary, he is always willing to help) down to the beach (sheltered, shady, a bit dirty), then following tracks north until you reach the golf course, from where you return along the west coast to Gros Islet. You will see cacti, wild scenery, Martinique and no tourists. The sea is too rough to swim. If exploring the Atlantic beaches by vehicle, make sure it is 4WD, check your spare tyre and tools, take OS map and water, be prepared to park and walk, and if possible take a local person with you. Always take local advice on the state of the roads, which change quickly.

The road to Monchy from Gros Islet is a pleasant drive inland through several small villages. You gradually leave the dry north part of the island and climb into forest. The ridge between Mount Monier and Mount Chaubourg gives particularly

Rodney Bay

Rodney Bay centre

*Related map
A Rodney Bay centre,
page 644*

N

0 metres 800
0 yards 800

■ **Sleeping**
1 Bay Gardens Inn
2 CAPri
3 Glencastle Resort
4 Harmony Marina Suites
5 Marlin Quay
6 MJI
7 Papillon
8 Rainbow
9 Rex St Lucian
10 Royal St Lucian
11 Windjammer Landing

● **Eating**
1 Big Chef
2 Breadbasket
3 Capone's
4 Captain's Cellar
5 Cat's Whiskers
6 Charthouse
7 Eagles Inn
8 Elena's
9 Jambe de Bois
10 Lime
11 Memories of Hong Kong
12 Razmataz
13 Rumours
14 Shamrock's Pub
15 Spinnakers
16 Triangle Pub
17 Tropicana

● **Bars & clubs**
18 Jazz Lounge & Roof Garden Restaurant

impressive views over the east coast. There are no road signs. Watch out for the names on schools and if in doubt at junctions bear west. At the larger village of Babonneau, you can turn right to follow the river down to the coast at Choc Bay or go straight on to Fond Cacao where a west turn will take you back to Castries.

East coast to Vieux Fort

The new road from Castries to Cul de Sac, known as the Millennium Highway, was immediately popular with cars and trucks. It is quite a straight road running along the sea and is a welcome relief from the hairpin curves of the old Morne Road. The Castries end starts at the roundabout on La Toc Road, goes through two short tunnels and comes out in the Cul de Sac valley, where a right turn takes you towards the beautiful Marigot Bay and the West Coast Road to Vieux Fort. A jog to the left and then a quick right takes the East Coast Road to the southern end of the island. The West Coast Road is full of mountain curves but has less traffic than the East Coast. Together they present a very scenic drive round the island.

The transinsular road goes through extensive banana plantations with the occasional packaging plant, through the village of Ravine Poisson before climbing steeply over the **Barre de l'Isle**, the mountain barrier that divides the island. There is a short, self-guided trail at the high point on the road between Castries and Dennery, which takes about 10 minutes and affords good views of the rainforest and down the Roseau valley. There is a small picnic shelter. It can be slippery after rain. The experience is rather spoilt by the noise of traffic. A longer walk to **Mount La Combe** can also be undertaken from this point. Be careful in this area as it is known as the drug growing region. Cyclists and hikers have reported that the locals are not particularly friendly and their stares can make you feel uncomfortable.

The road descends through Grande Rivière to Dennery where the vegetation is mostly xerophytic scrub. Dennery is set in a sheltered bay with Dennery Island guarding its entrance and dominated by the Roman Catholic church. Here you can see the distinctive St Lucia fishing boats pulled up on the beach. Carved out of single tree trunks, the bows are straight and pointed rather than curved and are all named with phrases such as 'God help me'. A US$6 mn fishing port has been built with improved moorings and cold storage, with Japanese assistance. There are lots of small bars but no other facilities. You can follow the Dennery River inland towards Mount Beaujolais. At Errard there is a photogenic waterfall. Permission should be obtained from the estate office before attempting this trip. ■ *Plantation tour Tue, Wed, Fri, with lunch and hotel transfers costs US$90. Book through Sailaway Tours, T4529842.* **Dennery**

Fregate Island's Nature Reserve, on the north side of Praslin Bay has two small islands, nesting sites for the frigate bird and the north promontory of Praslin bay gives a good vantage point. Birds nest on the offshore rocks and a trail runs down to the shore and back up by another route. The area is also of some historical interest as there was an Amerindian lookout point in the reserve. It was also the site of a battle between the English and the Brigands. It used to be known as Trois Islet and the nearby Praslin River is still marked as Trois Islet River on maps today. **Fregate Island** *See Flora and fauna, page 627*

Praslin is noted as a fishing community with traditional boat building. The road leaves the coast here and goes through banana plantations and the villages of **Mon Repos** and Patience. Mon Repos is a good place to see the flower festivals of La Rose and La Marguerite. Between Praslin and Mon Repos are the **Mamiku Gardens**: Botanical Gardens and Woodland Walks on an estate owned by Baron de Micoud when he was Governor of the island for France in the 18th century but later a British military post and site of a battle with brigands. There is an on-going excavation at Mamiku which is producing interesting finds from the ruins of the house where the British soldiers were surprised and massacred by the brigands. ■ *Daily 0900-1700. EC$15 for foreigners, EC$10 for locals, there is a snack bar and souvenir shop. T4528236,* www.mamiku.com The coast is regained at **Micoud**. There are one or two restaurants, a department store, post office and a branch of *FirstCaribbean International* bank. They make wine here: banana, guava, pineapple and sugar cane brewed and bottled under *Helen Brand* and available in some supermarkets. Their ginger wine is recommended, light, not too sweet, with just the right amount of 'bite'. One mile west of Micoud is **Latille Gardens** with fruit, flowers, trees and waterfalls. From Mahaut Road follow signs to the south. Tours can also be arranged through hotels and include a walk through the Descartes Rainforest Trail, T4540202.

Mangrove swamps can be seen at **Savannes Bay Nature Reserve**. The shallow bay is protected by a reef and is excellent for the cultivation of sea moss, an ideal breeding ground for conch and sea eggs. Scorpion island lies in the bay and to the north are more archaeological sites on Saltibus Point and Pointe de Caille.

Vieux Fort
Population: 14,000

After about three miles you reach Vieux Fort, the island's industrial centre, where the Hewanorra International Airport is situated. It is an active town with a good Saturday market and a lot of traditional housing. Traditional gaily painted trucks are still used on special occasions. The area is markedly less sophisticated than the north of the island. The town boasts two new supermarkets in malls, *JQs* and *Julian's*. The latter has a cinema. The police station and post office, on Theodore Street, are right in the middle of the town. Fishing boats are pulled up on the small beach but there is no proper beach here. On Clarke Street you will pass the square with a war memorial and band stand. The bus terminal is at the end of Clarke Street near the airport.

The perimeter road skirts Anse de Sables beach (no shade, good windsurfing), and looks across to the **Maria Islands**. The interpretative centre on the beach is not always open. If you want to visit **Cap Moule à Chique**, turn left at the T junction and follow the road to the banana loading jetty (on Wednesday you will pass truck after truck waiting to be weighed). Bear left and go up a badly maintained track. Finally go left again through the Cable and Wireless site up to the lighthouse. The duty officer will be glad to point out the views including the Pitons, Morne Gomier (1,028 ft) with Morne Grand Magazin (2,022 ft) behind it. Unfortunately Morne Gimie (3,118 ft) is largely obscured. Further to the east is Piton St Esprit (1,919 ft) and Morne Durocher (1,055 ft) near Praslin. The lighthouse itself is 730 ft above sea level and also has good views over the Maria islands and southwest to St Vincent.

West coast to Soufrière and the Pitons

The West Coast Road is in excellent condition with good signposting. It is a curvy, but spectacular, drive down to Soufrière. Take the transinsular highway out of Castries and instead of branching left at Cul de Sac bay carry straight on. The road quickly rises to La Croix Maingot with good views of the Roseau banana plantation.

Marigot Bay

On reaching the Roseau valley, one of the main banana growing areas, take the signposted road to Marigot Bay (plenty of 'guides' waiting to pounce), a beautiful inlet and natural harbour which provided the setting for *Dr Doolittle*. It supports a large marina and not surprisingly a large number of yachts in transit berth here to restock with supplies from the supermarket and chandler. You will notice a small strip of land jutting out into the bay. This has a little beach (not particularly good for swimming) and can be reached by the *Gingerbread Express* (a water taxi, EC$2 return, refundable at *Doolittle's* if you eat or drink there), either from the hotel or the customs post. It is a good place for arranging watersports. There is a police station and immigration post here, bars, disco, restaurants and accommodation.

Canaries

The main road continues to Soufrière and passes through the fishing villages of **Anse La Raye** and Canaries (no facilities). To the south of Anse La Raye, taking the last road to the left before you reach the bridge, a well-restored sugar mill, **La Sikwi**, can be visited, EC$5 or EC$15 with guide. It is near the river on the way to a waterfall, in a garden containing many regional crop species. Boa constrictor come here to be fed and with luck you will see one. The bar and restaurant open on demand. A narrow, steep, bad road branches off to the right just before Canaries and leads to a former restaurant at **Anse Jambette**. Half way along this road, before it gets really steep, you can park and climb down the hill towards Canaries. There is a man-made cave and oven used by escaped slaves. Difficult to find (as intended), you need a knowledgeable local to show you where it is. There are many waterfalls in the vicinity of Canaries, some of which are visited by organized tours. If you go independently you need a 4WD and a guide. The closest is right at the end of the road into the rainforest, others are 30 minutes to 2½ hours' walk away. It is safe to swim. South of Canaries is **Anse La Liberté**, a National Trust site and a hiking and camping site (see Camping, below), reached by water taxi from Canaries, EC$2, or on foot from Belvedere along a nature trail (10 minutes down, 15 minutes up). There are many brigand holes in the area.

After Canaries the road goes inland and skirts Mount Tabac (2,224 ft) before descending into Soufrière. This is the most picturesque and interesting part of the island, with marvellous old wooden buildings at the foot of the spectacular Pitons, surrounded by thick vegetation and towering rock formations looming out of the sea. Petit Piton is dangerous to climb (several people have fallen off in recent years) and it is restricted Crown Lands, so you need permission. This does not stop local guides offering to show visitors up, though, for about US$50. Because of its location, the town is a must for tourists although it is not geared for people wanting to stay there. There are no buses back to Castries after midday unless you make a round-about journey via Vieux Fort. To do this, leave Castries at 0800, 2 hours. After visiting Soufrière, wait at the corner opposite the church and ask as many people as possible if they know of anyone going to Vieux Fort; you will get a lift before you get a bus. Get off at Vieux Fort 'crossroads', where there are many buses returning to Castries by another route, 1¼ hours. Buses to Castries leave from the market area. If you arrive by boat head for the north end of the bay, you will find plenty of help to tie up your yacht (EC$5) and taxis will appear from nowhere. It is a much cheaper alternative to tying up at the jetty. ■ *Organized tours are available from the hotels further north, by sea or road, from around US$65-80 including lunch, drinks, transfers and a trip to Soufrière, Diamond Gardens and the Sulphur Springs (see below).*

Soufrière is a charming old West Indian town dating back to 1713 when Louis XIV of France granted the lands around Soufrière to the Devaux family. The estate subsequently produced cotton, tobacco, coffee and cocoa. During the French Revolution, the guillotine was raised in the square by the Brigands but the Devaux family were protected by loyal slaves and escaped. It is on a very picturesque bay totally dominated by the Pitons. The water here is extremely deep and reaches 200 ft only a few yards from the shore, which is why boats moor close in. To reach Anse Chastanet from here take the rough track at the north end of the beach (past the yacht club) about one mile. This is an absolute must if you enjoy snorkelling (the south end near the jetty is superb but keep within the roped off area, the north end is also good with some rocks to explore, but avoid the middle where boats come in). The hotel has a good and inexpensive restaurant (although if you are on a budget you may prefer to take a picnic) and the dive shop is extremely helpful, they will hire out equipment by the hour. The *Unicorn, Endless Summer* and day boats stop here for snorkelling and a swim in the afternoon on their return to Castries.

In Soufrière is the Butterfly House, the only one in the Windwards. Imported pupae are hatched and grown in a small house in Lovers' Lane behind the Catholic Church. Over 60 varieties are flying around freely in the tropical setting. ■ *Daily 1000-1700. US$4. T4597429.*

Most visitors come to see the Diamond Gardens and Waterfall and the Sulphur Springs. There are no road signs in Soufrière and locating these two places can be

Sidebar

Soufrière
Population: 9,000

Soufrière was severely damaged in November 1999 by Hurricane Lenny, which brought 20-ft waves and destroyed about 70 houses and infrastructure

Butterfly House

Diamond Gardens

Windward Islands

difficult (or expensive if forced to ask). From the square take Sir Arthur Lewis Street east past the church and look for a right hand turning to reach the Diamond Gardens. These were developed in 1784 after Baron de Laborie sent samples taken from sulphur springs near the Diamond River to Paris for analysis. They found minerals present which were equivalent to those found in the spa town of Aix-la-Chapelle and were said to be effective against rheumatism and other complaints. The French King ordered baths to be built. Despite being destroyed in the French Revolution, they were eventually rebuilt and can be used by the public. The gardens are better than ever; well maintained and many native plants can be seen. ■ *Daily 1000-1700. T4524759. EC$7, children EC$3, EC$7 to use the outdoor hot baths, EC$10 for private bath. Only official guides are allowed in, do not accept offers from those at the gates. All the car parks are free, no matter what some people may tell you.*

Sulphur Springs

It is extremely dangerous to stray onto the grey area. The most famous 'crater' was formed a few years ago when a local person fell into a mud pocket. He received third degree burns

Take the Vieux Fort road between wooden houses about halfway along the south side of Soufrière square. Follow the road for about two miles and you will see a sign on the left. On the way you can stop off to visit the **Morne Coubaril Estate**, an open-air farm museum, working family plantation, processes cocoa, copra, cassava, also hiking or horse riding. ■ *Guided tour daily 0900-1600. EC$15. Horse riding 0900-1500, 1-2 hrs or whole week, T4597340, coubaril@candw.lc* You will be able to smell the springs before you reach them. Originally a huge volcano about 3 miles in diameter, it collapsed some 40,000 years ago leaving the west part of the rim empty (where you drive in). The sign welcomes you to the world's only drive-in volcano, although actually you have to stop at a car park. The sulphur spring is the only one still active, although there are seven cones within the old crater as well as the pitons which are thought to be volcanic plugs. Tradition has it that the Arawak deity *Yokahu* slept here and it was therefore the site of human sacrifices. The Caribs were less superstitious but still named it *Qualibou*, the place of death. There is a small village of about 40 inhabitants located inside the rim of the volcano. Water is heated to 180°F and in some springs to 275°F. It quickly cools to about 87°F below the bridge at the entrance. There has been much geothermal research here since 1974. From the main viewing platform, you can see over a moonscape of bubbling, mineral rich, grey mud. There are good, informative guides (apparently compulsory) on the site but you must be prepared to walk over uneven ground. Allow approximately 30 minutes. ■ *Daily 0900-1700. EC$3.* **Stonefield Estate**, just south of Soufrière on the way to the Sulphur Springs, has very fine petroglyphs, but you will need to ask if someone will show you them in the bush. This is a working cocoa plantation, with luxurious accommodation, a spectacular view of the Pitons and a restaurant, the *Mango Tree*, T4530777.

South of Soufrière

In the valley between Petit Piton and Gros Piton, a luxury all-inclusive resort, *Jalousie Hilton Resort and Spa*, has been built despite complaints from ecological groups and evidence from archaeologists that it is located on a major Amerindian site. An important burial ground is believed to be under the tennis courts and there have been many finds of petroglyphs and pottery. A rather fine petroglyph is at the back of the beach in front of Lord Glenconner's *Bang Between the Pitons*. Lord Glenconner used to own much of the land here. Take the turning opposite the Morne Coubaril Estate on the unsigned concrete road. Halfway along the drive to *Jalousie* you will see a little sign to a small, warm waterfall on your left. Someone will collect about US$2 for access. Relax in the warm waters.

South of Soufrière, near Union Vale estate, is the **Gros Piton trail**. The village of **Fond Gens Libre** is at the base of the mountain, accessible by jeep or high-clearance car although you will have to ford a couple of streams. Enquire at Forestry, T4502231. Call *Fond Gens Libre Tour Guides Association*, T4593833, to arrange a guide. The trip up and back is about four hours with stops to look at brigand caves and tunnels. A guide costs about EC$20, but if you have your own transport you can do it on your own. It is strenuous, so you must be in good physical condition. It should not be attempted in wet weather. It is also possible to climb **Petit Piton**, an extremely steep ascent. A guide is essential, contact Cecil Hippolyte, 'Yellowman', a licensed water taxi operator at Soufrière, through the tourist office.

The road from Soufrière to Vieux Fort takes about 40 minutes by car. The branch of the road through **Fond St Jacques** (church painted by Dunstan St Omer) runs through lush rainforest and a track takes you to the west end of the rainforest trail. In a few miles the road rapidly descends from Victoria Junction (1,200 ft) to the coastal plain at **Choiseul**. Choiseul is a quaint old West Indian village, there is a fish market and church on the beach. **Caraibe Point** is the last place on St Lucia where Caribs still survive, a small community of potters living in simple thatched houses. North of Choiseul is a petroglyph, visible from the road, but you must park and then walk a little way. Outlined in white, under a protective roof, it is just down the cliff toward the sea. On the south side of Choiseul, the Art and Craft development centre teaching skills in bamboo handicrafts. You can buy pottery, baskets and carvings.

Southeast of Choiseul, there are Arawak petroglyphs on rocks in the Balenbouche River. You will probably need somebody to show you the way from Balenbouche or Saltibus. **Balenbouche Estate** is an old sugar plantation where you can stay in the estate home or in a cottage, good local food. A team from the University of Bristol did an archaeological dig here in 2001 and an exploratory trip along the River Doree, where there are a number of petroglyphs. There is also an ancient aqueduct connected in some way to the irrigation system at Balenbouche and the canal that carried water to the wheel at the sugar mill.

Essentials

Apart from around Rodney Bay, many of the hotels are remote resorts, providing everything their guests need. You will have to arrange car hire or expensive taxis to get around the island or go to restaurants. All-inclusive resorts (namely the three *Sandals* resorts, *Club St Lucia*, *Le Sport*, *East Winds Inn*, *St James' Club on Morgan Bay* and *Rendezvous*) are usually, but not always booked from abroad. Many smaller hotels have grouped themselves as *The Inns of St Lucia*, representing a third of the total number of rooms on the island.

Sleeping
There is a 10-15% service charge and a 8% government tax on all hotel bills, porters (US$1 a bag); taxi drivers and others in service expect tips

Working roughly north to south down the west coast: **Far north LL** *CAPri*, Smugglers Cove, T4500009, www.capristlucia.com 10 a/c rooms in a villa which used to be the Chinese embassy, British-run, peaceful location, 4-poster beds, fans, small pool, walking distance to Smugglers Beach (used by *Club St Lucia*), guests can use the facilities of *Le Sport*.
Gros Islet L-C *Tropical Breeze*, 38 Massie St, Massade, Gros Islet, T/F4500589. Guesthouse and 1-4 bedroomed apartments, fully equipped, TV, phone, kitchens, group rates on request, backs on to police station. **B** *Glencastle Resort*, Massade, on hillside overlooking Rodney Bay, T4500833, F4500857. New, luxurious, good value for money, a/c, pool, 17 rooms, restaurant. **B-D** *B&B/Anette's Hotel*, on Gros Islet highway, Massade, T4508689, F4508134, within walking distance of Marina, beaches and Pigeon Island causeway. A/c, fans, kitchenettes in some rooms, noisy at night with loud music, especially country and western. **C-E** *Alexander's Guesthouse*, T4508610, F4508014, a new building on Mary Thérèse St, 1 min from beach. Clean, safe, friendly, helpful, kitchen, credit cards accepted. **D** *Bay Mini Guest House*, Bay St, painted bright orange, on beach, T4508956. Minimum stay 2 nights, spacious rooms, fan, bathroom, 2 studios with kitchenettes, run by Klaus Kretz, speaks German and English. **D** *La Panache*, Cas-en-Bas Rd, T4500765, augustinh@candw.lc Run by Henry Augustin, helpful and friendly, also Roger Graveson, who is working with the Forestry Department to complete a listing of the plants of St Lucia, can give information on Atlantic beaches and coastal walking, birdwatching tours, includes tax and service, 7 rooms, 2-bed apt, own bathroom, fridge, some with cooking facilities, hot water, insect screens, clean, fans, gardens with plants labelled, good meals, breakfast daily US$3-8, tasty Creole dinners (Henry's grandmother's recipes) US$13 by reservation only, snacks during day, bar with excellent alcoholic and non-alcoholic cocktails. **D** *Nelson's Furnished Apartments*, Cas-en-Bas Rd, T4508275, 300 m uphill from main road to Castries. Run by Marilyn and Davy, hot water, fan, TV, mosquito net, balcony with nice view over Rodney Bay, towels and toilet paper supplied, free but slow

internet access. **D** *The Wall/Paradise Beach Hotel*, 1A St George St, behind the restaurant (see below), T4500388. Right on beach, rooms clean, fan, shower, very hospitable, run by Cletus Hippolyte.

Rodney Bay is the place to stay if you want the beach, restaurants and nightlife on your doorstep

Rodney Bay   LL-L *Rex St Lucian*, T4528351, rexstlucian@candw.lc Right on the beach, 120 a/c rooms, restaurants, pools, entertainment, good facilities, conveniently located, with *Papillon* all-inclusive section and the 98-suite *Royal St Lucian*, its sister property, next door. Facilities for wheelchair users at both hotels. **L-AL** *Rainbow*, T4520148, www.rainbowstlucia.com Further down same road as *Rex* and *Royal*, across the road from the beach, 76 a/c rooms, CP, tennis, fitness centre, pool, beach towels, snack bar, very colourful, pleasant, internet access, linked with Cap Estate Golf Course, golf packages offered. **AL** *Harmony Marina Suites*, on lagoon, close to beach, T4528756, F4528677. Studios and apartments, restaurant, bar, pool, mini-mart, watersports including canoeing. **AL-A** *Bay Gardens Inn*, T4528200, www.baygardensinn.com Well-managed, 2 pools, restaurant, a/c, TV, conference facilities. **AL-A** *MJI*, just off the main road opposite *Bay Gardens Inn*, T4528090, www.mjivilla.com Small hotel with self-contained apartments, studios and 2-room villa, a/c, pool, TV, 19 rooms, rates negotiable according to season. **C** *Sunny Isles Hotel*, T4580800. 18 rooms, a/c, cable TV, pool, some rooms have kitchenette and veranda. **D** *Villa Zandoli*, just down the road from *Rumours* restaurant, T4528898. Small, cheap.

Labrellotte Bay   LL-L *Windjammer Landing*, T4520913, www.wlv-resort.com A beautiful resort in a lovely hillside setting, but isolated, the best villa complex with hotel facilities, 1-bedroomed suites clustered together, 2/4-bedroomed villas spread out with own plunge pool, luxury resort, tennis and watersports, on a much-improved beach, honeymoon, family, diving packages, 30-min walk to a bus route or EC$20 taxi to Rodney Bay.

The three-lane highway is dangerous here; in 2002 a tourist was killed when crossing to catch a bus north

Gablewoods Mall   B *Friendship Inn*, T4524201, F4532635. Rooms with kitchenette and babysitting services, small pool, restaurant. **D-E** *Sundale Guest House*, T4524120. Very popular, CP, own bathroom, fan, TV in lobby, check availability. On highway to Gros Islet, **D-E** *The Golden Arrow*, T4501832, F4502329. 15 clean, pleasant rooms, all with private bathroom, walking distance from beach and bus, friendly host, breakfast and dinner available. **D** *Parrots Hideaway*, T/F4520726. 4 rooms with private bathroom, 5 rooms share 2 toilets, discounts for long stays, bar, restaurant, Creole menu, charming hostess.

Castries   AL-B *Auberge Seraphine*, Vigie Marina, T4532073, www.aubergeseraphine.com 22 rooms, pool, restaurant, a/c, TV, attractive and well-run, nice location on edge of harbour, flocks of egrets fly in to roost here. **A** *Cara Suites*, La Pansée, overlooking Castries, T4524767, www.carahotels.com 54 rooms, magnificent view, pool, tennis, a/c, TV, VCR, video library, minibar, good restaurant, complimentary internet access, excellent value for business or pleasure. **B-C** *t'bell Maison*, Vide Bouteille, T4517574, tbel@candw.lc Run by Basil Belazaire and his niece Florencia, friendly, helpful, rooms with fan or a/c, clean and white, quiet even though main road to Gros Islet is 100 yd below. **C** *Chesterfield*, southern end of Bridge St, T/F4521295. Central, 16 rooms, tropical garden, some rooms with balcony, great view, a/c, kitchen, excellent value. **C** *Harbour Light Inn*, City Gate, T4523506, F4519455. 3 min walk to Vigie Beach, parking, 16 rooms, a/c or fan, private bath, hot water, cable TV, balcony all round building, panoramic view, restaurant, bar. **E** *Chateau Blanc*, on Morne du Don Rd, 7 rooms with fan and bathroom, basic but good central location, food available, T4521851, F4527967; **E** *Thelma's Guesthouse*, Waterworks Rd, T4527313. No sign, white building, green awnings, shared bathroom, lounge, kitchen, central, owner Theresa Debique is warm and caring.

Morne Fortune (above Castries)   AL-A *Top of the Morne Apartments*, T4523603 F4590936. 1-2 bedrooms for 1-5 people, very friendly, spectacular view, car rental, pool. **C** *Bon Appetit*, T4522757, F4527967. Beautiful view, clean, friendly, cable TV, restaurant, 3 rooms with bathroom, CP, book early for evening meal, popular. **E** *Morne Fortune Guest House*, T4521742 Single rooms are big enough for 2, shared bathrooms, spacious, well-equipped kitchen for self-catering, very clean, restaurant, bakery close by, across the road from the Sir Arthur Lewis Community College campus, where there are 2 restaurants. Run by Mrs Regina Willie, helpful informative, monthly rates available, good access to public transport.

Marigot Bay On the north shore of the bay is **LL-A** *Marigot Beach Club*, T4514974 www.marigotbeach.com Waterfront restaurant and bar, *Café Paradis* open from 0800, sailing, kayaking, PADI dive shop run by Rosemond Clery, pool, sundeck, beach, studios with kitchenette, fans, bathrooms and patio or villas with 1-3 bedrooms on hillside. **AL** *Seahorse Inn*, T4514436, www.seahorse-inn.com 8 bedrooms, waterside cottage with own dock US$600-950 per week, beach short walk, pool, restaurants within walking distance, watersports arranged. **AL** *The Inn On the Bay*, T4514260, www.saint-lucia.com Only 4 rooms, spacious, overlooking Marigot Bay, great view from pool and balcony, CP, tours and car hire arranged, run by friendly Normand Viau and Louise Boucher. Next door and just before you fall off the cliff, is **AL-C** *Cliff House*, T4514241, www.cliff-house.com Owned by Alice Bagshaw of silk screen factory, 2 rooms, CP, spectacular view, can rent whole house, car hire and airport transfers arranged, both properties along half mile unpaved road, away from Marigot Bay activities, secluded, beautiful views. **A** *Villa de la Gratia*, T4583119, www.villdelagratia.com Overlooking the harbour, CP, 12 rooms, a/c, fans, TV, fridge, 2 mins walk to beach, convenient for sailing, pool, pool bar, email.

Soufrière LL-L *Anse Chastanet*, T4597000, www.ansechastenet.com Hillside and beachside suites, really special, romantic, luxurious, stunning views in all directions, open balconies, airy, only drawback is the walk uphill after overindulging at dinner, the best scuba diving on the island, consistently highly rated dive operation, diving packages available, watersports, tennis, spa, lovely beach setting, restaurant on the beach and halfway up the hill, live music in the evenings, walks and excursions available, isolated. **LL** *Ladera Resort*, T4597323, www.ladera-stlucia.com Spectacular setting between Gros Piton and Petit Piton, 1,000 ft up, 24 rooms, each lacking a west wall over a drop that only Superman could climb, providing an uninterrupted view of the Pitons, 1-3 bedroomed villas and suites, every luxury, very cold plunge pools, 60s-style swimming pools, used to film *Superman II*, good restaurant, lots of birds and mosquitoes. **LL-L** *Stonefield Estate*, T4597037, www.stonefieldvillas.com 15 villas sleeping 1-8 on 26-acre estate, 2 pools, Japanese garden, petroglyphs, cook and staff, beach shuttle, view of Pitons, beautifully furnished. **LL-AL** *Mago Estate Hotel*, T4595880, www.mago-hotel.com Originally a private home, built by an architect into the cliff and incorporating all the natural and geological features, now a small, luxury hotel with 6 beautiful open fronted rooms framed by bougainvillea overlooking bay, Pitons and mountains, 4-poster beds, roomy, open bathrooms, CP, MAP available, pool bar in the roots of a huge mango tree, tree house above, lounge bar built into rock formation and mango trees, Yin & Yang health farm if you need a detox. **AL-B** *Humming Bird Beach Resort*, T4597232, hbr@candw.lc Only 10 rooms and a hillside cottage, nice gardens, pool, beach, near Soufrière. **AL-B** *The Still Plantation and Beach Resort*, T4597261, duboulayd@candw.lc 400-acre plantation, apartments, studios on the plantation or beachfront rooms, popular, pool, beach restaurant, spectacular view of Pitons. **B** *Chez Camille*, 7 Bridge St, T4595379, clean and friendly, family room available, kitchen, good restaurant attached (does takeaways). **D-E** *Home Guesthouse*, T4597318, on the main square. Clean, pay cash, TCs not accepted. **E** Peter Jackson rents a double room in his house on the edge of Soufrière, T4597269. Basic but good, full cooking facilities, Peter is friendly and helpful. **D** *La Mirage Guesthouse*, T4597010. English owner of Jamaican descent, Gilroy Lamontaigne, 4 rooms sleep 3, with bathroom, fan and fridge, lounge with cable TV, restaurant.

Coubaril B-C (per person) The Benedictine nuns have 22 rooms with private bathrooms, a/c, fans, MAP, in a lovely wooded setting, tranquil, secluded, 15 min easy walk along wooded road to frequent public transport. To get there, head south to the Morne junction at the Shell station, then right turn down hill, take second right to the nunnery, T4521282, the chapel is packed for Christmas Eve mass.

Laborie A-B *Mirage Beach*, on the west edge of the bay, T4559763, miragebeachresort@hotmail.com 5 tasteful, cottage-style rooms, secluded.

East coast B-C *Foxgrove Inn*, T4553271, F4553271. 12-bedroomed hotel, on hillside with view of Praslin Bay and Fregate Islands, beach 2 km, pool, nature trails, riding stables, good food, CP, MAP available, discounts for long stay, owned by Mr and Mrs Louis-Fernand, new conference room for 100 has view to Atlantic. **C** *Manje Domí*, 5 km south of Micoud, T4550729. Guesthouse with restaurant and bar, turn at Anse Ger junction, 1½ km to guesthouse on top of hill. 4 rooms, each with patio, screens, fans, very low-key, countryside setting, CP, meals are seafood, fresh local vegetables, fruits, pleasant, the name means 'good eating, good sleeping' in Kweyol, and it lives up to its name.

Several hotels in this area enjoy fabulous views of the Pitons and the coast; perched on hillsides in beautiful tropical gardens and forests, truly peaceful

Windward Islands

Vieux Fort A-B *Sky Way Inn*, T4547111, F4547116. Restaurant, nightclub, pool, shuttle service to airport and beach. **B** *Juliette's Lodge*, Beanfield, Vieux Fort, T4545300, F4545305. 16 rooms, a/c, TV, bathroom, all with ocean view, restaurant, bar, 10 min to beach, close to airport, run by Juliette and Andrew Paul, friendly, helpful. **D-F** *St Martin*, T/F4546674, on main street. Clean, friendly, cooking and washing facilities.

Apartment hotels & villas
Full details from tourist offices

L-AL *Villa Beach Cottages*, Choc Beach, T4502884, www.villabeachcottages.com Beach-front cottages with gingerbread fretwork, wooden shutters and jalousies, 1 or 2 bedrooms with 4-poster beds, a/c, fans, TV, phone, data ports, kitchen, living room, balcony with hammocks, Derek Walcott used to spend his holidays in what is now called the 'Nobel Cottage', lovely honeymoon villa, 9 new villa suites, *Coconuts* restaurant with bar and grill, car rental, tours desk. Alternatively, or in combination, under same ownership is **LL-AL** *La Dauphine Estate*, a 4-bedroom Great House and 2-bedroom Chateau Laffitte on a 200-acre plantation 5 miles from Soufrière. Built in 1890 in gingerbread style, surrounded by lush gardens and hills, recently refurbished to modern standards, housekeeper/cook provided, good hiking along nature trails and through fruit plantation. *Marlin Quay*, Gros Islet, T4520393, F4520383. On the waterfront in Rodney Bay, a villa resort offering a variety of rooms, studios and 1-2 bedroomed terraced villas, very comfortable and spacious, well equipped, views over lagoon, some with jacuzzi on roof, decks, verandas. Highly recommended for families or couples, restaurants attached, 2 pools, one small, one 40 ft long for exercise swimming.

Camping

The National Trust has opened a campsite on a 133-acre site at Anse La Liberté (see above) with tents, raised wooden platforms or levelled bare sites, picnic tables, showers, black sand beach, trails and a central building with an unobstructed view of the west coast and a fantastic place from which to watch the sunset, T4537656, www.slunatrust.org Elsewhere camping is dangerous and there are no facilities.

Eating
All the large hotels have a selection of restaurants and there are snack bars and restaurants all along the west coast. Most places add a 10% service charge

Street vendors In Castries cold drinks are sold on street corners, EC$1 for a coke, drink it and return the bottle. Coconut water sold by vendors is always refreshingly cool and sterile. Vendors outside *Julian's* at Gablewoods Mall sometimes sell home made cassava bread and a local delicacy called permi made of cornmeal and coconut wrapped up in a banana leaf. For other foods such as bakes, floats, fish, chicken, dal rotis (split pea), be sure that they are freshly cooked for the best flavour.

Castries *Kimlans*, Derek Walcott Square, T4521136. Upstairs café and bar with veranda, cheap, serves local food, open 0700-2300 Mon-Sat. *Chung's*, on John Compton Highway opposite the playing field, T4521499. Open 1100-2000 or so, pleasant, good food, inexpensive, for EC$16.50 you get soup, 3 choices from the menu and coffee, MSG used in a few dishes, if you don't want it, say so, will also cater for allergies, such as wheat. *Flamingo*, William Peter Blvd. Favourite local place for a cheeseburger (EC$6.50) or roti, open until about 1600, closes about 1200 on Sat, for a chicken roti specify you want it without skin and bones. *Quick Bite*, on Mongiraud, adjacent to the S&S building, T4523063. Vegetarian salad bar and takeaway, specializes in soya meals. There are about 10 good value local eateries in the street adjoining the central market, tables outside, heaped plates of local food, lunchtime only.

South of Castries On the Top of the Morne, *Bon Appetit* is recommended for its daily specials and spectacular views, but is not cheap, meals from EC$35, T4522757. Also on the Morne, *The Green Parrot*, T4523399. 4-course dinner EC$95, serves excellent lunches daily, lots of Caribbean specialities and good selection of tropical vegetables, have a cocktail in the lounge before dinner, the chairs are worth it alone, shows Wed, Sat, Ladies' Night Mon.

North of Castries *BJ's Pepper Pot*, along the main road in Marisule, about halfway between Castries and Rodney Bay, T4501030. Jamaican cooking, prices up to EC$18, open Tue-Sat, from 1100. *Coal Pot*, outstanding, at Vigie Marina, T4525566. The place to eat, reservations essential, lunch and dinner except Sat when dinner only, closed Sun. *Friends* at Casa Vigie, first floor, just below the Venezuelan embassy. Patisserie and café, very good sandwiches attractive, open Mon-Thu, Fri 1000-2400, Sat 1000-1800, lovely walk from here to the Vigie lighthouse. *Froggie Jack's*, tucked away at Vigie Cove, T4581900, riouxj@candw.lc Open for lunch and dinner, try their home-smoked local fish, run by former executives at *Anse Chastenet* and *Jalousie*. **Miss Saigon**, Gablewoods Mall, T4517309. Serves full English breakfast, EC$18, Chinese and Oriental lunch and dinner, open daily. *The Wharf* restaurant, bar and dancing at Choc Bay, short distance past Gablewoods Mall. Beach setting, waiter service to your sunbed, varied menu, reasonable prices, beer EC$5-6, house wine EC$6, BLT EC$12, hamburger EC$15, happy hour 1800-1900 daily, open 0900-2400. *Tiggis*, Gablewoods Mall, T4524815, a/c, very good food and service, popular for lunch but dinner looks like leftovers, open Mon-Sat 0830-2200, soups, meals, baguettes, sandwiches, desserts, free salad bar with all dinners. *En Bas Bwapen Créole Kitchen*, behind a fence at the bend in the Castries to Gros Islet road as it runs by the airport runway, T4521971. Breakfast and lunch, most expensive meal EC$10.

   Rodney Bay *Big Chef*, just round the bend from Shamrock, T4500210. Owner/chef Peter Kouly from Denmark is a local character of note, popular steak house, open Mon-Sat from 1800. *Capone's*, is a restaurant in the speakeasy style of the 1920s, open for dinner only and quite expensive, but attached to a pizzeria, open from 1100, both closed Sun-Mon, with prices starting at EC$12, T4520284. *Charthouse*, T4528115. Closed Sun, known for its steak, seafood and spare ribs, excellent rib steak. *Memories of Hong Kong*, opposite *Royal St Lucian* hotel, T/F4528218. Chinese chef from Hong Kong, expensive but excellent, you can inspect the kitchens, open Mon-Sat 1700-2230. *Rumours*, opposite Scotia Bank, T4529249. Sports bar, pool tables, lots of TVs, burgers, fish'n'chips, steak, not pricey. *The Lime* serves good meals and snacks at moderate prices, T4520761. Friendly, open from 1100 till late, closed Tue. *Triangle Pub*, across from the *Lime*, T4520334. Open daily 1100-late, local food and barbecue, eat in or take out, live bands, pan, jazz. *Razmataz*, opposite *Royal St Lucian*, T/F4529800. Indian, good, friendly, open from 1600, happy hour 1700-1900, if you're still around after that, John plays guitar and sings romantic songs from the 60s and 70s, or on Sat a belly dancer weaves her way around the diners, closed Thu. *Shamrock's Pub*, T4528725. 6 TVs, pool tables, darts, pub grub, open daily. *Elena's* ice cream parlour, has tables under umbrellas outside in a small courtyard, home-made ice cream and local fruit sorbets, good cappuccino and snacks, also another outlet at the Marina called *Café Olé*. Directly on the beach at Reduit is *Spinnakers*, T4528491. Breakfast, lunch and dinner daily, with full English breakfast EC$26, happy hour 1800-1900, excellent location, though food and service suffer when it is busy, good too for coffee and desserts, they also hire out loungers for EC$5 per day. Just by *Spinnakers* is *The Cat's Whiskers*, T4528880. Traditional English pub food, Sun roast beef and Yorkshire pudding, steak and kidney pie, Cornish pasties, etc, closed Mon, open 0800-2300. *Eagles Inn*, at the entrance to Rodney Bay Marina. You can sit and watch the boats go by and enjoy good and not too expensive cuisine. Great fish. On the highway, just past Julian's supermarket, are *Key Largo*, good pizza from wood-fired oven, and *Tilly's 2x4*, T4584440. Built like a couple of quaint local chattel houses, good Creole food, open daily for lunch and dinner, entrance from the road on foot but around the back by car. *Tropicana*, at the marina, T4520351. Good menu, live jazz or karaoke some evenings. *Breadbasket*, at the marina, a favourite for breakfast and for home-made bread and pastries. At Pigeon Island, *Jambe de Bois*, serves breakfast and reasonably priced meals until 2130, offering cakes, salads, art gallery, book swap, internet access at EC$20 per hr. *Captain's Cellar*, tables outside with good view over the channel and Burgot Rocks , food simple and inexpensive.

   Gros Islet *The Wall*, corner of Marie Thérèse and Dauphin Streets. Excellent value, US$4.50 for huge plateful, rooms available, see above. See also *Panache* guesthouse, above, for local food. *Milo's*, next door to *Anette's* (see Sleeping, above). New, clean and very good restaurant in colonial house, Milo is a super host and prices are medium for the area.

   Cap Estate *The Great House Restaurant*, T4500450, greathouse@clubstlucia.com. Traditional tea from 1630-1730 and watch the sunset, happy hour 1730-1830, dinner expensive, 1830-2145, eat à la carte or Great House menu EC$100, closed Mon.

   Marigot Bay Several hotels for lunch and dinner, but *JJ's Restaurant and Bar* on the bay is a cheaper alternative, T4514076. Specializes in fresh local dishes, open from 1000 till late, reasonably priced crayfish, crab and lobster, Wed night crabs and a live band, Fri salsa, Sat live band. *Chateau Mago*, T4524772. St Lucian-Indian cuisine, open daily 0700-1100, serves traditional hot bakes and cocoa tea for breakfast, credit cards accepted, reservations advised. *Shack Bar & Grill*, T4514145. Built over the water, tie up for dinghies, burgers, steaks, seafood, open Mon-Fri from 1500, Sat-Sun from 1200, happy hour 1700-1900, reservations recommended for dinner 1830-2200.

Windward Islands

Soufrière *The Still* specializes in authentic St Lucian dishes, T4597224. Open daily 0800-1700 it is not cheap but serves local vegetables grown on site. *The Humming Bird*, T4597232, is a good place to eat and take a swim. French, Creole and seafood, daily specials, good but expensive, barman is a great fund of information on horoscopes, good views, open from 0700. *Dasheene*, at Ladera Resort, T4597323. Good food, chef cooks with local produce, wonderful views, worth coming here even if only for a drink just for the views. The *Purity Bakery* near the church in the main square serves breakfast with good coffee, rolls and cakes. *Le Haut Plantation* on the west coast road 1 km north of Soufrière. Huge TV in sports bar, open 1000-2100, excellent 3-course lunch US$9.50, dinner also delicious with good wine list, stunning views of Pitons and Sulphur Springs, also 6 rooms. At Étangs Soufrière, on the road to Vieux Fort, is *The Barbican* restaurant and bar, T4597888. Run by the very welcoming Mr and Mrs Smith, local food at local prices, good home cooking, clean, popular. *The Old Courthouse*, T4595002. Bar, restaurant, batik gallery, French Creole and Southeast Asian dishes, waterfront dining, good view but can be noisy, open daily, credit cards. On Market St there is a pleasant rasta eating place run by *Jalam*, in a wooden house up a couple of steps from street level, small, clean, cheap, EC$10 for a dal, a roti and 2 fresh juices.

Vieux Fort

Several places within walking distance of the airport for drinks, meal or a swim if you are passing time before a flight

Close to Hewanorra Airport is the *Annex*, T4546200. Open from 0900 to midnight weekdays, 1000-0200 weekends, good food. At Anse de Sables beach is *Reef*, owned by Cecile Wiltshire, pleasant bar, local drinks and delicacies, reasonable prices, tables out by the beach as well as inside the building. A bit further down is *Sandy Beach* restaurant and bar on the beach and on the highway. Excellent location, delightful stopping place, good food, a bit overpriced but not dreadful, have a swim and lunch. *Sapphire*, near bus station, opposite football pitch. Good local food at low prices, run by Frenchman who brought his mother from France to cook.

Festivals

There is lots of music, dancing and drinking. Everything goes on for hours, great stamina is required to keep going

Carnival is a high point in the island's cultural activities, when colourful bands and costumed revellers make up processions through the streets. After some debate it was decided to move Carnival in 1999 from February to **Jul**, partly so as not to conflict with Trinidad's Carnival. On the Sat are the calypso finals, on Sun the King and Queen of the band followed by J'ouvert at 0400 until 0800 or 0900. On Mon and Tue the official parades of the bands take place. Most official activities take place at Marchand Ground but warming-up parties and concerts are held all over the place. Tue night there is another street party.

Independence Day is **22 Feb** and is celebrated quite extensively. There is a large exhibition lasting several days from the various ministries, business and industry, and NGOs, such as the National Trust, and various sporting events, serious discussions and musical programmes. On the Sun preceeding **1 May**, the *Festival of Comedy* is held at Pigeon Point (Cultural Centre if it is raining), organized by the National Trust. The annual *St Lucia Jazz Festival* in **May** is now an internationally recognized event, drawing large crowds every year. Most concerts are open-air and take place in the evening, although fringe events are held anywhere, anytime, with local bands playing in Castries at lunchtime. As well as jazz, played by international stars, you can hear Latin, salsa, soca and zouk, steel drums or Bob Marley. For more details T4518566, www.stluciajazz.org Tickets from US$35 or a season pass US$230. Contact the Department of Culture for programmes as shows are often poorly advertised. Tickets available at the Department of Culture and *Sunshine Bookstore* (Gablewoods Mall). On **29 Jun** *St Peter's Day* is celebrated as the Fisherman's Feast, in which all the fishing boats are decorated. The *Feast of the Rose of Lima* (Fét La Wòz), on **30 Aug**, and the *Feast of St Margaret Mary Alacoque* (La Marguerite), on **17 Oct**, are big rival flower festivals. Members of the societies gather in various public places around the island to dance and sing in costume. The first Mon in **Oct** is *Thanksgiving*, held either to give thanks for no hurricane or for survival of a hurricane. *Jounen Kweyol* (Creole Day), on the last Sun in **Oct**, although activities are held throughout the month. Four or five rural communities are selected for the celebration. There is local food, craft, music and different cultural shows. Expect traffic jams everywhere as people visit venues across the island. A lot is in kweyol/patois, but you will still have a good time and a chance to sample mouth-watering local food. *St Cecilia's Day*, held on **22 Nov**, is also known as Musician's Day (St Cecilia is the patron saint of music). *St Lucy's Day*, **13 Dec**, used to be called Discovery Day, but as Columbus' log shows he was not in the area at that time, it was renamed. It is now known as the National Festival of Lights and Renewal. St Lucy, the patron saint of light, is honoured by a procession of lanterns. For details contact Castries City Council, T4522611 ext 7071.

Fri nights are big for going out. Highlight of the week for locals is currently **Seafood Friday**, at Anse La Raye, where you can get the cheapest lobster and crayfish on the island in season, but it tends to run out by 2100, so get there early. The entire street running parallel to the bay has chairs and tables under awnings, very friendly, no hassling, music at a bearable pitch, sometimes a local quadrille band. Later on, head for the jump up at Gros Islet (see page 637), where it is hard to resist getting involved and you can get beer, barbecued chicken legs, lambi/conch, accra (fish cakes) and floats from the street stalls.

Nightlife

In May, nightlife is dominated by the annual jazz festival with lots of outdoor concerts

Most of St Lucia's nightlife revolves around the hotels, while some restaurants host live bands. The choice varies from steel bands, jazz groups, folk dancing, crab racing, fire eating and limbo dancers. The hotels welcome guests from outside.

Around Rodney Bay, venues like **The Late Lime** (upstairs at *The Lime*) are popular places for those who just want to hang out. Behind *The Lime* is **Jazz Lounge**, with live music most nights and upstairs is *The Roof Garden* restaurant. **Big Wood**, above *Eagles Inn* at entrance to Rodney Bay Marina. Reasonable dance floor, mezzanine with comfortable chairs, 3 bars and restaurant service from downstairs, pool tables, TV, etc, in separate room, open Tue-Sun, age limit 21 for women, 24 for men, photo ID required. Under same ownership and adjacent is **Happy Day Bar**, gives 2 drinks for the price of one all day, clumsy system of vouchers for the second drink, lots of hassling of unaccompanied women. **Indies** is a nightclub and disco (over 21s) next to the *Bay Gardens Inn*, Rodney Bay, fairly low key except when they have a love show and then they are packed. **Back Door@Indies** is also good, a good selection of Caribbean and international music can be heard, depending on the night, look out for specials, Wed package for US$15 includes admission, free drinks and round trip taxi to nearby hotels, EC$20 cover charge Fri and Sat, free shuttle bus from major hotels, late night happy hour 2200-2400. **Annex** in Vieux Fort has live music regularly. **JJ's**, Marigot, T4514076, casual, good mixture of locals and tourists, Caribbean music in simple disco, Fri can be very busy, Sat pleasantly so, frequent shows, live bands, karaoke, taxi service can be arranged.

For a more cultural evening, tours are available to **La Sikwi**, patois for sugar mill, at Anse La Raye. There is a visit to the 150 year-old mill, followed by a full costume play reliving life in the village on a stage set into the hills with jazz bands and local acts. Gilland Adjhoda and his sons who organize events here can be contacted at the *Caribbean Hospitality Group*, T4516511, F4523714. There are (irregular) shows: concerts, drama, dance, comedy, at the **National Cultural Centre** (Castries), the **Light House Theatre** (Tapion) and the **Great House Theatre** (Cap Estate). They can give you a better taste of St Lucian culture than hotel shows.

Pointe Seraphine, next to the main port in Castries, is a designer-built, duty-free shopping centre (same opening hours as other shops, so closed Sat afternoon), with many tourist-oriented outlets, restaurants, entertainment and tour operators. Goods bought here can be delivered directly to the airport. Cruise ships can tie up at the complex's own berths. **JQ Mall** at Rodney Bay is also a duty-free facility. On the top floor there is a local arts and crafts outlet guaranteed 100% St Lucian. Batik fabrics and cotton clothing from **Caribelle Batik** on Old Victoria Rd, The Morne and Bridge St. **Bagshaw's** silk screening workshops at La Toc, T4522139, are very popular, studio open Mon-Fri 0830-1630, Sat 0830-1200, also shops at *Marigot* and *Windjammer*. High-quality local crafts and paintings from **Artsibit**, corner of Brazil and Mongiraud streets, open Mon-Fri 0900-1700, Sat 0930-1300. **Eudovics Art Studio**, T4522747, in Goodlands, coming down from the Morne heading south, sells local handicraft and beautiful large wood carvings. **Pieces of Eight**, in the Rodney Bay Marina next to the *Caribbean Art Gallery*, has a selection of Caribbean gifts and sailing books. It is also the HQ for the local animal protection society, SLAPS, which is campaigning against a proposed captive dolphin facility in St Lucia.

Shopping

Bookshops *Sunshine Bookshop*, *Gablewoods Mall* (open Mon-Fri 0900-1745, Sat 0900-1630), *JQ Mall* (open Mon-Sat 0900-1800, Sun 1000-1300), and *Point Seraphine*, books, foreign newspapers and magazines, open Mon-Fri 0830-1630, Sat half day; *Book Salon*, Jeremie St on corner of Laborie St, good selection of paperbacks, several books on St Lucia,

Windward Islands

also stationery. *Rodney Bay Shipping Services* runs a book exchange, 2 for 1, mostly spy thrillers and light novels, not a huge selection, but useful. *Jambe de Bois* on Pigeon Island also has a book swap.

Buy a cocoa stick or 10 for US$5. To make hot chocolate, put 2 tablespoons of grated cocoa in a pan with half a pint of water and boil for 15 minutes, strain, then add dry milk, sugar, cinnamon and nutmeg to taste

Market day in Castries is Sat, very picturesque (much quieter on other days, speakers of Patois pay less than those who do not). A new public market has been built on the Castries waterfront, with the old market building renovated and turned into a craft market. *Wire World*, booth 3, charming figures by the award-winning Paulinus Clifford, T4538727, also at *Pointe Seraphine*, he and the next artisan, Augustus Simon, a potter, T4521507, will craft to order. Buy a coal-pot (native barbecue) for EC$12 and bring it home on your lap. There is a *Fisherman's Co-operative Market* on the John Compton Highway at the entrance to *Pointe Seraphine*. Fish is also sold by a Martiniquan woman inside the public market, good variety, hygienically displayed, and at an outlet outside the supermarket at *JQ's Mall*, Rodney Bay. Many fishermen still sell their catch wherever they can. Fish is cheap and fresh. *JQ's* supermarket at the traffic lights at the end of the Vigie runway, open Mon-Fri 0800-1900, Sat 0800-1600, bank next door, fair range of goods, also supermarket on the William Peter Blvd. *Gablewoods Shopping Mall*, between Rodney Bay and Castries, has a selection of boutiques, gift shops, book shop, post office, pharmacy, deli, open-air eating places and *Julian's Supermarket*, open Mon-Thu 0800-2000, Fri, Sat until 2100, Sun 0800-1300. Next door is a delicatessen. A few doors away is the *Sea Island Cotton Shop*, the main outlet for Caribelle Batik clothes. *Garden Gate Flowers* has takeaway boxes (cargo transport) and bouquets (hand luggage) of ginger, heliconia, anthuriums, 48 hrs notice required for export, US$12-30, at Bois D'Orange T4529176, at Hewanorra T4547651, F4529023. At *Rodney Bay Shopping Centre*, is *Vibes Music Store*, T4580056, www.vibesmusicstore.com with all the latest releases in a variety of styles. On the way to Gros Islet from Castries turn left just after the Texaco station for the studio *Zaka's*, where masks and totems are carved from driftwood collected along the Atlantic coast or discarded lumber off-cuts found in the forest. Prices from EC$140, open Mon-Fri 1000-1500, T4520946, also available from *Jambe de Bois* at Pigeon Island. Llewellyn Xavier has opened a gallery, *Caribbean Art Gallery*, with inexpensive framed prints and antique maps as well as his own work and that of local artists, 0900-1700 Mon-Sat, T4528071. Soufrière has a market on the waterfront.

Sports

For diving and watersports, see pages 632 and 633

There is a 6,829-yd, par 71, 18-hole **golf** course and driving range at Cap Estate, the *St Lucia Golf & Country Club* (green fee US$70 for 9 holes, US$95 for 18 holes, golf carts mandatory, T4508523, www.stluciagolf.com) and a private course for guests at La Toc. **Cycling** has become popular, mostly in groups with a guide. *Carib Travel*, T4522151, have 15 Rockhoppers and offer a trip starting at Paix Bouche through mountain villages down to Gros Islet. *Island Bike Hikes*, T4580908, www.cyclestlucia.com, have vehicle-supported and tailor-made bike tours from US$58, a great way to explore the beaches of the northeast coast. *Bike St Lucia*, T4597755, www.bikestlucia.com, are on a beach just north of *Anse Chastenet* (linked to *Scuba St Lucia*) and offer off-road riding on trails through 400 acres of forest (jungle biking). They have a fleet of Cannondale F800 CAAD-3 bikes, which are not for use away from their trails. Accessible only by boat, they organize transfers from your hotel, lunch, snorkelling, etc, US$89.

Ask at Trim's Stables for information on horse racing, usually held on public holidays at Cas-en-Bas and in Vieux Fort

Horses for hire at *Trim's Stables*, Cas-en-Bas, T4508273, riding for beginners or advanced also offers lessons, 1-hr rides US$40, 2hrs US$50 and picnic trips to the Atlantic, US$75. *Country Saddles*, T4500197, highly recommended for a ride through the countryside and the seashore, US$55, good horses, guides are encouraging with beginners and give the more experienced lots of fun. The *International Riding Stables* in Gros llet also does trail rides and caters for all levels, T4528139, choice of English or Western style, US$35 1 hr, US$50 2hrs, US$70 half-day picnic trip. *North Point Riding Stables*, Cap Estate, takes groups to Cas-en-Bas Beach, Donkey Beach, Pigeon Point or Gros Islet, US$35 1½ hrs, min age 12, T4508853. *Fayolle Stables & Riding School* offers similar sessions, US$40 1 hr, US$50 2 hrs, US$75 half-day trip with beach barbecue. Prices usually include transfers.

Cricket and **football** are the main spectator sports. Basketball, netball and volleyball are also popular. Every village has a cricket game at weekends or after work in the season, using makeshift equipment such as sticks or palm frond bases as bats. St Lucia hosted its first Test Match in 2003 between the West Indies and Sri Lanka at the Beausejour Cricket Ground and more international matches are being held here.

Most hotels will arrange tours (US$40-80) to the island's principal attractions around **Tour operators** Soufrière either by road, boat or helicopter. Coach tours are cheaper and are usually daily in high season, falling to once or twice a week off season. Alternatives are to go by boat (easy between Castries and Soufrière, some hotels have their own boats: *Anse Chastanet, Jalousie Plantation, Windjammer Landing* and *Sandals*) or by helicopter (recommended for a spectacular view of the sulphur springs). From **Pointe Seraphine** a north island helicopter tour costs US$45, 10 mins; south island US$80, 20 mins; a heli-hike with tour of Atlantic beaches and Cactus Valley US$65, T4500806; helicopters can also be hired for airport transfers, US$100 from Pointe Seraphine to *Hewanorra*, also pick-up from some hotels. Local tour operators offer highly recommended plantation tours; *Errard and Balenbouche* offer fascinating insights into colonial history and local environments. A tour of a working banana plantation, US$50, is recommended, you see a lot of the country and see and taste a lot of native fruit and vegetables. There are now 10 sites which constitute the *St Lucia Heritage Tours*, T4516058 at Pointe Seraphine, T4515067 at La Place Carenage, sluheritage@candw.lc, including **Latille Falls** (20-ft waterfall and pools where you can swim), **Fond d'Or Nature and Historical Park** (hiking trails to plantation house ruins, Amerindian remains and the beach), **Fond Latisab Créole Park** (demonstrations of traditional methods of making cassava bread, catching cray fish, etc) and the **Folk Research Centre** (19th-century building on Mount Pleasant documenting kweyol culture and history). Costs vary from US$2-12, depending on the activities offered, a full-day tour booked through a tour agency will be around US$60. More are being developed. *St Lucia Distillers* has an excellent rum factory tour with tasting, shop for purchases, south towards Marigot, T4514258. *The National Trust* (PO Box 595, Castries, T4525005, natrust@candw.lc) runs excursions to Maria Island and Fregate Island Reserve, see Fauna and flora, above, US$75 to Maria Island if booked through a tour agency. You can take a carriage ride through the north of the island, or spend an evening cruising into the sunset with as much champagne as you can drink. There are also day trips to neighbouring islands: day sail to Martinique US$95, Dominica US$215, Grenadines including sail, US$199-245, Barbados US$230 and others. The main tour agencies are *St Lucia Reps/Sunlink Tours*, T4528232, www.stluciareps.com *Spice Travel*, T4520866, www.casalucia.com; *Solar Tours*, T4519041; *Barnards Travel*, T4522214; *Barefoot Holidays*, T4500507, www.travelfile.com/ get/baredays.html In Vieux Fort is *Rainbow Option Tours & Services*, run by Nadine Edwards (T4548202), Paula Edwards (T4549156) and Julius James (T4545014). *ATV Adventures* have guided ATV rides, T4526441, mctours@candw.lc *Wilderness Explorers*, based in Guyana, www.wilderness-explorers.com, specialize in nature and adventure travel.

Long distance Air From Europe The only direct scheduled services are with *BWIA, Virgin* **Transport** *Atlantic* or *British Airways* (via Antigua) from London. **From North America** *BWIA* has *Check in is three hours* flights, via Barbados from New York and Miami. *Air Jamaica* from New York and *USAir* from *before a flight, kill* Philadelphia. *Air Canada* flies from Toronto. **From the Caribbean** Lots of flights from *time on the beach* Anguilla, Antigua, Barbados, Dominica, Fort-de-France, Grenada, Montego Bay, *at Vigie or at the reef,* Pointe-à-Pitre, Port of Spain, St Kitts, St Vincent, San Juan and Tortola with *American Eagle*, *a short drive from* *LIAT, Caribbean Star, Air Caraïbes, BWIA* and *Air Jamaica*. *Hewanorra*

Airports St Lucia has 2 airports: **George F Charles Airport** (formely Vigie) (T4521156), mainly for inter-island flights (*Caribbean Star, Liat, BWIA, American Eagle* from San Juan, *Air Caraïbes* from the French Antilles with *Air France* connections) only (2 miles from Castries, taxi for US$7.50, no exchange facilities), and **Hewanorra International Airport** (T4546355) in the Vieux Fort district, where international flights land (*British Airways, Virgin Atlantic, BWIA, Air Canada, Air Jamaica* and charter flights); there is an air shuttle to Vigie by helicopter, 12 mins, US$90. Alternatively a taxi to Castries costs US$60 (though, out of season, you can negotiate a cheaper rate) and it will take you 1½-2 hrs to reach the resorts north of Castries. A cheaper service is the *St Lucia Air Shuttle*, run by *Paradise Tourist Services*, Rodney Bay, behind *Julian's Supermarket*, by reservation only, US$17.50 one way, US$33 round trip, per person, credit cards accepted, T4529329, www.stluciatip.com You can also negotiate a ride with one of the transfer buses from hotels for EC$40, enquire at *St Lucia Reps*, T4569100, www.sunlinktours.com If you are travelling light you can walk to the main road and catch the minibus or route taxi to Castries, or if you are staying in Vieux Fort you can walk there, but be careful of the fast traffic. No baggage storage yet available at Hewanorra. Try to arrange it with one of the Vieux Fort hotels.

Look out for schools of dolphins on the crossing to Martinique, good view from the upper deck

Boat *Express des Îles*, links St Lucia with the French Antilles and Dominica, reservations T4565000, www.express-des-isles.com, or *Cox & Co Ltd*, William Peter Blvd, T4522211. You cannot buy a ticket at the dock, so remember to buy weekend tickets in advance as the office is shut then. Tickets ordered in advance and collected at the dock can not be paid for by credit card. Departs Castries for Fort-de-France Mon 0700, Tue 1700, Wed 1300, Sat 0700, Sun 1300, 1hr 20 mins, return Tue 0800, Wed 0800, Fri 1630, Sat 1700, Sun 1830, EC$183 day return plus EC$24 departure tax, Sat is the only day a day trip is possible, recommended, you get there in time for coffee and a croissant, with plenty of time for sightseeing and eating well. Customs clearance can be tedious with several hundred passengers. On Wed, Sat and Sun, the boat continues to Roseau (3½ -4 hrs) and Pointe-à-Pitre (5 ¾-6 ¼ hrs), returning from Pointe-à-Pitre Fri 1200 and Sun 1400, and Roseau Fri 1415 and Sun 1615. Alternatively you can take a yacht or motor launch to Martinique, see Day sails, above. Many cruise lines call. Captain Artes of the S/H *Krios*, Rodney Bay Harbour, T4528531, runs a boat taxi (sailing): to Martinique, 3 days, US$315 plus customs charges, Customs officers will make contact for you. Highly recommended.

Local Bus Bus stands in Castries are at the bottom of Darling Rd on the west side of the gardens and extending back to the multi-storey car park on Peynier St. Route 1 is Castries to Gros Islet, Route 2 Castries to Vieux Fort, Route 3 Castries to Soufrière, Route 4 Vieux Fort environs, Route 5 Castries central zone. Each route then has sub-routes, eg Route 1a is Castries-Gros Islet-Massade-Cap Estate, Route 1b is Castries-Union-Balata-Babonneau-Garrand, etc. Short journeys are only EC$1-1.25, rising to EC$2 Castries to Gros Islet, or to Soufrière, EC$7; from Gros Islet to Rodney Bay EC$1; from Soufrière to Vieux Fort EC$4; children half price. Ask the driver to tell you when your stop comes up.

It is often cheaper to organize car hire from abroad. You can only hire a car if aged 25 or over

Car Car hire is about US$45-95 per day, with discounts for weekly rates . Some car hire companies are open to negotiation. Optional collision damage waiver is another US$10-22 per day. A 5% tax is added to everything. A one-day licence costs US$12, or US$21 for up to 3 months. If arriving at George F L Charles (formerly Vigie) Airport, get your international licence endorsed at the immigration desk (closed 1300-1500) after going through customs. Car hire companies can usually arrange a licence. Car rental agencies include *Avis*, Vide Bouteille (T4522700, F4531536) and lots of other locations; *Hertz* headquarters at Rodney Bay (T4520680, F4528980); *Budget*, in Castries, airport and Marisule T4520233, F4529362; *National*, just before the Gros Islet turn off, T4508721; *Courtesy*, Bay Gardens Inn, T4528140; at Rodney Bay are *Candida*, T4527076, and *TJ's*, T4520116. Most have offices at the hotels, airports and in Castries. Check for charges for pick-up and delivery. If dropping off a car at George F L Charles Airport you can sometimes leave the keys with the tourist desk if there is no office for your car hire company. *Wayne's Motorcycle Centre*, Vide Bouteille, T4520680, rents **bikes**; make sure you wear a helmet and have adequate insurance. Filling stations are open Mon-Sat 0630-2000, selected garages open Sun and holidays 1400-1800. They only sell unleaded fuel, at EC$7.75 per US gallon.

Ferries around the island include: *Rodney Bay Ferry* shuttles between the marina shops Marlin Quay, *St Lucian Hotel*, *Mortar and Pestle* and Pigeon Island, fares within the marina US$8 return, children under 12 half price, T4520087, also half-day trips to Pigeon Island including lunch, US$40, bookings at the yellow hut by the entrance to the *Lime Restaurant's* car park Jerome, T3841961, will take you from *Eagle's Inn* to Pigeon Island for EC$10. The *Gingerbread Express* in Marigot Bay costs EC$5 return, but is refunded by *Doolittle's Restaurant* if you eat or drink there and present your tickets. Water taxis and speedboats can be rented. Water taxis ply between Soufrière waterfront and Anse Chastenet, easier than driving the awful road.

Registered taxis have red number plates with the TX prefix. Minibuses have the T prefix

Taxi Fares are set by the Government, but the US$60 Castries-Soufrière fare doubles a unlucky tourists discover that there are no buses for the return journey. *Club St Lucia*, in the extreme north, to Castries, about 10 miles away, costs US$15-18 one way for 1-4 people US$3.75 per additional passenger. Fare from Castries to Gros Islet (for Fri evening street party), US$12; to Pigeon Island National Park, US$15.50 one way; to Vigie Airport, US$5; to Hewanorra Airport, US$56; Vigie Airport to Rodney Bay US$16; Marigot Bay to Hewanorra Airport US$45; to Vigie Airport US$22, to Castries US$20 (30 mins). If in doubt about the amount charged, check with the tourist office or hotel reception. You can see a copy of the fixed fares at the airport. At rush hour it is almost impossible to get a taxi so allow plenty of time, the traffic jams are amazing for such a small place. A trip round the island by taxi is about US$20 per hr for 1-4 people, with an additional US$5 per hr for a/c. Recommended taxi drivers are Kenneth James, T4536844, 4519778, Barnard Henry, T4501951, Samson Louis, T4500516 (or through the *Rex St Lucian* taxi stand) and Raymond Cepal, pager T4843583.

Airlines The following airlines have offices on Brazil St, Castries: *LIAT* (T4523051, Hewanorra Airport T4546341, Vigie Airport T4522348, F4536584); *Air Canada* (T4523051, Hewanorra T4546249); *Air Jamaica*, Hewanorra, T4548869, reconfirmations only; *British Airways*, Cox and Co Building, William Peter Blvd (T4523951, F4522900 Hewanorra T4546172); *Air Martinique*, George F Charles Airport, T4522463; *American Eagle* at George F Charles Airport, T4521820/1840; *American Airlines* ticket office on Micoud near Bridge St, no phone; *St Lucia Helicopters* at Pointe Seraphine, T4536950.

Directory

Banks *Bank of Nova Scotia* (T4522292), *Royal Bank of Canada* (T4522245), on William Peter Blvd, Castries; *FirstCaribbean International Bank* (T4523306), and the *St Lucia Co-operative Bank* (T4522881), on Bridge St, *National Commercial Bank*, Waterfront (T4522103), Castries. *CBC*, *National Commercial Bank* and *St Lucia Co-operative Bank* have branches in Vieux Fort, and *National Commercial Bank* in Soufrière; *FirstCaribbean International Bank* (T4529384) and *Royal Bank of Canada* (T4529921) at Rodney Bay marina. Banks opening hrs vary, but most are open 0800-1500 Mon-Thu, 0800-1700 Fri. *FirstCaribbean InternationalBank of Nova Scotia* (T4528805), *St Lucia Co-operative Bank* (JQ Mall, T4528882) and *Royal Bank of Canada* at Rodney Bay open Sat until 1200, as do the *National Commercial Bank* in Castries and in Gros Islet.

Communications Internet: Services at the *Gablewoods Mall* office of *Cable & Wireless*, EC$5 for 30 mins, at *Jambe de Bois* on Pigeon Island, EC$10 per hr, and also in the University Centre. Many hotels offer internet services to guests. **Post**: Main post office is on Bridge St, Castries, open Mon-Fri, 0830-1630, Sat, 0800-1200, poste restante at the rear. Other branches in Gablewoods and JQ's Malls. Postcards to Europe EC$0.50, to the USA EC$0.40; letters to Europe EC$1.10, to the USA and UK EC$0.95. The DHL office is on Bridge St. **Telephone**: *Cable and Wireless*, no longer has a monopoly and has been joined by *Digicell* and *AT&T*, all with offices on Bridge St, Castries. Hotels do not generally allow direct dialling, you will have to go through the operator, which can be slow and costly. Intra-island calls are EC$0.27 in the Castries zone, EC$0.45-0.75 to other zones, depending on time of day and day of week. Pay phones use EC$0.25 and EC$1 coins or cards. *Cable and Wireless* phone cards are sold for EC$10, EC$20, EC$40 or EC$53; with these you can phone abroad. There is a credit card phone at Vigie Airport operated via the boat phone network, open daily 0800-2200. Call USA T1-800-6747000; Sprint Express T1-800-2777468; BT Direct T1-800-3425284; Canada Direct T1-800-7442580; USA Direct phone at Rodney Bay Marina, or T1-800-8722881. If you want to dial a toll-free US number, replace the 800 with 400. You will be charged a local call.

Embassies and consulates *British High Commission*, NIS Building, Waterfront, Castries, T4522484, F4531543, open Mon-Fri 0830-1230. *Cuban* Embassy, Rodney Heights, T4584666. *Danish* Consulate, Cap Estate Golf Club, T4508522/3, F4508317. *Dominican Republic* Consulate, corner Brazil and Mongiraud Sts, T4521919. *French* Embassy, Casa Vigie, T452-2462/5877, F4527899. *Italian* Vice Consul, Reduit, T4520865, F4520869. *Netherlands* Consulate, M & C Building, Bridge St, Castries, T4522811, F4523592. *Norwegian* Consulate, Bridge St, Castries, T4522216. *Swedish* Consulate, Rodney Bay, T4500190. *Venezuelan* Embassy, Casa Vigie, T4524033, F4536747, Mon-Fri 0900-1430.

Medical services For emergency T911; *Aerojet Ambulance* for air evacuation, T4521600, F4532229; *Victoria Hospital*, Castries, T4522421/4537059; *St Jude's*, Vieux Fort, T4546041, *Soufrière Casualty*, T4597258, *Dennery*, T4533310; *Tapion*, T4592000. Larger hotels have resident doctors or doctors 'on call', visits cost about EC$50. If given a prescription, ask at the Pharmacy whether the medication is available 'over the counter', as this may be cheaper. Pharmacies in Castries, on the Gros Islet Highway, in Gablewoods Mall and in JQ Charles Mall, Rodney Bay.

As on most Caribbean islands, there is dengue fever so take anti-mosquito repellent

Background

Even though some St Lucians have claimed that their island was discovered by Columbus on St Lucy's day (13 December, the national holiday) in 1502, neither the date of discovery nor the discoverer are in fact known, for according to the evidence of Columbus' log, he appears to have missed the island and was not even in the area on St Lucy's Day. A Vatican globe of 1520 marks the island as Santa Lucía, suggesting that it was at least claimed by Spain. In 1605, 67 Englishmen en route to Guiana made an unsuccessful effort to settle, though a

History

▶ **Patois for beginners**

Until recently, Kweyol was not a written language but it has been developed to facilitate teaching.

For people interested in learning a few phrases of Creole, or Kweyol, there is a booklet, Visitors Guide to St Lucia Patois, *EC$14, and the* Kweyol Dictionary, *EC$10, available in* Valmont's Book Salon *on the corner of Jeremie and Laborie streets by the Tourist Office, and at* Sunshine Books *in Gablewoods Mall and Rodney Bay and other outlets.*

For the more ambitious reader there are traditional story booklets which explain a lot about country life. Short stories are written in a style a child can understand with an English translation at the back. Examples are Mwen Vin Wakonte Sa Ba'w *(I am going to explain it to you), which has a tale for every letter of the alphabet about an animal, or* Se'kon Sa I Fèt *(Know how it is done), a book about farm life. These books, part of a series of eight aimed at a St Lucian readership, are not available in shops. Contact the* Summer Institute of Linguistics, *Box 321, Vieux Fort, price around EC$5 each.*

The Folk Research Centre *(PO Box 514, Mount Pleasant, Castries, T4522279, F4517444, open Monday-Friday 0830-1630) preserves and documents the local culture and folklore and has published several books, a cassette (EC$30) and CD (EC$60):* Musical Traditions of St Lucia. A Handbook for Writing Creole *gives the main points and features, while a* Dictionary of St Lucian Creole *and* Annou Di-Y an Kweyol, *a collection of folk tales and expressions in Creole and English, accompany it well.*

In 1999 the New Testament was published in Kweyol.

With thanks to Ulrike Krauss.

Dutch expedition may have discovered the island first. At this time the island was inhabited by Caribs. There are Amerindian sites and artefacts on the island, some of which are of Arawak origin, suggesting that the Caribs had already driven them out or absorbed them by the time the Europeans arrived, as no trace of the Arawaks was found by them. The Indians called their island Iouanalao, which may have meant 'Where the iguana is found'. The name was later changed to Hiwanarau and then evolved to Hewanorra. In 1638 the first recorded settlement was made by English from Bermuda and St Kitts, but the colonists were killed by the Caribs about three years later.

In 1642 the King of France, claiming sovereignty over the island, ceded it to the French West India Company, who in 1650 sold it to MM Houel and Du Parquet. There were repeated attempts by the Caribs to expel the French, several governors were murdered. From 1660, the British began to renew their claim to the island and fighting for possession began in earnest. The settlers were mostly French, who developed a plantation economy based on slave labour. In all, St Lucia changed hands 14 times before it became a British Crown Colony in 1814 by the Treaty of Paris.

From 1838, the island was included in a Windward Islands Government, with a Governor resident first in Barbados and then Grenada. Universal adult suffrage was introduced in 1951. The St Lucia Labour Party (SLP) won the elections in that year and retained power until 1964. The United Workers' Party (UWP) then governed from 1964-79 and from 1982 onwards. In 1958 St Lucia joined the West Indies Federation, but it was short-lived following the withdrawal of Jamaica in 1961-62 (see page 220). In 1967, St Lucia gained full internal self-government, becoming a State in voluntary association with Britain, and in 1979 it gained full independence.

From 1964 until 1996 the UWP was led by Mr John Compton, who held power in 1964-79 and subsequently won elections in 1982, 1987 and 1992. In 1996 Mr Compton retired as leader of the UWP and was replaced as Prime Minister and leader of the party by Dr Vaughan Lewis, former Director General of the Organization of Eastern Caribbean States (OECS), who led the party into the 1997 elections. The May 1997 elections were a triumph for the SLP, who had been in opposition for 25 years apart from a brief period in 1979-82. Led by Dr Kenny Anthony they won 16 of the 17 seats, with the UWP gaining the single remaining seat, a result which took even the SLP by surprise. In the December 2001 election the Labour government was returned with a smaller majority (14 seats). Significantly, the two seats lost were in areas hard hit by the banana crisis, Micoud North and Dennery North, while the UWP retained Micoud

South. The world economic downturn, with its knock-on effects on tourism and the banana industry, has created considerable discontent and opposition to the government has grown.

St Lucia is the second largest of the Windwards, lying between St Vincent and Martinique **Geography** with an area of 238 sq miles. The scenery is of outstanding beauty, and in the neighbourhood of the Pitons, it has an element of grandeur. The highest peak is Morne Gimie, 3,118 ft, but the most spectacular are Gros Piton, 2,619 ft, and Petit Piton, 2,461 ft, which are old volcanic forest-clad plugs rising sheer out of the sea near the town of Soufrière on the west coast. A few miles away is one of the world's most accessible volcanoes with soufrières: vents in the volcano which exude hydrogen sulphide, steam and other gases and deposit sulphur and other compounds in pools of boiling water. The mountains are intersected by numerous short rivers which in places debouch into broad, fertile and well-cultivated valleys.

St Lucia is an independent member of the Commonwealth and the British monarch is the **Government** Head of State, represented by a Governor General (Dame Pearlette Louisy, the first woman to hold the post). The 17-member House of Assembly is elected every five years, while the 11 members of the Senate are appointed by the Governor General, six on the advice of the Prime Minister, three on the advice of the Leader of the Opposition and two of his own choice. The Constituency Boundaries Commission has recommended that the number of constituencies is increased from 17 to 19.

St Lucia's economy has historically been based on agriculture, originally sugar, but since the **Economy** 1920s particularly on bananas and also cocoa and coconuts. It has the largest banana crop in the Windward Islands, but production has slumped and the industry is in turmoil. Farmers have suffered because of low prices, storm damage and labour disputes. Greater competition in the European banana market, particularly after EC unification in 1992, is leading to diversification away from bananas; dairy farming, flowers and fisheries are being encouraged.

There is also some industry, with data processing and a diversified manufacturing sector producing clothing, toys, sportswear and diving gear, and 14% of the workforce is now engaged in manufacturing. However, unemployment in the manufacturing sector rose sharply in 1996 with the closure of three foreign-owned garment factories, which had been operating for nearly 10 years, the period during which tax-free concessions are granted. Since then, more companies have closed (garments, informatics) and jobs lost. Tourism is now the major foreign employer and foreign exchange earner, and some 250,000 visitors stay on the island each year, but this too is subject to the vagaries of the world economic situation.

There is a good deal of French cultural influence. Most of the islanders, who are predomi- **Culture** nantly of African descent (though a few Black Caribs are still to be found in certain areas), speak Creole/Kweyol, a similar language to French, and in rural areas many people, particularly the older generation, have great difficulty with English. There is a French provincial style of architecture; most place names are French; about 70% of the population are Roman Catholics. The French Caribbean also has an influence on music, you can hear zouk and cadance played as much as calypso and reggae. The Folk Research Centre (see box) has recorded local music. *Musical Traditions of St Lucia* has 32 selections representing all the musical genres, with information on the background of the various styles. *Lucian Kaiso* is an annual publication giving pictures and information on each season of St Lucian calypso. In the pre-Christmas period, small drum groups play in rural bars. Traditionally, singers improvise a few lines about people and events in the community and the public joins in. The singing is exclusively in Kweyol, wicked and full of sexual allusions.

One of the Caribbean's most renowned poets and playwrights in the English language, **Derek Walcott**, was born in St Lucia in 1930. He has published many collections of poems, an autobiography in verse, *Another Life*, critical works, and plays such as *Dream on Monkey Mountain*. Walcott uses English poetic traditions, with a close understanding of the inner magic of the language (Robert Graves), to expose the historical and cultural facets of the Caribbean. His books are highly recommended, including his narrative poem *Omeros*, which contributed to his winning the 1992 Nobel Prize for Literature. Other St Lucian writers worth reading are the novelists **Garth St Omer** (*The Lights on the Hill*) and Earl Long (an MD in the USA), and the poets Jane King-Hippolyte, Kendal Hippolyte, John Robert Lee (Artefacts) and Jacintha Lee, who has a book of local legends. New authors to emerge in the 21st century include Anderson Reynolds, with his novel *Death By Fire*, and Michael Aubertin (head of the Dept of Culture) with his period romance *Neg Maron*.

St Lucia has also produced painters of international renown. **Dunstan St Omer** was born in St Lucia in 1927 into a Catholic family and is best known for his religious paintings. He created the altarpiece for the Jacmel church near Marigot Bay, where he painted his first black Christ, and reworked Castries Cathedral in 11 weeks in 1985 prior to the Pope's visit. St Omer and his four sons have also painted other countryside churches (Monchy and Fond St Jacques) and a quarter of a mile of sea wall in Anse La Raye. **Llewellyn Xavier** was born in Choiseul in 1945 but moved to Barbados in 1961, where he discovered painting. Galleries in North America and Europe have exhibited his work and his paintings are in many permanent collections. Xavier returned to St Lucia in 1987, where he was shocked by the environmental damage. He has since campaigned vigorously for the environment through his art. *The Global Council for Restoration of the Earth's Environment* is a work created from recycled materials including prints, postage stamps and seals and logos of preservation societies. It is on display at the artist's studio, T4509155 for an appointment, but he also has a gallery at the Rodney Bay Marina.

Other outstanding artists include **Ron Savory**, *Ron's Atelier and Framing Co*, Vide Bouteille Industrial Park, just past the roundabout at the end of the airport runway (called La Clery junction), T4524412. His rich rainforest scenes and his dancing figures are impressive and he sells collectables, souvenir art, paintings from originals to limited prints to prints, expensive to inexpensive. **Sean Bonnett St Remy** paints wonderful local scenes, village scenes with nostalgic charm and accuracy, he can be contacted at *Photographic Images*, 42 Brazil Street. **Winston Branch** is splashy, modern abstract, and shows internationally from London to Brazil. A recent display of his at the *Alliance Française* was painted directly on the walls. He is currently teaching in the USA. **Chris Cox** paints St Lucian birds, such as the parrot and the nightjar. He won an award at the Arts Award ceremony in January 2000 and can be contacted at Forestry. **Arnold Toulon**'s *Modern Art Gallery* in Bois d'Orange, T4529079, also exhibits local artists including **Cedric George** and **Nancy Cole,** along with his own works. Daniel Jean-Baptiste makes hand-painted, limited edition, silk artwork, call T4508000 for a private studio visit. **Alcina Nolley**, an artist and teacher of art, can refer you to many artists and artisans, particularly of the *Arts and Crafts Association*, T4532338, nolleym@candw.lc

The last week in January is Nobel Laureate Week, with lectures celebrating the two Nobel prize winners produced by the island (Sir Arthur Lewis and Derek Walcott). They were both born on 23 January. Other events include the annual Arts Awards, during which the Cultural Centre is packed, www.stlucia-arts.com

St Vincent and the Grenadines

IDD code: 784
Colour map 4, grid C5

St Vincent is green and fertile with a lush rainforest and mountainous interior, beautiful volcanic beaches and fishing villages, coconut groves and banana plantations. It is widely known for the superb sailing conditions provided by its 32 sister islands and cays and most visitors spend some time on a yacht, even if only for a day. Bareboat and crewed yachts are available for wherever you want to go. There are also very competitive regattas and yacht races held throughout the year, accompanied by a lot of parties and social events. The Grenadines have a certain exclusivity, some of the smaller islands are privately owned and Mustique is known for its villas owned by the rich, royal and famous. There are some fabulously expensive and luxurious places to stay, but there are also more moderate hotels, guesthouses and rental homes for those who don't want to spend all their time afloat.

Things to do in St Vincent and the Grenadines

- **Hiking up the volcano** is great: demanding but rewarding exercise and visually spectacular, highly recommended for a day away from the sea.
- **The sea, the sea**… That's what its all about. No trip to St Vincent and the Grenadines is complete without a day under sail, whether you're the skipper or the sunbather.
- The Tobago Cays are a snorkeller's paradise, but don't touch, just enjoy the underwater scenery as you float on the surface.
- **Canouan's beaches** go on for ever, soft pale sand, clear blue sea, empty, perfect.
- **Bequia** is the best place for restaurants and bars and great as part of a two-centre holiday: a villa here and then a yacht to see the rest of the islands, or take the ferry and see how the other half lives.

Windward Islands

Ins and outs

Air There are no direct services from Europe or North America but same day connecting flights are available through Antigua, Barbados, Puerto Rico and Trinidad. Light aircraft connect some of the Grenadine islands with Barbados and provide an air taxi service. **Sea** Many people arrive on yachts, having sailed across the Atlantic or through the Caribbean. There is an informal international ferry on a wooden fishing boat between Union Island and Carriacou (Grenada).

Getting there
See Transport, page 671, for further details

Air Flights within the Grenadines are cheap and reliable. *SVG Air* and *Mustique Airways* fly daily from St Vincent to Bequia, Canouan and Union Island (20 mins), and also to Mustique. *Trans Island Air (TIA)*, of Barbados, also has a Grenadines service, which can be booked through *Liat*. **Sea** There are several ferries between St Vincent and Bequia, while the mail boat, the *Barracouda*, links St Vincent with Bequia, Canouan, Mayreau and Union Island with a twice weekly service. **Road** Most, but not all, of the islands have a cheap bus service, which can be a minibus or a pick-up truck with seats in the back. Car hire is available on St Vincent and Bequia.

Getting around
Air taxi services connect the islands with short hop flights lasting only a few minutes

Temperatures the year round average between 77°F and 81°F, moderated by the trade winds; average rainfall is 60 in on the coast, 150 in in the interior, with the wettest months May to Nov. Best months to visit are therefore Dec to May. You can expect a shower most days in the hills of St Vincent, but the Grenadines are less forested and therefore drier.

Climate
Low season is June to mid-December

St Vincent and the Grenadines Department of Tourism, 3rd floor, Finance Complex, Bay St, Kingstown, T4571502, www.svgtourism.com, open Mon-Fri 0800-1200, 1300-1615; helpful desk at ET Joshua Airport, T4584379, hotel reservation EC\$1; on Bequia (by the jetty), T4583286, open Sun-Fri 0900-1230, 1330-1600, Sat morning only; on Union Island, between the dock and the *Clifton Beach Hotel*, T4588350, open daily 0800-1200, 1300-1600. The Tourist Office and the Hotel Association publish *Ins and Outs of St Vincent and the Grenadines* in association with Miller Publishing, an informative magazine on the islands. Bequia publishes its own brochure, *Holiday Bequia*, and *Mustique Airways* also has a magazine. **Maps:** a map of St Vincent, 1:50,000 and Kingstown, 1:10,000), EC\$15, is available from the Ministry of Agriculture, Lands and Survey Department, Murray Rd. In 1992 the Ordnance Survey (Southampton, UK) brought out a tourist map of St Vincent, 1:50,000, with insert of Kingstown, 1:10,000, double sided with Grenadines on the reverse, with text giving information, but it is not available in St Vincent.

Tourist information

Flora and fauna

St Vincent has a wide variety of tropical plants, most of which can be seen in the **Botanical Gardens**, where conservation of rare species has been practised since they were founded in 1765. There you can see the mangosteen fruit tree and one of the few examples of *Spachea perforata*, a tree once thought to be found only in St Vincent but now found in other parts of the world, as well as the famous third

The Wildlife Protection Act covers most of the island's birds, animals and reptiles and carries penalties for infringements

Touching down

See also Directory, pages 671 and 678

Boat information Ports of entry (own flag) are Wallilabou, on the northwest coast, Kingstown, Bequia (police station), Mustique and Union Island (airport, EC$10 weekdays during working hours, EC$25 overtime, holidays and weekends). Yachtsmen often anchor at Blue Lagoon or Young island and bus/taxi to Kingstown to complete customs and immigration formalities. Fees are EC$10/US$4 per person (EC$25 on Sat on Union Island) and charter yachts are charged US$2 per foot per month. For an exit stamp, go to the airport customs and immigration one day before departure. On Bequia local businesses deliver water, fuel, laundry, beer and groceries. Men and boys meet yachts in the northern St Vincent anchorages and ask to assist in tying stern line to a tree or offer other services. EC$10 is the current fee for tying up; other services negotiable. Others meet boats in Bequia, Union and the Tobago Cays, offering to supply seafood and groceries as well as selling T shirts and jewellery. They can take 'no' for an answer, but will return if you say 'maybe tomorrow'. Anchorages at Wallilabou, Young Island, Petit Byahaut, Blue Lagoon, Bequia, Palm (Prune) Island, Mustique, Canouan, Mayreau (Salt Whistle Bay and two others), Tobago Cays, Union Island (Clifton, Frigate Island, Chatham Bay), Petit St Vincent. **Marinas** at Caribbean Charter Yacht Yard, Lagoon Marina, Bequia Slipway, Anchorage Yacht Club on Union Island. **Moorings** at Young Island, Blue Lagoon, Friendship Bay, Union Island, Palm Island, Petit Byahaut (US$10 fee is deducted if you have dinner), Mustique. For possibilities of crewing on yachts, see the noticeboard at the Frangipani Yacht Services, Bequia.

Business hours Banks: Mon-Fri 0800-1200 or 1300, plus 1400 or 1500-1700 on Thu or Fri. The bank at the airport is open Mon-Fri 0830-1230, 1530-1730; **Government offices:** Mon-Fri 0800-1200, 1300-1615; **Shops:** Mon-Fri 0800-1200, 1300-1600, Sat 0800-1200.

Clothing Wear light, informal clothes, but do not wear bathing costumes or short shorts in shops or on Kingstown's streets.

Currency The East Caribbean dollar, EC$. EC$2.67=US$1.

Departure tax There is a departure tax of EC$30, or US$12.50.

Documents All visitors must have a passport and an onward, or return, ticket. Nationals of the UK, USA and Canada may enter for up to six months on proof of

---

generation sucker of the original breadfruit tree brought by Captain Bligh of the *Bounty* in 1793 from Tahiti. Other conservation work taking place in the gardens involves the endangered St Vincent parrot, *Amazona guildingii*, which is the national bird. An aviary, originally containing birds confiscated from illegal captors, now holds 12 parrots. The main colonies are around Buccament, Cumberland-Wallilabou, Linley-Richmond and Locust Valley-Colonarie Valley. A parrot reserve is being established in the upper Buccament Valley.

Another protected bird unique to St Vincent is the whistling warbler, and this, as well as the black hawk, the cocoa thrush, the crested hummingbird, the red-capped green tanager, green heron and other species can be seen, or at least heard, in the Buccament Valley. There are nature trails starting near the top of the Valley, passing through tropical forest, and it is possible to picnic. The Forestry Department have prepared official trail plans. A pamphlet details the Vermont Nature Trails, Wallilabou Falls, Richmond Beach, Trinity Falls, Falls of Baleine, Owia Salt Pond and La Soufrière Volcano Trails.

Diving and marine life

The Tobago Cays receive around 150 yachts a day in high season; they anchor on sand, but the dinghies can be seen on the coral reef

The underwater wildlife around St Vincent and the Grenadines is varied and beautiful. There are many types and colours of coral, including black coral at a depth of only 30 f in places. On the New Guinea Reef (Petit Byahaut) you can find three types of black coral in six different colours. The coral is protected so do not remove any. There are 1(marine protected areas including the northeast coast and the **Devil's Table** in Bequia **Isle à Quatre**, all **Mustique**, the **east coast of Canouan**, all of **Mayreau**, the **Tobago Cays**, the whole of **Palm Island, Petit St Vincent** and the surrounding reefs.

citizenship only. Other visitors who not need a visa are citizens of all Commonwealth countries, all the EU countries (except Eire and Portugal), Chile, Finland, Iceland, Liechtenstein, Norway, Switzerland, Sweden, Turkey, Uruguay and Venezuela. You will be asked where you will be staying on the island and will need a reservation, which can be done through the Tourist Office at the airport, before going through immigration (or you can make one up). You will usually be given entry until the day of departure on your ticket. If you are only given entry of a few days and want to stay longer, extensions are easily obtained for EC$20.

Duty-free allowance *200 cigarettes, or 50 cigars, or 250 grams of tobacco, and 40 fl oz of alcoholic beverage may be imported duty free.*

Emergency numbers *T999.*

Media *Newspapers The Herald is daily and contains news from wire services, including pages in French, Italian, Spanish, etc. Three newspapers, The Vincentian, Searchlight and The News, are published weekly. The News is editorially independent and by far the best. Radio Four radio*

stations: AM 705kHz, Nice FM 96.3, Hitz FM 107.3, WE FM 99.9. Weather can be heard on SSB weather net 4001 at 0800, 8104 at 0830. TV Two TV stations and Karib cable (26 channels).

Official time *Atlantic Standard Time, four hours behind GMT, 1 hr ahead of EST.*

Public holidays *1 Jan, Discovery and National Heroes Day (22 Jan), Good Fri and Easter Mon, Labour Day in May, Whit Mon, Caricom Day and Carnival Tue (in Jul), Aug Bank Holiday first Mon in Aug, Independence Day (27 Oct), Christmas Day and Boxing Day.*

Tourist offices overseas *Canada: 32 Park Rd, Toronto, Ontario M4W 2N4, T416-9245796, svgcan@home.com UK 10 Kensington Court, London W8 5DL, T020-79376570, svgtourismeurope@aol.com USA: 801 2nd Av, 21st floor, New York, NY 10017, T212-6874981, svgtony@aol.com and 6505 Cove Creek Place, Dallas, Texas, 75240, T214-2396451, scubasvg@aol.com*

Voltage *220/240 volts, 50 cycles, except Petit St Vincent and Palm Island, which have 110 volts, 60 cycles.*

Weights and measures *Imperial.*

However, the protected areas are very poorly policed and there are no marine park fees. Spearfishing is strictly forbidden to visitors and no one is allowed to spear a lobster. Buying lobster out of season (1 May-30 September) is illegal as is buying a female lobster with eggs. Fishing for your own consumption is allowed outside the protected areas. Contact the Fisheries Department for more information on rules and regulations, T4562738.

There is reef diving, wall diving, drift diving and wrecks to explore. The St Vincent reefs are fairly deep, at between 55 to 90 ft, so scuba diving is more rewarding than snorkelling. Dive sites include **Bottle Reef**, **the Forest**, **the Garden**, **New Guinea Reef** and **the Wall**. In Kingstown Harbour there are three wrecks at one site, the *Semistrand*, another cargo freighter and an ancient wreck stirred up by Hurricane Hugo, as well as two cannons, a large anchor and several bathtubs. **Bequia** is also considered excellent, with a leeward wall and 30 dive sites around the island, reached by boat within 15 minutes. The **Devil's Table** is good for snorkelling as well as diving. Other dive sites are *M/S Lirero*, the Wall off West Cay, the Bullet, the Boulders and Manhole. The best snorkelling is found in the Tobago Cays and Palm Island. There is snorkelling and diving around most of the other islands with at least one dive shop on each inhabited island.

St Vincent is a whaling nation and each year two humpback whales are killed off Bequia (see below and Whale and dolphin watching, page 60). In addition, short-finned pilot whales, known as 'black fish' are caught in Vincentian waters for the local market. For those who would rather watch than eat these mammals, Hal Daize runs coastal boat tours of St Vincent visiting the Falls of Baleine as well as whale and dolphin watching. *Sea Breeze Nature Tours*, T4584969, www.vincy.com/seabreeze

Dive centres

A two-tank dive costs around US$70-90, snorkellers US$20, full scuba equipment rental US$45, open water certification US$435-500

On St Vincent: *Dive St Vincent* (Bill Tewes) at Young Island Dock, T4574714, www.divestvincent.com, NAUI, PADI certification courses, camera rental, trips to Bequia and the Falls of Baleine; *Dive Fantasea*, at Villa Beach, T4575560, www.divefantasea.com PADI certification, dives around St Vincent and tours to the Grenadines, also snorkelling. *Wallilabou Dive Experience*, at Wallilabou, convenient for yachties anchored in the bay, also hotel and diving packages, T/F4560355, walldivexp@caribsurf. com *Petit Byahaut*, mostly for guests, but visitors may use the facilities, T/F4577008, VHF68. There are other dive shops on **Bequia**, **Canouan** and **Union**, see below for details. Some operations offer 'yachties' discounts.

Beaches and watersports

Sea urchins are a hazard, as in many other islands, especially among rocks on the less frequented beaches

St Vincent has splendid, safe beaches on the leeward side, most of which have volcanic black sand. The lightest coloured sand can be found on the south coast in the Villa area, where there are several hotels, watersports and marinas. At Sunsail Lagoon in Calliaqua there is a lovely long, crescent-shaped beach, Canash, which is perfect for young children. Further round the rocks, there are two more beaches becoming progressively more golden the closer to the point you get. Just offshore is Young Island (see below), which has a small, golden sand, 'improved' beach. The windward coast is rockier with rolling surf and strong currents, making it dangerous for swimming. Brighton Salt Pond beach has lovely swimming conditions most days and magically clear water. Cruise ships sometimes bring their guests here. All beaches are public. Some are difficult to reach by road, but boat trips can be arranged to the inaccessible beauty spots such as Breakers Beach, Prospect. Nearly all the inhabited islands of the Grenadines have at least one golden beach, and often more, some fringed with palm trees, others without any sun protection. *Paradise Windsurfing* has five different locations and offers different levels of instruction, T4583222. Surfing is good on the reef off Lagoon Bay (Canash) and at Shipping Bay and Argyll on the Windward coast for strong surfers.

Sailing

Sailing is excellent, indeed it was yachtsmen who first popularized the Grenadines and it is one of the best ways to see the islands. You can take day charter boats, easily arranged through hotels, or charter your own boat. There is a variety of boats for skippered day charters. Talk to the operators about size and predicted wind conditions if you are inclined towards seasickness. The large catamarans are usually quite stable so that you will hardly know you are on a boat, but they take quite large groups. If you hire a local yacht or motor boat for a day, make sure that the captain has life jackets and other safety equipment (eg a radio) on board and that he is properly insured. This may seem obvious, but do not take anything for granted and be

St Vincent & the Grenadines

Georgetown
Barrouallie
ST VINCENT
Kingstown

Port Elizabeth *BEQUIA*
ISLE À QUATRE *PETIT NEVIS* *BATTOW*
BALICEAUX
THE PILLORIES
Lovell Village *MUSTIQUE*
PETIT MUSTIQUE
PETIT CANOUAN *SAVAN IS*

CANOUAN Charlestown
CATHOLIC IS
UNION MAYREAU
ISLAND *Tobago Cays*
Clifton PALM (PRUNE) IS
PETIT
ST VINCENT

THE GRENADINES

N

0 km   10
0 miles

prepared to ask lots of questions. A tourist and his son taking a short hop boat ride between islands recently found themselves drifting hopelessly off course when the boat's engine failed. The captain had no radio and they were eventually found several days later at death's door off the Venezuelan coast.

Yacht races include the **Bequia Easter Regatta**, an official Mount Gay Red Cap event. There are races for all sizes and types of craft, even coconut boats chased by their swimming child owners or model sailing yachts chased by rowing boats. Everyone is welcome and there are crewing opportunities. There are other contests on shore (sandcastle building) and the nights are filled with events such as dancing, beauty shows and fashion shows. The centre of activities is the *Frangipani Hotel*, which fronts directly on to Admiralty Bay. The Canouan Yacht Race is in August.

The main regattas are Bequia Easter Regatta, Union Island Easterval, SVG Game Fishing Tournament (May) and Fisherman's Day (May)

Day sails

Bareboat and crewed yachts are available through *Sunsail*, the largest sailing company in the world, at Blue Lagoon, T4584308, www.lagoonmarina.com *Barefoot Yacht Charters* (Blue Lagoon), an American Sailing Association (ASA) sailing school and the longest-established charter company, T4569526, www.barefootyachts.com *Blue Water Charters* at the *Aquatic Club*, Villa, T4561232. *Nicholson Yacht Charters* over 70 crewed yachts, in USA T800-6626066. *Passion Day Charters*, T4584308. *Grenadine Escape*, Blue Lagoon Marina, offer yachts, villas and resorts, run by Guy Hadley (St Vincentian captain) and Lara Cowan Hadley, T/F4586326, in Europe T44-1993-951662, www.grenadine-escape.com On Union Island at Clifton, there are *Moorings*, T4588777, *VPM DuFour Antilles*, T4588894, and *Star Voyage*, *Bambou Yachting* and *Overseas Sailing*. *Kathryn B*, a spectacular 105-ft, three-masted, gaff-rigged topsail schooner, is in the Grenadines Jan-Apr, offering 6-night cruises from St Vincent to the southern Grenadines and back, T800-5006077, Kathrynb@midcoast.com *Captain Yannis* has catamaran day tours starting in Union Island (early morning flights from other islands), visiting the Tobago Cays, Palm Island, etc, T4588513. *Passion Day Charters*, T4583884, operate out of Bequia. Heidi and Marty Pritchard offer a large catamaran for day trips, private parties, weddings, sailing, sport fishing and snorkelling. From Bequia they go to Mustique on Tue and Thu, Tobago Cays on Wed and Sun, to Falls of Baleine on Fri.

St Vincent

Kingstown

The capital, Kingstown, stands on a sheltered bay and is surrounded on all sides by steep, green hills, with houses perched all the way up. However, it is a generally unattractive port city with the waterfront dominated by the container port, cruise ship terminal, fish market and bus station. There is no promenade along the seafront and buildings along the reclaimed land look inland rather than out to sea. Nevertheless, an active beautification association is making huge strides in cleaning up the city, with overgrown bridges repaired or rebuilt, buildings painted and re-roofed and plants maintained. Some buildings have been demolished. The most attractive and historical buildings are inland along the three main parallel streets, Bay Street, Long Lane and Grenville/Halifax Street, also known as Front Street, Middle Street and Back Street.

IDD code: 784
Colour map 4, grid C5

The town is always busy as there are few shops in the rest of the island, but Friday is the busiest day

Kingstown is known as the 'city of arcades' and it is possible to walk around most of the centre under cover. There are even building regulations to encourage the practice in new construction. The shopping and business area is no more than two blocks wide, running between Bay Street and Halifax Street/Grenville Street, also called Front Street and Back Street. There are quite a lot of new buildings, none of them tall. The government financial services building in front of the police station is large, modern, concrete and not particularly pretty. The New Kingstown Fish Market, built with Japanese aid, was opened in 1990 near the Police Headquarters. This

The Centre

complex, known as Little Tokyo, has car parking and is the point of departure for minibuses to all parts of the island. On Halifax Street at the junction with South River Road is the Old Public Library, an old stone building with a pillared portico. It was supposed to be renovated with French aid and made into the Museum of St Vincent, but the project has been dormant for several years. *Alliance Française* is on the first floor. There are public toilets to the rear.

The Market Square in front of the Court House is the hub of activity. A new covered market with cream and brown horizontal stripes has been built from Upper Bay to Halifax Street. Fruit and vegetables are downstairs and clothing is upstairs, but the vendors upstairs are not doing any business and are moving back on to the streets where they came from, selling from the backs of cars. In the middle of the market building is a circular area where farmers sell their produce on Fridays.

St Vincent

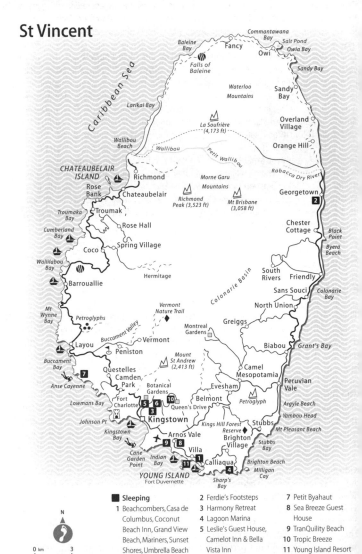

■ **Sleeping**

1 Beachcombers, Casa de Columbus, Coconut Beach Inn, Grand View Beach, Mariners, Sunset Shores, Umbrella Beach & Villa Lodge

2 Ferdie's Footsteps
3 Harmony Retreat
4 Lagoon Marina
5 Leslie's Guest House, Camelot Inn & Bella Vista Inn
6 New Montrose

7 Petit Byahaut
8 Sea Breeze Guest House
9 TranQuility Beach
10 Tropic Breeze
11 Young Island Resort

N

0 km   3
0 miles   3

The jetty

At the jetty where the boats for the Grenadines berth, you can see island schooners loading and unloading, all of which is done by hand. The men throw crates from one to the other in a human chain; the whole business is accompanied by much shouting and laughter. A new cruise ship terminal has been built alongside the rather unattractive container port, but the Government is cleaning up and beautifying the area, renovating old stone buildings and painting others.

Cathedrals

Kingstown has two cathedrals, St George's (Anglican) and St Mary's (Roman Catholic). **St George's**, consecrated in 1820, has an airy nave and a pale blue gallery running around the north, west and south sides. It became a cathedral in 1877 when the Diocese of the Windward Islands was constituted and the chancel and transepts date from 1880-87. The cupula was blown down by a hurricane in 1898 and after that battlements were added to the tower. There is an interesting floor plaque in the nave, now covered by carpet, commemorating a general who died fighting the Caribs. Other interesting features include a memorial to Sir Charles Brisbane (1772-1829) who captured Curaçao and a miniature of the action. A lovely stained glass window in the south transept was reputedly commissioned by Queen Victoria on the death

Kingstown

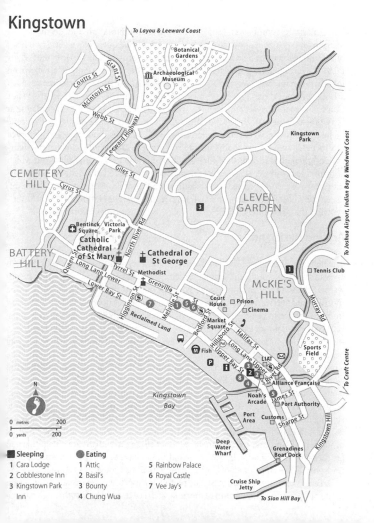

Sleeping ■
1 Cara Lodge
2 Cobblestone Inn
3 Kingstown Park Inn

Eating ●
1 Attic
2 Basil's
3 Bounty
4 Chung Wua
5 Rainbow Palace
6 Royal Castle
7 Vee Jay's

of her grandson. She took exception to angels in red rather than the traditional white and it was put into storage in St Paul's Cathedral. It was brought to St Vincent in the 1930s. **St Mary's** is of far less sober construction, with different styles, Flemish, Moorish, Byzantine and Romanesque, all in dark grey stone, crowded together on the church, presbytery and school. Building was carried out throughout the 19th century, with renovation in the 1940s. The exterior of the church is highly decorated but dark and grim, while the interior is dull in comparison but quite light and pretty. The **Methodist church**, dating from 1841, also has a fine interior, with a circular balcony. Its construction was financed largely through the efforts of freed slaves. There is a little bell tower at the south end, erected in 1907.

Botanical Gardens

Established in 1765, they are the oldest in the Western Hemisphere

In Kingstown the Botanical Gardens just below Government House and the Prime Minister's residence are well worth a visit (for a description see above under Fauna and flora). The **Nicholas Wildlife Complex** has parrots, agouti, Barbados green monkey and St Vincent parrot, but they aren't very well housed. ■ *Daily 0600-1800. The gardens are about a 20-min walk from the market square: go along Grenville St, past the cathedrals, turn right into Bentinck Square, right again and continue uphill to the gate. Or take a bus, EC$1 from the terminal.*

Fort Charlotte

The views of Kingstown and surroundings are spectacular. On a clear day the Grenadines and even Grenada are visible

Fort Charlotte (completed 1805) is on the promontory on the north side of Kingstown Bay, 636 ft above sea level, 15 minutes drive out of town (EC$1.50 from bus terminal to village below, if you ask the driver he might take you into the fort for EC$1-2, worth it if it is hot). Although the fort was designed to fend off attacks from the sea, the main threat was the Black Caribs and many of its 34 guns (some of which are still in place) therefore faced inland. The gatehouse, 1806, was where Major Champion of the Royal Scots Fusiliers was killed on 13 October 1824 (see plaque in St George's Cathedral) by Private Ballasty. The murderer was executed at the scene of the crime. In the old barrack rooms, a series of paintings shows the early history of St Vincent. Painted by William Linzest Prescott in 1972, they suffer from poor lighting and their condition is deteriorating. There is also a coastguard lookout which controls the comings and goings of ships entering the port. Below, the ruins of a military hospital can be seen, as well as a bathing pool at sea level on the end of the point, used when the fort housed people suffering from yaws. The National Trust of St Vincent and the Grenadines, PO Box 752, T4562591, has further information.

Around the island

La Soufrière & Mount St Andrew

Take water and insect repellent

The highest peak on the island, **La Soufrière** volcano, rises to about 4,000 ft. In 1970 an island reared up out of the lake in the crater: it smokes and the water round it is very warm. Hiking to the volcano is very popular, but you must leave very early in the morning and allow a full day for the trip. About two miles north of Georgetown (van from Kingstown to Georgetown EC$4, you can ask the driver to make a detour to the start of the trail for an extra charge) on the Windward side you cross the Dry River, then take a left fork and walk/drive through banana plantations to where the trail begins. It takes about three hours to reach the crater edge and it is a strenuous hike along a marked trail, the first three miles are through the Rabacca plantation, then up, along Bamboo Ridge and all the way to the crater's magnificent edge; the top can be cloudy, windy, cold and rainy, take adequate clothing and footwear. There is an alternative, unmarked and even more challenging four-hour route from the Leeward side starting from the end of the road after Richmond, but you will need a guide. There are guided tours which start on the Windward side and end on the Leeward side, about six or seven hours, around US$30 if there are about 10 of you, with the advantage that you are met at your destination by the driver and do not have to worry about scarce public transport. Leave an extra set of clothes in the van in case you get wet through.

An easier climb is up **Mount St Andrew**, near Kingstown. A tarmac track runs up to the radio mast on the summit of the peak, at 2,413 ft, passing first through banana and vegetable gardens and then through forest. There are no parrots but it is particularly good for the Antillean crested hummingbird and black hawks. The view from the summit covers the Grenadines and the Vermont and Mesopotamia valleys. To reach the track either take a van running along the Leeward Highway and ask to be put down at the junction with the Mount St Andrew road, or walk from Kingstown.

The Leeward Highway is a dramatic drive along the west coast towards La Soufrière; there are lush valleys and magnificent seaviews. It is a very crumpled landscape and the road is steep and twisty. The road leaves Kingstown and initially heads inland. There are views down into Campden Park Bay, to a deep water port complex and flour mill. The road passes through the small village of Questelles (good party at *Philo's Disco*, listen for them on the radio) before rejoining the coast briefly at Buccament Bay and down into Layou where there are a few excellent examples of gingerbread houses. About a mile after Questelles look for the **Vermont Nature Trail** sign, then turn right up the Buccament Valley to Peniston and Vermont. The car park at 975 ft is close to the Vermont Nature Centre. Buses from Kingston go to Peniston from where it is a long walk. Get a trail map from the information hut on the right. A guide is not necessary unless you want scientific information as you walk along this marvellous trail. There is a rest stop at 1,350 ft, and a Parrot Lookout Platform at 1,450 ft, probably the best place to see the St Vincent parrot. Be prepared for rain, mosquitoes and chiggars, use insect repellent.

> **The Leeward coast**
> *The drive from Kingstown to the end of the road at Richmond takes about two hours. Minibuses race along at great speed and some passengers complain of queasiness*

There are some interesting **petroglyphs** and **rock carvings** dating back to the Siboney, Arawak and Carib eras. The best known are just north of Layou, carved on a huge boulder next to a stream. They can only be visited on payment of US$2 for the owner, Mr Victor Hendrickson to open the gate to the fenced off area. Ask the local children to show you his house and the petroglyphs (for a tip), well worth a visit.

Passing Mount Wynne and Peter's Hope, **Barrouallie** is the next village of any size. It is a fishing village and on the beach are fishing boats, nets, pigs and chickens scratching about. The local speciality catch is 'black fish', in reality a short finned pilot whale, which grows to about 18 ft. Here there is a petroglyph known as the Ogham Stone, dated at 800 BC in the playground of the Anglican secondary school. There is a theory that it is in Celtic script. If the children are not in class they will highlight the picture in white chalk for you. The road also passes through the remains of a sugar mill (the furnace chimney is still standing) and then heads inland from the popular anchorage and restaurant at Wallilabou Bay. A stone gateway marks the entrance to the **Wallilabou Falls** (Wally-la-boo). You can swim here but the falls are not much more than a spurt (6 ft at the most). There are no changing rooms. On the opposite side of the road is a nutmeg plantation.

The road goes inland along the Wallilabou valley before quickly rising over the ridge into the North Leeward district. From here onwards all the villages are clearly marked with good road signs. The wooden pipeline from the hydroelectric scheme follows the road and is most visible at the aptly named Spring Village. Another pretty beach is reached at Cumberland and the road climbs quickly to Coulls Hill with perhaps the best view on the coast. The road through Chateaubelair (restaurant, use their facilities to change for a swim and have a snack), skirting Petit Bordel (drugs financed speed boats on the beach) with small islands offshore to **Richmond** and Wallibou beach is most attractive. There are some beach facilities at Wallibou.

Petit Wallibou Falls are a double waterfall in a very remote region 20 miles north of Kingstown; you can bathe at the bottom of the second fall. To get there, go through Richmond and turn right up the side road beside the (closed) Richmond Vale Academy; follow this road for one mile, it then turns into a track for two miles. At the river the top of the waterfall is on your left. There is a steep climb on the left hand side of the waterfall to reach the pool where you can swim. **Trinity Falls** are near Richmond in the Wallibou Valley, set deep in a canyon in the rainforest. The only known hot springs are in the canyon, having appeared since the last volcanic eruption. The road has been badly eroded and it is best to park about 40 minutes walk from the car park, except that there is a lot of loose gravel and you may fall. From the car park it is another 45 minutes walk to the falls (reasonable physical fitness required), through lovely rainforest. There is a sign down the river warning about undertow, this also applies to the pool by the falls. The current is very strong, swimmers have been sucked under and the sides are steep, with nothing to hold on to, while wind erosion has loosened boulders which are now potentially dangerous.

A boat trip to the falls of **Baleine** (on the northwest coast) is recommended. A few minutes up a river which originates on Soufrière, you come to the falls. At the base is a natural swimming pool. You can climb up the side behind the falls and then jump off into the pool. It is possible to reach the falls on foot, but the easiest way is to take an excursion by motor boat, which includes a stop for snorkelling, and a picnic lunch, for US$35-40. A new jetty and walkway were built in 2001.

The Windward coast

The Queens Drive takes you into the hills south of Kingstown and gives splendid views all around. The Marriaqua Valley with its numerous streams is particularly beautiful. In the Valley, beyond Mesopotamia (commonly known as Mespo), the lush, tropical gardens of **Montreal** are worth a visit; anthuriums are grown commercially for the domestic market. The owner, Timothy Vaughn, is a well-known landscape gardener in Europe and this is his first tropical garden, full of organic flowers and colourful foliage, with glorious views of Argyll and Mesopotamia Valley. It is designed in three sections, one of which includes a wild garden leading down to a river and a pool where you can swim. ■ *Open Dec-Aug 0900-1600, closed Sun and holidays. EC$5.*

Little waterfalls and pools, such as Kiss Me and Cheyne Spout, can be found on river walks from the Windward Highway

The road meets the **Windward Highway** at Peruvian Vale. It gets progressively drier as the road goes north hugging yellow sandstone cliffs which contrast with the white waves surging in towards the black volcanic beaches. A number of banana packaging stations are passed especially around Colonarie. There is a particularly impressive view of the coast just after the **Black Point tunnel**. The tunnel is 350 ft long and was constructed by Colonel Thomas Browne using Carib and African slaves in 1815. It was blasted through volcanic rock from one bay to the other and the drill holes are still visible, as are storage rooms and recesses for candles. It is very atmospheric and there are a few bats as well as people washing in the water which pours out of the rock. It provided an important link with the sugar estates in the north and sugar was hauled through the tunnel to be loaded on to boats in Byera Bay. Black sand Byera Beach is the longest in St Vincent and the sea is rough, but in the days of the sugar plantations the coast curved round more giving greater protection to shipping and there was a jetty. You cannot see the tunnel from the road, which goes over the top. Turn down towards the sea between the gas station and the river down a dirt road which leads to Black Point Recreation Site where cricket is played and hundreds of people gather for Easter Monday celebrations.

Georgetown is almost like a ghost town, with one or two quite well-maintained houses, the rest haven't been painted for years. It is an economically depressed area since the loss of sea cotton and arrowroot and now there are problems with bananas. A number of houses have been abandoned. The *St Vincent Rum Distiller*, a restaurant and guesthouse, does good business from visitors to the volcano, see above. North of here is parrot territory with cooling rivers and deep pools.

The road to **Sandy Bay** (beyond Georgetown), where St Vincent's remaining Black Caribs live, is now good, however, you have to cross the Dry River, a jumble of rocks, grit, rubbish and dead wood swept down from the mountains above, which sometimes is not dry and therefore not passable. Rocks and sand are extracted for the building industry. Sandy Bay is poor but beyond it is an even poorer village along a rough dirt road, **Owia**. Here is **Salt Pond**, a natural area of tidal pools filled with small marine life. The rough Atlantic crashes around the huge boulders and lava formations and it is very picturesque. The villagers have planted flowers and made steps down to the Salt Pond area. There is also an arrowroot processing factory which can be visited. Past Owia is **Fancy**, the poorest village on the island, also Black Carib and very isolated, reached by a rough jeep track which makes a pleasant walk. Baleine

Falls (see above) are a two-mile hike from here around the tip of the island, rugged and not recommended for the unadventurous. Fishing boats can be hired in Fancy to collect you (do not pay in advance).

The south

The airport is just southeast of Kingstown at **Arnos Vale**, a residential area where there is also a sports complex. The road runs round the runway and down towards the coast at Indian Bay. There are several hotels in this area, stretching along the seafront to Calliaqua Bay. It is very pleasant, with light sand beaches, Young Island just offshore, Bequia in the distance and dozens of moored yachts. Many people stay here rather than in the capital, as it is an easy commute into Kingstown if you need to go in, while there are marinas, dive shops, the best restaurants and watersports facilities here. The southeast of the island is drier and has different vegetation and birdlife. Take a van running to Stubbs and alight at the post office by the Brighton road junction. Walk into Brighton village and find a guide who can lead you to see, among others, the mangrove cuckoo, smooth-billed ani, broad-winged hawk and green heron. When tidal conditions are right it is possible to cross to Milligan Cay.

Young Island

A tiny, privately owned islet, 200 yd off the coast at Villa, with the only resort hotel on St Vincent. **Fort Duvernette**, on a 195-ft high rock just off Young Island, was built at the beginning of the 19th century to defend Calliaqua Bay. The 100 steps up to the fort have been partially washed away by hurricanes and rock falls have left it unsafe so you can no longer visit the fort. **LL** *Young Island Resort*, T4584826, www.youngisland.com; all accommodation in 30 cottages (MAP), yachts are US$500-650 per day, part sailing and honeymoon packages available. There is a lovely lagoon swimming pool, surrounded by tropical flowers and a golden sand beach overlooking Indian Bay.

Pick up the phone at the crossing to see if you will be allowed over

Essentials

Sleeping

Kingstown LL-L *Camelot Inn*, 14562100, caminn@caribsurf.com Originally the governor's residence and the oldest guesthouse on the island, 22 luxury rooms and 2 honeymoon suites, Camelot theme rigorously carried through with King Arthur's Restaurant, the Knight's room, etc, pool, tennis, gym, beauty salon, free transport to beach, quite a walk into town through an unsavoury area. **L-A** *Cara Lodge*, T4561897, www.carahotels.com The best place to stay in town, good for business travellers, within walking distance of the centre but up a hill away from the bustle, large rooms or excellent suites in a separate building across the road, email and other business facilities, good restaurant and bar, friendly and efficient service. **AL-C** *Harmony Retreat*, T4569113, harmonyretreat@ vincysurf.com Set in a beautiful, lush, hillside location, this peaceful Aparthotel offers a variety of accommodation options from studios to two bedroom apartments. On Upper Bay St, **A-B** *Cobblestone Inn*, T4561937, cobblestone@caribsurf.com Upstairs in a charming building which used to be a sugar and

Government tax of 7% on hotel rooms; most add a 10% service charge. Camping is not encouraged and there are no organized campsites

Windward Islands

arrowroot warehouse, violet and white decor, mostly quiet but avoid room 22, noisy from street below, rooms good, breakfast extra, restaurant and bar. **C** *Kingstown Park Inn*, T4572964. 7 rooms, fans, a/c in 1 room, TV. **D** *Bella Vista Inn*, behind *Camelot*, Kingstown Park, T/F4572757. 7 rooms, 3 with private bath, fans, run by Nzinga Miguel and her daughter Cleopatra, friendly, homely atmosphere, breakfast EC$10, dinner on request EC$15. **D-E** *Leslie's Guest House*, Kingstown Park, T4562863, 1 min from Camelot. 10-min walk downhill to town, shared bathroom, clean, cool, nice garden, large veranda, Leslie Waldron very friendly and helpful. Close to Kingstown: **AL-A** *Tropic Breeze Hotel*, Queen's Drive, T4584618, www.tropicbreezes-vg.com 17 rooms with balconies, 6 a/c, good views, restaurant, bar, pool. **B** *New Montrose Hotel*, T4570172, www.newmontrosehotel.com 25 modern rooms, some with kitchenettes, balcony, TV, phone, view of Kingstown and Grenadines, walking distance from Botanical Gardens.

There are lots of apartments close to the sea, contact the Tourist Office for a list

Villa and Indian Bay (3 miles from town, close to airport) **LL-AL** *Grand View Beach*, Villa Point, T4584811, www.grandviewhotel.com A former cotton plantation house, 19 rooms, 1st class, pool, tennis, squash, fully equipped gym, excursions arranged, restaurant, room service. **LL-AL** *Mariners Hotel*, T4574000, www.marinershotel.com 18 rooms, a/c, room service, TV, comfortable, jetty overlooks Young Island, Fri night barbecues. **LL-AL** *Sunset Shores*, T4584411, www.sunsetshores.com 32 rooms, a/c, TV, on the beach, snorkelling gear, pool, darts, dining room, bar. **AL** *Villa Lodge Hotel* and the adjacent *Breezeville Apartments*, Villa Point, T4584641, www.villalodge.com 10 rooms and 10 1-2 bedroom fully-equipped apartments overlooking Indian Bay, discounts for longer stay, a/c, fans, TV, internet access, pool with lovely view, restaurant, bar. **AL-A** *The Lagoon Marina and Hotel*, Blue Lagoon, Ratho Mill, T/F4584308, www.lagoonmarina.com 19 rooms with lovely view and beach, *Sunsail* yacht charter, full service marina, bar, happy hour 1730-1900, restaurant, mini-market, boutique, nice pool with slide and kids' pool, scuba diving, windsurfing. **AL-B** *Casa de Columbus*, T4584001, www.casadecolumbus.com Hotel on beach, nice veranda, good snorkelling just outside the hotel, daily or weekly rates, 2-bedroomed apartments available, sleep 3-4, a/c, kitchenettes, restaurant, watersports nearby. **A-B** *Beachcombers Hotel*, T4584283, www.beachcombershotel.com Small, family-run, CP, laundry service, restaurant and bar, also sauna and steam room. **A-B** *Coconut Beach Inn*, T/F4574900. Nice, clean, comfortable rooms, beautiful seaview, good restaurant (see below). **B-C** *Umbrella Beach*, T4584651. 9 double rooms with kitchen, bath, balcony, restaurant, pool, tennis, nice, simple, opposite Young Island. **C** *TranQuillity Beach Apartment Hotel*, Indian Bay, T4584021. Excellent view, 1, 2, 3- bedroom apartments, some a/c, kitchen facilities, fans, TV, laundry service, restaurant, clean, friendly, very helpful owners, Mr and Mrs Providence. **D** *Sea Breeze Guest House*, Arnos Vale, near airport, T4584969, seabreezetours@caribsurf.com Cooking facilities, 6 rooms with bath, noisy, friendly, helpful, bus to town or airport from the door.

Leeward coast **LL** *Petit Byahaut*, T/F4577008, VHF68, www.outahere.com/petitbyahaut, set in a 50-acre valley in a lovely secluded bay with a nice beach, very pretty. No road, TV or phones, luxury 10 ft x 13 ft tents with floors, queen-sized bed, shower, toilet, sink, sitting area and hammock in each tent, includes all meals, great snorkelling, sail and row boats, kayaks, hiking, scuba diving from beach or kayaks included but diver certification and first dive checkout (US$50) required, guided dives US$40 per person, you can hire the whole resort for 8-14 people, boat access only, ecological and conservation emphasis, solar powered.

Windward coast **D** *Ferdie's Footsteps*, on the main street in Georgetown, red pillars and blue walls, shop downstairs, entrance at the side on Cambridge St, T4586433. Food and accommodation, also 3-bedroom house for monthly rental.

Eating

Kingstown has several restaurants in the centre serving local food or fast food, but the better restaurants are in the Villa beach area several miles east

Kingstown *Vee-Jay's* restaurant on Lower Bay St is friendly and offers good local food, open Mon-Sat 1000-1900, Fri until late, also *Vee-Jay's Rooftop Diner & Pub* on Upper Bay St, T4572845, above Roger's Photo Studios. Open Mon-Sat 0900-2200, sandwiches, rotis, etc, for lunch, good local juices, cocktail bar, entrées EC$12-45, great steel band. *The Attic*, Pauls Av, West Indian/European, multi-screen sports broadcasts, a/c, buffet lunch Wed, open 1100 until late. *Bounty Restaurant and Art Gallery*, Egmont St, upstairs, T4561776. The oldest restaurant in town, windows open to catch the breeze, breakfast and lunch, patties, rotis, cakes and pastries, iced coffee/tea, Mon-Fri 0730-1700, Sat 0730-1330. *Rainbow Palace*, West Indian fast food, Grenville St, T4561763. Open Mon-Fri 0800-1630, Sat 0800-1400. For genuine West Indian food and local company *Basil's Bar and Restaurant* (see below) has a branch underneath the Cobblestone Inn, in Upper Bay St, T4572713. Buffet 1200-1400 Mon-Fri for hungry people, EC$32, acceptable but not startling, also à la carte lunch and dinner, open 0800-2200, pleasant for an evening drink and a chat. *Cobblestone Roof Top Restaurant*, belonging to the *Cobblestone Inn*, T4561937. West Indian lunches and hamburgers, open Mon-Sat 0700-1500, good place for breakfast. *Sweetie Pie Bakery and Café*, between the Grenadines dock and the shops, T4512168.

Fast food At the bus station (Little Tokyo) you can buy freshly grilled chicken and corn cobs, good value and tasty. Cafés on the jetty by ferry boats serve excellent, cheap, local food, eg salt cod rolls with hot pepper sauce. On market days fruit is plentiful and cheap, great bananas. *Stop-Light Restaurant and Bar*, Frenches Gate, opposite Karib Cable, T4562859. Extremely tasty rotis and other snacks and meals, good value. Takeaway food from *Pizza Party*, T4564932, in Arnos Vale by the airport. Delivery and takeaway of pizza, chicken, ice cream, snacks, until 2300, no credit cards. *Chung Wua*, Upper Bay St, T4572566. Open Mon-Sat 1100-2230, Sun 1700-2200, Chinese eat in or takeaway, no credit cards, from EC$10. *Royal Castle*, is on Grenville St. Chicken meal EC$8.10, veggie burger EC$5.25, veggie platter EC$8.75. *Tony's Original Pizza*, 2 locations, up town and down town, T4571506. Young crowd, god bar, great pizzas, EC$5 per slice, burgers (including veggie) EC$5 and up, no credit cards, open morning until late night.

Villa area *Ocean Allegro*, T4584972, VHF Channel 68. Canadian management, one of the best places for both service and food, open Mon-Sat 0900-2130, Sun 1700-2130 (in high season), prices EC$25-85 for main course, lovely beach view, gardens with beach bar, limbo games and good occasional salsa nights. The *Lime Restaurant & Pub* on the waterfront at Villa, T4584227. A casual menu and a dinner menu, reasonable prices, credit cards accepted, open 0930-2400. *Beachcombers* on Villa Beach, T4584283. Light fare and drinks, very casual, pizzas, samosas, burgers, popular with children, good value, or à la carte menu, open air, food 0700-2200, bar open later, happy hour 1700-1830. *Slicks*, T4575783. VHF68, moderate prices, building decorated with artwork of owner and other local artists, light meals or full dinners, lobster, steak, Italian, French, US and West Indian cuisine. *The Aquatic Club*, T4584205. West Indian and international, lunch 1100-1400, dinner 1800. The adventurous should try *Spin City* on the Callaquia playing field, T4574942, for inexpensive local lunches, beef, chicken, turkey, fish, all natural food served in calabash bowls. *Sunset Shores Restaurant*, overlooking Young Island, T4584411 for reservations. International, full English, West Indian or continental breakfast, open 0700-2130, buffet with live entertainment Wed, barbecue Sat, Sun brunch 1200-1500, credit cards. *Surfside Beachbar/Restaurant*, T4575362. Informal Continental/West Indian, pizza and seafood, 1000-2200, closed Mon. *Barefoot Bistro*, T4569880. International, waterfront pub-style restaurant with yachtsmen's specials and light meals available on the veranda, open 0800-2300 daily, dinghy dock. *Triangle Pub*, Villa Flat, Calliaqua, T4574270. Callaloo soup, curried conch, conch souse and other fishy features, barbeque and live music Fri night, open daily from 1100.

Leeward Coast *Buccama*, on Buccament beach, T4567855. Fabulous location, luxuriously designed, very spacious bar, restaurant and lounge, excellent food, not cheap but worth it, great pina coladas and fruit punch. Parties often hosted. *Wallilabou Anchorage*, T4587270. Caters mainly for yachties, mooring facilities, West Indian specialities, chicken, fish or veg lunch, juices, email access EC$5 per 15 mins. *Beach Front Restaurant & Bar*, Chateaubelair, T4582853. Eat inside or outdoors, roof terrace with shade, good view of bay, rotis and fish meals for lunch, happy hour Fri, there can be a swell here so if you are on a yacht it is sometimes better to stop at Wallilabou.

Windward Coast *Ferdie's Footsteps*, see Sleeping above, Georgetown. Local food, useful stop for lunch if you have climbed the volcano, inexpensive.

Emerald Valley Casino, T4567824. Call for transport, closed Tue, Ladies' Night Wed. *Basils Too*, T4584205. Offers lunch, dinner and dancing on Villa Beach. Check for happy hours at bars for lower-priced drinks, snacks and often entertainment. *Aquatic*, in Villa (see Eating). One of the main nightspots on the island, admission EC$20, more if there is

The local rum is Sunset, at around US$4-5, except for the very strong rum which will set you back about US$5-6 a bottle and blow your head off

Nightlife
Many hotels and restaurants have live music in the evenings

Windward Islands

a live band at weekends. *Calliaqua Culture Pot*, is a form of street party in the beach area, where you can find music and food, singing and dancing, arts and crafts, every Fri from 2000. In Kingstown, *Touch Entertainment Centre*, T4571825. Dance hall run by the Vincentian band, Touch. *The Attic*, see Eating above. Nightly live entertainment, jazz, karaoke, dancing, large screen video, music bar open 1200 till late. Other night time places are *Veejays* on Upper Bay St, *Dano's* on Grenville St and *Emotions*, a small nightclub on Grenville St. *Russell's Cinema*, Montrose, T4579308. *Cinerama*, Kingstown, T4856364. 3 screens, every night. *Cinemas Caribbean Ltd*, Georgetown, T4586669.

Festivals St Vincent's carnival, called *Vincy Mas* , is held in the last week of **Jun** and the 1st week of **Jul** for 10 days. Mas is short for masquerade, and the 3 main elements of the carnival are the costume bands, the steel bands and the calypso. During the day there is J'Ouverte, ole mas, children's carnival and steel bands through Kingstown's streets. At night calypsonians perform in 'tents', there is the King and Queen of the bands show, the steel bands competition and Miss Carnival, a beauty competition with contestants from other Caribbean countries (a talent contest, a beauty contest and local historical dress). Thousands of visitors come to take part, many from Trinidad. Independence Celebrations take place in **Oct**. From **16-24 Dec**, there is a *Carolling Competition* and *Nine Mornings Festival*, during which, for 9 mornings, people parade through Kingstown and dances are held from 0100. There is also an art and craft exhibition.

Shopping **Kingstown market** (do not take photos of the vendors) for excellent fresh fruit and vegetables and supermarkets. Several gourmet provisioning spots: *Gourmet Food*, Calliaqua, T4562983; *Stanley's Deli*, Kingstown, T4858585; *Basil's*, for good wine, T4562602. Supermarkets: The *St Vincent Philatelic Society* on Bay St, between Higginson St and River Rd, sells stamps in every colour, size and amount for the novice and collector alike. Service is helpful but slow in this second floor warehouse, complete with guard. *The Artisans Art & Craft Centre*, Bay St, T4562306. Upstairs in the Bonadie Building, sells handicrafts from about 70 artisans around the country, open Mon-Fri 0830-1600, Sat 0830-1200. For handicrafts, resort wear and books, *Noah's Arkade*, Blue Caribbean Building, Bay St, Kingstown (T4571513, Img@caribsurf.com), and at the *Frangipani* on Bequia (T4583424). *Nzimbu Arts & Craft*, McKies Hill, T4571677, www.gligli.com Goat skin drums, batik and banana leaf artwork, Nzimbu is often found on Bay St on Fri, selling his crafts on the roadside. Among the handful of fashion stores are *Images*, a boutique for locally made and imported linen and cotton wear in the Georges Plaza on Grenville St and *Isles Boutique*, James St, T4561063, for cheaper, trendy and sporty clothes.

Sports Many of the more expensive hotels have **tennis** courts but there are others at the *Kingstown*
For diving and *Tennis Club* and the *Prospect Racquet Club*. A new club house and floodlit courts have been
watersports, see built in Calliaqua, T4574090, Peter Lanten for reservations. Take the road opposite Howards
page 658 and 660 Marine before the bridge. **Squash** courts can be found at the *Cecil Cyrus Squash Complex* (St James Place, Kingston, reservations T4561805), the *Grand View Beach Hotel* and the *Prospect Racquet Club*. Spectator sports include **cricket** (Test Match cricket ground at Arnos Vale, near the airport), **soccer**, **rugby** (international – Amazonia Guildingii – and junior team practices, Wed, Sat, 1630, club secretary Jackie De Freitas, T4561590), **netball**, **volleyball** and **basketball**. Pick up games of basketball are played on St Vincent after 1700, or after the heat has subsided, at the Sports Complex behind the airport and Calliaqua (same times, right on the street). Everyone is welcome, although it can get very crowded, so arrive early. Players beware, fouls are rarely called, although travelling violations are. No one is deliberately rough but overall the game is unpolished, unschooled but spirited.

Tour operators *SVG Tours*, T4584534, svgtours@caribsurf.com Run by Dominique David, an agronomist by training and very interesting on farming and botany. Hikes up the volcano, tours of the rainforest, waterfalls, gardens and nature trails, day trips to other islands and sailing. *HazECO Tours*, T4578634, www.begos.com/hazecotour Similar tours, also with emphasis on nature.

Air *LIAT* and/or *Caribbean Star*, fly from Anguilla, Antigua, Barbados, Beef Island (BVI), Dominica, Grenada, Port of Spain (Trinidad), St Kitts, St Lucia and San Juan (Puerto Rico). *BWIA* flies from Barbados and Port of Spain. *American Eagle* and *American Airlines* fly from Puerto Rico. *Air Martinique* flies from Martinique. Inter-island charters are also operated by *SVGAir* and *Mustique Airways*. *SVGAir* has daily scheduled flights Barbados-Bequia as well as to/from Grenada and internal Grenadines flights. Their air taxi service will only fly for 2 or more passengers, but you may buy 2 seats. **Airport** ET Joshua Airport, small and rather chaotic, is 2 miles from Kingstown. The taxi fare to town is EC$20 (with other fares ranging from EC$15-40 for nearer or more distant hotels set by government); minibus to Kingstown EC$1.50, 10 mins. Frequent and easy minibuses also run east if you need to get to Young Island or Calliaqua. The airport currency exchange desk is open Mon-Fri 0830-1230, 1530-1730, and is more convenient and quicker than a bank, Visa/Mastercard accepted.

Transport

Not only do they weigh your luggage, but small planes also need to know the weight of their passengers, so be prepared to divulge this information

Local Road Minibuses from Kingstown leave from the Little Tokyo Fish Market terminal to all parts of St Vincent island, including a frequent service to Villa and Indian Bay, the main hotel area; they stop on demand rather than at bus stops. At the terminal they crowd round the entrance competing for customers rather than park in the bays provided. They are a popular means of transport because they are inexpensive and give an opportunity to see local life. No service on Sun or holidays. Fares start at EC$1, rising to EC$2 (Layou), EC$4 (Georgetown on the Windward coast), to EC$5 to the Black Carib settlement at Sandy Bay in the northeast (this is a difficult route, though, because buses leave Sandy Bay early in the morning for Kingstown, and return in the afternoon). The number of vans starting in Kingstown and running to Owia or Fancy in the north is limited. The best way is to take the early bus to Georgetown and try to catch one of the 2 vans running between Georgetown and Fancy (EC$10). To get to Richmond in the northwest take a bus to Barrouallie and seek onward transport from there. A day trip to Mesopotamia (EC$2.50) is worthwhile.

Car A local driving licence, costing EC$40, must be purchased at the airport, the police station in Bay St, or the Licensing Authority on Halifax St, on presentation of your home licence. However, there is no need to pay if you have an International Driving Permit and get it stamped at the central police station. **Car hire** Only jeeps may be used to go beyond Georgetown on the east coast. *Kim's* (T4561884, mail@kimsrentals.com) charges EC$100 per day for a car, with restrictions on where you drive in the north, EC$125 for a jeep, 60 miles free per day, EC$1 per mile thereafter, weekly rental gives one day free, EC$1,000 excess deposit in advance, delivery or collection anywhere on the island, phone from airport for collection to save taxi hassle, credit cards accepted. Among other agencies (all offering similar rates and terms) are *Ben's* T/F4562907, *David's* T/F4564026, *Star Garage* T4561743, *UNICO* T4565744, *Dac's* T4569739.

Driving is on the left. There are limited road signs

Bicycles Cycling is rewarding. The ride between Layou and Richmond is a strenuous 4 hrs one way, but absolutely spectacular. Expect long, steep hills and lots of them. *Sailors Cycle Centre*, Middle St, T4571712, owned by Trevor 'Sailor' Bailey, who also operates *Sailor's Wilderness Tours* for escorted hiking and biking.

Be careful in the north, which is a drug producing area

Taxi Taxi fares are fixed by the Government but you must check with the driver first to avoid overcharging. Late at night and early morning fares are raised. Kingstown to airport EC$20, Indian Bay EC$25, Mesopotamia EC$40, Layou EC$40, Orange Hill EC$80, Blue Lagoon EC$35, airport to Young Island EC$20, airport to Blue Lagoon EC$25. Hourly hire EC$40 per hr. *Vibie Taxi*, T4565288, 4565781 and *Clinton McCloud*, T4584573, both recommended, helpful. *Young Island Taxi Association* can be reached through Young Island on VHF 68.

Airlines *LIAT*, Halifax St, Kingstown, T4571821 for reservations, airport office T4584841, on Union Island T4588230; *Caribbean Star*, T4565800; *American Eagle*, T4565555; *American Airlines*, T4565000; *Mustique Airways*, T4584280; *SVGAIR*, Blue Lagoon, St Vincent, T4575777, www.svgair.com, air taxi service to Barbados, Martinique, St Lucia, Grenada and within the Grenadines; *Trans Island Air (TIA)*, T246-4181654. **Banks** *FirstCaribbean International Bank*, T4561706, exchange, Visa and Mastercard, ATM. *Scotia Bank*, T4571601, Visa and Mastercard, exchange, ATM. *National Commercial Bank of St Vincent*, T4571844, all on Halifax St. The *NCB*, opposite the market, is open Mon-Thu 0800-1300, Fri 0800-1700, Visa and Mastercard, exchange, but no ATM. Another *NCB* branch on Lower Bay St is open Mon-Fri 0900-1500 (Visa, MC). *Caribbean Banking Corporation*, 81 South River Rd on the corner with Middle St opposite the Old Library, Kingstown, is open Mon-Thu

Directory

Windward Islands

0800-1300, Fri 0800-1700, exchange and ATM facilities; also at Port Elizabeth, Bequia. *National Commercial Bank* has branches at ET Joshua Airport, Georgetown, Barrouallie and agencies at Layou and Chateaubeleair. When you cash TCs you can take half in US dollars and half in EC dollars as both currencies are widely used. Some banks have 24-hr ATMs, but they will not necessarily accept your card. **Embassies and consulates** *UK*, British High Commission, Grenville St, Kingstown, T4571701 (after hrs T4584381), F4562750; *Netherlands* Consulate, in the East Caribbean Group of Companies building in Campden Park, T4571918; *China*, Murray Rd, T4562431; *Venezuela*, Granby St, T4561374; *France*, Middle St, Box 364, Kingstown, T4561615; *Italy*, Queen's Drive, T4564774. **Communications** Internet: Some hotels, such as *Cara Lodge*, offer email and internet service for guests, while marinas (eg *The Lagoon* and *Mariners Hotel*) and other places frequented by yachties are good places to try. Post: Halifax St. Open 0830-1500 (0830-1130 on Sat, closed Sun). *St Vincent Philatelic Services Ltd*, General Post Office, T4571911, F4562383; for old and new issues, *World of Stamps*, Bay 43 Building, Lower Bay St, Kingstown. **Telephone**: operated by Cable and Wireless, on Halifax St; there is a 5% tax on international phone calls. Phone cards and fax available. Portable phones can be rented through *Boatphone* or you can register your own cellular phone with them upon arrival, T4562800. From many cardphones you can reach USA Direct by dialling 1-800-8722881. **Medical services** *Kingston General Hospital*, T4561185. *Emergency* T999.

The Grenadines

The Grenadines, divided politically between St Vincent and Grenada, are a string of 100 tiny, rocky islands and cays stretching across some 35 miles of sea between the two. They are still very much off the beaten track as far as tourists are concerned, but are popular with yachtsmen. The southern Grenadines are particularly beautiful, a cluster of picturesque, hilly islands with glorious white-sand beaches and rocky coves, excellent harbours and lots of opportunities for snorkelling, diving and other watersports.

Getting there

Island hopping by boat is easy and cheap, but be flexible in your schedule. Be prepared to get wet from the spray as the crossings are often rough

Sea All the ferries are cheap and cheerful and an excellent way of getting around if the sea is not too rough. Admiralty Transport Co Ltd, T4583348 for information, admiraltrans@caribsurf.com run 2 ferries: MV *Admiral 1* and MV *Admiral II*, with interchangeable schedules from Kingstown to Bequia, 1hr, EC$15 one way, EC$28 return on the same boat. They start in Bequia, leaving there at 0630, 0730, 1400 and 1700 Mon-Fri, departing Kingstown at 0900, 1030, 1630 and 1900. On Sat the ferry departs Bequia 0630, 1015 and 1700, departing Kingstown 0900, 1230 and 1900, on Sun and holidays it leaves Bequia at 0730 and 1700, departs Kingstown at 0900 and 1900. The MV *Bequia Express*, T4583472, bequiaexpress@caribsurf.com also runs on the same route, from Bequia 0630 and 0930 Mon-Fri, returning from Kingstown 0800 and 1300, with additional services on Mon, Wed and Fri at 1630 from Bequia and 1800 from St Vincent; on Sat it leaves Bequia at 0630 and returns from Kingstown at 1130; on Sun and holidays it departs Bequia at 0700 and 1630, returning at 0930 and 1800.

The Barracouda is the islands' main regular transport and carries everything, families and their goods, goats and generators; she rolls through the sea and the trip can be highly entertaining

MV *Barracouda* sails south on Mon and Thu from Kingstown at around 1030 to Bequia, Canouan, Mayreau and Union Island, arriving at around 1530-1600; on Tue and Fri she returns to St Vincent via Mayreau, Canouan and Bequia, leaving Union Island at 0630, arriving St Vincent 1200. On Sat she sails Kingstown-Union-Kingstown with no intermediate stops. All times are approximate, depending on the amount of goods to be loaded and schedules change frequently. Cargo takes priority and passengers are allowed on board once all the goods are stowed. On holidays day trips are often arranged, eg from Kingstown to the beach on Canouan. There are 3-4 cabins, 2 of which are used by the crew but you can negotiate for one quite cheaply if you need it. Fares: one stop EC$15, 2 stops EC$20, 3 stops EC$25, etc, eg Kingstown to Bequia EC$15, to Canouan EC$20, to Mayreau EC$25, to Union EC$30.

For other services, check at the Grenadines dock in Kingstown. There are often excursions from Kingstown to Bequia and Mustique on Sun. From Bequia you can take a boat trip to Mustique for US$40 per person by speedboat from Friendship Bay or by catamaran from Port Elizabeth, ask at Sunsports at *Gingerbread*. Throughout the Grenadines power boats can be arranged to take small groups of passengers almost any distance. Try to ensure that the boat is operated by someone known to you or your hotel to ensure reliability. Prices are flexible.

Cricket Grenadine style

Cricket is played throughout the Grenadines on any scrap of ground or on the beach. In Bequia, instead of the usual three stumps at the crease, there are four, and furthermore, bowlers are permitted to bend their elbows and hurl fearsome deliveries at the batsmen. This clearly favours the fielding side but batsmen are brought up to face this pace attack from an early age and cope with the bowling with complete nonchalance. Matches are held regularly, usually on Sundays, and sometimes internationals are staged. In Lower Bay v England, which Lower Bay usually wins, the visitors' team is recruited from cricket lovers staying in the area. Ask at De Reef; it is best to bat at number 10 or 11.

To travel further south to Carriacou (Grenada), you can catch a fishing boat ferry, the *Jasper*, from Ashton, Union Island to Carriacou 0700, 1 hr, Mon and Thu, although days vary according to demand and weather, returning Carriacou-Union Island from Hillsborough Pier, 1500, EC$15. You will probably have to sit on deck and hang on to whatever you can, as the hold is usually full of luggage and crates of soft drinks for sale in Carriacou. Although not absolutely essential, you should check out with immigration at the airport in Clifton the day before you travel. The boat captain will take you through Grenadian formalities on arrival at Hillsborough. In high season more frequent boat trips are organized, ask at hotels, take your passport and expect thorough searches of your luggage at Customs and Immigration.

Bequia

Named the island of the clouds by the Caribs (pronounced Bek-*way*), this is the largest of the St Vincent dependencies. Nine miles south of St Vincent and about seven miles square, Bequia attracts quite a number of tourists, chiefly yachtsmen but also the smaller cruise ships and, increasingly, land-based tourists. The island is quite hilly and well forested with a great variety of fruit and nut trees. Its main village is **Port Elizabeth** and here Admiralty Bay offers a safe anchorage. Boat building and repair work are the main industry. Experienced sailors can sometimes get a job crewing on boats sailing on from here to Panama and other destinations. When you get off the ferry you will find to your left the fruit and veg market, with some clothes stalls and souvenirs. Straight in front of you is the green-roofed **Tourist information**, run by the *Bequia Tourism Association*, 0830-1800 Mon-Fri, 0830-1400 Sat, 0830-1200 Sun, T4583286, F4583954, www.bequiasweet.com (They publish *Bequia This Week*, which has daily listings of what's on.) Across the road is the administration and finance building, and next to it is the Bayshore Mall, a new blue and white building which contains a bank, a few shops and airline offices. The Anglican **St Mary's Church** was built of local limestone and ballast bricks in 1829, replacing an earlier church which was destroyed by a hurricane in 1798. It is open and airy and has some interesting memorial stones. The southern part of the bay is known as **Belmont**, where a waterfront walkway runs past hotels, restaurants, bars and dive shops on the narrow strip of sand. Above Port Elizabeth a paved road runs to the **Hamilton Battery**, which used to guard the bay.

The nearest beach to Port Elizabeth is the pleasant **Princess Margaret beach** which shelves quickly into the clear sea. It was named after the princess in 1958 when she swam there while visiting the island by yacht. However, access is deliberately made difficult and there are no beach bars to spoil this stretch. At its south end there is a small headland, around which you can snorkel from **Lower Bay**, where swimming is excellent and the beach is one of the best on the island. Hurricane Lenny washed up extra sand in 1999 and the shore now shelves quite steeply into the sea. Damaged trees are further evidence of the swell but there are still trees for shade. Avoid the manchineel trees when it rains or you will get blisters. Local boys race their homemade, finely finished sailing yachts round the bay. In the village there are several places to stay as well as good restaurants and bars on the beach and up the hillside. Lower Bay gets very busy at holiday times.

Population: 6,000

Away from the west side of the island the beaches are empty. Take a taxi over the hills to the east coast and the wild beaches on that side of the island. There are bigger trees on the Windward side, including hard woods such as white cedar, used for making boats. Drive through coconut groves to **Spring Bay**, where there is a hotel and a beach bar (may be closed) and a pottery in a partially renovated sugar mill. The Spring Pottery and artist's studio produces domestic pottery and gardenware as well as local paintings. ■ *Daily 0730-1630. The Old Sugar Mill, Spring, T4573757.* **Industry Bay** is another nice beach surrounded by palms with a brilliant view across to Bullet Island, Battowia and Balliceaux where the Black Caribs were held before being deported to Roatán. Food and drink available at the *Industry Beach Bar*. Both beaches are narrow with shallow bays and a lot of weed, making them less good for swimming and snorkelling. In the wet season there can also be a lot of runoff from the hills. North of Industry at Park Beach, is **Old Hegg Turtle Sanctuary** in the northeast corner of the island. Not to be missed, an extremely worthwhile conservation project founded and maintained by a Bequian, a former fisherman, Orton 'Brother' King, to save the hawksbill turtle (*Eretmochelys imbricata*). Local people contact him if they see turtles hatching and he goes to the beaches to collect them, releasing them into the wild when they are about 2½ years old. There is only about a 50% success rate and a lot of injuries from the turtles biting each other, but it is still better than the natural survival rate. A few green (*Chelonia mydas*) and leatherback (*Dermochelys coriacea*) turtles can also be seen in the tanks. Larger tanks are needed if the enterprise is to improve its success rate. ■ *EC$10/US$5 entrance fee, but donations warmly welcomed. T4583245, oldhegg@vincysurf.com*

The walk up **Mount Pleasant** from Port Elizabeth is worthwhile (go by taxi if it is too hot), the shady road is overhung with fruit trees and the view of Admiralty Bay is ever more spectacular. There is a settlement of airy homes at the top, from where you can see most of the Grenadines. By following the road downhill and south of the viewpoint you can get to **Hope Bay**, an isolated and usually deserted sweep of white sand

Bequia

Sleeping
1 Bequia Beach Club
2 Blue Tropic
3 De Reef Apartments
4 Frangipani

5 Friendship Bay
6 Gingerbread & L'Auberge des Grenadines
7 Julie's Guest House
8 KingsVille Apartments

9 Old Fort
10 Plantation House
11 Spring on Bequia

and one of the best beaches. At the last house (where you can arrange for a taxi to meet you afterwards), the road becomes a rough track, after half mile turn off right down an ill-defined path through cedar trees to an open field, cross the fence on the left, go through a coconut grove and you reach the beach. The sea is usually gentle but sometimes there is powerful surf, a strong undertow and offshore current, take care. **Friendship Bay** on the south coast is particularly pleasant, with a long sandy beach; there is some coral but also quite a lot of weed. It takes about 30 minutes to walk from Port Elizabeth to the *Friendship Bay Hotel*, at the east end of the bay, or a taxi costs EC$15. Alternatively, take a dollar bus (infrequent) in the direction of Paget Farm, get out at the junction (EC$1.50) and walk down to the west end of the bay.

At **Paget Farm**, whale harpooning is still practised from February to May (the breeding season) by a few fishermen who use three 26-ft long cedar boats, powered by oars and sails. If you can arrange a trip to **Petit Nevis**, to the south, you can see the whaling station and find out more about Bequia's whaling tradition. Despite pleas from conservationists, a humpback mother and calf have been harpooned off Bequia each year for the last few years. Bequia has an annual quota of two whales and with traditional technology and power it is easier to kill a calf and then its mother than an adult male. There is a small whaling museum on the way to Paget Farm, **Athneal's petite museum**, which has a collection of whale bones, old photos and tools of the trade. ■ *US$2.*

The tourist office can help you visit the cliffside dwellings of **Moon Hole**, at the southwest, where a rocky arch frames the stone dwelling and the water comes up the front yard. People live here without any electricity or running water.

Essentials

Port Elizabeth LL *Plantation House Hotel*, T4583425, www.hotel-plantation.com Rebuilt **Sleeping** after 1988 fire, on beach at Admiralty Bay at the far end of the Belmont walkway, 27 rooms in pink and turquoise cottages with verandas, gingerbread style, all MAP, honeymoon packages, etc, restaurant in replica plantation house, tennis, swimming pool, watersports, jetty, Dive Bequia dive shop alongside, entertainment at weekends. **L-C** *Frangipani*, T4583255, www.frangipani.net Cheaper rooms share bathroom, Bequia suites have kitchen, good facilities and sea view, on beach along Belmont walkway, pleasant, bar, mosquito net provided, Noah's Arcade on site. **L-B** *Gingerbread*, T4583800, www.begos.com/gingerbread Added new luxury apartments with kitchens overlooking Admiralty Bay, old apartments at lower rates. 1-bedroomed with kitchen and bathroom, restaurant and bar upstairs, café downstairs, dive shop, tennis, waterskiing, Surf'n'Send internet/email access on site, on Belmont walkway by the beach, friendly. **A-C** *L'Auberge des Grenadines*, on Belmont Walkway, T/F4583201, frenchella@caribsurf.com French restaurant with 6 rooms to let, fans, TV, some but not all with en suite bathrooms. **C-D** *Julie's Guest House*, T4583304. 19 rooms with bath and shower, close to ferry dock, mosquito nets in rooms, good local food, good cocktails in noisy bar downstairs, meeting place for travellers to form boat charter groups. *The Whaleboner*, close to town, T4583233. A few sweet rooms with kitchenette and lively bar in front. **Mount Pleasant L-AL** *The Old Fort*, T4583440, www.oldfortbequia.com A 17th-century French built fortified farmhouse, probably oldest building on Bequia, magnificent views with a good breeze on top of the hill, quiet and peaceful, idyllic restaurant (must book), pool with view of 25 islands, beach within walking distance, 5/6 rooms, also available as a rental villa to sleep 10-14, excursions, diving, boat trips arranged. Highly recommended. Call Otmar Schaedle, multilingual. *Gipsy's Restaurant and Bar*, T4583337, specializes in local food, Mon-Sat 1100 - late. **Friendship Bay LL-AL** *Friendship Bay*, T4583222, www.friendship.com Lovely location, lush tropical gardens, 27 rooms, some renovated with a/c, ocean front or ocean view, boat excursions, dive shop, water and other sports facilities, friendly, Mosquito beach bar, food good but expensive, lobster barbecue Wed night, happy hour Sat, Sun 1700-1800, live music after that. **L-A** *Bequia Beach Club*, Friendship Bay, T4583248, www.bequiabeachclub.com 10 rooms, fans, mosquito nets, restaurant, bar, on the beach with trees for shade, casual and unsophisticated, diving, windsurfing, tennis nearby, day sails, weekly barbecues. **A** *Blue Tropic*, T4583573. Popular with

Germans, 10 rooms, view of bay, restaurant, bar, free bikes, 100 m to the beach, dive packages with Friendship Divers. Spring Bay **LL-AL** *Spring on Bequia*, T4583414, springonbequia@caribsurf.com Part of a 200-year-old working plantation, set among coconut palms, 10 rooms, pool, tennis, bar, restaurant, beach bar on unspoiled beach. **Lower Bay AL-A** *KingsVille Apartments*, Lower Bay, T4583404, kingsville@caribsurf.com Run by Bert and Kay King, 1-2 bedroom apartments in cottages, right by the beach, a/c, modern, convenient for restaurants. **A-B** *Keegan's Guesthouse*, T4583254. Lovely position on the beach, 11 rooms, fan, mosquito nets, includes breakfast and evening meal, will cater for vegetarians, also 1-2 bedroom apartments US$300-425 per week, table tennis, volley ball, no credit cards. **A-B** *Créole Garden Hotel*, T4583154, www.creolegardens.com above Corner Bay and Lower Bay beach, MAP, studios with bath, porch, refrigerator. **A-D** *De Reef Apartments*, Lower Bay, T4583484. 1-2 bedrooms in gardens by the beach, fans, kitchens, restaurant and bar.

Villas There are several villas for rent around the island, most of which are handled by letting agencies. The main agency is *Bequia Villa Rentals*, T4583393, beqvilla@caribsurf.com There is also *Friendship Bay Villa and Apartment Rentals*, T4583222, labambas@caribsurf.com; *Lime House Villas*, T4573092, www.limehousevillas.com for those who seek sanctuary up in the hills; and *Grenadine Escape Villa Rentals*, T/F4586326, www.grenadine-escape.com

Eating *Of the hotel restaurants, The Old Fort, see Sleeping, above, is one of the nicest and most romantic for a gourmet dinner up on Mount Pleasant*	**In Port Elizabeth** *Le Petit Jardin*, Back St, T4583318, VHF 16 and 68. French and international, open daily 1130-1400, 1830-2130, reservations preferred, EC$30-85 for entrées. *Porthole*, T4583458. Local Creole dishes, rotis, Mexican, fish. *Tantie Pearl's Café & Restaurant*, T4573160, VHF 68. West Indian cooking, lobster and conch sandwiches and light lunches from 1130, dinner from 1830, up on Cemetery Hill 2 mins by taxi above Port Elizabeth, nice breeze. *Daphne's*, just off the main street, T4583271. Cooks excellent Creole meals to eat in or takeaway, no credit cards. *Rainbow's End*, T4573688. Local and international snack menu, bar, disco, open 0900 until late, karaoke Tue, Band night Fri. *Lion Heart Roots Café and Boutique*, T4573917. Delicious vegetarian, Rasta food, home-made fruit juices and smoothies. Along Belmont walkway *L'Auberge de Grenadines*, T4583201. French with emphasis on lobster, large tank of live specimens, lobster lunch EC$28, lobster burgers very filling, entrées around EC$45, 3-course set dinner for EC$70, closed Thu, happy hour 1730-1830. *Mac's Pizzeria*, T4583474. Very popular, open 1100-2200, closed Mon, get there early or reserve in advance, also takeaways, try the lobster pizza, pricey at EC$60 for a small one, but covered with lobster, don't add other ingredients. *Green Boley*, T4583247. Local bar with fast food, rotis EC$5-10, burger and chips EC$12, fish and chips EC$18. The *Gingerbread Café* has sandwiches and snacks all day, open 0700-1800, also *Gingerbread BBQ*, outdoors on bayside 1200-1500, and *Gingerbread Restaurant & Bar*, T4583800, upper floor of Gingerbread complex, overlooking Admiralty Bay. Open 0800-2130, reservations recommended in season for dinner, West Indian and international, live music 3 nights a week. *Whaleboner*, T4583233. Food fresh from their own farm, EC$5-65, pizza and roti EC$8, open Mon-Sat 0800-2200, Sun 1400-2200. The *Frangipani* has sandwiches and snacks all day, slow service but friendly, good view, Thu night barbecue, buffet, steel band.

At Lower Bay *De Reef*. Lovely position on the beach, popular with yachties and locals, set meals and bar snacks, the place for Sun lunch. *Coco's Place*, T4583463, VHF 68. Fabulous view over harbour, up on hill at end of bay, lovely balcony, friendly pub and local kitchen, lunch and dinner daily, Fri lobster special EC$60, live music Tue, Fri. *Dawn's Créole Garden*, at the far end, T4583154. Open from 0800, breakfast, lunch and dinner, good home cooked food, fairly expensive, must book for dinner. *Keegan's*, T4583304, right on the beach. Local meals, open for breakfast, lunch and dinner, inexpensive 3-course meals and bar snacks all day, reservations advised in high season for dinner. *Fernando's Hideaway*, T4583758. Local-style fresh food, candlelit dinner Mon-Sat, special goat water soup.

Nightlife Jump ups and live music can be heard on different nights in the hotels, including *Plantation House*, *Frangipani*, *Friendship Bay*, and *Gingerbread*. Check bars for happy hours. There is something going on most nights either at Admiralty Bay or Friendship Bay. Look in *Bequia This Week* which has daily listings. Bands play reggae music in the gardens of several hotels.

Windward Islands

There is a market for fruit and veg by the jetty and there are small supermarkets in Port Elizabeth with improving selection of groceries and beverages but at higher prices than in St Vincent; for cash and carry purchases of items like soft drinks or beer (good for yacht provisioning), go to *Euro Shopper* up the hill in Belmont on the road to Paget, open Mon-Sat 0800-1800, T4573932, VHF 68; fish is sometimes on sale in the centre by the jetty. Overlooking Admiralty Bay on Belmont walkway, *Crab Hole*, T4583290 is a boutique where silk-screened fabrics are made downstairs and sewn into clothes upstairs, open 0800-1700 Mon-Sat in season, closing earlier out of season. *Noah's Arcade*, at the *Frangipani* on Belmont walkway, T4583424, is a branch of the enterprise on St Vincent, stocking gifts, books, handicrafts the artwork of resident artists, whatever their origin, open Mon-Fri 0900-1700, Sat-Sun 0900-1300. Also don't miss *Mauvin*'s and *Sargeant Brothers'* model boat shops (the latter up the hill going out of town), where craftsmen turn out replicas of traditional craft and visiting yachts. *Bequia Bookshop* in Port Elizabeth, T4583905, is run by Iain Gale, who keeps an excellent stock of books, particularly of Caribbean literature, maps and charts. Many of these shops stock Scrimshaw knives, intricately designed and engraved by Sam McDowell, whose studio is at the Banana Patch, Paget Farm. See also under St Vincent page 670.

Shopping
There are several marine stores & fishing tackle shops here

Sports

Tennis can be played at the Gingerbread, *Friendship Bay, Plantation House* and *Spring* hotels. Scuba diving with *Bequia Dive Adventures*, Belmont walkway, next to *Mac's Pizzeria*, T4583826, VHF68 and 16, www.BequiaDiveAdventures.com, full-service PADI dive centre. *Dive Bequia*, Belmont, T4583504, VHF16 or 68, www.dive-bequia.com, run by Bob and Cathy Sachs. In operation since 1984, this company has the biggest boats, with shade and more room to move around and manoeuvre tanks and gear. *Friendship Divers*, Friendship Bay, T4583422, bequia@friendshipdivers.de SSI/CMAS, 1-5 dives for US$39 each not including equipment. Diving is good around Pigeon Island, afternoon and night dives are usually on the leeward side of the southwest peninsula, there are a few sites around Isle à Quatre and shallow dives for training can be done around Petit Nevis. Sport fishing can be arranged on the *Ocean Catcher* T4583093, or *Passion*, T4583884, passion@caribsurf.com

Tour operators

Most tours of Bequia are little more than taxi tours taking around 3 hrs. For travel arrangements try *CITS*, in the Bayshore Mall, T4583062, cits@caribsurf.com or *Grenadine Travel* at the Gingerbread, Belmont, T4583795. *Sam's Taxi Tours* is based on St Vincent and in Bequia, T4583688. For tours by yacht to neighbouring islands and for snorkelling: the *Friendship Rose* is an 80-ft auxiliary schooner, T4583373; *Meteor* is a 51-ft yacht, T4583222; *Passion* is a 60-ft catamaran, offering day trips to Mustique, US$60, the Tobago Cays, US$75, or St Vincent and the Falls of Baleine, US$75, contact Heidi Pritchard, Belmont, T4583884, passion@caribsurf.com; *Quest* is a 44-ft centre cockpit yacht based at Paget, T4583917, owned by Johnny Ollivierre, who also has *Petrel*, a 47-ft Swan for day trips to Mustique; *SY Pelangi* is a 44-ft cutter, based at the *Frangipani Hotel*, T4583255. frangi@caribsurf.com; *SY Puka* is a 51-ft Beneteau, privately chartered to small parties (2-8), call Lara Cowan Hadley, T/F4586326, www.grenadine-escape.com

Transport

Air J F Mitchell Airport, named after the former Prime Minister, has been built on reclaimed land with a 3,200-ft runway, a terminal and night landing facilities, at the island's southwest tip. **Road Buses** (minivans and open pick-up trucks called dollar vans) leave from the jetty at Port Elizabeth and will stop anywhere to pick you up but do not cover the whole island, a cheap and reliable service. For about US$60, you can take a taxi tour around the island. **Car hire** is available at around EC$140/day, cheaper if you rent for a week, try *Phil's Car Rental*, T4583304, *Lubin's Car Rental*, T4583349, *Handy Andy Rentals*, T4583722, or *B & G Jeep Rentals*, T4583760. *Ryan & Gus's Rentals* have mokes, T4573238, short and long term rental, price negotiable. If staying in an apartment, your landlord may already have an agreement with a supplier and can offer you a good deal. **Cycling** is enjoyable, lots of gentle hills, great views and beaches. **Walking** is also rewarding. **Taxis** on Bequia, when not operating as buses, are pick-up trucks with benches in the back, brightly coloured with names like 'Messenjah'. **Sea Water taxis** scoot about in Admiralty Bay, Princess Margaret Beach and Lower Bay for the benefit of the many yachts and people on the beach, whistle or wave to attract their attention, fare EC$10 per trip.

For those arriving on yachts, there are anchorages all round either side of the channel in Admiralty Bay, Princess Margaret Beach, Lower Bay, Friendship Bay and off Petit Nevis by the old whaling station. Bequia Slipway has dockage, some moorings are available.

Directory **Banks** *National Commercial Bank*, T4583700, has an ATM for Visa and Mastercard. *Caribbean Banking Corp*, T4583845, does not. **Communications** Internet: plenty of places due to the number of yachties. *Surf'n Send*, downstairs at the *Gingerbread* complex, email, photocopying, computer accessories, open Mon-Fri 0800-1730, Sat 0800-1430, T4583577; *Sam Taxi & Tours Ltd*, behind the new Revenue Building, internet access EC$20 per hr, also printing, scanning, yacht clearance, brokerage and numerous other services for yachties, T4583686; *Icon*, in Port Elizabeth, T4573727; *RMS*, Port Elizabeth, T4583556; *Sailor Cyber Café*, Ocar Reform, T4573105. *Cyber City Internet Café* is upstairs in the *Bequia Bookshop*, Port Elizabeth, T4573161, F4856480. Non-member rates EC$5 per ¼ hr, EC$16.50 per hr. **Post**: The post office is on Back St behind *CBC*, open Mon-Fri 0830-1500, Sat 0830-1200. **Customs and immigration** On the main road by the dock, open Mon-Fri 0830-1600, Sat 0830-1200, Sun 0900-1200, 1500-1800. Overtime fee may be charged outside office hrs and on holidays. **Medical services** *Bequia Casualty Hospital*, Port Elizabeth, T4583294. See also under St Vincent. **Useful addresses** Police Turn up the road by the banks, past the hospital and the police station is on your right before you get to the *Clive Tannis Playing Field*, T4583350, VHF16.

Mustique

Lying 18 miles south of St Vincent, Mustique is 3 miles long and less than 2 miles wide. In the 1960s, Mustique was acquired by a single proprietor who developed the island as his private resort where he could entertain the rich and famous. It is a beautiful island, with fertile valleys, steep hills and 12 miles of white sandy beach, but described by some as 'manicured'. The whole of the island, its beaches and surrounding waters are a conservation area. It is no longer owned by one person and is more accessible to tourists, although privacy and quiet is prized by those who can afford to live there. Most visitors are day-trippers from Bequia or other neighbouring islands on private or chartered yachts, who stay on the beach and eat at *Basil's*. There is no intention to commercialize the island; it has only one petrol pump for the few cars.

Mustique

0 metres 500
0 yards 500

■ Sleeping
1 Cotton House   2 Firefly

You can walk, ride a horse or hire a moped to tour the island. The main anchorage *Jet skis and* is Britannia Bay, where there are 18 moorings for medium-sized yachts with waste *spear guns* disposal and phones. Take a picnic lunch to Macaroni Beach on the Atlantic side. *are banned* This white-sand beach is lined with small palm-thatched pavilions and a well-kept park/picnic area. Swimming and snorkelling is also good at Lagoon Bay, Gallicaux Bay, Britannia Bay and Endeavour Bay, all on the leeward side. L'Ansecoy Bay in the north is a wide beach, notable for the wreck of the French liner the *Antilles*, which went aground offshore in 1971.

Basil's Bar and Restaurant is *the* congregating spot for yachtsmen and the jet set. Snorkelling is good here too. From it there is a well beaten path to the *Cotton House Hotel*, which is the other congregating point. There is an honour system to pay for moorings at *Basil's Bar*, EC$50 a night, EC$20 second night.

LL *Cotton House*, T4564777, www.cottonhouse.com A 20-room refurbished (by Oliver **Sleeping** Messel) 18th-century cotton plantation house, very expensive, pool, tennis, windsurfers, sailfish, snorkelling, all complimentary, horse riding and scuba diving available, sailing packages tailor made. Smaller, slightly less expensive **LL** *Firefly*, T4563414, www.mustiquefirefly.com All 4 rooms with view overlooking the bay, CP, 2-tiered pool with a view, bar. 50 of the 82 private residences are available for rent, with staff, from US$3,500 per week in summer for a 2-bedroomed villa to US$30,000 per week in winter for a villa sleeping 14. Contact *The Mustique Company Ltd*, T4584621, www.mustique-island.com

Basil's Bar, T4584621 for reservations. For seafood and nightlife, open from 0800, entrées **Eating** EC$10-75. Locals' night on Mon with buffet for EC$35, Wed is good with barbeque and jump-up. On Sat go to the *Cotton House*. Reservations required at the *Cotton House* and *Firefly*. Up the hill from Basil's is the local *Piccadilly* pub, rotis and beer, and pool table; foreigners are welcome, but it is best to go in a group and girls should not go on their own.

Air International connections are best through Barbados, a 50-min flight with *Mustique Air-* **Transport** *ways*, although other connections are possible via Grenada and the neighbouring islands of St Vincent, Bequia, Canouan and Union with either *Mustique Airways* or *SVG Air*. The airstrip, being in the centre of the island is clearly visible, so check-in time is 5 mins before take off (that is after you've seen your plane land). **Sea** Fresh water is shipped in on Mustique boats *Robert Junior* (T4571918) and the *Geronimo*. Both take passengers and excursions on Sun (EC$20, 2-hr trip). Many people arrive on private or chartered yachts.

Canouan

A quiet, peaceful, crescent-shaped island, Canouan lies 25 miles south of St Vincent, with excellent reef-protected beaches. Evidence of human occupation dates back to 200BC, pendants and pottery shards having been found during construction work on the airport and hotels. The island was valuable for plantation crops during the colonial period, namely sugar then cotton, which was grown until 1924. The Snagg family who owned the land were unable to keep the plantation going and the north reverted to acacia scrub and thicket. The estate was sold to the government in 1946. Other local families include the Comptons and the Mitchells, shipwrights who arrived in the 19th century. At that time there was plenty of cedar (for the hull), mahogany (for planking) and bamboo (for masts) for ship building. In 1939 Reginald Mitchell built the largest schooner ever in the Lesser Antilles. The three-masted *Gloria Colita* was 165 ft long, 39 ft wide and weighed 178 tons. Unfortunately only two years later it was found abandoned and awash in the Gulf of Mexico and no one knows what happened to Capt Mitchell and his crew.

The village, on the leeward side in Grand Bay, is **Charlestown**, founded after a devastating hurricane destroyed the settlement at Carenage Bay in 1921. It is architecturally uninteresting, untidy and scruffy but the white-sand beach is superb, running the length of the bay and broken only by the jetty. On holidays, day trips are organized from St Vincent on the *Barracouda*, and then the beach is full of people.

Cricket matches are held on the sand, ranging from little boys to family groups to serious young men who carefully measure their wicket and dispute calls. Balls constantly go in the water and stumps are made of any sticks found on the beach. The beach at the *Canouan Beach Hotel* in the southwest is splendid with white sand and views of numerous islands to the south. Mahault Bay on the north coast is beautiful, isolated, with steep hills all around, and great for a picnic. Turtles come here to nest. Dive trips can be arranged through Blueway Diving at the *Tamarind Beach Hotel*. The hotels organize boat trips to the Tobago Cays and non-hotel guests are permitted to make up numbers if the boat is not fully booked.

Much of the north of the island, 800 of the island's 1,866 acres, is now taken up by the new, exclusive development, *Carenage Bay Resort*, built with Italian investment but closed since a management contract was terminated in 2002. There are two nice beaches, but being on the windward side the sea is often choppy and has a fair amount of weed. The centre of the bay is taken up with an 18-hole, par 72 golf course running up and over the hill. The development has not been without controversy. Although most residents appreciate the job opportunities, a vocal minority has occasionally mounted road blocks in protest at being denied access to beaches in the north, previously open to the public via public roads. The beaches are still open to the public, up to the high water mark, but access has to be from the sea, making a visit problematic.

Sleeping **LL** *Canouan Beach Hotel*, South Glossy Bay, T4588888, www.grenadines.net/canouan/ canouanbeachhotelhomepage.htm 32 deluxe bungalows and main building, in the south close to the airport, all-inclusive, French speaking, fabulous beach, very relaxing, daily excursions on their catamaran. **LL-L** *Tamarind Beach Hotel*, T4588044, www.tamarindbeach hotel.com Set in lovely mature gardens, green and lush, 42 comfortable rooms, all with sea view and right on beach, everything wood and wicker, no phones or TV, popular restaurant, humming with yachties at night, watersports, PADI dive shop on site, long dock for dinghies, moorings rather rolly, more comfortable sleeping to anchor in north corner of bay. They also provide water, ice, bread, showers, to yachties. Guests may use tennis courts and other facilities at the *Carenage Bay Resort*.

Canouan

■ Sleeping	2 Carenage Bay Resort
1 Canouan Beach	3 Tamarind Beach

A few local restaurants have opened in the village and are much cheaper than the hotels. *R&C Restaurant and Bar*, up the hill opposite the entrance to the *Tamarind Beach Hotel*, T4588264, VHF16. Run by Catherine and Roland Williams, open from 0730, seafood and local dishes such as roti, EC$8, good and filling, nice and breezy with good view over the harbour. There is a bar by the ferry dock but it does not always serve food. *Pompey*, on the main street, and *Honeycomb*, up the hill heading east out of town, also serve local food.

Eating
The hotel restaurants serve international food with local specialities

Air There is a new runway and terminal building built partly with finance from the *Carenage Bay Resort*, which persuaded *American Eagle* to fly in from San Juan and Barbados, allowing connections from the USA and Europe. *Air Caraïbe* flies in from Fort-de-France and Union Island. There is a good service from Barbados (55 mins) or Grenada (20 mins) with *SVGAir*, *TIA* or *Air Mustique*. These small planes also link Canouan with other islands nearby, Martinique (1hr), St Lucia (40 mins), St Vincent (15 mins). **Sea** The *Barracouda* calls here on its way from St Vincent to Union Island and back twice a week, with occasional day trips at holiday times. **Road** There is no public transport. Walking is rewarding and distances are not great although the island is hilly.

Transport
The main anchorage for yachts is Grand Bay. Others are at Canouan Beach Hotel and Rameau bays, South Glossy and Friendship Bays in settled weather

Banks *National Commercial Bank*, in centre of village at the road junction, T4588595, open Mon-Wed, Fri 0800-1300, Thu 0800-1300, 1430-1700, always busy with queues, not enough motivated staff, no ATM. **Communications** Internet: *Tamarind Beach Hotel*, US$7/hr. **Post office**: on the main street on the left heading south, no sign outside, the building used to be a bar and still looks like one.

Directory

Mayreau

A small privately owned island with deserted beaches and only one hotel and one guesthouse. The village is tightly packed on the hillside above the harbour. You can reach it only by boat and the *Barracouda* calls on its way from St Vincent to Union. There is no deep water dock, though, so goods and passengers are offloaded into little boats and dinghies which then struggle to the jetty in great danger of being swamped by a wave. The beaches are glorious and Mayreau is a popular stop-off point for yachties, particularly in **Salt Whistle Bay**, a perfect horseshoe-shaped bay in the northwest, on a spit of land with a long, wild beach on the other side, which is to windward. Several day charters include the bay as a useful lunch stop when

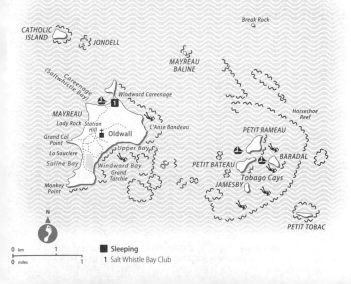

Mayreau & the Tobago Cays

■ **Sleeping**
1 Salt Whistle Bay Club

Windward Islands

visiting the Tobago Cays. The only disadvantage to its popularity is that it can be noisy at night in season with revellers enjoying entertainment at the restaurant and on board their yachts. Parts of Mayreau are within the Tobago Cays Marine Park and a marine environment interpretation centre is planned as a tourist attraction and to aid conservation by the *Mayreau Environmental Development Organization (MEDO)*, T4588458. This is one of the EC-funded pilot projects for sustainable development and community-based initiatives being carried out in the Eastern Caribbean, to encourage economic diversification through nature tourism.

Sleeping & eating **LL** *Salt Whistle Bay Club*, T4588444, VHF16. 10 rooms in rather gloomy cottages, MAP, yacht charters and picnics on nearby islands. Restaurant open to non-guests, entrées around EC$45-65, seafood and imported meat. **B-C** *Dennis' Hideaway*, T4588944. 5 rooms, bar, restaurant, good food and drinks at reasonable prices, yacht charter. *J & C Bar and Restaurant*, best view of the harbour with soft music, boutique, room for a large group, good lobster, fish and lambi, for parties of 4 and over the captain's dinner is free; *Island Paradise*, everything fresh, good lobster, fish and curried conch, half price happy hour 1800-1900, barbecue Fri with local band, free ride up the hill, skipper's meal free with more than 3 for dinner.

Communication There is a payphone in the village with an overseas operator for credit card calls.

Union Island

Arrival by air is spectacular as the planes fly over the hills and descend steeply to the landing strip

The most southerly of the islands belonging to St Vincent, Union Island is 40 miles from St Vincent and only three miles long by one mile wide. It has two settlements, **Clifton** and **Ashton**. The tourist office is on your left as you come off the ferry, T4588350, daily 0900-1600. 75% of the population live in Ashton, but 95% of the action takes place in Clifton. Union is distinguished by some dramatic peaks. Mount Olympus (637 ft) is in the northwest, while Mount Parnassus (920 ft) and Mount Taboi (1,002 ft) stand side by side in the centre-west and in the centre-east are the jagged Pinnacles (925 ft). The landscape around Ashton is more rugged and mountainous than around Clifton. **Parnassus**, or 'Big Hill', is a good hike. Take the upper level road in Ashton. In front of a clearing are some steps leading to a path. After two or three minutes, fork to the left. The path winds round the hill to the top, from where the views are as fine as you would imagine. North of the airport is Fort Hill (450 ft), where the site of a 17th-century French fort gives a panoramic view of dozens of islands. A walk around the interior of the island (about

Union Island

Sleeping	**2** Clifton Beach
1 Anchorage Yacht Club	**3** Palm Island Resort
	4 St Joseph's Guest House

two hours Clifton-Ashton-Richmond Bay-Clifton) is worth the effort, with fine views of the sea, half a dozen neighbouring islands, pelicans and Union itself. The Union Island Ecotourism Movement (UIEM) was created in 1996 with the aim of using community groups to encourage land-based tourism. Five guides have been trained with EC finance to maintain trails and escort visitors, although not a lot of progress has been seen so far. Contact Matthew Harvey, T4858317, or Ynolde Hutchinson, T4858486.

The beach at **Chatham Bay** is beautiful and deserted, but not particularly good for swimming as there is a coral ledge along most of it just off the beach. Snorkelling and diving are good though. It is one of the last undeveloped anchorages in the Grenadines. There is no road and you have to walk 30 minutes along a footpath through the bush from the end of the road just above Ashton down to the bay. Women should not go there alone, there have been reports of attacks. **Bloody Bay** has a long, sandy beach, best reached from the sea, although there is some surf. **Richmond Bay** is also pleasant, good for swimming and easily reached as the road runs alongside it. However, it is dirty and there is broken glass on the sand, so take care. Round the point, **Belmont Bay**, or Big Sands, is another sandy beach, with villas for rent.

Clifton serves as the south point of entry clearance for yachts. The immigration office and customs are at the airport, so if you arrive by boat you check in at the *Yacht Club* and the airport. Similarly on departure, check out at the airport, even if you are leaving by ferry from Ashton to Carriacou. For visiting yachts there are anchorages at Clifton, Frigate Island and Chatham Bay, while the *Anchorage Yacht Club* marina has some moorings. There is also a 20-berth marina at Bougainvilla, T4588678, bougainvilla@caribsurf.com, a smart new complex of businesses next to the *Anchorage*, offering apartment accommodation, a restaurant, a boutique, a wine shop, internet access and laundry at *Erika's Marine Services* (see below), the offices of *Moorings, VPM Dufour Yachting, Bamboo Yachting, Oversea Sailing, Star Voyage, Wind and Sea Ltd* (cruise ship agent and charter), and *Unitech Marine* supply and repair.

A good reason to visit Union Island is to arrange day trips to other islands or to find a ride on a yacht to Venezuela towards the end of the season (May-June). Day trip boats to other islands leave from Clifton around 1000 and are all about the same price, EC$120, including lunch. *Yannis Tours*, moored at the *Clifton Beach Hotel* arranges tours to the nearby Tobago Cays (see below), Palm Island, Petit St Vincent and other small islands. They have a comfortable catamaran, which is recommended if the sea is a bit rough, and provide breakfast, lunch, rum punch and soft drinks, T4588513. Alternatively, you can hire a local skipper to take you in a smaller boat wherever you want to go. This is recommended if the sea is calm so that you can spend the maximum time snorkelling at the Tobago Cays. The *SVG Water Taxi Association* sets prices, so don't be fooled into a 'good rate'. Check at the tourist booth, a water taxi to the Tobago Cays for three or four people is US$80 one way.

Sleeping

Apartments and villas are opening up and if you ask around you should find reasonable self-catering accommodation

L-B *Anchorage Yacht Club*, Clifton, T4588221, www.ayc-hotel-grenadines.com Beside the runway, full marina service, French restaurant, terrace bar, steel band or piano music, 15 rooms, special rates for yachties, small beach, boutique, very sad shark pool with very bored nurse sharks in very little water. **A-D** *Clifton Beach Hotel and Guest House*, T/F4588235, www.clifton beachhotel.com Rooms on the waterfront, cottages, guesthouse and apartment at other locations including Big Sands. Rather dilapidated and run down but comfortable, clean and friendly nonetheless, MAP available, restaurant overlooking water, a/c, dodgy electric showers, laundry, friendly service, water and ice for boats, bike, car and jeep rental. **A-D** *St Joseph's Guest House*, Clifton, T4588405, www.unionisland.com The nicest place to stay, new guesthouse built just above the new RC church, run by Father Andrew Roach, stupendous views of Palm Is, PSV, Petit Martinique and Carriacou, delightfully breezy and peaceful on the spacious balconies, 2 rooms share kitchen on balcony, 2-bedroomed cottage, 1-bedroom annex apartment on church, 2 dormitories for youth groups sleep up to 15 each at a squeeze, meeting facilities with computer room, access to beach at the bottom of the hill, good snorkelling, jeep rental. Father Andrew organizes classes in screen printing and computers for local youngsters and volunteer labour from guests is always welcome. You don't have to be religious to stay here, all

Windward Islands

are made to feel at home. **E** *Lambi's Guest House*, Clifton, T/F4588349. A/c, restaurant, bar, lively steel band every night. There is not much in Ashton, except the new *BBB Marine View Apartments*, which might be worth a try if you want to stay in that area.

Eating
Most places have a happy hour 1800-1900

In Clifton, *The West Indies*, at the Bougainvilla complex overlooking the sea, T4588311, VHF16. Probably the best restaurant for breakfast, EC$20-30, lunch (panini, burgers, chicken nuggets) or dinner, entrées EC$35-55, international style, local ingredients and imported meat, open air, pleasant, tropical fish tank with more than just fish. *Lambi's Restaurant*, next to the *Clifton Beach Hotel*, reached by alley from main street or from the sea, barn-like dining room with long tables for parties, steel band at night, get there by 1800 for the happy hour, EC$45 buffet starts around 1900, free water taxi service or free moorings if you eat there, also rooms to rent. *Sydney's Bar & Restaurant*, T/F4588320, VHF 16, Clifton, towards the airport. Owned by Sydney, who handpaints T-shirts for sale in Tobago Cays, food by Marin from Munich, local meals, snacks, seafood crêpes, happy hour 1800-1900, also guesthouse. *Jennifer's Restaurant*, West Indian food at reasonable prices, music at weekends. In Ashton, *Janti's*, T4588343, VHF16, is a small restaurant and bar on the left as you go into Ashton from Clifton. Snacks are available but dinner reservations required, good food, specializes in local fish, lobster in season, vegetarian meals, fruit juices and punches, free taxi if there are enough of you.

Festivals

At **Easter** there are sports, cultural shows and a calypso competition. In **May**, is the *Big Drum Festival*, an event which marks the end of the dry season, culminating in the Big Drum Dance, derived from African and French traditions. It is also performed on other occasions, for weddings or launching boats and even in times of disaster.

Shopping

Fruit and veg stalls line the road by the ferry dock, with the best of what's in season. There are a few supermarkets in Clifton, *Lambi's*, next to the *Clifton Beach Hotel*, T4588022, VHF68, and *Grand Union* (also a guesthouse), to your right as you come off the main dock, T4588178, will deliver to the dock, and 4-5 smaller groceries sell fresh produce and hardware. For luxury foodstuffs and the best steaks, *Captain Gourmet*, on the main street, T4588918, full of French yachties buying baguettes, croissants, cheese and other delicacies, good but expensive wine. Wine also sold at the *Grenadines Vine Shop*, in the Bougainvilla complex, T4588289, VHF16. There is also a nice boutique in the Bougainvilla, which sells gifts, cruising guides, cook books and fish guides, etc. More gift shops can be found all along the main street.

Sports

Grenadines Dive, T4588138, gdive@caribsurf.com and *The Dive Shack*, T4588508, offer scuba diving, mostly around the Tobago Cays.

Tour operators

Eagle's Travel Agency, opposite NCB just past *Grand Union* supermarket, T4588179, F4588095, eagtrav@caribsurf.com for reservations and ticketing for local airlines. *James Travel*, on the main street next to *Captain Gourmet*, T4858306, offers similar services.

Transport

Air *LIAT* flies from Carriacou and Mustique, with connections from Barbados and international carriers. *Air Caraïbe* flies from Fort-de-France via Canouan, making it possible to get from Paris in a day. Scheduled and charter services from St Vincent, Grenada, Barbados and St Lucia with *SVG Air*, *Air Mustique* and *TIA*. **Sea** There is an international ferry service between Ashton and Hillsborough on Carriacou. The *Jasper* is a wooden fishing boat which makes the 1-hr trip to Hillsborough at 0730, Mon and Thu, EC$15, returning same day around 1500. The captain takes you through immigration procedures, but you should check out at Immigration at Clifton Airport the night before. Expect to have your bags thoroughly searched on arrival at Customs and Immigration at Hillsborough. The *Barracouda* is the main link with the other islands in the St Vincent Grenadines, see above. The *SVG Water Taxi Association* sets rates for water taxis. From a yacht in harbour to land is US$2 per person during the day and US$3 per person at night. Clifton to Ashton or Palm Island is US$30 for 3-4 people one way, Chatham Bay, Mayreau, PSV or Petite Martinique US$60. **Land** Minibuses run between Clifton and Ashton, EC$2. They convert to a taxi on request. Bicycles can be hired from *Erika's Marine Services*, T4858335, US$18/day, US$64/week.

Directory

See under St Vincent, page 685. **Banks** The *NCB* is to your right as you come off the dock, open Mon-Thu 0800-1300, Fri 0800-1300, 1500-1700, T4588347. There is an ATM, but if it is broken try *Erika's*. **Communications** Internet: *Erika's Marine Services* at the Bougainvilla complex, run by Heather Grant (Canadian), T4858335, VHF68, erika@caribsurf.com, fast machines, EC$10/15 mins, open Mon-Sat 0900-1730, also Sun 0900-1400 in season. Additional services include bicycle hire, laundry, book exchange, telephone, fax, computer rental, *DHL*, cash advances on Visa, Mastercard and Eurocard with 10% commission, currency exchange at EC$2.50=US$1. Internet access at *Western Union*, upstairs on main street, Clifton, 4 terminals, some keyboards work better than others, EC$5/15 mins, open Mon-Fri 0800-1630, Sun 0800-1200, or later if you are already on the machine, also phone calls, EC$7/min to Europe, EC$5 to North and South America, EC$3 to the Caribbean and EC$10 elsewhere. *Union Island Communications Centre* (Unicom), is opposite the main gates to the *Anchorage* by the airport, T4588660, EC$0.50/min or EC$25/hr. Phone calls can be made via cardphone at *Anchorage Hotel*, the airport or in town. USA direct operator can also be reached by dialling 1-800-8722881 and credit card calls or operator assisted calls can be made. **Post**: The post office is on the main street in Clifton, on the right as you walk to Ashton. Stamps for postcards/letters to the Caribbean EC$0.60/0.70, Australia EC$0.75/1.40, to Canada/USA EC$0.65/0.90, to Europe EC$0.70/1.10. Federal Express, T4588843; DHL, T4858335. **Useful numbers** Fire, T999; Hospital, T4588339; Police, T4588229; *Harvey's Pharmacy*, T4588596; Doctor, T4588547/4588339; Customs, T4588360 (airport), T4588294 (seaport), Mon-Fri 0900-1800.

Tobago Cays

The Tobago Cays are a small collection of islets just off Mayreau, protected by a horseshoe reef and surrounded by beautifully clear water. The beaches are some of the most beautiful in the Caribbean and there is diving and snorkelling on Horseshoe reef and wall. Anchor damage, together with over-fishing and removal of black coral has killed some of the reef; hard coral lies broken on the bottom, but overall it is in remarkably good condition considering the volume of visitors it receives. Do not touch anything underwater, coral dies if you do. The Tobago Cays are crowded with unlimited charter boats, liveaboard boats or day charter catamarans out of St Vincent, Bequia, Canouan and Union Island which can number over 150 in high season. Mooring buoys have been put in to prevent anchoring on the reef, but there are not enough. Although the yachts anchor on sand, their dinghies do not and they are damaging the coral by putting down anchor wherever they want to snorkel. The flat, calm water within the reef has become popular as a place to kitesurf. Although exhilarating, it is extremely dangerous with so many snorkellers on the surface of the water. There are also anchorages in the cut between Petit Rameau and Petit Bateau, or to the south of Baradel. You can shop at your boat or on the beach. Ice, butter, fresh fish, lambi, lobster, T-shirts, even French designer clothes are brought to you by boat men. Don't give them your garbage though, or you'll be sunbathing next to it on the beach later.

The cays are a marine reserve, although nothing is done to police it

Petit St Vincent

Locally referred to as PSV, this is a beautiful, privately owned, 113-acre island with one of the Caribbean's best resorts. At the *Petit St Vincent* you will find laid-back luxury, casual and stylish, with an excellent standard of service. If relaxation is what you want, you can get it here in spades. There are lots of trees and flowers providing a peaceful atmosphere and you can see most of the southern Grenadines from one view or another, even Mustique on a really clear day. The island is owned and managed by Hazen Richardson, with help from his wife, Lynn, a staff of 80 (for 44 guests) and seven rather elderly labradors. Accommodation is in 22 secluded cottages mostly on the northeast side of the island, which have the most glorious views of the reef and the changing colours of the sea, encompassing all the blues and turquoises imaginable. Steps lead down the cliffs to the beach, where you can snorkel. There is a tennis court, fitness track and water toys: sunfish, hobie cats, windsurfers, glass-bottom kayaks. You can have room service (especially nice for breakfast) or eat in the central building. Picnics can be arranged on the south-facing beach (hammocks and shade

Communication is achieved with coloured flags hoisted outside your cottage; staff come round in golf carts to pick up your requests

thoughtfully provided) or on the tiny islet Petit St Richardson. You can snorkel and dive off the Mopion and Punaise sandbar islands to the northwest. The island can be reached by the resort's launch from Union Island. The resort will charter a flight from Barbados to Union Island for US$160 per person one way, children half price. The anchorage and jetty are on the south side opposite Petite Martinique, protected by a reef. Beaches are public, so don't be surprised to see local children from Petite Martinique swimming or playing cricket near the anchorage.

Sleeping **LL** *Petit St Vincent Resort*, T4588801, www.psvresort.com One of the Leading Hotels of the World. FAP, includes room service and all facilities, closed Sep-Oct.

Palm Island

Also known as Prune Island, is another privately owned, luxury resort, about a mile from Union Island, with coral reefs on three sides. The island was developed by John and Mary Caldwell, after they had made several ocean voyages. John is the author of *Desperate Voyage*, a book describing his first ocean crossing; with virtually no previous experience, he sailed from the USA to Australia to meet Mary. The boat was demasted, wrecked on a reef and John was stranded on an island and had to eat slime from his boat until he was rescued. The Caldwells later leased this low-lying, swampy island from the St Vincent government and the family still runs the resort.

There are four beaches, of which the one on the west coast, Casuarina, is the most beautiful, helped along with copious amounts of sand washed up by Hurricane Lenny in 1999. A casual bar and restaurant facing Union Island is open to yachties and passengers of small cruise ships, but the rest of the island is reserved for guests. Even access to the beach from the jetty is prevented by ropes and notices. Water purchase is possible for yachts, moorings available. Sailing, windsurfing, scuba diving, snorkelling, fishing, tennis, health club all available, snorkelling and diving is usually on the Mopion and Punaise sandbar islands. Shared charter flights can be arranged from Barbados to Union Island, where you will be met and brought over by the resort's launch, 10 minutes.

Sleeping **LL** *Palm Island Resort*, T4588824, www.palmislandresort.com Apartments and individual bungalows, FAP.

Background

History By the time Columbus discovered St Vincent on his third voyage in 1498, the Caribs were occupying the island, which they called Hairoun. They had overpowered the Arawaks, killing the men but interbreeding with the women. The Caribs aggressively prevented European settlement until the 18th century but were more welcoming to Africans. In 1675 a passing Dutch ship laden with settlers and their slaves was shipwrecked between St Vincent and Bequia. Only the slaves survived and these settled and mixed with the native population and their descendants still live in Sandy Bay and a few places in the northwest. Escaped slaves from St Lucia and Grenada later also sought refuge on St Vincent and interbred with the Caribs. As they multiplied they became known as 'Black Caribs'. There was tension between the Caribs and the Black Caribs and in 1700 there was civil war.

In 1722 the British attempted to colonize St Vincent but French settlers had already arrived and were living peaceably with the Caribs growing tobacco, indigo, cotton and sugar. Possession was hotly disputed until 1763 when it was ceded to Britain. It was lost to the French again in 1778 but regained under the Treaty of Versailles in 1783. However, this did not bring peace with the Black Caribs, who repeatedly tried to oust the British in what became known as the Carib Wars. A treaty with them in 1773 was soon violated by both sides. Peace came only at the end of the century when in 1796 General Abercrombie crushed a revolt fomented the previous year by the French radical Victor Hugues. In 1797, over 5,000 Black Caribs were deported to Roatán, an island at that time in British

Milton Cato 1915-1997

Milton Cato was a key figure in the development of democracy and independence in St Vincent and the Grenadines. From a poor family, he pulled himself up through a scholarship to grammar school, and after serving in the Canadian Volunteer Army in the War, was called to the bar in 1949. He returned from London to set up business in Kingstown and became involved in politics, then in its infancy, with plantation workers only recently having won the vote. In 1955 he founded the St Vincent Labour Party (SVLP), and when St Vincent became part of the West Indian Federation, he went in 1958 to Trinidad as one of his island's representatives. After the collapse of the Federation he entered St Vincent's

parliament in 1961 and led the SVLP to victory in the 1967 elections, becoming Chief Minister. In 1969 he participated in the negotiations which gave the island the status of Associated Statehood. He remained in power, with a brief interlude in 1972-74, and led St Vincent into independence in 1979. In the general elections of that year the SVLP won 11 of the 13 seats in the newly independent House of Assembly. However, economic stagnation, natural disasters and allegations of corruption hit the popularity of Cato's government and the SVLP was defeated in the 1984 elections which brought James Mitchell to power. Milton Cato retired a year later, shunning honours or public recognition of his service to his country.

Windward Islands

hands off the coast of Honduras. The violence ceased although racial tension took much longer to eradicate. In the late 19th century, a St Vincentian poet, Horatio Nelson Huggins wrote an epic poem about the 1795 Carib revolt and deportation to Roatán, called *Hiroona*, which was published in the 1930s.

In the 19th-century labour shortages on the plantations brought Portuguese immigrants in the 1840s and East Indians in the 1860s, and the population today is largely a mixture of these and the African slaves. Slavery was abolished in 1832 but social and economic conditions remained harsh for the majority non-white population. In 1902, La Soufrière erupted, killing 2,000 people, just two days before Mont Pelée erupted on Martinique, killing 30,000. Much of the farming land was seriously damaged and economic conditions deteriorated further. In 1925 a Legislative Council was inaugurated but universal adult suffrage was not introduced until 1951.

St Vincent and the Grenadines belonged to the Windward Islands Federation until 1959 and the West Indies Federation between 1958 and 1962. In 1969 the country became a British Associated State with complete internal self-government. Government during the 1970s was mostly coalition government between the St Vincent Labour Party (SVLP) and the People's Political Party. In 1979 St Vincent and the Grenadines gained full independence, but the year was also remembered for the eruption of La Soufrière on Good Friday, 13 April. Fortunately no one was killed as thousands were evacuated, but there was considerable agricultural damage. In 1980 Hurricane Allen caused further devastation to the plantations and it took years for production of crops such as coconuts and bananas to recover. Hurricane Emily destroyed an estimated 70% of the banana crop in 1987.

The National Democratic party (NDP), held power under Prime Minister James Mitchell (Sir James after receiving a knighthood in 1995) from 1984 until 2001. In the 1998 elections, the NDP won eight of the 15 seats in the House of Assembly, and its share of the vote fell. The United Labour Party (ULP) called for new elections because the ULP won 54.6% of the vote compared with only 45.3% for the winning NDP. The Government was often criticized for its handling of the economy and for failing to deal with drug trafficking and health and education issues. US officials believed that offshore banks in St Vincent were being used to launder drugs money and that the southern Grenadines were a transshipment point for cocaine. Marijuana is grown in the hills of St Vincent and the USA regularly carries out eradication exercises. Farmers complain they have no other crop to grow, particularly since the collapse in banana exports.

Political tensions in 2000 were defused by the mediation of the Caribbean Community (Caricom). Conflict arose when the government increased pension and gratuities for members of parliament. The ULP, trade unions and others organized strikes and called for the government's resignation. The Caricom agreement called for general elections to be brought forward by two years and held no later than end-March 2001. Sir James Mitchell (69) resigned the leadership of the NDP in August 2000. The 2001 elections resulted in a landslide victory for the ULP, which won all the seats in the House of Assembly. Ralph Gonsalves became Prime Minister.

Geography St Vincent, and its 32 sister islands and cays which make up the Grenadines were, until fairly recently, almost unknown to tourists except yachtsmen and divers. They remain uncrowded. St Vincent is very picturesque, with fishing villages, coconut groves, banana plantations and fields of arrowroot, of which the island is the world's largest producer. It is a green and fertile volcanic island, with lush valleys, rugged cliffs on the leeward and windward coasts and beaches of dark volcanic sand. The highest peak on the island is La Soufrière, an active volcano in the north rising to about 4,000 ft. It last erupted in 1979 but careful monitoring enabled successful evacuation before it blew. The mountain range of Morne Garu rises to 3,500 ft and runs southward with spurs to the east and west coasts. Most of the central mountain range and the steep hills are forested. St Vincent is roughly 18 miles long and 11 miles wide and has an area of 133 sq miles, while the Grenadines contribute another 17 sq miles all together.

People About 25% live in the capital, Kingstown and its suburbs, 8% live on the Grenadines; 66% of the population are black and 19% as mixed, while 2% are Amerindian/black, 6% East Indian, 4% white and the remainder are 'others'. In the north of the island there are people of Carib descent, see History above. Nelcia Robinson, above Cyrus Tailor Shop on Grenville Street, is an authority on Black Caribs/Garifuna and is the co-ordinator of the *Caribbean Organization of Indigenous People on St Vincent.*

Government St Vincent and the Grenadines is a constitutional monarchy within the Commonwealth. The Queen is represented by a Governor General. There is a House of Assembly with 15 elected representatives and six senators.

Economy The St Vincent economy is largely based on agriculture and tourism, with a small manufac-
Over half of all turing industry which is mostly for export. The main export is bananas, the fortunes of
exports are sold which used to fluctuate according to the severity of the hurricane season, but the fall in
to the UK prices brought about by the new European banana policy has hit hard. The Banana Growers Association is in debt and has been attempting to cut costs, but is also investing in improving land, irrigation and packing sheds. Quality, prices, planting and production have all recovered strongly. Nevertheless, the Government is encouraging farmers to diversify and reduce dependence on bananas with incentives and land reform. Arrowroot starch is the second largest export crop, St Vincent is the world's largest producer. Arrowroot is now used as a fine dressing for computer paper as well as the traditional use as a thickening agent in cooking. Other exports include coconuts, copra, anthurium lilies, orchids, sweet potatoes, tannias and eddoes. Fishing has received aid from Japan. In 1998 Japan gave the island a grant for the construction of fishery centres in Kingstown and elsewhere, having previously given aid for jetties and fish refrigeration facilities in St Vincent, Canouan and Bequia, for a coastal fisheries development project and the national fisheries development plan. In return, St Vincent supports Japan on whaling issues.

Tourism in St Vincent and the Grenadines is a major employer and source of foreign exchange. The Government has encouraged upmarket, often yacht-based tourism, mainly in the Grenadines. Expansion is limited by the size of the airport and the willingness of international airlines to fly into the islands. Stopover tourist arrivals are around 60,000 a year. Visitor expenditure is about US$50 mn a year.

Things to do in Grenada

★

- A rum punch with **nutmeg** is essential at sunset; nutmeg jelly for breakfast.
- For unsurpassed beauty, experience the rainforest with a **hike in the mountains**, cooling off in waterfalls and pools.
- Stroll around the harbour in **St George's**, watching the boats and the bustle.
- Take a day trip on the hovercraft to **Carriacou** watching out for dolphins along the way.
- Make the most of the **local food**, try callaloo, curry goat or oildown.

Grenada

Windward Islands

Known as the spice island because of the nutmeg, mace and other spices it produces, Grenada (pronounced 'Grenayda'), the most southerly of the Windward Islands, has a beautiful mountainous interior and is well endowed with lush forests and cascading rivers. Hikers and nature lovers enjoy the trails in the national parks, where many different ecosystems are found, from dry tropical forest and mangroves on the coast, through lush rainforest on the hillsides, to elfin woodland on the peaks. St George's, the capital, is widely acknowledged as the prettiest harbour city in the West Indies, blending the architectural styles of the French and English with a picturesque setting on steep hills overlooking the bay. The southern coast, with its sandy beaches, bays and rocky promontories, is being developed for tourism.

IDD code: 473
Colour map 4, grid C4

Ins and outs

Air links with Europe and North America usually involve a change of plane in San Juan, Trinidad or Barbados, although there are a few direct flights from London, Frankfurt and Philadelphia. There are charter services but these are seasonal. Unless you are on a yacht or a cruise ship it is not easy to get there by sea either, although there is a ferry between Union Island (St Vincent) and Carriacou, allowing island hopping from the north.

Getting there
See Transport, page 706, for further details

There is a good and colourful bus service connecting St George's with most parts of the island. It is cheap, but driving is fast and roads are twisty, so if you have a tendency to car sickness this may not be for you. One alternative is car hire, if you are good at finding your way around and are not intimidated by local drivers. Maps are often not accurate, so navigation becomes particularly difficult. Also be careful of the deep storm drains along the edges of the narrow roads. Cycling is good around Grenada, with accommodation conveniently spaced. The ride between Sauteurs and Victoria is peaceful with spectacular views. From Gouyave to St George's via Grand Étang is difficult but rewarding with some steep hills in the beautiful forest reserve and small, friendly communities. Allow 5-6 hrs. There are plenty of tours offered if you would prefer someone else to do the driving, usually by minibus and reasonably priced and informative.

Getting around
Driving is on the left. Be prepared for no road signs, few street names and no indication which way the traffic flows (just watch the other cars)

The average temperature is 26°C. Dec-Jan are the coolest months. The rainy season runs from Jun-Nov. In Nov 1999, the west coast of Grenada was hit badly by Hurricane Lenny and was declared a disaster area, as was the west coast of Carriacou and the whole of Petit Martinique. There was no storm and in fact the sun shone brightly as the hurricane passed much further north, but a tremendous swell caused flooding. Sea walls collapsed, taking coastal roads with them, cutting off some villages, while floods hit harbour front restaurants in St George's and beach hotels at Grand Anse. Damage has now been repaired.

Climate

Grenada Board of Tourism, Box 293, Burn's Point, St George's, T4402279/2001/1346, www.grenadagrenadines.com 0800-1600, very helpful, lots of leaflets. There is also a cruise ship office, T4402872, and tourist office at the airport, helpful, hotel reservation service, 4444140. The *Grenada Hotel Association* is at Ross Point Inn, Lagoon Rd, T4441353, www.grenadahotelsinfo.com **Maps** *Grenada National Parks* publishes maps and trail guides, worth having for the Grand Étang National Park and related walks. The *Overseas*

Tourist information

Windward Islands

► **Touching down**

See also Directory, page 707

Boat information Ports of entry (own flag) are Hillsborough on Carriacou, the site of the former Grenada Yacht Services at St George's, Grenada Marine, St David's Harbour, The Moorings at Lance aux Épines and Spice Island Marina at Prickly Bay. No port fees for clearing in or out of Prickly Bay, Lance aux Épines or St George's during normal working hours, Mon-Thu 0800-1145, 1300-1600, Fri until 1700, overtime charges will apply outside those hours. On Carriacou, moor in Tyrrel Bay and take bus to Hillsborough. Three crew and/or passenger lists, immigration cards for anyone going ashore, ships stores and health declaration, port clearance from the last country and valid passports. To clear out of the country take the boat to Prickly Bay (where they can see the boat), and four copies of the crew list. Firearms must be declared. Seal in a locker on board or take to an official locker on shore to be returned on departure. Yachting fees on Grenada are: less than 50 ft US$10, 50-100 ft US$12. Anchorages at Halifax Harbour (may have smoke from garbage burning), St George's Lagoon (security problems noted), True Blue Bay, Prickly Bay, Mount Hartman Bay, Clark's Court Bay, Port Egmont, Calivigny Harbour, Westerhall Bay. Hog Island can be used as a day anchorage; government and coast guard uncertain about overnight use; occasionally clear out all boats but then don't come back for a while. Can dinghy to Lower Woburn from Mount Hartman or Hog Island to catch bus to St George's, otherwise taxi from Secret Harbour. Prohibited anchorages : Grand Anse Bay, Prickly Bay (Lance aux Épines), Pingouin (Pink Gin) Beach, Point Salines, Tyrrel Bay (Carriacou), Mangrove Lagoon, the entire inner Lagoon and within 200 yd of any beach. The outer Lagoon is prohibited to yachts and other liveaboard vessels. The Mangrove Lagoon may only be entered to shelter from a hurricane. Marine weather for Grenada and the Windward Islands on VHF Ch 6 at 1000. **Spice Island Marine Services** in Prickly Bay (Lance aux Épines), T444-4257/ 4342, simsco@ caribaurf.com, has a small boatyard with bar, restaurant, ship's store, laundry and market, where boats can be stored or repaired on land as well as stern-to-dock, fuel and water. **Grenada Marine** at St David's harbour, east of Little Bacolet Bay, T4431667, www.grenadamarine. com has haulout facility with 70-ton, 30-ft wide lift, Customs and Immigration, repair services, storage, restaurant and bar, beach, internet, laundry, showers. The **Moorings Secret Harbour** base in Mount Hartman has stern-to-docks, fuel and water, a mart with food and drink, **Rum Squall** bar, will hold message/fax and mail for yachties, T4444449, www.secretharbour.com. Day charter services, bareboat or with captain, from the marina. **Blue Lagoon** (Grenada Yacht Services) on Lagoon Rd, T4406893. **True Blue Bay Marina**, T4438783, www.true bluebay.com Carriacou Yacht Services in Tyrrel Bay provide mail, phone, fax and message service to yachts.

Business hours Banks: Mon-Thu 0800-1300 or 1400; Fri 0800-1200 or 1300, 1430-1700. Shops: Mon-Fri 0800-1600, Sat 0800-1300. Government offices: Mon-Fri 0800-1145, 1300-1600, closed Sat.

Clothing Casual, lightweight summer clothes suitable all year. Bathing costumes not accepted off the beach.

Currency East Caribbean dollar, EC$.

Surveys Directorate, Ordnance Survey map of Grenada, published for the Grenada Government in 1985, scale 1:50,000, is available from the Tourist Office, from the Lands and Survey Department in the Ministry of Agriculture (at the Botanic Gardens) and from shops for EC$10.50-15 (it is not wholly accurate). Also available from Ordnance Survey, Southampton are 2 separate sheets, North (1979) and South (1988) at 1:25,000 scale.

Flora and fauna

At times of volcanic activity in the region, the water level in the crater lakes and lagoons on the island has risen sharply

A system of national parks and protected areas is being developed. Information is available from the Forestry Department, Ministry of Agriculture, Archibald Avenue, St George's. The focal point of Grenada's nature tourism is the **Grand Étang National Park**, 8 miles from the capital in the central mountain range. It is on the transinsular road from St George's to Grenville. The Grand Étang is a crater lake surrounded by

EC$2.67=US$1.

Departure tax For stays of over 24 hours, departure tax is EC$50, (EC$25 for children 2-12). EC$10 airport tax is charged on departure from Lauriston Airport, Carriacou.

Documents Citizens of the UK, USA and Canada need only provide proof of identity (with photograph) and an onward ticket (but note that if you go to Grenada via Trinidad, a passport has to be presented in Trinidad). For all others a passport and onward ticket are essential, though a ticket from Barbados to the USA (for example) is accepted. Departure by boat is not accepted by the immigration authorities. Citizens of certain other countries (not the Commonwealth, Caribbean – except Cuba –, South Korea, Japan and most European countries) must obtain a visa to visit Grenada. Check before leaving home. When you arrive in Grenada expect to have your luggage examined very thoroughly. It may take you at least 45 mins to get through passport control and customs. You must be able to give an accommodation address when you arrive.

Emergency numbers Ambulance T434 in St George's, T724 in St Andrew's and T774 on Carriacou.

Media Newspapers There are no daily papers, only weeklies, including Grenadian Voice, Indies Times, Grenada Guardian, The National, and The Informer. **Radio** There are four radio stations, on AM 535, AM 1400, FM 90, 96.3, 101.7, 105.5 kHz. **Television** There are three television stations but many hotels have satellite or cable reception.

Official time Atlantic Standard Time, 4 hrs behind GMT, 1 hr ahead of EST.

Public holidays New Year's Day (1 Jan), Independence Day (7 Feb), Good Fri and Easter Mon, Labour Day (1 May), Whit Mon (in May/Jun), Corpus Christi (Jun), Aug holidays (first Mon and Tue in Aug) and Carnival (second weekend in Aug), Thanksgiving (25 Oct), 25 and 26 Dec.

Safety On the Carenage in St George's, you may be pestered for money, particularly after dark, but it is no more than a nuisance. Unemployment and drug abuse are problems; over 75% of the prison population have been sentenced for drug-related crimes. Night police patrols operate in hotels and beach areas. In the countryside people are extremely helpful and friendly and there is no need anywhere for anything other than normal precautions against theft. If visiting St George's it is best to pick a day when there are no cruise ships in port, to avoid hassle from vendors and touts. Carriacou is generally safe, despite smuggling, but avoid deserted beaches. Two Swedish tourists were murdered on the beach in 2000 in the middle of the day, which just proves you can never be too careful.

Tourist offices overseas Austria c/o Discover the World Marketing, Stephans Platz 6/3/7, 1010 Vienna, T512-868640, discover_vie@compuserve.com **Canada** 439 University Av, Suite 920, Toronto, Ontario M5G 1Y8, T416-5951339, tourism@grenadaconsulate.com **Germany** Uhlandstrasse 30, D-53340 Mechenheim, T02225-947507, RMTours87@aol.com **UK** 1 Battersea Church Rd, London SW11 3LY, T020-77717000, grenada@cibgroup.co.uk **USA** 317 Madison Avenue, Suite 1522, New York, NY 10017, T212-6879554, noel@rfcp.com

Voltage 220/240 volts, 50 cycles AC.

Weights and measures Imperial.

---

lush tropical forest. A series of trails has been blazed which are well worth the effort for the beautiful forest and views, but can be muddy and slippery after rain. The **Morne Labaye** nature trail is only 15 minutes long, the return is along the same route; the shoreline trail around the lake takes 1½ hours and is moderately easy; much further, 1½ hours' walk, is **Mount Qua Qua**. The trail then continues for an arduous three hours to **Concord Falls**, with an extra 30-minute spur to **Fedon's Camp** (see page 698). From Concord Falls it is 25 minutes' walk to the road to get a bus to St George's. These are hard walks (Mount Qua Qua, Fedon's Camp, Concord); wet, muddy, it rains a lot and you will get dirty. Take food and water. A guide is not essential, but useful. There are two other trails in the Grand Étang area and one at Annandale. All hikes are graded for difficulty. An interpretation centre overlooking the lake has videos, exhibitions and explanations of the medicinal plants in the forest, T4406160. Leaflets about the trails can be bought here for EC$2-3 each. There is a bar, a shop and some amusing monkeys and parrots. ■ *The park is open 0800-1600, closed Sat. US$2. Accommodation at Lake House, T4427425 or enquire at forest centre, also for camping.*

The high forest receives over 160 in of rain a year. Epiphytes and mosses cling to the tree trunks and many species of fern and grasses provide a thick undergrowth. The trees include the gommier, bois canot, Caribbean pine and blue mahoe. At the

Grenada

Sleeping	10 La Sagesse Nature Centre
1 Allamanda Beach Resort & Spa	11 La Source
2 Blue Horizons Cottage	12 Lodge
3 Calabash	13 Morne Fendue Plantation House
4 Coral Cove Cottages	14 Patino's
5 Coyaba	15 Petit Bacaye Cottage
6 Flamboyant	16 Rendezvous Beach & Dive Resort
7 Gem Holiday Beach Resort	17 Rex Grenadian
8 Grenada Rainbow Inn	18 Sam's Inn
9 Laluna	19 Secret Harbour
	20 South Winds Holiday Cottages & Apartments
	21 Spice Island Beach Resort
	22 True Blue Bay Resort & Marina
	23 Victoria

summit, the vegetation is an example of elfin woodland, the trees stunted by the wind, the leaves adapted with drip tips to cope with the excess moisture. Apart from the highest areas, the island is heavily cultivated. On tours around the country look for nutmeg trees, cloves, cinammon, allspice, bay, turmeric and ginger. In addition there are calabash gourds, cocoa, coffee, breadfruit, mango, paw paw (papaya), avocado, sugar cane, bananas and coconuts.

In the northeast, 450 acres around **Levera Pond** was opened as a National Park in 1994. As well as having a bird sanctuary and sites of historic interest, Levera is one of the island's largest mangrove swamps; the coastal region has coconut palms, cactus and scrub, providing habitat for iguana and land crabs. There are white beaches where turtles lay their eggs and, offshore, coral reefs and the Sugar Loaf, Green and Sandy islands. You can swim at Bathway but currents are strong at other beaches. The coast between Levera Beach and Bedford Point is eroding rapidly, at a rate of several feet a year. South of Levera is **Lake Antoine**, another crater lake, but sunken to only about 20 ft above sea level; it has been designated a Natural Landmark.

Leatherback turtles come ashore here in April, May and June

On the south coast is **La Sagesse Protected Seascape**, a peaceful refuge which includes beaches, a mangrove estuary, a salt pond and coral reefs. In the coastal woodland are remains of sugar milling and rum distilleries. To get there turn south off the main road opposite an old sugar mill, then take the left fork of a dirt road through a banana plantation. Close to the pink plantation house (accommodation available), a few feet from a superb sandy beach, is *La Sagesse* bar and restaurant, good food, nutmeg shells on the ground outside. Walk to the other end of the beach to where a path leads around a mangrove pond to another palm-fringed beach, usually deserted. The snorkelling and swimming is good and there is a reef just offshore.

Marquis Island, off the east coast, can be visited; at one time it was part of the mainland and now has eel grass marine environments and coral reefs. Nearby is **La Baye Rock**, which is a nesting ground for brown boobies, habitat for large iguanas and has dry thorn scrub forest. It too is surrounded by coral reefs.

The only endemic bird is the Grenada dove, which inhabits scrubby woodland in some west areas. In the rainforest you can see the emerald-throated hummingbird, yellow-billed cuckoo, red-necked pigeon, ruddy quail-dove, cocoa thrush and other species. Wading and shore birds can be spotted at Levera and in the south and southwest. The endangered hook-billed kite (a large hawk) is found in the Levera National Park; the only place in the world. It uses its beak to pluck tree snails (its only food) out of their shells. A pile of shells with holes is evidence that a kite ate there.

There is little remarkable animal life: frogs and lizards, of course, and iguana, armadillo (tatoo) and manicou (possum), all of which are hunted for the pot. The tree boa (*Corallus enydris*) is known locally as a 'sarpint' and eats rodents. It grows to about 6 ft and sleeps during the day 50-70 ft above the ground in the trees. The higher they live the darker colour they become. They are quite common, but, being nocturnal, are rarely seen. A troop of Mona monkeys, imported from Africa over 300 years ago, lives around the Grand Étang. Once hunted for the pot (a male can weigh 50 lbs), they are now endangered. Another import is the mongoose.

Diving and marine life

The reefs around Grenada provide excellent sites for diving. A popular dive is to the wreck of the Italian cruise liner, *Bianca C*. Other dive sites include **Boss Reef**, **The Hole**, **Valley of Whales**, **Forests of Dean**, **Grand Mal Point** (wall dive), **Dragon Bay** (wall dive) ends at Molinière, **Happy Valley** (drift with current to Dragon Bay). Three wrecks from cargo ships off Quarantine Point, St George's, are in strong currents. **Molinière** reef for beginners to advanced has a sunken sailboat, the *Buccaneer*; **Whibble** reef is a slopey sand wall (advanced drift dive); **Channel** reef is a shallow reef at the entrance to St George's with many rusted ships' anchors; **Spice Island** reef is for resort dives and beginners as well as the wrecks *Red Buoy*, *Veronica L* and *Quarter Wreck*. Dive sites around Carriacou include **Kick Em Jenny** (a submarine volcano),

Dive sites
Reefs suffered some damage in 1999 from Hurricane Lenny, but diving is still good

Isle de Ronde, **Sandy Island**, **Sister Rocks** (to 100 ft, strong currents), **Twin Sisters** (walls to 180 ft and strong currents), **Mabouya Island**, **Saline Island** (drift dive).

The best **snorkelling** is around Molinière Point and up to Dragon Bay and Flamingo Bay. Flamingo Bay is named after a snail, not a bird. Snorkelling trips by boat will usually bring you to this area, often in the afternoons so that divers on board can do a shallow dive as well. You can see a wide variety of fish and invertebrates on the rocks and coral, even moray eels in holes if you look carefully.

Humpback whales can be seen off Grenada and Carriacou during their migrations in December-April. Pilot whales, dolphins and several other whales are also found in Grenadian waters (see Whale and dolphin watching, page 60). Contact Mosden Cumberbatch (see below) for whale watching tours, he has a boat especially designed for whale watching, taking up to 35 people on a four-hour trip.

Dive centres
5% tax is added to all diving and snorkelling rates

There is usually a dive company at any of the larger resorts but they change frequently. *Dive Grenada* is at the *Flamboyant Hotel*, T4441092, www.divegrenada.com, PADI courses, wreck dives for experienced divers, night dives, snorkelling (discounts for internet booking). *Aquanauts Grenada*, a PADI 5-star and BSAC operation, has 3 locations: at the *True Blue Bay Marina, Rendezvous Beach and Dive Resort* and *Spice Island Beach Resort/Blue Horizon Cottages*, offering easy access to a variety of dive sites, T4441126/4392500, www.aquanautgrenada.com Grenada's first live-aboard dive boat, *Seahawk*, operates out of *Rendezvous*, taking up to 12 guests on 6-night tours (US$1,750 per person including 5 dives a day and all food and drink), T4441126, www.seahawkcharters.net On Carriacou *Carriacou Silver Diving* at Main St, Hillsborough, T/F4437882, www.scubamax.com, run by Max and Claudia Nagel, an enthusiastic German couple who have been on the island since 1993, 2 boats, very professional.

The nearest recompression chamber is in Barbados or Trinidad, both 30 mins by air ambulance. Members of the *Grenada Scuba Diving Association* all carry oxygen on board their boats.

Beaches

There are 45 beaches on Grenada. The best are in the southwest, particularly **Grand Anse**, a lovely stretch of white sand which looks north to St George's. It can get crowded with cruise passengers, but there's usually plenty of room for everyone. Beach vendors have a proper market with 78 booths, washroom facilities, a tourist desk and a jetty for water taxis, to prevent hassling on the beach, but it is not working very well as not enough customers visit it. **Morne Rouge**, the next beach going southwest, is more private, has good snorkelling and no vendors. There are other nice, smaller beaches around **Lance aux Épines**. The beaches at **Levera** and **Bathway** in the northeast are also good, wild and unimproved.

Watersports

Windsurfing, **waterskiing** and **parasailing** all take place off Grand Anse beach. Windsurf board rental about US$7 for 30 mins, waterskiing US$15, parasailing US$25. The *Moorings Club Mariner Watersports Centre* at *Secret Harbour*, T4444439, has small sail boats, sunfish, windsurfing, waterskiing, speedboat trips to Hog Island including snorkelling. Inshore sailing on sunfish, sailfish and hobiecats is offered by Grand Anse and Lance aux Épines hotels and operators. Rates are about US$10 for 30 mins for sunfish rental.

Day sails
See Carriacou Tour operators, for day sails on that island

Sailing in the waters around Grenada and through the Grenadines, via Carriacou, is very good. *First Impressions* has catamarans for all types of charters, day, sunset, 14 different tours offered call Mosden Cumberbatch, T4403678, www.catamaranchartering.com *Carib Cats*, T4443222 offer full-day, snorkelling or sunset cruises. *Catch the Spirit*, T4444753, www.sanvics.com, offer customized trips for snorkellers, divers or fishermen. *Firefly* is a 38-ft sloop available for day sails or charters, T4438625, studio@caribsurf.net The *Moorings Secret Harbour* Watersports Centre has skippered charters at US$25 half day, US$50 whole day, minimum four people, T4444548, www.secretharbour.com. Trips go to Carriacou, Sandy Island, Calivigny Island and Hog Island or up the coast, stopping at beaches for barbecues or reefs for snorkelling. There are lots of other companies offering day sails, no shortage of choice.

On the first weekend in Aug is the **Carriacou Regatta** which has developed into a full-scale fes- **Regattas**
tival, with land as well as watersports and jump-ups at night (T4437930). **La Source Grenada**
Sailing Festival is held annually in Jan-Feb with several races and regattas, T4404809,
www.grenadasailingfestival.com At Easter there are yacht races and a power boat regatta off
Grand Anse as well as the Petite Martinique 2-day regatta. The **Grenada Summer Regatta** is a
4-day affair in July, with beach parties and other activities. Every month the *Grenada Yacht*
Club holds races off Grand Anse and there is usually an end-of-hurricane season yacht race at
the end of Nov (T4406826, www.grenadayachtclub.com).

Deep-sea fishing can be arranged through *Grenada Yacht Services*, *Bezo Charters*, **Fishing**
T4435477, westrum@caribsurf.com, *Evans Chartering Services*, T4444422,
bevans@caribsurf.com, and *Tropix* (T4404961). At the end of Jan each year, Grenada hosts
The Spice Island Billfish Tournament, T4402198 for information.

St George's

St George's is one of the Caribbean's most beautiful harbour cities. The town stands   *The tourist board*
on an almost landlocked sparkling blue harbour against a background of green and   *publishes a pamphlet,*
hazy blue hills, with its terraces of pale, colour-washed houses and cheerful red   *Historic Walking Tour*
roofs. The capital was established in 1705 by French settlers, and much of its charm   *of St George's, which*
comes from the blend of two colonial cultures: typical 18th-century French provin-   *is recommended*
cial houses intermingle with fine examples of English Georgian architecture. Unlike
many Caribbean ports, which are built around bays on coastal plains, St George's
straddles a promontory. It has steep hills with long flights of steps and sharp bends,
with police on point duty to prevent chaos at the blind junctions. At every turn is a
different view or angle of the town, the harbour or the coast.

The Carenage runs around the inner harbour, connected with the Esplanade on
the seaward side of Fort George Point by the **Sendall Tunnel**, built in 1895. There is
always plenty of dockside activity on the Carenage, with goods being unloaded from
wooden schooners. Cruise ships come in on the south side of the bay (although a
new deep water cruise ship port is being built on the western side of the city) and the
ferries and hovercraft from Carriacou and Petite Martinique dock in the middle.
Restaurants, bars and shops line the Carenage. The harbour is the crater of an old
volcano. In 1867 the water in the lagoon started to boil and the air stank of sulphur.
The water level in the harbour has on three occasions risen about 5 ft above sea level,
causing flood damage on the Carenage.

The small **National Museum**, in the centre of town (corner of Young and
Monckton Streets) is worth a visit. It used to be the *Antilles Hotel*, part of the former
French barracks built in 1704. From 1767-1880, the British used parts as a prison,
then the ground floor became a warehouse and upstairs a hotel. Note the cast iron
balcony, not many of which are left in St George's. Displays are rather dusty and
old-fashioned, but cover a wide range of historical topics, pre-Columbian, natural
history, colonial, military, independence, the Cuban crisis, some items from West
Africa, exhibits from the sugar and spice industries and of local shells and fauna.
■ *Mon-Fri 0900-1630, Sat 1030-1300. US$2. T4403725.*

Fort George (1706) on the headland is now the police headquarters, but public
viewpoints have been erected from which to see the coast and harbour. Photographs
are not allowed everywhere. Some old cannons are still in their positions and the views
all round are tremendous. The French called it Fort Royale but the British named it
Fort George. After the overthrow of Eric Gairy's government in 1979 it was briefly
renamed Fort Rupert, but reverted to George after the return of democratic rule in
1983. Just down from the Fort is St Andrew's Presbyterian Kirk (1830) also known as
Scot's Kirk. On Church Street are a number of important buildings: **St George's**
Anglican Church (1825), the **Roman Catholic Cathedral** (tower 1818, church 1884)
and the **Supreme Court** and **Parliament** buildings (late 18th, early 19th century). St
George's oldest religious building is the **Methodist Church** (1820) on Green Street.

The **Public Library** is in a renovated old government building on the Carenage. In this part of the city are many brick and stone warehouses, roofed with red, fishtail tiles brought from Europe as ballast. A serious fire on 27 April 1990 damaged six government buildings on the Carenage, including the Treasury, the Government Printery, the Storeroom and the Post Office, all now restored. Also on the Carenage is a monument to the Christi Degli Abbissi, or Christ of the Deep, moved from the entrance to the harbour, which commemorates "the hospitality extended to the crew and passengers of the ill-fated liner", *Bianca C*. It stands on the walkway beside Wharf Road. The **Market Square**, off Halifax Street (one of the main streets, one steep block from the Esplanade), is always busy. It is the terminus for many minibus routes and on Saturday holds the weekly market.

St George's

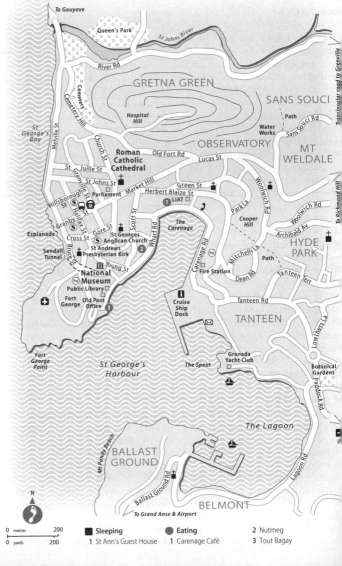

	Sleeping		Eating		2 Nutmeg
	1 St Ann's Guest House		1 Carenage Café		3 Tout Bagay

Just north of the city is **Queen's Park**, which is used for all the main sporting activities, carnival shows and political events. From **Richmond Hill** there are good views (and photo opportunities) of both St George's and the mountains of the interior. On the hill are Forts Matthew (built by the French, 1779), Frederick (1791) and Adolphus (built in a higher position than Fort George to house new batteries of more powerful, longer range cannon), and the prison in which are held those convicted of murdering Maurice Bishop.

Around the island

East of St George's

The Eastern Main Road heads east from Richmond Hill through numerous villages, twisting and turning, and there are a few places of interest for short excursions from St George's. To see a good selection of Grenada's flowers and trees, visit the **Bay Gardens** at Morne Delice (turn off the Eastern Main Road at St Paul's police station, the gardens are on your left as you go down). It's a pleasant place with a friendly owner; the paths are made of nutmeg shells. They will show you around if you want and explain the uses of all the fruits, herbs and spices. ■ *EC$5*. If you take the next turning off the Eastern Main Road, just before the Texaco station, you reach the **Morne Gazo Nature Trails** on your right. Morne Gazo (or Delice Hill) rises to 1,140 ft and the Forestry Department has created trails covered with nutmeg shells in the forest. At the summit a lookout platform gives a panoramic view of the island, down to the airport in the south, across to La Sagesse and up to the hills around Grand Étang. Information leaflets are available in several languages. ■ *Mon-Sat 0900-1600, Sun 1000-1500, closed public holidays. EC$5. Car park.* Further along the Eastern Main Road near Perdmontemps, is the turning for **Laura Spice and Herb Gardens**, where you can see nutmeg, cloves and all the other spices and herbs grown on the island. ■ *Closed Sat. EC$5.*

The southwest

The Lagoon is overlooked by a ruined hotel, taken over by the revolutionary government and subsequently destroyed in the intervention

From the Carenage, you can take a road which goes round the Lagoon, another sunken volcanic crater, now a yacht anchorage. Carrying on to the southwest tip you come to **Grand Anse**, Grenada's most famous beach. Along its length are many hotels, but none dominates the scene since, by law, no development may be taller than a coconut palm. Rather surprisingly, the St George's University School of Arts and Sciences has a campus here, right on the beach. Access to the beach and parking is at Camerhogue Park at the north end by the Spiceland shopping mall. From Grand Anse the road crosses the peninsula to a roundabout, from where roads lead off to the Point Salines Airport or the Lance aux Épines headland. The road to Portici and Parc à Boeuf beaches leads to the right, off the airport road; follow the signs to *Groomes* beach bar on **Parc à Boeuf** (food and drink available). **Portici** beach is virtually deserted, with good swimming despite a steeply shelving beach and excellent snorkelling around Petit Cabrits point at its northeast end. The next road to the right leads to Magazine Beach and the *Rex Grenadian Hotel*, then comes Pink Gin Beach and, practically as far as you can go, is the all-inclusive *La Source*, all very close to the airport. On the south side of the peninsula, at **Prickly Bay** (the west side of Lance aux Épines) are hotels, the Spice Island Marina and other yachting and watersports facilities. Luxury homes take up much of **Lance aux Épines** down to Prickly Point. There is a glorious stretch of fine white sand, the lawns of the *Calabash Hotel* run down to the beach, very nice bar and restaurant open to non-residents, steel bands often play there. The next bay west, **True Blue Bay**, is smaller and quieter, with no real beach, but also has a hotel and yachting facilities as well as the university's School of Medicine.

From the Point Salines/Lance aux Épines roundabout you can head east along a road which snakes around the south coast. At **Lower Woburn**, a small fishing community (bus from St George's), you can see vast piles of conch shells in the sea, forming jetties and islets where they have been discarded by generations of lambi divers. Stop at *Island View Restaurant* or a local establishment, *Nimrod and Sons Rum Shop*. Yachtsmen visit this spot to sign the infamous guest register and to be initiated with a shot of Jack Iron rum (beware, it is potent!). Past Lower Woburn is the **Clarks Court**

Windward Islands

Rum Distillery (tours available with rum sales, tip the guide). It is a steam-driven operation, unlike the river Antoine water-wheel system. Any number of tracks and paths go inland to join the Eastern Main Road, or run along the rias and headlands, such as Calivigny, Fort Jeudy, Westerhall Point or La Sagesse with its nature reserve (see above). Many of Grenada's most interesting and isolated bays are in the south-east, accessible only by jeep or on foot; taxis can drop you off at the start of a path and pick you up later.

The west coast

The beautiful west coast road from St George's hugs the shore all the way to Duquesne Bay in the north with lovely views

Heading north out of St George's, past Queen's Park stadium and Grand Mal Bay, you can turn inland to see petroglyphs, or rock carvings, near **Hermitage** (look for a sign on the road). Beauséjour Estate, once the island's largest, is now in ruins (except for the estate Great House). It is private, but from the road you can see the remains of the sugar mill and distillery on the opposite side of the road from the sports ground. Beyond Beauséjour is Halifax Bay, a beautiful, sheltered harbour, and the second most protected harbour in Grenada, but onland it is marred by a rubbish dump with smoke rising from it. Looking back over Halifax harbour is an old plantation house, Woodford Estate, a wooden building with pretty tiles, unfortunately falling apart.

At Concord, a road runs up the valley through nutmeg, cocoa, cashew, guava and clove trees to the First **Concord Falls** (45-minute hot walk from the main road or go by car, driving slowly, children and vendors everywhere). It is very busy at the end of the road with tour buses and spice stalls. There are toilets and changing facilities (small fee) if you want to bathe in the small cascade, but there is not much water in the dry season. The Second Concord Falls are a 30-40 minute walk (each way), with a river to cross seven times; there is no need for a guide but it is advisable. Three hours further uphill is **Fedon's Camp**, at 2,509 ft, where Julian Fedon (see page 714) fortified a hilltop in 1795 to await reinforcements from Martinique to assist his rebellion against the British. After fighting, the camp was captured; today it is a his-torical landmark. It is possible to hike from Concord to Grand Étang in five hours; it's a hard walk, but rewarding. The trail is hard to spot where it leaves the path to the upper falls about two-thirds of the way up on the left across the river.

North of Concord, just before Gouyave (pronounced *Gwarve*), is a turn-off to **Dougaldston Estate**. Before the revolution 200 people were employed here, culti-vating spices and other crops. Now there are only about 20, the place is run down, the buildings in disrepair, the vehicles wrecked. They still dry spices in the tradi-tional way on racks which are wheeled under the building if it rains and someone will explain all the spices to you. Samples cost EC$5 for a bag of cinnamon, cloves or nutmeg, or there are mixed bags; give the guide a tip.

Gouyave, 'the town that never sleeps', is a fishing port, nutmeg collecting point and capital of St John's parish. There are a few interesting old buildings; the post office, just past the shiny red fire engine, has an iron balcony. At the Nutmeg Pro-cessing Station, you can see all the stages of drying, grading, separating the nutmeg and mace and packing (give a tip here too). On the top floor **mace** is dried for four months in Canadian pine boxes before being graded. There are three grades, used for culinary spice, corned beef or cosmetics, and only Grenada produces grade one mace for cooking. On the first floor, **nutmeg** is dried on racks for two months, turned occasionally with a rake. The lighter ones are then used in medicine and the heavier ones for culinary spices. The husks are used for fuel or mulch and the fruit is made into nutmeg jelly (a good alternative to breakfast marmalade), syrup or liquor. The station is a great wooden building by the sea, with a very powerful smell. No photos. A little shop sells nutmeg products. ■ *A tour for US$1 is highly recom-mended.* There are two other processing plants, at Victoria and Grenville, but this is the largest. There is also a nutmeg oil distillery at Sauteurs. All are open to the public. Gouyave is the principal place to go to for the **Fisherman's Birthday** festival. On the last Friday in every month from May-December, Gouyave is open to tourists on a grand scale, with tours and walks during the day. In the evening the main street is closed to traffic, there is food, drink and music and dancing.

Just outside Victoria, another fishing port and capital of St Mark's Parish, is a rock in the sea with Amerindian petroglyphs on it (best to know where to look over the parapet). The road continues around the northwest coast, turning inland at Duquesne (pronounced *Duquaine*) where there is a beautiful grey sand beach (not particularly clean because of fishing), before returning to the sea at **Sauteurs**, the capital of St Patrick's parish, on the north coast. The town is renowned as the site of the mass suicide of Grenada's last 40 Caribs, who jumped off a cliff rather than surrender to the French (see page 714). Leapers Hill is appropriately in the cemetery by the church. There has been some sea erosion and the protective rail has disappeared, so make sure you are not next to go over the edge. In March Sauteurs celebrates St Patrick's Day with a week of events, exhibits of arts and crafts and a mini street festival. **Morne Fendue** plantation house is just south of Sauteurs and a popular place for tour groups to stop for lunch. The house was built in 1912 and still has all the old mouldings, cornices and light fittings of that time. Once owned by Betty Mascoll MBE, it is now run by Dr Jean Thompson, who has built a new accommodation wing with splendid views from Sauteurs on the coast to Mount Catherine inland, see Sleeping below. The buffet lunch features local specialities and is served in the large dining room of the old colonial house or on the veranda. Reservations essential.

The north

Windward Islands

From Sauteurs a road approaches **Levera Bay** (see above) from its west side. Turn left at *Chez Norah's* bar, a two-storey, green, corrugated-iron building (snacks available); the track rapidly becomes quite rough and the final descent to Levera is very steep, suitable only for 4WD. A better way to Levera approaches from the south. The road forks left about two miles south of Morne Fendue, passes through river Sallee and past Bathway Beach. The river Sallee Boiling Springs are an area of spiritual importance; visitors are inspired to throw coins into the fountain while they make a wish. **Bathway Beach** is a popular weekend spot when it can get busy. It is a huge dark golden stretch of sand, with cliffs at either end, trees for shade, a beach bar, picnic tables, and the **Levera National Park** visitors' centre. There is a ridge of rocks just offshore, parallel with the beach, which provides protection for swimming, almost like a swimming pool, but you must not swim beyond the rocks or you will be drowned. From here a dirt road leads past Levera Pond, where a wooden walkway allows you to walk out on to the water and a trail (1½ hours) runs round the pond. Birds are best seen early morning or late evening. Swimming is good at the beautiful and wild Levera Beach where leatherback turtles come to nest in April-June, and there is surf in certain conditions. It is not as busy as Bathway because not many people want to subject their vehicles to the dusty/muddy, potholed, dirt road. Do not swim far out as there is a current in the narrows between the beach and the privately owned Sugar Loaf Island.

The east coast

The word Bathway comes from a fish called the batwey

    A huge resort development is planned for Levera Beach, which will include an 18-hole championship golf course (nine holes already complete), a 600-room hotel and 200 villas, casino, medical centre and shops. The population explosion will completely change the character of the area.

    On the east side of the island, the coastal road runs south past the circular crater lake, **Lake Antoine** (see above) where, like St George's and Grand Étang, the water has risen at times of volcanic activity, notably in 1902. Nearby is the **River Antoine Rum Distillery**, driven by a water mill, the oldest in the Caribbean (guided tours, T4427109). The **Dunfermline Rum Distillery** can also be visited. There are no actual tours but the staff will show you around.

    Inland from here is the old **Belmont Estate**, which dates from the 17th century. The 400-acre estate is open to the public and you can tour the cocoa plantation and follow the beans from bush to export. A heritage museum is complemented by shows of traditional activities such as stick fighting, nation drumming, bele and pique dancing and games practised by the slaves. A lavish buffet is offered for lunch, with indoor or outdoor dining, reservations required by 0900. ■ *Sun-Fri. Tours from 0800 US$5, lunch 1200-1430 US$15. At Tivoli/La Poterie junction near Tivoli*

RC church, turn inland towards Sauteurs. At the next junction turn left and Belmont is on your right after a minute or so. T4429524, belmontestate@ caribsurf.com

Amerindian remains can be seen at an archaeological dig near the old **Pearls Airport**. Apparently it's so unprotected that lots of artefacts have been stolen. The airport is worth a quick visit to see the two old Cuban and Russian planes and the duty-free shop, a ghost town, although the runway is well used for driving lessons, cricket, biking, go-karting and social encounter in general.

Saturday is market day, worth seeing. Weavers turn palm fronds into hats, baskets and place mats

Grenville is the main town on the east coast and capital of St Andrew's Parish, the largest parish in Grenada with a population of about 25,000. It is a collection point for bananas, nutmeg and cocoa, and also a fishing port. You can tour the **Nutmeg Cooperative Processing Station**, US$1, with samples of nutmeg and mace (tip the guide). There are some well-preserved old buildings, including the Court House, Anglican Church, police station and post office. Funds are being raised to restore and convert the old Roman Catholic church into a library, museum, art gallery and cultural centre. Construction of the church began in 1841 and it was used as a church until 1915, when mosquitoes finally triumphed over worshippers. From 1923-72 it was used as a school, but then abandoned. The **Rainbow City Festival** is held here at the beginning of August, with arts and crafts displays, street fairs, cultural shows and a 10-km road race.

Two miles south of Grenville are the **Marquis Falls**, also called Mount Carmel Falls, the highest in Grenada. Trails are being improved, with signposts and picnic areas. Marquis village was the capital of St Andrew's in the 17th and 18th centuries. Nowadays it is the centre of the wild pine handicraft industry. Historical sites nearby are Battle Hill and Fort Royal. From here boats go to Marquis Island (see above).

The interior

Mount St Catherine can be climbed quite easily, contrary to popular opinion, although in places it is a climb rather than a walk

There are several routes up **Mount St Catherine**, perhaps easiest from Grenville. Take a minibus to the Mount Hope road, this is a 4WD track which becomes the path up the mountain. It takes about two hours from leaving the minibus. A guide is not necessary. Do not go alone, however, and do not go if you suffer from vertigo. Do not take chances with daylight either. For information on this and anything else, contact Mr and Mrs Benjamin at *Benjamin's Variety Store*, Victoria Street, Grenville. Mrs Benjamin is on the Tourist Board. Telfer Bedeau, from Soubise, is the hiking expert, T4426200.

Avoid the mountain roads around Grand Étang in the dark, although the night-time sounds of the dense jungle are fascinating

The transinsular, or hill road, from Grenville to St George's used to be the route from the Pearls Airport to the capital, which all new arrivals had to take. It is well surfaced, but twisty and narrow. The minibus drivers on it are generally regarded as 'maniacs', one bend is called 'Hit Me Easy'. The road rises up to the rainforest, often entering the clouds. If driving yourself, allow up to 1½ hrs from Levera to St George's. Shortly before reaching the Grand Étang (full details above), there is a side road to the St Margaret, or **Seven Sisters Falls**. They are only a 30-minute walk from the main road, but a guide is essential, or else get very good directions. A guide will show you a circular route, which is steep but more interesting than returning on the same path and takes two hours. The trail runs over private land, so a small fee is payable to the owners who keep the paths clear, at their place by the main road. After Grand Étang, there is a viewpoint at 1,910 ft overlooking St George's. A bit further down the hill is a detour to the **Annandale Falls** which plunge about 40 ft into a pool where the locals dive and swim. Tourists are pestered for money here, for diving, singing, information, whether requested or not. If coming from St George's on Grenville Road, fork left at the Methodist Church about half way to Grand Étang.

The peaks in the southeast part of the Grand Étang Forest Reserve can be walked as day trips from St George's. For **Mount Maitland** (1,712 ft), take a bus from the Market Place to Mardigras, or if there is none, get off at the junction at St Paul's and walk up. At the Pentecostal (IPA) church, turn left and immediately right. The paths are reasonably clear and not too muddy. The walk takes less than one hour each way. There are good views from the top over both sides, with some hummingbirds.

Mount Sinai (2,306 ft) is not as spectacular as Mount St Catherine, nor as beautiful as Mount Qua Qua, but is not as muddy either. Take a bus to Providence, then walk up (two hours) the particularly lovely road to Petit Étang and beyond, where the road turns into a track in the banana fields. The path up the mountain begins behind a banana storage shed and must be closely watched. The terrain is a bit tricky near the top. There is a path down the other side to Grand Étang. Local opinions vary as to how badly you would get lost without a guide as the paths are no longer maintained.

The highest point in the southeast is known on the Ordnance Survey map as **South East Mountain** (2,348 ft), but to locals as Mount Plima (Plymouth?). You can get up to the ridge, from where there are fine views, but both this summit and the nearby Mount Lebanon are inaccessible without a guide and machete. Here too it used to be possible to descend to Grand Étang but it is difficult now. For this area take a bus to the junction for Pomme Rose and walk up through the village. Mayhe Hazard lives near the top of the village and is the local expert on the trails (traces). He is good company and may be prepared to guide in the area; he will certainly show you the trail to the ridge, which you could never find alone.

Essentials

Grenada is particularly well served with good, mid-range, small hotels and guesthouses. Although large-scale tourism is starting to be developed, most of the hotels are still small enough to be comfortable and friendly even if they do cater for package tours. The majority of hotels are in the Grand Anse area. In St George's there are more guesthouses than hotels.

Sleeping
Hotel rooms are subject to a 10% service charge and 8% tax on accommodation, food and beverages

St George's LL *The Lodge*, on the Morne Jaloux ridge ½ mile south of Forts Matthew and Frederick, T4402330, www.thelodgegrenada.com Intimate, with only 2 rooms, luxuriously furnished, strictly vegan/vegetarian, full board, chemical-free pool, panoramic views of sunrise, sunset and mountains from veranda and garden terrace. **B** *Tropicana Inn*, Lagoon Rd, T4401586, tropicanainn@caribsurf.com 20 double rooms, bath, a/c, some with patio, cater to business as well as vacation traveller, family run, overlooks marina, on bus route.

Grand Anse LL *Spice Island Beach Resort*, T4444258, www.spicebeachresort.com Ocean-front suites, garden view, or pool suite, no children under 12 in pool suites, no children under 5 in winter, all inclusive available on request, lots of sports, diving and other facilities on offer, fitness centre, health spa. **LL-AL** *Allamanda Beach Resort and Spa*, T4440095, www.allamandaresort.com 50 rooms, 1 with wheelchair access, pool, bar, café, restaurant, games room, watersports, fishing, boating, tennis, massage, gym. **LL-AL** *Coyaba*, T4444129, www.coyaba.com Popular with package tours, but very comfortable, lots of facilities, 70 rooms on 5½ acres, 3 are wheelchair accessible, large pool with swim-up bar. **LL-AL** *The Flamboyant*, T4444247, www.flamboyant.com 60 units in rooms, suites and cottages, pool, free snorkelling equipment, diving, at the south end of Grand Anse, lovely views, steep walk down to beach but transport for people with mobility problems to restaurant and beach, quite a walk to bus stop. **L-AL** *Blue Horizons Cottage Hotel*, T4444316, www.bluegrenada.com 32 rooms, games room, parking, pool, its *La Belle Créole* restaurant is one of the island's best. **A-C** *South Winds Holiday Cottages and Apartments*, T4444310, www.south-winds.com Monthly rates on request, 1-2 bedrooms, electric mosquito killer, large kitchen, terrace or balcony, simple but clean, good restaurant, friendly staff and dogs, 5-10-min walk from beach, car hire.

Morne Rouge L-B *Gem Holiday Beach Resort*, T4444224, www.gembeachresort.com Rooms vary in quality, 1- or 2-bedroomed apartments, lovely beach, a/c nice and cool, enjoyable beachside lounge also popular with locals, restaurant limited.

Point Salines LL *Laluna*, T4390001, www.laluna.com The most expensive on the island, 16 1-2-bedroom cottages, height of luxury, open Italian/Indonesian style, computer outlets, private plunge pools as well as main pool, dining room on beach, children under 10 not welcome in high season. **LL-L** *Rex Grenadian*, T4443333, www.rexcaribbean.com 212 rooms, gym, pool, tennis, 2 beaches, watersports, scuba diving, 6 restaurants and bars, conference facilities, 5 rooms for handicapped guests. **LL** *La Source*, T4442556,

Windward Islands

www.lasourcegrenada.com At the extreme south of the island, 100 rooms, all-inclusive, steep hike to some rooms, pool, 9-hole golf course, health and leisure facilities, beaches not as good as Grand Anse, limited availability, popular, minimum age 16.

True Blue L-A *True Blue Bay Resort and Marina*, T4438783, www.truebluebay.com Close to medical school on pleasant south coast bay, quite remote, 25-min walk to nearest bus stop. Small, intimate, helpful and friendly, British-Mexican owners, large rooms, cottages and apartments, kitchenettes, a/c, fan, sea view, balconies with hammocks, child friendly, high chairs and play equipment, gym, car hire, dock facilities, boat charter available, dive shop on site, kayaks, hobie cats, sea sometimes murky, restaurant over water, good food, Mexican specialities and separate bar, *Stuart's Waterfront Bar*, see below.

Prickly Bay L-A *Rendezvous Beach and Dive Resort*, T4443040, www.rendezvousresort.com Grenada's first dedicated dive resort, dive and sail and stay packages, live-aboard dive boat, catamaran for guests, rooms and suites, some interconnect, some with kitchens, lots of variety, business centre, restaurant, cocktail bar and beach bar, pool, snorkelling off small beach.

Lance aux Épines LL *Calabash*, T4444334, www.calabashhotel.com Winner of a prestigious Golden Fork award for quality of food and hospitality, posh, MAP, 30 suites, 8 with private pool, 22 with whirlpool, expensive, on beach, nice grounds, tennis, games room, health and beauty facility. **L-AL** *Secret Harbour*, T4444439, www.secretharbour.com 20 luxury rooms, chalets built into the rock face overlooking the harbour, private, wonderful views, pool, friendly, steel band at times, no children under 12 accepted, this is a Club Mariner Resort and bareboat or crewed yacht charters are available from the marina. **AL-A** *Coral Cove Cottages*, T4444422, www.coralcovecottages.com Several, lovely, well-equipped cottages, beautiful view of Atlantic, 15 mins' walk to Lance aux Épines, own beach and jetty, good snorkelling, pool, very private, great for children.

South coast L-AL *Petit Bacaye Cottage Hotel*, on bay of same name, T/F4432902, www.petitbacaye.com Very desirable place to stay, romantic hideaway on beach, only 5 thatched self-catering cottages with kitchenettes, 1-2 bedrooms, mosquito nets over mahogany beds, no TV or radio, includes tax and service, restaurant on beach for breakfast, lunch and dinner, fisherman call daily, catch can be cooked to order, reef and own islet 200 yd offshore, jeep and guide hire arranged, sandy beach round the bluff. **AL-C** *La Sagesse Nature Centre* (see page 693), T/F4446458, www.lasagesse.com 14 rooms, of which 3 are ocean front, excellent, perfect setting, an old plantation house on a secluded, sandy bay (the sea may be polluted in the rainy season, seek the hotel's advice), child-friendly, good restaurant and bar by the beach, excursions.

Guesthouses St George's C *Mamma's Lodge*, Lagoon Rd, T4401623. Double, single and triple rooms, CP, pleasant, friendly, very clean, nice view, no credit cards, convenient for buses. **C-D** *St Ann's Guest House*, Paddock, beyond Botanic Gardens (some distance from centre), T4402717, pfrank@caribsurf.com CP, friendly, entrance forbidden to 'prostitutes and natty dreds', meals (communal) good value, a bit difficult to sleep because of dogs and roosters, take ear plugs. **D** *Mitchell's Guest House*, H A Blaize St, T4402803. Central, 9 double and 2 single rooms with fan, breakfast on request, downstairs rooms dark and not very private, no towels, town noises, ability to sleep through cock crowing essential. **E** Yacht's View Guest House, Lagoon Rd, T4403607. Fully furnished apartment, fan, no towels, no toilet paper, no TV, nice view from balcony of lagoon and yachts, 10-min walk into town, tin roof so rooms are hot during the day, cash only. **Grand Anse C** *Roydon's*, on busy Lagoon Rd T/F4444476, www.spiceisle.com/roydons EP or MAP, helpful staff, fans, private bathroom, very nice even if a bit overpriced, credit cards accepted, good restaurant, good for buses into town but 10 mins' walk from beach, run by Roy and Donnet De Freitas, also new apartments at Grand Anse. **Grenville A-C** *Grenada Rainbow Inn*, St Andrew's, T4427714, www.grenadarainbowinn.com Award-winning small hotel, run by Neitha Williams (Aunty Nits) and her daughter Yvonne Williams, 15 rooms or apartments (sleep 4), buses stop outside, organic food, fresh juices, earthen oven for barbecue, credit cards accepted. A few miles north at Dunfermline is **B-C** *Sam's Inn*, T4427313, F4427853. 16 a/c rooms in modern block, restaurant and bar, use of kitchen, hot water, balconies, country setting, view of Pearl's Airport, small store close by, Mrs Ellen Sam is very friendly owner. **Morne Fendue C-D** *Morne*

Fendue Plantation House, see page 699, T4429330, caribbean@caribsurf.com Good base for exploring the north, including Bathway beach and the Carib jump at Sauteurs. 8 rooms in new block with wonderful views or in old house, where guests have said it is like sleeping in a museum, real period pieces with old furniture and a cast-iron roll-top bath with eccentric plumbing. Evening meals on request and entertainment planned for high season. **Victoria C** *Hotel Victoria*, Queen St, on the waterfront, T4449367, F4448104. Basic rooms but nice location, 5 single and 5 double, fan, TV, balcony. **Gouyave E** *Patino's*, at the end of the town on the waterfront above a small bar. Does not look like a guesthouse so you may have to ask for directions, but worth the effort. 2-bedroom apartments with kitchens, Patino is very friendly, lived in Canada. Good base for nutmeg factory and Concord Falls.

Homestays Homestays Grenada, T4445845, www.homestaysgrenada.com All sorts of accommodation, living with families around the island in their homes or in self-catering apartments or villas, many hosts are retired, returned from living abroad. Prices from US$30 single, plus tax, including breakfast and one other meal, airport transfers if staying 2 nights or more, cleaning and linen change.

Villas and apartments There are many furnished villas and apartments for rent from various agents, daily or weekly rental. *Villas of Grenada*, T4441896, gpm&vog@caribsurf.com Luxury villas, some with pool, some with beach, up to 5 bedrooms, maid service, other staff available.

Camping is not encouraged as there are no facilities, but it is permitted in the Grand Étang National Park and in schools and church grounds on Carriacou.

Camping

Grenada's cooking is generally very good. Lambi (conch) is very popular, as is callaloo soup (made with dasheen leaves), souse (a sauce made from pig's feet), pepper pot and pumpkin pie. The national dish is 'oildown', a stew of salt meat, breadfruit, onion, carrot, celery, dasheen and dumplings, cooked slowly in coconut milk. There is a wide choice of seafood, and of vegetables. Goat and wild meat (armadillo, iguana, manicou) can be sampled. Nutmeg features in many local dishes, try nutmeg jelly for breakfast, ground nutmeg comes on top of rum punches. Of the many fruits and fruit dishes, try stewed golden apple, or soursop ice cream. There are three makes of rum, whose superiority is disputed by the islanders, *Clark's Court*, *River Antoine* and *Westerhall Plantation Rum*, made by Westerhall Distilleries. All three can be visited for a tour and sampling of rum and products for sale. Several readers have endorsed *Westerhall Plantation Rum* for its distinct flavour and aroma. The term 'grog', for rum, is supposed to originate in Grenada: taking the first letters of 'Georgius Rex Old Grenada', which was stamped on the casks of rum sent back to England. Grenada Breweries brew *Carib Lager*, *Guinness* and non-alcoholic malt beers.

Eating
Rum punches are excellent. Be sure to try the local sea-moss drink (a mixture of vanilla, algae and milk)

St George's *Tout Bagay*, on the Carenage near the Library, T4401500. Excellent location, upstairs and over the water, good view of all the boats in harbour, delicious food, not expensive but quite classy and currently the best place to eat in the city. *Nutmeg*, on the Carenage above the Sea Change Book Store, T4402539. Delicious local dishes and its own famous rum punch, very popular, but avoid if you do not want to see turtle on the menu, open Mon-Sat 0800-2300, Sun 1600-2300. *Carenage Café*, in the Otway building on the Carenage. Open 0800-1500 for breakfast, snacks and lunch, 2 computers for internet access make this the only cybercafé on the island - when they work - very popular, long queues for the terminals, EC$5/15 mins, sofas, book swap. *Tropicana*, on the Lagoon, T4401586. Popular, Chinese and local food, good, entrées from EC$10-45, excellent egg rolls and rotis, vast portions. Seating inside or out on covered patio, barbecues, open 0730-2400, reservations recommended in high season, also takeaway. *New Mamma's*, Lagoon Rd, T4401459. Multifarious local foods which the conservation-minded may not want to try (famous for wild meat dishes when in season but you don't always know what you are getting, you may not be told until you've finished that there is no wild game that night), need to book, full dinner EC$45, 1930-2100, bar open until 2400. *Patrick's*, T4400364, also on Lagoon Rd, is even better, with a greater variety and interesting combinations of local foods, breadfruit salad and green papaya salad are outstanding while Patrick is very entertaining, high camp. Very popular. On Melville St, near waterfront taxi stand,

Tax of 8% and service of 10% is usually added to the bill

Windward Islands

Deyna's, T4406795. New, modern, good local food at local prices, and lots of it, rotis, open Mon-Sat 0800-2100, Sun 1000-1600, crowded at lunch. *Pitch Pine Bar*, Esplanade, T4401976. Fun place on the waterfront for a drink or meal, curry mutton, fish broth.

At the St George's end of Grand Anse is *Coconut Beach Restaurant*, T4444644. French Creole food and fruit juices and punches, barbecues and live music Wed, Sun evenings in high season, open 1230-2200, closed Tue. *Fish 'n' Chick*, at Sugar Mill roundabout, T4444132. Barbecue and grilled fish and chicken, local fast food and takeaway. *Brown Sugar Restaurant*, Grande Anse, T4442374. New location following a devastating fire in 2002, thought by many to be the best place for callaloo, new ways of presenting traditional Grenadian cuisine, vegetarian and children's meal available, steel band on Tue, Fri, good musicians on Sun, open 1800-2300. *Aquarium Restaurant*, T4441410, Point Salines Beach. Open 1000-2300 except Mon, Wed specials, Sun barbeque, showers, toilets, snorkelling offshore, good food, lobster, fish, steak, sandwiches, live music and buffet from 1900 first Sat in month, dinner reservations requested. *Red Crab*, Lance aux Épines, T4444424. Excellent local seafood and international, entrées from EC$25, fabulous steak dinner EC$60, live music Mon, Fri in season, darts Wed nights, closed Sun. *Island View Restaurant and Nightclub*, Clark's Court Bay, Woburn, T4441878, VHF 16. Open 1000-2300, casual games room with pub food, pool tables, pinball machine, etc, disco from 2200 Fri and Sat, dinghy dock, boat outings arranged with food and drinks. *La Sagesse* (see page 693) fresh lobster, grilled tuna, outdoor restaurant, beautiful location, walk it off afterwards, good hiking over the mountain, T4446458 for reservations which are recommended, especially for dinner, US$30 for return transport, lunch, guided nature walk with exotic fruit tasting, dinner packages available, entrées EC$15-50.

Bars *Boatyard Bar* at Prickly Bay Marina. Happy hour 1730-1830, TV and live music several times a week in season, also good food at the Yacht Club. *Rum Squall Bar* at Secret Harbour Marina. Inexpensive weekly barbecue and daily happy hour 1600-1700. *Grenada Yacht Club* in St George's. Happy hour Wed, Fri, Sat 1800-1900, yachtsmen and others welcome, great place to sit and watch the boats entering the lagoon (and see if they are paying attention to the channel markers or run aground). *Stuart's Waterfront Bar*, at True Blue Bay, T4391377, moorings available. British-run, open daily, 1500-2300, happy hour 1700-1900, good cocktails and bar snacks or move on to the restaurant at the *True Blue Bay*, very popular Fri night when students come over from the medical school on the other side of the bay, but can be busy any time. *Casablanca Sportsbar*, Grand Anse, above the banks, T4441631. Games, pool, snooker, large TV, open until 0300.

Festivals **Independence Day** is *7 Feb*. **Easter** is a time for lots of events, both religious and otherwise. There are regattas, a kite flying competition at the old Pearls Airport, with music, food and drink, and other activities. Grenada holds a **Spice Jazz Festival** in *May or Jun*, with lots of music, cooking, sports. Concerts are mostly held in the big hotels, such as the *Rex*, or at the stadium, and tickets are quite expensive although a season ticket is better value. It doesn't yet have the reputation and popularity of St Lucia's jazz festival, but it is growing. Throughout the island, but especially at Gouyave, the **Fisherman's Birthday** is celebrated at the end of *Jun* (the feast of Saints Peter and Paul); it involves the blessing of nets and boats, followed by dancing, feasting and boat races. **Carnival** takes place over the 2nd weekend in *Aug*, although some preliminary events and competitions are held from the last week in Jul, with calypsos, steel bands, dancing, competitions, shows and plenty of drink. The Sun night celebrations, Dimanche Gras, continue into Mon, J'Ouvert; Djab Djab Molassi, who represent devils, smear themselves and anyone else (especially the smartly dressed) with black grease. On Mon a carnival pageant is held on the stage at Queen's Park and on Tue the bands parade through the streets of St George's to the Market Square and a giant party ensues. For information on playing Mas with a band contact Derrick Clouden (T4402551) or Wilbur Thomas (T4403545) of the Grenada Band Leaders Association. During Carnival it is difficult to find anywhere to stay and impossible to hire a car unless booked well in advance. Also in *Aug* over the first weekend, are the **Carriacou Regatta** (see above) and the **Rainbow City cultural festival** in Grenville which goes on for about a week.

The Boatyard at the marina on L'Anse aux Épines Beach has bands playing Wed and Fri nights with open-air dancing until 0300, soca, dance music. *Castaways*, L'Anse aux Épines, T4441250, www.grenadaguide.com/castaway Bar and restaurant from 1700-2200 and disco from 2200, popular with medical students at weekends, live music in season, closed Mon. *Fantazia Disco* on Morne Rouge Beach, T4444224, in a big shed, full of Grenadians, funky, soca, fast calypso, reggae, hot and steamy, starts midnight, until dawn, best night is Wed when they have old soul and reggae – 'oldies for goldies'. *Le Sucrier*, in the Sugar Mill at Grand Anse roundabout, behind the *Fish & Chick*, from midnight, Fri and Sat best nights, edgy feel, heavy dudes hang out outside the *Fish & Chick*, DJs or live music. The *Regal Cinema* is off Lagoon Rd, next to *Tropicana*, T4405368, movies nightly at 2030, EC$5 for double feature. *Deluxe Cinema* is in Grenville, T4426200. The *Marryshow Folk Theatre* in the University of the West Indies building on Tyrrel St, has concerts, plays and special events.

Nightlife
Hotels provide evening entertainment, including dancing, steelband and calypso music, limbo, etc. There are few discos and nightclubs outside the hotels and low season can be very quiet

Grenada prides itself on its spices, which are ideal souvenirs. They are cheaper in the supermarket than on the street or in the market. *Arawak Islands Ltd* make a range of spices, sauces, herbal teas, candied nutmeg pods, perfumes, soap, bath goodies and massage oils, scented candles and incense sticks; factory and retail outlet on the Upper Belmont Rd between Grand Anse and St George's, open Mon-Fri 0830-1630, mail order also available, T/F4443577, www.arawak-islands.com *De la Grenade Industries* make nutmeg jams, jellies, syrups, sauces and drinks, available in supermarkets and groceries, T4403241, www.dela grenade.com Their nutmeg syrup is an essential ingredient for a Grenadian rum punch, also delicious on pancakes. *The Grenada Co-operative Nutmeg Association* purchases nutmeg from its membership of 7,000 farmers and markets it worldwide. It sells nutmeg oil in 15 ml and 30 ml bottles, T4402117, gcnanutmeg@caribsurf.com *Spice Island Perfumes* on the Carenage sells perfumes and pots pourris made from the island's spices, as well as batiks, T-shirts, etc. *Grenada Craft Centre* on Lagoon Rd, next to the *Tropicana Inn* houses Grenadian craftspersons selling jewellery, pottery, batik, wood, basketry and T-shirts. *Art Fabrik*, 9 Young St, T/F4400568, batikart@caribsurf.com Batik clothing and gift shop, expensive, artisan demonstrating batik at table by door, 0830-1630 Mon-Fri, 0900-1300 Sat. *White Cane Industries* on the Carenage adjacent to the Ministry of Health, featuring a wide variety of arts and crafts. There is duty-free shopping at the airport and on the Carenage for cruise ships.

Shopping

There are several places where you can buy art by resident artists. *The Yellow Poui Art Gallery*, T4403001, sells Grenadian paintings, sculpture, photography, antique prints and engravings, above *Gifts Remembered* souvenir shop on Cross St, open Mon-Fri 0900-1600, Sat 0915-1215. *Art in Grenada*, on second floor Grand Anse Shopping Complex, T4442317, designco@caribsurf.com open Mon-Sat 1000-1700, fine art gallery, showcasing the work of Richard Buchanan, Susan Mains and others.

St George's Bookshop is on Halifax St, T4402309, reasonable selection of Caribbean and international literature as well as school texts; *Sea Change* , T4403402, is on the Carenage, beneath the Nutmeg bar, it has *USA Today* when cruise ships come in. *Fedon Books*, side entrance on Herbert Blaize St, open Mon-Fri 0900-1700, Sat 0900-1300, Caribbean novels, geography, cooking and children's books.

Cricket, the island's main land sport, is played from Jan-Jun. The locals play on any piece of flat ground or on the beaches, but international test matches are played at the Queen's Park Stadium. **Soccer** is also played. Hotels have **tennis** courts and public courts are found at Grand Anse and Tanteen, St George's. There is a 9-hole **golf** course at the *Grenada Golf and Country Club*, Woodlands, above Grand Anse; the club is open daily 0800 to sunset, but only till 1200 on Sun (T4444128). **Volleyball** can be played at the *Aquarium Beach Club* after snorkelling on the reef. It is a fun spot on a secluded beach just below Point Salines off the airport road, T4441410. The National Stadium at Queens Park, north of St George's, has a capacity for 15,000 people and hosts cricket, football, athletics, cycling, cultural events and exhibitions.

Sports
For diving and watersports, see page 693

Lots of companies offer day tours of the island, stopping to visit waterfalls, nutmeg processing plants, and have lunch at Morne Fendue or a picnic on Bathway beach. These are usually in minibuses or small buses and are primarily designed to give cruise ship passengers a taste of

Tour operators
There is a 5% tax on all tours

Windward Islands

the island, so they can seem rushed. Those offering something a bit different include *Ecotrek* (part of *Ecodive*), T4447777, for coastal and rainforest walks and island safaris, tailor-made tours for small groups or even a single person, US$45. *Mandoo Tours*, T/F4401428, www.grenadatours.com island tours US$40-55 and trekking, Concord Falls US$90per person full day, Mt Qua Qua US$40 half day, Seven Sisters Falls US$40. For guided hikes contact Telfer Bedeau in the village of Soubise on the east coast; you must ask around for him (or T4426200 or see if the Tourism Department can put you in touch). *Spice Island Trekking*, T4445985, www.spiceislandtrekking.com hiking half or full day, moderate to difficult, US$35-45, children half price, student reductions, also cycling tours and bike rental, US$15/day, US$65/week. Dennis Henry, of *Henry's Safari Tours* (T4445313, VHF channel 68, safari@caribsurf.com) conducts tours of the island and is very well informed on all aspects of Grenada. Henry's also services yachts, dealing with laundry, gas, shopping, etc. *Arnold's Tours*, Archibald Avenue, T4400531, F4404118, offers similar services to Henry's, also recommended, but in German as well.

Transport **Air From Europe** *British Airways*, *Virgin Atlantic* and *Monarch* direct from London, *BWIA* via Trinidad and *Air Jamaica* via Montego Bay. *Condor* flies weekly in Nov-Apr from Frankfurt. **From North America** *BWIA* flies from Miami, New York and Toronto via Trinidad. *Air Jamaica* from New York direct and from many other US cities via Montego Bay. *US Airways* weekly direct from Philadelphia. *American Eagle* from San Juan connects with American Airlines services from the USA. *Sky Service* has a seasonal charter flight from Toronto. **From the Caribbean** *BWIA* connects Grenada with Trinidad and Tobago. *LIAT* and/or *Caribbean Star* fly everywhere in the Eastern Caribbean with lots of flights from Barbados, and Trinidad and Tobago, with connecting flights from other islands. Charter or air taxi services such as *SVGAir* and *TIA* connect Grenada with Carriacou and neighbouring islands in the Grenadines. **Airport** The **Point Salines Airport** is 5 miles from St George's: taxis only, fixed rates to St George's, EC$30 (US$14), 15 mins; EC$25 (US$10) to Grand Anse and Lance aux Épines. Journeys within one-mile of the airport EC$7 (US$2.75). Add EC$10 (US$3.75) between 1800 and 0600. However, if you start walking down the road towards St George's the taxi changes into a bus and will pick you up for much less (only feasible with light luggage). If you are energetic, it takes an hour to walk to Grand Anse, longer to St George's. **Sea** Apart from cruise ships there are no international services. Grenada and Carriacou are linked by ferries, of which the best and quickest is a hovercraft, the *Osprey*.

Local **Buses** run to all parts of the island from the Market Square and the Esplanade in St George's; on the Esplanade look for the signs in the square, ask around. Fares are EC$1 within St George's, EC$3 to Grand Étang, and EC$5 to Grenville. There is also a regular bus service between Grenville and Sauteurs. It can be difficult to get a bus away from Grand Étang in either direction as most of them are full. The last buses tend to be in mid-afternoon and there are very few on Sun. **Taxi** Fares are set by the tourist board. EC$4 for the first 10 miles outside St George's, then EC$3 per mile thereafter (EC$10 charge extra 1800-0600). A taxi tour of Grenada costs about US$40-55 per person for a full day or US$15 per person per hour. Large speakers blast out steel bands or reggae music; taxi drivers will adjust the volume on request. A **water taxi** service runs from in front of the *Nutmeg* restaurant, St George's to the Grand Anse beach. **Hitchhiking** is quite easy though the roads are not very good.

Car hire Cars can be rented from a number of companies for about US$55 or EC$150 a day, plus US$2,500 excess liability and 5% tax (payable by credit card). You must purchase a local permit, on presentation of your national driving licence, for EC$30/US$12; a local permit is not required if you hold an international driving licence. Companies in St George's include *Spice Island Rentals* (Avis), Paddock and Lagoon Rd, T4403936; *Dollar Rent-a-Car* airport, T4444786; *David's*, at the airport and several hotels, T4443399; *McIntyre Bros*, car and jeeps, T4443944, macford@caribsurf.com; *Maitland's* (also rent motorcycles), Market Hill, T4444022, office at the airport which is often open for late arrivals when others are closed; Daily rates quoted over the phone are not always honoured when you pick up the car; check that the company does not operate a three-day minimum hire if you want a rate for one day only, this often applies in high season. **Bike** rentals can be arranged with *Ride Grenada*, T4441157. Bike parts, but no repairs, at *Ace Hardware*, Lagoon Rd, south end.

Airlines *LIAT*, T4405428 (4444121/2 Point Salines, 4437362 Carriacou), *British Airways*, T4441664, 0900-1700 at the airport; *BWIA*, Steele's Complex, Grand Anse, T4441221; *Air Jamaica*, T4445975; *American Eagle*, T4442222, at airport T4445151; *Caribbean Star* and *Condor*, both at *Carin Travel Services*, Grand Anse, T4444363; *Monarch*; *Sky Service*, at the airport, Dopco Ltd, T4444732; *SVGAir*, at the airport, T4443549.

Directory

Banks *FirstCaribbean International Bank* (branches in St George's-Halifax St, Grand Anse, Grenville and Carriacou), T4403232; *National Commercial Bank of Grenada* (Halifax St and Hillsborough St, St George's, Grand Anse, Grenville, Gouyave, St David's, Carriacou), T4403566; *Scotiabank* (Halifax St, St George's), T4403274; *Grenada Bank of Commerce* (Halifax and Cross St, St George's, and Grand Anse), T4404919; *Grenada Co-operative Bank* (Church St, St George's, Grenville and Sauteurs), T4402111.

Communications Internet: *Carenage Café*, in the Otway building on the Carenage. Open 0800-1500 for breakfast, snacks and lunch, 2 computers for internet access make this the only cybercafé on the island, very popular, long queues, EC$5/15 mins, sofas, book swap. *James Computer Service*, T4401600, Scott St at top of alley going up from Daihatsu on Carenage, side entrance to first floor for computers and internet access, pay downstairs at main entrance, EC$20/hr, a/c, functional, good and fast machines, no queues. Post: the General Post Office in St George's is at Burns Point near the pier, south of the Carenage, open 0800-1600 Mon-Fri, only postage stamps are sold during the lunch hr, 1200-1300. Villages have sub-post offices. **Telephone**: *Cable & Wireless Grenada Ltd*, T4401000, gndinfo@caribsurf.com, with offices on the Carenage, St George's, operates telephone services, including USA Direct and calls to USA on Visa card, etc, fax and cellular phones. Payphones take coins or phone cards, available at outlets near payphones. Home Direct Service can be made from any phone, if you have a credit or telephone charge card, and is available to the UK through BT Direct and to Canada through Teleglobe. Credit card holders and Visaphone card holders' access number is 1-800-8778000 for domestic and international calls. If you dial 1-800-8722881 at any public phone (no coin required), you get through to AT&T. A call to the UK costs approximately EC$37.50 for 5 mins. *Grentel Boatphone* provides mobile cellular phone service.

Embassies and consulates British High Commission, Grand Anse Shopping Centre on the main road in a new building by *FirstCaribbean International Bank*, on the other side from the *Grand Hotel* with its bright blue-roofed conference centre, T440-3222/3536, bhcgrenada@caribsurf.com; **Cuba**, Lance aux Épines, T4441884, ambacubagranada@caribsurf.com; **France**, T4406349; **Germany**, T4432156; **Netherlands**, T4403459; **Spain**, T4402087; **Sweden**, T4402765; **USA**, Lance aux Épines Stretch, St George's, T4441173, usembgnd@caribsurf.com; **Venezuela**, Lucas St, St George's, T4401721, embavengda@caribsurf.com.

Medical services St George's General Hospital is at Fort George's Point. There is also **Princess Alice Hospital** in Grenville, Princess Royal Hospital in Carriacou and the private **St Augustine Medical Centre**. **Black Rock Medical Clinic** in Grand Anse Shopping Centre has 24-hr emergency service. **Ambulance**: T434 in St George's, T724 in St Andrew's and T774 on Carriacou.

Carriacou

Carriacou (pronounced Carrycoo) is an attractive island of green hills descending to sandy beaches. It is less mountainous than Grenada, which means that any cloudy or rainy weather clears much quicker. Efforts are being made by the Government to curb contraband and drug smuggling in Carriacou, but a lot comes in around Anse la Roche, where there are picturesque smugglers' coves. Hurricane Lenny caused severe damage in 1999 because of the tidal surges it brought to the west side of the island. Repairs have been carried out, but evidence of the swell can still be seen.

Colour map 4, grid C4
Population: 6,800

There are flights from Barbados and Grenada in small planes, or you can get there by sea on a hovercraft, large ferries for cargo and passengers or yacht. It is a lovely route, following the length of Grenada's western coastline before crossing the channel to Carriacou and seeing the Grenadines coming into view. On the crossing look out for dolphins which follow the boats. The *Osprey* hovercraft is recommended for the most reliable service and the boat is in good condition. In heavy seas you may get seasick on any boat, said to be worse going to Carriacou than coming back.

Getting there
See Transport, page 712, for further details

Getting around Minibuses run to most parts of the island and will convert to a taxi to take you off route. Car hire is available, which is useful if you are staying in self-catering accommodation and need to shop. Cycling is recommended, the traffic is very light. Many of the roads are in very poor repair, giving the semblance of off-road cycling, although some of the main roads have recently been repaved. Potential for lots of flat tyres in the dry season as there is an abundance of cacti. Walking is equally rewarding, the heat being the main problem. There is good walking on the back roads and the woods are teeming with wildlife such as iguanas. Some beaches can only be reached on foot or by boat. Water taxis are on hand to take you to beaches in remote parts of the island, or to the islets offshore for picnics and snorkelling.

Tourist The *Board of Tourism* is on Patterson St, Hillsborough, beside the *Osprey* office, T4437948,
information carrgbt@caribsurf.com

Sights The islanders display Carriacou's capital is **Hillsborough** and has a population of about 1,000. It dates from a colonial settlement towards the end of the 18th century and was used by Admiral Ralph Abercrombie who came with 150 ships to launch an attack on the Spanish in 1796 and capture Trinidad. Main Street runs parallel to the sea and the hub of activity is the dock area where you find Customs, Immigration, Police, taxis, buses and fruit and vegetable stalls. Also along Main Street there are guesthouses, a few restaurants, bars, a supermarket, shops, internet access, banks and a dive shop. The town is also blessed with a lovely beach, a huge curve of white sand with good swimming, despite the presence of the jetty and large cargo ships. At the junction of Main Street and Paterson Street is the ticket office for the *Osprey* hovercraft. Along Paterson Street are the telephone office, the tourist office and the small museum. The **Carriacou Historical Society Museum** has exhibits from Amerindian settlements in the island and from later periods in its history. ■ *Mon-Fri 0930-1600, Sat 1000-1600.*

Carriacou

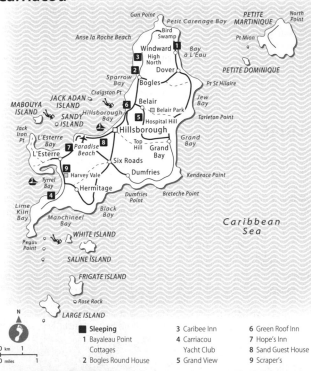

■ Sleeping	3 Caribee Inn	6 Green Roof Inn
1 Bayaleau Point Cottages	4 Carriacou Yacht Club	7 Hope's Inn
2 Bogles Round House	5 Grand View	8 Sand Guest House
		9 Scraper's

Small shop for gifts, cards, books and local music. The people maintain a strong adherence to their African origins and the annual Big Drum Dances, which take place around Easter, as well as those performed at weddings, wakes, tombstone feasts, boat launches and community gatherings, are almost purely West African. French traditions are still evident at L'Esterre and there is a vigorous Scottish heritage, especially at **Windward**, where the people are much lighter skinned than elsewhere on the island. Windward used to be the centre for the craft of hand-built schooners but in recent years the boat builders have expanded to Tyrrel Bay. Begun by a shipbuilder from Glasgow, the techniques are unchanged, but the white cedar used for the vessels is now imported from Grenada or elsewhere. The sturdy sailing vessels are built and repaired without the use of power tools in the shade of the mangroves at the edge of the sea. To demonstrate the qualities of these local boats, the Carriacou Regatta was initiated in 1965, see page 712. You can still see the boats being built and repaired along the beach at Windward overlooking Petite Martinique and Petit St Vincent, follow the paths through the mangroves, avoiding the huge crab holes.

Just north of Hillsborough, the Anglican Rectory is in what remains of the **Beausejour Great House**, on a slight hill so that the master could watch his slaves in the sugar and cotton fields below. The house is now single storey, having lost the second floor in Hurricane Janet in 1955. At **Belair Park** by a nature centre and a forest reserve, you can see the ruins of the old government house. The house was stripped bare during the US invasion of Grenada but the park is now used to hold the annual Maroon Festival. On Hospital Hill, Belair, northeast of Hillsborough, there is an old sugar mill, stunning views. The tower is well preserved, but not much else is left. The slaves had to carry the sugar cane all the way up the hill. The best views, however, are from the **Princess Royal Hospital** itself, built on top of the hill in 1907-09 because of an outbreak of malaria. The wind up on the hill is too strong for mosquitoes and it was also considered a nice, quiet spot for patients to recuperate. From here you get a fabulous view of Hillsborough, and most of the southern part of the island. A few old cannons were put here in 1948. Under the flamboyant tree in the courtyard there are some large, bored tortoises (*morrocoy*).

South of Hillsborough the road runs along the coast through Coconut Grove (Hurricane Lenny washed the palms away in 1999) and across the airport runway to Paradise Beach and L'Esterre. **Paradise Beach** is one of the nicest beaches on the island. The local painter, Canute Calliste, has his studio at **L'Esterre**. His naive style captures the scenes of Carriacou. The road then cuts across the peninsula to **Harvey**

Hillsborough

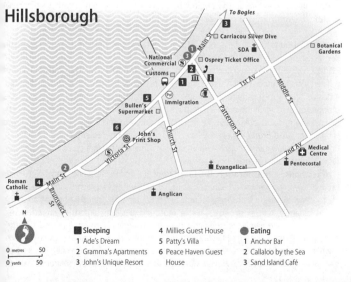

Windward Islands

To Bogles

Carriacou Silver Dive

SDA

Botanical Gardens

National Commercial

Osprey Ticket Office

Customs

Bullen's Supermarket

Immigration

John's Print Shop

1st AV

Middle St

Patterson St

Church St

Victoria St

2nd AV

Medical Centre

Pentecostal

Evangelical

Roman Catholic

Main St

Brunswick St

Anglican

N

0 metres 50
0 yards 50

■ Sleeping	4 Millies Guest House	● Eating
1 Ade's Dream	5 Patty's Villa	1 Anchor Bar
2 Gramma's Apartments	6 Peace Haven Guest	2 Callaloo by the Sea
3 John's Unique Resort	House	3 Sand Island Café

Vale, at Tyrrel Bay. Visitors should see the oyster beds at **Tyrrel Bay** where 'tree-oysters' grow on mangrove roots. Tyrrel Bay is an anchorage for yachts and the mangroves are a hurricane hole.

There are interesting underwater reefs and sandy islets with a few palms on them, ideal for snorkelling and picnicking

Sandy Island is a tiny, low-lying atoll in Hillsborough Bay off Lauriston Point, a sand spit with a few palm trees for shade and a bit of scrub. Excellent swimming and snorkelling, take food and drink. Boat from Paradise Beach, 5 minutes, or from Hillsborough EC$60, 30 minutes each way, pick a day when the islet is not swamped with cruise ship visitors. These small cruise ships offload 200 tourists to trample all round the islet and their anchor chains do untold damage to the coral. Yachts anchor here and there are no mooring buoys in place yet. Alternatively try **White Island**, a similar islet in Manchineel Bay off the south coast, ask for boats at *Cassada Bay Hotel*.

North of Hillsborough, Bogles is the most northerly village on the west side of the island and the end of the concrete road. From here 4WD or at least high clearance is necessary in the wet season. The Bogles emporium is an old building at the junction of the road to Windward, built in the mid-19th century by a merchant. Although desperately in need of renovation, the top floor overhang still has the original iron supports, denoting prosperity at the time of construction. A beautiful beach is **Anse La Roche**, which faces west and has a spectacular view across the strait to the mountains of rugged Union Island. Snorkelling is good, particularly among the rocks at the side. Take food and drink and no valuables of any sort, there are no facilities and few people. It is very easy to get lost walking to Anse La Roche beach and it is easier to take a water taxi there. Very peaceful, watch the yachts rounding the headland on their way to anchorage; at night turtles swim ashore to lay their eggs.

This end of the island has the highest elevation, High North Peak, which rises to 955 ft and is part of a protected area. The **Kido Ecological Research Station** is near Anse La Roche and High North Park, where you can go birdwatching, hiking, cycling, whale watching and even volunteering for one of the conservation projects. However, you should contact them in advance as their pack of dogs deters uninvited visitors. There has been local opposition to their plans to convert the whole of the north of the island into a national reserve, T/F4437936, kido-ywf@caribsurf.com

You can walk all round the north of the island. The British placed a cannon here in the 1780s. A path leads down (opposite a mauve-painted house) to the beach at Petit Carenage Bay, which has coarse, coral sand, good swimming and modest surf in some conditions. Returning to the road, Windward is a few minutes walk further on, a few shops and local bars. The Caribbean coast is spectacular in places and a walk from Windward to Dover, then following the coast road until it becomes a dirt road leading to Dumfries, is very pleasant and secluded.

Sleeping

Out of season the island is quiet. Not all the hotels are open

Hotels LL-L *Caribbee Inn*, Prospect, T4437380,www.caribbeeinn.com. Run by Robert and Wendy Cooper, a British couple and fount of all knowledge about what's happening on the island, as well as being known for their macaws, rescued from the illegal pet trade. Lovely but isolated setting on promontory above the sea, north of Bogles, spacious rooms, all different 4-poster beds with mosquito nets, hammocks on balcony or veranda, louvre windows propped open to catch the breeze, fans, thick gardens all around, lizards and biting insects take repellent, good but expensive food, path down to rocky bay for swimming and snorkelling. **A-B** *Grand View*, Belair Rd, overlooking Hillsborough, T4438659 www.carriacougrandview.com 14 room new apartment hotel high up on the hill, breezy fans, TV, restaurant, bar, pool, good views.

www.grenadines.net/ carriacou has details of several guesthouses and apartments

Guesthouses Hillsborough: B-C *Green Roof Inn*, on hillside overlooking sea, 10 mins north of town, just past the desalination plant, T/F4436399, www.greenroofinn.com 3 double rooms with private bathroom, 1 single and 1 double with shared bathroom, adjoining rooms for family suite, extra beds available, mosquito nets, fans, airport/jetty transfers, restaurant (see below), sandy area in front of hotel for swimming, day trips arranged. **C** *Patty's Villa*, Main St, Hillsborough, T4438412, pattysvilla@caribsurf.com. The nicest place to stay in town, on the beach, close to the dock, 2 apartments, sleep 2, mosquito net, fan, kitchen, bathroom, garden. **C** *Peace Haven Guest House*, south of pier on seafront, Main St

Hillsborough, T4437475. Rooms on first floor large, each with kitchenette, fridge, fan, contact Lucille Atkins. **C** *John's Unique Resort*, Main St, heading north, T4438345, junique@caribsurf.com Unmissable for its bright blue roof, good location and new, but standard of accommodation could have been better. **C-F** *Ade's Dream*, T4437317, adesdea@caribsurf.com, Main St, Hillsborough. 23 rooms or apartments, close to dock, well-equipped, own kitchenette or share large kitchen, clean and popular, run by the friendly Mrs Mills, supermarket downstairs open daily, restaurant across the road with sea frontage. **C-E** *Grammas Apartments*, Main and Patterson Streets, Hillsborough, above the bakery, T4437255, grammas@caribsurf.com. 7 rooms, singles and doubles, well-equipped, good. **AL-C** *Millies Guest House*, Main St, Hillsborough, T4437310, millies@caribsurf.com. Room or 1-, 2-, or 3-bedroomed apartments with kitchen, bathroom/shower, fans, a/c, ocean view. **D-E** *Sand Guest House*, T4437100, between Hillsborough and the airport. Quiet, basic but clean, nice beach across road, 11 rooms, with or without shared kitchen and bathroom, or apartment. **L'Esterre**: **C-E** *Hope's Inn*, T4437457. On bayfront close to Paradise Beach, quiet, basic, 6 rooms and an apartment, self-catering. **Harvey Vale/Tyrrel Bay**: **C** *Scraper's*, T/F4437403, scrapers@caribsurf.com Local restaurant and 6 rooms in cottages, across the road from the sea, with or without a/c. **C** *Carriacou Yacht Club*, T/F4436292, carriyacht@caribsurf.com. Designed for yachties to spend time on land, 4 rooms with self-catering facilities. **Bogles**: **B-C** *Bogles Round House*, T/F4437841, round-house@grenadunes.net. 3 cottages built around a round house, self-contained, sleep 2-3, comfortable, located away from the main tourist areas, path down to sea, excellent restaurant. **Windward**: **B-C** *Bayaleau Point Cottages*, T/F4437984, www.carriacoucottages.com 4 lovely, well-equipped cottages, clean, own little beach, good snorkelling, owners Ulla and Dave Goldhill are helpful, friendly, food and drink on request, good for children. **Villa and apartment rental LL-C** *Down Island Ltd*, villa rental agents, T4438182, www.islandvillas.com

Eating

The market near the pier in Hillsborough comes alive on Mon when the produce is brought in. 'Jack Iron' rum (180° proof) is a local hazard, it is so strong that ice sinks in it. It is distilled in Barbados but bottled in Carriacou; it costs around EC$10 per bottle and is liberally dispensed on all high days and holidays (fairly liberally on other days too). There are some basic local bar/restaurants but they often run out of food quite early or close in the evenings, check during the day if they will be open for dinner; finding cheap meals can be difficult at weekends.

In Hillsborough *Anchor Bar*, Main St. Owned by Bill Paterson, at the junction with Patterson St, rum shop facing the street but if you go round the side passage you find a café on a balcony overlooking the sea, cheap and cheerful, chicken, conch and fish meals, chicken wings and a cold beer make a good lunch/snack. *Callaloo by the Sea*, Main St, on the beach, T4438004. Probably the best restaurant in town, good drinks, nice veranda overlooking sea with view of dock, breezy, good for a swim before lunch, popular, entrées EC$16-50, plenty of choice, good value despite upmarket appearance, open daily. *E & A's*, very close to the pier. Good local cooking, ask for a large plate of vegetables. *Sand Island Café*, opposite Gramma's Bakery, T4436189. Set over the water, Grenadian chef, Jenson, seafood and pizzas, very local, closed Sun.

North of Hillsborough *The Green Roof Inn*, on hillside overlooking the sea, 10 mins' walk north of Hillsborough, T4436399. On second floor veranda with spectacular views of Hillsborough bay and sunset, roof, but no walls, Swedish owned, mainly seafood, lobster, barracuda, swordfish, Caribbean ingredients with European preparation, open Tue-Sun for dinner, lunch on request. *Bogles Round House*, in Bogles, T/F4437841. Kate Strobel, a New Yorker, cooks and serves excellent, tasty meals in the round house, evening reservations must be made in the morning and you have to choose your main course in advance, 3-course meal about EC$60, vegetarians welcome. *The Caribbee Inn*, at Prospect north of Bogles, T4437380. Candlelit dining in country house hotel, see Sleeping, above, Creole gourmet cooking, homemade bakeries, expensive meals priced in US$, reservations only.

Several small bars and restaurants in Tyrrel Bay which do takeaways and other services such as emails and faxes for visiting yachts. *Scraper's*, Tyrrel Bay, T4437403, scrapers@caribsurf.com Very good lunch but not much atmosphere, Mr Scraper and his family are very hospitable. The ice cream parlour just round Tyrrel Bay after Scrapers is recommended. *Poivre et Sel*, above Alexis Supermarket, difficult to find, T4438390, VHF 16. Excellent French food, French chef, try the lobster crêpe, a nice change from West Indian, casual but lively meeting place for the local French community. *Turtle Dove*, T4438322, VHF16. Pizzeria, bar, internet, fax, Italian food, lunch 1200-11400, dinner from 1900 by reservation, run by Luciana, Daniela and Scarlett.

Festivals Carriacou celebrates its **carnival** at the traditional Lenten time, unlike Grenada. It is not spectacular but it is fun and there is a good atmosphere. An interesting feature of Carriacou's carnival is the Shakespeare Mas, when participants, or 'pierrots' (*paywos*) dress up and recite from Shakespeare's plays. If they forget their lines or get something wrong, they are thumped by the others with a bull whip, so their costumes require a lot of padding and they wear a special cape which covers the back of the head. It is very competitive and carnival has traditionally been very violent, with battles between villages or between north and south of the island, led by their carnival 'kings'. The police have in the past frequently had to restore peace. At the end of *Apr* is the 3-day **Maroon Music Festival**, a recent revival of traditional customs held in the historic Belair Park. You can see a display of the Big Drum Nation Dance, string band music and quadrille dancing, as well as more modern entertainment such as reggae. There are also stalls selling local food, cultural and art exhibitions, www.grenadines.net/carriacou/maroon musicfestival.html In *Aug* is the **Carriacou Regatta** (see above), with races for work boats, yachts, model boats, donkeys and rowing boats, as well as the greasy pole, tug-o-war and cultural shows, contact the Carriacou Regatta Committee, T4437930, www.grenada explorer.com/events/carriacou_regatta.htm The *Parang* takes place in *mid-Dec* and runs over 3 evenings (Fri-Sun) from about 2100-0200 at the Tennis Club in Hillsborough (entrance EC$20 per night). It is a musical celebration: local groups perform on Fri, Sat is the most lively night with visiting Calypsonians and performers from Grenada and other islands judged by visiting dignitaries, and Sun is comedy day.

Tour operators Taxi drivers will offer to take you on a tour of the island, the Tourist Office will give you a recommendation if you want or contact the *Carriacou Owners and Drivers Association*, T4437386, VHF16. A full tour of the island is set at EC$150 for 2½ hrs, and a half tour for half that. Several captains offer tours of nearby islands by boat. Be sure to check safety equipment, they are not licensed. If the engine fails has he got oars or sails as an alternative? Is there a radio? Life jackets? A motor boat on its way to White Island for a picnic broke down and drifted for 3 days, eventually being found off the Venezuelan coast. *First Impressions* (see Grenada, above) has a 40-ft Morgan sloop, *Cinderella*, for tours of the Grenadines, T4437277, www.catamaranchartering.com Reggie Haemer or Captain Bubb, T4438468, has a 41-ft Morgan ketch, *Chaika*. Captain Carl McLawrence, T4437505, has a West Indies sloop, *Good Expectation III*. Water taxis will also take you on trips to the little islands offshore or to other Grenadines close by: *Snaggs* water taxi, T4438293, VHF16; *Scooby* water taxi, T4336622.

Transport **Air** Carriacou's airport is **Lauriston**, a EC$10 taxi ride from Hillsborough, EC$20 from Mount Pleasant. Disconcertingly, the main road goes straight across the runway, traffic is halted when aircraft are due. Every day *TIA* fly from Barbados and *SVG Air* from Grenada, linking with North American and European flights. *Liat* flies from Mustique and Union Island. **Sea** *Osprey Lines*, T4408126 (Grenada), T4438126 (Carriacou), osprey@caribsurf.com operate a punctual and efficient hovercraft service, the *Osprey Shuttle*, from Grenada to Carriacou and Petite Martinique. Office in Hillsborough on the corner of Main St and Paterson St, get ticket in advance if you want to catch the early morning boat, then you can just walk straight on with your luggage. On Mon-Fri the twice daily service starts in Petite Martinique 0530 and 1500, leaving Carriacou 0600 and 1530, arriving in St George's harbour opposite the fire station 1¼ hrs later. It returns from Grenada at 0900 and 1730, leaving Carriacou for Petite Martinique at 1030 and 1900. On Sat the 2 services to Grenada are the same but there is only one crossing back from Grenada, at 0900, then on Sun it starts in Grenada at 0800 and 1730, leaving Carriacou for Petite Martinique at 0930 and 1900, returning from Petite Martinique and Carriacou at 1500 and 1530 respectively. Fares are EC$15 Petite Martinique to Carriacou,

EC$30 return, EC$50 Grenada to Carriacou, EC$90 return. A second hovercraft service is the *Lexiana Jet Express*, T4436930, F443- 7179. It leaves Carriacou Mon-Sun at 0615 and 1515, returning from Grenada at 0915 and 1730 Mon-Sat and 0800 and 1730 on Sun, EC$40 one way, EC$75 return. A ferry (*Alexia II, Alexia III, Adelaide B)* also sails from the Carenage, St George's to Hillsborough, Carriacou, Tue 0930, Wed 1000, Fri 1100, Sat 0800, Sun 0700, returning Mon 1000, Wed 0930, Thu 1000, Sat 0900, Sun 1200, EC$20 one way, EC$ 30 return, weekends EC$35, 3-4 hrs. Cargo boats leave from the other side of the Carenage from the *Osprey Express*, normally EC$20, bicycles EC$10 or free, usually daily but enquire for times. There are also services between these islands; ask around. Carriacou is 1 hr by boat from Union Island; fishing boats leave irregularly, fare EC$15 between Hillsborough and Ashton. The ferry, *Jaspar*, runs twice a week (see above, Union Island).

Water taxis to beaches cost EC$60-100 depending on the length of the journey. Fishing and sailing trips from Hillsborough pier or ask at hotels. **Road** Buses go from Hillsborough to Bogles, Windward (EC$2.50) and to Tyrrel Bay. To get from Tyrrel Bay to Windward you would have to change buses in Hillsborough. Buses cost EC$1.50 for one mile, EC$2.50 for more than that. The same van may be a taxi and cost US$10, ask for "bus" and be prepared to wait. There are also plenty of **taxis**, which cost EC$15 from the airport to Hillsborough, up to a maximum fare of EC$30 to Petit Carenage. Other fares are EC$20-25. You can hire a **car** or jeep. *Desmond's*, T4437271; *Quality Jeep Rental*, T/F4438307; *Sunkey's Auto Rentals*, T4438382.

Airline offices See page 707. **Banks** *FirstCaribbean International Bank* is on Main St on the left as you head south. The *National Commercial Bank* is on Main St on the left as you head north, both open Mon-Thu 0800-1400, Fri 0800-1730. Currency exchange is quicker at *FirstCaribbean International*. **Communications** Internet: *John's Print Shop*, on the main street in Hillsborough, next to *FirstCaribbean International Bank*, T4438207, www.grenadines.net EC$10/30 mins including drink, also sells inter-island air tickets. *The Studio*, next to Alexis supermarket on Tyrrel Bay, T/F4438625, VHF 16, has email and internet access, mail drop, bookswap, bar, coffee shop, music, closed Sun, small and pleasant. **Useful numbers** Police and Immigration, Hillsborough, T4437482; Princess Royal Hospital, Belair, T4437400; Hillsborough Health Centre, T4437280; Charles Pharmacy, T4437933.

Directory

Petite Martinique

Petite Martinique is the only offshore island from Carriacou on which people live, descended from French fishermen, Glaswegian shipwrights, pirates and slaves. Its area is 486 acres, rising to a small, volcanic peak, and only a very small channel separates it from Petit St Vincent, where many people work at the resort. The principal legal occupations are boatbuilding and fishing, but for generations the islanders have been involved in smuggling and they are noticeably more prosperous than their neighbours. There was excitement in 1997 when the government proposed to build a house for 12 Coast Guard personnel in the campaign against drug smuggling. Half the population turned out to demonstrate against the arrival of government surveyors and clashed with armed police and the Special Services Unit. There is a dock with fuel, water, ice and other yachting supplies. Water taxis are available from Windward on Carriacou. The *Osprey Express*, the other ferries and the mailboat call here after Hillsborough coming from St George's.

Population: 1,000

Sleeping and eating D *Sea Side View Holiday Cottages*, T4439007, F4439210, 1 2-bedroomed and 2 1-bedroomed, self-contained cottages near beach, supermarket and boutique. **C** *Melodie's Guest House*, T4439052, www.spiceisle/melodies 10 rooms, some with balconies, ceiling fans, on the beach, tours and watersports offered. *Palm Beach Restaurant and Bar*, seafood, free water taxi service for those anchored in Petit St Vincent, Mon-Sat 1000-2200, Sun 1400-2200, T4439103, VHF 16.

Windward Islands

Background

History When Columbus discovered the island on his third voyage in 1498, it was inhabited by Caribs, who had migrated from the South American mainland, killing or enslaving the peaceful Arawaks who were already living there. The Amerindians called their island Camerhogue, but Columbus renamed it Concepción, a name which was not to last long, for shortly afterwards it was referred to as Mayo on maps and later Spaniards called it Granada, after the Spanish city. The French then called it La Grenade and by the 18th century it was known as Grenada. Aggressive defence of the island by the Caribs prevented settlement by Europeans until the 17th century. In 1609 some Englishmen tried and failed, followed by a group of Frenchmen in 1638, but it was not until 1650 that a French expedition from Martinique landed and made initial friendly contact with the inhabitants. When relations soured, the French brought reinforcements and exterminated the Amerindian population. Sauteurs, or Morne des Sauteurs, on the north coast, is named after this episode when numerous Caribs jumped to their death in the sea rather than surrender to the French.

The island remained French for about 100 years, although possession was disputed by Britain, and it was a period of economic expansion and population growth, as colonists and slaves arrived to grow tobacco and sugar at first, followed by cotton, cocoa and coffee. It was during the Seven Years' War in the 18th century that Grenada fell into British hands and was ceded by France to Britain as part of a land settlement in the 1763 Treaty of Paris. Although the French regained control in 1779, their occupation was brief and the island was returned to Britain in 1783 under the Treaty of Versailles. The British introduced nutmeg in the 1780s, after natural disasters wiped out the sugar industry. Nutmeg and cocoa became the main crops and encouraged the development of smaller land holdings. A major slave revolt took place in 1795, led by a free coloured Grenadian called Julian Fedon (see page 698), but slavery was not abolished until 1834, as in the rest of the British Empire.

In 1833, Grenada was incorporated into the Windward Islands Administration which survived until 1958 when it was dissolved and Grenada joined the Federation of the West Indies. The Federation collapsed in 1962 and in 1967 Grenada became an associated state, with full autonomy over internal affairs, but with Britain retaining responsibility for defence and foreign relations. Grenada was the first of the associated states to seek full independence, which was granted in 1974.

Political leadership since the 1950s alternated between Eric (later Sir Eric) Gairy's Grenada United Labour Party (GULP) and Herbert Blaize's Grenada National Party. At the time of independence, Sir Eric Gairy was Prime Minister, but his style of government was widely viewed as authoritarian and corrupt, becoming increasingly resented by a large proportion of the population. In 1979 he was ousted in a bloodless coup by the Marxist-Leninist New Jewel (Joint Endeavour for Welfare, Education and Liberation) Movement, which formed a government headed by Prime Minister Maurice Bishop. Reforms were introduced and the country moved closer to Cuba and other Communist countries, who provided aid and technical assistance. In 1983, a power struggle within the government led to Bishop being deposed and he and many of his followers were murdered by a rival faction shortly afterwards. In the chaos that followed a joint US-Caribbean force invaded the island to restore order. They imprisoned Bishop's murderers and expelled Cubans and other socialist nationalities engaged in building an airport and other development projects. Elections were held in 1984. They were won by the coalition New National Party (NNP), headed by Herbert Blaize, with 14 seats to GULP's one in the legislature. After the intervention, Grenada moved closer to the USA which maintains an embassy near the airport, but on 1 December 1999 diplomatic relations with Cuba were restored and embassies were opened in St George's and Havana.

Further reading on this era includes: *Grenada: Whose Freedom?* by Fitzroy Ambursley and James Dunkerley, Latin America Bureau, London, 1984; *Grenada Revolution in Reverse* by James Ferguson, Latin America Bureau, London, 1990; *Grenada: Revolution, Invasion and Aftermath* by Hugh O'Shaughnessy, Sphere Books, London, 1984; *Grenada: Revolution and Invasion* by Anthony Payne, Paul Sutton and Tony Thorndike, London, Croom Helm, 1984; *Grenada: Politics, Economics and Society,* by Tony Thorndike, Frances Pinter, London 1984.

In 1991 the Government decided to commute to life imprisonment the death sentences on 14 people convicted of murdering Maurice Bishop. Amnesty International and other organizations appealed for the release of Mrs Phyllis Coard, one of the 14 convicted, on grounds of ill-health following years of solitary confinement. She was allowed to go to Jamaica for cancer treatment in 2000, but was not pardoned.

Factionalism was rife in the 1980s and 1990s and political parties frequently divided until there were nine by 1999. Herbert Blaize died in 1989 and Sir Eric Gairy in 1997. The January 1999 general elections were a victory for the New National Party (NNP), which won all 15 seats. The opposition parties were too numerous and weak to provide a challenge, although the National Democratic Congress (NDC) received 24% of the vote. Keith Mitchell was sworn in for a second term as Prime Minister.

Geography

Grenada, the most southerly of the Windwards, has two dependencies in the Grenadines chain, Carriacou and Petit (often spelt Petite) Martinique. They, and a number of smaller islets, lie north of the main island. The group's total area is 133 sq miles. Grenada itself is 21 miles long and 12 miles wide. The highest point is Mount St Catherine, at 2,757 ft. The island seems to tilt on a northeast-southwest axis: if a line is drawn through ancient craters of Lake Antoine in the Northeast, the Grand Étang in the central mountains and the Lagoon at St George's, it will be straight. Northwest of that line, the land rises and the coast is high; south-east it descends to a low coastline of rias (drowned valleys). The island is green, well forested and cultivated and is blessed with plenty of rain in the wet season. Grenada is described as a spice island, for it produces large quantities of cloves and mace and about a third of the world's nutmeg. It also grows cacao, sugar, bananas and a wide variety of other fruit and veg-etables. Some of its beaches, especially Grand Anse, a dazzling two-mile stretch of white sand, are very fine. The majority of the tourist facilities are on the island's dry southwest tip, but the rest of the island is beautiful. With an area of 13 sq miles, Carriacou is the largest of the Grenadines. It lies 23 miles northeast of Grenada; 2½ miles further northeast is Petit Martinique, which is separated by a narrow channel from Petit St Vincent.

Government

Grenada is an independent state within the Commonwealth, with the British monarch as Head of State represented by a Governor General. There are two legislative houses, the House of Representatives with 15 members. and the Senate with 13 members.

People

The population of some 98,400 (of which 7,000 live on Carriacou and Petit Martinique) is largely of African (85%) or mixed (11%) descent. In contrast to other Windward Islands which have had a similar history of disputed ownership between the French and English, the French cultural influence in Grenada has died out. Nevertheless, it is a predominantly Catho-lic island, though there are Protestant churches of various denominations. Many people who emigrated from Grenada to the UK are returning to the island and are building smart houses for their retirement which are in stark contrast to the tiny shacks which are home to many of their countrymen. The population is young; 38% are under 15 years old and nearly 26% are in the 15-29 years' age bracket.

Economy

In the last decade, Grenada has seen a huge expansion of its tourism industry and the econ-omy has been driven by the construction sector meeting demand for new hotels, villas and infrastructure projects. Stopover visitors and cruise ship passengers have risen steadily and the yacht charter business has also expanded considerably. Agriculture accounts for about 12% of GDP but is falling. The number of farmers has fallen by 25% since 1961, with the area of prime farming land falling by 50% to about 30,000 acres in the same period. The major export crops are nutmeg, bananas and cocoa; nutmeg and mace account for about 14% of all exports and Grenada is a leading world producer of this spice. There is also a nutmeg oil distillation plant which produces oil.

Barbados

Introducing Barbados

Barbados has a long-established tourist industry and is highly experienced in providing efficient service to a wide clientele. Tourists who come here looking for the 'untouched' Caribbean are in for a disappointment. It hasn't got the best beaches in the Caribbean, there are no volcanoes, no rainforest, no virgin coral reef, but it has pleasantly rolling countryside with fields of sugar cane, brightly painted villages, flowering trees and open pastures and visitors come back time and time again. You can pay hundreds or thousands of dollars for a hotel room and be truly cosseted or rent a moderate apartment and look after yourself. You can play golf (the courses are very highly rated), tennis, squash and any number of other sports, or you can watch cricket, horse racing or polo. There is lovely walking along the rugged north and east coasts on the Atlantic side, while watersports are offered along the more protected west and south coasts on the Caribbean. For sightseeing, there are fortifications, plantation houses, museums, rum distilleries and gardens. Barbados' history as a British colony is evident in its political system and place names, but times are changing. You can still stand in Trafalgar Square and look at Nelson's statue; but the Lord High Admiral may soon be moved and the square now honours National Heroes.

Essentials

Before you travel

Visitors from North America, Western Europe, Commonwealth African countries, Argentina, Venezuela, Colombia, and Brazil need a passport but no **visa**. US visitors may get in on a driving licence, but the immigration officers are not keen on this. Visitors from most other countries are usually granted a short stay on arrival, and tourist visas are not necessary. Officially, you must have a ticket back to your country of origin as well as an **onward ticket** to be allowed in. Immigration officers do check. You will also need an accommodation address on arrival, they do not check your reservation but if you say you do not know where you will be staying, you will be sent to the back of the queue.

State the maximum period you intend to stay on arrival. Overstaying is not recommended if you wish to re-enter Barbados at a later date. Extending your stay is possible at the Immigration Office, Careenage House on the Wharf in Bridgetown (T4269912, 0830-1630 Mon-Fri), US$12.50 and is time consuming, take your passport and return ticket.

Documents
Work permits are very difficult to obtain; regulations are strictly enforced

Barbados

Currency The Barbados dollar, pegged at B$2.00 for US$1.00. Many tourist establishments quote prices in US dollars, if you are not careful a hotel room may end up costing twice as much as you bargained for. Banks will only change the US dollar, Canadian dollar, EC dollar, sterling and Euro. **Credit cards** are widely accepted.

Money

The climate is tropical, but rarely excessively hot because of the trade winds. Temperatures vary between 21°C and 35°C, the coolest and driest time being Dec-May, and a wet and hotter season Jun-Nov. Rain is heavy when it comes but Barbados has rarely been hit by hurricanes.

Climate

Getting there

Barbados' popularity as a tourist destination has resulted in good transport connections with many flights from Europe and North and South America. The Grantley Adams International Airport is 16 km from Bridgetown, near the resorts on the south coast and connected to the west coast beaches by the ABC Highway which bypasses the capital. Cruise ships call at Bridgetown and some passengers choose to start or break their journey here, but otherwise there is no passenger shipping.

Flights to Barbados are heavily booked at Christmas and for Crop Over (July-early August)

Touching down

The airport is modern and well equipped. Clearing Immigration can be slow but an expansion project to be completed by 2004 should cure congestion and triple shopping space. *Liat* has a connection desk before Immigration. There is a helpful Tourism Authority office, *Barbados National Bank* (bureau de change in the Arrivals and Departure areas is open from 0800-2400), a post office, car hire agencies and quite a wide range of shops including an Inbound Duty-Free Shop (very useful, saves carrying heavy bottles on the plane).

Across the car park there are two lively rum shops; the shop in the gas station is open when terminal shops are closed, selling food, papers etc. Taxis stop just outside customs. Check the notice board on the left as you come out of arrivals, as it gives the official taxi fares. Talk to the dispatcher if necessary. Drivers may attempt to charge more if you haven't checked. There is a bus stop just across the car park, with buses running along the south coast to Bridgetown, or (over the road) to the *Crane* and *Sam Lord's Castle*.

Airport information

Tourist office The Barbados Tourism Authority has its main office in Harbour Rd, Bridgetown, T4272623, www.barbados.org. There are also offices at the deepwater harbour, T4261718, and the airport, T4280937. Two good sources of information are *Visitor* and the *Sun Seeker*, published fortnightly and distributed free. *Sun Seeker* has an amazing listing of every possible club and society, down to Progressive Ballroom Dance and Clay Pigeon Shooting. Also lists where to worship, entertainment and daily events. *Signature* is a free magazine with articles on culture,

Tourist information

Barbados

▶ **Tourist offices overseas**

Australia, 10th floor, 1 Bligh St, Sydney 2000, T61-292-219800.

Benelux, Weekenstroo Public Relations, Breitnerlaan 298, 2596 Den Haag, The Netherlands, T3170-3280824, wpr@dutch.nl

Canada, 105 Adelaide St W, Suite 1010, Toronto, Ontario, M5H 1P9, T416-2149880, toll-free 1-800-268 9122, canada@barbados.org

France, c/o Tropic Consulting, 48 rue des Petites Écuries, 75010 Paris, T33-1 47 70 82 84, barbade@tropic-travel.com

Germany, Staatliches Fremdenverkehrsamt Barbados, Neue Mainzer Strasse 22, D-60311 Frankfurt/Main, T49-69-24269630, barbados@t-online.de

Italy, Via Gherardini 2, 20145 Milano,

T0233105841, thema.net@flashnet.it

Scandinavia, Soder Malerstrand 65A, S-118 25 Stockholm, T46(0)-84115066, inso@bridge-annons.se

UK, 263 Tottenham Court Rd, London W1P 0LA, T020-76369448/9, btauk@barbados.org

USA New York, NY, T212-9866516/8 or toll-free 800-2219831, btany@barbados.org; **Coral Gables,** FL, T305-4427471, btamiami@barbados.org; Los Angeles, CA, T213-380 2198/9, toll free 800-2219831, btala@barbados.org

Venezuela, Av Venezuela con Calle Mohedano, Hotel JW Marriot Local 4, El Rosal, Caracas, T0212-9512378, jrmccs@cantv.net

profiles, environment, business etc. *Sporting Barbados*, www.sportingbarbados.com, is another free glossy, with useful information. *Ins and Outs of Barbados*, www.insandouts-barbados.com, is published annually, a free glossy with lots of historical articles and useful year-round calendar, distributed by the *Barbados Hotel & Tourism Association*, 4th Av Belleville, St Michael, T4265041, bhta@inaccs.com.bb For US$32.75 you can buy an island pass to visit the Animal Flower Cave, Flower Forest, Banks Brewery Tour, Gun Hill, Andromeda Gardens, Sunbury Plantation, Orchid World and Malibu Visitors' Centre, available at any of these sites.

Maps *Ordnance Survey Tourist Maps* include Barbados in the series, 1:50,000 scale with inset of Bridgetown 1:10,000. *GeoCenter* publish a Holiday Map, 1:60,000 scale Bridgetown inset, 1:7,500, the Garrison, the west coast and the south coast with sites of tourist interest marked. *Insight* do the same map in a laminated edition. *Esso* distributes a road map with the free *Barbados in a Nutshell* booklet (advertising), with Bridgetown, west and south coast insets with hotels marked.

Safety   Take normal precautions against theft, which has risen in recent years. Do not leave your things unattended on the beach, shut windows and lock patio doors at night. There are some areas of Bridgetown, such as Nelson St, you would not want to walk round late at night. Baxters Rd is generally quite safe although it attracts cocaine addicts (paros). Take care along deserted beaches (avoid at night; there have been machete attacks) and watch out for pickpockets and bag snatchers in tourist areas. If hiring a car, watch out for people who wash the vehicle unasked and then demand US$5. Police have patrols on beaches and plain clothes officers around some rural tourist attractions.

Getting around

See also Transport,
page 743

The island is fairly small but it can take a surprisingly long time to travel as the rural roads are narrow and winding. The Adams Barrow Cummins highway runs from the airport to a point between Brighton and Prospect, north of Bridgetown. This road skirts the east edge of the capital, giving access by various roads into the city. The highway and roads into Bridgetown get jammed morning and afternoon; the city centre is worst in mIDD codele of the day.

Taxis are expensive. There are plenty at the airport, main hotels, and in Bridgetown. There are standard fares, displayed just outside 'arrivals' at the airport, and are also listed in the *Visitor* and the *Sunseeker*. You may have to bargain hard for tours by taxi but always agree a fare in advance. They will sometimes try to exceed the official rate per hr of US$16.

Touching down

Departure tax There is a departure tax of B$25, not payable for stays of less than 24 hrs. **Official time** Atlantic Standard Time, 4 hrs behind GMT, 1 hr ahead of EST. **Religion** Times of services can be found in The Visitor and Sunseeker. **Voltage** 120 volts and 50 cycles per second. Some houses and hotels also have 240-volt sockets for use with British equipment. **Weights and measures** Imperial.

See also Directory, page 745

Buses Flat fare of B$1.50 (B$1 for schoolchildren in uniform) per journey anywhere on the island. Almost all the routes radiate in and out of Bridgetown, so cross-country journeys are time-consuming if you are staying outside the city centre. However, travelling by bus can be fun. There are some circuits which work quite well; for example: 1) any south coast bus to Oistins, then cross country College Savannah bus to the east coast, then direct bus back to Bridgetown; 2) any west coast bus to Speightstown, then bus back to Bathsheba on the east coast, then direct bus back to Bridgetown. Out of town bus stops are marked simply 'To City' or 'Out of City'. For the south coast ask for Silver Sands route.

Buses are cheap, frequent and crowded

Barbados

Food and drink

Fresh fish is excellent. The main fish season is Dec-May, when there is less risk of stormy weather at sea. Flying fish are the national emblem and a speciality with 2 or 3 to a plate. Dolphin fish (*dorado*, not a mammal in spite of its name and now usually called *mahi mahi* on restaurant menus as in the USA) and kingfish are larger *steak-fish*. Snapper is excellent. *Sea eggs* are the roe of the white sea urchin, and are delicious but not often available. Fresh fish is sold at the fish markets in Oistins, Bridgetown and elsewhere in the late afternoon and evening, when the fishermen come in with their catch. **Oistins** lively Fri evening fish fry on the south coast is *the* place to eat the freshest of fish, or for something quieter, try **Half Moon Fort** in the north. *Cou cou* is a filling starchy dish made from breadfruit or corn meal. *Jug-jug* is a Christmas speciality made from guinea corn and supposedly descended from the haggis of the poor white settlers. Pudding and *souse* is a huge dish of pickled breadfruit, black pudding and pork.

Food

Barbados rum is probably the best in the English-speaking Caribbean, unless of course you come from Jamaica, or Guyana or… It is worth paying a bit extra for a good brand such as VSOP or Old Gold, or for Sugar Cane Brandy, unless you are going to drink it with Coca Cola. A rum and cream liqueur, *Crisma*, is popular in cocktails or on the rocks. *Falernum* is sweet, sometimes slightly alcoholic, with a hint of vanilla. *Corn and oil* is rum and falernum. Often refreshing *Mauby* is bitter, and made from tree bark. *Sorrel* is a bright-red Christmas drink made with hibiscus sepals and spices; very good with white rum. Banks beer has Bajan Light and other beers. Water quality is excellent, coming mostly from deep coral limestone wells.

Drink
Malibu, the rum and coconut drink, now also in a lime flavour, comes from Barbados

For rum tours, see page 744

Holidays and festivals

New Year's Day; Errol Barrow Day, 21 Jan; Good Fri; Easter Mon; National Heroes Day, 28 Apr; Labour Day' 1 May; Whit Mon, 7 weeks after Easter; Emancipation Day, 1 Aug; Kadooment Day, first Mon in Aug; Independence Day, 30 Nov; Christmas Day and Boxing Day.

Public holidays

Crop Over is the main festival (**Jul** to **early Aug**), with parades and calypso competitions over the weekend leading up to Kadooment Day (the first Mon in Aug), and calypso 'tents' (mostly indoors though) for several weeks beforehand. The celebrations begin with the ceremonial delivery of the last canes on a brightly coloured dray cart pulled by mules, which are blessed. There is a toast to the sugar workers and the crowning of the King and Queen of the crop (the champion cutter-pilers). The bands and costumes have improved but are a pale imitation of what Trinidad has to offer. However, even Trinidadians now take Barbadian soca and calypso seriously and talk of the Bajan invasion. The big crowd is on the Spring Garden Highway outside Bridgetown Mon afternoon, which has roadside music and places selling drinks for two weeks

Festivals
For a diary of events and festivals see http://barbados.org/eventcd.htm

before Kadooment. Next to the highway there is Festival village, an area for open-air parties with live music, small entry fee. Baxters Rd Mall runs for a couple of weekends beforehand; the road is closed off for fried fish, music and beer. For information contact the National Cultural Foundation, T4240909, http://barbados.org/cropover.htm

Many villages hold street fairs from time to time **The Holetown Festival**, in **Feb** (contact Alfred Pragnell, T4356264), commemorating the first settlers' landing in Feb 1627, and the **Oistins Fish Festival** at **Easter** (contact Dan Carter, T4286738), celebrating the signing of the Charter of Barbados and the history of this fishing town, are much less elaborate. There are competitions, parades and a big street party with music goes on until late at night. The **Holders Season** (**Mar**), is a popular festival started in 1992 with a season of opera, Shakespeare, cabaret with international performers and sporting events such as cricket, golf and polo. Performances are beautifully staged outdoors at Holders, an old plantation house overlooking the polo field. Take a picnic and an umbrella, tickets US$15-90. T4326385, www.holders.net

Congaline Street Festival is held in late **Apr**, finishing with a Mayday jump-up in the streets from Garrison Savanna to Spring Garden. Bajan and other Caribbean music. Contact the National Cultural Foundation, T4240909. NIFCA, the **National Independence Festival of Creative Arts** is a more serious affair, with plays, concerts and exhibitions in the four weeks before Independence on **30 Nov**.

There is a **Jazz Festival** held usually the second week of **Jan**, contact Gilbert Rowe, T4374537, www.barbadosjazzfestival.com, and Gospel fans the **Gospel Fest** is held in **May** (contact Adrian Agard, T4307300). Also in **May**, is the **Celtic Festival**, music, dance and sports.

Diving and marine life

A 2-km stretch of marine reserve from Coral Reef to Sandy Lane Hotel includes Dottin's Reef and Vauxhall Reef Scuba diving to the reefs or the wrecks around the coast can be arranged with any of a dozen companies on the south and west coasts (www.barbados.org/ diveops/htm). They offer PADI diving courses, equipment rental and other facilities. The only BSAC accredited school (also PADI and NAUI courses) is **Coral Isle Divers** on the Careenage in Bridgetown, T/F4319068, coralis@caribnet.net, who use a 40-ft catamaran dive boat. The **Barbados Sub Aqua Club**, a branch of the British Sub Aqua Club (BSAC) meets at 0800 on Sun at the *Boatyard Pub* on the waterfront on Bay St, Bridgetown. They don't hire out equipment but if you have your own they are welcoming to members from other branches, T4216020, Rob Bates. There is a recompression chamber at St Anne's Fort, T4278819, inform the operator of an emergency.

There is an extensive roped-off area for snorkelling at the **Folkestone Underwater Park** and equipment can be hired here, US$10, Mon-Sat 0900-1700. Life jackets, diving flags, lockers and children's equipment can also be hired. **Ocean Adventures** has 3½-hr kayak and turtle trip, also snorkelling trip, T4362088, Oceanadventure@sunbeach.net

Several **turtle- watching** tours are on offer as part of a day-sail to the area around Alleynes Bay and Gibbs Beach, where groups of them can be found. Individual turtles can also be found at snorkelling spots on the south coast. The hawksbill frequently nests on local beaches Jul-Oct, the leatherback occasionally in Feb-Jun. Green turtles are occasionally found in Bajan waters.

For those who want to see the underwater world without getting wet, the **Atlantis Submarine** is at Shallow Draft Harbour, T4368929, day and night dives at US$80, children aged 4 to 12 half price. The tour starts with a short video and then you go by bus to the deep water port or join the launch at the Careenage. The boat takes about 10 mins to get to the submarine, sit at the front to be first on the sub, an advantage as then you can see out of the driver's window as well as out of your own porthole. 2 divers on underwater scooters join the submarine for the last 15 mins, putting on a dive show. The weekly 1700 dive is the best as the submarine turns on its lights which bring out pretty colours not seen by daylight. Booking is necessary, check in 30 mins before dive time, whole tour takes 1½ hrs. They also offer snorkel tours, US$27.50.

Beaches and watersports

Beach vendors now have a licence and stall There are beaches along most of the south and west coasts. Although some hotels make it hard to cross their property to reach the sand, there are no private beaches in Barbados. For example, just north of Speightstown there is a narrow road between **Almond Beach** and the **Port St Charles Marina**, which ends in a small car park giving access to the good beaches which front these properties. The west coast beaches are very calm, and quite narrow, beach erosion is a serious worry and the Government's Coastal Conservation Unit is trying to sort it out. A swell can wash up lots of broken coral making it unpleasant underfoot. The south coast can be quite choppy, but there is more sand. The southeast, between the airport and East Point, has steep limestone cliffs with a series of small sandy coves with coconut trees, and waves which are big enough for surfing. **Bottom Bay** is currently *the* place to go. Be careful on the east side of the island, currents and undertow are strong in places. Don't swim where there are warning signs, or where there are no other bathers, even on a calm day. **Bathsheba**, on the east coast, is quite spectacular, with wonderful views. Some hotels sell day passes for the use of their facilities: pool, showers, deck chairs, etc. Work on the new *Sandals Resort* at **Paradise Beach** has been shelved and the site is for sale. Meanwhile, with no hotel, the beach is beautifully deserted and the hotel has thoughtfully left its sun loungers behind. Go to north end of Spring Gardens Highway, then up west coast road Highway 1 for about half a mile, then turn sharp left. Drive down to Batts Rock Beach, walk south to get to Paradise Beach. You can keep going along the shoreline as far as Deepwater Harbour, a nice walk, mostly beach. Near the south end of this stretch at **Brandon's Beach** and accessible also from Spring Gardens Highway, is *Weiser's Beach Bar*, T4256450, which has beach volleyball and an afternoon happy hour (Fri happy hours 1700-1900, 2200-2300), but it can be crowded if there's a cruise ship in. Just south of Bridgetown is **Bayshore** in the old police station site on Bay St, T4352909, set up as a beach facility for cruise passengers, Beach chairs US$5, lockers US$5, beach volleyball, small pool, internet café, *Joe's* bar and restaurant, dinner main course US$20 and up.

Sailing

There are a large number of **motor and sailing boats** available for charter by the week, day or for shorter periods. Large boats make you wear life vests for safety when you snorkel, smaller ones don't. Tall Ships Incorporated, T4300900, tallships@sunbeach.net runs *Excellence I* and *II*, *Irish Mist*, *Tiami* and *Spirit of Barbados* catamarans, US$61.50, *Harbour Master* and *Jolly Roger* (the last 2 being boozy fun cruises). *Heatwave*, T4299283, http://caribbean-connection.com/heatwave Usually takes about 30 passengers but will go out with only 10, good lunch, friendly crew, but not particularly eco-conscious, US$61.50, also runs *Wet'n'Wild Cruise*, a combination of cruise, snorkelling, jet skis, kayaks and banana boat rides. However, if you want something less crowded, try *Rubaiyat*, T4359913, lunch and dinner cruises, US$65, maximum 20 people, or 1 of the others with names like *Small Cats*, *Super Cats*, or *Wild Cats* (turtle and shipwreck adventure, US$43.50, T4363687), which take small groups. *Limbo Lady*, Patrick Gonsalves takes no more than 14 people on his 44-ft yacht and gives you a really good day/evening out, with snorkelling, sunset cruise US$55 with open bar, 5-hr lunch cruise US$34, T4205418, F4203254, limbolady@sunbeach.net (Patrick also runs *Ultimate Outback Tours* seeTour operators, page 743). *Ocean Mist*, 60-ft power catamaran, run by Ian and Jennifer Banfield, offers 1-day charters of 5-6 hrs, maximum 16 passengers, US$75 including food, drink, snorkelling gear, or the boat can be chartered, bareboat, for 7 days to the Grenadines, maximum 8 people, US$750 per day plus US$1,250 for fuel, clearances and licences. T4367639. *Wayzäro*, T4237196, is a glass-bottomed boat used for party cruises and snorkelling trips, eg 4-hr Sun-lunch trip with steel pan, sunset cruises from 1600 including drinks. Others are moored in the Careenage in Bridgetown, with a telephone number displayed. Most are equipped for fishing and snorkelling, and will serve a good meal on board. Rates and services offered vary widely.

The big sailing event is the *Mount Gay/Boatyard Regatta*, held in late May, contact the Barbados Yachting Association, T4356494. The *Barbados Sailing and Cruising Club* has its clubhouse and facilities at *Aquatic Gap*, St Michael, T4264434, and welcomes visitors.

Jetskis are allowed only on certain beaches: Brown's and Brandon's near Bridgetown, Dover on south coast, Mullins on west

Fishing

Deep-sea fishing can be arranged with *Fishing Charters Barbados* , T4292326, who run *Blue Marlin*, *Idyll Time*, *Blue Jay*.Others are *Cannon II*, T4246107, *Billfisher II*, T4310741, *IOU Charters*, T4322129 or *Honey Bea III*, T4285344. *The Barbados Game Fishing Association* (230 Atlantic Shores, Christ Church, T4286668, Dave Marshall, Secretary) runs an international tournament in Apr.

Barbados

Windsurfing & surfing The south coast is good for windsurfing and the International Funboard Challenge is held in Mar. The Barbados Windsurfing World Cup is in Jan. The best surfing is on the east coast and the Barbados International Surfing Championship is held at the Soup Bowl, Bathsheba, in late Nov. Contact the **Barbados Windsurfing Association** at Silver Sands, T4287277, or the **Barbados Surfing Association**, Roger Miller, T4265837

Bridgetown

IDD code:246
Colour map 4,
grid C6

The capital, Bridgetown, is on the southwest corner of the island. The city itself covers a fairly small area. It is busy and full of life. There are two interesting areas, downtown Bridgetown with National Heroes Square on the north side of the Careenage and the historic area at Garrison. There are no really large buildings except Tom Adams Financial Centre, which houses the central bank. Swan Street is now a lively pedestrian street where Barbadians do their shopping and street music is sometimes performed. On Broad St you will find a whole range of sophisticated shops for tourists, with large shopping malls and department stores. More developments are planned along the Careenage where old warehouses are being converted for other uses. The suburbs sprawl most of the way along the south and west coasts, and quite a long way inland. Many of the suburban areas are very pleasant, full of flowering trees and 19th-century coral stone gingerbread villas.

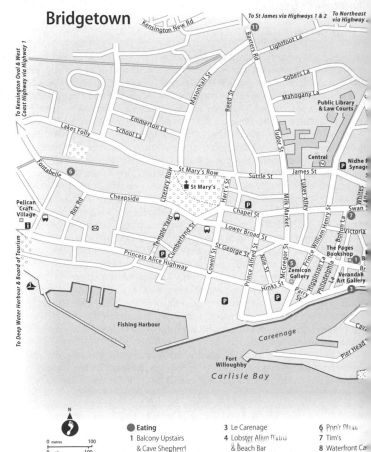

Bridgetown

Eating
1 Balcony Upstairs
  & Cave Shepherd
2 De Kitchen
3 Le Carenage
4 Lobster Alive Bistro
  & Beach Bar
5 Mustors Harbour
6 Pnn'r Place
7 Tim's
8 Waterfront Ca

Things to do in Barbados

★

- Don't miss a plate of **flying fish and chips**.
- **Explore** the east coast, where the Atlantic crashes against the cliffs.
- Tour a **rum plant**, taste, buy and enjoy.
- Experience British colonial military history at the **Garrison** and see the memorials around the race course.
- Take in a Sunday village **cricket match** or an international at the Kensington Oval.

Ins and outs

You can get a bus or taxi from the airport to Bridgetown. Minibuses and route taxis run around the capital, cheaply and efficiently, but are terribly slow in rush hour. The Tourism Authority does a useful free leaflet with map for a self-guided walking tour.

Getting there & around
*For details, see
Transport page 743*

Barbados

Sights

Bars & clubs
9 Boatyard
10 Penthouse
11 Pink Star

National Heroes Square was until 1999 called Trafalgar Square, with a statue of Lord Nelson, sculpted by Sir Richard Westmacott and predating its London equivalent by 36 years. It has recently been the subject of some controversy as it was thought to link Barbados too closely with its colonial past. First Nelson was turned through 180° so that he no longer looked down Broad Street, the main shopping area, but now he is to be removed, when a suitable home can be found. The square is now celebrating 10 official national heroes, including Sir Grantley Adams. There is a memorial to the Barbadian war dead and the fountain commemorates the piping of water to Bridgetown in 1861. To the north is the Parliament Building. Built in 1872, the legislature is an imposing grey building with red roof and green shutters. Built in gothic style, the clock tower is more reminiscent of a church. You can walk between the buildings (providing you are correctly dressed).

Take the northeast exit out of National Heroes Square along St Michael's Row to reach the 18th-century **St Michael's Cathedral**. It has a fine set of inscriptions and a single-hand clock. The first building was consecrated in 1665 but destroyed by a hurricane in 1780. The present cathedral is long and broad with a balcony. It has a fine vaulted ceiling and some tombs (1675) have been built into the porch. Completed in 1789, it suffered hurricane damage in 1831. If you continue east, you reach **Queen's Park**, a pleasant, restful park just outside the city centre. **Queen's Park House** is now a small theatre (Daphne Joseph Hackett Theatre) and art gallery. There is a small restaurant and bar, which does a good lunch and a buffet on Friday.

Jews in Barbados were granted the right to worship publicly even before Jews in London, and Barbados was the first British possession to grant Jews full political rights

The **synagogue** is an early 19th-century building on the site of a 17th-century one, one of the two earliest in the Western hemisphere. The original synagogue, was built in the late 1660s by Jews fleeing Recife, Brazil, who heard that Oliver Cromwell had granted freedom of worship for Jews and gained permission to settle in Barbados. The tomb of Benjamin Massiah, the famous circumciser of 1782 lies on the left hand side of the graveyard, just inside the entrance. The synagogue was out of religious use for 60 years, and in the 1950s was the office of the *Barbados Turf Club*. Recently painstakingly restored, it is now used for religious services again and is open to visitors. ■ *Mon-Fri 0900-1200, 1300-1600. T4320840.*

The **Harry Bayley Observatory** in Clapham is not far from *Banks Brewery*. A chance for northern visitors to look at the Southern Hemisphere stars. ■ *Fri 2030-2330. US$4 adults, US$2.50 children.T4245593.*

A short bus ride from town is **Tyrol Cot**, built in 1850, home of Sir Grantley Adams. There is a Heritage Village with craftwork on sale, plus chattel-house museum, gardens and restaurant in the old stables. Run by the National Trust. ■ *Mon-Fri 0900-1700. US$5.75, children US$2.90. T4242074.*

The Garrison Area

Cross the Careenage by the Charles Duncan O'Neale Bridge (one of the bus terminals and market area are just to the west) and follow Bay St around the curve of Carlisle Bay. You will pass St Patrick's Cathedral (Roman Catholic), the main government offices with St Michael's Hospital behind it before reaching the historic Garrison area. From here you can visit **Fort Charles** on Needham Point (turn right at the Pepsi plant). The fort was the largest of the many which guarded the south and west coasts, but is currently part of a building site because it forms part of the gardens of the *Hilton Hotel* which is being rebuilt. Only the ramparts remain but there are a number of 24 pounder cannons dating from 1824. There is a military cemetery here and the Mobil oil refinery was the site of the naval dockyard. Built in 1805, it was subsequently moved to English Harbour, Antigua. The buildings were then used as barracks before being destroyed in the 1831 hurricane.

Carry on up the hill to the **Garrison Historical Area**, which contains many interesting 19th-century military buildings, grouped around the Garrison Savannah parade ground, which is now a six furlong race course. The buildings that surround the racecourse were built out of brick brought as ballast on ships from England. They are built on traditional British colonial lines, the design can be seen throughout the Caribbean but also in India. Painted bright colours, some now contain government offices. There are several memorials around the oval race course, for instance in the southwest corner, the 'awful' hurricane which killed 14 men and one woman and caused the destruction of the barracks and hospital on 18 August 1831 and outside the Barbados Museum in the northeast corner to the men of the Royal York Rangers who fell in action against the French in Martinique, Les Saintes and Guadeloupe in the 1809-10 campaign.

Across the road is **St Anne's Fort** which is still used by the Barbados defence force. You cannot enter but look for the crenellated signal tower with its flag pole on top. It formed the high command of a chain of signal posts, the most complete of which is at Gun Hill (see below). The long, thin building is the old drill hall. **The Main Guard**, overlooking the savannah, has a nice old clock tower and a fine wide veranda. It has been turned into an information centre and houses exhibits about the West Indian Regiment. The Garrison Secretary of the Regiment is here, T4260982. Outside is the **National Cannon Collection** which he created, an impressive array of about 30 cannon, some are mounted on metal 'garrison' gun carriages. There are also a number of newer howitzers, dating from 1878.

The **Barbados Museum** is housed in the old military prison on the northeast corner of the savannah. Based on a collection left by Rev N B Watson (late rector of St Lucy Parish), it is well set out through a series of 10 galleries. It displays natural history, local history (in search of *Bim*), a fine map gallery including the earliest map of Barbados by Richard Ligon (1657), colonial furniture (Plantation House Rooms), military history (including a reconstruction of a prisoner's cell), prints and paintings which depict social life in the West Indies, decorative and domestic arts (17-19th-century glass, china and silver), African artefacts, a children's gallery and one to house temporary exhibits. The *Museum Café is* under the trees in the museum courtyard. ■ *Mon-Sat 0900-1700, Sun 1400-1800. US$5.75 (US$4 while renovation is in progress) children US$2.90. T4270201, www.barbmuse.org.bb* **Library** available for research purposes. ■ *Mon-Fri 0900-1300. US$10 for visitors, US$5 for locals, plus VAT.*

George Washington House, is where he stayed in 1751 for a few months when, as a 19-year old, he accompanied his sick brother Lawrence (who later died). This was George Washington's only excursion outside his homeland and Bridgetown was the largest town he had seen. He contracted smallpox but acquired immunity to the virus which enabled him to survive an outbreak of the disease during the American War of Independence. The Barbados National Trust is raising funds for restoration.

Nearby there are stables for the race course. Races go clockwise. A good place to watch is from the Main Guard. At other times, it is used as a jogging course for people in the mornings, when you can see the horses being exercised, or on weekday evenings. There is also rugby, basketball, etc, played informally in the Savannah; go and see what is going on on Sunday afternoons. There is a small children's playground in one corner. Later, at night, prostitutes parade here.

Also near Garrison is **Mallalieu Motor Collection**, with a Bentley, Vanden Plas Princess, Wolseley and Lanchester, etc. ■ *US$5, daily. T4264640.*

Around the island

Being the most easterly island and extremely difficult to attack, there are few defensive forts on Barbados. Instead the great houses of the sugar growing plantocracy give the island its historic perspective and most of its tourist attractions. Many parish churches are also impressive buildings. The island is divided into 11 parishes named after 10 saints, Christ Church being the 11th. Barbados is not large but it is easy to get lost when driving. There seem to be far too many narrow, winding roads threading their way through sugar cane fields. Deep gullies cut in the coral limestone which is the surface rock over most of the island. These are often full of wildlife and plants but make travelling around very confusing. A good map is essential. The bus service is cheap and efficient and recommended even for families with small children.

The west coast

The road north of Bridgetown on Highway 1 is wall to wall hotels and villas, but nothing high-rise. Highway 2a runs parallel inland and goes through the sugar cane heartland, with small villages and pleasant views.

For more information on west coast beaches, see page 722

Holetown today is a thoroughly modern town but was the place where the earliest settlers landed on 17 February 1627. The Holetown monument commemorates Captain John Powell claiming the island for England. Initially named Jamestown, it was renamed Holetown because of a tidal hole near the beach. It was quite heavily defended until after the Napoleonic Wars. Little trace of the forts can be seen now. Well worth visiting is **St James Church**. Originally built of wood in 1628, it was replaced by a stone structure in 1680. This building was extended 20 ft west in 1874 when columns and arches were added and the nave roof raised. You can see the

Holetown

(margin, rotated) Barbados

original baptismal font (1684) under the belfry and in the north porch is the original bell of 1696. Many of the original settlers are buried here (although the oldest tombstone of William Balston who died in 1659 is in the Barbados Museum). Church documents dating to 1693 have been removed to the Department of Archives. It was beautifully restored between 1983-86.

Barbados

■ Sleeping

1 Angler Apartments & Tamarind Cove
2 Calypso Rentals & Villa Marie
3 Casuarina Beach Club
4 Cobblers Cove & Sandridge
5 Coral Reef Club, Glitter Bay/Royal Pavilion, Lone Star Motel & Sandpiper Inn
6 Crane Beach
7 Edgewater Inn & Round House Inn
8 Just Home
9 Sandy Lane
10 Savannah
11 Sea-U, Atlantis & Bajan Surf Bungalow
12 Silver Sands
13 Sunswept Beach
14 Villa Nova

○ Sights

1 Andromeda Gardens
2 Animal Flower Cave
3 Aquatic Centre
4 Banks Brewery
5 Barclays Park
6 Clapham, Harry Bayley Observatory
7 Codrington College
8 Cotton Tower
9 Drax Hall
10 East Point Lighthouse
11 Farley Hill House & Wildlife Reserve
12 Flower Forest
13 Folkestone, Underwater Park & Marine Reserve & St James Church
14 Foursquare Rum Factory
15 Garrison
16 Graeme Hall Bird Sanctuary
17 Gun Hill Signal Station
18 Harrisons Cave
19 Holders
20 Morgan Lewis Mill
21 Mount Gay Distillery
22 Olympus Theatres Multiplex
23 Orchid World
24 Portvale Sugar Factory
25 St John's Church
26 St Nicholas Abbey
27 Sam Lord's Castle
28 Sunbury Plantation House
29 Turners Hall Woods
30 Tyrol Cot
31 Welchman Hall Gully

On the beach behind the church is the **Folkestone Park and Marine Reserve**. Here you can snorkel in a large area enclosed by buoys. The reef is not in very good condition but there are fish. Snorkelling equipment for hire as are glass bottomed boats which will take you over the reef to two small wrecks further down the coast. A diving platform about 100 yds offshore allows you to snorkel over the wrecks. There are lockers, toilets and a shower here. ■ *The small museum is open Mon-Fri 0900-1700. Buy ticket B$1.15 in gift shop alongside. Guide will take you upstairs to see some dusty exhibits, then show you a video of marine life along the US seaboard (not Barbados), then let you into the museum. Park open daily. T4222314.*

The **Sir Frank Hutson Sugar Machinery Museum** inland beside the **Portvale Sugar Factory** off Highway 2a has an interesting exhibition on the story of sugar and its products, guided tour recommended. ■ *Mon-Sat 0900-1700. US$7.50 when factory is running Feb-May, US$4 the rest of the time, children half price. T4320100. Jars of excellent molasses and sugar syrup for sale.*

Follow the coast road and glimpse the sea at Gibbes and Mullins Bays to reach Speightstown where William Speight once owned the land. An important trading port in the early days, when it was known as Little Bristol. Speightstown is now the main shopping centre for the north of the island. There are several interesting old buildings and many two-storey shops with Georgian balconies and overhanging galleries (sadly many have been knocked down by passing lorries). **Arlington** is a 17th-century structure built on the lines of an English late medieval town house.

The National Trust runs the **Arbib Nature and Heritage Trail**, starting in Speightstown. There are routes of 3½ miles and 4½ miles, starting from St Peter's church. ■ *Walks Wed, Thu and Sat 0900-1430. US$7.50. Reservations T4262421.*

A US$60 mn marina for nine mega-yachts and 140 yachts has been built at Heywoods Beach just north of Speightstown, known as **Port St Charles**. There are 145 residential units, a restaurant, a yacht club, heliport and watersports.

Speightstown
Pronounced Spitestown or Spikestong in broad dialect

Barbados

North of Speightstown

The road north of Speightstown is mercifully free of buildings and there is a good sandy beach on **Six Men's Bay**. Go through Littlegood Harbour and notice the boat building on the beach. The jetty you can see is at Harrison Point. Almost any of the roads off Highway 1B will take you to the north coast, at first green and lush around Stroud Point but becoming more desolate as you approach North Point. The northwest coast, being slightly sheltered from the Atlantic swells, has many sandy coves (Archers Bay). The cliffs are quiet and easy to walk. You may spot turtles in the sea.

The **Animal Flower Cave** at **North Point** is a series of caverns at sea level which have been eroded by the sea. The animals are sea anemones but there are now so few of them the cave should be renamed. There are various 'shapes' in the rock which are pointed out to you and a pool at the mouth of the cave where you can swim looking out to sea. The view from North Point over the cliffs and ledges is worth the trip even if (or particularly when) the cave is shut because of high seas. Eight miles of caverns have been created along the coast by the erosion of the waves. The main cave can be closed due to dangerous seas. The floor of the cave is very stoney and can be slippery. ■ *0900-1600 daily. US$5, children US$2.50.* Bar, toilets, souvenir shops outside.

Good walks along the cliffs can be enjoyed, for instance from River Bay to Little Bay along the Antilles Flat, but beware as there is no shade and there are shooting parties during the season. If driving, several back roads go through the attractive communities of Spring Garden and St Clements. At Pie Corner you can rejoin the coast and visit **Little Bay**. This is particularly impressive during the winter months with the swell breaking over the coral outcrops and lots of blowholes. Note the completely circular hole on the north edge of the bay. If you climb through this natural archway in the cliff, there is a big, calm pool, just deep enough to swim between the cliffs and a line of rock on which the enormous waves break and send up a wall of spray. Wear shoes to stop your feet getting cut to pieces on the sharp rock.

At **Paul's Point** is a popular picnic area. If the ground looks wet park at the millwall by the Cove Stud Farm as it is easy to get bogged down. You will get a good view of **Gay's Cove** with its shingle beach (safe to swim in the pools at low tide) and beyond it the 240-ft high **Pico Teneriffe**, a large rock (named by sailors who thought it looked like the mountain on Teneriffe in the Canaries) on top of a steeply sloping cliff. The white cliffs are oceanic rocks consisting of myriad tiny white shells or microscopic sea creatures. The whole of the coast to Bathsheba is visible and it is easy to see the erosion taking place in Corben's Bay. Indeed you get an excellent impression of the Scotland District, where the coral limestone has been eroded. The whole of this coast between North and Ragged Points has been zoned, no further development will be allowed along the seafront.

The Scotland District

Just to the northwest is **St Nicholas Abbey** which is approached down a long and impressive avenue of mahogany trees. Dating from around 1660, it is one of the oldest domestic buildings in the English-speaking Americas (**Drax Hall**, St George, open occasionally under the National Trust Open Houses programme, is probably even older). Three storied, it has a façade with three ogee-shaped gables. It was never an abbey, some have supposed that the 'St' and 'Abbey' were added to impress, there being lots of 'Halls' in the south of the island. Visitors are given an interesting tour of the ground floor and a fascinating film show in the stables behind the 400-year-old sand box tree. Narrated by Stephen Cave, the present owner and son of the film maker, its shows life on a sugar plantation in the 1930s. You will see the millwall in action and the many skilled workers from wheel wrights to coopers who made the plantation work. The importance of wind is emphasized. If the windmill stopped, the whole harvest halted, as the cane which had been cut would quickly dry out if it was not crushed straight away. The waste was used to fuel the boilers, as it is today in sugar factories. There is a collection of toy buses and lorries in the stables. ■ *US$5.*

Built around 1776, it is the largest, complete windmill in the Caribbean. You can climb to the top

Going back down the steep Cherry Tree Hill you come to the National Trust-owned **Morgan Lewis Mill**, a millwall with original machinery which the National Trust has restored. Note the 100-ft tail, this enabled the operators to position the mill to maximize the effect of the wind. It is on a working farm. ■ *Mon-Sat 0900-1700. US$5, children US$2.50. T4227429.* On the flat savannah at the bottom of the hill, the cricket pitch is a pleasant place to watch the game at weekends.

Most of the animals are not caged, you are warned to be careful as you wander around the shady paths

The **Barbados Wildlife Reserve**, established with Canadian help in 1985, is set in four acres of mature mahogany off Highway 2. They have a huge collection of the large red-footed Barbados tortoise, apparently the largest in the world, which roam slowly around all over the paths, while deer and agouti lounge about. There is an architecturally interesting bird house with snakes upstairs and you look down through the floor to the aviary. The population of the rabbit pen is seriously out of control and the lone wallaby kept with the rabbits and guinea pigs looks stunned. It is an excellent place to see lots of Barbados green monkeys close up if they haven't taken off to the forest next door. The primate research centre helps to provide farmers with advice on how to control the green monkeys who are regarded as a pest. The animals are fed near it at about 1600. The centre has also developed a nature trail in the neighbouring **Grenade Hall Forest**, with over a mile of coral pathways and interpretative signs. They can be rough, steep and slippery and are definitely not wheelchair friendly. An early 19th-century signal station next to Grenade Hall Forest which closed in 1884, rendered obsolete by the telephone, has been restored. The wonderful panoramic view conveys its original role in the communications network and an audio tape gives the history. ■ *Daily 1000-1700. US$11.50, children half price. Café and shop. Grenade Hall Forest and Signal Station and Wildlife Reserve, T4228826. Getting there: bus from Bridgetown, Holetown, Speightstown or Bathsheba.*

Farley Hill House, St Peter, is a 19th-century fire-damaged plantation house; a spectacular ruin on the other side of the road from the Wildlife Reserve, set in a pleasant park with spectacular views over the Scotland District. There is a large number of imported and native tree species, some labelled, planted over 30 acres of woodland. There are picnic benches under the trees and it is popular with Bajan families on Sun. ■ *Daily 0830-1800. US$1.75 per vehicle. T4223555.*

The Atlantic Parishes

The five-mile East Coast Road, opened by Queen Elizabeth on 15 February 1966 affords fine views. From Belleplaine, where the railway ended, it skirts Walker's Savannah to the coast at Long Pond and heads southeast to **Benab**, where there is **Barclays Park**, a good place to stop for a picnic under the shady casuarina trees. Walk up **Chalky Mount** for magnificent views of the east coast, easily reached at the end of the bus line from Bridgetown. If you ask locally for the exact path you are likely to be given several different routes. Walk down through the meadows to Barclays Park for a drink. Ask staff in the café for bus times to either Bathsheba or Speightstown. The East Coast Rd continues through **Cattlewash**, so named because Bajans brought their animals here to wash them in the sea, to Bathsheba.

The tiny hamlet of **Bathsheba** has an excellent surfing beach (see page 723). Guarded by two rows of giant boulders, the bay seems to be almost white as the surf trails out behind the Atlantic rollers. Surfing championships are often held here. Swimming here is not recommended due to the strong currents, only surfers usually venture out. Splashing around in the rock pools is a cooling alternative. A railway was built in 1883 (but closed in 1937) between Bridgetown and Bathsheba. Originally conceived as going to Speightstown, it actually went up the east coast to a terminus at Belleplaine, St Andrew. The cutting at My Lady's Hole, near Conset Bay in St John is spectacular, with a gradient of 1:31, which is supposed to have been the steepest in the world except for rack and pinion and other special types of line. The railway here suffered from landslides, wave erosion, mismanagment and underfunding so that the 37-mile track was in places in very bad condition. The crew would sprinkle sand on the track, the first class passengers remained seated, the second class walked and the third class pushed. There is good walking along the old railway track, through Bath to Conset Bay, although you have to scramble on some bits.

Above the bay at Hillcrest (excellent view) are the **Andromeda Gardens**. Owned by the Barbados National Trust, the gardens contain plants from all over Barbados as well as species from other parts of the world. There are many varieties of orchid, hibiscus and flowering trees. ■ *T4339261. US$6, children US$3. Every day, 0900-1700. The Hibiscus Café has good juices, closes 1645.* The *Atlantis Hotel*, T4339445, has traditionally been a good place for lunch especially on Sunday (US$25, 1300 sharp) when an excellent buffet meal containing several Bajan dishes is served (also Wed, US$22.50). Almost an institution and extremely popular with Bajans, so book ahead. Enid Maxwell, who ran it from 1945-2001, has now relinquished the reins.

From Bathsheba you can head inland to **Cotton Tower signal station** (National Trust owned. Not as interesting as Gun Hill). Then head south to Wilson Hill where you find Mount Tabor Church and **Villa Nova**, another plantation Great House (1834), which has furniture made of Barbadian mahogany and beautiful gardens. It was owned by the former British Prime Minister, Sir Anthony Eden, and until 1994 was part of the National Trust's heritage trail. Now a five-star country resort hotel, see below. You can continue from here via Malvern along the scenic **Hackleton's Cliff** (allegedly named after Hackleton who committed suicide by riding his horse over the cliff) or via Sherbourne to Pothouse, where **St John's Church** looks over the Scotland District. Built in 1660 it was a victim of the great hurricane of 1835. There is an interesting pulpit made from six different kinds of wood. You will also find the grave of Fernando Paleologus "descendant of ye imperial line of ye last Christian emperors of Greece". The full story is in Leigh Fermor's *The Traveller's Tree*.

Barbados

Turn left after a few miles for the downhill road to **Bath**. Here you will find a safe beach, popular with Barbadians and a recreation park for children. It makes a good spot for a beach barbecue and a swim and a beach bar does a good lunch.

Codrington College is one of the most famous landmarks on the island and can be seen from Highway 4b down an avenue of Cabbage (Royal) Palm trees. It is steeped in history as the first Codrington landed in Barbados in 1628. His son acted as Governor for three years but was dismissed for liberal views. Instead he stood for parliament and was elected speaker for nine years. He was involved in several wars against the French and became probably the wealthiest man in the West Indies. The third Codrington succeeded his father as Governor-General of the Leeward islands, attempted to stamp out the considerable corruption of the time and distinguished himself in campaigns (especially in taking St Kitts). He died in 1710, a bachelor aged 42, and left his Barbadian properties to the Society for the Propagation of the Gospel in Foreign Parts. It was not until 1830 that Codrington College, where candidates could study for the Anglican priesthood, was established. From 1875 to 1955 it was associated with Durham University, England. Apart from its beautiful grounds with huge lily pond (flowers close up in the middle of the day) and impressive façade, there is a chapel containing a plaque to Sir Christopher Codrington and a library. You can follow the track which drops down 360 ft to the sea at the beautiful Conset Bay. ■ *US$2.50. Getting there: you can take the Sargeant St bus as far as Codrington College, then walk 7 miles back along the Atlantic Coast to Bathsheba.*

At **Ragged Point** is the automatic **East Point lighthouse** standing among the ruined houses of the former lighthouse keepers. There are good views north towards Conset Point, the small Culpepper island, and the south coast. Note the erosion to the 80-ft cliffs caused by the Atlantic sweeping into the coves. An atmospheric station close to the shoreline measures air quality; this is the first landfall after blowing across the Atlantic from the coast of Africa.

The centre

Northeast of Holetown and reached from St Simon's Church are **Turners Hall Woods**, a good vantage point. It is thought that the wood has changed little to that which covered the island before the English arrived. The 50-acre patch of tropical mesophytic forest has never been clear-felled (although individual trees were often taken out). You can cross the steep paths and see species ranging from the sandbox tree to Jack-in-the-box and the 100-ft locust trees supported by massive buttresses.

On Highway 2, take the Melvin Hill road just after the agricultural station and follow the signs to the **Flower Forest**, a 50-acre, landscaped plantation, opened in 1983 with beautifully laid out gardens. Dropping downhill, the well-maintained paths afford excellent views over the valley to the east coast. To the west you can see **Mount Hillaby**, at 1,116 ft the island's highest point. It too contains species not only from Barbados but also from all over the world, they are beautifully arranged with plenty of colour all year round. There is a *Best of Barbados* shop, cafeteria and toilets. Good information sheet. ■ *Daily 0900-1700. US$7, children 5-16 half price. T4338152, ffl@sunbeach.net* Nearby is **Springvale Eco-Heritage Museum**, a folk museum on an 80-ha former sugar plantation with a presentation of historical rural Barbadian life. ■ *Mon-Sat 1000-1600. T4387011. Café.*

Roads in this area are often closed by landslides and circuitous routing may be necessary

Close by and to the south on Highway 2 is **Welchman Hall Gully**, a fascinating walk through one of the deep ravines so characteristic of this part of Barbados. You are at the edge of the limestone cap which covers most of the island to a depth of about 300 ft. There is a small car park opposite the entrance (despite the sign to the contrary). Maintained by the National Trust, a good path leads for about half a mile through six sections, each with a slightly different theme. The first section has a devil tree, a stand of bamboo and a judas tree. Next you will go through jungle, lots of creepers, the 'pop-a-gun' tree and bearded fig clinging to the cliff (note the stalactites and stalagmites); a section devoted to palms and ferns: golden, silver, macarthur and cohune palms, nutmegs and wild chestnuts; to open areas with tall leafy mahogany trees, rock balsam and mango trees. At the end of the walk are ponds with lots of frogs and toads. Best of all though is the wonderful view to the coast. On the left are some steps leading to a gazebo, at the same level as the tops of the cabbage palms. ■ *Daily 0900-1700. US$6, children US$3. T4386671.*

Harrison's Cave nearby has a centre with restaurant (fair), shop and a small display of local geology and Amerindian artefacts. You are taken into the cave on an electric 'train'. The visit takes about 20 minutes and you will see some superbly-lit stalactites and stalagmites, waterfalls and large underground lakes. There is a guide to point out the interesting formations and two stops for photo-opportunities. It is all rather overdone, you have to wear hard hats (to prevent complaints of bumped heads) and serviettes on your head despite the fact that the caves are totally stable. ■ *Daily 0830-1630. US$12.50, children US$5. T4386640. Getting there: the bus from Bridgetown to Chalky Mount stops near Harrison's Cave and the Flower Forest.*

If you take Highway 2 heading to Bridgetown you will pass **Jack-in-the-Box gully**, part of the same complex of Welchman Hall Gully and Harrison's Cave. **Coles Cave** (an 'undeveloped' cave nearby, which can easily be explored with a waterproof torch or flashlight) lies at its north end.

At **Gun Hill** is a fully restored signal tower. The approach is by Fusilier road and you will pass the Lion carved by British soldiers in 1868. The road was built by Royal Scot Fusiliers between September 1862 and February 1863 when they were stationed at Gun Hill to avoid yellow fever. The signal station itself had its origins in the slave uprising of 1816. It was decided that a military presence would be maintained outside Bridgetown in case of further slave uprisings. It was also intended for advance warning of attack from the sea. The chain of six signal stations was intended to give very rapid communications with the rest of the island. They quickly lost importance as military installations but provided useful information about shipping movements. The hexagonal tower had two small barrack rooms attached and would have been surrounded by a palisade. ■ *Mon-Sat 0900-1700. US$5 (children half price), guide book US$1. T4291358. The fusiliers' cookhouse has been converted to a snack bar.*

Near Gun Hill is the **Francia Plantation**, built in 1910 by a Frenchman who had lived in Brazil. The architecture is a blend of French and Bajan styles with Brazilian hardwoods. The beautiful house and gardens are open to the public, with old furniture, maps and prints, although the house is currently for sale and its future is open to doubt. ■ *Mon-Fri 1000-1600. US$5 including a drink. T4290474.*

Orchid World, at Groves, St George, is a 6½-acre orchid garden, 20,000 of them, mind-blowing, beautifully designed, don't miss it. ■ *0900-1700. US$7, children half price, discount if you visit Flower Forest. Gift shop, snack bar. T4330306.*

The southeast coast

The area around Six Roads was where the Easter Rebellion of 1816 took place. Turn north at Six Roads roundabout for **Sunbury Plantation**. Some 300 years old, the house is elegantly furnished in Georgian style, much of it with mahogany furniture, and you can roam all over it as, unusually, there is access to the upstairs rooms. In the cellars, you can see the domestic quarters. There is a good collection of carriages. The house and museum were damaged by fire in 1995 but have been restored and opened again. ■ *Daily 0930-1630. US$7.50. T4236270. Restaurant in the courtyard.*

Sam Lord's Castle on the southeast coast is the site of an all-inclusive hotel. It is high on the list of tourist attractions because of the reputation of Sam Lord who reputedly lured ships onto Cobbler's Reef where they were shipwrecked. There is supposed to be a tunnel from the beach to the castle's cellars to facilitate his operation. The proceeds made him a wealthy man although the castle was more likely to have been financed from his marriage to a wealthy heiress. The castle is not

Six Roads was called Six Cross Roads until they installed a roundabout

Barbados

Barbados

▶ **The National Trust**

The National Trust runs an Open House programme of visits to interesting private houses on Wednesday afternoons from January to April every year (B$15, children 5-12 half price, B$6 for members of foreign National Trusts, see below, Boyces Garage do a tour plus entrance for B$37, T4251103. A National Trust Heritage passport is available: pick up a free booklet and get it stamped at Andromeda Gardens (B$12), Welchman Hall Gully (B$11.50), Sir Frank Hutson Sugar Museum (B$15), Tyrol Cot (B$11.50) and then you get free admission to Gun Hill, Bridgetown Synagogue, Arbib Nature trail and Morgan Lewis. The National Trust Headquarters is at Wildey House, Wildey, open 0800-1600,

T4262421, natrust@sunbeach.net, which houses the Trust's collection of antique furniture and the Euchard Fitzpatrick and Edward Stoute photography collections. The Duke of Edinburgh Award Scheme (Bridge House, Cavans Lane, Bridgetown, T4369763) and National Trust joint scheme also arrange early Sunday morning walks to places of historical and natural interest. There is a reciprocal free entry to National Trust Properties for members of the National Trust in the UK, Australia, New Zealand, Fiji and Zimbabwe. The same arrangement applies to members of the National Trust for Historic Preservation in the USA and the Heritage Canada Foundation.

particularly old or castle-like, being in fact a regency building. Unfortunately the rooms are poorly lit making it difficult to appreciate the fine mahogany furniture or the paintings. Note the superb staircase, although you are not allowed upstairs. Wander down to the cove where there is a good example of a turtlecrawl, a salt water pond enclosed by a wall. Here turtles were kept alive until wanted for the kitchen. Today the hotel, in conjunction with the Barbados Wildlife park, keeps a few hawksbill turtles, a shark and a congor eel. ■ *US$5, children US$2.50, entrance charge even though the hotel reception forms part of the 2 rooms open to the public.*

Loungers, umbrellas, body boards for hire

Crane Bay, southwest of Sam Lord's Castle, is worth a detour. It is a pleasant cove with lovely pink sand and body-surfing waves, overlooked by 80-ft cliffs. *Crane Hotel* at the top of the southern cliffs charges US$2.50 for admission, redeemable against a drink, but it is worth it for the spectacular view over the bay from the cliff top restaurant. Popular for Sun buffet lunch as an interlude from the beach. You can access the beach from the north end without paying admission, but parking is tricky at weekends. Turn down a narrow lane off a little roundabout by Crane House.

The south coast

Oistins, the main town in the parish of Christ Church, was named after Edward Oistine, a plantation owner in the area. It was important in colonial times as the place where the 'Charter of Barbados' was signed in 1652, giving the island to the Commonwealth Parliament. It is now the main fishing port and has quite a large fish market where you can see and buy the recent catch. It is fascinating to watch the workers filleting flying fish at tremendous speed and efficiency and bagging them up for sale. Friday night 'fish fry' is the big event here (see Entertainment, page 739). Christ Church parish church overlooks the town and is notable for its cemetery containing the Chase Vault. When the vault was opened in 1812 for the burial of Colonel Thomas Chase, the lead coffins were found scattered around inside. It happened again in 1816, 1817, 1819 and 1820, whereupon the coffins were removed and buried separately in the churchyard.

The largest expanse of inland water in Barbados

Graeme Hall Bird Sanctuary, Worthing, near St Lawrence Gap, T4357078, has 80 acres of wetland and mangroves around a lake. It is a natural habitat for birds and there are 18 resident species and 150 migrants. A boardwalk is open to the public but the rest is to be a bird sanctuary for scientific research only. Three endangered Caribbean duck species are found here.

Essentials

Generally, the top hotels in the super luxury category costing well over US$300 a night are on the west coast, while cheap and cheerful places can be found on the south coast and 'getaways' on the east coast at Bathsheba. However, you can find an apartment to rent on the west coast for as little as US$25 a night if you are not too demanding. Self-catering is popular on Barbados, partly because restaurants are not cheap, and if there is a group of you, you can find good value places to stay. The Barbados Tourist Authority, www.barbados.org, has a range of brochures, including one on rates for hotels, guesthouses and apartments and a supplementary brochure on lodging with families and family apartments around the island.

West coast LL *Cobblers Cove*, St Peter, T4222291, www.cobblerscove.com 40 suites, small and exclusive, English country house style, run by Hamish Watson, wins lots of awards, high proportion of repeat business. **LL** *Coral Reef Club*, Holetown, St James, T4222372, www.coral reefbarbados.com Lovely landscaped gardens, lawn running down to sea, cottage style, very highly regarded; also in Holetown, under same management, **LL** *Sandpiper Inn*, T4222251, www.sandpiperbarbados.com Family-run, with award-winning restaurant, delicious but expensive food, both have large grounds and are on long beach. **LL** *Glitter Bay*, T4224555, and *Royal Pavilion*, T4225555, are very smart, next to each other in 30-acre grounds, www.fair mont.com The former is white 'Spanish Colonial Style', at right angles to quite a good beach (good for families or couples), the other a pink palace (couples only), built too close to the sea so the beach is eroding but every room has a sea view, faultless interior design and landscaping, tennis, fitness centre, swimming pools, beauty salon, internet access, watersports and boutiques also on offer at one or other of the sister hotels. **LL** *Little Good Harbour*, north of Speightstown, T4393000, www.littlegoodharbourbarbados.com Small wooden villas around pool, across the road from the sea, nicely laid out and furnished but a bit cramped, good restaurant. **LL** *Lone Star Motel*, on the beach next to restaurant of same name, by *Royal Pavilion*, T4190599, www.thelonestar.com 4 huge rooms, uncluttered, simple mahogany furniture building was originally a garage built in 1940s by Romy Reid, who ran a bus company and called himself the Lone Star of the west coast, then it was a nightclub and then a house, owned by Mrs Robertson, of the jam company, who waterskied offshore until her late 80s. **LL** *Sandy Lane*, T4442000, www.sandylane.com Most luxurious and pretentious hotel on the island and rates vary from US$1,200 to US$6,000 a night depending on season and category. Golf, tennis, state-of-the-art spa with everything from detox to pedicures. It is worth going to the *L'Acajou* French restaurant or *Bajan Blue* or for Sun brunch buffet, 1230-1500, just to see the place (good food and not all that expensive), but you have to book ahead to get past the gate, T4442030. **LL-A** *Sandridge*, 1 mile from Speightstown, T4222361, www.barbadostraveler.com Good-sized rooms or family apartments with cooking facilities, north-facing balconies overlook pool, friendly staff and management, watersports free for guests, barbecue evenings, excellent for families. **L-AL** *Sunswept Beach Hotel*, Holetown, T4322715, sunswept@ caribsurf.com On the beach, 23 comfortable rooms, a/c, fan, TV, kitchenettes and balcony, small pool with direct access to sea, very convenient, lots of restaurants close by, shopping centre across the road, bank alongside, sister hotel of all-inclusive Mango Bay along the beach.

West coast apartments A-B *Villa Marie*, Fitts Village, St James, T4321745, www.barba dos.org/villas/villamarie 3 large rooms, 2 apartments with kitchen (sleep 4), huge kitchen and dining room shared by all, well-equipped, huge showers, pleasant garden with loungers and mature trees, barbecue, 5 mins' walk from supermarket and beach, very quiet, up side road, lots of repeat guests, run by Peter (German) and friendly guard dog Booboo. **A-C** *Angler Apartments*, Derricks, T/F4320817, www.barbadosahoy.com/angler Owners live on premises, priority given to service, friendly, informal, family orientated, restaurant, freshly made Caribbean dishes, will prepare special meals on request, some home-grown vegetables. At the cheaper end of the market, *Calypso Rentals,* Paynes Bay, T4331787, http://calypso-rentals.com specializes in simple budget apartments and villas on the west coast from US$395 per week for an apartment for 2 people, to US$2,400 per week for a villa on the beach sleeping 8, run by Gay Taaffe (Scottish), contact her at Bombas Beach Bar. If you are travelling in a large group, it is possible to rent a property for as little as US$25 per person per day with a special group discount.

Sleeping
Most accommodation offered is very pleasant, if not particularly cheap. 15% VAT is levied on hotel services

Barbados

Inland LL *Villa Nova*, St John, T4331524, vilanova@sunbeach.net Formerly a plantation house, see above, the ultimate in luxury country living and perfect for a restful break away from the sea, 27 rooms, 15 acres of lush gardens, impeccable decor, elegant Terrace restaurant, MAP or CP.

Most of the South coast is wall-to-wall hotels from Hastings to Dover popular with package holiday makers. It's close to the airport, with plenty of watersports and nightlife

South coast LL-L *The Savannah*, Hastings, between Garrison Savannah and beach, T2283800, www.gemsbarbados.com/savannah 100 rooms, 21 in recently renovated historic building, antique furniture, each room different, the rest in new blocks in similar design, very smart, high quality facilities, earth-friendly bathroom goodies, gym, pool, short walk to beach at Hilton, recommended for business visitors. **LL-AL** *Casuarina Beach Club*, St Lawrence Gap, T4283600, www.casuarina.com On beach, 160 comfortable rooms with kitchenette and balcony, pool, tennis, well-managed, beautiful garden, tall trees obscure the hotel from the sea, environmentally conscious (Green Globe status), internet access. **LL-A** *Sandy Beach Island Resort*, Worthing, T4358000, www.sandybeachbarbados.com 128 rooms and 1-2 bedroom suites in pink concrete blocks, wide beach, enough sand for volleyball etc, calm water with reef just offshore, perfect for families. **C-E** *Shells Guest House*, First Av, Worthing, T4357253, www.shellsguest.com Just off Sandy Beach, CP, good value, well run (Swedish and Bajan), good location, 6 rooms with fan, 5 bathrooms, TV room, excellent food in restaurant, which is open 1200-1430 and 1800-2200. **D-E** *Beach House Cleverdale*, Fourth Av, Worthing, T4281035, www.barbados-rentals.com Looks like a chattel house from the outside, 15m from Sandy Beach. Rent rooms or whole house, 5 double rooms, 4 have washbasins, 2 bathrooms, mosquito screens, large living/dining room with TV, stereo, use of kitchen, veranda and barbeque, internet access arranged, help with finding alternative accommodation if full.

South coast apartments L-C *Chateau Blanc Apartments On Sea*, First Av, Worthing, T4357518, www.barbados.org Good value studios, well-equipped but old kitchen facilities, friendly management, also has 1-2 bedroomed apartments on beachfront. **AL-C** *The Nook Apartments*, Dayrells Rd in Rockley, T/F4276502, nookbdos@sunbeach.net Apartments with pool, maid service, clean, secure, convenient for shops and restaurants, discounts for airline staff and Caricom residents. **AL-C** *Venice Gardens & Bonanza Apartments*, 4th Av, Dover, T4289097, bonanza@sunbeach.net Studio, 1 or 2 bedrooms, helpful, quite convenient but not too clean. **B** *Melrose Beach Apartments*, Worthing, T4357985, http://melrosebeach-apts.com Good location, 2-min walk to beach, 14 1-bedroom units, a/c, kitchenette, living room, tiled floors, large bed, simple. **B-C** *Roman Beach Apartments*, Enterprise, near Oistins, T4287635, francesroman@sunbeach.net Friendly, simple, comfortable studios with kitchenette, across the road from beautiful beach. **C** *Tree Haven*, Rockley, T4356673, arturoolaya@caribsurf.com Excellent studio apartments opposite the beach, very clean, helpful and friendly owner. **C-E** *Just Home* (formerly Silverton), Aquatic Gap, T4273265, cpsilverton21@hotmail.com 6 rooms from single sharing bath and kitchen to studio apartment with kitchenette, next to *Grand Barbados* and *Brown Sugar* restaurant, clean and nice, run by Caroline Phillips.

Southeast coast LL-AL *Crane Beach*, T4236220, www.thecrane.com Fairly near the airport, but definitely a taxi ride away, spectacular cliff top setting, good beach, and good pool, tennis, luxury prices and usually fairly quiet with only 18 rooms, but an extra 250 timeshare units, have totally changed the character of the hotel. **LL-B** *Silver Sands Resort*, Christ Church, T4286001, www.silversandsbarbados.com A windsurfing resort with Club Mistral centre open Nov-Jun, 20 mins' drive from airport, on the sea at South Point, spacious and well-equipped, good service, food dull, good beach but waves strong and high, good for surfing but children and weak swimmers should use the pools.

Bathsheba AL-A *Sea-U*, T4339450, www.seaubarbados.com The nicest place to stay, 5 spacious guesthouse rooms with kitchenettes opening on to veranda with sea view, colonial-style wooden house on top of cliffs, run by Uschi (German), family style evening meal served 2-3 times a week, US$23, huge breakfast US$6.50, honour bar, lots of hammocks, quiet, peaceful, popular with active types who go to bed early. **L-A** *Edgewater Inn*, Bathsheba, T4339900, www.edgewaterinn.com Run-down, old-style hotel overlooking sea from top of cliffs, dark reception area, a couple of rooms are sought after, but otherwise nothing special, buffet lunch US$15 Mon-Sat, US$22.50 Sun, cards sold for internet access, US$10 per hr. **AL-B** *Atlantis*, Bathsheba, T4339445, www.atlantisbarbados.com Spectacular setting, opened 1884 alongside railway, now old and tired, feeling effects of Atlantic weather. **A** *Round House Inn*, Bathsheba, T4339678, roundhouse@sunbeach.net Building dates from 1832, 4 rooms in round part, all different, one considerably nicer than the others with roof terrace, others cramped, good restaurant, run by Robert and Gail Manley. **B-C** *Bajan Surf Bungalow*, T4339920, www.jorgen.com/surf The surfers' hangout, basic rooms, CP, restaurant and bar overlooking Soup Bowl, run by top female surfer, Melanie Welch, boards and tuition available.

Villa rental Agents and property managers including *Alleyne, Aguillar and Altman*, the most upmarket and a Christie's affiliate, T4320840, www.aaaltman.com. Also at the posh end, *Elegant Villas of Barbados*, has 400 short-term properties, US$300-400 a night range for beach cottage up to US$10,000 a night for 8-bedroom villa, www.elegantvillasbarbados.com *Rival Enterprises Ltd*, Flamboyant Av, Sunset Crest, St James, T4326457, rival@caribsurf.com 1-bedroom apartments to 3-bedroom villas in gardens, **LL-B** in season, cheaper in summer, well located, near restaurants, shops and beach.

Barbados has a very wide range of places to eat, many of them in an interesting setting and an open-air waterfront or garden terrace. The price range in a restaurant for a main course is US$12-40, but in cheap places you can get a filling lunch for US$6.

Eating

Eating out can be expensive, cheap local places are few and far between after lunchtime unless you want fried chicken every night

    Expensive (over US$20) **West coast**: *Amanda's*, 1st St, Holetown, T4327868. Creole cuisine, mostly seafood, around US$30, Mon-Sat 1800-2200, live jazz Sat night. *Angry Annie's*, 1st St, Holetown, T4322119. Very colourful, informal, brightly painted, sociable host, dinner only, main course from US$20, ribs, steak, lobster, rack of lamb, curries. *The Cliff*, Derricks, St James, T4321922. Dinner only, Mon-Sat, plus Sun in winter season, main course from US$27.50, worth the prices for a glimpse of the decor, stunning desserts, attractive and delightful meal, another recommended as the best food on the island. *Daphne's*, Payne's Bay, T4322731. Italian, chic and contemporary, try to get waterfront table when booking, 1200-1500, 1830-2130, cocktail bar open from 1200. *Emerald Palm*, at Porters, St James, T4224116, Tue-Sun 1830-2200, terribly smart, dine on the terrace on in a garden gazebo, only the finest ingredients will do. *The Fish Pot*, T4392604, at *Little Good Harbour Hotel*, north of Speightstown, in 18th century Fort Rupert. Imaginative menu, nice setting, main course lunch from US$13, dinner from US$20, reservations advised. *La Bella Collina*, Sugar Hill, Mount Standfast, T4190134. Inland but with view to the Caribbean, Italian chef, open daily 1200-1500, Mon-Sat 1630-2200. *La Mer*, at Port St Charles Marina, T4192000. German master chef, formerly at *Sandy Lane*, Tue-Fri lunch US$15, Tue-Sat dinner main course from US$25, Sun brunch. *Lone Star*, Mount Standfast, T4190599. With caviar bar, 3 types from Iran, lunch US$15-3,000, main courses from US$25, sushi, oriental and Asian dishes as well as Caribbean, wonderful setting, beach level, plenty of space, not ruinous if you choose carefully, open 1130-2230. *Mango's by the Sea*, Speightstown, T4220704. Nice waterfront setting, dinner only, 1800-2145, US$20-30 main course, complimentary shuttle from all points north of Holetown. *The Mews*, 2nd St, Holetown, T4321122. Daily from 18.30, quite expensive but superb food, mix of local and French dishes, dinner main course from US$14, very pretty house, tables on balcony or interior patio. Live jazz Fri. *Nico's Champagne Wine Bar*, Derricks, T4326386. Lunch and dinner, closed Sun, main courses US$12-25, lobster US$40, champagne US$14 a glass, good wine list. *Olives*, 1st St, Holetown, T4322112. Mediterranean/Caribbean, dinner only, main course from US$15, last orders 2230. *Raffles*, 1st St, Holetown, T4326557. Wonderful safari decor, huge zebra in dining room, cozy bar in bright colours, subtle lighting, looks like tiny shack from outside, but deceptively spacious inside, open 1700-2300. *Sakura*, 2nd St, Holetown, T4325187. 1800-2200 Mon-Sat, Japanese restaurant and sushi bar, dinner main course from US$18, reservations recommended. *Sasso*, Tamarind Cove, St James, T4321332. Tue-Sun 1900-2130, seafood. *Starfish*, Settlers' Beach, Holetown, T4223245. Seafood, breakfast 0700-1000, lunch 1200-1500, dinner 1830-2130. *Il Tempio*, Fitt's Village St James, T4322057. Italian owner and chef, open 1200-1400, 1830-2200. Happy hour at beach bar 1600-1800 daily.

Barbados

Bridgetown: central is *Le Carenage*, in Old Spirit Bond on the Careenage, T4343463. Lunch buffet US$12.50, evening main course from US$25, Tue-Sun 1130-1500, 1830-2130, Mon 1130-1500 only. To the east of the city are *Brown Sugar*, Bay St, Aquatic Gap, T4267684, www.brownsugarrestaurant.com All you can eat buffet lunch US$19-20 Sun to Fri 1200-1430, dinner daily from 1800. Main courses US$15-36, Bajan specialities, filling and hearty, attractive setting, lots of greenery and waterfall. *Lobster Alive Bistro & Beach Bar*, Carlisle Bay on beach, next to *Boatyard* on Bay St, T4350305. Mostly lobster flown in from the Grenadines, but also other seafood and delivery, 1200-2100 daily.

South coast: *Bellini's Trattoria*, *Little Bay Hotel*, St Lawrence Gap, T4357246. Italian menu, fresh pasta, but not just spaghetti and pizza, 1800-2230 daily, main course US$16-30. *Champers*, Hastings, T4356644. Waterfront bar and bistro downstairs, dining room upstairs on balcony, Mon-Sat 11.30-late, main course US$17-34, champagne from US$60. *Josef's*, St Lawrence Gap, T4358245. Dinner only, 1830-2200, small, delightful, is well used by Barbadians, you need to book well ahead, arrive early and have pre-dinner drinks on the lawn with the sea lapping the wall a few feet below you, candlelit elegance, delicious food. *Muscovado*, in Hotel Pommarine, Marine Gardens, T2280900. Hotel school. US$12.50-25 for meal, US$25 on Fri for 7-course gourmet evening. *Pisces*, St Lawrence Gap, T4356564. Perfect candlelit waterfront setting with waves lapping beneath you, good fish dishes, flying fish US$19, lobster US$38, excellent vegetarian platter, from 1830, very popular, staff rushed off their feet, service suffers. *Zafran*, El Sueño, Worthing Main Rd, Worthing, T4358995. Indian, Persian and Thai, 3-course lunch US$19 Tue-Sun, dinner Mon-Sat, main course US$18-30, croquet lawn and afternoon tea.

Mid-range (US$10-20) **West coast**: *Bombas Beach Bar*, Payne's Bay, St James, T4320569, www.bombasbeachbar.com Run by Rasta Wayne, lively, colourful and cheerful, deck on the beach, toilets and changing rooms, some pestering from beach bums, snacks and meals, organic salads, mostly veggie but some chicken and fishcakes, summer 1100-1800, winter 1100-2200 and Sun 1200-1500. *Bottoms Up*, Paynes Bay, St James, T4325737. Sun and Tue-Fri 1700 till last person leaves, Saturday from 1130, with traditional Bajan dishes like pudding and souse, cou cou, pickled breadfruit, red herring, plus Jamaican jerk chicken and pork, saltfish and ackee etc. Main course from US$15. *Café Indigo*, Highway 1, Holetown, opposite Methodist Church, T4320968. Upstairs in old building, open for breakfast and lunch 0800-1700, full English US$10, pub lunch, US$8-12.50 main course, well-stocked bar. *Cocomos*, Holetown, T4320134. On beach, varied and interesting menu, salads, seafood, steak, burgers and pasta, good solid food, spacious, airy, quick service, pleasant staff, nice atmosphere. Happy hour 1630-1830. *Groot's*, Porters, St James, T4327435. Open from 1200 till last person leaves Mon to Sat, from 1800 Sun. Curries US$13-17, other main courses US$15-23. *Jumbo's*, 1 Clarke's Gap, Derricks, T4328032. Chattel conversion with added veranda, lunch buffet US$12.50, main course for dinner US$15, good wine list, reasonable prices, adventurous food with Thai, Japanese and Bajan influences, closed Mon, Fri lunch only, Sat, Sun dinner only. *Sitar*, 2nd St, Holetown, T4322248. Indian, dinner main course from US$15, veg lunch buffet US$15. *Tam's Wok*, 1st St, Holetown, T4328000. Cheaper than most Holetown places, main course from US$12.50, dinner only, mainly Chinese and stir fry.

Bridgetown: *Waterfront Café* on the Careenage, T4270093. Interesting food, plenty to look at and a good social centre in the evenings, live entertainment some nights, food 1000-2200, drinks until 2400, closed Sun, main course US$11-35, good Caribbean Buffet Tue US$22.50. Live entertainment, mostly jazz.

South coast: *Café Sol*, St Lawrence Gap, T4359531. Grill and Margarita bar, 1800-2300, happy hours 1800-1900, 2200-2300, very popular, Mexican American, 10% discount for takeaway. *Carib Beach Bar*, Worthing, near former *Rydal Waters Guest House*, T4358540. Inexpensive meals (main course US$10-15) and drinks, barbecue and music twice a week, excellent rum punches, open from 0900, happy hour 1700-1800 Mon-Fri, great fun even if you are not eating. *Jambalayas*, St Lawrence Gap, T4356581. Lively, range of dishes from wider Caribbean including Hispanic, jerk chicken or pork, pasta, fish, dinner only. Live entertainment Tue-Sat. *Kapone's*, upstairs in grandstand at race course on Garrison, T4296782. Great view, open 1000-1500 Mon-Fri and on racing Sats, US$12.50 for 2 course lunch, Fri buffet. *39 Steps*, on the coast road near the Garrison, T4270715. Well run and lively, 1200-2400 Mon-Fri, 1800-2400 Sat, closed Sun and holidays, imaginative blackboard menu and choice of indoors or balcony, opened by Josef, previously of restaurant of that name, see above, popular, so book at weekends.

East coast: *Naniki*, Suriname, St Joseph, T4331300, www.lushlife.bb Difficult to get to but well worth the effort, car or strong legs required, take turning off Highway 3 just south of St Joseph's church, signs to Lush Life Nature Resort (Naniki), on hillside overlooking Atlantic coast, tremendous view over fields and palm trees, anthurium farm on property, cool and airy, eat on deck or inside, open 1000-sundown, lunch 1200-1500, tea 1600-1800, Sun buffet, closed Mon, full moon dinners by prior arrangement, local ingredients, much of it organic, Bajan style, a special place, run by Tom Hinds. *Roundhouse Inn*, Bathsheba (see Sleeping), good, lovely restored location, overlooks sea, the best place to eat at night in the area, 0800-1000, 1130-1500, 1830-2100, jazz Wed nights, reggae Sat, guitarist Sun lunch, closed Sun night.

Cheap (US$10 and under) **West Coast** *Fisherman's Pub* in Speightstown, T4222703. Good meal for US$7 and right on seafront, 1000-1600, happy time 1600-1800, dinner 1800-2130 except Sun 1800-2200, order and pay for food at bar, take ticket and hand in to kitchen, no frills, no table service, Wed night dinner from 1900 with steel band and floor show from 2000 on the deck over sea, diners US$17.50, non-diners US$2.50. **Bridgetown** *Balcony Upstairs*, in Cave Shepherd on Broad St, lunch Mon-Fri 1100-1500. *Christie's Canteen*, at Light and Power Company, on Bay St and at Spring Gardens, open to the public, huge traditional lunch. On Bay St near *Boatyard*, *De Kitchen*, T4272214, does combo plate US$7. *The Food Court* in the Imperial Plaza, Bridgetown, has veggie and salad bar sections as well as Chinese, Creole, etc. *Mustors Harbour*, McGregor St, T4265175. Third generation family business, snackette downstairs with Bajan fishcakes, etc, restaurant upstairs, 0900-1600 Mon-Fri, tasty, filling Bajan food, US$6-7 main course. *Pop's Place*, on Cheapside Rd, T4305979. Nice setting, very clean, only US$7 for good, filling lunch. *Port Hole*, Fontabelle, friendly bar near Board of Tourism Office, good solid lunch for US$6. *Tim's*, 43 Swan St. Local food, eat in or takeaway, on balcony or a/c, US$2-3 per portion, busy at lunchtime with office workers.

Lunch Club, at 1 Chattel Plaza, Hastings, T2283649, with takeaway T4258624, and at Earthworks Complex, Edgehill 2, St Thomas, T4252890. Delicious, imaginative sandwiches US$7 and up, build your own, soup and salads, quiche, will prepare picnics, etc. *Pot and Barrel*, just outside *Sam Lord's Castle*, T4234107. No name board, good inexpensive meals, worth a try. There are several decent beach bars on the **east coast** serving lunch, drinks and snacks: *Barclays Park Beach Bar*, *Sand Dunes*, Belleplaine, T4229427. Open 0900-2100, Fri pm fish fry, *Beach Bar* at Bath, *Lighthouse Restaurant & Bar*, at Ragged Point, *Bonito Bar*, Bathsheba.

Fast food places include Chefette, KFC, Pizza Man Doc and Chicken Barn. The cheapest meals are in supermarkets, around US$4

Cinemas *Globe* in Bridgetown, Upper Roebuck St, T4264692. *Olympus Theatres Multiplex* at Sheraton Mall, T4371000, 6 screens, plus *Globe drive-in* off ABC Highway, T4370479. **Entertainment**

Dances and fêtes For something less glossy and more Bajan, it might be worth trying one of the dances which are advertized in the *Nation* newspaper on Fri: ballroom dancing to slows and 'back in times'. People hire a dance hall, charge admission (usually US$5), provide a disco, and keep the profits. There are very few foreigners, but the atmosphere is friendly, and the drinks a lot cheaper than in the smarter nightclubs. There are also fêtes, younger crowd and Jamaican-style dub music, advertised by poster and sometimes on the radio. Venues include *Penthouse*, close to Parliament buildings in Bridgetown, *Cactus* in Silver Sands, *Liberty* in Black Rock, *De Base* on Bay St in Bridgetown, etc. Unfortunately, there have been a few fights at 'Dub' fêtes and they are no longer as relaxed as they were.

Shows Some of the better ones are: *Bajan Roots and Rhythms Tropical Spectacular Dinner Show* at the *Plantation Restaurant*, St Lawrence, US$75 with buffet dinner and transport from hotel, Wed and Fri, starts 1830, show and drinks US$37.50, T4285048. *1627 And All That*, Tyrol Cot, Thu, 1830, US$57.50, colourful show, bar, hors d'oeuvres, buffet dinner, tour of 17th-century market place and cultural village, steel band, complimentary transport, T4242074.

Barbados

Barbados

Theatres There are several good semi-professional theatre companies. Performances are advertised in the press. It is usually wise to buy tickets in advance. Most people dress quite formally for these performances. The *Daphne Joseph Hackett Theatre* in Queen's Park or the *Frank Collymore Hall* in the Central Bank are common venues.

Nightclubs, & bars
Look in Visitor and Sun Seeker or in Weekend Nation on Fri for information about what's on each night

There are quite a selection. Most charge US$12.50 or more for entry on 'free drinks' night, less when you are paying for the drinks. It's worth phoning in advance to find out what is on offer. There are live bands on certain nights in some clubs. Most do not get lively until almost midnight, and close around 0400. Some have a complicated set of dress codes or admission rules, which is another reason for phoning ahead.

The best place on the west coast is *Casbah*, in Holetown, otherwise known as *Baku*, same building as La *Terra* and *Baku* restaurants, billed as 'European style' and 'Moroccan themed', free drinks Thu, Latin beat Wed, excellent live music some nights with local bands, popular with those in their 20s and 30s, fewer teenage tourists, quieter than the other clubs although you still can't hear yourself think and its packed, glorious setting beside the sea, get a table lit by fairy lights overlooking the water, very romantic. The younger crowd go to *Harbour Lights*, Bay St, T4367225, harbourlights@sunbeach.net lots of tourists and expats, open-air on the beach, local and disco music, crowded on Wed, US$15 entry covers 'free' drinks Wed, Fri, 2130-0300 no cover charge Sun or Thu, beach party with dinner on Mon 1900-2230. The *Waterfront Café*, T4270093, is really a bar/restaurant, not a dance place, but has live entertainment Mon-Sat, most nights are jazz or steel pan. *The Boatyard*, T4362622, is the sailor's pub in front of the anchorage at Carlisle Bay, Bay St, free drinks on Tue, US$12.50 with live band, very lively all week, popular with landlubbers too. Happy hour 1700-1800 and 2000-2100 Wed, 1700-1900 and 2100-2300 Fri. *The Ship Inn*, St Lawrence Gap, T4356961, has a big outdoor area and is often packed, especially at weekends, live music, major parties and Thu and Sat, happy hours 1600-1800 and 2200-2300. *McBride's Irish Pub*, St Lawrence Gap, T4356352, has DJ, live music every night except Fri, which is karaoke. *Reggae Lounge* in St Lawrence Gap, T4356462, a bit sleezy but can be fun, US$10, happy hour 1000-2200 'free drinks' Mon, US$10 women US$5 men. *After Dark*, St Lawrence Gap, huge selection at the bar, very lively, live music quite often, more Bajans than tourists. *Chiller's*, in Worthing, north side of main road opposite *Sandy Beach*, is a lively pub with music and dancing, no entry charge. The beach bars can be lively (see listings above), but pick your night. *Bubba's Bar* in Rockley has 10-ft video screen plus 10 other TVs for watching sports while you drink. *Coach House*, Paynes Bay, St James, T4321163, lively pub. *Adriana's Entertainment Centre*, Queen St, Speightstown, T4190126. *Club Skyy* Brighton, T4217599, www.clubskyy.com Thu-Sat night, Sun afternoon.

Rumshops & party cruises
For Rum tours, see page 744

Baxters Rd in Bridgetown used to be the place to try but fewer people go there now. The one roomed, ramshackle, rumshops are open all night, and there's a lot of street life after midnight, although you might get pestered by cocaine addicts. Some of the rumshops sell fried chicken (the *Pink Star* is recommended, it has a large indoor area and the place also has clean lavatories) and there are women in the street selling fish, seasoned and fried in coconut oil over an open fire. Especially recommended if you are hungry after midnight. **Nelson St** rumshops are really houses of ill repute but have amazing larger-than-life naif paintings on the outside. Interior upstairs bar decor is a mix of girlie pix, fluorescent pointilliste and portraits of politicians **Oistins** on a Fri night is a major event for both Bajans and tourists. Lots of shops selling fish meals and other food, dub music one end and at the other a small club where they play oldies for ballroom dancing. It continues on Sat and Sun, though a bit quieter, some food places also stay open through the week. In the north of the island there is a smaller fish fry at Half Moon Fort, just north of Little Good Harbour, with tuna, barracuda, kingfish, next to the beach and under a breadfruit tree. US$7.50, Fri, Sat and Sun 1800 till very late. Also recommended is *Fisherman's Pub* on the waterfront in **Speightstown**, lots of music on Wed (see above).

If you drink in a rumshop, rum and other drinks are bought by the bottle. The smallest size is a mini, then a flask, then a full bottle. The shop will supply ice and glasses, you buy a mixer and serve yourself. The same system operates in dances, though prices are higher; nightclubs, of course, serve drinks by the glass like anywhere else. Wine, in a rumshop, usually means sweet British sherry. If you are not careful, it is drunk with ice and beer.

Party cruises The *Jolly Roger* run 4-hr daytime and evening cruises along the west coast to Holetown, near the Folkestone Underwater Park (where the fun and games take place) from the deepwater harbour. The drinks are unlimited (very). There is also a meal, music, dancing, etc, US$55 for the dinner cruise. On daytime cruises, there is swimming and snorkelling. The *Harbour Master*, which unlike the other cruises pulls up on the beach, 100 ft long, 40 ft wide with 4 decks, see above, Sailing.

Prices are generally high, but the range of goods available is excellent. Travellers who are going on to other islands may find it useful to do some shopping here. If coming from another Caribbean island there are strict controls on bringing in fresh fruit and vegetables.

Shopping
Street vendors are very persistent but generally friendly even when you refuse their wares

The best stocked **supermarket** is *JB's Mastermart* in Wildey. *Big B* in Worthing and *Supercentre* in Oistins and Holetown are also good, and are easier to reach by public transport. *Supercentre* will take orders on net and deliver, no delivery charge, minimum order B$50. Payment by credit card. Orders also by fax F4369820. Supermarkets open on Sun 0900-1300. *Big B* in Worthing is open 0800-1900 Mon-Tue, 0800-2000 Wed-Sat, 0900-1300 Sun, photocopying available. In Holetown in the Chattel Village is the *Gourmet Shop*, T4327711, thegourmetshop@caribsurf.com selling a lot of luxuries, excellent selection of food and wine, 0900-1800 Mon-Sat, 1000-1400 holidays and festivals. *Patisserie Flindt*, 1st St, Holetown, T4322626, patisserieflindt@caribsurf.com 0700-1700 Mon-Fri, 0700-1400 Sat, 0700-1200 Sun plus 1830-2130 Thu, Fri, full English breakfast weekends, US$10, also smaller outlet at Quayside Centre, Rockley, T4352600, 1000-1800 Mon-Wed, 1000-2130 Thu-Sat, *Savoy*-trained chef makes delicious (expensive) French pasties, cakes and chocolates (US$5 for a chocolate mousse, US$1.50 for one chocolate), very good coffee, good for a light meal, also do picnics for Holders Season.

Duty-free shopping is well advertised. Visitors who produce passport and air ticket can take most duty-free goods away from the store for use in the island before they leave, but not camera film or alcohol. Cameras and electrical goods may be cheaper in an ordinary discount store in the USA or Europe than duty free in Barbados. A duty-free shopping centre for cruise ship passengers is inside the deep water harbour, the *Bridgetown Cruise Terminal*.

Broad Street is dominated by enormous **jewellers**: *Colombian Emeralds*, *Diamonds International*, *Diamonds in Paradise*, *Jewelers Warehouse* and *Little Switzerland*. **Art galleries**: *The Kirby Gallery*, Hastings, T4303032, www.kirbyartgallery.com, opposite *Savannah Hotel*, has a bit of everything, paintings, prints, ceramics, used to be the best but now there is more competition with about 12 galleries on the island, 0900-1700 Mon-Fri, 0900-1300 Sat. *Queen's Park Gallery*, Bridgetown, T4272345. In Queen's Park, near the Daphne Joseph Hackett theatre, one-artist shows, variable quality but hung in a good space. Open Mon-Sat 1000-1800. *The Art Foundry*, Heritage Park, Foursquare, St Philip, Mon-Fri, 0900-1700, T4180714, has paintings, sculpture, prints, photographs, installation art and craft for sale. *Zemicon Gallery*, Hincks St, Bridgetown, T4300054, shows some of the best local artists, making a statement, Tue-Fri 1000-1600. The *Verandah Art Gallery*, Old Spirit Wharf, Bridgetown, Mon-Fri 0900-1630, Sat 0900-1300, T4262605, has a reasonable selection with some Haitian art and temporary exhibitions. The *Gallery of Caribbean Art*, Queen St, Speightstown, T4190858. A range of contemporary regional art work, Mon-Fri 0930-1630, Sat 0930-1400. *Whispers*, Horse Hill, Bathsheba, promotes new artists, young, dynamic, frequently changing exhibitions. **Crafts**: *Medford Craft World*, Whitehall Main Rd, T4251919, and *Medford Craft Shop*, Barbarees Hill, T4273179, have wooden carvings etc. Other good displays of craft items are at *Pelican Craft Centre*, over 30 shops on the Princess Alice Highway near the harbour, where you can watch artisans at work, Mon-Fri 0900-1700. *Red Clay Pottery* and *Fairfield Gallery* just outside Bridgetown sells very good ceramics, T4243800. *Earthworks Pottery*, Edgehill Heights No 2, St Thomas, T4250223, www.earthworks-pottery.com for solid houseware and pots in blues and greens with several different designs, used in local cafés, open Mon-Fri 0900-1700, Sat 0900-1300, VAT-free for visitors, also has restaurant/café, *Lunch Club*, T4253463, and gift shops with crafts from several local artists.

Bookshops are much better stocked than on other islands. *The Cloister* on Hincks St, T4262662, probably has the largest stock with a good range of Caribbean material and sells Footprint Handbooks. *The Book Place* on Probyn St specializes in Caribbean material and has a good secondhand section. *The Pages Bookshop* at Cave Shepherd (Broad St and West Coast Mall) also has a reasonable selection. *My Blue Heaven* bookshop and café, Brighton Beach Rd, is unusual, 1000-1400 daily.

Sports

For diving and watersports, see pages 722 and 722

Contact the National Sports Council, Blenheim, St Michael, T4366127, for information on any sport not mentioned here

Athletics A multi-purpose gymnasium is part of the *Sir Garfield Sobers Sports Complex* at Wildey, St Michael, T4376016. Badminton, bodybuilding, boxing, basketball, gymnastics, handball, judo, karate, netball, table tennis, volleyball and weightlifting, plenty of changing rooms and showers and also sauna and massage rooms, a medical room and warm-up/practice area. (**Badminton** is also played at the Community College, St Michael, Tue 1930, Sat 1300, equipment available.) Adjacent is the *Aquatic Centre*, with a 10-lane Olympic-size **swimming** pool, T4297946, tennis courts, hockey, football and cricket pitches outside. **Water Polo** is played at the *Aquatic Centre*, visitors are welcome to join in practice sessions with the team, which is sponsored by *Banks* beer. Training Mon, Wed 1830, while matches are played Sat 1400. Call Stephen Lewis, T4296767 (work), 4286042 (home).

Cricket Lots of village cricket all over the island at weekends. A match here is nothing if not a social occasion. For information about the bigger matches at Kensington Oval phone the Barbados Cricket Association, T4361397. If you and your local team want to tour Barbados, contact *Sporting Barbados*, T2289122, F2280243, www.sportingbarbados.com, for help with discounts and keeping the costs down.

Cycling is best on the east coast, but traffic is dangerously heavy everywhere and rush hour from 1600 makes cycling unpleasant almost anywhere on the island. Roads are narrow, potholed and twisty and lots of people lose their deposit because of damage. *Flex Bicycle Rentals*, T2311518 (mob), T4240321, gmgriff@sunbeach.net run by Paul Griffith, bike hire US$15, tours Fri, Sat. *Odyssey Tours*, offer ecological and historical excursions by bike, T2280003. Contact the *Mountain Bike Association*, Wayne Robinson, T4310419, or Robert Quintyne, T4293367.

Chess, draughts (checkers) and **dominoes** are played to a high standard. Join a rum shop match at your peril. Barbados has a world champion draughts player, Suki King. The island's Sports Person of the Year 2001 was the first Barbadian chess player to reach the rank of International Master, 34-year-old Kevin Denny.

The Barbados Open Golf Championship is held in November; the Senior PGA European Golf Tournament in March

Golf There are 3 championship courses, the best and most prestigious of which has traditionally been *Sandy Lane*, which now has a new 18-hole course, a 9-hole course and a second 18-hole course due for completion 2002, all on 600 acres of former sugar cane land next to the hotel, T4322946/4321311/4321145. An 18-hole, par 72, course at *Royal Westmoreland Golf and Country Club*, St James, T4224653, has 27 holes spread over 480 acres on a hilly site in St James with views over the west coast. To play here you must be staying in one of the villas or at a hotel with an access agreement. Members can use the hotel's beach club facilities 5 mins' drive away. Construction of 350 villas around one of the 9-hole loops has now started, 3 club houses, a swimming pool and 5 tennis courts. *Barbados Golf Club* is open to the public and will soon have 2 18-hole and 1 9-hole courses, with huge club house at Durants, Christ Church, T4288463. www.barbadosgolfclub.com Green fee US$115 in high season, US$79 in low season, also tuition, 3- and 7-day passes, etc. 2 9-hole courses are: the *Almond Beach Village*, built next to the Heywoods course in the northwest T4224900; *Rockley* has no clubhouse and is not highly rated, T4357880. The *Barbados Academy of Golf* is at Balls in Christ Church, T4207405, open 0800-2300, with happy hour and a half 1600-1730, putting green, driving range, 18-hole mini course (fun for families, not serious golfers), lessons and balls (US$6 per bucket).

Hockey is played on an astroturf hockey pitch at Wildey, near *Sir Garfield Sobers Gymnasium*. The *Banks International Hockey Festival* is the largest event of its type in the Americas and is held in Aug with 37 local teams and 26 from overseas. *Hockey Federation*, T4380732, or T4235442.

Horse racing The *Barbados Turf Club*, T4263980, holds meetings at the Garrison on Sat during 3 seasons (Jan-Mar, May-Oct and Nov-Dec). The biggest one being the *Sandy Lane Gold Cup* held in Mar, which sometimes features horses from neighbouring islands. Again this is something of a social occasion.

Polo National and international matches are played at Holders Hill, St James, between Nov and May, Thu and Sat at 1400, contact *Barbados Polo Club*, T4276022, 4321802.

Riding There are 8 riding schools offering beach and/or country rides. Some do not give instruction and cater for pleasure riding only. *Congo Road Riding Stables*, T4236180, 1-hr ride including lift to and from hotel is US$25, beginners or advanced; also *Brighton Stables* on west coast, T4259381; *Beau Geste Stables*, St George, T4290139; *Tony's Riding School*, St Peter, T4221549; *Caribbean Horseback Riding Centre*, St Joseph, T4227433, US$60 for 1½ hrs, US$82.50 for 2½ hrs, good for trail riding; *Trevena Riding Stables*, St James, T4326404, *Wilcox Stable*, Long Beach, T4283610 and *Big C Riding Stables*, Christ Church, T4374056. The *Barbados Equestrian Association*, Sandra Sampson, T4288857. Dressage information, Jean Ray, T4326404.

Road tennis is also a local game with defined rules, played with a low wooden 'net' on some minor (and some main) roads, contact Roger Cutting, Road Tennis Association, T4250446. The *World Road Tennis Series* is held at the end of Nov.

Running The *Run Barbados Series* is held in early Dec and comprises a 10 km race and a marathon. Contact Morris Greenidge at the Barbados Tourism Authority, T4272623, or Carl Bailey, *Runners Choice Promotions*, T4294199, www.runnerschoice.com Less ambitiously Hash Harriers, Sat, followed by barbecue and drinks, T4208113, www.barbadoshash.com

Squash *Rockley Resort* has 2 courts, T4357880, *Barbados Squash Club*, Hastings, 3 courts, T4277193, *Casuarina Hotel*, T4283600. *Squash Racquets Association*, Kristina Evelyn, T4372121.

Tennis There are good courts at *Royal Pavilion* and *Glitter Bay*, Peter Burwash Tennis Centre at *Royal Westmoreland Golf Course*, *Paragon*, T4272054, *Rockley Resort*, 5 courts, 3 lighted, T4357880, *Sam Lord's*, T4237350, *Crane Hotel*, T4326220.

Walking The most beautiful part of the island is the Scotland District on the east coast. There is also some fine country along the St Lucy coast in the north and on the southeast coast. There is a particularly good route along the old railway track, from Bath to Bathsheba and on to Cattlewash. The National Trust, together with the Duke of Edinburgh Award Scheme, and the Future Centre and Heart Foundation, organizes walks at 0600 Sun and either 1530 or 1730 (depending on moon). Details are usually printed in the *Visitor* and *Sunseeker* magazines or T4369033. Their walk to Chalky Mount in the Scotland District has been recommended. 3 speeds: 'stop and stare', 5-6 miles, 'here and there', 8-10 miles, 'grin and bear', 12-14 miles.

Tour operators

See also Rum tours, page 744

Bus tours *L E Williams*, T4271043, US$50-65 day tour (has a sign up in the bus: 'no 10 % service charge is paid with the tour price'), heavy pressure selling of tapes, limited drinks from bar; *Bajan Tours*, T/F4372389, cheaper and better value than some, no pressure on tipping, US$32.50 per half day, US$50 full day including lunch; *Island Safari*, T4325337, tour is with 4WD Landrovers so can get to some less accessible beaches, US$40 half day, US$57.50 full day with lunch, US$90 land and sea tour, kayaking also on offer; *Adventureland*, T4293687, also 4WD and same price; *Ultimate Outback Tours*, T4205418, limbolady@sunbeach.net, also 4WD charter with driver US$47 per hr, minimum 4 hrs, up to 6 passengers, children welcome, lunch at restaurant en route. Longer tours generally include lunch. A criticism of the tours with some companies is that it can take 1½ hrs to pick up everyone from hotels and those further north do not get the full tour through Bridgetown and Holetown. *Grenadine Tours*, T4358451, http://Barbados.org/tours/gttours, and *Caribbean Safari Tours*, Ship Inn, St Lawrence, T4275100, do day tours to Grenadines and other islands.

Transport

Air **From North America**: Miami (*American Airlines* and *BWIA*), New York (*American Airlines*, *Air Jamaica*, *BWIA*, *USAir*), Philadelphia (*USAir*), Washington DC (*BWIA*); *Air Canada* and *BWIA* from Toronto. *Air Canada* from Halifax. **From Europe** *British Airways*, *Virgin Atlantic* and *BWIA* have several flights a week from London. *BWIA* also from Manchester. *Condor* flies weekly from Frankfurt Nov-Apr. There are also lots of charter flights which are usually cheaper and recommended if you are staying only on Barbados. **From South America**: *Liat*, *Caribbean Star* and *BWIA* from Georgetown, Guyana; flights from Caracas, with connections from other countries, involve a change in Port of Spain. **From Caribbean islands**: *Liat*, *Caribbean Star*, *BWIA* and *Air Jamaica* have good connections from Antigua), Bequia, Carriacou, Dominica, Grenada, Kingston and Montego Bay, Jamaica, Mustique, Port of Spain, St Kitts, St Lucia, St Maarten, St Vincent, Tobago, Tortola, BVI and

Barbados

▶ ## Rum tours

The **Mount Gay Visitor Centre**, at Brandons, St Michael, does a very good 45-min tour of the blending and bottling plant, with an exhibition of rum, rum tasting and shop near the deep water port in Bridgetown on the Spring Garden Highway. Mon-Fri 0900-1545. US$6, or a special luncheon tour US$25. T4258757.

The **Mount Gay Rum Distillery** is reached off the road between the St Lucy church junction and Alexandra. Tours Mon-Fri at 1100 and 1400, must be arranged in advance, T4258757.

The **Malibu Beach Club**, Brighton, St Michael, is near the West India Rum Refinery. The adjacent beach has watersports. Mon-Fri 0900, last tour at 1545. US$7.50 , US$27.50 with lunch, US$37.50 day pass. Free hotel shuttle. T4259393.

Foursquare Rum Factory and **Heritage Park**, in an old sugar factory, with sugar machinery, craft market, pottery, bottling plant, folk museum, pet farm, pony stables and Foundry Art Gallery. Mon-Fri, 0900-1700, Fri-Sat 1000-2100, Sun 1200-1800. US$6 adults, children half price. Rum punch and miniature included. T4201977.

Banks Brewery has a tour and also does a 'beer trail', whereby you get your card stamped in participating bars and restaurants. With five stamps you are entitled to a free brewery tour, 15 get you a T-shirt. Tours Tue and Thu 1000 and 1300. US$5 adults, US$2.50 children 10-15, no children under 10, proceeds to charity. T4292113.

Union Island. **American Eagle**, flies to San Juan, Puerto Rico and Canouan. Check different airlines for inter-island travel, the Trinidad route is particularly competitive, **British Airways** often has good offers between Barbados, Antigua and St Lucia and a comfortable plane. It is usually worth organizing ticketing at the start of your journey so that Barbados appears as a stopover rather than as the origin for any side trips you make. **Helicopters** For those who want to make a lot of noise buzzing around the island, **Bajan Helicopters** do tours from US$75 per 20 mins, US$125 per 30 mins right round the coastline. The heliport is near the deep water harbour at Bridgetown, T4310069. Also **Barbados Light Aeroplane Club**, US$37.50 for 30-min flight. T4287102 ext 4676.

Petrol costs B$1.47 per litre. The speed limit is 80, 60 or 40 kmph. Drive on the left

Mini-mokes are fun but not recommended in the rainy season

Road Car hire: Drivers need a visitor's driving permit (Visitor Registration Certificate) from Hastings, Worthing, or Holetown police stations (cost US$5). You will need this even if you have an International Driving Licence. Car hire companies usually sort it out for you. A medium-sized car will cost on average US$105 per day, US$400 per week. **Sunny Isle Sixt Rent a Car**, Dayton, Worthing, T4357979, www.BarbadosTraveller.com; **Stoutes Car Rentals**, T4354456/7, F4354435; **Courtesy Rent a Car**, airport, T4182500, www.courtesyrentacar.com, are helpful, and will arrange to meet you at the airport if you telephone in advance, internet booking; **L E Williams**, T4271043; **Regency Rent-a-Car**, 77 Regency Park, Christ Church, T4275663, F4297735, free pick up and delivery. **Wander Auto Rentals & Taxi Services Inc** T4354813, www.wanderservices.com A smaller operator is **Eastmond's Car Rentals** T4287749, pick up and delivery wherever you want, 7 adequate cars, US$288 per week including VAT. Discounts available (including free driver's permit) and tourist magazines frequently contain 10-15% vouchers.

Bus: Around Bridgetown, there are plenty of small yellow privately owned minibuses and route taxis with ZR numberplates; elsewhere, the big blue and white Mercedes buses (exact fare required or tokens sold at the bus terminal) belong to the Transport Board, T4366820. Private buses tend to stick to urban areas while the public buses run half empty in rural areas and in evening. There is a **City Circle** route, clockwise and anti-clockwise round the inner suburbs of Bridgetown which starts in Lower Green. **Terminals for the south**: Fairchild St for public buses, clean, modern; Probyn St, or just across Constitution River from Fairchild St for minibuses; further east by Constitution River for ZR vans. **Terminals for the west**: Lower Green for public buses; west of post office for minibuses; Princess Alice Highway for ZR vans, but from 1800-2400 all leave from Lower Green. During the rush hour, all these terminals are chaotic, particularly during school term. On most routes, the last bus leaves at or soon after midnight and the first bus at 0500. There are 2 routes from the **airport**: Yorkshire buses go straight to Bridgetown, others go along the south coast past the hotels to Bridgetown.

Taxis: Between the airport and any point north of Speightstown, US$27.50, to Holetown, US$19, to Bridgetown Harbour US$15, to Garrison US$12, to Oistins US$8; between the city centre and *Sam Lord's Castle* US$19, to Oistins US$10, Dover US$9; between *Sandy Lane* and Oistins US$18. Fares are quoted also by mile (US$1.25) or km (US$0.75) but there are no taxi meters. Vehicles which look like route taxis but with ZM numberplates, are taxis plying for individual hire, and will charge accordingly. *VIP Limo Services*,T4294617, hire a vehicle with driver for a whole-day tour at a cost of US$150 for up to 4 passengers.

Sea Barbados is not well served by small inter-island schooners. You may be able to get a passage to another island on a yacht, ask at the harbour or at the *Boatyard* on Carlisle Bay. Mooring facilities are available at the Shallow Draft next to the Deep Water Harbour, or there are calm anchorages in Carlisle Bay. Several companies run mini-cruises based on Barbados.

The cruise ship passenger tax is US$8.50

Directory

Banks *FirstCaribbean International Bank*, the *Royal Bank of Canada*, *CIBC Caribbean Ltd*, *Scotiabank*, *Caribbean Commercial Bank*, *Barbados Mutual Bank* and *Barbados National Bank* all have offices in Bridgetown. The first 5 also have branches in the main south and west coast tourist centres. Opening hours for banks are 0800-1500 Mon to Thu, and 0800-1300 and 1500-1700 on Fri. *Caribbean Commercial Bank* in Hastings and Sunset Crest is also open on Sat from 0900 to 1200. All banks now have ATMs at most branches. Banking facilities in *JB's* and *Big B Supermarkets* are open 1000-1900 Mon-Thu, 1000-2000 Fri, 1000-1500 Sat. No banks on the east coast, but the supermarket at Belleplaine has a *Royal Bank* counter.

Communications Internet: Business services and internet access on the west coast at *Global Business Centre*, West Coast Mall, Holetown, T4326508, www.globalbizcentre.com Mon-Fri 0900-1700, Sat 0900-1300, B$5 per 10 mins, B$0.50 per min thereafter, also at Quayside Centre on south coast. *Web Café*, Sunset Crest, turn up by Royal Bank of Canada, parking outside, 0800-2000 Mon-Fri, 0900-1700 Sat, Sun, B$5 per 15 mins, internet phone calls B$1.50 per min to EU, USA, Caribbean, (B$4.50 for normal phone calls) fax B$1 per sheet locally, B$6 abroad, 6 terminals, lots of drinks, friendly service. In Bridgetown, *Netcafé*, Sogo Plaza, 20 Broad St, T4354736. Also in Broad St Mall, Bridgetown, opposite CIBC, US$3 for 15 mins, US$5 for 30 mins, US$10 for an hr, 4 terminals, Mon-Thu 0900-1700, Fri 0900-1800, Sat 0900-1400. *Connect*, just off Broad St, upstairs from *Windjammer* on Lancaster Lane opposite *Cave Shepherd*, US$1 for 7 mins, US$2 for 15 mins, US$7 for an hr, 8 terminals, free coffee, student rates with ID, net2phone calls, send photos, Mon-Thu 0900-1700, Fri 0900-1800, Sat 0930-1430, T2288648, toilets next door, also *Nelson's Arms* bar and restaurant. *Computer Internet Services*, in Broad St Mall, 8 terminals, no eating or drinking, US$1 for 10 mins, US$6 for an hr, 0900-1700 Mon-Thu, 0900-1800 Fri, 0900-1400 Sat. In St Lawrence Gap, *Bean 'n Bagel Café*, 'gourmet coffee', light meals under B$20, breakfast B$19.99, T420-4604, 0700-1730 for the café, 0800-1730 for computers, B$3 for 5 mins, B$10 for 30 mins, B$15 for an hr. *Happy Days*, Chattel Village, 0800-1500, burgers and sandwiches under B$15, 3 terminals, B$4 for 15 mins, B$8 for 30 mins, B$12 for an hr, B$20 for 2 hrs. *ICS Internet Café*, just east of *Ship Inn*, T4281513, B$3 for 5 mins, B$6 for 15 mins, B$18 for an hr, phone calls B$0.99 per min to USA, Canada, Caribbean, B$2 per min to South America, B$1.75 to UK, B$2 to Europe, 0830-2030 daily. *A&R Computer Services*, opposite Hastings Plaza in same complex as *Shak Shak*, B$4 for 15 mins, B$7 per 30 mins.

Lots of hotels have internet access for guests

    Post: The General Post Office Headquarters is in Cheapside, Bridgetown and there are District Post Offices in every parish. Collections from red post boxes on roadsides. Local postal rates are B$0.45 for priority, B$0.40 non-priority. Airmail rates to North America B$1.15 or B$0.45, to Europe B$1.40 or B$0.70, to the Caribbean B$0.90 or B$0.45. There is an express delivery service of 48 hrs worldwide: to the Caribbean B$28 per 1kg plus B$3 per 500gm extra, USA B$45 + B$8, Europe B$55 + B$12. A Philatelic Bureau issues first-day covers 4 times a year.

    Telephone: Calls from a pay phone cost 25 cents for 3 mins. Otherwise local calls are free. Many business places will allow you to use their telephone for local calls. International calls can be made from most hotels or (more cheaply) from *Cable & Wireless* (Wildey). Faxes can also be sent from and received at Cable & Wireless's office by members of the public. Cable & Wireless has a public office on the Wharf in Bridgetown for international calls and fax. Phone cards are available for Bds$10, 20 and 40 from airport arrivals duty-free shop, cruise terminal, phone company offices, and long list of other outlets; a cheaper way of making overseas calls than using hotel services, and can be used in most of the English-speaking Caribbean except Trinidad, Jamaica, Guyana, Bahamas. Cellphone rental is US$50 per week, T2340964. Roaming is possible with 800 Mhz analogue or digital TDMA phones, but is costly. Cellular service is to be opened to competition by end-2003, ending Cable & Wireless' monopoly.

Barbados

Media Newspapers: *The Advocate*, also publishes *The Sunday Advocate* and *Sun Seeker*. *The Nation* (also publishes *Sunday on Saturday*, *Sunday Sun*, *The Visitor* and *Barbados Business Authority*, Mon, US$0.50). *Broad Street Journal* is a free business weekly. **Radio** *CBC Radio*, medium wave 900 kHz; Starcom Gospel, medium wave 790 kHz; BBS, FM 90.7 MHz; Love FM, FM 104.1 MHz; Radio Liberty, FM 98.1 MHz, FAITH 102 FM. **Television** One terrestrial channel, *CBC*, mostly US imports. Also multi-choice TV with 30 channels and satellite-based *DirecTV* with 70 channels in several languages.

Virgin allows you to check in at your hotel and turn up at the airport only 50 minutes before departure, T4362110

Airline offices The *Liat* office is at St Michael's Plaza, St Michael's Row, T4345428. *BWIA*, T4262111, *British Airways*, T4366413, are all on Fairchild St. *American Airlines*, T4284170, and *Air Canada*, T4285077, have offices at the airport. *Virgin Atlantic* is in Hastings, T1800-744747. *Aeropostal*, Lower Bay St, T4361858, *Air Jamaica*, Bayside Plaza, T2286625. *Caribbean Star*, Lower Bay St, T4310540. *Surinam Airways*, Lower Bay St, T4361858.

Embassies and consulates Australia High Commission, Bishop's Court Hill, T4352843. **Brazil** Embassy, 3rd Floor, Sunjet House, Fairchild St, T4271735. **Canada** High Commission, Bishop's Court Hill, St Michael, T4283550. **Costa Rica**, Dayrells Court, T4310250. **Cuba**, Collymore Rock, T4352769. **France**, Hastings, Christ Church, T4356847. **Germany**, Banyan Court, Bay St, St Michael, T4271876. **Swedish**, Branckers Complex, Fontabelle, St Michael, T4274358. **UK** British High Commission, Lower Collymore Rock, St Michael, T4366694, F4365398. **US** Consular Section, Alico Building, Cheapside, Bridgetown, T4364950. **Venezuela**, El Sueño, Hastings, Christ Church, T4357619.

Background

History

There were Amerindians on Barbados for a thousand years or more. The first Europeans to find the island were the Portuguese, who named it 'Os Barbados' after the Bearded Fig trees which grew on the beaches, and left behind some wild pigs. These bred successfully and provided meat for the first English settlers, who arrived in 1627 and found an island which was otherwise uninhabited. It is not clear why the Amerindians abandoned the island, although several theories exist. King Charles I gave the Earl of Carlisle permission to colonize the island and it was his appointed Governor, Henry Hawley, who in 1639 founded the House of Assembly. Within a few years, there were upwards of 40,000 white settlers, mostly small farmers, and equivalent in number to about 1% of the total population of England at this period. After the 'sugar revolution' of the 1650s most of the white population left. For the rest of the colonial period sugar was king, and the island was dominated by a small group of whites who owned the estates, the 'plantocracy'. The majority of the population today is descended from African slaves who were brought in to work on the plantations; but there is a substantial mixed-race population, and there has always been a small number of poor whites, particularly in the east part of the island. Many of these are descended from 100 prisoners transported in 1686 after the failed Monmouth rebellion and Judge Jeffrey's 'Bloody Assizes'.

The two principal political parties are the Barbados Labour Party (BLP) and the Democratic Labour Party (DLP). The DLP held office in 1986-94. Economic difficulties in the 1990s eroded support for the government. The Prime Minister Erskine Sandiford narrowly lost a vote of confidence in June 1994, and stood aside for his Finance Minister David Thompson, who led the party into a general election on 6 September. The BLP won the elections with 19 seats, compared with eight for the DLP and one for a third party, the NDP. Mr Owen Arthur, then 44, an economist, became Prime Minister and took on the portfolios of Finance and Economic Affairs. In the January 1999 general elections, the BLP was returned with an overwhelming vote of confidence. It won 26 of the 28 seats, while the DLP won the other two. In the latest elections, on 21 May 2003, the BLP won a further landslide....

Geography

Barbados is 21 miles long and 14 miles wide, lying east of the main chain of the Leeward and Windward islands. Most of the island is covered by a cap of coral limestone, up to 600,000 years old. Several steep inland cliffs or ridges run parallel to the coast. These are the remains of old shorelines, which formed as the island gradually emerged from the sea. There are no rivers in this part of the island, although there are steep-sided gullies down which water runs in wet weather. Rainwater runs through caves in the limestone, one of which, Harrison's Cave, has been developed as a tourist attraction. The island's water supply is pumped up from the limestone. In the Scotland District in the northeast, the coral limestone has been eroded and older, softer rocks are exposed. There are rivers here, which have cut deep, steep-sided valleys. Landslides make agriculture and construction hazardous and often destroy roads.

Government

Barbados has been an independent member of the Commonwealth since November 1966. The British Monarch is the Head of State, represented by a Governor General. There is a strong parliamentary and democratic tradition. The House of Assembly is the third oldest parliament in the Western Hemisphere dating from 1639, although voting was limited to property owners until 1950. There are 21 senators appointed by the Governor General, of whom 12 are on the advice of the Prime Minister, two on the advice of the Leader of the Opposition and seven at his own discretion to reflect religious, economic and social interests. 28 single-member constituencies elect the House of Assembly.

A 1998 Commission on the constitution chaired by a former BLP leader and Attorney General, Sir Henry Forde QC, recommended abolition of the monarchy, with the Governor General replaced by a ceremonial president, changes in the composition of the Senate, and replacement of the London-based Privy Council as final appeal court by a Caribbean Court of Justice.

Economy

Natural resources are few. Sugar is still the main crop but many producers have abandoned the land, while trying to get planning permission for golf courses or housing developments. There is a well-established service sector and an expanding offshore financial sector with a good reputation. A range of light industries produce mainly for the local, regional, and North American markets. Manufacturing is the second largest foreign exchange earner. There is a small oil industry. Barbados National Oil Company's onshore field in St Philip produces enough for local requirements (although it is refined overseas). There is also enough natural gas for piped domestic supply to urban and suburban areas.

By far the main foreign exchange earner is now tourism, which accounts for 15% of GDP and employs 10,300 people. In 2002, 497,899 stopover tourists and 523,253 cruise ship passengers visited the island, slightly down from 2001 because of the international economic downturn. In contrast with most Caribbean islands, the UK is the main tourist market, accounting for 39% of arrivals compared with 25% from the USA. Barbados has no hotels with more than 330 rooms. The emphasis on small scale tourism may be an advantage in the British market, but has held back sales in North America, where customers prefer branded hotel chains.

Culture

People

Barbados has a population of 269,000. This is more than any of the Windwards or Leewards, and is considered enough to make the island one of the 'big four' in the Caribbean Community. With population density of 1,620 per square mile in 2002, Barbados is one of the most crowded countries in the world.

Because Barbados lies upwind from the main island arc, it was hard to attack from the sea, so it never changed hands in the colonial wars of the 17th and 18th centuries. There is no French, Dutch, or Spanish influence to speak of in the language, cooking or culture. People from other islands have often referred to Barbados as Little England, and have not always intended a compliment. Today, the more obvious outside influences on the Barbadian way of life are North American. Most contemporary Barbadians stress their Afro-Caribbean heritage and aspects of the culture which are distinctively 'Bajan'. There are extremes of poverty and wealth, but these are not nearly so noticeable as elsewhere in the Caribbean. This makes the social atmosphere relatively relaxed. However, there is a history of deep racial division. Although there is a very substantial black middle class and the social situation has changed radically since the 1940s and 50s, there is still more racial intolerance on all sides than is apparent at first glance. Barbadians are a religious people and although the main church is Anglican, there are over 140 different faiths and sects, including Baptists, Christian Scientists, Jews, Methodists, Moravians and Roman Catholics.

Literature Two Barbadian writers whose work has had great influence throughout the Caribbean are the novelist George Lamming and the poet Edward Kamau Brathwaite. Lamming's first novel, *In The Castle Of My Skin* (1953), a part-autobiographical story of growing up in colonial Barbados, deals with one of the major concerns of anglophone writers: how to define one's values within a system and ideology imposed by someone else. Lamming's treatment of the boy's changing awareness in a time of change in the West Indies is both poetic and highly imaginative. His other books include *Natives Of My Person*, *Season Of Adventure* and *The Pleasures Of Exile*.

Brathwaite is also sensitive to the colonial influence on black West Indian culture. Like Derek Walcott (see under St Lucia) and others he is also keenly aware of the African traditions at the heart of that culture. The questions addressed by all these writers are: who is Caribbean man, and what are his faiths, his language, his ancestors? The experience of teaching in Ghana for some time helped to clarify Brathwaite's response. African religions, motifs and songs mix with West Indian speech rhythms in a style which is often strident, frequently using very short verses. His collections include *Islands*, *Masks* and *Rights Of Passage*.

Heinemann Caribbean publish the *A to Z of Barbadian Heritage* which is worth reading (new edition in preparation). Macmillan publish *Treasures of Barbados*, by Harry S Fraser, an attractive guide to Barbadian architecture. *To Hell or Barbados - Irish Slavery in Barbados* by Sean O'Callaghan,Brandon Book Publishers 2000. *Barbados - Photos from Within*, Miller Publications, good photo book. *Geology of Barbados,* Hans Machel, Barbados Museum publication. *Art in Barbados*, Alissandra Cummins et al, Ian Randle Publishers and Barbados Museum and Historical Society, 1999, examines the work of Barbadian artists over six decades. Several books of old photos edited by Ann Watson Yates, of which the best is probably *Bygone Barbados*. *History of Barbados*, Schomburgk, 1848, has been reprinted, a natural history and geography of the island in early Victorian times.

Trinidad and Tobago

Introducing Trinidad and Tobago

Trinidad and Tobago are only just off the coast of Venezuela, yet they share little of the culture of South America. The people are a cosmopolitan mix of African, East Indian, Chinese, European and Syrian and the music, cuisine, culture, society and politics of the islands reflect this. Trinidad's ebullient carnival is world famous and attracts thousands of visitors but its wealth comes from oil, gas and manufacturing rather than tourism and many of its beaches remain empty and fairly unspoilt. Beach tourism has been developed on its smaller, sister island of Tobago, where hotels are spreading around the coastline, but there are still glorious bays and coves and resorts are low key. Both islands have a large area of rainforest, home to a huge array of flora and fauna, and birdwatching is a major attraction.

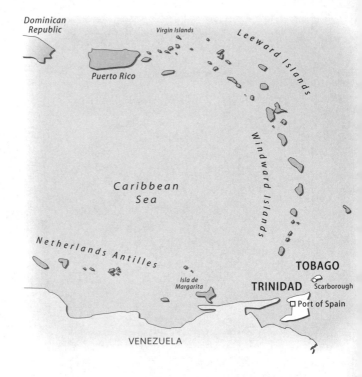

Essentials

Before you travel

Passports are required by all visitors. Visas are not required for visits of under 3 months by **Documents** nationals of most Commonwealth countries, West European countries, USA, Argentina, Brazil, Colombia, Israel, Iceland and Turkey; holders of OAS passports; and by Venezuelans for stays of up to 14 days. Citizens of some Commonwealth countries do need visas, however; these include Australia, New Zealand, India, Sri Lanka, Nigeria, South Africa, Uganda, Tanzania and Papua New Guinea. A visa normally requires 48 hours' notice. A waiver for those with no visa can be obtained at the airport, but it costs TT$50. Entry permits for 1-3 months are given on arrival; a 1-month permit can be extended at the immigration office at 67 Frederick St in Port of Spain, open 0700-1400. Your first visit is to make an appointment for a couple of days later; allow several hours for return visit, making sure you take all documents including ticket to home country plus TT$100 fee. Try and get a 3-month entry permit if planning a long stay. Business visitors are allowed to work without a work permit for 1 month in each calendar year.

Even though you may not get asked for it, all travellers need a return ticket to their country *Only those coming* of origin, dated, not open-ended, proof that they can support themselves during their stay and *from an infected area* an address at which they will be staying in Trinidad (the tourist office at the airport can help). A *need a yellow fever* ferry ticket to Venezuela has often satisfied immigration officials, but it is unwise to rely on this. *inoculation certificate*

Duty-free imports: 200 cigarettes or 50 cigars or 250g tobacco, 1 litre wine or spirits, and **Customs** TT$1,200 worth of gifts. Passengers in transit, or on short visits, can deposit goods such as liquor with customs at the airport and retrieve it later free of charge. Duty-free prices at the airport are low. Duty-free shops are accessible to arriving passengers.

The currency is the Trinidad and Tobago dollar, TT$. Notes are for TT$1, 5, 10, 20 and 100. **Money** Coins are for 1, 5, 10, 25 and (rarely) 50 cents.

Exchange The Trinidad and Tobago dollar was floated in Apr 1993, but the float is tightly managed and the exchange rate has remained around TT$6.30 = US$1 since 1996. Banks generally will change only certain currencies: Eastern Caribbean, US, Barbados and Canadian dollars, euros and sterling. On departure you can change TT$ back into US$ at *First Citizens Bank* at Piarco, open until 2200, but they charge US$10 minimum fee. Better to use small amounts of TT$ in the duty-free shops. It is difficult to exchange TT$ on other islands.

Travellers' cheques and major credit cards are accepted almost everywhere on Trinidad. On Tobago there are no banks outside Scarborough (except at Crown Point Airport); TCs are changed by large hotels but if you are travelling to the northern end of the island make sure you have enough TT$ as not everyone accepts US$. All banks charge a fee for cashing TCs, some more than others, so check first. ATMs are widely distributed and accept credit and debit cards with the Cirrus symbol. Royal Bank ATMs in West Mall, Park St, Maraval and the airport will give US$ as well as TT$.

The climate on the islands is tropical, but, thanks to the winds, rarely excessively hot. Tem- **Climate** peratures vary between 21 and 37°C, the coolest time being Dec-Apr. There is a dryish sea- *Trinidad and Tobago* son from Jan to mid-May and a wet season Jun-Nov. Rain is usually heavy. *are outside the* *hurricane belt*

Getting there

BWIA and other airlines have scheduled flights from Toronto, Washington DC, New York **Air** and Miami in North America and from London, but there are several charter flights from those and other cities such as Frankfurt, many of them straight to Tobago. There are some connections with the north of South America, with flights to Caracas, Paramaribo and Georgetown. There are many flights to other Caribbean islands if you want to island hop (see Transport, page 781).

Trinidad & Tobago

▶ **Tourist offices overseas**

Canada RMR Group, Taurus House, 512 Duplex Av, Toronto, M4R 2E3, T416-4858724, F416-4858256.

Germany Basic Service Group, Am Schleifweg 16, D-55128, Mainz, T49-06131-73337, F06131-73307.

Italy Ian Rocks, Via Sant Allessandro 688, Caronno Pertusella, 21042 VA, T392-96451070, F96564870.

UK Mitre House, 66 Abbey Rd, Bush Hill Park, Enfield, Middlesex EN1 2RQ, T020-83501009,

F020-83501011, anna@ttg.co.uk
USA Keating Communications, 350 Fifth Av, New York, NY10018, T1-888-595-4TNT, 212-7602400, F212-7606402.
Press information, 331 Almeria Av, Coral Gables, FL-33134, T305-4444033, F305-4470415.

TIDCO's website is www.tidco.co.tt, tourism-info@tidco.co.tt Alternatively visit www.visittnt.com

Sea There is a regular ferry service between Güiria, Venezuela, and Pier One, at Chaguaramas, see Transport, page 781, but from the north, cruise ships are the only passenger service calling at Port of Spain. The ferry service between Trinidad and Tobago is not cheap, quick or comfortable.

Crew will be admitted for 90 days; a 90-day extension costs US$30 per person

Yachts Chaguaramas, Trinidad, and **Scarborough**, Tobago are the ports of entry. In Chaguaramas, take the boat to the customs dock (open 24 hrs) to clear on arrival in Trinidad and fill in combined customs and immigration form. Overtime for after hours, 1600-0800, weekends and holidays is high, so it pays to arrive during normal working hours.

Departure by sea Clear out with customs and immigration. Pay port fees of US$8 for each month that the boat was in Trinidad and Tobago waters. To go from one island to the other clear out with Immigration and in on the new island. Clear customs only when making final departure. New arrivals must be signed aboard the vessel as crew by immigration in Chaguaramas.

Departure by air Boats can be left in storage; yacht yards will help with paperwork, present it to customs and clear with immigration within 24 hrs of departure for exemption from departure tax. When returning to Trinidad by air, go to third party line at airport to get paperwork to take with baggage to Chaguaramas customs to clear. Arriving outside office hrs leave boat parts for weekday review. Arriving guests should have return ticket and letter to Trinidad immigration stating vessel name and official number.

Information *The Boca* is a useful monthly 'yachtie' magazine available locally or at www.boatersenterprise.com The annual *Boaters Directory* (produced Dec) lists services for yachties: US$20 overseas, less locally. The editor, Jack Dawson, T6342044, is prepared to offer advice to potential visitors. The *Yacht Services Association* is also extremely helpful, T6344938.

There was a huge increase in facilities in the 1990s, principally to take advantage of Trinidad's location outside the hurricane belt

Marinas The Trinidad marinas are all west of Port of Spain along the coast to Chaguaramas *Trinidad and Tobago Yacht Club* (TTYC), Bayshore, T/F6374260, a private club, leases members' slips to visiting yachts when available, 60 in-water berths, security, restaurant, bar, laundry. *Point Gourde Yachting Centre*, T6275680, F6254083, 65 in-water berths, full service marina. *Trinidad and Tobago Sailing Association* (TTSA), Chaguaramas, T/6344519, a private members' association with moorings and anchorage available to visiting yachts, full service haul-out yard, 15-ton marine hoist, moorings, repair shed, bar, laundry. *Power Boats Mutual Facilities*, Chaguaramas, T6344303, F6344327, haul-out and storage 50-ton marine hoist, 23 in-water berths, boat storage, marine supplies, fibreglass repairs, welding, woodworking, apartments, grocery, restaurant, laundry. *Peake Yacht Services*, Chaguaramas, T6344423, F6344387, full service marina, 150-ton marine hoist capable of beams to 31 ft, 21 in-water berths, boat storage, 10-room hotel, restaurant Mini-Mart, laundry, skilled maintenance, recommended. *Industrial Marine Services*

Trinidad & Tobago

Touching down

Business hours *Banks: Mon-Thu 0800-1400, Fri 0800-1200, 1500-1700. Some banks have extended hours until 1800.*
Businesses and shops: *Mon-Fri 0800- 1600 or 1630 (shops 0800-1200 on Sat). Shopping malls usually stay open Mon-Sat until 2000.* **Government offices:** *Mon-Fri 0800-1600.*

Clothing *Beachwear is for the beach. In the evening people dress more smartly but are not formal.*

Departure tax *There is a TT$75 exit tax payable in local currency, or US$15, plus a TT$25 security fee. Passengers in transit do not have to pay, but are required to obtain an 'exempt' ticket from the departure tax window before being allowed through to the immigration officers on the way to the departure lounge. Visitors leaving by sea pay the departure tax to the shipping agent. Your immigration card must be presented on departure. See also page 752.*

IDD code *868.*

Official time *Atlantic Standard Time, 4 hrs behind GMT, 1 hr ahead of EST.*

Tipping *If no service charge on bill, 10% for hotel staff and restaurant waiters; taxi drivers, 10% of fare, minimum of 25 cents (but no tip in route taxis); dockside and airport porters, about 25 cents for each piece carried; hairdressers (in all leading hotels), 50 cents.*

Voltage *110 or 220 volts, 60 cycles AC.*

Weights and measures *Metric. Road signs are given in kilometres, but people still refer to miles.*

See also Directory, pages 782 and 793

(IMS), Chaguaramas, T6344328, F6344437, full service haul-out and storage yard, 70-ton marine hoist, paint shop, chandlery, sailmaker, fibreglass repair, welding, woodworking, sandblasting, restaurant, laundry. *Crews Inn Yachting Centre*, Chaguaramas, T6344384, is best equipped with on-shore facilities, including a 46-room hotel with pool and gym, *Lighthouse* restaurant, *Republic Bank* with ATM, *Econocar* car rental agency, T6342134, hair salon, *Travelsure* travel agency, T6344000, and duty-free liquor store. Tardieu Marine nearby will lift and dry storage. *Hummingbird Marina*, also nearby, has a restaurant. All locations charge a fee to anchored boats for use of shoreside facilities.

Touching down

Trinidad Piarco International Airport is 16 miles southeast of Port of Spain. An enormous new terminal opened in 2001. There is plenty of space, if few comfortable places to sit. Downstairs departure area has ATMs, several fast food restaurants (quiet one upstairs) and a *First Citizens Bank* foreign exchange office open 0600-2200, shops selling flowers and souvenirs. Inside departure area is a huge array of duty-free shops; upstairs for a fairly well-stocked bookshop, a bar and (very expensive) fast food. Try to avoid overnight connections here. Airline schedules ensure that it is possible to arrive at Piarco after the check-in counters have closed until next morning, so you cannot go through to the departure lounge. *Sky cap* has 24-hr left luggage service. If you are in transit always check that your bags have not been off-loaded at Piarco, some are not checked through despite assurances. Telephone (Companion) cards are for sale at the book stall close to Check-in (a long walk from Arrivals).

    Tobago Crown Point Airport is within walking distance of the hotels in the southwest. It is also uncomfortable for a long wait, often with no food available after you have been through immigration control. There are a few shops, snack bars and a bank with an ATM outside the terminal building but only a small duty-free inside.

Airlines offices *BWIA*, 30 Edward St, T6252470, F6252139, opens for reservations at 0800. Internet booking, www.bwee.com, is hassle-free but does not include some special deals so it can be more expensive. *BWIA* also at Piarco Airport, T6693000 (open later than Edward St office); at Carlton Centre, San Fernando, T6579712/6485; and at Crown Point Airport, Tobago, T6398741/2. *American Airlines*, 69 Independence Sq, T6277013, F6690261, at Piarco, T6694661. *Air Canada* is at Piarco, T6694065. *LIAT*, 9-11 Edward St, T6276274, at Piarco, T6695458, at Crown Point, T6390484. *Surinam Airways*, Cruise Ship Complex, Wrightson Rd, T6274747. *Caribbean Star* in Furness Building, Independence Sq. *Aeropostal*

Airport information
This is one of the few countries to charge departure tax to passengers arriving to change planes and leave same day; cheaper, therefore, to change planes in, say, Barbados

There is a 15% VAT on airline tickets purchased in Trinidad and Tobago

110-112 Frederick St, T6236641. *Rutaca* (to Maturin, Margarita, Barcelona, Puerto Ordaz), 16 Charles St, T6253708. *Air France* contact via *BWIA*, *Monarch Airlines* via *Tourist Services Ltd*, T6392285/6391103.

Safety

Care must be taken everywhere at night and walking on the beach after dark is not safe. Stick to main roads and look as if you know where you are going

The people of both islands are, as a rule, very friendly but several areas are no longer safe at night, especially for women. To the east of Charlotte St, Port of Spain becomes increasingly unsafe. You should avoid Laventille, Morvant and East Dry River at night. Central Port of Spain is fairly safe, even at night, as there are plenty of police patrols. Avoid the area around the port or bus terminal except when making a journey. Do not underestimate crime in Tobago. We have received reports of theft and muggings on the Pigeon Point road and parts of Scarborough are known to have crack houses. Do not walk in the Turtle Beach area after dark. There have also been attacks on tourists near waterfalls and in other beauty spots. Soft-top jeeps are at risk of theft. Leave nothing in them. If there is no safe where you are staying take your valuables (passport, tickets, etc) to a bank in Scarborough; the *Royal Bank* charges US$12 for 2 weeks. Women alone report feeling 'uncomfortable', particularly if they look like a tourist. Male and female prostitution has become a problem in Store Bay and elsewhere. HIV infection rates are high on both islands. Do not be tempted to dabble in narcotics. Penalties are severe and foreigners and their vehicles may be searched. 1 or 2 tourists have been killed as a result of suspected drug deals.

Where to stay

See pages 773 and 788 for further details

Hotels There are many hotels on the islands including some very good guesthouses and smaller hotels. Information about accommodation can be obtained from *TIDCO*, see Tourist information above. VAT (15%) is charged by all hotels and in most a 10% service charge is added to the bill. Some, like the *Hilton*, add a 2% surcharge.

Camping on **Trinidad** is unsafe and is not recommended. Try the Boca Islands to the west instead. On **Tobago**, it is possible near the Mt Irvine beach. Ask the taxi drivers for advice on where to head for.

Getting around

Air *BWIA*, T6272942, and *Tobago Express*, T6275162, fly the Trinidad to Tobago route offering lots of daily flights; the crossing takes 20 mins and costs US$35 return (check exchange rate; it's usually cheaper to pay in TT$). Departures, however, are often heavily booked at weekends and holidays, particularly Christmas and afterwards, also post-Carnival and Easter weekend (at other times tickets can often be bought the same day).

Road

Driving is on the left and the roads are narrow and winding

On **Trinidad** there are dual carriageways from Port of Spain south to San Fernando, west to Diego Martin and east to Arima, but other roads are not of a high standard. Neither is the driving. No-entry signs are misleadingly placed; some have a little notice underneath saying they apply only to public transport (private cars can enter). The rush hour on Trinidad starts early and ends late. Traffic is very heavy. Allow an hour or more to leave Port of Spain in the late afternoon. There are lots of pot-holes almost everywhere and traffic weaves about all over the place at high speed to avoid them. Allow a full day if going from Port of Spain to Toco in the northeast or to the far southwest, if you want to have time to see anything or relax before returning. On rural roads there are prominent kilometre posts. The older mile posts are still often there too and are used in some postal addresses (eg 21 mile post, Toco Road). In some of the more chaotic suburbs, light poles have a similar role (eg M Smith, opposite Light Pole 12, Smith Trace, Morvant). On **Tobago** the roads are fairly good in the south but badly maintained further north. The road between Charlotteville and Bloody Bay is no longer drivable even with 4WD vehicles. Speeds are such on this road that the butterflies overtake you; you are better off walking. Mountain bikes are fine if you can stand the hills and the heat.

International and most foreign driving licences are accepted for up to 90 days; after that you need to apply for a Trinidad and Tobago licence and take a written test. All drivers must always carry their licence and insurance with them. Documents are inspected at police road blocks.

which are frequent at night on many main roads. Do not leave anything in your car, theft is frequent. Be careful where you park in Port of Spain, police 'wreckers' are diligent and will tow the car away. It costs US$17 to retrieve it and you need to show every possible document. There are several car parks (eg Independence Sq and Pembroke St), mostly charging US$0.65 an hr.

Rental can be difficult on Trinidad, particularly at weekends and around Carnival, because of heavy demand. Best to make reservations in advance. Several companies do not accept credit cards, but require a considerable cash deposit. Small cars can be rented from US$25 a day upwards, unlimited mileage, check tyres before driving off. Deposit varies from company to company, as does method of payment, book in advance. Insurance (collision damage waiver) costs US$8. Many companies have offices at the airport.

Car hire
Some companies only rent for a minimum of three days

In Trinidad, the word 'taxi' includes most forms of public transport. The word 'travelling' means going by bus or taxi rather than by private car. Buses are run by the **PTSC**. A/c buses, **Express Commuter Service** (ECS), with a/c lounge for waiting passengers, run on main routes from City Gate Terminal to Arima, Chaguanas, Five Rivers and San Fernando, also from Arima to Sangre Grande. Rural buses are extremely infrequent. The *PTSC* office (T6237872) is located at the remodelled South Quay railway station, called City Gate, and is the main terminal for both buses and maxi taxis. You can get information showing how to reach the various sights by bus. **Unified Maxi Taxi Association** is T6243505.

Bus
On all routes, purchase your ticket at the kiosk before boarding the bus; you may have to tender the exact fare

On Tobago all buses originate in Scarborough. Schedules are changed or cancelled frequently. The route taxi system is difficult for the foreigner, being based on everyone knowing every car and therefore where it is going, but official route taxis have an H (for hire) at the start of the licence plate. Ask for directions for where to assemble for a particular route.

Taxis are expensive. **St Christopher's** taxis or airport taxis operate from the main hotels, *Ice House taxis*, T6276984, and **Independence Square Taxi Service**, T6253032, from Independence Sq. Helpful drivers approach all stray white people on Independence Sq, but this can be confusing if you are really looking for a route taxi (or a beer). There are fixed fares (eg US$20 to the airport during the day, US$30 after 2200), but agree on a price before the journey and determine whether the price is in TT$ or US$. Book ahead if you have a flight to catch. *Phone A Taxi* (T6288294 north, T6728294 central, T6588294 south), slightly cheaper day or night. Take a taxi if you have a complicated journey, or you have heavy baggage, or it is raining. At night it can be a lot cheaper than getting robbed. Route taxis (similar to colectivos) are very cheap but not as comfortable. These cannot easily be distinguished from ordinary taxis, so ask the driver. They travel along fixed routes, like buses, but have no set stops, so you can hail them and be dropped anywhere along the route. During rush hour they often pass full, however, and in general it takes time to master the system. They are the only means of transport on some suburban routes, such as to St Ann's, and in rural areas away from main roads. Travelling to remote areas may involve 3 or more taxis, not really a problem, just ask where the next 1 stops. Major routes run all night and are amazingly frequent during the day, others become infrequent or stop late at night. There are also 'pirate' taxis with the P registration of a private car, which cost the same as the ordinary taxis, although you can sometimes bargain with the drivers. Use these with caution; they are unlicensed and not insured for carrying paying passengers. Robberies have been reported. 'Ghost' taxis accept fares and drive off with your luggage as well – be warned.

Taxi
Look for cars with first letter H on licence plates (no other markings)

Hitchhiking is not common and is not advised anywhere – why take the risk when route taxis are cheap and frequent! Maxi-taxis are minibuses; they are frequent and go as fast as the traffic will allow, often a bit faster (see Transport, page 793).

Hitchhiking

Boats From Port of Spain to Tobago once a day at 1400 Mon-Fri and 1100 on Sun and public holidays, no crossings on Sat; return crossings from Scarborough at 2300 Mon-Fri and Sun, hrs. The trip can be rough. Tickets are sold at the Port Authority (T6392417 in Tobago or T6232901 ext 160 in Trinidad) on the docks, TT$50 economy class or TT$60 tourist class return, cabin for 2 TT$160 when available, children under 12 half price, under 3 free, office hrs Mon-Fri 0700-1500, 1600-1800, 1900-2200. Buy passage in advance, everyone will

Sea
Taking the ferry is time-consuming; it is easier to fly

Trinidad & Tobago

recommend you to queue at 0800, but 1000 is usually early enough. At peak times such as Christmas it is best to book several days ahead. You need a boarding pass and not just a ticket before you can board.

Keeping in touch

Media **Newspapers and books** The main daily papers are the Daily Express, the *Trinidad Guardian and Newsday*. The *Mirror* on Fri and Sun has interesting investigative journalism. *Tobago News* is weekly. There are several racier weekly papers which appear on Fri or Sat. *Punch, Bomb, Heat* and *Blast* are sensational tabloids. *Discover Trinidad and Tobago*, is published twice a year and distributed free to all visitors through hotels. **Radio** ICN Radio (610 AM), Radio Trinidad (730 AM), Music Radio (97 FM), 98.9 Yes FM, WABC (103 FM), ICN Radio (100 FM), Radio 95 FM, Radio Tempo (105 FM), Radio 96.1 FM, Rhythm (Radio 95.1 FM), Radio 1CN (91.1 FM), Sangeet (106.1 FM), Love Radio (94.1 FM), Gem Radio (93 FM), Central Radio (90.5 FM), Power (102 FM). **Television** 3 local TV stations: CCN TV is independent, TTT and The Information Channel are government-owned. There are 62 cable channels, mostly US, but also the BBC and Indian channels. Tobago has its own 56 channels, including Deutsche Welte TV.

Food and drink

Food Hotels and guesthouses serve a wide variety of European, American and traditional West
The variety of juices Indian (or Creole) dishes, including pork souse, black pudding, roast suckling pig, *sancoche*
and ice creams made and *callaloo* stews, and many others. There is also a strong East Indian influence and lots of
from local fruit is Chinese restaurants too. Seafood, particularly crab and shrimp, is excellent. Local oysters are
endless. Try the street cooked and sold around the Savannah (delicious, but a possible health risk). There is a local
vendors in St James fish called salmon, which is a white fish, no relation to the Scottish/Canadian variety. Smoked herring and salt cod are often eaten with a fried bake, especially for breakfast. The many tropical fruits and vegetables grown locally include the usual tropical fruits: large and juicy pineapples, pawpaws, very good sapodillas, and starchy eddoes and yam tanias. Citrus season is Jan-Mar, mangoes and avocados (locally called *zaboca*) come later in the year. Coconut water from a fresh nut is refreshing, usually sold around the Savannah, Port of Spain and on Independence Sq after dark, TT$3 per nut. A distinctive local herb is *chadon beni*.

The *roti*, a chapatti pancake which comes in various forms, filled with peppery stew, shrimp or vegetable curries, is very good, US$1.30 or so for vegetable, up to US$2.60 for shrimp. *Buss up shut* is a torn-up *paratha*, or Indian bread accompaniment to curries. *Pelau*, savoury peas and rice and meat cooked with coconut and pepper, is also good. Use the local pepper sauce in moderation unless you are accustomed to *chili* dishes. Try also *saheena*, deep-fried patties of spinach, dasheen, split peas and mango sauce. *Pholouri* are fritters made with split peas. *Buljol* is a salt fish with onions, tomatoes, avocado and pepper. *Callaloo* is a thick soup based on dasheen leaves. *Doubles* are curried chickpeas (*channa*) in 2 pieces of fried *barra* (mini pancakes). *Pastelles*, eaten at Christmas, are maize flour parcels stuffed with minced meat, olives, capers and raisins, steamed in a banana leaf. A *hops* is a crusty bread roll. If you go to Maracas Bay, have *shark-and-bake*, a spicy fried bread sandwich of fried shark with a variety of sauces such as tamarind, garlic, *chadon beni*; kingfish-and-bake, shrimp-and-bake are alternatives; also sugar cakes, made with grated coconut. Dumplings are a must on Tobago, particularly good with crab. A local sweet in Tobago is *benny balls*, made from sesame seeds.

Drink A local non-alcoholic drink is *mauby*, slightly bitter and made from the bark of a tree. Sorrel is a bright red Christmas drink made from hibiscus flowers. There is also ginger beer, and you can get sorrel and ginger beer shandy. Fresh lime juice is recommended; it is sometimes served with a dash of Angostura bitters. There are lots of rums to try, many of which are better without punch or Coke. Local beers are *Carib* and *Stag*, both owned by the same company, which also brews *Carlsberg, Mackeson, Royal Stout* and *Guinness*; *Samba* is a locally brewed independent. A good place to drink *Guinness* is the *Cricket Wicket*, in Tragarete Rd, opposite the Queen's Park Oval.

Holidays and festivals

New Year's Day, *Carnival* Mon and Tue before *Ash Wed* (not officially holidays), *Spiritual Shouter Baptist Liberation Day*, 30 Mar, *Good Fri*, *Easter Mon*, *Indian Arrival Day*, 30 May, celebrating the arrival of Indian labourers in 1845, *Corpus Christi*, *Labour Day*, 19 Jun, *Emancipation Da*y, 1 Aug, *Independence Day*, 31 Aug, *Republic Day*, 24 Sep, *Divali*, usually Nov (depends on Hindu religious calendar), *Eid ul-Fitr* (changes according to religious calendar, will be 24 Nov 2003 and 14 Nov 2004), *Christmas Day*, *Boxing Day*.

All Souls' Day (2 Nov) is not a holiday, but is celebrated, as is the Hindu festival of *Phagwa* (Feb/Mar) and the Shia Muslim festivals of *Hosay* (Feb or early Mar 2004-05).

Trinidad's carnival culminates each year on the 2 days before Ash Wed which marks the beginning of the Christian season of Lent (23-24 Feb 2004). In practice, the festivities start months ahead, with the *Mas' camps* abustle, the calypsonians performing most nights of the week and the impressive **Panorama** with competing steel bands at the Queen's Park Savannah stadium: preliminaries, semi-finals, then finals, which are held on Carnival Sat before Mas' proper. **Band launching parties**, where band leaders show off their costumes, start long before Christmas. **Calypso 'tents'**, where calypsoes are played, start in Jan. Try SWWTU Hall on Wrightson Rd, De Luxe Cinema on Keate St and Spektakula on Henry St. Panyards start practising every night even earlier. *Amoco Renegades* are at 17a Oxford St, Port of Spain; *Exodus* is at St John's Village on Eastern Main Rd, St Augustine; *Witco Desperadoes* are at Laventille Rd, Port of Spain; *BWIA Invaders* are opposite the Oval in Tragarete Rd. There are parties most of the time from then on. The biggest public fetes on successive weekends from Jan, then also midweek, at the fire service, flour mill, licensing authority, water authority (WASA), army, customs, etc, draw huge crowds. There is lots of crowd participation and flag-waving, a bit like a big football match. The largest is usually the PSA Caribbean Brass Festival in a sports field near Long Circular Rd. Getting a ticket in advance (slightly cheaper) from somewhere like *Rhyners Records* in Port of Spain or *Crosby's* in St James, or arriving early (eg 2130) saves a struggle at the gate; most go on until 0400-0500.

Fair-skinned visitors should avoid the skimpy costumes at carnival tramps. You will be two full days in the hot sun and sun block lasts about five minutes

Trinidad & Tobago

Panorama steel band finals are held on Carnival Sat before Dimanche Gras. Parties on Sun start early. The Dimanche Gras show at the Savannah that night has a little bit of everything. There are 2 main carnival shows for children: the Red Cross Kiddies Carnival 1 week before carnival proper, and the school-based children's carnival the following Sat. On Carnival Mon, the festivities start with *J'Ouvert* at 0400, which involves dressing up in the cheapest and most outlandish disguises available ('old mas'), including 'mud', which will inevitably be transferred to the spectators and is murder to wash out of your clothes. Starting mid-morning the *Parade of Bands* at the Savannah, features very large and colourful bands, portraying a wide sweep of historical and cultural events. Though the Savannah is the main venue, on Carnival Mon and Tue the bands march right around Port of Spain and are required to appear before the judges at other locations, including Independence Sq and Victoria Sq. Mon pm sees 'night mas' in St James, with few costumes but plenty of music; ditto on Tue until midnight. Ash Wed has big beach parties sponsored by radio stations, usually at Maracas and Manzanilla, very heavy traffic. (Big beach parties also at Easter.)

Night events and big pre-Carnival parties are fairly safe, but exercise caution; there is plenty of pickpocketing and a small number of stabbings, policing has been tighter since the murder of an American after a street robbery in 2002

Tickets for all National Carnival Commission shows (about US$10 for most events) are sold at the Queen's Park Savannah, where the shows are held. You can join one of the Mas' camps by looking in the newspaper for the times and locations of the camps (or use the internet, see below). If you are early enough you can get a costume, which will allow you to participate in one of the 'tramps' through town. The Tourist Office has a list of names and addresses of the bands you can contact in advance to organize a costume (US$120 and more). There is a lot of alcohol consumed during the road marches but no drunken brawls. Police are much in evidence on the streets. Note that it is illegal to sell tapes of carnival artists but 'bootleg' tapes and CDs are inevitably sold. If you have the strength, *Last Lap*, involves jumping up with a steel band around Port of Spain to squeeze the last ounce out of the festival, prior to its official end at midnight on Tue. Leave in time to beat the morning traffic ahead of the enormous beach parties at Manzanilla and Maracas on Ash Wednesday.

Useful contact details: *National Carnival Commission*, www.carnivalncc.com, T6271350; *National Carnival Bands Association*, T6271422; *Pan Trinbago*, www.pantrinbago.com, T6234486; *Trinbago Unified Calypsonians Association*, T6275912, truekaiso@hotmail.com

Tobago's carnival is very quiet compared with Trinidad's. On Easter Mon and Tue, there are crab, goat and donkey races at Buccoo Village (see box page 788).

Other festivals There is a festival or special event of some kind just about every week of the year in Trinidad. **Point Fortin Borough Week** is in late **Apr**, early **May**, with steel bands and street parties. **La Divina Pastora**, in the southern town of Siparia in May, celebrated by Catholics and Hindus. **St Peter's Day** in Carenage is the first weekend in **Jul**. **The Hosay**, or Hosein Festival, commemorating the murder of Mohammed's sons-in-law, Hussein and Hassan, starts 10 days after the first appearance of the new moon in the Moharrun month of the Moslem calendar (late-**Feb** or early-**Mar** 2004). These are Shia festivals, commemorating a defeat by the Sunni. Most Trinidad Muslims are Sunni and disapprove of the event; the drumming is increasingly late at night; in recent years this has sharply reduced the casual crowd. Although beer and rum are consumed, try not to flaunt it immediately around the *tajjas*. Also celebrated is the Muslim festival of **Eid ul-Fitr**, marking the end of Ramadan. 2 principal Hindu festivals are **Phagwa**, or Holi, the colour, or spring, festival on the day of the full moon in the month of Phagun (**Feb/Mar**), and **Divali**, the festival of lights, usually in **Nov**. At Phagwa everyone gets squirted with brightly coloured dyes (*abeer*); strict Hindus have their doubts about some of the dancing styles. The main event is usually at Tunapuna Hindu School. Divali is more of a family affair and involves a lot of rather good food in Indian homes, with pretty oil lamps or *deyas* burning outside. The display at Felicity in central Trinidad is spectacular, but go early to avoid the traffic. On 29 **Aug** in Arima the **Feast of St Rose of Lima** is celebrated; the parish church is dedicated to her. Descendants of the original Amerindians come from all over the island to walk in solemn procession round the church (see below, Arima).

The **Tobago Heritage Festival** lasts for the second fortnight of **Jul**, with historical re-enactments, variety shows and parades.

Flora and fauna

Trinidad combines the species of the Caribbean chain from Jamaica to Grenada with the species of the continental rainforests of South America The rainforests of the **Northern Range** running along the north coast and the wetlands on the east and west coast are more extensive, more dense and display a greater diversity of fauna and flora than any other ecosystems in the Caribbean. The **Forestry Division** (Long Circular Rd, St James, Port of Spain, T6227476, information on guided tours and hikes) has designated many parts of Trinidad and Tobago as national parks, wildlife reserves and protected areas. On Trinidad, the national parks are the Caroni and Nariva Swamps, Chaguaramas, and Madamas, Maracas and Matura in the north range of hills.

Wetlands Trinidad has mangrove swamps, fresh swamps, grassy freshwater marshes, palm marshes and water-logged savannah land, covering 7,000 acres of the Central Plain. A permit from the Forestry Division is necessary for trips into restricted areas such as the Nariva Swamp and Bush Bush Island in the Aripo Scientific Reserve; 72 hrs' notice is required; visit with a guide who can arrange it for you.

The **Nariva Swamp**, the largest freshwater swamp in Trinidad, is a Wetland of International Importance under the Ramsar Convention. It contains hardwood forest and is home to red howler monkeys and the weeping capuchin as well as 55 other species of mammal of which 32 are bats. Birds include the savannah hawk and the red-breasted blackbird. A tour by kayak is recommended (*Caribbean Discovery Tours*, T6247281) as you will see more than you would on a motor boat. You paddle silently across fields of giant water lilies, through channels in the thick forest of mangroves and towering silk cotton trees, with monkeys and parrots chattering overhead. The **Caroni Swamp** is usually visited in the late afternoon as it is the roosting place of scarlet ibis and egrets. No permit is necessary, see below, 'Around the island'.

The **Northern Range Sanctuary**, Maracas, or **El Tucuche Reserve**, is a forest on the second-highest peak, at 3,072 ft, covering 2,313 acres. The slopes are covered with forest giants such as the silk cotton trees, which carry creepers and vines. The thick forest canopy of mahogany, balata, palms and flowering trees like the poui and immortelle provides cover and maintains a cool, damp environment no matter the heat of the day. The interesting flora and fauna include giant bromeliads and orchids, the golden tree frog and the orange-billed nightingale-thrush. There are several hiking trails, the most popular of which is from Ortinola estate; guides can be hired. The 7-mile trek to the peak takes 5 hrs through dense forest; the views from the top are spectacular; for information contact the *Field Naturalists' Club* (see below).

Rainforests
Walking alone is not recommended in the northern hills; join a group or at least walk with someone who knows the trails well

The **Trinity Hills Wildlife Sanctuary** lies west of Guayaguayare and was founded in 1934. Its forests are home to a large variety of birds, monkeys, armadillos and opossums. Permits must be obtained from the Petroleum Company of Trinidad and Tobago (Petrotrin) in Pointe-a-Pierre.

The **Valencia Wildlife Sanctuary** contains at least 50 species of birds including antbirds and tanagers. Several mammals live here: deer, quenk, agouti, tatoo. Near Valencia is the **Arena Forest**, one of 10 recreation parks, while 5 areas have been designated scenic landscapes (Blanchisseuse, Maracas and Toco-Matelot on the north coast, Cocos Bay on the Atlantic, and Mount Harris on the Southern Rd, south of Sangre Grande). Permission to visit certain forests and watershed areas must be obtained from the *Water and Sewerage Authority* (WASA), Farm Rd, Valsayn, St Joseph. Permits for Hollis Reservoir have been suspended until further notice. Although about 46% of the island remains forested, there is concern about the loss of wildlife habitats, with damage from hunting, illegal logging and clearing of wetland for rice cultivation.

On Tobago, apart from 2 national parks (**Buccoo Reef** and the virgin and secondary forests of east Tobago), there are the **Goldsborough natural landmark**, the **Kilgwyn scientific reserve**, the **Grafton nature conservation area**, the **Parlatuvier-Roxborough scenic landscape**, and three recreation parks (including Mount Irvine). At the **Grafton Bird Sanctuary** some of the world's most beautiful birds, the blue crowned mot mots, are fed at 0800 and 1600 at the Old Copra House. They are not tame enough to be hand-fed but it is still a spectacular sight. Many of the small islands (Saut d'Eau, Kronstadt Island and Soldado Rock off Trinidad, and Little Tobago, see below, St Giles and Marble Islands off Tobago) are reserves for wildlife and are important breeding grounds for red-billed tropic birds, frigate birds, man-o-war and other seabirds.

It is possible to do voluntary work with Environment Tobago, Robinson St, Rollocks Building, Scarborough, T6607462

Many flowering trees can be seen: pink and yellow poui, frangipani, cassia, pride of India, immortelle, flamboyant, jacaranda. Among the many types of flower are hibiscus, poinsettia, chaconia (wild poinsettia – the national flower), ixora, bougainvillea, orchid, ginger lily and heliconia. The *Horticultural Society of Trinidad and Tobago* (PO Box 252) has its office on Lady Chancellor Rd, Port of Spain, T6226423.

Flora

The islands boast 60 types of bat, and other mammals include the Trinidad capuchin and red howler monkeys, brown forest brocket (deer), collared peccary (quenk), manicou (opossum), agouti, rare ocelot and armadillo. A small group of manatees is being protected in a reserve in the Nariva Swamp. Other reptiles include iguanas and 47 species of snakes, of which few are poisonous: the fer-de-lance (locally, *mapipire*), bushmaster and 2 coral snakes. The variety of fauna on Tobago is larger than on other similar-sized islands because of its one-time attachment to South America. It is home to 210 different bird species, 123 different butterfly species, 16 types of lizards, 14 kinds of frogs, 2 dozen species of snakes (all of them harmless), and it has some spectacled caymans at Hillsborough Dam.

Fauna

Trinidad and Tobago together have more species of birds than any other Caribbean island, although the variety is South American, not West Indian. No species is endemic, but Tobago has 13 species of breeding birds not found on Trinidad. Most estimates say that there are 433 species of bird, including 41 hummingbirds, parrots, macaws, the rare red-breasted blackbird, the nightingale-thrush and the mot mot. There are also 622 recorded species of butterfly. The most accessible birdwatching sites are the **Caroni Bird Sanctuary**, the **Asa Wright Centre**, the Caurita Plantation and the **Wild Fowl Trust**.

The aboriginal name for the island of Trinidad was leri, which just means 'island'

Trinidad & Tobago

Books Recommended is *A Guide to the Birds of Trinidad and Tobago*, by Richard ffrench (Macmillan Caribbean), with introductory information on rainfall, the environment and vegetation as well as birds. *Birds of Trinidad and Tobago*, also by Richard ffrench (M Caribbean Pocket Natural History Series), is a shorter guide with colour photos of 83 of the more common species. *Birds of Trinidad and Tobago – A Photographic Atlas*, by Russell Barrow (MEP Trinidad, 1994), has clear and striking pictures. *Views from the Ridge* by Prof Julian Kenny (MEP Trinidad, mep@wow.net), a respected local biologist, is beautifully produced and illustrated. *The Trinidad and Tobago Field Naturalists' Club Trail Guide*, by Paul Comeau, Louis Guy, Ewoud Heesterman and Clayton Hull, was published in 1992, 288 pages on 48 trails, difficult to obtain. ffrench and Bacon's *Nature Trails of Trinidad*, first published in 1982, has been revised by Dr Victor Quesnel and reissued by SM Publications Ltd under the auspices of the Asa Wright Nature Centre. Each Oct Trinidad and Tobago hold **Natural History Festivals** to foster understanding of the islands' flora and fauna. The **Trinidad Field Naturalists Club**, PO Box 642, Port of Spain (T6248017 evenings only), organizes walks on Sun.

Diving and marine life

Coral reefs flourish almost all round Tobago

The waters around Tobago are becoming known as an unspoilt diving destination and several dive shops have started operations. Most species of hard and soft corals can be found, and there is a huge brain coral, believed to be one of the world's largest, off Little Tobago, which you can see on a glass-bottom boat tour. The Guyana current flows round the south and east shores of Tobago and supports a large variety of marine life. Dive sites are numerous and varied, with walls, caves, canyons, coral gardens and lots of fish. There is exciting drift diving but it is not recommended for novices. You are swept along the coral reef at up to 5 knots while, high above, manta rays flap lazily to remain stationary in the current as they sieve out the plankton. Snorkelling is also excellent almost everywhere, with good visibility. Some of the most popular sites are **Arnos Vale**, **Pirate's Bay**, **Store Bay**, **Man O'War Bay** and **Batteaux Bay**. In 1997 a new site was added, with the sinking of the *Scarlet Ibis*, renamed the *Maverick*, a 350-ft roll-on/roll-off ship. This artificial reef lies 100 ft deep on a sandy bed and already coral is growing and schools of fish are being attracted to the wreck.

The most varied marine wildlife off Trinidad is found in the channels called the **Bocas**, between the islands off the northwest peninsula (The Dragon's Mouth). However, the currents are cold, so protective gear is essential. At many north coast beaches, particularly Macqueripe on the west peninsula, a few miles north of the marinas, the diving and snorkelling are safer, if less spectacular. The waters flowing from the Orinoco around Trinidad reduce visibility, but the sea is full of nutrients. There is lots to see but you may not be able to see it,

Turtle-watching tours are organized by the Asa Wright Nature Centre

especially in the rainy season. The leatherback turtle nests Mar-Sep on several beaches on Trinidad (Matura, Fishing Pond on east coast, Paria, Tacaribe and Grande Riviere on north coast) and Tobago (Great Courland Bay known as Turtle Beach, Stonehaven Bay, Bloody Bay and Parlatuvier), up to 8 times a season, laying 75 to 120 eggs each time about 10 days apart. Incubation is 60 days.

Dive centres

The Association of Dive Operators in Tobago, T639703/ 6391279, keeps a list of operators who meet their safety standards

There is a full list in *Discover Trinidad and Tobago*. **Tobago Dive Experience**, office T6397034, also at *Manta Lodge*, T6604888, and the *Turtle Beach*, T6350320, is the only company to offer both NAUI and PADI certification, www.tobagodiveexperience.com **Aquamarine Dive Ltd** (Keith and Alice Darwent) is at *Blue Waters Inn*, Speyside, T6605445, F6394416, amdtobago@trinidad.net *(Blue Waters Inn* tends to be full throughout the year so book early.)* This is a 5-star PADI facility, dives are around Little Tobago and all escorted by at least 2 dive masters because of the currents. Full range of courses available. **Man Friday Diving**, Charlotteville, T/F6604676, mfdiving@tstt.tt, covers the area from Charlotteville to Speyside. Other dive operators include **Pro Scuba**, *Rovanel's Resort*, Store Bay, T6397424, proscuba@tstt.net.tt Several more companies are involved in diving, fishing and other watersports, but are not listed here. A single tank dive costs on average US$35, night dives US$45, PADI Open Water course US$300, rental of BCD and regulator US$6-7, mask, fins and snorkel US$8-10.

Beaches and watersports

Close to Port of Spain, **Chaguaramas** is dirty, but if you drive north through Tucker Valley, **Macqueripe** is a small beach in a pretty, wooded bay, with surprisingly good snorkelling (car park TT$5 at weekends). **Scotland Bay**, near the northwest tip of the island, is very pretty but can only be reached by boat. **Maracas Bay**, 10 miles from the capital, has a sheltered sandy beach fringed with coconut palms; despite small waves there can be a dangerous undertow here and at other beaches, and drownings have occurred; do not swim far out and watch the markers. Swim at the east end away from the river mouth. Crowded on Sun but fairly quiet otherwise. Lifeguards are on duty until 1800; there are changing rooms, showers etc, car parking and cabanas for beach vendors. Try shark-and-bake, shark meat in a heavy fried dough, a Maracas speciality, very tasty, sold all along the beach. There are route taxis from Park St, but all transport is irregular and infrequent. Easy at weekends but less so during the week. Difficulties in catching the bus have led travellers to recommend car hire or taxis: from Port of Spain a hotel or *Ice House* taxi costs US$25.

Next to Maracas Bay is **Tyrico Bay** (surfing, lifeguard, another horseshoe-shaped beach with undertow). **Las Cuevas**, also on the north coast (changing rooms, showers, lifeguards, surfing is good here but beware of the sandflies in the wet season), is a picturesque bay with fishing boats moored at the east end. The west end is very beautiful, but take care of the current; no lifeguards. Even at weekends most of the beach is empty. There are smaller beaches at **La Fillette** and at **Blanchisseuse** where one beach has a sweet water lagoon where the river runs into the sea. The place is kept clean by the owners of *Cocos Hut* restaurant/*Laguna Mar Beach Resort*, who are establishing a 28-acre nature reserve on the banks of the river. Eric has kayaks to rent (TT$20, T6693032) which you can paddle up river. There are lots of birds but also mosquitoes and sandflies. Leatherback turtles come on to Blanchisseuse beach in the nesting season. The coast road ends at Blanchisseuse. At the northeast end of the island, near Toco, are a number of bays, including Balandra for good bathing, reached by a separate road via Sangre Grande and Toco.

The Atlantic coast from Matura to Mayaro is divided into three huge sweeping bays, with enormous palm trees in some places. Of these bays **Mayaro** and **Manzanilla** both have beautiful sandy beaches, but the Atlantic currents can make swimming dangerous. There are several beach houses to rent at Mayaro, heavily booked in peak holiday periods, some are poor, check beforehand. Manzanilla has public facilities and a hotel. From nearby Brigand Hill Lighthouse, a TSTT signal station, you can get a wonderful view of the east coast, the Nariva Swamp and much of Trinidad. Light patches of green are rice fields encroaching illegally on the swamp. In the southwest, near La Brea and the Pitch Lake, is the resort of Vessigny. The southwest, or Cedros, peninsula is a 3-hr car trip from Port of Spain to unspoilt beaches and miles of coconut palm plantations. Generally, the beaches are difficult to get to except by taxi or car.

Tobago is noted for its beaches, 2 of the best being only mins from the airport: **Store Bay**, popular with locals, lots of vendors, food stalls and glass-bottom boats; and **Pigeon Point**, a picture-postcard beach fringed with palms with calm, shallow water protected by **Buccoo Reef**. You have to pay to use the facilities at the beach (US$2), but you get changing space, umbrellas and beach bars. Here also there are lots of glass-bottom boats going out to Buccoo Reef and a catamaran for coastal tours and swimming in the Nylon Pool, a shallow area offshore. Other good beaches on the leeward side of the island are **Stone Haven Bay**, **Mount Irvine Bay** and **Courland Bay**, one of the longest. All have resort hotels and watersports. **Englishman's Bay** is another lovely bay, with the forest coming down to the beach and a river running into the sea. The east coast is more rugged and windswept. **Hillsborough Bay**, just outside Scarborough, has a glorious beach, but the sea is dangerous because of rip tides. Do not swim there. **Big Bacolet Bay**, also known as Minister Bay, is great for surfing, body surfing and boogie boarding, but watch out for the currents. In the northeast, **King's Bay** has a beach bar, toilets and huts for shade. There is a signpost to the beach, almost opposite the track to **King's Bay Waterfall**. **Speyside** and **Charlotteville** both have protected bays. From the former you can take glass-bottom boat trips to **Little Tobago** with birdwatching, walking and snorkelling included (about US$12.50) and from the latter you can walk to Pirate's Bay through the forest. Snorkelling is good on the reef here.

Trinidad & Tobago

Sailing Yachting has become big business in Trinidad and there are now several marinas attracting custom from other islands more at risk from hurricanes, with 2,850 visiting craft in 2001. Provisioning is excellent and there are boat repair and maintenance facilities; local teak costs a fraction of US prices, workmen are highly skilled, services are tax-free and spare parts can be imported duty free. Marinas have both dry storage and stern-to docks. Facilities have also been built at **Courland Bay**, Tobago, to attract the yachting crowd.

Every Jul/Aug, there is a power boat race from the *Trinidad and Tobago Yacht Club* (TTYC), Trinidad to Store Bay, Tobago. The **Trinidad and Tobago Sailing Association (TTSA)** T6344210 sponsors Carnival Fun Race and a weekly racing programme in winter and spring. Each year Tobago has a sailing week in May, sponsored by *Angostura and Yachting World* magazine; many crewing possibilities, lots of parties.

For surfing or windsurfing, contact the **Surfing Association of Trinidad and Tobago**, T6230920, and the **Windsurfing Association of Trinidad and Tobago**, T6288908.

Kayaking (including tuition) is available at many hotels on Tobago or at the **Chaguaramas Kayak Centre**, run by Merryl See Tai, 500 m after the Alcoa dock, just before Pier One, T6337871. You can hire kayaks for use in the bay or go on excursions along the coast, up rivers (eg at Blanchisseuse on Sun) or to the Bush Bush Sanctuary in the Nariva Swamp. Walking tours and overnight expeditions also arranged.

Fishing Charters can be arranged, for deep-sea fish or bonefish and tarpon in the mangroves and flats. Prices for deep-sea fishing are around US$250 for 4 hrs, US$400 for 8 hrs, maximum 6 people and for bonefishing US$150 for 4 hrs, maximum 3 people. On Tobago contact Capt Gerard 'Frothy' De Silva, Friendship Estate, Canaan, T6397108. He has a custom-built, 38-ft sports-fishing boat, *Hard Play*, and 2 23-ft skiffs for flats fishing. The annual International Game Fishing Classic is held Feb/Mar, the Kingfish Tournament in Jun and a Funfish Tournament in Nov. Contact the **Trinidad and Tobago Game Fishing Association**, T6245304, for information.

Trinidad

Port of Spain

IDD code: 868
Colour map 5, grid C6
Population: 51,000
(350,000 including
suburbs)

Port of Spain lies on a gently sloping plain between the Gulf of Paria and the foothills of the Northern Range. It is a busy port city with constant coming and going of shipping as well as being an important financial centre and business hub. All the multicultural aspects of Trinidad can be found here, it is full of life and an exciting city. Restaurants abound for every conceivable cuisine, the capital is renowned for its delicious food, while at night the clubs and bars offer a variety of music going on into the early hours. A little of the fretwork wooden architecture remains among the modern concrete and office towers; many of the main buildings of interest are within easy reach of the port.

Getting there
& around
See also pages
754 and 782

The taxi fare from **Piarco Airport** to Arouca is US$7 and to the centre of Port of Spain is US$20, to Maraval US$24, Diego Martin US$27, San Fernando US$31 (50% more after 2200). Taxi despatchers find taxis for new arrivals, ask to see the notice board or rate card for taxi fares. Unlicensed taxis outside the main parking area charge less, depending on the volume of business, at your own risk. Public transport is at some distance. From the roundabout at the end of the airport terminal approach road you can catch a route taxi to highway or to Arouca (US$0.30), then take a route taxi or maxi-taxi from the junction into Port of Spain (US$0.90). People are very helpful if you need to ask. There are also a few buses, see Transport page 781. Tickets are not available at the airport. From City Gate terminal you will have to walk to Independence or Woodford Sq for a route taxi. This is not advisable at night, especially if carrying luggage. Take a taxi.

You can see most of the sights of Port of Spain by walking around the town centre. For further afield, however, there are taxis, buses, route taxis and maxi-taxis.

Things to do in Trinidad

- Drive along the coast to **Blanchisseuse**; swim in the river and walk through the forest.
- See the winding roads of the **Central Range**. Lunch off fresh oranges and stop at a bar.
- Stroll round the **Savannah** at sunset. Drink the water from a coconut and eat oysters.
- Lime on the **Brian Lara Promenade** on a Friday evening or lime all day at a **cricket match** in the Oval.
- Get ready for **Carnival** – band launchings, big fetes, Panorama, J'Ouvert.

The Tourism and Industrial Development Company of Trinidad and Tobago Ltd (TIDCO), 10-14 Phillips St, 3rd Floor, Port of Spain, T6231932, 623-INFO, F6233848, tourism-info@tidco.co.tt, lists of hotels, restaurants, tour operators, monthly schedule of events, maps for sale, etc. The office at the airport, T6695196, is helpful with hotel or guesthouse reservations for your first night (maps of Trinidad and Port of Spain for sale). *The National Carnival Commission* is at Queen's Park W, Port of Spain, T6271350, nccmac@tstt.net.tt

   Maps Large-scale and island-wide maps of both Trinidad and Tobago can be bought from the *Lands and Survey Division*, 118 Frederick St, T6279204. Some areas are out of print.

Tourist information
For safety issues in Trinidad and Tobago, see page 754

On the south side of **Woodford Square**, named after former Governor Sir Ralph Woodford, is the fine **Anglican Cathedral Church of the Holy Trinity** (consecrated 1823), with an elaborate hammer-beam roof festooned with carvings. It was built during Woodford's governorship (1813-28) and contains a very fine monument to him. The **Red House** (completed 1907) contains the House of Representatives, the Senate and various government departments. It was the scene of an attempted overthrow of the Robinson Government by armed black Muslim rebels in July 1990. The rebels held the Prime Minister and several of his Cabinet captive for five days before surrendering to the Army. On the west side of the Red House, at the corner of St Vincent and Sackville Streets, the former Police Headquarters, which the rebels firebombed before launching their assault on the Red House, has been rebuilt. The first Red House on this site was destroyed by fire in 1903 during riots over an increase in water rates. On the opposite side of the square to the cathedral are the modern Hall of Justice and the City Hall, with a fine relief sculpture on the front. A new National Library is nearby.

   On **Independence Square** (two blocks south of Woodford Square) is the **Roman Catholic Cathedral of the Immaculate Conception**, built on the shore-line in 1832 but since pushed back by land reclamation. The central area of Independence Square, from the cruise ship complex to the cathedral, has been made into an attractive pedestrian area, known as the **Brian Lara Promenade** in honour of the Trinidadian cricketer and former West Indies captain. This is lively in the evening with people liming, drinking beer or playing chess. Behind the cathedral is **Columbus Square**, with a brightly painted statue of the island's European discoverer. South of Independence Square, between Edward and St Vincent Streets, is the financial complex, two tall towers and **Eric Williams Plaza**, housing the Central Bank and Ministry of Finance. A little to the south of the square, the old neoclassical railway station, now known as **City Gate**, is a transport hub for taxis and buses travelling between Port of Spain and eastern Trinidad. Close to the waterfront is the **San Andres fort**, built about 1785 to protect the harbour, and a lighthouse which has settled into the ground with a rakish tilt.

   To the north of the city is **Queen's Park Savannah**, a large open space with many playing fields and a favourite haunt of joggers. It was the site of Trinidad's main racecourse for decades, until racing was centralized in Arima. In the middle of the Savannah is the Peschier cemetery, still owned and used by the family who used to own the Savannah. Below the level of the Savannah are the Rock Gardens, with lily ponds and flowers. Opposite are the **Botanic Gardens**, founded in 1818 by Sir Ralph Woodford. There is an amazing variety of tropical and sub-tropical plants from Southeast Asia and South America, as well as indigenous trees and shrubs.

Sights
The 'University of Woodford Square' is Trinidad's equivalent to Speaker's Corner in London's Hyde Park

Fresh coconuts, oysters and Indian snacks are on sale in the afternoons and evenings around the Savannah

Trinidad & Tobago

Adjoining the gardens is the small Emperor Valley Zoo, dating from 1952, which specializes in animals living wild on the island. It has a number of reptiles, including iguanas, four species of boas and the spectacled caiman. ■ *0930-1800, no tickets after 1730. TT$4, children 3-12 TT$2.* Also next to the gardens is the presidential residence, a colonial-style building in an 'L' shape in honour of Governor James Robert Longden (1870-74). Just off the Savannah (on St Ann's Road) is **Queen's Hall**, where concerts and other entertainments are given.

For a history of Port of Spain buildings, with illustrations, read Voices In The Street, by Olga J Marrogordato (Inprint Caribbean Ltd 1977, but out of print)

There are several other Edwardian-colonial mansions along the west side of Queen's Park Savannah, built in 1904-10 and known as the **Magnificent Seven**. From south to north, they are Queen's Royal College; Hayes Court, the residence of the Anglican Bishop; Prada's House, or Mille Fleurs; Ambard's House, or Roomor; the Roman Catholic Archbishop's residence; White Hall, which has regained its status as the Prime Minister's office after a no-expense-spared restoration; and Killarney, also known as Stollmeyer's Castle (now owned by the Government). Apart from Hayes Court, which was built in 1910, all were built in 1904. A walk along the north and west sides of the Savannah is best in the early morning (before it gets too hot), arriving outside Queen's Royal College as the students are arriving and the coconut sellers are turning up outside. The Anglican Church of All Saints at 13 Queen's Park West is also worth a visit; its stained-glass windows are recently restored. Knowsley, another 1904 building, and the new headquarters of the BP

Trinidad

Amoco Oil Company, formerly the historic *Queen's Park Hotel* (1895), both on the south side of the Savannah, are interesting too.

Just off the Savannah, at the corner of Frederick and Keate streets, is the small **National Museum**, in the former Royal Victoria Institute. It has sections on petroleum and other industries, Trinidad and Tobago's natural history, geology, archaeology and history, carnival costumes and photographs of kings and queens, and art exhibitions (including a permanent exhibition of the work of the 19th-century landscape artist, M J Cazabon, see also page 796). ■ *Tue-Sat 1000-1800, Sun 1400-1800. Free. T6235941.*

Suburbs

The suburbs around Port of Spain vary considerably, some are desirable places to live, others are to be avoided (see Safety, page 754). To the east is Sea Lots, a rough squatter area on the shoreline. Beetham Estate is even rougher public housing along the highway. Laventille is a working-class hillside suburb, breezy with good views, two big water tanks, Our Lady of Laventille and the Desperadoes panyard (see Carnival, page 757). For a pleasant drive in the hills with attractive views of city, sea and mountains, go up Lady Young Road, about 2 miles from Savannah, to a lookout 563 ft above sea level (not on a taxi route, but some cars take this route from the airport), or Lady Chancellor Road (not always safe, even by car), or go up to the Laventille Hills to see the view from the tower of the shrine of **Our Lady of Laventille**. In the northeast,

Belmont is a rather run-down area of older housing. **Cascade** is a pretty valley with houses stretching up the hillsides. St Ann's is another pretty valley with the Prime Minister's residence (La Fantasie) and the psychiatric hospital. To the northwest, Newtown is crowded, commercial and run-down, while St Clair is spacious, expensive and quiet. Maraval is in the next valley with the road running through it to Maracas on the coast (heavy rush hour traffic). Away from the city centre, to the west of Port of Spain, is the suburb of **Woodbrook**; Ariapita Avenue, is full of restaurants and pubs, while **St James** is known as the city that never sleeps. In Ethel Street there is a large new Hindu temple, the Port of Spain Mandir, and on Nepaul Street is the childhood home of writer VS Naipaul. From **Fort George**, a former signal station at 1,100 ft, there are also excellent views. The fort was built around 1804 and formerly called La Vigie. Although it was never used to defend the island, in times of danger people from Port of Spain brought their valuables up here for safe keeping. To reach it take the St James route taxi from Woodford Square and ask to get off at Fort George Road. From there it is about one hour's walk uphill passing through some fairly tough residential territory. You can get a taxi from Bournes Road, St James, if you don't fancy the walk, or take a taxi up and walk down.

Port of Spain

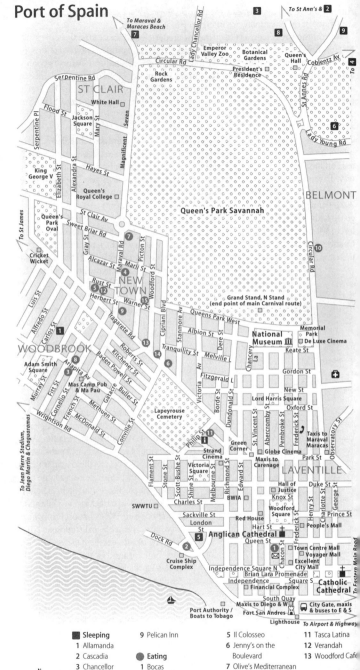

Trinidad & Tobago

N

0 metres 100
0 yards 100

■ Sleeping	9 Pelican Inn	5 Il Colosseo	11 Tasca Latina
1 Allamanda		6 Jenny's on the	12 Verandah
2 Cascadia	● Eating	Boulevard	13 Woodford Café
3 Chancellor	1 Bocas	7 Olive's Mediterranean	
4 Coblentz Inn	2 Breakfast Shed	Bistro	● Bars & clubs
5 Crowne Plaza	3 Chutney Rose &	8 Plantation House	14 Martin's & Syps
6 Hilton	Roxan's	9 Swan Chinese	15 Rafters
7 Kapok	4 Hot Shoppe &	10 Tamnak Thai	
8 Normandie	Jerk Pork Centre	& Apsara	

Around the island

Midway along the Western Main Road to Chaguaramas a road runs off to the north, through the residential area of Diego Martin. At the north end of the Diego Martin Valley, the **Blue Basin** waterfall and natural landmark, is about a five-minute walk along a path from the road. (Visit the falls in a group if possible to avoid being robbed and if you do leave your car to visit the fall, leave nothing of value in it.) At the nearby River Estate is a waterwheel which was once the source of power for a sugar plantation.

The Western Main Road offers many pretty views, especially of the Five Islands and the nearby Carrera island prison, and runs on past West Mall in Westmoorings, a featureless modern suburb. From here the road continues along the coast past the *Trinidad and Tobago Yacht Club (TTYC)* (opposite Goodwood Park, where the rich live) and to **Carenage**, where there is a fish market and a little church, St Peter's Chapel, on the waterside. **St Peter's Day festival**, the first weekend in July, is a mini-Carnival with street parties running late into the night, music and steel pan, but no costumes. On the Sunday there is a religious service, the original core of the celebration, but now barely visible. The Alcoa transhipment facility for Guyanese bauxite is next and then the *Kayak Centre*, T6337871, which also has mountain bikes, before you are into **Chaguaramas**, on the bay of the same name. On your left is Pier One, a small marina with restaurant and entertainment facilities, popular at weekends, and further along is Chagville, a dirty public beach opposite the Chaguaramas Convention Centre, with a KFC and some small bars. This area used to belong to the US Navy 1945-64 but is now under the control of the Chaguaramas Development Authority (CDA), T6344364. Most of the old military buildings are still there, with new uses.

Just after the police post which marks the start of the old military base, turn right for the **Tucker Valley**. The old village on the right was emptied to make way for US forces; a half-ruined church and a cemetery can still be seen. The main road leads to a car park, TT$5, with steps down to the Macqueripe beach. On a clear day you can see the Güiria peninsula of Venezuela. Turnings to the left from the main road lead to the Chaguaramas public golf course; the club house is a good place for a drink. Cliff-top paths from the car park run to the headland to the east and a longer one to the west leads eventually to the golf club. Also from the golf course is the short trail to **Edith Falls**, a nice walk, but there is barely a trickle of water in the falls except after heavy rain. Just south of the beach an asphalted road to the east is usually barred to vehicles. On foot, it leads to the cliff tops and eventually to the North Post at the head of the **Diego Martin Valley**. A good walk, but getting back is a problem unless you arrange for a car at the other end.

Further along the coast road, the **Chaguaramas Military History and Aviation Museum** has exhibitions on VE Day and Trinidad's role in both world wars with intricate models as well as relics. ■ *Entry through military checkpoint. TT$10 adults, TT$5 children. T6344391, knowledgeable staff.* Next you come to the Sailing Association, Power Boats, Peake's and Industrial Marine Services (IMS), all offering services to the yachting clientele; the area is packed with boats stacked on land or in the water. ■ *Buses from Port of Spain to Chaguaramas run about every 30 mins, TT$2.*

From *Island Property Owners Association* (T6344331 or 6344443), the last boatyard west of Chaguaramas, you can get a launch (known locally as a *pirogue*) to the offshore islands which dot the Bocas, between Trinidad and Venezuela. Usual return fares for a boat with up to 6 people are TT$100 per boat to **Gaspar Grande** (**Gasparee Caves**, TT$5), TT$120 to Scotland Bay beach (no road access), TT$400 to **Chacachacare** (a larger island with ruins of a former leper colony and several good beaches), or TT$150 per hour for just touring around. Extra passengers can be squeezed in for an extra charge, within safety limits. Pier One also does tours to Chacachacare, Sunday 1030-1630 TT$50 per person. The Gasparee Caves are certainly worth a visit. It is about a 20-minute boat ride from the Crews Inn marina. The landing stage is at the west end of Gaspar Grande which has many weekend homes.

Chaguaramas
Chaguaramas was the focus of international attention in May 1999, when the Miss Universe pageant was held there

Try to get a pirogue with a canvas shade as these are used to dealing with tourists and are likely to be more reliable

Trinidad & Tobago

The caves are about 15 minutes from the landing stage up a good path through woods, quite steep in places and hot. The caves are locked and it is necessary to have a guide from the house at the end of the path (drinks available). The complex of caves is large but you are only shown one, with good steps leading down and naturally lit from a blow hole. There is a beautiful lake (tidal) at the bottom with stalactites which the guide will light. Parts of the path around the cave are quite slippery. Despite what the boatman may tell you, there is now no swimming allowed in the cave. Be prepared for a wait at the landing stage as, despite all assurances, a number of boatmen will not wait for you, preferring to return to the island and then come back to pick you up (which they usually do). There are excellent views of the other islands making up the Dragon's Mouth. This is much frequented by boats and yachts at the weekend but is virtually deserted during the week. **Monos Island**, at the west tip of Trinidad, has many deep caves and white sandy beaches, popular with more affluent Trinidadians.

The north coast

It is possible to walk to Maracas from Port of Spain in about three hours; or take a maxi or route taxi to Maraval and then hike from there

North of Port of Spain is **Maraval**, just beyond which is the 18-hole St Andrews golf course at **Moka** (there is also a swimming pool, US$3 for non-members). From Maraval village (church, police station) 4WD taxis run to the hilltop village of Paramin, where several families still speak French Creole, and there is an annual Parang music festival before Christmas (see Culture). The North Coast Road branches left off Saddle Road (which runs through Maraval back over the hills to meet the Eastern Main Road at San Juan), leading to Maracas Bay, Las Cuevas and Blanchisseuse. There is a lookout point on the road to Maracas Bay at the *Hot Bamboo Hut*, where a track goes steeply down to a secluded beach. The stall-holder can call the toucans in the forest; take binoculars to see them fly close and answer him. There is a hiking route across the Northern Range from the Maracas Valley near St Joseph, but you will need a local guide. The Northern Range locations for hiking are best reached from the coastal villages.

East of Port of Spain

The east-west corridor from Port of Spain is a line of industrial and residential suburbs linked by the Eastern Main Road and, more quickly, by a dual carriageway or priority bus/taxi route. Although the flat bits are mostly unattractive, you are never more than a mile or two from the hills and both high- and low-income neighburhoods extend up the hillsides, with wonderful views of Central Trinidad and across to the Gulf of Paria. The older centres along the Eastern Main Road (San Juan, Curepe, Tunapuna, Arouca) are lively, with shops, small bars, Chinese

Trinidad northwest

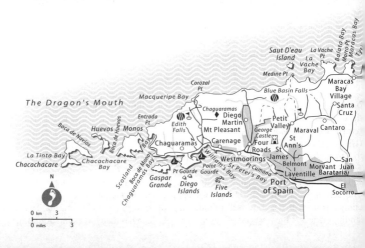

restaurants and fruit and vegetable markets, the latter jamming up the traffic even on Sunday morning. Just east of Port of Spain is the **Angostura rum distillery**. ■ *Tours Tue and Thu, 0830 and 1300, T6231841*. An old warehouse is now CCA7: artists' studio space, with occasional exhibitions. ■ *T6251889*. At Champs Fleurs is the **Carib brewery**, then the Mount Hope teaching hospital. **St Joseph** was once the seat of government, as San José de Oruña. The imposing Jinnah Memorial Mosque stands here. North of St Joseph is the **Maracas Valley** (no road to Maracas Bay, although there is a footpath), which has a 300-ft waterfall.

Further east, high on a hill, is **Mount St Benedict** monastery, reached through St Johns Road in St Augustine. Although the monastery was founded by a Belgian, the first Benedictine monks came from Bahia, Brazil, in 1912. It started with a tapia hut but construction of the main building on Mount Tabor began in 1918. The monastery has a retreat, lots of educational facilities, a drug rehabilitation centre, a farm and a guesthouse and is popular with birdwatchers and walkers. There are marvellous views over the Caroni Plain to the sea. A priority maxi-taxi from Port of Spain to St Augustine takes 20 minutes, TT$3, then a route taxi up St John's Road and then St Michael's Road will take you close to the monastery, but unless you pay to go off route it is still a stiff walk uphill. Otherwise take a private taxi all the way. From Caura Road, a little further east, a route taxi will take you up the valley of the **Caura River**, where the pools are popular spots for weekend picnics (river limes).

This is the oldest Benedictine complex in the Caribbean

A little further along the Eastern Main Road at Arouca, the road branches south to Piarco International Airport, or north winding 10 km up into the forested mountains to the **Lopinot Complex**, an estate built by the Comte de Lopinot (see page 794) at the turn of the 19th century. Originally called La Reconnaissance, it is now a popular picnic spot and destination for school trips; there is a small museum. There is a bar across the road, open, like most others in Trinidad, 'anyday, anytime'. It hosts a Parang music festival before Christmas.

High on a ridge in the Maracas Valley are the only known Amerindian (probably Arawak) petroglyphs in Trinidad, known as the **Caurita drawings**. They show a series of faces with curving lines indicating limbs. To get there it is a stiff climb of 1-1½ hours in the valley, with access from the main crossroads between San Juan and Tunapuna.

Arima is 25 km east of Port of Spain, reached by bus or route taxi. The landmark at the centre is the Dial, an old public clock. It has been repaired after an argument with a heavy truck, and plays the radio on Friday and Saturday nights. A few miles west of Arima is a small but interesting Amerindian museum at the Cleaver Woods Recreation Centre, housed in a reproduction Amerindian long house; entrance is free but donations are welcome. A group of people regard themselves as descendants of the original Amerindians of the area, although there are none left of pure blood. They have a figurehead Carib queen and call themselves the **Santa Rosa Carib Community**. West of the church in the centre of town is the Santa Rosa Carib Community Crafts Centre selling traditional crafts: cassava squeezers, serving trays, carvings, etc.

Arima
Population: 26,000

About 8 miles north of Arima, off the Blanchisseuse Road, you can get to the **Asa Wright Nature Centre**, an old plantation house overlooking a wooded valley and a must for bird-lovers (by car or taxi from Arima, US$7, the driver

North of Arima

Trinidad & Tobago

should wait for you, or a warm 2½-hour walk uphill through lovely forests). The nature centre now owns 700 acres of forest (not all of which are at the centre) and the annual Christmas bird count usually numbers 161-186 species. There is a beautiful man-made pool where you can swim, a network of trails and guided tours. Sit on the veranda and watch the hummingbirds. Take binoculars. The rangers are very knowledgeable and can tell you about the plants and insects (easier to see) as well as the birds. The rare oilbirds in **Dunstan Cave** (also called Diablotin Cave) can only be seen if you stay more than three nights. Field trips for guests are organized to the Caroni Swamp, Nariva Swamp, Aripo Savannah, Arena Forest and Blanchisseuse, while turtle-watching tours are also offered to the east and west coasts during leatherback nesting season (March to September). ■ *0900-1700. US$10 entrance and tour. US$9 or TT$50 for a good buffet lunch, or you can just have sandwiches, see below for accommodation. Give 48 hrs notice of your visit if possible.*

Do not enter the caves without a flashlight, rope and other equipment. A knowledgeable guide is recommended

This road carries on to Blanchisseuse. A 9-mile walk from the road are the **Aripo Caves** (the longest system in Trinidad) with spectacular stalagmites and stalactites (in the wet season, June to December, a river runs through the caves). Oilbirds can be seen at the entrance. Only fully equipped spelunkers should venture beyond the entrance. To get there, turn at Aripo Road off the Eastern Main Road, turn right at the 4-mile post, over the bridge into Aripo village. Keep left, continuing uphill to a wide bend to the left where you may park off the road and begin the walk uphill. Turn left at the small house. After a further 10 minutes take the trail to the right of the junction and to the left at the next junction, continuing uphill along the river. At a shelf of rock there is a well cleared trail away from the river. Keep to this trail heading north until the top of the hill. Go downhill for five minutes to the stream leading into the cave.

This town was named after the washerwomen who used to do their laundry in the Marianne River

Blanchisseuse has a population of about 3,000 and is divided between the Upper Village and Lower Village, with the Arima road as the dividing line. There is a post office, health centre, RC Church, government offices and police station in Lower Village, while Upper Village has the school, recreation field and several artisans working in wood and leather. All this part of the coast is very beautiful with the forest coming down to the sea. You can hike east all along the coast from here to Matelot and on to Grande Riviere, starting at the 100-year-old Silver Bridge just outside the village. It can be done in a day, or two if overnighting in Paria and a guide is useful; ask Fred (at *Laguna Mar*) or Barbara Zollna (at *Zollna House*) to arrange it.

From Arima you can drive, taxi or hitchhike to Brasso Seco and Paria. From here the trail runs to **Paria Bay**, possibly the best beach on the island, about 8 miles, ask directions, or see the *TIDCO Sites (trail guide)* book for the route. There is a primitive shelter on the beach but no other facilities so take provisions with you. At the beach, turn right to get to the bridge over the Paria River, from where it is a five-minute walk inland to the spectacular Paria waterfall. Another path from the beach leads west to Blanchisseuse (7 miles), where the track forks.

Northeast coast

The northeast coast is one of the most remote and unspoiled parts of the island, partly because the tarmac road does not extend along the whole of the north coast from Blanchisseuse. **Grande Riviere** lies in the middle of this area. It has a long and lovely beach, with accommodation and eco-tourism. Guesthouses can organize tours into the forest and along the path to Blanchisseuse, and in season you can watch the protected turtles laying their eggs in the sand.

Grande Riviere is easy to reach by private car but not easy by public transport. From Port of Spain take a bus (faster than a maxi) to Arima, TT$4. From Arima to Sangre Grande there are buses and maxis (ask around) but a route taxi may be easiest; turn left just past *Scotia Bank* and the third lot of route taxis is for Sangre Grande. At Sangre Grande buses, maxis and route taxis all stop in the same place. It is relatively easy to get a maxi to Toco and possibly on to Sans Souci, but this still means a 6-mile walk (very pleasant, no traffic) through the woods to Grande Riviere. There are some maxis and route taxis in the morning from Grande Riviere to Sangre

Grande, returning at about 1600. As a last resort a route taxi in Sangre Grande would very soon become a private taxi. Guesthouses at Grande Riviere can also arrange to pick you up, price negotiable. Whichever way you go, the effort is worthwhile.

If you are driving yourself, from Arima the road runs either to Toco at Trinidad's northeast tip (which is well worth a visit with a few small beaches nearby for bathing) or, branching off at Valencia, to the east coast. Left fork at Valencia, then left again at Honey Corner (where there are bottles of locally made honey on sale), through small villages, woods and, after Salybia, beaches a short distance off the road to the right. **The Salybia Waterfall** is close to the 13-mile post; cross the bridge and turn left after the old 14¼-mile post into the Salybia/Matura Trace. Follow a 20-minute, rather rough drive and park in front of two houses. Walk 15 minutes along the trail, turn left at the junction, continue about 10 minutes to a second junction where the path narrows on the right going slightly uphill into Mora Forest. Keep on the trail, crossing first a small stream and then a larger river. 10 minutes later at another junction you may bear right over a small hill or walk upstream. Either route will get you to Salybia Waterfall and pool in 10 minutes. The pool is 6 m deep and recommended for good swimmers. There is also a picnic area.

At **Galera Point**, reached off the road which goes to Toco, over a rickety wooden bridge, there is a small, pretty lighthouse. If you arrive before 1530 it is often open and you can climb to the top for a breathtaking view from the ramp. You can continue by car (quite a long drive) to **Grande Riviere** and the small hotels on a wide, sandy beach. There is a wide river, also good for bathing, and hiking trails in the hills behind. Staff at the hotels are very knowledgeable about the area and can help you arrange tours along the coast or hiking and camping in the forest.

South of Port of Spain

Driving south from Port of Spain along the highway (turn right at the Grand Bazaar shopping mall) or the old Southern Main Road (turn right opposite the big KFC/Pizza Hut), you will see sugar, citrus and rice fields, and maybe a few buffalypso (buffaloes which have been selectively bred for meat), Hindu temples and mosques. There are boat trips to the **Caroni Bird Sanctuary** (signposted from the highway), the home of scarlet ibis, whose numbers are dwindling as the swamp in which they live is encroached upon and polluted. Boats leave around 1600 from near the Visitor's Centre to take people to see the ibis returning to their roost at sunset. ■ *There are 2 boat operators in the swamp:* Moodoo Tours *and* Winston Nanan, *T6451305, US$10, group rates available. Nanan rarely guides now and not all his boatmen are informative; enquire at the Asa Wright Centre for more detailed tours. If possible take a cold bag with drinks, although Nanan sells drinks on board. Mosquito repellent is essential when you get off the boat at the end of your trip. To get there, take a bus or route taxi from Port of Spain or San Fernando to Bamboo Grove Settlement No 1, on the Uriah Butler Highway, from where the boats leave, TT$2.50 or TT$5 respectively. Maxi-taxi (green bands) from Independence Square. Ask to be dropped off at the Caroni Bird Sanctuary.*

On the left before you get to **Chaguanas**, a large blue statue of the Hindu god, Lord Shiva and a large white statue of Viveka Nanda, a Hindu philosopher, mark the site of the annual Divali Nagar exhibition in October/November. Chaguanas is a busy place, not an architectural must, but full of bargains for the shopper. At the centre is the imaginatively named junction Busy Corner. The Lion House (on the main road to the east, close to the police station) is the original for VS Naipaul's *A House for Mr Biswas*. Continuing south on the Southern Main Road parallel to the highway, **Carlsen Field** has several small potteries, using open wood-fired kilns. Most of the pots are a bit unwieldy, but wind chimes, etc are easily portable, as are the tiny lamps, or *deyas*, which are made for Divali. Turn off the Main Road at Chase Village, and 3 miles to the west is **Waterloo**, where a small Hindu temple has been built in the sea. It is reached by a short causeway and it is the successor of a structure built by Siewdass Sadhu, a sugar worker who selected his site in the shallow waters of the Gulf

Brechin Castle sugar factory is quite a landmark, although not open to the public

of Paria after being unable to find land to build on. Continuing south, the Southern Main Road leads to the Point Lisas industrial estate.

Alternatively, a left turn-off the highway at **Freeport**, or points south, takes you into the Central Range through sugar and citrus fields, then forests, with cocoa trees. There are cocoa houses with a sliding roof so that the beans can dry in the sun but go under cover when it rains. Pretty little villages with wooden houses and well-kept gardens overflow with hibiscus and bougainvillea. The roads are narrow and winding, so unless you are a map-reading wizard, you are bound to get lost. At **Chickland Village** near Freeport, the **Ajoupa Pottery**, T6730604 (see Shopping, page 780), with a wooden 19th-century estate house, is well worth a visit.

San Fernando
Population: 60,000

San Fernando on the southwest coast is a busy, hot city, as yet unspoilt by tourism but spoilt by just about everything else. A highway connects Port of Spain with San Fernando, making it a 30-minute drive (90 minutes in the afternoon rush hour, US$1 by a/c express, route taxi US$1.75). The waterfront area is a mess, in spite of continual talk of restoration, although Harris Promenade is pleasant. City Hall, the Our Lady of Perpetual Help church and the old railway engine are worth a look. Library Corner has the old Carnegie public library and is the main centre for maxis and route taxis. Coffee Street is also lively. Above the city is San Fernando Hill, oddly shaped as a result of quarrying and easily picked out from Northern Range viewpoints or from Chaguaramas. It is now landscaped, and you can either walk or drive to the top for a spectacular view.

North of San Fernando are the principal industrial area of **Point Lisas** and the **Pointe-a-Pierre** oil refinery. Within the oil refinery is the 26-ha **Wild Fowl Trust**, a conservation area with two lakes and breeding grounds for many endangered species. Many birds bred in captivity are later released into the wild. ■ *Mon-Fri 1000-1700, Sat 1200-1600, Sun 1030-1800. T6375145. Call 48 hrs in advance to get permission to enter the compound (many entrances, it can be confusing).*

The lake has been described by disappointed tourists, as looking like a parking lot, although others have pointed out that it is parking lots that look like the Pitch Lake

A famous phenomenon to visit on the southwest coast just after La Brea is **Pitch Lake**, about 116 acres of smooth surface of black tar; it is 135 ft deep. It is possible to walk on it, with care, watching out for air holes bubbling up from the pressure under the ooze. In the wet season, however, most of the area is covered with shallow fresh water. The legend is that long ago the gods interred an entire tribe of Chaima Indians for daring to eat sacred hummingbirds containing the souls of their ancestors. In the place where the entire village sank into the ground there erupted a sluggish flow of black pitch, which gradually became an ever-refilling large pool. The lake can be reached by taking a route taxi from San Fernando to La Brea (US$0.75). Insist on a professional guide, who should report to the security guard before taking you around, as locals who pose as guides harass tourists for large tips. Agree on a price in advance as there are no fixed rates. Sometimes there are crowds of guides who are difficult to avoid, but on the other hand it is difficult to understand the lake without explanation. Pompei, tall and stout and trained by the Tourist Board, is recommended.

Beyond La Brea the road continues to **Point Fortin**, a small but busy town with a liquefied natural gas plant and a small beach. The road carries on down the southwest peninsula, deteriorating as it goes, through Cedros (fishing village, beach) to **Icacos**, from which the mangroves of the Orinoco delta are clearly visible a few miles across the water. From the Point Fortin-Icacos road there are side roads leading to beaches such as Erin or Columbus Bay.

East of San Fernando

East of San Fernando the main road runs through rolling hills with sugar-cane fields, past the Usine Sainte Madeleine sugar mill to Princes Town, then continues to Rio Claro and Mayaro on the east coast. It runs parallel to the south coast, most of which is fairly inaccessible. Near Princes Town is the **Devil's Woodyard**, one of 18 mud volcanoes on Trinidad. This one is considered a holy site by some Hindus (it is also a natural landmark). It last erupted in 1852 and the bubbling mud is cool.

From St Julien, east of Princes Town, a road leads after 19 miles (slow driving) to the **The south** fishing village of **Moruga**. Every year around mid-July they have a celebration of **coast** Columbus' 1498 landing on the beach. Fishing boats are decked out as caravels, complete with the red Maltese cross. Columbus, a priest and soldiers are met by Amerindians (local boys, mostly of East Indian and African extraction); after the meeting everyone retires to the church compound where the revelry continues late into the night.

The **Karamat mud volcano** at Moruga, erupted in 1997. Thick mud spurted 150 ft into the air, killing one man, burying animals alive and engulfing houses, leaving 100 homeless. Seek local advice before visiting. To get there, from Penal Rock Road proceed west to the 8-mile post. On the right head down Haggard Trace driving south until the Moruga West oil field gate. Enter on the road and continue left for 1 mile. Pass a series of tank batteries, No 7, on the left, and continue to an oil pump on the right. Take the side road for 400 yds. Park near the oil pump at a well-head. Continue uphill. There is another mud volcano at **Piparo**, which erupted suddenly in 1994, destroying a section of the village and cutting off the approach by road from the northeast. What remains is a big expanse of dry mud. Nearby is a large and tasteless house, with adjoining Hindu temple. Now a drug rehabilitation centre, it was once the home of the notorious drug dealer and murderer, Dole Chadee, who was hanged in 1999 along with his associates. The eruption of the volcano was seen by some villagers as divine retribution for Chadee's activities.

It is quite difficult to get beyond Arima and San Fernando by bus, but there are route taxis, and privately operated maxi-taxis, or you can hire a car. A full-day circuit of the island can be driven from Port of Spain south to San Fernando, east to Mayaro then north to Sangre Grande and Arima. An alternative route back from Mayaro runs through Biche and the eastern fringe of the Central Range to Sangre Grande.

Essentials

If you intend to stay in Trinidad for Carnival you must book a hotel well in advance. Most **Sleeping** hotels raise their prices steeply and insist you stay for the full period. Some are booked a year *VAT of 15% will be* ahead. If arriving without accommodation arranged at Carnival time, the tourist office at the *added to your bill* airport may help to find you a room in a hotel, or with a local family, though both options will be expensive. Reservations are sometimes cancelled and hotels which have not sold their full package may make rooms available at the last min. You will probably find something, but not necessarily of the price or quality you would prefer. For most of the year, hotels in Port of Spain cater almost exclusively for business visitors and rooms can be hard to find if your visit coincides with a conference.

Port of Spain area **LL-L** *Hilton*, on a rise at the corner of Lady Young and St Ann's Rds, northeast Queen's Park Savannah, T6243211, www.hiltontrinidad.compos@wow.net Public areas and pool deck are on top and 394 rooms and 25 suites on lower levels, facilities for the disabled, all facilities, restaurants, bars, eating by the pool cheap, non-residents can eat/swim there (monthly membership US$28), tennis, badminton, gym, conference centre, ballroom, executive suite, frequent entertainment. **LL-B** *Cascadia*, 67 Ariapita Rd, St Ann's, T6234208, F6278046, up in the hills. 68 rooms, children under 12 free, rooms and suites vary, nice pool, chutes and waterslide (TT$25 for non-guests to use pool), sports and conference facilities, *Coconuts Club* disco, restaurant for conferences only, bar, busy at weekends. **L** *Crowne Plaza*, Wrightson Rd, T6253366, F6254166, in the business centre. All facilities very nice, friendly, small pool, restaurant 0630-2230. **L-AL** *The Chancellor*, 5a St Ann's Av, T6230880, www.thechancellorhotel.com. Small pool, *Waterfront Bistro*. **AL-A** *Kapok*, 16-18 Cotton Hill, St Clair, northwest Queen's Park Savannah, T6225765, www.kapokhotel.com 95 rooms, friendly, comfortable, light, big windows, some studios with kitchenette, excellent *Tiki Village* restaurant, T6225765, 0630-2215 daily, with Chinese and Polynesian cuisine, also light meals at bar downstairs, small pool, shopping arcade. **AL** *Coblentz Inn*, 44 Coblentz Av, T6210541, www.coblentzinn.com Well-run boutique hotel, 16 rooms, no pool, good restaurant,

Trinidad & Tobago

Battimamzelle. **AL-B** *Normandie*, off St Ann's Rd, at the end of Nook Av (No 10), T6241181, normandie@wow.net 53 standard, superior and loft rooms, a/c, reduced rates for businessmen, service quirky, swimming pool, in a complex with craft and fashion shops, art gallery and restaurants 1800-2200 daily, outdoor theatre 'Under the Trees', and *Breakfast Shed* for lunch.

Rooms for US$20 a night or less are few and far between in the capital and some are not recommended by TIDCO

Central Port of Spain **C** *Par-May*-La's Inn, 53 Picton St, T6282008, www.parmaylas.com Specially convenient for Carnival and cricket, double or triple rooms with bathroom, a/c, TV, phone, some cheap singles, facilities for the disabled, parking, local cuisine with roti, evening meals on request, credit cards accepted. Nearby the same owner has 15 apartments, **C** *Sun Deck Suites*, 42-44 Picton St, T6229560. A/c, with cooking facilities, sleep 2/3. **D-E** *Copper Kettle Hotel*, 66-68 Edward St, T6254381. Central, rooms with shower, price depends on a/c, restaurant. **D-E** *Gwen's Bed & Breakfast*, 7 First Roseway, Belmont, T6278032. 4 rooms, fan, towels, TV, shared bathroom, hot water, clean, cash only, short walk to Savannah. **E** *The Abercromby Inn*, 101 Abercromby St, T6235259, aberinn@ carib-link.net 17 rooms, a/c, TV, phone, laundry facilities, some large and some very small economy rooms, no food, 5 mins' walk to Queen's Park Savannah. **E** *Pearl's Guest House*, 3-4 Victoria Square East, T6252158. Access to kitchen, can prepare own meals, laundry room, excellent location for Carnival. **F** *Royal Guest House*, 109 Charlotte St, T6231042. Owners have coffee shop next door, shared bathroom.

Woodbrook **C-D** *Kitty Peters*, 26 Warren St. Immaculately clean, hot-water showers, fans. **D** *ML's Gingerbread House*, 25 Stone St, T6253663, mark@wow.net 3 double rooms with bathrooms, CP, other meals on request, varied cuisine, excursions arranged. **D** *La Calypso Guest House*, 46 French St, T6224077, F6286895. Kitchen, jacuzzi, car hire available, breakfast US$3, pool at their other guesthouse. **E** *Schultzi's Guest House and Pub*, 35 Fitt St, T/F6227521. CP, kitchen, hot shower, transport available to airport or dock. **E** *Allamanda*, 61 Carlos St, T6227719. 9 rooms, friendly, Spanish and Portuguese spoken.

St James **C** *Trini House*, 5A Lucknow St, T/F6287550. 3 rooms, CP, English, German, Italian and French spoken by owner Michael Figuera; steelpan tuition.

St Ann's **C** *Alicia's Guest House*, 7 Coblentz Gardens, T6232802, www.aliciashousetrinidad.com 17 rooms, some cheap, all a/c, fan, TV, phone, fridge, family rooms, suites, small pool, jacuzzi, exercise machine, meals available, excursions organized.

Cascade **C** *Pelican Inn*, 2-4 Coblentz Av, T/F6276271. 14 rooms, squash court, pub, very lively with music on Wed, Fri, Sun, great entertainment but not good for an early night. **E** *Scott's Guest House*, 5 Pomme Rose Av, Cascade, T6244105. Friendly, safe area, can be booked from airport.

The best guesthouses are in this area, only 10 mins by maxi-taxi from the Savannah

Maraval **B-C** *Zollna House*, 12 Ramlogan Terr, La Seiva, Maraval, T6283731, F6283737. Owned by Gottfried (Fred) and Barbara Zollna, small guesthouse, food varied with local flavour, special diets catered for, breakfast US$6 and dinner US$12, Barbara knows all about B&B places. **C** *Carnetta's House*, 28 Scotland Terr, Andalusia, Maraval, just off Saddle Rd, T6282732, www.carnettas.com Children under 12 free, a/c, all rooms different sizes, some fridges, some kitchenettes, TV, phone, ironing board, carpets, family room, laundry, nice gardens, grow some produce, meals on request, parking, family atmosphere, videos for TV, lots of repeat business, maxi-taxi will drop you at gate for extra US$0.50, run by Carnetta and Winston Borrell, who also own **C** *Carnetta's Inn*, 99 Saddle Rd, Maraval, T6225165/2884. 14 rooms in 2 adjacent properties, all rooms with mini-fridge, most with kitchenette, single, double, triple and connecting rooms, TV, a/c, phone, internet access, *Bamboo Terrace* restaurant serves local cooking, Shipwreck Bar for special cocktails. **C** *Monique's Guest House*, 114-116 Saddle Rd, Maraval, T6283334, www.moniquestrinidad.com, on way to golf course and north-coast beaches. Easy access from city, 10 rooms in main house, 10 more over the hill, large rooms, different sizes sleeping 4/5, a/c, TV, phone, some kitchenettes, *Pink Anthurium* restaurant serves good local food, clean, attractive, facilities for the disabled,

Monica and Michael Charbonné are helpful and hospitable. **C** *Tropical Hotel*, 6 Rookery Nook Rd, Maraval, T6225815, F6224249. A/c, pool, maid service, bar and restaurant attached, short walk from the Savannah, friendly, helpful.

Chaguaramas AL *Crew's Inn*, T6344384, www.crewsinn.com 46 rooms, clean and well-run, pool, gym, shops, bank, beauty salon and *Lighthouse* restaurant 0730-2300 daily on same marina site. **C** *The Bight*, Lot 5, Western Main Rd, T6344839, F6344387. 10 rooms, sports bar, marina, meals 0730-2330 daily. **C-D** *The Cove*, T6344319. Rather run-down, pool, maid and laundry, kitchenette, 1 3-bedroom apartment **B**, breakfast US$6, lunch/dinner US$10.

East of Port of Spain B *Pax Guesthouse*, Mt St Benedict, Tunapuna, T/F6624084, www.paxguesthouse.com Built 1932, original furniture made by monks, 18 rooms, popular with birdwatchers, 147 species of bird on estate, donkey trails into forest, rooms have high ceilings, no a/c necessary, 1 family room, most share showers, simple but wholesome food, lovely view of central Trinidad as well as of occasional monk. **C** *Sadila House*, run by Savitri and Dinesh Bhola, Waterpipe Rd, Five Rivers, Arouca, T6403659, F6401376, close to airport. 3 rooms, CP, credit cards accepted, weekly and group rates available, a/c, TV. **C-D** *Valsayn Villa*, 34 Gilwell Rd, Valsayn North, T/F6451193. Very large, modern, private house with beautifully furnished rooms and lovely garden, or fully furnished villas **B** and up, in one of the safest residential areas, close to university, 15 mins from airport, 20 mins by bus from downtown Port of Spain, excellent home-cooked Indian meals available. **D** *Airport View Guesthouse*, St Helena Junction, courtesy transport to and from Piarco Airport, T6694186. Convenient, a/c, hot water, double rooms have 2 double beds, breakfast US$5, restaurant nearby serving American-style food. **D-E** *The Caribbean Lodge*, 32 St Augustine Circular Rd, Tunapuna, T6452937 (15-30 mins to Port of Spain by bus on the priority route). Shared or private shower, a/c, single rooms available, comfortable, laundry facilities, breakfast room.

Northern Range LL-L *Asa Wright Nature Centre*, 7½-mile mark, Blanchisseuse Rd, Arima, T6674655, F6670493. Price includes all meals, rum punch, tax and service, 2 main-house rooms in colonial style, high ceilings, wooden furniture and floors, fan, bathroom, 24 standard rooms and bungalow in gardens, all designed to be private and secluded, facilities for the disabled, verandas for birdwatching, 80% of guests in high season are birdwatching groups. **A-E** *Aripo Cottage*, Hollier Trace, Aripo Estate, Heights of Aripo, 9 miles north of Arima, T/F6456736, www.aripocottage.com Cottage in converted cocoa house, or cabana with 3 units, each sleep 3-5 people, mostly in bunk beds, excellent value per person, full kitchens, new equipment, pool, birdwatching, pretty view of mountains, nature trails, river bathing. **E** *Alta Vista*, up the road from *Asa Wright*, no phone on premises but T6298030, F6293262 for reservations. 6 self-contained wooden cabins, meals with advance notice, attractive swimming pool, veranda overlooking forest, nice waterfall along a trail, TT$10.

Arima C *Chateau Guillaume*, 3 Rawle Circular, T6676670, joanwilliam@yahoo.com Run by Matthew and Joan William, 2 double and 2 triple rooms, bathroom, very clean, lower price for long stay, airport transfers, very helpful.

North coast Maracas **L-AL** *Maracas Bay Hotel*, T6691914, F6691643, west of beach. MAP, 36 a/c rooms with shower, each with porch overlooking bay, clean but rather characterless and spartan, nature trails, watersports. Blanchisseuse **B-C** *Laguna Mar Nature Lodge*, at milepost 65½ just before suspension bridge over Marianne River. *Cocos Hut* restaurant attached, owned by Fred Zollna, close to beach and lagoon, see Beaches and watersports, 10 rooms with 2 double beds, bathroom, jogging trail, write c/o *Zollna House*, 12 Ramlogan Terr, La Seiva, Maraval, or T6283731, F6283737. **C** *Second Spring*, 13 Damier Village, T6643909, F6234328. Cottage or 3 studios, CP, at milepost 67¾, rustic, comfortable, in gardens on clifftop with wooden walkway, spectacular views of coast, beaches within walking distance, restaurant 5 mins' walk, owned by Ginette Holder who is friendly and hospitable, excellent value. **C** *Surf's Country Inn*, Lower Village, T6692475. Good restaurant on hill above coast road, 3 rooms, CP, nice furnishings, picturesque, small beach below. **C** *The Almond Brook*,

Self-catering may be difficult, with few shops, no bank, no car rental

Trinidad & Tobago

Upper Village, Paria Main Rd, Blanchisseuse, T6420476. 2-bedroomed cottage on beach and 'couples retreat' up the hill, both same price but latter CP. **Grande Riviere B** *Mount Plaisir Estate Hotel & Spa*, Hosang St, on bay of same name at eastern end of north coast, T6708381, www.mtplaisir.com CP, 10 beachfront rooms right by the place where the leatherback turtles nest, nature trails, birdwatching, with excursions organized, overnight camping tours with local guide, restaurant 0800-2100, long drive through Toco. **B** *Le Grand Amandier*, 2 Hosang St, T/F6701013, www.legrandalmandier.com Also on the beach, cheaper, but no single rates, good standard of accommodation, CP, excellent food, 0700-2200 daily, cater to individual tastes including vegetarian, ask for the corn soup, meal plans available, a few suites sleep 4-5, knowledgeable and accessible proprietor. **C** *McEachnie's Haven*, T6701014, www.mchaventt.com 6 rooms on the beach.

Balandra Bay At milepost 23 on the Toco Main Rd, north of Balandra Bay is Mr Hugh Lee Pow's **E** *Green Acres Guest House*, on a farm backed by the ocean, FAP, good meals, very kind and restful. *Manzanilla Calypso Inn*, ¼ mile off main road where road joins beach, on Calypso Rd at south end of Manzanilla, T6685113. The only hotel, run by Meena Singh and her daughter Arisa, 10 motel-style rooms, large dining room overlooking scenic part of the beach, meals on request, nice place.

Beach houses to rent on the southeast coast but check their condition, some are unacceptable

Mayaro C *Azee's*, at 3½-mile mark Guayaguayare Rd, Grand Lagoon, Mayaro, T6309140, F6304619. 5 rooms, restaurant, not quite respectable. **C-E** *Harry's*, Grand Lagoon, south end of Mayaro. Right on beach (plastic litter), nice grounds, rather peculiar building, apartments range in size from tiny room with double bunk bed, kitchenette, bathroom, a/c, TV, to larger units, some with verandas, watch out for TT$50 service charge. **C** *Mrs Paria's*, guesthouse, just beyond the BP/Amoco compound. Self-contained room, TV, breakfast, beautiful modern home.

San Fernando L-A *Cara Suites Pointe-à-Pierre*, opened in 2002 in former *Farrell House Hotel*, Southern Main Rd, Claxton Bay, T6592230, www.carahotels.com 52 comfortable rooms and suites, pool, business centre with complimentary internet access and free bar drinks, view over muddy Gulf of Paria, restaurant, this West Indian hotel chain is highly regarded. **B** *Royal Hotel*, 46-54 Royal Rd, T6524881, www.royalhotelltt.com A/c, kitchenette, lovely hilltop garden. **AL-B** *Tradewinds*, 38 London St, St Joseph Village, San Fernando, T6529463, delia@tradewindshotel.net 13 rooms, kitchenette, bar, restaurant 0500-2300 daily, gym, pool, games room. **B-C** *Mikanne Hotel and Restaurant*, 15 Railway Av, Plaisance Village, Pointe-à-Pierre, T/F6592584. 13 rooms, a/c, private bath, meal plans, restaurant 0700-1800 daily, TV on request, pleasant, convenient for oil refinery and Wild Fowl Trust.

Eating

Plenty of choice west of city centre: Ariapita Avenue for smarter restaurants, Cipriani Blvd for mid-price and Maraval Road for cheap and cheerful

Opening hours are liable to change at short notice. Many places close on Sun, and some public holidays. They may close or reduce their hours over Carnival when most customers are too preoccupied to eat properly and staff are otherwise engaged.

Port of Spain *A La Bastille*, Ariapita Av and Verteuil St, T6221789. French-run, creative menu, good wine, evening main courses US$15 and over, excellent fixed-price lunch, Tue-Sat 0830-2230, Mon 1800-2230. *Olive's Mediterranean Bistro*, 22 Sweetbriar Rd, St Clair, T6229688. Good food, main courses from US$14, open Mon-Sat 1130-1500, 1800-2230. *Solimar*, 6 Nook Av, close to the *Normandie*, T6246267. International, prices US$25-40, very good service, outdoor dining, excellent food, reservations advisable and essential at weekends, 1830-2200 Mon-Sat. *Veni Mangé*, 67A Ariapita Av, T6244597. Small, friendly, good food, imaginative menu includes vegetarian dishes, around US$20. Open Mon-Fri 1130-1500, dinner Wed, Fri only 1930-2230. *Il Colosseo*, 16 Rust St, St Clair, T6281494. Good Italian food, main courses from US$14, 1130-1430 Mon Fri, 1830-2230 Mon-Sat. *Tamnak Thai*, 13 Queens Park East, T6250647. Excellent Thai restaurant, beautiful setting, 1830-2300 daily and 1100-1530 Tue-Fri, Sun. In same building is *Apsara*, T6237659. Very good food, Indian rather than Indo-Trini, prices US$25-40 for full meal, 1130-1530, 1800-2300 Mon-Sat. *Plantation House*, Ariapita Av and Cornelio St, T6285551. US-style Cajun food, main courses from US$12, open daily 1130-1430, 1830-2230. *Roxan's*, Corner Ariapita Av and O'Connor St, Woodbrook, T6224425. Arab restaurant, very good, especially for lunch, 0900-1800 Mon-Thu, 0900-2000 Sat. *Woodford Café*, 62 Tragarete Rd, T6222233. Creole fare, around US$20 for a meal. Open 1100-1530 Mon-Tue, 1100-2200 Wed Thu, 1100-2230 Fri Sat. *Joseph's*, T6225557, Rookery Nook, Maraval. Arab and other dishes, US$14 and upwards, excellent service, popular, run by a Lebanese, Joe, 1130-1430 Mon-Fri, 1830-2230 Mon-Sat. *Chutney Rose*, Fitt St and Ariapita Av, T6288541. Good, authentic Indian food, meals US$25-40, 1130-1400, 1830-2200 Mon-Sat. *Verandah*, 10 Rust St, St Clair, T6226287. Caribbean ingredients but not just the standard dishes, Mon-Fri lunch 1130-1345, Thu Sat dinner, 1900-2145. *Tasca Latina*, 16 Phillip St, T6253497. Good Venezuelan-style food, meals around US$10, Latin music sometimes, open 1100-2200 Mon-Fri, 1800-2200 Sat.

Chinese If you've a yen for the best pepper shrimps in the Caribbean, the Chinese restaurants in Trinidad are generally good, with chefs often direct from China. However, the standard can drop abruptly when the chef gets his US visa. There is plenty of choice, and the menus are fairly 'authentic', even in some cheap places, although others can be greasy and nasty. Some of the good ones are: *Tiki Village*, see page 773, *Kapok*, T6225765, 0630-2215 daily, Dim Sum buffet Sun, 1200-1430. *The Swan Chinese Restaurant*, Maraval Rd, T6222611. Unprepossessing interior but very good food, meals around US$10, 1100-1500, 1700-2200 Mon-Sat. *Jenny's on the Boulevard*, 6 Cipriani Blvd, T6251807. Wide variety of mainly Chinese dishes in elaborate setting, US$25-40, 1100-2200 Mon-Thu, 1100-2300 Fri-Sat, lively bar downstairs with light meals also Chinese, around US$10, open until 2400 Mon-Thu, 0100 Fri-Sat.

Fast food outlets where you can get a meal for around US$5: *Joe's Pizza*, St James. Good, also other Italian dishes, 1100-2200, Mon-Thu, 1100-2300 Fri-Sat, 3 other branches. *Pizza Burger Boys*, Frederick St, and Ellerslie Plaza, Boissiere Village, Maraval (T6282697, best of its type, will deliver to boatyards and marinas in Maraval, open until 2300, takeaway until 2200). The largest *Pizza Hut* in the world is *Pizza Hut Roxy*, which used to be a cinema, Tragarete Rd roundabout, T6285960, 1100-2400 daily. The world's busiest branch of *KFC* is on Independence Sq, open 24 hrs a day. *Royal Castle*, 49 Frederick St and other locations throughout Trinidad (Independence Sq is 24 hrs 7 days). Chicken and chips with a local flavour, also does fish and veggie burgers.

All along Western Main Rd in St James there are lots of cafés, snack bars and restaurants, all reasonably priced around US$5-10, lots of choice. *Breakfast Shed*, opposite *Crowne Plaza*, a big hall with several kitchens where locals eat, US$3.50 for very substantial lunch with juice. The best places for *roti* are *Patraj* at 159 Tragarete Rd, Port of Spain T6226219, 1000-1800 Mon-Sat (if you are watching cricket at the Oval come here and queue for food rather than buying anything other than nuts inside the ground), *Hot Shoppe*, in Maraval Rd and Mucurapo Rd, T6224073, 1000-2130 Mon-Sat, which are of a slightly heavier texture, and the lady in the street open late opposite *Smokey and Bunty* in St James. Next to the Maraval Rd branch of *Hot Shoppe*, the **jerk chicken/jerk pork** places have good, spicy Jamaican-style food. *Lawrence of Arabia*, in Shoppes of Maraval. Good Arabic food at around US$5, open until 2100, closed Sun. In central Port of Spain, the **Excellent City Mall** upstairs, **Town Centre Mall** and **Voyager Mall** on Frederick St have indoor halls with a varied and good selection of stands selling cheap food of different nationalities during the day, seating in the middle. Some booths stay open until 1800 but supplies become limited after 1330. **People's Mall**, between Frederick and Henry Sts, has small booths selling fish broth and similar. *The Bocas* on Chacon St is good for fish dishes, lunchtimes.

Chaguaramas *Lighthouse at Crew's Inn*, T6344384. Breezy, good view of yachts, 0700-2300. *The Bight*, Peake's, T6344839. Bar and restaurant overlooking the Chaguaramas anchorage, 0730-2330.

Popular with yachties, live entertainment some nights

East of Port of Spain *Botticelli's*, at the City of Brand Bazaar, Valsayn, T6458733. Italian, pricey at US$25-40 for a meal, good, 1100-2300 Mon-Fri, 1600-2300 Sat. *Valpark Chinese Restaurant*, Valpark Shopping Plaza, Churchill Roosevelt Highway, Curepe, T6624540. Meals for US$10, 1100-2300 daily. Going further east there are very few classy places, but plenty of Chinese restaurants. *Chinese Wok*, in Trincity Mall, T6403542, 1100-2100 Mon-Thu,

1100-2200 Fri, Sat, is good and also has branches in Tunapuna, T6625296, 1030-2300 Mon-Sat, 1100-2300 Sun, Chaguanas, T6656637, 1100-2200 Mon-Thu, to 2300 Fri, Sat, and Arima, T6672250, 1030-2200 Mon-Thu and to 2300 Fri, Sat. Very different and slow-paced is *Pax Guesthouse* on Mt St Benedict, above Tunapuna, T6624084. Tea is a tradition and all the bread, cakes, jam, honey etc are hand-made by the monks, wholesome and tasty, lovely views of Trinidad from patio. Also lunches and dinners, book 24 hrs ahead, enquire about opening times when booking, excellent value at TT$45.

Chaguanas A good Chinese restaurant is *Kam-Po*, 53 Ramsaran Park, T6654558, opposite Centre Pointe Mall. Also has high-quality imported US steaks and seafood, meals around US$10, 1100-2200 Mon-Wed, 1100-2300 Fri, Sat. *Buffet King*, Centre Pointe Mall, T6718795. Mid-price, mix of Chinese and non-Chinese dishes, with salad bar and dessert bar, 1200-1500 Mon-Sat, 1830-2130 Mon-Thu, 1830-2230 Fri-Sat. *Bougainvillea*, 85 Rivulet Rd, Brechin Castle, Couva, T6364837. Chef claims to specialize in 'American, Italian, Spanish, Creole, Chinese and seafood delights', 1100-2200 Mon-Sat.

San Fernando Not a lot of choice. For Chinese food *Soongs Great Wall*, 97 Circular Rd, T6522583, round the corner from the *Royal Hotel*. Very good reputation, but not as good as it used to be, meals around US$15, the distinctive, Trinidadian version of Chinese food, 1100-2200. Also *Canton Palace*, Cross Crossing shopping mall, T6525993. Prices around US$20, 1100-2200 Mon-Sat. *Pagoda*, Independence Av, T6576375. About US$10, 1000-2200 Mon-Sat. *Jenny's Wok*, Cipero Rd. T6521807. Around US$20 for US steak as well as Chinese food, 1100-2200 Mon-Thu, 1100-2300 Fri, Sat. *Spices*, 13 Sutton St, 6577809. Indian, recommended, 1030-2230 Mon-Thu, 1030-2400 Fri-Sat. More basic are *Charlie's Black Pudding*, on Ruth Av, and *Ali's Rotis*, on Hubert Rance St, both around US$5.

North coast *Surf's Country Inn*, North Coast Rd, Blanchisseuse, T6692475. Good value, delicious meals, beautiful setting, changing rooms available, 1000-1700 daily. *Cocos Hut*, also on coast road at Mile 65½ by Marianne River. Small, friendly, no menu, but usually a choice of fish or meat dishes, slow service but all food freshly cooked; both these restaurants offer rooms. Don't forget the shark-and-bake at Maracas, see Food, page 756.

Nightlife
Any opening hours listed are likely to vary at a moment's notice

Bars and clubs Trinidad has plenty of evening entertainment. For those wishing to visit the places where the local, rather than tourist population goes, anyone in the street will give directions. The atmosphere will be natural and hospitality generous; it will not be luxurious but the local rum is likely to flow feely. Places run late, starting to get lively around 2300-midnight and closing 0400-ish. Fri has a bigger crowd than Sat but no night is completely quiet.

Most of the smarter places are in **Chaguaramas**. The main places are *Pier One*, Thu-Sat 1200-0400, *The Base* and for special events, *MOBS Two* and *The Anchorage*; are all lively most weekends, sometimes big fetes, live music, etc. All-inclusives are 'free drinks' once you have paid the cover charge, or else free drinks up to a certain time. Less expensive are the 'cooler fetes', where you take a cooler with ice and your own drinks. Car parking can be a problem, and there are often traffic jams in and out on the road through Carenage. Other hazards include drivers who have been over-enthusiastic with the free drinks.

Closer to Port of Spain, **St James** is famously the 'city that never sleeps'. *Smokey and Bunty* is a lively rum shop, usually open until dawn or after at weekends. Most expats and tourists go at least once. However, it can irritatingly beset by crack addicts, prostitutes, etc. *Jazzy's*, just down the road, is lively on Fri. On Cipriani Blvd, close to the Savannah, *Jenny's*, see above, has a lively downstairs pub-style bar, with snacks, Fri lime starts after work around 1700. Across the road are *Martin's* T6237632, good simple meals as well as drinks, kitchen closes 2400 but bar open until 0100 Mon-Thu, 0200 Fri, Sat, not so smart as Jenny's but just as much fun, and *Syps*, T6245500, 1000-1630 Mon-Thu, 1000-2400 Fri, 1800-2400 Sat, 1800-2200 Sun. A couple of blocks away *Rafters*, 6a Warner St, is smart with better bar meals than *Jenny's*. *Mas Camp Pub*, Ariapita Av, Woodbrook. Nightly entertainment including calypso and steel band, best place to see live calypso out of season (cover charge usually US$4). *Cordials*, on Tragarete Rd and Picton St, T6288627. Open from 1100 for lunch weekdays (TT$40), then until 2400 for drinks, music, light meals. 1800-2400 Sat, Sun. Live music Fri, when entry is TT$15-20, sometimes with steel band on Picton St. Nearby on Maraval Rd is *Trotter's*, T6278768. 1130-2400 Sun-Thu, 1130-0200 Fri, Sat. Meals and drinks both hideously overpriced, but has interesting tabletops decorated with newsclippings of past corruption scandals. For a quiet drink in pleasant surroundings, *Poleska*, cocktail bar at Trinidad Country Club, Champs Elysees Maraval, T6222112, tcc@wow.net Meals, live entertainment Fri, Sat, open 1100-2300 Mon-Wed, 1100-0200 Thu-Sat, Sun closed. Pool and other club facilities, members only, but wine shop open in day, good selection. Pre-Carnival, *Rituals*, 5 Longden St, T6253262, has Fri pm session in pre-Carnival season, entry free, drinks on sale, where new and established artistes try out their acts. Small, friendly.

In **St Ann's/Cascade**, *The Pelican* (down hill from *Hilton*), 2-4 Coblentz Av, Cascade, T6247486. *Club Coconuts* in *Cascadia Hotel*, St Ann's, lively and crowded. Different styles of music on different nights, with noticeable effect on ethnicity of patrons attracted. Closed Mon, otherwise 2200-0400, entry around TT$40 except Wed, 'free drinks' and TT$60. Tue Hip Hop, Thu University specials, Sat ladies free before 2300, Sun reggae.

In central **Port of Spain**, clubs and bars tend to be fun but more rough and ready. Several lively bars on and close to Brian Lara Promenade, though some are very dirty. *Fast Lime*, on north side just east of *Royal Castle*, is clean and lively, especially Fri, open to around 2400, closed Sun. The *Bocas* on Chacon St is a bar by night. *Two Plus* on Henry St is busy on Fri with Laventille people and opens late, closing around 0400 Fri and Sat. Ballroom Thu night.

In **Barataria**, the poshest place is *Club Liquid*, Roundabout Plaza, glitzy, water running down the walls for decorative effect. On the other side of Barataria is *The Lair*, younger crowd and not nearly so posh, open to around 0400 weekends. In Grand Bazaar is *The Beer Garden*, T6621631, 1200-2400 Mon-Thu, 'a little later' Fri and Sat, 1500-2400 Sun, open-air and indoor sections, very busy. Also *The Parrot*, Grand Bazaar, Uriah Butler Highway, Valsayn, T6625631, 1000-2400 Mon-Thu, 1000-0400 Fri and Sat, 1600-2400 Sun. Meals around TT$60, older and richer crowd and extremely crowded.

Further east in **Tunapuna**, several small and lively bars, such as *The Sanctuary* and *The Palace*, lively at weekends and mostly open to around 0400 Fri, closing earlier in week. All along the Eastern Main Rd there are bars and restaurants with a busy crowd, especially on Fri, take your pick. The centre of **Arima** is full of life in the evenings, especially Fri after work. Lots of little bars, cheap Chinese restaurants, some of which open late. Liveliest are *Island Village*, on Hollis St, Fri night until 0400, and *Fifth Element*, close to Dial, Sat until 0400.

In **Chaguanas**, the *Matrix*, upstairs from *KFC*, open until around 0300 Fri and Sat. South of Chaguanas at **Edinburgh** and **Chase Village** are some fairly raunchy strip clubs which are frequently raided by the police. Risky and best avoided.

For nightclubs in **San Fernando**, *Club Celebs*, Gulf City Mall, La Romaine, T6527641, or *HiRPM*, same mall, T6523760, both until around 0400 weekends. For karaoke, try *The Lounge*, Carlton Centre, St James St, T6522719. Coffee St is lively, with plenty of bars.

There are several **casinos**, some of which run through the night. They are small and seedy by Bahamian or Aruban standards, but you can lose money just as effectively: slot machines, blackjack, roulette, etc, with 'free' sandwiches to keep you at it and 'free' drinks if you lose heavily. Best known are *Ma Pau*, in Ariapita Av and *Island Club*, at Grand Bazaar shopping mall, both open pretty much round the clock. Alternatively you can lose money in smaller amounts in most bars and neighbourhood shops through government-run gambling: *Play Whe*, which is based on traditional Chinese gambling, and the weekly *Lotto* draw.

Theatres *Queen's Hall*, 1-3 St Ann's Rd; *Little Carib*, White and Roberts Sts; *Central Bank Auditorium*, Eric Williams Plaza, Edward St. In San Fernando, *Naparima Bowl* has reopened after a lengthy period of renovation; for information on the folk theatre of the South National Institute of Performing Arts, T6535355. See Culture, page 797.

See press for details of performances

Cinemas See listing in daily papers. US-style multi-screens at **Movie Towne**, on highway west of Port of Spain (TT$35) and at **Trincity Mall**, near highway to Piarco (TT$15). Drive-in **Kay Donna**, Valsayn, also on highway to the east. 15 other cinemas, all very cheap, occasionally showing something good, beer, snacks, etc on sale. In Port of Spain, **Globe** and **Strand**, on Park St. **De Luxe,** at north end of Frederick St is only open for special showings, but worth visiting for glorious if run-down art deco design. Houses a calypso tent in Carnival season and also main venue for the Embassy-sponsored European film festival in Oct-Nov.

Shopping
Bargains can be found in fabrics, carvings, leather and ceramics

Most shops take US dollars but at a poor exchange rate. The main Port of Spain shopping areas are Frederick St, Queen St, Henry St and Charlotte St (fruit and vegetables), less exciting but more pleasant are Long Circular Mall at the junction of Long Circular Rd and Patna St, St James; West Mall, Cocorite, Port of Spain; Ellerslie Plaza on the way to Maraval, close to Savannah. There are also good but pricier local designers such as Meiling or Richard Young of *The Cloth*. Try shops in *Kapok* and *Normandie* hotels. Purchases can be made at in-bond shops in Port of Spain and at the airport. There is a huge selection of duty-free shops. *T-Wee* shop is recommended for **booze** and has the best aged rums, eg Guyanese El Dorado.

Watch expiry dates carefully when buying **food**. Expired food frequently remains on display. Scanner systems are inefficient, so shelf price is often different from price charged at checkout. Locally grown fruit and veg is often heavily sprayed, so wash thoroughly or peel. Markets offer a wide variety of fruit.

Handicrafts can also be purchased at some markets. In Port of Spain there are street vendors on Frederick St, Independence Sq and elsewhere selling hand-painted T-shirts, etc. *The People's Mall* between Frederick St and Henry St is a maze of booths selling clothes, shoes, etc along with bars and barbers' shops, lively especially Fri. Crafts also at *East Mall* on Charlotte St and at the cruise ship complex. There are several kilns in the Freeport area, turn off the Uriah Butler Highway before the Hindu temple for Chase Village. Good-quality local pottery in a variety of designs is available from *Ajoupa Pottery*, owned by Rory and Bunty O'Connor. You can get it in Port of Spain but a wider selection can be viewed at their kiln at Freeport, central Trinidad; T6225597 at Port of Spain shop at Ellerslie Plaza, or T6730604 at kiln/factory. Batik can be bought at many places including the Ajoupa Pottery shop at Ellerslie Plaza. The Central Market on the Beetham Highway is big, cheap fruit and veg, opens very early. Fresh fish by Western Main Rd in Carenage or on the highway near Valsayn.

For **music**, try *Crosby's Music Centre*, 54 Western Main Rd, St James, or *Rhyner's*, 54 Prince St, Port of Spain. Production costs are a problem so prices of local CDs are high, and despite being the main music outlets in this island of music they frequently have no stock. If you are going to Tobago, *Arcade Record Store*, Castries Rd, Scarborough, will make tape compilations to your specification, as will others, but check copyright status.

Metropolitan Books, Colsort Mall, has a good selection; *R I K Services Ltd*, Queen St, Port of Spain, and 104 High St, San Fernando, stocks mostly school books; *Ishmael M Khan and Sons*, 20 Henry St, Port of Spain is another good bookshop. Black literature at *Afrikan World Books* and *Kultural Items*, Park Plaza on Park St and St Vincent St, T/F6272128, good selection, history, contemporary issues. *Paper Chase* is a small shop with a good selection in the *Normandie* hotel. *A Different View* on Warren and Gallus St, Woodbrook, T6223648, has a good selection of Caribbean and Trinidad material, novels, New Age, good secondhand section. *Lexicon*, Boundary Rd, San Juan, T6753395, are wholesalers, but have very good selection and also do retail. There are secondhand bookshops in Town Centre Mall and various side streets.

Sports
For diving and watersports, see pages 760 and 761

Dwight Yorke is the best known of the dozen Trinidadian and Tobagonian footballers playing for top clubs internationally

Cricket is very popular. Test matches are played at Queen's Park Oval, west of Queen's Park Savannah, Port of Spain; take a cushion, sunhat/umbrella, whistle (!) and drinks if sitting in the cheap seats. It is a private club but a friendly gate guard might let you in for a look around. For information, ring **Queen's Park Cricket Club**, T6222295/6223787. There are smaller grounds for club cricket throughout both islands. Hockey and soccer are also played at the Oval (Football Association, T6245183/6247661) or at the Jean Pierre stadium, and rugby, basketball, cycling and marathon running are also popular. There is **horse-racing** at Santa Rosa Park, Arima, about 15 km outside Port of Spain. Horses for hire near Fort George.

Swimming at the *Hilton Hotel*, US$4 (US$2 children), or monthly season ticket US$28, *Cascadia Hotel* (chutes and waterslides, very busy at weekends and holidays) or *La Joya* at St Joseph, check first for availability, T6626929/6627492; see below for swimming and **golf** at **St Andrews (Moka) Golf Club** (T6290066); there are 5 other golf clubs on Trinidad, including a 9-hole public course at Chaguaramas (T6344349).

Tennis at Trinidad Country Club Maraval, T6223470, temporary membership, advance booking necessary, also at *Hilton Hotel*, **Tranquility Square Lawn Tennis Club** (T6254182) and public tennis courts at Princes Building Grounds, Upper Frederick St (T6231121). The *Cascadia Hotel*, Ariapita Rd, St Ann's has 2 **squash** courts with seating for 100 spectators per court, tennis courts, sauna and gym with lots of equipment and facilities, open for non-members, 0600-2100 Mon-Fri, 0900-1700 Sat, T6233511. Squash also at Pelican Squash Club, *Pelican Inn*, Cascade, T6276271, equipment for hire, and at Body Works Squash Courts, Long Circular Mall, T6221215, 0600-2200 (0900-1700 Sat), US$3/40 mins, advance booking essential.

Trinidad and Tobago Sightseeing Tours, run by Gunda Busch-Harewood, 12 Western Rd, St James, T6281051, F6229205. Speaks German, will arrange accommodation and car hire and has a representative on Tobago (Margaret Hinkson, T6397422, F6229205). Gunda also offers evening tours. She uses *Joy Tours* for sightseeing tours, deep-sea fishing, panyard visits, etc, T6337733, F6228974. *The Travel Centre Limited*, Level 2, Uptown Mall, Edward St, Port of Spain, T6235096, F6235101, is an American Express Travel Service Representative. Walking tours, cave exploration, horse riding in the Northern Range, kayaking expeditions and other trips off the beaten track can be arranged with *Caribbean Discovery Tours Ltd*, 9B Fondes Amandes Rd, St Ann's, T6247281, run by Stephen Broadbridge together with Merryl See Tai of the *Kayak Centre*, T6292680 (see page 762), camping (in basic-luxury tents or cabins) or lodging in guesthouses arranged for longer trips, tailor-made tours. *Banwari Experience Ltd*, 64 Prince St, Port of Spain, T624-TOUR, F6751619, banwari@tstt.net.tt, run by Andrew Welch, offers cultural and nature tours, hiking, birdwatching, Carnival. *Wilderness Explorers*, based in Guyana, www.wilderness-explorers.com, specialize in nature and adventure travel.

Tour operators
Trinidad and Tobago Tour Guide Association, president Dave Bostic, T6382423

Air From North America *Air Canada* and *BWIA* from Toronto; *American Airlines* from Miami and San Juan; *BWIA* from Miami, Washington DC and New York, all to Port of Spain. *North American Airlines* has charters from New York to Tobago and on to Trinidad. **From Europe** *BWIA* direct from London to Port of Spain; or go with *American* via Miami, or else *BA* (T1 800 7442997 toll free from Trinidad) or *Virgin* (T1 800 7447477) via Barbados or Tobago and change planes. *British Airways* and *Virgin Atlantic* from London Gatwick to Tobago. Several charters, including *Monarch Airlines* from London Gatwick to Tobago. **From South and Central America** To Port of Spain, *Aeropostal* from Caracas, *BWIA* from Caracas daily; *Rutaca* (T6238089) from Maturín, Margarita, Barcelona in Venezuela; *BWIA*, *Caribbean Star* and *Surinam Airways* from Georgetown, Guyana; *Surinam Airways* and *BWIA* from Paramaribo. *Air France* from Cayenne, on the way to Fort-de-France. *BWIA* twice weekly from Costa Rica. **From the Caribbean** *BWIA*, *Liat* and *Caribbean Star* connect Trinidad and Tobago with other Caribbean islands including Antigua, Barbados, Curaçao, Grenada, Jamaica (Kingston), St Lucia, St Maarten, St Vincent, San Juan, Puerto Rico. *Dutch Caribbean* flies from Curaçao. *BWIA* and *Tobago Express*, operate the domestic shuttle Trinidad-Tobago.

Transport
Charter flights can be difficult to book without an accommodation package

Sea See Getting around, page 755, for the ferry between Trinidad and Tobago. *Pier One*, Chaguaramas, T6344472 (Acosta Asociados, Güiria, T294-9820169), runs a ferry to **Venezuela** on Wed, 0900, 3½ hrs, leaves Güiria 1500, US$80 return plus VAT, departure tax TT$75, plus US$23 from Venezuela. Every Fri morning a boat carrying racing pigeons leaves for Güiria, Venezuela. Contact Francis Sagones, T6320040; or talk to Siciliano Bottini in the Agencia Naviera in Güiria for sea transport in the other direction. Fishing boats and trading vessels ply this route frequently and can often be persuaded to take passengers. A Trinidadian, Adrian Winter Roach, travels at least once a week with his boat *El Cuchillo*, and charges US$60 one way, US$100 return. He can be contacted in Venezuela through the *Distribuidora Beirut*, Calle Valdez 37, Güiria, T/F81677. From Cedros in southern Trinidad it is sometimes possible to travel by small boat to Tucupita in Venezuela. Lots of shipping lines have a service going north; go to Queen's Wharf and ask to speak to the captains. For Guyana, try *Abraham Shipping Company Ltd*, 10 Abercromby St, T6241138/1131, which handles 90% of the Guyana and Suriname trade. Be careful to get your passport stamped at both ends of the journey.

Drug dealers operate in these waters so behave with extreme caution. Small boats are likely to be intercepted by Venezuelan or Trinidad coast-guards, or both

Trinidad & Tobago

Bus *Express Commuter Service (ECS)* every 15-20 mins, 0600-2100 Mon-Sat, every 30 mins 0700-1900 Sun, from City Gate Terminal, Port of Spain, to San Fernando, US$1, or US$0.60 to other destinations: Arima, Chaguanas, Five Rivers. *PTSC* (T6237872) bus from City Gate to Chaguaramas every 60-90 mins, 0500-2200, US$0.30. Bus to airport from City Gate, 4 times daily, 0630, 0700, 1515, 1545, 45 mins, return 0715, 0745, 1600, 1630.

Car hire Car rental firms are numerous and include: *Auto Rentals Ltd*, Uptown Mall, Edward St, Port of Spain T6757368, Piarco Airport, T6692277, mail@autorentals.co.tt *Bacchus Taxi and Car Rental*, 37 Tragarete Rd, T6225588. *Kalloo*, 100 la Paille Village, Caroni, also airport, and Woodbrook, T6229073, T/F6695673, helpful, check tyres. *Singh's*, 7-9 Wrightson Rd, T6230150, and at airport, T6695417, F6643860, singhs1@tstt.net.tt *Southern Sales and Service Co Ltd*, El Socorro Extension Rd, San Juan, T6275623-4, 24-hr service. *Autocenter Ltd*, 6 Ariapita Av, T6284400. *Econo Car Rentals*, 191-193 Western Main Rd, T6228074, one of the cheapest. If you prefer a smarter car, contact *Executive Limousine Service*, 70 Sackville St, Port of Spain, T6278247. **Bicycles** Excellent bike shop, *Geronimo's Cycle and Sport Ltd*, 15 Pole Carew St, Woodbrook, Port of Spain, T6222453, owned and managed by former professional cyclist, Gene Samuel. *Bike Inn*, St James and 3 branches, T6455575, has new bikes from around US$125.

See also pages 754 and 762 **Maxi-taxi** These are colour-coded: yellow for Diego Martin and west, red for east, green for San Fernando, brown or black for maxis which start in San Fernando and travel south from there. The green and red ones set off mostly from the City Gate terminal; the yellow band from further west on South Quay; most Carenage and Chaguaramas maxis start from Green corner on St Vincent and Park Streets (*Globe* cinema); Maraval maxis start from Oxford and Charlotte Sts. Check route before starting, eg east taxis are either 'San Juan' or 'all the way up' the Eastern Main Rd to Arima, or 'highway', which is faster and closer to the airport but misses places like Tunapuna and Curepe. Fares start at US$0.30 and run to Arima, US$1; to Chaguanas, US$1; to San Fernando, US$1.75.

Route taxi In Port of Spain most sedan taxis (saloon cars, often rather beat up) set off from close to Independence Sq and use fast food restaurants as markers. They leave to the west from Chacon St on south side of square, for Chaguanas and San Fernando from near *KFC*, close to *Royal Castle* for Arima. Those for St Ann's and St James leave from Woodford Sq, for Carenage from Green Corner (St Vincent and Park Sts), and for Maraval, Belmont and Morvant from Duke and Charlotte Sts (also from here infrequently on to Maracas and the north coast). Fares in town US$0.50, further out US$0.75. If in a hurry you can pay for any empty seats and ask the driver to go. They will also go off-route for a little extra but going off-route to the *Hilton* costs US$7.

Directory **Banks** *Republic Bank Ltd*), 11-17 Park St, Port of Spain, T6254411, F6230371, open 0800-1100, 1200-1400, on Fri 0800-1200, 1500-1700. *Royal Bank of Trinidad and Tobago (RBTT)*, 3B Chancery Lane, Port of Spain, T6234291, and on Western Main Rd, Chaguaramas, not far from the marinas. *Bank of Nova Scotia*, Park and Richmond Sts, Port of Spain, T6253566. *Citibank*, Queens Park East, Port of Spain, T6251040. *Citicorp Merchant Bank*, same address, T6233344. *Western Union Money Transfer*, Uptown Mall, Edward St, Port of Spain, T6236000, and 10 other locations in Trinidad and Tobago. Bank branches in all major centres. Many suburban or shopping mall branches open 1000-1800. *Republic Bank* branch and ATM at *Crew's Inn Marina*. *Peake's Yacht Yard* has a branch with a 24-hr cash machine and a teller from 0900-1400.

A lot of places, eg University of the West Indies, are listed under 'T' for 'The' in the phone book **Communications** Internet cafés: *Interserve* (Chamber of Commerce building, near West Mall), *Mariner's Office* (Crew's Inn Marina). *Photo King*, at City Gate, Port of Spain, has computer access for email, TT$20 per hr. **Post:** *TT Post*, has a Port of Spain office on west side of Chacon St, north of Independence Sq. Stamps for Europe TT$4.50 upwards, USA TT$3.75. **Telephone** The main *Telecommunications Services of Trinidad and Tobago Ltd* (TSTT) offices on Frederick St and Independence Sq operate international telephone and fax. Charges for international calls are high. The fax number for the public is F6270856; they phone the recipient to say a fax is waiting. The fax service shuts outside working hrs except for urgent cases. This means no faxes for 3 days over

Carnival, so get it sent to your hotel. Companion phone cards are available for TT$10, 30, 60, or 100 plus 15% VAT, from TSTT offices, banks, airport, cruise ship complex, etc. Can be used from any touch tone phone. Home Direct Service for AT&T, Sprint and MCI, also Canada Direct and UK Direct available from TSTT, cruise ship complex in Port of Spain, TTYC, TTYA and Peake's Yacht Yard, also at Penitence St, San Fernando. To activate an overseas cellphone, visit a dealer (check yellow pages under 'cellular'), or the TSTT office in Frederick St, Port of Spain (Mon-Fri 0800-1600), West Mall or Trincity Mall (Mon-Sat 1100-1800), DSM Plaza, Chaguanas (Mon-Fri 0800-1600), St James St, San Fernando (Mon-Fri 0800-1600), Wilson Rd, Tobago (Mon-Fri 0800-1600), with passport. Allow 1 hr for service. The charge is TT$115 to activate for use with prepaid cards (which then cost TT$20-100 plus VAT). There is a 'roaming' agreement with some US cellphone systems, but per minute costs are very high. For a 'postpaid' service you will need a credit card.

Embassies and consulates Canada High Commission, 3-3A Sweet Briar Rd, St Clair (T6226232). **Denmark**, 20-22 Tragarete Rd, T6251156, F6238693. **Netherlands**, Life of Barbados Building, 69 Edward St, T6251210/1722, F6251704. **France** Embassy, 6th floor, Tatil Bldg, Maraval Rd, T6227446, F6282632. **Germany**, 7-9 Marli St, PO Box 828 (T6281630/2, F6285278). **Jamaica** High Commission, 2 Newbold St, St Clair, T6224995/7, F6289180. **UK** High Commission, 19 St Clair Av, St Clair, T6222748, F6224555. **USA**, 15 Queen's Park West, T6226371/6, F6285462, 0700-1700. **Venezuela**, 16 Victoria Av, T6279823/4, 0900-1300, 1400-1600, Consulate at same address, T6279773/4, visa section only open mornings.

Port of Spain, all listed on blue pages at beginning of phone book

Medical services There are hospitals in Port of Spain and San Fernando, as well as several district hospitals and community health centres. The **Port of Spain General Hospital** is at 169 Charlotte St, T6232951. Mount Hope, T6454673, has better facilities. **St Clair Medical Centre**, T6281451, is private, more comfortable, expensive, but not necessarily better equipped.

Tobago

Tobago is not as bustling as Trinidad but the island is ideal for people in search of relaxation. The tourist area is concentrated on the southwest end and about six miles from the capital, Scarborough. There are small hotels and guesthouses scattered all around the island, however, offering peace and quiet in beautiful surroundings. The forest on the central hills is quite wild and provides a spectacular backdrop for the many horse-shoe bays around the coast and there is good walking, sailing and diving. Tobago is 26 miles long and only 9 miles wide, shaped like a cigar with a central 18-mile ridge of hills in the north (the Main Ridge, highest point 1,890 ft), running parallel with the coast. These northeast hills are of volcanic origin and the southwest is flat or undulating and coralline. The population is concentrated in the west part of the island around Scarborough. The climate is generally cooler and drier, particularly in the southwest, than most parts of Trinidad.

IDD code: 868
Colour map 5, grid C6

Scarborough

Although there is a ferry from Trinidad, Tobago is best reached by air. Scarborough is only 15-25 mins' drive from Crown Point Airport and many beach hotels are within walking distance of the airport. Scarborough is small enough to walk around, but for trips to the suburbs or further afield take a route taxi or hire a car.

Ins & outs
See page 793 for further transport details

Division of Tourism kiosk is in NIB Mall, Scarborough, and the head office is on the 3rd level, next to *Buddy's Restaurant*, T6392125, F6393566, or at Crown Point Airport, T6390509, Tourbago@tstt.net.tt *TIDCO Tobago* is at Unit 12, TIDCO Mall, Sangster's Hill, Scarborough. Large-scale maps of Tobago can usually only be obtained in Trinidad (see page 763).

Tourist information
For safety issues in Tobago, see page 754

In Scarborough itself the **Botanic Gardens** on the hill behind the mall are worth a visit. There are also some interesting structures, such as the House of Assembly on James Park (built in 1825), and Gun Bridge, with its rifle-barrel railings. New development has included a new deep-water harbour and cruise ship terminal.

Sights
The town is pleasant but perhaps not worth an extended visit

Trinidad & Tobago

Things to do in Tobago

- Walk from **Anse Fourmi to Charlotteville** for spectacular scenery and birdwatching.
- Take a glass-bottom boat to **Little Tobago**, snorkel over the massive brain coral and see the nesting red-billed tropic birds.
- Try **crab and dumplings** at a local restaurant.
- Attend Sunday School on **Buccoo Beach** and party the night away.

Scarborough Mall is modern, concrete and rather tatty but most activity is around here: the tourist office, post office, library and bus station as well as the market, where you can find local varieties of fruit and vegetables, clothing, meat and fresh coconut water. There are banks on Main Street. Just off Main Street, George Leacock has turned his home into a museum that is quite interesting.

Above the town is **Fort King George**, which is well maintained and has good views along the coast. Building commenced in 1777 and continued under the French in 1786. Fort Castries was renamed Fort Liberté in 1790 after the garrison revolted, recaptured by the British in 1793, returned to France in 1801 and, after the island was ceded to Britain in 1802, named Fort King George after in 1804. It was decommissioned in 1854. The gardens are attractive and well kept and there are excellent views over Scarborough. There are a number of historic buildings here including the Officers' Mess, the Magazine (almost hidden under an enormous silk

Tobago

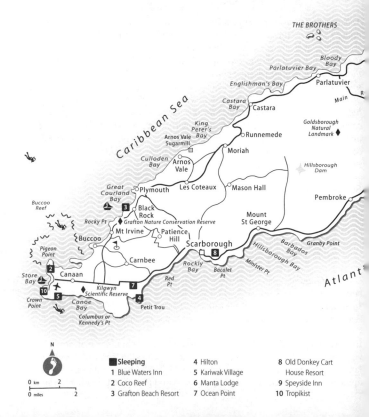

■ Sleeping		
1 Blue Waters Inn	4 Hilton	8 Old Donkey Cart
2 Coco Reef	5 Kariwak Village	House Resort
3 Grafton Beach Resort	6 Manta Lodge	9 Speyside Inn
	7 Ocean Point	10 Tropikist

cotton tree), the Bell Tank (still with water in it and an amazing echo), and a fine arts centre, which has displays by local artists as well as a permanent exhibition. A number of cannon mounted on metal garrison gun carriages can also be seen. There are two of artist Luise Kimme's huge wooden figures in the middle of the parade ground which are very attractive. You can visit her workshop on Sunday, T6390257. At the Barrack Guard House, the **Tobago museum** has an excellent display of early Tobago history including Amerindian pottery, military relics, maps and documents from the slave era. ■ *Mon-Fri 0900-1700, doors close 1630. US$0.50, children US$0.15. Drive through the hospital to get to the fort.*

Around the island

If you are driving around Tobago, the 1:50,000 map, usually available from the tourist office in Scarborough, at US$3.50, is adequate. Many of the minor roads are suitable only for 4WD. If you are hiking, get the three 1:25,000 sheets, not currently available in Tobago but obtainable from the Lands and Survey Division, Richmond St, Port of Spain, or from a good map shop. It is possible to walk anywhere. There is a book of trails.

Off the coastal road you can go to the Forest Reserve by taking a bus from Scarborough to **Mount St George** and then walking or hitching to **Hillsborough Dam**. The lake is the drinking-water supply for the island so swimming is not

East from Scarborough

allowed, but you may find a man to take you out in a rowing boat. It is a lovely forest setting. A 4WD vehicle is necessary if you want to drive but the walk there is recommended. From there continue northeast through the forest to **Castara** or **Mason Hall** on an unpaved, rough road. A guide is not necessary, as there is only one path. Birdwatching is excellent (oropendulas, mot-mots, jacamans, herons) and there are cayman in the lake, but look out for snakes (none of them poisonous). Alternatively, take a taxi to Mason Hall (ask the taxi to drop you at the road for the Hillsborough Dam) and walk to Mount St George via Hillsborough Dam, which is easier walking as the track is on the level or downhill, about 9 miles. By Mount St George (Tobago's first, short-lived principal town, then called George Town) is **Studley Park House** and **Fort Granby**, which guards Barbados Bay.

The road continues through **Pembroke** and **Belle Garden** and nearby is **Richmond Great House**, now a hotel. It has a lovely view but is not as 'great' as some of the plantation houses on other islands. **Roxborough**, the island's second town, also on the Windward coast, is worth a visit. The **Argyll River** waterfalls near Roxborough comprise four beautiful falls with a big green pool at the bottom, a 10-minute walk upstream from the road. You can't miss them because of all the rather overpriced and pushy guides standing in the road.

For a good walk take the road from Roxborough to Parlatuvier and Bloody Bay through the Main Ridge Forest Reserve. You go through singing forests with masses of birds including cocricos, collared trogon, mot-mots, jacamans, hummingbirds. After the 5-mile marker is a semi-circular trail in the forest called Gilpin's Trace. There are great views from the hut at the top of the road. Beyond Roxborough is **King's Bay**, with waterfalls near the road in which you can swim.

Speyside & Little Tobago

From the fishing village of Speyside you can visit Little Tobago, a forested islet off the northeast coast, and a sanctuary for birds. There are wild fowl and 58 species of other birds, including the red-billed tropic bird found here in the largest nesting colony in the north Atlantic. Boats across cost US$12.50 (includes a guided tour of the islet and snorkelling). There are lots of glass-bottomed boats and boatmen will find you fish and coral to see (see page 761). Go early in the morning to see the birds. If you want to camp, you are supposed to have prior permission from the Forestry Division at Studley Park, T6394468. They also have a rudimentary camp on the main ridge by the Roxborough-Parlatuvier road, which can be used by arrangement. At Speyside, you can sling a hammock near the government centre on the beachfront. It is well lit but it may be windy. A night-guard might keep your belongings under lock and key.

There are lurid, yet true, tales of tourists being lost up here for days

From Speyside you can climb **Pigeon Peak**, at about 1,900 ft the highest point on the island. There are two routes up the hill through the forest, the shorter one is steeper than the longer one, so both take about three hours. There is also a track on the Speyside Road from Charlotteville, 100 yd on the right before the turning to Flagstaff Hill. This is suitable for a 4WD to begin with. After about 30 minutes' walk you clamber down into a stream bed and up again, from which point it becomes a rough, steep path through old banana plantations and then woodland. There is no trouble following the path here, with markers cut into or painted on to trees, and there are many birds. However, when the ground becomes flatter, it becomes confusing. A guide is therefore essential. The actual summit is above the woodland, through grass and small shrubs, and has a trig point. From the top you can see the north and south coasts and offshore islets.

Scarborough

A trip to Charlotteville in the northeast is recommended. The easiest way to get there is by one of the seven buses a day from Scarborough, TT$8. There are maxi-taxis from Scarborough (TT$10, three a day but not on Saturday, when the Adventist drivers do not work, for the return journey you can arrange to be picked up). There are magnificent views on the way and the village itself is on a fine horseshoe bay with a good beach, lifeguard, good swimming and snorkelling and two dive shops. The Americans erected a radio tracking station in World War II on Flagstaff Hill overlooking Charlotteville (take the rough track off the main Speyside-Charlotteville road about ½ mile). There are several seats and a bandstand here. Half way along the rough road to Flagstaff Hill there is a cattle path to the right. Follow this as it descends and curves to the left. Near the bottom it meets another, wider trace (trail). Turn left and this will eventually bring you back to Charlotteville. It is a pleasant, shaded walk. From Charlotteville, it is a 15-minute walk to **Pirate's Bay**, which is magnificent and unspoilt and good for snorkelling. Also adjacent is **Man O'War Bay**. **Campbellton Bay** is a 30- to 40-minute walk from Charlotteville (ask for directions) through dense forest to a secluded beach, mostly used only by fishermen.

Charlotteville

The road between Charlotteville and Anse Fourmi along the Caribbean coast is no longer passable even with 4WD because of erosion. However, it is a wonderful hike and hikers are opposed to any repairs or paving of the road. The views are worth the trouble, with lots of lovely bays beneath you. Get a taxi to Anse Fourmi and walk (a comfortable four hours) along the track to Corvo Point, Hermitage (bush rum for sale), Man O'War Bay and Charlotteville. The terrain is undulating, bird life is plentiful, including parrots, and you may see iguanas. The stretch of road between Anse Fourmi and Moriah through Parlatuvier and Castara is smooth, traffic is light and it is very picturesque. Take water with you.

The north coast
Plymouth to Parlatuvier is not public transport route. You have to go via Roxborough

At the southwest end of the island there are many hotels and resorts, particularly in the Crown Point area. At **Store Bay** stand the ruins of small **Milford Fort**, and brown pelicans frequent the beautiful but crowded beach, which is a good place to watch the sunset. The fort was once Dutch (Bella Vista) but was overrun by the Indians. The British maintained a small battery here but it is now no more than a nice garden. **Pigeon Point** has the island's most beautiful beach, clean and with calm water. There are huts, tables and benches, lockers, bars, shopping, boat hire and watersports. It is another good place to watch the sunset. ■ *US$2, $0.50 children.*

The southwest

From **Mount Irvine Bay**, where there is an attractive, palm-fringed championship golf course (the hotel of the same name has a good beach for surfing), you can walk up to **Bethel** (about 2 miles), the island's highest village, for excellent views across the island. Another beach well worth a visit is **Turtle Bay**.

The main town on this coast is **Plymouth**, with **Fort James** overlooking **Great Courland Bay** (site of the Courlander settlement in the 17th century). Destroyed several times, the present fort was erected in 1800. Also here is the Latvian Monument. Designed by a local artist, it was erected in 1976 and represents 'Freedom'. A much-quoted attraction in Plymouth is the enigmatic tombstone of Betty Stevens (25 November 1783), which reads: "She was a mother without knowing it, and a wife, without letting her husband know, except by her kind indulgences to him."

Hidden in the forest some miles from **Arnos Vale** is the **Arnos Vale Sugarmill**, dating from 1880; a recommended excursion, it is possible to hitchhike. The Arnos Vale Waterwheel Park has a small museum, gift shop, restaurant and stage where shows are put on. The small village of **Castara** on the coast can be seen in 10 minutes but is a pleasant place to visit or stay. There is a small bay with a sandy beach and a snorkelling reef, and a 10-minute walk inland will take you to an easily accessible waterfall.

Trinidad & Tobago

▶ **Buccoo: goat-racing centre of the world**

Buccoo is the goat-racing centre of the world. The Buccoo Goat Race Festival was started in 1925 by Samuel Callendar and has taken place at several venues around the village before the current purpose-built track behind the beach facilities at Buccoo was constructed, in 1985. Easter Tuesday was chosen because Good Friday and Easter Saturday were already taken for marble pitching, Easter Sunday for the Moravian Love Feast and Easter Monday for horse racing.

The course is about 100 metres long and there is a maximum of 10 goats per race. Each jockey has to wear the silk of the goat's owner, white shorts and bare feet. Jockey and goat proudly walk around the ring with Mr Patterson giving the crowd helpful guidance on the form before walking down to the start. There is betting but it is all rather discreet. The goats are then loaded into the starting stall (accompanied by much banter from the commentators perched precariously in the judges' box). A yellow flashing light signifies that they are under starters orders,

the gates flip open and the race is on. Goats lead with the jockey running behind holding the goat on a short length of rope. This is no gentle jog, the goats are very fast and the jockeys would give Linford Christie a good run for his money. Of course, the jockey has little control over his goat and the best fun is had when the goat suddenly veers across the other runners. The finish is often chaotic with all 10 runners nearly ending in the grandstand at the end of the course. This may be one reason why the race was moved from the Battery, where the closeness of the cliffs overhanging the sea made it unpopular. The races are often very close and the judges have to study video evidence to find the winner.

The afternoon is interspersed with various cultural events and the occasional crab race. Huge sound rigs on the street above the course sometimes drown the commentators. The Prime Minister somtimes attends. Rum and beer flow and the whole day is topped off by an enormous jump up until late into the night.

Buccoo Reef
The reef is now protected by law; it is forbidden to remove or destroy the corals or other marine life

Glass-bottomed boats for visiting this undersea garden leave from Pigeon Point, Store Bay and Buccoo Bay. The charge is about US$15 for 2-2½ hours, with shoes and snorkel provided; wear a hat. Longer trips with barbecue cost around US$50-60, worth it if you eat and drink plenty. The dragging of anchors and greed of divers have tarnished the glory of this once marvellous reef (you may prefer to make the trip to Speyside where glass-bottomed boats make trips over a pristine reef). Elkhorn and other corals have been badly damaged by snorkellers and divers walking on them. Boat trips also include the **Nylon Pool**, an emerald-green pool in the Caribbean. Boats leave between 0900 and 1430, depending on the tide. Be selective in choosing which boat – and captain – you take for the trip; some are less than satisfactory.

Essentials

Sleeping
There are many cheap guesthouses and many people take in visitors; ask at any village store

Tobago Plantations, T6399377, www.tobagoplantations.com, is a 750-acre development around Petit Trou Lagoon, with hotel, villas, condominiums bungalows, championship Jack Nicklaus golf course, marina, shopping centre, wildlife refuge and tropical fruit plantation. On site, **LL** *Tobago Hilton*, T6608500, tobhilt@tstt.net.tt, all rooms with seaview and no more than 30 m from white, sandy beach.

Near Crown Point LL-AL *Coco Reef*, T6398571, cocoreef-tobago@trinidad.net Modelled on a Bermudan hotel, peach and white walls, red roof, 96 rooms, suites and villas on man-made beach, pretty view of Pigeon Point, height of luxury, close to airport and in main hotel area. **AL-A** *Kariwak Village*, T6398442, kariwak@tstt.net.tt Very nice, compact rooms in cabins, restaurant with excellent food, open 1230-1430, 1930-2130, meals around US$25 no beach, small pool, no radios or TV, meeting facilities, owners involved in the arts exhibitions held here, yoga and therapy, retreats. **AL-B** *Tropikist*, T6398512, F6390341. 53 good-sized a/c rooms with balcony, pool, loungers, large lawn, swings, restaurant overlooks sea, indifferent food, small beach but not suitable for swimming, painted white with lots of bougainvillea, right by airport. **A-C** *Belleviste Apartments*, Sandy Point, T/F6399351 bellevis@tstt.net.tt 20 self-contained apartments, kitchenette, pool, near airport.

B-C *Arthur's By The Sea*, Crown Point, T6390196, arthurs@trinidad.net   Kind and helpful, a/c, pool, 4-min walk from safe beach. **B-C** *Conrado Beach Resort*, Milford Extension Rd, between Store Bay and Pigeon Point, T6390145. CP, beachfront, standard or superior rooms, some small, some with balconies, TV, phone, some roadside view, priced accordingly, restaurant on beach for breakfast, inside for night-time, good snorkelling offshore on small reef, fishing boats moored outside, family-owned, excellent service. **B-C** *Crown Point Beach Hotel*, T6398781/3, crownpoint@trinidad.net   Studios and cabins, pool, *Best of Thymes* restaurant, excellent food. Guests at *Johnston Apartments*, T6398915, johnapt@tstt.net.tt, have use of *Crown Point* pool, restaurant and tennis court. **B-C** *Sandy Point Village*, T6398533, F6398534. 44 large rooms and suites, some split-level, TV, kitchenette, balcony, quiet a/c, in pleasant gardens, pool, beach rooms under restaurant open on to sea, poor beach, most people go to Store Bay, airless disco in basement, *The Deep*, music goes on until early hrs. If you turn right out of the airport, and take the first right, you come to **D-E** *Store Bay Holiday Resort*, T6398810, F6399733. 5-min walk, do not be fooled by taxi drivers who will charge US$5 for the ride, about the cheapest in this area, but self-catering only, 16 apartments, clean, well-furnished, kitchen, gardens, night-time security guard, small pool, friendly, good value. Close by is **B-C** *Toucan Inn*, T6397173, F6398933. Includes tax and service, African-style huts, good food and entertainment at *Bonkers* restaurant, open 0730-2230, main courses from US$12.

C-D *Jetway Holiday Resort*, 100 m from airport terminal, T/F6398504. Can be noisy until after 2200, 9 pleasant self-contained units with cooking facilities, friendly, helpful, a few mins' walk to Pigeon Point and Store Bay. **C-D** *James Holiday Resort*, Crown Point, T/F6398084. Standard room. 3-bedroom apartment maximum 12 people, car and jeep rental, credit cards accepted, 2-min walk from airport, TV, patio or balcony, restaurant. **C-D** *Surf Side Hotel*, Milford Rd Extension, Store Bay, T6399702, surfside@tstt.net.tt   30 self-contained apartments, a/c, walking distance to beaches. **D** *Serenity Apartments*, 14 Centre St, Canaan, T6390753, serenapt@tstt.net.tt   Run by Miss Selma Alfred, 5 double and triple rooms, kitchenette, a/c, balcony, daily cleaning, 2-min walk to buses, evening meals by arrangement, airport pick-up, tours arranged. **E** *Spence's Terrace*, Crown Point, T6398082. Room, kitchenette, bathroom, balcony, new and fresh. **F** *Doris Guest House*, and taxi service, John Gooram Trace, Milford Rd, Crown Point, T6608428. 15-min walk from airport and beach, nice, clean rooms with bathroom and cooking facilities, mosquito nets on windows, fan, quiet and safe, friendly owners. **F** *Lewis Villa*, T6398022. Small units with kitchen, good value.

There are lots of guesthouses and small hotels along the road between the airport and Pigeon Point

Lowlands area AL-C *Ocean Point*, Milford Rd, Lowlands, T/F6390973, www.oceanpoint.com   Studios sleep 3, suites fit 5, dive packages available, a/c, TV, pool, sundeck, 2-min walk from sea, transport needed, family-run, friendly. On the same road, **B-C** *Hampden Inn Guest House*, T/F6397522. CP, German spoken, standard or superior rooms all on ground floor, hammocks, large bathrooms, restaurant/bar, pool, bike hire, TV, dive packages, no pool. **C** *Viola's Place*, Birchwood Triangle, Hampden, T/F6399441, violasplace@hews-tours.com   14 self-contained rooms, kitchenette, pool, airport pick-up.

Scarborough About ½ mile south of Scarborough is the **B-C** *Old Donkey Cart House Resort*, 73 Bacolet St, T6396124. Run by Gloria Jones-Knapp, 2 mins from beach on hillside with seaview. CP, tax and service, charming rooms in old house or apartments in new building, restaurant, good food, pool. **A-B** *Horizons Tobago Apartments*, 89 Bacolet Point, T/F44-(0)121 7091648, www.toben.com   1- and 2-bedroomed apartments, a/c, large private pool, good amenities. **D** *Miriam's Bed and Breakfast*, or *Federal Villa*, 1-3 Crooks River, T6393926, F6393566. 3 rooms, shared bath, fan, modest but clean and comfortable, 7-min walk to harbour, run by friendly and helpful Miriam Edwards, secretary of the Bed and Breakfast Association. **E-F** *Hope Cottage*, Calder Hall Rd, corner of Ottley St, not far from hospital, T6392179, F6397550. 15 rooms, 3 with private bathroom, fan, pleasant, kitchen can be used, mini-market nearby, spacious public rooms, bar, restaurant, veranda, homely, peaceful, popular with students, entrance between 2 tamarind trees, brought from India and planted when original house was built in early 19th century.

The B&B Association lists 14 properties, mostly in the southwest or near Scarborough, about US$25

Trinidad & Tobago

Windward coast L-A *Blue Waters Inn*, Batteaux Bay, Speyside, T6602583, bwi@bluewatersinn.com An isolated and delightfully unsophisticated hotel, 38 rooms, 1- or 2-bedroom bungalows and self-catering units, caters for people who want to sit on the beach, birdwatchers and divers, includes tax and service, dive packages with *Aquamarine Dive* on site, tennis, very pretty bay, no other development, view of Little Tobago. **L-B** *Manta Lodge*, Windward Rd, Speyside, T6605268, info@mantalodge.com 22 standard, superior or loft rooms, rather sterile, loft has no view, a/c essential as hot under roof, superior rooms, though cheaper are better, with balcony, view and more air, small pool, bar, restaurant, caters mainly to divers, packages available with *Tobago Dive Experience*. **AL-B** *The Speyside Inn*, Windward Rd, Speyside, T/F6604852, speysideinn@trinidad.net 6 rooms, 2 cabins, lovely airy rooms, nicely furnished, excellent value, tax included, CP with home-made breads, dinner by reservation only, small beach across road, view of Little Tobago, close to *Jemma's* restaurant. One **F** guesthouse in Roxborough, ask for Mrs Carter, Police Station Rd, 2 rooms, kitchen, shower, quiet, friendly. *Top Ranking Hill View Guest House*, Top Hill St, Speyside, T6604904, toprank@tstt.net.tt 4 apartments with balcony view.

Accommodation here is expanding, particularly at the cheaper end

Charlotteville B *Man O'War Bay Cottages*, T6604327, pturpin@tstt.net.tt 10 cottages, sleep 4, minimum 2 nights, spacious, well-equipped kitchen, right on beach with tropical gardens behind, barbecue facilities, expensive shop with limited range, check your bill carefully. **C-E** *Cholson's Chalet* has rooms or 1 to 3-bedroomed apartments separated from the beach by the road, contact Hewitt Nicholson (T6392847) or Pat Nicholson (T/F6398553), the price sometimes rises after you have moved in. This place is very popular indeed and you may need to book in advance even in low season; in high season advance bookings of less than a week are not accepted. **D** *Morre's*, Bellaire Rd, Charlotteville, T6604799, contact Susan Simon. 4 double rooms, 1 2-bedroom self-contained apartment, all with kitchen facilities. **E** Mrs May Williams has ground-floor apartment, 2 rooms sleep 6, communal kitchen, bathroom, house faces jetty, between 2 shops painted blue, quite pleasant. **E** Marshall and Michelle Jack (twins), 13A Pirates Bay Rd, T6605923. Shared bathroom, no soap or towels but very clean, use of good kitchen, so close to sea that you could jump in from window, so don't stay there if the noise of the sea keeps you awake. **F** *Alyne*, very friendly, clean, comfortable. **F** *Dr P's Resort*, Belle Air St, T6605907. Double room or 2-room apartment, not the cleanest ever, kitchen, shower, toilet, fan, terrace, beautiful view of sea from hillside, accessible from track between Charlotteville and Pirate's Bay.

Castara A-C *Blue Mango*, T6392060. Owned by friendly Colin Ramdeholl, huts with kitchen, bathroom and fan, charming, good walking and swimming nearby, eating places in the village. **D-E** *The Naturalist Beach Resort*, Castara Village, T6395901, natural@trinidad.net 5 rooms, beach nearby, snorkelling.

Culloden Bay LL *Footprints Eco Resort*, T6600416, www.footprints ecoresort.com Set in 62 acres of nature reserve, 2 villas, 4 studio apartments and honeymoon retreat, more planned, all on stilts, well-equipped, palm roofs, wooden, solar powered with a/c, jacuzzi great views over sea, good fixed menu, saltwater pools at low tide, good snorkelling on reef very noisy cocrico birds at dawn calling across the valley, Mia Persad and staff willing to take you around if you have no transport. Get to it from Golden Lane, which passes the enormous silk cotton tree that is supposed to be the grave of Gan' Gan' Sarah.

Arnos Vale L-AL *Arnos Vale Hotel*, T6392881, F6393251. 38 rooms, beautiful surroundings in tropical forest, great birdwatching, mot mots and other birds come to be fed at 1600, afternoon tea-time, hospitable, dive shop, new 30-room complex at site of old water wheel. **D** *Arnos Vale Vacation Apartments*, Arnos Vale Rd, Plymouth, T/F6392881, trade-info@tidco.co.tt Run by Victor Forde, 1 or 2-bedroom apartments, kitchen, large living area, fully furnished, beautiful garden with fruit trees and tropical birds, transport to airport, car hire available.

Plymouth LL-L *Mount Irvine Bay Hotel and Golf Course*, T6398871, F6398800. Rooms, suites or garden cottage, luxury furnishings, TV, phone, pool, beach, sauna, gym, mediocre food a

Sugar Mill restaurant, tennis, gardens of 16 acres. **LL-L** *Grafton Beach Resort*, Stonehaven Bay, Black Rock, T6390191, grafton@trinidad.net 108 rooms, luxury. A/c, pool, TV, friendly and efficient service, good food, excellent beachfront location, facilities for the disabled. **LL** *Le Grand Courlan* is its sister resort next door, T6399667, legrand@trinidad.net 78 luxury rooms, 10 1-bedroom suites, 8 garden rooms with jacuzzis, all have phone, fan, a/c, hairdryers, minibar, handsome furnishings, shops, pools, restaurants, business centre, health spa, fully equipped gym, very upmarket compared with other hotels on Tobago. **AL** *Rex Turtle Beach Hotel*, Plymouth, T6392851, F6391495. 125 rooms, overlooking garden, railings on upperfloor balconies unsafe for children, pool, on beach, tennis, a/c, service and management good, Sun West Indian buffet highly recommended, especially the curried crab. **AL-D** *Cocrico Inn* and *Courland Bay Villa*, T6392961, cocrico@tstt.net.tt 16 rooms, kitchenette or 4-room villa and apartment, restaurant, swimming pool, friendly, clean, excellent meals, laundry service. **B** *La Belle Creole*, Mt Irvine, T6390908. Run by Mrs Gerhild Oliver, English, German, French and Italian spoken, right by golf course, 5-min walk from beach, CP, dinner on request, queen-sized beds. **B-C** *Old Grange Inn*, Buccoo Junction, Mt Irvine, T6399941, grangeinn@trinidad.net 18 rooms, pool, restaurant, bar, a/c. **B-D** *Blue Horizon*, Jacamar Drive, Mt Irvine, T6390432/3, F6395006. 14 self-contained rooms, kitchenette, pool. **E** *Green Acres*, Daniel Trace, Carnbee, T6398287. Clean rooms with shower, safe, some with kitchens, CP, delicious local food, friendly family, US$4-5 taxi service. **C-E** *King Solomon's Mine Holiday Resort*, T6392545. Owned by Leroy Solomon, at the end of George St off Shelbourne St where buses run, rooms or apartments, kitchen, beautifully furnished, good view from upstairs balcony, popular with Germans. **E** *Michael Baker's* apartments, Daniel Trace, Carnbee, T6398243. Owner is chief of lifeguards and singer. **E-F** *Rolita Tea Hut*, Old Grange Rd, Mt Irvine, opposite *Blue Horizon*. Small guesthouse run by Roy and Pat Cousins, rooms with shower and WC, pool, meals available 0700-2100 daily, also lunch boxes, 20-min walk from beach. T6397970. **F** *The Vibe*, right by the jetty in Buccoo, themillers1@hotmail.com Ask for Cecil, hostal beds or double room, peaceful, quiet, clean, fan, shower, breakfast US$5, Cecil also runs a bar.

Self-catering villas: *Sanctuary Villa Resort*, Grafton Estate, T6399556, www.sanctuaryvillas.com Luxury villa development just inland, fantastic views across island to Pigeon Point and Buccoo Reef from hill, bordered by 260-acre bird sanctuary. *Villas at Stonehaven*, Bon Accord, Black Rock, T6390361, stonehav@tstt.net.tt 14 3-bedroom villas each with 'infinity pool', restaurant, 20-acre wildlife sanctuary. *Plantation Beach Villas*, Stonehaven Bay, T6399377, villas@wow.net 6 3-bedroom houses with pool.

www.realestate tobago.com/villas has about 20 villas to let

Around Store Bay and Crown Point There are a number of restaurants, many with tables outside near the beach. *Blue Notes*, 2 mins walk from airport. Small bar and restaurant run by a jazz lover. Excellent local food. The *Beach Bar* has music all day on Sat, and a barbecue from 2000-2400, for US$17 per head for drinks and small portions of fish and chicken, poor value unless you drink a lot. *Miss Jean's*, T6390211. 0800-1900 daily, US$2 and less for all kind of 'ting', a full meal with drinks for 2 costs less than US$10, crab and dumplings are a speciality but the crabs are woefully small because of overfishing. *Miss Esme*, T6390163. Flying fish and bake, 0730-1730 daily. *Golden Star*, Crown Point, T6390873. Restaurant and bar, lobster thermidor and grilled king fish in Creole sauce, 0700-2300 daily. *Dillon's Seafood Restaurant*, Crown Point, T6398765. Open daily from 1800 except Mon. *Bonkers*, at Store Bay Local Rd, Crown Point, T6397173. Serves Creole food, live music, 0700-2200. *Joy's*, in Buccoo. Small, friendly, good local food for US$3.50, barbecue on Wed for US$2.50. *La Tartaruga*, Buccoo Bay, T6390940. Italian restaurant café-bar, Mon-Sat 1900-2130, excellent Italian food, limited menu, expensive, reservations essential. *Buccoo Place*, next door, same management, is simpler, 0930-1930 Tue-Sat, 0930-0200 Sun.

Patinos, Shirvan Rd, T6399481. Run by Kenneth and Marcia Patino with their son as chef, excellent food, delicious West Indian platter at lunchtime, evening steel band once a week, 1830-2230 daily, reservations needed. Good accommodation too. *Shirvan Watermill*, on Shirvan Rd, T6390000. Specializes in seafood and steaks, expensive and romantic, main courses from US$15, 1700-2200 daily. *Pelican Reef Bar & Grill*, T6608000. Main courses from US$9, open 1830-2230.

Eating

Most of the food from the huts on the beach is reheated

Trinidad & Tobago

The *Black Rock Café* on Black Rock main road, T6397625. Recommended for very good food, slow service, very busy, 1130-2300 Mon-Fri, 1500-2300 Sat, Sun. *Under the Mango Tree*, Black Rock. Very tasty local food, US$17 for full meal. *The Seahorse Inn*, beachfront, next to *Grafton Beach Resort*, T6390686. Excellent dinners, extensive menu, main course from US$16, 0745-1045, 1200-1530, 1830-2200 daily with happy hr 1730-1830 for drinks. *Indigo*, 2 Horseshoe Ridge, Pleasant Prospect, Grafton, T6310353, indigo2@tstt.net.tt Local and foreign dishes, very good food, garden setting, 1200-1500 Mon-Fri, plus 1900-2200 Mon-Sat, also accommodation.

Charlotteville *Sharon and Phebe's*, Charlotteville, T6605717. Nice view of the bay, very good and cheap meals, try the prawns if available, dumplings and curried crab also recommended, 0900-2300 Mon-Sat, Sun 1100-2300, very friendly, reopened after a fire, spotless, Phebe also has a laundry and special prices for people on yachts. *Gail's*, Charlotteville, on seafront as you walk to Pirate's Bay. Breakfast and dinner, no lunch, all fresh, very tasty, delicious vegetables and salad, Gail is a genius with fish, very friendly.

Speyside *Jemma's Sea View*, Speyside, T6604066, on a tree-top platform by the beach. Good, filling lunch or dinner, fixed menu but 2 choices, TT$40, slow service, nice atmosphere, no alcohol, 0900-2100 Sun-Thu, 0900-1600 Fri, closed Sat, you can get hassled here for boat trips.

Scarborough The *Blue Crab*, at the corner of Main St with Fort St, Scarborough, T6392737. Specializes in local food, very good lunch but slow service, reasonable prices, nice view over harbour, 1100-1500 Mon-Fri, will open for breakfast and Mon, Wed, Fri evenings by reservation. *Old Donkey Cart*, Bacolet, T6393551. Good food, European wines, nice shady garden setting or in old house if it is raining, 0800-2200, closed Wed except Dec-Apr.

Nightlife

The cinema in Scarborough is good value, US$1.10 for two films, but the audience can be a bit noisy

Though not as lively as Trinidad, Tobago does offer dancing in its hotels. The **Buccoo Folk Theatre** gives an attractive show of dancing and calypso every Thu at 2100. There is a *Tobago Folk Performing Company*. In **Scarborough**, *Golden Star Entertainment Centre*, nightly. *Crown Point*, T6390873, also bar-restaurant in day, 0700-0100, or until 0400 weekends/special events. *Michael's Bar*, Black Rock, recommended for friendly evening entertainment. The *Lush Pub*, Shirvan Rd, Store Bay, is recommended; busiest Fri 2300-0400. Good food, pool and table football, a bit sleazy but lively. Also nearby *Green Light*, busiest Fri, Sat, 2200-0400. Look in on the entertainment spots in the Crown Point area: *The Deep*, Sandy Point Village, and *Bonkers*, Store Bay Local Rd, T6397173, 0700-2200. Don't miss Sunday School on Buccoo Beach, a big party starting early every Sun evening with live music, followed at about 2300 by a DJ playing until early in the morning, TT$5, 2000-0400. Entertainment is available every night of Tobago Race Week, mostly at Crown Point but also at *Grafton Beach* or *Grand Courlan* hotels.

Shopping

On Tobago, you can get excellent handicrafts at the *Cotton House*, Bacolet St, just outside Scarborough (taxi US$2.50), batik studio, high standard, pictures and clothes at reasonable prices. They also have an outlet at Sandy Point. Local batiks also at the *Backyard*, Milford Rd, Crown Point and locally produced artefacts at *Shore Things*, Pigeon Point Rd. *Arcade Record Store*, Castries Rd, Scarborough, will make tape compilations to your specification. *Francis Supermarket* at Crown Point is not particularly well stocked but is open Mon-Sat 0800-1800, Sun and holidays 1000-1400. The main supermarket is *Penny Savers* on main road at Milford, good range including pharmaceuticals, open long hrs and holidays, has ATM (blue machine).

Sports

For diving and watersports, see pages 760 and 761

On Tobago, **golf** and **lawn tennis** at *Mount Irvine Bay*, T6398871: green fee US$20 per day, tennis US$3 daytime, US$6 at night. Squash at *Grafton Beach Resort*, 0800-2200, US$9.50 for 45 mins including court, ball and racket rental. Black Rock has a **basketball** league in late Aug, early Sep; you can play before or after the games. **Volleyball** at the *Turtle Beach Hotel*.

AJM Tours at the airport, T6390610, F6398918, day trips on Tobago and to Margarita, Angel **Tour operators**
Falls, Grenada and the Grenadines. Peter Gremli, T6398400 is a recommended tour guide,
friendly, knowledgeable and popular. Taxi drivers have set rates for sightseeing tours and
can be more flexible than an organized tour.

Air There are many seasonal and regular charters to Tobago in addition to the following **Transport**
scheduled flights: from Barbados (*BWIA*, *Liat*), Grenada (*BWIA*, *Liat*), London (*British Air-*
ways and *Virgin Atlantic*) and Miami (*BWIA*). Other flights connect through Port of Spain,
see Transport, page 781.

Car hire *Auto Rentals Ltd*, Crown Point Airport, T6390644, F6390313. *Peter Gremli Car*
Rental, Crown Point, T6398400. *Rodríguez Travel*, Clark Trace, Bethany, T6398507.
Banana Rentals at *Kariwak Village*, T6398441, cars and jeeps, US$21 per day, scooters US$10
per day (deposit US$60). *Suzuki Jeep Rental* and small cars, and *Cherry Scooter Rental* at
Sandy Point Beach Club scooters and deposit cheaper than *Banana*. *Tobago Travel*, Store Bay
Rd, Crown Point, T6398778/8105, F6398786, *Baird's*, Lower Sangster Hill Rd, T6392528.
Rollock's Car Rental Service, Lowlands, T6390328, after hrs T6397369, US$48 per day, rec-
ommended. *Hill Crest Car Rental Service*, 47 Mt Pelier Trace, Scarborough, T/F6395208.
Thrifty Car Rental, *Turtle Beach Hotel*, T6398111, and other agencies. **Bicycles** Bike repairs
and parts at *Numeral Uno* hardware store in Carnbee, a good contact for joining local riders
for some fun road riding. Bikes for hire from *Banana Rentals*, US$4 per day, see above.

Bus and route taxi Buses originate in Scarborough. Every hr on the hr between
Scarborough and Crown Point (airport), TT$2, 25 mins. Bus Scarborough-Plymouth hourly
on the hr, return on the ½ hr, half-hourly in busy times, via Carnbee, Buccoo junction, Mt
Irvine and Black Rock. To Charlotteville 7 buses a day, TT$8, first one at 0430, 1½ hrs and then
return. Also some maxis on this route. On Tobago, route taxis charge TT$4 and leave from
Republic Bank in Scarborough. The Crown Point Airport route is the best, every 15-30 mins,
0530-1830; Black Rock route is fair, every 30 mins Mon-Fri 0530-2030, every 60-75 mins Sat
and Sun until 2000. Route taxis to Charlotteville start from Burnett Sq, TT$9-10 depending on
whether vehicle is minibus or car, 1-1½ hrs.

Taxi Taxi fares are clearly displayed as you leave the airport: to Crown Point US$6, Pigeon
Point US$7, Scarborough US$10, Mt Irvine, Roxborough US$33, Speyside US$40,
Charlotteville US$45.

Banks On Tobago, there are no banks or ATMs in the north of the island. ATMs can be found at the **Directory**
airport, **Penny Savers Supermarket** on Milford Rd and in Scarborough. They accept Visa, Plus,
Mastercard and Cirrus. **Communications** Telephone There is a TSTT telephone office in
Scarborough. Home direct service for AT&T, Sprint and MCI available from TSTT office and at the
airport. Hospital Scarborough (T6392551). **Medical services** There is a hospital in Scarborough.

Background

History

Trinidad was discovered by Columbus and he claimed it for Spain on his third voyage in **Columbus'**
1498. Whether he named the island after the day of the Holy Trinity, or after a group of three **arrival**
hills that he spied from the sea is a matter of dispute. At that time there were probably seven
tribes of Amerindians living on the island. It was their hostility which prevented successful
colonization until the end of the 17th century when Catalan Capuchin missionaries arrived.
European diseases and the rigours of slavery took their toll on the Amerindian population
and by 1824 there were only 893 Amerindians left.

Trinidad & Tobago

Spanish rule

VS Naipaul's The Loss of El Dorado is a fascinating, if pessimistic, account of the early Spanish settlement, Sir Walter Raleigh's raid, and the early years of British rule

The first Spanish Governor was Don Antonio Sedeño who arrived in 1530 but who failed to establish a permanent settlement because of Indian attacks. In 1592 Governor Don Antonio de Berrio y Oruna, founded the town of San José de Oruna (now St Joseph). It was destroyed by Sir Walter Raleigh in 1595 and not rebuilt until 1606. In 1783 a deliberate policy to encourage immigration of Roman Catholics was introduced, known as the Royal Cedula of Population, and it was from this date that organized settlement began with an influx of mostly French-speaking immigrants, particularly after the French Revolution. Many also came from St Lucia and Dominica when these islands were ceded to Britain in 1784. Others came with their slaves from the French Caribbean when slavery was abolished and from Saint Domingue after the war of independence there (including the Compte de Lopinot, whose house in Lopinot has been restored, see page 769).

British rule

British rule in Trinidad began in 1797 when an expedition led by Sir Ralph Abercromby captured the island. It was formally ceded to Britain by Spain in 1802 under the Treaty of Amiens. African slaves were imported to work in the sugar fields introduced by the French, until the slave trade was abolished in 1807. After the abolition of slavery, in 1834, labour became scarce and the colonists looked for alternative sources of workers. Several thousands of immigrants from neighbouring islands came in 1834-48, and some Americans from Baltimore and Pennsylvania came in 1841 and Madeiran 'Portuguese' came seeking employment and were joined by small numbers of European immigrants – British, Scots, Irish, French, Germans and Swiss. There was also immigration of free West Africans in the 1840s. In 1844 the British Government gave approval for the import of East Indian labour and the first indentured labourers arrived in 1845. By 1917, when Indian immigration ceased, 141,615 Indians had arrived for an indentured period of five years, and although many returned to India afterwards, the majority settled. The first Chinese arrived in 1849 during a lull in Indian immigration. In 1866 the Chinese Government insisted on a return passage being paid which put an end to Chinese immigration. Labour shortages led to higher wages in Trinidad than in many other islands and from emancipation until the 1960s there was also migration from Barbados, Grenada and St Vincent. In the 1980s and 1990s there has been immigration from Guyana.

Colonial Tobago

Tobago is thought to have been discovered by Columbus in 1498, when it was occupied by Caribs. In 1641 James, Duke of Courland (in Latvia), obtained a grant of the island from Charles I and in 1642 a number of Courlanders settled on the north side. In 1658 the Courlanders were overpowered by the Dutch, who remained in possession of the island until 1662. In this year Cornelius Lampsius procured Letters Patent from Louis XIV creating him the Baron of Tobago under the Crown of France. After being occupied for short periods by the Dutch and the French, Tobago was ceded by France to Britain in 1763 under the Treaty of Paris. But it was not until 1802, after further invasions by the French and subsequent recapture by the British, that it was finally ceded to Britain, becoming a Crown Colony in 1877 and in 1888 being amalgamated politically with Trinidad. By some reckonings Tobago changed hands as many as 29 times and for this reason there are a large number of forts.

Dr Eric Williams

The first political organizations in Trinidad and Tobago developed in the 1880s, but in the 1930s economic depression spurred the formation of labour movements. Full adult suffrage was introduced in 1946 and political parties began to develop. In 1956, the People's National Movement (PNM) was founded by the hugely influential Dr Eric Williams, who dominated local politics until his death in 1981. The party won control of the new Legislative Council, under the new constitutional arrangements which provided for self-government, and Dr Williams became the first Chief Minister. In 1958, Trinidad and Tobago became a member of the new Federation of the West Indies, but after the withdrawal of Jamaica, in 1961, the colony, unwilling to support the poorer members of the Federation, sought the same independence rights for Trinidad and Tobago. The country became an independent member of the Commonwealth on 31 August 1962, and became a republic within the Commonwealth on 1 August 1976. Dr Williams remained Prime Minister until his death in 1981, his party drawing on the support of the ethnically African elements of the population, while the opposition parties were supported mainly by the ethnic Indians.

In 1986, the National Alliance for Reconstruction (NAR) ended 30 years' rule by the PNM, which had been hit by corruption scandals and the end of the oil boom of the 1970s, winning 33 of the 36 parliamentary seats in the general election.

The 1991 elections brought another about turn in political loyalties, with Patrick Manning, of the PNM, leading his party to victory, winning 21 seats. By mid-term the Government was suffering from unpopularity and lack of confidence. In 1995 the economy began to improve and the Prime Minister took a gamble in calling early general elections to increase his majority. His tactic failed, however, when the United National Congress (UNC), led by Basdeo Panday, and the PNM both won 17 seats. Although the PNM received 48.8% of the vote compared with 45.8% for the UNC, Basdeo Panday formed an alliance with the NAR, who again won the two Tobago seats, and he was sworn in as Prime Minister on 9 November 1995. A lawyer and trade union leader, he was the first head of government of Indian descent.

Elections were held in December 2000, after a bad-tempered campaign. The opposition PNM accused the Government of large-scale corruption. With high energy prices and continuing economic growth, the UNC claimed a record of strong 'performance' and attacked the personality of Patrick Manning (PNM leader). The UNC won 52% of the popular vote and 19 of the 36 seats. However, the PNM disputed this result in a number of court cases, alleging electoral malpractice.

In September 2001, three cabinet ministers were fired for speaking out against alleged government corruption. Accordingly, the UNC lost its parliamentary majority, and new elections were held in December 2001, in which both PNM and UNC won 18 of the 36 seats. With no constitutional mechanism for choosing a prime minister in a 'hung' parliament, both party leaders agreed after discussions that the choice should be made by President Robinson. On Christmas Eve, he appointed Mr Manning of the PNM as Prime Minister. However, the UNC then immediately said that while the President could choose, any choice other than Mr Panday was unconstitutional. With the UNC also reneging on an agreed choice of Speaker, parliament could not function. With a number of official inquiries into corruption allegations in progress, six people including a former UNC finance minister were charged formally with corruption and money laundering in March 2002. New elections in Oct 2002 gave the PNM a working majority, with 20 seats to 16 for the UNC. Although there is some continuing political tension, there appears to be no danger of political violence.

Government

Trinidad and Tobago became a republic within the Commonwealth on 1 August 1976 under a constitution which provides for a President and a bicameral Parliament comprising a 31-seat Senate and a 36-seat House of Representatives. Tobago has its own 12-seat House of Assembly, which runs many local services. In 2003 the presidential election was won by Max Richards, a former principal of the University of the West Indies. The electoral college which votes for the president is made up of the House of Representatives and the Senate.

Economy

Petroleum, natural gas and their products dominate the economy, providing about 25% of GDP, 20% of government current revenue and 75% of foreign exchange earnings. 75% of oil production comes from marine fields. Production is around 113,000 barrels a day but there have been new offshore discoveries in 2001-02. There is one refinery, at Pointe-à-Pierre, the other at Point Fortin having been mothballed. The island has substantial proven reserves of natural gas of 33 trillion cu ft, producing about 1.4 billion cu ft daily. These are used as a basic raw material for the production of petrochemicals such as methanol and ammonia, to provide liquefied natural gas for export and to provide electric power throughout the country. Trinidad's mineral deposits include asphalt from the pitch lake at La Brea on the southwest coast, gypsum, limestone, sand and gravel, which are mainly used for construction.

Agriculture now contributes only 1.4% of GDP and employs only 7.7% of the labour force. Coffee and cocoa production has fallen and the sugar industry makes heavy losses. However, fruits and vegetables are produced successfully.

Tourism is an important source of foreign exchange, but only really in Tobago. Of total stopover arrivals, only 21%, around 80,000, are tourists staying in hotels and guesthouses, most of whom go to Tobago. Business visitors make up 18% of the total and 55% are Trinidadians returning home to visit friends and relatives. Tobago now has 2,200 hotel rooms available, following an expansion in construction, notably a 200-room *Hilton* hotel, while Trinidad has slightly fewer. Although Port of Spain attracted 71,500 cruise passengers in 2001, with another 10,800 in Tobago, numbers have subsequently dipped because of a preference for short haul cruises out of Miami since September 2001.

Culture

People   Trinidad has one of the world's most cosmopolitan populations. The emancipation of the slaves in 1834 and the adoption of free trade by Britain in 1846 resulted in far-reaching social and economic changes. To meet labour shortages, over 150,000 immigrants were encouraged to settle here from India, China and Madeira. Of today's population of approximately 1,276,000, about 42% are black and 42% East Indian. The rest are mixed race, white, Syrian or Chinese. French and Spanish influences dominated for a long time (Catholicism is still strong) but gradually the English language and institutions prevailed and today the great variety of peoples has become a fairly harmonious entity, despite occasional political tension between blacks and those of East Indian descent. French patois is still spoken here and there, eg in the village of Paramin, just north of Port of Spain.

Tobago's population, mainly black, numbers about 51,000. The crime rate is catching up with Trinidad's but the people are still noticeably helpful and friendly.

Religion   Catholics are still the largest religious group but Hindus are not far behind. The Anglican Church and Methodists are also influential, as are many evangelical groups and the Muslim organisations. Spiritual Baptists blend African and Christian beliefs; the women wear white robes and head ties on religious occasions. They can be seen performing baptisms in the sea on the coast to the west of Port of Spain on Sunday nights. Orishas follow a more purely African tradition. Most East Indians are Hindu, some are Muslim, while others have converted to Christianity, particularly Presbyterianism (Canadian Presbyterian missionaries were the first to try converting the Indian population).

Carnival and   The most exciting introduction to the culture of this republic is the Carnival, or 'De Mas', as
visual arts   locals refer to the annual 'celebration of the senses'. Alongside a strong oral/literary tradition goes a highly developed visual culture, reflecting the islands' racial mix. The most obvious examples are the designs for the carnival bands, which often draw on craft skills like wire bending, copper beating, and the use of fibreglass moulds. A fabled, controversial Mas' designer is Peter Minshall, who designed the opening ceremony for the 1992 Barcelona Olympic Games and for the Atlanta Games in 1996. Michel Jean Cazabon, born 1813, was the first great local artist (an illustrated biography by Aquarela Gallery owner Geoffrey MacLean is out of print, but there is an illustrated book on the Lord Harris Collection with plenty of information). Contemporary work to look out for includes paintings and other artwork by Christopher Cozier, Irenée Shaw, Che Lovelace, Mario Lewis, Wendy Nanan, Emheyo Bahabba (Embah), Francisco Cabral, and Anna Serrao and Johnny Stollmeyer. Established artists include Pat Bishop, Isaiah Boodhoo, LeRoy Clarke, Kenwyn Crichlow and Boscoe Holder. A space with contemporary work on show is *CCA7* on Fernandes-Angostura distillery compound, T6251889, www.cca7.org Commercial galleries include 101 Tragarete Road, *1234* in the *Hotel Normandie*, and *Art Creators* in de Lima Apts, St Ann's, also close to the *Normandie*.

The extraordinary spectacle of Carnival (see page 757) is considered by many to be safer, more welcoming to visitors and artistically more stimulating than its nearest rival in Rio de Janeiro. Commercialization is undermining many of the greatest Mas' traditions but some of the historical characters like the Midnight Robber and the Moko Jumbies can be glimpsed at the Viey La Cou old-time Carnival street theatre at Queen's Hall a week before Carnival and often at J'Ouvert (pronounced joo-vay) on Carnival Monday morning, and in small, independent bands of players. But it's a great party, enlivened by hundreds of thousands of costumed masqueraders and the homegrown music, calypso and steel band (usually referred to as 'pan').

Calypsonians (or kaisonians, as the more historically minded call them) are the commenta- **Music &** tors, champions and sometime conscience of the people. This unique musical form, a mix- **theatre** ture of African, French and, eventually, British, Spanish and East Indian influences, dates back to Trinidad's first 'shantwell', Gros Jean, late in the 18th century. Since then it has evolved into a popular, potent force, with both men and women (also children, of late) battling for the Calypso Monarch's crown. This fierce competition takes place at the Sunday night Dimanche Gras show at the Queen's Park Savannah, which in turn immedi- ately precedes the official start of J'Ouvert at 0400 on the Monday morning, marking the beginning of Carnival proper. Calypsonians band together to perform in 'tents' (perform- ing halls) in the weeks leading up to the competition and are judged in semi-finals, which hones down the list to six final contenders. The season's songs blast from radio stations and sound systems all over the islands and visitors should ask locals to interpret the some- times witty and often scurrilous lyrics, for they are a fascinating introduction to the state of the nation. Currently, party soca tunes dominate, although some of the commentary calypsonians, like Sugar Aloes, are still heard on the radio. There is also a new breed of 'Rapso' artists, fusing calypso and rap music. Chutney, an Indian version of calypso, is also becoming increasingly popular, especially since the advent of radio stations devoted only to Indian music. Chutney is also being fused with soca, to create 'chutney soca'.

Pan music has a shorter history, developing this century from the tamboo-bamboo bands which made creative use of tins, dustbins and pans plus lengths of bamboo for per- cussion instruments. By the end of the Second World War (during which Carnival was banned) some ingenious souls discovered that huge oil drums could be converted into expressive instruments, their top surfaces tuned to all ranges and depths (the ping pong, or soprano pan, embraces 28 to 32 notes, including both the diatonic and chromatic scales). Aside from the varied pans, steel bands also include a rhythm section dominated by the steel, or iron men. For Carnival, the steel bands compete in the grand Panorama, playing calypsoes which are also voted on for the Road March of the Year. Biennally, the World Steel Band Festival highlights the versatility of this music, for each of the major bands must play a work by a classical composer as well as a calypso of their choice. On alternate years the National Schools Steel Band Festival is held, in late October/early November. A pan jazz festival is held annually in November, with solos, ensembles and orchestras all emphasizing the versatility of the steel drum.

Other musical forms in this music-mad nation include parang (pre-Christmas). Part of the islands' Spanish heritage, parang is sung in Spanish and accompanied by guitar, cuatro, mandolin and tambourine. The big annual parang competitions are at Paramin, in a natural hillside amphitheatre, and at Lopinot. For the Hindu and Muslim festivals, there are East Indian drumming and vocal styles such as chowtal, which is particularly associated with Phagwa in early March.

Throughout the year, there are regular performances of plays and musicals, often by Caribbean dramatists, and concerts by fine choirs such as the Marionettes Chorale and the Lydian Singers, sometimes accompanied by steel bands. There is a lot of comedy and some serious plays too, see press for details. Theatres include the Little Carib Theatre (T6224644), Space Theatre (T6230732), the Central Bank Auditorium (T6230845) and Queen's Hall (T6241284).

Books

Some authors to investigate are CLR James, Samuel Selvon, Shiva Naipaul, all now deceased, as well as Shiva's more famous brother, VS Naipaul, who in 2001 won the Nobel Prize for Literature. Also, look out for works by the historian and past prime minister Dr Eric Williams, Earl Lovelace and Valerie Belgrave (whose *Ti Marie* has been described as the Caribbean *Gone with the Wind*). Although the tradition of performance poetry is not as strong here as in, say, Jamaica (calypso fulfils some of its role), the monologues of Paul Keens-Douglas, some of which are on album or cassette, are richly entertaining and a great introduction to the local dialect or patois (if now somewhat dated).

Isla de Margarita

Introducing Isla de Margarita

Margarita is Venezuela's main Caribbean holiday destination and the largest of Venezuela' s 72 islands in the Caribbean. Some parts are crowded but there are also undeveloped beaches and colonial villages. Despite the property boom and frenetic building on much of the coast and in Porlamar, much of the island has been given over to natural parks. Of these the most striking is the Laguna La Restinga. Isla de Margarita is in fact one island whose two sections are tenuously linked by the 18-km sandspit which separates the sea from the Restinga lagoon. At its largest, Margarita is about 32 km from north to south and 67 km from east to west. Most of its people live in the developed eastern part, which has some wooded areas and fertile valleys. The western part, the Península de Macanao, is hotter and more barren, with scrub, sand dunes and marshes. Wild deer, goats and hares roam the interior, but 4WD vehicles are needed to penetrate it. The entrance to the peninsula is a pair of hills known as Las Tetas de María Guevara, a national monument covering 1,670 ha.

Essentials

Before you travel

Entry is by **passport** and **visa**, or by passport and **tourist card**. Tourist cards (*tarjetas de ingreso*) are valid only for those entering by air and are issued by most airlines to visitors from Andorra, Antigua and Barbuda, Argentina, Australia, Austria, Barbados, Belgium, Brazil, Canada, Chile, Costa Rica, Dominica, Denmark, Finland, France, Germany, Ireland, Italy, Iceland, Japan, Liechenstein, Luxembourg, Lithuania, Malaysia, Mexico, Monaco, Norway, Netherlands, Netherlands Antilles, New Zealand, Paraguay, Portugal, St Kitts/Nevis, St Lucia, San Marino, St Vincent, South Africa, Spain, Sweden, Switzerland, Taiwan, Trinidad and Tobago, UK, Uruguay and USA. Valid for 60 days, tourist cards are not extendable. Overstaying can lead to arrest and a fine when you try to depart. Nationals of countries not listed above must obtain a consular visa in advance. All travellers to Venezuela are advised to check with the consulate before leaving home as regulations are subject to change.

Documents

To enter the country overland or by sea, you must obtain a tourist visa in advance. Apply to a Venezuela consulate prior to arrival. For a tourist visa, you need 2 passport photos, passport valid for 6 months, references from bank and employer, onward or return ticket, completed and signed application form. The fee is US$30 (costs vary from country to country). Consuls may give a one-year visa if a valid reason can be given. It generally takes 2 days to issue any visa. Tourist visas are multiple entry within their specified period.

You may bring in free of duty, 25 cigars and 200 cigarettes, 2 litres of alcoholic drinks, four small bottles of perfume, and gifts at the inspector's discretion. New items up to US$1,000 may be brought in.

Customs

Currency The unit of currency is the bolívar, which is divided into 100 céntimos (owing to devaluation, céntimos not in use). There are coins for 1, 2, 5, 25, 50, 100 and 500 bolívares, and notes for 5, 10, 20, 50, 100, 500, 1,000, 2,000, 5,000 and 10,000 bolívares. There is a shortage of small coins and notes: many shops round up prices unless you have small change or notes.

Exchange Dollars cash and TCs can be changed in banks and *casas de cambio*. To convert unused bolívares back into dollars upon leaving, you must present the original exchange receipt (up to 30% of original amount charged); only banks and authorized *casas de cambio* can legally sell bolívares. *Casas de cambio* may change TCs more readily than banks, but they always insist on photocopying your passport, photographing you and may ask for proof of purchase.

Credit cards Visitors are strongly advised to use Visa or Mastercard. There are cash machines for Visa, Mastercard and Amex, although these may give a receipt but no cash. *Corp Banca* is affiliated with American Express, no commission; *American Express* travel services are handled by *Italcambio* and *Quo Vadis* agencies. *Banco Unión* and *Banco de Venezuela* handle Visa and ATM transactions, including cash advances, and *Banco Mercantil* handles Mastercard. *Mastercard* assistance T8001-002902. *Visa* assistance T08001-002167.

Money
5,000 and 10,000 bolívar notes; are often forged Beware of forged Amex TCs and US$ notes too

Tropical, with little change between season. Margarita is outside the hurricane belt. The climate is exceptionally good, but rain is scant. Water is piped from the mainland but water trucks also deliver to resorts to keep up with demand.

Climate

Getting there

From Europe You can fly direct to Porlamar, Margarita, from Frankfurt (*Condor*) and Madrid (*Avensa*) or you can connect in Caracas, Venezuela. There are regular flights to Caracas from London, Paris, Amsterdam, Frankfurt, Madrid, Milan and Lisbon. **From North America** There are no direct scheduled services. Cities which have direct flights to Caracas are New York, Miami, Chicago, Atlanta, Dallas and Houston. **From Latin America and the Caribbean** Flights from Central and South America go to Caracas, from where there are many daily flights. *Avior* has direct flights from Grenada and Port of Spain. In addition there are charter services, which come and go, depending on the season and demand, from Europe and North America.

Air

Isla de Margarita

▶ **Venezuelan embassies and consulates overseas**

Australia 5 Culgoa Circuit O'Malley, ACT 2606, Canberra, T61-2-62902967, www.venezuela-emb.org.au

Canada 32 Range Rd, Ottawa, ON-K1N8J4, T1-613-2355151, www.misionvenezuela.org

Denmark Holbergsgade 14, 3th, 1070 Copenhagen K, T33936311, http://home7.inet.tele.dk/emvendk/

France 11 rue Copernic, 75116 Paris, T33-1-45532998, www.embavenez-paris.com

Germany Schillstrasse 9-10, Berlin 10785, T49-331-8322400, F83224020.

Italy Via Nicolò Tartaglia 11, 00197 Roma, T39-6-8079797, http://users.iol.it/embaveit

Japan 38 Kowa Building, Room 703, 12-24, Nishi Azabu, 4 Chome, Minato-Ku, Tokyo-106,

T81-3-34091501, http://sunsite.sut.ac.jp/venemb/embvenez.html

Netherlands Nassaulaan 2, 2514 JS The Hague, T31-70-352 3851, embvene@xs4a11.nl

Spain Capitán Haya 1, 13, Torrre EuroCentro, 28020 Madrid, T34-91-598 1200, www.univernet.net/embavenez/index.htm

Sweden Engelbrektsgaten 35B, S-114, 31 Stockholm, T46-8-411 0996, venezuela.embassy@mbox300.swipnet.se

Switzerland Schlosshaldenstrasse 1, 3006 Bern, T41-31-3505757, embavenez@span.ch

UK 56 Grafton Way, London W1T 5DL, T44-020-73876727, www.venezlon.demon.co.uk

USA 1099 30th St, NW, Washington DC 20007, T1-202-3422214, www.embavenez-us.org

Isla de Margarita (left margin)

Sea
See Trinidad, page 781 and Aruba, page 857 for details of ferries

Ports of entry   Ferry: (very busy at weekends and Mon) From **Puerto La Cruz** to Margarita (**Punta de Piedras**): *Conferry*, Los Cocos terminal, Puerto La Cruz, T0281-2677847/2677129, www.conferry.com Ferries to Margarita, 3 daily (check times, extras when busy), 5 hrs, US$8 one-way, children under 3 free (proof required), cars US$15. Fast ferries, *Margarita Express* and *Cacique Express*, take 2 hrs. Also from Terminal Marítimo, La Guaira, near Caracas, T/F3312433. Fares are twice the price. Ferries not always punctual. Don't believe taxi drivers at bus terminal who may tell you there's a ferry about to leave. To get to terminal in Puerto La Cruz, take 'Bello Monte' *por puesto* from Libertad y Anzoátegui, 2 blocks from Plaza Bolívar. From **Cumaná**, Conferry Terminal, Puerto Sucre, T/F0293-4311462, twice a day, US$10 one way. *Conferry* freefone number for reservations 0800-3377900, in Porlamar T2616780, in Punta de Piedras T2398340. *Gran Cacique II* is a passenger-only hydrofoil service that also runs from Puerto La Cruz, T0800-2272600 (2 daily, US$19, 2 hrs), and Cumaná, T0293-4320011 (2 daily, US$16, 2hrs). A ferry operated by *Conferry* from Punta de Piedras to Coche sails once a day, US$1.50, 1 hr. **Yacht**: on arrival, take your dinghy to Vemesca (Venezuelan Marine Supply) in Porlamar which is the main anchorage. Clear in and out at the Port Captain's office. It can be very crowded in hurricane season and rolly with southeast winds. Lock up the boat, dinghy and motor as thefts are common. A few boats stop in Pampatar, and Juan Griego makes a good stopping point when coming from La Blanquilla. On Isla de Coche by *Paradise Speed* (move close to ferry dock at night and stay out of way of fishermen), El Saco, Cubagua. Dinghy thefts and other security problems at Porlamar, Coche and Cubagua. Fuel and water at Porlamar dock, fuel but no water at Juan Griego. Occasionally possible to get a slip at Concorde marina. Supplies at Vemesca and several local marine stores. Do not try to clear Customs and Immigration without an agent in commercial port, well worth the fee. Get your tourist card at a Venezuelan embassy before arriving, although if you arrive during a major storm officials may make an exception.

Security During the busy hurricane season security problems increase; thieves arrive by night in boats with bolt cutters and fast engines and steal dinghies, motors and other items left on deck. Best security is in marinas. Porlamar even has trouble with swimmers during the day. Take all precautions possible.

Touching down

Airport information
Airport General Santiago Mariño (PMV), between Porlamar and Punta de Piedra is comfortable and modern and has the international and national terminals at either end. There are many flights a day from Caracas, with *Aeropostal*, *Aserca*, *Laser*, 45-min flight; from

Touching down

◀

Business hours *Banks: 0830-1530 Mon-Fri only. Business firms generally start work about 0800, and some continue until about 1800 with a midday break.* **Government offices:** *hours vary, but 0800-1200 are usual morning hours. Government officials have fixed hours, usually 0900-1000 or 1500-1600, for receiving visitors.* **Shops:** *Mon-Sat 0900-1300, 1500-1900. Generally speaking, Venezuelans start work early, and by 0700 everything is in full swing. Most firms and offices close on Sat.*

Departure tax *Passengers on international flights pay a combined airport and exit tax of approximately US$36 (Bs38,800 airport tax, Bs19,400 exit tax) payable in bolívares, cash only.*

Minors under 15 years do not pay the exit tax. There is a 1% tax on the cost of all domestic flights, plus an airport tax .

IDD code *58-295*

Official time *Atlantic Standard Time, 4 hrs behind GMT, 1 hr ahead of EST.*

Safety *Cameras and other valuables should not be exposed prominently.*

Tipping *Taxi drivers are tipped if the taxi has a meter (hardly anywhere), but not if you have agreed the fare first. Hotel porters, US$0.50; airport porters US$0.50 per piece of baggage. Restaurants, between 5% and 10% of bill.*

Voltage *110 volts, 60 cycles.*

Weights and measures *Metric.*

Canaima and Los Roques with *Aereotuy* and*Rutaca*; tickets are much cheaper if purchased in Venezuela in local currency. Reservations made from outside Venezuela are not always honoured. Passengers leaving **Caracas** on international flights must reconfirm their reservations not less than 72 hrs in advance, it is safer to do so in person than by telephone; not less than 24 hrs for national flights (if you fail to do this, you lose all rights to free accommodation, food, transport, etc if your flight is cancelled and you may lose your seat if the plane is fully booked). Beware of counterfeit tickets; buy only from agencies. If told by an agent that a flight is fully booked, try at the airport anyway. International passengers must check in 2 hrs before departure or they may lose their seat to someone on a waiting list. Handling charge for your luggage US$0.50.

    Airport facilities 28 km from Caracas, near the port of La Guaira: **Maiquetía**, for national flights, **Simón Bolívar** for international flights, adjacent to each other (5-min walk – taxis take a circular route, fare US$2.25; airport authorities run a shuttle bus between the 2 every 10 mins from 0700). Many facilities close on 1 Jan, including duty and money exchangers. Several *casas de cambio* open 24 hrs (*Italcambio*, good rates, outside duty-free area; also *Banco Industrial*, branch in international terminal and another, less crowded, in baggage reclaim area). If changing TCs, you may be asked for your purchase receipt; commission 2.5%. There are cash machines for Visa, Amex and Mastercard. Pharmacy, bookshops, basement café (good value meals and snacks, open 0600-2400, hard to find; cafés and bars on 1st floor viewing terrace also good value), tourist office (see below). No official left luggage; ask for Paulo at the mini bar on the 1st floor of international terminal. Look after your belongings in both terminals. Direct dial phone calls to USA only, from AT&T booth in international departure lounge. CANTV at gates 15 and 24, open 0700-2100, long-distance, international and fax services.

From airport to Caracas Taxi fares from airport to Caracas cost US$18 minimum, depending on the quality of the taxi, the part of city, or on the number of stars of your hotel, regardless of distance. Overcharging is rife and taxi drivers can be aggressive in seeking passengers. Fares are supposedly controlled, but it is essential to negotiate with the drivers; find out what the official fare is first. After 2200 and at weekends a surcharge of 20% may be added, you may get charged up to US$40. Drivers may only surcharge you for luggage (US$0.50 per large bag). If you think the licensed taxi driver is overcharging you, make a complaint to Corpoturismo or tell him you will report him to the Departamento de Protección del Consumidor. The airport shuttle bus (blue and white with 'Aeropuerto Internacional' on the side) leaves from east end of terminal, left out of exit (in the city, under the flyover at Bolívar and Av Sur 17, 250 m from Bellas Artes metro, poorly lit at night, not recommended to wait here in the dark), regular service from 0700 to 2300, bus leaves when there are enough passengers; fare to international terminal US$3.50. The bus is usually crowded so first time visitors may find a taxi advisable.

Always allow plenty of time when going to the airport, whatever means of transport you are using; the route can be very congested (2 hrs in daytime, but only 30 mins at 0430). Allow at least 2 hrs checking-in time before your flight. Airport bus or *por puesto* to airport can be caught at Gato Negro metro station.

Tourist information

Local tourist office The state tourism department can be contacted on T2622322, corpoturmargarita@cantv.net A tourist information booth on Av 4 de Mayo, opposite the *Dugout* sports bar, has good map, coupon booklet, *La Vista* tourist magazine. The private *Cámara de Turismo*, T2639024, is located at the seaward end of Av Santiago Mariño. They have free maps and are very helpful. *MultiGuía de Margarita* (US$4) is published yearly and is a useful directory of tourist information and can be found in kiosks, *panaderías*, cafés, and bookshops. Travel agencies can also provide a tourist guide to Margarita. A good English-language newspaper, *Mira*, is published on the island; the editor/publisher acts also as a tour guide; Av Santiago Mariño, Ed Carcaleo Suites, Apdo 2-A, Porlamar, T613351. For information on the **national parks** system, and to obtain necessary (free) permits to stay in the parks, contact Instituto Nacional de Parques (Inparques), T2854859, Caracas, www.inparques.gov.ve

Maps and books The best map is available from Corpoven. *Venezuela Handbook*, by Alan Murphy and Dan Green (Footprint Handbooks). *GAM*, the monthly *Guía Aérea y Marítima de Venezuela*, gives details of all flights, but also of hotels, travel agents, car hire, etc. The *Guide to Venezuela* (925 pages), by Janice Bauman, Leni Young and others, in English (available in Caracas) is a mine of information and maps, US$11. *Elizabeth Kline's Guide to Camps, Posadas and Cabins/Guía de campamentos, posadas y cabañas in/en Venezuela* is published every other year and gives a comprehensive survey of these establishments. (Apdo 63089, Caracas 1067-A, Venezuela, T0212-9451543, ekline@cantv.net).

Useful websites: www.islamargarita.com and www.margaritaonline.com **Outside Venezuela**, tourist information also at Venezuelan embassies and consulates (for addresses, see box). The official government site is **www.venezuela.gov.ve**; Asociación Venezolana de Agencias de Viajes: **www.viajes-venezuela.com/avavit**

Where to stay

Officially controlled prices exist for 1-star and 2-star hotels. Hotels are often heavily booked up, especially in high season; advance reservations are advisable. Prices for singles are often not much less than doubles. There is a tax of 16.5% on hotel rooms; 10% service may also be added. Most hotels and tour operators work on a high season/low season price system on Margarita. High season prices (Christmas, Easter and Jun-Aug) can be as much as 25% higher. Flights and hotels are usually fully booked at this time. In low season, bargaining is possible. **Camping** In Venezuela camping is a popular recreation, spending a weekend at the beach or on the islands. If camping on the beach, for the sake of security, pitch your tent close to others.

Getting around

Air

Try to check in two hours before departure

Aeropostal, *Aereotuy*, *Air Venezuela*, *Aserca*, *Avensa*, *Avior*, *LAI*, *Laser*, *Santa Bárbara* and *Servivensa* fly to a variety of destinations. None is perfect. Internal airlines offer special family discounts and student discounts, but this practice is variable (photocopies of ISIC card are useful as this allows officials to staple one to the ticket).

Road

Bus Buses are relatively cheap, but the quality of long-distance travel varies a lot. There are numerous services between the major cities. Several bus companies in Caracas sell through tickets from Caracas to Porlamar, arriving about midday. Buses return from Porlamar from terminal at Centro Comercial Bella Vista, at bottom end of Calle San Rafael (it takes about 4 hrs). The colectivo taxis and minibuses, known in Venezuela as *por puesto*, seem to monopolize transport to and from smaller towns and villages. *Por puestos* serve most of Margarita; to Punta de Piedras, from Maneiro, Mariño a Arismendi; Airport, from Centro Comercial AB, Av Bolívar (0530 and 2000 every day); La Asunción, from Fajardo, Igualdad a Marcano;

Pampatar, from Fajardo y La Marina; La Restinga, from Mariño, La Marina a Maneiro; Playa El Agua, from Guevara, Marcano a Cedeño; Juan Griego, from Av Miranda, Igualdad a Marcano; El Valle, from Av Miranda, Igualdad a Marcano; Playa Guacuco, from Fraternidad, La Marina a Mérito (mornings), from Fajardo, Igualdad a Velásquez (afternoons); El Conejeros, Fraternidad, Igualdad a Velásquez.

Car The roads are generally good and most are paved. A bridge connects the 2 parts. Sign posts are often non-existent or poorly positioned. All visitors to Margarita can drive if they are over 18 and have a valid driving licence from their own country; an international driving licence is preferred. If you have an accident and someone is injured, you will be detained as a matter of routine, even if you are not at fault. Do not drive at night if you can help it. Self-drive tours, and fly-drive are available, the latter through *National Car Rental*, which has a wide network of offices. Basic rates for a car are US$35 per day depending on make; government tax of 16.5% is also added. If you book and prepay outside the country, most major companies give unlimited mileage. Car and personal insurance (US$10-17.50 per day) is recommended. There are 3 grades of gasoline: 87, 91 and 95 octane (average cost US$0.10-0.16 a litre).

Sea You can also charter a yacht and visit the Venezuelan islands for day sails or longer. A Venezuelan captain must be on board, even on a bareboat charter. He knows the rules, regulations and places to go, which makes it easier. A recommended yacht is *El Gato*, Captain Pinky can be contacted through Cumanagoto Marina. A typical 12-day cruise starts from the mainland with a downwind sail to Los Testigos for a few days of relaxation, snorkelling or diving, then to Juan Griego, on north coast of Margarita with a night in a hotel, on to La Blanquilla to visit 2 beautiful, white-sand beaches, spending the night ashore in tents, and back to Margarita.

Keeping in touch

Post *Ipostel*, the national postal service, offers an international express mail service (EMS), which guarantees delivery in 2-3 days depending on destination. It costs from US$20 for up to 1 kg. Normal airmail letters cost US$0.90 for up to 10 g and usually take 2-3 days to the USA. *Ipostel* also offer EEE, which is a domestic express service, guaranteeing delivery next day. An alternative to *DHL* and other courier companies is *Grupo Zoom*, who sell A5 or A4 envelopes for international postage, guaranteed delivery in 3-4 days, cost US$10-15.

Telephone & internet
IDD code: 58
7-digit phone numbers for all cities were introduced in 2002

All international and long-distance calls are operated by *CANTV* and can be dialled direct. Major cities are linked by direct dialling (*Discado Directo*), with a 3-figure prefix for each town in Venezuela. There are *CANTV* offices for long-distance and international calls. Collect calls are possible to some countries, at least from Caracas, though staff in offices may not be sure of this. Most public phones on prepaid *CANTV* cards (*tarjetas*) in denominations of 3,000 and 5,000 bolívares. Buy them from *CANTV* or numerous small shops bearing the *CANTV* logo, or a scrap of card reading "*¡Sí! ¡Hay tarjetas!*" They are also sold by street vendors. Make sure they are still in their clear plastic wrapper with an unbroken red seal. Many small shops impose a 25% handling charge and *tarjetas* may be out of stock. When making international calls from a public booth, ensure that it has a globe symbol on the side. International calls are cheaper with a *tarjeta*, minimum needed Bs5,000, but you get little more than 1 min to Europe. To make an international call, dial 00 plus country code, etc. Canada direct: 800-11100. For UK, BT Direct, 800-11440 (BT chargecard works from any phone). For collect calls to Germany T800-11490. International calls are charged by a series of bands, ranging from about US$1.50 per min to USA and Canada, to US$2.50 to UK, to US$2.15. There are various reduced and economy rates according to band. Mobile phones are 'pay as you go'. System dialling codes are usually 014 or 016. The systems available are AMPS analog and CDMA or GSM digital. **Fax** rates are as for phones. **Email** public access to the internet is fairly widespread with cybercafés, see page 813

Food and drink

Food
Venezuelans dine late

There is excellent local fish (*pargo* or red snapper), crayfish, small oysters and prawns. Of true Venezuelan food there is *sancocho* (a stew of vegetables, especially yucca, with meat, chicken or fish); *arepas*, a kind of white maize bread, very bland in flavour; toasted *arepas* served with a wide selection of relishes, fillings or the local somewhat salty white cheese are cheap, filling and nutritious; *cachapas*, a maize pancake (soft, not hard like Mexican *tortillas*) wrapped around white cheese; *pabellón*, made of shredded meat, beans, rice and fried plantains (vegetarian versions available); and *empanadas*, maize-flour pies containing cheese, meat or fish. At Christmas only there are *hallacas*, maize pancakes stuffed with chicken, pork, olives, etc boiled in a plantain leaf (but don't eat the leaf). A *muchacho* (boy) on the menu is a cut of beef. *Ganso* is also not goose but beef. *Solomo* and *lomito* are other cuts of beef. *Hervido* is chicken or beef with vegetables. *Contorno* with a meat or fish dish is a choice of chips, boiled potatoes, rice or yucca. *Caraotas* are beans; *cachitos* are *croissants* of bread. *Pasticho* is what the Venezuelans call Italian *lasagne*. The main fruits are bananas, oranges, grapefruit, mangoes, pineapple and papaya. Some Venezuelan variants of names for fruit: *lechosa* is papaya, *patilla* is water melon, *parchita* passion fruit, and *cambur* a small banana. Delicious sweets are *huevos chimbos* – egg yolk boiled and bottled in sugar syrup, and *quesillo* – milk, egg and caramel.

Drink
A lisa is a glass of keg beer; for a bottle of beer ask for a tercio

Venezuelan rum is very good; recommended brands are *Cacique*, *Pampero* and *Santa Teresa*. There are 5 good local beers: *Polar* (the most popular), *Regional* (with a strong flavour of hops), *Cardenal*, *Nacional* and Brazilian *Brahma* beer (lighter than *Polar*), now brewed in Venezuela. There are also mineral waters, gin and a good, local wine. The Polar brewery and Martell (France) built a winery in Carora. Wines produced are *Viña Altagracia* and *Bodegas Pomar*; the latter also produces a sparkling wine in the traditional champagne style. Liqueurs are cheap, try the local *ponche crema*. The coffee is very good (*café con leche*

Isla de Margarita

has a lot of milk, *café marrón* much less, *cafe negro* for black coffee. Try a *merengada*, made from fruit pulp, ice, milk and sugar; a *batido* similar but with water and a little milk; *jugo* is the same but with water.

Shopping

Venezuelan tourists were the first to take advantage of Margarita's duty-free status after a drastic devaluation of the bolívar forced them to take holidays at home. There are now dozens of duty-free shops, particularly in **Porlamar**; besides all duty-free shops, *Del Bellorín*, Cedeño, near Av Santiago Mariño is good for handicrafts. Good selection of jewellery at *Sonia Gems*, on Cedeño. When purchasing jewellery, bargain hard, don't pay by credit card (surcharges are imposed), get a detailed guarantee of the item. The trendy Av Santiago Mariño and surroundings are the place for designer labels, but decent copies can be found on Blvds Guevara and Gómez and around Plaza Bolívar in the centre. For super bargains on denims, T-shirts, shorts, swimming gear, bikinis, towels, etc take a bus to the *Conejeros* market.

Holidays and festivals

There are 2 sorts of national holidays, those enjoyed by everybody and those taken by employees of banks and insurance companies. Holidays applying to all businesses include: **1 Jan**, *Carnival* on the Mon and Tue before Ash Wed (everything shuts down Sat-Tue; book accomodation in advance), Thu-Sat of *Holy Week*, **19 Apr**, **1 May**, **24 Jun**, **5 Jul**, **24 Jul**, **12 Oct**, **25 Dec**. Holidays for banks and insurance companies include all the above and also: **19 Mar** and the nearest Mon to **6 Jan**, *Ascension Day*, **29 Jun**, **15 Aug**, **1 Nov** and **8 Dec**. There are also holidays applying to certain occupations such as *Doctor's Day* or *Traffic Policeman's Day*. From **24 Dec-1 Jan**, most restaurants are closed and there is no long-distance public transport. On *New Year's Eve*, everything closes. Business travellers should not visit during Holy week or Carnival. **19 Mar** at Paraguachí (*Feria de San José*, 10 days); **26 Jul** at Punta de Piedra; **31 Jul** (*Batalla de Matasiete*) and **15 Aug** (*Asunción de la Virgen*) at La Asunción; **1-8 Sep** at El Valle; **4-11 Nov** at Boca del Río, **4-30 Nov** at Boca del Pozo; **5-6 Dec** at Porlamar; **27 Dec-3 Jan** at Juan Griego.

Public holidays

Flora and Fauna

Despite the property boom and frenetic building on the coast and in Porlamar, much of the island has been given over to natural parks. Of these the most striking is the **Laguna La Restinga**. Launches provide lengthy runs around the mangrove swamps. The mangroves are fascinating, with shellfish clinging to the roots. Flamingoes live in the lagoon. There are mangroves also in the **Laguna de las Marites Natural Monument**, west of Porlamar. Other parks are **Las Tetas de María Guevara**, **Cerro El Copey**, 7,130 ha, and **Cerro Matasiete y Guayamurí**, 1,672 ha (both reached from La Asunción). Details of *Inparques*, the national parks office, are given on page 804. By boat from Porlamar you can go to the **Isla de los Pájaros** or **Morro Blanco** for bird-spotting.

Diving and marine life

The Venezuelan Islands are fast becoming new dive destinations with sites found off Margarita, La Blanquilla, Los Testigos, Las Frailes and Los Roques. There is good snorkelling and diving off **Cubagua** on a sunken barge and a ferry with cars still inside. At **Farallón**, near Pampatar, there is an underwater religious statue, large brain coral, large sea fans and fish, including barracuda. La **Macura** is a rock patch where holes in boulders are home to parrotfish. **Los Frailes**, 8 small islands northeast of Margarita are ideal for current dives and underwater life including moray eels, barracudas and oysters.

Dive centres Porlamar is a good place to book scuba diving and snorkelling trips: most go to Los Frailes, but it's also possible to dive at La Restinga National Park and Isla Cubagua. *Enomis' Divers*, at *Hotel Margarita Dynasty*, Los Uveros, and Caribbean Center Mall, Av Bolívar, T/F2622977 enomisdivers@hotmail.com; *Octopus*, at *Hotel Hilton*, Los Uveros, and Av Bolívar 13, T2646272, octopus@cantv.net; *Margarita Divers*, at the Marina Concorde, T2642350, all offer half and full-day dives and PADI courses. Prices from US$85 per person for an all-inclusive full day (2 dives), but bargaining is possible if you have a group of 4 or more. Snorkelling is always about half the price of scuba diving.

Beaches and watersports

Nude sunbathing is forbidden. Topless bathing is not seen, except at some resort pools and beaches, but the tanga (hilo dental – dental floss) is fairly common

There are wild, isolated beaches, long white stretches of sand bordered by palms, developed beaches with restaurants and sunshades for hire, and beaches where you can surf or snorkel. Sunscreen is essential. The beaches of Porlamar suffer from their popularity at weekends. The *Bella Vista* beach, although crowded, is kept clean and has lots of restaurants. *Playa Concorde* is small, sheltered and tucked away to the side of the marina. *Playa Morena* is a long, barren strip of sand serving the *Costa Azul hotel* zone to the east of the city. *La Caracola* is a very popular beach for the younger crowd.

The beaches on the east coast are divided into ocean and calm beaches, according to their location in relation to the open sea. The former tend to be rougher and colder. Water is clear and unpolluted. Restaurants, *churuatas* (bars built like native huts), sunshades and deckchairs are widespread. Hire charges are about US$5. For a more Venezuelan atmosphere go northeast to Pampatar, which is set around a bay favoured by foreign yachtsmen as a summer anchorage; jet skis for hire on a clean and pretty beach. A scale model of Columbus' *Santa María* is used for trips. A fishing boat can be hired for US$20 for 2½ hrs, 4-6 passengers; good fun and fishing. The private yachts *Viola Festival* and *Moon Dancer*, and the catamarans *Yemaya* and *Catatumbo* all can be hired for mini cruises to the island of Coche or Isla Cubagua. Contact *Viola Turismo*, Caribbean Center Mall, Av Bolívar, T2670552, *Enomis' Divers* (see above), or *Octopus* (see above). Expect to pay US$35-40 per person. Fishing trips also.

Health

*See also
Health page 48*

Water is heavily chlorinated, so safe to drink, although most people drink bottled water. Medical attention is good. State health care is free and said to be good. A doctor's consultation costs about US$10. Protection against mosquito bites is advised as dengue fever has been present since 1995.

Around the island

Porlamar

*Phone code: 0295
Population: 85,000*

Most of the hotels are at Porlamar, 20 km from the airport and about 28 km from **Punta de Piedra**, where most of the ferries dock. If you're seeking sun and sand, then head for the north coast towns. Porlamar's beaches are nothing special, but it makes up for what it lacks in this department with its shops. At Igualdad y Díaz is the **Museo de Arte**

> ## Things to do on Isla de Margarita
>
> - **Margarita** is a beach-lover's mecca. There are rough ones for surfing, calmer ones for windsurfing and quiet ones for swimming and sunbathing. Take bucket loads of sunscreen.
> - Watch the sunset at the little fort of La Galera on a promontory overlooking the fishing town of **Juan Griego**, where you can go for dinner afterwards at one of the many seafront restaurants.
> - Take a **yacht trip** to visit other more remote, Venezuelan islands and find your own deserted cay.
> - A launch into **La Restinga** lagoon and the mangrove swamps is an ideal way of getting close to nature.

Francisco Narváez, displaying the work of this contemporary local sculptor. At night everything closes by 2300; women alone should avoid the centre after dark. Note that in Porlamar there is a Calle Mariño and an Avenida Santiago Mariño in the centre.

Ferries go to the **Isla de Coche** (11 km by 6 km), which has over 4,500 inhabitants and one of the richest salt mines in the country. They also go, on hire only, to **Isla de Cubagua**, which is totally deserted, but you can visit the ruins of Nueva Cádiz (which have been excavated). Large yachts and catamarans take tourists on day sails to Coche.

La Asunción

The capital, La Asunción has several colonial buildings, a cathedral, and the fort of **Santa Rosa**, with a famous bottle dungeon. ■ *Mon 0800-1500, other days 0800-1800.* There is a museum in the Casa Capitular, and a local market, good for handicrafts. Nearby are the **Cerro Matasiete** historical site, where the defeat of the Spanish on 31 July 1817 led to their evacuation of the island, and the **Félix Gómez** look out in the Sierra Copuy.

Population: 30,000

Between La Asunción and Porlamar are the Parque Francisco Fajardo, beside the Universidad de Oriente, and **El Valle del Espíritu Santo**. Here is the church of the **Virgen del Valle**, a picturesque building with twin towers, painted white and pink. The adjoining museum opens at 1400, it displays costumes and presents for the Virgin, including the *Milagro de la pierna de perla*, a leg-shaped pearl. A pilgrimage is held in early September.

Throughout the island, the churches are attractive: fairly small, with baroque towers and adornments

Pampatar has the island's largest fort, **San Carlos Borromeo** (built 1662 after the Dutch destroyed the original fort), and the smaller **La Caranta**, where the cannon show signs of having been spiked. Visit also the church of Cristo del Buen Viaje, the Library/Museum and the customs house. There is an amusement park to the south-west of Pampatar, called **Isla Aventura**. ■ *Fri and Sat 1800-2400, Sun 1700-2400, and more frequently in peak holiday season. Peak season US$5, children US$3.35, includes all rides; low season entry US$0.50 and each ride US$0.30-0.60.* The beach at Pampatar is picturesquely circled with palm trees and kiosks selling local fresh fish. Limited local services and watersports; crowded at weekends. A scale model of Columbus' Santa María is used for taking tourists on trips. A fishing boat can be hired for US$20 for 2½ hours (four to six passengers); shop around for best price, good fun and fishing. La Caracola beach has an ultralight airport, kiosks and beachchairs. **Bella Vista**, near town, is calm, with restaurants and services.

Pampatar
Population: 25,000

On the eastern coast is **Playa Guacuco**, reached from La Asunción by a road through the Guayamurí reserve: a lot of surf, fairly shallow, restaurants and parking lot; excellent horse riding, US$30 for 2 hours, contact Harry Padrón at the ranch in Agua de Vaca, or phone travel agent on 2611311. Before Punta Cabo Blanco are **El**

East coast

Isla de Margarita

Cardón and **Puerto Fermín**/El Tirano (Lope de Aguirre, the infamous conquistador, landed here in 1561 on his flight from Peru), El Caserío handicrafts museum is nearby. Beyond the point is **Playa Parguito**, a long, open beach with strong waves, best for surfing, and full public services.

From the northern end of the beach, it is possible to see the island by Ultra light from here at the weekends; Contact Omar Contreras, T2617632

Playa El Agua, 45 minutes by bus from Porlamar is 4 km of stone-free white sand with many *kioskos*, which have palm-leaf shade areas. The sea is very rough for children, but fairly shallow (beware the strong cross current when you are about waist deep). This is the most popular beach on the island and is ideal for sunbathing and walking, but it gets overcrowded at Venezuelan holiday times. The fashionable part is at the southern end; the northern end, popular with younger people, is less touristy and has less shade. There is bungee jumping, parasailing and most watersports. Horse riding can be arranged with *Altos de Cimarrón*. Activities abound at weekends in peak season. **El Humo** is a nice, less crowded and not so well known, with deeper water and stronger currents. At **Manzanillo**, a picturesque bay between the mountains, fish sold on beach, there is accommodation and places to eat; **Playa Escondida** is at the far end.

North coast The coast road is interesting, with glimpses of the sea and beaches to one side, inland vistas on the other. There are a number of clifftop lookout points. The road improves radically beyond Manzanillo, winding from one beach to the next. **Playa Puerto la Cruz** (the widest and windiest beach) adjoins **Pedro González** (population: 3,700), with a broad sweeping beach, running from a promontory (easy to climb) to scrub and brush that reach down almost to the water's edge. **Playa Caribe** is a fantastic curve of white sand with moderate surf. Chairs and umbrellas can be hired from the many beach bars.

Further west is **Juan Griego**, a small, sleepy town whose picturesque bay is full of fishing boats, drawn up on the narrow beach or moored offshore. The little fort of **La Galera** is on a promontory at the northern side, beyond which is a bay with a narrow strip of beach, more fishing boats and many seafront restaurants. La Galera is a good place to watch the famous Juan Griego sunset. **Playas Caribe**, north of La Galera, has restaurants, deserted caverns at the south end and the water is usually rough.

Inland from Juan Griego South of Juan Griego, the road goes inland to **San Juan Bautista** (a pleasant colonial town ringed by hills; *por puesto* from Juan Griego), then to Punta de Piedra, the ferry dock, see below (a pleasant stretch through cultivated land and farms at regular intervals *por puesto* Juan Griego to ferry). Near San Juan is Fuentedueño park.

The south coast El Yaque, near the airport and the mouth of the Laguna de las Marites attracts windsurfers with its flat water and windy conditions. The best winds are mid-June to mid-October and the water is shallow enough to stand if you fall off. Most come on package deals and therefore accommodation is expensive, but cheaper places can be found. There is no public transport; a taxi from Porlamar costs US$8. Sailboards, kite surf and kayaks can be hired. Half day costs US$30, full day US$35-40 for sailboard; US$25 per hour for kite surf. English, German, French and Portuguese spoken. *Cholymar* travel agency will change money and there is *casa de cambio* in the *Hotel California*. Passages to Coche island cost US$14 from *Hotel Yaque Paradise*.

La Restinga La Restinga is a 22-km sandbar of broken seashells that joins the eastern and western parts of Margarita. Behind the *restinga* is the eponymous national park, designated a wetland of international importance. Over 100 species of birds live here, including the blue-crowned parakeet, which is endemic to Margarita. There are also marine turtle and other reptiles, dolphins, deer, ocelots, seahorses and oysters. Bus from Porlamar US$1. On La Restinga beach you can look for shellfish in the shallows (sun protection essential), the delicious oysters can be bought for around US$1 a dozen.

Lanchas can be taken into the lagoon and mangrove swamps at the eastern end (US$10 per person for one-hour trip, plus US$0.35 entrance fee to park)

This western part of the island over the road bridge from La Restinga is mountainous, **Península de** barely populated and a peaceful place to relax. Car hire is the best way to get here. It also has **Macanao** some good beaches. Punta Arenas, a pleasant beach with calm water is the most popular and has some restaurants. Further on is the wilder Playa Manzanillo. Boca del Río, near the road bridge, has a museum and a small aquarium. ■ *Daily 0900-1630. US$2, children US$1. T2913231, www.fpolar.org.ve/museomarino* Horse riding on the peninsula for US$35-45 at *Hato San Francisco, Cabatucan Ranch* (T0416-6819348, cabatucan@telcel.net.ve) and at El Saco with *Rancho Negro* (T2423197, T0414-9951103).

Essentials

La Asunción C-D *Ciudad Colonial*, La Margarita, T2423086. Upmarket, pleasant. **F** *de la* **Sleeping** *Asunción*, Unión, 2 blocks from Plaza Bolívar, T2420902. A/c, fridge (rooms with balcony cost more, rooms without window cost less). Frequent *por puesto* service stops in front of hotel.

　　Pampatar A-B *Flamingo Beach*, T2624822, F2620271. 5-star, all-inclusive, food, drinks, entertainment, service, taxes, casino, good value.

　　Porlamar A-B *Bella Vista*, Av Santiago Mariño, T2617222, www.hbellavista.com Luxury hotel *Almost all of the* with all expected services, also beach, car hire, French restaurant, and restaurant serving comida *luxury hotels are* criolla. **A-B** *Hilton*, Los Uveros, Costa Azul, T2621132, res-margarita@hilton.com Luxury services *grouped in the Costa* plus beach, parasailing, car hire, casino. **B-C** *Margarita Princess*, Av 4 de Mayo, T2618732, *Azul suburb to the* www.margaritaprincess.com Large, comfortable rooms, balcony, restaurant, small pool, *Highberg* *east of Porlamar* *Tours* (see below). **B-C** *For You*, Av Santiago Mariño, T2638635, F2618708. Large rooms, CP (and welcome cocktail), excellent service and roof restaurant, bar. **B-C** *Colibrí*, Av Santiago Mariño, T2616346, www.hotelcolibri.com.ve Good rooms, CP, cambio, car hire, travel agency. **E** *Imperial*, Prolongación de Marcano y Campos, T2616420, F2615056. Best rooms in front have sea view, comfortable, safe, a/c, hot water, parking, English spoken. **E** *Posada Lutecia*, Campos Cedeño a Marcano, T/F2638526. Lovely rooms with personal touch, a/c, hot water, TV, French-owned, café with outdoor seating. **E** *Tamaca*, Prolongación de Marcano y Campos, near the sea, T2611602. Popular, a/c, OK, **F** with fan, German-run tasca. **F** *Brasilia*, San Nicolás. Quiet, nice new rooms at back. **F** *Malecón*, Marina y Arismendi, T2635723. Sea view from front rooms, very helpful and generous, dangerous area at night, best to take a taxi. **F** *Porto Viejo*, La Marina y Fajardo, T2638480. Under US$5 per person, basic, not overly friendly, take care at night. Many others around Plaza Bolívar.

　　Playa Guacuco B-C *Guacuco Resort*, Sabana de Guacuco, T2423040, http://guacucoresort.com Apartments sleep 4 people, 1 km from the beach and 300 m off the road, a/c, self-catering facilities, tranquil, beautiful gardens, pool and bar. **F** (per person) *Posada Isla Dorada*, near *Guacuco*, well signposted, T4163132. Simple rooms with a/c, meals extra.

　　Playa El Agua B-C *Coco Paraíso*, Av Principal, T2490117, www.cocoparaiso.cjb.net Very pleasant, large rooms, a/c, pool, 3 mins from beach, German spoken. **B-C** *Costa Linda*, Miragua, T/F2491229, www.hotelcostalinda.com Very nice rooms in colonial-style house, CP, a/c, TV, safe, pool, restaurant and bar, accepts credit cards, changes TCs and US$, English and German spoken. **B-C** *Trudel's Garden Vacation Homes*, Miragua, www.islamargarita.com/trudel.htm 6 large 2-bedroom houses set in a beautiful garden, 200 m from beach, fully equipped kitchens. **C-E** *Chalets de Belén*, Miragua 3, next to El Agua, T2491707. 2 chalets for 4 and 6, kitchen facilities, good value, no towels provided, parking, laundry service, also 2 double rooms, discounts in low season. **C-D** *Residencia Miramar*, Av 31 de Julio-Carretera Manzanillo, esq Miragua. 3 mins from beach, 1 min from supermarket (expensive), family-run, self-catering apartments, comfortable, barbecue. **E-F** *Residencia Vacacional El Agua*, T2491975. Fully equipped, self-catering bungalows for 4, 6 and 8 with fan, run-down, but good value, 1 double room. **F** *Hostería El Agua*, Av 31 de Julio vía Manzanillo, T2491297, hosteriaelagua@hotmail.com Simple, a/c, hot water, safe, laundry facilities, restaurant/bar, 4 mins' walk from beach, English and Italian spoken.

　　Playa Caribe B *Casa Chiara*, contact through *Delfino Tours*, T Caracas 2675175, or http://web.tiscalinet.it/casa_chiara. 8 private luxury villas built with adobe and hardwood with small gardens that back on to a large pool, a huge *churuata* houses bar, restaurant and seating area, Italian owners, Paolo and Chiara, are great hosts, exceptional food.

　　Juan Griego C-D *El Yare*, El Fuerte, T2530835, 1 block from beach. Some suites with kitchen, owner speaks English. **D** *Nuevo Juan Griego*, next to beach. English spoken, book exchange.

Isla de Margarita

F *Aparthotel y Residencia El Apurano*, Calle La Marina y El Fuerte, T2530901. Friendly, English speaking manager, 2-bedroom apartments with bath, hot water, a/c, but no utensils or towels (because of theft). **F** *Patrick's*, El Fuerte, next to *Hotel Fortín*, T/F2534089. French-run, a/c rooms, excellent restaurant and bar. **F** *Residencia Carmencita*, Calle Guevara 20, T2535561. A/c, private bath. **F** *Fortín*, opposite beach, a/c, cold water, restaurant and tables on the beach. **F** *La Posada de Clary*, Los Mártires, T2530037. Restaurant, also apartments for 4, a/c, kitchen, parking.

El Yaque A-B *Yaque Paradise*, T2639810, yaque@grupoparadise.com Upmarket, good rooms, CP, English and German spoken. **E** *El Yaque Motion*, T2639742, www.elyaquemotion.com Next to *La Casa de Migelina*, 400 m from beach. Fan, kitchen, laundry, cheaper with shared bath, English and German spoken.**C-F** *La Casa de Migelina*, orange house behind the police checkpoint at entrance to town. A/c, rooms and self-catering apartments, for max 5, fully equipped kitchen, a/c, sitting room, TV, discounts for long stay. **F** *Sail Fast Shop*, T/F2637486, sailfastshop@hotmail.com Basic rooms 300 m from the beach, ask for Herbert Novak at the Sail Fast Shop opposite *Hotel Yaque Paradise*. Several other hotels with restaurants.

Península de Macanao There is no accommodation at the beaches, but in nearby Robledal is **C-D** *Auberge L'Oasis*, T2915339 charles@enlared.net A/c or fan, hot water, TV, sea view, garden, restaurant. Playa La Pared is an impressive beach bounded by steep cliff walls. There is a *parador turístico* at the top of the cliff and lodging at the **B-C** *Makatao*, T/F2636647, http://makatao.iespana.es Price includes transfer, food, natural drinks and lodging in the singular rooms. The doctor runs health and therapy programs, and there are mud baths at the *campamento*. At *Cabatucan Ranch*, 2 km from Guayacancito on the road to Punta Arenas, is the **B-C** *Posada Río Grande*, T4168111, www.posadariogrande.com Rooms with a/c, hot water, full board available, scuba diving (US$57) and snorkelling trips (US$27) to Isla Cubagua.

Eating

Upmarket dining such as Japanese food in Urb Costa Azul on Avenida Bolívar

Porlamar Plenty of eating places on Campos and 4 de Mayo, including *Mediterráneo Café*, Italian, and *Flaco's Ribs*, Tex-Mex. On 4 de Mayo: *El Picadilly*, good, cheap lunch; *Dragón Chino*, great Chinese food. *Doña Martha*, Velázquez near Hernández. Colombian food, good, inexpensive. *El Punto Criollo*, Igualdad near *Hotel Porlamar*. Excellent value *comida margariteña*. *Rancho Grande*, Guevara, near Playa El Agua bus stop. Colombian, good value. *El Pollo de Carlitos*, Marcano y Martínez. Nice location, live music most nights, good food and value. *Bahía* bar-restaurant, Av Raúl Leoni y Vía El Morro. Excellent value, live music. *Los 3 Delfines*, Cedeño 26-9. Good seafood. *La Isla*, Mariño y Cedeño. 8 fast food counters ranging from hamburgers to sausages from around the world. *Dino's Grill*, Igualdad y Martínez. Open 0700-1400, buffet lunch indoor/outdoor seating, grill, home-made sausages, wood-fired pizza oven, cheap, good service.

Pampatar *El Farallón*, seafood restaurant beside Castillo. Seafood soup recommended bowl of shellfish and meal on its own. Also beach restaurant *Antonio's* and *Trimar*, seafood.

Playa El Agua *Restaurant El Paradiso*, southern end. Rents out cabins, small but comfortable. *Kiosko El Agua*, helpful, English spoken. *Posada Shangri-Lá* is good, *Casa Vieja*, seafood, *La Dorada*, French-owned, good beach view, good value. *Mini Golf Café*, from the corner of *Miramar* turn left after 300 m. Run by Matthias, ask for special dishes cooked by Yvonne, internet access. Many beach restaurants stay open till 2200.

Juan Griego Many restaurants close out of season. *Restaurant Mi Isla* is good. *Viña de Mar*, opposite *Hotel Fortín*. A/c, attractive, excellent food. *Juan Griego Steak House*, same building as *Hotel El Yare*. Good value. Also *Viejo Muelle*, good restaurant, live music, outside beach bar. *El Buho* is a good French-run bar open until 0600.

El Yaque *Fuerza 6* and *Gabi's Grill*, main meals US$6. Several beach bars; best bar is *Los Surf Piratas*, drinks and dancing from 2130.

Nightlife

At night everything closes by 2300; women alone should avoid the centre after dark

Porlamar *Mosquito Coast Club*, behind *Hotel Bella Vista*. Good *merengue* and rock music bar outside. Also does excellent Mexican meals (beware of overcharging on simple items like water). *Village Club*, Av Santiago Mariño. Recommended disco for good music with a variety of styles but expensive drinks, cover charge. *Doce 34*, Av 4 de Mayo. 2 dance floors. Highly recommended. *Woody's Bar*, Av 4 de Mayo. A spit and sawdust venue that's good for a drink and a dance. In the Centro Comercial Costal Azul on Av Bolívar there are 3 bar/clubs, including the popular *Señor Frogs*. *Cheers*, Av Santiago Mariño y Tubores and *Dugout*, Av 4 de Mayo, are popular sports bars. Every Fri there is dancing at *Marlin Bar & Restaurant* on Blvd

Playa El Agua. Many of the hotels in Urb Costa Azul have relatively inexpensive **casinos**; the best are the *Casino del Sol* at the *Hotel Marina Bay*, and *Gran Casino Hilton*. Porlamar has many illegal casinos, too.

Esparta Tours, Final de Av Santiago Mariño, near *Hotel Bella Vista*, T2615524. **Jeep tours** around Margarita from: *Highberg Tours*, *Hotel Margarita Princess*, Av 4 de Mayo, T/F2631170, jeepsafari@telcel.net US$50 per person, guides in English, German, and Polish; *CC Tours*, El Colegio, T2642003, taking in Cerro El Copey and La Restinga national parks, off-roading in Macanao Peninsula, including food and drinks. *Moony Shuttle Service*, T2635418, runs **treks** in Cerro El Copey.

Tour operators

Car hire: *Ramcar*, at airport and *Hotel Bella Vista*, recommended as cheap and reliable, non-deductible insurance; others on Av Santiago Mariño. In all cases check the brakes and body-work, as well as conditions and terms of hire. Scooters can also be hired from, among others, *Maruba Motor Rentals*, La Mariña (English spoken, good maps, US$16 bike for 2, US$13 bike for 1). Motor cycles may not be ridden between 2000 and 0500. Make sure to fill up with fuel before leaving Porlamar as service stations become scarce the further away you get. **Bicycles** can be hired for US$6 per day from *Bicimanía*, Caribbean Center Mall, Av Bolívar, T/F2629116, bicimania@cantv.net **Taxi**: taxi fares are published by the magazine *Mira* but are not uniformly applied by drivers. If you want to hire a taxi for a day you will be charged US$10-15 per hr. Always establish the fare before you get in the car. There is a 30% surcharge after 2100.

Transport

Airline offices *Aeropostal*, *Hotel Hilton*, Los Uveros, T2645877, T0800-2846637. *Aereotuy*, Av Santiago Mariño, T2630367. *Air Venezuela*, *Hotel Plaza Royal*, Fermín, T2630367. *Aserca*, CC Margarita Plaza, Av Santiago Mariño, near *Hotel Bella Vista*, T2616186, T0800-6488356. *Avensa*, at airport, T2691315. *Avior*, at airport, T2691314. *LAI*, at airport, T2691352. *Laser*, Edif Bahía de Guaraguao, Av Santiago Mariño, T2691216, T0800-5273700. *Rutaca*, Galería La Rosa, Cedeño, T2699236. **Banks** on Avs Santiago Mariño and 4 de Mayo. **Casas de cambio**: *Cambio Cussco* at Velásquez y Av Santiago Mariño. *Italcambio*, CC Jumbo, Av 4 de Mayo, Nivel Ciudad. **Communications** Internet: *Cyber Café Jumbo Margarita*, CC Jumbo, Av 4 de Mayo, Nivel Fiesta. *Neon's Chat & Play*, Marcano, A Hernández y Narváez. *News Café*, 4 de Mayo, open 0800-2400. **Post office**: Calle Maneiro. **Telephone**: *CANTV*, Bolívar, entre Fajardo y Fraternidad.

Directory

Background

Christopher Columbus made landfall on the nearby Paria Peninsula in August 1498. Two years later, a settlement had been established at Santiago de Cubagua (later called Nueva Cádiz) to exploit the pearls which grew in its waters. Cubagua became a centre for pearling and slavery, as the local Indians were used, to dive into the oyster beds. By 1541, when Santiago was destroyed by an earthquake and tidal wave, the pearl beds had been almost exhausted, but the Greek for pearl, *margarita*, was kept for the main island.

History

Margarita, and the nearest town on the mainland, Cumaná, were strongholds of the forces for the independence of South America from Spain. Between 1810 and 1817, the island was the scene of revolts and harsh Spanish reprisals. The liberator Simón Bolívar declared the Third Republic, and was himself declared Commander in Chief of the Liberating Army, at Villa del Norte (now Santa Ana) in 1816. After the war, the name of Nueva Esparta (maintaining the Greek allusion) was conferred in recognition of the bravery of Margarita in the struggle. Subsequent events have been nothing like so heroic. After a regeneration of the the pearl industry at the end of the 19th century, it has gone into decline, the oyster beds having all but disappeared through disease.

When the Spaniards landed in East Venezuela in 1498, in the course of Columbus' third voyage, they found a poor country sparsely populated by Indians who had created no distinctive culture. Four hundred years later it was still poor, almost exclusively agrarian, exporting little, importing less. The miracle year which changed all that was 1914, when oil was discovered near Maracaibo. Today, Venezuela is one of the richest countries in Latin America and is one of the largest producers and exporters of oil in the world.

Geography

Venezuela has 72 island possessions in the Caribbean, of which the largest and the most visited is Isla de Margarita. This island, and two close neighbours, Coche and Cubagua, form the state of Nueva Esparta. Most of the other islands are Federal Dependencies (whose capital is Los Roques) stretching in small groups of keys to the east of Bonaire. Two other sets of islands are incorporated in the national parks of Morrocoy (west of the country's capital, Caracas) and Mochima, east of Caracas.

Economy   Margarita's tourism boom began in 1983, largely as a result of the fall in the value of the bolívar and the consequent tendency of Venezuelans to spend their holidays at home. Margarita's status as a duty-free zone has also helped. Venezuelan shoppers go in droves for clothing, electronic goods and other consumer items. Gold and gems are good value, but many things are not. There has been extensive building in Porlamar, with new shopping areas, hotels and beaches. All-inclusive resorts and timeshare have expanded on the northeast corner of the island and there is a glut of hotel rooms and apartments. The island's popularity means that various packages are sometimes on offer.

Local industries are fishing and fibre work, such as hammocks and straw hats. Weaving, pottery and sweets are being pushed as handicraft items for the tourists.

Isla de Margarita

Netherlands Antilles, the ABC Islands

Introducing the Netherland Antilles, the ABC Islands

The Netherlands Antilles consist of the islands of Aruba, Bonaire and Curaçao, popularly known as the 'ABCs' (60-80 km off the coast of Venezuela, south of the hurricane belt), and the '3 S's': Sint Eustatius (Statia), Saba, and the south part of Sint Maarten in what are generally known as the Leeward Islands, 880 km further north in the hurricane belt.

There is some confusion regarding which islands are Leeward and which are Windward: locals refer to the ABCs as 'Leeward Islands', and the other 3 S's 'Windward', a distinction adopted from the Spaniards, who still speak of the *Islas de Sotavento* and *Islas de Barlovento* with reference to the trade winds.

Each island is different from the others in physical features and the level of development and prosperity. However, they are all water playgrounds with excellent diving, sailing, windsurfing and any number of other toys available. Accommodation is of a very high standard and any visitor can feel extremely comfortable and relaxed or active and energized according to mood.

★

Things to do in Bonaire

- **Diving** and more diving, in pristine conditions and with excellent facilities.
- Some 11,000 **flamingoes** also think this is a top spot; see their conical nests on the salt pans and watch them taking off at sunset in a huge pink cloud to overnight in Venezuela.
- In this arid climate the springs at **Fontein** are a surprising sight, with fresh water pouring through the walls of a cave into pools where you can plunge and soak.
- You'll find cool jazz on warm Bonaire when the **Bonaire Jazz Club** meets.

Bonaire

The diving here is among the best in the Caribbean, with pristine reefs and wonderful visibility as there are no rivers to muddy the waters and it is out of the hurricane belt. The climate is dry and the vegetation little more than scrub and cactus but it is prized by birdwatchers. Once important as a salt producer, this Dutch island now makes its living out of tourism. Bonaire is the least densely populated of the ABC islands and the inhabitants are mostly of mixed Arawak, European and African descent. They are a very friendly and hospitable people. The island is clean, quiet, peaceful and very safe. As in Curaçao and Aruba, Dutch is the official language, Papiamentu the colloquial tongue, and Spanish and English are both widely spoken.

IDD code: 599
Colour map 5, grid B2
Population: 11,000

Ins and outs

Air Long distance regular direct flights are limited to only Amsterdam, although there are lots of connecting flights from the USA and Europe via Curaçao, Montego Bay and San Juan, Puerto Rico, and there are extra flights from other destinations in season, see Transport, page 827. **Sea** Connections can be made by ferry from Curaçao.

Getting there

There is no scheduled bus service, but so-called 'autobuses' (AB on the licence plate) pass at certain places in town and take you to the street or place you want to go for a few guilders. There are taxis at the airport but they are difficult to find around the island. Taxis do not 'cruise' so you must telephone for one, T7178100. The best way of getting about is to hire a car, scooter or mountain bike. Distances are not great but the heat is. Some hotels have a free shuttle service to town. Hitching is fairly easy and safe.

Getting around
See Transport, page 827, for further details

Local tourist office Kaya Simón Bolívar 12, Kralendijk, T7178322, www.Info Bonaire.com *The Bonaire Hotel and Tourism Association* (Bonhata) is at T7175134, info@bonhata.org The Bonaire tourist map shows all the dive and snorkelling sites. *The Official Roadmap with Dive Sites* is available in some shops. It gives a good street plan of Kralendijk, dive sites and points of interest on Bonaire and Klein Bonaire, but tends to indicate rocky cliffs as 'beach' areas. The *Bonaire Reporter* is the island's weekly English-language newspaper and is available free on Bonaire or on the internet at www.bonairereporter.com

Tourist information

Flora and fauna

An environmental awareness for preservation of the reefs and the island's natural state pervades society here like no other Caribbean destination. Nature and the environment is even a subject for study in the primary school system thanks to a grant given in 1996 by the World Wildlife Fund. It is also a United Nations Environmental Project (UNEP) demonstration location. All of the waters to 60 m deep and much of the countryside, fauna and flora of Bonaire is protected.

Bonaire has one of the largest Caribbean flamingo colonies in the Western Hemisphere (between 3,500 and 11,000 depending on the season), and these birds build their conical mud nests in the salt pans. The Salt Company has set aside an area of 56 ha for a flamingo sanctuary, with access strictly prohibited. The birds have settled

Netherlands Antilles, the ABC Islands

into a peaceful co-existence, so peaceful in fact that they are now laying two eggs a year instead of one. They can be seen from the roads in the south and in Goto Meer Bay in the northwest, in the salt lake near Playa Grandi, and in Lac Bay on the southeast coast of Bonaire, feeding on algae and crustaceans giving them their striking pink colour.

An annual Birdwatching Olympics and Nature Week is held in September, with prizes for those who spot the greatest number of species

There are also two smaller bird sanctuaries at the Solar Salt Works and Goto Meer. At Pos'i Mangel, in the Washington Park, thousands of birds gather in the late afternoon. Bronswinkel Well, also in the Park, is another good place to see hundreds of birds and giant cacti. The indigenous Bonaire green parrot (a conjure rather than a parrot) and the endangered yellow-shouldered Amazon (*Amazona barbarebdis rothschildi*) can be seen in the park and at other locations around the island. In 2002 a blue Amazonian parrot was observed mingling with its green-feathered brethren. About 190 species of birds have been found on Bonaire in addition to the flamingoes.

There are lots of iguanas and lizards of all shapes and sizes. The big blue lizards are endemic to Bonaire, while the Anolis, a tree lizard with a yellow dewlap, is related to the Windward Islands Anolis species rather than to the neighbouring Venezuelan species. The most common mammals you are likely to see are feral goats and donkeys. Try to resist feeding the friendly donkeys because this attracts them to the roadside where they are hit by vehicles too frequently. Bonaire's only native mammal is the bat, of which eight species have been identified.

Diving and marine life

A monthly underwater clean-up is organized by Green Submarine dive shop, T7172929, divers and snorkellers welcome

Bonaire's combination of low rainfall, little runoff, fringing reef and gin clear water with visibility of 30 m or more makes for diving that is unsurpassed in the Caribbean. Bonaire's reefs have been protected since 1971, the Marine Park celebrated its 25th anniversary in 2001 and was designated a National Park in 1999. Surrounding the island are corals harbouring over a thousand different species of marine creatures. Ranked as one of the three top dive spots in the world, and number one in the Caribbean (followed by Grand Cayman Island and Cozumel), Bonaire led the movement for preservation of underwater resources. Surrounding the whole island is a protected marine park from the high water mark down to 60 m. Two areas have been designated marine reserves, with no diving allowed; along Playa Frans, north to Boca Slogbaai, and west of Karpata. Lac Bay, a natural nursery for fish, is also part of the Marine Park because of its extensive mangroves and seagrass beds. Stringent laws passed in 1971 ban spearfishing and the removal of any marine life from Bonaire's waters. It is a serious offence to disturb the natural life of the coral reefs. Permanent anchors have been placed in all dive spots to avoid doing any unwarranted damage. Do not: touch the coral or other underwater life, such as sea horses; move anything to create a better photo; feed the fish, as it is not natural and encourages more aggressive species; or drop litter. Sea turtles can be seen at several sites around Bonaire and Klein Bonaire. Turtle spotters can report sightings to the *Sea Turtle Conservation Bonaire (STCB)* via a form available in all dive schools, or contact the Bonaire Marine Park, T7178444, www.bmp.org In January, suring the post-hatching season, the island's resident turtles are tagged. Visitors are invited to accompany the bilogists during their activities. Contact the STCB, T7172225 or T7900433 to arrange it.

On the east side of the island there is a shelf and a drop-off about 12 m from the shore down to a 30-m coral shelf and then another drop down to the ocean floor. The sea is rather rough on that side for most of the year although it sometimes calms down in October or November. Along the west side of the island the sea is calm and there are numerous dive sites of varying depths with wrecks as well as reefs. The most frequently dived sites include, **Rappel**, **Pink Beach**, **Small Wall**, **Angel City** and the **Town Pier**. There are also dozens of sites for boat dives off Klein Bonaire just 1½ km from Kralendijk. *Bonaire Diving Made Easy* is recommended and can be obtained from dive shops for US$10, or online from the *Bonaire Reporter*, the local English language newspaper, www.bonairereporter.com/divingguide.htm

Snorkelling is excellent at **Andreas**, **Oil Slick Leap**, **Tori's Reef**, **Windsock Steep** and along the east side of **Klein Bonaire**. Dive boats usually take snorkellers along for about US$12. The *Sea and Discover* marine education service, T7175322, seaandis@bonairelive.com, offers snorkelling excursions with a guide for US$30 per person. The *Skiffy* water taxi provides round trips to Klein Bonaire for US$10. There are also glass-bottom boats, *Bonaire Dream* (US$22.50, T7807838 or 5666061) or *Aquaspace* (US$30, T7172568). Tickets available at local hotels.

Snorkelling

According to the latest Reader Survey carried out by *Rodale's Scuba Diving Magazine*, **Buddy Dive**, T7175080, www.buddydive.com, and **Toucan Diving**, T7172500 at the *Plaza Resort Bonaire*, received top ratings from its readers. The **Dive Inn**, T7178761, was rated the No 2 resort in the Caribbean by the German magazine *Tauchen*. The other main schools are **Dive Bonaire**, T7178285, F7178238, at the *Divi Flamingo*, **Habitat Dive Center**, T7178290, F7177346, **Bon Bini Divers** at the *Coral Regency Resort*, T7175425, F7174425, www.bonbinidivers.com, **Green Submarine**, T/F7172929, dive@greensubmarine.com, **Blue Divers**, T7176860, F7176865, www.bluedivers.com, **Photo Tours Divers** at the *Caribbean Courts Resort*, T7175353, ext 328, www.bonairephototours.com, and the newest dive school, **WannaDive**, at the *Eden Park Resort*, T7908111. All dive schools can conduct lessons in English, Dutch, German, Spanish and sometimes other tongues. Prices are competitive, ranging from US$25-50 for a 2-tank dive if you have your own equipment. Add a 10% service charge on most diving and 5% sales tax on all training courses and rentals. All packages include tank,

Dive centres
For underwater images of the reef, see www.BonaireWeb-Cams.com, updated every two minutes

Bonaire

Netherlands Antilles, the ABC Islands

Sleeping
1 Bayside Resort
2 Black Durgon Inn
3 Bruce Bowker's Carib Inn
4 Buddy Beach & Dive Resort
5 Captain Don's Habitat
6 Caribbean Club Bonaire
7 Caribbean Court
8 Eden Beach
9 Lac Bay Resort
10 Lion's Dive
11 Plaza Resort Bonaire
12 Sand Dollar Condominium Resort
13 Sorobon Beach Resort

Netherlands Antilles, the ABC Islands

▶ Essentials

See also Directory, page 828

Departure tax *There is a departure tax of US$6 (NAf 10) on local flights and US$20 (NAf 36) on international flights.*

Hours of business *Shops: Mon-Sat 0800-1200, 1400-1800, until 2100 on Fri, and for a few hours on Sun if cruise ships are in port.* **Supermarkets:** *0800-2000, and some on Sun 0900-1400.*

Public holidays *New Year's Day, Good Fri, Easter Mon, Queen's Birthday and Rincon Day (30 Apr), Labour Day (1 May), Ascension Day, Bonaire Day (6 Sep), Christmas Day and Boxing Day.* **Carnival** *takes place over about 6 weeks from the end of Jan to the beginning of Mar, with parades, jump-ups and the election of King and Queen of the Carnival and 'Prince and Pancho'. Several days are devoted to the Tumba festival, a Tumba being a winning song. Carnival is organized by the Fundashon Karnival Boneiru (Fukabo). Dates for the main adult parade are 22 Feb 2004, 6 Feb 2005.*

Radio *The news is broadcast in Dutch on Voz di Bonaire, FM 94.7 MHz, Mon-Sat on the hour 0700-1800. Transworld Radio broadcasts in English on 800 KHz MW daily 0700-0830, 2200-2400, news 0700 Mon-Fri, 0800 and 2200 daily, 2300 Sat and Sun; Caribbean weather forecast 0730 Mon-Fri, 0800 Sat and Sun. Radio Nederland, 6020 KHz at 0630, 6165 and 15315 KHz at 2030, 9590 and 11720 KHz at 2330. The Papiamento broadcast is on 97.1 FM.*

Tipping *10-15% in restaurants, which is often added automatically to the bill. Tax is 10%. Dive shops 10%.*

Tourist offices overseas *Canada* **RMR Group Inc,** *Taurus House, 512 Duplex Av Toronto, Ontario, M4R 2E3, T416-4844864, 800-8266247, F416-4858256.*

Europe **Interreps BV,** *Visseringlaan 24, 2288 ER Rijswijk, The Netherlands, T31070-3954444, interrep@interrep.demon.nl* **USA Adams Unlimited,** *10 Rockefeller Plaza, Suite 900, New York, NY 10020, T212-9565912, 800-2662473, lisa@adams-pr.com* **Venezuela Flamingo Representaciones,** *Yazmín Pérez de Ramírez, Av Humboldt, Edif Humboldt, Piso 1 Apt 5, urb Bello Monte, Caracas, T9534653, F9511625.*

Voltage *127 volts, 50 cycles. 220 volts available at some resorts.*

---

air, weights and belt; equipment rental varies, US$6-11 for a BC jacket, US$6-11 for a regulator, US$6-10 for mask, snorkel and fins. Camera and other equipment rental widely available.

All dive operations are well equipped and well staffed with excellent safety records. If booking a package deal check whether their week-long dive packages include nightly night dives, or only 1 a week. For less experienced divers it is worth choosing a dive boat which keeps staff on board while the leader is underwater, in case you get into difficulties. Shore diving is available nearly everywhere, weather and sea conditions permitting. The guide book, *Bonaire Diving Made Easy*, details the entry and dive site conditions.

A US$10 per person levy for maintenance of the marine park has to be paid only once every calendar year. You will be given a marine park tag to wear on your gear when scuba diving. There is a **recompression chamber** at the San Francisco Hospital Emergency Room and doctors trained in hyperbaric medicine. An *Annual Dive Festival* is held in Jun.

Beaches and watersports

Be careful at east coast beaches; the surf is strong and it is dangerous to swim except within Lac Bay

Bonaire is not noted for its beaches; the sand is usually full of coral and rather hard on the feet, and those on the west coast are narrow, although beaches in front of some hotels have been helped with extra sand. They do offer peace and quiet, though, and you will not get pestered by people trying to sell you things. **Pink Beach**, at the southern tip of the island is popular, the water is shallow and good for swimming, but the sand is gritty. **Sorobon** is a private, nudist resort where non-guests pay US$10 for daily admission. Kai at **Lac Bay** has an area of mangroves at the north end of the bay, and in the northeast **Playa Chiquitu** is pleasant for sunbathing but has strong surf. In the Washington-Slagbaai National Park are two attractive bays: **Playa Funchi**, which is good for snorkelling, but has no sand and **Boca Slagbaai**, where the ruins of colonial buildings are being restored and you can see flamingoes wading in the salinja behind the beach.

La Dania's Leap

Divers and snorkelers can have a thrilling, yet safe, experience by doing a drift dive from shore. First drive north to the La Dania's leap dive site. Unload your gear. Have the driver continue another 2 km and park the car at the Karpata dive site. After he/she walks back to the group, proceed to the edge of the cliff. Don your gear and jump into the sea. It's less than a 2 m drop. Turn right and head north.

The coral here is especially beautiful and massive. Swim slowly because the slight current will push you along. You will know you are coming to your exit point when you pass an huge old ship's anchor. The exit at Karpata has an old concrete pier and steps carved in the cliff that will return you to the place where you parked your car. This adventure should take about 45 minutes.

Fishing
You can charter a fishing boat through your hotel and arrange half- or full-day trips with tackle and food included. Bonaire has good bonefishing and also deep-sea fishing. 2 independent charter companies are *Piscatur*, run by Captain Chris Morkos, T7178774, F7174784, half day US$275 for 4 people, US$425 full day in 38-ft diesel boat, or US$125 half day for 2 people, US$225 full day in 15-ft skiff; and *Big Game*, a 30-ft Bertram sport fisherman run by Captain Cees and his son Thomas, US$325 half day, US$450 full day for up to 5 people, T7176500, F7176500, www.bonairenet.com.biggame/indexbgs.htm Recreational boats can be chartered from *Nautico Bonaire*, Kaya Jan NE Craane 24, T7175800, F7175850. A wonderful motor sloop, *The Green Parrot*, can be chartered for US$140 per day, all-inclusive, from *Blonk Boatworks*, T7176800, 5670871. There is an annual **Bonaire International Fishing Tournament**, held at the end of Mar.

Sailing
The annual **Bonaire Sailing Regatta** is held in early Oct. This has grown into a world-class event with races for seagoing yachts, catamarans, sunfishes, windsurfers and local fishing boats. The smaller craft compete in Kralendijk Bay, while the larger boats race round Bonaire and Klein Bonaire. The windsurfers race in Lac Bay. Held over 5 days, the event attracts crowds and hotel reservations need to be made well in advance. For information call the Regatta office, T7177425, F7175576. There are also monthly regattas for several classes of small boats. In Dec the final event of the **World Freestyle Windsurfing Championship** is held in Lac Bay, contact Elvis Martinus, T7172288. The Marina at *Harbour Village* is the only full-service marina in Bonaire. There are 60 slips for boats up to 110 ft with showers, laundry, fuel, water, chandlery, etc, and a shop for repairs.

Day sails
Sailing trips with snorkelling and beach barbecue, often on Klein Bonaire, or sunset booze cruises, from US$38 per person plus 10% service, are offered on *Samur*, T7175592, samur@bonairelive.com), a 56-ft Siamese junk built in Bangkok in 1968, based at *Captain Don's Habitat*, with pick-up service from most resorts. Others include the 42-ft cutter, *Oscarina*, offering trips to the nearby Klein Curaçao and the Venezuelan Las Aves islands as well as day sailing around Bonaire T7907674; *Woodwind* is a 37-ft trimaran offering sailing and guided snorkelling around Bonaire and Klein Bonaire, T5607055. *Skiffy Water Taxi*, run by the amiable Henk Ram, offers a watertaxi service to Klein Bonaire from *Nautico Bonaire* and most hotels, T5607254. The *Baka de Laman* water taxi runs from *Karel's Beach Bar*, T5607126.

Windsurfing
Conditions are ideal for windsurfing with winds of 15-25 knots December to August and 12-18 knots September to November

On the leeward side, offshore winds allow you to sail in protected water. At Lac Bay on the windward side of the island, where the water is calm and shallow, there is a constant onshore wind making it safe and easy to learn the sport. The bay is about 8 sq km but a coral reef just outside the bay breaks up the waves. However, the adventurous can get out of the bay at one end where long, high waves enable you to wave ride, jump or loop. *Jibe City*, T7175233, www.jibecity.com (closed Sep), run by Ernst Van Vliet, is a BIC/TIGA Centre and has the latest models and Gaastra sails with retail shop and *Hangout Bar*. Lessons from US$45 per hr, rentals from US$55 per day, US$265 per week. *The Place*, managed by Elvis Martinus and Bonaire's first Olympian, Paun Sargosa, is also on Lac Bay, featuring top-notch gear, T7172288. Windsurfing rentals and instruction are available along with kayak, sunfish, mini speed boats, waterskiing, sea sausage rides, small Hobie cat, waterskiing, hydrosliding and paddle boats. *Parasail*, T7174998, has waterskiing and banana boat rides in addition to parasailing. A few dive shops rent kayaks, quite a good way of getting to Klein Bonaire without a boatload of other people, but remember that it is over 1 km back paddling into the wind. *Jibe City* (see above) rents kayaks in Lac Bay for a whole (US$30 single kayak, US$35 double) or half day (US$20/25) or a couple of hrs (US$10/15).

Kralendijk

Population: 1,690

Most people who work in the town live within walking distance in the suburbs of Antriol, Hato, Niki Boko and North Saliña

Kralendijk, meaning coral dike, the capital of Bonaire, is a small, sleepy town with colourful buildings one or two storeys high. It is often referred to locally as simply 'Playa', because of its historic position as the main landing place. The town is just a few blocks long with several streets projecting inland. In 2002 a seaside promenade project was completed along the Playa section of Kralendijk, south to the *Divi Flamingo* hotel. Most of the shops are in the small *Harbourside Shopping Mall* and on the main street, the name of which changes from J A Abraham Boulevard to Kaya Grandi to Kaya Gobornador Debrot. The **Museum** (Department of Culture), tucked away on a side street near the big Catholic church with the clock tower, houses snippets of folklore, art, archaeology, old photographs and a shell collection. Small enough for you to get personal attention if you want it. ■ *Weekdays 0800-1200, 1300-1700. Small donation requested. Kaya J van der Ree 7, or Kaya Sabana 14, T7178868.* The small **Fort Oranje** has been renovated and now houses the Bonairean court of justice as well as a permanent archaeological collection with items found during the renovation. The shorefront plaza, **Wilhelminaplein**, has a monument to the Bonaireans who were killed in the Merchant Marine in the Second World War, and a **vegetable market** built like a Greek temple

Kralendijk

Sleeping	**Eating**	4 Rendez-Vous
1 Divi Flamingo	1 Beefeater	5 Zeezicht
2 Dive Inn Beach Resort	2 Cozzoli's Pizzeria	
3 Rochaline	3 Mona Lisa	

N

Not to scale

Around the island

The island can be toured in a day if you start early but it is more pleasant to do a north tour on one day and a south tour another. Take food and drinks, there are rarely any available along the way, and aim to picnic somewhere you can swim to cool off. Dominating the skyline outside Kralendijk is a long hill or **Seru Largu**. A good paved road leads to the top for spectacular views of the town, the small island of Klein Bonaire, the salt hills and the surrounding sea and farmland. It's quiet and undeveloped except for a few benches, and is a favourite spot for a picnic.

North of Kralendijk the road passes most of the hotels, past the Power and Water Distillation Plant along the 'scenic' road, which offers several descents to the sea and some excellent spots for snorkelling along the rocky coastline. The first landmark is the Radio Netherlands station which has masses of aerials. Note that the road becomes one-way after the radio station, do not turn round. At the abandoned Karpata Landhuis, if you turn right you go directly to Rincon, climbing to the top of the hill for a steep descent and a good view of Rincon and the Windward coast. Alternatively, continue along to the Bonaire Petroleum Company Tank Farm (BOPEC) where the road turns inland to **Goto Meer Bay**, the best place to see flamingos close up, on another road to Rincon.

The north
The road is new and smooth but narrow; watch out for sunbathing iguanas and lizards

On the first Saturday of the month the sleepy village of **Rincon**, Bonaire's oldest settlement where the slaves' families lived, comes alive with a street market, the *Marshe Rincon*. It wasn't intended as a tourist attraction but has become one for the visitors lucky enough to find out about it (a less extensive street market is held on other Saturdays). Dozens of stands are set up to sell fresh produce, plants, handicrafts, pastries, local foods, clothing and assorted goods. It is the only scheduled time for the *Soldachi* (hermit crab) tours. The tours leave from the Marshe centre and are either on foot, with a guide who explains the architecture, history and culture of Rincon, or by bus, around Rincon, the Lourdes Grotto, the Altamira overlook, Ita's Garden and the museum at Washington Park. ■ *Walking tour 0900-1000, US$5.60; bus tour 1030-1200, US$8.50, T7172670 or 7176435, wilmari@bonairelive.com*

East of Rincon is a side road to the **Boca Onima** caves with their Arawak Indian inscriptions. Inscriptions can still be seen in several caves around the island. The springs of **Fontein** opened in 2000 after being off limits for a decade. On Bonaire it's very unusual to see fresh water pouring through the walls of a cave and flowing freely down the hill. The water has nurtured huge trees and tropical fruit groves along its path. You can tour the area, picnic and cool off in one of three pools fed by the spring water. ■ *Open Sun or by appointment, free, call Alejander Werner, T7905363 for information.*

The road leading north from Rincon takes you to Washington/Slagbaai National Park, established in 1969, which occupies the north portion of the island, about 5,460 ha, and contains more than 190 species of birds. ■ *Daily 0800-1700 (no entry after 1500). NAf17.50, US$10, children up to 15 NAf 5, US$3. Bicycles only on guided tours as per park rules, arrangements must be made in advance for bike entry. Toilet at the entrance. Bring food and water.* There is a small store selling food, drinks and souvenirs at the entrance. Behind the shop there are displays of traditional crafts of lime and charcoal making, a walking trail and a museum of local historical items plus a room with geological explanations, bird pictures and a shell collection. You can choose to drive a 34-km or a 24-km tour, the roads being marked by yellow or green arrows. You will get a route map when you pay to get in. The road is dirt, rough in parts, and the long route, which passes lovely beaches (including Playa Cocolishi, almost paved in tiny shells), can be hot and tiring. It is possible to drive round in an ordinary car but many car rental agencies discourage the use of their normal cars, especially after rain, and a pick-up or 4WD is preferable. Once you have chosen your route you have to stick to it. Even the short route takes a minimum of two hours. *Cycle Bonaire* is permitted to take cycling tours into the park and self-organized trips

Washington/ Slagbaai National Park

▶ **Bonaire Sky Park**

Bonaire's skies are usually clear and always free of pollution. Residents like to call the heavens at night the Sky Park; a place where there's no admission fee and nature holds sway. One of the best features of the Sky Park is the fact that it holds both northern and southern hemisphere stars. During the winter peak tourist season, just after dark, you'll see two bright stars winking emerald and white light at you. The brighter, although not by much, is Sirius, the Dog Star, the eye of Canis Major, familiar to those who live in the north. But the other is a true southern star, the wonderful Canopus, that bright star that most northerners have never seen. In fact it's the second brightest star visible from Earth. If you wait until midnight you'll easily spot the Southern Cross low in the southern sky. And if you can stay awake for a couple more hours you can spot Alpha Centauri, the star closest to Earth, rising just as Canopus sets.

are permitted provided a 'chase car' comes along, but other two-wheeled transport is not allowed. There are guided hiking excursions up **Mount Brandaris**, or you can do it on your own; hiking trails have been marked. An area has been set aside for rappelling. You can drive to view Goto Meer on the longer route but the view is better from the observation point outside the park. The return to Kralendijk is inland through the villages of **Noord Salinja** and **Antriol**.

The south
Remember the flamingos are easily frightened, so move quietly if near them

The tour south passes the airport and Trans World Radio's towering 213-m antenna which transmits 50,000 watts. The salt pier dominates the view along the coastal road and the salt pans are a stunning pink/purple colour. Further on are the snow-white salt piles and the three obelisks which guided the sailing ships coming to load salt: blue, white, and orange, dating from 1838, with the tiny huts that sheltered the slaves who worked the saltpans. The roofs of the slave huts reach only to waist level.

At the south tip of the island is **Willemstoren**, one of Bonaire's three main lighthouses, which dates from 1837. Pass Sorobon Beach and the mangrove swamps to **Boca Cai** at landlocked **Lac Bay**, with its clear water excellent for underwater exploration. The extensive seagrass beds and surrounding mangroves are an important nursery for marine creatures. Near the Sorobon Resort is the Sea Hatch Bonaire shrimp farming project. Take the road back to Kralendijk through the village of **Nikiboko**, or a straight route west to the airport area. There is a **Donkey Sanctuary** just south of the airport, founded in the mid-1990s by a Dutch woman, Marina Melis. At any one time she is likely to have 50 or more donkeys which are sick or disabled, and most stick around even after they are healed. It is a well-organized facility and visitors are welcome. ■ *Tue-Sun 1000-1600. Free entry but donations welcome. T5607607, donkeyshelp@bonairelive.com*

Essentials

Sleeping
A US$5.50 or US$6.50 per person per night government tax and 10-15% service charge must be added

High season rates (16 Dec to 2 weeks after Easter) are roughly double low-season rates in the more expensive hotels; the cheaper ones tend to charge the same all year round. Aug is 'family month' with lots of good deals. All the hotels with on-site dive shops, and some others besides, offer dive packages which give better value than the rack rates listed here. In addition there are lots of apartments and condos for rent, not mentioned here. Ask the tourist office for details.

South of Kralendijk **LL-AL** *Divi Flamingo Beach Resort & Casino*, J A Abraham Blvd 40, T7178285, www.divibonaire.com Totally renovated in 2000, 145 units, standard rooms or more luxurious, is on a small artificial beach, snorkelling or diving just off the beach is excellent, tennis, pools, jacuzzi. Next door is **L-A** *Bruce Bowker's Carib Inn*, J A Abraham Blvd 46, T7178819, bruce@caribinn.com Rooms, apartments and 3-bedroom house, a/c, cable TV, pool, dive shop. **LL-AL** *Plaza Resort Bonaire*, J A Abraham Blvd 80, T7172500, info@plazaresortbonaire.com 200 rooms, suites and villas, diving, tennis, racquet ball, watersports, casino, pool, beach, striving to be 5-star resort. Using all the same facilities is **LL-L** *Port Bonaire Resort*, part of the *Plaza Resort,* a condo-resort, villas and apartments, on waterfront, no beach, pool. **LL-AL** *Caribbean Court Bonaire*, J A Abraham Blvd, T7175353, www.caribbean court.com 21 apartments, 1-3 bedrooms, close to airport, fully equipped. **A-C** *Dive Inn*, Kaya L D Gerharts 22, T7178291, F7178118. Only 7 rooms, some rooms with kitchenettes, bicycle rental, near sea and town next to *Dive Inn* dive shop.

Kralendijk **B-C** *Hotel Rochaline*, Kaya Grandi 7, T7178286, F7178258. 10 rooms, a/c, functional, bar facing sea, restaurant. Popular and often full is the **B-C** *Palm Studios* attached to *Blue Divers Diveshop* on Kaya den Tera 2, T7176860, www.bluedivers.com 10 rooms, a/c, common shower and kitchen, big garden, clean, cosy, pool, recommended for budget travellers/divers.

North of Kralendijk **LL** *Bayside Resort*, Kaya Jan NE Craane 24, T7175800, F7175850. Short walk to town, 1-bedroom suites sleep 4, 2-bedroom penthouses sleep 6, fully equipped, balconies overlooking charter boats. **AL-A** *Eden Beach Apartment Resort*, Kaya Gobernador N Debrot 74, T7176720. Good value, new property, well-equipped, *WannaDive* dive shop and *Bongos Restaurant* on the premises. **LL-L** *Sand Dollar Condominium Resort*, Kaya Gobernador N Debrot 79, T7178738, sanddollar@bonairenet.com, 76 apartments, a/c, rocky shoreline, tennis, pool. **L-AL** *Buddy Beach and Dive Resort*, Kaya Gob N Debrot 85, T7175080, www.buddydive.com 68 rooms and apartments all with sea views, a/c, kitchen, pool, Buddy Watersports Center. **LL-AL** *Lions Dive Hotel Bonaire*, Kaya Gob N Debrot 91, T7175580, www.bonairenet.com Suites and apartments some sleep 6, diving with Bon Bini Divers, pool, sundeck, also sells time shares. **LL-AL** *Captain Don's Habitat*, Kaya Gob N Debrot 103, T7178290. 93 rooms, cottages and nice villas of differing standards, well laid out seafront bar and restaurant, dive packages, family packages, pool, dive shop, mountain bike rental. A little further along the coast is **AL-C** *Black Durgon Inn/Pilot Fish Apartments*, Kaya Gobernador N Debrot 145, T7175736, F7178846, 8-room inn, 1-bedroom apartments, 2/3-bedroom villa, with view of Klein Bonaire, non-commercial, dive shop. **A-B** *Caribbean Club Bonaire*, Kaya Gob N Debrot 200, T7177901, www.caribbeanclubbonaire.com 23 rooms, bungalow style with 1 and 2 bedroom apartments, good value, cosy, secluded, nice bar and snack restaurant, internet lounge, pool, renovated 2002.

Windward coast **LL-L** *Sorobon Beach Resort*, at Lac Bay, T7178080, F7176080, sorobon@ bonairenet.com Clothes optional, 30 chalets on the beach, restaurant for hotel guests, small shop for self-catering, free trips to town for shopping daily, snorkelling, kayaks, windsurfing. **LL-AL** *Lac Bay Resort*, Kaminda Sorobon 64, T7178198, F7175686. In protected nature area, studios, apartments and 3-bedroom villa, good view from *Kon Tiki* restaurant and bar.

International food at the major hotels varies on different nights of the week with barbecues, Italian or Indonesian nights, etc. Main courses in the upper-priced restaurants are about US$12-20, but several restaurants do bar snacks, 'Bar Hop', if you want to economize. **Water** comes from a desalinization plant, has an excellent taste and is safe to drink. Take water with you on excursions. Do not, however, wash in or drink water from outside taps. This is often *sushi* (dirty) water, treated sufficiently for watering plants but nothing more.

There are over 80 restaurants on this small island. The **hotels** mostly offer good restaurants with fine views over the sea. *The Lion's Den*, at the *Lion's Dive Hotel*, T7173400, has one of the most spectacular views and a stylish menu. *Rum Runners at the Reef* at *Captain Don's Habitat*, T7177303. Breakfast, lunch and dinner with theme nights, eg Bonairean food, Mexican or barbecue, with live music some nights. *Captain Wook's Marina Bar & Compadres Restaurant*, T7177500, at the *Harbour Village* marina. Tex-Mex specialities and you can use the cascade pool and outdoor pool table. *It Rains Fishes*, at the *Bayside Resort*, T7178780. Dinner only.

In Kralendijk *Rendez-Vous*, Kaya L D Gerharts 3, T7178454. Award-winning chef, dinner, seafood specials, vegetarian choice, good vegetables, small and friendly, closed Sun. *Mona Lisa*, on Kaya Grandi, T7178718. Closed Sat-Sun, bar and restaurant, interesting, imaginative food, Dutch chef enjoys discussing the menu, expect to pay NAf 25-35 for main

Eating

Food is imported, so market fruit and veg are pricey. Try local dishes such as salt fish, goat stew or fungi (corn meal polenta)

Netherlands Antilles, the ABC Islands

course, friendly service, popular with Europeans. *Croccantino*, Kaya Grandi 48, T7175025. Inspired, Italian, in historic town house, a/c dining room or garden dining, open daily for lunch and dinner. *Capriccio*, Kaya Isla Riba I, T7177230. Closed Tue, Italian, homemade pasta, pizza, lunch and dinner. *The Lost Penguin*, in the town centre. Street side bar and restaurant, breakfast, lunch and dinner, with sandwiches, cakes, coffee and juices. *Beefeater*, Kaya Grandi 12, T7177776. Open from 1100 daily, local and Venezuelan specialities, rich pastry counter, garden setting in rear. *Zeezicht*, Kaya JNE Craane 12, T7178434. On the waterfront, Bonaire's oldest restaurant, does breakfast, lunch and dinner, sandwiches and omelettes as well as fish, steak, pasta and some Indonesian, open daily. In the *Harbourside Shopping Mall* there is *Cozzoli's Pizzeria*, T7175195. For fast food, breakfast, lunch and dinner, *The Garden Café*, Kaya Gob Debrot 11, T7173410, features Middle Eastern and South American meals. *The Swiss Chalet*, Kaya Simon Bolivar 21, T7173366. International food and Swiss specialities, raclette, fondue, rostis. South of town, just past *Carib Inn* is *Richard's Waterfront Dining*, J A Abraham Blvd 60, T7175263. American owner, happy hour 1700-1900, dinner 1830-2230, closed Mon, seafood and steak specialities. *Blue Moon*, Kaya CEB Hellmund 5, T7178617. On waterfront, set menu or à la carte, French and international, open for food 1800-2200, happy hour 1700-1830, closed Wed. *Den Laman Seafood Restaurant*, at the roundabout near the northern hotels, T7178955. Open for lunch and dinner. *Maiky Snack Kaminda*, New Amsterdam 30, T09-5670078. An out-in-the-country spot to get home-made local food.

There are lots of Chinese restaurants. *Peking*, Kaya Korona 140, T7174999. Lunch and dinner, cheap, large portions of Chinese food. *Great China* , Kaya Grandi 39, T7178886; *Shanghai Bar Restaurant*, Kaya L D Gerharts 17, T7178838, all open for lunch and dinner. As in the other Dutch Antilles, Indonesian food is good and popular. *Old Inn*, on J A Abraham Blvd opposite *Plaza Resort*, T7176666. Indonesian Rijsttafel a speciality, also steak, fish and children's menu, dinner only, closed Wed. There is a Surinamese restaurant: *Surinaamse Bar Restaurant*, Kaya A Cecillia 31, T7172127. For pizza, try *Pasa Bon Pizza and Bar*, Kaya Gob Debrot 42, T7901111. Most restaurants can prepare food for takeaway.

Windward side of the island, *Beachclub Kontiki* next to the *Lac Bay Resort*, T7175369, kontiki@bonairelive.net Seafood, steaks, salads and a wide variety of international cuisine, friendly, casual, beautiful view, Caribbean decor, open 1200-1500, 1830-2200, closed Mon. Home of the *Bonaire Jazz Club*. The beach bar, *Hang Out*, at Jibe City is recommended for terrific sandwiches, drink, shade, rest and regaining energy for windsurfing.

Nightlife
Some contrived typically Caribbean entertainment and gambling, but Bonaire's real nightlife revolves around free slide and video shows at hotels and dive shops

Check schedule of Bonaire's *Weekly Happenings* update at tourist office, or in the free English language weekly, *The Bonaire Reporter*. *Karel's Beach Bar* has a live band, Kaya K Craane 12, from 2200 Fri and Sat. The Bonaire Latin Jazz Club meets on the first Sun of the month at the *Kon Tiki* and the *Sorobon Resort*, 3 hrs of music, US$5.60, informal, outdoors, visiting musicians from Europe and the USA join the regular musicians (Bonairean, Dutch and Venezuelan) and music ranges from standard jazz to selections from Broadway with a Latin beat, call *Kontiki*, T7175369, for details. There are casinos at the *Divi Flamingo Beach Resort* (open 2000 except Sun), T7178285, and *Plaza Resort*, T7172450. There is a **cinema** on Kaya Prinses Marie, *The Movies Bonaire*, T7172400, www.InfoBonaire.com/cinema, usually closed Mon and Tue.

Shopping
Bonaire is not a major shopping centre, though some shops do stock high quality, low duty goods. Sales tax is 5%

The *Harbourside Shopping Mall* contains small boutiques and a photo-processing shop *Kodalux*, T7178123. Local arts and crafts are largely sea-based and fabrics. The *Fundashon Arte Industri Bonairano* and the *Caribbean Arts and Crafts shop* are both in Kralendijk for souvenirs. *Palu Wiri*, which plays local, native instruments, has recorded 3 CDs, available locally, of Bonairean and Antillean songs. The largest supermarket is *Cultimara*, T7178278, with groceries and some household goods, or there are several minimarkets. *Sand Dollar Grocery*, open daily is located in a small plaza in front of the *Sand Dollar Beach Club* along with *Lovers Ice Cream Parlour*. Near the *Divi Flamingo* a turning opposite leads to *Joke's* grocery and mini-market.

Sports
For diving and watersports, see pages 818 and 820

There are **tennis** courts at the *Divi Flamingo Beach Resort*, open 0800-2200, T7178285, and the *Harbour Village Beach Resort* and *Sand Dollar Condominium Resort*, open 0900-2100, T7178738. There is also **horse riding**. *Kunuku Warahama* has horses and playgrounds for the children as well as lots of other animals. Lunch and dinner also available, T7175558, not alway open, so phone ahead. **Walking** and **birdwatching** are popular in the Washington/Slagbaai National Park, particularly climbing up Mt Brandaris, the highest point on the island. **Cycling** is popular and tours are organized or there is a cycling trails map if you want to go it alone. Bikes and mountain bikes can be rented at several hotels and outlets (see below). In May a **Mountain Bike Challenge Race** is held and in Oct a **Mountain Bike Speed Challenge Race**.

Tour operators

Bonaire Tours, T7178778, head office at the Harbour Village Marina, for large or small groups, 2-hr north or south tour, half- or full-day Washington Park tour, day trip to Curaçao. Taxis have fixed prices for sightseeing tours. *Discover Bonaire*, Kaya Gob N Debrot 79, T7175252, www.discover bonaire.com, for kayaking, nature tours, guided snorkelling and mountain biking, tours. *SkiffyWatertaxi*, T/F5607254, trips to Klein Bonaire Mon-Sat, US$14 per person, on Sun by appointment. Cruises Tue, Fri, Sat, and snorkel trips. *Bonaire Travel & Tours*, at the corner of the Lourdes Mall.

Transport

Flamingo Airport (BON) can accommodate 747 jumbo jets with a runway of over 4 km

Air *KLM* flies non-stop twice daily from Amsterdam and on to Quito or Lima. *Dutch Caribbean Express* flies in high season from Aruba, Curaçao and Miami, and Sint Maarten and Venezuela both via Curaçao. In low season services are drastically cut. Depending on the season, *Air Jamaica* flies from Boston, Chicago and Philadelphia via Montego Bay. *American Eagle* flies daily from San Juan, Puerto Rico, where you can make connections with US cities. Several other international airlines fly to Curaçao, 48 km away, from where frequent daily flights are available to Bonaire. A new airline, *BonairExel*, a joint venture between KLM and Dutch Eagle Express, was expected to start operations in 2003 with flights to other Dutch Caribbean islands and Venezuela.

Sea There is a fast ferry, *Chogogo*, making 1 round trip a day from Kralendijk to Willemstad, Curaçao, US$50 round trip, 2 hrs there, 2½ back, T7177001.

Road Bicycle Available to rent from most hotels' front desks (see above). *De Freeweiler*, on Kaya Grandi downtown, T7178545, sells, rents and repairs touring and mountain bikes. Bike hire from US$10 per day, US$40 per week. *Cycle Bonaire/Discover Bonaire*, has Trek mountain bikes and offers rentals, repairs and guided tours. Bike rental is US$15 per day or US$75 per week, while guided excursions are US$40 half day including drinks and US$65 whole day including lunch but not including bike rental. Also *Hot Shot*, see above, and *Bonaire Boating*, with an office in the *Divi Flamingo Hotel*, T7175353, ext 505, and some hotels. *Discover Bonaire* has tours through the kunuku and Washington/Slagbaai National Park. The roads in the south are flat and in good condition but there is no shade and you would need lots of water and sun screen. In the north it is more hilly and the roads are not as good. For mountain bikers there are lots of unpaved trails and goat paths.

Car hire *A B Car Rental* at the airport, T7178980, F7175034. *Budget*, T7174700, F7173325. *Trupial Car Rental*, Kaya Grandi No 96, T7178487. *Avis*, J A Abraham Blvd 4, Kralendijk, T7175795, F7175793. There are nearly a dozen other companies not listed here, plenty of choice, many have offices in the hotels. At the busiest times of the year, it is best to reserve a car in advance. 4WD vehicles are not easy to find, and it is best to order one in advance. Most cars are manual shift. There are lots of pick-ups and minivans for divers wanting to carry gear around for shore diving. Some companies prohibit the use of ordinary cars on unpaved roads and in Washington/Slagbaai Park. There is a government tax of US$4 per day plus 2% on the rental fee. The speed limit in built-up areas is 40 kmph, outside towns it is 60 kmph unless otherwise marked. Several of the streets in Kralendijk and the tourist road north of the Radio Netherlands towers are 1-way. There are 4 filling stations, open Mon-Sat 0700-2100. The Kralendijk station is also open Sun 0900-1530.

You must have a valid driver's licence. Minimum age for car rental varies between agencies from 21-26

Motorcycle Motorcycles and quad bikes can be rented from US$18 a day; shop around as there are several new scooter shops and rates are competitive: *Rent-O-Fun Drive*, T7173708; *De Freeweiler*, T7178545; *Macho Scooter Rentals*, T7172500; *Orlando's Bonaire Motorcycle Shop*, T7178429, 7904409, rent Harleys or other interesting motorcycles for US$50 a day.

Taxi Drivers carry a list of officially approved rates, including touring and waiting time, but be sure to agree a price beforehand. The short trip from the airport to the *Divi Flamingo Beach Resort* is US$10; fares increase by 50% from midnight-0600. Taxis have TX on their licence plates. Taxis are available at the airport but do not cruise for business elsewhere. Any hotel will call a taxi for you. To call a taxi yourself, T7178100 for the taxi stand at the airport.

Netherlands Antilles, the ABC Islands

Things to do in Curaçao

- Take in the **underwater world**, diving, snorkelling or by visiting the Seaquarium.
- Trace the **Jewish heritage** and visit the 1732 synagogue, museum and cemetery.
- Walk around historical **Punda** and **Otrobanda**, the two sides of the capital, Willemstad, and cross over the swing bridge for a spectacular view of the two halves.
- Join local office staff for a typical, filling lunch of **goat stew and funchi** at the Old Market, where cooks prepare tasty Curaçaoan meals in huge pots on charcoal fires.
- Stock up on the original **Curaçao liqueur** and tour the distillery.

Directory **Airlines** *Dutch Caribbean Airline*, at the airport, T7178500, 0600-2130, or Blvd J A Abraham 35, T7177447, F7178118, 0800-1200, 1330-1730 Mon-Fri, www.flydca.com *KLM, Air Jamaica, American Eagle*, T7178300. **Banks** Open 0800 or 0830-1530 or 1600, Mon-Fri. All have ATMs. TCs and credit cards are widely accepted. *Royal Bank of Trinidad & Tobago (ABN-AMRO)*, T7178417, F7178469; *Maduro & Curiel's Bank (Bonaire) NV*, T7177249, F7172645, is a full-service Antillean bank with a branch in Rincon, T7176266; *Banco di Caribe NV*, T7178295, F7175153. **Communications** Internet: *De Tuin Eetcafe*, T7172999, *Seahorse Cyber Café*, T7174888, and *City Cybercafé*, offer high speed internet access at downtown locations. Several hotels offer internet access to their guests as well. Internet service providers are *BonaireLive!*, T7175180, F7175181 and *BonaireNet*, T/F7177160, **Post**: J A Abraham Blvd, Kralendijk, on the corner of Plaza Reina Wilhelmina opposite the ABN bank, open 0730-1200, 1330-1700 for stamps and postage, 1330-1600 for money orders, etc. Airmail to the USA and Canada is NAf1.75 for letters, NAf0.90 for postcards. There is also Express Mail and Federal Express Mail. *Rocargo Services*, T7178922, F7175791, is the FedEx and cargo agent. **Telephone**: Direct dialling to the USA with a credit card is available at the airport and at Telbo in town. Avoid the 'blue' long distance credit card phones; even short conversations can cost US$25. The international code for Bonaire is 599, followed by a 7-digit number. For information on services, contact Telbo, T7177000, F7175007. You can rent cellular phones at several places at low rates. Many US system cell phones work on Bonaire with reprogramming. There is no GSM service. **Medical services** The *Hospitaal San Francisco* in Kralendijk has 60 beds, T7178900. There is an **air ambulance** for emergency evacuation and a recompression chamber. phone number is T911. Dentist: *Chirino Dental Clinic*, T7178106. Opticians: *Optica Antillana*, T7178815, and *Ram's Optica*, T7175612. **Useful numbers** Emergency, T911. Immigration, T7178000. **Government main number**, T7175300. **Police**, T7178000 or T911. **Stinapa** (Park Authority) and **Bonaire Marine Park**, T7178444.

Curaçao

IDD code: 599
Colour map 5, grid B1
Population: 170,000

Curaçao is the largest of the Netherlands Antilles and its capital, Willemstad, has some very fine Dutch colonial architecture painted in a variety of pastel colours, while in the countryside there are several beautiful plantation houses, called landhuisen. *It also has one of the most important historical sites in the Caribbean: a synagogue dating back to 1732, which is the oldest in continuous use in the Western Hemisphere. For most of the 20th century the island's fortunes, like Aruba, depended on its oil refinery, which processes Venezuelan crude oil, but more recently tourism has increased in importance. Diving has grown very popular since the establishment of an underwater park to preserve the reef and there are dive sites all along the Leeward side of the island.*

Ins and outs

Getting there
Airlines and their routes change frequently so check the latest flight guides

Flights from Europe originate in Amsterdam, while flights from North America connect in Miami or San Juan. Curaçao has good links with South America and it is easy to get to from Venezuela, Colombia and Ecuador. **Hato Airport** is about 12 km from Willemstad and if you don't want to pay for a taxi there are buses in to Punda and Otrobanda.

Touching down

Business hours Shops: Mon-Sat 0830-1200, 1400-1800; Sun morning and lunchtimes if cruise ships are in port.

Departure tax There is an airport tax of US$10 on departure to the Netherlands Antilles or US$20 to Aruba or other destinations. This must be paid at a separate kiosk after you check in.

Documents Most nationalities (including US and Canadian citizens) need a passport and onward/return ticket. Visas are needed by citizens of Colombia, Dominican Republic and Haiti. Transit visitors and cruise ship passengers must have proof of identity for a 24-hour, or less, stay on the island. Immigration procedures at the airport are quick and easy.

Health The climate is healthy and non-malarial; epidemic incidence is slight. Rooms without a/c or window and door screens may need mosquito nets during the wetter months of Nov and Dec and sometimes May and Jun, and, although some spraying is done in tourist areas, mosquitoes are a problem. Some anti-mosquito protection is recommended if you are outdoors any evening. Beware of a tree with small, poisonous green apples that borders some beaches. This is the manchineel (manzanilla) and its sap causes burns on exposed skin.

Money The currency is the guilder, divided into 100 cents. There are coins of 1, 2½, 5, 10, 25, 50 cents and 1 and 2½ guilders, and notes of 10, 25, 50, 100, 250 and 500 guilders. Old and new coins are in circulation. **Exchange** The exchange rate is US$1=NAf1.77 for bank notes, NAf1.79 for cheques, although the rate of exchange offered by shops and hotels ranges from NAf1.75-1.80. Credit cards and US dollars are widely accepted.

Official time Atlantic Standard Time, 4 hrs behind GMT, 1 hr ahead of EST.

Safety There is a drugs problem in Willemstad and you are advised to be careful in Otrobanda at night and avoid the outer stretches of Pietermaai even by day (crack houses). If strangers stop you on the street asking 'alles goed?' (everything OK?) be assured that they are not enquiring after your health.

Public holidays New Year's Day, Carnival Mon (Feb), Good Fri, Easter Mon, Queen's Birthday (30 Apr), Labour Day (1 May), Ascension Day, Flag Day (2 Jul), Antillean Day (21 Oct), Christmas on 25 and 26 Dec, half day holiday 31 Dec.

Tourist offices overseas Holland: Vasteland 82-84, 3011 BP Rotterdam, PO Box 23227, T3110-4142639, info@ctbe.nl UK: Axis Sales and Marketing, 421a Finchley Rd, London NW3 6HJ, T0207-431 4045, destinations@axissm.com USA: Toll free: T800-2703350, 800-4458266, joel@aventura.npipb.com **Venezuela**: Av Abraham Lincoln entre Negrin y Recreo, Torre la Piñata, Piso 3, Oficina 3-A, Blvd Sabana Grande, Caracas, T58-212-7616647, curacaoturismo@cantv.net

Voltage 110/130/127/220 volts AC, 50 cycles. **Weights and measures** Metric.

See also Directory, page 844

Netherlands Antilles, the ABC Islands

Willemstad is a great place to walk around and there are tours if you want a guide who can explain all the architecture and history to you. The 2 halves of the city are connected with a pontoon bridge, the Queen Emma Bridge, which you can walk across when it is not open for shipping. Collective taxis and buses will take you further afield to most parts of the island; alternatively rent a car and explore on your own. There are about 4 car rental agencies at the airport, all the offices are together so it is easy to pick up price lists for comparison. 1 or 2 companies usually have desks in each of the major hotels. Look in local tourist literature or newspapers for news of special deals on offer, there is lots of choice. There have been problems with unsafe cars, inadequate insurance and licensing. Those listed in the transport section are considered reputable. Taxis are easily identified by the signs on the roof and TX before the licence number. There are taxi stands at all hotels and at the airport, as well as in principal locations in Willemstad.

Getting around
See Transport, page 843, for further details

The main office of the **Curaçao Tourism Development Bureau** is at Pietermaai 19, Willemstad, PO Box 3266, T4616000, F4612305. There are information offices on Breedestraat, east of Hendrikplein, and at the airport. Information on the large hotels, restaurants and other tourist details are at www.curacao.com/tourism www.curacao-tourism.com The Curaçao Hotel and Tourism Association (CHATA), Kaya Junior Salas 1, downtown Punda, T4651005, offers information, maps and assistance in finding a hotel. Several visitor information centres and booths, some sponsored by resort hotels, are dotted

Tourist information

round Willemstad. **Maps** *Curoil nv* publishes a road map with a satellite photo of the island with superimposed information, town street plans and index, available in *Mensing* and other bookshops. For maps on the web, **www.cartocaribe.com**

Diving and marine life

The waters around Curaçao contain a wide variety of colourful fish and plant life and several wrecks (*Superior Producer*, near the water distillation plant, and a tugboat in Caracas Bay), which have foundered on the coral reef just offshore. The reef surrounds the island and consists generally of a gently sloping terrace to a depth of about 10 m, then a drop-off and a reef slope with an angle of about 45°. The coral formations are spectacular in places and there are many huge sponges; one in Boca Santa Martha is so big it is known as 'the double bed'. There are lots of fish and you are likely to see barracuda, moray eels, spiny lobsters, turtles, manta rays and maybe sharks. Underwater visibility averages 24 m and water temperature varies between 24-27°C. There are lots of opportunities for successful underwater photography.

Many of the large resort hotels have dive shops on site. They have been encouraged by the establishment in 1983 of the Curaçao Underwater Park managed by the Netherlands Antilles National Parks Foundation (Stinapa), which stretches from the *Princess Beach Hotel* to East Point. The park extends out from the shore to a depth of 60 m and covers 600 ha of reef and 436 ha of inner bays.

Over 40 permanent mooring buoys for boats have been placed at dive sites along the south coast as part of Stinapa's programme for sustained utilization of the reef. A few of the sites can be dived from the shore (West Point, Blauwbaa, Port Marie, Daaibooi, Vaersen Bay, San Juan, Playa Kalki), but most of the coastal strip is private property and boat dives are necessary. The *Guide to the Curaçao Underwater Park*, by Jeffrey Sybesma and Tom van't Hof, published in 1989 by Stinapa and available locally, describes the sites and discusses conservation. For independent divers and snorkellers without a boat

Curaçao

there is the *Complete Guide to Landside Diving and Snorkelling Locations in Curaçao*, by Jeffrey Sybesma and Suzanne Koelega. No harpoons or spear guns are allowed and make sure not to damage or remove coral or any other sea creatures.

Seaquarium

The Seaquarium, southeast of Willemstad, just beyond the *Lions Dive Hotel*, has a collection of undersea creatures and plants found around the island, which live in channelled sea water to keep them as close as possible to their natural environment. The Seaquarium was built in 1984, the lagoons and marina being excavated so as to leave the original coastline untouched and do minimal damage to the reef offshore. There is a shark (lemon and nurse) and animal (turtles, stingrays) encounter programme, where you get in the water with them to feed them, good for photography, poor for animal welfare, US$55 for diving (no previous experience necessary), US$30 snorkelling. An even more controversial attraction has been the recent introduction of a swim with the dolphins programme, where dolphins caught in the wild are kept in tanks for visitors' amusement. A Marine Awareness Center offers divers day-long courses on the balance of the marine ecosystem for US$70 with half price discovery programmes for children over six. ■ *0830-1700. US$13.25, children under 15 US$7.50; after 1600 US$3 and US$1.50 respectively. T4616666. There is a restaurant, snack bar and shops selling shells and coral in marked contrast to the conservation efforts of the Underwater Park administration. The Seaquarium can be reached by bus marked Dominguito from the post office at 35 mins past the hr (except for 1335), which passes the* Avila Beach Hotel.

Dive centres

There are many dive operators, not all of which are mentioned here, and it is worth shopping around before booking a package deal. Most operators offer a single boat dive for around US$30-35, a 2-tank dive for US$55-60 and snorkelling trips including equipment for about US$15-20, but check when booking whether 10% service is included in the quoted price. **Ocean Encounters** (T4618131,www.oceanencounters.com) at the *Lions Dive Hotel* next to the Seaquarium is a PADI 5-star Gold Palm Resort and one of the larger operations. Dive boats are fully equipped for emergencies and take no more than 16 divers each. It has a large air station, equipment rental, a retail shop and offers several courses. **Habitat Curaçao** is an offshoot of *Captain Don's Habitat* in Bonaire, at Rif St Marie, offering PADI, NAUI and SSI courses, boat dives, shore dives, snorkelling, photography, all equipment available for rent, lots of package deals, T8648200, curacao@habitatdiveresort.com **Dive School Wederfoort** has been in operation since 1966, very friendly, reputable, mostly shore dives, the drop starts 25 m from dive centre; a PADI open-water course is US$271, accommodation and restaurant available, contact Eric and Yolanda Wederfoort, *Marine Beach Club*, St Michielsbaai, T8884414, www.divewederfoort.com Out at Westpoint and Playa Kalki are **All West Diving**, T8640102, www.allwestcuracao.com, offering courses, boat dives, introductory dives (US$30) and equipment for rent. Students are given preferential rates.

Netherlands Antilles, the ABC Islands

Beaches and watersports

Topless sunbathing is prohibited on public beaches but is tolerated on a few private beaches

There are several good beaches on Curaçao. The northwest coast is rugged and rough, but the southwest coast has some sheltered bays and beaches with excellent swimming and snorkelling. Windsurfing, waterskiing, yachting and fishing are available at resorts. Many of the beaches are private and make a charge per car (amount depends on day of the week and popularity, US$3-6) but in return you usually get some changing facilities, toilets and refreshments. Public beaches are free but most have no facilities and some are rather dirty and smelly.

Heading south out of Willemstad are the two small, artificial beaches at the *Avila Beach Hotel*, where non-residents pay an entrance fee. The sand is imported and the sea is not calm enough to see much if you snorkel but the breakwaters make it pleasant for swimming. You can get to the beach at **Piscadera Bay** near the *Sheraton* hotel by catching one of their shuttle buses from beside the Rif Fort in Otrobanda. Southeast of Willemstad, by the *Princess Beach Hotel*, the *Lions Dive Hotel* and the Seaquarium (see above), is a 450-m, man-made beach and marina with all watersports available. It can be crowded and noisy with music; motorized watersports are all down one end. ■ *0830-1800. Entrance to the beach is US$2.25. Showers and toilets. Mambo Beach Club for night-time entertainment.* Past the Seaquarium is a residential area and private beach on **Jan Thiel Bay**, good swimming and snorkelling. ■ *Entrance NAf6 per car, changing facilities, drinks and snacks.* **Santa Barbara** located at the mouth of Spanish Water Bay on the Mining Company property, is a favourite with locals. Behind Spanish Water Bay rises **Mount Tafelberg**, where phosphate mining used to take place. ■ *0800-1800. Entrance US$2.25 per person. Changing rooms, toilets and snack bars. You can take a bus from the post office, get off at the Mining Company gate and hitch down to the beach, or take a taxi; it is too far to walk.* Across the bay, which is one of the island's beauty spots, is the Curaçao Yacht Club. There are four yacht clubs in Spanish Water. **Caracas Bay Island** offers biking, horse riding, a tour of the fort and watersports such as kayaking, canoeing, guided snorkelling tours, windsurfing and jet skis. The *Baya Restaurant on the Beach*, open 1200-2300, has French Oriental cuisine, while there is also the *Baya Beach Club*, for a daytime drinking spot or night-time entertainment. The new *Curaçao Howard Johnson* hotel in Willemstad has an agreement for its guests to be shuttled to *Baya Beach Club* for beach activities. ■ *T7470656, www.caracasbayisland.com*

Travelling northwest from Willemstad heading towards Westpoint, there are lots of coves and beaches worth exploring. A left turn soon after leaving town will take you to **St Michiel's Bay**, a fishing village and tanker-clearing harbour (free). **Daaibooibaai**, south of St Willibrordus is a public beach and gets very crowded on a Sunday. Further up the coast, **Porto Marie** is private and sandy and there are umbrellas for shade. A double reef here gives good snorkelling and diving. ■ *Mon-Sat US$2, Sun US$2.50, including soft drink, 0930-1830. Restaurant and dive area to change, rinse off equipment, etc.* **Cas Abao Beach** is pretty with good snorkelling and diving from shore in beautiful clear water. ■ *Changing facilities, showers, shade huts, lounge chairs cost US$3, US$3 per car per day, US$5 at weekends and holidays, snacks and beverages.* **San Juan**, a private beach with lots of coral is off to the left of the main Westpoint road, down a poor track, entrance fee charged. **Boca Santa Martha**, where the *Coral Cliff Resort* is located, is quiet with nice sea. ■ *Beach entrance US$4.50 for non-residents, no pets or food allowed on the beach, some shade provided.* **Lagun** is a lovely secluded beach in a small cove with cliffs surrounding it and small fishing boats pulled up on the sand. It is safe for children and good for snorkelling. ■ *There are facilities and some shade from trees. Some buses pass only 50 m from the beach.* **Jeremi**, a public beach with no charge, is of the same design, slightly larger sandy beach with a steep drop to deep water and boats moored here, protected by the cliffs. Further up the coast, **Knip** is a more open, larger, sandy beach again with cliffs at either end. Many people rate this the best beach on the island, but the stairway down to the beach was destroyed by the storms of 1999. There are some facilities here and it is very popular at weekends when there is loud music and it gets crowded and noisy. **Playa Abau** is big, sandy, with beautiful clear water, surrounded by cliffs. ■ *Some shade provided, toilets, well organized, popular at weekends and busy.* Nearing the west tip, **Playa Forti** has good swimming. There is a restaurant on the clifftop overlooking the sea. The beach at **Westpoint** below the church is stoney and littered, the only shade comes from the poisonous manchineel trees. Fishing boats tie up at the pier but bathers prefer to go to Playa Forti. Beyond Westpoint is **Kalki Beach** which is good for snorkelling and diving as well as bathing. Westpoint is the end of the road, about 45 minutes by car or 1 hour by bus from Otrobanda, US$1.

Many charter boats and diving operators go to **Klein Curaçao**, a small, uninhabited island off East Point which has sandy beaches and is good for snorkelling and scuba diving, a nice day trip with lunch provided. Sailing boats include *Mermaid*, T5601530, *Miss Ann*, T7671579 and *Bounty*, T5601887. There are snorkel, snorkel-picnic and sunset trips; also day sailing trips from Willemstad up the coast with barbecue lunches at, for example, Port Marie, for about US$55, to the East End with lunch at Santa Barbara, and weekend sailing trips to Bonaire, accommodation on board, for about US$225. One such sailing ship is the 120 ft *Insulinde*, T5601340, shore T8688710, F4616633, www.insulinde.com, beautiful trip, including lunch but not drinks. You can also go on hovercraft excursions to various beaches for snorkelling or for sunset tours, with *Neptune Hovercraft Tours*, T8641500. Deep-sea **fishing** charters can be booked with several companies including *Hemingway Fishing Charters*, T5630365.

Day sails

The **Curaçao International Sailing Regatta** is held end-Jan with competitions in 3 categories, short distance (windsurfers, hobie cats, sunfish etc), long distance and open boat (trimarans, catamarans, etc, race 32 km to Spanish Water and back), all starting from the *Santa Barbara Beach Resort*. For details, T5619292, www.curacaoregatta.com. The **Sami Sail Regatta** in Apr is organized by the village of Boca Sami, accompanied by local food and live music, T5618090. The **International Blue Marlin** tournament is held in Mar. The Yacht Club is at Brakkeput Ariba, z/n, T7673038 or contact Mr B van Eerten, T7675275. *Sail Curaçao* has sailing courses, rentals and boat trips, also surfing lessons, T7676003.

Sailing

Netherlands Antilles, the ABC Islands

Willemstad

Willemstad, capital of the Netherlands Antilles and of the island of Curaçao, is full of charm and colour. The architecture is a tropical adaptation of 17th-century Dutch, painted in storybook colours. Pastel shades are used for homes, shops and government buildings alike. Fanciful gables and bulging columns evoke the spirit of the Dutch colonial burghers.

Population: 140,000

The earliest buildings in Willemstad were exact copies of Dutch buildings of the mid-17th century, high-rise and close together to save money and space. Not until the first quarter of the 18th century did the Dutch adapt their northern ways to the tropical climate and begin building galleries on to the façades of their houses, to give shade and more living space. The chromatic explosion is attributed to a Governor-General of the islands, the eccentric Vice-Admiral Albert Kikkert ('Froggie' to his friends), who blamed his headaches on the glare of white houses and decreed in 1817 that pastel colours be used. Almost every point of interest in the city is in or within walking distance of the shopping centre in **Punda**, which covers about five blocks. Some of the streets here are only 5 m wide, but attract many tourists with their myriad shops offering international goods at near duty-free prices. The numerous jewellery shops in Willemstad have some of the finest stones to be found anywhere.

There is a red and white trolley train which takes 60 passengers around the streets of Punda several times a day

The **Floating Market**, a picturesque string of visiting Venezuelan, Colombian and other island schooners, lines the small canal leading to the Waaigat, a small yacht basin. Fresh fish, tropical fruit, vegetables and a limited selection of handicrafts are sold with much haggling. In the circular, concrete, public market building nearby there are straw hats and bags, spices, butcheries, fruit and vegetables for sale, while in the old market building behind, local food is cooked over charcoal and sold to office workers at lunchtime.

Synagogue Nearby on Hanchi Snoa, is one of the most important historical sites in the Caribbean, the **Mikvé Israel-Emanuel synagogue**, which dates back to 1732, making it the oldest in continuous use in the Western Hemisphere. In the 1860s, several families broke away from the Mikvé Israel congregation to found a Sephardi Reform congregation which was housed in the Temple Emanuel (1867-1964) on the Wilhelminaplein. In 1964, however, they reunited to form the Mikvé Israel-Emanuel congregation, which is affiliated with both the Reconstructionist Foundation and the World Union for Progressive Judaism. The big brass chandeliers are believed to be 300 years older than their synagogue, originating in Spain and Portugal, their candles are lit for Yom Kippur and special occasions. The names of the four mothers, Sara, Rebecca, Leah and Rachel are carved on the four pillars and there are furnishings of richly carved mahogany with silver ornamentation, blue stained glass windows and stark white walls. The traditional sand on the floor is sprinkled there daily, some say, to symbolize the wandering of the Israelites in the Egyptian desert during the Exodus. Others say it was meant to muffle the sound of the feet of those who had to worship secretly during the Inquisition period. ■ *Normally open 0900-1145 and 1430-1645, Mon-Fri, free. Services are held Fri 1830 and Sat 1000. Dress code for men is coat and tie and ladies equally conventional.*

In the courtyard is the **Jewish Cultural Historical Museum**, occupying two restored 18th-century houses, which harbours an excellent permanent exhibition of religious objects, most of which have been donated by local Jewish families. There are scrolls, silver, books, bibles, furniture, clothing and household items, many 18th-century pieces and family bequeathments. Outside are some tombstones and a ritual bath excavated during restoration work. A small shop sells souvenirs, the *Synagogue Guide Book* and *Our Snoa*, Papiamento for synagogue, produced for the 250th anniversary in 1982. ■ *Open the same hrs as the Synagogue, closed Jewish and public holidays. US$2, children US$1. Hanchi di Snoa 29, T4611633, www.snoa.com/350/*

Willemstad orientation

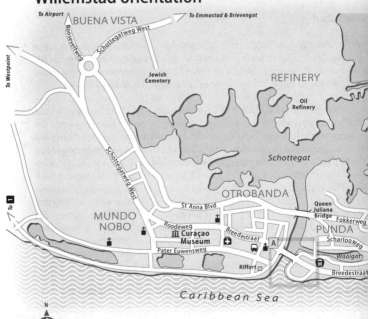

Related map:
A Willemstad centre,
page 844

N
Not to scale

■ Sleeping
1 Marriott

2 Trupial Inn

West of the city, on the Schottegatweg Nord, is one of the two **Jewish cemeteries**, Bet Chayim (or Beth Haim), consecrated in 1659 and still in use. There are more than 1,700 tombstones from the 17th and 18th centuries, with bas-relief sculpture and inscriptions, many still legible. It is a little out of the way but well worth a visit. It is also a fine example of what atmospheric pollution can do, as the tombstones have suffered from the fumes from the surrounding oil refinery.

Fortkerk, an 18th-century Protestant church at the back of the square behind **Fort Amsterdam**, the Governor's palace, still has a British cannonball embedded in its walls. It is not as large as the synagogue museum, but is well laid out, with some interesting items, like original church silver and reproductions of old maps and paintings of Curaçao. Note the clock in the ceiling of the church and the still-functioning rain water cistern inside the church. It was once the main source of fresh water for the garrison. ■ *Mon-Fri 0900-1200, 1400-1700. US$2/NAf3, children US$1, you get a guided tour of the church and the associated museum.T4611139, F4657181.*

Two forts, **Rif Fort** and **Water Fort** were built at the beginning of the 19th century to protect the harbour entrance and replace two older batteries. All that is left of Rif Fort is a guard house dating from about 1840 but you can walk on the walls and eat at the restaurants in the vaults. The Water Fort Arches have been converted to house shops, bars and restaurants.

Otrobanda

Parts of **Otrobanda** are being restored and there are many old houses here, both small, tucked away down alleys, and mansions or town houses. The Belvedere, an Otrobanda landmark, was restored in 1992-93. Breedestraat is the main shopping street. The **Basilica Santa Ana**, founded in 1752 and made a Basilica in 1975 by Pope Paul VI, is just off here. The houses fronting on to the Pater Euwensweg, once overlooked the Rifwater lagoon, now reclaimed land. Along St Anna Bay, past the ferry landing, is **Porto Paseo**, a restored area with bars and restaurants. The old hospital has been restored into the *Hotel and Casino Porto Paseo*. A new cruise ship pier has been built at Otrobanda for liners too big to reach the existing terminal in Willemstad harbour.

Scharloo

Another area within walking distance of Punda and worth exploring, is **Scharloo**, across the Wilhelmina bridge from the floating market. A former Jewish merchant housing area, now under renovation, there are many substantial properties with all the typical architectural attributes; note the green house with white trimmings known as the Wedding Cake House, at Scharlooweg 77. Reading matter of architectural enthusiasts includes the magnificently illustrated *Scharloo – A 19th-century Quarter of Willemstad, Curaçao: Historical Architecture and its Background*, by Pauline Pruneti-Winkel (Edizioni Poligrafico Fiorentino, Florence 1987), and a more general collection of essays with illustrations, *Building up the Future from the Past: Studies on the Architecture and Historic Monuments of the Dutch Caribbean*, edited by Henry E Coomans and others (De Walburg Pers, Zutphen, the Netherlands, 1990).

To Brievengat
Emancipatie Blvd
Curaçao Dry Dock
Venezuela Ferry Terminal
Schottegatweg Oost
To Santa Rosa
Landhuis Rooi Catootje
Centro Pro Arte
Rijkseenheid Blvd
Schottegatweg Oost
To Spanish Water
Caracas Baaiweg
SALIÑA
Berg Altena
Grebbelineweg
STEENRIJK
Oranjestraat
Penstraat
Dr ML King Blvd
To Seaquarium & Thiel Bay

The **S E L Maduro Library** is at the **Landhuis Rooi Catootje**, the site, in 1954, of the Round Table Conferences which led to the Statuut between the Dutch Kingdom and its Caribbean territories. The library, in the beautifully restored landhuis, contains all manner of things Caribbean and the conference table still stands in the dining room. ■ *Open by appointment, T7375119. Take the Rond minibus from Punda and ask to be let off next to the chicken factory, a site better known to most drivers than the house itself.*

Museums The **Maritime Museum** opened in 1998 in a 1729 colonial mansion on the Waaigat inlet near the Floating Market. It has permanent and temporary exhibitions of marine history relating to Curaçao and the Caribbean, with video presentations and multimedia displays. The museum has its own boat for tours of the harbour Wed and Sat and ferrying cruise ship passengers. ■ *Mon-Sat 1000-1700. US$8.50, US$4.50 for students and children under 12. Call for reservations for the tour of the museum, the harbour through the Annabaai, the Brionwerf and the refinery. Harbourside café and gift shop. Van Brandenburg, T4652327.* Another good museum in this area, opened in 1999, relates to Willemstad's maritime and trading history. The **Kurá Hulanda** has exhibits of the slave trade, tracing it back to the capture of slaves in Africa, their transatlantic crossing and eventual sale as commercial goods. Also exhibitions on the predominant cultures of the island, the origin of man, West African empires, pre-Columbian gold, Mesopotamian relics and Antillean art. ■ *1000-1700 daily. US$6, children US$3. Audio cassettes for rent; guided tours, photography and group rates available on request. Gift shop. Klipstraat 9, T4347765. www.kuruhulanda.com*

The **Philatelic Museum** is on the corner of Keukenstraat and Kuiperstraat in a recently restored building which is the oldest in Punda (1693). There is a comprehensive permanent display of Dutch Caribbean stamps, plus temporary exhibitions. ■ *Mon-Fri 0900-1200, 1330-1700, Sat 1000-1500. US$2/NAf3.50, NAf1.75 for children. T4658010, F4617851.*

Willemstad centre

Sleeping
1 Avila Beach

2 Kurá Hulanda
3 Otrobanda

4 Van der Valk Plaza

Not to scale

The *Central Bank of the Netherlands Antilles* owns and operates a **Numismatic Museum**, Breedestraat 1, Punda, with a collection of coins and notes from the Netherlands Antilles, as well as a display of precious and semi-precious gemstones. ■ *Mon-Fri 0830-1130, 1330-1630. Free. T4613600, F4615004.*

On the outskirts of Otrobanda, on van Leeuwenhoekstraat, is the **Curaçao Museum**, founded in 1946 (housed in an old quarantine station built in 1853) with a small collection of artefacts of the Caiquetio Indian culture, as well as 19th- and 20th-century paintings, antique locally made furniture, and other items from the colonial era. In the basement there is a children's museum of science. On the roof is a 47-bell carillon, named The Four Royal Children after the four daughters of Queen Juliana of the Netherlands. ■ *Mon-Fri 0900-1200, 1400-1700, Sun 1000- 1600. US$2.25/NAf5.30, children under 14 US$1.25/ NAf2.60. T4623873, F4623777.*

The swinging **Queen Emma Bridge** spans St Anna Bay, linking the two parts of the city, Punda and Otrobanda (the latter means 'the other side' in Papiamento, and people tend to refer to 'Punda' and 'Otrobanda' rather than 'Willemstad'). Built on 16 great pontoons, it is swung aside some 30 times a day to let ships pass in and out of the harbour. The present bridge, was built in 1939. While the bridge is open, pedestrians are shuttled across for free by small ferry boats. The bridge is closed to vehicular traffic.

The new **Queen Juliana** fixed bridge vaults about 50 m over the bay and connects Punda and Otrobanda by a four-lane highway. Taxis will often offer to stop at the bridge so you can get a panoramic view and photo of Willemstad on one side and the oil refinery on the other. Although you can reach it on foot it is not open for pedestrians; the wind and the way it shakes will explain why.

Bridges

Around the island

Set in 503 ha in the east part of the island is **Brievengat**. Its exact date of construction is unknown, but it is believed to date from the early 18th century. It was used in the 19th century to produce cattle, cochineal and aloe, but a hurricane in 1877 devastated the plantation and the house was gradually abandoned. Shell later took over the property to extract water from the subsoil, but in 1954 when it was in a state of ruin Shell donated it to the Government who restored it to its former grandeur. The windows and the roof are typical of the local style but unusual are the arches extending the length of the house and the two towers at either side, which were once used to incarcerate slaves. ■ *Daily 0915-1215, 1500-1800. US$2, children half price. Bar and snacks, live music on Wed and Fri and often on Sun, check beforehand; open house on Sun 1000-1500 with folklore show at 1700 on last Sun of the month. T5652156. Take the bus marked Punda-Hato from Punda at 15 mins past the hr and get off at the Sentro Deportivo Korsou.*

Chobolobo, at Salinja, came into the Senior family in 1948 and *Senior & Co* make the Curaçao liqueur here, using a copper still dating from 1896 and the original Valencia orange known locally as Laraha. The clear, orange, amber, red, green and blue are for cocktails and all taste the same; others are chocolate, coffee, rum-raisin. Chobolobo is worth visiting, but if you resist the temptation to buy *Senior & Co*'s products you will find them cheaper in the duty-free lounge at Hato Airport although they occasionally run out of some flavours. The original *Curaçao Liqueur* can only be purchased on the island. Copy cats are exported from Holland, etc. ■ *Mon-Fri 0800-1200, 1300-1700. Free and visitors may taste the liqueur. T4613526.*

Near the Hato International Airport on Rooseveltweg, are the **Hato Caves** which contain stalactites and stalagmites, a colony of longnose bats and pools among spectacular limestone formations. There are also some **Caquetio rock drawings** believed to be 1,500 years old. ■ *Tue-Sun 1000-1700. Guided tours every hr, the last one at 1600. US$6.25, children US$4.75. T8680379.*

Jan Kok is the oldest landhouse on the island, dating from 1654 and overlooking the salt flats where flamingoes gather. ■ *1100-2100 high season, 1100-1900 on Sun low season. Bar and restaurant, guided tour Tue, Thu 0900-1300 through the salt pans*

Country estate houses, or landhuizen, emerge here and there in the parched countryside

Netherlands Antilles, the ABC Islands

and the landhouse. T8648087. Take the bus marked Lagun and Knip from the Riffort, Otrobanda, at half past the even hr in the morning or half past the odd hr in the afternoon. **Santa Martha**, built in 1700 and restored in 1979, is used as a day-care centre for the physically and mentally handicapped but is open to visitors. ■ *Mon-Thu 0900-1200, 1300-1500, Fri 0900-1200, if you call in advance, T8641559.* **Ascension**, built in 1672 and restored in 1963, is used by Dutch marines stationed on the island. ■ *First Sun of the month 1000-1400 only. T8641950. Local music, handicrafts and snacks. Take bus marked Westpunt from Otrobanda (see below).* **Landhuis Kenepa** or **Knip**, near the beach of the same name, is a restored 17th-century landhouse where there was a slave rebellion in 1795. It has a collection of antique furniture and an exhibition about the Kenepa people. ■ *T8640244, F640385. On the same bus route as Jan Kok.*

The Christoffel Park covers an area of 1,860 ha in the west of the island, including Mount Christoffel at 375 m, which was formerly three plantations. These plantations Savonet, Zorgvlied and Zevenbergen, are the basis for a system of well-marked trails blue (9 km), green (7½ km or 12 km) and yellow (11 km), and there is a red walking trail up Mount Christoffel which takes about four to five hours there and back. You can see a wide range of fauna and flora, including orchids, the indigenous *wayacá* (*lignum vitae*) plant, acacias, aloe, many cacti, calabash and the tiny Curaçao deer. The ruins of the Zorgvlied landhouse can be seen off the green route. The Savonet route takes you to the coast and along to Amerindian rock drawings, painted between 500 and 2,000 years ago in terracotta, black and white. In this area there are also two caves, one of which is about 125 m long and you have to crawl in before you can stand up and walk to the 'white chamber' (stalactites and stalagmites) and the 'cathedral'.

The 17th-century **Savonet Plantation House** is at the entrance to the park on the Westpoint Road, but it is not open to the public. However, several outbuildings are used. There is a small museum with archaeological exhibits, Guided tours are available, special walks at dawn or dusk are organized at random, check in the newspapers, evening walking tours to see the Curaçao deer, maximum eight people reservations essential. Stinapa publishes an excellent *Excursion Guide to the Christoffel Park, Curaçao*, by Peer Reijns, 1984, which is available at the Park administration. A basic map of the trails is also provided. Rancho Alfin at the park also does tours, walking, mountain biking or horse riding, including night trips, sunrise trips and a romantic package for honeymooners, T8640535. ■ *Mon-Sat 0800-1600, Sun 0600-1500. T8640363. US$9. Admission to the mountain side closes at 1400 and to the ocean side at 1500, although you can stay in until later. On Sun the park opens at 0600 and closes at 1500, no admittance after 1300 and 1400 for inland or sea routes. Guided walking tours US$15. Horse riding tours US$40 for 2 hrs. Deer watching US$5, 1600-1830, reservations required. Jeep tours US$85, max 5 people, includes entrance fee. The bus Otrobanda-Westpunt passes the entrance to the park.*

Essentials

Sleeping   New hotels, villas or timeshare developments are springing up all over Curaçao and the number of hotel rooms is approaching 5,000. Be prepared for construction work. We have not included here the international chain hotels such as *Marriott*, *Hilton* or *Breezes*, for contact details see www.curacao-to urism.com. Several small hotels have organized themselves into the *Curaçao Apartments and Small Hotel Association (CASHA)*, www.curacaoweb.com/casha Many hotels have no hot water taps, only cold because the water pipes are laid overground, so the water them is warmed by the sun during the day and is cold at night. Time your shower accordingly

There is a 7% government tax and 12% service charge to be added to any quoted room rate

Willemstad   (hotels) **LL** *Kurá Hulanda*, Langestraat 8, Otrobanda, T434770, www.kurahulanda.com The newest, most luxurious hotel in town, 100 rooms and suites close to the Queen Emma bridge, in restored 18th- and 19th-century colonial building around several courtyards on a former slave trading site, marble bathrooms, a/c, fans, cable TV, phone with modem, spa and fitness centre, 2 pools, shuttle to beach club, several restaurants and cafés, business centre, anthropological museum on site and conference centre and Institute for Advanced Cultural Studies across the road. **LL-A** *Van der Valk Plaza Hotel and Casino*, on Punda seafront, T4612500, www.plazahotelcuracao.com Very central, huge tower dominates the skyline by the fortress walls, 224 rooms and 19 suites, most with sea or harbour view, price per room includes service, tax, bargain for a cheaper rate for several nights, popular with the Dutch, good food, shops, restaurants, diving, boat excursions, pool, child care. **L-AL** *Otrobanda Hotel & Casino*, Breedestraat, just by the bridge in Otrobanda, T4627400, www.otrobandahotel.com Excellent location, good for business travellers, rooms small but comfortable, suites and single rooms available, coffee shop and restaurant with good view of Punda and floating bridge, pool. 15 mins' walk east of the centre is the family-owned **LL-AL** *Avila Beach*, Penstraat 130, T4614377, www.avilahotel.com Built in 1811 as Governor's residence but most rooms in an old hospital wing, small and with no sea view, cool reception area, service friendly but slow, no pool, lovely bar shaped like a ship's prow on the beach, great for evening cocktails, pleasant outdoor dining, live music Wed. An extension has been built in an attractive colonial style, the other side of the pier (bar and restaurant, *Blues*, excellent fish, live jazz Thu, Sat, closed Mon) on another man-made beach, 40 hotel rooms, some apartments, all rooms and suites with sea view, ballroom, tennis, both the beaches are protected by breakwaters and have imported sand for pleasant swimming. **A-B** *Trupial Inn*, Groot Davelaarweg 5, T7378200, www.trupialinn.com In residential area, 74 rooms, a/c, newly decorated, pool, restaurant, tennis, open-air bar, entertainment, shuttle bus to downtown, suites available. **A-B** *Hotel San Marco*, Columbusstraat 5, Punda, T4612988, www.sanmarcocuracao.com 89 rooms, completely renovated, a/c, TV. **C-D** *Pelikaan Hotel*, Lange Straat 78, T4623555, F4626063. In the heart of Otrobanda, newly rebuilt, small, clean, 62 rooms, a/c, restaurant.

Willemstad (guesthouses and apartments) **C** *El Conde Hotel*, Roodeweg 74, near hospital, T/F4627875. Some rooms noisy, basic, 7 rooms, a/c. **C** *Douglas Apartments*, Salinja 174, T4614549, lizac@interneeds.net A/c, cots available, towels and linen provided, kitchenette, phone, fax facilities, on 1st floor of shopping gallery, bus stop outside. Outside town, **A-C** *Wayaca Apartments and Bungalows*, Gosieweg 153, T7375589, wimgonny@cura.net A/c, TV, phone, supermarket, launderette, tennis, minimum 1 week, car rental can be included; houses also available usually on weekly basis or longer. **A-B** *Art and Nature Inn*, 17 Valkensweg, T8682259, www.curacaoart.com 10 mins' drive from Willemstad, bungalow with kitchenette and bathroom, each of 9 studios is decorated with murals, mosaics and paintings by the proprietor, Geerdine Kuypers, an internationally known artist, speaks 6 languages, 5-min drive to supermarket. A good small hotel is **C** *Buona Sera (Bonacera) Inn*, Kaya Eilson Godett (Pietermaai)104, T4618286, F4658344. 16 rooms, sleeps 1-4, a/c, private bathroom, seaview restaurant and bar, English, Dutch, Spanish, French and Papiamento spoken. **C-E** *Mira Punda*, Van de Brandhofstraat 12, T4613995, joserosales@cura.net Near floating market, 11 rooms, fan, cold water, clean, private bath, in restored mansion, bar.

The tourist board's main office at Pietermaai 19 has a long list of guesthouses and apartments (not all of which it recommends)

East of Willemstad On Dr Martin Luther King Blvd is the **L-AL** *Lion's Dive*, T4348888, www.lionsdive.com Attractive Green Globe hotel on private beach next to Seaquarium (free entry), 72 rooms, CP, a/c, fan, TV, pool, dive shop on site, dive packages, fitness centre, windsurfing, *Rumours* restaurant, friendly staff, caters for hard-core diving fraternity, courtesy bus to town, internet access. **LL-A** *Seru Coral*, Koral Partier 10, T7678499, serucoral@cura.net In the east part of the island, in the middle of nowhere but great restaurant, nice pool, studios, apartments and villas, 5 km from beach, 29 km from airport, 22 km from town.

West of Willemstad 2 mins from the airport is **B** *Holland*, T8688044, www.hotelholland.com 45 rooms, a/c, TV, phone, business services, restaurant, pool, car rental, casino, diving. **B-C** *Bulado Inn*, in Boca St Michiel fishing village, Red A'Weg, T8695731, F8695487, www.iseeyou.com/buladoinn Family run, very nice, good value, call and check for deals, 17 a/c rooms, all ocean view, restaurant, bar, pool, nicely landscaped, tennis, meeting rooms, car rental, parking, 10 mins walk from beach. **LL-AL** *Habitat Curaçao*, linked to *Captain Don's Habitat* in Bonaire, at Rif St Marie, Willibrordus, T8648800,

Netherlands Antilles, the ABC Islands

www.habitatdiveresort.com 56 suites and cottages, expanded in 2001 with another 14 2-bedroom cottages around sea water pond, with meeting rooms, pool, restaurant, bar, beach, free town shuttle bus, dive centre, lots of packages available. **B-C** *Landhuis Daniel*, weg naar Westpunt, T/F8648400, www.landhuisdaniel.com Another landhuis guesthouse, built by Daniel Ellis in 1711 on extensive property leading to sea, used as an inn for travellers on the east-west route for centuries, renovated 1997, 4 rooms in plantation house, 4 more in small row house by pool, breezy French Caribbean restaurant, dive packages available. **AL-B** *Bahia Inn*, near Lagun beach, T8684417, F8641000. Small, basic, adequate, 6 studios with kitchenettes or 3 2-bedroom apartments, several beds available. At Westpoint, **A-B** *All West Apartments*, T4612310, www.curacaoweb.com A/c 4 rooms, 3 studios, caters to individuals, dive shop attached, adventure diving, PADI courses, boat and shore diving, small scale. **C-D** *Jaanchie Christian's*, West Point 15, T8640126. Popular restaurant with 4 rooms to let, a/c, bathroom, CP, double beds, can fit extras in, usually full, phone for reservation.

Eating

5% sales tax and 10% service is added to the bill in restaurants but an extra 5% is appreciated

Native food is filling and the meat dish is usually accompanied by several different forms of carbohydrate, one of which may be *funchi*, a cornmeal bread in varying thickness but usually looking like a fat pancake (the same as *cou-cou* in the Eastern Caribbean). Goat stew (*stoba di kabritu*) is popular, slow cooked and mildly spicey (milder and tastier than Jamaican curry goat), recommended. Soups (*sopi*) are very nourishing and can be a meal on their own, grilled fish or meat (*la paria*) is good although the fish may always be grouper, red snapper or conch (*karkó*), depending on the latest catch; meat, chicken, cheese or fish-filled pastries (*pastechi*) are rather like the *empanadas* of South America or Cornish pasties. While in the Netherlands Antilles, most visitors enjoy trying a *rijsttafel* (rice table), a sort of Asian *smørgasbørd* adopted from Indonesia, and delicious. Because *rijsttafel* consists of anywhere from 15 to 40 separate dishes, it is usually prepared for groups of diners, although some Curaçao restaurants will do a modified version of 10 or 15 dishes.

A selection of European, South American (mostly Chilean) and Californian wines is usually available in restaurants. Curaçao's gold-medal-winning *Amstel* beer, the only beer in the world brewed from desalinated sea water, is very good indeed and available throughout the Netherlands Antilles. *Amstel* brewery tours are held on Tue and Thu at 1000, T4612944 for information. Some Dutch and other European beers can also be found. Fresh milk is difficult to get hold of and you are nearly always given evaporated milk with your tea or coffee. Curaçao's tap water is excellent; also distilled from the sea.

Willemstad Expensive (over US$20): One of the most highly regarded restaurants in Willemstad is *The Wine Cellar* on Concordiastraat, T4612178. Owned by chef Nico Cornelisie, a master rotisseur, in small old house, only 8 tables, chilly a/c, very good food but unexciting wine list, local fish and meat (ostrich) particularly good, no shorts or sandals, reservations recommended, closed Sun. *Larousse*, in an old house on Penstraat 5, almost opposite the Avila Beach, T4655418. French menu with local and imported North Sea fish, quiet, no shorts or sandals, open 1800-2400, closed Mon. *Fort Nassau*, reservations T4613450. Spectacular location with a panoramic view from the 200-year old fort, open Mon-Fri 1200-1400, Mon-Sun 1830-2300, no shorts, sandals or sneakers. *Bistro Le Clochard*, in the Rif Fort walls overlooking the harbour, T4625666, www.bistroleclochard.com French and Swiss cuisine, choose fresh local fish rather than imported, open Mon-Fri 1200-1400, 1830 onwards, Sa evenings only, open Sun in Dec-Mar. *La Pergola*, in the Waterfort Arches, T4613482. Serves Italian food, fish, pizza, terrace or a/c dining, open 1200-1400 Mon-Sat, 1830-2230 daily. *Grill King*, in the Waterfort Arches, T4616870, www.waterfortterrace.com. Friendly and has good international food, open Mon-Sat 1100-2300, Sun 1700-2300. There are several restaurants in the Arches, good for a meal or just drinks. **Mid-range** (US$10-20): *Fort Waakzaamheid*, Seru Domi, T4623633. Lovely sunset views from the terrace on top of the fort, which is on a hill above Otrobanda, restaurant and tavern, good food and menu, open daily 1800-2230, reservations suggested, dinner US$15-20. *Green Mill*, Salinja Galleries, T4658821. Lunches o dinners, happy hour Mon-Thu 1800-1900, Fri 1700-1830, menu with good variety. *Hook Hut*, T4626575, between *Marriott* and *Hilton* hotels. Thatched tiki hut bar and restaurant next to the sea, good drinks, food OK, evening entertainment at weekends.

For an **Indonesian** meal it is best to make up a party to get the maximum number of dishes but this is not essential. The *Indonesia*, Mercuriusstraat 13, T4612606. Wonderful Javanese food specializing in 16 or 25-dish rijstaffel, essential to book, often several days ahead, open 1200-1400, 1800-2130 daily, dinner only on Sun, no shorts. *Mambo Beach* , at the Seaquarium, T4618999. Wed Indonesian buffets.

The best place to try local food in Willemstad is the old market building beyond the round concrete market tower by the floating market, open Mon-Fri 1100-1430. Here many cooks offer huge portions of good, filling local food cooked in huge pots on charcoal fires, at reasonably prices, choose what you want to eat and sit down at the closest bench or one of the nearby tables having first ordered, takeaway available, very busy at lunchtimes, the best dishes often run out, make sure you have the right money available. The best restaurant for local food is *The Golden Star*, Socratesstraat 2, T4654795. Informal, friendly, plastic table cloths, fun, TV showing American sport, home cooking, very filling, goat stew washed down by a couple of *Amstels* recommended, popular with locals and tourists, open daily 1200-2300, live music Sat 1900-2300, takeaway available.

On the **Westpoint** road, opposite the entrance to the Christoffel Park, is *Oasis*, Savonet 79, T8640085. Seafood and Creole dishes but also offering chicken and ribs, open 1200-2400, weekends 1030-0300, dinner served until 2100, dancing afterwards. *Jaanchie's*, Westpoint 15, T8640126. Popular, huge, filling portions, see the bananaquits eating sugar, parties catered for, takeaway service, bus stops outside for return to Willemstad.

A good fish restaurant is *El Marinero*, Schottegatweg Noord 87B, T7379833. Moderately priced seafood dishes, lunch 1200-1500, dinner 1830-2330. *Fisherman's Wharf*, Dr Martin Luther King Blvd 91-93, T4657558. Very good seafood, lunch and dinner. *Octopus*, Marinebadplaats, St Michielsbay, T8881244. Fresh fish, local food, bar, restaurant and terrace by the sea, run by Eric and Yolanda Wederfoort, see Diving and marine life, page 830. Chinese food at *Ho Wah*, Saturnusstraat 93, T4615745. *Lam Yuen*, Fokkerweg 25, T4613462, locals' favourite Chinese food. *Sawasdee*, Eyck Van Voorthuyzenweg 5, near Curaçao Museum, T4626361, Thai restaurant, takeaway available, open 1830-2200.

For drinks, snacks or cheap lunches and dinner, *Downtown Terrace*, Gomezplein 4, T4616722. You can hear the chimes from the Spritzer and Fuhrmann bells, great selection of Belgian beers. There is plenty of fast food to cater for most tastes, including pancake houses, *Pizza Hut, Domino's Pizza, McDonalds, Burger King, KFC*, etc. Late night fast food, local fashion, can be found at truk'i pans, bread trucks which stay open until 0400-0500 and sell sandwiches filled with conch, goat stew, salt fish and other Antillean specialities. Great fruit shakes at *Trax's*, a van at the Otrobanda side of the Queen Emma bridge. Wonderful home-made ice cream, large variety, at *Vienna Ice Café*, on Handelskade in Punda.

For 'night-owls', there are **casinos**. All the large hotels have them, with many gaming tables and rows and rows of fruit machines, open virtually all hours, but usually 1400-0500. There are many nightclubs and discos, several of which are in the **Salinja area**: *Façade*, Lindberghweg 32-34, T4614640, open 2200-0400 except Mon and Thu, happy hour on Fri from 1800, and *Studio 99*, Lindberghweg, are favoured by wealthy locals of all ages, you will not be let in wearing jeans or trainers. *The Living Room*, Salinja 129, T4614433, thelivingroom@cura.net, has a restaurant, dance floor and lounge, DJ playing latest hits. Latin music and dance is very popular here. *La Paix*, T8881600 and *De Fles* (the *Flask*) have been recommended for salsa and merengue, take local currency; other places for Latin music are *Salsipuedes*, at De Ruyterkade 5, Punda, T461090, salsa dancing, classes, concerts, and *Tututango*, at Plaza Mundo Merced, T4654633. If you want to improve your salsa or merengue, you can take lessons at *Salsa City*, T5610782, at the *Danzarte Academy*, T6674616, or at Landhuis Brievengat, T5603645, 1900, Wed, Thu. *The Music Factory*, Salinja 131, T4610631. Open Mon-Sat 1700-0300, Fri live music, Sat DJ, special drinks nights with half-price brand names 2200-2400. On the Seaquarium beach is the *Mambo Beach Club*, a good nightspot with happy hour and dancing weekends, restaurant during the week, T4618999. At Caracas Bay Island is the *Baya Beach Club*, T470777, Latin night Fri, best on Sat night, disco and drinking spot. Live music and dancing most nights at *Octopus*, see Eating, above, happy hour 1800-1900. *Mirage*, a 'gentleman's club', has an 'adult entertainment' show Mon, Thu, Sat 2300, T8681170. *Habana Vieja*, T5686340, also has exotic

Nightlife
K-Pasa is a weekly dining and entertainment guide, widely available, check for happy hours, www.k-pasa.com

female dancers, Cuban style. **Cinema** *The Movies Curaçao*, T4651000, www.themoviescuracao.com One of the most bizarre sights of Curaçao, not dealt with in the tourist brochures, is the government-operated red-light area. Close to the airport, it resembles a prison camp and is guarded by a policeman.

Festivals Curaçao, Aruba and Bonaire all hold the traditional *pre-Lent Carnival*. On the **Sun**, a week before, is the children's parade. Curaçao's main parade is on the Sun at 1000 and takes 3 hours to pass, starting at Otrobanda. The following Mon most shops are closed. On the Mon at 1500 there is a children's farewell parade and there is a **Farewell Grand Parade** on the Tue evening when the Rey Momo is burned. *Curaçao Carnival Foundation*, T4612717.

Several **music festivals** are held throughout the year. You can hear *tumba* around carnival time and a competition is held in **Feb** at the Festival Center, T7376343. Contact the *Curaçao Jazz Foundation*, T4658043, www.curacaojazz.com for details of the May and Nov jazz festivals, and the *Festival Center*, T7376343, for details of *salsa* (**Aug**) and *merengue* (**May**) festivals. For the *Golden Artists Music Festival* in **Oct**, T4655777.

A *Kite Festival* with kite-flying competitions is held around **Easter** when the winds pick up, T7331127, kasdicultura@curinfo.an

Shopping The main tourist shopping is in Punda (see above) where you can pick up all sorts of
Willemstad's duty-free bargains in fashion, china, etc. *Arawak Craft Products*, Mattheywerf 1, Otrobanda
jewellery shops T4627249, F4628394, near cruise ship dock and ferry, tiles, reliefs of Dutch style houses and
are noted for the other ceramics, you can watch the potters and artists and even make your own, *Arawak Art*
quality of *Gallery* upstairs, open 0900-1800, on Sun also if cruise ship in dock.
their stones

Bookshops *Boekhandel Mensing* in Punda has a limited selection of guide books and maps. Larger and more well stocked bookshops are out of the centre of Willemstad, *Mensings' Caminada* and *Schottegatweg and Van Dorp* in the *Promenade Shopping Centre*, good maps and guide book section. *Van Dorp* shops are also located in most large hotels, they stock *Footprint Handbooks*. The public library is a modern building in Scharloo, cross the bridge by the floating market, turn right along the water and it is on your left. *The Reading Room* has books in Dutch, English, Spanish, French and Papiamento, T4617055.

Sports *Rancho Alegre*, T8681181, does **horse riding** for US$20 per hr, including transport. *Ashari'. Ranch* offers horses for hire by the hr inland (US$20), or 1½ hrs including a swim at the beach (US$30), open 1000-1900, Groot Piscadera Kaya A-23, T8690315, beginners as well as experienced riders, playground for children. *Rancho Alfin*, T8640535, has guided rides through the Christoffel Park, no experience necessary or, alternatively they offer **mountain biking** guided or alone. Biking is also available at Caracas Bay Island. There is **bowling** on the island, *Curaçao Bowling Club*, Chuchubiweg 10, T7379275, 6 lanes, US$11 per hr, reservation advised. The *Curaçao Golf and Squash Club* at Wilhelminalaan, Emmastad, has a 9-hole sand **golf** course open 0800-1230, green fee US$15 for 18-hole round, and 2 **squash** courts, US$7, open 0800-1800, T7373590. The 18-hole *Blue Bay Golf and Beach Resort* championship course opened in 2000, T7373590, www.bluebay-golf.com. *Santa Catharina Sport and Country Club*, T7677028, F7677026, has 6 hard **tennis** courts, a **swimming** pool, bar and restaurant. The large hotels have tennis courts and some have a pro. For information about **running**, particularly for the marathon, half marathon and 10-km run in Nov, contact *Road Runners Club*, T8682317. **Triathlons** are sometimes organized, with sea swimming, mountain biking and trail running, contact *Vista Bike and Body Beach*, Boca Sint Michiel, T8682576.

Tour operators One of the best island tours available is with *Casper Tours*, T5610721/4653010, informative, fun, covers east to west, 0900-1600 including lunch at a local restaurant for US$35 (cruise ships' tours from US$15) in a/c mini buses, English, Dutch and Spanish spoken. *Taber Tours*, http://curacao.com/tabertours (branch at airport and many hotels) do a variety of tour, usually in large Greyhound-type buses. *Old City Tours* do a walking tour of Otrobanda, 1715-1900, US$5.55 including a drink, T4613554. *Dornasol Tours*, T8682735, highly recommended local guide with minibus, full- or half-day eco-tours by biologist and historian Lie van de Kar, English, Dutch, German and Spanish spoken, also tours of Jewish sites.

Netherlands Antilles, the ABC Islands

Air From Europe *KLM* and *Dutch Caribbean Express* fly direct from Amsterdam several times   **Transport**
a week and KLM has connecting flights to Guayaquil and Quito. *Sobelair* flies from Brussels. **From
North America** There are flights from Miami with *American Airlines* and *Dutch Caribbean
Express*; connecting flights from other US cities generally go through Miami, San Juan or
Montego Bay (*Air Jamaica*) although *Delta* has direct flights from Atlanta. **From South Amer-
ica** *Aires* flies from Barranquilla; *Avianca* flies from Bogotá; *Dutch Caribbean Express* and
Aeropostal fly from Caracas; *Dutch Caribbean Express* also flies from Valencia, Maracaibo, Coro
and Las Piedras. *Surinam Airways* and *Dutch Caribbean Express* fly from Paramaribo. **From the
Caribbean** *Dutch Caribbean Express* from Aruba, Bonaire, Kingston, Port-au-Prince, Port of
Spain, Santo Domingo and Sint Maarten. *Air Jamaica* from Kingston, Montego Bay and New
York. *American Eagle* from San Juan. *Aeropostal* from Havana and Santo Domingo.

Road Bus There are collective taxis, called buses, and identified by an AC prefix on their
licence plates, which charge about US$1 anywhere. *Konvoois* are big buses which run to a
schedule and serve outlying areas of Curaçao. There is a terminal at the post office by the circular market in Punda and another near the Rif Fort in Otrobanda. To the airport get a bus
marked Hato from Punda at 15 mins past the hr from 0615 to 2315, or from Otrobanda at 15
mins past the hr from 0615 to 2320, returning on the hr, usually full. Buses to Westpunt leave
from Otrobanda on the odd hr, last bus 2300, return on the even hr. Buses and minibuses to
Dominguito (the Seaquarium) and Caracas Bay run from Punda. A bus marked Schottegat
runs from Punda via the *Trupial Inn Hotel*, the *Curaçao Golf and Squash Club*, the Jewish cemetery and the Curaçao Museum to Otrobanda. The Lagun and Knip bus route leaves
Otrobanda at half past the even hr in the mornings and on the odd hr in the afternoons via
the Curaçao Museum, the University, Landhuis Jan Kok, Santa Cruz beach, Jeremi beach,
Lagun Beach and Bahia beach, returning from Knip on the alternate hr. While the service in
and around Willemstad is efficient, the service to Westpunt is erratic and planning is needed
to avoid getting stranded. The standard city bus fare is NAf1 with no apparent timetables or
bus stops. Outside town you may get charged a variety of fares, particularly on minibuses.
Check beforehand or ask what others are paying.

   Car hire Foreign and international driving licences are accepted. Traffic moves on the
right. Companies include *Budget* (best rates, ask for specials or coupons, T8683466,
www.curacao-budgetcar.com), *Europcar/ National* (T8694433, www.nationalcuracao.com),
Avis (T4611255, www.avis.com), *Star Rent a Car* (T4627444), *Vista Rent-a-Car* (T7378871).
Prices start at about US$30 daily, US$180/week; jeeps, minimokes, buggies, scooters and bikes
also available. You can rent a Harley Davidson at FD Rooseveltweg 411, T5643284,
www.bikersworldcuracao.com

   Taxi It is not always possible to get a taxi to the airport early in the morning or late at
night so if you are going to a night club arrange your taxi in advance (sometimes the driver
will turn up a little early and join you on the dance floor). Taxis do not have meters but fares
are fixed. Fares from the airport to *Van der Valk Plaza* or *Avila Beach* US$18, *Lion's Dive* US$20,
Coral Cliff US$27. Airport displays taxi fares to main hotels. Try and pay in guilders as taxi driv-
ers do not always have the right change for dollars. Fares for sightseeing trips should be
established at beginning of trip, the usual price is US$20 for the 1st hr and US$5 for each subsequent 15 mins. Tipping is not strictly obligatory. The high price of taxis is a common complaint. Taxis do not always go looking for business and it can be difficult to hail one. Best to
telephone from a hotel lobby or restaurant/bar, one will arrive in a couple of mins. For taxi
fares or complaints T8690747, or go to a taxi stand and just get into an empty car, the driver
will then turn up. Drivers do not always know the area as well as they should, even restaurants can sometimes be tricky for them to find. The rear windows of many taxis do not work,
making car journeys hot. Courtesy vans operated by the hotels can be more comfortable.

Sea There is a fast ferry, *Chogogo*, making 2 round trips a day from Kralendijk to Willemstad,
US$50 round trip, see Bonaire, above. It is possible for the adventurous and persistent to get a
boat from Muaco at La Vela. You have to contact the captains direct as the practice of taking
passengers is discouraged. The *capitanía* is not much help, try the maritime agency 2 blocks
from Plaza Bolívar for help in contacting captains. The journey takes 9 hrs, head seas all the way.

Netherlands Antilles, the ABC Islands

Things to do in Aruba

· Blow your mind away **windsurfing** in the shallow waters off the northeast coast.
· Pay for your next holiday indulging your urges in the many **casinos**.
· Explore the **bat-filled caves** of the east coast where there are huge chambers, long tunnels and Amerindian drawings.
· Lie on the beach - an antidote to stress and adrenalin rushes - but don't just stay by your hotel, explore some of the less-frequented **beaches in the south**.

Directory **Airlines** *Dutch Caribbean Airline/Express* at the airport, ticket office open 0330-2100, T8338157, telephone sales 0800-2000, T8695533, in Punda, ticket office at Gomezplein 5, 0800-1700 Mon-Fri, 0900-1300 Sat, T4612255, www.flydce.com or www.fly-dca.net *KLM*,T4652737, offices are also at Gomezplein. *American Airlines* at the airport, T800-4337300; *Avianca*, T8680122. *Aeropostal*, T8882818, *Delta*, T8886644. **Banks** *ABN-AMRO Bank*, *Antilles Banking Corp* , *Maduro & Curiel Bank* on Plaza Jojo Correa, T4611100, *Banco di Caribe* on Schottegatweg Oost, T4616588. Banking hrs are 0800-1530 Mon-Fri. At the airport the bank is open 0800-2000 Mon-Sat, 0900-1600 Sun. ATMs at *ABN-AMRO Bank* and *Maduro & Curiel Bank* (Visa, Mastercard and Cirrus, issuing either US$ or NAf). **Communications** **Internet**: There is a *cybercafé* in the Salinja Galleries, and the *public library* has 2 public internet terminals. **Telephone**: Prepaid phone cards are available for international calls from Antelecom, Belvédère House, T124. Telephone rates abroad are published in the telephone book, but beware if phoning from a hotel, you can expect a huge mark up, check their rates before you call. To Europe, US$3.05 per min, to the USA US$1.60, to Australia and Africa US$5.55, to the Netherlands Antilles US$0.55, Central America US$3.90, Venezuela US$1.10, Leeward and Windward Islands US$1.75. There are other companies offering lower rates, so shop around, eg TS charges US$0.70 per min to the Netherlands, US$0.50 to the USA (T8696590, 5601988) and Amtel charges US$0.61 and US$0.49 respectively (T7375327, 4610304). You can rent a mobile phone from the post office already programmed for the local system with a prepaid card, no roaming or excess charges. There is a booth in the airport arrivals hall and you can return the phone at the PO opposite the entrance to the departure hall. **Medical services** The 550-bed **St Elisabeth Hospital** is a well-equipped and modern hospital with good facilities including a coronary unit and a recompression chamber (T462-4900). For emergencies, T110 (hospital), 112 (ambulance). The **Sentro Mediko Santa Rosa**, at Santa Rosaweg 329, is open 7 days a week, 0700-0000, laboratory on the premises. **Useful addresses** Police and fire: T114.

Aruba

IDD code: 297
Colour map 5, grid B1

Aruba is the smallest of the 'ABC' group of islands, only 25 km north of Venezuela. It has been closely linked with the Venezuelan oil industry for most of the 20th century but when times were hard, a decision was made to diversify into mass tourism. The coastal strip on the Leeward side of the island with the best beaches is now wall-to-wall hotels, with all those of more than 300 rooms allowed to have a casino. A wide range of watersports is on offer, including excellent windsurfing, which is world class. On land there is a golf course among the sand dunes in the north.

Ins and outs

Getting there Like the other Dutch islands, there is a scheduled flight from Amsterdam with *KLM*, but otherwise poor connections with Europe. Many more flights, bringing sun-worshippers, honeymooners and gamblers, come from North and South America.

Getting around
See Transport, page 857, for further details
There are buses and taxis, otherwise you can hire a car, motorcycle or bicycle. Most people don't bother and simply book a seat on a tour bus if they want to get away from the beach and hotel for a while but a car is useful for dining at restaurants away from your hotel. The airport is only 3.5 km south of Oranjestad, the capital, but nearly all the hotels hug the coast north of town; there are buses on the route from Oranjestad to San Nicolas in the extreme southeast, and taxis, which have a set charge for each hotel based on distance.

Netherlands Antilles, the ABC Islands

Aruba is out of the hurricane belt and the climate is dry. The hottest months are Aug-Oct and the coolest are Dec-Feb, but the temperature rarely goes over 32°C or below 26°C. A cooling trade wind can make the temperature deceptive. Average rainfall is 51 cm a year, falling in short showers during Oct-Dec.

Climate

Aruba Tourism Authority, L G Smith Boulevard 172, Oranjestad, near the harbour, T5823777, www.aruba.com Also at airport (open daily until about 1900) and cruise dock. Another very good site on Aruba is www.visitaruba.com

Tourist information

Flora and fauna

Aruba has 48 different types of native trees, 11 of which are now very scarce and in some cases have only five examples left. The loss of native trees is due to wood cutting, changing weather and marauding goats. A tree-planting programme is under way and negotiations with goat owners are in progress to keep them out of protected areas. About 170 species of bird can be found on Aruba, and about 50 species breed on the island but if you include the migratory birds which come in November-January the total rises to around 300 species. The most common birds are the trupiaal (bright orange), the chuchubi, the prikichi (a little parrot) and the barika geel (the little yellow-bellied bird you will find eating the sugar on the table in your hotel). The shoco, a burrowing owl, is endangered. An interesting place to see waterfowl is the **Bubali Plassen**, opposite the Olde Molen. Here you can often find cormorants, herons and fish eagle. Brown pelicans can be found along the south shore. Two kinds of snake can be found on Aruba: the harmless little Santanero (however, be careful when you pick it up, because it defecates in your hand) and the not-so-harmless rattle snake. Aruba's rattle snake, the cascabel, is a nearly extinct subspecies that does

As well as various kinds of lizards, Aruba has large iguanas, that are hunted to prepare a typical Arubian soup

Netherlands Antilles, the ABC Islands

Aruba

▶ **Tourist offices overseas**

Canada, T905-2643434, ata.canada@aruba.com **Germany, Austria, Switzerland**, Postfach 1204, D064333 Seeheim, T49-6257-962921, ata.germany@aruba.com **The Netherlands**, Schimmelpenninncklaan 1, 2517 JN, Den Haag, T31-70-3028040, ata.europe@aruba.com **UK**, The Copperfield, 25 Copperfield St, London SE1 0EN, T44-20-79281600, geoff@saltmarshpr.co.uk; **USA**, 199 14th Street, NE, Suite 2008, **Atlanta**, GA 30309-3688, T404-8927822, ata.atlanta@aruba.com; I Financial Plaza, Suite 136, **Fort Lauderdale**, FL 33394, T954-7676477, ata.florida@aruba.com; 5901 N Cicero, Suite 301, **Chicago**, Il 60646, T773-2025054, ata.chicago@aruba.com; 10655 Six Pines Drive, Suite 145, **Houston**, Tx 77380-3416, T281-3621616, ata.houston@aruba.com; 1000 Harbor Blvd, Ground level, Weehawken, NJ 07087, T201-3300800, ata.newjersey@aruba.com **Venezuela**, Centro Ciudad Comercial Tamanaco, Torre C, Piso 8, Oficina C-805, Chuao, Caracas, T0602-9599166, ata.venezuela@aruba.com

not use its rattle. Rattle snakes live in the triangular area between the Jamanota, Fontein and San Nicolas. The best place to go looking for rattle snakes, if you really want to, is the area south of the Jamanota mountain. In the unlikely event that you get bitten, go immediately to the hospital. They have anti-serum.

The **Arikok National Park**, www.arubanationalparks.com, covers a triangle o land between Boca Prins and San Fuego and bounded on the east by the sea as far as Boca Keto. After decades of discussion the plan converts 17% of the island into a protected park area. Work is continuing to provide trails, clean up and upgrade the park, clearing litter and reconstructing benches and a stairway built at Fuerte Prins in the 1960s. The three centres will be linked by trails for cars and walkers. Arikok Centre contains the 184.5 m Arikok hill, the second highest point in Aruba. Prins Centre in the northeast includes the former Prins Plantation, the functioning Fontein Plantation and the Fontein Cave. The Jamanota Centre in the south includes the 189 m Jamanota hill, the highest point of the island, and the old gold-mining operation at Miralamas. The Spanish Lagoon area is also included.

Diving and marine life

Visibility in Aruban waters is about 30 m in favourable conditions and snorkelling and scuba diving are very good, although not as spectacular as in the waters around Bonaire. A coral reef extends along the west side of the island from California reef in the north to Baby Beach reef in the south, with dives varying in depth from 5 m to 45 m. There are lots of dive sites suitable for beginners where you can see morays, grouper, eagle rays, manta rays and sting rays, as well as lobsters, parrot fish, ange fish and others. The northwest of the island has fields of seagrass which attrac leatherback turtles during the nesting season and are home to hawksbill, green and loggerhead turtles all year. The other side of the island is only for experienced diver as there are strong currents. Organized boat trips regularly visit two wrecks wortł exploring, although they can get a bit crowded and then visibility deteriorates. On is a German freighter, the *Antilla*, which was scuttled just after the Second Worl War was declared and is found in 20 m of water off Malmok beach on the west coast You can see quite a lot just snorkelling here as parts of the wreck stick up above th water. Snorkelling boat trips usually combine Malmok beach and the wreck. Th other wreck is nearby in 10 m of water, the *Pedernales*, a flat-bottomed oil tanke which was hit in a submarine attack in May 1941, while ferrying crude oil from Ven ezuela to Aruba. The *Aruba Watersports Association* recently sunk a DC-3 aeroplan near the *Pedernales*, to be another wreck dive site only 10 m deep, and the *Sta Gerren* tanker was sunk in 2000 at a similar depth for snorkellers and divers opposit the hotel strip by Hadicurari. Be careful not to touch anything underwater; not a

Essentials

◀

Documents US and Canadian citizens only require **proof of identity**, such as passport, birth certificate, certificate of naturalization, with photo ID if not using a passport. Other nationalities need a **passport** and some, such as citizens of former Communist bloc countries, need a **visa**, unless they are legally residing in a country whose citizens do not need a visa. A return or onward ticket and proof of adequate funds are also required for all visitors. Dogs and cats are permitted entry if they have a valid rabies and health certificate; no pets are allowed from South or Central America. Check with your hotel to see if they are allowed to stay.

Customs People over 18 are allowed to bring in one-fifth of liquor, 200 cigarettes, 50 cigars and 250 grammes of tobacco.

Currency Aruba has its own currency, the Aruban florin, not to be confused with the Antillean guilder, which is not accepted in shops and can only be exchanged at banks. The **exchange rate** is Afl1.77=US$1, but shops' exchange rate is Afl1.80. US dollars and credit cards are widely accepted, even on buses, and the Venezuelan bolívar is also used.

Departure tax US$23, usually included in the price of your flight ticket, or US$10 to Bonaire, but a general usage tax of US$7 still has to be paid. If flying out to the USA, you will clear US customs and immigration in Aruba, which saves you time at the other end (US Immigration, T831316). There are 2 terminals for international and US-bound flights, with restaurants, duty-free shops and other services.

Clothing Swimsuits are not permitted in the shopping area. Most casinos require men to wear jackets, and smart clothes (but no ties) are expected at expensive restaurants; otherwise casual summer clothes worn all year. Nudity of any kind is illegal although topless sunbathing is tolerated on most resort beaches.

Public holidays New Year's Day, GF Betico Croes Day (25 Jan), Carnival Mon (beginning of Feb), Flag Day (18 Mar), Good Fri, Easter Sun and Mon, Queen's Birthday (30 Apr), Labour Day (1 May), Ascension Day (May), Christmas Day, Boxing Day.

Voltage 110 volts 60 cycle AC same as USA.

Weights and measures Metric.

Netherlands Antilles, the ABC Islands

the dive masters warn you of the dangers of fire coral and hydroids. An annual Aruba Perrier Reef Care Project takes place over a weekend in June or July when everyone gets together to preserve the underwater environment and clean up debris and pollution from the main dive sites and beaches.

There are several scuba diving operations and prices start from about US$35 for a single tank dive. **Aruba Pro Dive** is at about 5 resorts, T5825520, but tries to keep groups small at an average of 6 divers. **Red Sail Sports**, L G Smith Blvd 83, T5861603, and at hotels, sailing, snorkelling, diving with PADI, SSI, IDEA, HSA certification courses, windsurfing, waterskiing, hobie cats, etc, accommodation packages available, this is a large, reputable but expensive international operation. Others include **Pelican** (PADI, NAUI, SSI, T5872302); **Unique Sports of Aruba** (PADI, T/F5860096, uniquesports@visitaruba.com); **SEAruba** (T/F5838759), who offer diving in the southeast and to Venezuela; **Native Divers** (IDD, PADI, T/F5864763); **Dax Divers** (PDIC, T/F5851270); and **Dive Aruba** (PADI, T5827337). Snorkelling from a dive boat varies from US$15-30, although a longer trip with lunch will cost from US$40-55. On these trips you will visit around 3 sites, usually including the *Antilla*, and snuba is often available for one of these stops.

Dive centres
For further information on diving and marine news contact the Aruba Tourism Authority

Atlantis Submarines, T5836090, operate a US$75, 2-hour trip, including the boat ride to the *Atlantis VI*, which descends to 30 m and explores the *MI Dushi I* and *Morgenster* shipwrecks or the *Sonesta* aeroplane wreck. A semi-submersible, **Seaworld Explorer**, T5862416, offers a tour along the Arashi Reef and the *Antilla* wreck, at 1130, 1330 and 1630 daily.

Beaches and watersports

There are good, sandy beaches on both sides of the island although fewer on the east side which is rough and not so good for swimming. Travelling north along the west coast from Oranjestad an excellent road takes you to the main resort areas where nearly all the hotels are gathered. **Druif Beach** starts at the *Tamarijn Aruba Beach*

Of the three ABC islands, Aruba stands out as having the best beaches, all of which are public and free

Resort, extending and widening along the coast to the sister hotel, the *Divi Aruba*, with good windsurfing. At the *Manchebo* there is a huge expanse of sand, often seen in advertisements. North of here is **Eagle Beach** where the 'low rise' hotels are separated from the beach by the road, and then **Palm Beach** where the 'high rise' hotels front directly on to the beach. These three sandy beaches extend for several kilometres, the water is calm, clear and safe for children, although watch out for watersports and keep within markers where provided.

The California Lighthouse area was originally called Hudishibana, but acquired this name after the California steamship was wrecked here one stormy night in 1891

A residential area and the new golf course stretches up from Arashi to the lighthouse and the coast is indented with tiny rocky bays and sandy coves, the water is good for snorkelling, while shallow and safe for children. It is also a fishing ground for the brown pelicans. There is a blow hole, where water sometimes spouts up more than 5 m.

At the other end of the island is **Seroe Colorado**, known as 'the colony', which used to be a residential area for Exxon staff. You have to enter the zone through a guard post, but there is no entrance fee and no hindrance. There are two west facing beaches here worth visiting. **Rodgers Beach** has a snack bar, showers, yachts and is protected by a reef but is in full view of the refinery. **Baby Beach**, on the other hand, is round the corner, out of sight of the refinery, in a lovely sandy bay, protected by the reef, nice swimming and snorkelling, very busy on Sun, with toilets but little shade. **Sea Grape Grove** and **Boca Grandi**, on the east coast of the south tip has good snorkelling and swimming, being protected by a reef, and is popular with tours who come to see the largest elkhorn coral. Experienced windsurfers come here to wave jump. The prison is near here, remarkable for the pleasant sea view from the cells. Other beaches on the east side of the island are **Boca Prins**, where there are sand dunes, and further north from there, reached by a poor road, is **Dos Playa** where there is good surf for body surfing. The beach here is closed to vehicles because of nesting turtles. **Andicouri** is also popular with surfers, note that you may not approach it through the coconut grove which is private property.

For excellent windsurfing, head north of Palm Beach to an area of shallow water, known as **Fisherman's Huts** (next to the *Marriott*). Although speeds are high and there is a strong offshore wind, surfing is safe and there are several rescue boats. Kitesurfing can also be arranged at Fisherman's Huts, but is done before 1000 and after 1630 so as not to conflict with windsurfers. This beach is called **Malmok** (south end) or **Arashi** (north end) and there are many villas and guesthouses around. There are several high-quality operators offering windsurf packages, boards, sails and accommodation. For information about the Aruba Hi-Winds Pro/Am competitions, contact *ATA Special Events*, T5860440 They usually take place in June. At the same time a Windsurfing Festival combines a consumer trade show, with all the latest gear, and music and food on the beach.

Watersports Virtually every type of watersport is available and most hotels provide extensive facilities. Activities which are not offered on site can be arranged through several tour agencies such as *De Palm Watersports*, T5824545, *Pelican Watersports*, T5831228 and *Red Sail Sports*, T5824500. You can hire jetskis, waterskis, wave runners, banana boats, snorkelling equipment and other toys. Parasailing can be done from the high-rise hotels. Glass-bottomed-boat trips from various locations are around US$20-25, but can be more for a sunset cruise.

Day sails Several yachts and catamarans offer cruises along the coast with stops for snorkelling and swimming. A **morning cruise** often includes lunch (about US$40-50), an afternoon trip will be drinks only – and then there are the **sunset booze cruises** (about US$20-30). The largest catamaran is *Red Sail Sports'* (see above) *Fiesta*, which carries 90 passengers, while its sister ship, *Balia*, a 53-ft racing catamaran, does all the usual cruises, T5864500; *Pelican I* is a 50-ft catamaran running along the west coast from Pelican pier, T5872302; *Wave Dancer*, another catamaran, departs from *Holiday Inn* beach, T5825520; *Octopus* is a 40-ft trimaran, departing from *Holiday Inn* pier also available for private charter, snorkelling and sailing cruises, T5833081; *Mi Dushi* is an old sailing ship built in 1925 which starts cruises from the *Aruba Grand Beach Resort* pier, T5823513.

Near Spanish Lagoon is the **Aruba Nautical Club** complex, with pier facilities offering safe, **Sailing**
all-weather mooring for almost any size of yacht, plus gasoline, diesel fuel, electricity and
water. For information, write to PO Box 161, T5853022. They also organize an annual 'catch
and release' deap-sea fishing tournament every October. A short sail downwind from there is
the **Bucuti Yacht Club** with clubhouse and storm-proofed pier providing docking, electricity,
water and other facilities. Write to PO Box 743. A **Catamaran Regatta** is held annually in Nov
in front of the Palm Beach hotels, with competitors from the USA, Europe and Venezuela. For
information contact the *Aruba Tourism Authority*, T5823777. Also in Nov is the **Seaport Yacht
Race** with races from Havana to Seaport Marina, around the island and from Punto Fijo in
Venezuela. For details contact Mr Henk Grim at the Seaport Marina, T5839190.

Many charter boats are available for deep-sea fishing. You can fish for red snapper and **Fishing**
triggerfish with *Rainbow Runner*, T5831689, www.rainbowseekers. com or there is
deep-sea fishing with *Driftwood Fishing Charters* from Seaport Marina, T5832515, and others. The tourist office has a list so you can contact the captain direct, or else go through *De
Palm Tours*. Whole-day trips including meals range from US$350-500, half days around
US$250, depending on the number of people on board. A deep-sea fishing tournament is
held in October at the *Aruba Nautical Club*, T5853022 for information.

Oranjestad

Oranjestad, the capital of Aruba, is a busy little town where 'duty-free' generally *Population: 21,000*
implies a discount rather than a bargain. The main shopping area is on Caya G F
(Betico) Croes, and streets off it. Many of the buildings in the colourful Antillean style
are actually modern and do not date from colonial times as in Willemstad, Curaçao.
The former fruit market area on the harbour opposite the Royal Plaza Mall is now a
Plaza Cultural, a market place for arts, crafts and food, with performance artists.
    There is a small museum in the restored 17th-century Fort Zoutman/Willem III
Tower, Zoutmanstraat. Named the **Musco Arubano**, it contains items showing the
island's history and geology, with fossils, shells, tools, furniture and products. It is
not particularly well laid out, the displays are unimaginative and old-fashioned but it
is still worth going if only to see the building. The fort, next to the Parliament buildings, opposite the police station, dates from 1796 and marks the beginning of
Oranjestad as a settlement. Built with four guns to protect commercial traffic, in
1810-1911 it sheltered the government offices. The tower was added around 1868
with the first public clock and a petrol lamp in the spire, which was first lit on King
Willem III's birthday in 1869 and served as a lighthouse. The Fort was restored in
1974 and the tower in 1980-83. ■ *Mon-Fri 0900-1200, 1330-1630. US$2. T5826099.*
The **Archaeological Museum** is small, but cleverly laid out in three parts,
Preceramic, Ceramic (from AD 500) and Historic (from AD 1500-1800 when the
Indians used European tools). The two main sites excavated are Canashitu and
Malmok and most objects come from these. There are some interesting publications
available in English. Recommended, the best museum in the ABCs. ■ *Mon-Fri
0800-1200, 1300-1600. J E Irausquin 2-AT5, 828979.* A numismatic museum,
Mario's Worldwide Coin Collection, also known as the **Museo Numismatico**,
not far from Fort Zoutman and the *Central Bank of Aruba* has a large collection of
coins from over 400 countries and coins from ancient Greece, Rome, Syria and
Egypt. A bit cramped, but with a lot of fascinating material, the museum is run by the
daughter of the collector, Mario Odor; donations welcomed. ■ *Mon-Fri 0730-1200,
1300-1600.* Zuidstraat 27. The **Aloe Museum** is a museum factory of aloe and its
products in Hato. The aloe has long been important in Aruba, where growing conditions are ideal, and the aloe even figures in the national coat of arms. Cosmetics and
other products are for sale. ■ *Mon-Fri 0800-1600. Tours available. Pitastraat 115,
Hato. T5883222, www.arubaaloe.com*

Netherlands Antilles, the ABC Islands

Around the island

Aruba is the smallest and most westerly of the ABC group lying 25 km north of Venezuela and 68 km west of Curaçao. Like Curaçao and Bonaire, Aruba has scant vegetation, its interior or *cunucu* is a dramatic landscape of scruffy bits of foliage, mostly cacti, the weird, wind-bent divi divi (*watapana*) trees and tiny bright red flowers called *fioritas*, plus huge boulders, caves and lots of dust. Flashes of colour are provided by bougainvillea, oleanders, flamboyant, hibiscus and other tropical plants. You will need a couple of days to see everything on offer inland without rushing. The Esso Road Map marks all the sites worth seeing and it is best to hire a car (4WD if possible) as you have to go on dirt roads to many of them and there is no public transport. Tour agencies do excursions, about US$20-30 for a half-day tour of the island, see page 857.

The village of **Noord** is known for the **Santa Anna Church**, founded in 1766, rebuilt in 1831 and 1886, the present stone structure was erected in 1916 by Father Thomas V Sadelhoff, whose portrait is on the twelfth station of the Cross. It has

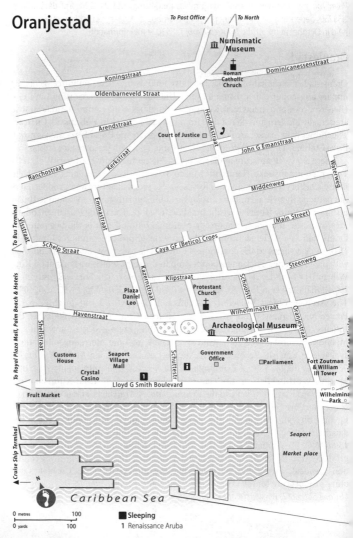

Oranjestad

To Post Office · To North

Numismatic Museum

Roman Catholic Chruch

Koningstraat

Dominicanessenstraat

Oldenbarneveld Straat

Arendstraat

Court of Justice

Hendrikstraat

John G Emanstraat

Waterweg

Kerkstraat

Ranchostraat

Middenweg

Emmastraat

(Main Street)

To Bus Terminal

Schelp Straat

Caya GF (Betico) Croes

Steenweg

Kazenstraat

Klipstraat

Plaza Daniel Leo

Protestant Church

Schoolstr

Wilhelminastraat

Oranjestraat

Havenstraat

Zoutmanstraat

Archaeological Museum

To Royal Plaza Mall, Palm Beach & Hotels

Shellstraat

Customs House

Seaport Village Mall

Schuttestr

Government Office

Parliament

Fort Zoutman & William lll Tower

Crystal Casino

1

Lloyd G Smith Boulevard

Wilhelmina Park

Fruit Market

Cruise Ship Terminal

Seaport

Market place

N

Caribbean Sea

| 0 metres | 100 |
| 0 yards | 100 |

■ **Sleeping**
1 Renaissance Aruba

heavily carved neo-Gothic oak altar, pulpit and communion rails made by the Dutchman, Hendrik van der Geld, which were the prize work shown at the Vatican Council exhibition in 1870. They were then housed in St Anthony's Church at Scheveningen in Holland, before being given to Aruba in 1928. The church is popular for weddings, being light and airy with a high vaulted ceiling and stained glass windows. ■ *Services are held Mon, Wed and Fri at 1830, Sat at 1900 and Sun at 0730 and 1800*. Not far from Noord on the north coast is the tiny **Chapel of Alto Vista**, dating from 1952 but on the site of the chapel built by the Spanish missionary, Domingo Antonio Silvester in 1750. It is in a spectacular location overlooking the sea and is so small that stone pews have been built in semi circles outside the Chapel.

Also on the north coast are the ruins of a gold mine at **Seroe Gerard** and a refinery at **Bushiribana** in a particularly bleak and sparsely vegetated area. The machinery at the mill, right on the coast, was damaged by sea spray and moved to Frenchman's Pass in 1824. A partly paved road leads to the natural bridge where long ago the roof of a cave collapsed, leaving only the entrance standing. It is actually fairly low and not as spectacular as tourist brochures would have you believe. There is a souvenir shop.

Inland, extraordinary rock formations can be seen at **Casibari** and **Ayó**, where huge, diorite boulders have been carved into weird shapes by the wind. At Casibari steps have been made so that you can climb to the top, from where you get a good view of the island and the Haystack. There is a snack bar and souvenir shop. Ayó does not have steps, you have to clamber up, but a wall is being built up around the rocks to keep out the goats. There are some Indian inscriptions. Toilets, a snack bar and souvenir shop are planned. The 541 ft **Hooiberg**, or Haystack, has steps all the way up. Very safe, even with children, the view is worth the effort.

At the village of **Santa Cruz**, just southeast of the Haystack, a cross on top of a boulder marks the first mission on the island. Travelling east from here you pass the **Arikok National Park**, where there are some well laid out trails for easy, but hot, walking. There are some interesting rock formations, indigenous fauna and flora and Amerindian art. See 'Flora and fauna' above. The road leads to Boca Prins (dune sliding) and the **Fontein** cave. Work has been completed to restore the Amerindian drawings in the cave, clean up the more recent graffiti and install a car park and picnic benches. The cave is open to visitors during daylight hours only. There is a large chamber at the entrance, with natural pillars, and a 100-m tunnel leading off, halfway down which are Indian paintings. Despite the desolation of the area, there is a well near the caves with brackish water, which a Japanese man uses to cultivate vegetables for the Chinese restaurants on the island. Further along the coast are the **Guadirikiri** caves, two large chambers lit by sunlight, connected by passages and pillars, with a 100 m tunnel, for which you need a torch. Bats live in this cave system. The road around the coast here is very bumpy and dusty, being used by quarry trucks. A third cave, **Huliba**, is known as the Tunnel of Love. Again, no entry fee but helmets (US$7) and torches available. The walk through the tunnel takes 20-30 minutes with a 10-minute return walk overground. Be prepared for a certain amount of scrambling and rock climbing in the dark, you are told to follow the arrows.

The road then takes you to **San Nicolas** where there is a strong smell of oil. The Lago Oil Refinery (*Exxon*) was built in 1928 and was the largest refining plant in the world during the Second World War, when it supplied the allies. The effect on San Nicolas was dramatic. It drew immigrant workers from 56 countries and the community thrived. However, after the war a steady decline set in. After the closure of the oil refinery in 1985, San Nicolas was a ghost town, but now that Coastal Oil has taken over the refinery, activity is beginning to pick up. Old wooden houses are being demolished and new concrete houses built instead. A landmark is *Charlie's Bar*, which has been in operation since 1941; a good place to stop for refreshment to see the souvenirs hanging everywhere. Efforts are being made to rejuvenate the town and attract tourism.

Returning northwest towards Oranjestad you pass through Savaneta, where the Dutch marines have a camp. Turn off to the left to *Brisas del Mar*, a good seafood restaurant open to the sea and very popular. At **Pos Chiquito**, a walkway leads through mangroves to *Isla di Oro*, a restaurant built like a ship where there is dancing at weekends and pedalos and watersports. A little further on, a bay with shallow water and mangroves is ideal for snorkelling beginners. The view is not spectacular but you can see many colourful fish. **Spanish Lagoon**, once a pirates' hideout, is a seawater channel, at the mouth of which is the Aruba Nautical Club and the water desalination plant. At the other end is a bird sanctuary where parakeets breed and the ruins of the Balashi gold mill dating from 1899, where the machinery is better preserved than at Bushiribana. There is quicksand in the area around the bird sanctuary, so it is not advisable to walk there. Nearby is **Frenchman's Pass** where the French attacked the Indians in 1700. From here you can turn east again to drive up **Jamanota**, at 189 m the highest elevation on the island.

Essentials

Sleeping
A 17.66% tax/ service charge is added; some hotels also add a US$1.50-5.75 per day energy surcharge

Glittering luxury hotels jostle for space along Druif Bay, and Eagle and Palm beaches, many of them all-inclusive. Decent, cheap accommodation is now very difficult to find unless you rent an apartment and share with friends. The *Aruba Apartment Resort and Small Hotel Association (ARASA)* members offer accommodation at less than US$100 but to get a double room at that price at one of the large hotels you will have to negotiate a package deal in advance. Summer rates are substantially less, sometimes half high-season winter rates (16 Dec-15 Apr).

Oranjestad On the waterfront is the **LL-AL** *Renaissance Aruba Beach Resort & Casino*, at L G Smith Blvd 9 and 82, T5836000, www.renaissancehotels.com 560 rooms, Seaport Village shops and Crystal casino.

Druif Bay The low-rise resort hotel development starts on Punta Brabo Beach, Druif Bay, all hotels are on the beach and offer swimming pools, tennis, watersports, shops, restaurants, etc. Several are managed by Divi: **LL** *Tamarijn Aruba Beach Resort*, J E Irausquin Boulevard 41, T5824150, www. tamarijnaruba.com **LL** *Divi Aruba Beach Resort Mega All-inclusive*, J E Irausquin Blvd 45, T5823300, www.diviaruba.com *Divi Village*, at J E Irausquin Blvd 47, T5835000. Next is the **L-AL** *Manchebo Beach Resort*, J E Irausquin Blvd 55, Manchebo, T5823444, www.manchebo.com Run by *Best Western*, 71 rooms with balcony or terrace, dive shop and windsurfing on huge expanse of beach. **LL-AL** *Bucuti Beach Resort*, J E Irausquin Blvd 55-B, T5831100, www.bucuti.com Attractive design, pleasant resort, 63 rooms, some with kitchenette, some suites, fitness centre. **LL-AL** *Casa del Mar*, J E Irausquin Blvd 51-53, Punta Brabo Beach, T5827000,

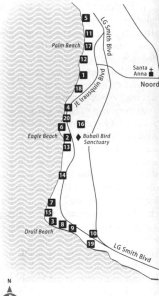

Northwest coast

Palm Beach

Santa Anna

Noord

Eagle Beach

◆ Bubali Bird Sanctuary

Druif Beach

LG Smith Blvd

N

Not to scale

■ **Sleeping**
1 Allegro Resort Aruba
2 Amsterdam Manor
3 Aruba Beach Club
4 Aruba Grand Beach
  Resort & Casino
5 Aruba Marriott Resort
  & Stellaris Casino
6 Aruba Phoenix Beach
  Resort
9 Bucuti Beach Resort
10 Casa del Mar
11 Divi Aruba Beach Resort
  Mega All-Inclusive

12 Divi Village
13 Holiday Inn Aruba
  Beach Resort & Casino
14 Hyatt Regency Aruba
  Beach Resort & Casino
15 La Cabana
16 La Quinta
17 Manchebo Beach
  Resort
18 Mill Condominium
  Resort & De Olde
  Molen Restaurant
19 Playa Linda Beach Res
20 Radisson Aruba
21 Tamarijn Aruba Beach
  Resort
22 Wyndham Aruba
  Beach Resort & Casinc

www.casa delmar-aruba.com 147 luxury 2-bedroom (time-share) apartments on the beach and 1-bedroom suites not on the beach, children's play area, tennis, pool, minimarket, laundromats. **LL-AL** *Aruba Beach Club*, same address, T5823000, mshipabccdm@setarnet.aw shared facilities, 131 rooms with kitchenette, for up to 4 people.

Eagle Beach LL-AL *La Cabana*, J E Irausquin Blvd 250, T5879000, www.lacabana.com Massive resort, 803 studios and suites, tennis, squash, fitness centre, waterslide, children's pool and playground, casino and condominiums. **LL-AL** *Amsterdam Manor*, J E Irausquin Blvd 252, T5871492, www.amsterdam manor.com Low-rise, pleasant, 72 painted Dutch colonial-style studios and apartments with sea view, kitchen, pool, bar and restaurant. **LL-AL** *La Quinta*, J E Irausquin Blvd 228, T5875010. Timeshare with rentals, 54 apartments with kitchenette, pools, tennis.

Palm Beach After the sewage treatment plant and Pos Chiquito the road curves round Palm Beach where all the high-rise luxury hotels are. All have at least 1 smart restaurant and another informal bar/restaurant, some have about 5, all have shops, swimming pools, watersports, tennis and other sports facilities on the premises and can arrange anything else. The first is **LL-AL** *Aruba Phoenix Beach Resort*, J E Irausquin Blvd 75, T5861170, www.diviphoenix.com Once the *Aruba Royal*, but resurrected by Divi, 101 a/c studios and apartments, fitness centre, 2 pools, jacuzzi, watersports. **LL-L** *Wyndham Aruba Beach Resort and Casino*, J E Irausquin Blvd 77, T5864466. 444 rooms, behind it is the restaurant *De Olde Molen*, an imported windmill around which **LL-A** *The Mill Condominium Resort* has been built, J E Irausquin Blvd 330, T5867700. 200 rooms and suites with kitchens, sauna, excercise room, tennis, 2 pools, beach club membership across the road. **LL-L** *Aruba Grand Beach Resort & Casino*, T5863900. 200 rooms and suites, Olympic-size swimming pool. The oldest hotel along here is the renewed and extended **LL-L** *Radisson Aruba*, J E Irausquin Blvd 81, T5866555, arubasales@radisson.com Covers 14 acres, 372 rooms and suites, not all with sea view, new pool area with 2 freeform pools, tennis, fitness centre, games room, watersports, conference centre, resort spa, golf putting, usual luxury facilities. **LL-L** *Allegro Resort Aruba*, J E Irausquin Blvd 83, T5864500. 421 rooms and suites with sea view and balcony, full service, deluxe, *Red Sail* diving and watersports on site. The next hotel along is the **LL** *Hyatt Regency Aruba Beach Resort & Casino*, J E Irausquin Blvd 85, T5861234. 360 rooms and suites, designed for a luxury holiday or for business meetings and incentive trips, built around a huge 3-level pool complex with waterfalls, slides and salt water lagoon, in beautiful gardens, health and fitness centre, *Red Sail* diving and watersports, very popular, great for children or business travellers, always full. **LL** *Playa Linda Beach Resort*, J E Irausquin Blvd 87, T5861000, www.playalinda.com A timeshare resort of suites and efficiencies, health club, games room, *Spa del Sol* in lobby area for lots of treatments, 0900-1800. **LL-AL** *Holiday Inn Aruba Beach Resort & Casino*, J E Irausquin Blvd 230, T5863600, www.holidayinn-aruba.com 600 rooms with balcony, dated concrete block style, pools, tennis, diving, casino, lots of facilities. **LL** *Aruba Marriott Resort and Stellaris Casino*, L G Smith Blvd 101, T5869000. 413-room hotel next to the *Holiday Inn*, lots of facilities and luxuries, *Vela Windsurf Centre*, *Red Sail Watersports*.

Apartments and guesthouses The Aruba Tourism Authority publishes a list of apartments and guesthouses. Weekly or monthly rates are more advantageous. **LL-A** *Boardwalk Vacation Retreat*, Bakval 20, Noord, T5866654, www.theboardwalk-aruba.com Right by the *Marriott*, 150 m to the beach, 1 or 2-bedroom casitas with living room and kitchen, hammocks, fans, a/c, well equipped, nice furnishings, mini market, pool with jacuzzi, gardens with flowering plants, palm trees and hummingbirds. **LL-B** *Aruba Beach Villas* (*Sailboard Vacations*), 462 LG Smith Blvd, ½ mile north of *Marriott*, T5862527, www.arubasailboardvacations.com Windsurfing resort with large board and sail shop, 31 villas with 1-2 bedrooms across the road from the sea, CP, pool, sundeck, jacuzzi, kayaks, beach towels, internet, multilingual staff. **L-B** *Aruba Millennium Resort*, Palm Beach Rd, T5861120, www.arubamillenniumresort.com 12 studios and 10 1-bedroom apartments, price reflects 50% cut in summer, light, bright, nice furnishings, kitchen, TV, whirlpool outside suite, also pool, sundeck, minimarket, car rental arranged, 2 mins walk from beach.

Hotels with over 300 rooms have casinos

If you arrive at a weekend the tourist office in town will be shut and you cannot get any help except at the airport

Netherlands Antilles, the ABC Islands

A-B *Coconut Inn*, Noord 31, T5866288, www.coconutinn.com Walking distance from supermarket, banks and restaurants, 40 a/c studios and 1-bedroom apartments, TV, balcony, kitchenette, pool, near beach. **A-B** *Aruba Harmony Apartments*, Palmitastraat 9, Ponton, Oranjestad, T5886787, www.arubaharmony.com New in 2001, in residential area, Dutch management, all tax and service included, good value, all furnishings crisp, bright and new, tiled floors, kitchen, TV, quiet a/c, daily maid service, good beds, free form pool in garden, internet, car rental, parking. **A-C** *Arubiana Inn*, T5877700, www.arubianainn.com 12-min walk to Eagle Beach, 16 studios with fridge and microwave, TV, phone, small living room, pool, beach towels, mini-market, cocktail lounge. **A-C** *Vistalmar*, Bucutiweg 28, T5828579 daytime, T5847737 evenings. One-bedroom apartments with car run by Alby and Katy Yarzagaray, friendly, wooden jetty for swimming and sunbathing, near airport, laundry facilities. **C** *Andicuri Inn*, Oranjestad, T5821539. Apartments with a/c bedroom, living room, kitchenette, TV, balcony, sleep 2 plus 1 child, pool, convenient for nightlife but nothing special. **C** *Seabreeze Apartments*, Malohistraat 5, Pos Chiquito, 8 km southeast of Oranjestad, T/F5857657, www.sea-breezeappartments.com Well away from tourist conglomeration, 9 studios and 1-bedroom suites, a/c, kitchenette, patio, TV, clean and smart, dive packages available, snorkelling offered on owner's boat, free airport pick-up, cool boxes provided for picnics, special deals on car hire, short walk to beach, supermarket or *Marina Pirata* restaurant. In the district of Noord, also Mr and Mrs Kemp, **C** *A1 Apartments*, Pagaaistraat 5, T5828963, www.visitaruba.com/a1apts Fully furnished a/c rooms with kitchenette, 10 mins walk from main shopping centre, TV, well-stocked fridge, car hire arranged.

Camping Permit needed from police station, on Arnold Schuttrstraat, Oranjestad. It can take 10 days to get a permit and you must have a local address (ie hotel room).

Eating

Drinking water is distilled from sea water and is safe

With few exceptions, meals on Aruba are expensive and generally of the beef-and-seafood variety, but you can get some excellent food

Service charge on food and drinks is 15% at the hotels but at other places varies from 10% to 15%. The *Aruba Gastronomic Association* (AGA), www.arubadining.com has a dine around programme at 27 restaurants, but there is a surcharge on many items you might want to eat. Try Balashi beer, brewed by the award winning Brouwerij Nacional Balashi. It is the island's first fully-automated brewery and uses no artificial additives.

For Aruban specialities, *Gasparito*, Gasparito 3, T5867044, www.gasparito.com. Aruban and seafood, wins awards for cuisine, average price US$25, daily except Wed 1730-2200, art gallery attached exhibiting Aruban works. *The Old Cunucu House*, Palm Beach 150, T5861666. In a typical, low Aruban house, serving Aruban and international food, average price US$20, open 1800-2230, closed Sun. *Brisas del Mar*, Savaneta 222A, T5847718. Seafood specialities, on deck right on the sea, cool and airy, reasonable prices, catch of the day US$12, open 1200-1430, 1830-2200, closed Mon. *La Nueva Marina Pirata*, at Spanish Lagoon, T5857150. Seafood and Aruban dishes, around US$20, open 1800-2300, Sun 1200-2300, closed Tue, follow the main road to San Nicolas, turn right at *Drive Inn*. If you are in San Nicolas and want to try a local Aruban establishment serving Creole food, try *Freddy's Snack*, Mauritsstraat 4A, T5847888, open 0730-2330, main dishes around US$6, nothing fancy, no credit cards.

There are a few excellent steak restaurants. *El Gaucho*, Wilhelminastraat 80, T5823677, www.elgaucho-aruba.com 1130-1430, 1800-2300, some say this is the best, with excellent Argentine tenderloin, others complain about crowding and noise, go early for best service. Steak and a glass of wine around US$30 per person. Have an aperitif beforehand at the *Garufa Cigar & Cocktail Lounge* across the street and they will page you when your table is ready. A more relaxed atmosphere can be found at the *French Steak House*, in the Tam complex by the *Manchebo*, T5823444, www.manchebo.com/steakhouse, where there is less noise, it is less expensive, very good steak and piano player, US$29.95 for 5-course steak dinner with bottle of wine between 2 people and coffee. 1 of the most recent places to open is the Brazilian restaurant, *Amazonia*, JE Irausquin Blvd 374, Palm Beach, T5864444, www.amazonia-aruba.com Meat and more meat, waiters bring it round all the tables as they do in Brazil, huge salad bar to die for, US$35 for all you can eat, but go there really hungry, open Tue-Sun, 1800-2300. *Texas de Brasil*, opposite *Playa Linda*, upstairs above *Amici's*, T5864686. Lots of meat like at *Amazonia*, great salad bar and good wine list.

For surf'n'turf, *Twinkletone's*, Turibana Plaza, Noord 124, T5869806. Mon-Sat 1600-2300, prices around US$18 for main course, prime rib, great lobster and shrimp, singing chefs and waiters. *Madame Janette*, 5 mins east of the high rise hotels, T5870184, www.madamejanette.com Tenderloin good, also fish, garden dining, one of the in places to eat so reservations needed. *Le Petit Café*, at Royal Plaza Mall, second floor overlooking cruise ship dock, T5823166. Cook your own steak on hot coals, reasonable prices. An excellent seafood restaurant is *Flying Fishbone*, near *Brisas del Mar*, T5842506, www.flying-fishbone.com Tables on the beach, some seating on deck, lobster tank, reserve well in advance as very popular, seafood menu, about US$25. *Driftwood*, Lipstraat 12, Oranjestad, T5832515, open 1700-2300, meal for 2 with wine around US$50-60, good fresh sea food. *The Buccaneer*, Gasparito 11 C, T5866172. Seafood, giant aquariums, around US$20-25, open Mon-Sat from 1730-2230, no reservations.

The hotels have some very good gourmet restaurants. Otherwise, the best French restaurant is *Chez Mathilde*, Havenstraat 23, T5834968. Open for lunch and dinner, expect to pay around US$40 per person. *Le Dome*, near the *Divi*, T5871517. Belgian restaurant with indoor and outdoor seating, open for lunch and dinner, fine dining, 3-course dinner with wine and coffee around US$130-140 for 2. Sun brunch recommended, 1100-1500 US$38 fixed price, order from menu for breakfast dishes, hot or cold appetizers, entrées and desserts, in any order, as many helpings as you want, better than a buffet. Champagne and mimosas included. *Cuba's Cookin'*, Wilhelminstraat 27, T5880627. Cuban cuisine, accompanied by a live trio playing Cuban music, a cigar salon where you can enjoy a *cohiba*, open Mon-Sat 1130-2230, Sun 1700-2200, meals around US$20-25. *Villa Germania*, Seaport Market Pl, T5836161. German food for breakfast, lunch and dinner, around US$13, open 0800-2200. *Qué Pasa?*, T5834888. A good, intimate restaurant in the centre of Oranjestad, with prices around US$20, open 1800-0100, Italian/international. The best Japanese restaurant is currently *Blossom's*, at the *Wyndham Hotel*. Japanese food on 1 side and Chinese on the other, also excellent sushi bar, early-bird special US$16 1730-1830, good value. Several Oriental restaurants, *Warung Djawa*, Wilhelminastraat 2, T5834888. Serves Indonesian and Surinamese food, open Mon-Fri, 1130-1400 for weekday rijstafel buffet lunch, and Wed-Mon 1800-2300, all you can eat. For Japanese food try *Sakura*, Wilhelminastraat, 4, T5824088, also Thai, quite cheap at around US$15, open 1200-2300 Mon-Sat, *Sake House* , Caya Betico Croes 9, T5830405, the most expensive at an average US$25, open 1200-2300, or *Benihana*, Sasakiweg, T5826788, around US$20, open 1200-2300. Most restaurants have vegetarian options on the menu, but the only vegetarian restaurant is *The Green House*, Palm Beach 29, T5865241, fairly cheap at around US$15 but only open for lunch 1100-1400.

Charlie's Bar, Zeppenfeldtstraat 56, San Nicolas, T5871517, international, Aruban and seafood, has become more expensive at around US$20-25, open 1200-2130, bar until 2200. *Eetcafé The Paddock* on L G Smith Blvd 13, T5832334. Outside or indoor seating, sea view, very good, great saté, inexpensive for Aruba, Amstel on draught and the *daghap* (dish of the day) for US$7, live music on Sun. Sun brunch is good at *Promenade*, San Nicolas, 2 blocks from *Charlie's*, unlimited amount of food, good choice of appetizers and entrées. *Café The Plaza* at the Seaport Market Pl, T5838826, has a nice terrace and you can get a good, reasonably priced meal there, daily specials, food 1000-2400, but open until 0200. For night owls in need of food the white trucks (mobile restaurants) serve local food and snacks from 2100- 0500 at around US$5, located at Wilhelmina Park, the post office and the courthouse.

Most action takes place in Oranjestad and doesn't get going until around midnight. Start the night at *Carlos'n'Charlies*, www.carlosandcharlies.com Mexican, the hottest place at the moment, then when they close, 0100 weekdays, 0300 weekends, move on to *Mambo Jambo*, for Latin, salsa and merengue. *Club 2000*, has lots of dance music and techno. *Cellar Bar*, close to Benetton, behind Renaissance, is a small, cosy bar downstairs but upstairs it is *The Music Factory (TMF)*, popular with gays at weekends (gets going after 0100), empty weekdays, trance, club, house music, also salsa and merengue. *Choose A Name*, behind Royal Plaza Mall, is the cool place for the more sophisticated crowd, with a bar/restaurant and live music. Dancing spots include *La Bahia*, Weststraat, Oranjestad, *Club City One*, Sasakiweg, Eagle Beach, *E-Zone*, Weststraat, Oranjestad, *La Fiesta*, Aventura Mall, Oranjestad, and plenty of others in hotels or elsewhere. *Garufa Cigar & Cocktail Lounge*,

Nightlife

The legal age for consumption of alcohol and entry to nightclubs is 18

Wilhelminastraat 63, Oranjestad, T5823677, catches the clientele of *El Gaucho* before and after their meal for aperitifs or coffee and cigars. Places open late for drinking include *Café The Plaza*, in Seaport Market Pl, and *Eetcafé The Paddock*, LG Smith Blvd 13, see restaurants, above, both open until 0200. If you want to bar hop book a seat on *Kukoo Kunuku*, an open-sided bus, which takes you to 5 stops including an Aruban dinner and a champagne beach halt, US$55, 1800-2400 Mon-Sat, *Aruba Adventures*, Turibana Plaza 124, T5862010. Another party bus is *Yabbadabbadoo*, which starts with a barbecue at *Monte Blanco Ranch* and carries on with carnival music, dancing, free draft beer and snacks, 1900-2400, US$55, T5870115. *Tattoo* is a floating nightclub, a double-deck boat with rope swing, sunset and dinner dance cruise, US$55, all drinks US$1, www.arubaadventures.com A major attraction is gambling and there are 11 **casinos** on the island. Hotels must have 300 rooms before they can build one; those that do usually start at 1100 and operate 2 shifts. A few are open 24 hrs. The *Seaport Cinema* in Oranjestad has 6 screens showing US films. The *Drive-In Theatre* in Balashi occasionally shows European or Latin American films.

Festivals The most important festival of the year is the pre-Lenten *Carnival*, which gets earlier and earlier every year with supplementary parades and festivities preceding the event itself. There are colourful parades and competitions for best musician, best dancer, best costume, etc. The culmination is the Grand Parade on the Sun preceding Lent. Other festive occasions during the year include *New Year*, when fireworks are let off at midnight and musicians and singers go round from house to house (and hotel to hotel); *National Anthem and Flag Day* on 18 Mar, when there are displays of national dancing and other folklore, and *St John's Day* on 24 Jun, which is another folklore day: 'Derramento di Gai'. Local dance music, such as the fast, lively *tumba* is very influenced by Latin America. Arubans are fond of *merengue*. Throughout the year there are several different music and dance festivals. The *International Theatre Festival* takes place every other year; for information contact CCA, Vondellaan 2, T5821758. There is also a 2-day *Music Festival* in Oct with R&B, rock, Latin musicians, T5823777.

Shopping In addition to Caya G F (Betico) Croes shopping, areas include the Port of Call Market Pl, Seaport Village Mall, Royal Plaza Mall, Harbour Town, The Galleries, Strada I and II and the Holland Aruba Mall. A wide range of luxury items are imported from all over the world for resale to visitors at cut-rate prices. Liquor rates are good, but prices for jewellery, silverware and crystal are only slightly lower than US or UK prices. There is no sales tax. There are also local handicrafts such as pottery and artwork, try *Artesanía Arubiano*, on LG Smith Blvd 178, opposite *Tamarijn Hotel*, T5837494, or ask the Institute of Culture, T821010, or the Aruba Tourism Authority, T823777, for more information. *Galería Harmonia*, Main St, St Nicolas, exhibits and sells local artists' work, T5842969. Bookshops include *Van Dorp* in Caya G F (Betico) Croes, which is the main town centre bookshop. The light and airy *Captains Log* in the new Harbour Town development has a few books and reading material but is mostly souvenirs. Many bookshops in the hotels have some paperbacks.

Sports
See also diving and watersports, pages 846 and 847

Golf In 1995 the 18-hole, par 71, *Tierra del Sol Golf Course* opened near the lighthouse, designed to fit in with the natural landscape and with the sea. A community of homes and villas has also been designed to blend in with the surrounding vegetation with a full-service clubhouse, swimming pool, golf practice range and tennis and fitness complex. It took over 30 years to get the golf course built because of difficulties with the barren landscape and the lack of water, but now it is 1 of the best golf courses in the Caribbean. Many hotels are signing up for preferential rates for their guests, otherwise contact Tierra del Sol on T5860978, www.tierradelsol.com Green fees US$68-133 depending on time of day and time of year. There is a 9-hole golf course with oiled sand greens and goats near San Nicolas, golf clubs for rent US$6, green fee US$10 for 18 holes, US$7.50 for 9 holes, T842006, Sat and Sun members only, open daily 0800-1700. *Divi Aruba* is also building a 9-hole golf course which will have restaurants and villas around it. At the *Holiday Inn* is an 18-hole mini-golf course. A mini golf course has been built opposite *La Cabana*. Aruba Golf and Leisure is a golf driving range on Sasakiweg just east of *The Mill Resort*, open daily 0700-2300, with pro-shop, family centre, Chinese restaurant and café with internet, T5864590.

There are **tennis** courts at most major hotels. The *Aruba Racquet Club*, Rooi Santo 21, Palm Beach area, has 8 lit courts, an exhibition centre court, pro-shop, pool, aerobics classes, fitness centre, bar and restaurant. 0800-2300, for reservations, T5860215. There is usually an **international tennis tournament** in Sep. **Horse riding** at *Rancho El Paso*, Washington 44, near Santa Ana Church, T5873310, daily rides except Sun, 1 hr through countryside, US$15, or 2 hrs part-beach, part-*cunucu*, US$30, special trips on paso fino horses for experienced riders. The National Horse Fair, a 3-day international competition for paso fino horses is held here in Apr. *Rancho Daimari* also has paso fino horses and offers 2½-hr rides with snorkelling, daily at 0900 and 1500, a/c transport from your hotel included, T5860239. *Rancho del Campo* takes riders into the national park or to the natural bridge, 2½ hrs, 0930 or 1530, US$45 including transport and snorkelling, T5850290. *Rancho Notorious*, T5860508, has a choice of 3 trails, to the Alto Vista chapel, the California Lighthouse or a sunset beach ride.

Bowling The *Eagle Bowling Palace* at Pos Abou, T5835038, has 16 lanes, 6 of which are for reservation, 1000-0200, US$9 from 1000-1500, US$10.50 from 1500-0200, US$1.20 shoe rental; also 3 racquetball courts. There is an international bowling tournament in Apr, T5826443 for details, and an international youth tournament in Jul. **Triathlons** and **marathons** are held periodically, contact the tourist office for details or IDEFRE, JG Emanstraat, Oranjestad, T5824987.

De Palm Tours, L G Smith Blvd 142, T5824400, www.depalm.com, also with offices in many **Tour operators** hotels, sightseeing tours of the island and excursions to nearby islands or Venezuela. Their Mar-Lab Biological Tour costs US$25 including a visit to Seroe Colorado, and snorkelling at Boca Grandi. *Aruba Transfer Tours and Taxi*, Pos Abou z/n, T5822116. Julio Maduro, *Corvalou Tours*, T5821149, specializes in archaeological, geological, architectural, botanical and wildlife tours. For a combination 6-hr tour with lunch, US$35, call archaeologist Egbert Boerstra, T5841513, or Julio Maduro, or *Private Safaris* educational tour, T834869. Mr Boerstra has been involved in excavation work at Ser'l Noka, Malmok, Savaneta, Tanki Flip and Canashito and has worked with the project to establish the Arikok National Park. There are lots of companies offering tours of the island by minibus with a swimming and snorkelling stop at Baby Beach, about US$35.

Air **From Europe** *KLM* has direct flights from Amsterdam, going on to Lima. *Martinair* has **Transport** a flight from Amsterdam. **From North America** Atlanta (*Delta*), Boston (*American Airlines*), Charlotte (*US Air*), Chicago (*United Airlines*), Dallas (*American Airlines*), Miami (*American Airlines*, *Martinair*), New York (*American Airlines*, *Continental*), Philadelphia, Pittsburgh and St Louis (*US Air*). There are also charter services. Scheduled services from Canada involve a change of plane in Miami. Charter service from Canada is available through *Air Canada*, *Royal Air*, *Canada 3000* and *Skyservice* on a seasonal basis. **From South America** Lots of flights from Venezuela: Barcelona, Caracas, Las Piedras, Maracaibo, Porlamar and Valencia with *Servivensa*, *Aeropostal*, *Aserca*. From Colombia, *Avianca* fly from Bogotá and *Aires* from Barranquilla. *KLM* from Lima. **From the Caribbean** From San Juan with *American Airlines* and *American Eagle*, from Santo Domingo with *Aeropostal*, as well as flights from Bonaire and Curaçao with *Dutch Caribbean Airlines*.

Road **Bus** The bus station is behind the Public Works Department and the Royal Plaza Mall. Route 1 starts in San Nicolas and runs through Oranjestad via the hospital to Malmok, Mon-Sat, 0455-2255 hourly, returning from Malmok on the hr, journey time 55 mins. Route 2 also runs from San Nicolas on a slightly different route to Oranjestad and Palm Beach, more or less hourly, 0525-2200. Route 3 runs between Oranjestad and San Nicolas, 0550-2030 and Route 4 runs from Oranjestad through Noord to Palm Beach almost hourly on the ½ hr. There are also extra buses running between Oranjestad and the *Holiday Inn* (schedules available at the hotels and the tourist office). One-way fare is US$1. Otherwise there are 'jitney cars' which operate like *colectivos*; the fare is US$1.25. A jitney or bus from Oranjestad to San Nicolas will drop you at the airport.

Car hire There are some 23 car hire companies. *Airways* (Sabana Blanco 35, T5821845, airport T5829112), *Hertz* (L G Smith Blvd 142, T5824545, airport T5824886), *Avis* (Kolibristraat 14, T5828787, airport T5825496), *Budget* (Kolibristraat 1, T5828600, airport T5825423), *Dollar* (Grenedaweg 15, T5822783, airport T5825651) and *Toyota* (L G Smith Blvd 114, T5834832, airport, T5834902, toyota.rentacar@setarnet.aw) have offices in Oranjestad and at the airport. Many companies also have desks in the hotels. Prices begin at US$35 daily, US$215 weekly, with unlimited mileage. Often when you rent a 4WD vehicle you cannot take out all risks insurance. You must have a valid foreign (held for at least 2 yrs) or international driver's licence and be at least 21 to rent a car. Requirements vary between companies with a minimum age of 21-25 and a maximum of 65-70. Driving is on the right and all traffic, except bicycles, coming from the right should be given right of way, except at T-junctions.

Motorcycle A rental 50cc moped or scooter costs around US$30 a day, a 250cc motorcycle US$40, a Harley Davidson SP1100 US$90 and insurance is US$8-15 a day, depending on the size of engine. *Big Twin* rents Harley Davidson, T5839322. *Pablito's Bikes Rental*, L G Smith Blvd 228, T5878300, at *La Quinta Beach Resort*, Eagle Beach, men's, ladies, children's **bicycles**, US$3 per hr, US$8 half day, US$12 per 24 hrs. Other companies include *Donata*, T5878300, *Dream Cycles*, T5824329, *George*, T5825975, *Nelson*, T5866801, *New York*, T5863885, *Semver*, T5866851 and *Ron's* T5862090.

Taxis do not have meters **Taxi** Telephone the dispatcher at Pos Abao 41 behind the Eagle Bowling Palace on the Sasaki road, T5822116. Drivers speak English and individual tours can be arranged. Ask for flat-rate tariffs. From the airport to Oranjestad is US$9, to the low-rise hotels US$12 and to the high-rise hotels US$14 per taxi, not per person, maximum 4 passengers.

Sea Boat The harbour is 5 mins' walk from the town, there is a tourist information centre and some souvenir shops which open if a cruise ship is in. A fruit boat leaves once a week for Punto Fijo, Venezuela; check with Agencia Marítima La Confianza, Braziliëstraat 6 (T823814), Oranjestad. A new ferry *Josefa Camejo* started in 2002 to Coro, Venezuela, tickets from *Maduro Travel*, Rockefellerstraat 1, Oranjestad, T5825995, travel@selmaduro.com Daily in high season, 5 days a week in summer, first-class round trip US$90, other classes US$70, children and senior citizens US$60 first class, US$40 others, a car costs US$150, capacity 400 passengers, 45 cars, departs Aruba 1100, 3 hrs, returns next day 0700, check-in 2 hrs in advance.

Directory **Airline offices** Airline offices for all airport lines T5824800. *American Airlines*, T5822700. *Dutch Caribbean Airline*, open daily, T5838080, www.flydca.com *Avianca/SAM*, T5826277. *KLM*, T5823546/7. *Viasa*, T5836526. *Servivensa*, T5827779. *Aeropostal*, T5837799. *Vasp*, T5825995. **Banks** *ABN/AMRO Bank*, Caya G F (Betico) Croes 89, T5821515, at the Port of Call shopping centre on L G Smith Blvd; ATMs at these offices and at Sun Plaza Building, L G Smith Blvd 160 and Dr Horacio Oduber Hospital, for Cirrus or Mastercard. *Aruba Bank NV*, Caya G F (Betico) Croes 41, T5821550, and at L G Smith Blvd 108, T5831318. *Banco di Caribe NV*, Caya G F Croes 90-92, T5832168. *Caribbean Mercantile Bank NV*, Caya G F (Betico) Croes 51, T5823118, ATM for Cirrus or Mastercard here and also at Palm Beach 48 (Noord), Zeppenfeldstraat 35 (San Nicolas), Santa Cruz 41 (Santa Cruz), L G Smith Blvd 17, Seaport Village Mall. *Interbank*, Caya G F (Betico) Croes 38, T5831080. *First National Bank*, Caya G F (Betico) Croes 67, T5833221. *Western Union Money Transfer Service*, T5824400. *American Express* representative for refunds, exchange or replacement of cheques or cards is *SEL Maduro & Sons*, Rockefellerstraat 1, T5823888, open Mon-Fri 0800-1200, 1300-1700. *Aruba Bank*, *Caribbean Mercantile Bank* and *Interbank* are Visa/Mastercard representatives with cash advance. Aruba Bank at the airport is open daily 0800-1600. **Communications** Internet: There is an internet café at Royal Plaza Mall, Oranjestad, with access for US$7 per 30 mins. Email services at some hotels are complimentary for guests. *Post*: The post office at J E Irausquinplein is open 0730-1200, 1300-1630. Postal rates to the USA, Canada and the Netherlands are Afl 1.40 for letters and Afl0.60 for postcards. Letters to Europe Afl 1.50, postcards Afl 0.70. Collectors can subscribe for new issues by contacting the Philatelic Service, T5821900. **Telephone**: Modern telephone services with direct dialling are available. In 2003 phone numbers changed from 6 to 7 digits, all beginning with 5. Mobile phone numbers also changed to 7 digits, beginning with 9. Hotels add a service charge on to international calls. The IT office is on Boecoetiweg 33, T5821458. Phone and fax calls, email and mariphone calls at Servicio di Telecommunicacion di Aruba (Setar), at Palm Beach opposite *Hyatt Regency Aruba Beach Resort*, in Oranjestad just off the Plaza and next to the Post Office Building at Irausquinplein, Oranjestad. **Embassies and consulates** Denmark, L G Smith Blvd 82, T5824622. **Dominican Republic**, J E Emanstraat 79, T5836928. **Germany**, Scopetstraat 13, T5821767. **Italy**, Caya G F Betico Croes 7 T5822621. **Spain**, Madurostraat 9, T5823163. **Sweden**, Havenstraat 33, T5821821. **Venezuela**, Adriane Lacle Blvd 8, T5821078. **Medical services** All the major hotels have a doctor on call. *Dr Horacio Oduber Hospital*, LG Smith Blvd, T5874300, 280-bed hospital near the main hotel area.

Background

History

The first known settlers of the islands were the Caiquetios, a tribe of peaceful Arawak Indians. They survived principally on fish and shellfish and collected salt from the Charoma saltpan to barter with their mainland neighbours for supplements to their diet. There are remains of Indian villages on Curaçao at Westpunt, San Juan, de Savaan and Santa Barbara, and on Aruba near Hooiberg. The Arawaks in this area had escaped attack by the Caribs but soon after the arrival of the Spaniards most were transported from Curaçao to work on Hispaniola. Although some were later repatriated, more fled when the Dutch arrived. The remainder were absorbed into the black or white population, so that by 1795, only five full-blooded Indians were to be found on Curaçao. On Aruba and Bonaire the Indians maintained their identity until about the end of the 19th century, but there were no full-blooded Indians left by the 20th century.

The islands were encountered in 1499 by a Spaniard, Alonso de Ojeda, accompanied by the Italian, Amerigo Vespucci and the Spanish cartographer Juan de la Cosa. The Spanish retained control over the islands throughout the 16th century, but because there was no gold, they were declared 'useless islands'. After 1621, the Dutch became frequent visitors looking for wood and salt and later for a military foothold. Curaçao's strategic position between Pernambuco and New Amsterdam within the Caribbean setting made it a prime target. In 1634, a Dutch fleet took Curaçao, then in 1636 they took Bonaire, which was inhabited by a few cattle and six Indians, and Aruba which the Spanish and Indians evacuated. Curaçao became important as a trading post and as a base for excursions against the Spanish. After 1654, Dutch refugees from Brazil brought sugar technology, but the crop was abandoned by 1688 because of the dry climate. About this time citrus fruits were introduced, and salt remained a valuable commodity. Much of Curaçao's wealth came from the slave trade. From 1639-1778 thousands of slaves were brought to Willemstad, and sold to the mainland and other colonies. The Dutch brought half a million slaves to the Caribbean, most of which went through Curaçao.

Wars between England and the Netherlands in the second half of the 17th century led to skirmishes and conquests in the Caribbean. The Peace of Nijmegen in 1678 gave the Dutch Aruba, Curaçao, Bonaire and the three smaller islands in the Leeward group, St Eustatius, Saba and half of St Martin. Further conflicts in Europe and the Americas in the 18th century led to Curaçao becoming a meeting place for pirates, American rebels, Dutch merchants, Spaniards and Creoles from the mainland. In 1800 the English took Curaçao but withdrew in 1803. They occupied it again from 1807 until 1816 (when Dutch rule was restored), during which time it was declared a free port. From 1828 to 1845, all Dutch West Indian colonies were governed from Surinam. In 1845 the Dutch Leeward Islands were joined to Willemstad in one colonial unit called Curaçao and Dependencies. The economy was still based on commerce, much of it with Venezuela, and there was a ship building industry, some phosphate mining and the salt pans.

In the 20th century oil was discovered in Venezuela and the Dutch-British Shell Oil Company set up a refinery on Curaçao because of its political stability, its port facilities and its better climate. The Second World War was another turning point as demand for oil soared and British, French and later US forces were stationed on the islands. The German invasion of Holland encouraged Dutch companies to transfer their assets to the Netherlands Antilles leading to the birth of the offshore financial centre.

Government

The organization of political parties began in 1936 and by 1948 there were four parties on Curaçao and others on Aruba and the other islands, most of whom endorsed autonomy. In 1948, the Dutch constitution was revised to allow for the transition to complete autonomy of the islands. In 1954 they were granted full autonomy in domestic affairs and became an integral part of the Kingdom of the Netherlands. The Crown continued to appoint the Governor. Nevertheless, a strong separatist movement developed on Aruba and the island finally withdrew from the Netherlands Antilles in 1986, becoming an autonomous member of the Kingdom of the Netherlands.

Netherlands Antilles, the ABC islands

The Netherlands Antilles now form two autonomous parts of the Kingdom of the Netherlands. The main part, comprising all the islands except Aruba, is a parliamentary federal democracy, the seat of which is in Willemstad, Curaçao, and each island has its own Legislative and Executive Council. Parliament (Staten) is elected in principle every four years, with 14 members from Curaçao, three from Bonaire, three from Sint Maarten and one each from Saba and St Eustatius.

Separate status for some or all of the islands has been a political issue with a breakaway movement in Curaçao and St Maarten. The Netherlands Government's previous policy of encouraging independence has been reversed. In November 1993 a referendum was held in Curaçao on its future status within the Federation. The Government was defeated when the electorate voted to continue the island's present status as a member of the Antillean federation (73.6%), rejecting the other options of separate status (11.9%), incorporation in the Netherlands (8.0%) and independence (0.5%). Referenda were also held on the other islands, Saba, Statia, St Maarten and Bonaire with the aim of restructuring the Antilles. The vote in October 1994 was in favour of the status quo, with 90.6% support in Statia, 86.3% in Saba, 88.0% in Bonaire and 59.8% in Sint Maarten.

Economy

Bonaire Bonaire's economy is heavily dependent on tourism, with small operations for solar salt mining, oil trans-shipment, a rice mill and radio communications industry. Cargill Corporation, the world's largest private company, operates the salt industry, which benefits so greatly from the constant sunshine (with air temperatures averaging 27°C and water 26°C), scant rainfall, and refreshing trade winds. A shrimp farm started operations in 1999. *Sea Hatch Bonaire* is near Sorobon and offers tours.

Tourism is specialized and most visitors are divers. The USA is the largest single market, followed by the Netherlands, Venezuela and Germany. Accommodation for tourists is split fairly evenly between hotels and condominiums or villas, amounting to about 1,100 rooms and still growing. Financial assistance for the development of tourism has been provided by the EU and Holland, which have financed the expansion of the airport and development of other infrastructure.

Curaçao Curaçao has a more diversified economy than the other islands, yet even so, it suffered severe recession in the 1980s and unemployment is around 13% of the labour force. The major industry is the oil refinery dating back to 1917, now one of the largest in the world, to which the island's fortunes and prosperity are tied. Imports of crude oil and petroleum products make up two-thirds of total imports, while exports of the same are 95% of total exports. That prosperity was placed under threat when Shell pulled out of the refinery in 1985, but the operation was saved when the island government purchased the plant, and leased it to Venezuela for US$11 mn a year. Despite the need for a US$270 mn reconstruction, principally to reduce pollution, the Venezuelan company, PDVSA, signed a 20-year lease agreement which came into effect in 1995, ending its previous system of short-term operating leases. Bunkering has also become an important segment of the economy, and the terminal at Bullenbaai is one of the largest bunkering ports in the world. The island's extensive trade makes it a port of call for a great many shipping lines.

Coral reefs surrounding the island, constant sunshine, a mean temperature of 27°C (81°F), lure visitors. Curaçao used to be a destination for tourists from Venezuela, but a devaluation of the bolívar in 1983 caused numbers to drop by 70% in just one year. A restructuring of the industry has led to a change of emphasis towards attracting US and European tourists, as well as South Americans, and numbers have now increased. Cruise visitor numbers have been boosted by the arrival of the megaship *Rhapsody of the Seas*, which carries 2,000 and calls 26 times a year. The single largest market for visitors to Curaçao is Holland, with 30% of stayover arrivals, followed by the USA with 15% and Venezuela with 14%. Diving has been promoted and Curaçao now registers about 10,000 visiting divers a year.

A major foreign currency earner, the offshore financial sector, is seeking new areas of business, including captive insurance and mutual funds, in a highly competitive market.

Gold was discovered in 1825, but the mine ceased to be economic in 1916. In 1929, black **Aruba** gold brought real prosperity to Aruba when *Lago Oil and Transport Co*, a subsidiary of *Exxon*, built a refinery at San Nicolas at the east end of the island. At that time it was the largest refinery in the world, employing over 8,000 people. In March 1985 *Exxon* closed the refinery, a serious shock for the Aruban economy, and one which the Government has striven to overcome. In 1989, *Coastal Oil of Texas* signed an agreement with the Government to reopen part of the refinery by 1991, with an initial capacity of 150,000 barrels a day, but despite plans to increase it, present capacity is only about 140,000 b/d.

The economic crisis of 1985 forced the Government to turn to the IMF for help. The fund recommended that Aruba promote tourism and increase the number of hotel rooms by 50%. The Government decided, however, to triple hotel capacity to 6,000 rooms, which it was estimated would provide employment for 20% of the population. In 1995 the opening of the *Marriott* raised the total to 6,626 rooms in hotels, a figure which rose to 7,103 by 1996. Total employment in tourism absorbs 35% of the workforce. The economy is dependent on tourism for income and in 2000 combined stayover and cruise ship passengers exceeded 1 million for the first time with more than 25 cruise lines visiting each month and even more airlines adding Aruba to their routes from the USA.

Efforts are being made to diversify away from a single source of revenues into areas such as re-exporting through the free trade zone, and offshore finance. Aruba is still dependent on the Netherlands for budget support and aims to reduce financial assistance.

Unemployment is rare on Aruba and labour is imported for large projects such as the refinery and construction work. The Government is encouraging skilled Arubans to return from Holland but is hampered by a housing shortage.

Netherlands Antilles, the ABC Islands

Netherlands Antilles, the ABC Islands

Footnotes

Index

Shorts

Advertisers' index

Map Index

Footnotes

Credits

Footnotes

Footprint credits
Text editor: Felicity Laughton
Map editor: Sarah Sorensen

Publishers: James Dawson
and Patrick Dawson
Editorial Director: Rachel Fielding
Editorial: Alan Murphy, Sophie Blacksell,
Sarah Thorowgood, Claire Boobbyer,
Caroline Lascom, Davina Rungasamy,
Laura Dixon
Production: Jo Morgan, Mark Thomas
Cartography: Robert Lunn,
Claire Benison, Kevin Feeney
Design: Mytton Williams
Marketing and publicity:
Rosemary Dawson, La-Ree Miners
Advertising: Debbie Wylde,
Lorraine Horler
Finance and administration:
Sharon Hughes, Elizabeth Taylor,
Leona Bailey

Photography credits
Front cover: Imagestate
Inside colour section: Claire Boobbyer,
Robert Harding, Impact, JD, Nature Pl,
Stone, Travelink, Trip

Print
Manufactured in Italy by LegoPrint
Pulp from sustainable forests

Footprint feedback
We try as hard as we can to make each
Footprint guide as up to date as possible
but, of course, things always change. If you
want to let us know about your experiences
– good, bad or ugly – then don't delay, go
to www.footprintbooks.com and send in
your comments.

Publishing information
Caribbean Islands 2004
Fifteenth edition
© Footprint Handbooks Ltd
September 2003

ISBN 1 903471710
CIP DATA: A catalogue record for this
book is available from the British Library

® Footprint Handbooks and the Footprint
mark are a registered trademark of
Footprint Handbooks Ltd

Published by Footprint
6 Riverside Court
Lower Bristol Road
Bath BA2 3DZ, UK
T +44 (0)1225 469141
F +44 (0)1225 469461
discover@footprintbooks.com
www.footprintbooks.com

Distributed in the USA by
Publishers Group West

Neither the black and white nor coloured
maps are intended to have any political
significance.

Every effort has been made to ensure that
the facts in this guidebook are accurate.
However, travellers should still obtain
advice from consulates, airlines etc about
travel and visa requirements before
travelling. The authors and publishers
cannot accept responsibility for
any loss, injury or inconvenience
however caused.

Acknowledgements

Specialist contributors

We are fortunate to have had contributions to the Essentials section from a number of writers who are specialists in their field, notably:

Whale and dolphin watching by Erich Hoyt, consultant for the Whale and Dolphin Conservation Society, marine ecologist and author of 12 books including The Whale Watcher's Handbook, Collins Whales and Dolphins and Seasons of the Whale. **Scuba Diving** and **Hurricanes** by Martha Watkins Gilkes, a freelance diving journalist based in Antigua and author of The Scuba Diving Guide to the Caribbean (Macmillan). **Windsurfing** by Nicolette Clifford, formerly based in Tortola, British Virgin Islands. **Watersports** by Rosie Mauro, formerly of Barbados. **Sailing** by Kathy Irwin, an experienced yachtie from Heath, Texas. **Walking** by Mark Wilson, geographer and journalist, currently based in Trinidad. **Cycling** by Patricia Thorndike de Suriel, formerly of *Iguana Mama*, in the Dominican Republic. **Cricket** by Jeremy Cameron, peripatetic correspondent. **Flora and fauna** and **Responsible travel** by Mark Eckstein with additional information from Mark Wilson

Health by Dr Charlie Easmon who has worked as a medical adviser to the Foreign and Commonwealth Office and as a locum consultant at the hospital for tropical diseases travel clinic, as well as being a specialist registrar in Public Health. He now also runs Travel Screening services (www.travelscreening.co.uk) at 1 Harley Street.

Thanks also to Nigel Gallop for **Music**, Puerto Rico.

Correspondents

We are indebted to all our regular and not so regular correspondents in the Caribbean region who help us update each year: Antigua and Barbuda, Martha Watkins Gilkes; Barbados, Mark Wilson; Bonaire, George de Salvo; Cayman Islands, Amanda George; Cuba, Juan Carlos Otaño, Julio César Muñóz; Dominica, Steve McCabe; Dominican Republic, Wendy Coward, Mara Strahm and Urs Zumbuehl, Maribel at *Iguana Mama*; French Antilles, Graham Gendall Norton with thanks to Guy-Claude Germain (Guadeloupe), Jacques Bajal (Martinique) and Elise Magras (St-Barts); Jamaica, Robert Kerr; Montserrat Richard Aspin; St Kitts and Nevis, Maria Vendiese James; St Lucia Maria Grech; St Vincent and the Grenadines, Lara Hadley; Sint Maarten, Saba and Statia, Mireille Hermans; Trinidad and Tobago, Mark Wilson; Turks and Caicos Islands, Kathi Robertson; US Virgin Islands, Martha Watkins Gilkes.

During the year of research for this edition, Sarah Cameron visited the Dominican Republic, Antigua, Barbuda, St Kitts, Nevis, Montserrat, Anguilla, St-Martin and Sint Maarten and is most grateful to all the people who helped her on those islands. In the Dominican Republic thanks go to Kim Beddall, Estela Rodríguez, Mara Strahm and Urs Zumbuehl, as well as staff at the tourist office who helped tremendously in the planning and execution of the visit. Tourist office personnel in the Leeward Islands were also extremely attentive and helpful, particularly Nicole Liburd (Nevis) Randolph Hamilton and Cliff Hamilton (St Kitts), Bernadette Davis and Erica Beaujour (St-Martin), William Bell (Sint Maarten), Rosetta West (Montserrat), Candis Niles (Anguilla) and Annette Michael (Antigua). Our local correspondents pulled out all the stops and helped Sarah research restaurants and sundowners with enthusiasm, particularly Martha Watkins Gilkes, whose hospitality in Antigua and company on Barbuda were greatly appreciated. Thanks also to Claire Frank for taking the time to chat about Barbuda. In addition, the following hotels are to be thanked for their hospitality: *Old Manor*, Nevis; *Ottley Plantation Inn*, St Kitts; *Anguilla Great House*, Anguilla; *Les Alizés*, St-Martin; *Holland House*, Sint Maarten; *Hawksbill Beach Resort*, Antigua, *Tree Tops*, Antigua, *Island Chalet*, Barbuda, *Montserrat Moments Inn*, Montserrat.

We are very grateful to all the travellers who have written to us over the last year: Paola Amadei and Jorge Garzon, USA; John Bosworth, UK; Ariel and Xen, Israel; Ariel ben Hur, Israel; Carla Burshtein, Canada; Mike Esposito, USA; Michael Hall and Catherine Fouquet, UK; John and Diana Jones, Grand Cayman; Jan Meissner, Germany; Frank and Christine Mueller, Germany; Alison Perkins and Cameron Russo, Australia; Ricardo Poppeliers and John de Ridder, Netherlands; Scott Rasmussen, USA; David Richardson, USA; Jean Claude Rouanet, email; Stephen Thorpe, UK; Urtzi Urrutikoetxea, Spain; Guillaume Vadevoncoeur, Canada; Beate Weber, Germany.

Footnotes

Complete title listing

Footprint publishes travel guides to over 150 destinations worldwide. Each guide is packed with practical, concise and colourful information for everybody from first-time travellers to travel aficionados. The list is growing fast and current titles are noted below.

Available from all good bookshops and online

www.footprintbooks.com

(P) denotes pocket guide

Latin America & Caribbean

Argentina
Barbados (P)
Bolivia
Brazil
Caribbean Islands
Central America & Mexico
Chile
Colombia
Costa Rica
Cuba
Cusco & the Inca Trail
Dominican Republic
Ecuador & Galápagos
Guatemala
Havana (P)
Mexico
Nicaragua
Peru
Rio de Janeiro
South American Handbook
Venezuela

North America

Western Canada
Vancouver (P)
New York (P)

Africa

Cape Town (P)
East Africa
Libya
Marrakech & the High Atlas
Marrakech (P)
Morocco
Namibia
South Africa
Tunisia
Uganda

Middle East

Egypt
Israel
Jordan
Syria & Lebanon

Australasia

Australia
East Coast Australia
New Zealand
Sydney (P)
West Coast Australia

Asia

Bali
Bangkok & the Beaches
Cambodia
Goa
India
Indian Himalaya
Indonesia
Hong Kong (P)
Laos
Malaysia
Myanmar (Burma)
Nepal
Pakistan
Rajasthan & Gujarat
Singapore
South India
Sri Lanka
Sumatra
Thailand
Tibet
Vietnam

Europe

Andalucía
Athens (P)
Barcelona
Barcelona (P)
Berlin (P)
Bilbao (P)

Bologna (P)
Britain
Copenhagen (P)
Croatia
Dublin
Dublin (P)
Edinburgh
Edinburgh (P)
England
Glasgow
Glasgow (P)
Ireland
Lisbon (P)
London
London (P)
Lyon (P)
Madrid (P)
Marseille (P)
Naples (P)
Northern Spain
Paris (P)
Reykjavík (P)
Seville (P)
Scotland
Scotland Highlands & Islands
South Italy
Spain
Tallinn (P)
Turin (P)
Turkey
Valencia (P)
Verona (P)

Also available

Traveller's Handbook (WEXAS)
Traveller's Healthbook (WEXAS)
Traveller's Internet Guide (WEXAS

Footnotes

What the papers say...

"I carried the South American Handbook from Cape Horn to Cartagena and consulted it every night for two and a half months. I wouldn't do that for anything else except my hip flask."
Michael Palin, BBC Full Circle

"My favourite series is the Handbook series published by Footprint and I especially recommend the Mexico, Central and South America Handbooks."
Boston Globe

"If 'the essence of real travel' is what you have been secretly yearning for all these years, then Footprint are the guides for you."
Under 26 magazine

"Who should pack Footprint-readers who want to escape the crowd."
The Observer

"Footprint can be depended on for accurate travel information and for imparting a deep sense of respect for the lands and people they cover."
World News

"The guides for intelligent, independently-minded souls of any age or budget."
Indie Traveller

Mail order
Available worldwide in bookshops and on-line. Footprint travel guides can also be ordered directly from us in Bath, via our website www.footprintbooks.com or from the address on the imprint page of this book.

Footnotes

BWIA have changed the distance to the Caribbean

Our largest seat pitch ever, up to a staggering 60″ in Business Class and up to a generous 34″ in Economy Class – Who says size doesn't matter?

BWIA welcomes you onboard the Airbus A340-300 with the quietest and most luxurious cabin in the sky.

What other airlines call Premium Economy - BWIA provides as standard. You now get the longest seat pitch ever on our Europe to Caribbean route – up to a generous 34″ in economy and a staggering 60″ in business/first class. You can also enjoy the finest Caribbean food and drink served with the warmth of a Caribbean smile.

BWIA's new connecting service with LIAT now gives you seamless hassle-free transfers whatever your Caribbean destination.

PARTNERS

BWIA
IN THE CARIBBEAN

liat
AND BEYOND

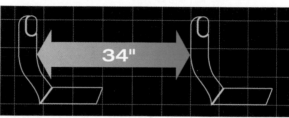
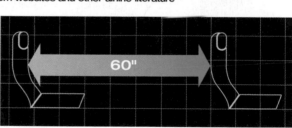

Map symbols

Administration

- - - International border
- State/province border
- □ Capital/principal city
- ○ Other city/town

Roads and travel

— Main road (National highway)
— Other road
- - - Track
...... Footpath
⊢■— Railway with station

Water features

River
Lake
Marshland
Beach
Ocean
Waterfall
~~ Reef
Ferry
Dive site
Boat anchorage
Windsurfing

Cities and towns

□ Sight
■ Sleeping
① Eating
Building
Main through route
Main street
Minor street
Pedestrianized street
Tunnel
→ One way street

⋈ Bridge
IIIIIIII Steps
Park, garden, stadium
Fortified wall
✈ Airport
Ⓢ Bank
Bus station
Hospital
Market
Museum
Police
Post office
Tourist office
Cathedral, church
Synagogue
Fort
Petrol
Internet
Telephone office
Golf
Parking
A Detail map
A Related map

Topographical features

Contours (approx), rock outcrop
Mountain
Volcano
Escarpment

Other symbols

Archaeological site
National park/wildlife reserve
Viewing point
Deciduous/palm trees
Mangrove

Caribbean Islands

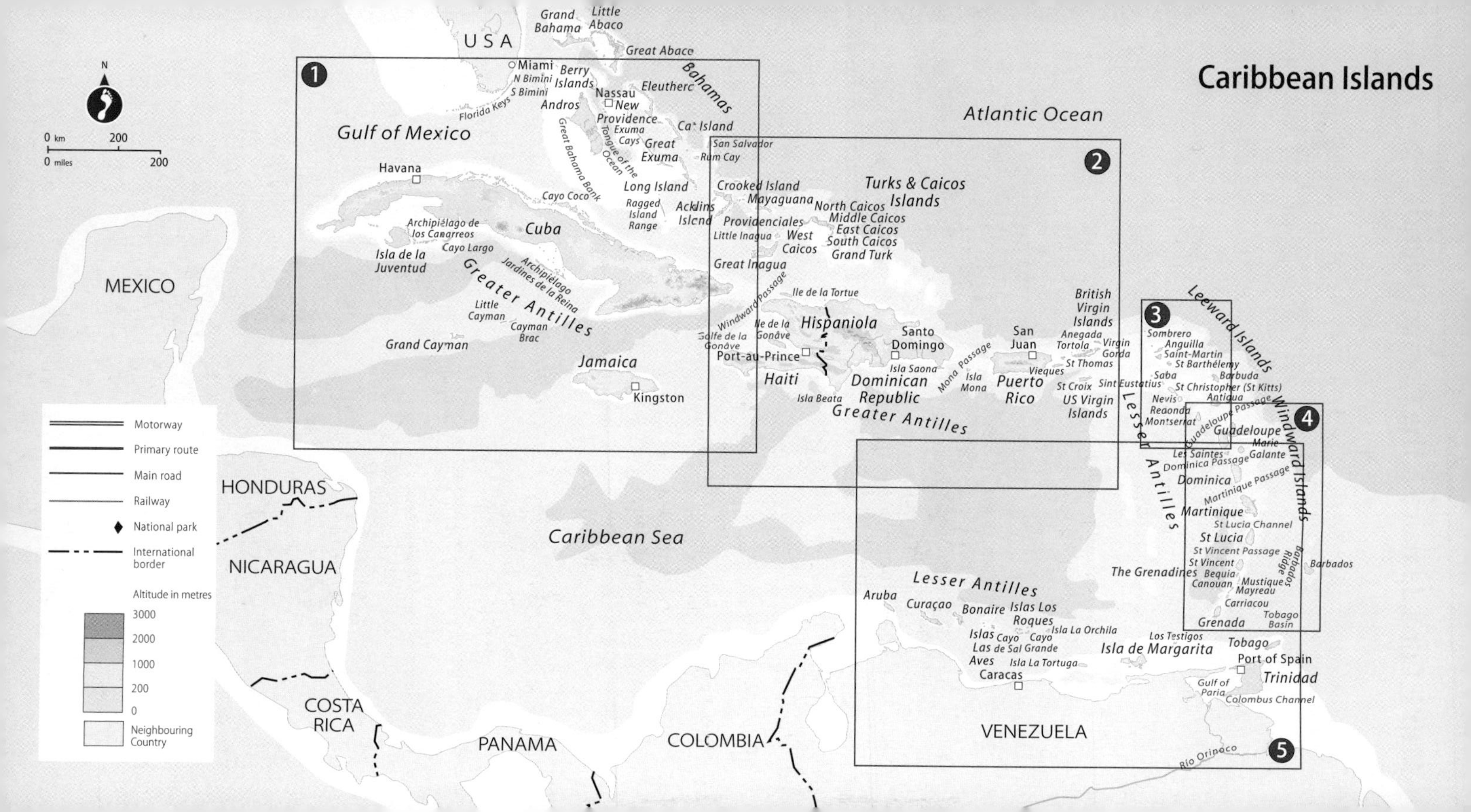

Atlantic Ocean

Gulf of Mexico

Caribbean Sea

MEXICO

USA

Miami
Florida Keys

Bahamas
Grand Bahama
Little Abaco
Great Abaco
N Bimini Islands
S Bimini
Berry Islands
Nassau
New Providence
Eleuthera
Cat Island
Andros
Exuma Cays
Great Exuma
Long Island
Tongue of the Ocean
Great Bahama Bank
Ragged Island Range
San Salvador
Rum Cay
Crooked Island
Acklins Island
Mayaguana
Great Inagua
Little Inagua

Havana

Cuba
Isla de la Juventud
Archipiélago de los Canarreos
Cayo Largo
Cayo Coco
Archipiélago Jardines de la Reina

Grand Cayman
Little Cayman
Cayman Brac

Jamaica
Kingston

Greater Antilles

Turks & Caicos
Providenciales
North Caicos
Middle Caicos
West Caicos
East Caicos
South Caicos
Grand Turk

Île de la Tortue
Haiti
Port-au-Prince
Île de la Gonâve
Windward Passage
Golfe de la Gonâve
Isla Beata
Hispaniola
Dominican Republic
Santo Domingo
Isla Saona
Isla Mona
Mona Passage

Puerto Rico
San Juan
Vieques
Mona Passage

British Virgin Islands
Anegada
Virgin Gorda
Tortola
St Thomas
US Virgin Islands
St Croix

Lesser Antilles

Sombrero
Anguilla
Saint-Martin
St Barthélemy
Saba
Barbuda
Sint Eustatius
St Christopher (St Kitts)
Nevis
Redonda
Montserrat
Antigua

Leeward Islands

Guadeloupe
Marie-Galante
Les Saintes
Dominica Passage
Dominica
Martinique Passage
Martinique
St Lucia Channel
St Lucia
St Vincent Passage
St Vincent
Bequia
Mustique
Canouan
Mayreau
Carriacou
The Grenadines
Grenada

Windward Islands

Barbados
Barbados Ridge
Tobago Basin
Tobago
Trinidad
Port of Spain
Gulf of Paria
Columbus Channel

Lesser Antilles

VENEZUELA
Caracas
Los Testigos
Isla de Margarita
Islas Los Roques
Islas Los
Cayo Grande
La Orchila
Isla La Tortuga
Aves
Bonaire
Curaçao
Aruba
Río Orinoco

COLOMBIA
PANAMA
COSTA RICA
NICARAGUA
HONDURAS

Legend

Motorway
Primary route
Main road
Railway
National park
International border
Altitude in metres

3000
2000
1000
200
0
Neighbouring Country

0 km   200
0 miles   200

N

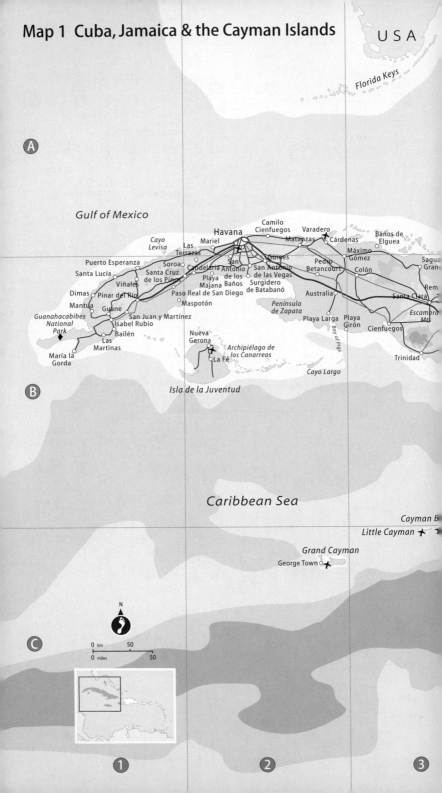

Map 1 Cuba, Jamaica & the Cayman Islands

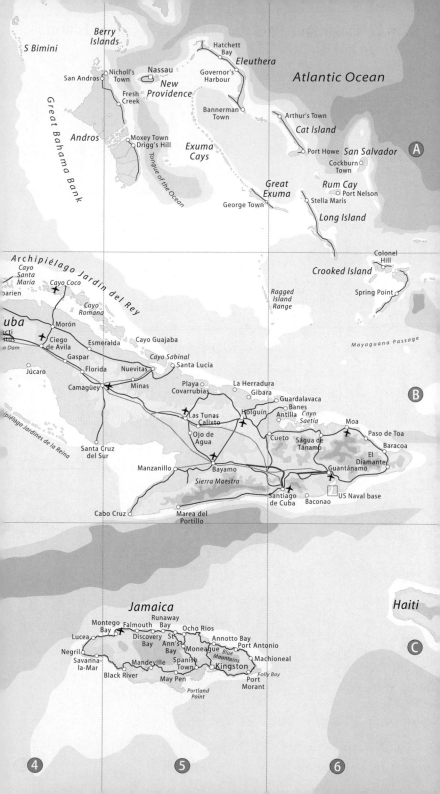

Map 2 Hispaniola, Puerto Rico, Turks & Caicos Islands & the Virgin Islands

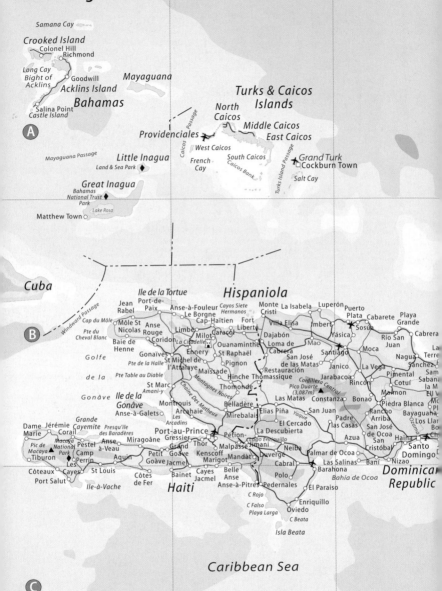

A

Samana Cay

Crooked Island
Colonel Hill
Richmond

Long Cay
Bight of
Acklins
Goodwill

Mayaguana

Turks & Caicos
Islands

Acklins Island
Bahamas

Salina Point
Castle Island

North
Caicos

Providenciales

Middle Caicos
East Caicos

Mayaguana Passage

West Caicos

Little Inagua
Land & Sea Park ◆

Caicos
Passage

South Caicos

French
Cay

Caicos Bank

Grand Turk
Cockburn Town

Salt Cay

Great Inagua
Bahamas
National Trust
Park
Lake Rosa

Matthew Town ○

Turks Island Passage

B

Cuba

Windward Passage

Ile de la Tortue
Port-de-
Paix

Jean
Rabel

Cap du Môle
Pte du
Cheval Blanc

Môle St
Nicolas

Baie de
Henne

Anse
Rouge

Coridon

Golfe

Gonaïves

Pte de la Halle

de la

Pte Table au Diable

Gonâve
Ile de la
Gonâve

Hispaniola

Anse-à-Fouleur
Le Borgne
Cap-Haïtien
Fort
Liberté

Limbé
Milot
Caracol
La Citadelle▲
Ouanaminthe

Monte
Cristi

La Isabela

Luperón

Puerto
Plata

Cabarete

Playa
Grande

Villa Elisa

Dajabón
Loma de
Cabrera

Imbert

Yásica

Sosúa

Río San
Juan

Cabrera

Ennery

St Raphaël
Pignon

San José
de las Matas

Mao

Santiago

Moca

La Vega

Janico

Nagua

Sanchez

St Michel de
l'Attalaye

Hinche
Thomassique

Restauración

Jarabacoa

Rincón

Pimental

Cotuí

Sam
Sanchez
la M

Ell V
Mc

Maissade

Thomonde

Cordillera Central
Pico Duarte
(3,087m)▲

Constanza

Bonao

Piedra Blanca

Bayaguana
Los Llan
Bo

St Marc
Amani-y

Chaîne Des Matheux

Montagnes Noires

Belladère

Elías Piña

San Juan

Las Matas

Rancho
Arriba

Maimon

Grande
Cayemite

Montrouis

Arcahaie
Les
Arcadins

Mirebalais

El Cercado

Padre
las Casas

San José
de Ocoa

Pi

Jérémie
Corail

Presqu'île
des Baraderes

Anse-à-Galets

Port-au-Prince

Pétion-
ville

La Descubierta

Azua

San
Cristóbal

Haina

Ch

Dame
Marie

Pestel

Anse
à-Veau

Miragoâne
Gressier

Grand
Goave

Thor

Malpasse
Jimani

Neiba

Palmar de Ocoa

Baní

Santo
Domingo

Pic de
Macaya
National ▲
Park

Camp
Perrin

Aquin

Petit
Goave
Jacmel

Kenscoff
Marigot

Mandat
Duverge

Cabral

Las Salinas

Nizao

Tiburon

Les
Cayes

St Louis

Côtes
de Fer

Bainet

Belle
Anse

Polo

Barahona

Dominica
Republic

Côteaux
Port Salut

Ile-à-Vache

Cayes
Jacmel

Haiti

Anse-à-Pitres
Pedernales

C Rojo

El Paraiso

Bahía de Ocoa

C Falso
Playa Larga

Enriquillo
Oviedo

C Beata

Isla Beata

C

Caribbean Sea

1   **2**   **3**

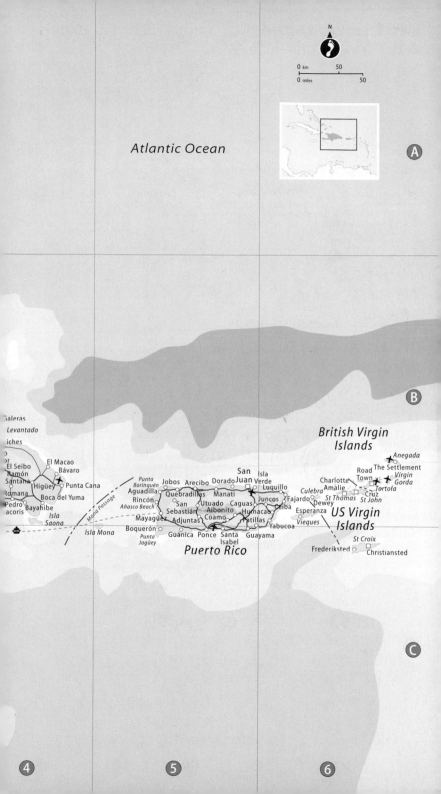

Atlantic Ocean

A

B

British Virgin
Islands

C

Galeras
Levantado
iches
or
El Macao
Ramón
Bávaro
Santana
Higüey
Punta Cana
Romana
Boca del Yuma
Pedro
acoris
Bayahibe
*Isla
Saona*

Mona Passage

Isla Mona

Punta
Borinquén
Aguadilla
Rincón
Añasco Beach
Mayagüez
Boquerón
*Punta
Jagüey*

San
Jobos
Arecibo
Dorado
Juan
Quebradillas
Manatí
San
Utuado
Caguas
Sebastián
Aibonito
Adjuntas
Coamo
Guánica
Ponce
Santa
Isabel

Isla
Verde
Luquillo
Juncos
Humacao
Patillas
Guayama
Yabucoa

Ceiba
Fajardo
Dewey
Esperanza
Vieques

Anegada
Road
The Settlement
Town
*Virgin
Gorda*
Charlotte
Culebra
Amalie
Cruz
St Thomas
Tortola
St John

US Virgin
Islands

Puerto Rico

St Croix
Frederiksted
Christiansted

4

5

6

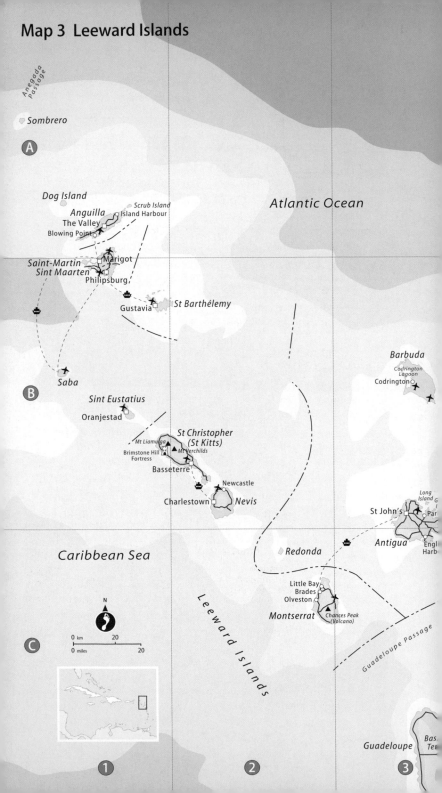

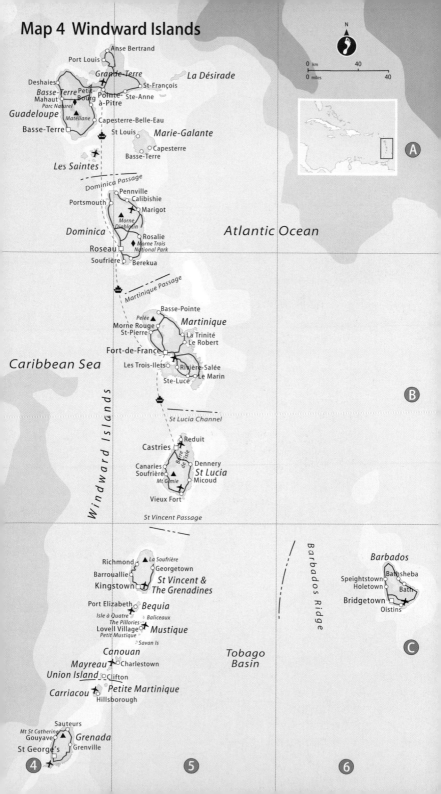

Map 5 Lesser Antilles & Trinidad

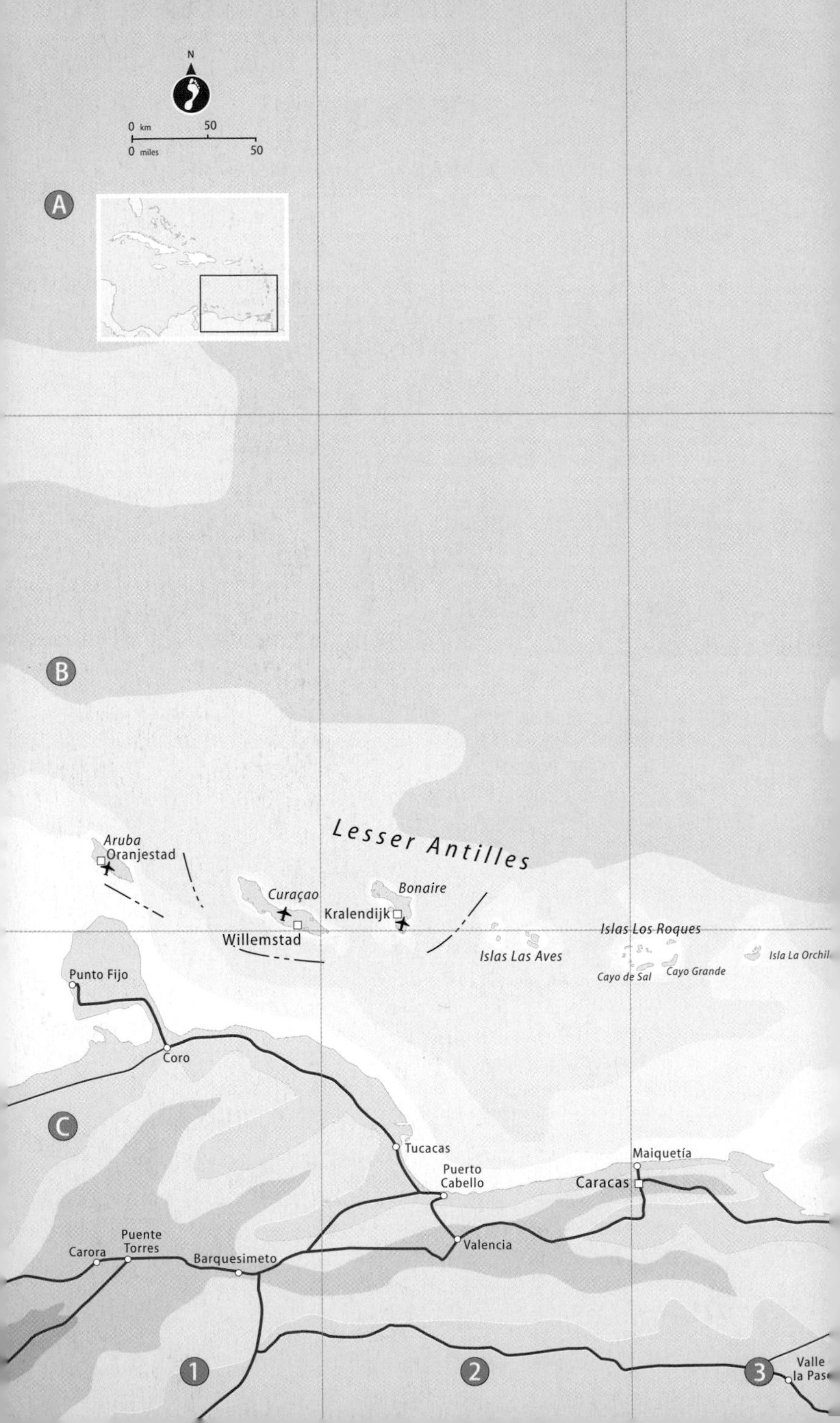

N

0 km 50

0 miles 50

A

B

Lesser Antilles

Aruba
Oranjestad

Curaçao
Willemstad

Bonaire
Kralendijk

Islas Los Roques

Islas Las Aves

Cayo de Sal *Cayo Grande*

Isla La Orchil

Punto Fijo

Coro

C

Tucacas

Puerto
Cabello

Maiquetía

Caracas

Carora

Puente
Torres

Barquesimeto

Valencia

1

2

3

Valle
la Pas

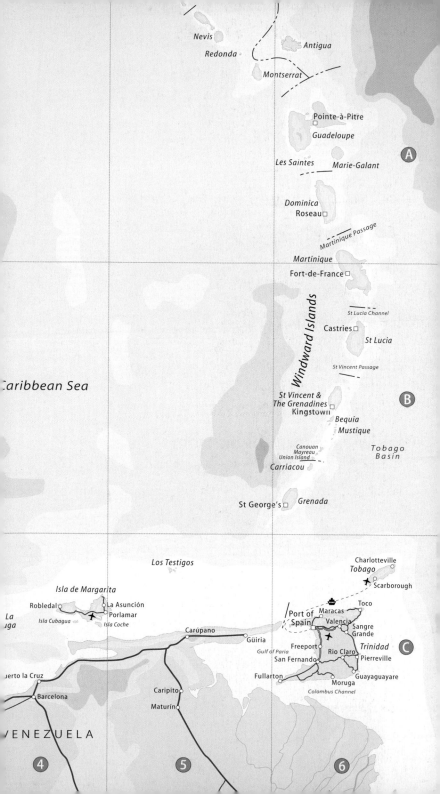

Check out...

WWW...

100 travel guides, 100s of destinations,
5 continents and 1 Footprint...
www.footprintbooks.com